Pacific Rim edition
STRATEGIC MANAGEMENT

Pacific Rim edition
STRATEGIC MANAGEMENT

COMPETITIVENESS and GLOBALISATION

dallas hanson

peter dowling

michael a. hitt

r. duane ireland

robert e. hoskisson

NELSON
THOMSON LEARNING

Australia · Canada · Mexico · Singapore · Spain · United Kingdom · United States

102 Dodds Street
Southbank Victoria 3006

Email nelson@nelson.com.au
Website http://www.nelson.com.au

First published by South-Western College Publishing as *Strategic Management: Competitiveness and Globalization* (4th edition), by Michael A. Hitt, R. Duane Ireland & Robert E. Hoskisson. Authorised adaptation of the original edition by South-Western College Publishing, Cincinnati, Ohio.

First published in 2002
10 9 8 7 6 5 4 3 2 1
06 05 04 03 02

Copyright © 2001 South-Western College Publishing.

Copyright © 2002 Nelson, a division of Thomson Learning.
Thomson Learning is a trademark used herein under licence.

COPYRIGHT
Apart from fair dealing for the purposes of study, research, criticism or review, or as permitted under Part VB of the Copyright Act, no part of this book may be reproduced by any process without permission. Copyright owners may take legal action against a person who infringes on their copyright through unauthorised copying. Enquiries should be directed to the publisher.

National Library of Australia
Cataloguing-in-Publication data

Strategic management: competitiveness and globalisation.

   Includes index.
   ISBN 0 17 010274 2.

   1. Industrial management, 2. Strategic planning,
   3. Competition. I. Hanson, Dallas.

658.401

Editor: Robyn Flemming
Project editor: David Parnham
Publishing editor: Lachlan McMahon
Text designer: Andrew Burgess
Illustrators: Modern Art Production Group and Shelly Communications
Photo and permissions researcher: Pam Underwood
Indexer: Fay Donlevy
Typeset in Sabon 10/13 by Modern Art Production Group
Production controller: Sally Chick
Printed in Singapore by Markono

Nelson Australia Pty Limited ACN 058 280 149 (incorporated in Victoria) trading as Nelson Thomson Learning.

Contents in Brief

Part 1
Strategic Management Inputs

Chapter 1 Strategic management and strategic competitiveness 2

Chapter 2 The external environment: Opportunities, threats, industry competition and competitor analysis 38

Chapter 3 The internal environment: Resources, capabilities and core competencies 78

Part 2
Strategic Actions: Strategy Formulation

Chapter 4 Business-level strategy 120

Chapter 5 Competitive dynamics 154

Chapter 6 Corporate-level strategy 193

Chapter 7 Acquisition and restructuring strategies 228

Chapter 8 International strategy 269

Chapter 9 Cooperative strategy 309

Part 3
Strategic Actions: Strategy Implementation

Chapter 10 Corporate governance 346

Chapter 11 Organisational structure and controls 385

Chapter 12 Strategic leadership 423

Chapter 13 Corporate entrepreneurship and innovation 454

Part 4
Cases

Glossary G–1

Name index I–1

Subject index I–7

Photo credits I–16

Contents

Cases grid xvi
Preface xviii
About the authors xxiii

Part 1
Strategic Management Inputs

Chapter 1
Strategic Management and Strategic Competitiveness 2

Opening Case: E-commerce strategy: Changing the nature of competition 3
The challenge of strategic management 7
    Strategic Focus: The difficulties of success 9
The 21st-century competitive landscape 11
    The global economy 11
    The march of globalisation 12
    Technology and technological changes 15
    Strategic Focus: Compaq is flailing against Internet technological trends 16
The I/O model of above-average returns 18
The resource-based model of above-average returns 20
Strategic intent and strategic mission 22
    Strategic intent 22
    Strategic mission 23
Stakeholders 23
    Classification of stakeholders 24
Organisational strategists 29
    The work of effective strategists 30
The strategic management process 31
Summary 33
Review questions 34
Application discussion questions 34

Ethics questions 34
Internet exercise 35
Notes 35

Chapter 2
The External Environment: Opportunities, Threats, Industry Competition and Competitor Analysis 38

Opening Case: Rio Tinto and the global challenge 39
The general, industry and competitor environments 41
External environmental analysis 43
    Scanning 44
    Monitoring 45
    Forecasting 45
    Assessing 45
Segments of the general environment 46
    The demographic segment 46
    The economic segment 48
    The political/legal segment 50
    The socio-cultural segment 51
    The technological segment 53
    The global segment 55
    Strategic Focus: Dell's direct business model leads to strategic success in China 56
Industry environment analysis 58
    Threat of new entrants 59
    Bargaining power of suppliers 61
    Bargaining power of buyers 62
    Threat of substitute products 63
    Intensity of rivalry among competitors 63
    Strategic Focus: Amazon.com and Barnesandnoble.com: A continuing rivalry 64
Interpreting industry analyses 67
Strategic groups 68
    The value of strategic group analysis 69
Competitor analysis 69
    Strategic Focus: Competitive intelligence and the Internet 72
Summary 73
Review questions 74
Application discussion questions 74
Ethics questions 74
Internet exercise 74
Notes 75

Chapter 3
The Internal Environment: Resources, Capabilities and Core Competencies 78

Opening Case: Brands as a source of competitive advantage 79
The importance of internal analysis 85
    The challenge of internal analysis 89

Resources, capabilities and core competencies 91
    Resources 91
    Capabilities 94
    Strategic Focus: Knowledge management and sustainable competitive advantage 95
    Core competencies 98
Building core competencies 99
    Criteria of sustainable competitive advantage 99
    Strategic Focus: Trust: Is it valuable, rare, costly to imitate and non-substitutable? 102
    Value chain analysis 105
    Strategic Focus: Adding value at Flight Centre 107
Outsourcing 109
Core competencies: Cautions and reminders 111
Strategic inputs and strategic actions 112
Summary 113
Review questions 114
Application discussion questions 114
Ethics questions 114
Internet exercise 115
Notes 115

Part 2
Strategic Actions: Strategy Formulation

Chapter 4
Business-level Strategy 120

Opening Case: The Internet, customer (buyer) power and business-level strategy 121
Customers: Who, what and how 126
    Who: Determining the customers to serve 127
    What: Determining the customer needs to satisfy 130
    How: Determining core competencies necessary to satisfy customers' needs 130
Types of business-level strategy 131
    Cost leadership strategy 132
    Competitive risks of the cost leadership strategy 136
    Differentiation strategy 136
    Strategic Focus: Sony Corporation's use of the differentiation business-level strategy 137
    Competitive risks of the differentiation strategy 141
    Focus strategies 141
    Competitive risks of focus strategies 143
    Integrated cost leadership/differentiation strategy 144
    Competitive risks of the integrated cost leadership/differentiation strategy 146
    Strategic Focus: Merrill Lynch compromises its differentiation strategy by implementing an on-line strategy 147
Summary 149
Review questions 150
Application discussion questions 150
Ethics questions 151
Internet exercise 151
Notes 151

Chapter 5
Competitive Dynamics 154

Opening Case: The global competitive landscape is changing: Wal-Mart is on the move 155
Increased rivalry in the new competitive landscape 157
    Strategic Focus: Food retailing in Australia 157
Model of competitive dynamics and rivalry 161
    Market commonality 162
    Strategic Focus: Air Wars: Competitive rivalry in Australia 163
    Resource similarity 164
    Strategic Focus: Cola wars, water wars and going for the jugular vein 165
Likelihood of attack 167
    First, second and late movers 167
Likelihood of response 169
    Type of competitive action 170
    Actor's reputation 170
    Strategic Focus: Car wars: The battle for survival 171
    Dependence on the market 172
Firms' abilities to take action and respond 174
    Relative size of firm 174
    Speed of competitive actions and competitive responses 175
    Innovation 176
    Quality 177
Outcomes of inter-firm rivalry 180
    Competitive market outcomes 180
    Competing in fast-cycle markets 182
    Competitive dynamics and industry evolution outcomes 184
Summary 187
Review questions 188
Application discussion questions 188
Ethics questions 189
Internet exercise 189
Notes 189

Chapter 6
Corporate-level Strategy 193

Opening Case: Wesfarmers: A diversified West Australian conglomerate 194
History of diversification 197
Levels of diversification 199
    Low levels of diversification 200
    Moderate and high levels of diversification 200
Reasons for diversification 201
Related diversification 203
    Operational relatedness: Sharing activities 204
    Corporate relatedness: Transferring of core competencies 205
    Strategic Focus: Williams Companies transfers its skills from natural-gas pipelines to Internet pipelines 206
    Market power 207
Unrelated diversification 210
    Efficient internal capital market allocation 210
    Strategic Focus: Refocusing large diversified business groups in emerging economies 211
    Restructuring 214

Diversification: Incentives and resources 214
    Incentives to diversify 214
    Resources and diversification 218
    Extent of diversification 219
Managerial motives to diversify 219
    Strategic Focus: AOL's diversification merger with Time Warner 221
Summary 223
Review questions 224
Application discussion questions 224
Ethics questions 224
Internet exercise 224
Notes 225

Chapter 7
Acquisition and Restructuring Strategies 228

Opening Case: The Internet: Driving mergers and acquisitions in the global economy 229
The increasing use of merger and acquisition strategies 231
    Mergers, acquisitions and takeovers: What are the differences? 232
    Reasons for acquisitions 233
    Strategic Focus: BP Amoco and Atlantic Richfield Co.: A case of intentions and realities in the world of acquisitions 235
    Strategic Focus: Daimler-Benz and Chrysler Corporation: Will it be a successful union? 238
    Problems in achieving acquisition success 243
Effective acquisitions 250
Restructuring 252
    Strategic Focus: Successful acquisitions the Cisco Systems way 252
    Downsizing 254
    Downscoping 254
    Leveraged buyouts 256
    Restructuring outcomes 257
    Strategic Focus: BHP Billiton: A resources giant is created 259
Summary 263
Review questions 264
Application discussion questions 264
Ethics questions 265
Internet exercise 265
Notes 265

Chapter 8
International Strategy 269

Opening Case: Technology and globalisation: A changing landscape in the 21st century 270
Identifying international opportunities: The incentive to pursue an international strategy 273
Increased market size 276
    Return on investment 277
    Economies of scale and learning 278
    Location advantages 279
    Strategic Focus: The decade of Europe: 2000–2010 279
International strategies 281
    International business-level strategy 281

International corporate-level strategy 286
   Strategic Focus: Awakening of the Asian tiger 289
Environmental trends 291
   Regionalisation 291
Choice of international entry mode 292
   Exporting 292
   Licensing 293
   Strategic alliances 294
   Acquisitions 295
   New wholly owned subsidiary 296
   Dynamics of mode of entry 296
Strategic competitiveness outcomes 297
   International diversification and returns 297
   International diversification and innovation 298
   Complexity of managing multinational firms 299
Risks in an international environment 299
   Strategic Focus: Foster's worldwide wine 300
   Political risks 301
   Economic risks 301
   Limits to international expansion: Management problems 302
   Other management problems 303
Summary 304
Review questions 305
Application discussion questions 305
Ethics questions 305
Internet exercise 305
Notes 306

Chapter 9
Cooperative Strategy 309

Opening Case: Using cooperative strategies in the global automobile industry 310
Types of cooperative strategies 313
   Reasons firms develop strategic alliances 315
Business-level cooperative strategies 317
   Complementary alliances 318
   Strategic Focus: Horizontal alliances among airline companies: A route to increased strategic competitiveness? 320
   Competition reduction strategies 323
   Competition response strategies 324
   Uncertainty reduction strategies 325
   Assessment of competitive advantage for business-level cooperative strategies 326
Corporate-level cooperative strategies 327
   Diversifying strategic alliances 327
   Synergistic strategic alliances 328
   Franchising 328
   Assessment of competitive advantage for corporate-level cooperative strategies 329
International cooperative strategies 330
   Strategic intent of partner 332
   Strategic Focus: The relationship between partner selection and strategic alliance success 332
Network cooperative strategies 333

Strategic Focus: Alliance networks: Benefits and issues 334
Competitive risks with cooperative strategies 335
Trust as a strategic asset 337
Strategic approaches to managing alliances 337
Summary 339
Review questions 340
Application discussion questions 340
Ethics questions 340
Internet exercise 341
Notes 341

Part 3
Strategic Actions: Strategy Implementation

Chapter 10
Corporate Governance 346

Opening Case: Are CEOs worth their weight in gold? 347
Separation of ownership and managerial control 351
    Agency relationships 352
    Product diversification as an example of an agency problem 353
    Agency costs and governance mechanisms 354
Ownership concentration 355
    The growing influence of institutional owners 356
    Strategic Focus: Institutional investors: ASA 358
    Shareholder activism: How much is possible? 359
Boards of directors 361
    International differences in board structures 362
    Enhancing the effectiveness of the board of directors 364
    Strategic Focus: The top and bottom of American boards of directors 365
Executive compensation 366
    A complicated governance mechanism 367
    The effectiveness of executive compensation 368
The multi-divisional structure 369
Market for corporate control 370
    Managerial defence tactics 370
    Strategic Focus: Corporate governance: Do shareholders' interests really matter? 371
International corporate governance 373
    Corporate governance in Australia 373
    Corporate governance in Germany 376
    Corporate governance in Japan 377
    Global corporate governance 378
Governance mechanisms and ethical behaviour 379
Summary 380
Review questions 381
Application discussion questions 381
Ethics questions 382
Internet exercise 382
Notes 382

Chapter 11
Organisational Structure and Controls 385

Opening Case: The new structure of Microsoft 386
Evolutionary patterns of strategy and organisational structure 389
    Simple structure 389
    Functional structure 391
    Multi-divisional structure 392
Implementing business-level strategies: Organisational structure and controls 394
    Using the functional structure to implement the cost leadership strategy 394
    Using the functional structure to implement the differentiation strategy 396
    Using the functional structure to implement the integrated cost leadership/differentiation strategy 397
    Using the simple structure to implement focused strategies 398
    Movement to the multi-divisional structure 398
Implementing corporate-level strategies: Organisational structure and controls 399
    Using the cooperative form to implement the related-constrained strategy 399
    Strategic Focus: IBM implements the cooperative M-form structure, facilitating e-commerce services 401
    Using the strategic business unit form to implement the related-linked strategy 402
    Using the competitive form to implement the unrelated diversification strategy 405
The effect of structure on strategy 407
Implementing international strategies: Organisational structure and controls 407
    Using the worldwide geographic area structure to implement the multi-domestic strategy 408
    Using the worldwide product divisional structure to implement the global strategy 409
    Strategic Focus: Procter & Gamble restructures and implements a worldwide product divisional structure 410
    Using the combination structure to implement the transnational strategy 412
    Strategic Focus: Ford implements the combination structure 412
Implementing cooperative strategies: Organisational structure and controls 414
    Implementing business-level cooperative strategies 415
    Implementing corporate-level cooperative strategies 416
    Implementing international cooperative strategies 417
Contemporary organisational structures: A cautionary note 418
Summary 419
Review questions 420
Application discussion questions 420
Ethics questions 420
Internet exercise 420
Notes 421

Chapter 12
Strategic Leadership 423

Opening Case: Strategic leaders: The good, the bad and the ugly 424
Strategic leadership 427
Managers as an organisational resource 428
    Top management teams 430
Managerial labour market 433
    Strategic Focus: Shattering the glass ceiling: Women top executives 435
Determining strategic direction 436

Exploiting and maintaining core competencies 437
Developing human capital 438
> Strategic Focus: Competitive advantage powered by human capital 438

Sustaining an effective organisational culture 441
> Entrepreneurial orientation 441
> Changing the organisational culture and business reengineering 443

Emphasising ethical practices 444
> Strategic Focus: Lies, managed earnings and conflicts of interest – the ethics of strategic leaders 445

Establishing balanced organisational controls 447
Summary 448
Review questions 449
Application discussion questions 449
Ethics questions 450
Internet exercise 450
Notes 450

Chapter 13
Corporate Entrepreneurship and Innovation 454

Opening Case: Innovation, competition and competitive success in the global automobile industry 455

Innovation, entrepreneurship, corporate entrepreneurship and entrepreneurs 457
> Innovation 459
> Strategic Focus: Surprise, surprise, surprise! What might be tomorrow's innovative products, and what will be the source of their development? 459
> Entrepreneurship 461
> Corporate entrepreneurship 462
> Entrepreneurs 462

International entrepreneurship 463
Internal corporate venturing 465
> Autonomous strategic behaviour 465
> Induced strategic behaviour 467
> Strategic Focus: Product innovations and induced strategic behaviours: Personal computers, video games and other delights 467

Implementing internal corporate ventures 468
> Using product development teams to achieve cross-functional integration 469
> Appropriating (gaining) value from innovation 471

Strategic alliances: Cooperating to produce and manage innovation 472
Acquisitions and venture capital: Buying innovation 474
> Acquisitions 474
> Venture capital 475

Entrepreneurship in small businesses and entrepreneurial ventures 476
> Strategic Focus: Innovation as a key source of value creation 477
> Producing more innovation in large organisations 478

Summary 479
Review questions 480
Application discussion questions 480
Ethics questions 480
Internet exercise 480
Notes 481

Part 4
Cases

INTRODUCTION: Preparing an effective case analysis C-3

CASE 1 ABB in China, 1998 C-16
Suzanne Uhlen and Michael Lubatkin

CASE 2 Ansett Airlines and Air New Zealand: A flight to oblivion? C-31
Megan Woods, Peter Dowling and Dallas Hanson

CASE 3 BP–Mobil and the restructuring of the oil refining industry C-44
Karel Cool, Jeffrey Reuer, Ian Montgomery and Francesca Gee

CASE 4 Compaq in crisis C-67
Adrian Elton

CASE 5 Gillette and the men's wet-shaving market C-76
Lew G. Brown and Jennifer M. Hart

CASE 6 Incat Tasmania's race for international success: Blue-Riband strategies C-95
Mark Wickham and Dallas Hanson

CASE 7 Kiwi Travel International Airlines Ltd C-105
Jared W. Paisley

CASE 8 Beefing up the beefless Mac: McDonald's expansion strategies in India C-120
Nitin Pangarkar and Saroja Subrahmanyan

CASE 9 Nucor Corporation and the US steel industry C-128
Brian K. Boyd and Steve Gove

CASE 10 Pacific Dunlop: Caught on the half volley C-157
Stuart Crispin, Mark Wickham and Dallas Hanson

CASE 11 Philip Morris C-173
Rhonda Fronk, Bill Pilgrim, Bill Prosser, Regan Urquhart and Monte Wiltse

CASE 12 Pisces Group of Singapore C-188
Siah Hwee Ang and Kulwant Singh

CASE 13 Raffles, Singapore's historic hotel C-194
Kulwant Singh, Nitin Pangarkar, Gaik Eng Lim and Ng Seok-Hui

CASE 14 Southwest Airlines, 1996 C-205
Andrew Inkpen and Valerie DeGroot

Glossary G-1
Name index I-1
Subject index I-7
Photo credits I-16

Cases grid

Case Title	Manufacturing	Service	Consumer Goods	Industrial Goods	International Perspective
ABB in China, 1998	■			■	■
Ansett Airlines and Air New Zealand		■			
BP–Mobil and the restructuring of the oil refining industry	■			■	■
Compaq in crisis	■		■		
Gillette and the men's wet-shaving market	■		■		■
Incat Tasmania's race for international success	■				■
Kiwi Travel International Airlines Ltd		■			■
Beefing up the beefless Mac: McDonald's expansion strategies in India		■	■		
Nucor Corporation and the US steel industry	■			■	
Pacific Dunlop	■				■
Philip Morris	■		■		■
Pisces Group of Singapore					
Raffles, Singapore's historic hotel		■			
Southwest Airlines, 1996		■			

Cases grid

High Technology	Sports/ Entertainment	Food/Retail	Social/Ethical Issues	Entrepreneurial/ Small–Medium Size	Industry Perspective	Chapters
			■			2,3,8,11
■					■	2,3,4,9
					■	5,6,7
■						7,10,12
					■	7,8,10
■						2,3,13
				■		5,8,12,13
		■				2,8
					■	2,3,4
					■	2,3,4,6,7,9
		■	■		■	2,6,11,12
		■		■		6
						1
					■	1,3,4,5

PREFACE

The Australian edition of *Strategic Management: Competitiveness and Globalisation* is based on the 2001 fourth edition of the American text of the same name by Hitt, Ireland and Hoskisson. It continues the tradition from previous US editions of integrating 'cutting edge' with an engaging writing style and includes significant Australian material.

Features

- Australian and Asia-Pacific material in all chapters.
- Chapter Opening Cases and Strategic Focus segments.
- Company-specific examples that are integrated with each chapter's topic.
- Substantial emphasis on use of the Internet and e-commerce.
- Coverage of strategic issues in the 21st-century competitive landscape, including a strong emphasis on the competition created through e-commerce ventures and start-ups.
- Global coverage with an emphasis on the international context.
- New and current research integrated throughout the chapters' conceptual presentations.
- Review questions, application discussion questions and ethics questions at the end of each chapter that include issues suggested by the e-commerce phenomenon.
- Internet exercises and e-projects at the end of each chapter. These exercises and projects encourage readers to use the Internet as an information source and problem-solving tool.
- Case analysis guide.

The book emphasises a global advantage with comprehensive coverage of Australian and international concepts and issues. In addition to comprehensive coverage of international strategies in Chapter 8, references to and discussions of the international context and issues are included in every chapter. The Opening Cases, Strategic Focus segments and individual examples in each chapter cover numerous global issues and markets.

The book contains a wealth of references. Drawn from the business literature and academic research, these materials are used to present current and accurate descriptions of how firms use the strategic management process. Our goal while preparing this book has been to present you, our readers, with a complete, accurate and up-to-date explanation of the strategic management process as it is used in the global economy. We have sought to include enough local content to stimulate interest, and enough international content to reflect the nature of current strategic management.

The book's focus

The strategic management process is the focus of our textbook. Described in Chapter 1, organisations (both for-profit companies and not-for-profit agencies) use the strategic management process to understand competitive forces and develop competitive advantages. The magnitude of this challenge is greater today than it has been historically. A new competitive landscape is developing in the 21st century as a result of the technological revolution (especially in e-commerce) and increasing globalisation. The technological revolution has placed greater importance on product innovation and the ability to rapidly introduce new goods and services to the marketplace. The global economy, one in which goods and services flow relatively freely among nations, continuously pressures firms to become more competitive. By offering either valued goods or services to customers, competitive firms increase the probability of earning above-average returns. Thus, the strategic management process helps organisations to identify what they intend to achieve and how they will do it.

This Australian edition remains focused on core topics that were the foundation for the first three American editions. In addition, we use a wide range of company-specific examples to discuss e-commerce applications of the strategic management process. E-commerce examples are presented in each chapter to show the pervasive effect of the Internet and e-commerce on competition in the global economy. Through these examples, our text is clearly differentiated from others regarding e-commerce applications of the strategic management process.

This book is intended for use primarily in strategic management and business policy courses. The materials presented in the 13 chapters have been researched thoroughly. Both the academic, scholarly literature and the business, practitioner literatures were studied and then integrated to prepare this edition. The academic literature provides the foundation to develop an accurate, yet meaningful description of the strategic management process. The business practitioner literature yields a rich base of current domestic and global examples to show how the strategic management process's concepts, tools and techniques are applied in different organisations.

The strategic management process

Our discussion of the strategic management process is both traditional and contemporary. In maintaining tradition, we examine important materials that have historically been a part of understanding strategic management. For example, we thoroughly examine how to analyse a firm's external environment and internal environment.

Contemporary treatment. To explain the aforementioned important activities, we try to keep our treatments contemporary. In Chapter 3, for example, we emphasise the importance of identifying and determining the value-creating potential of a firm's resources, capabilities and core competencies. The strategic actions taken as a result of understanding a firm's resources, capabilities and core competencies have a direct link with the company's ability to establish a competitive advantage, achieve strategic competitiveness and earn above-average returns.

Our contemporary treatment is also shown in the chapters on the dynamics of strategic change in the complex global economy. In Chapter 5, for example, we discuss how the dynamics of competition between firms, dynamics that are often 'hyper-competitive', affect strategic outcomes. Chapter 5's discussion suggests that in most industries, a firm's strategic actions are influenced by its competitors' actions and reactions. Thus, competition in the global economy is fluid, dynamic and fast-paced. Similarly, in Chapter 7, we explain the dynamics of strategic change at the corporate level, specifically addressing the motivation and consequences of mergers, acquisitions and restructuring (for example, divestitures) in the global economy.

We also emphasise that the set of strategic actions known as strategy formulation and strategy implementation (see Figure 1.1 in Chapter 1) must be integrated carefully if a firm is to achieve strategic competitiveness and earn above-average returns. Thus, this book shows that competitive success occurs when firms use implementation tools and actions that are consistent with the previously chosen business-level (Chapter 4), corporate-level (Chapter 6), acquisition (Chapter 7), international (Chapter 8) and cooperative (Chapter 9) strategies.

Contemporary concepts. Contemporary topics and concepts are the foundation for our in-depth analysis of strategic actions firms take to implement strategies. In Chapter 10, for example, we describe how different corporate governance mechanisms (for example, boards of directors, institutional owners, executive compensation, and so on) affect strategy implementation. Chapter 11 explains how firms gain a competitive advantage by effectively using organisational structures that are matched properly to different strategies. The vital contributions of strategic leaders are examined in Chapter 12. Chapter 13 addresses the important topic of corporate entrepreneurship and innovation through internal corporate venturing, strategic alliances, and external acquisition or venture capital investments.

Key features of this text

To increase our book's value for you, several features are included.

Learning objectives. Each chapter begins with clearly stated learning objectives. Their purpose is to emphasise key points you will want to master while studying each chapter. To both facilitate and verify learning, you can revisit individual learning objectives while preparing answers to the review questions appearing at the end of each chapter.

Opening cases. An Opening Case follows the learning objectives in each chapter. The cases describe current strategic issues in modern companies such as Rio Tinto, Sony, General Motors, DaimlerChrysler and Dell Computer Corporation, among others. The purpose of the Opening Cases is to demonstrate how specific firms apply individual chapters' strategic management concepts. Thus, the Opening Cases serve as a direct and often distinctive link between the theory and application of strategic management.

Key terms. Key terms that are critical to understanding the strategic management process are boldfaced throughout the book. Definitions of these key terms appear in chapter margins as well as in the text. The glossary at the end of the book conveniently gathers all the key terms and definitions together for ease of reference. Other terms and concepts throughout the text are italicised, signifying their importance.

Strategic focus segments. A number of Strategic Focus segments are presented in each chapter. As with the Opening Cases, the Strategic Focus segments highlight a variety of high-profile organisations, situations and concepts. Each segment describes issues that can be addressed by applying a chapter's strategy-related concepts.

End-of-chapter summaries. Closing each chapter is a summary that revisits the concepts outlined in the learning objectives. The summaries are presented in a bulleted format to highlight a chapter's concepts, tools and techniques

Review questions. Review questions are pointedly tied to the learning objectives, prompting readers to re-examine the most important concepts in each chapter.

Application discussion questions. These questions challenge readers to directly apply the part of the strategic management process highlighted in that chapter. The questions are designed to stimulate thoughtful classroom discussions and to help readers develop critical thinking skills.

Ethics questions. At the end of each chapter, readers are challenged by questions about ethical issues requiring careful thought and analysis. Preparing answers to these questions helps readers to recognise and confront ongoing ethical issues facing management teams. Discussing these difficult issues in class heightens awareness of the ethical challenges encountered in today's global organisations and markets.

Internet exercises. The Internet is an invaluable source for exchanging information worldwide. For this reason, we present a set of Internet exercises at the end of each chapter. Each exercise is designed to help readers develop an ability to recognise information sources that can aid in problem solution. Following each Internet exercise is a unique *e-project module that can be used as a more comprehensive assignment – an assignment that challenges people to use the Internet for strategic purposes.

Examples. In addition to the Opening Cases and Strategic Focus segments, each chapter is filled with real-world examples of companies in action. These examples illustrate key strategic management concepts and provide realistic applications of strategic management.

Indices. The book contains Subject and Name indices.

Format. The format of the book provides the foundation for an interesting and visually appealing treatment of all parts of the strategic management process. Figures, tables, exhibits and photos further enhance the presentation by giving visual insight into the workings of companies competing in the global business environment.

The strategic advantage

The strategic management process is critical to organisational success. As described in Chapter 1, strategic competitiveness is achieved when a firm develops and exploits a sustained competitive advantage. Attaining such an advantage results in the earning of above-average returns – that is, returns that exceed those an investor could expect from other investments with similar amounts of risk. For example, the Australian firm Cochlear has developed and sustained a competitive advantage over time because of its significant emphasis on innovation.

The competitive advantage

Success in the 21st-century competitive landscape requires specific capabilities, including the abilities to (1) use scarce resources wisely to maintain the lowest possible costs, (2) constantly anticipate frequent changes in customers' preferences, (3) adapt to rapid technological changes, (4) identify, emphasise and effectively manage what a firm does better than its competitors, (5) continuously structure a firm's operations so objectives can be achieved more efficiently, and (6) successfully manage and gain commitments from a culturally diverse workforce.

The global advantage

Critical to the approach used in this text is the fact that all firms face increasing global competition. Firms no longer operate in relatively safe domestic markets, as Australian supermarkets have discovered. In the past, many companies produced large quantities of standardised products. Today, firms typically compete in a global economy that is complex, highly uncertain and unpredictable. To a greater degree than in a primarily domestic economy, the global economy rewards effective performers, whereas poor performers are forced to restructure significantly to enhance their strategic competitiveness. As noted earlier, increasing globalisation and the technological revolution have produced a new competitive landscape in the 21st century. This landscape presents a challenging and complex environment for firms, but one that also has opportunities. The importance of developing and using these capabilities in the 21st century should not be underestimated.

Cases

Included in this book are 14 cases. These are basically international in focus, and six are concerned principally with the Asia-Pacific environment. The cases cover many different strategic issues and a range of industries.

To help you refer easily to the coverage of the cases a matrix is presented on pp. xvi–xvii. This matrix will enable you to select cases that address issues in which you are interested. The matrix also indicates the chapter or chapters within the book to which each case relates.

Writing new cases is a little like sticking a foot in a river; once we had written the Ansett and Pacific Dunlop cases the companies changed as their environmental challenges altered. The cases are as up-to-date as a book publication schedule allows – a fact of which we are proud. In future editions we will update cases and add new cases so that the book keeps pace with a fast-changing world.

Support material

The CD-ROM Instructor's Manual that supplements this book comprises Case Solutions and PowerPoint® Presentation (ISBN: 0 17 010479 6). Also available for the instructor is a CD-ROM Testbank (ISBN: 0 17 010478 8). The accompanying website contains additional case studies, along with multiple-choice tests and the PowerPoint® Presentation. Visit the site at: www.nelson.com.au/hanson.

Acknowledgements

We want to thank those who helped us prepare this Australian edition of Strategic Management. Dr John Steen had the major responsibility for adapting Chapter 3; Stuart Crispin adapted Chapter 6, with a substantial contribution from Frank McCann; John Darby adapted Chapter 8; and Mark Wickham adapted Chapter 9. Ms Wahu Sutiyono made a substantial contribution to Chapter 10. Stuart Crispin and Mark Wickham also helped with reviews of chapters and supported all the authors by providing information and Australian material. It was a big job, which everyone tackled in a great spirit.

Final comment

Organisations face exciting and dynamic competitive challenges in the 21st century. These challenges, and effective responses to them, are explored in *Strategic Management: Competitiveness and Globalisation*. The strategic management process conceptualised in this text offers valuable insights and knowledge to those committed to meeting successfully the challenge of dynamic competition. Thinking strategically, as this book challenges you to do, increases the likelihood that you will help your company to achieve strategic success. In addition, continuous practice with strategic thinking and the use of the strategic management process gives you skills and knowledge that will contribute to career advancement and success. Finally, we want to wish you all the best and nothing other than complete success in all of your endeavours.

ABOUT THE AUTHORS

Dallas Hanson

Dallas Hanson is Senior Lecturer in Strategic Management at the University of Tasmania. His PhD was from the University of Tasmania and concerned the strategic management of ecological issues by organisations. He believes that strategic management is a multidisciplinary area and takes a multidisciplinary approach to issues. He publishes in a variety of journals, including the *Scandinavian Journal of Management*, *Prometheus*, the *International Journal of Innovation Management*, *Greener Management International*, the *European Journal of Marketing* and the *Journal of Marketing Management*. He reviews for a similar variety of journals and does a range of strategy consulting. Currently, his main academic interest is in corporate communication, and he is undertaking a major investigation into the arational nature of much corporate activity.

Peter J. Dowling

Peter J. Dowling (who received his PhD from Flinders University of South Australia) is Foundation Professor of Management at the University of Tasmania. Previous teaching appointments include Monash University, the University of Melbourne and California State University, Chico. He has also held visiting appointments at Cornell University and Michigan State University (in the United States), and the University of Paderborn and the University of Bayreuth (in Germany).

His current research interests are concerned with international human resource management and strategic management. Professor Dowling has co-authored three books (*International Human Resource Management: Managing People in a Multinational Context*, with Denice Welch and Randall Schuler; *Human Resource Management in Australia*, with Randall Schuler, John Smart and Vandra Huber; and *People in Organizations: An Introduction to Organizational Behaviour in Australia*, with Terence Mitchell, Boris Kabanoff and James Larson). He has also written or co-authored over 50 journal articles and book chapters and serves on the editorial boards of *Management International Review*, *Asia Pacific Journal of Human Resources*, *Journal of International Management*, *Human Resource Planning*, *International Journal of Human Resource Management*, *Journal of World Business* and *Thunderbird International Business Review*.

Professor Dowling is a former National Vice-President of the Australian Human Resources Institute, past editor of *Asia Pacific Journal of Human Resources* (1987–96) and a Life Fellow of the Australian Human Resources Institute. He was recently appointed as a Senior Research Affiliate of the Center for Advanced Human Resource Studies at Cornell University and as a member of the Australian Defence College Advisory Board.

Michael A. Hitt

Michael A. Hitt is a Professor of Management and holds the Weatherup/Overby Chair in Executive Leadership. He received his PhD from the University of Colorado in the United States. He has authored or co-authored several books and book chapters and numerous journal articles in such journals as the *Academy of Management Journal*, *Academy of Management Review*, *Strategic Management Journal*, *Organization Studies*, *Journal of Management Studies* and *Journal of Management*, among others. His recent publications include the books *Downscoping: How to Tame the Diversified Firm* (Oxford University Press) and *Creating Value Through Mergers and Acquisitions* (Oxford University Press). He has served on the editorial review boards of multiple journals, including the *Academy of Management Journal*, *Academy of Management Executive*, *Journal of Applied Psychology*, *Journal of World Business* and *Journal of Applied Behavioral Sciences*. Furthermore, he has served as consulting editor (1988–90) and editor (1991–3) of the *Academy of Management Journal*. He was co-editor of a 1995 special issue for the *Strategic Management Journal* on 'Technological Transformation and the New Competitive Landscape' and is a consulting editor of a series of graduate-level books on strategic management for South-Western Publishing Co. He is the Past President of the Academy of Management, a 10 000-member international organisation dedicated to the advancement of management knowledge and practice. Following Michael Porter (1994) and C. K. Prahalad (1995), he received the 1996 Award for Outstanding Academic Contributions to Competitiveness from the American Society for Competitiveness. He is a Fellow in the Academy of Management.

R. Duane Ireland

Dr R. Duane Ireland is the W. David Robbins Chair of the Department of Management Systems at the University of Richmond in the United States. Interested in research questions related to both the entrepreneurship and strategic management disciplines, his work has been published in an array of journals, including the *Academy of Management Journal*, *Administrative Science Quarterly*, *Strategic Management Journal*, *Academy of Management Executive*, *Journal of Management*, *Journal of Management Studies*, *Decision Sciences*, *Human Relations*, *Entrepreneurship: Theory & Practice*, *Business Horizons*, *British Journal of Management*, *Journal of Small Business Management* and *American Journal of Small Business*. Dr Ireland has also served in various editorial capacities. He has been, or is serving as, a member of the editorial review boards for *Academy of Management Review*, *Academy of Management Journal*, *Academy of Management Executive*, *Journal of Management* and *Entrepreneurship: Theory & Practice*. Additionally, he previously completed terms as an associate editor for *Academy of Management Executive* and as consulting editor for *Entrepreneurship: Theory & Practice*. He is the co-author of seven books.

Robert E. Hoskisson

Robert E. Hoskisson is the Rath Chair in Strategic Management at the Michael F. Price College of Business in the United States. He received his PhD from the University of California, Irvine. He teaches courses in strategic management at graduate and undergraduate levels. His research focuses on topics in technology strategy, international and product diversification, corporate restructuring, corporate governance and strategic alliances, especially in the international arena. He is currently on the Board of Governors of the Academy of Management. He has served on the editorial review board of the *Academy of Management Journal*, including one term as consulting editor. He also has served on the boards of the *Strategic Management Journal*, *Organisation Science* and *Journal of Management*. His articles have appeared in journals such as the *Academy of Management Journal*, *Strategic Management Journal*, *Academy of Management Review*, *Academy of Management Executive*, *Journal of Management* and *California Management Review*. He has co-authored several books, including *Downscoping: How to Tame the Diversified Firm* (Oxford University Press, 1994).

Part 1

Strategic management inputs

Chapter 1
Strategic management and strategic competitiveness

Chapter 2
The external environment: Opportunities, threats, industry competition and competitor analysis

Chapter 3
The internal environment: Resources, capabilities and core competencies

Chapter 1

Strategic management and strategic competitiveness

Objectives

After reading this chapter, you should be able to:

1. Define strategic competitiveness, competitive advantage and above-average returns.
2. Discuss the challenge of strategic management.
3. Describe the 21st-century competitive landscape and how global and technological changes shape it.
4. Use the industrial organisation (I/O) model to explain how firms can earn above-average returns.
5. Use the resource-based model to explain how firms can earn above-average returns.
6. Describe strategic intent and strategic mission, and discuss their value to the strategic management process.
7. Define stakeholders, and describe the three primary stakeholder groups' ability to influence organisations.
8. Describe strategists' work.
9. Explain the strategic management process.

E-commerce strategy: Changing the nature of competition

Electronic commerce (e-commerce) is changing strategic management practices in many industries. The competition in the frenetic e-commerce environment often creates paranoia among CEOs. In his book *Only the Paranoid Survive*, Intel's former CEO, Andrew Grove, suggests that continual change and quick strategic decisions are essential if a firm is to be successful in the new world of hyper-competition. Continuous change and rapid strategic decisions are particularly important for e-commerce firms such as Dell, Amazon.com, Yahoo and eBay.

The conditions facing e-commerce firms call for E-CEOs (CEOs of electronic-commerce firms) to evangelise, continuously making clear their vision as it changes. In addition, these CEOs must encourage employees consistently and meaningfully. Because the e-commerce world is so intangible, the E-CEO must spend a significant amount of time to position the company in the minds of customers, employees, the press and numerous strategic alliance partners. A key reason for this is that a change of expectations in the minds of business analysts can diminish significantly an e-commerce firm's capital base in a short time.

The problems of the e-commerce sector in 2000 reveal the fragility of this situation. World markets turned against the market relatively quickly and the value of shares in dotcom companies declined worldwide. Yahoo!, the world's most consistently successful Internet company, provides an indication of the scale of the problem. In October 2000, shares were trading at US$76 (approximately A$152 at time of writing), down from US$130 in January. The biggest Internet retailer, Amazon.com, also reached a 52-week low in mid-October, while technology stocks such as Apple, Intel and Dell also fell sharply. In Hong Kong, the dotcom frenzy of early 2000 slowed even more remarkably. In early 2000, a crowd of more than 10 000 almost rioted when trying to get application forms for shares in tom.com, the Internet venture of Hong Kong's richest man, Li Ka-shing. The initial public offer for tom.com was 669 times over-subscribed. Shares in the company reached HK$7.75 on the first day of trading, but by early October they were HK$3.27. The fall occurred despite confident predictions about the Chinese market on which tom.com is focused.

Despite this mini-collapse of dotcom companies in 2000, the use of the Internet remains basic to much world business, changing the patterns of competition among companies, creating new opportunities and simultaneously affecting the way well-established firms traditionally conduct their business. Australia Post is a prime example. The Australian public-sector mail-focused organisation has an established infrastructure – 10 000 vehicles, 8.8 million mail delivery points and 80 000 square metres of warehousing. It is now attempting to use this to become Australia's largest e-commerce delivery network. Their retail outlets now double as e-commerce payment and parcel pick-up centres for customers unwilling or unable to pay for products on-line.

Because the Internet also makes it easier for new companies to enter markets, it amplifies the market weaknesses of the existing companies. For example, Dell's approach of selling direct to customers has revealed weaknesses in a number of computer firms, such as Compaq, Hewlett-Packard and IBM, that primarily use resellers. Dell's strategy requires fewer resources to implement and provides better customer satisfaction.

In addition, the Internet creates new strategic opportunities. For example, NextCard offers direct marketing services to sell financial products such as credit cards. NextCard has found that it attracted roughly US$30 million in new revenues in one month; these revenues were acquired at 70 per cent lower cost relative to traditional methods. Furthermore, those who have the sophistication to use the websites to apply for credit cards are the target customer group. These individuals tend to be professionals who pay their debts rapidly and maintain a good credit rating. The target customers represent an advantage for NextCard as it seeks to attract card users for its customers.

Amazon.com's Internet strategy also provides substantial customer service opportunities. For example, it makes recommendations for its customers based on their previous purchases and provides fast, quality service in regard to mailing its books and other items, such as CDs and videos. These services have created a loyal customer group for Amazon.com. More than 60 per cent of the company's sales are from repeat business.

The Internet is also changing how firms manage strategy implementation through their traditional operations. For example, Australia Post now has on-line billing for consumers and future plans include use of the Internet to expand the scope of their retail operations.

Sun Microsystems uses the Internet to remain abreast of its hiring needs in the incredibly intense competition for knowledge workers in California's Silicon Valley. The firm examines websites and advertises on them to hire qualified people for critical engineering jobs. Also, Sun provides an incentive for current employees to refer high-potential candidates to it for possible employment.

Ford Motor Company is using its intranet (internal Web-based system) to allow better utilisation of information among its group of approximately 100 000 employees. Top executives have supported and championed the intranet Web-only publication of divisional business plans, to engineer best practices and to prepare more precise product-development specifications. Their commitments and actions indicate clearly that Ford relies on its intranet. Approximately 80 per cent of Ford's employees are connected to it on a daily basis. The average employee can check every car and truck model to examine and track design, production, quality control and delivery processes. Through the company's information technology (IT) system, employees can examine whether a new dashboard will slow assembly, or find out how many blue fenders are needed in tomorrow's shipment. A central information group tracks the intranet's performance and keeps its search engines operating effectively. The group also maintains over 700 web page applications and servers. At Norska Skog's Boyer paper mill in Tasmania's south, a less sophisticated intranet is basic to the factory's operations. This intranet has been a fundamental tool in the ongoing 'greening' of the organisation, demonstrating how intranet/Internet technology can be used in complex organisational change.

In summary, e-commerce has changed technology-based businesses and has greatly affected traditional businesses in the way they manage their suppliers, customers and internal operations. Furthermore, and equally important, it has changed the way strategic leadership is practised in all types of businesses.

www.amazon.com
www.apple.com
www.australiapost.com
www.compaq.com
www.dell.com
www.ebay.com
www.ford.com
www.hp.com
www.ibm.com
www.intel.com
www.nextcard.com
www.sun.com
www.tom.com
www.yahoo.com

Sources: T. Petzinger, Jr, 2000, 'There's a new economy out there, and it looks nothing like the old one', *Wall Street Journal*, 1 January, p. R31; L. Armstrong, 1999, 'The rise and fall of an Internet star', *Business Week*, 26 April, pp. 88–94; E. Brown, 1999, 'Nine ways to win on the Web', *Fortune*, 24 May, pp. 112–25; G. Colvin, 1999, 'How to be a great E-CEO', *Fortune*, 24 May, pp. 104–10; H. Green, 1999, 'Throw out your old business model', *Business Week*, 22 March, pp. EB22–3; R. D. Hof, 1999, 'What every CEO needs to know about electronic business: A survival guide', *Business Week*, 22 March, pp. EB9–12; A. Reinherd, M. Moeller and R. Siklos, 1999, 'As the Web spins', *Business Week*, 24 May, p. 31; J. Davidson, 2000, 'Yahoo profits fail to impress', *Australian Financial Review*, 12 October, p. 27; M. Bryan, 2000, 'Australia Post, ready to put stamp on e-commerce', *Australian Financial Review*, 2 November, p. 14; M. Dwyer, 2000, 'Internet boom goes bust in HK', *Australian Financial Review*, 25 October, p. 41; S. Chadwick and D. Hanson, 2001, 'Environmental management, structure, networks, and information exchange: The case of a Tasmanian pulp mill', *Prometheus*, forthcoming.

Electronic commerce (e-commerce) is changing strategic management practices. These changes are seen in e-commerce firms such as Amazon.com, Dell and Yahoo!, and in what are thought of as more traditional organisations, such as Australia Post.

The expansion of on-line retailing efforts by major firms can affect the industry's competitive dynamics. This was the case when US grocery giant Wal-Mart formed an agreement with Fingerhut to handle many of its e-commerce orders. Wal-Mart, however, has failed to profit from four years of trying to get on-line sales going. Despite this, because of its size and global reach, Wal-Mart remains a feared opponent in retailing.[1] Of course, all actions taken in firms are intended to help companies achieve strategic competitiveness and earn above-average returns. *Strategic competitiveness* is achieved when a firm successfully formulates and implements a value-creating strategy. When a firm implements such a strategy that other companies are unable to duplicate or find too costly to imitate,[2] this firm has a **sustained, or sustainable, competitive advantage** (hereafter called simply competitive advantage). A firm is assured of a competitive advantage only after others' efforts to duplicate its strategy have ceased or failed. Even if a firm achieves a competitive advantage, it normally can sustain it only for a certain period.[3] The speed with which competitors are able to acquire the skills needed to duplicate the benefits of a firm's value-creating strategy determines how long a competitive advantage will last.[4] Understanding how to exploit its competitive advantage is necessary for a firm to earn above-average returns.[5]

By achieving strategic competitiveness and successfully exploiting its competitive advantage, a firm is able to accomplish its primary objective: the earning of above-average returns. **Above-average returns** are returns in excess of what an investor expects to earn from other investments with a similar amount of risk. **Risk** is an investor's uncertainty about the economic gains or losses that will result from a particular investment.[6] Returns are often measured in terms of accounting figures, such as return on assets, return on equity or return on sales. Alternatively, returns can be measured on the basis of stock market returns, such as daily, weekly or monthly returns (the beginning stock price minus the end-of-period stock price, divided by the beginning stock price). Firms that are without a competitive advantage or that are not competing in an attractive industry earn, at best, only average returns. **Average returns** are returns equal to those an investor expects to earn from other investments with a similar amount of risk. In the long run, an inability to earn at least average returns results in failure. Failure occurs because investors will choose to invest in firms that earn at least average returns and will withdraw their investments from those earning less.[7]

Dynamic in nature, the **strategic management process** (see Figure 1.1) is the full set of commitments, decisions and actions required for a firm to achieve strategic competitiveness and earn above-average returns.[8] Relevant *strategic inputs*, from analyses of the internal and external environments, are necessary for effective strategy formulation and implementation. In turn, *effective strategic actions* are a prerequisite to achieving the desired outcomes of strategic competitiveness and above-average returns. Thus, the strategic management process is used to match the conditions of an ever-changing market and competitive structure with a firm's continuously evolving resources, capabilities and competencies (the sources of strategic inputs). Effective *strategic actions* that take place in the context of carefully integrated strategy formulation and implementation result in desired *strategic outcomes*.[9]

A sustained, or sustainable, competitive advantage occurs when a firm implements a value-creating strategy of which other companies are unable to duplicate the benefits or find it too costly to imitate.

Above-average returns are returns in excess of what an investor expects to earn from other investments with a similar amount of risk.

Risk is an investor's uncertainty about the economic gains or losses that will result from a particular investment.

Average returns are returns equal to those an investor expects to earn from other investments with a similar amount of risk.

The strategic management process is the full set of commitments, decisions and actions required for a firm to achieve strategic competitiveness and earn above-average returns.

Figure 1.1 | The strategic management process

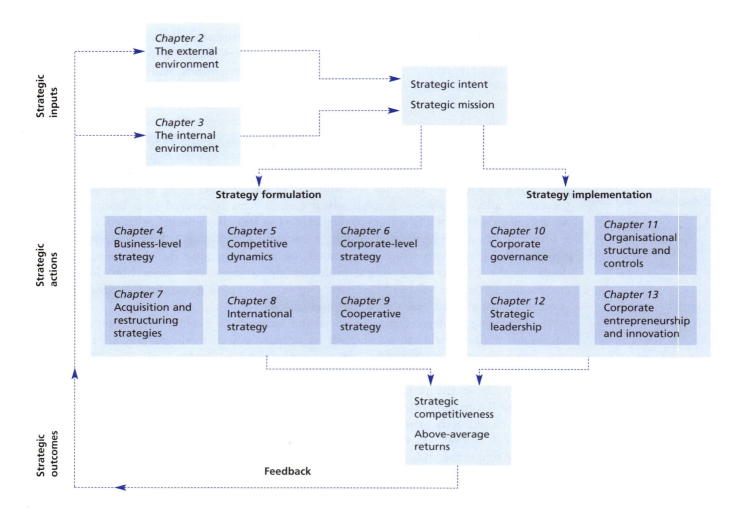

In the remaining chapters of this book, we use the strategic management process to explain what firms should do to achieve strategic competitiveness and earn above-average returns. Through these explanations, it becomes clear why some firms consistently achieve competitive success and others fail to do so.[10] As you will see, the reality of global competition is a critical part of the strategic management process.[11]

Several topics are discussed in this chapter. First, we examine the challenge of strategic management. This brief discussion highlights the fact that the strategic actions taken to achieve and then maintain strategic competitiveness demand the best of managers, employees and their organisations on a continuous basis.[12] Second, we describe the 21st-century competitive landscape, created primarily by the emergence of a global economy and rapid technological changes. The 21st-century competitive landscape establishes the context of opportunities and threats within which the strategic management process is used by firms striving to meet the competitive challenge raised by demanding global standards.

We next examine two models that suggest conditions which organisations should study to gain the strategic inputs needed to select strategic actions in the pursuit of strategic competitiveness and above-average returns. As we explain, the emphases of these two models differ. The first model (industrial organisation) suggests that the *external environment* should be the primary determinant of a firm's strategic actions. The key to this model is identifying and competing successfully in an attractive (that is, profitable) industry.[13] The second model (resource-based) suggests that a firm's unique resources and capabilities are the critical link to strategic competitiveness.[14] Comprehensive explanations of these two models appear in this chapter, and the next two chapters show that through the combined use of these models, firms obtain the full set of strategic inputs needed to formulate and implement strategies successfully.

Analyses of its external and internal environments provide a firm with the information required to develop its strategic intent and strategic mission. (Intent and mission are defined later in this chapter.[15]) As shown in Figure 1.1, strategic intent and strategic mission influence strategy formulation and implementation actions.

The chapter's discussion then turns to the stakeholders that organisations serve. The degree to which the stakeholders' needs can be met increases directly with enhancements in a firm's strategic competitiveness and its ability to earn above-average returns. Closing the chapter are introductions to organisational strategists and the elements of the strategic management process.

The challenge of strategic management

The goals of achieving strategic competitiveness and earning above-average returns are challenging, not only for firms as large as IBM, but also for those as small as your local computer retail outlet or dry cleaners. The performance of some companies, of course, more than meets strategic management's challenge. For example, in the Australian biotechnology industry, Biota Holdings has managed to get the anti-influenza drug Relenza on to the world market. Any new drug successfully entering the world market is rare, and this emerging company (revenue $30 million) stands out in an industry where research is the lifeblood but profits are usually hard to find.[16] At the other end of the financial spectrum, the US company Microsoft in 1999 became the first company to exceed U$500 billion in market value. At that time, this value equalled that of the world's ninth-largest economy.

The rigours of change and competition catch many, however. In Australia, only 10 of the year 2000's largest 100 enterprises were in business at the beginning of this century – Westpac (then the Bank of New South Wales), BHP, National Australia Bank, Colonial and Australia Post among them. *Business Review Weekly*'s annual list of the 'Top 1 000' companies (see Table 1.1) provides a good indication of attrition. More than 30 per cent of companies drop off the list each decade, and only around 40 per cent of those in the 2000 list were in the 1980 list. In the 2000 list, 12 per cent were running at a loss – more troubles for these firms will no doubt follow. Of the big corporations, BHP is engaged in a difficult turnaround after several years of financial difficulty and several highly publicised disasters, while Pacific Dunlop has experienced a decade of decline and North Limited has been taken over by Rio Tinto.[17]

Table 1.1 | From the 'Top 1 000': Best and worst performing stocks of 2000

**The most and least profitable:
Return on shareholders' funds, after tax**

Most		%	Least		%
1	Insurance Commission WA	12 686	1	Reinsurance Australia	−883
2	TNT	1 229	2	Golden West Refining	−313
3	NSW Lotteries	450	3	Mitsubishi Motors	−205
4	AAP Information Services	449	4	Allianz Australia	−184
5	Gascor	403	5	Normandy Yandal	−154
6	SA Lotteries	337	6	Resolute	−147
7	RESI Utilities	290	7	Tomen	−146
8	TAB South Australia	281	8	Astre German Automotive	−105
9	Lotteries Commission WA	273	9	Chubb Security	−79
10	TAB Western Australia	152	10	Oakridge	−73
11	Employment National	139	11	Fluor	−63
12	Swift & Moore	107	12	MacMahon Holdings	−61
13	Pharmacia & Upjohn (Perth)	105	13	Acer Computers	−60
14	Optima Energy	100	14	Airservices Australia	−58
15	Comcare	100	15	Hitachi Construction Machinery	−52
16	Vodafone Pacific	97	16	Isuzu	−51
17	BT Australia	94	17	National Jet Systems	−45
18	Hays Personnel	91	18	Australian Hospital Care	−45
19	Microsoft	86	19	Franklins	−44
20	Motorola	82	20	Toshiba	−39
21	TIAS	79	21	Avater Industries	−38
22	WA Newspapers	78	22	MCK Holdings	−37
23	NSW Treasury Corporation	73	23	Monsanto	−36
24	Normandy Mount Leyshon	72	24	Centaur Mining	−36
25	Australian Air Express	71	25	Amrad Corporation	−32

Source: *Business Review Weekly*, 17 November 2000, p. 24.

It is interesting to note that, in a US survey, CEOs did not place 'strong and consistent profits' as their top priority; in fact, it was fifth. A 'strong and well-thought-out strategy' was the top concern that will make a firm the most respected in the future. This was followed by maximising customer satisfaction and loyalty, business leadership and quality products and services, and then concern for consistent profits.[18] This is consistent with the view that no matter how good a product or service is, the firm must select the 'right' strategy and then implement it effectively.[19]

CEOs' concern for strategy is well founded. Some firms create their own problems by formulating the wrong strategy or implementing a strategy poorly. Such is the case with Pacific Dunlop and Levi Strauss. Because of strategic errors, recent years have found these firms failing to earn the returns that shareholders expect. Pacific Dunlop's strategic errors led to the company share price close to a 15-year low in October 2000. At Levi Strauss, poor performance resulted in a decision to reduce costs substantially. It is interesting to note that Levi Strauss could not achieve its socially responsible ideals because it was not creating the customer value that had long resulted from implementation of its strategies. The experiences of these firms are described in the Strategic Focus.

Strategic Focus Corporate

The difficulties of success: Pacific Dunlop and Levi Strauss

Pacific Dunlop, a diversified conglomerate, was formed out of the business units centred on the long-established Dunlop company in the mid-1980s. It has a history of strategic moves that ultimately led to further difficulties.

The number and variety of divisions that made up Pacific Dunlop in early 2000 provides an idea of the management challenges posed in this corporation. The star was Ansell International, their most profitable business and a world leader in condom and rubber glove production. Pacific Brands (including household names such as Bonds, Malvern Star and Sleepmaker) struggled, as did Pacific Distribution, which mainly included automotive and electrical businesses (including Repco). Their cable division struggled in a rapidly globalising industry where economies of scale are vital but unavailable to Pacific Dunlop. Their South Pacific Tyres division operates in highly competitive mature markets, and GNB Batteries were consistent under-performers. The overall picture was bleak, with only Ansell looking solid.

Pacific Dunlop was once even more diversified. In the early 1990s, it purchased and then subsequently sold significant food holdings, including well-known brands such as Peters and Edgells. It also had a history of selling businesses that went on to become very successful. Petersville-sleigh is one example, but an even better one is Cochlear, the world leader in ear-implant hearing aid technology. This was sold by Pacific Dunlop only to become one of the best performers on the Australian Stock Exchange – $1 000 invested in Cochlear in 1999 was worth over $6 000 in early 2000. In contrast, Pacific Dunlop peaked in value at $5.90 in 1994 and in April 2000 was worth $1.43.

The strategic errors that have led to this position are, in retrospect, easy to detect. The company is too diversified, and its managers have been unable to manage the portfolio. Instead of selling poor businesses, it has sold good ones. It now has only one division in a promising market; all the rest operate in highly competitive mature markets that have relatively gloomy outlooks. Finally, the company has a knack for making things hard for itself – for example, its Telectronics business distributed 42 000 pacemakers, and enough of these proved faulty for the company to be hit with a number of class actions and a bill of around $400 million.

Pacific Dunlop is likely to survive, however; under CEO Rod Chadwick it has sold Telectronics and GNB Batteries. Chadwick is also attempting to reorganise Pacific Brands and to change the whole Pacific Dunlop culture.

Beginning in 1997, Levi Strauss announced plans to close 29 factories in North America and Europe, thereby eliminating 16 310 jobs. Its 1998 sales dropped 13 per cent from the year before, to just under US$6 billion. In comparison, its cross-town (San Francisco) rival, Gap, Inc., grew much more rapidly during the same period. In 1996, Levi Strauss went through a leveraged buyout (LBO). Its stock had grown from US$2.53 per share in 1985 to over US$265 (adjusted for splits) per share in 1996. Robert Haas and other family shareholders decided to take the firm private to ensure that the company would be driven largely by social values and that it would not be hostage to profits alone.

Evidence suggests that Levi Strauss has not satisfied either its profit target or its social goals. In fact, many claim that it has mismanaged the Levi brand since 1990. Levi Strauss has always been a strong advocate of corporate philanthropy and social responsibility. In 1993, it embarked on a project it called its customer-service supply-chain initiative. However, this supply-chain initiative changed over time to emphasise improving service to all retail customers. The initiative produced a reengineering team whose budget had swollen 70 per cent by 1995, to over US$850 million. While engaged in this restructuring, the company became overly focused on one brand for all customers.

During the period of Levi's restructuring efforts, other brands (for example, Tommy Hilfiger) took some market share from Levi Strauss. Selling their clothing in new store-concept outlets, such as Hot Tropic, Pacific Sunwear and Gap, contributed to these other brands' success. In contrast to these new concept stores, Levi's clothing was being sold through channels (such as traditional department stores) that were less popular with the firm's target customers. Although Levi Strauss has now started a multi-brand strategy, something its competitors have done for years, it is in a catch-up phase. Gap, for example, has its high-end Banana Republic stores, its mid-level brand Gap, and its low-priced Old Navy store concepts and associated brands. Although Gap has had some problems as well (see Strategic Focus in Chapter 4), they pale in comparison to Levi's mismanagement.

Another area where Levi Strauss fell behind was in its Web strategy. While Levi's market share shrank to 14 per cent in 1998 from 16.9 per cent in 1990, many direct-sale Internet sites were appearing. Levi's executives flirted with creating a site in 1994, but it wasn't until 1995 that the firm's first site was operational. Even then, the company was focused on giving customers a place to 'hang, chat, and read about graffiti art and South African street styles'. Feedback indicated that the site's capabilities frustrated customers, who expressed their desire to have an opportunity to buy jeans electronically. This interest troubled Levi personnel, who were concerned that such a site would offend its traditional retail outlet customers. These concerns may have surfaced because Levi did not launch its direct-sales strategy in collaboration with its retail outlets. Thus, while Lee jeans can be purchased at jcpenney.com and Calvin Klein jeans at macy.com, buying Levi's jeans from these retailers requires customers to visit 'bricks and mortar' retail stores. Although Levi Strauss's Web approach is generating acceptable sales numbers, it is not clear how the firm's traditional customer – retailers – will react. Affecting this reaction could be Levi's position that its e-commerce approach serves the public customer, not the retailer.

Sources: A. Ferguson, 1999, 'Time's up at Pacific Dunlop', *Business Review Weekly*, 1 February, pp. 28–31; A. Ferguson, 2000, 'Pacific Dunlop skids towards the parts yard', *Business Review Weekly*, 1 January, p. 36; J.. Durkie, 2000, 'Pacific Dunlop has to get moving', *Australian Financial Review*, 3 October, p. 44; D. Rees, 2000, 'Pacific Dunlop', *Shares*, September, p. 59; L. Himelstein and R. Siklos, 1999, 'The rise and fall of an Internet star', *Business Week*, 26 April, pp. 88–94; L. Kroll, 1998, 'Digital denim', *Forbes*, 28 December, pp. 102–3; N. Munk, 1999, 'How Levi's trashed a great American brand', *Fortune*, 12 April, pp. 83–90.

In recognition of strategic management's challenge, Andrew Grove, Intel's former CEO, observed that only paranoid companies survive and succeed. Intel is the number-one computer chip manufacturer in the world, with market capitalisation greater than all the top US vehicle manufacturers combined. Such firms know that current success does not guarantee future strategic competitiveness and above-average returns. In fact, in 1998, Intel lost ground to competitors. 'It's fighting battles on many fronts, including the popular sub-[US]$1,000 PC sector. Rather than cede this area to clone makers such as National Semiconductor, Intel plans to win back lost market share through the introduction of the Intel Celeron Processor.'[20] By mid-1999, Intel had regained a great deal of the share it had lost.

As this example indicates, Intel strives continuously to improve in order to remain competitive. For Intel and others that are competing in the 21st century's competitive landscape, Andrew Grove believes that a key challenge is to try to do the impossible – namely, to anticipate the unexpected.[21]

The 21st-century competitive landscape[22]

The fundamental nature of competition in many of the world's industries is changing.[23] The pace of this change is relentless and is increasing. Even determining the boundaries of an industry has become challenging. Consider, for example, how advances in interactive computer networks and telecommunications have blurred the definition of the television industry. The near future will find companies such as The Nine Network and Foxtel competing not only among themselves, but also with AT&T, Microsoft and Sony.

The blurring of boundaries is most obvious in petrol retailing and groceries. Woolworths, apart from selling some 30 000 grocery lines, can also handle petrol through the Petrol Plus chain which has petrol bowsers at some Woolworths stores. Woolworths also provides in-store banking, called Ezybanking, through a joint venture with the Commonwealth Bank. At the same time, it is becoming almost conventional for large petrol stations in Australia to put in major grocery lines and compete with the local convenience stores, making use of their late hours to gain market share.[24]

Still other characteristics of the 21st-century competitive landscape are noteworthy. Conventional sources of competitive advantage, such as economies of scale and huge advertising budgets, are not as effective in the 21st-century competitive landscape. Moreover, the traditional managerial mind-set cannot lead a firm to strategic competitiveness in the competitive landscape. In its place, managers must adopt a new mind-set; one that values flexibility, speed, innovation, integration and the challenges that evolve from constantly changing conditions. The conditions of the competitive landscape result in a perilous business world, one where the investments required to compete on a global scale are enormous and the consequences of failure are severe.[25]

Hyper-competition is a term that is often used to capture the realities of the 21st-century competitive landscape. (Mentioned briefly here, hyper-competitive environments are discussed further in Chapter 5.) According to Richard A. D'Aveni, hyper-competition results from the dynamics of strategic manoeuvring among global and innovative combatants. It is a condition of rapidly escalating competition based on price–quality positioning, competition to create new know-how and establish first-mover advantage, competition to protect or invade established product or geographic markets, and competition based on deep pockets and the creation of even deeper pocketed alliances.[26]

Several factors have created hyper-competitive environments and the 21st-century competitive landscape. The two primary drivers are the emergence of a global economy and technology, specifically rapid technological changes.

The global economy

> A global economy is one in which goods, services, people, skills and ideas move freely across geographic borders.

A **global economy** is one in which goods, services, people, skills and ideas move freely across geographic borders. Relatively unfettered by artificial constraints, such as tariffs, the global economy significantly expands and complicates a firm's competitive environment.[27]

Interesting opportunities and challenges are associated with the global economy's emergence. For example, Europe, instead of the United States, is now the world's largest single market. The European market, with 700 million potential customers, has a gross domestic product (GDP) of US$8 trillion, which is comparable to that of the United States.[28] In addition, by 2015, China's total GDP will be greater than Japan's, although its per capita output will be much lower.[29] In recent years, the Japanese economy has lagged behind that of the United States and some European countries. However, other Asian countries – in particular, Singapore and Hong Kong (now part of China) – have maintained their rankings. This is interesting, considering the severe Asian financial crisis of 1997.³⁰ Achieving improved competitiveness allows a country's citizens to have a higher standard of living. Some believe that entrepreneurial activity will continue to influence living standards during the 21st century. For example, a report describing European competitiveness concluded that 'it is only through the creation of more new businesses and more fast-growing businesses that Europe will create more new jobs and achieve higher levels of economic well-being for all of its citizens'. (We discuss the role of entrepreneurship further in Chapter 13.³¹)

A country's competitiveness is achieved through the accumulation of individual firms' strategic competitiveness in the global economy. Increasingly, to accomplish this, a firm must view the world as its marketplace. For example, US firm Procter & Gamble believes that it still has tremendous potential to grow internationally because, globally, the demand for household products is not as mature as it is in the United States. For shipbuilder Incat Australia, the demand for high-speed ferries worldwide has fuelled the company's growth. Incat vessels are now in service in the UK, Scandinavia and South America.³²

Although a commitment to viewing the world as a company's marketplace creates a sense of direction, it is not without risks. For example, Whirlpool Corporation, the world's largest manufacturer of major home appliances, intends to maintain its global leadership position. It has production facilities in 13 countries and marketing efforts in 140 nations.³³ Recently, Whirlpool bought the white goods business of Gentrade of South Africa. The acquisition provides Whirlpool with a sales and manufacturing base in that country. Whirlpool also has joint ventures with firms in various countries, including China, Taiwan and India. However, with the global financial crisis initiated in Asia and spreading to Latin America, sales declined. For example, sales decreased by about 25 per cent in Brazil in 1998. Furthermore, Whirlpool has been able to achieve only a 12 per cent market share in Europe, compared with its goal of 20 per cent, due to increased competition from firms such as Electrolux. Internet-ready products such as refrigerators and ovens may help the firm in its efforts to reach its goals in various world markets. A Web-savvy oven, offered initially in Europe, was introduced in the US market in 2000. Also introduced in the United States in 2000 was an Internet-ready refrigerator. Focusing on customer convenience, consumers can download a recipe from the Internet through a touch screen on the refrigerator and then automatically program the oven to cook the recipe.³⁴

The march of globalisation

Globalisation is the spread of economic innovations around the world and the political and cultural adjustments that accompany this diffusion. Globalisation encourages international integration, which has increased substantially during the last generation. In globalised markets and industries, financial capital might be obtained in one national market and used to buy raw materials in another. Manufacturing equipment bought from a third national market can be used to produce products that are sold in yet a fourth market. Thus, globalisation increases the range of opportunities for firms competing in the 21st-century competitive landscape.

For example, the US firm Wal-Mart is trying to achieve boundaryless retailing with global pricing, sourcing and logistics. Most of Wal-Mart's international investments have been in Canada and Mexico, in close proximity to the United States. However, recently the company moved into Argentina, Brazil, Indonesia and China. Supercentre stores in Buenos Aires sell as many as 15 000 items in a day, twice as many as in comparable US superstores. Wal-Mart plans to export its North American dominance to other regions of the world as well. For instance, it recently made a large acquisition of stores in Germany and Europe.³⁵ One of Wal-Mart's objectives is to offer lower-priced goods to the world's citizens.

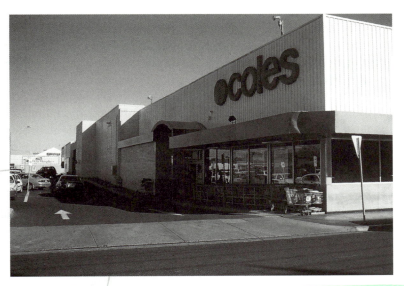

In comparison to the world giant Wal-Mart, does the Australian Coles Myer organisation match up in terms of size and buying power?

The internationalisation of markets and industries makes it increasingly difficult to think of some firms as domestic companies. For example, Daimler Benz, the parent company of Mercedes Benz, merged with Chrysler to create DaimlerChrysler. Moreover, even before these firms were integrated, Jürgen E. Schrempp, DaimlerChrysler CEO, tried to acquire cash-strapped Nissan Motor Co. The company needed better partnering arrangements in Asia. However, after the stock price declined, DaimlerChrysler's board decided that the deal was premature. DaimlerChrysler has now focused on getting the companies integrated around the world. In a similar move, Ford announced an acquisition of Volvo's car division. Ford now has six brands around the world: Ford, Lincoln, Mercury, Jaguar, Mazda and Aston Martin. It can use these brands to spread its economies of scale in the purchase and sourcing of components that make up 60 per cent of the value of a car.[36]

There are a number of other car companies that remain independent, such as Honda. However, Honda has become a target firm to be acquired.[37] Currently, Honda has a number of plants throughout the world. For instance, it produces in the United States over 70 per cent of the cars it sells in the US domestic market.

Most automobile firms should not be thought of as European, Japanese, Australian or American. Instead, they can be classified more accurately as global companies striving to achieve strategic competitiveness in the 21st-century competitive landscape. Some believe that because of its enormous economic benefits, globalisation will not be stopped. It has been predicted, for example, that genuine free trade in manufactured goods among the United States, Europe and Japan would add 5–10 per cent to the triad's annual economic output; free trade in the triad's service sector would boost aggregate output by another 15–20 per cent. Realising these potential gains in economic output requires a commitment from the industrialised nations to cooperatively stimulate the higher levels of trade necessary for global growth. Eliminating national laws that impede free trade is an important stimulus to increased trading among nations.[38]

Global competition has increased performance standards in many dimensions, including those of quality, cost, productivity, product introduction time, and smooth, flowing operations. Moreover, these standards are not static; they are exacting, requiring continuous improvement from a firm and its employees. As they accept the challenges posed by these increasing standards, companies improve their capabilities and individual workers sharpen their skills. Thus, in the 21st-century competitive landscape, strategic competitiveness will be earned only by those capable of meeting, if not exceeding, global standards. This challenge exists for all companies that develop cooperative relationships (such as joint ventures) in order to capitalise on international growth opportunities.[39]

The development of emerging and transitional economies also is changing the global competitive landscape and significantly increasing competition in global markets. The economic development of Asian countries outside of Japan is increasing the significance of Asian markets. Firms in the emerging economies of Asia, such as South Korea, however, are becoming major competitors in global industries. For instance, Samsung has become a market leader in the semiconductor industry, taking market share away from Japanese and American firms. With increasing globalisation and the spread of information technology, other countries are likely to develop their industrial bases as well. For instance, Taiwan's semiconductor industry has grown through firms such as United Microelectronics and Taiwan Semiconductor Manufacturing Co., which pursue a strategy of flexible contracting with other chip producers.[40] As this occurs, global markets will expand, but competition in those markets will also become more intense.

Firms such as Wal-Mart and Motorola are moving more boldly into international markets. In particular, each of these firms is making important investments in Asia. Of course, there are also Australian firms – such as Pratt Industries, Brambles and BHP – that have made investments in North America and Latin America. Thus, international investments come from many directions and are targeted for many different regions of the world. There are risks with these investments, however, as Burns Philp's sad fate in the US yeast market indicates. We discuss a number of them in Chapter 8. Some people refer to these risks as the 'liability of foreignness'.[41] Recent research suggests that firms are challenged in their early ventures into international markets and can have difficulties if they enter too many different or challenging markets. In other words, performance may suffer in early efforts to globalise until the skills required to manage it are developed.[42] Moreover, performance may suffer with substantial amounts of globalisation. In this instance, firms may over-diversify internationally beyond their ability to manage the diversified operations that have been created.[43] The outcome can sometimes be quite painful to these firms.[44] Thus, entry into international markets, even for firms with substantial experience in such markets, requires careful planning and selection of the appropriate markets to enter and the most effective strategies to operate successfully in those markets.

Global markets are attractive strategic options for some companies, but they are not the only source of strategic competitiveness. In fact, for most companies – even for those capable of competing successfully in global markets – it is critical to remain committed to the domestic market.[45] In the 21st-century competitive landscape, firms are challenged to develop the optimal level of globalisation, a level that results in appropriate concentrations on a company's domestic and global operations.

In many instances, strategically competitive companies are those that have learned how to apply competitive insights gained locally (or domestically) on a global scale.[46] These companies do not impose homogeneous solutions in a pluralistic world. Instead, they nourish local insights so that they can modify and apply them appropriately in different regions around the world. Moreover, they are sensitive to globalisation's potential effects. For example, a report issued by the World Health Organization and the International Labor Organization suggests that the 'continuing shift of industrial production to low-cost sites in developing countries where worker protection is lower is likely to increase the global incidence of occupational disease and injury'.[47] Firms with strong commitments to global success evaluate these possible outcomes in making their strategic choices. One interesting feature of globalising firms is impact on employment. In 2000, the world's largest 1 000 corporations controlled 14.2 per cent of global revenue but were responsible for only 2 per cent of employment.[48]

Technology and technological changes

There are three categories of trends and conditions through which technology is significantly altering the nature of competition.

Increasing rate of technological change and diffusion

Both the rate of change of technology and the speed at which new technologies become available and are used have increased substantially over the last 15 to 20 years. *Perpetual innovation* is a term used to describe how rapidly and consistently new, information-intensive technologies replace older ones. The shorter product life cycles resulting from these rapid diffusions of new technologies place a competitive premium on being able to introduce new goods and services quickly into the marketplace. In fact, when products become somewhat indistinguishable because of the widespread and rapid diffusion of technologies, speed to market may be the only source of competitive advantage (see Chapter 5).[49]

There are other indicators of rapid technology diffusion. Some evidence suggests that after only 12 to 18 months, companies likely will have gathered information about their competitors' research and development and product decisions.[50] In the global economy, any idea that works can sometimes be imitated in a matter of a few days. Consider, for example, that approximately 75 per cent of the product-life gross margins for a typical PC are earned within the first 90 days of sales.[51]

Once a source of competitive advantage, today's rate of technological diffusion stifles the protection firms possessed previously through their patents. Today, patents are thought by many to be an effective way of protecting proprietary technology only in the pharmaceutical and chemical industries. Indeed, many firms competing in the electronics industry often do not apply for patents to prevent competitors from gaining access to the technological knowledge included in the patent application!

The information age

Dramatic changes in information technology have occurred in recent years. Personal computers, cellular (mobile) phones, artificial intelligence, virtual reality and massive databases (for example, Lexis/Nexis) are a few examples of how information is used differently as a result of technological developments. Intel's former CEO Andrew Grove believes that electronic mail (e-mail) systems are the first manifestation of a revolution in the flow and management of information in companies throughout the world. In Grove's view, 'The informed use of e-mail has two simple but startling implications: It turns days into minutes, and allows each person to reach hundreds of co-workers with the same effort it takes to reach just one.'[52] An important outcome of these changes is that the ability to access and use information effectively has become an important source of competitive advantage in virtually all industries.

Companies are now being wired to build electronic networks linking them to customers, employees, vendors and suppliers. IBM has made this a major thrust in its drive to reorient and revive its business. These networks are often referred to as e-businesses by IBM and others.[53] E-business is big business. For example, Internet trade was predicted to reach US$105 billion by 2000, up from only US$7.8 billion in 1997. It is even predicted that e-business will eventually represent 75–80 per cent of the US gross domestic product. This means that most transactions will be accomplished electronically. It is interesting to note that e-commerce between businesses, about US$43 billion in 1998, is five times larger than consumer e-business. By 2003, Forrester Research, Inc. estimates that it will balloon to US$1.3 trillion.[54]

As the Opening Case suggests, e-businesses have a different form of competition and require a different leadership approach. Both the pace of change in information technology and its diffusion will continue to increase. It is predicted, for example, that the number of personal computers in use will grow from over 150 million today to 278 million in 2010. The declining costs of information technologies and the increased accessibility to them are also evident in the 21st-century competitive landscape. The global proliferation of relatively inexpensive computing power and its linkage on a global scale via computer networks combine to increase the speed and diffusion of information technologies. Thus, the competitive potential of information technologies is now available to companies throughout the world, rather than only to large firms in Europe, Japan and North America. This provides major opportunities for small to medium-sized firms in Australia's regional areas – as long as they are able to make use of the technologies and stay open to new ideas.

Strategic Focus Corporate

Compaq is flailing against Internet technological trends

In January 1998, Compaq Computer Corporation acquired Digital Equipment Corporation (DEC). This was ostensibly a defining moment for Compaq, showing that it was moving into a different league of competitors; ones offering larger machines and services as well as PCs. Eckhard Pfeiffer, then Compaq's CEO, was quoted as saying, 'We want to do it all, and we want to do it now.' However, a little over a year later, on 18 April 1999, Compaq chairman Benjamin M. Rosen, although praising Pfeiffer, announced through a press release that Pfeiffer was being asked to step down.

Pfeiffer had brought the company back from the precipice after Rod Canion, Compaq's founder, was deposed in 1991. Pfeiffer built the company from US$3.3 billion to over US$40 billion in sales since his 1991 ascent to the CEO position. In the process, Compaq became number one in overall PC sales in August 1995. How did Pfeiffer's precipitous fall at Compaq happen? What went wrong?

In 1996, Compaq bought Tandem Computers, a minicomputer manufacturer focused on workstations. As already mentioned, in January 1998, it also purchased DEC, for US$8.4 billion. The latter transaction was to help Compaq move into services, although DEC's business in workstations was declining. Thus, Compaq was moving into the territory of formidable competitors such as Sun Microsystems and IBM. IBM is excellent in services, but Compaq executives felt that acquiring DEC would help develop Compaq's services business in a growing high-tech world where services are the drivers that often foster sales in hardware and software. However, in so doing, Compaq executives lost focus on their main business, PCs, and were unable to execute Web-based direct selling as effectively as their main competitor, Dell Computer Corporation.

Compaq announced in February 1994 that by 1996 it would be implementing a build-to-order strategy that was similar to Dell's. At the time of the announcement, 55 per cent of Compaq's PC sales were generated through direct and Web-based sales efforts. When Compaq announced a more significant move towards Internet sales, friction surfaced between the firm and its numerous resellers. This friction became especially pronounced when Compaq decided to sell its new Prosignia model exclusively on the Web. This decision was reversed in March

1999, following the initial announcement in November 1998. The reversal was due to an inventory buildup and an 8 per cent drop in Compaq's stock price in 1998. Compaq subsequently announced that it would downsize the number of its resellers to four dominant distributors from approximately 20 major ones. This strategic decision was intended to provide Compaq with more control over its resellers and allow the company to concentrate on its strategy of direct selling.

To add to Compaq's problems, the main strategist in charge of its service business, John Rando, resigned three weeks after Pfeiffer's forced departure. Compaq's service business ranked third behind IBM and EDS, just ahead of Hewlett-Packard (HP) and Andersen Consulting, when Compaq acquired DEC in early 1998. Rando's departure created still additional uncertainty about the shape of Compaq's future.

Before Rando's replacement was chosen, many high-tech customers changed from DEC and Tandem technology-based workstations to systems from formidable competitors such as HP, IBM and Sun Microsystems.

It is not unusual for an acquiring firm to encounter problems when it tries to integrate high-tech acquisitions into its operations. Silicon Graphics had trouble with its acquisition of Cray Research, while AT&T's acquisition of NCR and HP's acquisition of Apollo Computers never resulted in the positive outcomes executives expected when they decided to buy these other companies. Thus, as an acquirer, Compaq may be learning what some others in this industry (such as Silicon Graphics, AT&T and HP) learned previously: it is difficult to compete successfully on several major fronts in an industry in which change is constant and dynamic.

Sources: P. Burrows, I. Sager and M. Moeller, 1999, 'Can Compaq catch up?', *Business Week*, 3 May, pp. 162–6; L. Kehoe, 1999, 'Compaq at the crossroads after Pfeiffer's departure', *Financial Times*, 20 April, p. 17; G. McWilliams, 1999, 'Head of Compaq services unit resigns in third recent high-level departure', *Wall Street Journal Interactive Edition*, 12 May, www.interactive.wsj.com; G. McWilliams and J. S. Lublin, 1999, 'Compaq Computer's board removes Chief Executive Officer Eckhard Pfeiffer', *Wall Street Journal Interactive Edition*, 19 April, www.interactive.wsj.com; M. R. Zimmerman, 1999, 'Compaq and the road not taken', *PCWeek Online*, 3 May, www.zdnet.com; J. G. Auerbach and W. M. Bulkeley, 1998, 'Compaq seeks Digital's prized asset: its world-famous service business', *Wall Street Journal Interactive Edition*, 28 January, www.interactive.wsj.com; *Fortune*, 1998, 'Where Compaq went wrong', 23 April, www.fortune.com.

Combined, the Internet and the World Wide Web create an infrastructure that allows the delivery of information to computers in any location. Access to significant quantities of relatively inexpensive information yields strategic opportunities for a range of industries and companies. Retailers, for example, use the Internet to provide abundant shopping privileges to customers in multiple locations. To begin the competitive thrust into e-commerce, Nordstrom Inc. formed a partnership with venture capital firms.[55] Thus, as the Opening Case indicates, the power of this means of information access and application results in an almost astonishing array of strategic implications and possibilities.

Increasing knowledge intensity

Knowledge (information, intelligence and expertise) is the basis of technology and its application. In the 21st-century competitive landscape, knowledge is a critical organisational resource and is increasingly a valuable source of competitive advantage. Because of this, many companies now strive to transmute the accumulated knowledge of individual employees into a corporate asset. Some argue that the value of intangible assets, including knowledge, is growing as a proportion of total shareholder value.[56] The probability of achieving strategic competitiveness in the 21st-century competitive landscape is enhanced for the firm that realises that its survival depends on the ability to capture intelligence, transform it into usable knowledge and diffuse it rapidly throughout the company.[57] Firms that accept this challenge shift their focus from merely *obtaining* the information to *exploiting* the information to gain a competitive advantage over rival firms.[58]

Strategic flexibility is a set of capabilities firms use to respond to various demands and opportunities that are a part of dynamic and uncertain competitive environments.

Our discussion of conditions in the 21st-century competitive landscape shows that firms must be able to adapt quickly to achieve strategic competitiveness and earn above-average returns. The term *strategic flexibility* describes a firm's ability to do this. **Strategic flexibility is a set of capabilities firms use to respond to various demands and opportunities that are a part of dynamic and uncertain competitive environments.**[59] Firms should develop strategic flexibility in all areas of their operations. Such capabilities in terms of manufacturing allow firms to 'switch gears – from, for example, rapid product development to low cost – relatively quickly and with minimum resources'.[60] As suggested in the Strategic Focus, one of Compaq's problems in the late 1990s was a lack of strategic flexibility.[61]

To achieve strategic flexibility, many firms have to develop organisational slack. Slack resources allow the firm some flexibility to respond to environmental changes.[62] When the changes required are large, firms may have to undergo strategic reorientations. Such reorientations can drastically change a firm's competitive strategy.[63] Strategic reorientations are often the result of a firm's poor performance. For example, when a firm earns negative returns, its stakeholders (discussed later in this chapter) are likely to place pressure on the top executives to make major changes.[64] To be strategically flexible on a continuing basis, a firm has to develop the capacity to learn. The learning continuously provides the firm with new and current sets of skills. This allows the firm to adapt to its environment as it encounters changes.[65] As illustrated in the Strategic Focus, Compaq has had difficulties adjusting to the on-line selling approach pioneered by Dell. Although Compaq has maintained strategic flexibility in the past, its acquisition of Digital Equipment Corporation has created some difficult adjustment challenges. In addition, the firm has not adapted quickly in other strategic areas.

Next, we describe two models used by firms to generate the strategic inputs needed to successfully formulate and implement strategies and to maintain strategic flexibility in the process of doing so.

The I/O model of above-average returns

From the 1960s to the 1980s, the external environment was thought to be the *primary* determinant of strategies firms selected to be successful.[66] The industrial organisation (I/O) model explains the dominant influence of the external environment on firms' strategic actions. The model specifies that the industry in which a firm chooses to compete has a stronger influence on the firm's performance than do the choices managers make inside their organisations.[67] The firm's performance is believed to be determined primarily by a range of an industry's properties, including economies of scale, barriers to market entry, diversification, product differentiation and the degree of concentration of firms in the industry.[68] (These industry characteristics are examined in Chapter 2.)

Grounded in economics, the I/O model has four underlying assumptions. First, the external environment is assumed to impose pressures and constraints which determine the strategies that would result in above-average returns. Second, most firms competing within a particular industry or within a certain segment of an industry are assumed to control similar strategically relevant resources and to pursue similar strategies in light of those resources. The I/O model's third assumption is that resources used to implement strategies are highly mobile across firms. Because of resource mobility, any resource differences that might develop between firms will be short-lived. Fourth, organisational decision makers are assumed to be rational and committed to acting in the firm's best interests, as shown by their profit-maximising behaviours.[69]

The I/O model challenges firms to locate the most attractive industry in which to compete. Because most firms are assumed to have similar strategically relevant resources that are mobile across companies, competitiveness generally can be increased only when the firms find the industry with the highest profit potential and learn how to use their resources to implement the strategy required by the structural characteristics in that industry. The *five forces model of competition* is an analytical tool used to help firms with this task. The model (explained in detail in Chapter 2) encompasses many variables and tries to capture the complexity of competition.[70]

The five forces model suggests that an industry's profitability (that is, its rate of return on invested capital relative to its cost of capital) is a function of interactions among five forces (suppliers, buyers, competitive rivalry among firms currently in the industry, product substitutes and potential entrants to the industry).[71] Using this tool, a firm is challenged to understand an industry's profit potential and the strategy that should be implemented to establish a defensible competitive position, given the industry's structural characteristics. Typically, the model suggests that firms can earn above-average returns by manufacturing standardised products or producing standardised services at costs below those of competitors (a cost–leadership strategy) or differentiated products for which customers are willing to pay a price premium (a differentiation strategy). Cost–leadership and differentiation strategies are described fully in Chapter 4.

As shown in Figure 1.2, the I/O model suggests that above-average returns are earned when firms implement the strategy dictated by the characteristics of the general, industry and competitor environments. Companies that develop or acquire the internal skills needed to implement strategies required by the external environment are likely to succeed, while those that do not are likely to fail. Hence, above-average returns are determined by external characteristics rather than by the firm's unique internal resources and capabilities.

Figure 1.2 | The I/O model of superior returns

1. Study the external environment, especially the industry environment.

The external environment
- The general environment
- The industry environment
- The competitor environment

2. Locate an industry with high potential for above-average returns.

An attractive industry
An industry whose structural characteristics suggest above-average returns

3. Identify the strategy called for by the attractive industry to earn above-average returns.

Strategy formulation
Selection of a strategy linked with above-average returns in a particular industry

4. Develop or acquire assets and skills needed to implement the strategy.

Assets and skills
Assets and skills required to implement a chosen strategy

5. Use the firm's strengths (its developed or acquired assets and skills) to implement the strategy.

Strategy implementation
Selection of strategic actions linked with effective implementation of the chosen strategy

Superior returns
Earning of above-average returns

Recent research provides support for the I/O model. The research showed that approximately 20 per cent of a firm's profitability was explained by the industry. In other words, 20 per cent of a firm's profitability is determined by the industry(ies) in which it chooses to operate. This research also showed, however, that 36 per cent of the variance in profitability could be attributed to the firm's characteristics and actions.[72] The results of the research suggest that both the environment and the firm's characteristics play a role in determining the firm's specific level of profitability. Thus, there is likely a reciprocal relationship between the environment and the firm's strategy, and this interrelationship affects the firm's performance.[73]

As the research results suggest, successful competition in the 21st-century competitive landscape mandates that a firm build a unique set of resources and capabilities. This should be done, however, within the framework of the dynamics of the industry (or industries) in which a firm competes. In that context, a firm is viewed as a bundle of market activities and of resources. Market activities are understood through the application of the I/O model. The development and effective use of a firm's resources, capabilities and competencies is understood through the application of the resource-based model. Through an effective combination of results gained by using both the I/O and the resource-based model, firms dramatically increase the probability of achieving strategic competitiveness and earning above-average returns.

The resource-based model of above-average returns

The resource-based model assumes that each organisation is a collection of unique resources and capabilities that provides the basis for its strategy and that is the primary source of its returns. In the 21st-century competitive landscape, this model argues that a firm is a collection of evolving capabilities that is managed dynamically in pursuit of above-average returns.[74] Thus, according to the model, differences in firms' performances across time are driven primarily by their unique resources and capabilities rather than by an industry's structural characteristics. This model also assumes that over time, a firm acquires different resources and develops unique capabilities. Therefore, not all firms competing within a particular industry possess the same strategically relevant resources and capabilities. Another assumption of the model is that resources may not be highly mobile across firms. The differences in resources form the basis of competitive advantage.

Resources are inputs into a firm's production process, such as capital equipment, the skills of individual employees, patents, finances and talented managers. In general, a firm's resources can be classified into three categories: physical, human and organisational capital.[75] Described fully in Chapter 3, resources are either tangible or intangible in nature. With increasing effectiveness, the set of resources available to the firm tends to become larger.[76]

Individual resources alone may not yield a competitive advantage. For example, a sophisticated piece of manufacturing equipment may become a strategically relevant resource only when its use is integrated effectively with other aspects of a firm's operations (such as marketing and the work of employees). In general, it is through the combination and integration of sets of resources that competitive advantages are formed. A **capability** is the capacity for a set of resources to integratively perform a task or an activity. Through continued use, capabilities become stronger and more difficult for competitors to understand and imitate. As a source of competitive advantage, a capability 'should be neither so simple that it is highly imitable, nor so complex that it defies internal steering and control'.[77]

Resources are inputs into a firm's production process, such as capital equipment, the skills of individual employees, patents, finance and talented managers.

A **capability** is the capacity for a set of resources to integratively perform a task or an activity.

Amazon.com has taken the retail book market by storm. It was the first firm to sell books on the Internet. Because of this, Amazon.com has developed important capabilities for marketing and distributing books on-line. The firm has shown that a large inventory and beautiful facilities are not necessary to sell books. However, Amazon.com's capabilities may be imitable. In fact, the large and powerful Barnes & Noble sought to do just that when it opened its own on-line bookshop in 1997. Although developing web pages and taking orders on-line are copied easily, Amazon.com had a 20-month lead, which, in Internet time, is significant. Barnes & Noble's strategic action could have had a significantly negative effect on Amazon.com, but the early evidence does not indicate this to be the case. In fact, the 1998 Christmas season was strong for Amazon.com: the firm realised one million new on-line customers, while Barnes & Noble achieved only 320 000. Accordingly, the firm's stock price skyrocketed, while Barnes & Noble's decreased. However, it remains to be seen whether the Internet resources of Amazon.com will continue to enjoy first-mover advantages against the bricks and mortar of Barnes & Noble. (See Chapter 5 for a full discussion of first-mover advantages.) Although Amazon.com has won round one, the competitive battle will continue because Barnes & Noble has the resources to remain engaged in substantial competition.[78]

The resource-based model of superior returns is shown in Figure 1.3. In contrast to the I/O model, the resource-based view is grounded in the perspective that a firm's internal environment, in terms of its resources and capabilities, is more critical to the determination of strategic actions than is the external environment. Instead of focusing on the accumulation of resources necessary to implement the strategy dictated by conditions and constraints in the external environment (I/O model), the resource-based view suggests that a firm's unique resources and capabilities provide the basis for a strategy. The strategy chosen should allow the firm to best exploit its core competencies relative to opportunities in the external environment.

Figure 1.3 | The resource-based model of superior returns

1. Identify the firm's resources. Study its strengths and weaknesses compared with those of competitors.

   Resources
   Inputs into a firm's production process

2. Determine the firm's capabilities. What do the capabilities allow the firm to do better than its competitors?

   Capability
   Capacity of an integrated set of resources to integratively perform a task or activity

3. Determine the potential of the firm's resources and capabilities in terms of a competitive advantage.

   Competitive advantage
   Ability of a firm to outperform its rivals

4. Locate an attractive industry.

   An attractive industry
   An industry with opportunities that can be exploited by the firm's resources and capabilities

5. Select a strategy that best allows the firm to utilise its resources and capabilities relative to opportunities in the external environment.

   Strategy formulation and implementation
   Strategic actions taken to earn above-average returns

   Superior returns
   Earning of above-average returns

Not all of a firm's resources and capabilities have the potential to be the basis for competitive advantage. This potential is realised when resources and capabilities are valuable, rare, costly to imitate and non-substitutable.[79] Resources are *valuable* when they allow a firm to take advantage of opportunities or to neutralise threats in its external environment; they are *rare* when possessed by few, if any, current and potential competitors; they are *costly to imitate* when other firms either cannot obtain them or are at a cost disadvantage in obtaining them compared with the firm that already possesses them; and they are *non-substitutable* when they have no structural equivalents.

When these four criteria are met, resources and capabilities become core competencies. **Core competencies** are resources and capabilities that serve as a source of competitive advantage for a firm over its rivals. Often related to a firm's functional skills (for example, the marketing function is a core competence at Philip Morris, the diversified tobacco-based corporation which also owns Kraft Foods, producer of the Australian icon, Vegemite), core competencies, when developed, nurtured and applied throughout a firm, may result in strategic competitiveness. Managerial competencies are important in most firms. For example, they have been shown to be critically important to successful entry into foreign markets.[80] Such competencies may include the capability to effectively organise and govern complex and diverse operations, and to create and communicate a strategic vision.[81] Another set of important competencies is product-related. Included among these competencies is the capability to develop innovative new products and to reengineer existing products to satisfy changing consumer tastes.[82] Competencies must also be under continuous development to keep them up to date. This requires a systematic program for updating old skills and learning new ones.[83] Dynamic core competencies are especially important in rapidly changing environments, such as those that exist in high-technology industries.[84] Thus, the resource-based model argues that core competencies are the basis for a firm's competitive advantage, its strategic competitiveness and its ability to earn above-average returns.

> **Core competencies** are resources and capabilities that serve as a source of competitive advantage for a firm over its rivals.

Strategic intent and strategic mission

Resulting from analyses of a firm's internal and external environments is the information required to form a strategic intent and develop a strategic mission (see Figure 1.1). Both intent and mission are linked with strategic competitiveness.

Strategic intent

Strategic intent is the leveraging of a firm's internal resources, capabilities and core competencies to accomplish the firm's goals in the competitive environment.[85] Concerned with winning competitive battles and obtaining global leadership, strategic intent implies a significant stretch of an organisation's resources, capabilities and core competencies. When established effectively, a strategic intent can cause people to perform in ways they never imagined possible.[86] Strategic intent exists when all employees and levels of a firm are committed to the pursuit of a specific (and significant) performance criterion. Some argue that strategic intent provides employees with the only goal worthy of personal effort and commitment: to unseat the best or remain the best, worldwide.[87] Strategic intent has been formed effectively when people believe fervently in their product and industry and when they are focused totally on their firm's ability to outperform its competitors.[88]

> **Strategic intent** is the leveraging of a firm's internal resources, capabilities and core competencies to accomplish the firm's goals in the competitive environment.

The next few examples are expressions of strategic intent. Phillips Petroleum Company seeks 'to be the top performer in everything' the company does. Intel intends to become the premier building-block supplier to the computer industry. Microsoft believes that its 'holy grail' is to be the Yellow Pages for an electronic marketplace of on-line information systems. Canon desires to 'beat Xerox', and Honda strives to become a second Ford (a company it identified as a pioneer in the automobile industry). A new Australian biotechnology company, GroPep, develops novel factors to increase cell growth and manufactures and commercialises them. Its strategic intent is to establish a world reputation in its targeted area of biotechnology.

But it is not enough for a firm only to know its own strategic intent: to perform well demands that the firm also identify its competitors' strategic intent. Only when the intentions of others are understood can a firm become aware of the resolve, stamina and inventiveness (traits linked with effective strategic intents) of those competitors.[89] A company's success may be grounded in a keen and deep understanding of the strategic intent of customers, suppliers, partners and competitors.[90] But more is needed: a mechanism that catalyses intent into action.[91] An organisation must be able to perform. BHP's recent efforts to change its organisation culture and organisation structure provide an excellent example of a major corporation reshaping itself so that it can perform better.[92]

Strategic mission

As the preceding discussion shows, strategic intent is internally focused. It is concerned with identifying the resources, capabilities and core competencies on which a firm can base its strategic actions. Strategic intent reflects what a firm is capable of doing as a result of its core competencies and the unique ways they can be used to exploit a competitive advantage.

> The **strategic mission** is a statement of a firm's unique purpose and the scope of its operations in product and market terms.

Strategic mission flows from strategic intent. Externally focused, the **strategic mission** is a statement of a firm's unique purpose and the scope of its operations in product and market terms.[93] A strategic mission provides general descriptions of the products a firm intends to produce and the markets it will serve using its internally based core competencies.

An effective strategic mission establishes a firm's individuality and is exciting, inspiring and relevant to all stakeholders.[94] Together, strategic intent and strategic mission yield the insights required to formulate and implement the firm's strategies.

Basing their decisions partially on a firm's strategic intent and mission, top executives develop a *strategic orientation* – a predisposition to adopt a certain strategy or strategies over others.[95] Strategic orientation is also affected by the national culture in an executive's home country and the institutional environment where the firm's operations are located.[96]

When a firm is strategically competitive and earning above-average returns, it has the capacity to satisfy its stakeholders' interests. The stakeholder groups a firm serves are examined next.

Stakeholders

An organisation is a system of primary stakeholder groups with whom it establishes and manages relationships.[97] **Stakeholders** are the individuals and groups who can affect, and are affected by, the strategic outcomes achieved and who have enforceable claims on a firm's performance.⁹⁸ Claims against an organisation's performance are enforced through a stakeholder's ability to withhold participation essential to a firm's survival, competitiveness and profitability.⁹⁹ Stakeholders continue to support an organisation when its performance meets or exceeds their expectations.

Stakeholders are the individuals and groups who can affect, and are affected by, the strategic outcomes achieved and who have enforceable claims on a firm's performance.

Shareholders, like those shown here at a BHP shareholder meeting, have invested capital in the firm and expect at least an average return on their investments. However, short-term enhancement of shareholders' wealth can have a negative effect on a firm's future.

Thus, organisations have dependency relationships with their stakeholders. Firms, however, are not equally dependent on all stakeholders at all times; as a consequence, not every stakeholder has the same level of influence. The more critical and valued a stakeholder's participation is, the greater a firm's dependency on it. Greater dependence, in turn, results in more potential influence for the stakeholder over a firm's commitments, decisions and actions. In one sense, the challenge strategists face is to either accommodate or find ways to insulate the organisation from the demands of stakeholders controlling critical resources.¹⁰⁰

Classification of stakeholders

The parties involved with a firm's operations can be separated into three groups.¹⁰¹ As shown in Figure 1.4, these groups are the *capital market stakeholders* (shareholders and the major suppliers of a firm's capital), the *product market stakeholders* (the firm's primary customers, suppliers, host communities and unions representing the workforce), and the *organisational stakeholders* (all of a firm's employees, including both non-managerial and managerial personnel).

Each stakeholder group expects those making strategic decisions in a firm to provide the leadership through which its valued objectives will be accomplished.¹⁰² But these groups' objectives often differ from one another, sometimes placing managers in situations where trade-offs have to be made.

Grounded in laws governing private property and private enterprise, the most obvious stakeholders, at least in firms operating in OECD countries, are *shareholders* – those who have invested capital in a firm in the expectation of earning at least an average return on their investments. Shareholders want the return on their investment (and, hence, their wealth) to be maximised. This often can be accomplished at the expense of

Figure 1.4 | The three stakeholder groups

investing in a firm's future. Gains achieved by reducing investment in research and development, for example, could be returned to shareholders (thereby increasing the short-term return on their investments). However, a short-term enhancement of shareholders' wealth can negatively affect the firm's future competitive ability. Sophisticated shareholders, with diversified portfolios, may sell their interests if a firm fails to invest in its future. Those making strategic decisions are responsible for a firm's survival in both the short and the long term. Accordingly, it is in the interests of neither the organisational stakeholders nor the product market stakeholders for investments in the company to be unduly minimised.

In contrast to shareholders, customers prefer that investors receive a minimum return on their investments. In that way, customers could have their interests maximised when the quality and reliability of a firm's products are improved, but without a price increase. High returns to customers might come at the expense of lower returns negotiated with capital market shareholders.

Because of potential conflicts, each firm is challenged to manage its stakeholders. First, a firm must carefully identify all-important stakeholders. Second, it must prioritise them in case it cannot satisfy all of them. In doing this, power is the most critical criterion. Other criteria might include the urgency of satisfying each particular stakeholder and the degree of importance to the firm.[103] When the firm earns above-average returns, this challenge is lessened substantially. With the capability and flexibility provided by above-average returns, a firm can more easily satisfy all stakeholders simultaneously.

When earning only average returns, however, a firm may find the management of stakeholders to be more difficult. In these situations, trade-offs must be made. With average returns, the firm is unable to maximise the interests of all stakeholders. The objective then becomes one of at least minimally satisfying each stakeholder. Trade-off decisions are made in light of how dependent the firm is on the support of the stakeholder groups. An example of how stakeholders can demand satisfaction of their claims on a firm's performance is provided in the next subsection. A firm earning below-average returns does not have the capacity to minimally satisfy all stakeholders. The managerial challenge in this case is to make trade-offs that minimise the amount of support lost from stakeholders.

Societal values influence the general weightings allocated among the three stakeholder groups. Although all three groups are served by firms in at least the major industrialised nations, the priorities in their service vary somewhat because of cultural differences. These differences are shown in the following commentary:

> In America [and Australia] … shareholders have a comparatively big say in the running of the enterprises they own; workers … have much less influence. In many European countries, shareholders have less say and workers more … In Japan … managers have been left alone to run their companies as they see fit – namely for the benefit of employees and of allied companies, as much as for shareholders.[104]

> A **global mind-set** is the capacity to appreciate the beliefs, values, behaviours and business practices of individuals and organisations from a variety of regions and cultures.

Thus, it is important that those responsible for managing stakeholder relationships in a country outside their native land use a global mind-set. A **global mind-set** is the 'capacity to appreciate the beliefs, values, behaviors, and business practices of individuals and organizations from a variety of regions and cultures'.[105] The use of a global mind-set allows managers to better understand the realities and preferences that are a part of the world region and culture in which they are working. Thus, thinking globally means 'taking the best [that] other cultures have to offer and blending that into a third culture'.[106]

In the next three subsections, additional information is presented about the stakeholder groups that firms manage.

Capital market stakeholders

Both shareholders and lenders expect a firm to preserve and enhance the wealth they have entrusted to it. The returns expected are commensurate with the degree of risk accepted with those investments (that is, lower returns are expected with low-risk investments, and higher returns are expected with high-risk investments).

If lenders become dissatisfied, they can impose stricter covenants on subsequent borrowing of capital. Shareholders can reflect their dissatisfaction through several means, including selling their shares. When a firm is aware of potential or actual dissatisfactions among capital market stakeholders, it may respond to their concerns. The firm's response to dissatisfied stakeholders is affected by the nature of its dependency relationship with them (which, as noted earlier, is also influenced by a society's values). The greater and more significant the dependency relationship is, the more direct and significant the firm's response becomes.

The power of capital market shareholders has become more obvious in Australia in recent time. The Australian Shareholders Association (ASA) has become active; for example, they ran a campaign against Pacific Dunlop chairman John Ralph in 2000. Major institutional shareholders have also flexed their muscles. At the October 2000 AGM of News Corporation, a proposal to grant a considerable quantity of options to some senior News Corp. executives was passed with 392.7 million votes for and 253.4 million against (the millions reflect number of shares). This was a relatively close vote compared to previous exercises of News Corp. executive power and reflected a strong feeling among investors that executive remuneration was too loosely controlled.[107] These issues are discussed in more depth in Chapter 10.

Product market stakeholders

Initial thoughts about customers, suppliers, host communities and unions representing workers might suggest little commonality among these parties' interests. However, close inspection indicates that all four groups can benefit as firms engage in competitive battles. For example, depending on product and industry characteristics, marketplace competition may result in lower product prices being charged to a firm's customers and higher prices paid to its suppliers. (The firm might be willing to pay higher supplier prices to ensure delivery of the types of goods and services that are linked with its competitive success.)

As is noted in Chapter 4, customers, as stakeholders, demand reliable products at the lowest possible prices. Suppliers seek loyal customers who are willing to pay the highest sustainable prices for the goods and services they receive. Host communities want companies willing to be long-term employers and providers of tax revenues, without placing excessive demands on public support services. Union officials are interested in secure jobs, under highly desirable working conditions, for the employees they represent. Thus, product market stakeholders are generally satisfied when a firm's profit margin yields the lowest acceptable return to capital market stakeholders (that is, the lowest return lenders and shareholders will accept and still retain their interests in the firm).

All product market stakeholders are important in a competitive business environment. However, in many firms, customers are being emphasised. Dennis Eck, CEO of Coles Myer, is known for his position that satisfied customers are the only source of job security for the firm's organisational stakeholders. Although a firm's boundaries can be redrawn through the power of capital market stakeholders, the ultimate test of performance is customer satisfaction. The relationship between satisfaction of customers' needs and strategic competitiveness is examined in Chapter 4.

Organisational stakeholders

Organisational employees expect the firm to provide a dynamic, stimulating and rewarding working environment. As stakeholders, employees are usually satisfied working for a company that is growing and is actively developing their skills, especially those required to be effective team members and to meet or exceed global work standards. Workers who learn how to productively use their rapidly developing knowledge are thought to be critical to organisational success. In a collective sense, the education and skills of a nation's workforce may be its dominant competitive weapon in a global economy.[108]

In the next section, we describe the people responsible for the design and execution of strategic management processes. These individuals are variously named, including top-level managers, executives, strategists, the top management team and general managers. Throughout this book, these names are used interchangeably. But, in each case, the name is used to describe the work of persons responsible for designing and implementing a successful strategic management process.

As is discussed in Chapter 12, top-level managers can be a source of competitive advantage. The decisions and actions these people make to combine resources to create capabilities often result in a competitive advantage. In fact, it may be that those ranked by *Business Week* as the world's top business leaders (see Table 1.2) are individually a source of competitive advantage to their firms.

Table 1.2 | Business Week's 25 top managers of the year, 1999

Name	Company	Strategic accomplishment
Minoru Arakawa	Nintendo America	Scored huge hit by bringing Pokemon to the US over objections of co-workers and negative market research
Bernard Arnault	LVMH	From just 23 in October 1998, LVMH's US shares have vaulted 280 per cent, to about 87
Arthur Blank	Home Depot	Profits should jump 46 per cent, to US$2.3 billion for fiscal year 1999. Sales are expected to grow 25 per cent, to US$38 billion
Peter Bijur	Texaco	After his company was labelled racist, attracted minorities to key jobs, including treasurer Ira Hall, a former IBM executive
Gordon Binder	Amgen	Boosted stock price by around 100 per cent last year, to about US$54
Steve Case	America Online	Deals to broaden AOL's availability and services will help boost income 102 per cent this fiscal year, to US$800 million
John Chambers	Cisco Systems	Broadened Cisco into strategic businesses such as software, consulting and fibre-optic communications
Jim Curvey	Fidelity Investments	Reduced internal conflicts and spurred growth through management changes
Thierry Desmarest	Totalfina	Acquired rival French oil company ELF Aquitaine for US$44 billion. Shares up about 35 per cent in 1999, as profits expected to grow 20 per cent, to US$3.1 billion
Bernie Ebbers	MCI WorldCom	Turned towards more profitable data, Internet and international operations
Tom Engibous	Texas Instruments	Jump-started growth by focusing on key digital signal processing chip market
Chris Gent	Vodafone Airtouch	Shares have skyrocketed 243 per cent, to around US$48, in two years
Irwin Jacobs	Qualcomm	Developed digital technology that was adopted in 1999 as a global standard for next-generation wireless cell phones
Steve Jobs	Apple Computer, Pixar	Apple's stock increased roughly 140 per cent in 1999, to about US$99
Mel Karmazin	CBS/VIACOM	Arranged the US$80 billion merger of CBS with Viacom
Jim Kelly	United Parcel Service	Made UPS the leader in e-commerce deliveries, with 55 per cent market share
T. K. Koogle	Yahoo!	Yahoo should earn US$131.6 million – a rare profit maker in the Net world
Ken Lay	Enron	Shares rose about 50 per cent last year, quadruple the S&P Natural Gas Index
Jenny Ming	Old Navy	Opened 135 locations in 1999, bringing the total to more than 500
Thomas Siebel	Siebel Systems	Landed key deal for IBM to push Siebel's customer-relationship software; increased stock price more than 400 per cent last year, to about US$88

Masayoshi Son	Softbank	Created a powerful Net empire by forging links between his 100-plus Net companies in the US and Japan
Martha Stewart	Martha Stewart, Omnimedia	A splashy October IPO gave her empire a market capitalisation of US$1.1 billion
Keiji Tachikawa	NTT DoMoCo	Turned 'i-mode' Net access service for wireless phones into smash hit in Japan
Jack Welch	General Electric	Profits should rise 15 per cent, to US$11 billion, on sales up 10 per cent, to US$110 billion
Yun Jong Yong	Samsung Electronics	Profits up tenfold in 1999, to US$2.4 billion, on sales up 24 per cent, to US$22 billion

Source: Special Report, 2000, 'The top 25 managers of the year', *Business Week*, 10 January, pp. 60–78.

Organisational strategists

Small organisations may have a single strategist. In many cases, this person owns the firm and is involved deeply with its daily operations. At the other extreme, large, diversified firms have many top-level managers. In addition to the CEO and other top-level officials (for example, the chief operating officer and chief financial officer), other managers of these companies are responsible for the performance of individual business units.

Top-level managers play a critical role in firms' efforts to achieve their desired strategic outcomes. Organisational failure is often attributed to those who are responsible for the quality and effectiveness of a firm's decisions and actions.

Top-level managers play critical roles in firms' efforts to achieve their desired strategic outcomes. In fact, some believe that every organisational failure is actually a failure of those who hold the final responsibility for the quality and effectiveness of a firm's decisions and actions. Failure can stem from the strategic assumptions changing, and the strategic mission may become a strategic blinder. The firm's method of operating may become routines that create strategic inertia. Established relationships may create shackles that prevent change. Finally, a shared set of beliefs could become dogmas that prevent a change in corporate culture.[109] This is arguably the reason for the difficulties Pacific Dunlop and BHP now have in changing their organisation culture.[110] Strategic managers need to stop and ask the right questions to overcome the inertia that is often created by success itself, a lesson apparently not learned by managers of the world paint pigment company Tioxide, which had to close plants worldwide (including one in northwest Tasmania) because of environmental problems associated with a commercially successful product.[111]

Decisions for which strategists are responsible include how resources will be developed or acquired, at what price they will be obtained and how they will be used. Managerial decisions also influence how information flows in a company, the strategies a firm chooses to implement and the scope of its operations. In making these decisions, managers must assess the risk involved in taking the actions being considered. This risk is then factored into the decision.[112] The firm's strategic intent will affect the decisions managers make. Also, managers' strategic orientations, which include their personal values and beliefs, will affect their decisions.[113] Additionally, how strategists complete their work and their patterns of interactions with others significantly influence the way a firm does business and affect its ability to develop a competitive advantage.

How a firm does business is captured by the concept of organisational culture. Critical to strategic leadership practices and the implementation of strategies, **organisational culture** refers to the complex set of ideologies, symbols and core values shared throughout the firm and that influences the way it conducts business. Thus, culture is the 'social energy that drives – or fails to drive – the organization'.[114] Accenture's (previously Andersen Consulting) core values include the requirement that employees attend company-sponsored training classes in professional attire, an expectation of hard work (up to 80 hours per week), and a willingness to work effectively with others to accomplish all tasks that are parts of the company-wide demanding workload.[115] These core values at Accenture provide a particular type of social energy that drives the firm's efforts. As discussed in Chapters 3, 12 and 13, organisational culture is a potential source of competitive advantage.[116]

After evaluating available information and alternatives, top-level managers must frequently choose from among similarly attractive alternatives. The most effective strategists have the self-confidence necessary to select the best alternatives, allocate the required level of resources to them, and effectively explain to interested parties why certain alternatives were selected.[117]

When choosing among alternatives, strategists are accountable for treating employees, suppliers, customers and others with fairness and respect. Evidence suggests that trust can be a source of competitive advantage, thereby supporting an organisational commitment to treat stakeholders fairly and with respect.[118] Nonetheless, firms cannot succeed without people who, following careful and sometimes difficult analyses, are willing to make tough decisions – the types of decisions that result in strategic competitiveness and above-average returns.[119]

The work of effective strategists

Perhaps not surprisingly, hard work, thorough analyses, a willingness to be brutally honest, a penchant for always wanting the firm and its people to accomplish more, and common sense are prerequisites to an individual's success as a strategist.[120] In addition to possessing these characteristics, effective strategists must be able to think clearly and ask many questions. Their strategic effectiveness increases as they find ways for others also to think and enquire about what a firm is doing and why. But, in particular, top-level managers are challenged to 'think seriously and deeply ... about the purposes of the organizations they head or functions they perform, about the strategies, tactics, technologies, systems and people necessary to attain these purposes and about the important questions that always need to be asked'.[121]

Organisational culture refers to the complex set of ideologies, symbols and core values shared throughout the firm and that influences the way it conducts business. It is the social energy that drives – or fails to drive – the organisation.

However, just as e-commerce is changing the nature of competition, it is also changing strategic decision making. Speed is becoming a much more prominent competitive factor, and it makes strategic thinking even more critical. Most high-tech firms operate in hyper-competitive industry environments. The intense competition in these industries has caused some product life cycles to decrease from a period of one to two years to a period of six to nine months, leaving precious little time for a company's products to generate revenue. For companies competing in these industries, speed and flexibility have become key sources of competitive advantage. For example, Sun Microsystems, a leading manufacturer of high-end workstations and networking systems, has made reducing product development times its key operational focus.[122] Thinking strategically, in concert with others, increases the probability of identifying bold, innovative ideas. When these ideas lead to the development of core competencies – that is, when the ideas result in exploiting resources and capabilities that are valuable, rare, costly to imitate and non-substitutable – they become the foundation for taking advantage of environmental opportunities.

Our discussion highlights the nature of a strategist's work. The work is filled with ambiguous decision situations – situations for which the most effective solutions are not always easily determined. However, the opportunities suggested by this type of work are appealing. These jobs offer exciting chances to dream and to act. The following words, given as advice by his father to Steven J. Ross, the former chairman and co-CEO of Time-Warner, describe the opportunities in a strategist's work: 'There are three categories of people – the person who goes into the office, puts his feet up on his desk, and dreams for 12 hours; the person who arrives at 5 a.m. and works for 16 hours, never once stopping to dream; and the person who puts his feet up, dreams for one hour, then does something about those dreams.'[123] The organisational term used for a dream that challenges and energises a company is strategic intent.[124]

Strategists have opportunities to dream and to act, and the most effective ones provide a vision (the strategic intent) to effectively elicit the help of others in creating a firm's competitive advantage.

The strategic management process

The pursuit of competitiveness is at the heart of strategic management and the choices made in designing and using the strategic management process. Firms are in competition with one another; to gain access to the resources needed to earn above-average returns and to provide superior satisfaction of stakeholders' needs. Effective use of the interdependent parts of the strategic management process results in selecting the direction the firm will pursue and the means it utilises to achieve the desired outcomes of strategic competitiveness and above-average returns.

As suggested by Figure 1.1, the strategic management process is intended to be a rational approach to help a firm respond effectively to the challenges of the 21st-century competitive landscape. This process calls for a firm to study its external (Chapter 2) and internal (Chapter 3) environments to identify its marketplace opportunities and threats and determine how to use its core competencies in the pursuit of desired strategic outcomes. With this knowledge, the firm forms its strategic intent so that it can leverage its resources, capabilities and core competencies and win competitive battles in the global economy. Flowing from strategic intent, the strategic mission specifies, in writing, the products a firm intends to produce and the markets it will serve when leveraging its resources, capabilities and competencies.

The firm's strategic inputs provide the foundation for its strategic actions to formulate and implement strategies. Both formulating strategies and implementing them are critical to achieving strategic competitiveness and earning above-average returns.

As suggested in Figure 1.1 by the horizontal arrow linking the two types of strategic actions, formulation and implementation must be integrated simultaneously. In formulating strategies, thought should be given to implementing them. During implementation, effective strategists seek feedback that allows them to improve the selected strategies. The separation of strategy formulation from strategy implementation in the figure is for discussion purposes only. In reality, these two sets of actions allow the firm to achieve its desired strategic outcomes only when they are integrated carefully. Some believe, for example, that Kodak's decline in performance in the late 1990s could be attributed partly to poor execution in terms of actions taken to implement the firm's strategies.[125]

Figure 1.1 shows the topics we examine to study the interdependent parts of the strategic management process. In Part 2 of this book, actions related to the formulation of strategies are explained. The first set of actions studied is the formulation of strategies at the business-unit level (Chapter 4). A diversified firm – one competing in multiple product markets and businesses – has a business-level strategy for each distinct product market area. A company competing in a single product market has but one business-level strategy. In all instances, a business-level strategy describes a firm's actions designed to exploit its competitive advantage over rivals. But, as is explained in Chapter 5, business-level strategies are not formulated and implemented in isolation. Competitors respond to, and try to anticipate, each other's actions. Thus, the dynamics of competition are an important input to the formulation and implementation of all strategies, but especially to business-level strategies.

For the diversified firm, corporate-level strategy (Chapter 6) is concerned with determining the businesses in which the company intends to compete, how resources are to be allocated among those businesses and how the different units are to be managed. Other topics vital to strategy formulation, particularly in the diversified firm, include the acquisition of other companies and, as appropriate, the restructuring of the firm's portfolio of businesses (Chapter 7) and the selection of an international strategy that is consistent with the firm's resources, capabilities, core competencies and external opportunities (Chapter 8). Chapter 9 examines cooperative strategies. Increasingly important in a global economy, these strategies are used by a firm to gain competitive advantage by forming advantageous relationships with other firms.

To examine more direct actions taken to implement strategies successfully, we consider several topics in Part 3 of the book. First, the different mechanisms used to govern firms are considered (Chapter 10). With demands for improved corporate governance voiced by various stakeholders, organisations are challenged to manage in ways that will result in the satisfaction of stakeholders' interests and the attainment of desired strategic outcomes. Finally, the matters of organisational structure and actions needed to control a firm's operations (Chapter 11), the patterns of strategic leadership appropriate for today's firms and competitive environments (Chapter 12), and the link among corporate entrepreneurship, innovation and strategic competitiveness (Chapter 13) are addressed.

As noted earlier, competition requires firms to make choices to survive and succeed. Some of these choices are strategic in nature, including those of selecting a firm's strategic intent and strategic mission, determining which strategies to implement to offer a firm's products to customers, choosing an appropriate level of corporate scope, designing governance and organisation structures that will properly coordinate a firm's work, and, through strategic leadership, encouraging and nurturing organisational innovation.[126]

When made successfully, choices in terms of any one of these sets of actions have the potential to result in a competitive advantage for a firm over its rivals.

Primarily because they are related to how a firm interacts with its stakeholders, almost all strategic decisions have ethical dimensions.[127] Organisational ethics are revealed by an organisation's culture – that is to say, a firm's strategic decisions are a product of the core values that are shared by most or all of a company's managers and employees. Especially in the turbulent and often ambiguous 21st-century competitive landscape, those making strategic decisions are challenged to recognise that their decisions do affect capital market, product market and organisational stakeholders differently, and to evaluate the ethical implications of their decisions. As the executives of Levi Strauss discovered, socially responsible actions are interwoven with their abilities to satisfy all stakeholders in the organisation (see the first Strategic Focus).

As you will discover, the strategic management process examined in this text calls for disciplined approaches to the development of competitive advantage. These approaches provide the pathway through which firms will be able to achieve strategic competitiveness and earn above-average returns in the 21st century. Mastery of this strategic management process will effectively serve readers and the organisations for whom they choose to work.

Summary

- Through their actions, firms seek strategic competitiveness and above-average returns. Strategic competitiveness is achieved when a firm has developed and learned how to implement a value-creating strategy. Above-average returns – returns in excess of what investors expect to earn from other investments with similar levels of risk – allow a firm to simultaneously satisfy all of its stakeholders.
- A 21st-century competitive landscape – one in which the fundamental nature of competition is changing – has emerged. This landscape challenges those responsible for making effective strategic decisions to adopt a new mind-set, one that is global in nature. Through this mind-set, firms learn how to compete in what are highly turbulent and chaotic environments that produce disorder and a great deal of uncertainty. The globalisation of industries and their markets, and rapid and significant technological changes, are the two primary realities that have created the 21st-century competitive landscape. Globalisation – the spread of economic innovations around the world and the political and cultural adjustments that accompany this diffusion – is likely to continue. Globalisation also increases the standards of performance companies must meet or exceed to be strategically competitive in the 21st century. Developing the ability to satisfy these global performance standards also helps firms to compete effectively in their critical domestic markets.
- There are two main models of what a firm should do to earn above-average returns. The I/O model argues that the external environment is the primary determinant of the firm's strategies. Above-average returns are earned when the firm locates an attractive industry and successfully implements the strategy dictated by the characteristics of that industry. The resource-based model assumes that each firm is a collection of unique resources and capabilities that determines a firm's strategy. In this model, above-average returns are earned when the firm uses its valuable, rare, costly-to-imitate and non-substitutable resources and capabilities (that is, core competencies) to establish a competitive advantage over its rivals.
- Strategic intent and strategic mission are formed in light of the information and insights gained from studying a firm's internal and external environments. Strategic intent suggests how resources, capabilities and core competencies will be leveraged to achieve desired outcomes in the competitive environment. The strategic mission is an application of strategic intent. The mission is used to specify the product markets and customers a firm intends to serve through the leveraging of its resources, capabilities and competencies.
- Stakeholders are those who can affect, and are affected by, a firm's strategic outcomes. Because a firm is dependent on the continuing support of

stakeholders (shareholders, customers, suppliers, employees, host communities, and so on), they have enforceable claims on the company's performance. When earning above-average returns, a firm can adequately satisfy all stakeholders' interests. However, when earning only average returns, a firm's strategists must carefully manage all stakeholder groups in order to retain their support. A firm earning below-average returns must minimise the amount of support it loses from dissatisfied stakeholders.

- Organisational strategists are responsible for the design and execution of an effective strategic management process. Today, the most effective of these processes are grounded in ethical intentions and conduct. Strategists themselves – people with opportunities to dream and to act – can be a source of competitive advantage. The strategist's work demands decision trade-offs, often among attractive alternatives. Successful top-level managers work hard, conduct thorough analyses of situations, are brutally and consistently honest, and ask the right questions, of the right people, at the right time.

Review questions

1. What are strategic competitiveness, competitive advantage and above-average returns? Why are these terms important to those responsible for an organisation's performance?
2. What is the challenge of strategic management?
3. What are the two factors that have created the 21st-century competitive landscape? What meaning does this landscape have for those interested in starting a business firm in the near future?
4. According to the I/O model, what should a firm do to earn above-average returns?
5. What does the resource-based model suggest a firm should do to achieve strategic competitiveness and earn above-average returns?
6. What are the differences between strategic intent and strategic mission? What is the value of the strategic intent and mission for a firm's strategic management process?
7. What are stakeholders? Why can they influence organisations? Do stakeholders always have the same amount of influence over an organisation? Why or why not?
8. How would you describe the work of organisational strategists?
9. What are the parts of the strategic management process? How are these parts interrelated?

Application discussion questions

1. As suggested in the Opening Case, the outcomes in e-commerce are uncertain. Using the Internet, study Yahoo!'s current performance. Based on analysis, do you judge Yahoo! to be a success? Why or why not?
2. Choose several firms in your local community with which you are familiar. Describe the 21st-century competitive landscape to them, and ask for their feedback about how they anticipate that the landscape will affect their operations during the next five years.
3. Select an organisation (for example, a school or club) that is important to you. Who are the organisation's stakeholders? What degree of influence do you believe each has over the organisation, and why?
4. Are you a stakeholder at your university? If so, of what stakeholder group, or groups, are you a part?
5. Think of an industry in which you want to work. In your opinion, which of the three primary stakeholder groups is the most powerful in that industry today? Why? Which do you expect to be the most powerful group in five years? Why?
6. Do you agree or disagree with the following statement? 'I think managers have little responsibility for the failure of business firms.' Justify your view.
7. Do strategic intent and strategic mission have any meaning in your personal life? If so, describe it. Are your current actions being guided by an intent and mission? If not, why not?

Ethics questions

1. Can a firm achieve a competitive advantage and, thereby, strategic competitiveness without acting ethically? Explain.
2. What are a firm's ethical responsibilities if it earns above-average returns?
3. What are some of the critical ethical challenges to firms competing in the global economy?
4. How should ethical considerations be included in analyses of a firm's internal and external environments?
5. Can ethical issues be integrated into a firm's strategic intent and mission? Explain.
6. What is the relationship between ethics and stakeholders?
7. What is the importance of ethics for organisational strategists?

Internet exercise

Internet-based services depend heavily on continuous change and rapid strategic decision making. Companies such as Amazon.com that rely on Internet users for their customer base have demonstrated a distinct competitive advantage in serving their customers well. Barnes & Noble (www.bn.com) and Borders Books (www.borders.com) are some of Amazon.com's new competitors in the on-line book and music markets. How does this Web-based expansion affect the stakeholders of each? How does the entrance of these profitable retailers into the on-line market affect Amazon.com's competitive advantage?

e-project: Using other Web resources such as current business press and financial reports, discuss Amazon.com's continued growth despite recording no profits.

Notes

1. W. Zellner, 2000, 'Wal-Mart tries to make e-commerce work', *Business Review Weekly*, 10 November, pp. 59–61.
2. J. B. Barney, 1999, 'How firm's capabilities affect boundary decisions', *Sloan Management Review*, 40(3), pp. 137–45; J. B. Barney, 1991, 'Firm resources and sustained competitive advantage', *Journal of Management*, 17, pp. 99–120.
3. K. M. Eisenhardt and S. L. Brown, 1999, 'Patching: Restitching business portfolios in dynamic markets', *Harvard Business Review*, 77(3), pp. 72–84; D. J. Collis and C. A. Montgomery, 1995, 'Competing on resources: Strategy in the 1990s', *Harvard Business Review*, 73(4), pp. 118–28.
4. D. Abell, 1999, 'Competing today while preparing for tomorrow', *Sloan Management Review*, 40(3), pp. 73–81; D. J. Teece, G. Pisano and A. Shuen, 1997, 'Dynamic capabilities and strategic management', *Strategic Management Journal*, 18, pp. 509–33.
5. R. Coff, 1999, 'When competitive advantage doesn't lead to performance: The resource-based view and stakeholder bargaining power', *Organization Science*, 10, pp. 119–33; R. A. D'Aveni, 1995, 'Coping with hyper-competition: Utilizing the new 7S's framework', *Academy of Management Executive*, IX(3), p. 54; D. Schendel, 1994, 'Introduction to the Summer 1994 special issue; Strategy: Search for new paradigms', *Strategic Management Journal*, 15 (Special Summer Issue), p. 3.
6. P. Shrivastava, 1995, 'Ecocentric management for a risk society', *Academy of Management Review*, 20, p. 119.
7. J. G. March and R. I. Sutton, 1998, 'Organizational performance as a dependent variable', *Organization Science*, 8, pp. 698–706.
8. D. Lei, M. A. Hitt and R. Bettis, 1996, 'Dynamic core competences through meta-learning and strategic context', *Journal of Management*, 22, pp. 549–69; R. P. Rumelt, D. E. Schendel and D. J. Teece (eds), 1994, *Fundamental Issues in Strategy* (Boston: Harvard Business School Press), pp. 527–30.
9. Schendel, 'Introduction to the Summer 1994 special issue', pp. 1–3.
10. Rumelt, Schendel and Teece, *Fundamental Issues in Strategy*, pp. 543–7.
11. S. A. Zahra, R. D. Ireland and M. A. Hitt, 2000, 'International expansion by new venture firms: International diversity, mode of market entry technological learning and performance', *Academy of Management Journal*, in press; M. E. Porter, 1994, 'Toward a dynamic theory of strategy', in R. P. Rumelt, D. E. Schendel and D. J. Teece (eds), *Fundamental Issues in Strategy* (Boston: Harvard Business School Press), pp. 423–5.
12. J. Lee and D. Miller, 1999, 'People matter: Commitment to employees, strategy and performance in Korean firms', *Strategic Management Journal*, 20, pp. 579–93.
13. A. M. McGahan and M. E. Porter, 1997, 'How much does industry matter, really?', *Strategic Management Journal*, 18 (Summer Special Issue), pp. 15–30.
14. Barney, 'Firm resources and sustained competitive advantage'.
15. Associated Press, 1999, 'Microsoft's now worth more than most countries', *Dallas Morning News*, 17 July, p. F1.
16. B. Quinlivan, 2000, 'The promise of miracles', *Business Review Weekly*, 27 October, pp. 94–7.
17. N. Hooper, 1999, 'A world of new winners', *Business Review Weekly*, 12 November, pp. 92–4.
18. V. Marsh, 1998, 'Attributes: Strong strategy tops the list', *Financial Times*, 30 November, www.ft.com.
19. J. Nocera, 1999, 'Five lessons from Iomega', *Fortune*, 2 August, pp. 251–4.
20. E. Schonfeld, 1999, 'The morphing of Intel', *Fortune*, 15 February, p. 78.
21. A. Reinhardt, 1997, 'Paranoia, aggression, and other strengths', *Business Week*, 13 October, p. 14; A. S. Grove, 1995, 'A high-tech CEO updates his views on managing and careers', *Fortune*, 18 September, pp. 229–30.
22. This section is based largely on information featured in two sources: M. A. Hitt, B. W. Keats and S. M. DeMarie, 1998, 'Navigating in the new competitive landscape: Building competitive advantage and strategic flexibility in the 21st century', *Academy of Management Executive*, XII(4), pp. 22–42; R. A. Bettis and M. A. Hitt, 1995, 'The new competitive landscape', *Strategic Management Journal*, 16 (Special Summer Issue), pp. 7–19.
23. D. B. Yoffie and M. A. Cusumano, 1999, 'Judo strategy: The competitive dynamics of internet time', *Harvard Business Review*, 77(1), pp. 70–81.
24. L. Schmidt, 1999, 'Crunch time at Woolworths', *Business Review Weekly*, 5 November, pp. 78–81.
25. R. D. Ireland and M. A. Hitt, 1999, 'Achieving and maintaining strategic competitiveness in the 21st century: The role of strategic leadership', *Academy of Management Executive*, XIII(1), pp. 22–42.
26. D'Aveni, 'Coping with hyper-competition', p. 46.
27. T. P. Murtha, S. A. Lenway and R. Bagozzi, 1998, 'Global mind-sets and cognitive shifts in a complex multinational corporation', *Strategic Management Journal*, 19, pp. 97–114.
28. S. Koudsi and L. A. Costa, 1998, 'America vs. the new Europe: By the numbers', *Fortune*, 21 December, pp. 149–56.
29. T. A. Stewart, 1993, 'The new face of American power', *Fortune*, 26 July, pp. 70–86.
30. K. Schwab, M. E. Porter, J. D. Sachs, A. W. Warner and M. Levinson, 1999, *The Global Competitiveness Report* 1999 (New York: Oxford University Press).
31. E. Tucker, 1999, 'More entrepreneurship urged', *Financial Times*, 22 June, p. 2.
32. Incat Australia, 2001, *Incat Australia Home Page*, 19 February: www.incat.com.au.
33. *Whirlpool Home Page*, 1999, 'Important company stuff', 24 September: www.whirlpoolcorp.com.
34. S. Thurm and M. Tatge, 2000, 'Whirlpool to launch Internet-ready refrigerator', *Wall Street Journal*, 7 January, p. B6; I. Katz, 1998, 'Whirlpool: In the wringer', *Business Week*, 14 December, pp. 83–7; G. Steinmetz and C. Quintanilla, 1998, 'Whirlpool expected easy going in Europe and it got a big shock', *Wall Street Journal*, 10 April, pp. A1, A6.
35. J. Kahn, 1999, 'Wal-Mart goes shopping in Europe', *Fortune*, 7 July, pp. 105–12.
36. *Economist*, 1999, 'Business: Ford swallows Volvo', *Economist*, 30 January, p. 58.
37. E. Thornton, K. Kerwin and K. Naughton, 1999, 'Can Honda go it alone?', *Business Week*, 5 July, pp. 42–5.
38. R. Ruggiero, 1997, 'The high stakes of world trade', *Wall Street Journal*, 28 April, p. A18.
39. S. A. Zahra, 1999, 'The changing rules of global competitiveness in the 21st century', *Academy of Management Executive*, 13(1), pp. 36–42; R. M. Kanter, 1995, 'Thriving locally in the global economy', *Harvard Business Review*, 73(5), pp. 151–60.
40. D. P. Hamilton, 1999, 'As global chip industry reinvents itself again, Taiwan stands to gain', *Wall Street Journal*, 17 February, p. A19.
41. S. Zaheer and E. Mosakowski, 1997, 'The dynamics of the liability of foreignness: A global study of survival in financial services', *Strategic Management Journal*, 18, pp. 439–64.
42. J. S. Black and H. B. Gregersen, 1999, 'The right way to manage expats', *Harvard Business Review*, 77(2), pp. 52–63; H. B. Gregersen, A. J. Morrison and J. S. Black, 1998, 'Developing leaders for the global frontier', *Sloan Management Review*, 40(1), pp. 21–32.
43. M. A. Hitt, R. E. Hoskisson and H. Kim, 1997, 'International

diversification: Effects on innovation and firm performance in product-diversified firms', *Academy of Management Journal*, 40, pp. 767–98.

44 R. W. Moxon and C. Bourassa-Shaw, 1997, 'The global free-trade dilemma: Can you control the personal gale of creative destruction?', *Business*, 18 (Spring), pp. 6–9.

45 T. Nakahara, 1997, 'Innovation in a borderless world economy', *Research-Technology Management,* May–June, pp. 7–9.

46 N. Dawar and T. Frost, 1999, 'Competing with giants: Survival strategies for local companies in emerging markets', *Harvard Business Review*, 77(2), pp. 119–29.

47 F. Williams, 1999, 'Globalization bad for health, say UN agencies', *Financial Times*, 10 June, p. 7.

48 P. Ruthven, 2000, 'Here's to a long corporate life', *Business Review Weekly*, 12 November, pp. 96–7.

49 K. M. Eisenhardt, 1999, 'Strategy as strategic decision making', *Sloan Management Review*, 40(3), pp. 65–72.

50 C. W. L. Hill, 1997, 'Establishing a standard: Competitive strategy and technological standards in winner-take-all industries', *Academy of Management Executive*, XI(2), pp. 7–25.

51 R. Karlgaard, 1999, 'Digital rules', *Forbes*, 5 July, p. 43.

52 Grove, 'A high-tech CEO', p. 229.

53 B. Morris, 1997, 'IBM really wants your E-business', *Fortune*, 10 November, pp. 36–8.

54 R. D. Hof, 1999, 'What every CEO needs to know about electronic business: A survival guide', *Business Week*, 22 March, pp. EB9–12.

55 W. Zellner, S. Anderson Forest, K. Morris and L. Lee, 1999, 'The big guys go online', *Business Week*, 6 September, pp. 30–2.

56 B. L. Simonin, 1999, 'Ambiguity and the process of knowledge transfer in strategic alliances', *Strategic Management Journal*, 20, pp. 595–624.

57 T. H. Davenport and L. Prusak, 1998, Working Knowledge: *How Organizations Manage What They Know* (Boston: Harvard Business School Press); C. A. Bartlett and S. Ghoshal, 1995, 'Changing the role of top management: Beyond systems to people', *Harvard Business Review*, 73(3), p. 141.

58 T. K. Kayworth and R. D. Ireland, 1998, 'The use of corporate IT standards as a means of implementing the cost leadership strategy', *Journal of Information Technology Management*, IX(4), pp. 13–42.

59 R. Sanchez, 1995, 'Strategic flexibility in product competition', *Strategic Management Journal* (Special Summer Issue), 16, pp. 135–59.

60 S. Kotha, 1995, 'Mass customization: Implementing the emerging paradigm for competitive advantage', *Strategic Management Journal*, 16, p. 21.

61 J. Browning and S. Reiss, 1999, *Wall Street Journal*, 23 April, p. A14.

62 J. L. C. Cheng and I. F. Kesner, 1997, 'Organizational slack and response to environmental shifts: The impact of resource allocation patterns', *Journal of Management*, 23, pp. 1–18.

63 C. Markides, 1998, 'Strategic innovation in established companies', *Sloan Management Review*, 39(3), pp. 31–42; V. L. Barker III and I. M. Duhaime, 1997, 'Strategic change in the turnaround process: Theory and empirical evidence', *Strategic Management Journal*, 18, pp. 13–38.

64 W. Boeker, 1997, 'Strategic change: The influence of managerial characteristics and organizational growth', *Academy of Management Journal*, 40, pp. 152–70.

65 R. T. Pascale, 1999, 'Surviving the edge of chaos', *Sloan Management Review*, 40(3), pp. 83–94; E. D. Beinhocker, 1999, 'Robust adaptive strategies', *Sloan Management Review*, 40(3), pp. 95–106; N. Rajagopalan and G. M. Spreitzer, 1997, 'Toward a theory of strategic change: A multi-lens perspective and integrative framework', *Academy of Management Review*, 22, pp. 48–79.

66 R. E. Hoskisson, M. A. Hitt, W. P. Wan and D. Yiu, 1999, 'Swings of a pendulum: Theory and research in strategic management', *Journal of Management*, 25, pp. 417–56.

67 D. Schendel, 1994, 'Introduction to competitive organizational behavior: Toward an organizationally-based theory of competitive advantage', *Strategic Management Journal*, 15 (Special Winter Issue), p. 2.

68 A. Seth and H. Thomas, 1994, 'Theories of the firm: Implications for strategy research', *Journal of Management Studies*, 31, pp. 165–91.

69 Seth and Thomas, 'Theories of the firm', pp. 169–73.

70 Porter, 'Toward a dynamic theory of strategy', p. 428.

71 M. E. Porter, 1985, *Competitive Advantage* (New York: Free Press); M. E. Porter, 1980, *Competitive Strategy* (New York: Free Press).

72 A. M. McGahan, 1999, 'Competition, strategy and business performance', *California Management Review*, 41(3), pp. 74–101; A. M. McGahan and M. E. Porter, 1997, 'How much does industry matter, really?', *Strategic Management Journal*, 18 (Special Summer Issue), pp. 15–30.

73 R. Henderson and W. Mitchell, 1997, 'The interactions of organizational and competitive influences on strategy and performance', *Strategic Management Journal* (Special Summer Issue), 18, pp. 5–14; C. Oliver, 1997, 'Sustainable competitive advantage: Combining institutional and resource-based views', *Strategic Management Journal*, 18, pp. 697–713; J. L. Stimpert and I. M. Duhaime, 1997, 'Seeing the big picture: The influence of industry, diversification, and business strategy on performance', *Academy of Management Journal*, 40, pp. 560–83.

74 C. C. Markides, 1999, 'A dynamic view of strategy', *Sloan Management Review*, 40(3), pp. 55–72; Abell, 'Competing today while preparing for tomorrow'; J. R. Williams, 1994, 'Strategy and the search for rents: The evolution of diversity among firms', in R. P. Rumelt, D. E. Schendel and D. J. Teece (eds), *Fundamental Issues in Strategy* (Boston: Harvard Business School Press), pp. 229–46.

75 Barney, 'Firm resources'; Grant, 'Resource-based theory'.

76 J. Kay, 1999, 'Total war and managers from Mars', *Financial Times*, 4 August, p. 8.

77 P. J. H. Schoemaker and R. Amit, 1994, 'Investment in strategic assets: Industry and firm-level perspectives', in P. Shrivastava, A. Huff and J. Dutton (eds), *Advances in Strategic Management* (Greenwich, Conn.: JAI Press), p. 9.

78 N. Munk, 1999, 'Title fight', *Fortune*, 21 June, pp. 84–94.

79 J. B. Barney, 1995, 'Looking inside for competitive advantage', *Academy of Management Executive*, IX(4), p. 56.

80 A. Madhok, 1997, 'Cost, value and foreign market entry mode: The transaction and the firm', *Strategic Management Journal*, 18, pp. 39–61.

81 A. A. Lado, N. G. Boyd and S. C. Hanlon, 1997, 'Competition, cooperation, and the search for economic rents: A syncretic model', *Academy of Management Review*, 22, pp. 110–41.

82 A. Arora and A. Gambardella, 1997, 'Domestic markets and international competitiveness: Generic and product specific competencies in the engineering sector', *Strategic Management Journal*, 18 (Special Summer Issue), pp. 53–74.

83 Teece, Pisano and Shuen, 'Dynamic capabilities'.

84 D. Lei, M. A. Hitt and R. A. Bettis, 1996, 'Dynamic core competences through meta-learning and strategic context', *Journal of Management*, 22, pp. 547–67.

85 G. Hamel and C. K. Prahalad, 1989, 'Strategic intent', *Harvard Business Review*, 67(3), pp. 63–76.

86 S. Sherman, 1995, 'Stretch goals: The dark side of asking for miracles', *Fortune*, 13 November, pp. 231–2; G. Hamel and C. K. Prahalad, 1994, *Competing for the Future* (Boston: Harvard Business School Press), pp. 129–36.

87 Hamel and Prahalad, 'Strategic intent', p. 66.

88 S. Sherman, 1993, 'The secret to Intel's success', p. 14.

89 Hamel and Prahalad, 'Strategic intent', p. 64.

90 M. A. Hitt, D. Park, C. Hardee and B. B. Tyler, 1995, 'Understanding strategic intent in the global marketplace', *Academy of Management Executive*, IX(2), pp. 12–19.

91 J. Collins, 1999, 'Turning goals into results: The power of catalytic mechanisms', *Harvard Business Review*, 77(4), pp. 70–82.

92 D. Hanson and H. Stuart, 2000, 'Failing the reputation test: BHP', *Proceedings of the Corporate Reputation Conference*, Copenhagen, Denmark.

93 R. D. Ireland and M. A. Hitt, 1992, 'Mission statements: Importance, challenge, and recommendations for development', *Business Horizons*, 35(3), pp. 34–42.

94 W. J. Duncan, 1999, *Management: Ideas and Actions* (New York: Oxford University Press), pp. 122–5.

95 N. Rajagopalan, 1992, 'Strategic orientations, incentive plan adoptions, and firm performance: Evidence from electric utility firms', *Strategic Management Journal*, 18, pp. 761–85.

96 M. A. Geletkanycz, 1997, 'The salience of culture's consequences: The effects of cultural values on top executive commitment to the status quo', *Strategic Management Journal*, 18, pp. 615–34, M. A. Hitt, M. T. Dacin, B. B. Tyler and D. Park, 1997, 'Understanding the differences in Korean and U.S. executives' strategic orientation', *Strategic Management Journal*, 18, pp. 159–67.

97. J. Frooman, 1999, 'Stakeholder influence strategies', *Academy of Management Review*, 24, pp. 191–205.
98. T. M. Jones and A. C. Wicks, 1999, 'Convergent stakeholder theory', *Academy of Management Review*, 24, pp. 206–21; R. E. Freeman, 1984, *Strategic Management: A Stakeholder Approach* (Boston: Pitman), pp. 53–4.
99. G. Donaldson and J. W. Lorsch, 1983, *Decision Making at the Top: The Shaping of Strategic Direction* (New York: Basic Books), pp. 37–40.
100. Rumelt, Schendel and Teece, *Fundamental Issues in Strategy*, p. 33.
101. Donaldson and Lorsch, *Decision Making at the Top*, p. 37.
102. D. A. Gioia, 1999, 'Practicality, paradigms, and problems in stakeholder theorizing', *Academy of Management Review*, 24, pp. 228–32.
103. R. K. Mitchell, B. R. Agle and D. J. Wood, 1997, 'Toward a theory of stakeholder identification and salience: Defining the principle of who and what really count', *Academy of Management Review*, 22, pp. 853–86.
104. Donaldson and Preston, 'The stakeholder theory of the corporation', citing a quote from *The Economist*, 1994, Corporate governance special section, 11 September, pp. 52–62.
105. 'Don't be an ugly-American manager', 1995, *Fortune*, 16 October, p. 225.
106. G. Dutton, 1999, 'Building a global brain', *Management Review*, May, pp. 23–30.
107. J. Kavanagh, 2000, 'Shareholders bare their teeth', *Business Review Weekly*, 3 November, pp. 68–77.
108. P. F. Drucker, 1999, *Management Challenges for the 21st Century* (New York: HarperCollins).
109. D. N. Sull, 1999, 'Why good companies go bad', *Harvard Business Review*, 77(4), pp. 42–52.
110. D. Hanson and H. Stuart, 2000, 'Failing the reputation test: BHP', *Proceedings of the Corporate Reputation Conference*, Copenhagen, Denmark.
111. D. Hanson, J. Steen and P. Liesch, 1999, 'Reluctance to innovate: A case study of the titanium dioxide industry', *Prometheus*, 14, pp. 251–63.
112. G. McNamara and P. Bromiley, 1997, 'Decision making in an organizational setting: Cognitive and organizational influences on risk assessment in commercial lending', *Academy of Management Journal*, 40, pp. 1063–88.
113. L. Markoczy, 1997, 'Measuring beliefs: Accept no substitutes', *Academy of Management Journal*, 40, pp. 1228–42.
114. M. A. Hitt and R. E. Hoskisson, 1991, 'Strategic competitiveness', in L. W. Foster (ed.), *Advances in Applied Business Strategy* (Greenwich, Conn.: JAI Press), pp. 1–36.
115. Bartlett and Ghoshal, 'Changing the role of top management', p. 139.
116. K. Weigelt and C. Camerer, 1988, 'Reputation and corporate strategy', *Strategic Management Journal*, 9, pp. 443–54; J. B. Barney, 1986, 'Organizational culture: Can it be a source of sustained competitive advantage?', *Academy of Management Review*, 11, pp. 656–65.
117. R. D. Ireland, M. A. Hitt and J. C. Williams, 1992, 'Self-confidence and decisiveness: Prerequisites for effective management in the 1990s', *Business Horizons*, 35(1), pp. 36–43.
118. J. H. Davis, F. D. Schoorman, R. C. Mayer and H. H. Tau, 2000, 'The trusted general manager and business unit performance: Empirical evidence of a competitive advantage', *Strategic Management Journal*, in press; R. C. Mayer, J. H. Davis and F. D. Schoorman, 1995, 'An integrative model of organizational trust', *Academy of Management Review*, 20, pp. 709–34; J. B. Barney and M. H. Hansen, 1994, 'Trustworthiness as a source of competitive advantage', *Strategic Management Journal*, 15 (Winter Special Issue), pp. 175–90.
119. E. Cohen and N. Tichy, 1999, 'Operation leadership', *Fast Company*, September, pp. 278–86.
120. W. C. Taylor, 1999, 'Whatever happened to globalization', *Fast Company*, September, pp. 288–94.
121. T. Leavitt, 1991, *Thinking About Management* (New York: Free Press), p. 9.
122. T. Minahan, 1997, 'Buyers tap suppliers to help them trim cycle times', *Purchasing*, 27 November, pp. 30–33.
123. M. Loeb, 1993, 'Steven J. Ross, 1927–1992', *Fortune*, 25 January, p. 4.
124. Hamel and Prahalad, *Competing for the Future*, p. 129.
125. R. Waters, 1999, 'Fisher to step down as Kodak chief executive', *Financial Times*, 10 June, p. 17.
126. Rumelt, Schendel and Teece, *Fundamental Issues in Strategy*, pp. 9–10.
127. Our discussion of ethics and the strategic management process, both here and in other chapters, is informed by materials appearing in J. S. Harrison and C. H. St. John, 1994, *Strategic Management of Organizations and Stakeholders: Theory and Cases* (St. Paul, Minn.: West Publishing Company).

Chapter 2

The external environment: Opportunities, threats, industry competition and competitor analysis

Objectives

After reading this chapter, you should be able to:

1. Explain the importance of studying and understanding the firm's external environment.
2. Define and describe the general environment and the industry environment.
3. Discuss the four activities of the external environmental analysis process.
4. Name and describe the general environment's six segments.
5. Identify the five competitive forces and explain how they determine an industry's profit potential.
6. Define strategic groups and describe their influence on the firm's competitive actions.
7. Describe what firms need to know about their competitors and different methods used to collect intelligence on their competitors.

Rio Tinto and the global challenge

At Rio Tinto the belief is that mining companies will look very different within five years. The right kind of growth is essential to survival.

Rio Tinto is an international mining group made up of Rio Tinto plc (incorporated in England and Wales) and Rio Tinto Limited (incorporated in Australia). The assets are managed as one group with six product groups that operate in more than 20 countries. Industrial Mining owns companies that mine borate, titanium dioxide and talc in places as diverse as California and Lake MacLeod in Western Australia. The copper group owns major companies worldwide. The minerals and energy group handles coal and uranium dioxide (including holdings in Namibia). Gold and other minerals include zinc, lead, silver and nickel mining among other globally spread activities. The iron ore group, among other holdings, operates Brazilian and Columbian mines and large mines such as Mt Tom Price in Australia. The final group is the Comalco group, a recent acquisition that manufactures aluminium and mines bauxite (the base ore).

At the end of 1999, the Rio Tinto group employed 26 983 people directly and declared US$1 282 million in adjusted earnings. CEO Leigh Clifford believes that the mining industry is increasingly competitive and that companies must be innovatively managed. The recent takeovers of Comalco and later North Ltd were expressions of this interest. The Comalco takeover led to a more unified aluminium group and the North takeover offers, according to Clifford, were opportunities to effectively manage the now combined iron ore operations.

The company has many of its significant assets in Australia and the United States, politically stable countries with mining-friendly taxation. In comparison, as Clifford points out, despite excitement after the break-up of the Soviet Union, no significant mining operation has managed to proceed.

In early 2001, Rio was still reviewing its North operations and is expected to find a buyer for North Forest Products (NFP), a major landholder in Tasmania and a leading woodchip exporter. Divesting NFP is consistent with keeping a focus on mining.

The group is also aware of the need to display social and environmental sensitivities. They produce a detailed and extensive social and environment report centrally and similar reports by 15 of their businesses for their local public. In the central report there are lists of policies, targets and progress. In the 1999 report, performance on four out of seven goals was on track. Clifford (who only took the CEO position in April 2000) is keen to build the reputation of the mining industry. Rio is involved in the Global Mining Initiative, a project that is considering the sustainability of mining, its costs as well as benefits.

Major changes in the business environment represented by the Internet are part of the company's activities. Rio Tinto has used e-business technologies in procurement of supplies. In May 2000, they announced that resources would be put into a 13-company strong Mining and Minerals e-Marketplace. The project team were to report by late 2000.

Rio Tinto is less successful in handling the union movement. It has had a volatile relationship with the Australian Construction, Forestry, Mining and Energy Union (CFMEU), is the target of the Brussels-based international union organisation ICEM and in 1999 had significant industrial problems at the Kaltin Prima Mine in Indonesia.

Understanding the global, political, technological and socio-cultural segments of their environment is obviously critical to Rio Tinto's success. They have acquired companies in order to consolidate global mining, operate in 20 countries, seek to display environmental and social responsibility, must seek to understand unions and must deal with communications technology. They take advantage of opportunities in this environment and at the end of 2000 were also a company with many challenges – the unions, the need to deal innovatively with new acquisitions, the problem of reframing the public's view of mining and the ongoing challenge of the highly competitive global industries that collectively make up their mining operations. Clifford explains the communication challenge, making clear the global nature of their operations: 'We have to explain ourselves better to the wider community, governments and the population at large.'

www.riotinto.com.au

Sources: Jon McCallum, 2000, 'Rio Tinto shape up', *Business Review Weekly*, 29 September, pp. 32–3; Rio Tinto, 1999, *Annual Report*; Rio Tinto, 2000, *Social and Environment Report*; Rio Tinto, 2000, *Half Year Report*.

Companies' experiences across time and research evidence suggest that the external environment affects firm growth and profitability.[1] Changes in political/legal realities, the strength of different nations' economies at different times, and the emergence of new technologies are a few examples of conditions in the external environment that are affecting Rio Tinto and other firms throughout the world, such as the US giant, GE, one of the world's largest corporations. The former CEO of GE, Jack Welch, believes, for example, that the capabilities of the Internet will change everything, including relationships with employees, customers and suppliers. Regarding suppliers, Welch decided that those supplying GE would be allowed no more than 18 months to gain the skills necessary to supply the firm on the Internet. Those failing to satisfy this expectation 'won't do business with us', Welch declared.[2] One technique GE uses to impress the criticality of the Internet to each employee is to send materials about the need to change the way each unit conducts its business across the company under the heading 'destroyyourbusiness.com'.

The practice of using the Internet to work with suppliers is becoming common. In Australia, 14 of the country's largest businesses have set up corProcure, an Internet site designed to facilitate business-to-business (B2B) transactions between member companies. It is thought that corProcure will generate significant cost savings and increase the efficiency of B2B transactions.

This chapter focuses on what firms do to analyse and understand the external environment. As the discussion of Rio Tinto shows, the external environment influences the firm's strategic options, as well as the decisions made in light of them. The firm's understanding of the external environment is matched with knowledge about its internal environment. (The internal environment is discussed in the next chapter.) Matching the conditions of the two environments is the foundation the firm needs to form its strategic intent, to develop its strategic mission, and to take strategic actions in the pursuit of strategic competitiveness and above-average returns (see Figure 1.1 in Chapter 1).

As noted in the first chapter, the environmental conditions facing firms in the global economy today differ from those firms faced previously. Technological changes and the explosion in information-gathering and processing capabilities demand more timely and effective competitive actions and responses.[3] The rapid sociological changes occurring in many countries affect labour practices and the nature of products demanded by increasingly diverse consumers. Governmental policies and laws affect where and how firms choose to compete.⁴ Deregulation and local government changes, such as those being witnessed in the global electric utilities industry, affect the general competitive environment, as well as the strategic decisions that will be made by companies competing globally. Victoria Power is now the owner of important sections of the Victorian infrastructure. This US-based corporation is an example of the hundreds of energy marketers, utilities and banks seeking a share of the US$300 billion global gas and power business that is rapidly consolidating as a result of deregulation activities around the world.⁵ Privatisation, a form of deregulation, is a process in which ownership of an enterprise is transferred from the public sector to the private sector. To achieve strategic competitiveness, when dealing with all situations, including privatisation activities, companies must be aware of and understand the implications of the realities of the external environment's different parts.

Firms attempt to understand the external environment by acquiring information about competitors, customers and other stakeholders. In particular, firms seek to gain information to build their own base of knowledge and capabilities.⁶ Firms may attempt to imitate the capabilities of able competitors or even successful firms in other industries, or they may build new knowledge and capabilities to develop a competitive advantage. On the basis of this new information, knowledge and capabilities, firms may take actions to buffer environmental effects on them or to build relationships with stakeholders in their environment.⁷ To build up their knowledge and capabilities, and to take actions that buffer or build bridges to external stakeholders, organisations must effectively analyse the external environment.

The general, industry and competitor environments

Through an integrated understanding of the external and internal environments, firms gain the information they need to understand the present and predict the future.⁸ As shown in Figure 2.1, a firm's external environment is divided into three main areas: the general, industry and competitor environments.

Figure 2.1 | The external environment

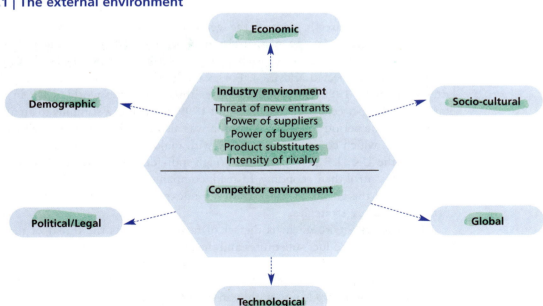

> The **general environment** is composed of elements in the broader society that influence an industry and the firms within it.

The **general environment** is composed of elements in the broader society that influence an industry and the firms within it.[9] We group these elements into six environmental segments: demographic, economic, political/legal, socio-cultural, technological and global. Examples of elements analysed in each of these segments are shown in Table 2.1.

Table 2.1 | The general environment: Segments and elements

PESTDG

Segment	Elements	
Demographic segment	• Population size • Age structure • Geographic distribution	• Ethnic mix • Income distribution
Economic segment	• Inflation rates • Interest rates • Trade deficits or surpluses • Budget deficits or surpluses	• Personal savings rate • Business savings rates • Gross domestic product
Political/legal segment	• Antitrust laws • Taxation laws • Deregulation philosophies	• Labour training laws • Educational philosophies and policies
Socio-cultural segment	• Women in the workforce • Workforce diversity • Attitudes about the quality of work life	• Concerns about the environment • Shifts in work and career preferences • Shifts in preferences regarding product and service characteristics
Technological segment	• Product innovations • Applications of knowledge • New communication technologies	• Focus of private and government-supported R&D expenditures
Global segment	• Important political events • Critical global markets	• Newly industrialised countries • Different cultural and institutional attributes

Firms cannot directly control the general environment's segments and elements. Accordingly, successful companies gather the types and amounts of data and information that are required to understand each segment and its implications so that appropriate strategies can be selected and used. For example, the 'red-hot' US economy during the latter part of the 1990s surprised countries throughout the world. GDP in the United States grew 4.1 per cent between 1995 and 1999, providing a stimulus to an ailing global economy. In the period 1989–99, Australia was also a healthy economy with a growth of 3.4 per cent, which compares favourably with major nations such as Germany (0.6 per cent) and the UK (1.9 per cent).[10] Although individual firms were affected differently, none could control their economy. Instead, companies around the globe were challenged to understand the effects of this economy's unexpectedly strong growth on their firm's current and future strategies.

The **industry environment** is the set of factors, such as the threat of new entrants, suppliers, buyers, product substitutes and the intensity of rivalry among competitors, that directly influences a firm and its competitive actions and responses. In total, the interactions among these five factors determine an industry's profit potential. The challenge is to locate a position within an industry where a firm can favourably influence

> The **industry environment** is the set of factors – the threat of new entrants, suppliers, buyers, product substitutes and the intensity of rivalry among competitors – that directly influences a company and its competitive actions and responses.

those factors or where it can successfully defend against their influence. The greater a firm's capacity to favourably influence its industry environment, the greater is the likelihood that the firm will earn above-average returns.

How companies gather and interpret information about their competitors is called *competitor analysis*. Understanding the firm's competitor environment complements the insights provided by studying the general and industry environments.

In combination, the results of the three analyses that are used to understand the external environment influence the development of the firm's strategic intent, strategic mission and strategic actions. Analysis of the general environment is focused on the future; analysis of the industry environment is focused on understanding the factors and conditions influencing a firm's profitability; and analysis of competitors is focused on predicting the dynamics of competitors' actions, responses and intentions. Although we discuss each analysis separately, performance improves when the firm integrates the insights gained from analyses of the general environment, the industry environment and the competitor environment.

External environmental analysis

Most firms face external environments that are growing more turbulent, complex and global, conditions that make interpretation increasingly difficult.[11] To cope with what are often ambiguous and incomplete environmental data and to increase their understanding of the general environment, firms engage in a process called external environmental analysis. The process, which should be conducted on a continuous basis, includes four activities: scanning, monitoring, forecasting and assessing (see Table 2.2). Those analysing the external environment should understand that completing this analysis is a difficult, yet significant, activity.[12]

Table 2.2 | Components of the external analysis

Scanning	• Identifying early signals of environmental changes and trends
Monitoring	• Detecting meaning through ongoing observations of environmental changes and trends
Forecasting	• Developing projections of anticipated outcomes based on monitored changes and trends
Assessing	• Determining the timing and importance of environmental changes and trends for firms' strategies and their management

> An **opportunity** is a condition in the general environment that may help a company achieve strategic competitiveness.

An important objective of studying the general environment is identifying opportunities and threats. An **opportunity** is a condition in the general environment that may help a company achieve strategic competitiveness. General Motors believes that in the not-too-distant future, a person's car will be a mobile node on 'the world-wide communications grid, plugged in by satellites and cellular links to digital audio, video, telecommunications and the Internet'. GM executives see the possibility of selling billions of dollars of ancillary services to customers after they have purchased their automobiles as an 'enormous opportunity'.[13] An early action taken to exploit this perceived opportunity was the use of GM's OnStar satellite-based service to deliver e-mail, traffic reports and other information to drivers of certain 2000-model luxury cars. Essentially, the OnStar system was being used as the portal for basic Internet services.[14] The fact that no more than one billion of the world's total population of six billion has anything close to cheap access to a telephone appears to be a huge opportunity for global telecommunications companies.[15] And General Electric believes that 'e-business represents a revolution that may be the greatest opportunity for growth that [the] Company has ever seen'.[16]

A **threat** is a condition in the general environment that may hinder a company's efforts to achieve strategic competitiveness.[17] In light of the Internet's growing use and promise, many business schools are offering an MBA degree focusing on electronic commerce. IBM is even offering such a degree in partnership with ESC Grenoble, a French business school.[18] For business schools lacking modern technology and a faculty that is fully conversant with the use of electronic commerce as a means of competitive survival and the development of a competitive advantage, the emergence of electronic commerce MBA degrees could appear threatening.[19] As our examples and discussion indicate, opportunities suggest competitive *possibilities*, while threats are potential *constraints*.

Several sources are used to analyse the general environment, including a wide variety of printed materials (for example, trade publications, newspapers, business publications, and the results of academic research and public polls); attendance at and participation in trade shows; the content of conversations with suppliers, customers and employees of public-sector organisations; and business-related 'rumours'.[20] An additional source of data and information is people in 'boundary-spanning' positions who interact with external constituents such as salespersons, purchasing managers, public relations directors and human resource managers. As discussed in sections to come, the Internet is increasingly a vital source of data and information for the purpose of understanding the general environment. In each case, though, the firm should verify the validity and reliability of the sources on which its environmental analyses are based.[21]

Scanning

Scanning entails the study of all segments in the general environment. Through scanning, firms identify early signals of potential changes in the general environment and detect changes that are already under way.[22] When scanning, the firm often deals with ambiguous, incomplete or unconnected data and information. Environmental scanning is critically important for firms competing in highly volatile environments.[23] In addition, scanning activities must be aligned with the organisational context; a scanning system designed for a volatile environment is inappropriate for a firm in a stable environment.[24]

As the 1990s closed, a trend towards early retirement was emerging in Western societies. One reason for this was the difficulty people aged 50 and over were having locating work. Magnifying this difficulty was the virtual disappearance of some jobs. For example, the door-to-door collector of insurance premiums is being outsourced, and the numbers of bank tellers are decreasing. 'Over-the-counter relationships are disappearing as customers are given electronic and Internet alternatives.'[25]

Some analysts expect the pressure brought to bear by the early retirement trend on countries such as France, Germany, Australia and Japan to be quite significant and challenging. Governments in these countries appear to be offering future elderly populations state-funded pensions that cannot be met with the present taxes and social security contribution rates.[26] In Australia, the challenge of organising income support for older people has been a focus of activity for successive federal governments, with a range of incentives being offered for individuals to undertake superannuation. The numbers are revealing. In June 1998 there were 2.3 million people, or 12 per cent of the population, aged 65 and over in Australia. Only 6 per cent were in the labour force. In the period 1996–7, government pensions were the principal source of income for 74 per cent of

---

A **threat** is a condition in the general environment that may hinder a company's efforts to achieve strategic competitiveness.

households where the main income earner was over 65. However, between 1986 and 1997, the proportion of people over 45 holding superannuation rose from 35 per cent to 58 per cent.[27] Those selling financial planning services and options should observe trends such as this to determine whether it represents an opportunity to help governments find ways to meet their previously agreed-upon responsibilities. Early retirees might also be an important customer segment for those providing education through electronic means.[28]

Monitoring

When *monitoring*, analysts observe environmental changes to see if an important trend is emerging from among those spotted by scanning.[29] Critical to successful monitoring is the ability to detect meaning in different environmental events. For example, a new law permitting shopping on Sunday for 'touristic items' was introduced recently in eastern Germany. The limited Sunday store openings were a challenge to the nation's restrictive rules on shopping hours. Popular initially with consumers, the Sunday openings, said some analysts, might spread beyond the economically stricken east, even though the move towards longer hours was strongly opposed by the service sector union.[30] German retailers should monitor this change in their selling environment to determine if an important trend in shopping patterns might emerge.

Forecasting

Scanning and monitoring are concerned with events in the general environment at a point in time. When *forecasting*, analysts develop feasible projections of what might happen, and how quickly, as a result of the changes and trends detected through scanning and monitoring.[31] For example, analysts might forecast the time that will be required for a new technology to reach the marketplace, the length of time before different corporate training procedures are required to deal with anticipated changes in the composition of the workforce, or how much time will elapse before changes in governmental taxation policies affect consumers' purchasing patterns.

The increasing use of the Internet by new companies called *infomediaries* is affecting business practices in the global economy. Infomediaries use technology to bring buyers and sellers together on-line. The company called E-Chemicals brokers 55-gallon (250-litre) drums of manufacturing chemicals between DuPont and thousands of heavy manufacturers located in the upper Midwest and east coast of the United States. PaperExchange.com maintains its website to enable paper suppliers and buyers from 40 countries to negotiate for products ranging from containerboard to writing paper. The firm's revenue source is the 3 per cent commission it charges for each transaction completed by parties using its website.[32]

Assessing

The objective of *assessing* is to determine the timing and significance of the effects of environmental changes and trends on the strategic management of a firm.[33] Through scanning, monitoring and forecasting, analysts are able to understand the general environment. Going a step further, the intent of assessment is to specify the implications of that understanding for the organisation. Without assessment, the firm is left with data that are interesting, but of unknown competitive relevance.

In the US automobile industry, Ford, General Motors and DaimlerChrysler are selling increasing numbers of trucks, sport utility vehicles and minivans. However, all three firms have lost market share in car sales to competitors such as Honda, Toyota, Volkswagen,

Audi and BMW. These three firms understand that if petrol costs were to rise substantially, or if consumer preferences shift from trucks to cars, they could be in trouble. However, shifting some production capacity to cars is a difficult decision for these companies, in that profits per unit on trucks, sport utility vehicles and minivans vastly exceed those earned on cars.[34] Thus, the challenge for those firms is to continually assess the significance of possible decreases in demand for their most profitable products and to understand changes that would be necessary in their strategies to deal successfully with shifts in consumer preferences.

Segments of the general environment

The general environment is composed of segments (and their individual elements) that are external to the firm (see Table 2.1). Although the degree of impact varies, these environmental segments affect each industry and the firms within it. The challenge is to scan, monitor, forecast and assess those elements in each segment that are of the greatest importance. In addition, the results of an external environmental analysis should recognise environmental changes, trends, opportunities and threats. Opportunities are then matched with a firm's core competencies. (The matching process is discussed further in Chapter 3.) Through proper matches, the firm achieves strategic competitiveness and earns above-average returns.

The demographic segment

> The **demographic segment** is concerned with a population's size, age, structure, geographic distribution, ethnic mix and income distribution.

The **demographic segment** is concerned with a population's size, age structure, geographic distribution, ethnic mix and income distribution.[35] As previously noted, the firm analyses demographic segments on a global basis rather than a domestic-only basis.

Population size

In October 1999, the world's population reached six billion (growing from five billion in 1987). Combined, China and India accounted for one-third of the six billion. Experts speculate that the population might stabilise at 10 billion after 2200 if the deceleration in the rate of increase in the world's head count continues. By 2050, India (with over 1.5 billion people) and China (with just under 1.5 billion people) are expected to be the most populous countries.[36]

Observing demographic changes in populations highlights the importance of this environmental segment. For example, in some advanced nations there is negative population growth (discounting the effects of immigration). For example, in Australia the birth rate in 1998 was 1.76 for each woman, and according to the Australian Bureau of Statistics about 28 per cent of woman will remain childless. The replacement level for a population is estimated at 2.1, allowing for early mortality.[37] The birth rate in Australia is below that of the United States (2.0) and New Zealand (2.0), but above that of Britain (1.70), Germany (1.5) and Italy (1.2).

In contrast to advanced nations, the rapid growth rate in the populations of some developing countries (for example, in Nigeria it is 6.0) is depleting natural resources and reducing citizens' living standards. In the words of one writer, 'If poor countries develop their economies in the same wasteful way industrial nations have, population growth will put an increasing burden on food and water supplies and the habitat of endangered species.'[38] These projections suggest major challenges and business opportunities in the 21st century.

Age structure

In some countries, the population's average age is increasing. In the United States, for example, the percentage of the population aged 55 and older is expected to increase from roughly 6 per cent in 1995 to approximately 37.5 per cent in 2019.[39] In Australia, the over 65s are expected to increase from 12 per cent of the total population in 1998 to 24 per cent by 2051.[40] Contributing to this change are declining birth rates and increasing life expectancies. Among others, these trends may suggest numerous opportunities for firms to develop goods and services to meet the needs of an increasingly older population.

It has been projected that up to one-half of the females and one-third of the males born at the end of the 1990s in developed countries could live to be 100 years old, with some of them possibly living to be 200 or more.[41] If such life spans become a reality, a host of interesting business opportunities and societal issues will emerge. For example, the effect on individuals' pension plans will be significant and will create potential opportunities for financial institutions, as well as possible threats to government-sponsored retirement and health plans.[42]

Many countries in addition to Australia are witnessing a trend towards an older workforce. By 2030, the proportion of the OECD's total labour force of 45–59-year-olds is projected to increase from 25.6 to 31.8 per cent and the share of workers aged 60 and over is expected to increase from 4.7 to 7.8 per cent.

Geographic distribution

For decades, the Australian population has been shifting to the coast, while the interior regions of the country are depopulating. As a consequence, there has been a lessening of service provision for rural areas, with banks, post offices and hospitals being withdrawn from these areas. A study by the National Institute of Economic and Industry Research (NIEIR) divided Australia up into 57 geographical/economic regions and found two economies. In the 'global cities' of Melbourne and Sydney, unemployment is low and incomes are rising; while in most country regions, unemployment is high (over 10 per cent) and property values are static or falling. In the Wide Bay/Burnett region of Queensland, the average household income is already less than half that of inner Sydney. In the Mersey-Lyell region of Tasmania, the 1996 unemployment rate was 11.2 per cent, the constrained employment rate (that is, the percentage of the adult working-age population that cannot work for various reasons) was 23.7 per cent, and the average household income slipped from $32 759 in 1986 to $30 941 in 1996, while average net household wealth (non-superannuation financial assets plus housing and business worth) was $87 314. In the 12 harbourside/middle-class suburbs of Sydney (referred to by the NIEIR as 'Global Sydney'), unemployment was 4.1 per cent, constrained employment 8.5 per cent, average household income rose from $42 683 in 1986 to $53 080 in 1996, and household wealth was $393 381.[43]

The progress of Australian states also differs. Melbourne and Sydney are centres of new industry and their states therefore benefit. Of these two, Sydney has by far the higher number of new industries. State by state, rating the 50 fastest-growing industries, New South Wales has 30, Victoria 8, Queensland 5, Western Australia 5, South Australia 1 (wine), Northern Territory 1 (uranium mining) and Tasmania has none. The NSW economy has 86 per cent of the national output of contract staff services industry and 75 per cent of information services, and it also dominates film and video distribution, cotton, computer wholesales, computer consulting, building construction and telecommunications. Overall, New South Wales dominates the 'new age' industries. The two old-economy states, South Australia and Tasmania, are therefore likely to suffer as a new-age economy based on services, telecommunications and computers takes hold.[44]

Ethnic mix

The ethnic mix of countries' populations continues to change. For business firms, the challenge is to be aware of and sensitive to these changes. Through careful study, firms can develop and market goods and services intended to satisfy the unique needs and interests of different ethnic groups. Because a labour force can be critical to competitive success, firms across the globe, including those competing in OECD countries, must learn to work effectively with labour forces that are becoming more diverse, as well as different (for example, in terms of proportions along the dimensions of age and race), than they were previously.[45]

Changes in the ethnic mix also affect a workforce's composition. In Australia, the workforce will continue to be ethnically diversified. In 1999, the proportion of Australian residents born overseas was around 23 per cent. People born in the UK made up 6 per cent of the total population and those born in New Zealand accounted for 2 per cent, but there are also large populations born in other European and Asian nations. In 1997–8, the most rapidly growing birthplace groups were those born in Singapore and Indonesia.[46]

Workforce diversity is also a socio-cultural issue. Effective management of a culturally diverse workforce can produce a competitive advantage. For example, heterogeneous work teams have been shown to produce more effective strategic analyses, more creativity and innovation, and higher-quality decisions than homogeneous work teams.[47] However, evidence also suggests that work team diversity and team performance are complex.[48] Because of this complexity, a number of companies promote cultural diversity in their workforces and facilitate effective management of such diversity through specialised management training.

Income distribution

Understanding how income is distributed within and across populations informs firms of different groups' purchasing power and discretionary income. Studies of income distributions suggest that while living standards have improved over time, variations exist within and between nations.[49] Of interest to firms are the average incomes of households and individuals. For instance, a notable change is the increase in dual-career couples. For example, in Australia, 22.4 per cent of households are two-income families.[50] Although, in general, real income has been declining, dual-career couples have increased their income. The actual figures yield strategically relevant information.

The economic segment

The health of a nation's economy affects the performance of individual firms and industries. Because of this, companies study the economic environment to identify changes, trends and their strategic implications.

> The **economic environment** refers to the nature and direction of the economy in which a firm competes or may compete.

The **economic environment** refers to the nature and direction of the economy in which a firm competes or may compete.[51] Because of the interconnectedness among nations that is resulting from the global economy, firms must scan, monitor, forecast and assess the health of economies outside their host nation. Brazil's recent experiences highlight the need to do this.

In the mid- to late 1990s, Brazil was one of Latin America's fastest-growing economies and 'was the darling of the international investment community'. In particular, the country's middle class was experiencing significant work-related opportunities to improve its standard of living. However, the effects of economic 'meltdowns' in Russia and Asia in the late 1990s were crippling for the Brazilian economy. For example, the global economic turmoil resulted in a decline in sales of 27.5 per cent from 1997 to 1998 for Brazil's automobile industry alone. In response to the nation's crisis, the country's president instituted a major currency devaluation. In 1998, employers eliminated over 580 000 jobs. The fortunes of the middle class became bleak as job losses found them unable to cope with the demands of financial purchases they made during the 'good time'. In turn, Brazil's economic crisis affected companies throughout the world, including both large and small US firms. Ford and General Motors decided to lay off workers in their facilities in Argentina because of the economic fallout from Brazil's devaluation.[52] Thus, any uncertainty in the world's interdependent economies affects firms of all types and sizes.

The cost of reversing the fortunes of an economy (such as Brazil's) once problems are encountered can be significant. For example, recent times found two-thirds of Indonesian and a quarter of Thai companies to be virtually insolvent. According to a World Bank official, 'cost estimates of financial-sector restructuring range[d] from a low of 18 percent of GDP in Indonesia to 30 percent in Thailand'.[53] These estimated costs highlight the importance of a nation being able to govern itself and its business organisations in ways that facilitate continuous, uninterrupted economic success.

In light of the increasing interdependencies among the world's economies, some believe that it is in the best interests of all nations to create truly global markets. Doing this, it is argued, can create a future in which the common goals of creating wealth and fostering economic stability are achievable. Comments by members of the World Trade Organization (WTO) speak to this matter: 'A broad range of empirical studies conclude that open trade policies are conducive to growth. The conclusion appears to hold regardless of the level of development of the countries concerned, challenging the notion that a certain level of development is required before the benefits from trade can be fully realized.'[54] In another camp, radical groups, such as S11, argue that incomes in global trade are socially divisive because the major consequence is that wealthy regions and countries become even wealthier. They also argue that the growth that accompanies increases in world trade is environmentally unsustainable.

DaimlerChrysler's CEO, Jürgen E. Schrempp, who is a strong proponent of completing a transatlantic integration between Europe and North America, appears to support the position taken by the WTO regarding the benefits of unrestricted trade. Schrempp believes that an integration between Europe and North America is logical in that 'Europe and the United States each account for close to 20 percent of the other's trade in goods while services account for more than 38 percent of bilateral trade'. Principles developed by the Transatlantic Business Dialogue (a group of businesspersons and politicians) could support an integration effort. Among the principles are the removal of all trade barriers and differing regulatory controls, and the acceptance of a product in all parts of the transatlantic marketplace once it has been approved.[55] The vice president of the European Commission believes that the Asian and Russian financial crises make it necessary to quickly integrate multiple economies, including those of Europe and the United States. In his view, 'We must inject greater urgency into opening up world markets. And we must resist any moves to return to crippling pre-war protectionism.'[56] For relatively isolated countries such as Malaysia, Singapore and Australia, the challenge is to remain in touch with such large integrated economies. These three countries are founding members of the Asia-Pacific Economic Co-operation Group (APEC), which is working towards a free trade agreement in the Pacific region. However, APEC is not as advanced as either the European Union (EU) or the North American Free Trade Agreement (NAFTA) in terms of economic integration between members.

Creating the truly 'borderless commerce' that free trade among nations would permit is proving to be a significant challenge. Using the Internet to purchase books in Europe is an example of the barriers to borderless electronic commerce. A teacher of foreign languages living in Berlin purchases books from Amazon.com's website in the United Kingdom, rather than from the firm's German website. In his words, 'If you buy from the UK site, it's much cheaper. Even if you include the shipping, it's a better deal in the UK.' The reason for the price differentials is that governments in Germany, France and some other European nations allow publishing cartels to influence business practices. A group of book publishers, each cartel can legally dictate retail prices to booksellers, both in stores and on-line.⁵⁷ Thus, the selling of books in Europe via electronic commerce appears to be an example of a business transaction that could benefit a firm through the use of the principles designed by the members of the Transatlantic Business Dialogue group.

As our discussion of the economic segment suggests, economic issues are intertwined closely with the realities of the external environment's political/legal segment.

The political/legal segment

> The **political/legal segment** is the arena in which organisations and interest groups compete for attention, resources and a voice in overseeing the body of laws and regulations guiding the interaction among nations.

The **political/legal segment** is the arena in which organisations and interest groups compete for attention, resources and a voice in overseeing the body of laws and regulations guiding the interactions among nations.⁵⁸ Essentially, this segment represents how organisations try to influence government and how governments influence them. Constantly changing, the segment influences the nature of competition (see Table 2.1). Because of this, firms must carefully analyse a new administration's business-related policies and philosophies. Antitrust laws, taxation laws, industries chosen for deregulation, labour training laws and the degree of commitment to educational institutions are areas in which an administration's policies can affect the operations and profitability of industries and individual firms. Often, how the firm intends to interact with the political/legal segment is captured through the development and use of a political strategy. The effects of a host of global governmental policies on the firm's competitive position increase the importance of forming an effective political strategy.⁵⁹

In these early years of the 21st century, business firms across the globe confront an interesting array of political/legal questions and issues. For example, the debate continues over trade policies. Some believe that a nation should erect trade barriers to protect products manufactured by its companies. Others argue that free trade across nations serves the best interests of individual countries and their citizens. The International Monetary Fund (IMF) classifies trade barriers as restrictive when tariffs total at least 25 per cent of a product's price. At the other extreme, the IMF stipulates that a nation has *open trade* when its tariffs are between zero and 9 per cent. To foster trade, New Zealand initially cut its tariffs from 16 to 8.5 per cent, and then to 3 per cent in 2000. Some measure of the subsequent health of the New Zealand economy in late 2000 came with the NZ dollar's value of 38 cents to the US dollar. Major NZ firms, such as Lion Nathan (brewing), now do more than 80 per cent of their business in Australia. Columbia reduced its tariffs to less than 12 per cent. The IMF classifies this percentage as 'relatively open'.⁶⁰ In a cooperative spirit, the EU, Japan, Australia, Hong Kong, Singapore, Mexico and Chile were among the countries that, beginning in January 2000, initiated a new round of global trade talks to try to develop multilateral negotiations that would reduce or eliminate trade barriers. Resulting from these actions, the countries hoped, would be a significant increase in the amount of free trade completed among their economies.⁶¹

An interesting debate occurring in the United States concerns the regulation of e-commerce. In part, laws regulating e-commerce are an attempt to prevent fraud, violations of privacy and poor service. Beyond this, some think that governmental policies should be developed to influence the nature of Internet gambling.⁶² Thus, as the 21st century started, US government officials were trying to devise policies on a 'host of knotty issues ranging from on-line pornography to Internet taxation'. A concern of all parties is for government officials to develop policies that will not stifle the legitimate growth of e-commerce.[63]

Across the globe, governments are trying to develop policies that are in their countries' best economic interests. Japan's government is working actively to find policies that can stimulate economic growth. US energy firms are investing heavily in Mexico as a result of recent favourable regulatory changes. Germany's government is seeking ways to support an entrepreneurial spirit that seems to have the potential to reduce the nation's unemployment rate. In the United Kingdom, regulators were working to end British Telecommunications plc's dominance of local services as 1999 came to a close. Central America, once a proving ground for guerrilla-warfare tactics, is joining most of the rest of Latin America as a proving ground for free-market reform. Guatemala, for example, is implementing one of the most aggressive telecommunication reform laws in Latin America. It is essentially opening its market to full competition in all segments – local, long-distance, paging and cellular services. Motorola and 14 other foreign telecommunications companies are negotiating to provide these services. The Australian government's program of deregulation and privatisation, which included the partial sale of Telstra, is timid (or wise) by comparison. Furthermore, Guatemala has already privatised railroad, radio and electrical utility companies and has begun the process of privatising its telecommunications company, Guatel. Other Central American countries are taking similar, if not identical, actions.[64]

The socio-cultural segment

> The **socio-cultural segment** is concerned with a society's attitudes and cultural values.

The **socio-cultural segment** is concerned with a society's attitudes and cultural values. Because attitudes and values form the cornerstone of a society, they often drive demographic, economic, political/legal and technological conditions and changes.

Socio-cultural segments differ across countries. For example, in the United States, 14 per cent of the nation's GDP is spent on health care. This is the highest percentage of any OECD country. Germany allocates 10.4 per cent of GDP to health care, while Switzerland allocates 10.2 per cent, Australia 8.4 per cent and New Zealand 7.6 per cent.[65] Countries' citizens have different attitudes about retirement savings as well. In Italy, just 9 per cent of the citizenry say that they are saving primarily for retirement, while the figures are 18 per cent in Germany and 48 per cent in the United States.[66] Attitudes regarding one's savings for retirement affect a nation's economic and political/legal segments. Differences in attitudes about work seem to exist between France and some other nations, including the United States. In Australia and the United States, boundaries between work and home are becoming blurred, as employees' workweeks continue to be stretched, whereas working long hours has become a crime in France. Commenting about the situation in France, a business writer noted that 'at a time when employees around the globe toil more and more, France is cutting the legal workweek to 35 hours from 39, even for white-collar staff. And after decades of ignoring the working habits of this workaholic group of employees known in France as *cadres*, labour inspectors are clamping down on companies where managers, engineers and researchers burn the midnight oil.' Those supporting control of work hours suggest that doing so would reduce France's overall unemployment rate. From the strategic management perspective, a French company seeking to establish an operation in the United States, or an Australian firm attempting to do the same in France, should fully understand the effects of the socio-cultural environment on expectations they can have of employees.[67]

Describing a culture's effect on a society, columnist George Will suggested that it is vital for people to understand that a nation's culture has a primary effect on its social character and health.⁶⁸ Thus, companies must understand the implications of a society's attitudes and its cultural values before they can expect to offer goods and services that will meet consumers' needs and interests.

The number of female workers is an important indicator of increased workforce diversity. In Australia, women now account for approximately 41 per cent of the workforce.

As mentioned earlier, a significant trend in many countries is increased diversity of the workforce. The number of female workers is an important indicator of increasing workforce diversity, and women are a valuable source of highly productive employees. Some argue, for example, that 'educated hardworking women double the talent pool in the U.S. and give the nation a big competitive advantage over countries that deny women full participation in their economies'.⁶⁹ However, across multiple global workforces, women comprise an increasing percentage of employees. In the United States, women now account for approximately 47 per cent of the workforce. In Sweden, they account for roughly 52 per cent, in Japan 44 per cent, in France 40 per cent, in Australia and Germany 41 per cent, and in Mexico 37 per cent. In the United States, women hold 43 per cent of the managerial jobs. In Sweden, they hold 17 per cent of managerial positions, while in Japan the figure is only 9.4 per cent.⁷⁰

In some instances, women hold high-profile executive positions. For example, the retiring head of Cochlear, Australia's leading-edge hearing implant company, is Catherine Livingstone, while the new chair of Qantas is Margaret Jackson, who resigned from her board positions at BHP and Pacific Dunlop to concentrate on Qantas. In 2000, Jill Ker Conway was appointed as the chairperson of Lend Lease Corporation.

Pay differentials between men and women still exist, too, although because of equal pay and equal opportunity legislation in many countries, relative pay for women is increasing continuously. Among Western European countries, the pay gap between men and women is greatest in the United Kingdom, where men earn 34 per cent more than women do, and lowest in Sweden, where a 17 per cent gap exists.⁷¹ In Australia, the gap is somewhat pronounced, where the average wage of a full-time male worker is $885 per week, compared to $715 for a female worker.⁷²

The influx of women into the workforce and the increasing ethnic and cultural diversity yield exciting challenges and significant opportunities.⁷³ Included among these are the needs to combine the best of both men's and women's leadership styles for a firm's benefit and to identify ways to facilitate all employees' contributions to their firms. An example of a firm attempting to meet these challenges and take advantage of such opportunities is Avon, where Andrea Jung was appointed CEO and four of the 11 board members and more than 40 per cent of global managers are women.⁷⁴ Some companies now provide training to nurture women's and ethnic minorities' leadership potential. Changes in organisational structure and management practices often are required to eliminate subtle barriers that may exist. Learning to manage diversity in the domestic workforce can increase a firm's effectiveness in managing a globally diverse workforce as the firm acquires more international operations. These commitments to promote and manage diversity enhance the firm's performance.

Another manifestation of changing attitudes towards work is the continuing growth of contingency workers (part-time, temporary and contract employees) throughout the global economy. Parts of the world in which this trend is significant include Australia, Canada, Japan, Latin America, Western Europe and the United States. The fastest-growing segment of contingency workers is in the technical and professional area. Because of tight labour markets for technical and professional workers, agencies providing contingency workers to companies are offering multiple inducements to those they hire. Snelling Personnel Services, in the United States, for example, offers points to their employees for hours worked. The points can be used to purchase items from a gift catalogue.⁷⁵ In Japan, analysts believe that the entire service sector, including the part dealing with contingency workers, is going to grow substantially. Creating this growth are corporate restructurings and a breakdown of lifetime employment practices. Pasona, Japan's largest temporary staffing agency, is moving quickly to take advantage of increasing demand for its services.⁷⁶

Participating often in the workforce as contingency workers, cross-border electronic telecommuters are an interesting socio-cultural trend. 'Commuting' frequently from developing countries to work in developed countries, the number of electronic telecommuters is expected to increase rapidly this century. This work-style option is feasible because of changes in the technological segment, including the Internet's rapid growth and evolution.⁷⁷

The technological segment

Pervasive and diversified in scope, technological changes affect many parts of societies. Their effects occur primarily through new products, processes and materials. The **technological segment** includes the institutions and activities involved with creating new knowledge and translating that knowledge into new outputs, products, processes and materials.

> The **technological segment** includes the institutions and activities involved with creating new knowledge and translating that knowledge into new outputs, products, processes and raw materials.

The knowledge and capabilities that are created by developing or using new technologies sometimes transform or revitalise an entire industry. This appears to be the case with the yo-yo. Stuck in an up-and-down cycle since being introduced in the United States in 1930, yo-yos have benefited from a technological innovation that created a demand which exceeds the industry's supply capacity. Recently, yo-yos were the second-largest-selling toy in the United States, and a 'minor' yo-yo craze was in full swing in Australia. The transaxle, which is a sleeve around the yo-yo axle that reduces friction, is the technology contributing to the yo-yo's increase in popularity. This technology makes it possible for average users to easily perform more complicated tricks, such as the 'long sleeper', in which the yo-yo spins at the bottom of the string for at least 15 seconds. The original technology allowed only 'masters' to perform the trick.⁷⁸

Given the rapid pace of technological change, it is vital for firms to study the technological segment quickly and thoroughly. The importance of such efforts is suggested by the finding that firms which are early adopters of new technology often achieve higher market shares and earn higher returns. Thus, executives must verify that their firm is continuously scanning the external environments to identify potential substitutes for technologies that are in current use, as well as to spot newly emerging technologies from which their firm could derive competitive benefits.[79]

As mentioned in Chapter 1 and highlighted in other chapters throughout the book, the Internet is a technology with important strategic implications for firms of all types and sizes. Sometimes referred to as 'the information superhighway', the connectivity among different technologies and media that the Internet makes possible is thought by many to be at least as significant as were the changes brought about by the Industrial Revolution.[80]

Numerous surveys suggest that executives are aware of the Internet's potential. A survey completed by Booz Allen & Hamilton in partnership with *The Economist* revealed that: (1) 92 per cent of executives who participated in the survey believed that the Internet would continue to reshape their companies' markets; (2) 61 per cent thought that effective use of the Internet would facilitate efforts to achieve their firms' strategic goals; and (3) 30 per cent noted that their competitive strategies had already been altered because of the Internet's influence.[81] The growing number of university and other tertiary students pursuing degrees in electronic commerce suggests that tomorrow's businesspeople also recognise the Internet's importance and potential.[82] In contrast, the results of a survey of manufacturing executives suggest an opposite reaction: these respondents believe that on-line sales growth to 2003 will not be enough for the Internet to become a major force in the manufacturing industry. Commenting about the survey results, an industry analyst suggested that the manufacturing CEOs may be 'missing the boat' in terms of the Internet's potential and influence.[83]

Among other valuable uses, the Internet is an excellent source of data and information for a firm to use in understanding its external environment. Using the Internet for this purpose supports the firm's efforts to complete an effective external environmental analysis. Access to experts on such topics as chemical engineering and semiconductor manufacturing, and even to satellite photographs, is available through the Internet. Other information available through this incredibly powerful and significant technology includes Australian Bureau of Statistics data, *The Economist* magazine, *The Age* and *The Australian* newspapers (among many others), annual reports of listed companies and stock market updates.

As a technology, the Internet is used to conduct business transactions between companies, as well as between a company and its customers. In late 1999, e-commerce between businesses accounted for the bulk (approximately 84 per cent) of all Internet transactions. Projected to increase to 92 per cent by 2003, the total value of B2B on-line commerce is expected to reach US$1.3 trillion in the same year. This figure substantially dwarfs the estimated US$108 billion in goods and services companies will sell on-line to consumers in 2003.[84] As an indication of the uncertainty associated with understanding how rapidly Internet business transactions with consumers will grow, another firm predicts that 'the global consumer market for products and services ordered over the Internet may balloon to [US]$380 billion by 2003'.[85] The differences in these projections of Internet sales to consumers in 2003 (US$108 billion versus US$380 billion) could have important strategic implications (for example, in terms of opportunities and threats) for firms competing in a variety of industries.

According to Dell Computer Corporation's CEO Michael Dell, the Internet also has great potential as a business-organisation system. We discussed this point briefly in Chapter 1, where we noted that Dell reduces its paperwork flow, schedules its payments more efficiently, and is able to coordinate its inventories efficiently and effectively through the use of this technology. Dell accomplishes all of this by linking personal computers with network servers, which the firm's CEO believes have the potential to revolutionise business processes 'in a way that blurs traditional boundaries between supplier and manufacturer, and manufacturer and customer. This will eliminate paper-based functions, flatten organization hierarchies, and shrink time and distance to a degree not possible before.'[86] Thus, a competitive premium may accrue to the company that is capable of deriving full value from the Internet in terms of both e-commerce activities and transactions taken to process the firm's workflow.

When coupled with Michael Dell's opinion, the sales volume data presented above suggest that the Internet's power is recognised by today's successful firms, as well as by those seeking to enter an industry or to compete in ways that define a new market space.[87] Some companies are using the Internet to create new market space in the global music industry. It may be that digital distribution of music via the Internet will account for at least 8 per cent (US$4 billion in sales volume) of all recorded music sold worldwide in 2004 and up to 20 per cent by 2010.[88] Some analysts believe that these expectations are stimulating the music industry to recognise the Internet as the key driver of its global future.[89] These examples suggest that companies which understand the Internet's potential and the business opportunities it creates embrace change and seek to use the Internet to increase their flexibility so that they can move rapidly when engaging in marketplace competition.[90]

The global segment

The **global segment** includes relevant new global markets, existing ones that are changing, important international political events, and critical cultural and institutional characteristics of global markets. Although the segments we have examined so far are analysed in terms of their domestic and global implications, some additional specific global factors should be analysed as well. For example, firms must attempt to identify critical new global markets, as well as those that are changing. Many global markets (for example, those in some South American nations and in South Korea and Taiwan) are becoming borderless and integrated.[91] In addition to contemplating opportunities, firms should recognise potential threats in these countries and their marketplaces.

As explained in the Strategic Focus about Dell Computer Corporation, China is a nation with a business environment with both opportunities and threats. Creating additional opportunities is China's recent admission to the WTO. A Geneva-based organisation, the WTO establishes rules for global trade. China's membership in this organisation suggests the possibility of increasing and less-restricted participation by the country in the global economy.[92] In return for gaining entry to the WTO, China agreed to cut duties on foreign goods from 22.1 per cent to an average of 17 per cent. Trade barriers were reduced in multiple industries, including telecommunications, banking, automobiles, movies and professional services (such as the services of lawyers, doctors and accountants).[93] The immediate reaction to the reduced barriers in China was positive among a host of countries. However, caution was also expressed, because most of the terms to which China agreed in order to gain entry to the WTO were to be phased in over roughly a five-year period. Also, an analyst noted that conducting business in China would challenge firms throughout the world, as China's environment and markets are 'very unique' and really beyond easy comparison.[94]

> The **global segment** includes relevant new global markets, existing ones that are changing, important international political events, and critical cultural and institutional characteristics of global markets.

Strategic Focus International

Dell's direct business model leads to strategic success in China

According to a business writer, 'One thing's for certain: The Dell model is working in China. And as long as China's PC market continues to grow, Dell is ready to grow with it, provided it sticks to that model and continues to execute it better than anyone else.'

Dell's success in China is being achieved in spite of economic conditions that some believe are unfavourable. Examples of these conditions include the fact that only 40 per cent of China's industrial output comes from private ventures and the reality that China suffers from a number of the symptoms that contributed to the trouble of neighbouring Asian countries during the latter part of the 1990s. These symptoms include government interference with the economy and a host of traditional personal business arrangements that often require padding of egos and wallets. What is the Dell model, and why does it allow the firm to succeed when confronting conditions that do not necessarily predict success?

Commenting about Dell's origins, one writer noted that 'Michael Dell began in 1984 with a simple business insight: he could bypass the dealership channel through which personal computers were then being sold. Instead, he would sell directly to customers and build products to order.' Using this model, Dell has become the world's leading direct computer systems company, with recent annual revenues of over US$22 billion. As the largest seller of personal computers in the United States, Dell does approximately two-thirds of its business with large corporations, government agencies and educational institutions.

Manufacturing facilities are located in Round Rock, Texas; Nashville, Tennessee; Limerick, Ireland; Penang, Malaysia; and Xiamen, China. The company's direct business model allows it to sell personal computer systems directly to the consumer. Innovative when initially developed, the model allows Dell to better understand consumers' requirements and to reduce costs by eliminating the need for a group of wholesale and retail dealers between the firm and its customers. The model also allows Dell to maintain extremely low inventory levels of component parts, as it custom-manufactures products according to individual customers' specifications.

Dell's business transactions through the Internet continue to expand. The firm maintains country-specific sites in close to 50 countries. In the last quarter of 1999, Internet sales exceeded US$14 million daily. Convinced that the Internet was turbo-charging his firm's business, founder Michael Dell wanted at least 50 per cent of total revenue to be from Internet sales by the end of 2000.

An economy with huge potential, China was already the world's fifth-largest PC market (behind the United States, Japan, Germany and Britain) at the start of the 21st century. Along with competitors such as Compaq, IBM and Hewlett-Packard, Dell concluded that the Chinese PC market was simply too large to ignore. Avoiding the consumer retail market (almost two years of a citizen's savings are required to buy a PC in China), Dell decided to sell directly to corporations instead. In contrast, its competitors relied largely on resellers. Avoiding the costs of middlemen, Dell believed that it could deliver products to customers at lower, more competitive prices. The fact that Dell's Chinese market share tripled in 1999 to 1.2 per cent, while Compaq's declined from 3.5 to 2.7 per cent, and the firm's ability to become the eighth-largest PC seller in China in a mere eight months, may be preliminary evidence supporting this belief.

To the surprise of competitors and analysts alike, Dell learned quickly how to sell to China's state-owned enterprises (SOEs). Contributing to this success was Dell's ability to gain support from these firms' chief information officers, company officials who were found to place high value on the speed, convenience and service associated with Dell's products. In addition, Dell's salespeople learned that information managers in SOEs were far more 'tech-savvy' than originally thought. Because of their increasing ability to solve many of their own technical problems, these managers and those working for them did not need the extensive (and more expensive) technical service support offered by Dell's competitors. In the words of Xiao Jian Yi, deputy general manager of China Pacific Insurance (a fast-growing state-owned insurance company), 'We may still need some consulting services, but in our front offices we know how to choose our equipment.' Speaking to Dell's advantages, he indicated that 'Dell provides exactly what we need, and with Dell we can choose exactly what we want'.

As noted by analysts, Dell intends to continue relying on the direct business model as it pursues strategic success. 'By taking its direct business model and its associated customer experience to even higher levels, through the Internet and value-added services, Dell intends to continue to grow its business at a multiple of the high-growth rate anticipated for the computer-systems industry as a whole. Dell still has significant opportunity for expansion in all parts of the world, especially in markets outside of the U.S.' Continuous scanning, monitoring, forecasting and assessing of its external environment will help Dell to identify opportunities for using the direct business model. In addition, these activities will help it to identify conditions indicating that the model should be adapted to cope successfully with shifts in one or more of the external environment's segments.

Sources: N. Chowdhury, 1999, 'Dell cracks China', *Fortune*, 21 June, pp. 120–4; Dell Computer Corporation, 2000, 17 January: www.dell.com; L. Kraar, 1999, 'Five Chinese myths', *Fortune*, 10 May, p. 30; M. B. Regan, 1999, 'Industries adjust to e-commerce', *Waco Tribune-Herald*, 11 April, pp. B6, B7; J. Magretta, 1998, 'The power of virtual integration: An interview with Dell Computer's Michael Dell', *Harvard Business Review*, 76(2), pp. 73–84.

Following an analysis of the conditions in the external environment and their implications, Dell decided to apply its direct business model in a market that sceptics suggested would not respond favourably to it. However, Dell thought that China was a market with potential that simply could not be overlooked, and therefore, deciding to compete in China was a strategic decision with acceptable risk.

The commitment to carefully evaluate its external environment before making strategic decisions is part of the pattern Dell follows when using its direct business model. The firm believes that its external environment is composed of a group of factors (for example, general economic and industry conditions; competitors; international activities; product, customer and geographic mixes; and seasonal trends) that are beyond its direct control. As a result, Dell examines these factors intensely to identify opportunities and threats.[95]

Firms must also have a reasonable understanding of the different socio-cultural and institutional attributes of global markets in which they do compete or in which they hope to compete. Dell Computer Corporation, for example, continues to study China's political/legal and economic structures, as well as the attitudes and values that form and influence the nation's evolving culture.

Companies operating in South Korea must understand the value placed on hierarchical order, formality and self-control, as well as on duty rather than rights. Furthermore, Korean ideology emphasises communitarianism, a characteristic of many Asian countries. Korea's approach differs from those of Japan and China with its focus on *Inhwa*, or harmony. *Inhwa* is based on a respect of hierarchical relationships and an obedience to authority. Alternatively, the approach in China stresses *Guanxi*, personal relationships or good connections, while in Japan, the focus is on *Wa*, or group harmony and social cohesion.[96] The institutional context of Korea suggests a major emphasis on centralised planning by the government. Indeed, the emphasis placed on growth by many South Korean firms is the result of a government policy to promote economic growth.[97]

A key objective of analysing the general environment is identifying anticipated significant changes and trends among external elements. With a focus on the future, the analysis of the general environment allows firms to identify opportunities and threats. Also critical to a firm's future operations is an understanding of its industry environment and its competitors; these issues are considered next. A good CEO will constantly monitor the external environment for new ideas. For example, BHP's CEO Paul Anderson states that changes in the external environment, such as privatisation of government mining activities, reductions in mining leases on Aboriginal lands, and consolidation of mining companies around the world, mean that a new competitive dynamic will emerge in the mining industry. Increasingly, this will mean a focus on making money, not just building better production facilities.[98]

Industry environment analysis

An **industry** is a group of firms producing products that are close substitutes.

An **industry** is a group of firms producing products that are close substitutes. In the course of competition, these firms influence one another. Typically, industries include a rich mix of competitive strategies that companies use in pursuing strategic competitiveness and above-average returns. In part, these strategies are chosen because of the influence of the effects of an industry's characteristics.[99] Some believe that technology-based industries in which e-commerce is a dominant means of competing differ from their more traditional predecessors. An important difference may be the virtually free exchange of information among e-commerce firms, partly to seek advice about how to improve their firms' operations. With a 'communal bent', the belief is that sharing information allows each firm to learn how to improve its competitiveness.[100]

Compared to the general environment, the industry environment has a more direct effect on strategic competitiveness and above-average returns. The intensity of industry competition and an industry's profit potential (as measured by the long-run return on invested capital) are a function of five competitive forces: the threats posed by new entrants, suppliers, buyers, product substitutes, and the intensity of rivalry among competitors (see Figure 2.2).

Figure 2.2 | The five forces model of competition

The five forces model of competition expands the arena for competitive analysis. Historically, when studying the competitive environment, firms concentrated on companies with which they competed directly. However, today competition is viewed as a grouping of alternative ways for customers to obtain the value they desire, rather than as a battle among direct competitors. This is particularly important, because in recent years industry boundaries have become blurred. For example, in the electrical utilities industry, co-generators – firms that also produce power – are competing with regional utility companies. Moreover, telecommunications companies now compete with broadcasters, software manufacturers also provide personal financial services, airlines sell mutual funds, and automobile manufacturers sell insurance and provide financing.[101] In addition, in order to focus on customers rather than specific industry boundaries to define markets, geographic boundaries should be considered. The reason for this is that research evidence suggests that different geographic markets for the same product can have considerably different competitive conditions.[102]

The five forces model recognises that suppliers could become a firm's competitor (by integrating forward), as could buyers (by integrating backward). The former strategy was illustrated graphically in the pharmaceuticals industry when Merck & Company acquired Medco Containment Services, a mail-order pharmacy and prescription benefits management company. In so doing, Merck integrated forward and became a competitor of other pharmacies and prescription benefits management companies. Perhaps most importantly, Merck guaranteed a major source of distribution for its products. Shortly after Merck's acquisition, SmithKline Beecham and Eli Lilly announced plans to acquire similar companies and integrate forward as well.[103] In addition, firms choosing to enter a new market and those producing products that are adequate substitutes for existing products could become competitors of a company.

Threat of new entrants

Evidence suggests that companies have always found it difficult to identify new competitors.[104] This is unfortunate, in that new entrants often have the potential to be quite threatening to incumbents. One reason new entrants pose such a threat is that they bring additional production capacity. Unless the demand for a good or service is increasing, additional capacity holds consumers' costs down, resulting in less revenue and lower returns for an industry's firms. Often, new entrants have substantial resources and a keen interest in gaining a large market share. As a result, new competitors may force existing firms to be more effective and efficient and to learn how to compete on new dimensions (for example, an Internet-based distribution channel).

The likelihood that firms will enter an industry is a function of two factors: barriers to entry and the retaliation expected from current industry participants. When firms find entry into a new industry difficult, or when they are at a competitive disadvantage entering a new industry, *entry barriers* exist.

Barriers to entry

Existing competitors try to develop barriers to market entry. In contrast, potential entrants seek markets in which the entry barriers are relatively insignificant. The absence of entry barriers increases the probability that a new entrant can operate profitably. There are several kinds of potentially significant entry barriers.

Economies of scale. An important characteristic of each production technology, *economies of scale* are 'the marginal improvements in efficiency that a firm experiences as it incrementally increases its size'.[105] From an operational perspective, economies of scale mean that as the quantity of a product produced during a given period increases, the costs of manufacturing each unit decline.

Economies of scale can be gained through most business functions (for example, marketing, manufacturing, research and development, and purchasing). New entrants face a dilemma when confronting current competitors' scale economies. Small-scale entry places them at a cost disadvantage. However, large-scale entry, in which the new entrant manufactures large volumes of a product to gain economies of scale, risks strong competitive retaliation.

Also important (for example, for automobile manufacturers) are instances of current competitive realities that reduce the ability of economies of scale to create an entry barrier. Many companies now customise their products for large numbers of small customer groups. Customised products are not manufactured in the volumes necessary to achieve economies of scale. Rather, customisation is made possible by new, flexible manufacturing systems. In fact, the new manufacturing technology facilitated by advanced computerisation has allowed the development of mass customisation in some industries. Mass customised products can be individualised to the customer in a very short time (for example, within a day). Mass customisation may become the norm in manufacturing products.[106] Companies manufacturing customised products learn how to respond quickly to customers' desires, rather than developing scale economies.

Product differentiation. Over time, customers may come to believe that a firm's product is unique. This belief can result from service to the customer, effective advertising campaigns, or the firm being the first to market a good or service. Companies such as Coca-Cola, PepsiCo and the world's automobile manufacturers spend a great deal of money on advertising to convince potential customers of their products' distinctiveness. Customers valuing a product's uniqueness tend to become loyal to both the product and the company producing it. Typically, new entrants must allocate many resources across time to overcome customer loyalties. To combat the perception of uniqueness, new entrants frequently offer products at lower prices. Doing this, however, may result in lower profits or even losses.

Capital requirements. Competing in a new industry requires resources to invest. In addition to physical facilities, capital is needed for inventories, marketing activities and other critical business functions. Even when competing in a new industry is attractive, the capital required for successful market entry may not be available to pursue an apparent market opportunity.

Switching costs. *Switching costs* are the one-time costs customers incur when buying from a different supplier. The costs of buying new ancillary equipment and of retraining employees, and even the psychic costs of ending a relationship, may be incurred in switching to a new supplier. In some cases, switching costs are low, such as when the consumer switches to a different soft drink. Switching costs can vary as a function of time. For example, in terms of hours towards graduation, the cost to a student to transfer from one university to another as a first year is much lower than it is when the student is entering the final year. Occasionally, a decision made by manufacturers to produce a new, innovative product creates high switching costs for the final consumer. This was the case for the consumer who had to decide to switch from cassette tapes to CDs and for the customer contemplating switching from analog to digital cellular telephones. If switching costs are high, a new entrant must offer either a substantially lower price or a much better product to attract buyers. Usually, the more established the relationship between parties, the greater is the cost incurred to switch to an alternative offering.

Access to distribution channels. Over time, industry participants can develop effective means of distributing products. Once a relationship with distributors is developed, firms nurture it in order to create switching costs for them. Access to distribution channels can be a strong entry barrier for new entrants, particularly in consumer non-durable goods industries (for example, in grocery stores, shelf space is limited). Thus, new entrants have to persuade distributors to carry their products, either in addition to or in place of those already being stocked. Price breaks and cooperative advertising allowances may be used for this purpose; however, those practices reduce the new entrant's profit potential. As explained in the Strategic Focus, Dell uses its distribution channels to create value for customers in China, as well as throughout the world. To maintain the direct business model's advantage, Dell nurtures relationships with its customers by offering them services and responding to their needs.

Cost disadvantages independent of scale. In some instances, established competitors have cost advantages that new entrants cannot duplicate. Proprietary product technology, favourable access to raw materials, favourable locations and government subsidies are examples. Successful competition requires new entrants to find ways to reduce the strategic relevance of these factors. Delivering purchases directly to the buyer can counter the favourable location advantage; new food establishments in an undesirable location follow this practice. Similarly, automobile dealerships located in unattractive areas (for example, in a city's downtown area) can provide superior service (for example, picking up and returning the car to be serviced to the customer) to overcome a competitor's location advantage.

Government policy. Through licensing and permit requirements, governments can control entry into an industry. Liquor retailing, banking and airlines are examples of industries in Australia in which government decisions and actions affect entry possibilities. Also, governments restrict entry into some utility industries because of the need to provide quality service to all and the capital requirements necessary to do so.

Expected retaliation

Firms seeking to enter an industry also anticipate the reactions of firms in the industry. An expectation of swift and vigorous responses reduces the likelihood of entry. Vigorous retaliation can be expected when the firm has a major stake in the industry (for example, having fixed assets with few, if any, alternative uses), when it has substantial resources, and when industry growth is slow or constrained.

Locating market niches not being served by incumbents allows the new entrant to avoid entry barriers. Small entrepreneurial firms are generally best suited for searching out and serving neglected market segments. When Honda first entered the US market, it concentrated on small-engine motorcycles, a market that firms such as Harley-Davidson ignored. By targeting this neglected niche, Honda avoided competition. After consolidating its position, Honda used its strength to attack rivals by introducing larger motorcycles and competing in the broader market. Competitive actions and responses between firms such as Honda and Harley-Davidson are discussed fully in Chapter 5.

Bargaining power of suppliers

Increasing prices and reducing the quality of products sold are potential means through which suppliers can exert power over firms competing within an industry. If a firm is unable to recover cost increases through its pricing structure, its profitability is reduced by its suppliers' actions. A supplier group is powerful when:
- it is dominated by a few large companies and is more concentrated than the industry to which it sells;
- satisfactory substitute products are not available to industry firms;
- industry firms are not a significant customer for the supplier group;
- suppliers' goods are critical to buyers' marketplace success;
- the effectiveness of suppliers' products has created high switching costs for industry firms; and

- **suppliers** are a credible threat to integrate forward into the buyers' industry (for example, a clothing manufacturer might choose to operate its own retail outlets). Credibility is enhanced when suppliers have substantial resources and provide the industry's firms with a highly differentiated product.

As a result of its success, initially in its US domestic market and now globally as well, Wal-Mart is an example of a company over which few suppliers have power. The sheer size of its purchases and the relatively low switching costs it faces when choosing among suppliers often combine to yield significant power for the firm.

Bargaining power of buyers

Firms seek to maximise the return on their invested capital. Buyers (customers of an industry or firm) want to buy products at the lowest possible price, at which the industry earns the lowest acceptable rate of return on its invested capital. To reduce their costs, buyers bargain for higher quality, greater levels of service and lower prices. These outcomes are achieved by encouraging competitive battles among the industry's firms. Customers (buyer groups) are powerful when:

- they purchase a large portion of an industry's total output;
- the product being purchased from an industry accounts for a significant portion of the buyers' costs;
- they could switch to another product at little, if any, cost; and
- the industry's products are undifferentiated or standardised, and the buyers pose a credible threat if they were to integrate backward into the sellers' industry.

Iceland is a niche frozen-food retailer operating in the United Kingdom. Recently, the firm announced that it was banning the use of genetically modified ingredients to manufacture its private-label products. This decision was in reaction to consumer demands for products to be prepared with unaltered food items. A recent poll taken in the United Kingdom showed that '40 percent of people had no trust in what scientists said on the safety of modified food' and that '56 percent thought modified foods were unsafe to eat, more than double the percentage thinking them safe'. Initially, competitors' reaction to Iceland's decision was one of disdain. Separating modified from unmodified crops, they alleged, was virtually impossible. However, only 13 months after Iceland took its action, some giant manufacturers, including Unilever and Nestlé, began to phase out gene-altered ingredients from their food stocks. Actions taken by these companies were perhaps influenced by the size of the consumer group expressing concerns about the safety of items made with genetically altered crops.[107] An individual buyer lacks the degree of influence necessary to produce these responses; collectively, however, a large group of food consumers can account for a significant portion of the food manufacturing and retailer industries' output. Certainly this has been the case in both the British, and now European, beef industry, where consumers have refused, en masse, to purchase beef over fears it may be contaminated with Bovine Spongiform Encephalopathy, commonly known as BSE or mad cow disease.

Armed with greater amounts of information about the manufacturer's costs and the power of the Internet as a shopping and distribution alternative, the consumer appears to be stimulating a shift in power in the automobile industry. One reason for this shift is that individual buyers incur virtually zero switching costs when they decide to purchase from one manufacturer rather than another, or from one dealer as opposed to a second or third one. These conditions are forcing companies in the automobile industry to become more focused on the needs and desires of the people actually buying cars, trucks, minivans and sport utility vehicles. To retain a more direct relationship with their customers and possibly to reduce the power of their buyers, automobile companies are acting swiftly. General Motors, for example, has developed a new national on-line buying service.[108]

Threat of substitute products

Substitute products are different goods or services from outside a given industry that perform similar or the same functions as a product that the industry produces. For example, as a sugar substitute, Nutrasweet places an upper limit on sugar manufacturers' prices (that is, Nutrasweet and sugar perform the same function, but with different characteristics). Other product substitutes include fax machines instead of overnight deliveries, plastic containers rather than glass jars, paper bags in place of plastic bags, and tea substituted for coffee.[109]

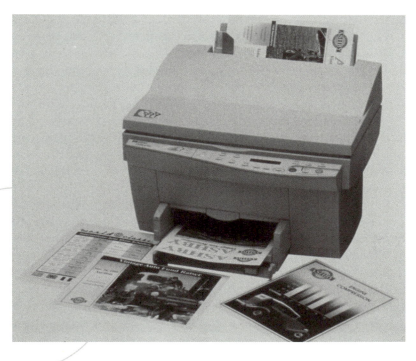

Fax machines are substitutes for surface mail. E-mail has now become a substitute for faxes. Within the communications industry, the probability of substitutes for products, given technological dynamism, is high.

In general, product substitutes are a strong threat to a firm when customers face few, if any, switching costs and when the substitute product's price is lower or its quality and performance capabilities are equal to or greater than those of the competing product. Differentiating a product along dimensions that customers value (for example, price, quality, service after the sale, and location) reduces a substitute's attractiveness.

Intensity of rivalry among competitors

Because an industry's firms are mutually dependent, actions taken by one company usually invite competitive retaliation. Thus, in many industries, firms compete actively and vigorously as they pursue strategic competitiveness and above-average returns. Competitive rivalry intensifies when a firm is challenged by a competitor's actions or when an opportunity to improve a market position is recognised. Visible dimensions on which rivalry is based include price, quality and innovation. Typically, firms seek to differentiate their products from competitors' offerings in terms of dimensions that customers value and in which the firms have a competitive advantage. As explained in the Strategic Focus, the rivalry between competitors Amazon.com and Barnesandnoble.com has been intense. However, given Amazon.com's recent strategic decisions, the nature of the rivalry may change.

The remainder of this section describes the various factors influencing the intensity of the rivalry between firms.

Strategic Focus Corporate

Amazon.com and Barnesandnoble.com: A continuing rivalry

With a mission of using the Internet to transform book buying into the fastest, easiest and most enjoyable shopping experience possible, Amazon.com opened its electronic doors in July 1995. The firm is credited widely for virtually creating the on-line retailing industry.

Businesspeople and business analysts alike consider Amazon.com's growth to be phenomenal. This perspective is highlighted by the following commentary from a business writer: 'Amazon's four-year rise from upstart on-line bookseller to one of the largest retailers on the Web is now legendary. The company has defined e-commerce as we know it.' Amazon's path-breaking success and its competitive aggressiveness is captured by the term 'getting Amazoned', which is used to describe what happens when a conventional business is damaged severely by an on-line competitor.

In contrast to Amazon.com, Barnes and Noble's (B&N's) origins are in the 'bricks and mortar' portion of book retailing. B&N was started in 1965 with a US$5 000 investment in one bookstore. Len Riggio purchased the company six years later. At the time, B&N was a single 100-year-old bookstore on lower Fifth Avenue in New York City. In the mid-1980s, Riggio acquired the B. Dalton chain with a loan and junk bond financing. With these units as a foundation, Riggio developed his concept of a superstore for a retail bookseller. The concept was framed around the belief that independent bookstores were too small to be efficient. By stocking thousands of titles and placing sofas and coffee bars in large stores, Riggio was able to transform the book-retailing industry. The concept worked, analysts believe, because it 'not only attracted traditional readers but tapped a whole new market, those who purchase the 53 percent of American books sold through supermarkets, mail-order clubs, or large wholesalers like Wal-Mart'. Recently, Barnes & Noble, Inc., operated over 520 B&N units, as well as over 470 B. Dalton bookstores. Offering books from more than 50 000 publisher imprints, and with an emphasis on small, independent publishers and university presses, the company provides access to more than a million titles.

Amazon.com quickly became a serious, yet different, type of competitor for B&N. Because of the success of Amazon.com, a company that some believe B&N views as its 'dreaded enemy', Barnes and Noble, Inc. established barnesandnoble.com in 1997. Claiming that its website was built by booksellers for book lovers, B&N considers its on-line retailing operation to be one of the world's largest and most focused on-line booksellers. When the on-line aspect of the company started, Steve Riggio, founder Len Riggio's brother, predicted that barnesandnoble.com would use its national brand identity, its superstores and its publisher network to make a 'quantum leap beyond the current level of online bookselling'. Roughly two-and-a-half years after this prediction, data showed that Amazon.com commanded 75 per cent of the on-line bookselling market, while barnesandnoble.com controlled only 15 per cent. During the first 30 months or so of head-to-head competition, Amazon.com and barnesandnoble.com established a new rivalry in the marketplace. However, recent strategic decisions may change the nature and intensity of the rivalry.

Following a study of the external environment and its internal environment, Amazon.com decided that its future would differ from the firm's origins. In late 1999, founder and CEO Jeff Bezos observed that 'sixteen months ago Amazon.com was a place where you could find books. Tomorrow Amazon.com will be a place where you can find anything.' With this announcement, Amazon.com indicated its intention of being at the centre of the e-commerce world. In Bezos's vision, customers will be able to use Amazon.com as a portal to purchase virtually any item, pet food, pharmaceuticals, flowers, tennis shoes and banjos, as well as books and thousands of other items. In total, Amazon.com offers over half a million items on its sites. Almost any item can be found in this assortment. However, a line of respectability does exist: no live animals, no pornography and no contraband. To reflect its capabilities in terms of e-commerce, Amazon.com claims to have 'the Earth's Biggest Selection of products, including free electronic greeting cards, online auctions, and millions of books, CDs, videos, DVDs, toys and games, and electronics'.

B&N is keenly aware of competitor Amazon.com's intention of becoming the centre of the e-commerce world. Seeing its competitor's decision as an opportunity, B&N quickly suggested that 'as Amazon becomes the place to sell anything on-line, it presents an opportunity for barnesandnoble.com to own books' by gaining a larger share of the retail book market. The perceived opportunity to 'own books' is highly consistent with the firm's original mission of 'bringing books and bookstores into the mainstream of American life'. Thus, future competition between Amazon.com and barnesandnoble.com will differ from what it has been in the past. The difference is a product of Amazon.com's desire to be at the centre of the e-commerce universe, while barnesandnoble.com views its future as one in which it becomes the dominant portal for the delivery of information. While remaining highly competitive, the competition between these two on-line retailers may not be as direct and intense as it previously was.

Sources: K. Brooker, 1999, 'Amazon vs. everybody', *Fortune*, 8 November, pp. 120–8; D. Carvajal, 1999, 'Amazon asks court to clear use of Times Best-Seller lists', *New York Times*, 5 June, p. C3; K. Li, 1999, 'Big wheels & (maybe) big deals', *Daily News*, 12 July, p. 23; J. Oleck, 1999, *Business Week*, 24 May, p. 6; J. McHugh, 1999, 'The $29 billion flea market', *Forbes*, 1 November, pp. 66–8; J. Robins, 1999, 'Media: Sell first, print later', *The Independent*, 19 October, p. 13; W. St. John, 1999, 'Barnes & Noble's epiphany', *Wired*, June, pp. 132–44; B. Stavro, 1999, 'The cutting edge special report: E-commerce', *Los Angeles Times*, 30 September, p. 6; D. Streitfeld, 1999, 'Barnes & Noble looses marketing virus', *The Washington Post*, 15 July, p. E5.

Numerous or equally balanced competitors

Intense rivalries are common in industries with many companies. With multiple competitors, it is common for a few firms to believe that they can take actions without eliciting a response. However, evidence suggests that other firms generally are aware of competitors' actions, often choosing to respond to them. At the other extreme, industries with only a few firms of equivalent size and power also tend to have much rivalry. The large and often similar-sized resource bases of these firms permit vigorous actions and responses. The competitive battles between fast-food chains (for example, McDonald's versus Burger King) and footwear companies (for example, Nike versus Reebok) exemplify intense rivalries between relatively equivalent competitors.

Slow industry growth

When a market is growing, firms try to use resources effectively to serve an expanding customer base. Growing markets reduce pressures on firms to take customers from competitors. However, rivalry in non-growth or slow-growth markets becomes more intense as firms battle to increase their market shares by attracting competitors' customers.

Typically, battles to protect market shares are fierce. Certainly, this has been the case with the battle between Amazon and Barnes and Noble for control of the Internet book retailing market. The instability in the market that results from these competitive engagements reduces profitability for firms throughout the industry, as is demonstrated by the fast-food industry. Relative to past performance, the market for the industry's products in the United States is growing more slowly. To expand market share, fast-food companies (such as McDonald's) compete aggressively in terms of pricing strategies, the introduction of new products, and product and service differentiation. Promoting products through low-pricing options appeals to customers and may increase a firm's market share; however, these actions tend to reduce profits for individual firms, and they make it difficult for all competitors to stabilise their promotions around price categories that create profits.

High fixed costs or high storage costs

When fixed costs account for a large part of total costs, companies try to maximise the use of their productive capacity. Doing this allows the company to spread costs across a larger volume of output. However, when many firms attempt to maximise their productive capacity, excess capacity is created on an industry-wide basis. To then reduce inventories, individual companies typically cut the price of their product and offer rebates and other special discounts to customers. These practices, however, often intensify competition. The pattern of excess capacity at the industry level followed by intense rivalry at the firm level is observed frequently in industries with high storage costs. Perishable products, for example, lose their value rapidly with the passage of time. As their inventories grow, producers of perishable goods often use pricing strategies to sell products quickly.

Lack of differentiation or low switching costs

When buyers find a differentiated product that satisfies their needs, they frequently purchase the product loyally over time. Industries with many companies that have successfully differentiated their products are less rivalrous, resulting in less competition for individual firms.[110] However, when buyers view products as commodities (that is, as products with few differentiated features or capabilities), rivalry intensifies. In these instances, buyers' purchasing decisions are based primarily on price and, to a lesser degree, service.

The effect of switching costs is identical to that described for differentiated products. The lower the buyers' switching costs, the easier it is for competitors to attract buyers (through pricing and service offerings). High switching costs, however, at least partially insulate the firm from rivals' efforts to attract customers.

Capacity augmented in large increments

In some industries (for example, in the manufacture of vinyl chloride and chlorine), the competitive importance of economies of scale dictates that production capacity be added only on a large-scale basis. Substantial increases in capacity can be disruptive to a balance between industry supply and demand. Price cutting is often used to bring supply and demand back into balance. Achieving balance this way, though, has a negative effect on a firm's profitability.

Diverse competitors

Not all companies seek to accomplish the same goals, nor do they operate with identical cultures. These differences make it difficult to identify an industry's competitive rules. Moreover, with greater diversity, it becomes increasingly difficult to be aware of the primary outcomes a competitor seeks through industry competition. Diversity among firms sometimes causes a company to take certain competitive actions just to see what competitors' responses will be. Doing this can improve the firm's ability to predict competitors' future actions.

High strategic stakes

Competitive rivalry is more intense when achieving success in a particular industry is important to many companies. For example, the success of a diversified firm in one industry may influence its effectiveness in other industries. This can be the case when the firm uses a related diversification corporate-level strategy. (Chapter 6 presents a detailed discussion of this strategy.)

High strategic stakes can also exist in terms of geographic locations. For example, Japanese automobile manufacturers are committed to a significant presence in the US marketplace. A key reason for this is that the United States is the world's single largest market for automobile manufacturers' products. Because of the stakes involved in this country for Japanese and US manufacturers, rivalry among firms in the US and global automobile industry is highly intense.

High exit barriers

Sometimes companies continue competing in an industry even though the returns on their invested capital are low or negative. Firms making this choice face high exit barriers, which include economic, strategic and emotional factors causing companies to remain in an industry when the profitability of doing so is questionable. Common exit barriers are:

- **specialised assets** (assets with values linked to a particular business or location);
- **fixed costs of exit** (for example, labour agreements);
- **strategic interrelationships** (relationships of mutual dependence between one business and other parts of a company's operations, such as shared facilities and access to financial markets);
- **emotional barriers** (aversion to economically justified business decisions because of fear for one's own career, loyalty to employees, and so forth); and
- **government and social restrictions**. These restrictions often are based on government concerns for job losses and regional economic effects.

Interpreting industry analyses

Effective industry analyses are products of careful study and interpretation of data and information from multiple sources. A wealth of industry-specific data is available for analysing an industry. Because of globalisation, international markets and rivalries must be included in the firm's analyses. In fact, research shows that in some industries, international variables are more important than domestic ones as determinants of strategic competitiveness. Furthermore, because of the development of global markets, a country's borders no longer bound industry structures.[111]

Following study of the five industry forces, a firm has the insights required to determine an industry's attractiveness in terms of the potential to earn adequate or superior returns on its invested capital. In general, the stronger competitive forces are, the lower the profit potential for an industry's firms. An *unattractive industry* has low entry barriers, suppliers and buyers with strong bargaining positions, strong competitive threats from product substitutes and intense rivalry among competitors. These industry characteristics make it very difficult for firms to achieve strategic competitiveness and earn above-average returns. Alternatively, an attractive industry has high entry barriers, suppliers and buyers with little bargaining power, few competitive threats from product substitutes and relatively moderate rivalry.[112]

Strategic groups

The term *strategic group* is used to capture competitive patterns that are visible across a set of firms competing against each other either on an industry-wide basis or within a segment (for example, a set of customers with unique needs) of an industry. The term originated when a researcher discovered that not all firms within the same industry were using the same strategy. This finding was a little surprising, in that conventional wisdom at the time was that an industry's characteristics forced firms to compete in the same way. (We talk about this view in greater detail in Chapter 3.) Groups of firms following similar strategies were labelled strategic groups.[113] Formally, a **strategic group** is 'a group of firms in an industry following the same or a similar strategy along the same strategic dimensions'.[114] Examples of strategic dimensions that firms in a strategic group treat similarly or identically include the extent of technological leadership, the degree of product quality, pricing policies, the choice of distribution channels, and the degree and type of customer service the firms offer. Evidence suggests that 'organizations in a strategic group occupy similar positions in the market, offer similar goods to similar customers, and may also make similar choices about production technology and other organizational features'.[115] Thus, membership in a particular strategic group defines the essential characteristics of the firm's strategy.[116] The strategies of firms within a group are similar, but they differ from strategies being implemented by companies in the industry's other strategic groups.

A **strategic group** is a group of firms in an industry following the same or a similar strategy along the same strategic dimensions.

The notion of strategic groups is popular for analysing an industry's competitive structure.[117] Contributing to its popularity is the assertion that strategic group analysis is a basic framework that should be used in diagnosing competition, positioning and the profitability of firms within an industry.[118]

The use of strategic groups for analysing industry structure requires that dimensions relevant to the firms' performances within an industry (for example, price and image) be selected. Plotting companies along these dimensions helps to identify groups of firms competing in similar ways. For example, there are unique radio markets because consumers prefer different music formats, as well as different kinds of programming (news hours, talk radio, and so forth). It is estimated that approximately 30 different radio formats exist. These formats suggest 30 strategic groups. Typically, a format is created through choices made regarding music or non-music style, scheduling and announcer style.[119] The strategies within each of the 30 formats are similar, while the strategies across the total set of formats are dissimilar.

Strategic groups have several implications. Because firms within a group are selling similar products to the same customers, the competitive rivalry among them can be intense. The more intense the rivalry, the greater is the threat to each firm's profitability. Second, the strengths of the five competitive forces (that is, the threats posed by new entrants, suppliers, buyers and product substitutes, and the intensity of rivalry among competitors) differ across strategic groups. Third, the closer the strategic groups are in terms of strategies followed and dimensions emphasised, the greater is the likelihood of rivalry between the groups. For example, two radio stations with a classical music format, but different announcer styles, are relatively close competitors, so the rivalry between them in a local market could be intense. In the Sydney and Melbourne radio market there is intense rivalry between Triple J and Triple M, each vying for position as premium radio station for the youth market. However, one station is government-owned and has no advertisements, while the other is a commercial operation.

The value of strategic group analysis

Opinions vary about the value of strategic group analysis as a tool for understanding industry dynamics and structure. Some even argue that there is no convincing evidence that strategic groups exist or that a firm's financial performance is influenced by membership within a certain strategic group.[120] Another criticism is that studying the actions of companies within a strategic group may not yield any information that would not be captured by analysing an entire industry and individual firms within it. However, recent research shows that there is 'limited evidence that a rigorous search for strategic groups may prove fruitful'.[121] This evidence suggests that caution should be taken in studying strategic groups, but that the analysis can help a firm in efforts to understand the industry in which it competes and to identify its most relevant competitors. Thus, as with all tools, the benefits and limitations of strategic group analysis should be recognised before the firm uses it to better understand an industry's structure.

Competitor analysis

The *competitor environment* is the final part of the external environment requiring study. Competitor analysis focuses on each company against which a firm competes directly. Important in all industries, competitor analyses are conducted energetically by companies competing in an industry with just a few companies possessing relatively equal capabilities. For example, Nike and Reebok are keenly interested in understanding each other's objectives, strategies, assumptions and capabilities, as are Coles and Woolworths. Furthermore, intense rivalry and desires to understand competitors characterise industries in which supply exceeds demand, such as retailing. In the United States, 'retailers are in the throes of a crisis. There are too many retail outlets and too few consumers – experts estimate 20% to 30% excess retail capacity – and the competition for eyes, ears, and dollars is downright savage'. To better understand both competitors' customers and their own, some prominent retailers (for example, Coca-Cola, McDonald's and Starbucks) are using the services of Envirosell.[122] Viewing themselves as a group of 'retail anthropologists', employees of Envirosell physically observe tens of thousands of shoppers across firms to determine why they buy what they buy. Thus, when engaged in a competitor analysis, the firm seeks to understand:

- what drives the competitor, as shown by its future objectives;
- what the competitor is doing and can do, as is revealed by its current strategy;
- what the competitor believes about itself and the industry, as shown by its assumptions; and
- what the competitor's capabilities are, as shown by its capabilities.[123]

Information about these four issues helps the firm to prepare an anticipated response profile for each competitor (see Figure 2.3). Thus, the results of an effective competitor analysis help a firm to understand, interpret and predict its competitors' actions and initiatives.[124]

Figure 2.3 | Competitor analysis components

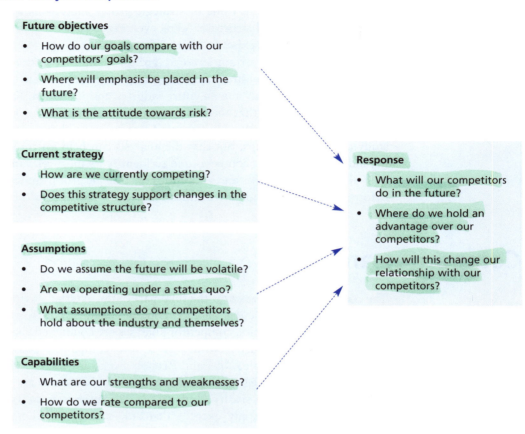

Critical to effective competitor analysis is the gathering of data and information that can help the firm to understand competitors' intentions and the strategic implications resulting from them.[125] Useful data and information combine to form **competitor intelligence**: the set of data and information the firm gathers to better understand and better anticipate competitors' objectives, strategies, assumptions and capabilities.[126] In competitor analysis, the firm should gather intelligence not only about its competitors, but also regarding public policies in countries across the world. Intelligence about public policies 'provides an early warning of threats and opportunities emerging from the global public policy environment, and analyzes how they will affect the achievement of the company's strategy'.[127] Through effective competitive and public policy intelligence, the firm gains the insights it requires to help create a competitive advantage and to increase the quality of the strategic decisions it makes when choosing how to compete against its major rivals.[128]

Firms should follow generally accepted ethical practices in gathering competitor intelligence. Industry associations often develop lists of these practices that firms can adopt. Practices considered both legal and ethical include: (1) obtaining publicly available information (for example, court records, competitors' help-wanted advertisements, annual reports and financial reports of publicly held corporations); and (2) attending trade fairs and shows to obtain competitors' brochures, view their exhibits and listen to discussions about their products. In contrast, certain practices (for example, blackmail, trespassing, eavesdropping, and stealing drawings, samples or documents) are viewed widely as unethical and often are illegal.

> **Competitor intelligence** is the ethical gathering of needed information and data about competitors' objectives, strategies, assumptions and capabilities.

Breaking into PCs used by a competitor's personnel is an example of an illegal intelligence-gathering activity. In spite of this, the frequency with which such activity occurs seems to be increasing. A variant of this practice is trying to read the screen on a person's laptop computer during an airplane flight. Aware of the practice, a media consultant who travels frequently loads an interesting file if he finds that another person is trying to read his laptop's screen. The message reads, 'If you can read this, you ought to be ashamed of yourself.' Commenting about the message's effectiveness, the person said, 'It works every time. It's a nice, polite two-by-four between the eyes.'[129] To protect themselves from digital fraud or theft that occurs through breaking into employees' PCs, some companies are buying insurance to protect against PC hacking. Chubb's new ForeFront plan offers up to US$10 million coverage against digital fraud, theft and extortion. Cigna's information asset protection division sells anti-hacker policies that cover up to 10 per cent of a firm's revenues. The number of clients making claims seems to suggest the value of having one of these policies.[130]

Some competitor intelligence practices are legal, but a firm must decide whether their use is ethical, given its culture and the image it desires as a corporate citizen. Especially with electronic transmissions, the line between legal and ethical practices can be difficult to determine. For example, some firms develop website addresses that are very similar to those of competitors. Occasionally, the firm then receives e-mail transmissions that were intended for its competitor. Is e-mail snagging legal? According to legal experts, the answer to this question remains unclear.[131] Nonetheless, the practice is an example of what companies face when determining how to gather intelligence and how to protect themselves from having too much of their own intelligence fall into competitors' hands.

Open discussions of intelligence-gathering techniques that a firm will use go a long way towards ensuring that people understand the firm's convictions about what is ethical and acceptable for use and what is not when gathering competitor intelligence. An appropriate guideline about competitor intelligence practices that can frame these discussions is for the firm to respect the principles of common morality and the right of competitors not to reveal certain information about their products, operations and strategic intentions.[132]

Despite the importance of studying competitors, evidence suggests that a relatively small percentage of firms use formal processes to do so. In fact, some believe that 'only 10–15 percent of all businesses actually have a systematic process for collection and dissemination of competitive intelligence information'.[133] Beyond this, some firms forget to analyse competitors' *future objectives* as they try to understand their current strategies' assumptions and capabilities. As previously stated, it is important to study the present *and* the future in examining competitors. Failure to do so yields incomplete insights about those competitors.[134]

Earlier in the chapter, we discussed the value of the Internet as a tool to help a firm scan, monitor, forecast and assess the external environment. In the Strategic Focus, we discuss how the Internet's extensive capabilities may cause the firm to divulge too much about itself to competitors. Thus, through websites, the Internet creates interesting *opportunities* for the firm (for example, to entice sales from current and future customers), as well as *threats* (such as giving too much competitive intelligence to competitors through its website) to the firm's survival.

Strategic Focus Corporate

Competitive intelligence and the Internet

The Internet is an excellent technology for distributing information to current and prospective customers. The tool appears to be effective, in that for many companies, customers are becoming increasingly comfortable with the practice of buying products through electronic commerce.

Interested in being recognised for the superiority of their websites, as well as selling to current customers and attracting new ones, a growing number of companies are offering a 'digital cache of press releases and executive bios, job postings and research papers, price lists and details on strategic alliances', among other types of information, via their websites. For firms competing through e-commerce only, it is vital that they develop an effective website, because it is their single distribution channel. For example, started by Louis H. Borders, who also founded Borders Books & Music, Webvan sells groceries, meat and fish, and non-prescription drugs over the Internet. Strictly a Web-based business, Webvan has no operations from a 'bricks and mortar' facility. The company is attractive to investors, and its stock price surged 66 per cent on the day of its initial public offering. With a resulting market capitalisation of US$8 billion, Webvan immediately had one-half of the capitalisation of Safeway, Inc. and Kroger Co., the industry's traditional leaders. Webvan's competitors continue to increase, however, as the entry barriers to this type of business are low. In Dallas, Texas, GroceryWorks.com uses part of its website to emphasise, in an attractive manner, the superior freshness of its perishable items relative to those available through on-line competitors.

Providing competitive intelligence to competitors that historically was difficult for them to obtain is a downside to comprehensive websites. The seriousness of this problem is highlighted by the fact that the entry barriers to starting a Web-based business are very low. Commenting about the issue of providing intelligence to competitors through one's website, an analyst suggested that 'Boeing's Web site is a gold mine for a competitor that would like to hire away staff who come with lots of sensitive information. And you know who[m] to talk to about each person. You can call their boss, work your way up the organizational chart and find out information about an executive, his background, how he is to work for.' Other companies study the backgrounds of competitors' CEOs and top management teams. Knowing the functional backgrounds of a competitor's key decision makers yields valuable insights. For example, knowing that a CEO is from a marketing rather than, say, a finance background allows a firm to predict how the CEO 'views the world' and the issues that likely have major effects on his or her strategic decisions. Corporations are well aware that others are studying their websites to develop competitor intelligence. One company official observed that 'we know our competitors check out our Web site ... And, of course, we do the same to them.'

Another indicator of the value of competitor intelligence that is available from another firm's website is highlighted by the fact that new ventures have surfaced to provide what is called 'Web-spying services'. The need these companies satisfy is to help firms deal with 'infoglut', a term used to describe the vast amount of intelligence to which firms can gain access to study competitors. Called corporate intelligence firms, the charges for these firms' services can be over US$1 million for a large project. One firm studied competitors' websites (and other publicly available information) to help Dow Chemical determine if there was a market for a promising new heat-resistant, super-strong composite of clay and plastic that it had developed (the answer was 'yes') and if any of Dow's competitors were too far ahead in producing and distributing a competing product (the answer from the corporate intelligence firm was 'maybe').

What should the firm do about Web spying? An obvious action is for the company to exercise caution about the type and level of information that is included on its website. The level of scrutiny devoted to assessing what is to be featured on a website should parallel the scrutiny an annual report undergoes before being published. The firm might also wish to verify, if it chooses to study competitors' sites, that any information included on a competing company's site about its own firm is accurate. According to a business writer, one firm has become 'quite adept at spreading myths through its Web site' about the raw materials used to manufacture a competitor's product. Thus, if a firm chooses to study a competitor's website, it may also want to assess the accuracy of any information on that site that the competitor is providing about it.

Sources: G. Anders and R. Berner, 1999, 'Webvan's splashy stock debut may shake up staid grocery industry', *Wall Street Journal*, 8 November, pp. B1, B4; M. Fumento, 1999, 'Tampon terrorism', *Forbes*, 17 May, pp. 170–2; M. Halkias, 1999, 'New online grocer wants to grow with market', *Dallas Morning News*, 9 November, pp. D1, D6; K. Labich, 1999, 'Attention shoppers: This man is watching you', *Fortune*, 19 July, pp. 131–4; A. L. Penenberg, 1999, 'Is there a snoop on your site?', *Forbes*, 17 May, pp. 323–6; 'Two new tech offerings are hits on Wall Street', *Dallas Morning News*, 6 November, p. F11.

As explained in Chapter 1, a firm's strategic actions are a product of its external and internal environments. Thus, to attain the outcomes of strategic competitiveness and above-average returns, the firm must integrate the insights gained by studying its external environment with those acquired by analysing its internal environment. In this chapter, we discussed the insights the firm develops by studying the external environment. In the next, we describe what the firm seeks to understand about its internal environment and the tools that are used to develop those understandings.

Summary

- The firm's external environment is challenging and complex. Because of the effect the external environment has on performance, the firm must develop the skills required to identify opportunities and threats existing in that environment.
- The external environment has three major parts: (1) the general environment (elements in the broader society that affect industries and their firms); (2) the industry environment (factors that influence a firm, its competitive actions and responses and the industry's profit potential; the threats of entry, suppliers, buyers and product substitutes; and the intensity of rivalry among competitors); and (3) the competitor environment (in which the firm studies each major competitor's future objectives, current strategies, assumptions and capabilities).
- Effective environmental analyses assume a nationless and borderless (that is, global) business environment.
- The external environmental analysis process has four steps: scanning, monitoring, forecasting and assessing. Through environmental analysis, the firm identifies opportunities and threats.
- The general environment has six segments: demographic, economic, political/legal, socio-cultural, technological and global. For each segment, the firm wants to determine the strategic relevance of environmental changes and trends.
- Compared to the general environment, the industry environment has a more direct effect on the firm's strategic actions.
- The five forces model of competition includes characteristics that determine the industry's profit potential. By studying these forces, the firm finds a position in an industry whereby it can influence the forces in its favour or whereby it can isolate itself from the power of the forces to reduce its ability to earn above-average returns.
- Industries are populated with different strategic groups. A strategic group is a collection of firms that follow similar strategies along similar dimensions. Competitive rivalry is greater within a strategic group than it is between strategic groups.

- Competitor analysis informs the firm about the future objectives, current strategies, assumptions and capabilities of the companies with whom it competes directly.
- Different techniques are used to create competitor intelligence: the set of data, information and knowledge that allows the firm to better understand those with whom it directly competes. At a minimum, the firm must use only legal practices to gather intelligence. Increasingly, the firm is being called on to determine that those practices it will use are ethical as well as legal. The Internet's capabilities allow the firm to gather insights quickly about competitors and their intentions.

Review questions

1. Why is it important for a firm to study and understand the external environment?
2. What are the differences between the general environment and the industry environment? Why are these differences important?
3. What is the external environmental analysis process? What does the firm want to learn as it scans, monitors, forecasts and assesses its external environment?
4. What are the six segments of the general environment? Explain the differences among them.
5. Using information in the chapter, can you justify the following statement? 'There are five competitive forces that determine an industry's profit potential.' Explain.
6. What is a strategic group? Of what value is the strategic group concept in choosing a firm's strategy?
7. Why do firms want to understand how data and information about competitors are collected and interpreted? What practices should a firm use to gather competitor intelligence and why?

Application discussion questions

1. Given the importance of understanding the external environment, why do some firms fail to do so? Using the Internet, find an example of a firm that did not understand its external environment. What were the implications of the firm's failure to understand that environment?
2. Select a firm and describe its external environment. Suppose you are about to enter the business world. What actions do you believe the firm should take, given its external environment, and why?
3. How is it possible that one firm could see a condition in the external environment as an opportunity while a second firm sees it as a threat?
4. Select a firm in your local community. What materials would you read to understand the firm's external environment? How could the Internet help you to complete this activity?
5. Select an industry that is of interest to you. What actions could firms take to erect barriers of entry to this industry?
6. What conditions would cause a firm to retaliate aggressively against a new entrant to the industry?

Ethics questions

1. How can a firm use its 'code of ethics' to analyse the external environment?
2. What ethical issues, if any, may be relevant to a firm's monitoring of its external environment? Does use of the Internet to monitor the environment lead to additional ethical issues? If so, what are they?
3. Think of each segment in a firm's general environment. What is an ethical issue associated with each segment? Are firms across the globe doing enough to deal with the issue?
4. What is the importance of using ethical practices between a firm and its suppliers?
5. In an intense rivalry, especially one that involves competition in the global marketplace, how can the firm gather competitor intelligence ethically while maintaining its competitiveness?
6. What do you believe determines whether an intelligence-gathering practice is or is not ethical? Do you see this changing as the world's economies become more interdependent? If so, why? Do you see this changing because of the Internet? If so, how?

Internet exercise

Firms rely on gathering and analysing the general, industry and competitor environments to assess their potential for global growth and profitability. Go to the website for Rio Tinto (www.riotinto.com). List how each of the six segments of the general environment prompted them to expand into the markets and launch takeovers that it has.

Notes

1. D. J. Ketchen, Jr and T. B. Palmer, 1999, 'Strategic responses to poor organizational performance: A test of competing perspectives', *Journal of Management*, 25, pp. 683–706; V. P. Rindova and C. J. Fombrun, 1999, 'Constructing competitive advantage: The role of firm-constituent interactions', *Strategic Management Journal*, 20, pp. 691–710; J. A. Wagner and R. Z. Gooding, 1997, 'Equivocal information and attribution: An investigation of patterns of managerial sense-making', *Strategic Management Journal*, 16, pp. 497–518.
2. N. Shirouzu and R. L. Simison, 2000, 'Toyota holds talks about joining GM in online market for suppliers' goods', *Wall Street Journal*, 6 January, p. A4; T. A. Stewart, 1999, 'See Jack. See Jack run', *Fortune*, 27 September, pp. 124–36.
3. 'The great convergence: An introduction', 1999, *Forbes ASAP*, 4 October, pp. 15–16; C. M. Grimm and K. G. Smith, 1997, *Strategy as Action: Industry Rivalry and Coordination* (Cincinnati: South-Western); C. J. Fombrun, 1992, *Turning Point: Creating Strategic Change in Organizations* (New York: McGraw-Hill), p. 13.
4. T. E. Ricks and A. M. Squeo, 1999, 'Pentagon urges caution on big defense mergers', *Wall Street Journal*, 22 October, p. A2.
5. This is still a controversial ownership situation, as is the corporatisation of the (at the moment still state-owned) power infrastructure in Tasmania. See L. Nelson, 2001, 'An analysis of the Hydro-Electric Corporation in Tasmania: A case study in organisational change', unpublished PhD thesis, University of Tasmania.
6. S. A. Zahra, A. P. Nielsen and W. C. Bogner, 1999, 'Corporate entrepreneurship, knowledge, and competence development', *Entrepreneurship: Theory and Practice*, 23(3), pp. 169–89; M. Farjoun and L. Lei, 1997, 'Similarity judgments in strategy formulation: Role, process, and implications', *Strategic Management Journal*, 18, pp. 255–73.
7. M. A. Hitt, J. E. Ricart I Costa and R. D. Nixon, 1998, 'The new frontier', in M. A. Hitt, J. E. Ricart I Costa and R. D. Nixon (eds), *Managing Strategically in an Interconnected World* (Chichester: John Wiley & Sons), pp. 1–12.
8. W. C. Bogner and P. Bansal, 1998, 'Controlling unique knowledge development as the basis of sustained high performance', in M. A. Hitt, J. E. Ricart I Costa and R. D. Nixon (eds), *Managing Strategically in an Interconnected World* (Chichester: John Wiley & Sons), pp. 167–84; D. J. Teece, G. Pisano and A. Shuen, 1997, 'Dynamic capabilities and strategic management', *Strategic Management Journal*, 18, pp. 509–33.
9. L. Fahey, 1999, *Competitors* (New York: John Wiley & Sons); B. A. Walters and R. L. Priem, 1999, 'Business strategy and CEO intelligence acquisition', *Competitive Intelligence Review*, 10(2), pp. 15–22; L. Fahey and V. K. Narayanan, 1986, *Macro-environmental Analysis for Strategic Management* (St. Paul: West Publishing Company), pp. 49–50.
10. OECD, 2000, *OECD in Figures*.
11. R. D. Ireland and M. A. Hitt, 1999, 'Achieving and maintaining strategic competitiveness in the 21st century: The role of strategic leadership', *Academy of Management Executive*, 13(1), pp. 43–57; M. A. Hitt, B. W. Keats and S. M. DeMarie, 1998, 'Navigating in the new competitive landscape: Building strategic flexibility and competitive advantage in the 21st century', *Academy of Management Executive*, 12(4), pp. 22–42.
12. J. Kay, 1999, 'Strategy and the delusion of grand designs', Mastering Strategy (Part One), *Financial Times*, 27 September, p. 2.
13. G. L. White and J. B. White, 1999, 'At GM, Pearce returns to lead a push into high tech', *Wall Street Journal*, 23 April, pp. B1, B4.
14. J. Hyde, 1999, 'GM plans to offer car connected to Web', *Dallas Morning News*, 3 November, pp. D1, D12; G. L. White, 1999, 'GM will connect drivers to the World Wide Web', *Wall Street Journal*, 3 November, pp. B1, B4.
15. R. Karlgaard, 1999, 'Digital rules: Technology and the new economy', *Forbes*, 17 May, p. 43.
16. GE Overview, 2000, *General Electric Home Page*, 12 January: www.ge.com.
17. V. Prior, 1999, 'The language of competitive intelligence: Part four', *Competitive Intelligence Review*, 10(1), pp. 84–7.
18. F. Beckett, 1999, 'IBM high technology meets European class', *Financial Times*, 10 May, p. 12.
19. D. Kunde, 1999, 'Higher tech ed: Colleges focus on building e-commerce MBAs', *Dallas Morning News*, 9 June, pp. D1, D10.
20. G. Young, 1999, '"Strategic value analysis" for competitive advantage', *Competitive Intelligence Review*, 10(2), pp. 52–64.
21. D. N. Sull, 1999, 'Why good companies go bad', *Harvard Business Review*, 77(4), pp. 42–52; H. Courtney, J. Kirkland and P. Visuerie, 1997, 'Strategy under uncertainty', *Harvard Business Review*, 75(6), pp. 66–79.
22. D. S. Elenkov, 1997, 'Strategic uncertainty and environmental scanning: The case for institutional influences on scanning behavior', *Strategic Management Journal*, 18, pp. 287–302.
23. S. D. Hilmetz and R. S. Bridge, 1999, 'Gauging the returns on investments in competitive intelligence: A three-step analysis for executive decision makers', *Competitive Intelligence Review*, 10(1), pp. 4–11; I. Goll and A. M. A. Rasheed, 1997, 'Rational decision-making and firm performance: The moderating role of environment', *Strategic Management Journal*, 18, pp. 583–91.
24. R. Aggarwal, 1999, 'Technology and globalization as mutual reinforcers in business: Reorienting strategic thinking for the new millennium', *Management International Review*, 39(2), pp. 83–104; M. Yasai-Ardekani and P. C. Nystrom, 1996, 'Designs for environmental scanning systems: Tests of contingency theory', *Management Science*, 42, pp. 187–204.
25. R. Donkin, 1999, 'Too young to retire', *Financial Times*, 2 July, p. 9.
26. Ibid.
27. Australian Bureau of Statistics, 1999, *Older Persons and Australia* (Canberra: Australian Bureau of Statistics).
28. K. Morris, 1999, 'Wiring the ivory tower', *Business Week*, 9 August, pp. 90–2.
29. Fahey, *Competitors*, pp. 71–3; Fahey and Narayanan, *Macro-environmental Analysis*, p. 39.
30. H. Simonian, 1999, 'Germans buy new Sunday shopping laws', *Financial Times*, 3 August, p. 2.
31. Fahey, *Competitors*; Fahey and Narayanan, *Macro-environmental Analysis*, p. 41.
32. Karlgaard, 'Digital rules', p. 43; M. B. Regan, 1999, 'Industries adjust to e-commerce', *Waco Tribunal Herald*, 11 April, pp. B6, B7.
33. Fahey, *Competitors*, pp. 75–7; Fahey and Narayanan, *Macro-environmental Analysis*, p. 42.
34. T. Box, 1999, 'Keep on truckin'', *Dallas Morning News*, 22 April, pp. D1, D4.
35. Fahey and Narayanan, *Macro-environmental Analysis*, p. 58.
36. D. Fishburn, 1999, 'The world in 1999', *The Economist Publications*, p. 9; 'Six billion ... and counting', 1999, *Time*, 4 October, p. 16.
37. Australian Bureau of Statistics, 1999, *Population Proportions* (Canberra: Australian Bureau of Statistics).
38. 'Six billion', p. 16.
39. R. Stodghill, II, 1997, 'The coming job bottleneck', *Business Week*, 24 March, pp. 184–5.
40. Australian Bureau of Statistics, *Older Persons and Australia*.
41. D. Stipp, 1999, 'Hell no, we won't go!', *Fortune*, 19 July, pp. 102–8; G. Colvin, 1997, 'How to beat the boomer rush', *Fortune*, 18 August, pp. 59–63.
42. Colvin, 'How to beat the boomer rush', p. 60.
43. National Institute of Economic and Industry Research, 1999, *State of the Regions*.
44. Statistics based on IBISWORD, 1999.
45. J. R. W. Joplin and C. S. Daus, 1997, 'Challenges of leading a diverse workforce', *Academy of Management Executive*, XI(3), pp. 32–47; G. Robinson and K. Dechant, 1997, 'Building a business case for diversity', *Academy of Management Executive*, IX(3), pp. 21–31.
46. Australian Bureau of Statistics, 1999, *Overseas Population Makes up Half Our Population Growth* (Canberra: Australian Bureau of Statistics).
47. G. Dessler, 1999, 'How to earn your employees' commitment', *Academy of Management Executive*, 13(2), pp. 58–67; S. Finkelstein and D. C. Hambrick, 1996, *Strategic Leadership: Top Executives and Their Effect on Organizations* (Minneapolis: West).
48. L. H. Pelled, K. M. Eisenhardt and K. R. Xin, 1999, 'Exploring the black box: An analysis of work group diversity, conflict, and performance', *Administrative Science Quarterly*, 44, pp. 1–28.
49. E. S. Rubenstein, 1999, 'Inequality', *Forbes*, 1 November, pp. 158–60; J. Landers, 1997, 'Incomes rising around world', *Dallas Morning News*, 15 September, pp. D1, D4.
50. Australian Bureau of Statistics, 2001, *Income and Welfare – Household Income*, 20 February: www.abs.gov.au.
51. Fahey and Narayanan, *Macro-environmental Analysis*, p. 105.
52. T. Robberson, 1999, 'Brazil's middle class scrambles to survive amid economic woes', *Dallas Morning News*, 10 April, pp. F1, F11.
53. J. Wolfensohn, 1999, 'The world in 1999, A battle for corporate honesty', *The Economist Publications*, p. 38.

54 World Trade Organization, 1998, *Annual Report*, pp. 5–6.
55 J. E. Schrempp, 1999, 'The world in 1999, Neighbours across the pond', *The Economist Publications*, p. 28.
56 L. Brittan, 1999, 'The world in 1999, The millennium round', *The Economist Publications*, p. 50.
57 M. E. Boudette, 1999, 'In Europe, surfing a Web of red tape', *Wall Street Journal*, 29 October, pp. B1, B4.
58 Fahey and Narayanan, *Macro-environmental Analysis*, pp. 139–57.
59 A. J. Hillman and M. A. Hitt, 1999, 'Corporate political strategy formulation: A model of approach, participation, and strategy decisions', *Academy of Management Review*, 24, pp. 825–42.
60 M. Carson, 1998, *Global Competitiveness Quarterly*, 9 March, p. 1.
61 Brittan, 'The millennium round', p. 50.
62 R. L. Riley, 1999, 'Will Uncle Sam trump Internet gamblers?', *Wall Street Journal*, 14 May, p. A14.
63 'Cyberspace: Who will make the rules?', 1999, *Business Week*, 22 WTO, pp. 30D–F.
64 S. Calian and S. Gruner, 1999, 'UK regulators move to open local phones to competition', *Wall Street Journal*, 9 July, p. A14; J. Friedland and K. Kranhold, 1999, 'Mexico's energy reforms lure U.S. investors', *Wall Street Journal*, 29 June, p. A8; P. Landers, 1999, 'Government involvement has boosted Japan's recovery', *Wall Street Journal*, 15 June, p. A12; C. Murphy, 1999, 'Will the future belong to Germany?', *Fortune*, 2 August, pp. 129–36; T. Vogel, 1997, 'Central America goes from war zone to enterprise zone', *Wall Street Journal*, 25 September, p. A18.
65 J. MacIntyre, 1999, 'Figuratively speaking', *Across the Board*, May, p. 11.
66 A. R. Varey and G. Lynn, 1999, 'Americans save for retirement', *USA Today*, 16 November, p. B1.
67 D. Kunde, 1999, 'Survey finds technology blurring lines of work, home', *Dallas Morning News*, 13 October, pp. D1, D10; D. Woodruff, 1999, 'In France, working long hours becomes a crime', *Wall Street Journal*, 25 June, p. A15.
68 G. F. Will, 1999, 'The primacy of culture', *Newsweek*, 18 January, p. 64.
69 'Woman power!', 1999, *Worth Magazine*, September, pp. 100–1.
70 B. Beck, 1999, 'The world in 1999, Executive, thy name is woman', *The Economist Publications*, p. 89; P. Thomas, 1995, 'Success at a huge personal cost: Comparing women around the world', *Wall Street Journal*, 26 July, p. B1.
71 R. Taylor, 1999, 'Pay gap between the sexes widest in W. Europe', *Financial Times*, 29 June, p. 9.
72 Australian Bureau of Statistics, 2001, *Average Weekly Earnings: May 2000*, Cat. No. 6302.0 (Canberra: Australian Bureau of Statistics).
73 Associated Press, 1999, 'Women-owned businesses making gains', *Dallas Morning News*, 28 April, p. D2; N. Enbar, 1999, 'What do women want? Ask 'em', *Business Week*, 29 March, p. 8.
74 S. Branch, 1999, 'Avon names Andrea Jung to CEO post', *Wall Street Journal*, 5 November, p. A3; B. Morris, 1997, 'If women ran the world it would look a lot like Avon', *Fortune*, 21 July, pp. 74–9.
75 D. Kunde, 1999, 'Temporary shortage', *Dallas Morning News*, 28 September, pp. D1, D6.
76 N. Nakamae, 1999, 'Service sector shining in land of the rising sun', *Financial Times*, 27 July, p. 4.
77 'Trends and forecasts for the next 25 years', 1999, *World Future Society*, p. 3.
78 P. Hochman, 1999, 'Yo-yos are back. This time they mean it', *Fortune*, 24 May, p. 64.
79 X. M. Song, C. A. Di Benedetto and Y. L. Zhao, 1999, 'Pioneering advantages in manufacturing and service industries', *Strategic Management Journal*, 20, pp. 811–36.
80 C. Newman, 1999, 'Pearson to double Internet investment', *Financial Times*, 3 August, p. 15.
81 'Business ready for Internet revolution', 1999, *Financial Times*, 21 May, p. 17.
82 K. S. Mangan, 1999, 'Business students flock to courses on electronic commerce', *The Chronicle of Higher Education*, 30 April, p. A25.
83 K. Fairbank, 1999, 'CEOs downplay effect of Net sales', *Dallas Morning News*, 12 November, pp. D1, D10.
84 Regan, 'Industries adjust', p. B7.
85 A. Goldstein, 1999, 'E-commerce may soar to $380 billion', *Dallas Morning News*, 13 October, pp. D1, D10.
86 M. Dell, 1999, 'The world in 1999, The virtual firm', *The Economist Publications*, p. 99.
87 W. C. Kim and R. Mauborgne, 1999, 'Creating new market space', *Harvard Business Review*, 77(1), pp. 83–93; R. D. Nordstrom and R. L. Pinkerton, 1999, 'Taking advantage of Internet sources to build a competitive intelligence system', *Competitive Intelligence Review*, 10(1), pp. 54–61.
88 A. Rawsthorn, 1999, 'Global Internet music sales to reach $4bn in five years', *Financial Times*, 26 May, p. 8.
89 R. La Franco, 1999, 'Record companies, awake!', *Forbes*, 15 November, pp. 76–80.
90 D. B. Yoffie and M. A. Cusumano, 1999, 'Judo strategy: The competitive dynamics of Internet time', *Harvard Business Review*, 77(1), pp. 71–81.
91 A. K. Gupta, V. Govindarajan and A. Malhotra, 1999, 'Feedback-seeking behavior within multinational corporations', *Strategic Management Journal*, 20, pp. 205–22.
92 'China and the U.S. sign trade deal, clearing hurdle for WTO entry', 1999, *Wall Street Interactive Journal*, 15 November: www.interactive.wsj.com.
93 J. Cox, 1999, 'USA could get billion Chinese customers', *USA Today*, 16 November, p. B1; 'In historic pact, U.S. opens way for China to finally join WTO', 1999, *Wall Street Journal*, 16 November, pp. A1, A19.
94 'U.S. companies eager for business in China', 1999, *Dallas Morning News*, 16 November, pp. D1, D9.
95 *Dell Home Page*, 2000, 12 January: www.dell.com.
96 E. W. K. Tsang, 1998, 'Can guanxi be a source of sustained competitive advantage for doing business in China?', *Academy of Management Executive*, 12(2), pp. 64–73; M. A. Hitt, M. T. Dacin, B. B. Tyler and D. Park, 1997, 'Understanding the differences in Korean and U.S. executives' strategic orientations', *Strategic Management Journal*, 18, pp. 159–67.
97 T. Khanna and K. Palepu, 1999, 'The right way to restructure conglomerates in emerging markets', *Harvard Business Review*, 77(4), pp. 125–34; Hitt, Dacin, Tyler and Park, 1997, 'Understanding the differences in Korean and U.S. executives' strategic orientations'.
98 R. Gottliebsen, 2001, 'Playing mine games', *The Weekend Australian*, 17–18 February, p. 44.
99 T. H. Brush, P. Bromiley and M. Hendrickx, 1999, 'The relative influence of industry and corporation on business segment performance: An alternative estimate', *Strategic Management Journal*, 20, pp. 519–47.
100 E. O. Welles, 1999, 'Not your father's industry', *Inc.*, January, pp. 25–6.
101 Hitt, Ricart, Costa and Nixon, 'The new frontier'.
102 Y. Pan and P. S. K. Chi, 1999, 'Financial performance and survival of multinational corporations in China', *Strategic Management Journal*, 20, pp. 359–74; G. R. Brooks, 1995, 'Defining market boundaries', *Strategic Management Journal*, 16, pp. 535–49.
103 A. M. McGahan, 1994, 'Industry structure and competitive advantage', *Harvard Business Review*, 72(5), pp. 115–24.
104 P. A. Geroski, 1999, 'Early warning of new rivals', *Sloan Management Review*, 40(3), pp. 107–16.
105 R. Makadok, 1999, 'Interfirm differences in scale economies and the evolution of market shares', *Strategic Management Journal*, 20, pp. 935–52.
106 R. Wise and P. Baumgartner, 1999, 'Go downstream: The new profit imperative in manufacturing', *Harvard Business Review*, 77(5), pp. 133–41; J. H. Gilmore and B. J. Pine, II, 1997, 'The four faces of mass customization', *Harvard Business Review*, 75(1), pp. 91–101.
107 J. Willman, 1999, 'Consumer power forces food industry to modify approach', *Financial Times*, 10 June, p. 11.
108 J. Muller, K. Naughton and L. Armstrong, 'Old carmakers learn new tricks', 1999, *Business Week*, 12 April, pp. 116–18; O. Port, 1999, 'Customers move into the driver's seat', 1999, *Business Week*, 4 October, pp. 103–6.
109 S. Browder, 1997, 'Tea is bagging a bigger crowd', *Business Week*, 25 August, p. 6.
110 D. L. Deephouse, 1999, 'To be different, or to be the same? It's a question (and theory) of strategic balance', *Strategic Management Journal*, 20, pp. 147–66.
111 G. Lorenzoni and A. Lipparini, 1999, 'The leveraging of interfirm relationships as a distinctive organizational capability: A longitudinal study', *Strategic Management Journal*, 20, pp. 317–38.
112 M. E. Porter, 1980, *Competitive Strategy* (New York: Free Press).
113 M. S. Hunt, 1972, 'Competition in the major home appliance industry, 1960–1970' (doctoral dissertation, Harvard University).
114 Porter, *Competitive Strategy*, p. 129.
115 H. R. Greve, 1999, 'Managerial cognition and the mimetic adoption of market positions: What you see is what you do', *Strategic Management Journal*, 19, pp. 967–88.
116 R. K. Reger and A. S. Huff, 1993, 'Strategic groups: A cognitive perspective', *Strategic Management Journal*, 14, pp. 103–23.

117 J. B. Barney and R. E. Hoskisson, 1990, 'Strategic groups: Untested assertions and research proposals', *Managerial and Decision Economics*, 11, pp. 198–208.
118 M. Peteraf and M. Shanely, 1997, 'Getting to know you: A theory of strategic group identity', *Strategic Management Journal*, 18 (Special Issue), pp. 165–86.
119 Greve, 'Managerial cognition', pp. 972–3.
120 D. Nath and T. Gruca, 1997, 'Covergence across alternatives for forming strategic groups', *Strategic Management Journal*, 18, pp. 745–60.
121 D. Dranove, M. Peteraf and M. Shanley, 1998, 'Do strategic groups exist? An economic framework for analysis', *Strategic Management Journal*, 19, pp. 1029–44.
122 K. Labich, 1999, 'Attention shoppers: This man is watching you', *Fortune*, 19 July, pp. 131–4.
123 Porter, *Competitive Strategy*, p. 49.
124 Young, '"Strategic value analysis"', p. 52.
125 P. M. Norman, R. D. Ireland, K. W. Artz and M. A. Hitt, 2000, 'Acquiring and using competitive intelligence in entrepreneurial teams', Working paper, Baylor University.
126 Nordstrom and Pinkerton, 'Taking advantage of Internet sources', p. 54.
127 C. S. Fleisher, 1999, 'Public policy competitive intelligence', *Competitive Intelligence Review*, 10(2), p. 24.
128 Young, '"Strategic value analysis"', p. 52.
129 E. de Lisser, 1999, 'Hearing and seeing business travel blab and laptop lapses', *Wall Street Journal*, 8 November, pp. A1, A20.
130 V. Drucker, 1999, 'Is your computer a sitting duck during a deal?', *Mergers & Acquisitions*, July/August, pp. 25–8; J. Hodges, 1999, 'Insuring your PC against hackers', *Fortune*, 24 May, p. 280.
131 M. Moss, 1999, 'Inside the game of e-mail hijacking', *Wall Street Journal*, 9 November, pp. B1, B4.
132 J. H. Hallaq and K. Steinhorst, 1994, 'Business intelligence methods, How ethical?', *Journal of Business Ethics*, 13, pp. 787–94.
133 Nordstrom and Pinkerton, 'Taking advantage of Internet sources', p. 55.
134 L. Fahey, 1999, 'Competitor scenarios: Projecting a rival's marketplace strategy', *Competitive Intelligence Review*, 10(2), pp. 65–85.

Chapter 3

The internal environment: Resources, capabilities and core competencies

Objectives

After reading this chapter, you should be able to:

1. Explain the need for firms to study and understand their internal environment.
2. Define value and discuss its importance.
3. Describe the differences between tangible and intangible resources.
4. Define capabilities and discuss how they are developed.
5. Describe four criteria used to determine whether resources and capabilities are core competencies.
6. Explain how value chain analysis is used to identify and evaluate resources and capabilities.
7. Define outsourcing and discuss the reasons for its use.
8. Discuss the importance of preventing core competencies from becoming core rigidities.
9. Explain the relationship between strategic inputs and strategic actions.

Brands as a source of competitive advantage

A set of differentiating features that link a good or service to its customers, a brand is recognised widely by businesspeople and academic researchers alike as one of the most sustainable, and hence valuable, of all competitive advantages. The world's leading marketer of juices and owner of many drinks, including Fruitopia, Fanta, Sprite and Mello Yello, as well as its soft drinks, the Coca-Cola Company owns one of the world's most famous and, some think, most valuable brands. As an indicator of the brand's value, consider that in the early 1990s, some analysts suggested that if all of Coca-Cola's tangible assets were destroyed simultaneously, the company could borrow at least US$100 billion with only its brand name as collateral. Because of concerns that surfaced in mid-1999 about the quality of some of its products in a few European countries, some estimated that the value of this brand had fallen to approximately US$84 billion, a staggering 59 per cent of its market capitalisation and an amount that still ranked Coca-Cola as the most valuable brand name in the world. At the same time, Microsoft was second with a brand value of almost US$57 billion (21 per cent of its market capitalisation).

The top 60 global brands by value in 1999 are shown in Table 3.1. Absent from this list are financial sector organisations. In the words of an analyst, 'The great failure of financial institutions has been their inability to create any relevant differentiation for themselves, other than at the edges.' Of such institutions, Goldman Sachs is recognised as having one of the best brands in the global investment banking business. Citibank and American Express are thought to have strong brand identities in the general financial sector. Given that demand for savings and investment products is increasing on a worldwide basis, AMP is striving to become a global 'financial services' brand. Initially the brand will be rolled out in the United Kingdom with plans to leverage its stake in the powerful Virgin brand to expand into Japan and South Africa.

Contributing to the sustainability of brand as a competitive advantage is the fact that a brand is an intangible resource. Discussed later in the chapter, intangible resources are less visible and more difficult for competitors to understand and imitate than are tangible resources. The importance of intangible resources to Australian firms has been demonstrated in a study that traced the growth of intangible capital in companies listed on the Australian Stock Exchange. That study showed that the ratio of intangible capital to all capital in Australian publicly listed companies has increased annually by 1.3 per cent since 1948 and is currently at about 28 per cent. Increasingly, firms agree that, as an intangible resource or asset, a brand generates an identifiable stream of earnings over time. Once this perspective is adopted, brand value can then be defined and a net present value for future profits can be established for a brand.

Table 3.1 | Banking on a ranking: Top 60 global brands by value

	Brand name	Country of origin	Industry	Value (US$m)		Brand name	Country of origin	Industry	Value (US$m)
1	Coca-Cola	US	Beverages	83 845	31	Volkswagen	Ger	Automobiles	6 603
2	Microsoft	US	Software	56 654	32	Pepsi-Cola	US	Beverages	5 932
3	IBM	US	Computers	43 781	33	Kleenex	US	Pers. care	4 602
4	General Electric	US	Diversified	33 502	34	Wrigley's	US	Food	4 404
5	Ford	US	Automobiles	33 197	35	AOL	US	Software	4 329
6	Disney	US	Entertainment	32 275	36	Apple	US	Computers	4 283
7	Intel	US	Computers	30 021	37	Louis Vuitton	Fra	Fashion	4 076
8	McDonald's	US	Food	26 231	38	Barbie	US	Toys	3 792
9	AT&T	US	Telecoms	24 181	39	Motorola	US	Telecoms	3 643
10	Marlboro	US	Tobacco	21 048	40	Adidas	Ger	Sports goods	3 596
11	Nokia	Fin	Telecoms	20 694	41	Colgate	US	Pers. care	3 568
12	Mercedes	Ger	Automobiles	17 781	42	Hertz	US	Car hire	3 527
13	Nescafé	Swit	Beverages	17 595	43	Ikea	Swe	Housewares	3 464
14	Hewlett-Packard	US	Computers	17 132	44	Chanel	Fra	Fashion	3 143
15	Gillette	US	Pers. care	15 894	45	BP	UK	Oil	2 985
16	Kodak	US	Imaging	14 830	46	Bacardi	Cuba	Alcohol	2 895
17	Ericsson	Swe	Telecoms	14 766	47	Burger King	US	Food	2 806
18	Sony	Jap	Electronics	14 231	48	Moet & Chandon	Fra	Alcohol	2 804
19	Amex	US	Fin. services	12 550	49	Shell	UK	Oil	2 681
20	Toyota	Jap	Automobiles	12 310	50	Rolex	Swit	Luxury	2 423
21	Heinz	US	Food	11 806	51	Smirnoff	Russ	Alcohol	2 313
22	BMW	Ger	Automobiles	11 281	52	Heineken	Neth	Alcohol	2 184
23	Xerox	US	Office equipmt	11 225	53	Yahoo!	US	Software	1 761
24	Honda	Jap	Automobiles	11 101	54	Ralph Lauren	US	Fashion	1 648
25	Citibank	US	Fin. services	9 147	55	Johnnie Walker	UK	Alcohol	1 634
26	Dell	US	Computers	9 043	56	ampers	US	Pers. care	1 422
27	Budweiser	US	Alcohol	8 510	57	Amazon.com	US	Books	1 361
28	Nike	US	Sports goods	8 155	58	Hilton	US	Leisure	1 319
29	Gap	US	Apparel	7 909	59	Guinness	Ire	Alcohol	1 262
30	Kellogg's	US	Food	7 052	60	Marriott	US	Leisure	1 193

Source: R. Tomkins, 1999, 'Assessing a name's worth', *Financial Times*, 22 June, p. 12.

Some of the world's most powerful brands result from the labour of inspired men and women who are leaders with visions of global expansion and dominance. (See Table 3.2 for a listing of such 'one-person brands'.) These individuals' actions were founded on the belief that 'while the day to day business might be about profits, brand building is about giving a single, often mundane product an identity that inspires loyalty and passion'. For instance, when he became president of Coca-Cola in 1923, Robert Woodruff observed that his job was 'to sell Coca-Cola, to see that as many people as possible are able to enjoy it'. To inspire loyalty and to create a passion for his firm's products, Woodruff sent 64 portable bottling plants to follow American troops during their Second World War travels. Following the war's end, these plants became part of the beachhead on which Coca-Cola began its global expansion – an expansion and operation that remains vital today to the firm's ability to earn above-average returns.

Table 3.2 | One-person brands

SOME OF THE CENTURY'S GREAT BRANDS HAVE BEEN INSEPARABLE FROM THEIR BUILDERS

Richard Branson	Virgin Atlantic	Adventurer, beard wearer
Walt Disney	Disney	Cartoonist, ideas person
Hugh Hefner	Playboy Enterprises	Dirty-mag mogul, pyjama wearer
R. M. Williams	R. M. Williams	Australian outback legend
Reg Ansett	Ansett Airlines	Travel entrepreneur
Lindsay Fox	Linfox	Trucking magnate
Colonel Sanders	KFC	Fast-food entrepreneur

Source: Adapted from S. Branch, 1999, 'The brand builders', *Fortune*, 10 May, p. 134.

Other great 'brand mechanics' include Sony Corporation's Akio Morita, McDonald's' Ray Kroc, Nike's Phil Knight and Virgin's Richard Branson. Each of these leaders is credited with at least one key action that helped to create a powerful brand for his firm. Phil Knight, for example, pioneered celebrity sports marketing by signing athletes such as Michael Jordan and Tiger Woods to endorse his firm's products. In the ongoing brand war with Nike, Adidas has responded by signing glamour athletes such as Anna Kournikova and Ian Thorpe. Ray Kroc made fast food a global way of life by tirelessly building his company on the mantra of quality, service, cleanliness and value. Kroc was famous for visiting McDonald's units unannounced to verify that the actions demanded to fulfil his mantra were in place. Richard Branson's adventurous lifestyle and celebrity status has done much to raise the profile of the Virgin brand. Virgin operates across a broad scope of industries, such as railways, airlines, retailing, mobile phones, banking, soft drinks, radio and clothing. The only common thread is the brand association with youth culture and good value. Akio Morita's decision to build a tiny portable stereo (a product that was to become known as the Walkman) over his engineers' objections caused Sony, which already had a formidable brand name, to become a global icon for innovation in consumer electronics products.

Individuals can also be a powerful brand. This is the case with Michael Jordan, the retired Chicago Bulls superstar and now president of the Washington Wizards National Basketball Association (NBA) franchise. Chosen by the ESPN television network as the athlete of the 20th century, Jordan is thought to have transcended the sport of basketball. Viewed as a 'powerbrand', Jordan is recognised as 'a player whose popularity and reach is peerless in the history of sports business'. The significance of Jordan as a powerbrand is evidenced by the fact that the NBA and the television networks broadcasting the league's games expressed serious concerns about how to retain fan interest when Jordan decided to retire after 13 'extraordinary years of skywalking across the NBA'.

Only carefully managed brands are a source of competitive advantage. Coca-Cola, R. M. Williams, Country Road, McDonald's and Nike, for example, devote a significant amount of time and energy to managing their brand name to gain a competitive advantage. How a brand is managed varies from company to company. For instance, shelf space for cigarettes in convenience stores is critical to the management of the Philip Morris cigarette brand. In the United States, the firm has developed the Retail Leaders sales-incentive program to support its brand in the thousands of convenience stores that have displaced grocery stores, thus becoming the country's largest seller of cigarettes. The Retail Leaders program compensates retailers for favouring Philip Morris brands over competitors' offerings. In the world of fine food, King Island Dairy improves the recognition of its dairy products in key Melbourne and

Sydney markets by using small refrigerated trucks, painted with the corporate logo, to offer product samples to and deal directly with restaurateurs.

For large global branded firms, the challenge is to engage frequently in brand rationalisation, a process that is 'an opportunity to cut costs and improve purchasing efficiencies', as well as to improve products' positions in various global markets. Based in Switzerland, Nestlé SA offers more than 8000 brands across the globe, including Nescafe instant coffee and Perrier mineral water. To manage the diversity of its brands, Nestlé relies on what it calls a 'brand umbrella'. Grouped as parts of the umbrella are World-Wide Corporate, World-Wide Strategic, Regional Strategic and Local. Each umbrella part features multiple brands. Unit managers are responsible for managing and continuously rationalising their brands in ways that contribute to strategic competitiveness and the earning of above-average returns.

Some preliminary evidence suggests that a brand name creates little, if any, value for young Internet users. In place of brand, perceived product utility is a key source of value. To date, Amazon.com has been quite successful in terms of demonstrating the utilities of its products to customers. Thus, companies with strong brand names may find it necessary to describe the actual utility of their products more precisely in terms of their functionality, at least to young Internet users, in order to earn their business. On the other hand, studies on dotcom retailers after the sobering April 2000 'tech wreck' on world stock exchanges have shown that brands may be particularly important in cyberspace.

www.amazon.com
www.americanexpress.com
www.bestfoods.com
www.citibank.com
www.coca-cola.com
www.fidelity.com
www.goldmansachs.com
www.kidairy.com.au
www.mcdonalds.com
www.microsoft.com
www.nba.com
www.nestle.com
www.nike.com
www.philipmorris.com
www.sony.com

Sources: G. Anders, 2000, 'Investing for the new millennium', *Wall Street Journal*, 1 January, p. R20; E. Beck, 1999, 'Nestlé sticks to strategy of broad categories of brands', *Wall Street Journal*, 14 September, p. B4; S. Branch, 1999, 'Bestfoods aims to spice up North American business', *Wall Street Journal*, 10 November, p. B6; S. Branch, 1999, 'The brand builders', *Fortune*, 10 May, pp. 132–4; B. Copple, 1999, 'If you build it, will they sit down?', *Forbes*, 29 November, pp. 132–4; T. Corrigan, 1999, 'Weighing up the value of one of banking's best brands', *Financial Times*, 19 March, p. 28; R. O. Crockett, 1999, 'Yikes: Mike takes a hike', *Business Week*, 25 January, pp. 74–6; R. Heller, 1999, 'Gucci's $4 billion man', *Forbes*, 8 February, pp. 108–9; S. Lubove, 1999, 'Brand power', *Forbes*, 9 August, pp. 98–104; E. I. Schwartz, 1999, 'Brands aren't everything', *Industry Standard*, 30 April, pp. 27–30; R. Tomkins, 1999, 'Assessing a name's worth', *Financial Times*, 22 June, p. 12; S. Reed, M. L. Clifford, B. Bremner and G. Smith, 1998, 'Fidelity takes on the world', *Business Week*, 18 May: www.businessweek.com; D. Jackson, 2000, 'Brand affinity', *The Australian*, 22 August, pp. 35–7; D. Uren, 2001, 'Today's corporations just want to be your friend', *The Weekend Australian*, 24–25 February, pp. 43–5; S. Creedy, 2000, 'Brand loyalty', *The Australian*, 28 November, pp. 37–8; 'Valuing system gives a brand new days', 2000, *Australian Financial Review*, 17 October, p. 4.

The firms mentioned in the Opening Case have resources, capabilities and core competencies (see Chapter 1) that have been used to create brand as a source of competitive advantage. Even cities can use resources, capabilities and competencies to form a brand that is a source of competitive advantage. For example, the city of New Orleans in the United States historically has leaned 'on its carnival reputation as a brand name' to attract tourists. Some believe, though, that the city's future growth depends on its ability to form a business brand identity. Officials and citizens hope to develop a business brand by emphasising education and highlighting the quality of the city's scientific and technological business communities.[1]

Organisations that rely on brand as a competitive advantage want that advantage to be *sustainable*. However, as discussed in the first two chapters, several attributes of the global economy, including the rapid emergence of the Internet's capabilities, are making it increasingly difficult to develop a competitive advantage that can be sustained for any reasonable period of time. In these instances, firms try to create advantages that can be sustained longer than can others. Regardless of the period for which it can be sustained, a *sustainable competitive advantage* is achieved when firms implement a value-creating strategy that is grounded in their own unique resources, capabilities and core competencies.

A key indicator of understanding the importance of the relationship between advantage and value-creating strategies is the fact that 'competitive advantage continues to provide the central agenda in strategy research'.[2] The reason for this is that 'the basic notion behind strategy is that a successful, high performing business requires a distinctive (or core) competence or competitive advantage'.[3] To identify and use successfully its competitive advantages across time, firms must think constantly about their strategic management process and how to increase continuously the value it creates as it is used throughout the company.[4] Thus, as the discussion in this chapter indicates, firms achieve strategic competitiveness and earn above-average returns when their unique core competencies are leveraged effectively to take advantage of opportunities in the external environment. Increasingly, employees or associates are an important source of competitive advantage for firms competing in the 21st century's global economy.[5] For example, Ericsson believe that people and their ideas are an important competitive advantage for their widely globalised firm.[6]

Over time, the benefits of every firm's value-creating strategy can be duplicated. In other words, there are no absolutes or guarantees, in that all competitive advantages have a limited life.[7] The question of duplication is not *if* it will happen, but *when*. Speaking to the essence of this reality, General Electric CEO Jack Welch argues that 'to be vital, an organization has to repot itself, start again, get new ideas, renew itself'.[8] Being brutally honest is a prelude to accepting the need for the firm to reinvent itself to develop new competitive advantages. In this context, failing to communicate fully and honestly with all people in the firm to make certain that the limited life of competitive advantages is fully understood can create problems. One such problem is that, without full understanding of an advantage's limited life, organisational change that is vital to continuously developing new advantages may be stifled.[9] This may have been the case at David Jones.

David Jones, the retailer that is legendary for its competitive advantage of traditional up-market *customer service*, was refloated in 1995. However, the share price has since languished well below the $4 initial offer in the face of weak earnings, and the company is now the subject of takeover speculation.[10] Part of David Jones's problems stem from the changing nature of its customers and the ability of focused retailers such as Harvey Norman to outflank David Jones's competitive advantage. In a business with increasingly fickle customers who do not like waiting weeks for delivery and do not like being told that 'we don't have your size', the ability to adapt rapidly to changes in consumer demands has become more important for competitive advantage than the old-style customer service. Specialists know their niche and adapt faster than the big department stores, such as David Jones, which cannot move as rapidly. In an attempt to reinvent itself, David Jones has sacked many old-school sales assistants, replaced non-performing merchandise buyers, updated outmoded inventory control systems and is moving through an expensive rollout of refurbishments.[11] These refurbishments include a move towards more flexible building formats, so that space can be quickly allocated to boom segments, such as telecommunications and homewares, and less space allocated to slower-moving stock, such as men's clothing. In an attempt to adapt to customer tastes, David Jones introduced over 100 new brands in the first half of 1999 while replacing private labels. Other initiatives include a move into on-line retailing. After abandoning the Web in 1997, David Jones re-entered the world of e-commerce in 2000 armed with technology from failed e-tailer TheSpot. After buying TheSpot's infrastructure and customer database, as well as retaining TheSpot's e-commerce integrator, Cortex, to handle the larger product range, David Jones has reported promising signs of success with popular products such as hampers. However, sceptical analysts fear that e-commerce will not provide lasting competitive advantage and will instead divert David Jones's attention away from future core business.[12]

Effective duplication by competitors may have contributed to Apple Computers' mid-1990s performance difficulties which nearly finished the company. Apple has made two revolutionary contributions to the computer industry, which have gradually been duplicated in both cases. Steve Jobs and Steve Wosniak's original 1970s' insight into the potential importance of the personal computer market and Wosniak's invention of the computer 'Volkswagen', in the form of the Apple II, sustained Apple's meteoric growth until IBM and IBM clones entered the PC market during the early 1980s. Apple's counter to the declining margins caused by IBM's entry was the development of the Macintosh with its innovative windows-based operating system. However, this too has been duplicated by Microsoft's Windows operating system. Critics have accused Apple of being too reliant on superior technology for competitive advantage while ignoring the larger strategic picture. A prime example of this is the failure to license its technology during the 1980s in an effort to retain control over its technology. However, licensing could have turned Apple's technology into an industry standard, creating barriers to entry that may have left Microsoft as a minor player in the software business. Since the dumping of Steve Jobs in 1985, professional managers with little understanding of the industry have failed to position Apple competitively. But Steve Jobs's recent reappointment has brought back the clarity of focus that the company had lacked during the 1990s. He has replaced the bewildering array of product lines with a four-cornered structure of powerful high-end desktops and portables, and a colourful range of mass-market desktops and portables. Software development has been rationalised and Apple's more esoteric research projects have been shut down. Most importantly, Jobs has recognised the opportunity in the rapidly expanding Internet user market. Brightly hued, sleekly designed and reasonably priced iMac computers, without a floppy disk drive, have become so popular with Internet users that Apple has had difficulty in keeping up with demand. Despite Apple's remarkable turnaround, the long-term prospects for competitive advantage remain uncertain.[13]

In general, the sustainability of a competitive advantage is a function of three factors: (1) the rate of core competence obsolescence due to environmental changes; (2) the availability of substitutes for the core competence; and (3) the imitability of the core competence.[14] The challenge in all firms – a challenge that can be met through proper use of the strategic management process – is to manage current core competencies effectively while simultaneously developing new ones to use when the competitive advantage derived from the application of current ones has been eroded.[15] In the words of Michael Dell, CEO of Dell Computer Corporation, 'No [competitive] advantage and no success is ever permanent. The winners are those who keep moving. The only constant in our business is that everything is changing. We have to be ahead of the game.'[16] Thus, as with Dell Computer, only when firms are able to develop a continuous stream of competitive advantages (as explained further in Chapter 5) do they achieve strategic competitiveness, earn above-average returns and remain ahead of competitors.

In Chapter 2, we examined the general, industry and competitor environments. Armed with knowledge about the realities and conditions of their environments, firms have a better understanding of marketplace opportunities and the goods or services through which they can be pursued.

In this chapter, we focus on the firm. Through an analysis of the internal environment, a firm determines *what it can do* – that is, the actions permitted by its unique resources, capabilities and core competencies. As discussed in Chapter 1, core competencies are a firm's source of competitive advantage. The magnitude of that competitive advantage is a function primarily of the uniqueness of those competencies compared to competitors' competencies.[17] The proper matching of what a firm *can do* with what it *might do* allows the development of strategic intent, the pursuit of a strategic mission and the formulation of strategies. When implemented effectively, a value-creating strategy leads to strategic competitiveness and above-average returns. Outcomes resulting from internal and external environmental analyses are shown in Figure 3.1.

Figure 3.1 | Outcomes from external and internal environmental analyses

By studying the external environment, firms identify	By studying the internal environment, firms determine
• what they *might* choose to *do*	• what they *can do*

We examine several topics in this chapter. First, the importance and challenge of studying a firm's internal environment are addressed. We then discuss the roles of resources, capabilities and core competencies in the development of sustainable competitive advantage. Included here are descriptions of the techniques used to identify and evaluate resources and capabilities and the criteria firms use to select core competencies from among them. While studying these materials, it is important to recall that resources, capabilities and core competencies are not *inherently* valuable; they have value only because they allow the firm to perform certain activities that result in a competitive advantage. To create a *sustained* competitive advantage, these activities must be unique.[18]

As shown in Figure 1.1 in Chapter 1, strategic intent and strategic mission, coupled with insights gained through analyses of the internal and external environments, determine the strategies a firm will select and the actions it will take to implement those strategies successfully. In the final part of this chapter, we describe briefly the relationship between intent and mission and a firm's strategic actions in terms of formulation and implementation.

The importance of internal analysis

In the 21st-century competitive landscape, traditional conditions and factors, such as labour costs, access to financial resources and raw materials, and protected or regulated markets, can still be a source of competitive advantage, but to a lesser degree than in the past.[19] One important reason for this decline is that the advantages created by these sources can be overcome through an international strategy (discussed in Chapter 8) and by the relatively free flow of resources throughout the global economy. In economist Lester Thurow's words, 'Raw materials can be bought and moved to wherever they are needed. Financial capital is a commodity that can be borrowed in New York, Tokyo or London. Unique pieces of equipment that cannot be obtained or are too expensive for one's competitors to buy simply don't exist.'[20] One of the outcomes of these conditions is a significant amount of excess capacity. In fact, it seems that over-capacity is the norm in a host of industries, increasing the difficulty of forming competitive advantages.[21] In this challenging competitive environment, few firms are able consistently to make the most effective strategic decisions. To improve the quality of decisions across events and time, 21st-century firms must develop the capability to change rapidly. A key challenge to developing this capability is fostering an organisational environment in which experimentation and learning are expected and promoted.[22]

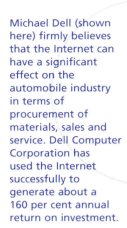

Michael Dell (shown here) firmly believes that the Internet can have a significant effect on the automobile industry in terms of procurement of materials, sales and service. Dell Computer Corporation has used the Internet successfully to generate about a 160 per cent annual return on investment.

The demands of the 21st-century competitive landscape make it necessary for top-level managers to rethink the concept of the corporation. Michael Dell, for example, believes that automobile executives should do this by learning how to use the Internet to streamline procurement and to reshape service and sales.[23] Dell is not the only person convinced about the Internet's significance to the automobile industry. In the words of Lee Sage, the global leader of Ernst & Young LLP's automotive-consulting practice, 'The Internet is going to have as much of an impact on the automobile industry as Henry Ford's mass-merchandising and production methods did in the 1920s.'[24] One reason car companies are intrigued by Dell's proposal and the Internet's potential is that, by following some of the principles that Michael Dell thinks could be used successfully by automobile manufacturers, Dell Computer Corporation has generated an annual return on its investment of approximately 160 per cent.[25]

Although corporations are difficult to change, achieving strategic competitiveness in the 21st-century landscape requires development and the use of a different managerial mind-set.[26] This is true both for those leading some of the world's automobile manufacturers and for people leading a host of companies throughout the global economy.

Most top-level managers recognise the need to change their mind-sets, but many hesitate to do so. In the words of a European CEO of a major US company, 'It is more reassuring for all of us to stay as we are, even though we know the result will be certain failure ... than to jump into a new way of working when we cannot be sure it will succeed.'[27] However, Jacques Nasser, Ford Motor Company's CEO in the United States, is not hesitating to call for the adoption of a new mind-set throughout his firm. In fact, Nasser believes that all employees, but especially senior-level executives, must change their mind-set from one that concentrates on their own area of operation to one that encompasses a view of the company in its entirety. This is necessary, in Nasser's view, to generate the type of rapid decision making required for Ford to be successful in a 'world driven by rapidly changing consumer needs and tastes'.[28] Similarly, mining giant Rio Tinto has transformed itself into a highly profitable business after decades of missed opportunities. Traditionally, miners, including Rio Tinto, have given lip-service to profits, because the companies tended to be run by engineers who were motivated by the challenge of assembling large projects. The mind-set of many of these engineer–managers was that the ability of these projects to make money would depend upon the price of the commodity, and that was outside the control of the chief executives and board. According to business commentator Robert Gottliebsen, Rio Tinto is the first international mining company to realise that profits are important. In an address to the Securities Institute in Melbourne during 1999, Rio Tinto CEO, Robert Wilson, pointed to the abysmal returns on capital that the mining industry had achieved and delivered a strong attack on past management and board practices in the industry.

The renewed Rio Tinto is focusing on competitive advantage by lowering production costs through better process integration. Other strategic initiatives include plans for alliances with other miners to coordinate shipping of global minerals, and coordination of purchasing whereby miners will individually forward their requirement to the electronic marketplace in a business-to-business exchange.[29] Critical to the required mind-set is the view that a firm is a bundle of heterogeneous resources, capabilities and core competencies that can be used to create an exclusive market position.[30] This view suggests that individual firms possess at least some resources and capabilities that other companies do not have – at least not in the same combination. Resources are the source of capabilities, some of which lead to the development of a firm's core competencies.[31] By using their core competencies, firms perform activities *better* than competitors or perform activities that competitors are unable to duplicate. Essentially, the mind-set needed in the 21st-century competitive landscape requires decision makers to define their firm's strategy in terms of a unique competitive position, rather than *strictly* in terms of operational effectiveness. For instance, Michael Porter argues that quests for productivity, quality and speed from a number of management techniques (total quality management, benchmarking, time-based competition and reengineering) have resulted in operational efficiency, but not strong sustainable strategies.[32] As we discussed in Chapter 1, strategic competitiveness results when the firm satisfies the operational efficiency demands of its external environment, while simultaneously using its own unique capabilities to establish a viable competitive position.

Increasingly, managers are being evaluated in terms of their ability to identify, nurture and exploit their firm's core competencies.[33] A part of these evaluations is framed around the understanding that an effective internal environmental analysis includes the recognition of both what *are* and what *are not* the firm's core competencies.[34] By emphasising the acquisition and development of competencies, organisations *learn how to learn*.[35] Being able to learn is a skill that is linked with the development of competitive advantage. This skill has been called *metalearning*.[36] Learning how to learn requires commitment, time and the active support of top-level executives. At Deere & Co., a global firm operating in over 160 countries, through commitments to product quality, customer service, and business integrity and a high regard for the contributions of individuals, managers have created an 'in-house Yellow Pages' to help them find an expert inside or outside the firm.[37] The system is quite inexpensive – about the cost of one engineer to operate it – but it has paid for itself annually at least six times over, especially when there is a crisis, say, in production, and an expert is needed to solve it. In the final analysis, a corporate-wide obsession with the development and use of knowledge, together with broader core competencies, may characterise companies that are able to compete effectively on a global basis.[38]

By exploiting their core competencies and meeting the demanding standards of global competition, firms create value for customers. **Value** consists of the performance characteristics and attributes companies provide in the form of goods or services for which customers are willing to pay.[39] At Flight Centre, operational excellence is treated as non-negotiable. Apart from the guarantee of lowest-price airfares, a strong emphasis is placed on service quality because of the belief that it doesn't matter how cheap your prices are – you won't get business in the long run if your service isn't good. With a combined attention to customer service and competitive pricing, Flight Centre has

---

Value consists of the performance characteristics and attributes provided by companies in the form of goods or services for which customers are willing to pay.

achieved stellar financial performances by delivering value to its clients.[40] Ultimately, customer value is the source of a firm's potential to earn average or above-average returns. What the firm intends to do to create value affects its choice of business-level strategy (see Chapter 4) and its organisational structure (see Chapter 11).[41] In Chapter 4's discussion of business-level strategies, we note that value is created by a product's low cost or highly differentiated features, or by a combination of low cost and high differentiation, compared to competitors' offerings. For R. M. Williams, the Australian clothing designer and manufacturer, the distinctive value of their clothing is found in its quality, design, durability and link to Australia's 'outback' heritage.[42] Thus, the firm creates value through a differentiation business-level strategy (described in detail in the next chapter). At R. M. Williams, core competencies such as craftsmanship and quality materials are actually a value-creating system through which the company seeks strategic competitiveness and above-average returns. (The various relationships are shown in Figure 3.2.) In the 21st-century competitive landscape, firms must continually evaluate the degree to which their core competencies create customer value.[43]

Figure 3.2 | Components of internal analysis leading to competitive advantage and strategic competitiveness

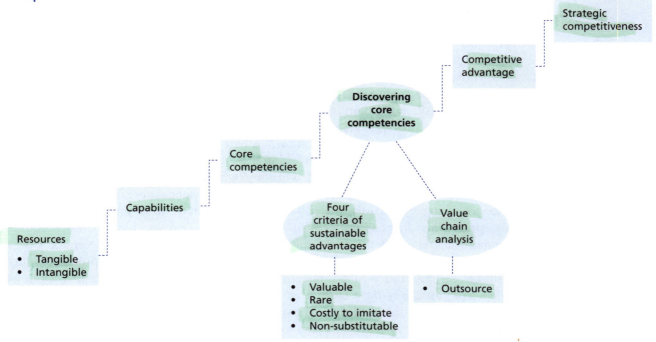

During the last several decades, the strategic management process was concerned largely with understanding the characteristics of the industry in which a firm was competing and, in light of those characteristics, determining how the firm should position itself relative to competitors. The emphasis on industry characteristics and competitive strategy may have understated the role of organisational resources and capabilities in developing competitive advantage. A firm's core competencies, in addition to the results of an analysis of its general, industry and competitor environments, should drive the selection of strategies. In this regard, core competencies, in combination with product-market positions or tactics, are the most important sources of competitive advantage in the 21st-century competitive landscape.⁴⁴ Emphasising core competencies when formulating strategies is how companies learn to compete primarily on the basis of firm-specific differences, rather than seeking competitive advantage solely on the basis of an industry's structural characteristics.⁴⁵

The challenge of internal analysis

The decisions managers make in terms of resources, capabilities and core competencies have a significant influence on a firm's ability to develop competitive advantages and earn above-average returns.⁴⁶ Making these decisions – that is, identifying, developing, deploying and protecting resources, capabilities and core competencies – may appear to be a relatively easy task. In fact, however, this work is as challenging and difficult as any other with which managers are involved; and it is becoming increasingly internationalised and linked with the firm's success.⁴⁷ The challenge and difficulty of making effective decisions is implied by preliminary evidence suggesting that one-half of organisational decisions fail.⁴⁸ Recognising the firm's core competencies is required before the firm can make important strategic decisions, including those related to entering or exiting markets, investing in new technologies, building new or additional manufacturing capacity, and forming strategic partnerships.⁴⁹ Patterns of interactions between individuals and groups that occur as strategic decisions are made affect decision quality as well as how effectively and quickly they are implemented.⁵⁰

Sometimes, mistakes are made when a firm conducts an internal analysis. Managers might, for example, select resources and capabilities as the firm's core competencies that do not, in fact, yield a competitive advantage (see Figure 3.5). When this occurs, decision makers must have the confidence to admit the mistake and take corrective actions. A firm can still grow through well-intended errors. Indeed, learning generated by making and correcting mistakes can be important to the creation of new competitive advantages.⁵¹ Moreover, from the failure resulting from mistakes, firms learn what *not* to do when seeking competitive advantage.⁵²

To facilitate the development and use of core competencies, managers must have courage, self-confidence, integrity, the capacity to deal with uncertainty and complexity, and a willingness to hold people accountable for their work *and* to be held accountable themselves. It is now widely believed that upper-level executives should empower managers throughout the firm to take charge of their units to achieve stretch goals while expecting to be judged on the results accomplished by those units.⁵³ Thus, effective strategists try to create an organisational environment in which those working in operating units feel empowered to use core competencies to pursue marketplace opportunities.

Difficult managerial decisions concerning resources, capabilities and core competencies are characterised by three conditions: uncertainty, complexity and intra-organisational conflicts (see Figure 3.3).⁵⁴

Figure 3.3 | Conditions affecting managerial decisions about resources, capabilities and core competencies

Source: Adapted from R. Amit and P. J. H. Schoemaker, 1993, 'Strategic assets and organizational rent', *Strategic Management Journal*, 14, p. 33.

Managers face *uncertainty* in terms of the emergence of new proprietary technologies, rapidly changing economic and political trends, transformations in societal values and shifts in customer demands.[55] Environmental uncertainty increases the *complexity* and the range of issues to examine when studying the internal environment. Biases about how to cope with uncertainty affect decisions about the resources and capabilities that will become the foundation of the firm's competitive advantage. Finally, *intra-organisational conflict* surfaces when decisions are made about core competencies that are to be nurtured and about how the nurturing is to take place.

In making decisions affected by these three conditions, judgement should be used. *Judgement* is the capability of making successful decisions when no obviously correct model or rule is available or when relevant data are unreliable or incomplete.[56] In this situation, one must be aware of possible cognitive biases. For instance, one must compare internal firm resources and make a judgement as to whether a resource is a strength or a weakness. When exercising judgement, decision makers demonstrate a willingness to take intelligent risks in a timely manner. In the 21st-century competitive landscape, executive judgement can be a particularly important source of competitive advantage. One reason for this is that, over time, effective judgement allows a firm to retain the loyalty of stakeholders whose support is linked to above-average returns.[57]

Significant changes in the value-creating potential of a firm's resources and capabilities can occur in a rapidly changing global economy. Because these changes affect a company's power and social structure, inertia or resistance to change may surface. Even though that happens, decision makers should not deny the changes needed in their firm to assure its strategic competitiveness. *Denial* is an unconscious coping mechanism used to block out and not initiate painful changes.[58] It has been observed that top-level executives must demonstrate unflinching candour when making strategic decisions. Part of this candour demands that decision makers cause their firms and their people to face reality, as it is not as it once was or as they want it to be.[59] Successful firms learn that involving many people when making decisions about organisational change reduces denial as well as intra-organisational conflict.[60] Involving a range of individuals and

Resources, capabilities and core competencies

Our attention now turns to a description of resources, capabilities and core competencies – characteristics that are the foundation of competitive advantage. As shown in Figure 3.2, combinations of resources and capabilities are managed to create core competencies. This subsection defines and provides examples of these internal aspects.

Resources

Defined in Chapter 1, *resources* are inputs into a firm's production process. Capital equipment, the skills of individual employees, patents, finances and talented managers are all resources. Broad in scope, resources cover a spectrum of individual, social and organisational phenomena.[62]

Typically, resources alone do not yield a competitive advantage.[63] A professional football team may benefit from employing the league's most attacking winger, but it is only when he integrates his play with the forwards that the team's competitive advantage may develop. A competitive advantage is actually created through the *unique bundling of several resources*.[64] Dell Computer Corporation, for example, combines technological and human resources to use what analysts believe is a highly efficient business model. (See the discussion about these actions in a Strategic Focus in Chapter 2.) This model results in Dell selling PCs directly to customers, bypassing retailers and other middlemen. Thus, the model has created a unique distribution channel that is the company's main competitive advantage.[65] As with Dell, Frito-Lay's (sellers of potato chips) distribution system in the United States has long been cited 'as the company's most important competitive advantage'. Recently, though, the firm changed its distribution methods to better integrate its marketing capabilities with the physical delivery and support of products. A new emphasis is to have its army of 15 000-plus salespeople spend more time merchandising and selling chips in retail outlets, rather than loading and sorting products in their trucks.[66]

> **Tangible resources** are assets that can be seen and quantified.
>
> **Intangible resources** include assets that are rooted deeply in the firm's history and that have accumulated over time.

Some of a firm's resources are tangible, while others are intangible. **Tangible resources** are assets that can be seen and quantified. Production equipment, manufacturing plants and formal reporting structures are examples of tangible resources. **Intangible resources** include assets that are rooted deeply in the firm's history and that have accumulated over time. Because they are embedded in unique patterns of routines, intangible resources are relatively difficult for competitors to understand and imitate. Knowledge, trust between managers and employees or associates, ideas, the capacity for innovation, managerial capabilities, organisational routines (the unique ways people work together), scientific capabilities, and the firm's reputation for its goods or services and the ways it interacts with people (such as employees, customers and suppliers) are examples of intangible resources.[67]

The four types of tangible resources are financial, organisational, physical and technological (see Table 3.3). The three types of intangible resources (human, innovation and reputational) are shown in Table 3.4.

Table 3.3 | Tangible resources

Financial resources	• The firm's borrowing capacity • The firm's ability to generate internal funds
Organisational resources	• The firm's formal reporting structure and its formal planning, controlling and coordinating systems
Physical resources	• Sophistication and location of a firm's plant and equipment • Access to raw materials
Technological resources	• Stock of technology, such as patents, trademarks, copyrights and trade secrets.

Source: Adapted from J. B. Barney, 1991, 'Firm resources and sustained competitive advantage', *Journal of Management*, 17, p. 101; R. M. Grant, 1991, *Contemporary Strategy Analysis* (Cambridge, UK: Blackwell Business), pp. 100–2.

Table 3.4 | Intangible resources

Human resources	• Knowledge • Trust • Managerial capabilities • Organisational routines
Innovation resources	• Ideas • Scientific capabilities • Capacity to innovate

Reputational resources	• Reputation with customers
	  – Brand name
	  – Perceptions of product quality, durability and reliability
	• Reputation with suppliers
	  – For efficient, effective, supportive and mutually beneficial interactions and relationships

Source: Adapted from R. Hall, 1992, 'The strategic analysis of intangible resources', *Strategic Management Journal*, 13, pp. 136–9; R. M. Grant, 1991, *Contemporary Strategy Analysis* (Cambridge, UK: Blackwell Business), pp. 101–4.

Tangible resources

As tangible resources, a firm's borrowing capacity and the status of its plant and equipment are visible to all. The value of many tangible resources can be established through financial statements, but these statements do not account for the value of all of a firm's assets, because they disregard some intangible resources.[68] As such, each of the firm's sources of competitive advantage may not be reflected fully in corporate financial statements. The value of tangible resources is also constrained because it is difficult to leverage them – that is, it is hard to derive additional business or value from a tangible resource. Consider the case of an airplane as a tangible resource or asset: 'You can't use the same airplane on five different routes at the same time. You can't put the same crew on five different routes at the same time. And the same goes for the financial investment you've made in the airplane.'[69]

Decision makers are challenged to understand fully the strategic value of their firm's tangible and intangible resources. The *strategic value of resources* is indicated by the degree to which they can contribute to the development of capabilities, core competencies and, ultimately, a competitive advantage. For example, as a tangible resource, a distribution facility will be assigned a monetary value on the firm's balance sheet. The real value of the facility as a resource, however, is grounded in other factors, such as its proximity to raw materials and customers and the manner in which workers integrate their actions internally and with other stakeholders (for example, suppliers and customers).[70]

Resources are the source of a firm's capabilities (see Figure 3.2). Capabilities, in turn, are the source of a firm's core competencies, which are the basis of competitive advantages. Compared to tangible resources, intangible resources are a superior and more potent source of core competencies.[71] In fact, in the global economy, 'the success of a corporation lies more in its intellectual and systems capabilities than in its physical assets. [Moreover], the capacity to manage human intellect and to convert it into useful products and services is fast becoming the critical executive skill of the age.'[72] There is some evidence that the value of intangible assets is growing relative to that of tangible assets. John Kendrick is a well-known economist studying the main drivers of economic growth. His findings indicate that there has been a general increase in the contribution of intangible assets to US economic growth since the early 1900s: 'In 1929, the ratio of intangible business capital to tangible business capital was 30 percent to 70 percent. In 1990, that ratio was 63 percent to 37 percent.' As was mentioned in the Opening Case for this chapter, similar patterns in the growth of intangible capital have occurred in Australia.[73]

Intangible resources

Because they are less visible and more difficult for competitors to understand, purchase, imitate or substitute for, firms prefer to rely on intangible resources as the foundation for their capabilities and core competencies. In fact, the more unobservable (that is, intangible) a resource is, the more sustainable will be the competitive advantage that is based on it.[74] Another benefit of intangible resources is that, unlike the case with most tangible resources, their use can be leveraged. For instance, sharing knowledge among employees does not diminish its value for any one person. On the contrary, two people sharing their individualised knowledge sets often can leverage them to create additional knowledge that is new to each of them and relevant to helping the firm pursue strategic competitiveness. With intangible resources, the larger the network of users, the greater is the benefit to each party.[75]

As illustrated in the Opening Case, brand names are an intangible resource that helps to create a firm's reputation and are recognised widely as an important source of competitive advantage for many companies, especially those manufacturing and selling consumer goods and services.[76] When effective, brand names inform customers of a product's performance characteristics, attributes and value.[77] As part of an effort to revitalise Hewlett-Packard (H-P) in the United States, CEO Carly Fiorina allocated US$200 million to an advertising campaign. The campaign's primary purpose was to advance and support an overarching corporate image and brand name for the company itself. Historically, people managing the firm's 100-plus individual product lines (including personal computers and LaserJet printers) have been responsible for developing advertising programs to support their products. Fiorina believes that H-P would be served better if it were to use its advertising budget to develop a strong brand name as a company that is dedicated to producing a wide diversity of innovative products that are oriented towards providing solutions for customers.[78]

When a brand name yields a competitive advantage, some companies seek additional ways to exploit it in the marketplace. The Harley-Davidson brand name now has such cachet that it adorns a limited-edition Barbie doll, a popular restaurant in New York City and a line of L'Oreal cologne. Moreover, Harley-Davidson Motorclothes annually generates over US$100 million in revenue for the firm. The Harley brand adorns a broad range of clothing items, from black leather jackets to fashions for tots and French-cut women's undergarments.[79] In Australia, Country Road Limited has been able to leverage its strong brand name developed in high-fashion clothing into a range of products, including crockery, tea towels, napkins, quilt covers, cushions and vases.[80]

As a source of capabilities, tangible and intangible resources are a critical part of the pathway to the development of competitive advantage (see Figure 3.2). As discussed previously, the strategic value of resources is increased when they are integrated or combined. Unique combinations of the firm's tangible resources (see Table 3.3) and intangible resources (see Table 3.4), capabilities are what the firm is able to do as a result of teams of resources working together.

Capabilities

Capabilities are the firm's capacity to deploy resources that have been purposely *integrated* to achieve a desired end state.[81] As the glue that binds an organisation together, capabilities emerge over time through complex interactions among tangible and intangible resources. Capabilities enable the firm 'to create and exploit external opportunities and develop sustained advantages when used with insight and adroitness'.[82] Critical to the pursuit of competitive advantage and strategic competitiveness, capabilities are often based on developing, carrying, and exchanging information and knowledge through the firm's human capital.[83] In the view of some representing one of the world's leading consultancies, greater numbers of executives 'recognize that people's skills and commitment are [their firm's] best route to competitive advantage and stellar business results'.[84] In competitively successful organisations, the firm's knowledge base is embedded in, and reflected by, its capabilities and is a key source of advantage in the 21st-century competitive landscape.[85] Because a knowledge base is grounded in organisational actions that may not be understood explicitly by all employees, the firm's capabilities become stronger and more valuable strategically through repetition and practice.

The foundation of many capabilities lies in the skills and knowledge of a firm's employees and, often, their functional expertise. Hence, the value of human capital in the development and use of capabilities and, ultimately, core competencies cannot be overstated. Australian biotechnology company GroPep, which specialises in a novel class of pharmaceutical peptides called insulin-like growth factors (IGF), has considerable intellectual expertise in the form of research staff who have been involved in international IGF research for many years. GroPep's products are still in the clinical trial phase, but the real potential of the company lies with their extensive knowledge of the biochemistry of IGFs which is likely to provide a platform for further applications of these enigmatic peptides. This specialised knowledge is reflected in GroPep's share price in February 2001 of over $6 with a tangible asset backing of 11 cents/share.[86] Similarly, Microsoft believes that its best asset is the 'intellectual horsepower' of its employees. To assure continued development of this capability and the core competence that flows from it, the firm strives continuously to hire people who are more talented than the current set of employees. Doing this facilitates satisfying Microsoft's desire to defend and extend the domain of its intellectual property.[87]

Thus, increasingly, global business leaders support the view that the knowledge possessed by the firm's human capital is among the most significant of an organisation's capabilities and may ultimately be at the root of all competitive advantages. In the words of a business writer, 'Today dominance rarely comes to the owner of a stockpile; in fact, it's not usually an issue of goods at all. Power is in the hands of people who hold valuable knowledge.'[88] Similarly, researchers have suggested that 'in the information age, things are ancillary, knowledge is central. A company's value derives not from things, but from knowledge, know-how, intellectual assets, competencies – all of it embedded in people.'[89] Given this reality, the firm's challenge is to create an environment that allows people to fit their individual pieces of knowledge together so that, collectively, each employee will have command of as much organisational knowledge as possible.[90]

A firm's human capital – the skills and knowledge of employees – is a key source of advantage in the 21st-century competitive landscape.

To help firms develop an environment in which knowledge is widely spread across all employees, organisations in many different industry settings (for example, professional services, government, health care and manufacturing) have created a new upper-level managerial position. As the chief learning officer (CLO), this person is expected to find ways for the organisation to acquire, internalise and share knowledge in competitively relevant manners. Another way of saying this is that the CLO is responsible for determining how the firm should manage knowledge to derive maximum competitive value from it. Similar trends are evident in Australia with the emergence of chief knowledge officers (CKO) in many private and public organisations.[91] How to manage the capability called knowledge so that it can be a source of competitive advantage is discussed in the Strategic Focus. Gaining an ability to manage knowledge is critical, in that 78 per cent of US companies indicated recently that they are moving towards becoming knowledge-based enterprises, enterprises that view knowledge as their primary source of competitive advantage.[92] In general, knowledge should be managed in ways that will support the firm's efforts to create value for customers.[93]

Strategic Focus Corporate

Knowledge management and sustainable competitive advantage

If compensation is used as an indicator, organisations appear to place high value on the expected contributions of individuals serving as their chief knowledge officer (CKO) or, somewhat more commonly, chief learning officer (CLO). In 1999 in the United States, for example, the average salary for CLOs across seven industries (professional services;

transportation, communications and utilities; government; finance, insurance and real estate; manufacturing; health care; and wholesale and retail sales) was US$134 550. In management consulting firms, the average CLO salary that year was US$225 000. Combining attractive stock options with these salaries, as is often the case, suggests the importance firms attach to the CLO's work – work that is completed to help their firms' employees learn how to acquire, develop, share and exploit knowledge.

What is knowledge? As a social construct, knowledge emerges through interaction. Knowledge is not data, nor is it information. *Data* are objective facts, presented without any judgement or context. When categorised, analysed, summarised and placed into a context, data become *information*. As data that are endowed with relevance and purpose, information is of competitive value to organisations. Information develops into more competitively relevant knowledge when it is used to establish value-creating connections with the marketplace. *Knowledge*, then, is information that is laden with experience, judgement, intuition and values. In the final analysis, most knowledge resides within individuals. Because of this, successful organisations provide continuous opportunities for employees to increase their stock of data and information.

At its core, knowledge management is concerned with identifying the valuable knowledge residing within the firm so that it can be catalogued for continuous and effective dissemination and use throughout the company. Developing the type of 'corporate memory' that results from these activities is linked with the firm's ability to adapt and modify knowledge and its use in ways that are consistent with changing environmental conditions. Sometimes, as with Siemens, a firm's knowledge management process has a very specific customer focus. A global powerhouse in electrical engineering and electronics, Siemens argues that, for it, 'knowledge management entails gathering in-depth information about customers' needs and immediately channeling the knowledge into development, production, logistics and sales processes to maximize customer benefit'. To channel knowledge that is relevant to unique projects, Siemens must effectively disseminate catalogued information regarding its product development, production, logistics and sales functions across the firm.

Two prominent researchers who study knowledge and its management, Ikujiro Nonaka and Hirotaka Takeuchi, believe that there are 'four interrelated processes by which knowledge flows throughout the firm and transmutes into different forms'. These four processes are the primary means through which firms can manage knowledge.

Socialisation is the process of communicating an individual's tacit knowledge to others. Tacit knowledge is knowledge that can be acquired only through observation and practice. Using apprenticeships and assigning mentors to employees are knowledge management methods that firms employ to help people acquire another's skills by watching and practising. *Externalisation* is the process used to convert tacit knowledge into explicit concepts. Metaphors are used often for this purpose to express complex tacit knowledge in more easily understood terms. *Combination* involves the study of sets of knowledge that are held by different individuals. The purpose of combination is to integrate what are often unique tacit knowledge sets to create explicit knowledge that can be shared readily across the firm. Through *internalisation*, people throughout the firm absorb explicit knowledge that has been created through socialisation, externalisation and combination. This newly generated and explicit knowledge becomes the foundation from which employees are able to create new forms of tacit knowledge, knowledge that then initiates a new round of the fourfold knowledge management process.

Sources: J. Byrne, 1999, 'The search for the young and gifted', *Business Week*, 4 October, pp. 108–16; L. Empson, 1999, 'The challenge of managing knowledge', Mastering Strategy (Part Two), *Financial Times*, 4 October, pp. 9–10; B. Fryer, 1999, 'Get smart', *Inc. Tech 1999*, 3, pp. 61–70; J. Pfeffer and R. L. Sutton, 1999, 'Knowing "what" to do is not enough: Turning knowledge into action', *California Management Review*, 42(1), pp. 83–108; J. Webber, 1999, 'School is never out', *Business Week*, 4 October, pp. 164–8; 'Top teachers', 1999, *Wall Street Journal*, 30 November, p. B16; P. Clarke, 1998, 'Implementing a knowledge strategy for your firm', *Research-Technology Management*, March–April, pp. 28–31; Siemens, 1998, *Siemens Annual Report*; I. Nonaka and H. Takeuchi, 1995, *The Knowledge Creating Company* (New York: Oxford University Press).

As illustrated in Figure 3.4 and Table 3.5, and as suggested by the description of Siemens in the Strategic Focus, capabilities are often developed in specific functional areas (for example, manufacturing, R&D and marketing) or in a part (for example, advertising) of a functional area. Research results suggest a relationship between distinctive competencies (or capabilities) developed in particular functional areas and the firm's financial performance at both the corporate and business-unit levels.[94] Thus, firms should seek to develop functional-area core competencies in individual business units and at the corporate level in the case of diversified firms (as explained in Chapter 6). Table 3.5 shows a grouping of organisational functions and the capabilities certain companies are thought to possess in terms of all or parts of those functions.

Figure 3.4 | Capabilities

Table 3.5 | Examples of firms' capabilities

Functional areas	Capabilities	Examples of firms
Distribution	Effective use of logistics management techniques	Aldi Supermarkets
Human resources	Motivating, empowering and retaining employees	The Body Shop
Management information systems	Effective and efficient control of inventories through point-of-purchase data collection methods	Coles Myer (especially 1998–2000)
Marketing	Effective promotion of brand-name products	Gillette
		Country Road
		R. M. Williams
	Effective customer service	McDonald's
		Singapore Airlines
	Innovative merchandising	Mambo
Management	Effective execution of managerial tasks	Hewlett-Packard
	Effective organisational structure	PepsiCo
Manufacturing	Design and production skills yielding reliable products	Blundstone Boots
	Product and design quality	R. M. Williams
	Production of technologically sophisticated automobile engines	Mazda
	Miniaturisation of components and products	Sony
Research & development	Unique papers recycling capacity	Pratt Industries (Mulligator)
	Exceptional, focused R&D	Cochlear
	Exceptional technological capability	Corning
	Deep knowledge of silver-halide materials	Kodak
	Innovative household cleaning technology	Dyson

Core competencies

Armed with knowledge about resources and capabilities, firms are prepared to identify their core competencies. Defined in Chapter 1, *core competencies* are resources and capabilities that serve as a source of competitive advantage for a firm over its rivals. As the source of competitive advantage for a firm, core competencies distinguish a company competitively and reflect its personality. Core competencies emerge over time through an organisational process of accumulating and learning how to deploy different resources and capabilities. As the capacity to take action, core competencies are the activities that the company performs especially well compared to competitors and through which the firm adds unique value to its goods or services over a long period of time.[95]

Not all of a firm's resources and capabilities are strategic assets – that is, assets that have competitive value and the potential to serve as a source of competitive advantage.[96] Some resources and capabilities may result in incompetence, because they represent competitive areas in which the firm is weak compared to competitors. Thus, some resources or capabilities may stifle or prevent the development of a core competence. Firms with insufficient financial capital, for example, may be unable to purchase facilities or hire the skilled workers required to manufacture products that yield customer value. In this situation, financial capital (a tangible resource) would be a weakness. Armed with an in-depth understanding of their resources and capabilities, firms must locate external environmental opportunities that can be exploited through their capabilities while avoiding competition in areas of weakness.

In addition, an important question is: 'How many core competencies are required for the firm to have a competitive advantage?' Responses to this question vary. McKinsey & Co. recommends that clients identify three or four competencies around which their strategic actions can be framed.[97] Trying to support and nurture more than four core competencies may prevent the firm from developing the focus it needs to exploit fully its competencies in the marketplace.

Many companies' actions are consistent with McKinsey's advice. With competencies in real estate, restaurant operations, marketing and its global infrastructure, for example, McDonald's has exactly four competencies, as does Ford Motor Company. With the actual manufacturing of automobiles and trucks expected to become a declining part of its operations, Ford intends to frame its 21st-century competitive success around competencies in the areas of design, branding, sales and service operations. Acquired recently by AlliedSignal, Honeywell, Inc. long relied on its technology and customer service core competencies to achieve strategic competitiveness. To restore its performance, Michael Capellas, Compaq Computer Corporation's newly appointed CEO and president, intends to use the firm's strong technology core and innovative culture. Brady Corporation is an international manufacturer and marketer of safety, graphics, speciality tape and industrial identification products. Selling primarily to other companies rather than to end users, Brady relies on its expertise in adhesives and material conversion as the competencies through which it designs, manufactures and sells a wide variety of special labels and tapes for many different industries. CSL's important resources in its key staff's deep knowledge of immunology have created competencies in plasma products, pharmaceuticals (which include the flu vaccine), and animal health diagnostics to protect livestock and pets.[98]

As long as core competencies contribute to strategic competitiveness, it is important that the firm not deviate from their use. Sizzler International, Inc., for example, achieved initial success through competencies (for example, expertise in purchasing products and the use of cost control systems) that allowed the firm to develop a low-cost steakhouse concept. Sizzler's performance declined as it abandoned the competencies on which this concept was developed and moved towards what eventually became an undistinguished buffet-court approach. To reverse its fortunes, the firm's CEO is taking actions so that Sizzler can return to its heritage of offering 'a great streak grill concept and a great salad bar'. Purchasing expertise, and product storage and preparation skills, are competencies to be emphasised in Sizzler's turnaround effort.[99]

Not all resources and capabilities are core competencies. The next section discusses two approaches for identifying core competencies.

Building core competencies

Two tools help the firm to identify and build core competencies.[100] The first tool consists of four specific criteria that firms use to determine which of their resources and capabilities are core competencies. Because they have satisfied the four criteria of affording sustainable competitive advantage, the capabilities shown in Table 3.5 are core competencies for the firms possessing them. The second tool is the value chain analysis. Firms use this tool to select the value-creating competencies that should be maintained, upgraded or developed, and those that should be outsourced.

Criteria of sustainable competitive advantage

As shown in Table 3.6, capabilities that are valuable, rare, costly to imitate and non-substitutable are strategic capabilities. Strategic capabilities are also known as core competencies and hence serve as a source of competitive advantage for the firm over its rivals. Capabilities failing to satisfy the four criteria of sustainable competitive advantage are not core competencies. Thus, as shown in Figure 3.5, every core competence is a capability, but not every capability is a core competence. Operationally, for a capability to be a core competence, it must be 'valuable and non-substitutable, from a customer's point of view, and unique and inimitable, from a competitor's point of view'.[101]

Table 3.6 | Four criteria for determining strategic capabilities

Valuable capabilities	• Help a firm to neutralise threats or exploit opportunities
Rare capabilities	• Are not possessed by many others
Costly-to-imitate capabilities	• Historical: A unique and valuable organisational culture or brand name
	• Ambiguous cause: The causes and uses of a competence are unclear
	• Social complexity: Interpersonal relationships, trust and friendship among managers, suppliers and customers
Non-substitutable capabilities	• No strategic equivalent

Figure 3.5 | Core competence as a strategic capability

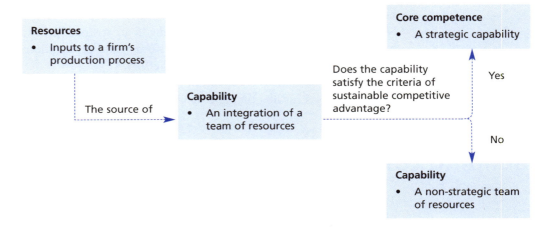

A sustained competitive advantage is achieved only when competitors have tried, without success, to duplicate the benefits of the firm's strategy or when competitors lack the confidence to attempt imitation. For some period of time, the firm may earn a competitive advantage through the use of capabilities that are, for example, valuable and rare, but are imitable.[102] In such an instance, the length of time a firm can expect to retain its competitive advantage is a function of how quickly competitors can successfully imitate a good, service or process. It is only through the combination of conditions represented by all four criteria that a firm's capabilities have the potential to create a sustainable competitive advantage.

Valuable

Valuable capabilities are those that create value for a firm by exploiting opportunities or neutralising threats in the firm's external environment. Valuable capabilities enable a firm to formulate and implement strategies that create value for specific customers. Sony Corp. has used its valuable capabilities dealing with the designing, manufacturing and selling of miniaturised electronic technology to exploit a range of marketplace opportunities, including those for portable disc players and easy-to-hold eight-millimetre video cameras. Identifying 21st-century opportunities that are a product of rapidly emerging technologies, Sony wants customers to enter its 'digital world', whether that entry is through a television, PC or cell (mobile) phone.[103] Relying initially on its distribution capabilities to pursue an opportunity, Wal-Mart started its business in the United States by offering startlingly low prices on a vast selection of brand-name goods. Analysts believe that Wal-Mart changed the way consumers thought about value, letting them know that they did not have to pay the prices charged by most retailers.[104] J. Boag and Son Brewery's capability at brewing and marketing premium beer is proving to be very valuable, with the company's Boag's Premium being the second best selling premium beer in the Australian beer market. The company has also won a number of awards for this beer, including being the Grand Champion Beer at the 1998 Australian International Beer Awards.[105]

> **Valuable capabilities** are those that create value for a firm by exploiting opportunities or neutralising threats in the firm's external environment.

Rare

Rare capabilities are those possessed by few, if any, current or potential competitors. A key question managers seek to answer when evaluating this criterion is: 'How many rival firms possess these valuable capabilities?' Capabilities possessed by many rival firms are unlikely to be a source of competitive advantage for any one of them. Instead, valuable,

> **Rare capabilities** are those possessed by a few, if any, current or potential competitors.

but common (that is, not rare), resources and capabilities are sources of competitive parity. Competitive advantage results only when firms develop and exploit capabilities that differ from those they share with competitors. For example, Dell's business model through which it sells directly to customers allows it to be more efficient than its competitors and to record growth rates that outpace those of the industry. Thus, the capabilities Dell uses to shape and deploy its business model appear to be rare.[106] Computershare Limited also possesses capabilities that are rare. Computershare developed and now operates the world's largest share registry, and is the only global share registry in existence. As such, their software has come to be the accredited industry standard, effectively excluding alternative software companies from this lucrative industry.[107]

Costly to imitate

Costly-to-imitate capabilities are those that other firms cannot develop easily. Capabilities that are costly to imitate can occur because of one or a combination of three reasons (see Table 3.6).

> **Costly-to-imitate capabilities** are those that other firms cannot develop easily.

First, a firm sometimes is able to develop capabilities because of *unique historical conditions*. 'As firms evolve, they pick up skills, abilities and resources that are unique to them, reflecting their particular path through history.'[108] Another way of saying this is that firms sometimes are able to develop capabilities because they were in the right place at the right time.[109]

A firm with a unique and valuable organisational culture that emerged in the early stages of the company's history 'may have an imperfectly imitable advantage over firms founded in another historical period',[110] one in which less valuable (or competitively useful) values and beliefs strongly influenced the development of the firm's culture. This may be the case for the consulting firm McKinsey & Co. Discussed briefly in Chapter 1, organisational culture is 'something that people connect with, feel inspired by, think of as a normal way of operating. It's in their hearts and minds, and its core is voluntary behavior.'[111] An organisational culture is a source of advantage when employees are held together tightly by their belief in it.[112]

McKinsey's culture is thought by competitors, clients and analysts alike to be a primary source of competitive advantage. As testimony to the intangibility of culture – even to some of those familiar with it – consider the following description of culture as McKinsey's source of advantage: 'It is that culture, unique to McKinsey and eccentric, which sets the firm apart from virtually any other business organization and which often mystifies even those who engage [its] services.' Marvin Bower, the company's founder, established the historical foundation for McKinsey's culture. In fact, 'much of what McKinsey is today harks back to the early 1930s', when Bower entered the consulting business. Bower's concept of how his consulting firm would operate was that it should provide advice about effective managerial practices to top-level executives. As guidance for McKinsey's consultants, Bower developed a set of principles. Cited frequently and intensely, these principles actually define what McKinsey was and is today. They are the backbone of the company's unique, and what some think is an enigmatic, culture. According to Bower's principles, a McKinsey consultant should (1) put the interests of the client ahead of increasing the company's revenues, (2) remain silent about the client's business operations, (3) be truthful and not fear challenging a client's opinion, and (4) perform only work that she or he believes is in the client's best interests and is something McKinsey can do well.[113] It would seem that McKinsey's culture is able to create a relentless, yet positive, dissatisfaction among those working within it to challenge themselves to perform in ways that will continuously generate greater levels of value for clients.

A second condition of being costly to imitate occurs when the link between the firm's competencies and its competitive advantage is *causally ambiguous*.[114] In these instances, competitors are unable to understand clearly how a firm uses its competencies as the foundation for competitive advantage. As a result, competitors are uncertain about the competencies they should develop to duplicate the benefits of a competitor's value-creating strategy. *Social complexity* is the third reason that capabilities can be costly to imitate. Social complexity means that at least some, and frequently many, of the firm's capabilities are the product of complex social phenomena. Examples of socially complex capabilities include interpersonal relationships, trust and friendships among managers and between managers and employees, and a firm's reputation with suppliers and customers. In part, the success of Mushroom Records has been due to the close ties between founder Michael Gudinski and performers, the media, agents, promoters and venue managers.[115] Firms such as General Electric, Hewlett-Packard, Merck, Sony, Harvey Norman and Walt Disney Co. rely on their socially complex capabilities as the foundation for a vision of their role in the global economy, their responsibilities to stakeholders (including customers, suppliers and local communities) and their commitment to employees. Important to how those firms operate, 'these socially complex visions have profoundly affected the decisions made by these firms and the strategies they have pursued'.[116]

Non-substitutable

> **Non-substitutable capabilities** are those that do not have strategic equivalents.

Non-substitutable capabilities are those that do not have strategic equivalents. This final requirement for a capability to be a source of competitive advantage 'is that there must be no strategically equivalent valuable resources that are themselves either not rare or imitable. Two valuable firm resources (or two bundles of firm resources) are strategically equivalent when they each can be exploited separately to implement the same strategies.'[117] In general, the strategic value of capabilities increases the more difficult they are to substitute for.[118] The more invisible capabilities are, the more difficult it is for firms to find substitutes and the greater the challenge is to competitors trying to imitate a firm's value-creating strategy. Firm-specific knowledge and trust-based working relationships between managers and non-managerial personnel are examples of capabilities that are difficult to identify and for which finding a substitute is challenging. Additional comments about trust as a capability that can be a core competence are offered in the Strategic Focus.

Strategic Focus Corporate

Trust: Is it valuable, rare, costly to imitate and non-substitutable?

Trust has long been thought to have an important link with organisational success. When trust exists, for example, it is less necessary for firms to establish formal contracts to specify expected actions and interaction patterns. In addition, when parties trust one another, it is less necessary for the firm to rely on organisational structures (see Chapter 11 for a study of different types of structures) to monitor and control individual and group behaviours. Thus, through trust-based working relationships, the firm's transaction costs, as measured by formal contracts and organisational structures, are reduced. Another way of saying this is that trust reduces the costs the firm incurs to manage or govern itself.

Various attributes are associated with trust. Perhaps the most prominent of these is risk. In terms of capabilities and core competencies, the study of trust is concerned with managerial and individual risk rather than organisational risk. *Managerial risk* speaks to the reality of uncertain outcomes that are associated with managerial decisions. In contrast, *organisational risk* is a characteristic of firms experiencing volatile and often unpredictable income streams. The logic of managerial risk applies at the level of each individual, in that 'all trusting relationships have meaningful incentives at stake and the trusting party must understand the risks involved in the relationship'. In essence, managerial risk creates vulnerability, because to trust another party makes a person vulnerable to the outcomes of that party's actions. Combining these perspectives with others about risk, Davis, Schoorman, Mayer and Tan comprehensively define trust as 'the willingness of a party (trustor) to be vulnerable to the actions of another party (trustee) based on the expectation that the trustee will perform an action important to the trustor, regardless of the trustor's ability to monitor or control the trustee'.

Evidence is emerging to suggest that trust, as just explicated, is a source of competitive advantage for the firm when it exists between the general manager and her or his employees. This type of trust is based on the trustor's perception of the trustee's ability, benevolence and integrity. *Ability* is the composite of skills and attributes through which a party is able to influence outcomes in a specific situation. *Benevolence* is the extent to which the trustee perceives that the trustor intends to perform in ways that serve the trustor's good in a particular situation. *Integrity* deals with the trustor's belief that the trustee will follow a set of principles that are not only acceptable, but also desirable, given the trustor's value set. A reputation for honesty and fairness influences the trustee's perception of the trustor's integrity.

As the foundation for a study that was conducted to determine whether trust could be a source of competitive advantage, Davis and his colleagues hypothesised that 'the level of trust a general manager is able to garner from his/her employees is contingent upon the employee's perceptions of the general manager's ability, benevolence and integrity'. The researchers found trust to be significantly related to sales, profits and turnover in a corporation consisting of a chain of nine restaurants. More broadly, the study concluded that the ability of a general manager to earn higher trust from her or his employees likely creates a competitive advantage for a firm over its rivals.

Thus, the results from the Davis et al. study suggest that trust satisfies at least three, and seemingly all four, of the criteria of sustainable competitive advantage. Trust is *valuable* because it allows a firm (for example, the restaurants in the study's sample) to better serve its customers and to improve its performance as a result. Trust is *rare* because few rivals have the relationship between managers and employees that trust denotes. Trust is *costly to imitate* because it is causally ambiguous and socially complex. As such, it is difficult for competitors to understand what trust is and how to establish it in their firms. Is trust *non-substitutable*? It may very well be, in that trust is a capability that is difficult for competitors to observe. As we have noted, capabilities that cannot be observed at least somewhat easily are hard to imitate. Although devices such as the use of strict performance benchmarks can be used to monitor employees' work, these mechanisms are costly relative to trust.

Placing these expectations about trust into the context of information included in Table 3.7 suggests that the firm that has trust as a valuable, rare, costly-to-imitate, and likely non-substitutable capability has a sustainable competitive advantage that can be expected to contribute to the earning of above-average returns. Thus, trust has the potential to reduce the costs that are required to monitor employees' behaviours, as well as to improve revenue streams through the efforts of employees who are motivated by the trust between themselves and their managers.

The suggestion that trust is a capability that can be a competitive advantage is supported by other firms' experiences. Anderson & Associates, for example, operates through what it calls 'open-book management'. Among other operational principles, this system is one through which all of the firm's financial information, including information about salaries, is placed on its intranet. The foundation on which open-book management is based is trust. As the firm's CEO says, 'We do have a great deal of trust here, and our employees stick with us.' In his view, the trust-based open-book management system contributes to the firm's profitability, although quantitative measures are not in place to verify this belief.

SecureNet is a Melbourne-based global provider of secure e-commerce solutions for Internet applications, remote banking, virtual private networks (VPNs) and data-critical activities. As a broad-based security business, Securenet's core competencies are in the form of smart card technology, public key infrastructure, and firewalls to secure payments and security consultancy. SecureNet has experienced rapid growth that has been supported by three pillars of expansion. One of these is the normal path of internal growth, while the other two have been adopted to keep pace with the changing e-commerce market – namely, acquisitions and partnering with established, high-profile organisations such as Telstra and Richard Li's PCCW in Hong Kong. In recognition of the strategic importance of trust in these alliances, SecureNet has developed a trusted partner program. The criteria for partners in this program are simple and reflect a clear strategic intent on the part of SecureNet. These include: global reach, best-of-breed technology; credibility; and trustworthiness. The importance of trustworthiness in alliances will be discussed in more detail in Chapter 9.

Our discussion of these firms suggests that the abilities of Anderson & Associates and SecureNet to earn above-average returns are increased because their respective trust capabilities are valuable, rare, costly to imitate and non-substitutable.

Sources: J. H. Davis, F. David Schoorman, R. C. Mayer and H. H. Tan, 2000, 'The trusted general manager and business unit performance: Empirical evidence of a competitive advantage', *Strategic Management Journal*, in press; G. Imperato, 2000, 'Their specialty? Teamwork', *Fast Company*, January–February, pp. 54–6; K. Anderson, 1999, 'By the (open) book', *Inc. Tech 1999*, 3, pp. 33–4; P. Martin, 1999, 'Lessons in humility', *Financial Times*, 22 June, p. 18; T. B. Palmer and R. M. Wiseman, 1999, 'Decoupling risk taking from income stream uncertainty: A holistic model of risk', *Strategic Management Journal*, 20, pp. 1037–62; J. Rosenfeld, 1999, 'MTW puts people first', *Fast Company*, December, pp. 86–8.

Table 3.7 | Outcomes from combinations of the criteria for sustainable competitive advantage

Is the resource or capability valuable?	Is the resource or capability rare?	Is the resource or capability costly to imitate?	Is the resource or capability non-substitutable?	Competitive consequences	Performance implications
No	No	No	No	Competitive disadvantage	Below-average returns
Yes	No	No	Yes/no	Competitive parity	Average returns
Yes	Yes	No	Yes/no	Temporary competitive advantage	Above-average returns to average returns
Yes	Yes	Yes	Yes	Sustainable competitive advantage	Above-average returns

To summarise this discussion, we reiterate that sustainable competitive advantage results only through the use of capabilities that are valuable, rare, costly to imitate and non-substitutable. Table 3.7 shows the competitive consequences and performance implications resulting from combinations of the four criteria of sustainability. The analysis suggested by the table helps managers to determine the strategic value of a firm's capabilities. Resources and capabilities falling into the first row in the table (that is, resources and capabilities that are neither valuable nor rare and that are imitable and for which strategic substitutes exist) are ones the firm should not emphasise to formulate and implement strategies. Capabilities yielding competitive parity and either temporary or sustainable competitive advantage, however, will be supported. Large competitors such as Coca-Cola and PepsiCo may have capabilities that can yield only competitive parity. In such cases, the firms will nurture these capabilities while simultaneously emphasising those that can yield either a temporary or sustainable competitive advantage.

In the next section, we discuss another framework firms use to examine their resources and capabilities to identify their core competencies. Value chain analysis allows the firm to understand the parts of its operations that create value and those that do not. Understanding these issues is important because the firm earns above-average returns only when the value it creates is greater than the costs incurred to create that value.[119]

Value chain analysis

The value chain is a template that the firm uses to understand its cost position and to identify the multiple means that might be used to facilitate the implementation of its business-level strategy.[120] As shown in Figure 3.6, a firm's value chain is segmented into primary and support activities. **Primary activities** are involved with a product's physical creation, its sale and distribution to buyers, and its service after the sale. **Support activities** provide the support necessary for the primary activities to take place. The value chain shows how a product moves from the raw material stage to the final customer. For individual firms, the essential idea of the value chain 'is to add as much value as possible as cheaply as possible, and, most important, to capture that value'. In a globally competitive economy, 'the most valuable links on the chain tend to belong to people who own knowledge – particularly about customers'.[121] This locus of value-creating possibilities applies just as strongly to retail and service firms as it does to manufacturers. Thus, for organisations in all sectors, the effects of e-commerce make it increasingly necessary for companies to develop value-adding knowledge processes to compensate for the value and margin that the Internet strips from physical processes.[122]

> **Primary activities** are involved with a product's physical creation, its sale and distribution to buyers, and its service after the sale.
>
> **Support activities** provide the support necessary for the primary activities to take place.

Figure 3.6 | The basic value chain

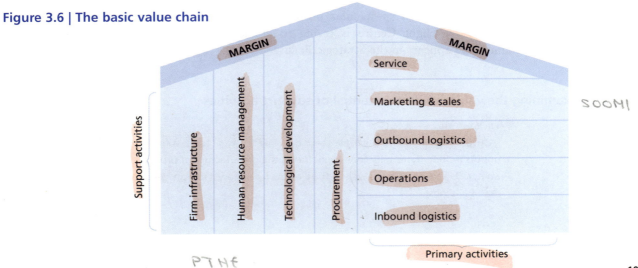

Table 3.8 | Examining the value-creating potential of primary activities

Inbound logistics
Activities, such as materials handling, warehousing and inventory control, used to receive, store and disseminate inputs to a product.

Operations
Activities necessary to convert the inputs provided by inbound logistics into final product form. Machining, packaging, assembly and equipment maintenance are examples of operations activities.

Outbound logistics
Activities involved with collecting, storing and physically distributing the final product to customers. Examples of these activities include finished-goods warehousing, materials handling and order processing.

Marketing and sales
Activities completed to provide means through which customers can purchase products and to induce them to do so. To market and sell products effectively, firms develop advertising and promotional campaigns, select appropriate distribution channels, and select, develop and support their sales force.

Service
Activities designed to enhance or maintain a product's value. Firms engage in a range of service-related activities, including installation, repair, training and adjustment.

Each activity should be examined relative to competitors' abilities. Accordingly, firms rate each activity as *superior*, *equivalent* or *inferior*.

Source: Adapted with the permission of The Free Press, a division of Simon & Schuster, from Michael E. Porter, *Competitive Advantage: Creating and Sustaining Superior Performance*, pp. 39–40, Copyright © 1985 by Michael E. Porter.

Table 3.8 lists the items to be studied to assess the value-creating potential of primary activities. In Table 3.9, the items to consider when studying support activities are shown. As with the analysis of primary activities, the intent in examining these items is to determine areas where the firm has the potential to create and capture value. All items included in both tables are to be evaluated with competitors' capabilities in mind. To be a source of competitive advantage, a resource or capability must allow a firm (1) to perform an activity in a manner that is superior to the way competitors perform it, or (2) to perform a value-creating activity that competitors cannot complete. Only under these conditions does a firm create value for customers and have opportunities to capture that value. Sometimes, this requires firms to reconfigure or recombine parts of the value chain in unique ways. Flight Centre has, by adding value in both support activities and primary activities, achieved spectacular profits in an unattractive industry. Further discussion about how Flight Centre is trying to create value in the 21st-century competitive landscape appears in the Strategic Focus.

Table 3.9 | Examining the value-creating potential of support activities

Procurement
Activities completed to purchase the inputs needed to produce a firm's products. Purchased inputs include items fully consumed during the manufacture of products (for example, raw materials and supplies, as well as fixed assets machinery, laboratory equipment, office equipment and buildings).

> *Technological development*
> Activities completed to improve a firm's product and the processes used to manufacture it. Technological development takes many forms, such as process equipment, basic research and product design, and servicing procedures.
>
> *Human resource management*
> Activities involved with recruiting, hiring, training, developing and compensating all personnel.
>
> *Firm infrastructure*
> Firm infrastructure includes activities such as general management, planning, finance, accounting, legal support and governmental relations that are required to support the work of the entire value chain. Through its infrastructure, the firm strives to effectively and consistently identify external opportunities and threats, identify resources and capabilities, and support core competencies.
>
> Each activity should be examined relative to competitors' abilities. Accordingly, firms rate each activity as *superior*, *equivalent* or *inferior*.
>
> Source: Adapted with the permission of The Free Press, a division of Simon & Schuster, from Michael E. Porter, *Competitive Advantage: Creating and Sustaining Superior Performance*, pp. 40–3, Copyright © 1985 by Michael E. Porter.

Strategic Focus | Corporate

Adding value at Flight Centre

Flight Centre is a good example of how firms with the right core competencies can achieve strong profit growth in unattractive industries. Indeed, Flight Centre's reporting of an eighth consecutive profit increase in 1999 attracted the attention of Sydney-based management academics Richard Dunford and Ian Palmer to find out how such returns could be obtained by a firm in such an unattractive industry.

Flight Centre is an Australian-based, international travel agency with 490 retail outlets (1999) and other businesses across Australia, New Zealand, South Africa and the United Kingdom. A 'five forces' analysis of the industry indicates that all forces are working against the generation of high returns. Competitive rivalry within the industry is high. Based upon outlet per capita, the Australian industry is twice as competitive as its industry equivalent within the United Kingdom and the United States. This rivalry has indeed translated into low margins, as Porter suggests it should, with 1996–7 figures showing that the industry generated a combined operating profit before tax of $37 million, representing a margin of just 2 per cent. The large number of travel agency businesses (3266 in 1997) indicates low barriers to entry. Furthermore, e-commerce has lowered barriers to entry by media conglomerates and software/technology companies that were not previously market participants. The threat of substitutes is also high, as travel agents are threatened with disinter-mediation. This can be seen particularly clearly with budget domestic airlines Virgin Blue and Impulse, who sell cut-price tickets directly through their own websites. Suppliers, through an accreditation process, have the power to choose which agencies they will authorise to sell their services. Greater access to information has meant that many consumers are no longer reliant on agents to design and book travel. The consumers are price sensitive, with negligible costs involved with switching between one agent and another, which gives a high degree of bargaining power to the consumer.

Despite the unpromising nature of the industry, Flight Centre has been able to perform well with a 1999 net profit after tax figure (NPAT) of $27.9 million. This compares with well-known competitors Harvey World Travel with a NPAT of $2.12 million, STA Travel with $1.3 million and Traveland with a loss of $2.9 million. Flight Centre is earning returns that are well above average and must therefore have core competencies that enable them to add value where their competitors cannot. This is achieved in four areas: organisation, marketing, operating systems and 'people policies'. The organisation is lean and team-based, with staff working in small teams of three to seven members. New stores are opened in preference to existing stores expanding to meet demand. There is a strong egalitarian culture, which is maintained with the idea of no privileges, such as secretaries and offices, unless everybody has them. This has created a situation where staff are empowered to make decisions in an environment of 'total information sharing'. Flight Centre promises never to lose a booking over price and manages its brand carefully so that when the company expands into new niches, new brands have been used to maintain a clear focus of each brand on its specific market. Service quality also adds value to the marketing capability. Operational standardisation is used to achieve centralisation in a decentralised company. Such standardisation reduces costs and gives suppliers a clearly identifiable market share, which enables Flight Centre to negotiate better prices. In terms of 'people policies', Flight Centre is not concerned with industry experience or travel qualifications and instead looks for people with a tertiary education who have travelled widely and who appear to be highly motivated and likeable. These people are trained intensively by the company and remunerated on the basis of their performance. Apart from a few specialised positions, such as accounting, promotion at Flight Centre is from within the firm. The profitability of Flight Centre is based on a bundling of capabilities, rather than just one or two.

Sources: Flight Centre, 2001, Flight Centre Home Page: www.flightcentre.com.au; I. Palmer and R. Dunford, 2000, paper presented at ANZAM 2000, Macquarie Graduate School of Management.

Rating a firm's capability to execute the primary and support activities is challenging. Earlier in the chapter, we noted that identifying and assessing the value of a firm's resources and capabilities requires judgement. Judgement is equally necessary in using value chain analysis. The reason for this is that there is no obviously correct model or rule available to help in the process. Moreover, most data that are available for these evaluations are largely anecdotal, sometimes unreliable or difficult to interpret.

As with Flight Centre, an effective value chain analysis results in the identification of new ways to perform activities that create value. Recently, Pirelli SpA unveiled a tyre-manufacturing process that it expects will eventually allow the company to reduce its production costs by 25 per cent while simultaneously increasing product quality. Called a modular integrated robotised system, this new technology is an automated process through which Pirelli 'will be able to reduce the steps in manufacturing a tire from 14 to just three, while cutting the lead time from six days to just 72 minutes'.[123] Thus, this change is intended to help Pirelli create more value in the operation's primary activity. In the financial service sector, large broking houses J. B. Were and Ord Minnett are altering how they create value in terms of primary activities. As a stockbroking service, Ord Minnett and J. B. Were were being affected by banks' and on-line brokers' efforts to encourage customers to make their own share and managed fund purchases via the Internet, and by the reductions in commissions the broker receives for purchases. In the face of these competitive threats, Ord Minnett and J. B. Were are now offering more diverse wealth management services which build on the capability of managing equities portfolios for clients. These brokers are now more focused upon servicing top-end clients who wish to make investments in the order of millions of dollars.

What should a firm do with respect to primary and support activities in which its resources and capabilities are not a source of competence and competitive advantage? In these instances, firms should study the possibility of outsourcing the work associated with primary and support activities in which they cannot create and capture value.

Outsourcing

> **Outsourcing** is the purchase of a value-creating activity from an external supplier.

Concerned with how components, finished goods or services will be obtained, **outsourcing** is the purchase of a value-creating activity from an external supplier.[124] In multiple global industries, the trend towards outsourcing continues at a rapid pace.[125]

Sometimes, virtually all firms within an industry seek the strategic value that can be captured through effective outsourcing. The automobile-manufacturing industry is an example of this. Ford Motor Company, for example, has decided to outsource key parts of its final assembly operations. Initially, the plan is for machine tool suppliers and equipment manufacturers to take over assembly operations at Ford's new US$1.3 billion Brazilian car plant. Although the outcome of Ford's move is too early to determine with certainty, some analysts suggest that this outsourcing foray may signal the firm's gradual withdrawal from final assembly activities as a core function. Nissan Motor Co. has signed a US$1 billion contract with IBM. Covering a nine-and-a-half-year period, the arrangement calls for IBM to manage Nissan's North American computer systems. To fulfil its contractual obligations, IBM will handle software and hardware for various functions, including payroll, human resources and car distribution. Nissan expects its outsourcing decision to reduce its costs.[126] Automotive components manufacturer Tripac International (Australia) has outsourced the entire workforce for its Sydney factory, leasing their staff from EL Blue. For Tripac, outsourcing has improved the company's productivity and increased its profitability.[127]

The main reason outsourcing is used prominently is that few, if any, firms possess the resources and capabilities required to achieve competitive superiority in all primary and support activities. With respect to technologies, for example, research suggests that few companies can afford to develop internally all the technologies that might lead to competitive advantage in the future. By nurturing a small number of core competencies, the firm increases its probability of developing a competitive advantage. In addition, by outsourcing activities in which it lacks capabilities, the firm can concentrate fully on those areas in which it can create value.[128] Dell Computer Corporation, for example, outsources most of its manufacturing and customer service activities, so that it can concentrate on creating value through its distribution channels. Nike and Reebok both focus on design and marketing, areas in which those firms believe that they have core competencies. Outsourcing almost all of their manufacturing in order to control costs generates resources that can be used to nurture and support those firms' design and marketing competencies.[129]

Outsourcing by large firms such as the Commonwealth Bank, Ansett, Nike and Reebok creates opportunities for smaller firms. Using focused business-level strategies (discussed fully in Chapter 4), these companies concentrate on providing superior service to their customers in terms of specific functions.

Spotless Services Limited (part of the Spotless Group Limited) is an example of a business that has prospered from the outsourcing activities of other companies. Spotless specialises in providing a range of support services to over 20 000 businesses in Australia and New Zealand. The types of services provided by Spotless include cleaning, building maintenance, ground maintenance and food services, with clients ranging in size from small offices through to large venues, such as Melbourne's Colonial Stadium.¹³⁰ Similarly, Stax Research, Inc., in the United States, concentrates on providing business research and due-diligence support to its clients. Large companies contract with Stax to have the firm conduct the research needed for them to complete due-diligence processes related to possible merger and acquisition transactions. Unlike its competitors, Stax contracts with clients to conduct research only; it does not offer advice to its clients based on the results of its research. In the words of an analyst, 'Stax has carved out a niche by stubbornly focusing on the research end of the business, packaging itself as an analyst group such as those at traditional consulting firms and investment banks but without the advisory component and costs'.¹³¹

When outsourcing, a firm seeks the greatest value. In other words, a company wants to outsource only to firms possessing a core competence in terms of performing the primary or support activity that is being outsourced. This is the case between Nissan and IBM. In fact, IBM's services division, the group to which Nissan outsourced some of its computer operations, is the fastest-growing part of the company.

IBM recently sold its Global Network division to AT&T at a price of US$5 billion. As part of this transaction, IBM agreed to pay AT&T Solutions US$5 billion to run its global telecom network to the end of 2004. According to analysts, 'This swap was a watershed in the corporate outsourcing world. IBM says it got fed up trying to maintain and understand a global telecom network.' As a measure of the complexity of business operations in a technologically intensive global environment, the transaction is thought to allow AT&T and IBM to concentrate their efforts on different operations, operations in which the companies have core competencies.¹³² For companies to whom others outsource, such as IBM from Nissan and AT&T Solutions from IBM, being able to create value is the pathway through which they achieve strategic competitiveness and earn above-average returns.

When evaluating resources and capabilities, firms must be careful not to outsource activities in which they can create and capture value. In addition, companies should not outsource primary and support activities that are used to neutralise environmental threats or complete necessary ongoing organisational tasks. Called a 'non-strategic team of resources' in Figure 3.5, firms must verify that they do not outsource capabilities that are critical to their success, even though the capabilities are not actual sources of competitive advantage.

Another risk that is part of outsourcing concerns the firm's knowledge base. As discussed earlier in the chapter, knowledge continues to increase in importance as a source of competence and competitive advantage for firms in the competitive landscape. In part, organisations learn through a continuous and integrated sharing of experiences that employees have as they perform primary and support activities. One reason for the success of a learning organisation is that, with continuous and integrated sharing of experiences, the firm is able to evaluate thoroughly the ongoing validity of the key assumptions it holds about the nature and future of its business operations. Outsourcing activities in which the firm cannot create value can have the unintended consequence of damaging the firm's potential to continuously evaluate its key assumptions, learn, and create new capabilities and core competencies. Therefore, managers should verify that the firm does not outsource activities that stimulate the development of new capabilities and competencies.¹³³

The next section discusses some important cautions about core competencies.

Core competencies: Cautions and reminders

An attractive attribute of a firm's core competencies is that, unlike physical assets, they tend to become more valuable through additional use. A key reason for this is that they are largely knowledge-based.[134] Sharing knowledge across people, jobs and organisational functions often results in an expansion of that knowledge in competitively relevant ways.[135] At Chaparral Steel, in the United States, for example, the CEO believes that one of his firm's 'core competencies is the rapid realization of new technology into steel products'.[136] As a learning organisation, Chaparral expends a significant effort on verifying that learning is shared across the entire firm. Thus, in a manner that is consistent with the most effective learning organisations, Chaparral Steel appears to have a healthy 'disrespect' for the status quo. Resulting from this 'disrespect' is a commitment to continuous self-examination and experimentation.[137]

Evidence and company experiences show that the value of core competencies as sources of competitive advantage should never be taken for granted. Moreover, the ability of any particular core competence to provide competitive advantage on a permanent basis should not be assumed. The reason for these cautions is the central dilemma that is associated with the use of core competencies as sources of competitive advantage – namely, that all core capabilities simultaneously have the potential to be *core rigidities*. This reality is captured by the following comment from Leslie Wexner, CEO of The Limited, Inc.: 'Success doesn't beget success. Success begets failure because the more that you know a thing works, the less likely you are to think that it won't work. When you've had a long string of victories, it's harder to foresee your own vulnerabilities.'[138] Thus, each capability is both a strength and a weakness – a strength because it is the source of competitive advantage and, hence, strategic competitiveness; and a weakness because, if emphasised when it is no longer competitively relevant, it can be a seed of organisational inertia.[139]

Events occurring in the firm's external environment create conditions through which core competencies can become core rigidities, generate inertia and stifle innovation. 'Often the flip side, the dark side, of core capabilities is revealed due to external events when new competitors figure out a better way to serve the firm's customers, when new technologies emerge, or when political or social events shift the ground underneath.'[140] It really isn't changes in the external environment that cause core capabilities to become core rigidities; rather, it is strategic myopia and inflexibility on the part of a firm's managers that results in core competencies being emphasised to the point that strategic inertia strangles the firm's ability to grow and to adapt to environmental changes through innovations.[141]

Steel manufacturers, for example, need to approach major customers' intended actions with a great deal of flexibility. As suggested in other parts of the chapter, GM and Ford are launching Web-based networks that will force their suppliers to work together and cut costs. These two companies have aggressive objectives with their electronic networks: 'Both auto-makers hope to save billions by replacing an elaborate network of personal contacts and triplicate forms with a global electronic forum where deals can be done almost instantly. And both want their suppliers to use the Web sites to make their own purchases or sell excess inventory.'[142] Describing the potential effects of the electronic programs on steel manufacturers, a business writer suggested that the automobile manufacturers' actions point 'to yet another round of cost cuts and slimmer profits. Their best hope is to make up in volume what they will lose from lower prices.'[143] Attempts by key customers to reduce their costs are an important issue to US steel manufacturers, in that GM and Ford alone combine to buy roughly 17 per cent of the industry's output. To cope with this environmental change, steel manufacturers may need to develop new competencies required to deal successfully with Web-based purchasing and delivery practices. Steel manufacturers' existing competencies may be less valuable, given the increase in the power of buyers (GM and Ford, for example) that the Internet is creating relative to the power of suppliers (for example, steel manufacturers). Thus, domestic steel manufacturers should take actions necessary to prevent existing core competencies from becoming core rigidities in light of changes being brought to bear on their operations by major customers.

This chapter closes our discussion of strategic inputs as a primary part of the strategic management process. As shown in Figure 1.1, results gained from analysing a firm's external and internal environments provide the strategic inputs the firm needs to develop its strategic intent and strategic mission. Beginning with the next chapter, our focus turns to explanations of the strategic actions firms take to achieve strategic competitiveness and earn above-average returns. However, before starting that important stream of discussions, we offer a few final comments on strategic intent and strategic mission. As mentioned in Chapter 1, the primary value of intent and mission is that they reflect what the firm wants to accomplish in light of its external opportunities and internal competencies.

Strategic inputs and strategic actions

Defined in the first chapter, *strategic intent* is the leveraging of a firm's resources, capabilities and core competencies (hereafter called capabilities for the purpose of this discussion) to accomplish the firm's goals in the competitive environment.[144] Recent evidence suggests that, indeed, successful companies competing in the global economy have learned how to leverage their capabilities to reach challenging goals.[145] How Chaparral Steel seeks to leverage its resources, capabilities and competencies is suggested by the following statement: '[T]he goal for every hour, the criterion for every person's activity, is crystal clear: make ever more steel, increasingly better than anyone else.'[146] The intent of Cochlear, the Australian hearing implant company, is to provide the world's best products and services in the cochlear implant industry. At 3M, the intent indicates that the firm 'must be the company [that] innovates, [that] changes the basis of competition.' Coca-Cola Company wants to leverage its competencies to have a 'Coke within arm's reach of everyone on the planet'.[147] The challenge expressed by strategic intent can also apply to individuals. Some upper-level executives believe that, when committed to the dreams and aspirations that are suggested by the firm's intent, 'quite ordinary people consistently do extraordinary things'.[148]

Strategic intent defines the framework for a firm's strategic mission, which is a statement of a firm's unique purpose and the scope of its operations in product and market terms.[149] The mission of Cochlear is for clinical teams and recipients to embrace Cochlear as their partners in hearing for life.[150] An effective mission is formed when the firm has a very strong sense of what it wants to do and of the ethical standards that will guide behaviours in the pursuit of its goals.[151] Because it specifies the products a firm will offer in particular markets and presents a framework within which the firm will work, the strategic mission is an application of strategic intent.[152] In a small private school, the strategic intent may be the vigorous pursuit of excellence. The strategic mission flowing from this intent is to use a curriculum that is grounded in the liberal arts to serve intellectually gifted or highly motivated students living within a region who seek success in pre-university education.

In the case of all firms and organisations, once formulated, the strategic intent and strategic mission are the basis for the development of business-level, corporate-level, acquisition, restructuring, international and cooperative strategies (see Chapters 4 and 6 to 9). Business-level strategy is discussed in the next chapter.

Summary

- In the 21st-century landscape, traditional conditions and factors, including labour costs and superior access to financial resources and raw materials, can still create a competitive advantage for the firm. However, these factors now lead to a competitive advantage in a declining number of instances. In the new landscape, the resources, capabilities and core competencies that make up the firm's internal environment may have a relatively stronger influence on the firm's performance than do conditions in the external environment. The most effective firms recognise that strategic competitiveness and above-average returns result only when core competencies (as identified through the study of the firm's internal environment) are matched with opportunities (as determined through the study of the firm's external environment).
- No competitive advantage lasts forever. Over time, rivals use their own unique resources, capabilities and core competencies to form different, yet effective, value-creating propositions that duplicate the value-creating ability of the firm's competitive advantages. In general, the Internet's capabilities are reducing the sustainability of many competitive advantages. Thus, because competitive advantages are not sustainable on a permanent basis, firms must exploit their current advantages while simultaneously using their resources and capabilities to form new core competencies that can serve as relevant competitive advantages in the future.
- Effective management of core competencies requires careful analysis of the firm's resources (inputs to the production process) and capabilities (capacities for teams of resources to perform a task or activity in an integrative manner). To manage core competencies successfully, individuals must be self-confident, courageous, and willing both to hold others accountable for their work and to be held accountable for the outcomes of their own efforts.
- Individual resources are usually not a source of competitive advantage. Capabilities, which are groupings of tangible and intangible resources, are a more likely source of competitive advantages, especially sustainable ones. A key reason for this is that the firm's nurturing and support of core competencies that are based on capabilities is less visible to rivals and, as such, is harder to understand and imitate.
- Increasingly, employees' knowledge is viewed as perhaps the most relevant source of competitive advantage. To gain maximum benefit from knowledge, firms commit to finding ways for individuals' unique knowledge sets to be shared throughout the firm. The Internet's capabilities affect both the development and the sharing of knowledge.
- Only when a capability is valuable, rare, costly to imitate and non-substitutable is it a core competence and a source of competitive advantage. Over time, core competencies must be supported, but they cannot be allowed to become core rigidities. Core competencies are a source of competitive advantage only when they allow the firm to create value by exploiting opportunities in the external environment. When this is no longer the case, attention shifts to selecting or forming other capabilities that do satisfy the four criteria of sustainable competitive advantage.
- Firms use value chain analysis to identify and evaluate the competitive potential of resources and capabilities. By studying their skills relative to those associated with primary and support activities, firms are able to understand their cost structure and identify the activities through which they can create value.
- When the firm cannot create value in either a primary or support activity, outsourcing is considered. Used commonly in the 21st-century landscape, outsourcing is the purchase of a value-creating activity from an external supplier. The firm must outsource only to companies possessing a competitive advantage in terms of the particular primary or support activity under consideration. In addition, the firm must verify continuously that it is not outsourcing activities from which it could create value.
- Results obtained from analysing the external environment (see Chapter 2) and the internal environment provide the inputs needed for the firm to develop its strategic intent and strategic mission.

With the intent and mission formed, the firm is prepared to choose the strategies it will follow to pursue strategic competitiveness and above-average returns.

Review questions

1. Why is it important for a firm to study and understand its internal environment?
2. What is value? Why is it critical that a firm be able to create value, and how does it do so?
3. What are the differences between tangible resources and intangible resources? Why is it important for those making strategic decisions to understand these differences? Are tangible resources linked more closely to the creation of competitive advantages than are intangible resources, or is the reverse true? Why?
4. What are capabilities? What must firms do to create capabilities?
5. What are the four criteria firms use to determine which of their capabilities are core competencies? Why is it important for these criteria to be used?
6. What is value chain analysis? What insight or understanding does a firm gain when it uses this tool successfully?
7. What is outsourcing and why do firms engage in the practice? Will outsourcing's importance grow in the 21st century? If so, why?
8. What are core rigidities? Why is it vital that firms prevent core competencies from becoming core rigidities?
9. What is the relationship between strategic inputs and strategic actions, and why is it important to understand it?

Application discussion questions

1. Several companies that have brand as a competitive advantage are discussed in the Opening Case. Given your knowledge about the global economy, which of these brands do you believe has the strongest likelihood of remaining as a source of advantage in the 21st century? Why? What effects do you believe the Internet's capabilities will have on this brand, and what should the owner of the brand do in light of them?
2. Visit the manager of a store with which you conduct business in your local community. Using the definition presented in the chapter, define value for the manager. Ask the manager if the definition is consistent with how her or his firm thinks of value. If there is a difference, ask the manager to assess why the difference exists.
3. Think of a group (for example, Toastmaster's or a voluntary organisation) in which you hold membership. Using the categories shown in Tables 3.3 and 3.4, list what you believe are the group's tangible and intangible resources. Show the list to another member of your group. Does the person agree with your assessment of the group's resources? If not, what might account for the differences? If differences do exist between you and your colleague, what is the meaning of such differences in terms of trying to form the group's capabilities?
4. Refer to the third question. Was it easier for you to list the tangible or the intangible resources? Why? How confident are you with your assessments?
5. What competitive advantage does your university or TAFE college possess? What evidence can you provide to support your opinion? Share what you think the competitive advantages are with a colleague. Does this person agree with your assessment? If not, why not?
6. What effects do you believe the Internet will have on your university or TAFE college within the next five years as it seeks to develop new competitive advantages? In your view, do the strategic decision makers in your educational institution understand the Internet's capabilities? If not, why not?
7. Trust is identified in the chapter as a potential source of competitive advantage. Have you ever been involved in a situation in which trust was instrumental in accomplishing an organisation's goals? If so, what outcomes were made possible because of trust?

Ethics questions

1. Can efforts to develop sustainable competitive advantages result in employees using unethical practices? If so, what unethical practices might be used to compare a firm's core competencies with those held by rivals? How do the Internet's capabilities affect actions taken to form competitive advantages that will help the firm in efforts to outperform its rivals?
2. Do ethical practices affect a firm's ability to develop brand as a source of competitive advantage? If so,

how does this happen? Can you think of brands that are a source of competitive advantage at least in part because of the firm's ethical practices?

3. What is the difference between exploiting a firm's human capital and using that capital as a source of competitive advantage? Are there situations in which the exploitation of human capital can be a source of advantage? If so, can you name such a situation? If the exploitation of human capital can be a source of competitive advantage, is this a sustainable advantage? Why or why not?

4. Are there any ethical dilemmas associated with outsourcing? If so, what are they? How would you deal with outsourcing ethical dilemmas that you believe exist?

5. What ethical responsibilities do managers have if they determine that a set of employees has skills that are valuable only to a core competence that is becoming a core rigidity?

6. Through the Internet, firms sometimes make a vast array of data, information and knowledge available to competitors as well as to customers and suppliers. What ethical issues, if any, are involved when the firm finds competitively relevant information on a competitor's website?

7. Firms are aware that competitors read information that is posted on their websites. Given this reality, is it ethical for a firm to include false information – for example, about its sources of competitive advantage – on its website in hopes that the information will influence competitors to take certain actions as a result of viewing it?

Internet exercise

A recent global development in the automobile industry has been the mergers and acquisitions going on among firms. These include the coupling of Daimler-Benz with Chrysler; VW with Audi, Rolls-Royce and Bentley; and GM with Saab; as well as, most recently, Ford's acquisition of Volvo. The new partnerships have allowed firms to combine resources and capabilities to build a new breed of universal car. Explore the websites of these firms. Do you still see a specific brand identification associated with each type of car? How important do you think branding will be in the future for these products?

e-project: Imagine that you are able to purchase your dream car from among the current year's models. Before buying, though, you would like to learn something about how the car is produced. (For example, is your Rolls-Royce being assembled alongside a Beetle?) Using Internet sources, attempt to trace the origins of the car's major components, technology, and performance-testing resources, as well as the production and advertising or marketing facilities.

Notes

1. J. Clinton, 2000, 'Brand New Orleans', *Fast Company*, January/February, p. 33.
2. M. J. Rouse and U. S. Daellenbach, 1999, 'Rethinking research methods for the resource-based perspective: Isolating sources of sustainable competitive advantage', *Strategic Management Journal*, 20, pp. 487–94.
3. D. Schendel, 1999, 'Fresh challenges for the future', Mastering Strategy (Part Twelve), *Financial Times*, 13 December, p. 14.
4. C. K. Prahalad, 1999, 'Changes in the competitive battlefield', Mastering Strategy (Part Two), *Financial Times*, 4 October, pp. 3–4; W. J. Duncan, P. M. Ginter and L. E. Swayne, 1998, 'Competitive advantage and internal organizational assessment', *Academy of Management Executive*, 12(3), pp. 6–16.
5. J. Lee and D. Miller, 1999, 'People matter: Commitment to employees, strategy and performance in Korean firms', *Strategic Management Journal*, 20, pp. 579–93; M. A. Huselid, S. E. Jackson and R. S. Schuler, 1997, 'Technical and strategic human resource management effectiveness as determinants of firm performance', *Academy of Management Journal*, 40, pp. 171–88.
6. G. Colvin, 1999, 'The ultimate manager', *Fortune*, 22 November, pp. 185–7.
7. J. G. Covin and M. P. Miles, 1999, 'Corporate entrepreneurship and the pursuit of competitive advantage', *Entrepreneurship: Theory and Practice*, 23(3), pp. 47–64; D. J. Teece, G. Pisano and A. Shuen, 1997, 'Dynamic capabilities and strategic management', *Strategic Management Journal*, 18, pp. 509–34; R. G. McGrath, I. C. MacMillan and S. Venkataraman, 1995, 'Defining and developing competence: A strategic process paradigm', *Strategic Management Journal*, 16, pp. 251–75.
8. Colvin, 'The ultimate manager', p. 187.
9. G. Colvin, 1999, 'How to be a great eCEO', *Fortune*, 24 May, pp. 104–10.
10. B. Clegg, 2000, 'Market does stocktake on DJ's', *Australian Financial Review*, 10 August, pp. 21–2.
11. M. Carr, 2000, 'To be or not to be: David Jones & Co.', *Australian Financial Review*, 12 March, pp. 3–7.
12. J. Boyle, 2000, 'Merrill to direct DJ's growth', *Australian Financial Review*, 28 August, pp. 28–30.
13. J. R. Hagerty, 2000, 'Home Depot strikes at Sears in tool duel', *Wall Street Journal*, 24 January, pp. B1, B4; B. Upbin, 2000, 'Profit in a big orange', *Forbes*, 24 January, pp. 122–7; N. Byrnes, W. C. Symonds and D. Foust, 1999, 'The best performers', *Business Week*, 29 March, pp. 98–107.
14. P.-L. Yeoh and K. Roth, 1999, 'An empirical analysis of sustained advantage in the U.S. pharmaceutical industry: Impact of firm resources and capabilities', *Strategic Management Journal*, 20, pp. 637–53; P. C. Godfrey and C. W. L. Hill, 1995, 'The problem of unobservables in strategic management research', *Strategic Management Journal*, 16, pp. 519–33.
15. D. F. Abell, 1999, 'Competing today while preparing for tomorrow', *Sloan Management Review*, 40(3), pp. 73–81; D. Leonard-Barton, 1995, *Wellsprings of Knowledge: Building and Sustaining the Sources of Innovation* (Boston: Harvard Business School Press); McGrath, MacMillan and Venkataraman, 'Defining and developing competence', p. 253.
16. K. M. Eisenhardt, 1999, 'Strategy as strategic decision making', *Sloan Management Review*, 40(3), pp. 65–72.
17. Rouse and Daellenbach, 'Rethinking research methods', pp. 487–9; Godfrey and Hill, 'The problem of unobservables', p. 522.
18. J. B. Barney, 1999, 'How a firm's capabilities affect boundary decisions', *Sloan Management Review*, 40(3), pp. 137–45; J. B. Barney, 1996, 'The resource-based theory of the firm', *Organization Science*, 7, pp. 469–80; M. E. Porter, 1996, 'What is strategy?', *Harvard Business Review*, 74(6), pp. 61–78.

19 D. Stauffer, 1999, 'Why people hoard knowledge', *Across the Board*, September, pp. 17–24; 'Changes in the competitive battlefield (Introduction)', 1999, Mastering Strategy (Part Two), *Financial Times*, 4 October, p. 1; A. Mehra, 1996, 'Resource and market based determinants of performance in the U.S. banking industry', *Strategic Management Journal*, 17, pp. 307–22.

20 L. Thurow, 1999, *Creating Wealth* (London: Nicholas Brealey Publishing), p. 117.

21 Prahalad, 'Changes in the competitive battlefield', pp. 3–4.

22 R. T. Pascale and A. H. Miller, 1999, 'The action lab: Creating a greenhouse for organizational change', *Strategy & Business*, 17, pp. 64–72.

23 K. Kerwin, P. Burrows and D. Brady, 1999, 'A new era of bright hopes and terrible fears', *Business Week*, 4 October, pp. 84–98.

24 S. Kirsner, 2000, 'Collision course', *Fast Company*, January/February, pp. 118–44.

25 G. McWilliams and J. B. White, 1999, 'Dell to Detroit: Get into gear online!', *Wall Street Journal*, 1 December, pp. B1, B4.

26 C. C. Markides, 1999, 'A dynamic view of strategy', *Sloan Management Review*, 40(3), pp. 55–63; R. Henderson and W. Mitchell, 1997, 'The interaction of organizational and competitive influences on strategy and performance', *Strategic Management Journal*, 18 (Summer Special Issue), pp. 5–14; J. B. Barney, 1995, 'Looking inside for competitive advantage', *Academy of Management Executive*, IX(4), pp. 59–60.

27 S. Ghoshal and C.A. Bartlett, 1995, 'Changing the role of top management: Beyond structure to processes', *Harvard Business Review*, 73(1), p. 96.

28 S. Wetlaufer, 1999, 'Driving change: An interview with Ford Motor Company's Jacques Nasser', *Harvard Business Review*, 77(2), pp. 77–81.

29 D. Uren, 2001, 'CRA-Rio dance to a new tune', *The Australian*, 14 February, p. 32.

30 V. P. Rindova and C. J. Fombrun, 1999, 'Constructing competitive advantage: The role of firm-constituent interactions', *Strategic Management Journal*, 20, pp. 691–710; M. A. Peteraf, 1993, 'The cornerstones of competitive strategy: A resource-based view', *Strategic Management Journal*, 14, pp. 179–91.

31 T. H. Brush and K. W. Artz, 1999, 'Toward a contingent resource-based theory: The impact of information asymmetry on the value of capabilities in veterinary medicine', *Strategic Management Journal*, 20, pp. 223–50.

32 Porter, 'What is strategy?', pp. 61–78.

33 T. J. Dean, R. L. Brown and C. E. Bamford, 1998, 'Differences in large and small firm responses to environmental context: Strategic implications from a comparative analysis of business formations', *Strategic Management Journal*, 19, pp. 709–28; K. E. Marino, 1996, 'Developing consensus on firm competencies and capabilities', *Academy of Management Executive*, X(3), pp. 40–51.

34 Colvin, 'How to be', p. 107.

35 S. A. Zahra, R. D. Ireland and M. A. Hitt, 2000, 'International expansion by new venture firms: International diversity, mode of market entry, technological learning and performance', *Academy of Management Journal*, 43(5), pp. 925–50.

36 D. Lei, M. A. Hitt and R. A. Bettis, 1996, 'Dynamic core competencies through metalearning and strategic context', *Journal of Management*, 22, pp. 247–67.

37 Deere & Company, 2000, *Deere & Company Home Page*, 21 January: www.deere.com; T. A. Stewart, 1997, 'Does anyone around here know...?', *Fortune*, 29 September, p. 279.

38 G. Lorenzoni and A. Lipparini, 1999, 'The leveraging of interfirm relationships as a distinctive organizational capability: A longitudinal study', *Strategic Management Journal*, 20, pp. 317–38; C. M. Christensen, 1997, 'Making strategy: Learning by doing', *Harvard Business Review*, 75(6), pp. 141–56; C. E. Helfat, 1997, 'Know-how and asset complementarity and dynamic capability accumulation: The case of R&D', *Strategic Management Journal*, 18, pp. 339–60; Lei, Hitt and Bettis, 'Dynamic core competencies'.

39 Pocket Strategy, 1998, 'Value', *The Economist Books*, p. 165.

40 I. Palmer and R. Dunford, 2000, paper presented at ANZAM 2000, Macquarie Graduate School of Management.

41 R. Ramirez, 1999, 'Value co-production: Intellectual origins and implications for practice and research', *Strategic Management Journal*, 20, pp. 49–65.

42 R. M. Williams, 2001, *R. M. Williams Home Page*, 19 February: www.rmwilliams.com.au.

43 S. W. Floyd and B. Wooldridge, 1999, 'Knowledge creation and social networks in corporate entrepreneurship: The renewal of organizational capability', *Entrepreneurship: Theory and Practice*, 23(3), pp. 123–43; A. Campbell and M. Alexander, 1997, 'What's wrong with strategy?', *Harvard Business Review*, 75(6), pp. 42–51.

44 M. A. Hitt, R. D. Nixon, P. G. Clifford and K. P. Coyne, 1999, 'The development and use of strategic resources', in M. A. Hitt, P. G. Clifford, R. D. Nixon and K. P. Coyne (eds), *Dynamic Strategic Resources* (Chichester: John Wiley & Sons), pp. 1–14.

45 Rouse and Daellenbach, 'Rethinking research methods', p. 9; C. Oliver, 1997, 'Sustainable competitive advantage: Combining institutional and resource-based view', *Strategic Management Journal*, 18, pp. 697–713; D. J. Collis and C. A. Montgomery, 1995, 'Competing on resources: Strategy in the 1990s', *Harvard Business Review*, 73(4), pp. 118–28; B. Wernerfelt, 1995, 'The resource-based view of the firm: Ten years after', *Strategic Management Journal*, 16, pp. 171–4.

46 P. Chattopadhyay, W. H. Glick, C. C. Miller and G. P. Huber, 1999, 'Determinants of executive beliefs: Comparing functional conditioning and social influence', *Strategic Management Journal*, 20, pp. 763–89; J. H. Dyer, 1996, 'Specialized supplier networks as a source of competitive advantage: Evidence from the auto industry', *Strategic Management Journal*, 17, pp. 271–91; R. L. Priem and D. A. Harrison, 1994, 'Exploring strategic judgment: Methods for testing the assumptions of prescriptive contingency theories', *Strategic Management Journal*, 15, pp. 311–24; R. Amit and P. J. H. Schoemaker, 1993, 'Strategic assets and organizational rent', *Strategic Management Journal*, 14, pp. 33–46.

47 R. Gertner and A. Rosenfield, 1999, 'How real options lead to better decisions', Mastering Strategy (Part Five), *Financial Times*, 25 October, pp. 14–15; H. R. Greve, 1998, 'Managerial cognition and the mimetic adoption of market positions: What you see is what you do', *Strategic Management Journal*, 19, pp. 967–88; W. Boeker, 1997, 'Executive migration and strategic change: The effect of top manager movement on product-market entry', *Administrative Science Quarterly*, 42, pp. 213–36; C. R. Schwenk, 1995, 'Strategic decision making', *Journal of Management*, 21, pp. 471–93.

48 P. C. Nutt, 1999, 'Surprising but true: Half the decisions in organizations fail', *Academy of Management Executive*, 13(4), pp. 75–90.

49 Eisenhardt, 'Strategy as strategic decision making', p. 70.

50 R. S. Dooley and G. E. Fryxell, 1999, 'Attaining decision quality and commitment from dissent: The moderating effects of loyalty and competence in strategic decision-making teams', *Academy of Management Journal*, 42, pp. 389–402.

51 D. A. Aaker and E. Joachimsthaler, 1999, 'The lure of global branding', *Harvard Business Review*, 77(6), pp. 137–44; R. G. McGrath, 1999, 'Falling forward: Real options reasoning and entrepreneurial failure', *Academy of Management Review*, 24, pp. 13–30; McGrath, MacMillan and Venkataraman, 'Defining and developing competence', p. 253.

52 Schendel, 'Fresh challenges', p. 15.

53 Colvin, 'The ultimate manager', p. 187.

54 Amit and Schoemaker, 'Strategic assets and organizational rent', p. 33.

55 W. S. Lovejoy, 1999, 'How many decisions should you automate?', Mastering Strategy (Part Eleven), *Financial Times*, 6 December, pp. 12–13.

56 M. Farjoun and L. Lai, 1997, 'Similarity judgments in strategy formulation: Role, process and implications', *Strategic Management Journal*, 18, pp. 255–73.

57 S. Bishop, 1999, 'The strategic power of saying no', *Harvard Business Review*, 77(6), pp. 50–61; H. W. Vroman, 1996, 'The loyalty effect: The hidden force behind growth, profits and lasting value' (book review), *Academy of Management Executive*, X(1), pp. 88–90.

58 R. T. Pascale and A. H. Miller, 1999, 'The action lab: Creating a greenhouse for organizational change', *Strategy & Business*, 17, pp. 64–72; W. Kiechel, 1993, 'Facing up to denial', *Fortune*, 18 October, pp. 163–5.

59 Colvin, 'The ultimate manager', p. 187; P. Sellers, 1996, 'What exactly is charisma?', *Fortune*, 15 January, pp. 68–75.

60 Wetlaufer, 'Driving change', p. 79.

61 N. Tichy, 1999, 'The teachable point of view', *Harvard Business Review*, 77(2), pp. 82–3.

62 J. G. Combs and D. J. Ketchen, Jr, 1999, 'Explaining interfirm cooperation and performance: Toward a reconciliation of predictions from the resource-based view and organizational economics', *Strategic Management Journal*, 20, pp. 867–88; Teece, Pisano and Shuen, 'Dynamic capabilities', pp. 513–14; Barney, 1995, 'Looking inside for competitive advantage', p. 50.

63 D. L. Deeds, D. DeCarolis and J. Coombs, 2000, 'Dynamic capabilities and new product development in high technology ventures: An empirical

analysis of new biotechnology firms', *Journal of Business Venturing*, 15, pp. 211–29; T. Chi, 1994, 'Trading in strategic resources: Necessary conditions, transaction cost problems, and choice of exchange structure', *Strategic Management Journal*, 15, pp. 271–90; R. Reed and R. DeFillippi, 1990, 'Causal ambiguity, barriers to imitation, and sustainable competitive advantage', *Academy of Management Review*, 15, pp. 88–102.

64. Yeoh and Roth, 'An empirical analysis', p. 638; McGrath, MacMillan and Venkataraman, 'Defining and developing competence', p. 252.

65. A. Goldstein, 1999, 'Dell outpaces Compaq in U.S. sales of PCs', *Dallas Morning News*, 25 October, pp. D1, D4.

66. K. Yung, 1999, 'An expanding palate', *Dallas Morning News*, 15 October, pp. D1, D12.

67. Deeds, DeCarolis and Coombs, 'Dynamic capabilities', p. 213; Hitt, Nixon, Clifford and Coyne, 'The development and use of', p. 2; M. de Miranda Oliveira, Jr, 1999, 'Core competencies and the knowledge of the firm', in M. A. Hitt, P. G. Clifford, R. D. Nixon and K. P. Coyne (eds), *Dynamic Strategic Resources* (Chichester: John Wiley & Sons), pp. 17–42; P. R. Hall, 1991, 'The contribution of intangible resources to business success', *Journal of General Management*, 16(4), pp. 41–52.

68. S. A. Zahra, A. P. Nielsen and W. C. Bogner, 1999, 'Corporate entrepreneurship, knowledge, and competence development', *Entrepreneurship: Theory and Practice*, 23(3), pp. 169–89; T. A. Stewart, 1996, 'Coins in a knowledge bank', *Fortune*, 19 February, pp. 230–3.

69. A. M. Webber, 2000, 'New math for a new economy', *Fast Company*, January/February, pp. 214–24.

70. S. J. Marsh and A. L. Ranft, 1999, 'Why resources matter: An empirical study of knowledge-based resources on new market entry', in M. A. Hitt, P. G. Clifford, R. D. Nixon and K. P. Coyne (eds), *Dynamic Strategic Resources* (Chichester: John Wiley & Sons), pp. 43–66.

71. Brush and Artz, 'Toward a contingent resource-based theory', p. 225; McGrath, MacMillan and Venkataraman, 'Defining and developing competence', p. 252; Porter, 'What is strategy?'.

72. J. B. Quinn, P. Anderson and S. Finkelstein, 1996, 'Making the most of the best', *Harvard Business Review*, 74(2), pp. 71–80.

73. Webber, 'New math', p. 217.

74. Lee and Miller, 'People matter'; Godfrey and Hill, 'The problem of unobservables', pp. 522–3.

75. Webber, 'New math', p. 218.

76. V. Griffith, 1999, 'Branding.com: How bricks-and-mortar companies can make it on the Internet', *Strategy & Business*, 15, pp. 54–9; S. I. Hill, J. McGrath and S. Dayal, 1998, *Strategy & Business*, 11, pp. 22–34.

77. S. Ward, L. Light and J. Goldstine, 1999, 'What high-tech managers need to know about brands', *Harvard Business Review*, 77(4), pp. 85–95.

78. D. P. Hamilton, 1999, 'H-P to relaunch its brand, adopt new logo', *Wall Street Journal*, 16 November, p. B6.

79. G. Rifkin, 1998, 'How Harley-Davidson revs its brand', *Strategy & Business*, 9, pp. 31–40.

80. Country Road Limited, 2001, *Country Road Limited Home Page*, 19 February: www.countryroad.com.au.

81. Hitt, Nixon, Clifford and Coyne, 'The development', p. 3.

82. C. L. Lengnick-Hall and J. W. Wolff, 1999, 'Similarities and contradictions in the core logic of three strategy research streams', *Strategic Management Journal*, 20, pp. 1109–132.

83. B. McEvily and A. Zaheer, 1999, 'Bridging ties: A source of firm heterogeneity in competitive capabilities', *Strategic Management Journal*, 20, pp. 1133–56.

84. W. C. Rappleye, Jr, 1999, 'Human capital management', *Fortune* (Special Advertising Section), 14 October, p. S2.

85. D. G. Hoopes and S. Postrel, 1999, 'Shared knowledge: "Glitches," and product development performance', *Strategic Management Journal*, 20, pp. 837–65; Lei, Hitt and Bettis, 'Dynamic core competencies'; J. B. Quinn, 1994, *The Intelligent Enterprise* (New York: Free Press).

86. GroPep Limited, 2001, *GroPep Home Page*, 18 February: www.gropep.com.au.

87. Thurow, *Creating Wealth*, p. 117; Stross, 1997, 'Mr. Gates builds his brain trust'; E. M. Davies, 1996, 'Wired for hiring: Microsoft's slick recruiting machine', *Fortune*, 5 February, pp. 123–4.

88. T. A. Stewart, 1999, 'Grab the knowledge and squeeze', *Fortune*, 8 November, p. 322.

89. G. G. Dess and J. C. Picken, 1999, *Beyond Productivity* (New York: AMACOM).

90. D. Stauffer, 1999, 'Why people hoard knowledge', *Across the Board*, September, pp. 17–24.

91. P. Roberts, 1998, 'Information gives today's edge', *Australian Financial Review*, 13 March.

92. L. Empson, 1999, 'The challenge of knowledge management', Mastering Strategy (Part Two), *Financial Times*, 4 October, pp. 9–10.

93. M. T. Hansen, N. Nhoria and T. Tierney, 1999, 'What's your strategy for managing knowledge?', *Harvard Business Review*, 77(2), pp. 106–16.

94. M. A. Hitt and R. D. Ireland, 1986, 'Relationships among corporate level distinctive competencies, diversification strategy, corporate structure, and performance', *Journal of Management Studies*, 23, pp. 401–16; M. A. Hitt and R. D. Ireland, 1985, 'Corporate distinctive competence, strategy, industry, and performance', *Strategic Management Journal*, 6, pp. 273–93; M. A. Hitt, R. D. Ireland and K. A. Palia, 1982, 'Industrial firms' grand strategy and functional importance', *Academy of Management Journal*, 25, pp. 265–98; M. A. Hitt, R. D. Ireland and G. Stadter, 1982, 'Functional importance and company performance: Moderating effects of grand strategy and industry type', *Strategic Management Journal*, 3, pp. 315–30; C. C. Snow and E. G. Hrebiniak, 1980, 'Strategy, distinctive competence, and organizational performance', *Administrative Science Quarterly*, 25, pp. 317–36.

95. Hitt, Nixon, Clifford & Coyne, 'The development', p. 3; Zahra, Nielsen and Bogner, 'Corporate entrepreneurship', p. 171; D. Leonard-Barton, H. K Bowen, K. B. Clark, C. A. Holloway and S. C. Wheelwright, 1994, 'How to integrate work and deepen expertise', *Harvard Business Review*, 72(5), p. 123; C. K. Prahalad and G. Hamel, 1990, 'The core competence of the corporation', *Harvard Business Review*, 68(3), pp. 79–93.

96. Brush and Artz, 'Toward a contingent resource-based theory', pp. 224–5; T. Chi, 1994, 'Trading in strategic resources: Necessary conditions, transaction cost problems, and choice of exchange structure', *Strategic Management Journal*, 15, pp. 271–90.

97. C. Ames, 1995, 'Sales soft? Profits flat? It's time to rethink your business', *Fortune*, 25 June, pp. 142–6; S. Fatsis, 1993, 'Bigger is not necessarily better', *Waco Tribune-Herald*, 17 January, pp. B1, B6.

98. M. Pachacz, 2000, 'CSL's bloody coup', *Australian Financial Review*, 1 September, pp. 31–3.

99. A. Palazzo, 1999, 'Sizzler restaurants are returning to their roots', *Wall Street Journal*, 15 November, p. B13A.

100. This section is drawn primarily from three sources: Barney, 'How a firm's capabilities'; Barney, 'Looking inside for competitive advantage'; J. B. Barney, 1991, 'Firm resources and sustained competitive advantage', *Journal of Management*, 17, pp. 99–120.

101. C. H. St. John and J. S. Harrison, 1999, 'Manufacturing-based relatedness, synergy, and coordination', *Strategic Management Journal*, 20, pp. 129–45.

102. Barney, 'Looking inside for competitive advantage'.

103. I. M. Kunii, W. Thornton and J. Rae-Dupree, 1999, 'Sony's shakeup', *Business Week*, 22 March, pp. 52–3; Barney, 'Looking inside for competitive advantage', p. 50.

104. R. Tomkins, 1999, 'Marketing value for money', *Financial Times*, 14 May, p. 18.

105. J. Boag and Son Breweries, 2001, *J. Boag and Son Home Page*, 19 February: www.boags.com.au.

106. L. B. Ward, 2000, 'Dell sales overtake Compaq', *Dallas Morning News*, 24 January, pp. D1–2; A. Goldstein, 1999, 'Dell shareholders celebrate gains', *Dallas Morning News*, 17 July, pp. F1, F3.

107. Computershare Limited, 2001, *Computershare Limited Home Page*, 19 February: www.computershare.com.au.

108. Barney, 'Looking inside for competitive advantage', p. 53.

109. Barney, 'How a firm's capabilities', p. 141.

110. Barney, 'Firm resources', p. 108.

111. J. Kurtzman, 1997, 'An interview with Rosabeth Moss Kanter', *Strategy & Business*, 16, pp. 85–94.

112. R. Burt, 1999, 'When is corporate culture a competitive asset?', Mastering Strategy (Part Six), *Financial Times*, 1 November, pp. 14–15.

113. J. Huey, 1993, 'How McKinsey does it', *Fortune*, 1 November, pp. 56–81.

114. Reed and DeFillippi, 'Causal ambiguity'.

115. C. Eliezer, 1999, 'Gudinski is back for a second act', *Business Review Weekly*, 12 November, pp. 161–5.

116. Barney, 'How a firm's capabilities', p. 141.

117. Barney, 'Firm resources', p. 111.

118. Amit and Schoemaker, 'Strategic assets', p. 39.

119. M. E. Porter, 1985, *Competitive Advantage* (New York: Free Press), pp. 33–61.

120. G. G. Dess, A. Gupta, J.-F. Hennart and C. W. L. Hill, 1995, 'Conducting and integrating strategy research at the international corporate and

business levels: Issues and directions', *Journal of Management*, 21, p. 376; Porter, 'What is strategy?'.
121 T. A. Stewart, 1999, 'Customer learning is a two-way street', *Fortune*, 10 May, pp. 158–60; T. A. Stewart, 1995, 'The information wars: What you don't know will hurt you', *Fortune*, 12 June, pp. 119–21.
122 C. Batchelor, 1999, 'Logistics aspires to worldly wisdom', *Financial Times*, 17 June, p. 13; Stewart, 'Customer learning', p. 158.
123 D. Ball, 1999, 'Pirelli expects new tire-making plan to lower costs, increase market share', *Wall Street Journal*, 6 December, p. A29A.
124 J. Y. Murray and M. Kotabe, 1999, 'Sourcing strategies of U.S. service companies: A modified transaction-cost analysis', *Strategic Management Journal*, 20, pp. 791–809.
125 S. Jones, 1999, 'Growth process in global market', *Financial Times*, 22 June, p. 17.
126 Burt, 'Ford expects to farm out', p. 1; P. Landers, 1999, 'Nissan retains IBM to manage its computers', *Wall Street Journal*, 29 October, p. A15.
127 N. Tabakoff, 1999, 'The go between', *Business Review Weekly*, 8 October.
128 B. H. Jevnaker and M. Bruce, 1999, 'Design as a strategic alliance: Expanding the creative capability of the firm', in M. A. Hitt, P. G. Clifford, R. D. Nixon and K. P. Coyne (eds), *Dynamic Strategic Resources* (Chichester: John Wiley & Sons), pp. 266–98.
129 Dess and Picken, *Beyond Productivity*, p. 23.
130 Spotless Group Limited, 2001, *Spotless Service Limited Home Page*, 19 February: www.spotless.com.au.
131 Jones, 'Growth process', p. 17; K. Tan, 1999, 'Firms needing data in a hurry seek out Stax', *Wall Street Journal*, 23 March, p. B10.
132 S. Woolley, 1999, 'Ma Bell at your service', *Forbes*, 17 May, pp. 54–5.
133 N. A. Wishart, J. J. Elam and D. Robey, 1996, 'Redrawing the portrait of a learning organization: Inside Knight-Ridder, Inc.', *Academy of Management Executive*, X(1), pp. 7–20; D. Lei and M. A. Hitt, 1995, 'Strategic restructuring and outsourcing: The effect of mergers and acquisitions and LBOs on building firm skills and capabilities', *Journal of Management*, 21, pp. 835–59.
134 Zahra, Nielsen and Bogner, 'Corporate entrepreneurship', pp. 171–7; J. C. Spender and R. M. Grant, 1996, 'Knowledge and the firm: Overview', *Strategic Management Journal*, 17 (Winter Special Issue), pp. 5–10.
135 Lei, Hitt and Bettis, 'Dynamic core competences'; Leonard-Barton, *Wellsprings of Knowledge*, pp. 59–89.
136 Leonard-Barton, *Wellsprings of Knowledge*, p. 7.
137 Wishart, Elam and Robey, 'Redrawing the portrait', p. 8.
138 G. G. Dess and J. C. Picken, 1999, 'Creating competitive (dis)advantage: Learning from Food Lion's freefall', *Academy of Management Executive*, 13(3), pp. 97–111.
139 M. Hannan and J. Freeman, 1977, 'The population ecology of organizations', *American Journal of Sociology*, 82, pp. 929–64.
140 Leonard-Barton, *Wellsprings of Knowledge*, pp. 30–1.
141 Junior, 'Core competencies', pp. 20–1; R. Sanchez and J. T. Mahoney, 1996, 'Modularity, flexibility, and knowledge management in product and organization design', *Strategic Management Journal*, 17 (Winter Special Issue), pp. 63–76; C. A. Bartlett and S. Ghoshal, 1994, 'Changing the role of top management: Beyond strategy to purpose', *Harvard Business Review*, 72(6), pp. 79–88.
142 G. L. White, 1999, 'How GM, Ford think Web can make splash on the factory floor', *Wall Street Journal*, 3 December, pp. A1, A8.
143 R. G. Matthews, 1999, 'Steelmakers face online threat from auto industry', *Wall Street Journal*, 26 November, p. B4.
144 G. Hamel and C. K. Prahalad, 1989, 'Strategic intent', *Harvard Business Review*, 67(3), pp. 63–76.
145 R. Gulati, 1999, 'Network location and learning: The influence of network resources and firm capabilities on alliance formation', *Strategic Management Journal*, 20, pp. 397–420; DeCarolis and Deeds, 'The impact of stocks and flows'; P. Almeida, 1996, 'Knowledge sourcing by foreign multinationals: Patent citation analysis in the U.S. semiconductor industry', *Strategic Management Journal*, 17 (Winter Special Issue), pp. 155–65.
146 Leonard-Barton, *Wellsprings of Knowledge*, p. 8.
147 'Action item', 2000, *Fast Company*, January/February, p. 86; 3M, 2000, *3M Home Page*, 16 January: www.3m.com; Herb Kelleher, 1998, *Financial Times*, 30 November, p. 36; C. E. Smith, 1994, 'The Merlin factor: Leadership and strategic intent', *Information Access*, 5(1), pp. 67–85.
148 M. M. Waldrop, 1996, 'Dee Hock on organizations', *Fast Company*, October, p. 84.
149 D. Roth, 1999, 'The value of vision', *Fortune*, 24 May, p. 285; R. D. Ireland and M. A. Hitt, 1992, 'Mission statements: Importance, challenge and recommendations for development', *Business Horizons*, 35(3), pp. 34–42.
150 Cochlear Limited, 2000, *Annual Report*.
151 P. Martin, 1999, 'Lessons in humility', *Financial Times*, 22 June, p. 18.
152 C. Marshall, 1996, 'A sense of mission', *The Strategist*, 7(4), pp. 14–16.

Part 2

Strategic actions: Strategy formulation

Chapter 4
Business-level strategy

Chapter 5
Competitive dynamics

Chapter 6
Corporate-level strategy

Chapter 7
Acquisition and restructuring strategies

Chapter 8
International strategy

Chapter 9
Cooperative strategy

Chapter 4

Business-level strategy

Objectives

After reading this chapter, you should be able to:

1. Define strategy and explain business-level strategies.
2. Describe the relationship between customers and business-level strategies.
3. Discuss the issues firms consider when evaluating customers in terms of importance in the 21st-century competitive landscape.
4. Describe the capabilities necessary to develop competitive advantage through the cost leadership, differentiation, focused cost leadership, focused differentiation and integrated cost leadership/differentiation business-level strategies.
5. Explain the risks associated with each of the five business-level strategies.

The Internet, customer (buyer) power and business-level strategy

The Internet is spawning new companies and even new industries. Yahoo! Inc. is a start-up Internet-based venture. Initially, Yahoo! Inc. was thought by many to be an unusual name for a company that was founded by two graduate school dropouts. However, the firm's success is suggested by the fact that its recent market capitalisation was approximately US$40 billion.

The Internet is a marketplace phenomenon that already features more than US$1 trillion worth of network connections, computer power and databases full of information. The Internet is largely free to anyone in the world who has a phone line and a personal computer. It can be used day or night, and it offers an opportunity to the founders of virtually any start-up venture to enter a range of industries and market segments within them. The Internet's significant effect is highlighted by the fact that Amazon.com's birth has been cited as one of the 10 moments that shaped and defined the 1990s.

To date, the strategies that are being implemented by Internet companies are still undefined. Jacques A. Nasser, the US Ford Motor Company's CEO, joked recently that Amazon.com's strategy 'boils down to buy at 100 and sell at 80'. This comment hints at the fact that many Internet companies, including Amazon.com, are not profitable. However, the potential of e-commerce to generate above-average returns in the long term (see Opening Case in Chapter 1) encourages large firms, such as Ford, to pursue business through this medium.

Because of the immense flow of information through it, the Internet allows customers with access to have greater control over their buying behaviour than ever before. Prior to the Internet, buyers faced considerable obstacles when trying to make an optimal purchase. In addition, finding information about products was usually time consuming. Compounding the issue for buyers in pre-Internet days were sellers' efforts to guard against extensive distribution of product-related information. Restricting information flows tends to increase sellers' power relative to that of buyers (see Chapter 2). Today, however, buyers use the Internet to access a wealth of information about goods and services that are of interest to them. It should be noted, however, that there is inequality in Internet access across countries. For example, in Australia, there are 60.8 people in every 1 000 head of population with access to the Internet, while in Turkey only 2.7 people in 1 000 have Internet access. It is only when this inequality is rectified that the full potential of the Internet may be realised.

In Australia, these benefits extend from large purchases such as housing and cars to groceries. For example, gofish.com lists new and used cars and gives prices, models, and details on condition and availability. A buyer can find out from the site what the best price for their chosen model is. In the groceries market, there are numerous companies in search of the e-shopper – Coles Myer and Woolworths compete with specialists such as GreenGrocer.com.au which has 50 000 registered customers.

The Internet also makes it possible for sellers to identify consumers and to collect an unprecedented amount of information about their purchasing patterns. Sophisticated software programs analyse this information and compare it with that of other customers. These sophisticated practices make it possible for companies to sell additional products to consumers. For example, based on a purchase profile, companies such as Amazon.com and barnesandnoble.com can suggest a specific book or CD for a customer to consider buying to complement the product that was ordered. This capability is generating significant levels of customer satisfaction for firms selling via the Internet and increases the viability of the differentiation and integrated cost leadership/differentiation business-level strategies. (Both strategies are discussed fully in the chapter.)

The Internet is also creating different pricing options to which customers are responding favourably. Auctions, for example, traditionally resulted in pricing outcomes that favoured sellers. In the Internet age, however, firms such as priceline.com organise the option in favour of the buyer. This allows buyers to pool as groups and purchase products at a lower price.

Amazon.com's Internet-based strategy has put traditional 'bricks and mortar' businesses such as the American bookseller Barnes & Noble at a significant cost disadvantage. Even virtual upstarts can reach customers faster than 'bricks and mortar' businesses with stores and full sales staffs can, and for a fraction of the cost. Amazon.com recently reached US$1.2 billion in annual sales revenue. This amount equals the revenue Barnes & Noble generated from 200 of its superstores. While Barnes & Noble has spent US$472 million to renovate and upgrade its 1000-plus stores, Amazon.com carries only US$56 million in fixed assets on its books. This amount of assets accounts primarily for the firm's warehouses and computers. Furthermore, the future portends an even worse situation for Barnes & Noble, because Amazon.com's new investment in warehouses can support US$15 billion in sales. For these reasons, it has a US$21.2 billion market capitalisation, compared to US$1.8 billion for Barnes & Noble. This suggests that the low-cost competitive advantage, an advantage that is pursued through the cost leadership business-level strategy, can shift from traditional 'bricks and mortar' stores to those pursuing cost leadership through an Internet-based strategy. In recognition of this shift, Barnes & Noble has formed an Internet operation (barnesandnoble.com) in partnership with Bertelsmann AG, the German media giant that paid US$200 million to purchase a 50 per cent stake in the Web-based venture. Although, as suggested in a Strategic Focus in Chapter 2, the competition between Amazon.com and Barnes & Noble may be changing, it has still caused a significant shift in the business-level strategy of Barnes & Noble.

In addition, large traditional firms are being challenged on the cost side in terms of where value can be captured along the value chain (see Chapter 3). This challenge is a result of the fact that many firms are reconfiguring the value chain to generate additional value by purchasing through suppliers' Web-based business models. For instance, Cisco Systems handles 78 per cent of its sales via the Internet, a practice that results in the firm never physically touching at least US$4 billion in customers' orders. Cisco develops products and manufacturing and specifications, but uses the Internet to forward orders directly to contract manufacturers. Cisco owns only two of the 30 plants that produce the networking switches and routers that are sold to its telecommunications customers.

As previously noted, many large traditional companies are responding to Web-based competition by establishing their own Internet presence. The main problem, however, is that these large firms' Web businesses have a tendency to cannibalise their company's existing businesses. In turn, cannibalisation can increase rivalry inside the firm between those involved with 'traditional' sales activities and those generating revenues via the newly formed Internet operation.

Whirlpool Corporation has established a business-to-business (B2B) Web-based strategy. In the last several years, Whirlpool developed 3300 customised Web pages for its dealers. By logging on to one of these pages, a dealer can order products and check on their delivery status. Whirlpool is also using the Internet to form start-up ventures. The initial concept is a venture called brandwise.com. This site serves as a portal to shop for appliances such as washing machines, clothes dryers, refrigerators, microwave ovens, and so forth. Featuring other brands in addition to its own, Whirlpool owns only 37 per cent of brandwise.com. The risk that customers using brandwise.com will buy a competitor's product is acceptable, given Whirlpool's commitment to establishing a viable Internet distribution channel and its belief in the competitive superiority of its products. Another benefit from brandwise.com is the opportunity for Whirlpool to obtain valuable data that the company can use to design products in the future that can meet customers' emerging needs. Furthermore, the same data will allow Whirlpool to learn about buying patterns by tracking buyer demographics. Retailers who receive revenue referred from brandwise.com will pay a flat fee each time a sale is consummated that originated from the site. Revenues will also be generated through those advertising on the website and through commissions earned from sales of accessories, warranties and service contracts. However, Whirlpool's rivals may be able to get the same information from the site and thereby compromise Whirlpool's differentiation business-level strategy. Thus, although there are opportunities, there are also significant risks involved with Whirlpool's decision to integrate the Internet into the formulation and implementation of its business-level strategy.

The strategic changes resulting from use of the Internet are profound. Firms such as Hewlett-Packard and IBM have sold plants because they were increasingly regarded as a liability. In fact, in 1998, firms in the United States outsourced 15 per cent of all manufacturing. It is estimated that as much as 40 per cent of manufacturing will be outsourced in the future. In addition, this approach allows much more customisation in a shorter period of time: instead of taking months or weeks to receive a customised car, Toyota and other Japanese automobile manufacturers are pioneering the five-day car. This capability generates more value for customers and dealers. Customers receive products that satisfy their unique needs. Value is created for dealers in that the customised and direct sales approach prevents cars from being carried in their inventories for long periods of time.

In sum, the Internet has the potential to create more value for customers in the form of lower costs and additional differentiated features. Increasingly, the Internet is influencing a firm's choice of a business-level strategy. In other instances, the Internet affects how companies implement a business-level strategy once it has been selected. Thus, as our discussion will show, the Internet is having major effects on business-level strategy, the topic of this chapter.

www.amazon.com
www.bn.com
www.brandwise.com
www.cisco.com
www.colesmyer.com.au
www.ford.com
www.gofish.com.au
www.GreenGrocer.com.au
www.hp.com.au
www-7.ibm.com.au
www.s-central.com.au
www.toyota.com
www.whirlpool.com
www.woolworths.com.au
www.yahoo.com

Sources: A. Goldstein, 2000, 'Online merchants seek to improve e-commerce', *Dallas Morning News*, 14 January, pp. D1–2; E. Brown, 1999, 'Big business meets the e-world', *Fortune*, 8 November, pp. 88–98; R. D. Hof, K. Kerwin, P. Burrows and D. Brady, 1999, 'A new year of bright hopes and terrible fears', *Business Week*, 4 October, pp. 84–98; B. Marvel, 1999, 'The '90s: Cultural trends that shaped a decade', *Dallas Morning News*, 19 December, p. C1; O. Port, 1999, 'Customers move into the driver's seat', *Business Week*, 4 October, pp. 103–6; P. Timmers, 1998, 'Business models for electronic markets', in Y. Gadient, B. F. Schmid and D. Selz, 'Electronic commerce in Europe', *EM – Electronic Markets*, 8, 2, July: www.electronicmarkets.org/netacademy/publications.nsf/all_pk/949; E. Ross, 2000, 'Shoppers are yet to click with e-grocers', *Business Review Weekly*, 4 August, pp. 63–4; OECD, 2000, *OECD in Figures*.

It is clear from the Opening Case that the Internet's capabilities are yielding a rich array of opportunities for companies throughout the global economy. In terms of market potential, it is important to note that in Australia, it is estimated that a mere 5 000 individuals purchase items regularly via the Internet, while a further 200 000 have made purchases in a 'one-off' situation.[1] This nevertheless vast untapped market is enticing to both established firms and start-up ventures.

An established and dominant retailer in the United States, Wal-Mart is pursuing the Internet's opportunities largely through partnerships. One of the agreements it has formed is with Books-A-Million. The cooperative arrangement calls for Books-A-Million to supply and deliver books for Wal-Mart's on-line store, which will compete with Amazon.com and barnesandnoble.com, among others. Initial plans called for this venture to offer bestsellers at a 50 per cent discount, with hardbacks being sold at a 30 per cent discount. Wal-Mart intends to form alliances with still other companies to pursue its cost leadership business-level strategy through Internet sales. Within Australia, B2B use of the Internet became very topical in mid-2000 with the formation of CoreProcure, an alliance of 14 major companies (including ANZ and Coles Myer). This is basically a 'buying club' that facilitates procurement of goods and services. Peter Lavis, Australia Post's nominee on the steering committee, said of it: 'There are savings in searching for the product you want, ordering it, delivery, electronic invoicing and having it reconciled back to your ERP [Enterprise Resource Planning] system.' Balancing this optimism, a 365-page report on B2B said: '[Companies] are now desperately grasping at the B2B Holy Grail in the hope of being spirited with the magic dust of a high tech multiple.'[2] According to a US analyst, 'Business-to-business e-commerce is poised to soar, and GM and Ford are at the vanguard of this movement. Both companies are exercising their enormous buying power to jump start trading exchanges on the Internet.'[3] As shown by the examples, the Internet is becoming an increasingly important aspect of firms' business-level strategies. Moreover, as noted previously, for firms in general, 'the Internet is reshaping the global marketplace and it will continue to do so for some time to come'.[4]

To achieve strategic competitiveness and earn above-average returns, a company analyses its external environment, identifies opportunities in it, determines which of its internal resources and capabilities are core competencies, and selects an appropriate strategy to implement.[5] This array of actions is required of *all* companies — those competing through more traditional means, as well as those seeking above-average returns as Internet-based ventures.

A **strategy** is an integrated and coordinated set of commitments and actions designed to exploit core competencies and gain a competitive advantage. Strategies are purposeful, precede the taking of actions to which they apply, and demonstrate a shared understanding of a firm's strategic intent and mission.[6] An effectively formulated strategy marshals, integrates and allocates the firm's resources, capabilities and competencies so that it can cope successfully with its external environment.[7] An effective strategy also rationalises the firm's strategic intent and strategic mission and what will be done to achieve them.[8] Information about a host of variables, including markets, customers, technology, worldwide finance and the changing world economy, must be collected and analysed to formulate and implement strategies properly.[9] As the Opening Case illustrates, the Internet creates a more competitive strategic situation in which to select strategies to use in the pursuit of strategic competitiveness and above-average returns.

Recall from Chapters 1 and 3 that *core competencies* are resources and capabilities that serve as a source of competitive advantage for a firm over its rivals. Strategic competitiveness and the earning of above-average returns hinge on a firm's ability to develop and exploit new core competencies faster than competitors can mimic the competitive advantages yielded by current ones.[10] Firms that focus on the continuous need to develop new core competencies are able to drive competition in the future as well as the present.[11] Thus, especially in the 21st-century competitive landscape, with its continuing globalisation and rapid technological changes, only firms with the capacity to improve, innovate and upgrade their competitive advantages over time can expect to achieve long-term success.[12]

As explained in this chapter, successful firms use their core competencies to satisfy customer needs. The relationship between appropriate strategic actions and the achievement of strategic competitiveness is increasingly important in today's turbulent and competitive environment.[13] These relationships are shown in Figure 1.1 in Chapter 1. The figure shows that a firm's *strategic inputs* (gained through studying the external and internal environments) are used to select the *strategic actions* (the formulation and implementation of value-creating strategies) that will yield desired *strategic outcomes*.

A **strategy** is an integrated and coordinated set of commitments and actions designed to exploit core competencies and gain a competitive advantage.

At a broader level, companies that are committed to the importance of competing successfully in the global economy constantly scan developments in the world's markets to identify emerging opportunities to exploit their competitive advantages. The segments most closely linked with strategic competitiveness vary by the type of business-level strategy the firm is using.[14] Consider, for example, Taiwanese PC manufacturers. Collectively, PC manufacturers in Taiwan maintain the third-largest market share position behind the United States and Japan. The low-priced segment of the PC market is targeted by many of Taiwan's PC manufacturers. Competition among firms seeking to serve this segment through the use of the cost leadership business-level strategy is severe. To drive their costs lower and to exploit the competitive advantage their low-cost structures provide, Taiwanese companies are relying more and more on suppliers from mainland China to supply low-priced components. Chinese component suppliers can offer less expensive parts to the Taiwanese PC manufacturers because of lower costs, made possible by relatively inexpensive land and labour expenses. Because the Taiwanese firms rely on export to fulfil global demand, completing business transactions with firms in China is not seen as risky: Taiwan does not rely on sales to Chinese customers and hence does not have to worry about the associated credit risks.[15]

> A **business-level strategy** is an integrated and coordinated set of commitments and actions designed to provide value to customers and gain a competitive advantage by exploiting core competencies in specific, individual product markets.

Business-level strategy, this chapter's focus, is an integrated and coordinated set of commitments and actions designed to provide value to customers and gain a competitive advantage by exploiting core competencies in specific, individual product markets.[16] Thus, a business-level strategy reflects a firm's belief about where and how it has an advantage over its rivals.[17] The essence of a firm's business-level strategy is 'choosing to perform activities differently or to perform different activities than rivals'.[18] Related to the firm's competitive environment and the interactions the firm has with that environment is the necessity that all employees understand what the firm's advantage is relative to rivals.[19] Questions about the firm's strategy in the future and the competitive advantages on which it would be based should be resolved quickly to permit effective strategic actions.

Customers are the foundation of successful business-level strategies. Increasingly, firms are emphasising the importance of the link between building relationships and delivering service to customers and the firm's financial performance. One CEO captures this sentiment by observing that in his firm, 'the central question is, What kind of initiatives will help us strengthen the customer relationships we have and encourage new ones to form?'.[20] This emphasis is consistent with the perspective that, at its core, business-level strategy is 'the ability to build and maintain relationships to the best people for maximum value creation, both internally (to firm representatives) and externally (to customers)'.[21]

Because of their strategic importance, we begin this chapter with a discussion of customers. Three issues are considered in this analysis. Each firm determines (1) *whom* it will serve, (2) *what* needs target customers have that it will satisfy, and (3) *how* those needs will be satisfied through the implementation of a chosen strategy. Following the discussion on customers, we describe four generic business-level strategies. These strategies are called *generic* because they are implemented in both manufacturing and service industries.[22] Our analysis of the generic strategies includes descriptions of how each one allows a firm to address the five competitive forces discussed in Chapter 2. In addition, we use the value chain (see Chapter 3) to show examples of primary and support activities that are necessary to implement each generic strategy. Risks associated with each generic strategy are also presented. Organisational structures and controls required for the successful implementation of business-level strategies are explained in Chapter 11.

A fifth business-level strategy that both manufacturing and service firms are implementing more frequently is considered in the chapter's final section. Some believe that this integrated strategy (a combination of attributes of the cost leadership and differentiation strategies) is essential to establishing and exploiting competitive advantages in the global economy – an economy with growth possibilities that are being expanded and changed because of the Internet's capabilities.[23]

Customers: Who, what and how

Organisations must satisfy some group of customers' needs to be successful. *Needs* refers to the benefits and features required of a good or service that customers seek to purchase. A basic need of all customers is to buy products that provide value for money.

A key reason that firms must be able to satisfy customers' needs is that, in the final analysis, returns earned from relationships with customers are the lifeblood of all organisations.[24] Relationships with customers are strengthened when the firm is committed to providing superior value to those it serves. Superior value is often created when a firm's product helps a customer to enhance the business's own competitive advantage.[25]

The challenge of identifying and determining how to satisfy the needs of what some business analysts believe are increasingly sophisticated, knowledgeable and fickle customers is difficult.[26] However, products are now available to assist companies in their efforts to better understand customers and suppliers and to manage their relationships with them. Through its acquisition of Smart Technologies, for example, i2 Technologies offers software to companies that support the management of Internet-based customer relationships. Additionally, i2's flagship product manages information related to manufacturers' customers and suppliers. GM's recent decision to use i2's software and services was seen by analysts as a significant affirmation of the firm's strategy to foster training hubs on the Internet.[27]

It is also important for firms to recognise that it is only through total satisfaction of their needs that customers develop the type of firm-specific loyalty companies seek. To improve the chances that its products will totally satisfy customers, Whirlpool in the United States now uses what it calls the 'Real Whirled' training program. This program is intended to generate insights that can be passed on to the firm's sales trainers, personnel who work with employees at retail establishments to teach them how to sell Whirlpool products. Real Whirled places eight company employees into a 'retro-décor' house near a beach on Lake Michigan. These people 'spend two months living, baking, washing, cooking, and cleaning with the products their company sells. Then they take what they've learned as real-world consumers, and use those insights and experiences to train Whirlpool retailers to sell products in terms that buyers understand.'[28] In addition to serving customers currently, being able to move towards total need satisfaction increases the likelihood that the firm will retain customers' interest and earn repeat business from them. It is also important to consider the strategic value of the finding that 'companies reap far greater economic rewards from highly satisfied customers than they do from merely satisfied customer[s]'.[29] This finding seems to offer important evidence of the need for the firm to provide goods or services through which customers will reach high levels of satisfaction. Increasingly, databases are linked with customer retention rates. Among other useful outcomes, information gleaned from these databases allows the firm to tailor its offerings more precisely to satisfy individualised customer needs.[30]

Evidence suggests that strategically competitive organisations in the 21st century – those that concentrate on customers in selecting and implementing business-level strategies – will (1) seek to solve customers' problems with the goods or services they sell, (2) remain focused on the need to innovate continuously, even when their current offerings are selling well, (3) determine how to use their core competencies in ways that competitors cannot imitate, and (4) design their strategies to allow them to satisfy customers' current, anticipated and even unanticipated needs.[31] Consistent with these practices, Caterpillar, Inc., has developed a technology-based process that has customer needs as the starting point. As the driver of this process, customer needs are expected to help the firm remain a leader in developing innovative and customer-centred product technologies. Similarly, in an attempt to improve the reputation and competitive health of its brand, the Commonwealth Bank of Australia implemented its 'Make it Happen' campaign. This campaign was designed as part of its commitment to improving its understanding of customers' needs so that it can produce and deliver products that provide additional levels of satisfaction.[32]

However, to achieve strategic competitiveness in what seems to be a rapidly developing Internet-based economy, 21st-century firms will need to do even more than is called for by the four actions listed in the previous paragraph. The reason for this is that attention on the Internet is shifting from *claiming* virtual space to *defending* and *capturing* it. Three dimensions have been defined relative to customers that may facilitate competitive advantage in this context. The *reach* dimension is about access and connection to customers. For instance, the largest physical retailer in American bookstores, Barnes & Noble, carries about 200 000 titles. In Singapore, the Kinkonya bookstore claims 500 000 titles, while the typical Dymocks in Australia has around 25 000 titles. By contrast, Amazon.com offers some 4.5 million titles and is located on roughly 25 million computer screens, with additional customer connections expected in the future. Thus, its reach is significantly magnified relative to that associated with Dymocks' physical bookstores.

Reach is the most obvious difference between electronic and physical businesses. The second dimension, *richness*, is the depth and detail of information that the firm can deliver to customers, as well as collect from them. The richness dimension is causing traditional brokers to move on-line, because on-line brokers such as E*Trade and Charles Schwab are moving into the area that has been held by traditional brokerages. (See the Strategic Focus on Merrill Lynch and other on-line brokers later in the chapter.) Richness holds enormous potential for building close relationships with customers in a future dominated by e-commerce. Gaining access to rich information was prohibitively expensive before the e-commerce information era.

Affiliation is the third dimension and focuses on relationship with the customer. Gofish.com creates affiliation by creating a network of usable information for the potential car buyer. They can take the potential buyer through the specifications of the model, the options, the pricing, finance options, insurance and delivery. The buyer can be referred to the nearest dealer with the right car, and will know the right price. The next dealer in line is also known and can be used if the first one does not turn out to be satisfactory.[33]

Who: Determining the customers to serve

Customers can be divided into groups based on differences in their needs. Called **market segmentation**, this is a process through which people with similar needs are clustered into individual and identifiable groups. Market segmentation is a two-step process of naming broad product markets and segmenting them in order to select target markets and

> **Market segmentation** is a process through which people with similar needs are clustered into individual and identifiable groups.

develop suitable marketing mixes.[34] Compared to the decision that the firm will serve the needs of the 'average customer', marketing segmentation creates a framework that is important to the selection of a business-level strategy. The reason for this is that averages sometimes do not provide the type of in-depth insights about issues that are relevant to the firm's strategic actions.

Almost any identifiable human or organisational characteristic can be used to subdivide a market into segments that differ from one another in terms of a given characteristic. In the ultra-luxury automobile market, for example, Rolls-Royce Motor Cars Ltd suggests that its Bentleys and Rolls-Royces satisfy different customer needs, in that the Bentley is more of a car for people who want to drive the product, while the Rolls is intended to serve those who have a need to be driven by a chauffeur.[35] Common characteristics on which customers' needs vary are illustrated in Table 4.1. These characteristics can be used as the basis for market segmentation.

Table 4.1 | Basis for customer segmentation

Consumer markets
1. Demographic factors (age, income, sex, etc.)
2. Socio-economic factors (social class, stage in the family life cycle)
3. Geographic factors (cultural, regional and national differences)
4. Psychological factors (lifestyle, personality traits)
5. Consumption patterns (heavy, moderate and light users)
6. Perceptual factors (benefit segmentation, perceptual mapping)

Industrial markets
1. End-use segments
2. Product segments (based on technological differences or production economics)
3. Geographic segments (defined by boundaries between countries or by regional differences within them)
4. Common buying factor segments (cut across product market and geographic segments)
5. Customer size segments

Source: Adapted from S. C. Jain, 2000, *Marketing Planning and Strategy* (Cincinnati: South-Western College Publishing), p. 120.

Recently, some British pubs redesigned their facilities, and the experiences offered within them, in a manner that is intended to appeal to gender-related differences between customers (that is, men's needs versus women's needs). Industry analysts have observed that these actions, which are intended to better serve female customers' needs, have resulted in more 'female friendly' outlets. In addition, start-up ventures have surfaced to meet women's needs. These pubs are viewed as quite 'trendy'. Thus, through their analysis of demographic variables, British pub operators concluded that two market segments exist. According to one pub manager, '[W]omen have higher expectations, and are more demanding and discerning. They want staff to be welcoming and a pub to be clean and comfortable.' To meet women's needs, pubs are now providing (1) toilets that are easy to find and that are clean, well lighted and apportioned, with a full-length mirror, (2) staff with a more positive attitude towards women, especially those entering the pub alone, (3) good ventilation, and (4) airy interiors. Data showing that the number of women entering pubs once a month or more increased 8 per cent between 1991 and 1998 are seen by analysts and pub operators alike as evidence that the new approach to market segmentation has been successful.[36] It would appear that similar segmentation may be a so-far untapped opportunity in the Australian market.

Increasing segmentation of markets

In the 21st-century competitive landscape, many firms are adept at identifying precise differences among customers' needs. Armed with this understanding, companies segment customers into *competitively relevant groups*, each with its own unique needs. Thus, Australian market research, dealing with the possibilities of e-shopping for groceries, has determined that there are five types of shopper. The 'traditional' shopper includes most of the population. They shop several times a week, are not excited by new technology and have low rates of Internet usage. 'Passing shoppers' hate grocery shopping, tend to use smaller supermarkets, are brand loyal and are attracted to the e-grocery possibility. 'Value shoppers' tend to be younger, shop around, are in search of a place that meets their needs but are sceptical about e-grocers. 'Modern responsibility' shoppers work full-time, have a high income, like to spend time with the family, tend to have Internet access and are attracted to e-grocers. The 'time starved' are from a higher socio-economic group, have high weekly grocery expenditure, have Internet access, are 'time poor' and look on e-grocers as a viable alternative to traditional shopping.[37]

A range of Australian firms are now targeting one-person households. Single people make up 37 per cent of the total adult population. The numbers living alone have increased 4 per cent since 1986, fed by a rising divorce rate and increases in the number of people who defer marriage. The group is diverse – for example, the age ranges from around 20 to 80; some own houses, others do not; most work, but some don't. Nevertheless, opportunities exist. Heinz-Watties have a 'Heinz Big Eat' range of canned bean and pasta meals targeted at single men aged between 15 and 40 who cannot cook well or can't be bothered cooking. Simplot also market to single people. Their Leggo's Stir Through Pasta Sauce is aimed at reluctant single cooks, while their Big Sister brand of puddings is now available in single serves.[38]

Particularly in instances in which focused business-level strategies are being used to serve unique market segments, companies may wish to capitalise on the fact that product uniqueness exists within categories, as well as in terms of the absolute number of available goods and services. For example, in comparison to the past's somewhat standardised soft drinks, consumers now choose from among different brands and different versions – sugar-free drinks, caffeine-free beverages, bottled water (flat or sparkling), and so forth. However, companies' efforts to create a huge set of goods and services that is intended to satisfy unique needs may be confusing to some customers. This confusion can result from the sheer number of goods and services that are available to consumers across the globe.[39] Selecting a business-level strategy that is called for by conditions in the firm's external and internal environments and then implementing that strategy effectively reduces the likelihood that the firm will confuse its customers through its product offerings.

The teenage population in all OECD countries is a major segment for marketers to aim at. They have special needs and, increasingly, have money to spend in satisfying them.

What: Determining the customer needs to satisfy

As a firm decides whom it will serve, it must simultaneously identify the targeted customer group's needs that its goods or services can satisfy. Top-level managers play a critical role in efforts to recognise and understand these needs. Their capacity to gain valuable insights from listening to and studying customers influences product, technology and distribution decisions. For example, upper-level executives at Volkswagen AG heard concerns from customers about the firm's decision to base several Volkswagen and Audi models on the same chassis and to use the same transmissions. Some consumers asked the firm why they should pay for the premier Audi brand when they could obtain much of the technology at a lower cost by purchasing a Volkswagen product. In response to these concerns, Volkswagen AG 'intends to invest six billion marks ([US]$3.32 billion) during the next few years to ensure that each of its brands retains a separate identity'.[40]

An additional competitive advantage accrues to firms that are capable of anticipating and then satisfying needs that were unknown to target customers. Firms that are able to do this provide customers with unexpected value – that is, a product performance capability or characteristic they did not request, yet do value.[41] Moreover, anticipating customers' needs yields opportunities for firms to shape their industry's future and gain an early competitive advantage (called a **first-mover advantage** and discussed in Chapter 5).

> **First-mover advantage** is an early competitive advantage that allows firms to anticipate customers' needs and shape their industry's future.

How: Determining core competencies necessary to satisfy customers' needs

Firms use their *core competencies* to implement value-creating strategies and satisfy customers' needs. One of the strategic imperatives at IBM is to convert the firm's technological core competence more quickly into commercial products that customers value. In addition, IBM's intensive knowledge of its customers' businesses has helped it to turn its historical focus on customer service into a mainline business. In this context, since the beginning of Lou Gerstner's tenure as the firm's CEO, IBM has focused on providing customer 'solutions' to clients. Historically, customer solutions were built around IBM's hardware. However, Gerstner has engineered a remarkable transformation, making services rather than products the firm's growth engine. For instance, fitting in with its focus, IBM's software division is competing quite effectively, earning in excess of 20 per cent pre-tax profit margins. The computer sales division is now the one encountering performance problems. For example, IBM's PC division lost US$992 million in 1998, although server computers were still yielding 25.7 per cent pre-tax profit margins. Monitors, storage equipment and memory chips were far less profitable, recording pre-tax profit margins of 5.8 per cent. With increases of 22 per cent in services revenue, this segment accounted for 28 per cent of IBM's 1998 sales of US$82 billion. It is also interesting to point out that IBM's services growth, which is expected to increase as the 21st century proceeds, has also helped the company to sell its hardware. This suggests that a focus on customers' needs can help a business across a number of competitive dimensions.[42]

One of the most solid and trusted suppliers in the electronics and computer industries, Hewlett-Packard (HP), uses its engineering core competence to manufacture products that are renowned for their quality.[43] But changes such as those at IBM have sparked the interest of HP and other companies. In fact, HP has created an e-services division. Instead of selling multimillion-dollar computers, this division sells computing power over a network for a monthly fee. For purchasers, the value created by buying HP's services lies in avoiding the trouble and expense of operating their own systems. In running an e-commerce site for a client, HP can charge its customers a percentage of the client's transaction revenues. Ann Livermore, CEO of HP's US$14 billion Enterprise Computing Solutions (the e-service division), estimates that such a fee may account for 80 per cent of the division's revenues.[44]

Next, we discuss the business-level strategies firms use when pursuing strategic competitiveness and above-average returns.

Types of business-level strategy

Business-level strategies are concerned with a firm's industry position relative to those of competitors.[45] Companies that have established favourable industry positions are better able to cope with the five forces of competition (see Chapter 2). To position itself, a firm must decide whether its intended actions will allow it to perform activities differently from the way its rivals do, or to perform different activities from those of its rivals.[46] Thus, favourably positioned firms may have a competitive advantage over their industry rivals. This is, of course, important in that the universal objective of all companies is to develop and sustain competitive advantages.[47] Improperly positioned firms encounter competitive difficulties and may fail to sustain competitive advantages.

Earlier, we mentioned that firms choose from among four generic business-level strategies to establish and exploit a competitive advantage within a particular competitive scope: *cost leadership*, *differentiation*, *focused cost leadership* and *focused differentiation* (see Figure 4.1). A fifth generic business-level strategy, the integrated cost leadership/differentiation strategy, has evolved through firms' efforts to find the most effective ways to exploit their competitive advantages.

Figure 4.1 | Four generic strategies

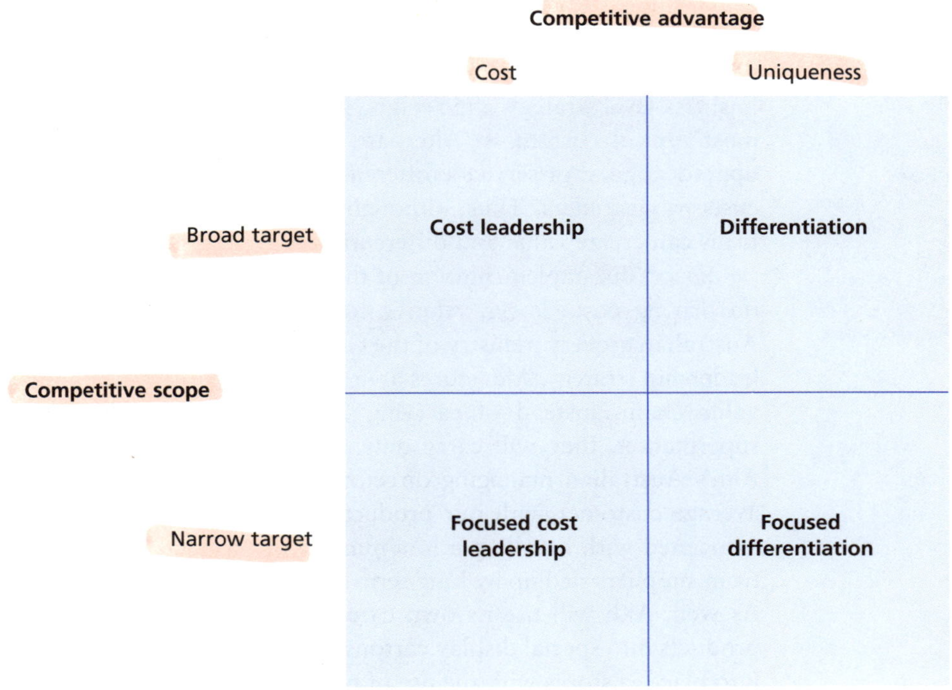

	Competitive advantage	
Competitive scope	Cost	Uniqueness
Broad target	Cost leadership	Differentiation
Narrow target	Focused cost leadership	Focused differentiation

Source: Adapted with the permission of The Free Press, a Division of Simon & Schuster, Inc., from Michael E. Porter, *Competitive Advantage: Creating and Sustaining Superior Performance*, Figure 1-3, p. 12. Copyright © 1985, 1998 by Michael E. Porter.

In selecting a business-level strategy, firms evaluate two types of competitive advantage: 'lower cost than rivals, or the ability to differentiate and command a premium price that exceeds the extra cost of doing so'.⁴⁸ Having lower cost than rivals derives from the firm's ability to perform activities differently than rivals; being able to differentiate indicates a capacity to perform different activities.⁴⁹ Competitive advantage is achieved within some scope. Scope has several dimensions, including the group of product and customer segments served and the array of geographic markets in which a firm competes. Competitive advantage is sought by competing in many customer segments when implementing either the cost leadership or the differentiation strategy. In contrast, through the implementation of focus strategies, firms seek either a cost advantage or a differentiation advantage in a *narrow competitive scope* or *segment*. With focus strategies, the firm 'selects a segment or group of segments in the industry and tailors its strategy to serving them to the exclusion of others'.⁵⁰

None of the five business-level strategies is inherently or universally superior to the others.⁵¹ The effectiveness of each strategy is contingent on the opportunities and threats that exist in a firm's external environment *and* the possibilities permitted by the firm's unique resources, capabilities and core competencies. It is critical, therefore, for the firm to select a strategy that is appropriate in light of its competencies and environmental opportunities; once selected, the strategy should be implemented carefully and consistently.

Cost leadership strategy

A **cost leadership strategy** is an integrated set of actions designed to produce or deliver goods or services at the lowest cost, relative to that of competitors, with features that are acceptable to customers. A **differentiation strategy** is an integrated set of actions designed to produce or deliver goods or services that customers perceive as being different in ways that are important to them.⁵² The differentiation strategy calls for firms to sell non-standardised products to customers with unique needs. The cost leadership strategy should achieve low cost relative to that of competitors, while not ignoring means of differentiation that customers value. Firms seeking competitive advantage through this business-level strategy often sell no-frills, standardised goods or services to the industry's most typical customers. Alternatively, the differentiation strategy should consistently upgrade a good or service's differentiated features that customers value without ignoring costs to customers. Thus, although cost leadership and differentiation strategies differ, firms can create value and differentiation strategies through either one.⁵³

Successful implementation of the cost leadership strategy requires a consistent focus on driving costs lower, relative to competitors' costs. The entry into the profitable Australian grocery industry of the German discount supermarket Aldi is based on the cost leadership strategy. Aldi stores are organised in order to minimise costs at all levels in the value chain. Instead of carrying 30 000 products, like the typical large Australian supermarket, they will carry only around 600 of the most popular lines of groceries. Aldi's Australian managing director believes that 'we can cover the daily needs of the average customer with our product range'. Costs are minimised because of economies associated with handling a low number of products, and also because they are sourced from suppliers tied up by long-term contracts that agree to supply to Aldi's specifications. As well, Aldi will use its own carefully designed warehouses and place its own brand products into special display cartons that can be stocked directly on to shelves or wheeled into place in stores with the use of pallets. The bays in Aldi stores are organised the same

---

A **cost leadership strategy** is an integrated set of actions designed to produce or deliver goods or services at the lowest cost, relative to competitors, with features that are acceptable to customers.

A **differentiation strategy** is an integrated set of actions designed to produce goods or services that customers perceive as being different in ways that are important to them.

way as in their warehouses but in the opposite order – this makes stocking easy. Cashiers use the latest scanning technology and, in order to minimise fatigue, sit in the best possible chairs at the end of long conveyor belts that are designed to minimise queues. However, simply reducing costs is not equivalent to implementing the cost leadership strategy. Aldi's products are of high quality and consumer satisfaction is a central aim of the Aldi approach. They therefore expect to retain their customers.[54]

Firms that are fully committed to using the cost leadership strategy therefore drive their costs lower through investments in efficient-scale facilities, tight cost and overhead control, and cost minimisations in such areas as service, sales force, and research and development. The Australian managing director of Aldi summarises this position well: 'We think about the whole process between manufacturers and consumers. We think about every single step and how we can streamline that step and be more efficient.' One of the lowest-cost steel producers in the world, the US firm Nucor Corporation has also relied on investments in efficient-scale facilities to achieve strategic competitiveness (the firm has operated profitably every year since 1966) through its cost leadership strategy.[55] Similarly, Unifi, Inc., a company that is one of the world's largest texturisers of filament polyester and nylon fibre, makes significant investments in its manufacturing technologies to drive its costs lower in an environment of upward pressure on prices for raw materials and packaging supplies. Already one of the most efficient producers in its industry, the company recently completed a modernisation program for texturising polyester. Unifi also intends to modernise and expand its nylon, covered-yarn, and dyed-yarn operations. Combined, these actions are expected to increase the firm's technological lead over its rivals and further reduce its production costs.[56]

As described in Chapter 3, firms use the value chain to determine the parts of the company's operations that create value and those that do not. Shown in Figure 4.2 are primary and support activities that allow a firm to create value through the cost leadership strategy. Companies that cannot link the activities mentioned in this figure lack the resources and capabilities (and hence the core competencies) that are required to use the cost leadership strategy successfully.

In using the cost leadership strategy, firms must be careful not to completely ignore sources of differentiation (for example, innovative designs, service after the sale, product quality, and so on) that customers value.

Effective implementation of the cost leadership strategy allows a firm to earn above-average returns in spite of the presence of strong competitive forces.

Rivalry with existing competitors

Having the low-cost position serves as a valuable defence against rivals. Because of the cost leader's advantageous position, rivals hesitate to compete on the basis of price. Instead, competitors try to compete against cost leaders through some means of differentiation. In South America, for example, top-level executives at Disco SA concluded that they could not compete against giant retailers Wal-Mart and Carrefour of France on the basis of price alone. Offering products at prices nearly as low as its largest competitors, Disco believes that it provides more convenience and service to customers. Carrying a wide range of brands and perishables, Disco stores offer home delivery, telephone ordering and childcare. Strategically, the firm's executives believe that customers will accept a slight increase in the cost of the product in return for the store's conveniences and services.[57] However, if rivals challenge the firm to compete on the basis of price, the low-cost firm can still earn at least average returns, while competitors may experience below-average returns through competitive rivalry.[58]

Figure 4.2 | Examples of value-creating activities associated with the cost leadership strategy

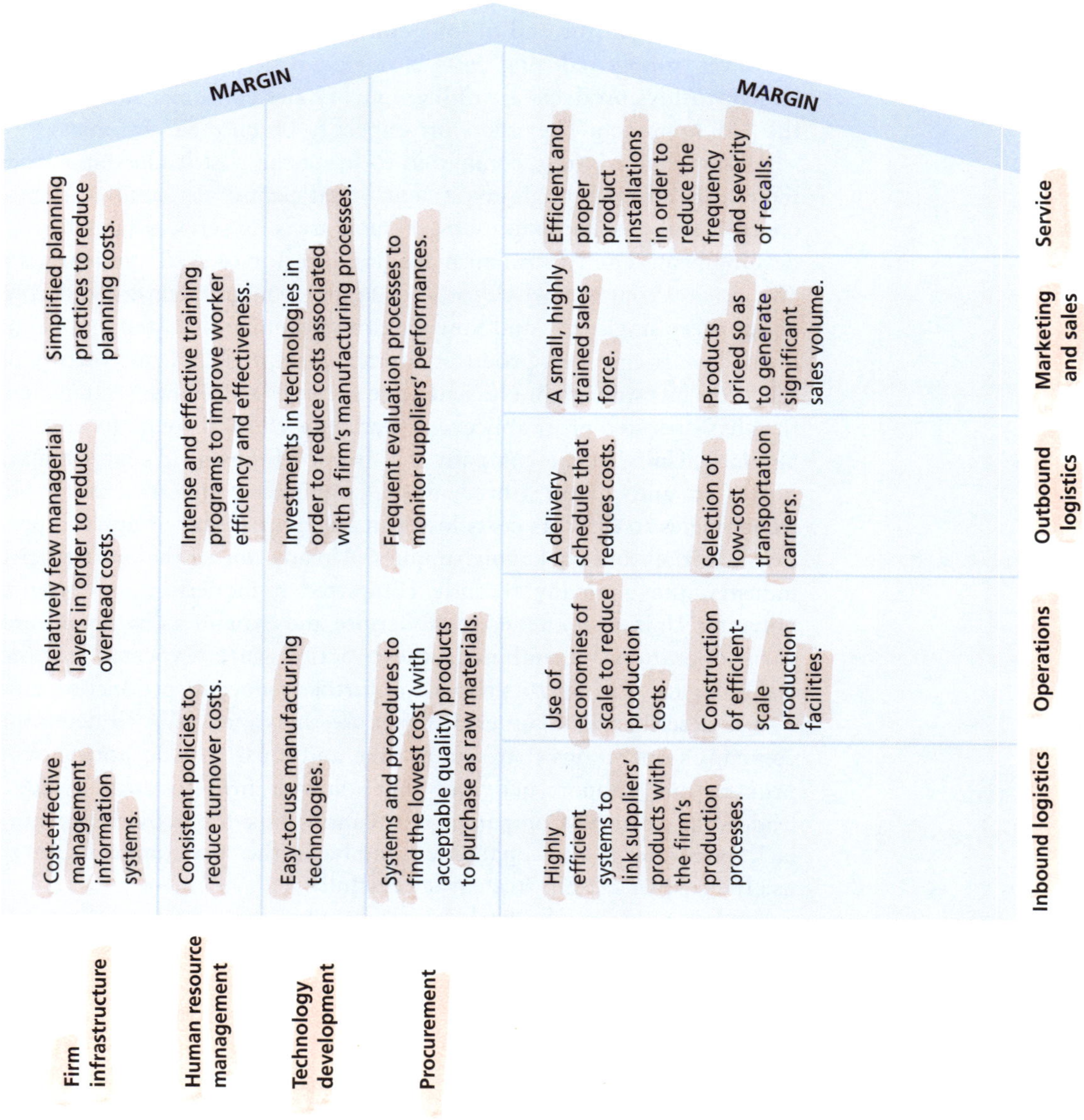

	Inbound logistics	Operations	Outbound logistics	Marketing and sales	Service
Firm infrastructure	Cost-effective management information systems.	Relatively few managerial layers in order to reduce overhead costs.		Simplified planning practices to reduce planning costs.	
Human resource management	Consistent policies to reduce turnover costs.			Intense and effective training programs to improve worker efficiency and effectiveness.	
Technology development	Easy-to-use manufacturing technologies.			Investments in technologies in order to reduce costs associated with a firm's manufacturing processes.	
Procurement	Systems and procedures to find the lowest cost (with acceptable quality) products to purchase as raw materials.			Frequent evaluation processes to monitor suppliers' performances.	
	Highly efficient systems to link suppliers' products with the firm's production processes.	Use of economies of scale to reduce production costs. Construction of efficient-scale production facilities.	A delivery schedule that reduces costs. Selection of low-cost transportation carriers.	A small, highly trained sales force. Products priced so as to generate significant sales volume.	Efficient and proper product installations in order to reduce the frequency and severity of recalls.

Source: Adapted with the permission of The Free Press, a Division of Simon & Schuster, Inc., from Michael E. Porter, *Competitive Advantage: Creating and Sustaining Superior Performance*. Copyright © 1985, 1998 by Michael E. Porter.

Bargaining power of buyers (customers)

Powerful customers can force the cost leader to reduce its prices, but price will not be driven below the level at which the next-most-efficient industry competitor is able to earn average returns. Although powerful customers could force the cost leader to reduce prices even below this level, they probably would not choose to do so. Still lower prices would prevent the next-most-efficient competitor from earning average returns, resulting in its exit from the market and leaving the cost leader in a stronger position. Customers lose their power and pay higher prices when they are forced to purchase from a firm operating in an industry without rivals.

Occasionally, a firm's bargaining power allows it to transfer increased costs to customers. For example, when Unifi incurred substantially higher costs for raw materials and packaging products, it was able to pass the costs on to customers because the firm is a dominant supplier in many of its markets (with up to a 70 per cent share in some markets).[59]

Bargaining power of suppliers

The cost leader operates with margins greater than those of competitors. Among other benefits, higher margins relative to competitors' make it possible for the cost leader to absorb suppliers' price increases. When an industry is faced with substantial increases in the cost of its supplies, the cost leader may be the only one able to pay the higher prices and continue to earn either average or above-average returns. Alternatively, powerful cost leaders may be able to force suppliers to hold down their prices, reducing their margins in the process.

Potential entrants

Through continuous efforts to reduce costs to levels that are lower than competitors', cost leaders become very efficient. Because they enhance profit margins, ever-improving levels of efficiency serve as a significant entry barrier to potential entrants. New entrants must be willing to accept no better than average returns until they gain the experience required to approach the efficiency of the cost leader. To earn even average returns, new entrants must have the competencies required to match the cost levels of other competitors.

The cost leader's low profit margins (relative to margins earned by firms implementing the differentiation strategy) make it necessary for the cost leader to sell large volumes of its product to earn above-average returns. Founded in 1976, headquartered in Taiwan, and selling its products in over 100 countries, including Singapore, Malaysia and Australia, Acer Computer Corporation follows the cost leadership strategy. In describing Acer's strategy, a business analyst noted that the firm's 'core competency is building cutting edge personal computers faster and cheaper than the competition'.[60] According to Acer's CEO, margins on his company's products, including its personal computers, are 'shell-thin'. 'But sell enough of them,' he believes, 'and a formula emerges: Low margins and high turnover can be a recipe for success.'[61] The cost leadership strategy and the resulting emphasis on high volume and low margins are the foundation for the firm's 20-plus-year effort to become Taiwan's first global brand-name powerhouse, similar to IBM or Sony Corp.[62] However, firms striving to be the cost leader must avoid pricing their products at a level that precludes them from earning above-average returns and encourages new industry entrants.

Product substitutes

Compared to its industry rivals, the cost leader holds an attractive position in terms of product substitutes. When faced with the possibility of a substitute, the cost leader has more flexibility than its competitors. To retain customers, the cost leader can reduce the price of its good or service. With still lower prices and features of acceptable quality, the cost leader increases the probability that customers will prefer its product rather than a substitute. As an example, there are still millions of cassette tapes sold in world markets because of lower prices, even though CDs have taken over leadership as a substitute. MP3.com and other on-line distributors now sell music over the Internet through a digital-format substitute, but CDs are still dominant, partly because of legal and ownership problems that need to be resolved regarding the new format.[63] At the same time, another market has emerged in Europe and Australia for vinyl-driven music, with DJs and serious music aficionados returning to the long playing record. In the latter case, the 'warm' quality of vinyl-driven jazz and elite 1970s' rock music is attracting increasing numbers of the cognoscente.

Competitive risks of the cost leadership strategy

The cost leadership strategy is not risk free. One risk is that the cost leader's manufacturing equipment could become obsolete because of competitors' technological innovations. These innovations may allow rivals to produce at costs lower than those of the original cost leader.

A second risk is that too much focus on cost reductions may occur at the expense of trying to understand customers' needs or concerns regarding issues and other competitive dimensions. An emphasis on continuous cost reductions is somewhat legendary at Britain's Lloyds TSB Group plc. The chairman, Sir Brian Pitman, takes the second-class train to work, whereas his counterparts are driven to their offices. When travelling on business, the bank's employees are expected to book stays only at 'cheap' hotels. If a taxi is used, the employee, not the bank, pays for the service. According to analysts, though, the bank earns above-average returns through its use of the cost leadership strategy. Evidence for that assertion is provided by the fact that Lloyds recently earned a net 33.5 per cent return on shareholders' investments. This performance is quite attractive compared to those of major competitors Wells Fargo & Co. (17.4 per cent) and Deutsche Bank AG (19.6 per cent). However, Lloyds TSB Group may be risking an understanding of customer needs in that, according to analysts, some of the bank's customers 'complain that they bear the brunt of Lloyds' bottom-line focus'.[64] Note that, because of their focus on continuously driving costs lower, firms that follow the cost leadership strategy sometimes fail to detect significant changes in customers' needs or in competitors' efforts to differentiate what has traditionally been an undifferentiated, commodity-like product.

A final risk of the cost leadership strategy concerns imitation. Using their own core competencies (see Chapter 3), competitors sometimes learn how to successfully imitate the cost leader's strategy. When this occurs, the cost leader must find ways to increase the value that its good or service provides to customers. Commonly, value is increased by selling the current product at an even lower price or by adding features that customers value while maintaining price. Even cost leaders must be careful when reducing prices to a still lower level. If the firm prices its good or service at an unrealistically low level (a level at which it will be difficult to retain satisfactory margins), customers' expectations about what they envision to be a reasonable price become difficult to reverse.

Differentiation strategy

With the differentiation strategy, the *unique* attributes and characteristics of a firm's product (other than cost) provide value to customers. Because a differentiated product satisfies customers' unique needs, firms following the differentiation strategy usually charge premium prices. To do this successfully, a 'firm must truly be unique at something or be perceived as unique'.[65] The ability to sell a good or service at a price that exceeds what was spent to create the product's differentiated features allows the firm to outperform its rivals and earn above-average returns.

Rather than costs, the differentiation strategy's focus is on continuously investing in and developing features that differentiate a good or service in ways that customers value. Overall, a firm using the differentiation strategy seeks to be different from its competitors along as many dimensions as possible. The less similarity between a firm's goods or services and those of competitors, the more buffered the firm is from rivals' actions. Commonly recognised differentiated goods include Porsche motorcars, Country Road clothing and Caterpillar's heavy-duty earth-moving equipment. Thought by some to be the world's most expensive and prestigious consulting firm, McKinsey & Co. is a well-known example of a firm that offers differentiated services.

A product can be differentiated in an almost endless number of ways. Unusual features, responsive customer service, rapid product innovations and technological

Dick Smith's food products satisfy needs for local identity. The success of this business rests on the strength of this need in Australia. The established nature of the generic Australian Dick Smith (glasses and mop of hair) brand helped the food business establish itself quickly.

leadership, perceived prestige and status, different tastes, and engineering design and performance are examples of approaches to differentiation. In fact, virtually anything a firm can do to create real or perceived value for customers is a basis for differentiation. The challenge is to identity features that create value for the customer. For example, Mambo produces irreverent and colourful designs for surf and street-wear that are highly distinctive in youth-oriented clothing. These designs help Mambo to achieve a healthy market share in a competitive industry.[66] Dick Smith Foods delivers on the promise that it is 'as Australian as you can get', running against Kraft Foods, whose parent company is the cigarette giant Philip Morris, with a distinctively nationalist and anti-smoking message. Both companies are strongly differentiated from competitors along strong, locally Australian dimensions.

The Strategic Focus on Sony Corporation shows how a firm can consistently create value for customers by identifying and then providing desired features. Through this strategy, which is implemented through use of the firm's core competencies, Sony earns above-average returns.

Strategic Focus Corporate

Sony Corporation's use of the differentiation business-level strategy

Sony has long used differentiation as its business-level strategy. Frequently, the firm's core competence of product miniaturisation is the foundation on which its products are differentiated. Miniaturised radios, televisions, transistors, the Camcorder and the Walkman cassette recorder are examples of products that Sony developed through the use of this core competence. More recently, the miniaturisation competence has been used to manufacture the firm's laptop computers. The success of Sony's laptop, the Vaio, is somewhat remarkable, considering that only four major PC brands remain on US retailer shelves because of the intensity of rivalry among competitors (see Chapters 2 and 5). Furthermore, the company's success with this product is noteworthy in that Sony is the only firm with three digital devices – the PC, the TV and the video-game machine – that are becoming wired into networks.

The most recent version of the Vaio, the 505 series, is slim and silvery in colour with grey-toned accents. Teiyu Goto, a Sony engineer, originally designed the model so that it was 22 millimetres in thickness. Instead of using a standard plastic body, Goto designed the 505 series to be sheathed in a glossy magnesium alloy. To attract customers, Sony originally chose to sacrifice function for style. Ultimately, however, as the components advanced and became smaller, Sony was able to improve the Vaio's performance and memory capacity. The combination of the product's differentiated features, including style, then satisfied the needs of customers who were willing to pay a slightly higher price for the Sony PC.

The digital camera is another example of Sony's ability to design and produce products with differentiated features that customers value. Introduced in 1997, Sony's digital camera (called the Mavica) does not use film. As with competitors' offerings, the Mavica etches images on to electronic sensors, translating them into computer-readable binary data to create photos that can then be printed through the use of a PC. Digital cameras designed and sold by Eastman Kodak and Casio Computer Company were the original leaders in this segment of the photography market. The feature that differentiates the Mavica from competitors' products and that provides value to customers is ease of use. With the Mavica, the customer uses a standard floppy disk to take photographs. The disk is then removed from the camera and inserted into a PC to print pictures. Through this differentiated feature's capabilities, even novices are able to use the Mavica successfully. Also contributing to the product's ease-of-use feature is the fact that no additional cable hookups or adapters are required to view the images, in contrast to Kodak's and Casio's digital cameras.

Compared to Kodak's and Casio's digital cameras, the Mavica is more expensive and produces pictures that are not as clear. However, in 1998, sales of the Mavica were 50 per cent higher on a year-to-year basis. This result suggests that customers value the ease-of-use differentiated feature more than the clarity-of-picture differentiated feature that is associated with Sony's competitors' digital cameras. The Mavica accounted for US$1.2 million of the estimated US$12 million point-and-shoot photographs sold in the United States in 1998 and helped Sony to gain prominence as a brand name in digital cameras and as a major player in photography.

As noted earlier, the differentiation strategy yields long-term competitive success when the firm invests continuously to offer customers differentiated features that provide value to them. Now the market leader, Sony intends to improve the quality of the images that are generated by its digital cameras. One step the company has already taken is the introduction of a new camera that uses a 'memory cap stick', a removable device with lots of storage space and higher resolution. Sony's intention is to reduce the value of competitors' clarity-of-picture differentiated feature by inducing current customers to purchase the firm's more advanced digital cameras. This strategic action is consistent with Sony's practices. For example, once consumers became familiar with the firm's camcorder, Sony began to move to the smaller, non-VHS format, with better picture and sound quality. Thus, Sony has effectively used the differentiation business-level strategy to design and sell multiple products.

Sources: P. Beamish, 1999, 'Sony's Yoshihide Nakamura on structure and decision making', *Academy of Management Executive*, 13(4), pp. 12–16; R. A. Guth and E. Ramstad, 1999, 'How Sony turned a skinny laptop into an unlikely PC success', *Wall Street Journal*, 12 November, pp. B1, B6; A. Klein, 1999, 'How Sony beat digital-camera rivals', *Wall Street Journal*, 25 January, pp. B1, B4.

As his next strategic challenge, Sony's CEO, Nobuyuki Idei, expects to make money by linking Web-based products and media to provide interactive versions of music, movies and games that can be downloaded on to Sony-made devices. 'The hardware business is peanuts,' he says. 'But the distribution of programs will be big.'[67] However, such a strategy will require that Sony change its value chain significantly.

A firm's value chain can be used to determine whether it can link the activities required to create value through implementation of the differentiation strategy. Examples of primary and support activities that are commonly used to differentiate a good or service are shown in Figure 4.3. Companies without the core competencies needed to link these activities cannot expect to implement the differentiation strategy successfully.

As explained next, the successful use of the differentiation strategy allows a firm to earn above-average returns in spite of the presence of strong competitive forces.

Figure 4.3 | Examples of value-creating activities associated with the differentiation strategy

Support activities	Primary activities – examples
Firm infrastructure	Highly developed information systems to better understand customers' purchasing preferences. — A company-wide emphasis on the importance of producing high-quality products.
Human resource management	Compensation programs intended to encourage worker creativity and productivity. — Superior personnel training.
Technology development	Strong capability in basic research. — Investments in technologies that will allow the firm to produce highly differentiated products.
Procurement	Systems and procedures used to find the highest-quality raw materials. — Purchase of highest-quality replacement parts.
Inbound logistics	Superior handling of incoming raw materials so as to minimise damage and improve the quality of the final product.
Operations	Consistent manufacturing of attractive products. Rapid responses to customers' unique manufacturing specifications.
Outbound logistics	Accurate and responsive order-processing procedures. Rapid and timely product deliveries to customers.
Marketing and sales	Extensive granting of credit buying arrangements for customers. Extensive personal relationships with buyers and suppliers.
Service	Extensive buyer training to assure high-quality product installations. Complete field stocking of replacement parts.

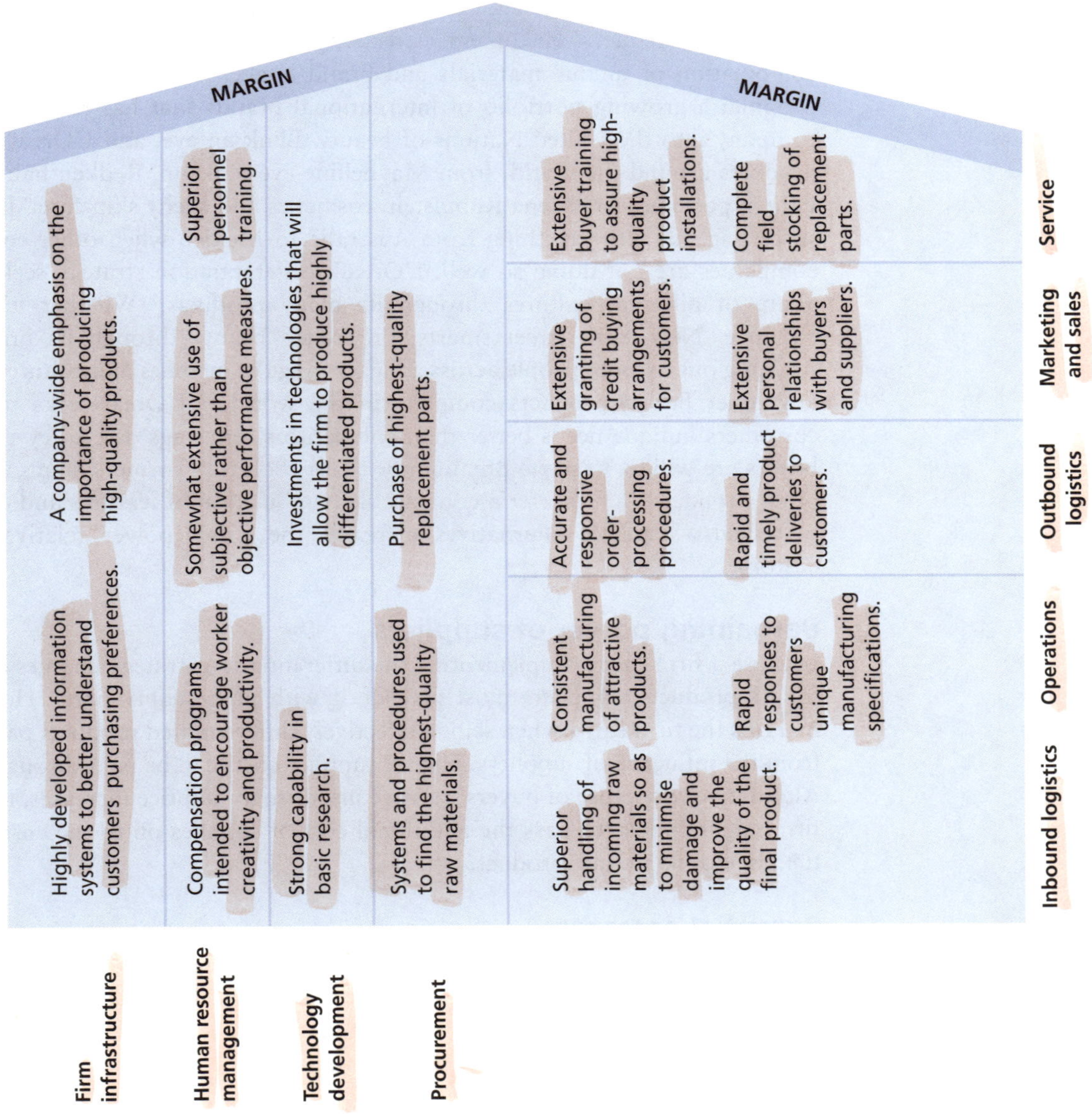

Source: Adapted with the permission of The Free Press, a Division of Simon & Schuster, Inc., from Michael E. Porter, *Competitive Advantage: Creating and Sustaining Superior Performance*, Figure 4-1, p. 122. Copyright © 1985, 1998 by Michael E. Porter.

Rivalry with existing competitors

Customers tend to be loyal purchasers of products that are differentiated in ways that are meaningful to them. As their loyalty to a brand increases, customers' sensitivity to price increases is reduced. This relationship between brand loyalty and price sensitivity insulates a firm from competitive rivalry. Thus, McKinsey & Co. is insulated from its competitors, even on the basis of price, as long as it continues to satisfy the differentiated needs of what appears to be a loyal customer group. The same is true of Mambo as long as they can continue to deliver the fun/irreverent message. This may become more difficult with the March 2000 sale of the company to Gazal Corp. The creative centre of Mambo will remain with the label, but may struggle with the relocation to a more conventional company.[68]

Bargaining power of buyers (customers)

The uniqueness of differentiated goods or services insulates a firm from competitive rivalry and reduces customers' sensitivity to price increases. On the basis of a combination of unique materials and brand image, 'L'Oreal has developed a winning formula: a growing portfolio of international brands that has transformed the French company into the United Nations of beauty. Blink an eye, and L'Oreal has just sold 85 products around the world, from Maybelline eye makeup, Redken hair care and Ralph Lauren perfumes to Helena Rubinstein cosmetics and Vichy skin care.' L'Oreal is finding success in markets stretching from Australia to Mexico when other consumer product companies are not doing so well. L'Oreal's differentiation strategy seeks to convey the allure of different cultures through its many products: 'Whether it's selling Italian elegance, New York street smarts, or French beauty through its brands, L'Oreal is reaching out to more people across a bigger range of incomes and cultures than just about any other beauty-products company in the world.'[69] L'Oreal seeks to satisfy certain customers' unique needs better than competitors' offerings do. A key reason that some buyers are willing to pay a premium price for the firm's cosmetic items is that, for them, other products do not offer a comparable combination of features and cost. The lack of perceived acceptable alternatives increases the firm's power relative to that of its customers.

Bargaining power of suppliers

Because a firm that is implementing the differentiation strategy charges a premium price for its products, suppliers must provide it with high-quality parts. However, the high margins the firm earns when selling effectively differentiated products partially insulate it from the influence of suppliers. Higher supplier costs can be paid through these margins. Alternatively, because of buyers' relative insensitivity to price increases, the differentiated firm might choose to pass the additional cost of supplies on to the customer by raising the price of its unique product.

Potential entrants

Customer loyalty and the need to overcome the uniqueness of a differentiated product are substantial entry barriers faced by potential entrants. Entering an industry under these conditions typically demands significant investments of resources and a willingness to be patient while seeking the loyalty of customers.

Product substitutes

Firms selling brand-name goods and services to loyal customers are positioned effectively against product substitutes. In contrast, companies without brand loyalty are more subject to their customers switching either to products which offer differentiated features that serve the same function as the current product (particularly if the substitute has a lower price) or to products which offer more features that perform more attractive functions.

Competitive risks of the differentiation strategy

Like the other business-level strategies, the differentiation strategy is not risk free. One risk is that customers might decide that the price differential between the differentiator's and the cost leader's product is too large. In this instance, a firm may be providing differentiated features that exceed customers' needs. When that happens, the firm is vulnerable to competitors that are able to offer customers a combination of features and price that is more consistent with their needs.

Another risk of the differentiation strategy is that a firm's means of differentiation no longer provide value for which customers are willing to pay. The differentiation strategy becomes less valuable if imitation by rivals causes customers to perceive that competitors offer the same good or service, sometimes at a lower price. For example, in the early 1990s, the Tasmanian optometrical industry changed as a result of the entry of the Australian giant, OPSM. The new entrant offered a similar (professional) optometrical consultation, but a wider range of frames and other services than the traditional owner/operator firms. Traditional operators differentiated between each other mainly on the basis of a traditional offering of professional services – OPSM offered more services and lower prices while apparently matching the core service of vision assessment.

A third risk of the differentiation strategy is that learning can narrow customers' perceptions of the value of a firm's differentiated features. The value of the IBM name on personal computers was a differentiated feature for which some customers were willing to pay a premium price as the product emerged. However, as customers familiarised themselves with the standard features, and as a host of PC clones entered the market, IBM brand loyalty began to fail. Clones offered customers features similar to those of the IBM product at a substantially lower price, reducing the attractiveness of IBM's product. Even currently, IBM's relatively new Aptiva line is failing to meet company expectations. In assessing the situation, one dealer observed that while the Aptiva is a 'cool' machine, it simply costs too much for the features that it provides relative to the combination of features and prices of products from competitors such as Compaq and Hewlett-Packard.[70]

A fourth risk is concerned with counterfeiting. Increasingly, counterfeit goods – products that attempt to convey differentiated features to customers at significantly reduced prices – are a concern for many firms that use the differentiation strategy. In the United Kingdom, for example, 'It has been estimated that the market for parallel imports, cars, toiletries and clothing imported to the UK without the brand owners' consent and sold at substantial discounts to retail prices, is worth 1.3 billion pounds a year.'[71] Companies often seek help from governments and their import regulations to curb the problem that can surface because of this particular risk of the differentiation strategy.

Focus strategies

In contrast to firms that employ the cost leadership and differentiation strategies, a company that implements a focus strategy seeks to use its core competencies to serve the needs of a certain industry segment: a particular buyer group (for example, youths or senior citizens), a different segment of a product line (for example, products for professional painters or those for 'do-it-yourselfers'), or a different geographic market (for example, the different states in Australia).[72] Thus, a **focus strategy** is an integrated set of actions that is designed to produce or deliver goods or services that serve the needs of a particular competitive segment. Although the breadth of a target is clearly a matter of degree, the essence of the focus strategy 'is the exploitation of a narrow target's differences from the balance of the industry'.[73] As an example, Cisco Systems, mentioned

> A **focus strategy** is an integrated set of actions designed to produce or deliver goods and services that serve the needs of a particular competitive segment.

in the chapter's Opening Case, has shifted increasing percentages of its sales to smaller companies – a particular buyer group.[74] Through successful implementation of a focus strategy, firms such as Cisco Systems can gain a competitive advantage in chosen target market segments, even though they do not possess an industry-wide competitive advantage.[75]

As our discussion implies, the foundation of the focus strategy is that a firm can serve a particular segment of an industry more effectively or efficiently than can industry-wide competitors. Success with a focus strategy rests on a firm's ability either to find segments whose unique needs are so specialised that broad-based competitors choose not to serve them, or to locate a segment being served poorly by the industry-wide competitors.[76] For instance, the US firm Station Inn serves the needs of a particular buyer group that does not appear to be of interest to industry-wide competitors such as Hilton and Sheraton, among others. Through its focus strategy, the Station Inn serves the unique needs of railroad buffs. Instead of getting mints on their pillows and pay-per-view movies in their rooms, these railroad devotees stay in a hotel that is located a mere 35 metres from major rail tracks. Through the night, guests sleep 'next to thundering freight trains, more than 60 of them every 24 hours'.[77]

As noted at the beginning of the chapter, the Internet is having a significant influence on business-level strategies. This is clearly the case with focus business-level strategies. Some analysts believe that the Internet allows market segments to be refined with greater and greater specificity in terms of unique customer needs. In particular, start-up ventures seek to serve what often are very narrow market segments or niches. Frequently, the name of these companies gives the focus: Just-socks.com; Raremaps.com; Mustardstore.com; Uglies.com (ugly boxer shorts); and Steelofthenight.com (steel drums).[78] For each of these ventures, as is the case for every company using the focus business-level strategy, the intention is to serve the needs of a specific market segment better than the industry-wide competitor can.

Firms can create value for customers in specific and unique market segments by using one of two different focus strategies: focused cost leadership and focused differentiation.

Focused cost leadership strategy

The global furniture retailer Ikea seeks to provide customers with 'affordable solutions for better living' through use of the focused cost leadership strategy.[79] Young buyers desiring style at a low cost make up Ikea's market segment. For these customers, the firm offers home furnishings that combine good design, function and quality with low prices. Several practices are used to keep costs low. For example, instead of relying primarily on third-party manufacturers, Ikea's engineers design low-cost, modular furniture that is ready for assembly by customers. Inside the stores, Ikea uses a self-service model rather than having sales associates trail customers from one room of furniture to the next. Typically, competitors' furniture stores display multiple varieties of a single item in single rooms. Thus, customers examine dining room tables in one room, living room sofas in another room, and beds in yet another room. In contrast to this approach, Ikea displays its products in room-like settings. Viewing different living combinations (with sofas, chairs, tables, and so forth) eliminates the need for sales associates or decorators to help the customer imagine how a batch of furniture will look when placed in its setting (a living room, for example). Fewer sales personnel are required with this approach, allowing Ikea to keep its costs low. Expecting customers to pick up and deliver their purchased items also reduces the firm's costs. Although a cost leader, Ikea offers some features that appeal to customers in addition to products' low prices. Among these features are in-store childcare and extended hours. These services, it is argued, 'are uniquely aligned with the needs of Ikea's customers, who are young, are not wealthy, are likely to have children (but no nanny), and, because they work for a living, have a need to shop at odd hours'.[80]

Focused differentiation strategy

Other firms implement the focused differentiation strategy. The number of ways products can be differentiated to serve the unique needs of particular market segments is virtually endless. Consider the following examples.

Upscale apartment buildings in various inner city locations are being designed to serve the needs of technologically savvy city dwellers. Included as part of these apartments' differentiated features are high-speed digital Internet access and other sophisticated telecommunications services. Having their needs satisfied by their differentiated features in an apartment is expensive. In yet another example, several automobile manufacturers, including Ferrari, Aston Martin and Lamborghini, compete in the tiny super-car category. With prices in Australia beginning at $300 000 and increasing to as high as $1.2 million, one company official suggested that these cars are about passion, not transportation.[81] The Holden Special Vehicle firm (owned by a division of the British Tom Walkinson Group) prepares enhanced Holdens for a large following. They turn over almost $100 million per year, mainly selling to 'middle Australians' who follow motor sport. The questionnaire they send to buyers gets a 92 per cent response rate, indicating great buyer loyalty.[82]

Firms must be able to complete various primary and support activities in a competitively superior manner to achieve strategic competitiveness and earn above-average returns when using a focus strategy. The activities that must be completed to implement the focused cost leadership and the focused differentiation strategies are virtually identical to those shown in Figures 4.2 and 4.3, respectively. Similarly, the manners in which the two focus strategies allow a firm to deal successfully with the five competitive forces parallel those described with respect to the cost leadership and the differentiation strategies. The only difference is that the competitive scope changes from an industry-wide to a narrow industry segment. Thus, a review of Figures 4.2 and 4.3 and the text regarding the five competitive forces yields a description of the relationship between each of the two focus strategies and competitive advantage.

Competitive risks of focus strategies

When using either type of focus strategy, the firm faces the same general risks as does the company pursuing the cost leadership or the differentiation strategy on an industry-wide basis. However, focus strategies have three additional risks beyond these general ones. First, a competitor may be able to focus on a more narrowly defined competitive segment and 'out-focus' the focuser. For example, The Body Shop is the leading company to focus on that group of women who want chemical-free cosmetics made from 'natural ingredients' and without being tested on animals. Within Australia, the company is perceived as being British because of the high profile of the founder and media star, Anita Roddick. In fact, Body Shop Australia is a franchise owned by Australians. The perception of 'Britishness' has not inhibited their appeal to the natural cosmetics market, but within this broad market firms such as Tonic and Red Earth have been able to focus on the group that prefers Australian-sourced materials in their natural cosmetics. As one of the founders of Tonic stated, 'People now really like to buy Australian.'[83]

Second, a firm that is competing on an industry-wide basis may decide that the market segment being served by the focus-strategy firm is attractive and worthy of competitive pursuit. This motive appears to be behind the purchase of Red Earth by Hong Kong-based Esprit, who wished to extend into the natural cosmetics industry.[84]

The Body Shop is a leading firm in the cosmetics industry. It uses its reputation for environmental work based on the generation of publicity in that area to differentiate itself from other firms in a tight market.
It works: people shop with the firm in many parts of the world.

The third risk of a focus strategy is that the needs of customers within a narrow competitive segment may become more similar to those of customers as a whole. When this occurs, the advantages of a focus strategy are either reduced or eliminated.

Integrated cost leadership/differentiation strategy

Particularly in global markets, a firm's ability to blend the cost leadership and differentiation approaches may be critical to sustaining competitive advantages. Compared to firms that rely on one dominant generic strategy for their success, a company that is capable of successfully using an integrated cost leadership/differentiation strategy should be in a better position to adapt quickly to environmental changes, learn new skills and technologies more quickly, and effectively leverage its core competencies across business units and product lines.

A growing body of evidence supports the relationship between the implementation of an integrated strategy and the earning of above-average returns.[85] Some time ago, for example, a researcher found that the most successful firms competing in low-profit-potential industries were able to combine effectively the low-cost and differentiation strategies.[86] In a more recent comprehensive study, it was discovered that 'businesses which combined multiple forms of competitive advantage outperformed businesses that only were identified with a single form'.[87] Other research found that the highest-performing companies in the Korean electronics industry were those that combined both the differentiation and cost leadership strategies, suggesting the viability of the integrated strategy in different nations.[88]

A key reason why firms capable of successfully implementing the integrated strategy can earn above-average returns is that the benefits of this strategy are additive: 'Differentiation leads to premium prices at the same time that cost leadership implies lower costs.'[89] Thus, the integrated strategy allows firms to gain competitive advantage by offering two types of value to customers: some differentiated features (but fewer than those provided by the product-differentiated firm) and relatively low cost (but not as low as the products of the cost leader). For example, Coca-Cola has operated with this strategy successfully for several generations.

Firms must be strategically flexible to use the integrated cost leadership/ differentiation strategy successfully. Discussed next are three approaches to organisational work that can increase the strategic flexibility that is associated with this strategy's use.

Flexible manufacturing systems

Made possible largely as a result of the increasing capabilities of modern information technologies, flexible manufacturing systems increase the 'flexibilities of human, physical and information resources'[90] that are integrated to create differentiated products at low costs. A *flexible manufacturing system* (FMS) is a computer-controlled process used to produce a variety of products in moderate, flexible quantities with a minimum of manual intervention.[91]

The goal of an FMS is to eliminate the low-cost-versus-product-variety trade-off that is inherent in traditional manufacturing technologies. The flexibility provided by an FMS allows a plant to change quickly and easily from making one product to making another one.[92] Used properly, an FMS can help a firm become more flexible in response to changes in its customers' needs, while retaining low-cost advantages and consistent product quality. Because an FMS reduces the lot size needed to manufacture a product efficiently, a firm's capacity to serve the unique needs of a narrow competitive scope is increased. Thus, FMS technology is a significant technological advance that allows firms to produce a large variety of products at a low cost. Levi Strauss, for example, uses an FMS to make jeans for women that meet their exact measurements. Motorola successfully uses an FMS to customise pagers in different colours, sizes and shapes.[93]

The effective use of an FMS is linked with a firm's ability to understand the constraints these systems may create (in terms of materials handling and the flow of supporting resources in scheduling, for example) and to design an effective mix of machines, computer systems and people.[94] As a result, this type of manufacturing technology facilitates the implementation of complex competitive strategies, such as the integrated cost leadership/differentiation strategy, that lead to strategic competitiveness in global markets.[95]

A *manufacturing execution system* (MES) is a type of FMS. An MES is able to simulate and model everything that takes place in a factory, including the routing of products and the direction of processes. With an MES, changes can be made quickly to alter how a product is manufactured. An MES is in use in Unifi, the producer of synthetic yarn discussed earlier in the chapter. With MES software, Unifi transformed its newest plant from a commodity yarn producer to a maker of much more profitable speciality yarns. Importantly, this change was made without increasing the firm's costs.

Information networks across firms

New information networks linking manufacturers with their suppliers, distributors and customers are another technological development that increases a firm's strategic flexibility and responsiveness.[96] Companies have invested significant amounts of resources (in terms of dollars and people) to install elaborate enterprise resource planning (ERP) software systems that are intended to improve the firm's efficiency. These improvements result from the use of systems through which financial and operational data are moved rapidly from one department to another. In addition, the systems support the exchange of data between the firm and its suppliers and distributors.

The largest of the five major ERP software producers is SAP. This firm generated ERP revenue of US$5 billion in 1998. The remaining four prominent ERP manufacturers, with the amount of revenue they generated in 1998, are Oracle (US$2.4 billion), PeopleSoft (US$1.3 billion), J. D. Edwards (US$979 million) and Baan (US$743 million). However, these firms are encountering significant competition from product substitutes, in that many of their customers are using new ERP modules designed specifically for manufacturing companies. These dedicated systems have specialised features that contrast with those associated with the large, traditional ERP systems. Partly accounting for the differences between those systems could be the functional background of the companies' founders. Many SAP founders have expertise in financial software. In contrast, some of those developing the more specialised ERP modules come from manufacturing backgrounds. This is the case with Steve Haley, Pivotpoint's CEO, who spent 17 years in manufacturing companies. Pivot.Man, Pivotpoint's principal ERP program, is built around a flexible business-modelling strategy that does not force a company to change its operations to suit the software.[97] This product, compared to its more generalised predecessors, may increase the ability of users to differentiate their products more sharply while driving costs lower. Thus, the new ERP generation of software may facilitate even more the implementation of the integrated cost leadership/differentiation strategy.

Total quality management systems

Although total quality management (TQM) systems are sometimes difficult to implement,[98] many firms have established such systems (see also Chapter 5). Important objectives sought through the use of TQM systems include increases in the quality of a firm's product and the productivity levels of the entire organisation.[99] Enhanced quality focuses customers' attention on improvements in the performance of products and on the utility and reliability of features. This allows a firm to achieve differentiation and, ultimately, higher prices and market share. An emphasis on quality in production techniques lowers manufacturing and service costs through savings in reworking, scrap and warranty expenses. These savings can result in a competitive advantage for a firm over its rivals. Thus, TQM programs integrate aspects of the differentiation and cost leadership strategies.

Four key assumptions are the foundation of TQM systems. The first assumption is that 'the costs of poor quality (such as inspection, rework, lost customers, and so on) are far greater than the costs of developing processes that produce high-quality products and services'.[100] The second assumption is that employees naturally care about their work and will take initiatives to improve it. These initiatives are taken only when the firm provides employees with the tools and training they need to improve quality and when managers pay attention to the employees' ideas. The third assumption is that 'organizations are systems of highly interdependent parts'.[101] Problems encountered in such systems often cross traditional functional (for example, marketing, manufacturing, finance, and so on) lines. Solving interdependent problems requires integrated decision processes with participation from all affected functional areas. The fourth assumption is that the responsibility for an effective TQM system rests squarely on the shoulders of upper-level managers. These people must openly and totally support the use of a TQM system and accept the responsibility for an organisational design that allows employees to work effectively. In addition, managers must learn the rhetoric that facilitates the application of the rather clearly defined rules for using and analysing information that constitutes TQM's technical aspects.[102]

Competitive risks of the integrated cost leadership/differentiation strategy

The potential of the integrated strategy, in terms of above-average returns, is significant, but this potential comes with substantial risk. Selecting a business-level strategy calls for firms to make choices about how they intend to compete.[103] Achieving the low-cost position in an industry or a segment of an industry (for example, a focus strategy) demands that the firm be able to reduce its costs consistently relative to competitors' costs. The use of the differentiation strategy, with either an industry-wide or a focused competitive scope (see Figure 4.1), results in above-average returns only when the firm provides customers with differentiated goods or services they value and for which they are willing to pay a premium price.

The firm that fails to establish a leadership position in its chosen competitive scope, as the cost leader or as a differentiator, risks becoming 'stuck in the middle'.[104] Being stuck in the middle prevents the firm from dealing successfully with the five competitive forces and from earning above-average returns. Indeed, some research results show that the lowest-performing businesses are those lacking a distinguishable competitive advantage. Not having a clear and identifiable competitive advantage results from a firm being stuck in the middle.[105] Such firms can earn average returns only when an industry's structure is highly favourable or when the firm is competing against others that are in the same position.[106]

As is explained in the Strategic Focus, Merrill Lynch is at risk of becoming stuck in the middle. If this were to occur, the outcome would be primarily a product of the brokerage industry's competitive dynamics.

Strategic Focus International

Merrill Lynch compromises its differentiation strategy by implementing an on-line strategy

As on-line competitors create lower cost structures in the retail brokerage industry, they force high-cost differentiators such as Merrill Lynch into a compromised position. Merrill Lynch and other full-service brokerage firms have been under siege from Internet firms such as E*Trade, as well as Charles Schwab & Co. In 1998, 20 per cent of equity trading done by individuals was via Web-based brokers. By 2000, around 49 per cent of retail brokerage trades were completed on-line. Because Merrill Lynch is the largest diversified brokerage company, it is taking the brunt of this swift change in consumers' approach to executing security trades. Merrill Lynch's recognition of the swift changes that have taken place and its realisation that it let the competition jump ahead in the retail on-line market have led the company to reshape its strategy.

Merrill Lynch's traditional strategy has been to differentiate the company by customising its research and products to allow it to price on a premium basis. The approach is a traditional broad differentiation business-level strategy. This strategy is based on the advantage that Merrill has had in the private information produced by its analysts, traders and brokers. Against on-line brokers, the strategy suggests that, at some point, on-line technology will become ubiquitous and that the information produced by Merrill Lynch's people will become the battleground. At this point, however, Merrill Lynch faces the technological battle not only from portals such as Yahoo!, but also from other traditional brokers such as Morgan Stanley Dean Witter and Donaldson Lufkin & Jenrette, which have been rolling out on-line systems.

Besides the external competition from discount brokers such as Charles Schwab, portals such as Yahoo!, using information that is available publicly, and other traditional brokers, Merrill Lynch has inside battles. In particular, the change necessary to meet the sweeping technological and cost focuses will be difficult to implement without significant disruption for the brokers and their client relationships. However, the internal momentum necessary to make the change inside occurred when Schwab's US$25.5 billion market capitalisation topped Merrill Lynch's US$25.4 billion. This suggested to Merrill Lynch employees that the firm's current approach was coming up short. Merrill Lynch also has preached that it needs to gather assets so that customers will desire to put all their assets in accounts such as the cash management account (CMA) at the company. Even on this measure, however, Merrill Lynch was coming up short: Schwab increased its asset base by 39 per cent in 1998, while Merrill Lynch's grew by only 18 per cent. The message was clear: Merrill had to offer on-line-only accounts, or it would lose many assets, not to mention a whole generation of investors.

The main problem is that Merrill's 17 000 commissioned brokers would find it difficult to embrace the Internet, relative to the 7 000 salaried brokers at Schwab. The leaders at Merrill know that their brokers can go to another firm and take their clients with them. Without the support of the brokers to go on-line, it would be almost impossible to change to an on-line strategy without destroying the company's earnings and losing its sales force. Thus, to implement any Internet strategy, Merrill needs to enlist its brokers' support. If Merrill 'hits a home run' on a low-cost on-line trading system and loses thousands of its best brokers in the process, it would be a Pyrrhic victory, with the battle won, but the war lost.

Merrill decided to roll out its retail on-line strategy with a US$29.95 commission rate on transactions. To increase customer loyalty, it has also launched an elaborate e-commerce offering, signing on 40 electronic retailers from Barnes & Noble, Inc., to e-toys to sell through its portal. The firm wants customers to do some of their spending via Merrill Lynch, ideally through their Merrill Visa Signature cards, which gives credit or points towards discount purchases. In addition, Merrill is including business news and Merrill research reports to draw new customers and hold them.

The company is also building up the institutional side of its business. Represented are financial institutions (for example, banks and insurance firms), corporations and public organisations that operate retail or pension fund accounts. Merrill's strategy is to participate in a multi-dealer system, such as TradeWeb, wherein corporate clients see not only Merrill's offerings, but also those of competitors. With this new portal approach at the institutional level, Merrill's goal is to attract some 20 000 middle-market corporate accounts, well beyond its current 2 000 institutional clients, which are generally larger institutions. Merrill is currently not serving these middle-market companies, because it is not cost effective to hire conventional salespeople and traders to do so. Of course, the large institutions can pick up the phone and attract personal attention from Merrill traders and salespeople, and they have far more access to research on-line than do retail clients currently. Still, at the end of 1998, 26 per cent of institutional customer trading was done electronically, and that amount was estimated to have risen to 44 per cent in 2000. Thus, Merrill Lynch will need a better system for large traders anyway. Moreover, with the institutional customer portal, the firm would not only have the ability to reach the smaller institutional segment, but would also have the ability to attract new institutional clients overseas. In Internet-savvy countries such as Sweden and Japan, there is no reason why Merrill Lynch could not cover the medium-to-large institutional customers.

This approach, however, will deeply affect how Merrill Lynch is organised. Currently, the company is a loose confederation of 'territories', from foreign exchange to municipal bonds. Each office has its own managers, computer systems and clients. With the portal systems, both retail and institutional, Merrill Lynch will have to rationalise its products and services into a single system. The main risk of this approach is that in the transition period the company will cannibalise its thriving off-line business.

Firms such as Merrill Lynch that have used a differentiation strategy to build up their product image are confronting the new economics of information created by the Internet. Their customers have been able to exploit more direct information, which causes the firms to lower their pricing strategy. Furthermore, focused competitors are picking off the more profitable parts of their value chain. Alternatively, as in the Merrill Lynch case, the Internet opens new opportunities to markets that these companies have been unable to serve in the past using their current strategy. This opportunity is no more prevalent than the opportunity for Merrill Lynch to offer a broader range of products to smaller institutional investor clients such as small companies and foreign businesses. The main pitfalls to the changes are the internal systems that developed over time in these firms. The challenges will force significant changes upon the lives of the people involved if they are to be successful. Merrill's bureaucracy and culture will be hard to change as the firm tries to meet the low-margin on-line business, which will require deep cuts in company costs. Furthermore, the change will force cannibalisation of Merrill Lynch's current strategies, which will also be difficult. However, all people in these companies realise that this strategy needs to take place for the company to meet the competition. Otherwise, an even worse disaster may follow.

Sources: R. Buckman, 1999, 'Merrill, an online skeptic, now plans an internet lure', *Wall Street Journal*, 15 October, pp. C1, C11; P. Evans and T. S. Wurster, 1999, 'Getting real about virtual commerce', *Harvard Business Review*, 77(6), pp. 84–94; J. M. Laderman, 1999, 'Wall Street's frenzy over fees', *Business Week*, 22 November, pp. 140–1; L. N. Spiro, 1999, 'Merrill's e-battle', *Business Week*, 15 November, pp. 256–68.

Once a firm has selected its business-level strategy, it must both anticipate and be prepared to respond to competitors' actions and responses. Merrill Lynch had to respond to the onslaught of on-line brokers. Although this change is difficult, it must take the risk. However, it has a very real risk of compromising its differentiation strategy in trying to implement the cost leadership strategy required to meet the on-line competition.

Competitive dynamics between firms, such as those illustrated by Merrill Lynch and Blockbuster and their on-line competitors, are examined in the next chapter. These dynamics take place with respect to all types of strategies (see Chapters 6 to 9), but the majority of competitive actions and competitive responses are initiated in order to implement a firm's business-level strategy.

Summary

- A business-level strategy is an integrated and coordinated set of commitments and actions designed to provide value to customers and gain a competitive advantage by exploiting core competencies in specific, individual product markets. Five business-level strategies are examined in this chapter. The Internet's capabilities are affecting firms' strategic actions in terms of both selecting a business-level strategy and determining how to implement it. A firm's strategic competitiveness is enhanced when it is able to develop and exploit new core competencies faster than competitors can mimic the competitive advantages yielded by the firm's current competencies.
- Customers are the foundation of successful business-level strategies. When considering customers, a firm simultaneously examines three issues: who, what and how. These issues, respectively, refer to the customer groups it will serve, the needs those customers have that the firm seeks to satisfy, and the core competencies the firm possesses that can be used to satisfy customers' needs. The increasing segmentation of markets now occurring throughout the world creates multiple opportunities for firms to identify unique customer needs.

- Firms seeking competitive advantage through the cost leadership strategy often produce no-frills, standardised products for an industry's typical customer. Above-average returns are earned when firms continuously drive their costs lower than those of their competitors, while providing customers with products that have low prices and acceptable levels of differentiated features.
- Competitive risks associated with the cost leadership strategy include: (1) a loss of competitive advantage to newer technologies; (2) a failure to detect changes in customers' needs; and (3) the ability of competitors to imitate the cost leader's competitive advantage through their own unique strategic actions.
- The differentiation strategy enables firms to provide customers with products that have different (and valued) features. Because of their uniqueness, differentiated goods or services are sold at a premium price. Products can be differentiated along any dimension that is valued by some group of customers. Firms using this strategy seek to differentiate their products from competitors' goods or services along as many dimensions as possible. The less similarity with competitors' products, the more buffered a firm is from competition with its rivals.

- Risks associated with the differentiation strategy include: (1) a customer group's decision that the differences between the differentiated product and the cost leader's good or service are no longer worth a premium price; (2) the inability of a differentiated product to create the type of value for which customers are willing to pay a premium price; (3) the ability of competitors to provide customers with products that have features similar to those associated with the differentiated product, but at a lower cost; and (4) the threat of counterfeiting, whereby firms produce a cheap 'knock-off' of a differentiated good or service.
- Through the cost leadership and differentiated focus strategies, firms serve the needs of a narrow competitive segment (for example, a buyer group, product segment or geographic area). This strategy is successful when firms have the core competencies required to provide value to a narrow competitive segment that exceeds the value available from firms serving customers on an industry-wide basis.
- The competitive risks of focus strategies include: (1) a competitor's ability to use its core competencies to 'out-focus' the focuser by serving an even more narrowly defined competitive segment; (2) decisions by industry-wide competitors to serve a customer group's specialised needs that the focuser has been serving; and (3) a reduction in differences of the needs between customers in a narrow competitive segment and the industry-wide market.
- Firms using the integrated cost leadership/ differentiation strategy strive to provide customers with relatively low-cost products that have some valued differentiated features. The primary risk of this strategy is that a firm might produce products that do not offer sufficient value in terms of either low cost or differentiation. When this occurs, the company is 'stuck in the middle'. Firms stuck in the middle compete at a disadvantage.

Review questions

1. What is a strategy and what are business-level strategies?
2. What is the relationship between a firm's customers and its business-level strategy? Why is this relationship important?
3. In studying customers in terms of who, what and how, what questions are firms trying to answer?
4. What is the integrated cost leadership/differentiation strategy? Why is the number of firms using this strategy continuing to increase?
5. How is competitive advantage achieved through successful implementation of the cost leadership strategy? The differentiation strategy? The focused cost leadership strategy? The focused differentiation strategy? The integrated cost leadership/ differentiation strategy?
6. What risks are associated with selecting and implementing each of the five strategies mentioned in question 5?

Application discussion questions

1. You are a customer of your university. What actions does it take to recognise and satisfy your needs? Be prepared to discuss your views with your classmates.
2. Select a firm in your local community that interests you. Based on interactions with this company, which business-level strategy do you think the firm is implementing? What evidence can you provide to support your opinion? Is the Internet affecting the firm's strategic actions? If so, how?
3. Assume that you have decided to establish and operate a restaurant in your local community. What market segment would you intend to serve? What needs do these customers have that you could satisfy with your restaurant? How would you satisfy those needs? Be prepared to discuss your responses.
4. What business-level strategy is your school implementing? What core competencies are being used to implement this strategy?
5. Suppose you overheard the following comment: 'It is impossible for a firm to produce a relatively low-cost, yet somewhat highly differentiated, product.' Is this statement true or false? What is the reasoning behind your decision?
6. Is the Internet potentially of more value for firms implementing either the differentiation strategy or the focused differentiation strategy than for those using either the cost leadership or focused cost leadership strategy? If so, why?
7. Is it possible for a traditional firm to become too reliant on the Internet? If so, why? If not, why not?

Ethics questions

1. Can a commitment to ethical conduct on issues such as the environment, product quality and fulfilling contractual agreements affect a firm's competitive advantage? If so, how?
2. Is there more incentive for differentiators or cost leaders to pursue stronger ethical conduct? Think of an example to support your answer.
3. Can an over-emphasis on cost leadership or differentiation lead to ethical challenges (such as poor product design and manufacturing) that create costly problems (for example, product liability lawsuits)?
4. Re-examine the assumptions about effective TQM systems presented in the chapter. Do these assumptions urge top-level managers to maintain higher ethical standards than they now have? If so, how?
5. As discussed in Chapter 3, a brand image is one way a firm can differentiate its good or service. However, many questions are now being raised about the effect brand images have on consumer behaviour. For example, considerable concern has arisen about brand images that are managed by tobacco firms and their effect on teenage smoking habits. Should firms be concerned about how they form and use brand images? Why or why not?
6. What ethical issues do you believe are associated with use of the Internet to implement the firm's business-level strategy?
7. If ethical issues do exist regarding Internet use, who do you believe should be responsible for addressing them – governments or companies themselves? Why?

Internet exercise

Universities use different strategies to draw a wider customer base as well as to serve the needs of their current students and staff. Explore the websites of major Australian universities. Decide what type of strategy each pursues. How does each university determine its customer groups and utilise its core competencies to attract and retain its customers? With on-line course offerings increasing, do some of the institutions' target markets overlap?

e-project: Go to the website of the university you currently attend. Based on your knowledge of students, staff and curricula, what steps can be taken to improve customer satisfaction?

Notes

1. T. Thomas, 1998, 'E-commerce poses huge challenge', *Business Review Weekly*, 13 April: www.brw.com.au/content/130498/brw24.htm.
2. S. Magnunon, 2000, 'B2B or not 2B', *Australian Financial Review*, 21 September, pp. 29–30.
3. J. Pepper, 1999, 'GM and Ford are poised to take commanding lead in B2B e-commerce', *The Detroit News*, 13 December, pp. B3, B9.
4. C. V. Callahan and B. R. Pasternack, 1999, 'Corporate strategy in the digital age', *Strategy & Business*, 15, pp. 10–14.
5. C. A. Lengnick-Hall and J. A. Wolff, 1999, 'Similarities and contradictions in the core logic of three strategy research streams', *Strategic Management Journal*, 20, pp. 1109–32; A. Campbell and M. Alexander, 1997, 'What's wrong with strategy?', *Harvard Business Review*, 75(6), pp. 42–51.
6. J. G. Covin and M. P. Miles, 2000, 'The strategic use of corporate entrepreneurship', Working paper, Indiana University; D. P. Slevin and J. G. Covin, 1997, 'Strategy formation patterns, performance, and the significance of context', *Journal of Management*, 23, pp. 189–209.
7. M. M. Crossan, H. W. Lane and R. E. White, 1999, 'An organizational learning framework: From intuition to institution', *Academy of Management Review*, 24, pp. 522–37; C. E. Helfat, 1997, 'Know-how and asset complementarity and dynamic capability accumulation: The case of R&D', *Strategic Management Journal*, 18, pp. 339–60; A. Seth and H. Thomas, 1994, 'Theories of the firm: Implications for strategy research', *Journal of Management Studies*, 31, p. 167.
8. T. J. Dean, R. L. Brown and C. E. Bamford, 1998, 'Differences in large and small firm responses to environmental context: Strategic implications from a comparative analysis of business formations', *Strategic Management Journal*, 19, pp. 709–28; N. Rajagopalan and G. M. Spreitzer, 1997, 'Toward a theory of strategic change: A multi-lens perspective and integrative framework', *Academy of Management Journal*, 22, pp. 48–79.
9. P. F. Drucker, 1999, *Management in the 21st Century* (New York: Harper Business); H. Courtney, J. Kirkland and P. Viguerie, 1997, 'Strategy under uncertainty', *Harvard Business Review*, 75(6), pp. 67–79.
10. D. Abel, 1999, 'Competing today while preparing for tomorrow', *Sloan Management Review*, 40(3), pp. 73–81; C. C. Markides, 1999, 'A dynamic view of strategy', *Sloan Management Review*, 40(3), pp. 55–72.
11. R. T. Pascale, 1999, 'Surviving the edge of chaos', *Sloan Management Review*, 40(3), pp. 83–94.
12. P. Lane and M. Lubatkin, 1998, 'Relative absorptive capacity and interorganizational learning', *Strategic Management Journal*, 19, pp. 461–78; W. Wiggenhorn, 1997, 'The evolution of learning strategies in organizations: From employee development to business redefinition', *Academy of Management Executive*, 11(4), pp. 47–58; D. Lei, M. A. Hitt and R. Bettis, 1996, 'Dynamic core competences through meta-learning and strategic context', *Journal of Management*, 22, pp. 549–69.
13. R. A. D'Aveni, 1999, 'Strategic supremacy through disruption and dominance', *Sloan Management Review*, 40(3), pp. 117–35; C. M. Christensen, 1997, 'Making strategy: Learning by doing', *Harvard Business Review*, 75(6), pp. 141–56.
14. B. A. Walters and R. L. Priem, 1999, 'Business strategy and CEO intelligence acquisition', *Competitive Intelligence Review*, 10(2), pp. 15–22.
15. R. Flannery, 1999, 'Taiwan PC makers rely more on China', *Wall Street Journal*, 21 October, p. A16.
16. V. P. Rindova and C. J. Fombrun, 1999, 'Constructing competitive advantage: The role of firm-constituent interactions', *Strategic Management Journal*, 20, pp. 691–710; G. G. Dess, A. Gupta, J.-F. Hennart and C. W. L. Hill, 1995, 'Conducting and integrating strategy research at the international, corporate, and business levels: Issues and directions', *Journal of Management*, 21, pp. 357–93.
17. M. E. Porter, 1998, *On Competition* (Boston: Harvard Business School Press).
18. M. E. Porter, 1996, 'What is strategy?', *Harvard Business Review*, 74(6), pp. 61–78.
19. D. L. Deephouse, 1999, 'To be different, or to be the same? It's a question (and theory) of strategic balance', *Strategic Management Journal*, 20, pp. 147–66.
20. R. A. Smith, 1999, 'Retailing: Confronting the challenges that face bricks-and-mortar stores', *Harvard Business Review*, 77(4), pp. 164–5.
21. B. Lowendahl and O. Revang, 1998, 'Challenges to existing strategy theory in a postindustrial society', *Strategic Management Journal*, 19, pp. 755–73.

22. M. E. Porter, 1980, *Competitive Strategy* (New York: The Free Press).
23. P. S. Adler, B. Goldoftas and D. I. Levin, 1999, 'Flexibility versus efficiency? A case study of model changeovers in the Toyota production system', *Organization Science*, 10, pp. 43–68.
24. A. Afuah, 1999, 'Technology approaches for the information age', in Mastering Strategy (Part One), *Financial Times*, 27 September, p. 8.
25. D. Peppers, M. Rogers and B. Dorf, 1999, 'Is your company ready for one-to-one marketing?', *Harvard Business Review*, 73(5), pp. 59–72.
26. H. D. Rozanski, A. G. Baum and B. T. Wolfsen, 1999, 'Brand zealots: Realizing the full value of emotional brand loyalty', *Strategy & Business*, 17, pp. 51–63; T. A. Stewart, 1997, 'A satisfied customer isn't enough', *Fortune*, 21 July, pp. 112–13.
27. A. Goldstein, 2000, 'GM to use i2 software; stock soars', *Dallas Morning News*, 20 January, pp. D1–2; A. Goldstein, 1999, 'i2 acquiring Smart for $68 million', *Dallas Morning News*, 13 May, p. D2.
28. R. Balu, 1999, 'Whirlpool gets real with customers', *Fast Company*, December, pp. 74–6.
29. N. G. Carr, 1999, 'The economics of customer satisfaction', *Harvard Business Review*, 77(2), pp. 15–18.
30. P. Evans and T. S. Wurster, 1999, 'Getting real about virtual commerce', *Harvard Business Review*, 77(6), pp. 84–94; S. F. Slater and J. C. Narver, 1999, 'Market-oriented is more than being customer-led', *Strategic Management Journal*, 20, pp. 1165–8.
31. W. Bounds and R. Quick, 1999, 'The secret of Ursula Andress's bikini', *Wall Street Journal*, 10 November, pp. B1, B6; T. Connor, 1999, 'Customer-led and market-oriented: A matter of balance', *Strategic Management Journal*, 20, pp. 1157–63.
32. S. Lloyd, 1999, 'Which bank can make it happen?', *Business Review Weekly*, 2 July, pp. 44–5.
33. B. Tuckley, 2000, 'Auto Alley meets Infobarn', *Business Review Weekly*, 4 August, pp. 84–5.
34. S. C. Jain, 2000, *Marketing Planning and Strategy* (Cincinnati: South-Western College Publishing), pp. 104–25.
35. Associated Press, 1999, 'Rolls Bentley targets U.S. drivers', *Dallas Morning News*, 2 May, p. H5.
36. S. Jones, 1999, 'Women customers win warmer welcome at the bar', *Financial Times*, 12 April, p. 7.
37. E. Ross, 2000, 'Shoppers are yet to click with e-grocers', *Business Review Weekly*, 4 August, pp. 63–4.
38. M. Hannen, 2000, 'Choosing the single dollar', *Business Review Weekly*, 22 September, pp. 68–72.
39. V. Griffith, 1999, 'branding.com: How bricks-and-mortar companies can make it on the Internet', *Strategy & Business*, 15, Second Quarter, pp. 54–9.
40. S. Miller, 1999, 'VW sows confusion with common pattern for models', *Wall Street Journal*, 25 October, pp. A25, A38.
41. J. Kurtzman, 1997, 'An interview with Gary Hamel', *Strategy & Business*, 9, Fourth Quarter, pp. 89–97.
42. D. Kirkpatrick, 1999, 'IBM: From big blue dinosaur to e-business animal', *Fortune*, 26 April, pp. 116–27.
43. Hewlett-Packard, 1999, *Hewlett-Packard Home Page*, 20 December: www.hp.com.
44. P. Burrows, 1999, 'The hottest property in the valley?', *Business Week*, 30 August, pp. 69–77.
45. M. E. Porter, 1985, *Competitive Advantage* (New York: The Free Press), p. 26.
46. Porter, 'What is strategy?'.
47. B. McEvily and A. Zaheer, 1999, 'Bridging ties: A source of firm heterogeneity in competitive capabilities', *Strategic Management Journal*, 20, pp. 1133–56.
48. M. E. Porter, 1994, 'Toward a dynamic theory of strategy', in R. P. Rumelt, D. E. Schendel and D. J. Teece (eds), *Fundamental Issues in Strategy* (Boston: Harvard Business School Press), pp. 423–61.
49. Porter, 'What is strategy?', p. 62.
50. Porter, *Competitive Advantage*, p. 15.
51. G. G. Dess, G. T. Lumpkin and J. E. McGee, 1999, 'Linking corporate entrepreneurship to strategy, structure, and process: Suggested research directions', *Entrepreneurship: Theory and Practice*, 23(3), pp. 85–102; P. M. Wright, D. L. Smart and G. C. McMahan, 1995, 'Matches between human resources and strategy among NCAA basketball teams', *Academy of Management Journal*, 38, pp. 1052–74.
52. Porter, *Competitive Strategy*, pp. 35–40.
53. Dess, Lumpkin and McGee, 'Linking corporate entrepreneurship to strategy', pp. 88–9.
54. S. Mitchell, 2000, 'German giant has time, money to win Australia', *Australian Financial Review*, 3 April, p. 23.
55. Nucor Corporation, 1999, *Nucor Home Page*, 20 December: www.nucor.com; Nucor Corporation, 1999, *Better Investing*, July, p. 76.
56. Unifi, Inc., 1999, *Unifi Home Page*, 20 December: www.unifi.com; C. Sirois, 1997, 'Unifi, Inc.', *Value Line*, 22 August, p. 1640.
57. J. Friedland, 1997, 'Latin American retailer fights giants', *Wall Street Journal*, 19 September, p. A10.
58. Porter, *Competitive Strategy*, p. 36.
59. Sirois, 'Unifi, Inc.', p. 1640.
60. Acer Computer Corporation, 2000, *Acer Computer Corporation Home Page*, 12 January: www.acer.com.
61. L. Kraar, 1995, 'Acer's edge: PCs to go', *Fortune*, 30 October, p. 192.
62. J. Moore and P. Burrows, 1997, 'A new attack plan for Acer America', *Business Week*, 8 December, pp. 82–3.
63. M. France, 1999, 'This lawsuit is cranking up the volume over MP3', *Business Week e-biz*, 13 December: www.businessweek.com.
64. E. Portanger, 1999, 'One way Lloyds TSB earns so much money is by not spending it', *Wall Street Journal*, 13 December, pp. A1, A8.
65. Porter, *Competitive Advantage*, p. 14.
66. A. Lucas, 2000, 'Mambo duo get shirty with cut and thrust of business', *Australian Financial Review*, 7 March, p. 3.
67. I. R. Kunii, 1999, 'Here comes the Sony netman', *Business Week e-biz*, 1 November: www.businessweek.com.
68. Lucas, 'Mambo duo get shirty'.
69. G. Edmondson, E. Neuborne, A. L. Kazmin, E. Thornton and K. N. Anhalt, 1999, 'L'Oreal: The beauty of global branding', *Business Week e-biz*, 28 June: www.businessweek.com.
70. I. Sager and P. Burrows, 1997, 'I'm not gonna pay a lot for this Aptiva', *Business Week*, 13 October, p. 59.
71. P. Hollinger, 1999, 'Big rise reported in counterfeiting of luxury goods', *Financial Times*, 16 April, p. 3.
72. Porter, *Competitive Strategy*, p. 38.
73. Porter, *Competitive Advantage*, p. 15.
74. S. Thurm, 1999, 'For Cisco, focus on smaller companies pays off', *Wall Street Journal*, 27 May, p. B8.
75. Porter, *Competitive Advantage*, p. 15.
76. Ibid., pp. 15–16.
77. D. Machalaba, 1999, 'There's a small hotel where happy guests see screamin' demons', *Wall Street Journal*, 22 March, pp. A1, A8.
78. E. De Lisser, 1999, 'Online retailers slice and dice niches thinner than Julienne fries', *Wall Street Journal*, 29 November, pp. B1, B6.
79. Ikea, 2000, *Ikea Home Page*, 14 January: www.ikea.com.
80. Porter, 'What is strategy?', p. 65.
81. P. Lkebnikov, 1999, 'The $600,000 car', *Forbes*, 17 May, pp. 94–9.
82. B. Tucky, 2000, 'HSV's new surge', *Business Review Weekly*, 6 October, p. 48.
83. S. Lloyd, 2000, 'The natural approach pays off for body and soul', *Business Review Weekly*, 6 October, pp. 32–3.
84. Ibid.
85. Dess, Lumpkin and McGee, 'Linking corporate entrepreneurship to strategy', p. 89.
86. W. K. Hall, 1980, 'Survival strategies in a hostile environment', *Harvard Business Review*, 58(5), pp. 75–87.
87. Dess, Gupta, Hennart and Hill, 'Conducting and integrating strategy research', p. 377.
88. L. Kim and Y. Lim, 1988, 'Environment, generic strategies, and performance in a rapidly developing country: A taxonomic approach', *Academy of Management Journal*, 31, pp. 802–27.
89. Porter, *Competitive Advantage*, p. 18.
90. R. Sanchez, 1995, 'Strategic flexibility in product competition', *Strategic Management Journal*, 16 (Summer Special Issue), p. 140.
91. Ibid., p. 105.
92. L. J. Krajewski and L. P. Ritzman, 1999, *Operations Management: Strategy and Analysis*, 5th edition (Reading, MA: Addison-Wesley), pp. 161–3.
93. J. Martin, 1997, 'Give them exactly what they want', *Fortune*, 10 November, pp. 283–5.
94. R. S. Russell and B. W. Taylor III, 2000, *Operations Management*, 3rd edition (Upper Saddle River, NJ: Prentice Hall), pp. 262–4.
95. J. B. Dilworth, 2000, *Operations Management: Providing Value in Goods and Services*, 3rd edition (Fort Worth, TX: The Dryden Press), pp. 286–9; D. Lei, M. A. Hitt and J. D. Goldhar, 1996, 'Advanced manufacturing technology, organization design and strategic flexibility', *Organization Studies*, 17, pp. 501–23.

96 C. V. Callahan and J. Nemec, Jr, 1999, 'The C.E.O.'s information technology challenge: Creating true value', *Strategy & Business*, 14, pp. 78–89.
97 G. Bylinsky, 1999, 'Challenges are moving in on ERP', *Fortune*, 6 December, p. 250C.
98 R. K. Reger, L. T. Gustafson, S. M. DeMarie and J. V. Mullane, 1994, 'Reframing the organization: Why implementing total quality is easier said than done', *Academy of Management Review*, 19, pp. 565–84.
99 J. D. Westphal, R. Gulati and S. M. Shortell, 1997, 'Customization or conformity: An institutional and network perspective on the content and consequences of TWM adoption', *Administrative Science Quarterly*, 42, pp. 366–94.
100 J. R. Hackman and R. Wageman, 1995, 'Total quality management: Empirical, conceptual, and practical issues', *Administrative Science Quarterly*, 40, p. 310.
101 Ibid., p. 311.
102 M. J. Zbaracki, 1998, 'The rhetoric and reality of Total Quality Management', *Administrative Science Quarterly*, 43, pp. 602–36.
103 C. H. St John and J. S. Harrison, 1999, 'Manufacturing-based relatedness, synergy, and coordination', *Strategic Management Journal*, 20, pp. 129–45.
104 Porter, *Competitive Advantage*, p. 16.
105 A. Miller and G. G. Dess, 1993, 'Assessing Porter's (1980) model in terms of its generalizability, accuracy and simplicity', *Journal of Management Studies*, 30, pp. 553–85.
106 Porter, *Competitive Advantage*, p. 17.

Chapter 5

Competitive dynamics

Objectives

After reading this chapter, you should be able to:

1. Define the conditions for undertaking competitive actions.
2. Identify and explain factors affecting the probability that a competitor will initiate a response to competitive actions.
3. Describe first, second and late movers, and the advantages and disadvantages of each.
4. Understand the factors that contribute to the likelihood of a response to a competitive action.
5. Explain the effects of the size of a firm, the speed with which it makes strategic decisions, and implementation, innovation and quality on the firm's ability to take competitive action.
6. Understand three basic market situations as outcomes of competitive dynamics.
7. Discuss the types of competitive actions most relevant for each of the three stages of an industry evolution.

The global competitive landscape is changing: Wal-Mart is on the move

Sam Walton, the American retailing king, perhaps defied conventional wisdom more than any other executive in the 20th century. He focused on locating large stores in rural areas, while rivals built large stores in urban cities and suburbs. In so doing, he built the largest retailing company in the world and the fourth largest of all companies behind GM, DaimlerChrysler and Ford. Walton carefully chose the store sites, and the company distributed its goods in a highly efficient manner. Essentially, Walton started a revolution in retailing. As noted in Chapter 3, prior to Wal-Mart's existence, most retailers carried the merchandise they were provided by suppliers, and consumers bought the merchandise that was available. However, Walton squeezed the suppliers for better prices on merchandise and gave the savings to the consumer. Most large competitors ignored Wal-Mart, until it was so large and well-established that it began to compete on their turf (in large cities and suburbs).

Wal-Mart's total annual sales of more than US$160 billion and market capitalisation of over US$200 billion are both more than double the sales and capitalisation of the closest rivals. This is why rivals in other parts of the world are worried about Wal-Mart's global expansion. In fact, analysts suggest that retailers across the European continent are running scared. Wal-Mart first entered Europe with the acquisition of 21 stores from Wertkauf GmbH in 1997. In 1998, Wal-Mart acquired 74 hypermarkets from Spar Handels AG in Germany. In 1999, it bought Asda of Great Britain with 229 supermarkets. Wal-Mart's entry into Europe has prompted price wars in Germany and England. Soon Wal-Mart is expected to make acquisitions in France and Italy as well. Wal-Mart already has operations in Canada, Mexico and China and has targeted other global regions outside of North America. Thus, Wal-Mart is spreading its revolution to Europe and elsewhere around the world. It has suggested that Wal-Mart has already looked at Australia and rejected it as a target for expansion because of the small size of the market. Nevertheless, given the expansionary behaviour and relative size of Wal-Mart compared to Coles (shown above) and Woolworths (their market capitalisation is around A$6 billion each), the value of the Australian dollar, and the track record at the Foreign Investment Review Board which routinely approves foreign entry to Australia, a move on one of the Australian 'giants' seems probable. (See the Strategic Focus for more on the Australian retailing industry and its current competitive rivalry.)

George Wallace, director of a prominent retail consulting firm based in London, speaking of the British experience, suggests that 'Wal-Mart's arrival will be the catalyst for a battle in Europe between the juggernauts of the industry'. The rivalry is exemplified by British retailer Tesco's price reductions on goods amounting to US$414 million. Metro AG, the largest retailer in Germany, changed its logo, started opening earlier, and developed the slogans 'honestly low prices' (similar to Wal-Mart's 'everyday low prices') and 'permanently reasonable'. To reinforce its customer service, Real, another competitor, gives shoppers five Deutschmarks if they have to wait more than five minutes at a cashier. German shoppers stated that they are encountering improved customer service.

In one of the boldest responses to Wal-Mart's European invasion, Carrefour acquired Promodes in late 1999. The merger of the two French firms created Europe's number-one retailer and number two in the world behind Wal-Mart. In addition, Carrefour is now able to challenge Wal-Mart in global markets, with 8 800 stores in 26 countries. Carrefour has 20 per cent of the Brazilian market, versus 1.4 per cent for Wal-Mart. Carrefour has been operating in Latin America for 25 years. Its annual revenues are over US$65 billion. Size is important in order to obtain lower prices from suppliers. To compete with Wal-Mart, Carrefour has reduced prices drastically, remodelled stores and relocated other stores. One executive of a rival described Carrefour as 'relentless, the toughest competitor I've ever seen anywhere'. In addition to its presence in Latin America, Carrefour is strong in Asia.

The pressure is on other major European retailers, such as Royal Ahold, based in the Netherlands, and Great Britain's Sainsbury's. In fact, because of Wal-Mart's move into Great Britain, the stock prices of several of England's prominent retailers began to slide in late 1999. While Wal-Mart's road to success in Europe is not paved with gold, it is likely to revolutionise retailing there and in other regions of the world that it enters. Thus, Wal-Mart is spawning a global revolution.

www.ahold.com
www.asda.co.uk
www.carrefour.fr
www.colesmyer.com.au
www.daimler-chrysler.com
www.ford.com
www.gm.com
www.metro.de
www.promodes.com
www.sainsbury.co.uk
www.spar.de
www.tesco.co.uk
www.walmart.com
www.woolworths.com.au

Sources: A. Barrett and J. Carreyrou, 1999, 'French retailers Carrefour, Promodes agree to join in $16.3 billion accord', *Wall Street Journal Interactive Edition*, 30 August: www.interactive.wsj.com/articles; E. Beck and E. Nelson, 1999, 'As Wal-Mart invades Europe, rivals rush to match its formula', *Wall Street Journal Interactive Edition*, 6 October: www.interactive.wsj.com/articles; H. Dawley, 1999, 'Watch out Europe: Here comes Wal-Mart', *Businessweek Online*, 28 June: bwarchive.businessweek.com; C. Matlack, I. Resch and W. Zellner, 1999, 'Engarde, Wal-Mart', *Businessweek Online*, 13 September: bwarchive.businessweek.com; E. Nelson and E. Beck, 1999, 'Wal-Mart seeks supermarket firm', *Wall Street Journal*, 15 June, pp. A3–4; P. Sellers, 1999, 'Category killers: They left their competitors with nowhere to hide', *Fortune*, 27 September, pp. 223–6; S. Voyle, 1999, 'Wal-Mart casts shadow over gloomy retailers', 20 November: www.ft.com/nbearchive; D. Woodruff and J. Carreyrou, 1999, 'French retailers create new Wal-Mart rival', *Wall Street Journal*, 31 August, pp. A14, A19.

Wal-Mart's entry into European markets and competitors' reactions represent examples of changes in the 21st-century competitive landscape. Companies competing in this more volatile and unpredictable landscape must learn how to cope successfully with the challenges presented by discontinuous environmental changes, the increasing globalisation of their industries, and the array of competitive actions and responses that are being taken by aggressive rivals.[1] In addition, top-level managers must be willing to make the type of difficult decisions that are called for by the nature of competitors' actions and responses. In fact, some believe that one of the most important skills that will be linked to strategic competitiveness in the 21st century will be managers' willingness, and perhaps even eagerness, to make significant and sometimes painful decisions.[2] Many of these decisions will be necessitated by the competitive dynamics affecting the firm's operations.

Wal-Mart's entry into European markets, along with its moves into Latin America and China, also exemplify the globalisation of markets. The competition's reactions, particularly the acquisition of Promodes by Carrefour, exemplify the trend towards consolidation in many industries to compete effectively in global markets. Wal-Mart's volume of sales provides tremendous leverage with suppliers because of large purchases of merchandise. Thus, Wal-Mart's market power continues to grow as it expands into global markets. Some fear Wal-Mart's power; thus, a few states in the United States, such as Arizona, California and Nevada, have passed legislation limiting the size of retail establishments, thereby targeting supercentres.[3] However, Wal-Mart has responded by flexing its cyber-muscles: it is starting to focus on selling merchandise through e-commerce. Granted that its sales over the Internet are considerably smaller than Amazon.com's, but with Wal-Mart's brand name, market power and considerable resources, its e-commerce venture has a high probability of success.[4]

Increased rivalry in the new competitive landscape

Conditions in the new competitive landscape are increasing competitive rivalry and require many companies to compete differently in order to achieve strategic competitiveness and earn above-average returns. (Recall the description of European retailers preparing to compete with Wal-Mart as it enters their markets.) C. K. Prahalad refers to the environment as a competitive battlefield. He suggests that the strategic discontinuities a firm encounters can be positive. For example, the political changes in Eastern Europe opened markets and provided opportunities for firms from Western countries and Asia. And the Asian financial crisis represented a less-than-positive strategic discontinuity for many Australian, US and Western European firms. Prahalad suggests that the competitive landscape in the 21st century requires a new strategic approach and managerial mind-set.[5] For instance, the increased competitive rivalry requires that firms bring new goods and services to the market more quickly.[6] Compaq has discovered this necessity. In the mid-1990s, Compaq won the competitive battle to become the number-one manufacturer and marketer of personal computers. However, in 1999, Dell overtook Compaq to become number one in this market. In fact, Compaq reported a major loss in 1999. Compaq not only lost its leadership in the PC market, it also lost major users of Compaq servers to competitors (for example, Volkswagen and America Online). In addition, Compaq was criticised for having an undeveloped Internet strategy. As a result, Compaq made a number of managerial changes and increased investment in the development of its product line.[7]

Strategic Focus Corporate

Food retailing in Australia

Two firms dominate food retailing in Australia: Woolworths has more than 40 per cent of market share and Coles about 30 per cent. Before it was split up and sold by its Hong Kong owners in mid-2001, Franklins had about 11 per cent.

Price competition in the industry is interesting. A report by Taylor Research Services and Roy Morgan Research in 1998 indicated that price variation depends on the presence of a third competitor in specific regional markets – where there is a discount supermarket grocery, prices fall on average by 9 per cent, and fresh food prices by 16 per cent, in major supermarkets. There is also variation by location – for example, the study found that the most expensive Coles store (in Darwin) had prices 23 per cent higher than the cheapest (in Belmont, Newcastle). Some of this can be explained by changes in operating costs, but variations such as that of 9 per cent between Coles stores in Newcastle can only be explained in terms of patterns of micro-regional competition (or lack of it).

Coles and Woolworths have both extended their dominance in the market in the past few years, Coles with a takeover of Bi-Lo, previously a major discount chain, and Woolworths with the takeover of Davids. The chairman of the National Association of Retail Groups of Australia claimed in 1999 that the big three were buying out competition: '[S]ome 26 to 30 independent retailers have been approached by the major supermarket companies and have been made an offer that they simply couldn't refuse – in some cases, at least double the market value of the business.'

Competition between the big chains is strong in other aspects of the grocery buying experience. New competitive moves from Woolworths include petrol retailing (although their Petrol Plus business lost $8.9 million in 1998–9) and banking via a joint Commonwealth Bank/Woolworths initiative called 'Ezy-banking'. Woolworths have also continued a successful emphasis on fresh food and attractive store layout. Coles, led by American Dennis Eck since 1997, have revitalised their supermarket division with a range of new retailing ideas and much better synergies with other units in the Coles Myer corporation. In March 2000, Eck launched a major electronic commerce initiative which will have significant implications for the whole corporation.

Major new competition is looming for both Coles Myer and Woolworths supermarkets. The definite new entrant is the German-based 'no frills' chain, Aldi. Run by two brothers, they offer a far smaller range of items than is conventional in Australia (600 compared to about 30 000), use high-quality 'own brand' goods supplied by mainly local providers tied up by carefully constructed contracts, and reduce costs through rigorous examination of the value chain and elimination of non-essential activities. Their international success indicates that they will be very significant discounters and will provide solid competition to the big two in Australia.

Sources: M. Bryan, 2000, 'Coles Online finally clicks', *Australian Financial Review*, 4 August, p. 14; James Kirby, 1999, 'Supermarkets in a double-bind', *Business Review Weekly*, 29 March, pp. 40–1; T. Condon, 1999, 'Retailers adapt to a new environment', *Business Review Weekly*, 15 October, pp. 98–101.

The competitive landscape is undergoing fundamental changes, with new entrants transforming industries, often by using new technology.[8] For example, a recent, but now classic, case of such change occurred with Amazon.com's entrance into the retail book market. In previous chapters, we saw the profound effects of Amazon.com on the retail book market, and indeed, the success of Amazon.com began the revolution in e-commerce. Before Amazon's entry into the market, analysts were predicting that Barnes & Noble would become the 'master' of the retail book market. It had the most bookstores, the largest market share in the industry and the promise of more growth. However, Barnes & Noble was 'Amazoned', according to *Fortune* magazine. It was almost a year before Barnes & Noble responded with its own on-line book sales, and thus its growth slowed.[9] In America, small bookstores are truly struggling, trying to compete against both Amazon.com and Barnes & Noble. Several have argued that it is a 'jungle' in on-line book sales. Amazon.com offered 50 per cent discounts on its books, forcing Barnes & Noble and other booksellers to match the prices at which they were selling the same items.[10] Amazon.com also obtained an injunction against Barnes & Noble, barring it from using Amazon.com's patented one-click system for on-line orders from its barnesandnoble.com website.[11]

Barnes & Noble recently expanded its on-line sales to include music as a catalyst to increase its growth.[12] But Amazon.com has been in the on-line music business for some time. In fact, Amazon now sells many products in addition to books. In 1999, it even purchased a stake in an on-line grocery firm.[13] Interestingly, Amazon.com may face its largest competition from Wal-Mart. Some have described Amazon.com as the Wal-Mart of the Internet. In fact, it is probably the significant presence of Amazon and other growing 'e-tailers' that has led Wal-Mart and other 'bricks and mortar' retailers to respond to their growing presence. As noted in the Opening Case, however, Wal-Mart has moved into on-line sales of its merchandise. In late 1999, it announced an alliance with America Online to further its presence in on-line sales.[14]

Competitive advantages may come from non-traditional areas in the evolving competitive landscape. For example, hiring trucks at very low rates and making a profit out of accessories to the hiring prices.[15]

Another phenomenon in the 21st-century landscape is the consolidation of industries. There are many reasons for this, but among them is the need to be large in order to achieve economies of scale to compete effectively in global markets. With freer access to markets in many countries, foreign companies are entering at increasing rates. The enhanced competition has emphasised the need for efficiency, both to offer low prices and, at the same time, to differentiate a firm's products through innovation. Consolidation has occurred in industries ranging from the petroleum industry (for example, the merger of Exxon and Mobil) and the communications industry (for example, the merger of Carlton Communications and United News and Media, both from the United Kingdom) to the on-line computer electronics industry. On-line sales competition in the US computer hardware industry had become so fierce that firms were selling products below their wholesale costs. Their only hope to make a profit was to sell on-line advertising. Thus, consolidation became necessary to reduce some of the competitive rivalry.[16]

On-line retailing is growing dramatically; on-line sales in the United States in 1999 were 2.5 times the amount in 1998. Some still believe that there is a need and demand for physical stores where customers can see, feel and operate the products as they desire. They also believe that the opportunity to have a salesperson work directly with the consumer provides an advantage to physical stores. However, analysts suggest that the environment is too different and uncertain to make definitive predictions at this time.

Both significant advances in communication technologies that allow more effective coordination across operations in multiple markets and faster decision making and competitive responses facilitate the changes occurring in many industries' competitive landscapes.[17] In addition, new technology and innovations, particularly in the information technology and computer industries, have helped small and medium-sized businesses to compete effectively. Finally, the increasing number of agreements allowing free trade across country borders is facilitating a growing cross-border focus.[18]

The changing competitive landscape even has former competitors cooperating in such areas as the development of new technology and forming strategic alliances to compete against other competitors (as discussed in Chapter 9).[19] For example, global alliances also have been formed among many of the world's telephone companies to pursue business in Europe and Asia. Telstra's foray into Asia via an alliance with Hong Kong company Pacific Century CyberWorks (PCCW) provides an example.[20] At the same time, PCCW is so eager to enter a telecommunications partnership that it has a 'plan B' for a possible merger with AT&T should the Telstra deal fail to eventuate.[21]

Increasingly, cooperative R&D arrangements are being developed in the competitive landscape as well. These arrangements are vehicles through which firms overcome their resource constraints by acquiring skills and capabilities from partners.[22]

This chapter focuses on competitive dynamics. The essence of this important topic is that a firm's strategies and their implementation (see Figure 1.1 in Chapter 1) are dynamic in nature. Actions taken by one firm often elicit responses from competitors that, in turn, typically result in responses from the original firm. This chain of events is illustrated by the Opening Case, which is concerned with the competitive actions being taken by European retailers competing with Wal-Mart. The series of actions and responses among firms competing within a particular industry creates **competitive dynamics**. This competitive interaction often shapes the competitive position of firms undertaking the business-level strategies described in the previous chapter and, to some extent, the corporate strategies described in Chapters 6, 8 and 9. Thus, because of competitive dynamics, the effectiveness of any strategy is determined not only by the initial move, but also by how well the firm 'anticipates and addresses the moves and countermoves of competitors and shifts in customer demands over time'.[23]

> **Competitive dynamics** results from a series of competitive responses among firms competing within a particular industry.

To explain competitive dynamics more effectively, we introduce a model of the phenomenon (see Figure 5.1). The remainder of the chapter then describes this model. After the overall model is introduced, we examine the factors that lead to competitive attack and potential responses. We follow this examination with a discussion of the incentives of market leadership (first-mover advantages) and its disadvantages. We also discuss the advantages and disadvantages of second and late movers. After a competitive action is taken, a number of factors affect the potential response. These factors are discussed, and we then examine firms' capabilities to attack and respond, including the size of the firms, the speed of decision making, innovation, and product and process quality. Following this analysis is a discussion of three different types of competitive markets (slow cycle, standard cycle and fast cycle) that result from competitive interaction. In particular, we explore the nature of rivalry and propose strategies for competition in fast-cycle markets where competitive rivalry has escalated to an intense level. This discussion examines the strategy of competitive disruption, in which firms capitalise on temporary, compared to sustainable, competitive advantage by cannibalising their past new-product entries to introduce the next product or process innovation. Finally, we describe competitive rivalry outcomes as industries move through the emerging, growth and maturity stages.

Figure 5.1 | A summary model of inter-firm rivalry: The likelihood of attack and response

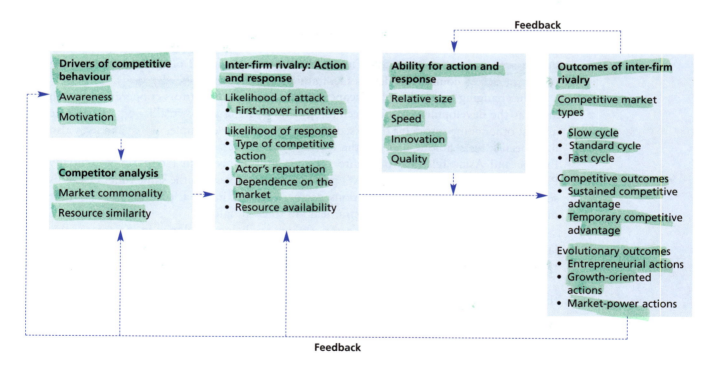

Source: Adapted from M. J. Chen, 1996, 'Competitor analysis and inter-firm rivalry: Toward a theoretical integration', *Academy of Management Review*, 21, pp. 100–34.

Model of competitive dynamics and rivalry

Competitive rivalry exists when two or more firms jockey with one another in the pursuit of an advantageous market position.

Over time, firms competing in an industry employ a number of competitive actions and responses.[24] **Competitive rivalry** exists when two or more firms jockey with one another in the pursuit of an advantageous market position. Competitive rivalry takes place among firms because one or more competitors feel pressure or see opportunities to improve their market position. Rivalry is made possible by *competitive asymmetry*, which exists when firms differ from one another in terms of their resources, capabilities and core competencies (see Chapter 3) and in terms of the opportunities and threats in their industry and competitive environments (see Chapter 2). Strategies – especially business-level ones – are formed to exploit the asymmetric relationships among competitors.[25]

In most industries, a firm's competitive actions have observable effects on its competitors and typically cause responses designed to counter the action.[26] In early 1998, for instance, Renault, France's largest car and truck manufacturer, announced plans to increase its output by 500 000 units a year to 2002. In addition, the car maker indicated that it was committed to improving the efficiency of its manufacturing operations to reduce its overall costs. Renault's competitive decisions were made partly in response to Toyota's previously announced intention to build a new small-car manufacturing plant in France. Renault officials believed that the firm's response was required for it to become more competitive in its home market and to prevent Renault from falling behind more efficient rivals such as Toyota.[27] As noted in the Strategic Focus later in the chapter, Renault must respond to Toyota's strategic action. It is predicted that by the year 2010, only six major automobile manufacturers will be operating globally. Although Renault will be a formidable competitor for any firm entering European markets, it is not expected to be among the surviving 'global six' identified in the Strategic Focus.[28]

Competitive rivalry can have a major effect on a firm's profitability. As rivalry in an industry increases, the average profitability of firms competing in the industry decreases.[29] The intensity of the rivalry is affected not only by the number of competitors, but by many other factors as well. It is affected by the market structure and the firm's strategy. Thus, firms that develop and implement more effective strategies (recall the discussion of business-level strategies in Chapter 4) will fare better than others.[30] For example, in the Victorian beer market, Carlton United has been able to head off challenges by Bond Brewing in the 1980s and Lion Nathan in the 1990s. Both tried to establish Tooheys beer in a market fiercely loyal to Victoria Bitter. In 2000, Lion Nathan tried again, buying hotels, signing sponsorship deals and pushing Hahn beers.[31]

As the example of the competitive actions and competitive responses among the beer marketers demonstrates, firms and their competitors are mutually interdependent.[32] **Mutual interdependence** among firms means that strategic competitiveness and above-average returns result only when companies recognise that their strategies are not implemented in isolation from their competitors' actions and responses. The pattern of pricing and other competitive actions in the Australian airline industry in early 2000 illustrates this. As Impulse and Virgin entered the market, Ansett and Qantas changed fare structures. Impulse's use of Internet selling also forced further actions out of the other players, all of whom were increasingly concerned about the age and appearance of their aircraft.[33] Because they affect strategic competitiveness and returns, the pattern of competitive dynamics and the rivalry it creates are obviously a major concern of firms.[34]

Mutual interdependence among firms means that strategic competitiveness and above-average returns result only when companies recognise that their strategies are not implemented in isolation from their competitors' actions and responses.

Figure 5.1 illustrates a summary model of inter-firm rivalry and the likelihood of attack and response. As is seen in the figure, competitor analysis begins with an examination of competitor awareness and motivation to attack and respond to competitive action. *Awareness* refers to whether or not the attacking or responding firm is aware of the competitive market characteristics, such as the market commonality and the resource similarity of a potential attacker or respondent. (These terms are defined in a subsequent section.³⁵) Managers may have 'blind spots' in their industry and competitor analyses, due to underestimation or an inability to analyse these factors.³⁶ Of course, such errors are likely to harm the managers' firms and the industry as well. For example, this lack of awareness may lead to industry over-capacity and excessive competition.³⁷ Firms in an industry are likely to exhibit several different types of competitive responses. The reasons for these differences are several, but include the number of common markets in which the firm competes with the firm to whose action it is responding, as well as its resources to respond. Also, the response may depend partially on the similarity of the resources among the competitors.³⁸ *Market commonality* and *resource similarity* both affect a firm's motivation to respond to a competitive action. *Motivation* relates to the incentives a firm has to attack and respond if attacked. A firm may perceive advantages to moving first, given the potential for interaction.

As Figure 5.1 suggests, both market commonality and resource similarity mediate the awareness and motivation to undertake actions and responses. The likelihood of action and response will result in the competitive outcomes which, however, will be moderated by a firm's ability to undertake strategic actions and responses. Furthermore, Figure 5.1 illustrates that feedback from the nature of a particular rivalry will also influence a competitor's awareness and motivation to take future actions or responses.

Market commonality

Many firms – for example, those in the airline, chemical, pharmaceutical, breakfast cereal and electronics industries – compete in the same multiple markets. In the brewery industry, many beer producers compete in the same regional markets.³⁹ Regional competition is also evident in international markets through 'triad' competition, or the necessity for multinational corporations to have businesses in Asia (traditionally Japan), Europe and North America.⁴⁰ Multi-market overlap presents opportunities for **multi-point competition**, a situation in which firms compete against each other simultaneously in several product or geographic markets.⁴¹ In the airline industry, for instance, there are many opportunities for multi-point competition. The large airlines, such as Qantas and Ansett, have substantial market overlap and therefore substantial awareness and motivation to respond to competitive actions. Research has shown that such commonality reduces the likelihood of competitive rivalry in the industry.⁴² Because the major airlines operate in many common markets, peace will reign until one firm makes a competitive move; the competitive response is likely to be swift, as explained in the Strategic Focus on air wars in Australia.⁴³

Multi-point competition occurs when firms compete against each other simultaneously in several product or geographic markets.

The largest Australian airlines compete in the same multiple markets, which can lead to multi-point competition. The firms must be continually aware of their competitors and be motivated to respond quickly to their competitive actions.

Strategic Focus Corporate

Air wars: Competitive rivalry in Australia

The Australian airline industry in 2000 provides a good illustration of complex rivalry. The basic situation in early 2000 featured two major players with significant resources. Qantas had a proud Australian history, 107 aircraft in their core fleet and 44 in a regional network, about 30 000 staff, and 115 Australian and overseas destinations. Ansett, in the middle of change related to a takeover (frequently referred to in the media as a merger) by Air New Zealand, had 73 aircraft in their core fleet and 32 in their regional airlines, 13 500 staff, and about 60 local and four international destinations. Competition between the two was genteel, routes and times of flights were very close, and prices were nearly identical. For example, the full economy one-way fare from Melbourne to Sydney (the most frequently travelled route) was $320.10 for both airlines, while Brisbane to Sydney was $353.10 for Qantas and $353 for Ansett. Both airlines had good access to terminals at major airports (a major resource). Both were struggling because of a sharp rise (44 per cent) in fuel costs during the 1999–2000 period.

Into this situation two new airlines were launched: Impulse (backed by major institutions, including the ANZ Bank) and Virgin Blue (part of Richard Branson's organisation). Impulse launched with a short-term offer of $33 for Internet-booked fares from Melbourne to Sydney. Qantas and Ansett responded with equally low fares, and both provided more seats at the low fare than Impulse. Virgin Blue then entered the market (after considerable Branson-focused publicity) and also offered low fares on major routes.

The rivals are also competing in other ways. Virgin Blue flights are 'fun experiences'. A flight attendant will read out horoscopes for travellers, their in-flight music is popular/contemporary, and considerable effort is put into making the flight entertaining for each passenger. On a Sydney to Brisbane flight, as the passengers were about to board in wet weather, two flight attendants started singing:

> We're boarding in the rain,
> Just boarding in the rain
> We know it's not a nice day
> But we'll get you on the plane.

The passengers applauded. Virgin also keeps costs low, using only one type of plane (new Boeing 737s) and concentrating on (for them) cheap on-line bookings (about 35 per cent of fares). Richard Branson has guaranteed $50 million to fund the early period of airline competition and is confident of success.

Impulse was also confident. They had major backing – $120 million from AMP and the Singapore government. This was also an experienced airline that had a culture of hard work established over the 18 years they had operated as a freight airline. They used a low-cost approach similar to the successful US firm Southwest. CEO McGowan said, 'Careful attention to costs have meant that the cost per seat is 40 per cent of Qantas.' They offered no in-flight meals, used one type of plane (new Boeing 717s) and ran the organisation with only five executives. Around 60 per cent of their fares were booked on the Internet. Their failure in 2001 was related to the fierce competition they engendered.

The established players have responded aggressively. Qantas spent $7 million on advertising in September 2000, well above their usual expenditure. Both Ansett and Qantas claim that they can continue to match the low Impulse and Virgin fares and make good profits because of their sophisticated yield management systems. These may include five levels of fare: business, full-fare economy, small discount, middle discount and deep discount. Ansett has claimed that the new entrants attack only the deep discount market and that the lucrative business market remains Ansett–Qantas territory.

In April 2001, Ansett had a major public relations and reputational disaster when the Civil Aviation Safety Authority (CASA) grounded their 767 aircraft on safety grounds. CASA then insisted on a complete overhaul of the Ansett maintenance process, as well as a change in the communication process in the company. Qantas also suffered, although less badly, when a critical report on a landing error by the crew of a jet that landed at Bangkok airport in 2000 was released the same month. The aircraft had aquaplaned off the end of the runway and into a golf course as a result of communication and pilot error.

The airline battle will continue. The established firms have major resources, but so has Virgin Blue. All have clear ideas on the winning strategy – fun/low-cost Virgin, and solidity/convenience/history Ansett and Qantas. Virgin has an excellent brand and reputation to support its positioning, but so does Qantas. (For a full account of the background, see Case 2 in the cases section.)

Sources: J. Eastway, 1999, 'Qantas keep in service for the flying kangaroo', *Business Review Weekly*, 22 October, pp. 105–9; L. Colquohoun, 2000, 'Newcomers score in dog-fight's early rounds', *Business Review Weekly*, 13 October, pp. 80–5; Qantas, 2001, *Qantas Home Page*: www.qantas.com.au..

Interestingly, research suggests that market commonality and multi-market competition may begin almost by chance. However, the same research also suggests that after it begins, the multi-market competition becomes intentional.[44] Such intentional actions may provide incentives to reduce product lines and avoid entering certain markets.[45] Thus, multi-market competition can become a deterrent to competitive rivalry. However, most multi-market contact is highly complex, as in the airline industry. As a result, competitive interactions are likely to be more complex than was even suggested in the Strategic Focus on the airlines.

Recent work suggests that firms may take one or more of three different actions in multi-market contact with competitors. First, they may make a *thrust*, which is a direct attack on a specific competitive market niche, forcing competitors to withdraw resources. The second action that firms may take is a *feint*, which is an attack on a focal area that is important to a competitor, but not vital to the firm taking the action. The intent is to get the focal firm to commit more resources to the market in question. Given the absence of visible outcomes from a recent American and British Air alliance, it might have been intended as a feint by one or both firms. The final type of action firms may take is a *gambit*, from the game of chess. In a business gambit, a position is sacrificed to entice a competitor to divert resources to a certain niche.

Resource similarity

The intensity of competitive rivalry often is based on a potential response and is of great concern for an attacker. An attacker may not be motivated to target a rival that is likely to retaliate. This is especially true of firms with strategic resources similar to those of a potential attacker.[46] *Resource similarity* refers to the extent of resource overlap between two firms.[47] *Resource dissimilarity* also plays a vital role in a competitor's motivation to attack or respond. In fact, 'the greater is the resource imbalance between the acting firm and competitors or potential responders, the greater will be the delay in response'.[48] Although the degree of market commonality is obvious to both firms, strategic resources are difficult to identify because of their causal ambiguity and social complexity (as described in Chapter 3). The difficulty in identifying and understanding the competing firms' resources (including its capabilities and core competencies) also contributes to response delays, especially in instances of resource dissimilarity.

Coca-Cola and Pepsi's decisions to compete in the American bottled-water market (as explained in the Strategic Focus) demonstrate an imbalance in resources between the acting firms (Coke and Pepsi) and their competitors (Perrier Group, Suntory International, McKesson, Great Brands of Europe and Crystal Geyser). However, the resource dissimilarity between firms such as the Perrier Group on the one hand and Coca-Cola and Pepsi on the other made it difficult for the smaller and less resource-rich companies to implement effective competitive responses.[49]

Strategic Focus International

Cola wars, water wars and going for the jugular vein

Coca-Cola is the dominant firm in the global soft-drink market. It has the largest market share in the United States and in many other markets as well. For example, Coca-Cola has approximately 75 per cent of the soft-drink market in Chile and just under 70 per cent in Mexico. In fact, it has over 50 per cent of the soft-drink market in many of the European countries (for example, France, Germany and Spain). Its share of the global soft-drink market is about 50 per cent. Because of Coca-Cola's dominant position, along with those of several other competitors (mostly local or regional, except for Pepsi), many of these markets have become saturated. Thus, competitors can no longer enjoy a growing market and must target their competitors' market share. Competitors have largely targeted Coca-Cola.

Coca-Cola withdrew from the Indian market in 1987 because of a nationalist government that wanted it to sell to local firms. It returned to India in 1993, but by that time Pepsi was well entrenched without Coca-Cola as a competitor. A local cola firm also gained a major foothold in the market during Coca-Cola's absence. The stakes are high in India, because it is one of the few remaining large markets that are not saturated. Recently, the government approved the use of artificial sweeteners in carbonated drinks. Coca-Cola and Pepsi moved swiftly to introduce their diet colas. In fact, Pepsi introduced Diet Pepsi to the market within two days of the approval. Coca-Cola responded with prominent advertising announcing the arrival of Diet Coke. However, within a week, the Indian Health Ministry announced that it would enforce an old regulation requiring all carbonated drinks to contain at least 5 per cent sucrose. Pepsi blamed Coca-Cola for bringing this regulation to the attention of the Indian government. Pepsi believed that Coca-Cola took its action to delay Pepsi so that Coca-Cola could catch up. Pepsi then sought and obtained a court waiver to avoid having to add the sucrose and also won a temporary injunction that allows it to keep selling Diet Pepsi until the court rules on its case. Coca-Cola also sought a waiver and then launched its Diet Coke into the market. Neither company may gain much, even if they win the right to sell their diet drinks: Indians generally do not like the taste of diet drinks and are suspicious of artificial sweeteners.

Pepsi and Coca-Cola are competing in another market as well. In 1994, Pepsi introduced its brand of bottled water, Aquafina. Since that time, Aquafina has become the top-selling brand of bottled water in US convenience stores. Five years after Pepsi's introduction of bottled water, Coca-Cola announced that it was entering this market as well. In 1999, Coca-Cola declared that it would begin marketing bottled water under the brand name Dasani. The product will be purified, non-carbonated water fortified with minerals to enhance its taste.

Coca-Cola was reluctant to add bottled water to its line of products, preferring instead to encourage consumption of its carbonated soft drinks. However, the popularity of bottled water and Pepsi's success probably lured Coca-Cola into the market, although belatedly. A large number of smaller competitors offer similar bottled-water products. Naya, another brand of water, is distributed by Coca-Cola, but probably will not be for much longer. Pepsi and Coca-Cola are expected to battle for sales of their water products. However, both will need to be careful not to substitute sales of water for soft-drink sales (because their margin is much higher on soft drinks).

In the 1990s, consumption of Pepsi's soft drinks increased by only 2 per cent, while Coca-Cola's consumption increased by 30 per cent in the same decade. Thus, Pepsi managers decided to invest heavily in advertising. In 1999, Pepsi spent almost as much as did Coca-Cola on advertising, even though Pepsi is much smaller, after spinning off its bottlers and restaurant operations, now called Tricon. Pepsi used the approximately US$4 billion that it received from the spin-offs to help finance the new campaign.

While Coca-Cola is the clear global leader, all is not well in the company. In 1999, it experienced embarrassing and costly lapses in quality that caused short-term bans of its products in Belgium and France. It also had to withdraw 180 000 bottles of water in Poland after coliform bacteria were discovered in the drink. In addition, Italy's competition authority fined Coca-Cola for anticompetitive practices. Given all of these problems and slow and ineffective reactions to them, Coca-Cola's CEO, Douglas Ivestor, resigned his position. Coca-Cola also recently announced employee layoffs and a restructuring of its management. Managers at Pepsi are probably revelling over Coca-Cola's problems.

Sources: M. Benson, 1999, 'In New York, battle is over city-owned property', *Wall Street Journal Interactive Edition*, 29 September: www.interactive.wsj.com/archive; J. Blitz and B. Liu, 1999, 'Coca-Cola: $16 million fine from Italian authorities', 18 December: www.ft.com/sea; N. Deogun and E. Williamson, 1999, 'Coke, in new breakdown, recalls more water products in Poland', *Wall Street Journal Interactive Edition*, 6 July: www.interactive.wsj.com/articles; D. Foust, 1999, 'Coke and Pepsi want to make a splash in water', *Businessweek Online*, 1 March: bwarchive.businessweek.com; D. Foust, G. Smith and D. Rocks, 1999, 'Coke's man on the spot', 3 May: bwarchive.businessweek.com; 'Going for broke', 1999, *The Economist*, 16 August: www.economist.com/editorial; 'It's the real thing: Coca Cola preparing for dive into bottled water market', *Dallas Morning News*, 20 February, p. F12; L. Light, 1999, 'The Pepsi generation', *Businessweek Online*, 22 March: bwarchive.businessweek.com.

Because of the intense competition experienced in a number of industries, many firms have inadequate resources to be competitive. For example, Packard Bell NEC, owned jointly by NEC of Japan and Groupe Bull of France, announced in 1999 that it was closing most of its US operations in the personal computer market. In 1995, Packard Bell was the largest retail PC marketer in the United States. However, its fortunes changed quickly with substantial competition from Hewlett-Packard and Compaq, particularly in the low-cost PC market. In 1998 and 1999, Packard-Bell NEC experienced significant net losses. As a result, it no longer had adequate resources to compete in that market.[50] The difficulties of the Tasmanian-owned milk producer Betta Milk, in its battle with the nationally based Pura Milk, provides a further example. Following deregulation of the milk industry, prices dropped and the small Tasmanian has experienced problems in trying to match its bigger rivals' prices for milk.[51]

Inadequate resources, whether financial, technical or important capabilities, have forced firms to form alliances to compete in specific markets. Thus, one of the primary reasons for strategic alliances is the opportunity for partners to share resources. Also, alliances help firms to acquire certain types of resources. For instance, firms may enhance their capabilities by learning from partners, thereby improving their resource base.[52] NEC formed an alliance with Mitsubishi Electric with the purpose of improving the firm's ability to compete. The 50/50 joint venture is designed to develop, manufacture and market computer monitors and displays. The venture is expected to sell 10 million units annually by 2002, generating revenue of 350 billion yen. NEC has also established a joint venture with GE to manufacture and market medical equipment.[53] Likewise, Global Crossing, based in Bermuda, has established a joint venture with Hutchison Whampoa, based in Hong Kong. The venture will integrate Hutchison's local fixed phone line network with Global Crossing's international telecommunications capabilities. Global Crossing has also formed a joint venture with Japan's Softbank and Microsoft to build a fibre-optic network in Asia.[54] In each of these ventures, both partners contribute a unique set of resources. It is this complex competitive environment that Telstra is trying to enter, and the obvious way to try to match the resources and capabilities of such powerful competitors is via an alliance strategy.

Competitive dynamics have caused firms to move beyond simple alliances to develop more complex networks of relationships. Networks of organisations can provide greater value to consumers, as well as draw on resources from multiple partners. Networks are particularly useful with smaller businesses and in international markets. In fact, the use of networks may allow smaller entrepreneurial businesses to compete with larger and more resource-rich firms. However, managing the networks of relationships is difficult: firms must formulate and implement network strategies.[55] (We discuss these network-based businesses further in Chapters 9 and 11.) Next, we examine the likelihood that firms will take strategic actions or respond to them from competitors.

Likelihood of attack

> A **competitive action** is a significant competitive move made by a firm that is designed to gain a competitive advantage in a market.

Although awareness and motivation to respond are derived largely from competitors' analyses of market commonality and resource similarity, there are strong incentives to be the first mover in a competitive battle if the attacking firm believes it has the potential to win. This was the basis of Impulse Airline's radical low-cost entry into Australia's domestic airline industry. A **competitive action** is a significant competitive move made by a firm that is designed to gain a competitive advantage in a market.[56] Some competitive actions are large and significant; others are small and designed to help fine-tune or implement a strategy. The first mover in a competitive interaction may be able to gain above-average returns while competitors consider potential countermoves. Furthermore, the first mover may be able to deter a counterattack, given enough time. As a result, there are significant incentives to be a first mover, and the order of each competitive action and response influences an industry's competitive dynamics. Of greatest importance are first movers, second movers and late movers.

First, second and late movers

> A **first mover** is a firm that takes an initial competitive action.

A **first mover** is a firm that takes an initial competitive action. The concept of first movers has been influenced by the work of economist Joseph Schumpeter. In particular, he believed that firms achieve competitive advantage through entrepreneurial and innovative competitive actions.[57] In general, first movers 'allocate funds for product innovation and development, aggressive advertising, and advanced research and development'.[58] Through competitive actions such as these, first movers hope to gain a competitive advantage. For example, Disco SA was the first supermarket chain to offer on-line shopping in Argentina. Royal Ahold of the Netherlands and Velox Investment Co. of Argentina jointly own Disco. The on-line service alliance represented a natural extension of Disco's shop-by-phone service initiated in 1996. Also in 1996, Disco had a website that clients in the company's frequent shopper program could consult about the points they had accumulated and their eligibility for prizes. Disco sells a minimum of 3 million pesos per month to non-traditional shoppers (by phone or on-line) and reached 2 billion pesos during 1999. Importantly, 72 per cent of the on-line shoppers previously were customers of other supermarkets. Thus, the on-line service is attracting a significant new clientele to Disco. In addition, the average purchase of a Disco in-store shopper is 14 pesos, while the average purchase of an on-line customer is 100 pesos. As a result, the new service offered by Disco appears to be an unqualified success in all dimensions.[59]

Several competitive advantages can accrue to the firm that is first to initiate a competitive action. Successful actions allow a firm to earn above-average returns until other competitors are able to respond effectively. In addition, first movers have the opportunity to gain customer loyalty, thereby making it difficult for responding firms to capture customers. For instance, Harley-Davidson has been able to maintain a competitive lead in large motorcycles due to intense customer loyalty. Across time, though, the competitive advantage of a first mover begins to erode. (Recall from Chapter 1 that every competitive advantage can be imitated eventually.) The advantages and their duration vary by the type of competitive action and industry. First-mover advantages also vary on the basis of the ease with which competitors can imitate the action. The more difficult and costly an action is to imitate, the longer a firm may receive the benefits of being a first mover. When core competencies are the foundation of a competitive action, first-mover advantages tend to last longer. Core competence-based competitive actions have a high probability of resulting in a sustained competitive advantage.

However, potential disadvantages may result from being the first firm to initiate a competitive action. Chief among these is the degree of risk taken by first movers. The risk of a first move is high, because it is not easy to predict the amount of success a particular competitive action will produce prior to its initiation.[60] Often, first movers have high development costs. Second movers can avoid these costs through reverse engineering (taking apart a new product and then reassembling it to learn how it works). Another potential disadvantage of being a first mover is the dynamic and uncertain nature of many markets in which a firm may compete. In other words, the extent and range of marketplace competition heighten the potential risk. In fact, in a highly uncertain market, it may be more appropriate to be a second or late mover.

A **second mover** is a firm that responds to a first mover's competitive action, often through imitation or a move designed to counter the effects of the action. When the second mover responds quickly to a first mover's competitive action, it may earn some of the first-mover advantages without experiencing the disadvantages. For example, a fast second mover may gain some of the returns and obtain a portion of the initial customers, and thereby customer loyalty, while avoiding some of the risks encountered by the first mover. The firm taking a second action as a competitive response to the first mover can do so after evaluating customers' reactions to the first mover's action.[61] To be a successful first mover or fast second mover, a company must be able to analyse its markets and identify critical strategic issues.[62] Firms have different capabilities of obtaining information on markets and analysing that information after it is obtained. These differences explain why some firms are faster to adopt market innovations than are others.[63]

Being second to the market also allows a firm to conduct market research to learn the first mover's actions and improve on them. Thus, being a second mover allows a firm to introduce directed innovation to better meet consumer needs. A second mover has information that is unavailable to a first mover and thus can direct its strategy on the basis of observing what happens to the first mover. Furthermore, being second provides time to perfect the good or service, eliminating potentially irritating 'bugs'. Hence, the second-mover strategy gains time for R&D to develop a superior product.[64] Sometimes, being first to the market means that the firm will be the first to fail! It is difficult to conduct definitive market research before introducing a new good or service. First, it may

> A **second mover** is a firm that responds to a first mover's competitive action, often through imitation or a move designed to counter the effects of the action.

be difficult to define precisely the market for a highly innovative product. Second, some market pioneers fail because they lack either sufficient vision for how the product can be used or the commitment to persist for the long term. Time may be required to convince consumers to accept a new good or service.[65]

In some instances, it may not be possible to move quickly in response to a first mover's action. For example, if the first mover introduces a sophisticated new product and competitors have not undertaken similar research and development, considerable time may be required to respond effectively. Therefore, some risks are involved in being a follower in the market. There are no blueprints for first-mover success. Followers may be able to respond without significant market development costs by learning from a first mover's successes and mistakes. Thus, the actions and outcomes of the first firm to initiate a competitive action may provide a more effective blueprint for second and later movers.[66]

New Balance, Inc. is a second mover in the athletic shoe industry. As mentioned in Chapter 2, accounting for New Balance's success as a second mover is its ability to satisfy baby boomers' needs. The firm's target market is demonstrated by customers' average ages – 25 for Nike, 33 for Reebok and 42 for New Balance. As a second mover's product, the firm's shoes are not particularly innovative compared to those of the industry leader, Nike. In contrast to many competitors that introduce new models roughly every six weeks, New Balance introduces a new one approximately every 17 weeks. New Balance's competitive success as a second mover appears to be based on its ability to offer high-quality products at moderate prices, but in multiple-sized widths. Unlike most companies, which produce shoes in two widths – medium and wide – New Balance offers customers multiple choices, ranging from a narrow AA to an expansive EEEE. The varying widths are a valued competitive feature, as many Australians have either narrower- or wider-than-average feet.

A **late mover** is a firm that responds to a competitive action, but only after considerable time has elapsed after the first mover's action and the second mover's response. Although some type of competitive response may be more effective than no response, late movers tend to be poorer performers and often are weak competitors. Avon is a late mover in e-commerce. It implemented its Internet-based marketing and sales efforts in 2000, using IBM as a consultant to help in the design and implementation of its system. While analysts think that the change may be a good one for Avon in helping to attract a more upscale customer, Avon is alienating its direct-sales force. The company's Internet sales compete with its sales representatives who provide direct-sales' service. Furthermore, at least six major competitors established Internet sales before Avon did. It will be difficult for Avon to gain a reasonable share of this market with the formidable competition.[67]

Like Avon, Dell was a late mover in providing Internet access, but it has achieved a measure of success in the European market. Its free Internet access service probably benefits from the Dell brand name (see Chapter 2) that many other new ventures do not enjoy. In late 1999 and early 2000, Dell launched a free Internet access service in the United States as well.[68]

> A **late mover** is a firm that responds to a competitive action, but only after considerable time has elapsed after the first mover's action and the second mover's response.

Likelihood of response

> A **competitive response** is a move taken to counter the effects of an action by a competitor.

After firms take a competitive action, the success of the action often is determined by the likelihood and nature of the response by competitors. A **competitive response** is a move taken to counter the effects of an action by a competitor. Firms considering offensive action need to evaluate the potential responses from competition in making their decision to act. An offensive action may escalate rivalry to a point where actions become self-defeating and an alternative strategy may be necessary. A *de-escalation strategy* is an attempt to reduce overly heated competition that has become self-defeating. As Figure 5.1 shows, the probability of a competitor's response to a competitive action is based on the type of action, the reputation of the competitor taking the action, the competitor's dependence on the market and the availability of resources to the competitor.

Type of competitive action

The two types of competitive actions are strategic and tactical.[69] A **strategic action** represents a significant commitment of specific and distinctive organisational resources; it is difficult to implement and to reverse. Wal-Mart's entry into European markets is an example of strategic action, as is Woolworths' Ezy-Banking alliance with the Commonwealth Bank.

In contrast to strategic actions, a **tactical action** is taken to fine-tune a strategy; it involves fewer and more general organisational resources and is relatively easy to implement and reverse. A price increase in a particular market (for example, in airfares) is an example of a tactical action. This action involves few organisational resources (for example, communicating new prices and changing prices on products), its implementation is relatively easy, and it can be reversed (through a price reduction, for example) in a relatively short period of time.

Compared to a tactical action, responses to a strategic action are more difficult, because they require additional organisational resources and time. Compared to strategic actions, tactical actions usually have more immediate effects. The announcement of a price increase in a price-sensitive industry such as airlines could have immediate effects on competitors. Therefore, it is uncommon for airlines not to respond quickly to a competitor's price change, particularly if the announced change represents a price reduction, because without a response, the competing airline may lose market share.[70] The price war in the Australian airlines industry in 2000 clearly demonstrates this.[71]

Not all competitive actions elicit or require a response from competitors. On the whole, there are more competitive responses to tactical than to strategic actions.[72] It is usually easier to respond to tactical actions, and sometimes it is necessary, at least in the short term. For example, responding to changes in a competitor's frequent-flier program is much easier and requires far fewer resources than responding to a major competitor's decision to upgrade its fleet of jets and to form strategic alliances to enter new markets.

Actor's reputation

An action (either strategic or tactical) taken by a market leader is likely to serve as a catalyst to a larger number of and faster responses from competitors and to a higher probability of imitation of the action. In other words, firms are more likely to imitate the actions of a competitor that is a market leader. For instance, if Coca-Cola enters a new market or introduces a new product, competitors are likely to respond (if they have adequate resources to do so). Schweppes is the most likely competitor to respond in Australia, because it has adequate resources and because it is second behind Coca-Cola. Most market leaders have market power and enjoy special advantages because of their strong positive reputation.[73] Coca-Cola, for instance, enjoys a brand name that is well known globally and has considerable market power (as described in Chapter 3). These advantages create formidable barriers for competitors to overcome in trying to imitate Coca-Cola's actions. For example, Coca-Cola has an extensive bottling and distribution system. Many of the smaller competitors' products are bottled and distributed by Coca-

Cola's bottlers. Thus, a smaller competitor may have difficulty introducing a new product to the market that is competitive with Coca-Cola's products, as Coca-Cola's distributors may refuse to distribute the new product.

Firms also often react quickly to imitate successful competitor actions. For example, in the personal computer market, IBM quickly dominated the market as a second mover, but was imitated by Compaq, Dell and Gateway. By contrast, firms that take risky, complex and unpredictable actions are less likely to solicit responses to, and imitations of, their actions.[74] Finally, firms that are known to be price predators (frequently cutting prices to hurt competitors and obtain market share, only to raise prices later) also do not elicit a large number of responses or imitation. In fact, there is less imitation and a much slower response to price predators than to either of the other two types of firms (market leader and strategic player).[75]

As suggested in the Strategic Focus on the automobile industry, there is no single dominant company in the industry. GM was once dominant, but its share of the large US automobile market decreased from 36 per cent to 29 per cent in the 1990s. GM, Ford, DaimlerChrysler and Toyota have the strongest reputations globally. Any firm in the industry is likely to carefully observe a major strategic action by any of those four. If resources allow, other automobile companies are likely to respond to the action. However, their response is not only because of the actor's reputation: most automobile firms are highly dependent on the industry, so they have no choice but to try to respond to strategic actions of competitors in order to remain viable.

Strategic Focus International

Car wars: The battle for survival

The number of automobile manufacturers continues to shrink. The acquisition of Chrysler by Daimler, Ford's purchase of Volvo, and GM's alliance with Honda may foretell the future of the industry. Toyota's CEO, Hiroshi Okuda, suggested that in the 21st century there will be only five or six major automobile manufacturers. He proposes that a firm's sales volume needs to be at least five million vehicles annually in order for the company to compete in global markets. Consolidation is occurring in the automobile industry, as it is in others. Most of the consolidation crosses country borders. Thus, national identity is becoming obsolete. It is predicted that by 2010, each major automobile market in the world will have two automobile manufacturers. Some analysts believe that six firms will remain: Ford and GM in the United States, DaimlerChrysler and Volkswagen in Europe, and Toyota and Honda in Asia. Currently, only GM and Ford sell more than five million vehicles annually.

The major firms will acquire the healthy, but smaller, firms in Europe (for example, Renault) and the distressed firms in Asia (for example, Nissan). Still, this is only speculation as the dynamism in the competitive landscape makes prediction difficult. As the likely survivors, the 'big six' automobile manufacturers noted above must continue to develop and implement effective strategies and respond effectively to competitors' strategic actions to be able to operate successfully and have the resources to acquire and win their battles with competitors. If they do not, they will not survive. For example, DaimlerChrysler is desperately seeking an ally in Asia to help it penetrate Asian markets. Ford owns a significant interest in Mazda and Volvo, and GM is aligned with Honda. Both also have relationships with other Asian firms (for example, GM is working on a deal to help improve Daewoo's automobile unit). However,

DaimlerChrysler does not have alliances with firms from this region, nor are there many available. Nissan has rejected Daimler's overtures. Of course, Renault owns a stake in Nissan, and Mitsubishi is engaged in talks with Volvo because of a previous relationship between the firms. But Daimler finally acquired a stake in Mitsubishi.

Toyota has announced that it is increasing its manufacturing capacity in North America. Toyota currently sells approximately 1.5 million vehicles in North America despite a capacity to produce only about 1.2 million vehicles. Such expansion may allow Toyota to better serve the lucrative North American market. The company is expected to increase its production of light trucks (for example, SUVs), which account for about 50 per cent of the North American market for motor vehicles. This is a highly contested market because of its popularity. In late 1999, for example, Ford and DaimlerChrysler both announced rebates on some of their most profitable light trucks. GM had already offered rebates on some of its light trucks (for example, the Chevrolet Venture minivan). The actions of all three firms have been prompted by competition, particularly from Japanese and European manufacturers.

Volkswagen is another concern in the survival war. While VW has about 19 per cent of the Western European automobile market, up from 15 per cent in 1994, it is experiencing stagnation. Expectations are that it will continue to have problems over the foreseeable future and may be the most vulnerable of the 'big six'. Concerns grow as the European Union allows freer competition across European country borders and less control over automobile dealers. GM's Opel expects to increase its market share in Germany, likely at the expense of VW, which may need a partner in Europe and elsewhere to be among the survivors. On the positive side, VW's sales in the large US market are quite strong.

Thus, the 21st-century competitive landscape is likely to produce exciting battles and outcomes in the global automobile industry.

Sources: J. Ball, 1999, 'Ford, DaimlerChrysler boost rebates on some very profitable light trucks', *Wall Street Journal Interactive Edition*, 17 November: www.interactive.wsj.com/articles; 'Chrysler in battle of minivan', 1999, *Houston Chronicle*, 26 November, p. 4D; J. Ewing, K. Kerwin and K. N. Anhalt, 1999, 'VW: Spinning its wheels?', *Businessweek Online*, 22 November: bwarchive.businessweek.com; J. Ewing, E. Thornton and M. Ihlwan, 1999, 'DaimlerChrysler: Desperately seeking an ally', *Businessweek Online*, 13 December: bwarchive.businessweek.com; 'Ford: Faith in high prices', 1999, 24 December: www.ft.com/sea; K. Naughton, K. L. Miller, J. Muller, E. Thornton and G. Edmondson, 1999, 'Autos: The global six', *Businessweek Online*, 25 January: bwarchive.businessweek.com; N. Shirouzu, 1999, 'Toyota considers boosting capacity in North America', *Wall Street Journal Interactive Edition*, 29 June: www.interactive.wsj.com/articles

Dependence on the market

Firms with a high dependency on a market in which a competitive action is taken are more likely to respond to that action. For example, firms with a large amount of their total sales from one industry are more likely to respond to a particular competitive action taken in that industry than is a firm with businesses in multiple industries (for example, a conglomerate). Thus, if the type of action taken has a major effect on them, firms are likely to respond, regardless of whether the action is strategic or tactical.

In the Australian cinema screen industry, the major competitors – Hoyts (purchased by Kerry Packer's Consolidated Press in July 1999), Greater Union (part of Amalgamated Holdings) and Village Roadshow compete for the cinema goer in a number of ways. They continue to build more cinema complexes (despite the fact that this is becoming more expensive – in 1996, $750 000 and in 2000, $1 million). Within cinemas they offer an ever better service – better seats, bar service, good coffees and better sound systems. All are pursuing the older cinema goer, an under-exploited segment. All are concerned about challenges from the Internet, pay television and the old video threat in the new form of DVD.[76]

Worldwide the cinema screen industry is considering how new technology will change the business. For example, within five years digital cinema will be possible, and movies will be downloaded to a screen from a satellite or via fibre-optic cable. This will be costly but will yield better screen resolution and, because it is a secure technology, reduce movie piracy.[77]

The battle between McDonald's and Burger King, in the American market, also exemplifies a pattern of competitive actions and responses occurring between two firms that are highly dependent on their core market. Burger King and McDonald's are both completely dependent on sales in the fast-food industry. Hence, it is not surprising that the two firms monitor each other's strategic and tactical actions quite carefully. Moreover, competitive actions taken by one of these companies, whether strategic or tactical, almost certainly will result in a competitive response. McDonald's and Burger King have battled over which has the crispest and best-tasting French fries and hamburgers, but have now decided that they need to be more creative and better serve the customer. In addition, they have decided against growing primarily through the development of more restaurants; rather, they are concentrating on growth through increases in average restaurant sales. To do so, Burger King returned to its flame-broiled hamburgers customised to each customer. The return to the older strategy has been successful. In addition, Burger King began to redesign all of its restaurants in 1999 and to introduce innovations such as interactive video games at tables (an initiative that will spread internationally in this intensely competitive industry). In response, McDonald's implemented a 'made for you' cooking system in each of its kitchens. The flexible kitchens allow McDonald's to experiment with new foods and recipes. For example, it has pilot tested such novelties as steak, egg and cheese bagels for breakfast in some of its restaurants. The number-three hamburger restaurant chain, Wendy's, has also reorganised its kitchens to provide more flexible menus. The results have been positive; in 1999, McDonald's market share in the United States increased from 42.2 to 42.7 per cent, Burger King increased its market share from 19.4 to 20.2 per cent, and Wendy's market share increased from 11.3 to 11.5 per cent. These increases have come at the expense of smaller chains and independent hamburger restaurants.[78]

Similarly, retail chains in Europe are responding to Wal-Mart's entry into their markets. For example, Tesco and Sainsbury in the UK have implemented initiatives to capture the home-shopping market. Tesco Direct, Tesco's e-commerce effort, is profitable and is predicted soon to become the world's largest Internet grocery business. The effort may be highly important for Tesco, because Wal-Mart's entry into Britain's grocery market has driven down prices, thereby reducing the margins earned from physical-store sales.[79]

Boeing has other businesses, but its core business is the manufacture and marketing of commercial aircraft. Its only global competitor, Airbus Industrie, has decided to develop a super jumbo aircraft that will hold up to 600 passengers. While a few years ago Boeing considered and decided against developing a larger version of its 747, it is now reconsidering this option as a competitive response to Airbus. Unfortunately, there are only six airlines that could use such a large aircraft profitably, thereby limiting the market size. Thus, one or both firms could lose money on a super jumbo aircraft.[80] Of course, Boeing has the resources to develop such an aircraft (said to cost about US$3 billion) to respond to Airbus, but not all firms have the resources to respond effectively to competitors' strategic actions.

Competitors' availability of resources

A competitive response to a strategic or tactical action requires organisational resources. Firms with fewer resources are more likely to respond to tactical actions than to strategic ones, because responses to tactical actions require fewer resources and are easier to implement. In addition, a firm's resources may dictate the type of response it makes. For example, local video stores have relatively limited resources to respond to competitive actions taken by Blockbuster, a dominant firm in the video industry. Typically, a local store cannot imitate a Blockbuster strategic action to establish multiple units within a particular geographic area. In contrast, the smaller local firm is far more likely to respond to a Blockbuster tactical action of reduced prices. However, because of its lower volume and lack of purchasing power relative to the large chains, initiating a tactical price reduction can also be difficult for the local store. To compete against Blockbuster, the local video store often relies on personalised customer service and willingness to stock or search for hard-to-find videos as the sources of its competitive advantage. Focusing instead on mass availability of the most popular titles and holding operating costs as low as possible, a large video chain such as Blockbuster is unlikely to respond to the local store's service-oriented competitive actions, even though it has the resources to do so.[81] However, Internet technology firms such as Blockbuster may be able to customise rentals more easily for the consumer. As this suggests, small firms can respond effectively to their larger counterparts' competitive actions, but this may be more difficult to accomplish in a future dominated by electronic markets.

Firms' abilities to take action and respond

As indicated earlier, resource availability and ability to respond affect the probability of a company's response to a competing firm's competitive actions. Firms' abilities therefore moderate the relationship between inter-firm rivalry and the competitive outcomes (see Figure 5.1). In general, four characteristics of firms influence competitive interaction within a market or industry: (1) the relative size of the firm within a market or industry; (2) the speed at which competitive actions and responses are made; (3) the extent of innovation by firms in the market or industry; and (4) the quality of the firm's product.

Relative size of firm

The size of a firm can have two important, but opposite, effects on an industry's competitive dynamics. First, the larger the firm, the greater is its market power. Of course, the extent of any firm's market power is measured relative to the power of its competitors. Boeing Company (with roughly a 65 per cent share of the world's commercial aircraft market) and Airbus Industries (with approximately a 33 per cent market share) both have substantial market power. Relatively, however, Boeing's market power exceeds that of Airbus. Thus, Boeing hopes that developing a larger 747 will limit the ability of Airbus to capture the super jumbo aircraft market niche.[82] In the global automobile manufacturing industry, the four major competitors identified earlier – GM, Ford, DaimlerChrysler and Toyota – are large; hence, no individual firm has critical market power over the others. Nonetheless, it is difficult for small firms to enter the market because the sheer size of those four firms creates substantial entry barriers. Relative to them, Renault is smaller and has less market power, which is why it is predicted that the firm will not survive over the long term competing against the 'big six'.

Size usually reflects more than market power: Often, a firm's market share reflects the general level of its resources, which may even include its R&D capabilities and the perceived quality of its products.[83] The market power and resources of competitors also shape a focal firm's responses.[84] A firm competing against weaker competitors may ignore their actions. However, it may also take actions to which its competitors are unlikely to be able to respond. Indeed, it can even drive them out of the market. For example, in

1999, Intel implemented a tactical reduction of 41 per cent in the price of its Pentium III chips to take sales from its competitors. Actions like these caused National Semiconductor to exit the PC microprocessor business. The company fell behind in the technology and did not have the resources to increase its technology development.[85]

Problems created by a firm's size are demonstrated by events – both historical and current – in the computer industry. Although the giant in the industry, IBM, was highly successful, it did not invent or even first introduce the microcomputer, which is the primary basis of the industry today. Entrepreneurial ventures, such as Apple Computer, Dell Computer and Compaq, introduced the innovations in goods and services that revolutionised the industry. Small firms often do this by fostering what Joseph Schumpeter referred to as 'creative destruction'.[86] As Steven Jobs and his partner Steve Wozniak revolutionised the computer industry, Michael Dell, who was in high school when Apple introduced its computers, revolutionised the way computers were produced and distributed. The microcomputer market is highly dynamic. Compaq became the number-one manufacturer and seller of personal computers in the 1995–6 period. In 1999, however, Compaq was overtaken by Dell as the top producer of personal computers.[87] Thus, often the smaller competitor is more innovative and eventually overtakes the top firm. The moral is that it may not be best to grow too large, but rather to find a way to continue to operate using a small-firm culture even though the firm is actually large.

A quote attributed to Herbert Kelleher, co-founder and CEO of Southwest Airlines in the United States, best describes the approach needed by large firms. In Kelleher's words, 'Think and act big and we'll get smaller. Think and act small and we'll get bigger.'[88] This aphorism suggests that large firms should use their size to build market power, but that they must think and act like a small firm (for example, move quickly and be innovative) in order to achieve strategic competitiveness and earn above-average returns over the long run. A commitment to the value of each employee and to the use of organisational structures that encourage individuals to demonstrate initiative appears to facilitate large firms' efforts to act entrepreneurially.[89] Thermo Electron and Xerox are large companies that appear to be following Kelleher's prescription to overcome the liabilities of size through the creation and support of entrepreneurship.[90]

Speed of competitive actions and competitive responses

Time and speed are important in the 21st-century competitive landscape. The speed with which a firm can initiate competitive actions and competitive responses may determine its success. In the 21st-century competitive landscape, speed in developing a new product and moving it to the marketplace is becoming critical to establish a competitive advantage and earn above-average returns.[91]

Tesco and Sainsbury in Britain and Carrefour in France had to respond quickly to Wal-Mart's entry into their markets. Failure to do so could make them highly vulnerable to Wal-Mart's market power once it became established in their markets. In each country, the firms chose a different way to respond. Carrefour responded by acquiring a major competitor to increase its size, resource base, economies of scale, and breadth and depth of market power. In contrast, Tesco and Sainsbury chose to focus on a market niche in which Wal-Mart has not exhibited strength – e-commerce. Their actions were swift and helped the firms continue to be important competitors in their respective markets.

Speed in bringing their products to the marketplace is one of the problems US automobile manufacturers have experienced in competing with Japanese firms. Some time ago, Japanese automobile companies were able to design a new product and introduce it to the market within three years. In comparison, US firms required between five and eight years to complete these activities. This time differential made it possible for Japanese firms to design two or three new automobiles and move them to the market in the same time it took a US automobile manufacturer to do one. Thereafter, Ford, GM and DaimlerChrysler all reduced their development time to three to four years. However, Toyota responded by reducing its development time to a minimum of 15 months. In a global economy, although time is a critical source of competitive advantage, managing for speed requires more than attempting to have employees work faster. Essentially, it requires working smarter, using different types of organisational structures, and shortening the time it takes to bring a car to completion, as primary work-related goals.[92] Research has shown that the pace of strategic decision making may be affected by an executive's cognitive ability, use of intuition, tolerance for risk and propensity to act.[93] Executives who use intuition and have a greater tolerance for risk are predisposed to make faster strategic decisions than do those without such characteristics. Also, decisions are likely to occur faster in centralised organisations because they will not have to go through as many levels or get approval from as many people. More formalised and bureaucratic organisations, however, may find it difficult to make fast strategic decisions[94] because they require more layers of approval.

Innovation

In some industries, such as pharmaceuticals and computers, a third general factor, innovation, has long been known to have a strong influence on a firm's performance.[95] Innovation is increasing in importance in many industries in the 21st-century landscape. The strategic importance of innovation is explored further in Chapter 13. In today's global economy, research suggests that innovation, in both products and processes, is becoming linked with above-average returns in a growing number of industries.[96]

In general, the dynamics of competition among firms in high-tech industries encourage significant allocations to each company's R&D operations.[97] Within Australia, the leading companies for R&D expenditure are BHP, Telstra and Rio Tinto, all very large companies involved in high-tech areas in some of their operations.[98] Such companies require R&D in order to continue competing in the global marketplace. As the number of competitors increases in an industry, so does the amount of innovation usually produced.[99] In particular, innovation is often a strength of small firms and acts to equalise the competitiveness between large and small firms (see Chapter 13). Innovation is especially important in the computer software industry. While there are different niches, and while separate companies have achieved significant market shares in these niches, Microsoft is probably the best-known and most dominant firm in the software industry. However, Sun Microsystems has targeted Microsoft. Sun acquired the Star Division Corporation, which makes a series of office software known as Star Office. Sun's primary purpose in acquiring Star is to attack Microsoft with Web-based word-processing and spreadsheet applications. Sun plans to build Star Office into a free Internet-based service that can be run directly with a Web browser, without the need to load large programs on to the PC. Sun's stated intention is to change the 'rules of the game'. Given that Microsoft earns approximately 40 per cent of its revenue from sales of Office, this new challenge could present significant problems for the firm.[100] It also shows the need to continuously bring innovation to the market in the software industry.

In another industry in which innovation is important, mobile phones, Ericsson has fallen behind Nokia. Ericsson's problems stem primarily from being slow to bring innovations to the market. As a result, Nokia has moved ahead of the Swedish company. In 1999, the CEO of only 15 months was forced to resign. However, his supporters argue that he was treated unfairly because he was given a company with a poor product life cycle that could not be corrected in a short period of time. While Ericsson's problems can be solved, some analysts have predicted that the firm will need to embark on a process of managed decline.[101]

Firms competing in industries in which the pattern of competitive dynamics calls for innovation-related abilities should recognise that implementing innovations effectively can be difficult. Some researchers believe that a failure of implementation, not innovation, increasingly is the cause of many firms' inability to derive adequate competitive benefits from product and process innovations.[102] Among other capabilities, a firm requires executives who are able to integrate its innovation strategy with other strategies (such as the business-level strategies discussed in Chapter 4) and to recruit and select high-tech workers to implement innovations successfully.[103]

Procter & Gamble is a well-known company that has operated successfully in many global markets. However, it has suffered greatly from price competition and has been unable to differentiate itself through innovations. In fact, its new CEO in 1999, Durk Jager, suggested that the firm's last important innovation was its feminine-hygiene product, 'Always', which was introduced in 1982. Thus, Jager has taken actions to triple the rate of Procter & Gamble's innovation and reduce the time it takes to introduce new products to the market by 50 per cent. Of course, its competitors are likely to maintain or increase their own rates of innovation in response.[104]

Earlier, we suggested that large firms with significant market power that act like small firms – making strategic decisions and implementing them speedily – and that are innovative are strong competitors and are likely to earn above-average returns. However, no matter how large, fast or innovative an organisation is, the quality of its products and services also affects its industry's competitive dynamics and influences the firm's ability to achieve strategic competitiveness in domestic and global markets.

Quality

Product quality has become a universal theme in the global economy and continues to shape competitive dynamics in many industries.[105] Today, product quality is important in all industry settings and is a necessary, but not sufficient, condition for implementing a firm's strategy successfully. Without quality goods or services, strategic competitiveness cannot be achieved. Quality alone, however, does not guarantee that a firm will achieve strategic competitiveness or earn above-average returns. In the words of the president of the National Center for Manufacturing Sciences, a non-profit research consortium in the United States, 'Quality used to be a competitive issue out there, but now it's just the basic denominator to being in the market.'[106]

Quality involves meeting or exceeding customer expectations in the goods or services a firm offers.[107] The quality dimensions of goods and services are shown in Table 5.1. As a competitive dimension, quality is as important in the service sector as it is in the manufacturing sector.[108]

> **Quality** involves meeting or exceeding customer expectations in the goods or services offered.

Table 5.1 | Quality dimensions of goods and services

Product quality dimensions
1. *Performance* – Operating characteristics
2. *Features* – Important special characteristics
3. *Flexibility* – Meeting operating specifications over some period of time
4. *Durability* – Amount of use before performance deteriorates
5. *Conformance* – Match with pre-established standards
6. *Serviceability* – Ease and speed of repair or normal service
7. *Aesthetics* – How a product looks and feels
8. *Perceived quality* – Subjective assessment of characteristics (product image)

Service quality dimensions
1. *Timeliness* – Performed in promised period of time
2. *Courtesy* – Performed cheerfully
3. *Consistency* – Giving all customers similar experiences each time
4. *Convenience* – Accessibility to customers
5. *Completeness* – Fully serviced, as required
6. *Accuracy* – Performed correctly each time

Sources: Adapted from J. W. Dean, Jr and J. R. Evans, 1994, *Total Quality: Management, Organization and Society* (St. Paul, MN: West Publishing Company); H. V. Roberts and B. F. Sergesketter, 1993, *Quality is Personal* (New York: The Free Press); D. Garvin, 1988, *Managed Quality: The Strategic and Competitive Edge* (New York: The Free Press).

Quality begins at the top of the organisation. Top management must create values for quality that permeate the entire organisation.[109] These values should be built into strategies that reflect long-term commitments to customers, shareholders and other important stakeholders.[110]

Quality and total quality management are closely associated with the philosophies and teachings of W. Edwards Deming (and, to a lesser extent, Armand Feigenbaum and Joseph Juran).[111] These individuals' contributions to the practice of management are based on a simple, yet powerful, insight: the understanding that it costs less to make quality products than defect-ridden ones.

Total quality management (TQM) is a 'managerial innovation that emphasizes an organization's total commitment to the customer and to continuous improvement of every process through the use of data-driven, problem-solving approaches based on empowerment of employee groups and teams'.[112] Actually a philosophy about how to manage, TQM combines the teachings of Deming and Juran on statistical process control and group problem-solving processes with Japanese values concerned with quality and continuous improvement.[113] Statistical process control (SPC) is a technique used to continually upgrade the quality of the goods or services a firm produces. SPC benefits the firm through the detection and elimination of variations in processes used to manufacture a good or service.[114]

Although there are sceptics, when applied properly, the principles of total quality management can help firms achieve strategic competitiveness and earn above-average returns.[115] Three principal goals sought when practising total quality management are boosting customer satisfaction, reducing the amount of time required to introduce products into the marketplace, and cutting costs. These are accomplished in several ways, but most importantly, by empowering workers to achieve continuous improvements in all aspects of their tasks.[116] British Telecommunications (BT) uses a TQM system in order to be competitive with US firms. In fact, BT implemented the system in 1986, so it has considerable experience with it. BT managers believe that the firm's TQM system has helped it to compete effectively in global markets.[117] Ironically, Deming's and Juran's

---

Total quality management is managerial innovation that emphasises an organisation's total commitment to the customer and to continuous improvement of every process through the use of data-driven, problem-solving approaches based on empowerment of employee groups and teams.

ideas on quality and continuous improvement were adapted and implemented by Japanese firms long before many US firms acknowledged their importance. For this reason, a host of Japanese companies developed a competitive advantage in product quality that was difficult for US firms to overcome.[118] By implementing TQM systems effectively, many US, Australian and Western European firms have overcome the original competitive advantage enjoyed by Japanese firms related to the quality of their products. Deming's 14 points for managing and achieving quality (see Table 5.2) have become a watchword in businesses around the world.

Table 5.2 | Deming's 14 points for management

1. Create and publish to all employees a statement of the aims and purposes of the company or other organisation. The management must demonstrate constantly their commitment to this statement.
2. Learn the new philosophy, top management and everybody.
3. Understand the purpose of inspection, for improvement of processes and reduction of costs.
4. End the practice of awarding business on the basis of price tag alone.
5. Improve constantly and forever the system of production and service.
6. Institute training.
7. Teach and institute leadership.
8. Drive out fear. Create trust. Create a climate for innovation.
9. Optimise towards the aims and purposes of the company – the efforts of teams, groups and staff areas.
10. Eliminate exhortations for the workforce.
11. (a) Eliminate numerical quotas for production. Instead, learn and institute methods for improvement. (b) Eliminate management by objective. Instead, learn the capabilities of processes and how to improve them.
12. Remove barriers that rob people of pride of workmanship.
13. Encourage education and self-improvement for everyone.
14. Take action to accomplish the transformation.

Source: Reprinted from W. Edwards Deming, *Out of the Crisis*, by permission of MIT and The W. Edwards Deming Institute. Published by MIT, Center for Advanced Engineering Study, Cambridge, MA 02139. Copyright © 1986 by W. Edwards Deming.

Embedded within Deming's 14 points for management is the importance of striving continuously to improve both the operation of a firm and the quality of its goods or services. In fact, Deming did not support use of the term 'TQM', arguing that he did not know what total quality was and that it is impossible for firms to reach a goal of total quality. The pursuit of improvements in quality, Deming believed, should be a never-ending process.

Newer methods of TQM use benchmarking and emphasise organisational learning.[119] Benchmarking facilitates TQM by developing information on the best practices of other organisations and industries. This information is often used to establish goals for the firm's own TQM efforts. Benchmarking is a process by means of which a company can learn from the outcomes of other firms.[120] Because of the importance of quality (of both goods and services) in achieving competitive parity or a competitive advantage, many firms emphasise TQM and integrate it with their strategies.

In sum, relationships between each of the four general abilities (size, speed, innovation and quality) influence a firm's competitive actions and outcomes. Those responsible for selecting a firm's strategy should understand these relationships and anticipate that competitors will take competitive actions and competitive responses designed to exploit the positive relationships depicted in Figure 5.2. In the next section, we describe the different outcomes of competitive dynamics.

Figure 5.2 | Effects of firm size, speed of decision making and actions, innovations and quality on sustainability of competitor actions and outcomes

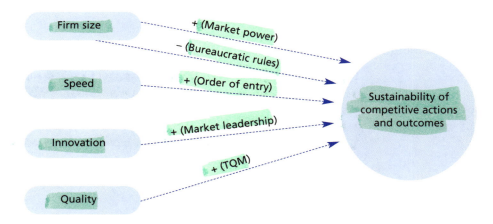

Outcomes of inter-firm rivalry

Figure 5.1 illustrates various potential outcomes of inter-firm rivalry. In some competitive environments, building a sustainable competitive advantage may be more likely than in others. As discussed in Chapter 3, one of the key determinants of sustainability is whether a firm's products are costly to imitate. Sustainability, therefore, might focus on different markets in which product imitability is largely or partially shielded.[121] In countries whose markets are largely open to international competitors, foreign rivals have made inroads into most major markets. However, even with strong rivalry and an increasing potential for imitability, some markets have been shielded from such competition. These markets are referred to as slow-cycle or sheltered markets. In other markets, product imitability is moderate, so they are labelled standard-cycle markets and are sometimes described as oligopolistic. In still other markets, firms operate in rapid, dynamic and often entrepreneurial environments. These markets are identified as fast-cycle markets.[122]

Competitive market outcomes

Products in **slow-cycle markets** reflect strongly shielded resource positions wherein competitive pressures do not readily penetrate the firm's sources of strategic competitiveness.

Products in **slow-cycle markets** reflect strongly shielded resource positions wherein competitive pressures do not readily penetrate the firm's sources of strategic competitiveness. In economics, this situation is often characterised as a monopoly position. A firm that has a unique set of product attributes or an effective product design may dominate its markets for decades, as did IBM with large mainframe computers. This type of competitive position can be established even in markets where there is significant technological change; an example is Microsoft's position with respect to difficult-to-imitate, complex software systems. Of course, conditions have changed for IBM and also for Microsoft, as competitors such as Sun Microsystems close in on Microsoft and the government prosecutes the firm for anticompetitive practices. Regulations or laws prohibiting competition may protect other firms. For example, for a long time, the utilities industries were largely protected as legal monopolies. However, that stance has changed and competition is now allowed. In contrast, pharmaceutical manufacturers still maintain a legally protected position under patent laws. Note that shielded advantages may be geographic; thus, the opening of huge emerging markets in Eastern Europe, Russia, China and India offers strong motivation for firms to pursue such opportunities.

Effective product designs may enable the firms that produced them to dominate their markets for many years, as the examples of Microsoft and IBM show. These firms' advantages are drawn largely from their special core competencies, because their resources and capabilities are difficult to imitate. The sustainability of competitive action associated with a slow-cycle market is depicted in Figure 5.3. Because these markets (and hence the firms that operate in them) are largely protected, they usually enjoy the highest average price increase over time. Alternatively, price increases in standard-cycle markets often vary closely around zero.[123]

Figure 5.3 | Gradual erosion of a sustained competitive advantage

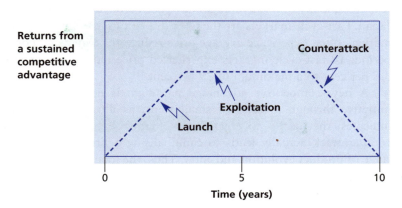

Source: Adapted from I. C. MacMillan, 1988, 'Controlling competitive dynamics by taking strategic initiative', *Academy of Management Executive*, II(2), pp. 111–18.

Products in standard-cycle markets reflect moderately shielded resource positions where competitive interaction penetrates a firm's sources of strategic competitiveness; but with improvement of its capabilities, the firm may be able to sustain a competitive advantage.

Standard-cycle markets are more closely associated with the industrial organisation economics approach exemplified in Porter's five forces model of competitive strategy (see Chapter 2). In these firms, strategy and organisation are designed to serve high-volume or mass markets. The focus is on coordination and market control, as in the automobile and appliance industries.[124] Even though these firms may be able to sustain world-class products for decades (for example, Coca-Cola), they may experience severe competitive pressures. Extended dominance and, in fact, world leadership are possible through continuing capital investment and superior learning, as was the case with Coca-Cola. However, as described in the Strategic Focus on the cola wars, Coca-Cola is now experiencing substantial competitive pressures in several of its markets. In particular, Pepsi is taking strategic actions much more quickly than Coca-Cola. In contrast, less investment is made in innovation in protected markets. Although it may be difficult to enter standard-cycle markets because of the competitive intensity, if a firm is successful and if its strategy is duplicated by competitors, more intense competitive pressures can be brought to bear. In that case, the competition may be similar to that found in fast-cycle markets.[125]

Standard-cycle markets that are intensely competitive may also require innovation (as discussed earlier). For example, a firm can capture market share in the standard-cycle market of brewing by offering innovative products. Cascade and Boags premium beers have captured good market share by offering a new beer experience to the Australian market. Coopers Beer of Adelaide has also prospered with its traditional 'cloudy' beer, a product that has been available for generations but has recently been successfully relaunched in the eastern states of Australia as an innovative boutique beer.[126, 127]

Competing in fast-cycle markets

Achieving a sustained competitive advantage is possible in slow- and, possibly, standard-cycle markets. However, it is largely impossible to gain a sustained competitive advantage in a **fast-cycle market**. Figure 5.3 focuses on sustainable competitive advantage. Usually, there is an entrepreneurial launch stage of the strategy, then a period of exploitation and, ultimately, a period of counterattack wherein the competitive advantage erodes. In fast-cycle markets, a competitive advantage can even create inertia and expose a firm to aggressive global competitors. Even though GM has economies of scale, a huge advertising budget, an efficient distribution system, cutting-edge R&D and slack resources, many of its advantages have been eroded by global competitors in Europe and Japan. Fast-cycle markets are the most difficult to manage and are the most volatile. Such markets often experience average price reductions over time. For example, over a recent period, 10 fast-cycle markets experienced price reductions ranging from a minimum of 3.5 per cent to a maximum of 29 per cent.[128]

A new competitive advantage paradigm is emerging in which a firm seizes the initiative through a series of small steps, as illustrated in Figure 5.4. As the figure indicates, the idea is to create a counterattack before the advantage is eroded. The counterattack actually leads to cannibalising a firm's own products through the next stage of product evolution and entry. Thus, the focus of this new paradigm is competitive disruption.[129] However, a firm can escalate competition in areas such as price and quality only so far before the dominant competitor seeks to achieve another level of competition focused on factors such as speed and know-how or innovation.

> In **fast-cycle markets** a competitive advantage cannot be sustained; firms attempt to gain temporary competitive advantages by strategically disrupting the market.

Figure 5.4 | Obtaining temporary advantages to create sustained advantage

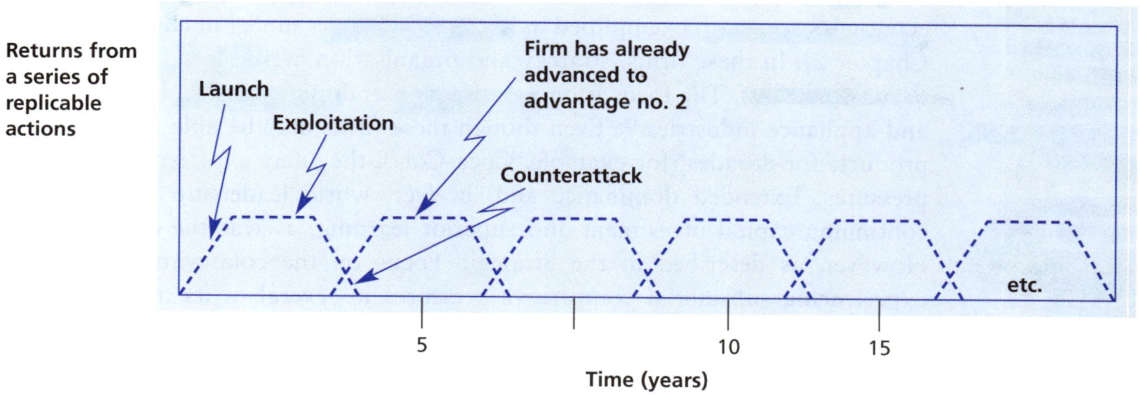

Source: Adapted from I. C. MacMillan, 1988, 'Controlling competitive dynamics by taking strategic initiative', *Academy of Management Executive*, II(2), pp. 111–18.

The telecommunications industry reflects a fast-cycle market. It is global in nature and highly dynamic. Firms in the industry have acquired cable companies and are now focusing on wireless communications companies. Most firms in the industry believe that the next generation of telecommunications will be based on wireless transmission. In 1999, Vodafone, a telecommunications firm based in Great Britain, acquired AirTouch Communications, a US-based firm. Vodafone also has acquired Mannesman, a fast-growing wireless operator based in Germany. For similar reasons, MCI WorldCom acquired Sprint. The expectation is that telephone calls and access to the Internet are likely to be provided by wireless networks. Many of the firms in this industry are forming alliances to compete more effectively in global markets. Telstra, by late 2000, was following a policy of multiple alliances in its attempt to get into the competitive Asian market.[130]

In an allied industry, telecommunications equipment, Nortel recently counterattacked Cisco Systems, which has been an especially effective competitor. Nortel announced that it was introducing new software and dramatically reducing hardware prices. The firm established licensing agreements with Intel and Microsoft. Cisco, a fast-growing data communications equipment manufacturer, developed the router that controls traffic on the Internet. Nortel was slow to respond to the Internet and is trying to make up lost ground. Cisco managers referred to Nortel's actions as a fire sale. They suggested that it indicated that the firm was desperate.[131]

The array of competitive actions and competitive responses occurring over time in the telecommunications industry demonstrates the four strategic steps shown in Table 5.3. At different times and with different products, several telecommunications firms have been able to: (1) identify a competitive opportunity that disrupted the status quo; (2) create a temporary advantage that was eroded through aggressive responses by their competitors; (3) seize the initiative from their competitors through effective competitive actions; and (4) sustain their momentum by continually offering new products and entering new markets. Thus, firms must exhibit strategic flexibility if they are to compete successfully in fast-cycle markets. When operating under these market conditions, firms must learn to respond quickly to technological change and market opportunities by offering more new products, broader product lines and product upgrades more rapidly.[132]

Table 5.3 | Strategic steps for seizing the initiative in fast-cycle markets

1 Disrupting the status quo
Competitors disrupt the status quo by identifying new opportunities to serve the customer and by shifting the rules of competition. These moves end the old pattern of competitive interaction between rivals. Disrupting the status quo requires speed and variety in approach.

2 Create temporary advantage
Disruption creates temporary advantages that are based on better knowledge of customers, technology and the future. Derived from customer orientation and employee empowerment throughout the entire organisation, these advantages are short lived and eroded by fierce competition.

3 Seizing the initiative
By moving aggressively into new areas of competition, acting to create a new advantage or undermining a competitor's old advantage, the company seizes the initiative. This throws the opponent off balance and puts it at a disadvantage for a while. The opponent is forced to play catch-up, reacting rather than shaping the future with its own actions to seize the initiative. The initiator is proactive, whereas competitors are forced to be reactive.

> **4 Sustaining the momentum**
>
> Several actions in a row are taken to seize the initiative and create momentum. The company continues to develop new advantages and does not wait for competitors to undermine them before launching the next initiative. This succession of actions sustains the momentum. Continually offering new initiatives is the only source of sustainable competitive advantage in fast-cycle environments.
>
> Source: Adapted from R. A. D'Aveni, 1995, 'Coping with hyper-competition: Utilizing the new 7's framework', *Academy of Management Executive*, IX(3), pp. 45–60.

Competitive dynamics and industry evolution outcomes

Because industries and markets evolve over time, so do the competitive dynamics between firms in an industry. We have examined how firms interact in a short span of time using an action–response framework, but we have not yet considered how competitive interaction evolves over longer periods of time. Three general stages of industry evolution are relevant to our study of competitive dynamics: the emerging, growth and mature stages. These are shown in Figure 5.5.

Figure 5.5 | An action-based model of the industry life cycle

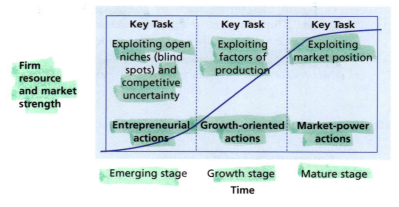

Source: Adapted from C. M. Grimm and K. G. Smith, 1997, *Strategy as Action: Industry Rivalry and Coordination* (St. Paul, MN: West Publishing Co.).

Firms entering emerging industries attempt to establish a niche or an initial form of dominance within an industry. Competitive rivalry for the loyalty of customers is serious. In these industries, depending on the types of products, firms often attempt to establish product quality, technological superiority or advantageous relationships with suppliers in order to develop a competitive advantage in the pursuit of strategic competitiveness. These firms are striving to build their reputation. As a result, a variety of different competitive strategies may be employed in such an industry. This diversity can be beneficial to many of the firms in the industry, helping them to avoid direct competition and gain dominance in market niches.¹³³ Although speed is important in emerging industries, access to capital is often the critical issue. Therefore, it is not uncommon to have strategic alliances develop between a new firm entering the market and a more established firm that wishes to gain a foothold in the new industry.¹³⁴

Firms in emerging industries often rely on top management to develop market opportunities. Steve Jobs and Bill Gates were able to foresee the future possibilities of the microcomputer and the standardised microcomputer operating system. Their vision of an uncertain environment gave rise to Apple Computer and Microsoft, respectively. Thus, firms in an emerging stage take *entrepreneurial actions* that focus on entrepreneurial discovery in uncertain environments.

Firms in growth-oriented industries are survivors from the emerging-industry stage. In the growth stage, *growth-oriented actions* are emphasised, which tend to create product standardisation as consumer demand creates a mass market with growth potential. Thus, many of these firms are more established, but no less competitive. In fact, as the industry begins to mature, the variety of strategies that are implemented tends to decrease. Entrepreneurial actions are indeed still taking place, but there is more emphasis on growth-oriented actions. Often, groups of firms will follow a similar strategy and thus become directly competitive. However, the rivalry between groups may be more indirect.¹³⁵ In industries in which there is considerable rivalry both within strategic groups and between firms in separate strategic groups, firms frequently earn below-average returns.¹³⁶

Some of these industries may also be fragmented. Fragmented markets, such as fast-food restaurants, tend to offer standardised facilities and products, but leave decentralised decision making to the local units. The standardisation allows for low-cost competition. The primary value added comes from the services that are provided. These markets offer a prime opportunity for franchising, because of the ability to standardise facilities, operations and products.¹³⁷

The Internet access market has become relatively fragmented, but remains an emerging growth industry as well. America Online (AOL) is the market leader, particularly after acquiring its chief competitor, CompuServe. However, there is considerable rivalry in this market, with at least eight other major competitors, primary among which is Microsoft, with Microsoft Net (MSN), and Prodigy. While AOL is the dominant force in the Internet access business, Microsoft cannot be ignored. In particular, Bill Gates once threatened to buy or bury AOL. Although he has not been able to do that, Microsoft is a formidable foe. As stated by one author, 'Microsoft's past is littered with the corpses of old enemies.'¹³⁸ AOL is strengthened with its acquisition of Netscape and its alliance with Sun Microsystems, another old nemesis of Microsoft.

In response, Microsoft has devised a three-pronged attack on AOL. First, it has developed and brought to market an

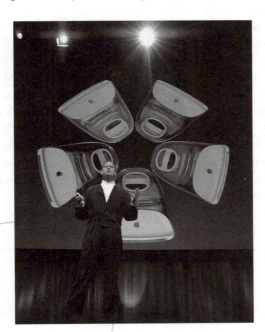

Steve Jobs of Apple Computer foresaw the future possibilities of the microcomputer and the need for user-friendly software.

instant messaging system to compete directly with AOL's. Second, Microsoft is preparing the way for low-cost or free Internet access in the United States. This move could be particularly damaging to AOL, as the firm receives 77 per cent of its revenues from Internet subscriptions. Third, Microsoft is trying to emphasise broadband communication to revolutionise the Internet as a platform for 'infotainment' and commerce. Both firms are successful and powerful. AOL is in a good position in the markets it serves; however, it must be careful because Microsoft has the capability to win competitive battles and harm AOL.[139] AOL's recent merger with Time Warner has increased its strength and reduced the likelihood that Microsoft will be able to 'bury it'. In non-fragmented industries, the speed with which new products are developed and introduced to the marketplace becomes an important competitive weapon. Consumers tend to be more sophisticated and expect not only quality products, but also product designs that meet their needs. Firms that can move new products that better meet consumers' needs to the market more quickly than competitors are likely to gain a competitive advantage.

In mature industries, there are usually fewer surviving competitors. Those that do survive tend to be larger and hold dominant market share positions. Therefore, firms in the mature stage emphasise *market-power actions*, which focus the firm's attention on offering product lines that are profitable and producing those products in an efficient manner. Product innovations and entrepreneurial actions continue, but are greatly de-emphasised. Process innovations are emphasised more, because they maintain dominance through cost efficiencies and the quality of the product manufactured and provided to customers.[140] Finally, firms in industries in the mature stage frequently seek to expand into international markets or increase their emphasis on international operations and sales to extend a product's life. Thus, growth-oriented actions also continue, even though the primary emphasis is on market-power actions.

In sum, once mature firms have a dominant market share, they seek to exploit their market power and extensive resources and capabilities to maintain dominance. The PC/server operating system market exemplifies a mature industry. Microsoft rather quickly became the dominant force in this industry and has held a virtual monopoly for the last decade. Because of its position, Microsoft provides incremental innovation of its Windows system. However, recently, a challenge to Microsoft's dominance developed from an operating system called Linux, which is distributed free by Red Hat and a few other entrepreneurial firms. These firms obtain their revenue by providing support operations for those who adopt the Linux operating system. Microsoft is concerned enough to develop an 'attack team' designed to monitor and analyse Linux and its distributors. The purpose of this team, as described by Microsoft's director of marketing for Windows 2000, is 'Getting inside the head of our competitor'. Linux is targeted for the server market, of which it has captured approximately 17 per cent, while Windows holds about 36 per cent. The Linux advantage, besides the fact that the software is free, is that it is about 50 per cent faster than Windows.[141] It will be interesting to observe the competitive battle between the rivals as it plays out.

This chapter concludes our emphasis on business-level strategy, although some business-level issues are discussed in subsequent chapters (for example, Chapters 8, 9 and 11). The next chapter begins our discussion of corporate-level strategy.

Summary

- Competitive rivalry entails actions and responses to competitive actions taken by other firms. Competitive attack and response are more likely when awareness, motivation, and abilities to attack or respond are present.
- Market commonality, as determined by multi-market contact in such industries as airlines, is likely to lead to the dampening of a potential attack. However, if an offensive action is taken, a response is more likely in the presence of market commonality.
- Awareness of competitors' ability to attack or respond is facilitated by resource similarity among competitors. Those with similar resources are more likely to attack and respond than are those with less overlap in resources.
- First movers can gain a competitive advantage and customer loyalty in the market. First movers also take more risks; however, they often are higher performers. Second movers, particularly those that are larger and faster, can also gain a competitive advantage and earn at least average returns because they imitate first movers, but do not take some of the risk that first movers do. In fact, some second movers may gain significant market share and outperform the first movers. They do this when they carefully observe the market's reaction and are able to improve the product introduced by the first mover and correct or avoid its mistakes. However, the longer the time required for the second mover to respond, the higher is the probability that the first mover will enjoy strong performance gains. Late movers (those that respond a long time after the original action was taken) tend to be lower performers and much less competitive.
- The probability of a response by a competitor to a competitive action is based partially on the extent to which the competitor is dependent on the particular market in which the action was taken. In addition, the probability of response is based on the type of action, the reputation of the firm taking the strategic action (which affects the expectation of the firm's success) and the resources available to the competitor contemplating the response.
- The two types of competitive actions are strategic and tactical. Strategic actions are more long term in nature, require many specific resources and are difficult to reverse. By contrast, tactical actions tend to be more short term in orientation, require fewer and more general resources, and can be reversed more easily. More tactical, rather than strategic, actions are taken, and more responses are made to tactical than to strategic actions. It is easier to respond to a tactical action, partly because doing so requires fewer resources. In addition, a tactical action is likely to have a shorter-term effect than a strategic action. Responses to strategic actions are more difficult, require more resources and require a longer-term investment.
- When competitors are highly dependent on a market in which competitive actions are taken, there is a high probability that they will respond to such actions. However, firms that are more diversified across markets are less likely to respond to a particular action that affects only one of the markets in which they compete.
- The highest probability of a response comes when a market leader takes action. Furthermore, when a market leader takes an action, a competitor is more likely to imitate it. Alternatively, if the firm has a reputation for taking more complex and risky actions, there is a lower probability of response. A price predator is also less likely to elicit a response from competitors.
- Those with a larger resource base are more likely to respond to strategic actions than are those with fewer resources. Furthermore, the probability of response is determined not only by the amount of resources, but by the ability to use those resources in taking competitive actions.
- Characteristics important to engaging in competitive actions and responses include the relative size of the acting and responding firms, the function of speed in the market or industry, the importance of innovation in competitive moves and the quality of the competing firms' products.
- Large firms often have strong market power. However, as firms grow larger, they frequently institute bureaucratic rules, procedures and structures that have the effect of reducing the probability that a firm will take actions and respond to others' actions. In addition, they reduce the speed with which a firm may be able to implement an action or respond to competitors' actions.
- Speed is becoming increasingly important in many industries in order to gain and hold a competitive advantage. In fact, many large firms must act like small firms (that is, be flexible and agile) to be competitive. This may require that they decentralise many responsibilities and decisions and that they create cross-functional teams in order to speed a number of processes (for example, the innovation process).
- Both product and process innovation are becoming

increasingly important in the competitive posture of many industries. Some research has shown that firms that invest more in R&D and create more innovation tend to have higher performance in multiple industries. Product innovation tends to be more important in emerging and growth industries, process innovation in mature industries.

- Product quality has become critical to maintaining competitive parity in most industries. Total quality management must be infused throughout the organisation by top management and integrated with firm strategies. Benchmarking is used to help make comparative judgements about quality relative to other firms' best practices.
- There are three basic market outcomes of competitive rivalry among firms. Slow-cycle markets allow a firm to establish competitive advantage in a near-monopoly situation. Until recently, many utility firms were in this position. Standard-cycle markets allow market situations in which sustainability is possible. Firms that have multi-market contact may dampen competition somewhat. Fast-cycle markets create a situation in which only temporary competitive advantage is possible, such as that in the electronics and pharmaceutical industries.
- In fast-cycle markets, competitive disruption, a new paradigm of competitive action, may be necessary. This usually involves cannibalisation of a previous product by reducing prices, while establishing a new product at the high end of the market, with increased performance at a premium price.
- Industry evolution is important in determining the type of competition and competitive actions that are emphasised by a firm. For example, firms in an emerging industry attempt to establish a reputation and develop a market niche in technology or the quality of products they provide. Their main task is to establish an entrepreneurial action, usually in an uncertain environment. In growth industries, the firm may place special emphasis on innovation to increase economies of scale. The speed of competitive actions taken is also important. The key task is to pursue growth-oriented actions by exploiting factors of production to increase the firm's dominance. In mature industries, with fewer competitors, special emphasis is placed on market-power actions designed to defend the most profitable product lines and processes in order to produce and distribute those products with the greatest efficiency (lowest cost). Entrepreneurial, growth-oriented and market-power actions are taken at all stages, but the emphasis is different at each stage.

Review questions

1. What two factors contribute to awareness, motivation and ability in competitor analysis?
2. What are the advantages and disadvantages of being a first mover? a second mover? a late mover?
3. On what four factors is the likelihood of a response to a competitive action based?
4. What is the likelihood of response to a tactical action? a strategic action? actions taken by market leaders? Explain why in each of these cases.
5. How does size affect strategic actions and responses?
6. Why is speed important in many industries? What can firms do to increase their speed in making and implementing strategic decisions?
7. In what types of industries is innovation important in gaining competitive advantage? Explain the importance of product and process innovations for success in different industries.
8. What are the three types of markets and the nature of rivalry in each?
9. How does industry evolution affect inter-firm rivalry? Identify three stages of industry evolution, and briefly explain the types of competitive actions emphasised in those stages.

Application discussion questions

1. Read the popular business press (for example, *Business Review Weekly*, *Australian Financial Review*) and identify a strategic action and a tactical action taken by firms approximately two years ago. Next, use the Internet to search the popular business press to see if, and how, competitors responded to those actions. Explain the actions and the responses, linking your findings to the discussion in this chapter.
2. Why would a firm regularly choose to be a second mover? Likewise, why would a firm purposefully be a late mover?
3. How did Wal-Mart's strategic actions affect its primary European competitors? How will Wal-Mart's new e-commerce strategy affect competitors?
4. Choose a large firm and examine the popular business press to identify how its size, speed of actions, level of innovation, and quality of goods or services have affected its competitive position in its industry. Explain your findings.
5. Identify a firm in a fast-cycle market. What strategic actions account for its success or failure over the last several years? How has the Internet affected the firm?

Ethics questions

1. Are there some industries in which ethical practices are more important than in other industries? If so, name the industries that are ethical, and explain how the competitive actions and competitive responses might differ for these industries compared with a typical industry.
2. When engaging in competitive rivalry, firms jockey for a market position that is advantageous, relative to competitors. In this jockeying, what types of competitor intelligence-gathering approaches are ethical? How has the Internet affected competitive intelligence activities?
3. A second mover is a firm that responds to a first mover's competitive actions, often through imitation. Is there anything unethical about how a second mover engages in competition? Why or why not?
4. Standards for competitive rivalry differ in countries throughout the world. What should firms do to cope with these differences? How do the differences relate to ethical practices?
5. Could total quality management practices result in firms operating more ethically than before such practices were implemented? If so, what might account for an increase in the ethical behaviour of a firm using TQM principles?
6. What ethical issues are involved in fast-cycle markets?

Internet exercise

With an offer of around 270 billion Deutschmarks (about A$295 billion), Chris Gent, the head of Britain's telecommunications giant Vodafone, planned to acquire the traditional German firm, Mannesmann AG, by February 2000. In a last-minute effort in January 2000 to stave off the hostile takeover, Mannesmann attempted to acquire NetCologne to strengthen its position against Vodafone. Look up Vodafone (www.vodafone.co.uk) and Mannesmann (www.mannesmann.de) on the Web to see how the merger progressed and how each company's stocks reacted to the news. How did MCI WorldCom (www.wcom.com), Vodafone's lead competitor, respond to these competitive actions?

*e-project: Discuss how the Internet has become a vital component in increasing the speed, ease and frequency of today's large mergers and acquisitions.

Notes

1. J. Kurtzman, 1998, 'An interview with C. K. Prahalad', in J. Kurtzman (ed.), *Thought Leaders* (San Francisco: Jossey-Bass), pp. 40–51; C. M. Grimm and K. G. Smith, 1997, *Strategy as Action: Industry Rivalry and Coordination* (Cincinnati: South-Western College Publishing); A. Y. Illinitch and R. A. D'Aveni, 1996, 'New organizational forms and strategies for managing in hypercompetitive environments', *Organization Science*, 7, pp. 211–20.
2. G. Colvin, 1997, 'The most valuable quality in a manager', *Fortune*, 29 December, pp. 279–80.
3. 'Target: Wal-Mart', 1999, *Wall Street Journal Interactive Edition*, 21 October: www.interactive.wsj.com/articles.
4. N. Byrnes and L. Armstrong, 1999, 'When Wal-Mart flexes its cybermuscles', *Business Week*, 26 July, pp. 82–3.
5. C. K. Prahalad, 1999, 'Changes in the competitive battlefield', Mastering Strategy (Part Two), *Financial Times*, 4 October, pp. 2–4.
6. J. Fox, R. Gann, A. Shur, L. Von Glahn and B. Zaas, 1999, 'Process uncertainty: A new dimension for new product development', *Engineering Management Journal*, 10(3), pp. 19–27.
7. G. McWilliams, 1999, 'Compaq's losses of big clients may foster plummeting profits', *Wall Street Journal Interactive Edition*, 22 July: www.interactive.wsj.com/articles.
8. D. L. Deeds, D. DeCarolis and J. Coombes, 2000, 'Dynamic capabilities and new product development in high technology adventures: An empirical analysis of new biotechnology firms', *Journal of Business Venturing*, 15, pp. 211–29; C. V. Callhan and B. A. Pasternack, 1999, 'Corporate strategy in the digital age', *Strategy & Business*, 15, pp. 10–14; B. H. Clark, 1998, 'Managing competitive interactions', *Marketing Management*, 7(4), pp. 8–20.
9. N. Munk, 1999, 'Title fight', *Fortune*, 21 June, pp. 84–94.
10. E. Noonan, 1999, 'Small booksellers struggle to beat out Internet retail', *Bryan-College Station Eagle*, 14 June, p. A7.
11. S. Thurm and R. Quick, 1999, 'Amazon.com is granted an injunction in barnesandnoble.com patent dispute', *Wall Street Journal Interactive Edition*, 3 December: www.interactive.wsj.com/articles.
12. P. M. Reilly, 1999, 'Barnesandnoble.com's redesign yields new online music store', *Wall Street Journal Interactive Edition*, 7 July: www.interactive.wsj.com/articles.
13. G. Anders, 1999, 'Amazon.com buys 35% stake of Seattle online grocery firm', *Wall Street Journal*, 18 May, p. B8.
14. B. Wysocki, Jr, 1999, 'The outlook', *Wall Street Journal Interactive Edition*, 28 June: www.interactive.wsj.com/articles; W. Zellner, S. Anderson and K. Morris, 1999, 'The big guys go online', *Business Week*, 6 September, pp. 30–2.
15. O. Gadiesh and J. L. Gilbert, 1998, 'Profit pools: A fresh look at strategy', *Harvard Business Review*, 76(3), pp. 139–42.
16. N. Wingfield, 1999, 'Merger shows retailers can't cut prices forever', *Wall Street Journal Interactive Edition*, 15 July: www.interactive.wsj.com/articles; J. Harding and P. T. Larsen, 1999, 'Carlton and United News set to merge', 25 November: www.ft.com/hippocampus; J. Bennett, 1999, 'A torrent of competition drives consolidation of Web companies', *Wall Street Journal Interactive Edition*, 14 July: www.interactive.wsj.com/articles.
17. E. K. Clemons, 1997, 'Technology-driven environmental shifts and the sustainable competitive disadvantage of previously dominant companies', in G. S. Day and D. J. Reibstein (eds), *Wharton on Dynamic Competitive Strategy* (New York: John Wiley & Sons), pp. 99–126.
18. B. S. Silverman, J. A. Nickerson and J. Freeman, 1997, 'Profitability, transactional alignment, and organizational mortality in the U.S. trucking industry', *Strategic Management Journal*, 18 (Special Summer Issue), pp. 31–52.
19. R. Gulati, 1999, 'Network location and learning: The influence of network resources and firm capabilities', *Strategic Management Journal*, 20, pp. 397–420; A. C. Inkpen and P. W. Beamish, 1997, 'Knowledge, bargaining power, and the instability of international joint ventures', *Academy of Management Review*, 22, pp. 177–202; J. Stiles, 1995, 'Collaboration for competitive advantage: The changing world of alliances and partnerships', *Long Range Planning*, 28, pp. 109–12.
20. A. Ferguson, 2000, 'Ziggy's big call', *Business Review Weekly*, 8 September, pp. 46–51.
21. S. Evans and S. Lewis, 2000, 'PCCW plans Telstra alternative', *Australian Financial Review*, 2 October, p. 12.

22. D. B. Holm, K. Eriksson and J. Johanson, 1999, 'Creating value through mutual commitment to business network relationships', *Strategic Management Journal*, 20, pp. 467–86; M. Sakakibara, 1997, 'Heterogeneity of firm capabilities and cooperative research and development: An empirical examination of motives', *Strategic Management Journal*, 18 (Special Summer Issue), pp. 143–64.
23. G. S. Day and D. J. Reibstein, 1997, 'The dynamic challenges for theory and practice', in G. S. Day and D. J. Reibstein (eds), *Wharton on Competitive Strategy* (New York: John Wiley & Sons), p. 2.
24. S. J. Marsh, 1998, 'Creating barriers for foreign competitors: A study of the impact of anti-dumping actions on the performance of U.S. firms', *Strategic Management Journal*, 19, pp. 25–37; K. G. Smith, C. M. Grimm and S. Wally, 1997, 'Strategic groups and rivalrous firm behavior: Towards a reconciliation', *Strategic Management Journal*, 18, pp. 149–57.
25. R. A. Klavans, C. A. Di Benedetto and J. J. Prudom, 1997, 'Understanding competitive interactions: The U.S. commercial aircraft market', *Journal of Managerial Issues*, IX(1), pp. 13–36.
26. Day and Reibstein, *Wharton on Competitive Strategy*; M. E. Porter, 1980, *Competitive Strategy* (New York: The Free Press), p. 17.
27. H. Simonian, 1998, 'Renault expands horizons', *Financial Times*, 2 January, p. 10.
28. 'Autos: The Global Six', 1999, *BusinessWeek Online*, 25 January: www.businessweek.com/bwarchive.
29. K. Cool, L. H. Roller and B. Leleux, 1999, 'The relative impact of actual and potential rivalry on firm profitability in the pharmaceutical industry', *Strategic Management Journal*, 20, pp. 1–14.
30. W. P. Putsis, Jr, 1999, 'Empirical analysis of competitive interaction in food product categories', *Agribusiness*, 15(3), pp. 295–311.
31. J. McCallum, 2000, 'To sell beer, buy the pub', *Business Review Weekly*, 12 September, pp. 60–3.
32. Porter, *Competitive Strategy*.
33. L. Colquhoun, 2000, 'Newcomers score in dogfight's early rounds', *Business Review Weekly*, 13 October, pp. 80–4.
34. J. A. C. Baum and H. J. Korn, 1999, 'Dynamics of dyadic competitive interaction', *Strategic Management Journal*, 20, pp. 251–78; C. R. Henderson and W. Mitchell, 1997, 'The interactions of organizational and competitive influences on strategy and performance', *Strategic Management Journal*, 18 (Special Summer Issue), pp. 5–14.
35. W. Ocasio, 1997, 'Towards an attention-based view of the firm', *Strategic Management Journal*, 18 (Special Summer Issue), pp. 187–206.
36. Grimm and Smith, *Strategy as Action*, pp. 75–102; K. Krabuanrat and R. Phelps, 1998, 'Heuristics and rationality in strategic decision making: An exploratory study', *Journal of Business Research*, 41, pp. 83–93.
37. G. P. Hodgkinson and G. Johnson, 1994, 'Exploring the mental models of competitive strategists: The case for a processual approach', *Journal of Management Studies*, 31, pp. 525–51; J. F. Porac and H. Thomas, 1994, 'Cognitive categorization and subjective rivalry among retailers in a small city', *Journal of Applied Psychology*, 79, pp. 54–66.
38. N. J. Vilcassim, V. Kadiyali and P. K. Chintagunta, 1999, 'Investigating dynamic multi-firm market interactions in price and advertising', *Management Science*, 45(4), pp. 499–518.
39. N. Houthoofd and A. Heene, 1997, 'Strategic groups as subsets of strategic scope groups in the Belgian brewing industry', *Strategic Management Journal*, 18, pp. 653–66; G. P. Carroll and A. Swaminathan, 1992, 'The organizational ecology of strategic groups in the American brewing industry from 1975–1988', *Industrial and Corporate Change*, 1, pp. 65–97.
40. L. C. Thurow, 1999, *Building Wealth: The New Rules for Individuals, Companies and Nationals in a Knowledge-Based Economy* (New York: Harper Collins); K. Ohmae, 1985, *Triad Power* (New York: The Free Press).
41. J. Gimeno and C. Y. Woo, 1999, 'Multi-market contact, economies of scope, and firm performance', *Academy of Management Journal*, 42(3), pp. 239–59.
42. J. Gimeno, 1999, 'Reciprocal threats in multi-market rivalry: Staking out spheres of influence in the U.S. airline industry', *Strategic Management Journal*, 20, pp. 101–28; N. Fernandez and P. L. Marin, 1998, 'Market power and multi-market contact: Some evidence from the Spanish hotel industry', *Journal of Industrial Economics*, 46(3), pp. 301–15.
43. M. J. Chen, 1996, 'Competitor analysis and inter-firm rivalry: Toward a theoretical integration', *Academy of Management Review*, 21, pp. 100–34.
44. H. J. Korn and J. A. C. Baum, 1999, 'Chance, imitative, and strategic antecedents to multi-market contact', *Academy of Management Journal*, 42, pp. 171–93.
45. S. Javachandran, J. Gimeno and P. R. Varadarajan, 1999, 'Theory of multi-market competition: A synthesis and implications for marketing strategy', *Journal of Marketing*, 63, pp. 49–66.
46. J. A. Chevalier, 1999, 'When it can be good to burn your boats', Mastering Strategy (Part Four), *Financial Times*, 25 October, pp. 2–3; M. A. Peteraf, 1993, 'Intra-industry structure and response toward rivals', *Journal of Managerial Decision Economics*, 14, pp. 519–28.
47. Grimm and Smith, *Strategy as Action*, p. 84; Chen, 'Competitor analysis'.
48. Grimm and Smith, *Strategy as Action*, p. 125.
49. B. Horovitz, 1997, 'Coca-Cola, Pepsi tap bottled water market', *USA Today*, 27 August, p. B10.
50. P. Abrahams and L. Kehoe, 1999, 'NEC and Bull pull out of US market', 4 November: www.ft.com/hippocampus.
51. C. Waterhouse, 2000, 'Milk war spills over', *The Mercury*, 11 September, p. 1.
52. W. Mitchell, 1999, 'Alliances: Achieving long-term value and short-term goals', Mastering Strategy (Part Four), *Financial Times*, 18 October, pp. 6–11.
53. P. Abrahams, 1999, 'NEC/Mitsubishi: Competition forces joint venture', 1 October: www.ft.com/hippocampus.
54. 'Global crossing and Hutchison form telecom, web joint venture', 1999, *Wall Street Journal Interactive Edition*, 15 November: www.interactive.wsj.com/articles.
55. K. P. Coyne and R. Dye, 1998, 'The competitive dynamics of network-based businesses', *Harvard Business Review*, 76(1), pp. 99–109.
56. Smith and Grimm, *Strategy as Action*, pp. 53–74.
57. A. A. Lado, N. G. Boyd and S. C. Hanlon, 1997, 'Competition, cooperation, and the search for economic rents: A syncretic model', *Academy of Management Review*, 22, pp. 110–41.
58. J. L. C. Cheng and I. F. Kesner, 1997, 'Organizational slack and response to environmental shifts: The impact of resource allocation patterns', *Journal of Management*, 23, pp. 1–18.
59. M. Wallin, 1999, 'Supermarket chain to bring online shopping to Argentina', *Wall Street Journal Interactive Edition*, 30 July: www.interactive.wsj.com/articles.
60. M. B. Lieberman and D. B. Montgomery, 1988, 'First-mover advantages', *Strategic Management Journal*, 9, pp. 41–58.
61. K. G. Smith, C. M. Grimm and M. J. Gannon, 1992, *Dynamics of Competitive Strategy* (Newberry Park, CA: Sage).
62. A. Ginsberg and N. Venkatraman, 1992, 'Investing in new information technology: The role of competitive posture and issue diagnosis', *Strategic Management Journal*, 13 (Special Summer Issue), pp. 37–53.
63. H. R. Greve, 1998, 'Managerial cognition and the mimetic adoption of market positions: What you see is what you do', *Strategic Management Journal*, 19, pp. 967–88.
64. M. Zetlin, 1999, 'When it's smarter to be second to market', *Management Review*, March, pp. 30–4.
65. G. J. Tellis and P. N. Golder, 1996, 'First to market, first to fail? Real causes of enduring market leadership', *Sloan Management Review*, Winter, pp. 57–66.
66. Smith, Grimm and Gannon, *Dynamics of Competitive Strategy*.
67. E. White, 1999, 'Avon tries to exploit internet without alienating its ladies', *Wall Street Journal Interactive Edition*, 28 December: www.interactive.wsj.com/articles.
68. K. J. Delaney, 1999, 'Dell launches internet access free of charge in Europe', *Wall Street Journal Interactive Edition*, 9 June: www.interactive.wsj.com/articles.
69. G. S. Day, 1997, 'Assessing competitive arenas: Who are your competitors?', in G. S. Day and D. J. Reibstein (eds), *Wharton on Competitive Strategy* (New York: John Wiley & Sons), pp. 25–6.
70. K. Labich, 1994, 'Air wars over Asia', *Fortune*, 4 April, pp. 93–8.
71. R. Gluyas, 2000, 'Qantas deploys air defences', *The Weekend Australian*, 25–26 March, pp. 31–2.
72. Grimm and Smith, *Strategy as Action*, p. 134.
73. W. J. Ferrier, K. G. Smith and C. M. Grimm, 1999, 'The role of competitive actions in market share erosion and industry dethronement: A study of industry leaders and challengers', *Academy of Management Journal*, 42, pp. 372–88.
74. Smith, Grimm and Gannon, *Dynamics of Competitive Strategy*.
75. Ibid.
76. Village Roadshow, 2000, *Annual Report*.
77. J. Thompson, 2000, 'Village risks the family silver', *Business Review Weekly*, 9 February, pp. 66–71.
78. 'Burger with fries and videos to go', 1999, *Financial Times*, 18 April, p. 7.

Chapter 5 Competitive dynamics

79. N. Cope, 1999, 'Tesco and Sainsbury battle for home-shopping market', *Independent News*, 1 December: www.independent…inessother/tescoonline.
80. 'Boeing could make bigger 747 models', 1999, *Houston Chronicle*, 21 September, p. 4C.
81. B. Pinsker, 1997, 'Rental block', *Dallas Morning News*, 14 June, pp. C5, C8.
82. J. Cole, 1999, 'Airbus prepares to bet the company as it builds a huge new jet', *Wall Street Journal*, 3 November, pp. A1, A10; M. Skapinker, 1998, 'Airbus boasts year of record orders', *Financial Times*, 8 January, p. 6.
83. L. Krishnamurthi and V. Shankar, 1998, 'What are the options for later entrants?', Mastering Marketing (Part Six), *Financial Times*, 19 October, p. 4.
84. Baum and Korn, 'Dynamics of dyadic competitive interaction'.
85. 'Intel reduces prices on Pentium III chips', 1999, *New York Times Online*, 24 August: www.nytimes.com/library.
86. J. A. Schumpeter, 1961, *Theory of Economic Development* (New York: Oxford University Press).
87. M. A. Hitt, 2000, 'The new frontier: Transformation of management for the twenty-first century', *Organizational Dynamics*, 28 (Winter), pp. 7–17.
88. B. A. Melcher, 1993, 'How Goliaths can act like Davids', *Business Week* (Special Issue), p. 193.
89. J. Kurtzman, 1998, 'An interview with Charles Handy', in J. Kurtzman (ed.), *Thought Leaders* (San Francisco: Jossey-Bass), pp. 134–49; J. Birkinshaw, 1997, 'Entrepreneurship in multinational corporations: The characteristics of subsidiary initiatives', *Strategic Management Journal*, 18, pp. 207–29.
90. Harvard Business Review Perspectives, 1995, 'How can big companies keep the entrepreneurial spirit alive?', *Harvard Business Review*, 73(6), pp. 183–92.
91. R. E. Krider and C. B. Weinberg, 1998, 'Competitive dynamics and the introduction of new products: The motion picture timing game', *Journal of Marketing Research*, 35, pp. 1–15.
92. C. E. Lucier and J. D. Torbilier, 1999, 'Beyond stupid, slow and expensive: Reintegrating work to improve productivity', *Strategy & Business*, 17, pp. 9–13; R. R. Nayyar and K. A. Bantel, 1994, 'Competitive agility: A source of competitive advantage based on speed and variety', *Advances in Strategic Management*, 10A, pp. 193–222.
93. S. Wally and J. R. Baum, 1994, 'Personal and structural determinants of the pace of strategic decision-making', *Academy of Management Journal*, 37, pp. 932–56.
94. Ibid.
95. Kurtzman, 'An interview with Gary Hamel'; J. Wind, 1997, 'Preemptive strategies', in G. S. Day and D. J. Reibstein (eds), *Wharton on Dynamic Competitive Strategy* (New York: John Wiley & Sons), pp. 256–76; S. C. Wheelwright and K. B. Clark, 1995, *Leading Product Development* (New York: The Free Press).
96. S. A. Zahra, A. P. Nielsen and W. C. Bogner, 1999, 'Corporate entrepreneurship, knowledge, and competence development', *Entrepreneurship: Theory and Practice*, 23(3), pp. 169–89; B. N. Dickie, 1998, 'Foreword', in J. Kurtzman (ed.), *Thought Leaders* (New York: Jossey-Bass), pp. x–xvii; J. Kurtzman, 1998, 'An interview with Paul M. Romer', in J. Kurtzman (ed.), *Thought Leaders* (New York: Jossey-Bass), pp. 66–83.
97. D. L. Deeds, D. DeCarolis and J. Coombes, 1999, 'Dynamic capabilities and new product development in high technology ventures: An empirical analysis of new biotechnology firms', *Journal of Business Venturing*, 18, pp. 211–29; K. J. Klein and J. S. Sorra, 1996, 'The challenge of innovation implementation', *Academy of Management Review*, 21, pp. 1055–80.
98. Industry Research and Development Board, 1999, *R&D Scorecard* (Canberra: AGPS).
99. N. Kim, E. Bridges and R. K. Srivastava, 1999, 'A simultaneous model for innovative product category sales diffusion and competitive dynamics', *International Journal of Research in Marketing*, 16, pp. 95–111.
100. D. P. Hamilton, 1999, 'Sun to challenge Microsoft's Office with purchase of software maker', *Wall Street Journal Interactive Edition*, 31 August: www.interactive.wsj.com/articles.
101. N. George, 1999, 'Ericsson drifts in Nokia's wake', *Financial Times*, 22 July, p. 13.
102. Klein and Sorra, 'The challenge of innovation implementation'.
103. N. Dunne, 1998, 'American goldmine for high-tech workers', *Financial Times*, 15 January, p. 4; V. Griffith, 1998, 'Learning to wear two hats', *Financial Times*, 5 January, p. 20; N. Timmins, 1998, 'Manufacturers face skills shortfall', *Financial Times*, 9 January, p. 4.
104. 'Procter's gamble', 1999, *The Economist Online*, 6 December: www.economist.com/editorial.
105. J. W. Dean, Jr and D. E. Bowen, 1994, 'Management theory and total quality: Improving research and practice through theory development', *Academy of Management Review*, 19, pp. 392–419.
106. J. Aley, 1994, 'Manufacturers grade themselves', *Fortune*, 21 March, p. 26.
107. J. Heizer and B. Render, 1996, *Production and Operations Management*, 4th edition (Upper Saddle River, NJ: Prentice Hall), pp. 75–106.
108. M. van Biema and B. Greenwald, 1997, 'Managing our way to higher service-sector productivity', *Harvard Business Review*, 75(4), pp. 87–95.
109. S. Chatterjee and M. Yilmaz, 1993, 'Quality confusion: Too many gurus, not enough disciples', *Business Horizons*, 36(3), pp. 15–18.
110. J. Heizer and B. Render, 1999, *Operations Management*, 5th edition (Upper Saddle River, NJ: Prentice Hall).
111. W. S. Sherman and M. A. Hitt, 1996, 'Creating corporate value: Integrating quality and innovation programs', in D. Fedor and S. Ghoshal (eds), *Advances in the Management of Organizational Quality* (Greenwich, CT: JAI Press), pp. 221–44.
112. J. D. Westphal, R. Gulati and S. M. Shortell, 1997, 'Customization or conformity: An institutional and network perspective on the content and consequences of TQM adoption', *Administrative Science Quarterly*, 42, pp. 366–94.
113. E. E. Lawler, III, 1994, 'Total quality management and employee involvement: Are they compatible?', *Academy of Management Executive*, VIII(1), p. 68.
114. R. S. Russell and B. W. Taylor, III, 2000, *Operations Management*, 3rd edition (Upper Saddle River, NJ: Prentice Hall), pp. 130–65.
115. A. M. Schneiderman, 1998, 'Are there limits to total quality management?', *Strategy & Business*, 11, pp. 35–45; R. Krishnan, A. B. Shani and G. R. Baer, 1993, 'In search of quality improvement: Problems of design and implementation', *Academy of Management Executive*, VII(3), pp. 7–20.
116. S. Sanghera, 1999, 'Making continuous improvement better', *Financial Times*, 21 April, p. 28.
117. Ibid.
118. H. V. Roberts and B. F. Sergesketter, 1993, *Quality is Personal* (New York: The Free Press).
119. S. B. Sitkin, K. M. Sutcliffe and R. G. Schroeder, 1994, 'Distinguishing control from learning in total quality management: A contingency perspective', *Academy of Management Review*, 19, pp. 537–64.
120. J. R. Hackman and R. Wageman, 1995, 'Total quality management: Empirical, conceptualization and practical issues', *Administrative Science Quarterly*, 40, pp. 309–42.
121. J. R. Williams, 1999, *Renewable Advantage: Crafting Strategy through Economic Time* (New York: The Free Press); J. R. Williams, 1992, 'How sustainable is your competitive advantage?', *California Management Review*, 34, Spring, pp. 29–51.
122. G. S. Day, 1997, 'Maintaining the competitive edge: Creating and sustaining advantages in dynamic competitive environments', in G. S. Day and D. J. Reibstein (eds), *Wharton on Dynamic Competitive Strategy* (New York: John Wiley & Sons), pp. 48–75.
123. J. R. Williams, 1999, 'Economic time', *Across the Board*, September, p. 11.
124. A. D. Chandler, 1990, 'The enduring logic of industrial success', *Harvard Business Review*, 68(2), pp. 130–40.
125. J. L. Bower and T. M. Hout, 1988, 'Fast-cycle capability for competitive power', *Harvard Business Review*, 66(6), pp. 110–18.
126. S. Lloyd, 2000, 'To be sure, Guinness', *Business Review Weekly*, 15 September.
127. 'San Miguel to push Boags in Asia', 2000, *Australian Financial Review*, 22 June, p. 27.
128. Williams, 'Economic time'.
129. K. R. Conner, 1995, 'Obtaining strategic advantage from being imitated: When can encouraging "clones" pay?', *Management Science*, 41, pp. 209–25; R. A. D'Aveni, 1995, 'Coping with hyper-competition: Utilizing the new 7's framework', *Academy of Management Executive*, IX(3), pp. 45–60; K. R. Conner, 1988, 'Strategies for product cannibalism', *Strategic Management Journal*, 9 (Special Summer Issue), pp. 135–59.
130. C. Lacy, 2000, 'Telstra seeks third partner', *Australian Financial Review*, 18 October, pp. 20–1.
131. A. Cane, G. Bowley and R. Taylor, 1999, 'Nortel counter attack launched against Cisco', 9 November: www.ft.com/hippocampus.

132. R. Sanchez, 1995, 'Strategic flexibility in product competition', *Strategic Management Journal*, 16 (Special Summer Issue), pp. 9–26.
133. M. A. Hitt, B. B. Tyler, C. Hardee and D. Park, 1995, 'Understanding strategic intent in the global marketplace', *Academy of Management Executive*, IX(2), pp. 12–19.
134. M. A. Hitt, M. T. Dacin, E. Levitas, J. L. Arregle and A. Borza, 2000, 'Partner selection in emerging and developed market contexts: Resource-based and organizational learning perspectives', *Academy of Management Journal*, in press.
135. R. E. Miles, C. C. Snow and M. Sharfman, 1993, 'Industry variety and performance', *Strategic Management Journal*, 14, pp. 163–77.
136. K. Cool and I. Dierickx, 1993, 'Rivalry, strategic groups and firm profitability', *Strategic Management Journal*, 14, pp. 47–59.
137. S. A. Shane, 1996, 'Hybrid organizational arrangements and their implications for firm growth and survival: A study of new franchisers', *Academy of Management Journal*, 39, pp. 216–34.
138. 'Pricks and kicks', 1999, *The Economist Online*, 16 August: www.economist.com/editorial.
139. Ibid.
140. D. M. Schroeder, 1990, 'A dynamic perspective on the impact of process innovation upon competitive strategies', *Strategic Management Journal*, 11, pp. 25–41.
141. L. Gomes, 1999, 'Upstart Linux draws interest of a Microsoft attack team', *Wall Street Journal Interactive Edition*, 21 May: www.interactive.wsj.com/articles.

Chapter 6

Corporate-level strategy

Objectives

After reading this chapter, you should be able to:

1. Define corporate-level strategy and discuss its importance to the diversified firm.
2. Describe the advantages and disadvantages of single-business and dominant-business strategies.
3. Explain three primary reasons why firms move from single-business and dominant-business strategies to more diversified strategies.
4. Describe how related diversified firms use activity sharing and the transfer of core competencies to create value.
5. Discuss the two ways an unrelated diversification strategy can create value.
6. Discuss the incentives and resources that encourage diversification.
7. Describe motives that can encourage managers to over-diversify a firm.

Wesfarmers: A diversified West Australian conglomerate

Wesfarmers' origins can be traced back to 1914, when a cooperative of West Australian farmers formed with a strategy to focus on the provision of services and merchandise to the rural community in Western Australia. The cooperative operated for some 70 years before it listed on the Australian Stock Exchange (ASX) in 1984 as Wesfarmers Incorporated. At this time, Wesfarmers was considered a 'pastoral agency with, at best, moderate growth prospects'.

Since listing, however, Wesfarmers has been named as one of Australia's best performing stocks, especially during the 1990s, and indeed was recently quoted as the 'leading Australian conglomerate', generating net profit in excess of $100 million in 2000. The interesting aspect of Wesfarmers' growth strategy is that it has used a classic diversification strategy to realise its increase in value. As an ASX company, Wesfarmers is in the business of creating shareholder value through a myriad of rural operations in seven key areas: hardware retailing, coal production, fertilisers and chemicals, gas production, rural services, forestry products and transport.

Wesfarmers' hardware retailing division was established after the company purchased the Bunnings Buildings Supply and Warehousing Property Trust. Bunnings Building Supplies Pty Ltd provides Wesfarmers with a specialist retailer of home and garden improvement products and building materials, catering mainly for the do-it-yourself customer, small to medium-size builders and owner-builders. In addition to its chain of traditional hardware stores, Wesfarmers (through their Bunnings subsidiary) pursued a strong expansion program to develop a nationwide chain of warehouse superstores in all mainland states and territories. Wesfarmers established the Bunnings Warehouse Property Trust in 1998 to acquire hardware warehouse stores tenanted by Bunnings Building Supplies Pty Ltd. This initiative was taken to separate the operational and property aspects of the Bunnings hardware business and to limit the call on Wesfarmers' capital which the warehouse expansion program would otherwise have entailed. In order to capture a greater proportion of the market's potential, the company also purchased WA Salvage Pty Ltd, a firm that specialises in selling a broad range of discounted building materials and variety merchandise. It is one of the largest merchandisers of its type in Australia.

Wesfarmers' coal production division comprises Wesfarmers' Coal, which operates the Premier open-cut mine near Perth as well as the Curragh mine in Rockhampton, Queensland. These two mines produce in excess of eight million tonnes of coal for Wesfarmers annually, 4.5 million tonnes of which is already contracted to be purchased annually (until 2016) by the Stanwell Power Station in Queensland. In an effort to extend their mining interests beyond Western Australia and Queensland, Wesfarmers undertook a 40 per cent interest in the Bangalla open-cut mine in New South Wales. The Bangalla mine will produce approximately 5.5 million tonnes of coal for export revenue until it reaches its full capacity in 2003.

The fertiliser and chemicals division is represented by two Wesfarmers subsidiaries: Wesfarmers CSBP Ltd and Australian Gold Reagents Pty Ltd. Wesfarmers CSBP Ltd is the major supplier of fertilisers and chemicals to Western Australia's agricultural, mining and industrial sectors. CSBP operates a large fertiliser and chemicals complex at Kwinana in Western Australia. It employs a network of agricultural advisers who make on-farm visits each year to advise farmers on soil fertility, farm productivity and fertiliser use. The company operates one of the country's most respected soil and plant testing laboratories which more than 2000 farmers use each year. Thorough their 75 per cent holdings in Gold Reagents' operations, Wesfarmers manufactures and sells sodium cyanide solution for use in gold extraction processes.

Wesfarmers' gas production division is likewise made up of three major subsidiaries: Kleenheat, Wesfarmers LPG and Air Liquide WA. Kleenheat is a major distributor of LPG and gas appliances to a broad range of domestic, commercial, auto-gas and industrial companies. Kleenheat provides Wesfarmers with an extensive Australia-wide branch/franchise network, as well as gas storage and distribution facilities. Wesfarmers LPG owns and operates a plant at Kwinana, in Western Australia, and extracts LPG from the natural gas stream in the Dampier to Bunbury pipeline. Product from this operation supplies much of Western Australia's domestic market, the balance being exported to Japan for further revenue dollars. Wesfarmers also has a 40 per cent share of Air Liquide WA, a company that produces a large range of industrial and medical gases and welding products.

Wesfarmers Dalgety and Wesfarmers Federation Insurance are two subsidiary companies that provide rural services for Wesfarmers customers. Wesfarmers Dalgety Ltd is one of Australia's largest suppliers of services to the rural sector. The company services over 100 000 clients from almost 300 outlets throughout Australia. It provides clients with livestock, wool, merchandise, insurance, real estate and rural financial services. The company handles approximately 30 per cent of Australia's wool clip and about 20 per cent of the livestock trading in Australia. It is also a leading supplier to the live cattle export trade to Southeast Asia and the Middle East.

Sotico Pty Ltd, a major forest products company based in Western Australia, represents Wesfarmers' forestry division. Its activities include hardwood saw milling, contract forest harvesting and timber processing to supply local, national and international markets. Sotico produces sawn timber from Western Australia's jarrah and karri hardwood species. It buys logs from the state government agency responsible for all aspects of native forest management. Sotico has a 50 per cent share in Wespine Industries Pty Ltd, which operates a world-scale pine sawmill at Dardanup. The mill's main product is machine-graded pine used in roof frames and other building construction.

Wesfarmers' transport division consists of Wesfarmers Transport and Niteroad Express. Wesfarmers Transport Ltd has an extensive transport and logistics operation involved in supply chain management for commerce and industry in Western Australia and other states in Australia. The specialised services business offers specialist expertise, equipment and resources for bulk haulage of chemicals, fertiliser, grain, fuel, mineral sands and other bulk commodities throughout Western Australia and increasingly in other Australian states. In addition, specialised services operates heavy haulage services throughout Australia. Niteroad Express provides an overnight express freight service to more than 350 country destinations in the southwest of Western Australia.

Wesfarmers' high profitability and considerable return to its shareholders (averaging approximately 30 per cent per annum over the last decade) is widely attributed to the disciplined manner in which its management coordinates and diversifies the conglomerate. Wesfarmers management undertakes careful targeting of potential acquisitions, and only after complex net present valuations of these target firms are completed does the company commence its purchasing processes.

Firms such as Wesfarmers, however, are not risk-free ventures. Although the company's performance between 1984 and 2000 has been exceptional, recently Wesfarmers has moved to simplify what has now become described as a 'somewhat cumbersome' structure. The move results from a decline in the firm's liquidity and appeal to potential investors. CEO Michael Chaney believes that Wesfarmers has reached such a size that it is now at a 'disadvantage compared to other companies because of the way institutions, and investors in general, view the company's ownership as complex'. Only time will tell whether Wesfarmers will be able to retain this business model in their efforts to attract further equity investments.

www.wesfarmers.com.au

Sources: Wesfarmers Ltd, 2001, *Wesfarmers' History and Corporate Structure*, 20 February: www.wesfarmers.com.au; T. Thomas, 1998, 'Wesfarmers shareholders get benefit of discipline', *Business Review Weekly*, 5 October: www.brw.com.au; P. Rennie, 2000, 'Diversified industries', *Business Review Weekly*, 28 April: www.brw.com.au; G. Price, 2001, 'Wesfarmers begins shake-up', *The Australian*, 14 February; Wesfarmers Ltd, 2000, *Wesfarmers Limited Annual Report*.

As indicated in the Opening Case, top-level managers at Wesfarmers decided that their firm should be more diversified than other 'rural service' companies. Wesfarmers is following a related linked diversification strategy (see Table 6.2) wherein the businesses function in a way that creates added value for each other.

Disney, a large diversified entertainment company, has also sought to leverage its resources and capabilities to forge a set of on-line businesses. Its main portal, go.com, was seeking to compete with Yahoo!, Excite and other major service portals. In 1999, Disney acquired the rest of Infoseek Corporation to incorporate the Infoseek search engine more fully with Disney's other on-line businesses. However, the firm was too late getting into the portal business to compete with Yahoo! and AOL, so it has shifted the focus of go.com to that of an entertainment and leisure site. ABC.com is the news and entertainment website associated with the Disney TV network. Disney.com is the main e-commerce site that sells Disney-associated products on-line. ESPN.com is the sports information and entertainment site associated with the Disney-owned cable sports network. Disney also has a stake in e-companies that serve as an incubator for Internet start-ups similar to NaviSite, a CMGI affiliate. Thus, Disney is using its Internet diversification to build on the strengths that it already has in entertainment and associated products (for example, toys created from its animated movie figures).[1]

Our discussions of different business-level strategies (Chapter 4) and the competitive dynamics associated with their use (Chapter 5) were focused primarily on firms competing in a single industry or product market.[2] When a firm chooses to diversify its operations beyond a single industry and to operate businesses in several industries, it is pursuing a corporate-level strategy of diversification. As is the case with business-level strategies, a corporate-level strategy of diversification allows a firm to adapt to conditions in its external environment.[3] As influential strategic choices that companies make, diversification strategies play a major role in the behaviour of large firms.[4] Strategic choices regarding diversification are, however, fraught with uncertainty.[5]

A diversified company has two levels of strategy: a business-level (or competitive) strategy and a corporate-level (or company-wide) strategy.[6] In diversified firms, each business unit chooses a business-level strategy to implement to achieve strategic competitiveness and earn above-average returns. But diversified firms must also choose a strategy that is concerned with the selection and management of their businesses. Defined formally, a **corporate-level strategy** is an action taken to gain a competitive advantage through the selection and management of a mix of businesses competing in several industries or product markets. In essence, a corporate-level strategy is what makes 'the corporate whole add up to more than the sum of its business unit parts'.[7] Corporate-level strategy is concerned with two key questions: what businesses the firm should be in, and how the corporate office should manage its group of businesses.[8] In the current complex

A **corporate-level strategy** is an action taken to gain a competitive advantage through the selection and management of a mix of businesses competing in several industries or product markets.

global environment, top executives should view their firm's businesses as a portfolio of core competencies when seeking answers to these critical questions.[9]

Relating back to Figure 1.1 in Chapter 1, our focus herein is on the formulation of corporate-level strategy that evolves from the firm's strategic intent and mission. Also, as with business-level strategies, corporate-level strategies are expected to help the firm earn above-average returns (create value).[10] Some have suggested that few corporate-level strategies actually do create value.[11] In the final analysis, the value of a corporate-level strategy 'must be that the businesses in the portfolio are worth more under the management of the company in question than they would be under any other ownership'.[12] Thus, the corporate-level strategy should be expected to contribute a given amount to the returns of all business units that exceeds what those returns would be without the implementation of such a strategy.[13] When managed effectively, corporate-level strategies enhance a firm's strategic competitiveness and contribute to its ability to earn above-average returns.[14] In the 21st century, corporate-level strategies will be managed in a global business environment characterised by high degrees of risk, complexity, uncertainty and ambiguity.[15]

A primary approach to corporate-level strategy is diversification, which requires corporate-level executives to craft a multi-business strategy. One reason for the use of a diversification strategy is that managers of diversified firms possess unique general management skills that can be used to develop multi-business strategies and enhance a firm's strategic competitiveness.[16] To derive the greatest benefit from their skills, managers must focus their energies on the tasks associated with managing a diversification strategy.[17] The prevailing theory of diversification suggests that firms should diversify when they have excess resources, capabilities and core competencies that have multiple uses.[18] Multi-business strategies often encompass many different industry environments and, as discussed in Chapter 11, require unique organisational structures.

This chapter begins by addressing the history of diversification. Included in that discussion are descriptions of the advantages and disadvantages of single-business and dominant-business strategies. Next, the chapter describes different levels of diversification (from low to high) and the reasons why firms pursue a corporate-level strategy of diversification. Two types of diversification strategies that denote moderate to very high levels of diversification – related and unrelated – are then examined.

Large diversified firms often compete against each other in several markets. This type of rivalry is called multi-point competition. For instance, RJR Nabisco competes against Philip Morris in both cigarettes and consumer foods. The chapter also explores vertical integration strategies designed to exploit market share and gain power over competitors. Closing the chapter is a brief discussion of issues firms should consider when examining the possibility of becoming more diversified.

History of diversification

In 1950, only 38.1 per cent of the *Fortune* 500 US industrial companies generated more than 25 per cent of their revenues from diversified activities. By 1974, the figure had risen to 63 per cent. In 1950, then, more than 60 per cent of the largest *Fortune* 500 industrial companies were either single-business or dominant-business firms; by 1974, the percentage had dropped to 37 per cent.[19]

Beginning in the late 1970s and especially through the middle part of the 1980s, a significant trend towards refocusing on core businesses and divesting of business units unrelated to core business occurred in many firms. In fact, approximately 50 per cent of the *Fortune* 500 companies refocused on their core businesses from 1981 to 1987.[20] As a result, by 1988, the percentage of single- or dominant-business firms on the *Fortune* 500 list of industrial companies had increased to 53 per cent.[21]

In Australia, the diversification boom occurred during the 1980s, with many of the country's leading firms, such as BHP, Pacific Dunlop, Brambles and CSR, diversifying away from their core operations. The 1990s, however, saw a steady 'de-conglomeration' or 'de-mergering' of Australian companies. Such a move seems justified given that the findings of a study by IBIS World found that 'the more diversified a company is, the less impressive its performance'.[22]

Although many diversified firms have become more focused, this trend is somewhat masked because extensive international diversification (as opposed to product diversification) has taken place that is not included in these statistics. As Chapter 8's discussion reveals, international strategy has been increasing in importance and has led to greater financial performance relative to product diversification.[23]

The trend towards product diversification has been most significant among US firms. Nonetheless, large business organisations in Europe, Asia and Australia have also implemented diversification strategies. For Australia, in particular, see Table 6.1 for a list of diversified industrials.

Table 6.1 | Australian diversified industrials

	Company name	Net profit ($000)	Return on revenue (%)
1	Wesfarmers	100 079	8.3
2	SouthCorp	91 548	9.7
3	Howard Smith	61 955	6.2
4	Pacific Dunlop	60 700	3.3
5	Smorgon Steel	40 005	5.0
6	Futuris Corporation	30 888	1.9
7	Austrim Nylex	30 756	9.0
8	Email	24 028	3.6
9	GWA International	21 618	10.7
10	Pacifica Group	17 867	5.7
11	Hills Industries	8 962	8.0
12	McPherson's	6 959	5.7
13	Steamships Trading	6 889	11.8
14	Coventry Group	3 958	3.8
15	Hancock and Gore	3 488	11.5

Source: *Business Review Weekly*, 28 April 2000: www.brw.com.au/newsadmin/stories/brw/20000428/5414.htm.

These trends towards more diversification, which have been partially reversed due to restructuring (see Chapter 7), indicate that learning has taken place regarding corporate diversification strategies. The main lesson learned is that firms performing well in their dominant business may not want to diversify. Moreover, firms that diversify should do so cautiously, choosing to focus on a relatively few, rather than many, businesses.[24]

However, in some emerging economies, as well as in many industrialised countries, such as Germany, Italy and France, diversification has been the norm for the most successful firms (see the Strategic Focus later in this chapter). Subsequently, though, many of these diversified firms began to restructure. This sequence of diversification followed by restructuring mirrors actions of firms in the United States, the United Kingdom and Australia.

In Germany, for example, many of the largest conglomerates are restructuring as a result of the effects of three elements. First, deregulation both in Germany and across Europe is creating more competition, and the emergence of the European Union has caused firms to pursue pan-European strategies. Second, the realities of global competition are becoming prominent in Europe, and firms in several sectors are responding by restructuring. Finally, increasingly, shareholders are pressuring management to be more transparent and show separate business performances rather than reporting only overall results. One way to obtain this transparency is to spin off unrelated businesses and focus on core businesses. Two German conglomerates that have begun refocusing are Mannesmann in mobile telephone networks and Siemens, which makes multiple products from light bulbs to locomotives and has now sold one-seventh of its operations. Hoechst, one of the large chemical producers, and utilities such as Viag and Veba also have restructured. Most of these restructurings are intended to streamline the companies, focusing on a narrow set of businesses and short-term cost-cutting objectives.

Levels of diversification

Diversified firms vary according to their level of diversification and the connections between and among their businesses. Figure 6.1 lists and defines five categories of businesses according to increasing levels of diversification. In addition to the single- and dominant-business categories, more fully diversified firms are classified into related and unrelated categories. A firm is related through its diversification when there are several links between business units – for example, units may share products or services, technologies or distribution channels. The more links among businesses, the more 'constrained' is the relatedness of diversification. Unrelatedness refers to the absence of direct links between businesses.

Figure 6.1 | Levels and types of diversification

Low levels of diversification

- **Single business:** More than 95 per cent of revenue comes from a single business.
- **Dominant business:** Between 70 and 95 per cent of revenue comes from a single business.

Moderate to high levels of diversification

- **Related constrained:** Less than 70 per cent of revenue comes from the dominant business, and all businesses share product, technological and distribution linkages.
- **Related linked (mixed related and unrelated):** Less than 70 per cent of revenue comes from the dominant business, and there are only limited links between businesses.

Very high levels of diversification

- **Unrelated:** Less than 70 per cent of revenue comes from the dominant business, and there are no common links between businesses.

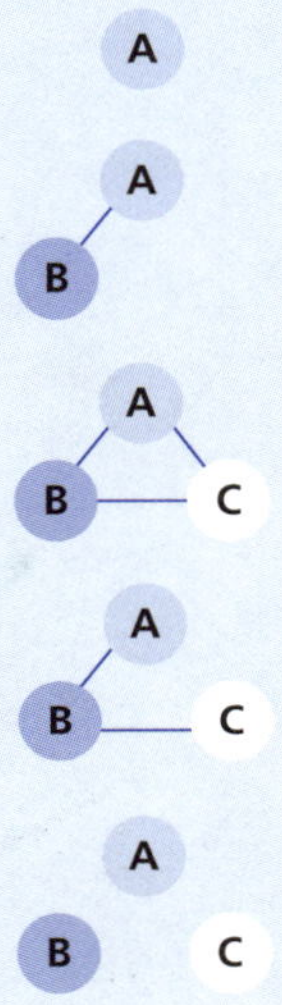

Source: Adapted from R. P. Rumelt, 1974, *Strategy, Structure and Economic Performance* (Boston: Harvard Business School).

Low levels of diversification

A firm pursing a low level of diversification focuses its efforts on a single or a dominant business. The Wm Wrigley Jr Company is an example of a firm with little diversification. Its primary focus is on the chewing-gum market.[25] A firm is classified as a single business when revenue generated by the dominant business is greater than 95 per cent of the total sales.[26] Dominant businesses are firms that generate between 70 per cent and 95 per cent of their total sales within a single category. Because of the sales it generates from breakfast cereals, Kellogg is an example of a dominant business firm. Recently, Kellogg has been pushing its cereal products as a snack food, because sales have lagged in the breakfast cereal market.[27]

Cadbury Schweppes (the largest Australian producer of chocolate and non-chocolate confectionery items) is another dominant business firm. Although Cadbury Schweppes manufactures some food products (principally under brand names such as Cottee's, Maxwell House Coffee, Pioneer and Monbulk), the bulk of the firm's revenue is earned through the selling of its confectionery and beverage items. To generate interest in its core products across time, the company introduces new products carefully and deliberately. A recent example of this was with the Yowie chocolate line, a decidedly Australian product that generated such excitement and sales in the Australian market that it was to be launched in Britain. Commenting about this approach, an analyst suggested: 'The success of this Australian-born creature has been such that the company has started selling it in Britain, Cadbury's second-biggest market. Yowies hit British shelves on April 26, 1999 after considerable marketing hype, and in the first five days more than 95,000 units were sold in Tesco supermarkets alone. Impressive results for a product that began as an idea by two authors and their business associate.'[28]

Moderate and high levels of diversification

When a firm earns more than 30 per cent of its sales volume outside a dominant business, and when its businesses are related to each other in some manner, the company is classified as a related diversified firm. With more direct links between the businesses, the firm is defined as related constrained. Examples of related constrained firms are Campbell Soup, Procter & Gamble, Xerox and National Australia Bank. If there are only a few links between businesses, the firm is defined as a mixed related and unrelated business, or a related linked firm (see Figure 6.1). Johnson & Johnson and General Electric are examples of related linked firms. Related and constrained firms share a number of resources and activities between businesses. Related linked firms have less sharing of actual resources and assets and relatively more transfers of knowledge and competencies between businesses. Highly diversified firms, which have no relationships between businesses, are called unrelated diversified firms. An example of a firm pursuing an unrelated diversification strategy is Samsung, which has been restructuring its operations after the 1997 Asian financial crisis.[29]

Although a number of unrelated diversified firms in the United States have refocused to become less diversified, a number continue to have high levels of diversification. General Electric is an example of a company that remains highly diversified. In Latin America and other emerging economies such as Korea and India, conglomerates (firms following the unrelated diversification strategy) continue to dominate the private sector.[30] For example, typically family controlled, these corporations account for more than two-thirds of the 33 largest private business groups in Brazil. Similarly, the largest business groups in Mexico, Argentina and Colombia are family-owned, diversified enterprises.[31]

Consistent with a global trend of refocusing, some companies decide to become less diversified. Cited historically as perhaps the world's most successful follower of the unrelated diversification strategy, Hanson plc nonetheless decided in the mid-1990s to become less diversified and streamline its operations. Thus, Hanson either sold or spun off a number of its operating businesses; those remaining were structured into four independent business units.[32]

As a more-than-100-year-old industrial manufacturer, Westinghouse Electric Corp. implemented a related linked diversification strategy for many years. The significant reduction in the amount of this firm's diversification began with its acquisition of CBS for US$5.4 billion in cash in August 1995. Convinced that the firm's future was in broadcasting, then CEO Michael H. Jordan initiated a process that culminated in the official changing of the firm's name to CBS Corporation (CBS Corp.). To create its broadcasting focus, two business units, Thermo King and Westinghouse Power Generation, were sold in 1997. Jordan completed the sales of the remaining major business units – energy systems, process control and government operations – by mid-1998.

During these divestitures, CBS Corp. acquired American Radio Systems' radio broadcasting operations. Calling the transaction 'strategically attractive', a top-level CBS executive stated, 'This investment will significantly strengthen CBS's position in the fast growing radio industry. It will enable CBS Radio to expand into new top 50 markets and increase its position in its existing markets.' Thus, to expand its single product line of broadcasting – a line that includes the CBS Network, CBS radio, the TV station group, and cable and 'other' broadcasting – CBS Corp. was committed to making selective acquisitions.

Ultimately, Mel Karmazin became CEO of CBS. In talking with Sumner M. Redstone, Viacom's 76-year-old CEO, about taking advantage of a US Federal Communications Commission ruling that allowed one company to own two television stations in one market, these CEOs decided to merge their two firms. Viacom bought the assets of CBS and agreed to pay US$37 billion in stock to combine the two companies into a new megamedia empire with capabilities comparable to Disney, News Corporation and AOL Time Warner.[33] Thus, over time, Westinghouse first increased its diversification, then decreased its diversification and became CBS Corporation, and finally increased its diversification when it merged with Viacom.

Reasons for diversification

Firms use a diversification strategy as their corporate-level strategy for many reasons. A partial list is shown in Table 6.2. These reasons are discussed throughout the remainder of the chapter in relation to related and unrelated diversification strategies, incentives and managerial motives to diversify.

Most firms implement a diversification strategy to enhance the strategic competitiveness of the entire company. This reason describes the strategic actions of Wesfarmers, as explained in the Opening Case. When a diversification strategy enhances strategic competitiveness, the firm's total value is increased. Value is created through either related diversification or unrelated diversification when that particular strategy allows a company's business units to increase revenues or reduce costs while implementing their business-level strategies. Another reason for diversification is to gain market power relative to competitors. As discussed later in more detail, this is often done through vertical integration.

Table 6.2 | Motives, incentives and resources for diversification

Motives to enhance strategic competitiveness

- Economies of scope (related diversification)
  Sharing activities
  Transferring core competencies
- Market power (related diversification)
  Blocking competitors through multi-point competition
  Vertical integration
- Financial economies (unrelated diversification)
  Efficient internal capital allocation
  Business restructuring

Incentives and resources with neutral effects on strategic competitiveness

- Antitrust regulation
- Tax laws
- Low performance
- Uncertain future cash flows
- Risk reduction for firm
- Tangible resources
- Intangible resources

Managerial motives (value reduction)

- Diversifying managerial employment risk
- Increasing managerial compensation

Other reasons for implementing a diversification strategy may not enhance strategic competitiveness; in fact, diversification could have neutral effects or actually increase costs or reduce a firm's revenues. These reasons include diversification (1) to neutralise a competitor's market power (for example, to neutralise the advantage of another firm by acquiring a distribution outlet similar to those of the competitors), and (2) to expand a firm's portfolio to reduce managerial employment risk (for example, if one of the businesses fails, the top executive remains employed in a diversified firm). Because diversification can increase a firm's size and thus managerial compensation, managers have motives to diversify a firm. This type of diversification may reduce the firm's value. Diversification rationales that may have a neutral effect or that may reduce a firm's value are discussed in a later section.

To provide an overview of value-creating diversification strategies, Figure 6.2 illustrates the two dimensions as sources of relatedness. Researchers have studied these independent dimensions of relatedness[34] and have found that resources and key competencies are critical. The vertical dimension of the figure relates to sharing activities (operational relatedness), while the horizontal dimension represents corporate capabilities for transferring knowledge (corporate relatedness). The upper left quadrant has to do with the firm that has a high degree of capability in managing operational synergy, especially in sharing assets between its businesses. It also represents vertical sharing of assets through vertical integration. The lower right quadrant of the figure represents a highly developed corporate capability of transferring a skill to other businesses. This skill is located primarily in the corporate office. Whichever type of relatedness is used, it is based on some kind of knowledge asset that the firm can either share or transfer.[35] Unrelated diversification may also be illustrated here, but its source of value does not come through either operational or corporate relatedness among business units; rather, it comes through financial economies or the restructuring of businesses the firm acquires. The next section examines related diversification.

Figure 6.2 | Value-creating strategies of diversification: Operational and corporate relatedness

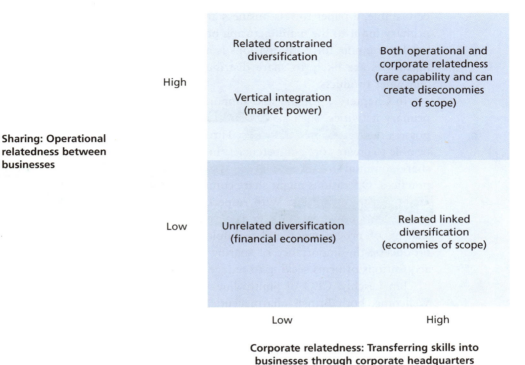

Related diversification

As suggested earlier in the chapter, related diversification is a strategy through which the firm intends to build upon or extend its existing resources, capabilities and core competencies in the pursuit of strategic competitiveness.[36] Thus, firms that have selected related diversification as their corporate-level strategy seek to exploit economies of scope between business units. Available to firms operating in multiple industries or product markets,[37] economies of scope are cost savings attributed to transferring the capabilities and competencies developed in one business to a new business.

As illustrated in Figure 6.2, firms seek to create value from economies of scope through two basic kinds of operational economies: sharing activities (operational relatedness), and transferring skills or corporate core competencies (corporate relatedness). The difference between sharing activities and transferring competencies is based on how separate resources are used jointly to create economies of scope. Tangible resources, such as plant and equipment or other business-unit physical assets, often must be shared to create economies of scope. Less tangible resources, such as manufacturing know-how, also can be shared. However, when know-how is transferred between separate activities and there is no physical or tangible resource involved, a corporate core competence has been transferred, as opposed to operational sharing of activities having taken place.

Economies of scope are cost savings attributed to transferring the capabilities and competencies developed in one business to a new business.

Operational relatedness: Sharing activities

Sharing activities is quite common, especially among related constrained firms. At Procter & Gamble, a paper towels business and a nappy business both use paper products as a primary input to the manufacturing process. Having a joint paper production plant that produces inputs for both divisions is an example of a shared activity. In addition, these businesses are likely to share distribution sales networks, because they both produce consumer products.

In Chapter 3, primary and support value-chain activities were discussed. In general, primary activities, such as inbound logistics, operations and outbound logistics, might possess multiple shared activities. Through efficient sharing of these activities, firms may be able to create core competencies. In terms of inbound logistics, the business units may share common inventory delivery systems, warehousing facilities and quality assurance practices. Operations might share common assembly facilities, quality control systems or maintenance operations. With respect to outbound logistics, two business units might share a common sales force and sales service desk. Support activities could include the sharing of procurement and technology development efforts. Among pharmaceutical producers, the importance of sharing of activities is driving a number of mergers and acquisitions of firms seeking to reduce their costs.

Jan Leschly, CEO of SmithKline Beecham plc, and Richard Sykes, CEO of Glaxo Wellcome, both British pharmaceutical firms, have signalled that the two huge firms intend to merge. The merger is valued at US$70 billion and will create the world's number-one drug-maker, to be called Glaxo SmithKline plc. This transaction is one of many that have been signalled among pharmaceutical firms recently. The anticipated acquisition of Warner-Lambert Co. by several suitor companies and the proposed merger of Monsanto Co. and Pharmacia & Upjohn, Inc. are two similar deals. The R&D costs of producing new drugs is forcing these firms to think about sharing laboratories and the capabilities they house. As one business writer said, 'Part of what is driving companies to join together is the need to finance the enormous effort required to turn a revolution in human biology into a steady flow of new medicines.'[38]

However, in 1996, when Swiss drug-makers Ciba-Geigy Ltd and Sandoz Ltd joined in a US$63 billion merger to form Novartis, CEO Daniel Vasella stated that Novartis was 'in a unique position to apply technologies learned from plant genetics to both pharmaceuticals and agricultural businesses'. He staked the company's future on genetic engineering. However, especially in Europe, a backlash over genetically modified crops has been undermining the life-sciences concept upon which Novartis is based. In 1999, the whole firm required restructuring because of poor performance in its agribusinesses.[39] Thus, there are risks associated with basing two businesses on a single value proposition to create economies of scope.

Sandoz president Marc Monet (left) and Ciba president Alex Krauer (right) announced the merger of their firms on 7 March 1999. The new company, Novartis, is now one of the biggest drug and agrochemical concerns in the world.

Firms expect the sharing of activities across units to result in increased strategic competitiveness and improved financial returns. Other matters, however, affect the degree to which these outcomes will be achieved through activity sharing. For example, firms should recognise that sharing activities requires sharing strategic control over business units. Moreover, one business-unit manager may feel that another is receiving more benefit from the activity sharing. Such a perception could create conflicts between division managers. Activity sharing also is risky because business-unit ties create links between outcomes. For instance, if demand for the product of one business is reduced, there may not be sufficient revenues to cover the fixed costs of running the joint plant. Shared activities create interrelationships that affect the ability of both businesses to achieve strategic competitiveness, as is illustrated in the aforementioned case of Novartis. Activity sharing may be ineffective if these costs are not taken into consideration.

The costs of activity sharing notwithstanding, research shows that the sharing of activities and resources across business units can increase the firm's value. For example, research examining acquisitions of firms in the same industry (referred to as horizontal acquisitions), such as the banking industry, has found that sharing resources and activities (thereby creating economies of scope) contributed to post-acquisition increases in performance and higher returns to shareholders.[40] Research also found that firms which sold off related units in which resource sharing was a possible source of economies of scope produced lower returns than those which sold off businesses unrelated to the firm's core business.[41] Still other research found that firms with more related units had lower risk.[42] These results suggest that gaining economies of scope by sharing activities and resources across businesses within a firm may be important in reducing risk and in earning positive returns from diversification efforts. Further, more attractive results are obtained through the sharing of activities when a strong corporate office facilitates the sharing.[43]

Corporate relatedness: Transferring of core competencies

Over time, a strategically competitive firm's intangible resources, such as its know-how, become the foundation for competitively valuable corporate capabilities and core competencies. Thus, as illustrated in Figure 6.2, corporate core competencies are complex sets of resources and capabilities that link different businesses, primarily through managerial and technological knowledge, experience and expertise.[44]

Marketing expertise is an example of a core competence that could be used in this way. Because the expense of developing such a competence has already been incurred, and because competencies based on intangible resources are less visible and more difficult for competitors to understand and imitate, transferring these types of competencies from an original business unit to another one may reduce costs and enhance a firm's strategic competitiveness.[45] A key reason Philip Morris decided to acquire the Miller Brewing Company was that it believed that a competitive advantage could be achieved by transferring its marketing core competence to Miller. One interesting aside on Philip Morris's diversification into foods is that it has created a new Australian brand as opposition: The Dick Smith Foods Company. Dick Smith's Foods was developed in direct response to the knowledge that Philip Morris, best known as a tobacco corporation, now owns the Australian icon Vegemite. Dick Smith's Foods Company now produces a range of products that include jellies, breakfast cereals, ice cream and soft-drinks.

As a cigarette company, Philip Morris developed a particular expertise in marketing. When Philip Morris purchased Miller Brewing, the beer industry had efficient operations, but no firm in the industry had established marketing competence as a source of competitive advantage. The marketing competence that was transferred from Philip

Morris to Miller resulted in the introduction of improved marketing practices to the brewing industry. These practices, especially in terms of advertising, proved to be the source of competitive advantage that allowed Miller Brewing to earn above-average returns for a period of time. In fact, several years passed before Anheuser-Busch, the largest firm in the brewing industry, developed the capabilities required to duplicate the benefits of Miller's strategy. A strong competitive response from Anheuser-Busch was predictable, however, in that beer is the firm's core business.

A number of firms have been exceptional in transferring skills across businesses. Besides Philip Morris, in tobacco, food and beer, Virgin Industries has been able to transfer its marketing skills across travel, cosmetics, music, drinks and a number of other businesses. Similarly, Honda has developed and transferred its expertise in small and now larger engines for a number of types of vehicles, from motorcycles and lawn-mowers to its range of automotive products.[46] The Strategic Focus, on Williams Companies, shows how this firm has transferred its skills in building and operating natural-gas pipelines to building and operating fibre-optic Internet pipelines.

Strategic Focus Corporate

Williams Companies transfers its skills from natural-gas pipelines to Internet pipelines

Williams Companies built its size and reputation on constructing large natural-gas pipelines in the United States. In the process, it learned how to manage large capital-intensive projects for a small number of vital business customers. Williams has now begun to transfer this skill to communication projects. Williams helps to connect businesses to other businesses in energy and communications. The company tries to deliver innovative, reliable products and services through its extensive networks of energy-distributing and high-speed fibre-optic cable pipelines. Williams also offers comprehensive services, including commodity trading and risk management on the energy side, and business communications systems and international satellite and fibre-optic video services through its communication business.

As it examined its wholesale role in energy and services, Williams found an analogous business in fibre-optic pipelines that were built to carry Internet traffic. The company felt that the two businesses were similar. As traffic increases in the pipeline, costs drop steeply. Williams felt that, as it had done in natural gas, it could ride this declining cost curve to profit from wholesale Internet traffic through a fibre-optic pipeline.

Accordingly, in the early 1980s, the firm started building a huge network of Internet pipelines that it ultimately sold to MCI WorldCom, Inc. in 1995. Williams is now in the process of building a second, more advanced 53 000-kilometre fibre-optic network. As it funded this network, Williams had a successful IPO that was partially financed by large potential customers who also became investors.

Even though telecommunication prices are declining, Williams believes that it can build volume and cut costs and still be 'enormously profitable'. Furthermore, its expertise in building pipelines will allow the company to move more rapidly and cheaply than other competitors who might produce similar large fibre-optic pipelines. Williams has already lined up SBC Communications, Teléfonos de Mexico and its own subsidiary company, Williams Communications, as customers. Furthermore, SBC Communications and Williams Communications are also investors in the project. Thus, through these ties with large customers (who also are committed through their investments), Williams expects to make the project successful.

Other firms have not been as effective as Williams in seeking to transfer their competencies. For instance, Johnson & Johnson (J&J) recently was criticised in this regard. J&J has three main businesses: professional health care devices, such as coronary stints and other wound-closure products associated with surgery; pharmaceuticals; and consumer health care products, such as Tylenol painkillers, Band-Aids, Johnson baby products and Neutrogena skin products. Because J&J has not been very successful in keeping up its stock price in relationship to those of other pharmaceutical companies, investors and Wall Street analysts have been calling for a breakup of the firm into its three separate businesses.

The company's CEO, Ralph Larsen, nonetheless argues that J&J is a health care company and not a pharmaceutical firm in particular. One of the problems is that J&J's strategy is implemented through decentralisation, an approach allowing each operating unit to manage itself independently. This makes it more difficult to transfer expertise from the corporate headquarters and between independent units. It is chiefly for this reason that many Wall Street analysts are suggesting that J&J should be broken up into three distinct units. In fact, to shore up its abilities in these separate areas, the company has been making acquisitions to allow each business to improve its competitiveness. Accordingly, J&J's approach has been to seek new knowledge from outside the firm, rather than trying to increase its ability to transfer knowledge from headquarters or across business units within the firm. Thus, relative to Williams Companies, J&J has been less successful in transferring its skills and knowledge within the company.

Sources: Williams Companies, Inc., 2000, *Williams Companies Home Page*: www.williams.com; R. King, 1999, 'Too much long distance', *Fortune*, 15 March, pp. 106–10; R. Langreth and R. Winslow, 1999, 'At J&J, a venerable strategy faces questions', *Wall Street Journal*, 5 March, pp. B1, B4; A. Stone, 1999, 'Why Williams Cos. mixes gas with fiberoptics', *Business Week Online*, 11 March: www.businessweek.com; B. Wysocki, Jr, 1999, 'Corporate America confronts the meaning of a "core" business', *Wall Street Journal*, 9 November, pp. A1, A4.

As the Strategic Focus suggests, Johnson & Johnson has discovered that some firms are either unable to transfer competencies, or they transfer competencies that do not help a business unit establish a competitive advantage. One way managers facilitate the transfer of competencies is to move key people into new management positions. Still, although Philip Morris accomplished a transfer of competence to Miller Brewing in this way, a business-unit manager of an older division may be reluctant to transfer key people who have accumulated corporate knowledge and experience. Thus, managers with the ability to facilitate the transfer of a core competence may come at a premium or may not want to transfer, and the top-level managers from the transferring division may not want the competencies transferred to a new division to fulfil the firm's diversification objectives. Research suggests that transferring expertise in manufacturing-based businesses often does not result in improved performance.[47] However, those businesses in which performance does improve often exhibit a corporate passion for pursuing skill transfer and appropriate coordination mechanisms for realising economies of scope.

Market power

> **Market power** exists when a firm is able to sell its products above the existing competitive level or reduce the costs of its primary and support activities below the competitive level, or both.

Related diversification can also be used to gain market power. Market power exists when a firm is able to sell its products above the existing competitive level or reduce the costs of its primary and support activities below the competitive level, or both.[48]

One approach to gaining market power through diversification is multi-point competition. *Multi-point competition* exists when two or more diversified firms compete in the same product areas or geographic markets.[49] For example, when Philip Morris moved into foods by buying General Foods and Kraft, RJR's competitive response was the acquisition of another food company, Nabisco. Alternatively, when Coles Myer moved into electronic commerce with its ColesOnline service, Woolworths responded by setting up Woolworths Homeshop.

If the diversified firms compete 'head to head' in each market, multi-point competition will not create potential gains; instead, it will generate excessive competitive activity. Over time, if the firms refrain from competition and, in effect realise mutual forbearance, they are engaged in a form of related diversification that creates value for each firm through less competitive activity (see Chapter 5). *Mutual forbearance* is a relationship between two or more firms in which excessive competition leads to a situation whereby the firms see that such competition is self-destructive and, without formal agreement, cease engaging in it. Again, as the discussion in Chapter 5 indicated, this is a good summary of the relationship between Coles Myer and Woolworths, one that is perhaps going to change as Aldi enters the market.

Actions taken by Vodafone Airtouch and Mannesmann are an example of multi-point competition. Mannesmann began as a German producer of steel piping, but moved into telecommunications services in 1996 with the purchase of a telecommunications network formerly owned by the German railroad, Deutsche Bahn. By 1997, Mannesmann had more mobile-phone customers than Deutsche Telekom. In 1999, Mannesmann purchased a number of mobile assets across Europe. The company paid US$1.2 billion for o.tel.o, owned by Veba and RWE, which exited the telecommunications business. Furthermore, Mannesmann purchased the cellular business of Olivetti, OmniTel, for US$7.8 billion, because Olivetti was trying to take over Telecom Italia. Then, in a surprise move, Mannesmann acquired British mobile-phone company Orange for US$34 billion in October 1999.

However, in November 1999, Vodafone Airtouch launched a hostile bid for Mannesmann. Headquartered in Britain, Vodafone realised that it had to make this deal because Mannesmann would be the firm's biggest competitor in Europe, especially after it took over Orange, a leading mobile-phone service provider in Britain. Mannesmann paid a significant premium of US$6 000 per subscriber for Orange, which is 70 per cent above the industry average cost per subscriber. However, Mannesmann shares had increased 145 per cent in 1999, a performance that satisfied shareholders.[50]

In 1998, Christopher Gent, Vodafone's CEO, paid US$60 billion in stock and cash for San Francisco-based Airtouch, beating out a rival offer from Bell Atlantic. However, Gent later structured a transaction with Bell Atlantic, which had acquired GTE's cellular business. The partnership creates a network of 20 million cellular customers that would cover 90 per cent of the population of the United States. AT&T would be in second place in market share, with 12 million wireless customers. As investors viewed the transaction, they not only approved of the American deal, but also could see the cellular global strategy in the combination of Vodafone and Airtouch. Accordingly, the takeover price appreciated 25 per cent. Bell Atlantic's stock price did not appreciate significantly, compared to the increases in Vodafone-Airtouch stock price. The reason for the difference is the international opportunity seen by shareholders in the Vodafone Airtouch deal. Anticipating an advantage in the future of international cellular calls, Gent decided to pursue the Mannesmann deal.[51]

The preceding example illustrates the potential negative side of multi-point competition. Vodafone Airtouch's actions represent a counterattack mode, an exceptional strategic action when multi-point competition exists.[52] Counterattacks are not common in multi-point competition because the threat of a counterattack may prevent strategic actions from being taken, or, more likely, firms may retract their strategic actions with the threat of counterattack.[53]

Vertical integration exists when a company is producing its own inputs (backward integration) or owns its own source of distribution of outputs (forward integration).

Another approach to creating value by gaining market power is the strategy of vertical integration (see Figure 6.2). Vertical integration exists when a company is producing its own inputs (backward integration), as for example with BHP Steel, or owns its own source of distribution of outputs (forward integration), as for example with Pacific Dunlop's ownership of the Beaurepaire tyre outlets. It is also possible to have partial vertical integration, wherein some inputs and outputs are sold by company units, while others are produced or sold by outside firms.

A company pursuing vertical integration is usually motivated to strengthen its position in its core business by gaining market power over competitors. This is done through savings on operations costs, avoidance of market costs, better control to establish quality and, possibly, the protection of technology. It also happens when firms have strong ties between their assets for which no market prices exist. Establishing a market price would result in high search and transaction costs, so firms seek to vertically integrate rather than remaining separate businesses.[54]

Of course, there are limits to vertical integration. For example, an outside supplier may produce the product at a lower cost. As a result, internal transactions from vertical integration may be expensive and reduce profitability. Also, bureaucratic costs are incurred in implementing this strategy. And because vertical integration can require that substantial sums of capital be invested in specific technologies, the strategy may be problematic when technology changes quickly. Finally, changes in demand create capacity balance and coordination problems. If one division of a firm is building a part for another internal division, but achieving economies of scale requires the first division to build the part at a scale beyond the capacity of the internal buyer to absorb demand, sales outside the company would be necessary. However, if demand slackens, over-capacity would result because the internal users cannot absorb the total demand. Thus, although vertical integration can create value and contribute to strategic competitiveness, especially in gaining market power over competitors, it is not without risks and costs.

As Figure 6.2 suggests, some firms may try to seek both operational and corporate forms of economies of scope.[55] Firms that attempt to do this often fail and create diseconomies of scope, because trying to manage two sources of knowledge is extremely difficult. However, if successful, this strategy can create value that is difficult for competitors to imitate. For example, General Electric has been successful both in realising operational synergy and in transferring knowledge between business units. GE had long possessed the ability to develop operational synergies inside its business groups. Through the use of 'sharing best practices' and 'boundary-less behavior', the firm also possesses the ability to transfer knowledge among its units.[56] In describing the achievements resulting from these abilities, business analysts suggest that 'GE is truly firing on all cylinders'. For instance, 'GE Capital, the world's largest non-bank finance company, boasts investments in 45 e-business companies. And NBC has allied with a host of Net players to capitalize on the convergence of the media, entertainment, and technology industries.'[57]

Because knowledge management is so important in consulting firms such as McKinsey and Company and Accenture (formerly known as Andersen Consulting), each of these companies tries to manage both operational and corporate relatedness.[58] Accenture Consulting originally focused on consulting in the field of information system implementation, but now the company consults on information systems and technology and provides strategic services and outsourcing (wherein Accenture becomes the computer-processing department for a large firm). Accenture also has diversified industry lines of consulting businesses (financial services, government, oil and gas, and so on). The firm does a lot of sharing across these lines, but also has a large knowledge base from which consultants draw and seek to transfer information across lines of industry consulting engagements. Consulting is a business that requires both the sharing and transfer of skills in order to remain profitable, especially if business declines and consulting projects become more competitive.⁵⁹

Disney has also been successful in using both operational and corporate relatedness. Disney's strategy is especially successful in comparison to that of Sony, at least as measured by revenues generated from blockbuster movies. Through the use of both operational and corporate relatedness, Disney made US$3 billion on the 150 products that came out simultaneously with its movie *The Lion King*. Sony's *Men in Black* was a super hit at the box office and earned US$600 million, but box-office and video revenues were practically all of the success story. Disney was able to accomplish its great success by sharing knowledge within its movie and distribution divisions, while at the same time transferring knowledge into its retail and product divisions, creating a music CD, *Rhythm of the Pride Lands*, and producing a video, *Simba's Pride*. In addition, there were *Lion King* themes at Disney resorts and Animal Kingdom parks.⁶⁰

The next corporate-level strategy considered, unrelated diversification, lacks both operational and corporate relatedness, but, when used appropriately, also creates value.

Unrelated diversification

Financial economies are cost savings realised through improved allocations of financial resources based on investments inside or outside the firm.

An unrelated diversification strategy (see Figure 6.2) can create value through two types of financial economies. Financial economies are cost savings realised through improved allocations of financial resources based on investments inside or outside the firm.⁶¹

The first type of financial economy involves efficient internal capital allocations. This approach seeks to reduce risks among the firm's business units – for example, through the development of a portfolio of businesses with different risk profiles. The approach thereby reduces business risk for the total corporation. The second type of financial economy is concerned with purchasing other corporations and restructuring their assets. This approach allows a firm to buy and sell businesses in the external market with the intent of increasing the total value of the firm.

Efficient internal capital market allocation

Capital allocation is usually distributed efficiently in a market economy by capital markets. Capital is distributed efficiently because investors seek to purchase shares of firm equity (ownership) that have high future cash-flow values. Capital is allocated not only through equity, but also through debt, by means of which shareholders and debt-holders seek to improve the value of their investment by investing in businesses with high growth prospects. In large diversified firms, however, the corporate office distributes capital to divisions to create value for the overall company. Such an approach may provide gains from internal capital market allocation, relative to the external capital market.⁶² The corporate office, through managing a particular set of businesses, may have access to more detailed and accurate information regarding those businesses's actual and prospective performance.

Compared with corporate office personnel, investors have relatively limited access to internal information and can only *estimate* divisional performance and future business prospects. Although businesses that seek capital must provide information to those who will supply the capital (for example, banks or insurance companies), firms with internal capital markets may have at least two informational advantages. First, information provided to capital markets through annual reports and other sources may not include negative information, but rather emphasise positive prospects and outcomes. External sources of capital have limited ability to know specifically what is taking place inside large organisations. Even owners who have access to information have no guarantee of full and complete disclosure.[63]

Second, although a firm must disseminate information, that information becomes available to potential competitors simultaneously. With insights gained by studying such information, competitors might attempt to duplicate a firm's competitive advantage. Without having to reveal internal information, a firm may protect its competitive advantage through an internal capital market.

If intervention from outside the firm is required to make corrections, only significant changes are possible, such as forcing the firm into bankruptcy or changing the dominant leadership coalition (for example, the top-management team described in Chapter 12). Alternatively, in an internal capital market, the corporate office may fine-tune corrections by choosing to adjust managerial incentives or suggest strategic changes in a division. Thus, capital can be allocated according to more specific criteria than is possible with external market allocation. The external capital market may fail to allocate resources adequately to high-potential investments, compared with corporate office investments, because it has less accurate information. The corporate office of a diversified company can more effectively perform such tasks as disciplining under-performing management teams and allocating resources.[64]

Some firms still follow the unrelated diversification strategy.[65] Many of these large diversified business groups are found in southern European countries and throughout the emerging economies of the world. The Strategic Focus on diversified business groups in emerging economies speaks to how many of those business groups are becoming less diversified. As our discussion of these strategic actions suggests, choosing not to use the unrelated diversification strategy may actually decrease a firm's strategic competitiveness.

Strategic Focus International

Refocusing large diversified business groups in emerging economies

Large firms with portfolios of unrelated businesses throughout the world's emerging economies, as well as in some developed economies, are seeking to refocus their portfolios on a 'core'. The intention of this type of strategic action is to improve performance. These large diversified business groups, known as *Chaebols* in South Korea, are actually quite typical of those in capitalist countries that have industrialised since the Second World War. Many such firms from Asia and Latin America are using a model of Western corporate-level strategies and are refocusing their diversified operations: 'Companies are mimicking Corporate America by refocusing, downsizing, merging, and spinning off faltering businesses to become globally competitive.' But, at times, this refocusing may not be wholly appropriate in an emerging economy. Nonetheless, many of the firms have followed the pattern in the United States and Australia, where high levels of diversified operations have been refocused. A number of refocused firms specialise in managing businesses with core technology families to realise related diversification.

However, in emerging economies and in many highly developed economies such as France, Germany and Italy, these diversified business groups have dominated the competitive landscape for several reasons. Some have argued that the underlying reason for having these conglomerates in the first place has not changed that much, especially in regard to emerging economies. Tarun Khanna and Krishna Palepu, accordingly, argue that the total restructuring of these diversified business groups is flawed. However, the recent financial crises in Asia and Latin America have reinforced the idea among politicians that these large business groups in emerging economies should refocus. In fact, in Korea, for instance, President Kim Dae Jung pressed the *Chaebols* to downscope and invited foreign investors to help in the process by buying some of the assets that the *Chaebols* were forced to spin off. The change of path to a new structure has not been smooth. In late February 2001, the workers at Daewoo Automotive rioted over the plant's closure, burning buses and stoning the factories.

Nevertheless, in a broad range of emerging economies, such as in Chile, India and South Korea, it has taken longer than a decade to build institutions that support well-functioning infrastructure markets for capital, management, labour and technology. The reason these diversified business groups evolved is that the markets for capital, management, labour and international technology have been internalised in firms in those groups. The main problem is unequal (that is, asymmetric) information and potential conflicts of interest between buyers and sellers in these markets. Where advanced markets exist, effective intermediaries, sound regulations and contract laws can minimise the unequal information and any conflicts between buyers and sellers. For instance, in the Australian financial market, investment bankers play an intermediary role in the allocation of capital to businesses. Furthermore, the Australian Stock Exchange and Australian Competition and Consumer Commission help to ensure that investors can rely on corporate disclosure and, thereby, adequate information. In addition, well-developed contract law helps to resolve conflicts between buyers and sellers, and dozens of business schools provide graduates who possess the knowledge required to manage firms successfully through the use of the strategic management process.

However, in emerging economies, these institutional mechanisms are often missing, creating additional transaction costs between businesses. The existence of a 'soft infrastructure' (laws, regulatory bodies and financial intermediaries that facilitate the transactional environment) is as important as that of a hard physical infrastructure such as roads, ports and telecommunications systems, because the former reduces transaction costs. China, for example, has invested heavily in its physical infrastructure, but has made little progress in creating a strong institutional infrastructure. Instead, China has been fostering large diversified business groups, such as the Baoshan Iron and Steel Group Corporation in steel-making, the Haier Group in appliances, the Sichuan Chang Hong Group in televisions, the North China Pharmaceutical Group Corporation in drugs, the Jiangnan Shipyard Group Co. in shipbuilding and the Peking University Founder Group Corporation in computer software. Although Western journalists have been disappointed with the formation of these large diversified corporations because unrelated diversification is often viewed as inefficient in more developed economies, they may be necessary because of the lack of a 'soft infrastructure' in China. As in other emerging economies, these large diversified business groups serve as internal capital markets for the allocation of capital by a strong corporate headquarters. Furthermore, they function as a way to manage transactions, often through their own subsidiaries, when the country does not have a well-developed legal infrastructure. The transactions are effective because the corporation has a way of managing them equitably within the firm and through family members or closely affiliated partners. In addition, these diversified companies serve as training grounds for managers in the labour market system, because educational institutions often are unable to train managers via distinctive business programs such as those found in Western educational institutions.

Although large diversified firms such as the *Chaebols* in Korea have been identified as the main cause of that country's economic problems, they in fact were necessary, given the absence of structure in the economy when those firms were first developing. Chile was one of the first emerging economies to seriously pursue market liberalisation, and it has succeeded in developing one of the most efficient capital markets. However, the process of reform took more than 25 years and is still not complete. Although financial deregulation began in 1974 with the banking crisis, which was similar to the events in Asia in 1997, it was not until 1990 that the benefits of Chile's reforms started to take effect, when the first American Depository Receipt, La Compañia de Teléfonos de Chile, was listed on an American exchange. In comparison, the Korean and Indian governments have both used banks as instruments of economic development, in a manner similar to bank lending policies in Malaysia and Indonesia. However, without a sharp-edged capital market such as that found in Chile, when a financial crisis develops, government interference has curtailed the development of basic financial intermediation expertise such as credit analysis.

As an example, Thai Petrochemical Industry, PCL, headquartered in Bangkok, Thailand, was recently forced to reorganise because of the Asian financial crisis and high levels of debt. This company and a number of others are sewn together in a large conglomerate owned by Prachai Leophairatana. Leophairatana was having a hard time understanding that when a company goes bankrupt, its lenders, not its owners, have first claims over the remains of the firm. In Thailand, this sort of reasoning seemed unfair to the debtor and his employees. In fact, the government agreed, and the International Monetary Fund relaxed the requirement to pass foreclosure legislation as part of a bail-out package for Thailand. Without appropriate legislation or suitable bankruptcy laws, it is unlikely that Thailand's financial difficulties can be resolved quickly. Traditionally, conglomerates in emerging economies have been controlled by families, and their main form of financing typically has been through debt, because debt allows family owners to control large business groups with a relatively small amount of equity capital. This approach has been used in Korean companies, and thus they are heavily indebted, even for very risky ventures. In theory, such risky ventures, such as diversifying into semiconductors, should be based on more long-term equity capital because debt requires short-term cash flow.

To restructure these firms in emerging economies, it may be necessary first to change their internal orientation rather than pursue drastic action, as was chosen by the Korean government. Most of these firms have adopted a growth orientation towards financial goals, forgoing some profits. Taking a stronger orientation towards profitability would help to make individual firms or divisions more accountable for their operating performance. In addition, the corporate office should take a role in management development by delegating operational authority to large affiliate corporations. Group-wide recruiting, training and job rotation programs would be helpful as well. These programs would allow executives to receive the training they need, but also enable them to be responsible for a greater profit orientation at the business or division level. Such an orientation would create better financial information internally and ultimately would lead to more transparent transactions in the economy. Rather than placing the blame on Korea's *Chaebols*, which have responded to government policy in the past, the Korean government should focus on building more effective institutions, a result of which would be a weeding out of inefficient groups. Simply blaming the *Chaebols* for the crisis is not helpful. The government should invite foreign competitors and, thereby, stronger product market competition. Effective intermediaries would then develop, and they would not be isolated from foreign competition. They could familiarise themselves with investment banking, venture capitalists and new business school techniques. Thus, focusing on developing the 'soft infrastructure' may be better for a government than blaming firms that helped them to achieve the foundation of economic development, even though the current weaknesses have been exposed by the Asian financial crisis.

Sources: T. Khanna and K. Palepu, 1999, 'The right way to restructure conglomerates in emerging markets', *Harvard Business Review*, 77(4), pp. 125–34; M. Schuman and J. L. Lee, 1999, 'Dismantling of Daewoo shows how radically Korea is changing', *Wall Street Journal*, 17 August, pp. A1, A10; J. Webber, H. Dawley, E, Malkin, M. Tanikawa and I. Katz, 1999, 'International: As the world restructures', *Business Week Online*, 14 June: www.businessweek.com; L. Chang, 1998, 'Big is beautiful', *Wall Street Journal*, 30 April, p. R9; D. McDermott, 1998, 'Asian recovery focus shifts to Thailand', *Wall Street Journal*, 9 December, p. A19.

Implementing the unrelated business strategy continues to make sense in many economies of the world, as the Strategic Focus points out, especially among emerging economies such as that of China. But research also indicates that the conglomerate or unrelated strategy has not disappeared in Europe, where the number of firms using this strategy has actually increased.⁶⁶ Although many conglomerates (for example, ITT and Hansen Trust) have refocused, other unrelated diversified firms have replaced them. The Achilles heel of the unrelated strategy is that conglomerates in developing economies have a fairly short life cycle because financial economies are more easily duplicated than in the case of operational and corporate relatedness. This is less of a problem in emerging economies, where the absence of a 'soft infrastructure' (for example, effective financial intermediaries, sound regulations and contract laws) supports and encourages the pursuit of the unrelated diversification strategy.

Restructuring

Another alternative, similar to the internal capital market approach, focuses exclusively on buying and selling other firms' assets in the external market.⁶⁷ As in the real-estate business, profits are earned by buying assets low, restructuring them, and selling them as high as possible. This restructuring approach usually entails buying the firm, selling off its assets, such as corporate headquarters, and terminating corporate staff members.

Selling under-performing divisions and placing the remaining divisions under the discipline of rigorous financial controls is an additional restructuring action that is often used. Rigorous controls require divisions to follow strict budgets and account regularly for cash inflows and outflows to corporate headquarters. A firm that pursues this approach may have to use hostile takeovers or tender offers. Hostile takeovers have the potential to increase the resistance of the target firm's top-level managers. In these cases, corporate-level managers often are dismissed, while division managers are retained.

Creating financial economies through the purchase of other companies and the restructuring of their assets requires an understanding of significant trade-offs. Success usually calls for a focus on mature, low-technology businesses. Otherwise, resource allocation decisions become too complex because the uncertainty of demand for high-technology products requires information-processing capabilities that are beyond those of the smaller corporate staffs of firms employing the unrelated diversification strategy. Service businesses are also difficult to buy and sell in this way, because of their client or sales orientation. Sales staffs of service businesses are more mobile than those of manufacturing-oriented businesses and may seek jobs with a competitor, taking their clients with them. This is especially so in professional service businesses such as accounting, law, advertising, consulting and investment banking. These businesses probably would not create value if they were acquired by a firm restructuring using an unrelated diversification strategy.

Diversification: Incentives and resources

Incentives to diversify

Incentives to diversify come from both the external environment and a firm's internal environment. The term 'incentive' implies that managers have some choice regarding whether to pursue the incentive or not. Incentives external to the firm include antitrust regulation and tax laws. Internal firm incentives include low performance, uncertain future cash flows and an overall reduction of risk for the firm.

Competition regulations and tax laws

Government competition policies and tax laws provided incentives for Australian firms to diversify. The application of competition laws to prevent mergers that created increased market power (via either vertical or horizontal integration) was stringent in the 1970s and onwards, particularly so through the enforcement of the *Trade Practices Act 1974* and the *Prices Surveillance Act 1983*. As a result, many of the mergers during this time were unrelated – that is, they involved companies pursuing different lines of business. Thus, the merger wave of the 1980s was 'conglomerate' in character.

In addition to the external incentive to diversify based on antitrust regulation and tax laws, a number of incentives internal to the firm increase the likelihood that diversification will be pursued.

Low performance

It has been proposed that 'high performance eliminates the need for greater diversification',[68] as in the example of the Wm Wrigley Jr Co. Conversely, low performance may provide an incentive for diversification. Firms plagued by poor performance often take higher risks.[69] Interestingly, though, some researchers have found that low returns are related to greater levels of diversification.[70] Poor performance may lead to increased diversification, especially if resources exist to pursue that tack. Continued poor returns following additional diversification, however, may slow the pace of diversification and even lead to divestitures. Thus, an overall curvilinear relationship, as illustrated in Figure 6.3, may exist between diversification and performance.[71]

Figure 6.3 | The curvilinear relationship between diversification and performance

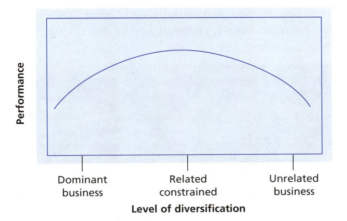

Lockheed Martin may have diversified beyond its capabilities to manage its level of diversification. The company is the largest defence contractor in the world, primarily because it chose to buy post-Cold War defence assets when other firms were selling them. However, the American government has grown uncomfortable with so much power being centred in one defence contractor. When Lockheed Martin was forced to drop its US$11.6 billion bid for Northrop Grumman, another defence contractor, in the face of government objections, it sought to acquire Comsat Corporation, which launches and delivers satellites. Lockheed Martin has also been interested in General Electric plc, a British defence company, and other transatlantic deals, to diversify away from the United States. Financial analysts, however, have driven down Lockheed's stock as it ponders these potential deals, because the firm has become so diversified, that one analyst questioned, 'Has this company just gotten too big and too complex?' In a period when the stock prices of most companies have been increasing, Lockheed Martin's price plummeted to a 52-week low at the beginning of the millennium. Although Lockheed's diversification creates strength when it can integrate its various divisions to bid for contracts, Lockheed's CEO, Peter B. Teets, suggests, 'My biggest challenge is to learn how to harness that strength.' Evidence suggests that Lockheed Martin's diversification is currently on the downside of the diversification-performance curve in Figure 6.3.[72]

Recent evidence suggests that Jürgen Schrempp, CEO of DaimlerChrysler, is struggling with the challenges that were created partly by the firm's failed attempts to diversify. Since assuming leadership of DaimlerChrysler, Schrempp has taken decisive actions. Money-losing operations, including the firm's electronics business and its 24 per cent stake in Cap Gemini, the French software services company, were sold. Fokker, the Dutch airplane manufacturer, was liquidated. (Interestingly, when he was serving as head of Daimler's aerospace division, Schrempp himself orchestrated the acquisition of Fokker.[73]) In addition, Schrempp eliminated a layer of upper-level executives and is trying to instill a culture of responsibility and entrepreneurship in the company. Thought of as a cultural revolution in which each of Daimler's 23 remaining business units is expected to earn at least 12 per cent on its invested capital, innovation is the driving force being used to create the new culture.

With the resources from the sales of more diversified operations, Schrempp decided to focus on cars and organised a revolutionary merger with Chrysler Corporation. The transaction set off a wave of consolidations in the global automobile industry.[74] DaimlerChrysler is now at a more optimal level of diversification on the curve shown in Figure 6.3. However, DaimlerChrysler does not want to stop there; rather, the German–American company now hopes to be the 'largest transportation company in the world'. To achieve this it will need to overtake Volkswagen, Toyota, Ford and General Motors, currently the fourth-largest to largest, respectively. This means that the firm will have to form one or two partnerships with other automobile manufacturers or else acquire them outright. In fact, DaimlerChrysler had discussions with Honda Motor Co.,

When Jürgen Schrempp (shown here) became CEO of Daimler-Benz, he had to take decisive actions to counteract the company's failed acquisitions. Money-losing operations were sold or liquidated and an upper layer of executives was eliminated. Deciding to focus on cars, Schrempp proposed a revolutionary merger with Chrysler Corporation.

Fiat SpA and Peugeot Citroen. In 2000, DaimlerChrysler acquired a 34 per cent stake in Mitsubishi Motors.⁷⁵ The reasons for the purchase include the firm's need to be a prominent small-car manufacturer, given the increasing size of that market on a global basis. Thus, DaimlerChrysler will likely continue using focused diversified growth to gain access to the Asian market.⁷⁶

Uncertain future cash flows

As a firm's product line matures or is threatened, diversification may be perceived as an important defensive strategy. Small firms and companies in mature or maturing industries sometimes find it necessary to diversify to survive over the long term.⁷⁷ Certainly, this was one of the dominant reasons for diversification among railroad firms during the 1960s and 1970s. Railroads diversified primarily because the trucking industry was perceived to have significant negative effects on the demand for rail transportation. Uncertainty, however, can be derived from both supply and demand sources.

For decades, Reuben Central Design Bureau was a secretive brain trust behind Russia's successful and renowned submarine industry. The Bureau created the *Typhoon*, the world's largest and most silent and lethal submarine. The group's work earned two coveted Orders of Lenin, which are still prominently displayed near the bust of the man himself. However, after 1989, this Soviet military design bureau needed to change. When it did change, the Bureau used a diversification strategy and became Russia's first international business centre. With its world-class design engineers, it beat Russian rivals competing to design an oil platform for a group of Russian companies working in the oil-rich waters around Sakhalin Island, off the nation's Pacific coast. With this success in 1992, the Bureau subsequently caught the eye of a consortium of firms, including the US firm Marathon Oil Company and the Royal Dutch/Shell Group, which needed help in customising an enormous drilling platform transported from Alaska and used off Sakhalin. This work proved that the firm could do more than design submarines. Besides continuing its marine business, the Bureau was able to secure contracts in other areas, such as developing an experimental high-speed rail train and link. In addition, it won a contract to develop a floating sea launch for three rocket companies in Russia and Ukraine, with venture partners Boeing and a Norwegian company, Kvaerner ASA. In addition to executing these ventures and maintaining its focus on non-nuclear (that is, diesel-powered) submarines, the Bureau has pursued real-estate development through its business centre. It also has six restaurants and many other projects in St Petersburg. It entered the tea business when tea was used as barter for some of its submarines sold in Asia. In many of these projects, the Bureau has used its connections with local and federal government leaders to gain the bureaucratic approvals needed. The Bureau's diversification strategy has allowed it to survive in the chaotic Russian economic environment.⁷⁸

Firm risk reduction

Because diversified firms pursuing economies of scope often have investments that are too inflexible to realise synergy between business units, a number of problems may arise. **Synergy** exists when the value created by business units working together exceeds the value those same units create working independently. But, as a firm increases its relatedness between business units, it also increases its risk of corporate failure, because synergy produces joint interdependence between business units and the firm's flexibility to respond is constrained. This threat may force two basic decisions.

First, the firm may reduce its level of technological change by operating in more certain environments. This behaviour may make the firm risk averse and thus uninterested in pursuing new product lines that have potential, but are not proven.

Synergy exists when the value created by business units working together exceeds the value those same units create when working independently.

Alternatively, the firm may constrain its level of activity sharing and forgo the benefits of synergy. Either or both decisions may lead to further diversification. The former would lead to related diversification into industries in which more certainty exists. The latter may produce additional, but unrelated, diversification.[79] Research suggests that a firm which pursues a related diversification strategy is more careful in its bidding for new businesses, whereas a firm which pursues an unrelated diversification move may more easily overprice its bid. An unrelated bidder may not be aware of all the informational dilemmas that the acquired firm faces.[80]

Boeing, for example, has been diversifying to reduce its dependence on commercial airlines and the frequent cycles in this business line. In 1998, Boeing acquired Rockwell's space division and McDonnell Douglas. Both acquisitions were designed to help Boeing improve its position in commercial space activities. In 2000, Boeing agreed to purchase Hughes Electronics' space operations. Hughes divested this unit so that it could better focus on DirectTV and other future Internet operations.[81] Boeing also invested in a long-range project with McCaw Cellular and Microsoft to create an Internet-in-the-sky satellite system called Teledesic. The Teledesic system would be the first satellite system with the capability of handling any kind of communication, from voice calls to Internet browsing to video and interactive multimedia. The system would be analogous to throwing a fibre-optic net around the world, but in space. Teledesic is different from Motorola's Iridium network, which has been in financial difficulty. The Iridium network was designed to handle only voice communication via mobile phones. These ventures are positioning Boeing as an aerospace firm for the next economic frontier – space. Once it has the Teledesic system in place, Boeing will be a world-class satellite producer and launcher.[82] However, the results of the firm's diversification strategy are as yet uncertain.

Resources and diversification

Although a firm may have incentives to diversify, it must possess the resources required to make diversification economically feasible.[83] As mentioned earlier, tangible, intangible and financial resources may facilitate diversification. Resources vary in their utility for value creation, however, because of differences in rarity and mobility; that is, some resources are easier for competitors to duplicate because they are not rare, valuable, costly to imitate and non-substitutable. For instance, free cash flows may be used to diversify the firm. Because these resources are more flexible and common, they are less likely to create value compared with other types of resources.[84] The earlier-mentioned diversification on the part of steel firms was significantly facilitated by the presence of free cash flows.

Tangible resources usually include the plant and equipment necessary to produce a product. Such assets may be less flexible: any excess capacity often can be used only for very closely related products, especially those requiring highly similar manufacturing technologies. Excess capacity of other tangible resources, such as a sales force, can be used to diversify more easily. Again, excess capacity in a sales force would be more effective with related diversification, because it may be utilised to sell similar products. The sales force would be more knowledgeable about related-product characteristics, customers and distribution channels. Tangible resources may create resource interrelationships in production, marketing, procurement and technology, defined earlier as activity sharing.

Intangible resources are more flexible than tangible physical assets in facilitating diversification. Although the sharing of tangible resources may induce diversification, intangible resources could encourage even more diversification.

Extent of diversification

If a firm has both the incentives and the resources to diversify, the extent of its diversification will be greater than if it has incentives or resources alone.[85] The more flexible it is, the more likely it is that the resources will be used for unrelated diversification; the less flexible it is, the more likely it is that the resources will be used for related diversification. Thus, flexible resources (for example, free cash flows) are likely to lead to relatively greater levels of diversification.[86] Also, because related diversification requires more information processing to manage links between businesses, more unrelated units can be managed by a small corporate office.[87]

Managerial motives to diversify

Managerial motives for diversification may exist independently of incentives and resources and include managerial risk reduction and a desire for increased compensation.[88] For instance, diversification may reduce top-level managers' *employment risk* (the risk of job loss or income reduction). That is, corporate executives may diversify a firm in order to diversify their employment risk, as long as profitability does not suffer excessively.[89] Diversification also provides an additional benefit to managers that shareholders do not enjoy. Diversification and firm size are highly correlated, and as size increases, so does executive compensation.[90] Large firms are more complex and harder to manage; thus, managers of larger firms are better compensated.[91] This increased compensation may serve as a motive for managers to engage in greater diversification. Governance mechanisms, such as the board of directors, monitoring by owners, executive compensation and the market for corporate control may limit managerial tendencies to over-diversify. These mechanisms are discussed in more detail in Chapter 10.

On the other hand, governance mechanisms may not be strong, and in some instances managers may diversify the firm to the point that it fails to earn even average returns.[92] Resources employed to pursue each line of diversification are most likely to include financial assets (for example, free cash flows), but may also involve intangible assets. Thus, this type of diversification is not likely to lead to improved performance. The loss of adequate internal governance may result in poor relative performance, thereby triggering a threat of takeover. Although this threat may create improved efficiency by replacing ineffective managerial teams, managers may avoid takeovers through defensive tactics (for example, golden parachutes and poison pills). Therefore, an external governance threat, although having a restraining influence on managers, does not provide flawless control of managerial motives for diversification.[93]

Most large publicly held firms are profitable because managers are positive agents and many of their strategic actions (for example, diversification moves) contribute to the firm's success. As mentioned, governance devices are designed to deal with exceptions to the norms of achieving strategic competitiveness and increasing shareholder wealth in the process. Thus, it is overly pessimistic to assume that managers usually act in their own self-interest as opposed to their firm's interest.[94]

Managers may also be held in check by concerns for their reputation in the labour market. If positive reputation facilitates power, a poor reputation may reduce power. Likewise, a market for managerial talent may deter managers from pursuing inappropriate diversification.[95] In addition, some diversified firms police other diversified firms, acquiring those poorly managed companies in order to restructure their asset base. Knowing that their firms could be acquired if they are not managed successfully, managers are encouraged to find ways to achieve strategic competitiveness.

In summary, although managers may be motivated to increase diversification, governance mechanisms are in place to discourage such action merely for managerial gain. However, this governance is imperfect and may not always produce the intended consequences. Even when governance mechanisms cause managers to correct a problem of over-diversification, these moves are not without trade-offs. For instance, firms that are spun off may not realise productivity gains, although spinning them off is in the best interest of the divesting firm.[96] Accordingly, the assumption that managers need disciplining may not be entirely correct, and sometimes governance may create consequences that are worse than those resulting from over-diversification.[97]

In general, the level of diversification the firm chooses should be based on the optimal levels indicated by market and strategic characteristics (resources) owned or available to each company. In turn, optimality may be judged in terms of resources, managerial motives and incentives.

As shown in Figure 6.4, the level of diversification that can be expected to have the greatest positive effect on performance (that is, strategic competitiveness and the earning of above-average returns) is based partly on how the interaction of resources, managerial motives and incentives affects the adoption of particular diversification strategies. As indicated earlier, the greater the incentives and the more flexible the resources, the higher is the level of expected diversification. Financial resources (the most flexible) should have a stronger relationship to the extent of diversification than either tangible or intangible resources. Tangible resources (the most inflexible) are useful primarily for related diversification.

Figure 6.4 | Summary model of the relationship between firm performance and diversification

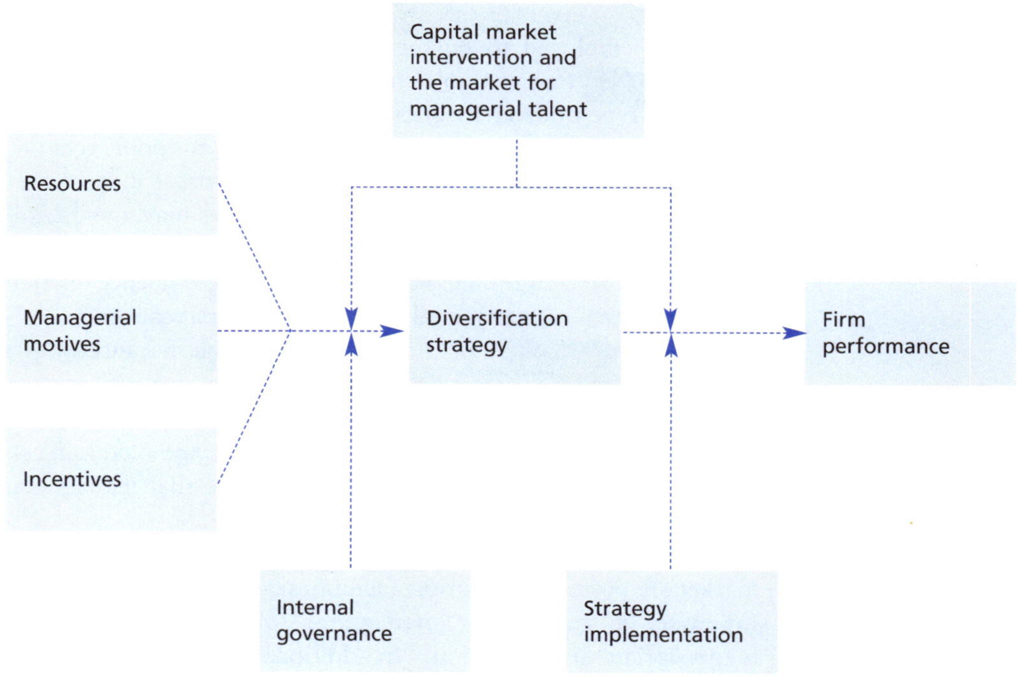

Source: R. E. Hoskisson and M. A. Hitt, 1990, 'Antecedents and performance outcomes of diversification: A review and critique of theoretical perspectives', *Journal of Management*, 16, p. 498.

The model suggests that implementation issues are important to whether diversification creates value (see Chapter 11). The model also suggests that governance mechanisms are important to the level and type of diversification implemented (see Chapter 10).

As mentioned in this chapter, diversification strategies can enhance a firm's strategic competitiveness and help it to earn larger financial returns. However, as the model shows, diversification must be kept in check by governance devices, because managers also have motives (for example, seeing their salaries increased) to grow the firm excessively through diversification. This appears to be the case, at least partially, with Philips Electronics NV.

Cor Boonstra has managed Philips, a large, widely diversified Dutch consumer electronics firm, since 1996. Although Boonstra has sold off or discontinued 40 of the company's businesses and has reorganised the company into eight groups called 'building blocks', he has also added new businesses, such as ATL Ultrasound in medical equipment. Philips currently has 80 businesses, compared with 120 when Boonstra assumed the CEO position. However, some of the company's businesses continue to perform poorly. Philips recently had a charge against its earnings because of a failed cellular phone venture with Lucent Technologies. In this industry, Philips is a second-tier player behind leaders Nokia, Telefon ABLM Erikkson of Sweden and Motorola of the United States. The firm's overall strategy is to compete in high-volume electronics businesses using the related linked diversification strategy. However, these businesses are very competitive, and Philips is competing against rivals such as Sony, which is much more focused and generates 44 per cent more revenue than Philips with 59 000 fewer employees. (Philips has a total of 234 000 employees.)

To understand why Philips has not restructured, one must understand the relationship between diversification strategy and corporate governance practices in the Netherlands. The board of directors at Philips is governed by a complex set of bylaws of the Philips Foundation, which includes most of the firm's directors and executives and gives them the power to make binding recommendations about appointments to the board. In effect, the foundation decides who runs Philips, and ordinary shareholders have little say in the matter. In fact, shareholders can do little to get rid of management if they feel that managers are not doing a good job. The main way that Philips' investors have to express their concerns is to sell the company's stock. Corporate bylaws and custom in most Dutch-incorporated companies do not allow shareholders to vote for directors or fire under-performing managers. Neither do shareholders have the right to launch proxy fights and vote on takeover bids. Although pension funds and the Dutch government are starting to push for change, shareholders are still rarely consulted when it comes to large mergers or acquisitions. However, because Philips is internationally traded, analysts believe that it is still undervalued, although its shares have increased in value during Boonstra's tenure. In sum, Philips Electronics is over-diversified and undervalued primarily because there are no strong corporate governance procedures to force its restructuring.

Strategic Focus Corporate

AOL's diversification merger with Time Warner

On 11 January 2000, a merger agreement was announced between AOL, an Internet service provider (ISP), and the media content company Time Warner, with businesses that include movies, magazines and music, as well as significant cable TV operations. Both companies have resources and incentives to become more diversified, as Figure 6.4 suggests. In fact, additional levels of diversification solve a number of problems for each firm, but especially for AOL. First, there is much opportunity for resource synergy between the two firms. AOL will be able to advertise *Time* magazine and other Time Warner publications on AOL's Internet sites. Furthermore, Time Warner owns the Book-of-the-Month Club, which gives AOL an opportunity to connect with many new subscribers to its service. In addition, Time Warner music and movies could be made available over the Internet. However, the primary reason for the acquisition is the cable TV assets that provide AOL with broadband speed: Time Warner currently owns the Roadrunner cable modem ISP service. When AT&T bought MediaOne and developed the TCI cable modem service, AOL's stock price decreased significantly, because, at the time, AOL did not appear to have a high-speed Internet service option. When the merger with Time Warner is complete, this problem will be solved. Accordingly, many resources will allow for synergistic improvement with both firms.

Some have questioned whether AOL and Time Warner are taking the best course of action. Because AT&T owns 25 per cent of Time Warner, AOL must finalise an arrangement with AT&T to get more access to the broadband approach through AT&T's cable operations. The problem is that many service providers have been offering regular modem Internet service for free so that they can get households to spend money on bundled cable TV and local and long-distance telephone services. This development may be especially problematic for AOL because it generates most of its money from its ISP service.

At the time of the announcement of the AOL–Time Warner merger, Yahoo! did not feel that it would need to purchase a company like Disney; instead, Yahoo! decided that it would rather buy services from a range of media providers, such as Disney and News Corporation, as well as from television stations and movie producers. Yahoo! believes that its media needs may be much cheaper to satisfy through purchase on the open market rather than through vertical integration. In addition, Yahoo! can achieve more flexibility that way. Yahoo! feels that the AOL–Time Warner merger is an unproved strategy for an ISP: 'It may be more viable for AOL rivals to strike different contract and distribution deals with a number of companies rather than to tie themselves inextricably to one partner.'

A number of implementation details also will influence the degree of success that is gained from the diversification created by the AOL–Time Warner merger. Gerald Levin, current CEO of Time Warner, will be the CEO of the new company, while Steve Case, current CEO of AOL, will be the chairman. Case apparently felt that the transaction would not be consummated unless Levin, a very powerful and politically astute individual, was in charge of operations. Fortunately, this plan fitted in with Case's leadership style, in that he is more of a strategic thinker than an operations manager. It remains to be seen how successful the efforts to assimilate the two diverse cultures will be: AOL is quite entrepreneurial, while, in contrast, the culture at Time Warner is stodgier and not focused on running on 'Internet time'.

AOL's stock price depreciated considerably shortly after the merger was announced, while that of Time Warner increased significantly. This combination of events, in which the acquiring firm's stock price declines while that of the target increases, is not unusual. However, how the diverse set of investors will mesh is also an important issue, in that AOL and Time Warner investors have different investment criteria and risk preferences. Nonetheless, several analysts suggested that institutional investors supported the merger. The board of directors will also have an influence on what happens, but only time will tell how the situation will evolve. Eight directors from each firm will be on the board. AOL shareholders will own 55 per cent of the newly formed company, Time Warner shareholders 45 per cent.

In the long run, the product market and rivals' strategic positioning will influence the effectiveness of the merger. AT&T has said that it will not seek to get into media content through such an acquisition. However, the prices of its main products, telecommunications services, are rapidly decreasing, and one wonders whether the company may need to pursue content deals to earn higher profit margins. As mentioned, Yahoo! signalled that it would not get into content in the near future, preferring instead the flexibility to contract for opportunities in that regard with a broad range of providers.

In sum, a number of resources and incentives support the diversification merger between AOL and Time Warner. There also may be managerial motives, especially on the part of Ted Turner (Turner Broadcasting was purchased by Time Warner) and Gerald Levin, who own significant amounts of stock in the new company. Indeed, their net worth has increased with the acquisition. However, the success of the acquisition will depend on a number of leadership, cost and restructuring issues. Furthermore, how well synergy is realised through the combination of resources will have a significant impact on the well-being of the firm. The reaction by capital and product market players will also play into the success or failure of the diversification move. Finally, whether the transaction is approved by regulators will influence the success or failure of the merger. Usually, media combinations take longer to pass through the regulatory process, creating at least short-term uncertainty for all parties.

Sources: G. Farrell, 2000, 'Deal forms multimedia marketer', *USA Today*, 17 January: www.usatoday.com; M. Murray, N. Deogun and N. Wingfield, 2000, 'Can Time Warner click with AOL? Here are eight things to watch', *Wall Street Journal*, 14 January, pp. A1, A16; M. Rose, 2000, 'Database of merged AOL brings cheers and chills', *Wall Street Journal*, 14 January, p. B6; D. Solomon, 2000, 'AOL's path to broadband now clear', *USA Today*, 11 January: www.usatoday.com; K. Swisher, 2000, 'Yahoo! posts a loud message: we're not next', *Wall Street Journal*, 12 January, pp. B1, B4.

To receive positive outcomes from a diversification strategy, a company must use a proper amount and type of diversification.[98] The chapter's final Strategic Focus is a recent example of diversification, with final outcomes that are yet to be determined. The transaction is between an Internet provider (AOL) and a media content provider (Time Warner).

As the Strategic Focus on the AOL–Time Warner merger suggests, a number of issues are involved in creating an effective diversification strategy. The firm must prepare forthright answers to questions of leadership, the synergistic use of combined resources and competitive reactions in order for the strategy to improve the company's performance. If the answers to these questions are in the direction opposite to that which suggests an ability to create value through diversification, then a decision not to become more diversified is required. At the corporate level, value is created through the selection and management of a particular group of businesses that is worth more under the ownership of the acquiring company than it would be under any other ownership.[99]

Summary

- Pursuing a single- or dominant-business, corporate-level strategy may be preferable to seeking a more diversified business strategy, unless a corporation can develop economies of scope or financial economies between businesses, or unless it can obtain market power through additional levels of diversification. These economies and market power are the main sources of value creation when the firm diversifies.
- The primary reasons a firm pursues increased diversification are value creation through economies of scope, financial economies or market power; some actions are taken because of government policy, performance problems, uncertainties about future cash flow or managerial motivations (for example, to increase compensation).
- Managerial motives to diversify can lead to over-diversification. On the other hand, managers can also be good stewards of the firm's assets.
- The level of a firm's diversification is a function of the incentives the firm has to diversify, its resources, and the managerial motives to diversify.
- Related diversification can create value by sharing activities or transferring core competencies.
- Sharing activities usually involves sharing tangible resources between businesses. Transferring core competencies involves transferring the core competencies developed in one business to another business. It also may involve transferring

competencies between the corporate office and a business unit.
- Sharing activities is usually associated with related constrained diversification. Activity sharing is costly to implement and coordinate, may create unequal benefits for the divisions involved in the sharing, and may lead to fewer managerial risk-taking behaviours.
- Successful unrelated diversification is accomplished by efficiently allocating resources or restructuring a target firm's assets and placing them under rigorous financial controls.

Review questions

1. What is corporate-level strategy? Why is it important to a diversified firm?
2. What are the advantages and disadvantages of single- and dominant-business strategies, compared with those of firms with higher levels of diversification?
3. What are three reasons that firms choose to move from either a single- or a dominant-business position to a more diversified position?
4. How do firms share activities and transfer core competencies to obtain economies of scope while pursuing a related diversification strategy?
5. What are the two ways to obtain financial economies when a firm pursues an unrelated diversification strategy?
6. What incentives and resources encourage diversification in firms?
7. What motives might encourage managers to engage a firm in more diversification than seems appropriate?

Application discussion questions

1. This chapter suggests that there is a curvilinear relationship between diversification and performance. How can this relationship be modified so that the negative relationship between performance and diversification is reduced and the downward curve has less slope or begins at a higher level of diversification?
2. The *Fortune* 500 firms are very large, and many of them have significant product diversification. Are these large firms over-diversified? Do they experience lower performance than they should?
3. What is the primary reason for over-diversification? Is it industrial policies, such as taxes and antitrust regulation, or do firms over-diversify because managers pursue their own self-interest through increased compensation and a reduced risk of job loss? Why? Explain.
4. One rationale for pursuing related diversification is to obtain market power. In Australia, however, too much market power may result in a challenge by the Australian Competition and Consumer Commission (because it may be perceived as anti-competitive). Under what situations might related diversification be considered unfair competition?
5. Suppose you have two job offers, one from a dominant-business firm and one from an unrelated diversified firm. (Suppose the beginning salaries are virtually identical.) Which offer would you accept and why?
6. Do you believe that by the year 2010 large firms will be more or less diversified than they are today? Why? Will the trends regarding diversification be identical in Australia, the United States and Japan? Explain.
7. Will the Internet make it easier for firms to diversify? Why or why not?

Ethics questions

1. Suppose you overheard the following statement: 'Those managing an unrelated diversified firm face far more difficult ethical challenges than do those managing a dominant-business firm.' Based on your reading of this chapter, is this statement true or false? Why?
2. Is it ethical for managers to diversify a firm rather than return excess earnings to shareholders? Provide reasoning in support of your answer.
3. What unethical practices might occur when a firm restructures? Explain.
4. Do you believe that ethical managers are unaffected by the managerial motives to diversify discussed in this chapter? If so, why? In addition, do you believe that ethical managers should help their peers learn how to avoid making diversification decisions on the basis of the managerial motives to diversify? Why or why not?

Internet exercise

Search the websites of CMGI (www.cmgi.com), Cisco Systems (www.cisco.com), EMC (www.emc.com) and ICG (www.internetcapital.com). Compare their business models, and explain the type of strategy and level of diversification that describes each one. In the extremely fast-cycle Internet economy, these companies run exceptional risks. Track the success of each company's shares over the past six months. Can you pinpoint changes within the industry that have affected the rise and fall of share prices? What advancements in information technology and e-commerce have had the greatest effect on the continuing strategies of these companies? Does this type of collaboration among Internet companies foster growth and value within the industry?

e-project: In the second Strategic Focus, the refocusing of large diversified groups in emerging economies was discussed. In late January 2000, the top three *Chaebols* in South Korea – Hyundai (www.hyundai.com), Samsung (www.samsung.com) and LG Group (www.lg.co.kr) – were fined by the government's Fair Trade Commission for illegally allocating funds to their failing subsidiaries. Using the information provided on the company websites, choose one of these companies and provide alternative strategies for it to better compete in international markets.

Notes

1. B. Orwell, 2000, 'Disney to recast Go network Web property as entertainment destination', Dow Jones.com archives, 27 January: www.dowjones.com.
2. M. E. Porter, 1980, *Competitive Strategy* (New York: The Free Press), p. xvi.
3. T. B. Palmer and R. M. Wiseman, 1999, 'Decoupling risk taking from income stream uncertainty: A holistic model of risk', *Strategic Management Journal*, 20, pp. 1037–62; K. Ramaswamy, 1997, 'The performance impact of strategic similarity in horizontal mergers: Evidence from the U.S. banking industry', *Academy of Management Journal*, 40, pp. 697–715.
4. M. A. Hitt, R. E. Hoskisson and H. Kim, 1997, 'International diversification: Effects on innovation and firm performance in product-diversified firms', *Academy of Management Journal*, 40, pp. 767–98; W. G. Rowe and P. M. Wright, 1997, 'Related and unrelated diversification and their effect on human resource management controls', *Strategic Management Journal*, 18, pp. 329–38.
5. D. D. Bergh and M. W. Lawless, 1998, 'Portfolio restructuring and limits to hierarchical governance: The effects of environmental uncertainty and diversification strategy', *Organization Science*, 9, pp. 87–102; W. Boeker, 1997, 'Executive migration and strategic change: The effect of top manager movement on product-market entry', *Administrative Science Quarterly*, 42, pp. 213–36; H. A. Haverman, 1993, 'Organizational size and change: Diversification in the savings and loan industry after deregulation', *Administrative Science Quarterly*, 38, pp. 20–50.
6. M. E. Porter, 1987, 'From competitive advantage to corporate strategy', *Harvard Business Review*, 65(3), pp. 43–59.
7. Ibid., p. 43.
8. Boeker, 'Executive migration and strategic change'; C. A. Montgomery, 1994, 'Corporate diversification', *Journal of Economic Perspectives*, 8, pp. 163–78.
9. B. Wysocki, Jr, 1999, 'Corporate America confronts the meaning of a "core" business', *Wall Street Journal*, 9 November, pp. A1, A4; J. Kurtzman, 1998, 'An interview with C. K. Prahalad', in J. Kurtzman (ed.), *Thought Leaders* (San Francisco: Jossey-Bass), pp. 40–51; D. Lei, M. A. Hitt and R. Bettis, 1996, 'Dynamic core competences through meta-learning and strategic context', *Journal of Management*, 22, pp. 547–67.
10. C. C. Markides, 1997, 'To diversify or not to diversify', *Harvard Business Review*, 75(6), pp. 93–9.
11. C. C. Markides and P. J. Williamson, 1996, 'Corporate diversification and organizational structure: A resource-based view', *Academy of Management Journal*, 39, pp. 340–67; M. Goold and K. Luchs, 1993, 'Why diversify? Four decades of management thinking', *Academy of Management Executive*, VII(3), pp. 7–25.
12. A. Roseno and C. Nokkentved, 1997, *Management Processes and Corporate-Level Strategy* (Copenhagen: Management Process Institute); A. Campbell, M. Goold and M. Alexander, 1995, 'Corporate strategy: The question for parenting advantage', *Harvard Business Review*, 73(2), pp. 120–32.
13. T. H. Brush, P. Bromiley and M. Hendrickx, 1999, 'The relative influence of industry and corporate on business segment performance: An alternative estimate', *Strategic Management Journal*, 20, pp. 519–47; T. H. Brush and P. Bromiley, 1997, 'What does a small corporate effect mean? A variance components simulation of corporate and business effects', *Strategic Management Journal*, 18, pp. 825–35.
14. J. B. Barney, 1997, *Gaining and Sustaining Competitive Advantage* (Reading, MA: Addison-Wesley).
15. M. A. Hitt, B. W. Keats and S. DeMarie, 1998, 'Navigating in the new competitive landscape: Building strategic flexibility and competitive advantage in the 21st century', *Academy of Management Executive*, XII(4), pp. 22–42; T. Mroczkowski and M. Hanaoka, 1997, 'Effective rightsizing strategies in Japan and America: Is there a convergence of employment practices?', *Academy of Management Executive*, XI(2), pp. 57–67.
16. D. J. Collis and C. A. Montgomery, 1998, 'Creating corporate advantage', *Harvard Business Review*, 76(3), pp. 70–83.
17. R. Simons and A. Davila, 1998, 'How high is your return on management?', *Harvard Business Review*, 76(1), pp. 71–80.
18. B. S. Silverman, 1999, 'Technological resources and the direction of corporate diversification: Toward an integration of the resource-based view and transaction cost economics', *Administrative Science Quarterly*, 45, pp. 1109–24; D. Collis and C. A. Montgomery, 1995, 'Competing on resources: Strategy in the 1990s', *Harvard Business Review*, 73(4), pp. 118–28; M. A. Peteraf, 1993, 'The cornerstones of competitive advantage: A resource-based view', *Strategic Management Journal*, 14, pp. 179–91.
19. R. P. Rumelt, 1974, *Strategy, Structure and Economic Performance* (Cambridge, MA: Harvard University Press).
20. C. C. Markides, 1995, 'Diversification, restructuring and economic performance', *Strategic Management Journal*, 16, pp. 101–18.
21. R. E. Hoskisson, M. A. Hitt, R. A. Johnson and D. S. Moesel, 1993, 'Construct validity of an objective (entropy) categorical measure of diversification strategy', *Strategic Management Journal*, 14, pp. 215–35.
22. N. Tabakoff, 2000, 'Big spreads get down and focused', *Business Review Weekly*, 21 January: www.brw.com.au.
23. Hitt, Hoskisson and Kim, 'International diversification'; M. A. Hitt, R. E. Hoskisson and R. D. Ireland, 1994, 'A mid-range theory of the interactive effects of international and product diversification on innovation and performance', *Journal of Management*, 20, pp. 297–326.
24. W. M. Bulkeley, 1994, 'Conglomerates make a surprising come-back with a '90s twist', *Wall Street Journal*, 1 March, pp. A1, A6.
25. A. Bary, 1999, 'Who wants gum?', *Barron's*, 27 September, pp. 21–2.
26. Rumelt, *Strategy, Structure, and Economic Performance*; L. Wrigley, 1970, 'Divisional autonomy and diversification' (PhD dissertation, Harvard Business School).
27. S. Thompson, 1999, 'Kellogg pushes portable snacks as cereal biz lags', *Advertising Age*, October, 18(4), p. 78.
28. S. Lloyd, 1999, 'Cadbury's little winner turns two', *Business Review Weekly*, 21 January: www.brw.com.au.
29. M. Ihlwan, P. Engardio, I. Kunii and R. Crockett, 1999, 'Samsung: How a Korean electronics giant came out of the crisis stronger than ever', *Business Week Online*, 20 December: www.businessweek.com.
30. T. Khanna and K. Palepu, 1997, 'Why focused strategies may be wrong for emerging markets', *Harvard Business Review*, 75(4), pp. 41–50.
31. 'Inside story', 1997, *The Economist*, 6 December, pp. 7–9.
32. L. L. Brownlee and J. R. Dorfman, 1995, 'Birth of U.S. industries isn't without complications', *Wall Street Journal*, 18 May, p. B4.
33. R. Siklos, 1999, 'Viacom-CBS: "They Have It All Now"', *Business Week Online*, 20 September: www.businessweek.com.
34. M. Farjoun, 1998, 'The independent and joint effects of the skill and physical bases of relatedness in diversification', *Strategic Management Journal*, 19, pp. 611–30.

35 R. Morck and B. Yeung, 1999, 'When synergy creates real value', Mastering Strategy (Part Seven), *Financial Times*, 8 November, pp. 6–7.

36 L. Capron, 1999, 'The long term performance of horizontal acquisitions', *Strategic Management Journal*, 20, pp. 987–1018; D. J. Teece, G. Pisano and A. Shuen, 1997, 'Dynamic capabilities and strategic management', *Strategic Management Journal*, 18, pp. 509–33.

37 M. E. Porter, 1985, *Competitive Advantage* (New York: The Free Press), p. 328.

38 S. D. Moore, M. Waldholz and A. Raghavan, 2000, 'Glaxo Wellcome to buy SmithKline', *Wall Street Journal Interactive Edition*, 17 January: www.wsj.com.

39 K. Capell and H. Dawley, 1999, 'Healing Novartis: As agribiz sours, it shifts to health care', *Business Week Online*, 1 November: www.businessweek.com.

40 T. H. Brush, 1996, 'Predicted change in operational synergy and post-acquisition performance of acquired businesses', *Strategic Management Journal*, 17, pp. 1–24; H. Zhang, 1995, 'Wealth effects of U.S. bank takeovers', *Applied Financial Economics*, 5, pp. 329–36.

41 D. D. Bergh, 1995, 'Size and relatedness of units sold: An agency theory and resource-based perspective', *Strategic Management Journal*, 16, pp. 221–39.

42 M. Lubatkin and S. Chatterjee, 1994, 'Extending modern portfolio theory into the domain of corporate diversification: Does it apply?', *Academy of Management Journal*, 37, pp. 109–36.

43 T. Kono, 1999, 'A strong head office makes a strong company', *Long Range Planning*, 32(2), p. 225.

44 Barney, *Gaining and Sustaining Competitive Advantage*, 367; A. Mehra, 1996, 'Resource and market based determinants of performance in the U.S. banking industry', *Strategic Management Journal*, 17, pp. 307–22; S. Chatterjee and B. Wernerfelt, 1991, 'The link between resources and type of diversification: Theory and evidence', *Strategic Management Journal*, 12, pp. 33–48.

45 N. Argyres, 1996, 'Capabilities, technological diversification and divisionalization', *Strategic Management Journal*, 17, pp. 395–410.

46 M. Maremont, 2000, 'For plastic hangers, you almost need to go to Tyco International', *Wall Street Journal*, 15 February, pp. A1, A10; R. Whittington, 1999, 'In praise of the evergreen conglomerate', Mastering Strategy (Part Six), *Financial Times*, 1 November, pp. 4–6; W. Ruigrok, A. Pettigrew, S. Peck and R. Whittington, 1999, 'Corporate restructuring and new forms of organizing: Evidence from Europe', *Management International Review*, 39 (Special Issue), pp. 41–64.

47 C. St. John and J. S. Harrison, 1999, 'Manufacturing-based relatedness, synergy, and coordination', *Strategic Management Journal*, 20, pp. 129–45.

48 W. G. Shepherd, 1986, 'On the core concepts of industrial economics', in H. W. deJong and W. G. Shepherd (eds), *Mainstreams in Industrial Organization* (Boston: Kluwer Publications).

49 J. Gimeno and C. Y. Woo, 1999, 'Multimarket contact, economies of scope, and firm performance', *Academy of Management Journal*, 42, pp. 239–59; K. Hughes and C. Oughton, 1993, 'Diversification, multi-market contact and profitability', *Economica*, 60, pp. 203–24.

50 R. Heller, 2000, 'The man with the big footprint', *Forbes*, 24 January, pp. 116–20.

51 J. Ewing and S. Reed, 2000, 'Can Mannesmann wriggle away?', *Business Week*, 17 January, pp. 52–4.

52 A. Karnani and B. Wernerfelt, 1985, 'Multipoint competition', *Strategic Management Journal*, 6, pp. 87–96.

53 F. I. Smith and R. L. Wilson, 1995, 'The predictive validity of the Karnani and Wernerfelt model of multipoint competition', *Strategic Management Journal*, 16, pp. 143–60.

54 O. E. Williamson, 1996, 'Economics and organization: A primer', *California Management Review*, 38(2), pp. 131–46.

55 K. M Eisenhardt and D. C. Galunic, 2000, 'Coevolving: At last, a way to make synergies work', *Harvard Business Review*, 78(1), pp. 91–111.

56 J. A. Byrne, 1998, 'How Jack Welch runs GE', *Business Week Online*, 8 June: www.businessweek.com.

57 'Live wire Welch', 2000, *Business Week*, 10 January, p. 71.

58 M. Sarvary, 1999, 'Knowledge management and competition in the consulting industry', *California Management Review*, 41(3), pp. 95–107.

59 T. D. Schellhardt, E. McDonald and P. Hennessey, 1998, 'Consulting firms get an unexpected taste of their own medicine', *Wall Street Journal*, 20 October, pp. A1, A10.

60 Eisenhardt and Galunic, 2000, 'Coevolving', p. 94.

61 Bergh, 'Predicting divestiture of unrelated acquisitions'; C. W. L. Hill, 1994, 'Diversification and economic performance: Bringing structure and corporate management back into the picture', in R. P. Rumelt, D. E. Schendel and D. J. Teece (eds), *Fundamental Issues in Strategy* (Boston: Harvard Business School Press), pp. 297–321.

62 O. E. Williamson, 1975, *Markets and Hierarchies: Analysis and Antitrust Implications* (New York: Macmillan Free Press).

63 R. Kochhar and M. A. Hitt, 1998, 'Linking corporate strategy to capital structure: Diversification strategy, type, and source of financing', *Strategic Management Journal*, 19, pp. 601–10.

64 Ibid.; P. Taylor and J. Lowe, 1995, 'A note on corporate strategy and capital structure', *Strategic Management Journal*, 16, pp. 411–14.

65 D. J. Denis, D. K. Denis and A. Sarin, 1999, 'Agency theory and the reference of equity ownership structure on corporate diversification strategies', *Strategic Management Journal*, 20, pp. 1071–6; R. Amit and J. Livnat, 1988, 'A concept of conglomerate diversification', *Journal of Management*, 14, pp. 593–604.

66 Whittington, 1999, 'In praise of the evergreen conglomerate', p. 4.

67 S. J. Chang and H. Singh, 1999, 'The impact of entry and resource fit on modes of exit by multibusiness firms', *Strategic Management Journal*, 20, pp. 1019–35.

68 Rumelt, 'Strategy, structure and economic performance', p. 125.

69 R. M. Wiseman and L. R. Gomez-Mejia, 1998, 'A behavioral agency model of managerial risk taking', *Academy of Management Review*, 23, pp. 133–53; E. H. Bowman, 1982, 'Risk seeking by troubled firms', *Sloan Management Review*, 23, pp. 33–42.

70 Y. Chang and H. Thomas, 1989, 'The impact of diversification strategy on risk–return performance', *Strategic Management Journal*, 10, pp. 271–84; R. M. Grant, A. P. Jammine and H. Thomas, 1988, 'Diversity, diversification, and profitability among British manufacturing companies, 1972–1984', *Academy of Management Journal*, 31, pp. 771–801.

71 L. E. Palich, L. B. Cardinal and C. C. Miller, 2000, 'Curvilinearity in the diversification-performance linkage: An examination of over three decades of research', *Strategic Management Journal*, 21, pp. 155–74.

72 S. Crock, 1999, 'A lean, mean fighting machine it ain't', *Business Week*, 11 January, p. 41.

73 Taylor, 'Revolution at Daimler-Benz', p. 147.

74 'Jurgen E. Schrempp: Deal of the decade', 1999, *Business Week*, 11 January, p. 61.

75 B. Tuckey, 2000, 'Upheaval costs car retailers marques and money', *Business Review Weekly*, 4 July: www.brw.com.au.

76 J. Ball and S. Miller, 2000, 'DaimlerChrysler is aiming for top spot', *Wall Street Journal*, 14 January, pp. A2, A10.

77 J. C. Sandvig and L. Coakley, 1998, 'Best practices in small firm diversification', *Business Horizons*, 41(3), pp. 33–40; C. G. Smith and A. C. Cooper, 1988, 'Established companies diversifying into young industries: A comparison of firms with different levels of performance', *Strategic Management Journal*, 9, pp. 111–21.

78 N. King, Jr, 1998, 'A Soviet defense giant saw the inevitable and decided: Diversify', *Wall Street Journal*, 2 January, p. A4.

79 N. M. Kay and A. Diamantopoulos, 1987, 'Uncertainty and synergy: Towards a formal model of corporate strategy', *Managerial and Decision Economics*, 8, pp. 121–30.

80 R. W. Coff, 1999, 'How buyers cope with uncertainty when acquiring firms in knowledge-intensive industries: Caveat emptor', *Organization Science*, 10, pp. 144–61.

81 J. Cole and A. Pasztor, 2000, 'Boeing moves closer to satellite-based telecom niche', *Wall Street Journal*, 14 January, p. B4.

82 D. Field, 1999, 'Boeing diversifies to avoid turbulence', *USA Today*, 28 February: www.usatoday.com; K. Maney and D. Field, 1999, 'Boeing joins Internet-in-the-sky venture', *USA Today*, 28 February: www.usatoday.com.

83 Chatterjee and Singh, 'Are tradeoffs inherent in diversification moves?'; S. J. Chatterjee and B. Wernerfelt, 1991, 'The link between resources and type of diversification: Theory and evidence', *Strategic Management Journal*, 12, pp. 33–48.

84 R. Kochhar and M. A. Hitt, 1998, 'Linking corporate strategy to capital structure', *Strategic Management Journal*, 19, pp. 601–10.

85 R. E. Hoskisson and M. A. Hitt, 1990, 'Antecedents and performance outcomes of diversification: Review and critique of theoretical perspectives', *Journal of Management*, 16, pp. 461–509.

86 Chatterjee and Singh, 'Are tradeoffs inherent in diversification moves?'.

87 C. W. L. Hill and R. E. Hoskisson, 1987, 'Strategy and structure in the multiproduct firm', *Academy of Management Review*, 12, pp. 331–41.

88 W. Grossman and R. E. Hoskisson, 1998, 'CEO pay at the crossroads of Wall Street and Main: Toward the strategic design of executive compensation', *Academy of Management Executive*, 12(1), pp. 43–57;

A. A. Cannella, Jr and M. J. Monroe, 1997, 'Contrasting perspectives on strategic leaders: Toward a more realistic view of top managers', *Journal of Management*, 23, pp. 213–37; S. Finkelstein and D. C. Hambrick, 1996, *Strategic Leadership: Top Executives and Their Effects on Organizations* (St Paul, MN: West Publishing Company).

89 P. J. Lane, A. A. Cannella, Jr and M. H. Lubatkin, 1998, 'Agency problems as antecedents to unrelated mergers and diversification: Amihud and Lev reconsidered', *Strategic Management Journal*, 19, pp. 555–78; D. L. May, 1995, 'Do managerial motives influence firm risk reduction strategies?', *Journal of Finance*, 50, pp. 1291–308; Y. Amihud and B. Lev, 1981, 'Risk reduction as a managerial motive for conglomerate mergers', *Bell Journal of Economics*, 12, pp. 605–17.

90 S. R. Gray and A. A. Cannella, Jr, 1997, 'The role of risk in executive compensation', *Journal of Management*, 23, pp. 517–40; H. Tosi and L. Gomez-Mejia, 1989, 'The decoupling of CEO pay and performance: An agency theory perspective', *Administrative Science Quarterly*, 34, pp. 169–89.

91 S. Finkelstein and R. A. D'Aveni, 1994, 'CEO duality as a double-edged sword: How boards of directors balance entrenchment avoidance and unity of command', *Academy of Management Journal*, 37, pp. 1070–108.

92 R. E. Hoskisson and T. Turk, 1990, 'Corporate restructuring: Governance and control limits of the internal market', *Academy of Management Review*, 15, pp. 459–77.

93 J. K. Seward and J. P. Walsh, 1996, 'The governance and control of voluntary corporate spin offs', *Strategic Management Journal*, 17, pp. 25–39; J. P. Walsh and J. K. Seward, 1990, 'On the efficiency of internal and external corporate control mechanisms', *Academy of Management Review*, 15, pp. 421–58.

94 Finkelstein and D'Aveni, 'CEO duality as a double-edged sword'.

95 E. F. Fama, 1980, 'Agency problems and the theory of the firm', *Journal of Political Economy*, 88, pp. 288–307.

96 R. A. Johnson, 1996, 'Antecedents and outcomes of corporate refocusing', *Journal of Management*, 22, pp. 439–83; C. Y. Woo, G. E. Willard and U. S. Dallenbach, 1992, 'Spin-off performance: A case of overstated expectations', *Strategic Management Journal*, 13, pp. 433–48.

97 H. Kim and R. E. Hoskisson, 1996, 'Japanese governance systems: A critical review', in S. B. Prasad (ed.), *Advances in International Comparative Management* (Greenwich, CT: JAI Press), pp. 165–89.

98 Markides, 'To diversify or not to diversify'.

99 Collis and Montgomery, 'Creating corporate advantage'.

Chapter 7

Acquisition and restructuring strategies

Objectives

After reading this chapter, you should be able to:

1. Describe the popularity of acquisition strategies in firms competing in the global economy.
2. Discuss reasons firms decide to use an acquisition strategy to achieve strategic competitiveness.
3. Describe seven problems that work against developing a competitive advantage when a firm uses an acquisition strategy.
4. Name and describe attributes of acquisitions that increase the probability of competitive success.
5. Define the restructuring strategy and distinguish among its common forms.
6. Describe the short- and long-term outcomes resulting from the use of the different types of restructuring strategies.

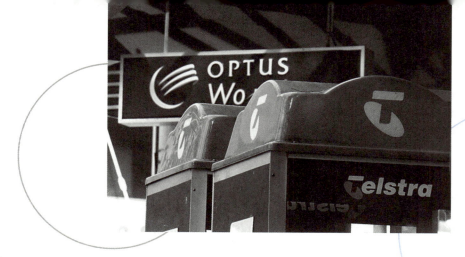

The Internet: Driving mergers and acquisitions in the global economy

Now freed from many regulatory constraints in multiple global markets, telecommunications companies are using merger and acquisition strategies to develop the economies of scale that are important to their competitive success in rapidly changing and cost-sensitive markets and to enter new markets. For example, Telstra is, in world terms, a small to medium-sized telecommunications company and needs to grow in order to survive in the globalising telecommunications industry. In order to help achieve this, Telstra has formed a strategic alliance with Hong Kong-based Pacific Century CyberWorks (PCCW), one of Asia's leading telecommunications companies. This alliance is intended to give Telstra a vital foothold in the lucrative Asian market.

Despite the collapse of many Internet companies, the Internet is still a driver of what is seen as a frenzy of merger and acquisition activity among telecommunications companies. For example, MCI WorldCom, Inc.'s attempted US$115 billion acquisition of Sprint was necessary, according to MCI's CEO, for the combined company to be a viable competitor in a global arena in which size has an important relationship to profitability. In addition, the acquisition would have allowed the new firm to become an important participant in Internet-related business transactions. Interestingly, MCI WorldCom is a product of World Com's 1998 acquisition of MCI.

The price of MCI WorldCom's acquisition of Sprint paled in comparison to the cost of the proposed transaction between two of the world's leading wireless communications companies. In early 2000, at a cost of US$190.5 billion, Vodafone AirTouch PLC of Britain acquired Mannesmann AG of Germany. The combined firm promised to dominate the European market with a global base of more than 50 million customers. Reviewing this combination, an analyst stated that 'the power that this company has to call the shots in wireless Internet is enormous'.

The Internet's commercial potential is also one factor associated with America Online, Inc.'s acquisition of Time Warner. (Recall the discussion of this merger in a Chapter 6 Strategic Focus.) According to some analysts, the ability to bundle services together for customers may be the core reason for the acquisition. Describing this possibility, business writers suggested that 'Time Warner's extensive cable network can help AOL compete with giants and fast-moving start-ups for the grand prize: the estimated [US]$100 to $150 a month a middle-class household is willing to spend on cable TV, local and long-distance telephone service, and Internet access. Bundling all of that on a single network has become a central strategy of the country's biggest telecom and Internet companies.' Moreover, it is likely that the commercial potential of bundling 'will drive mergers and acquisitions across several industries'.

The financial services industry is another industry in which merger and acquisition activity may be stimulated by bundling possibilities. Within Australia, even small financial institutions such as Tasmania's Connect Credit Union can handle a customer's bank account, retirement savings, credit cards, home mortgage, car loan and insurance on a single monthly statement. They also now provide complex financial advice to customers. All of these transactions can be completed via the Internet. Because acquisitions result in quicker market entry compared to developing a firm's capabilities internally (a point that is discussed in the chapter), it is likely that financial services firms will merge with or acquire other companies to have access to at least competitive, if not superior, Internet-based skills to facilitate customer-related transactions.

A second way the Internet is influencing merger and acquisition activity is through the large number of transactions taking place among Internet companies themselves. An interest in having first-mover advantages influences some of these transactions. By purchasing Internet ventures with strong brand names, the Internet-based firm that acquires them gains access to a critical mass of customers to whom products may be cross-sold. In addition, a firm with a strong brand name is harder to dislodge from its market share than are competitors without established brands. Examples of acquisitions involving Internet firms acquiring other Internet ventures include Yahoo! Inc.'s acquisition of Broadcast.com, Inc. (an Internet broadcaster), Excite@Home Corp.'s purchase of iMall, Inc. (an Internet retailer), and eBay, Inc.'s acquisition of Butterfield & Butterfield, Inc. (an auction house).

As discussed in earlier chapters, Amazon.com continues to acquire a host of Internet ventures, including Pets.com and Drugstore.com, to expand and diversify its operations. Facilitating high levels of acquisition activity among Internet ventures are the high valuations of many Internet-based companies, which allow the use of company stock as acquisition currency. In addition, venture capital funding is available at record rates to support growth via acquisitions. In general, experts predict that the torrent of merger and acquisition activity among Internet companies, as well as the number of transactions completed to gain access to an acquired firm's Internet capabilities, will likely continue, at least in the foreseeable future.

www.aol.com
www.mannesmann.com
www.sprint.com
www.timewarner.com
www.vodafone.com
www.wcom.com

Sources: R. Blumenstein, 2000, 'MCI WorldCom seeks to demonstrate Sprint deal will boost competition', *Wall Street Journal*, 13 January, p. B10; C. Hill and L. Landro, 2000, 'Does everybody have to own everything?', *Wall Street Journal*, 12 January, pp. B1, B4; R. MacLean, 2000, 'What business is Amazon.com really in?', *Inc.*, February, pp. 86–8; Wire Reports, 2000, 'Mannesmann to accept Vodafone's takeover bid', *Dallas Morning News*, 4 February, pp. D1, D2; J. Harrison, 1999, 'Dynamics driving Internet deals', *Mergers & Acquisitions*, September/October, pp. 49–51; R. Rivlin, 1999, 'Europeans lift M&A activity in US', *Financial Times*, 28 July, p. 20. P. Armstrong, Chairman, Connect Credit Union; A. Ferguson, 2000, 'Telstra's Asian mess', *Business Review Weekly*, 6 October, pp. 50–5.

In Chapter 6, we studied corporate-level strategies, focusing on types and levels of product diversification strategies that can build core competencies and create competitive advantage. As noted in that chapter, diversification allows a firm to create value by productively using excess resources.[1] For each strategy we discuss in this book, including diversification strategies and merger and acquisition strategies, the firm creates value only when its resources, capabilities and core competencies are used productively.[2]

In this chapter, which is related closely to Chapter 6, we explore acquisitions as the dominant means firms use to develop a diversification strategy. In one sense, diversification is a risk management tool, in that its successful use reduces a firm's vulnerability to the consequences of competing in a single market or industry.[3] As suggested in Chapter 1, risk plays a role in the strategies a firm selects to earn above-average returns. In addition, continuous evaluations of risk are linked with a firm's ability to achieve strategic competitiveness.[4]

The purpose of this chapter is to explore acquisition and restructuring strategies. Firms from different industries decide to use an acquisition strategy for several reasons, some of which are mentioned in the following commentary: 'Pharmaceutical companies are looking for new products, telecommunications companies are seeking faster ways to get into more households, finance companies want to burst into new services quickly, and high-tech money is constantly chasing creativity.'[5] However, acquisition strategies are not without problems. Before describing attributes that evidence suggests are associated with effective acquisitions, we discuss the most prominent problems companies experience when using an acquisition strategy. When acquisitions contribute to poor performance, a firm may deem it necessary to restructure its operations. Closing the chapter are descriptions of three restructuring strategies, as well as the short- and long-term outcomes resulting from their use. Setting the stage for our consideration of all of these topics are brief descriptions of the differences among mergers, acquisitions and takeovers.

The increasing use of merger and acquisition strategies

Acquisitions have been a popular strategy among firms for many years. Some believe that the strategy played a central role in an effective restructuring of US businesses during the 1980s and 1990s.[6] Increasingly, acquisition strategies are becoming more popular with firms in other nations and economic regions, including Australasia and Europe.[7] In fact, in the third quarter of 1999, for the first time the dollar volume of merger and acquisition transactions announced in Europe exceeded the value announced in the United States.[8] As is the case with all strategies, acquisitions indicate a choice a firm has made regarding how it intends to compete.[9] Because each strategic choice affects a firm's performance, the possibility of diversification merits careful analysis.[10] The successful use of an acquisition strategy is another way a firm can differentiate itself from competitors.[11] Being differentiated effectively may benefit the firm in that less direct competition with competitors is experienced when this is the case.[12]

An indicator of the popularity of the acquisition strategy is the labelling of the 1980s as the 'merger mania' decade. During that time, depending on whether only acquisitions of entire firms or partial (ownership) acquisitions are counted, the number of acquisitions completed in the United States varied from slightly over 31 000 to as many as 55 000. The total value of these acquisitions exceeded US$1.3 trillion.[13] However, the merger and acquisition activity of the 1980s pales in comparison to what occurred in the 1990s.[14] In 1999 alone, US$3.4 trillion was spent worldwide on mergers and acquisitions, up from US$2.5 trillion in 1998 and US$464 billion in 1990. In the United States in 1999, US$1.75 trillion in deals were announced, compared to US$1.6 trillion in 1998 and US$195 billion in 1990. As discussed in the Opening Case, 'the Internet is one key force driving this activity, merger experts say. With the Internet wrecking the traditional sales and distribution formulas for everything from cars to computers, even established companies believe they are at risk.'[15]

Another trend in acquisition strategies is the rapid increase in the number of acquisitions completed between firms based in different countries.[16] These transactions are called *cross-border acquisitions*.[17] In Chapter 9, we discuss cross-border alliances. Sharing similar characteristics, cross-border acquisitions and cross-border alliances are strategic alternatives firms consider in the pursuit of strategic competitiveness and above-average returns, as are domestic alliances and acquisitions.

The strategic management process (see Figure 1.1 in Chapter 1) calls for an acquisition strategy to increase a firm's strategic competitiveness as well as its returns to shareholders. Thus, an acquisition strategy should be used only when the acquiring firm will be able to increase its economic value through ownership and the use of an acquired firm's assets.[18]

Evidence suggests, however, that at least for acquiring firms, acquisition strategies may not result in these desirable outcomes. Recently, for example, a survey by accounting and consulting firm KPMG estimated that 83 per cent of mergers failed to increase shareholder value in acquiring firms; indeed, in 53 per cent of the transactions, shareholder value in acquiring firms was actually reduced![19] In the words of KMPG personnel, 'Mergers that didn't work out as promised have helped sink the stocks of Federal-Mogul Corp., Mattel Co., and Clorox Co., among others.'[20] In Australia, Pacific Dunlop's stock price has been severely reduced by a series of acquisitions that failed to create value and earn above-average returns for the company.[21] (See the Pacific Dunlop case in the case section of this text.)

These results are consistent with those obtained through studies by academic researchers who have found that *shareholders of acquired firms* often earn above-average returns from an acquisition, while *shareholders of acquiring firms* are less likely to do so, typically earning returns from the transaction that are close to zero.[22] Apparently, investors anticipate this state of affairs, as is indicated by the fact that, in approximately two-thirds of all acquisitions, the acquiring firm's stock price falls immediately after the intended transaction is announced. This negative response is viewed by some as an indication of 'investors' skepticism about the likelihood that the acquirer will be able both to maintain the original values of the businesses in question and to achieve the synergies required to justify the premium'.[23]

Mergers, acquisitions and takeovers: What are the differences?

A **merger** is a strategy through which two firms agree to integrate their operations on a relatively co-equal basis because they have resources and capabilities that together may create a stronger competitive advantage. The transaction between accounting firms Coopers and Lybrand and Price Waterhouse is an example of a merger. The deal joined firms with complementary services and geographical penetration. This merger created one of the world's largest accounting firms, with substantial market power and an ability to offer its clients an extensive range of accounting services on a global scale.[24] An **acquisition** is a strategy through which one firm buys a controlling, or 100 per cent, interest in another firm with the intent of using a core competence more effectively by making the acquired firm a subsidiary business within its portfolio.[25] Usually, the management of the acquired firm reports to its counterparts in the acquiring firm. Most mergers are friendly transactions, whereas acquisitions include unfriendly takeovers. A **takeover** is a type of acquisition strategy wherein the target firm did not solicit the acquiring firm's bid. One of the most acrimonious takeovers in Australian corporate history was AMP's takeover of the GIO. When AMP launched its takeover bid in 1998 it caught management at the GIO by surprise. Faced with a takeover bid, the board of the GIO advised shareholders to reject AMP's offer, which led to a very hostile dispute between the two companies. Over the following months, this dispute was played out before the public in the Australian media. Because of the hostility of the takeover, AMP was unable to make proper assessments of the financial position of the GIO. Consequently, it wasn't until after the takeover was complete that AMP was to discover the considerable problems that would emerge from GIO's reinsurance business, a fact that would cost AMP billions of dollars.[26, 27]

In early 2000, a generally favourable worldwide economic climate and a strong stock market in key countries created an environment in which few firms were safe from the possibility of a hostile takeover. According to some analysts, in the global economy, 'the ability to use stock as a currency and finance enormous transactions means a company can run, but it can't hide' from an unsolicited takeover bid.[28] Even a firm the size of General Motors is not immune from takeover speculation. The reason for this is that, primarily because of the value of its majority stake in Hughes Electronics, GM's assets are worth substantially more than its market capitalisation.[29]

On a comparative basis, acquisitions occur more commonly than mergers and takeovers. Accordingly, this chapter focuses on acquisitions.

Reasons for acquisitions

In this section, we discuss reasons that support the active use of an acquisition strategy, as well as a decision to occasionally acquire another company.[30] In contrast to these appropriate reasons, managerial ego does not justify a decision to merge with or acquire another firm. For example, an out-of-control ego might cause a manager to acquire other companies to increase the firm's size, even when doing so may be at the expense of profitability. Hard to detect as a decision criterion in individual transactions, egos nonetheless may influence a number of merger and acquisition decisions, as the results of a survey by the US Federal Trade Commission (FTC) of Wall Street professionals suggests.[31]

Increased market power

A primary reason for acquisitions is to achieve greater market power.[32] Defined in Chapter 6, *market power* exists when a firm is able to sell its goods or services above competitive levels or when the costs of its primary or support activities are below those of its competitors. Many companies may have core competencies but lack the size to exercise their resources and capabilities. Market power usually is derived from the size of the firm and its resources and capabilities to compete in the marketplace. Therefore, most acquisitions designed to achieve greater market power entail buying a competitor, a supplier, a distributor, or a business in a highly related industry to allow exercise of a core competence and gain competitive advantage in the acquiring firm's primary market. This is the case with Brambles Industries Limited. Brambles is one of Australia's leading companies, operating as an international provider of business-to-business industrial services. Through a series of acquisitions both within Australia and internationally, Brambles has been able to become a market leader in a number of industrial services, such as the provision of pallets for transportation, and in waste management.[33] Because of the relatively small size of the Australian economy, such potential for market power is relatively easy compared to similar actions in the European Union or the United States.

Firms use horizontal, vertical and related acquisitions to increase their market power.

Horizontal acquisitions. The acquisition of a firm competing in the same industry that a competitor competes in is referred to as a *horizontal acquisition*.[34] Horizontal acquisitions increase a firm's market power by exploiting cost-based and revenue-based synergies.[35] For example, the purchase by Mildara Blass (the wine division of Foster's Brewing Group) of other wine producers such as Magileri Wines and Rothbury Estate was intended to increase the company's market power and achieve revenue synergies.[36]

Research suggests that horizontal acquisitions of firms with similar characteristics result in higher performance than when firms with dissimilar characteristics combine their operations. Examples of important similar characteristics include strategy, managerial styles and resource allocation patterns. Similarities in these characteristics make the integration of the two firms proceed more smoothly.[37] Sterling Software, Inc. and Computer Associates International, Inc. were rivals in the business of selling software solutions to corporations and governments. Recently, Sterling agreed to be acquired by Computer Associates in a US$4 billion stock swap. Comments from the firms' executives suggested that the two formerly independent firms were similar in various respects, including their business philosophies.[38]

Vertical acquisitions. A *vertical acquisition* refers to a firm acquiring a supplier or distributor of one or more of its goods or services. A firm becomes vertically integrated through this type of acquisition, in that it controls additional parts of the value chain (see Chapter 3). In the beer industry, for example, Foster's Brewing Group purchased Pubco (later to become the Australian Leisure and Hospitality Group within Foster's). Pubco controlled a chain of hotels and clubs across Australia, which allowed Foster's to create more value by controlling part of its distribution chain. Over time, Foster's has purchased more hotels, which it has integrated into its Australian Leisure and Hospitality Group (ALH).[39]

Although promising in terms of increasing the firm's performance, vertical acquisitions have the potential to alienate some of a company's customers. PepsiCo discovered this effect after acquiring Pizza Hut, Taco Bell and KFC. One objective of these acquisitions was to use the three restaurant chains as distribution channels to sell Pepsi's drinks. Aware of this, Coca-Cola convinced Wendy's and other fast-food chains that selling Pepsi in their stores indirectly benefited those of their competitors that PepsiCo owned.[40] Later, PepsiCo spun off its three food units to form Tricon, a separate entity. Thus, firms must balance anticipated benefits of a vertical acquisition with potential risks.[41]

Related acquisitions. The acquisition of a firm in a highly related industry is referred to as a *related acquisition*. Carnival Corp., the large cruise-line firm, intended to acquire Fairfield Communities, Inc., a rapidly growing American company competing in the time-share vacation business. The transaction was to be completed through a stock swap valued initially at US$693 million. Carnival executives envisioned synergies by attaching the company's well-known brand name to Fairfield's properties in an effort to cross-sell products; cruise customers were to be offered time-share opportunities, while time-share customers were to be given chances to take a Carnival cruise. Also supporting Carnival's interest in this related acquisition was the belief that the firm faced a 'dearth of opportunities in cruise-line acquisitions'.[42]

However, roughly a month after the initial announcement, Carnival abandoned its attempt to acquire Fairfield. Influencing this decision was the stock market's reaction to Carnival's strategic intentions. Following the announcement that it sought to acquire Fairfield, the value of each firm's stock dropped dramatically (41 per cent in Carnival's case, 27 per cent for Fairfield). Thus, especially when stock swaps are involved, companies must anticipate a careful scrutiny of their merger and acquisition strategies by

Impulse Airlines CEO Gerry McGowan, shown here at Mascot Airport. Impulse was a horizontal acquisition by Qantas because of a loss of confidence in them by their major institutional backer (in Singapore). The term *merger* could also be used to describe the situation – at many points such as this, the theory becomes difficult to use with precision.

investors and financial analysts.[43] In this instance, investors apparently were not persuaded that an acquisition based on the firms' apparent relatedness would be in shareholders' best interests.

Acquisitions intended to increase market power are subject to regulatory review, as well as to analysis by financial markets (as in Carnival's intended acquisition of Fairfield). For example, in January 2001, the Australian Competition and Consumer Commission (ACCC) rejected proposals by both Qantas and Ansett to purchase regional carrier Hazelton Airlines. Hazelton operates an extensive flight network in New South Wales, and the ACCC held that attempts by the larger national carriers to purchase Hazelton were anti-competitive. Their concern stemmed from the limited number of departure 'slots' available from Sydney airport. If one of the larger carriers were to purchase Hazelton, they would gain access to Hazelton 'slots'. They would then be able to move regional service out of peak times and provide additional interstate services, lessening competition in both regional and interstate markets.[44] (See the Air New Zealand/Ansett case in the case section of this text.) The ACCC also blocked Mayne Nickless's bid for Australian Hospital Care. These firms are the two largest for-profit operators of hospitals in Australia, and the ACCC was concerned that any takeover of Australian Hospital Care by Mayne Nickless would significantly decrease competitiveness in the industry.[45]

Legal measures have also been used to stop acquisitions in the United States. In early 2000, the US FTC voted to sue BP Amoco, PLC, to block its US$30 billion acquisition of Atlantic Richfield Co. BP Amoco was the world's third-largest oil company when the intended acquisition was announced on 30 March 1999. BP Amoco was created when British Petroleum and Amoco merged in 1998. The foundation for the FTC's suit was the agency's assessment that the proposed transaction was anticompetitive and against consumers' interests, in that the combined company would dominate oil prices on the West Coast of the United States. Some analysts concluded that the suit showed the limits of the federal government's tolerance of steadily larger mergers. One observer suggested that monitoring agencies had seen the 'merger wave just go on and on, get larger and larger and more and more complicated, and they feel they have to stop some of these things in order to have any ability to maintain a competitive economy'.[46] Thus, firms seeking growth and market power through acquisitions must understand the political/legal segment of the external environment (see Chapter 2) in order to use an acquisition strategy successfully. Additional comments about BP Amoco PLC's intended acquisition of Atlantic Richfield Co. appear in the Strategic Focus.

Strategic Focus International

BP Amoco and Atlantic Richfield Co.: A case of intentions and realities in the world of acquisitions

One of the world's three biggest oil companies and the largest company in the United Kingdom, BP Amoco has a reputation as an important and consistent driving force for change among the oil majors. Given its history, it is perhaps not surprising that BP Amoco announced in 1999 that it intended to acquire Atlantic Richfield Co. (Arco). The key purpose of the intended horizontal acquisition was to increase the acquiring firm's market power. In addition, buying Arco was thought of as an integral step in taking BP Amoco to the next level of becoming a 'super major', wherein the firm would be in a position to compete directly against Exxon, Mobil and Royal Dutch/Shell, the world's other super major oil companies.

The transaction was to be completed through an all-stock deal valued at approximately US$25.6 billion. If completed, the acquisition will create the second-largest global oil firm, with 59 per cent of refining capacity in the United States and 28 per cent in Europe. In some analysts' view, this acquisition 'would be the latest integration in a rapidly consolidating oil industry and the second acquisition for the former British Petroleum Co., which completed its [US]$57.6 billion merger with Chicago-based Amoco Corp.' in December 1998. Growing quickly, the intention of acquiring Arco was announced only 60 working days after British Petroleum concluded what was at the time one of the world's biggest industrial mergers with US Amoco.

As a measure of the commitment between the acquiring and target firm, the parties agreed that the transaction was in the best interests of both companies' shareholders. From an industry-wide perspective, the announcement of this intended acquisition should not have been too surprising, in that it was the eighth major merger or acquisition in the global oil and gas business in a six-month period during 1999. Partly driving these transactions were rapidly declining oil prices and increasing demands that energy companies produce and distribute cleaner fuels. Interestingly, shortly after the acquisitions were completed, the price of oil increased.

Although the transaction was of keen interest to BP Amoco officials, who thought that it was a logical decision to support the firm's growth and market power objectives, regulators took a contrary view: by a three-to-two vote, the US FTC concluded that the market power that would result from the transaction was anticompetitive in nature (as we noted earlier). Describing the agency's position, the FTC's bureau of competition director said, 'We will prove in federal court that BP has market power and that it has used that market power to maintain higher (crude oil) prices on the West Coast by exporting crude oil to the Far East.' Thus, for US regulatory officials, allowing BP Amoco to further increase its market power was undesirable, given the FTC's mandates. However, BP Amoco and Arco officials strongly disagreed with the regulators' assessment. Describing their position, executives from the two firms said, 'We regret [that] the only course now open to us is to resolve the issue through litigation, but we believe we have a compelling case.'

Time will determine the outcome of this intended acquisition. However, the situation among BP Amoco, Arco and the US FTC demonstrates the effect government policies and regulations have on horizontal acquisitions in particular and firms' efforts in general to use an acquisition strategy as a means of increasing their market power.

Sources: M. A. Hitt, J. S. Harrison and R. D. Ireland, 2001, *Creating Value through Mergers and Acquisitions: A Complete Guide to Successful M&As* (New York: Oxford University Press); T. Barker and H. Durgin, 2000, 'BP Amoco: Company faces Arco battle', *Financial Times*, 3 February: www.ft.com; H. Durgin, 2000, 'BP Amoco: US regulator moves to block Arco deal', *Financial Times*, 4 February: www.ft.com; Associated Press, 1999, 'BP Amoco, Arco close to announcing merger', *Dallas Morning News*, 29 March, pp. D1, D4; R. Corzine, 1999, 'BP Amoco: UK's biggest company drills out of Alaskan trouble spot', *Financial Times*, 9 November: www.ft.com; N. Know, 1999, 'Oil companies confirm talks', *Dallas Morning News*, 30 March, pp. D1, D4; V. Marsh, T. Barker and H. Durgin, 1999, 'BP Amoco set to restructure to meet "aggressive" targets', *Financial Times*, 16 July; M. White, 1999, 'Arco, BP make deal official', *Dallas Morning News*, 2 April, pp. D1, D11.

Overcoming of entry barriers

Barriers to entry (introduced in Chapter 2) are factors associated with the market or firms operating currently in it that increase the expense and difficulty new ventures face when trying to enter a particular market. For example, well-established competitors may be producing their goods or services in quantities through which significant economies of scale are gained. In addition, enduring relationships with customers often create product loyalties that are difficult for new entrants to overcome. When facing differentiated products, new entrants typically must spend considerable resources to advertise their goods or services and may find it necessary to sell at a price below that of its competitors to entice customers. Facing the barriers created by economies of scale and differentiated products, a new entrant may find the acquisition of an established company to be more effective than attempting to enter the market as a competitor offering a good or service that is unfamiliar to current buyers. In fact, the higher the barriers to market entry, the greater is the probability that a firm will acquire an existing firm to overcome them. Although an acquisition can be expensive, it does provide the new entrant with immediate market access.

Entry barriers firms face when trying to enter international markets (that is, markets outside of their home country) are often quite steep. In response, acquisitions are commonly used to overcome those barriers. Being able to compete successfully in international markets is becoming increasingly critical, in that, in general, global markets are growing at more than twice the rate of domestic markets.[47] For large multinational corporations, another indicator of the importance of entering and then competing successfully in international markets is the fact that five emerging markets (China, India, Brazil, Mexico and Indonesia) are among the 12 largest economies in the world, with a combined purchasing power that is already half that of the Group of Seven (G7) industrial nations (United States, Japan, Britain, France, Germany, Canada and Italy).[48]

Cross-border acquisitions. Acquisitions made between companies with headquarters in different countries are called *cross-border acquisitions*. These kinds of acquisitions are often made to overcome entry barriers. In Chapter 9, we examine *cross-border alliances* and the reason for their use. Cross-border acquisitions and cross-border alliances are strategic alternatives firms consider while pursuing strategic competitiveness. Compared to a cross-border alliance, a firm has more control over its international operations through a cross-border acquisition.[49]

Historically, US firms have been the most active acquirers of companies outside their domestic market. However, in the global economy, companies throughout the world are choosing this strategic option with increasing frequency. Based on what seems to be a general conviction among corporate executives – namely, that 'if you are in the big leagues, you have to be big in the United States' – the activity through which foreign companies acquire US firms is growing rapidly. During the first nine months of 1999, for example, non-US companies acquired US$256 billion of US firm assets. In contrast, US firms spent US$121.9 billion to buy foreign entities during the same period. Because of relaxed regulations, the amount of cross-border activity among nations within the European community also continues to increase. Accounting for this growth in a range of cross-border acquisitions, some analysts believe, is the fact that 'Many large European corporations seem to have come to the conclusion in recent years that they had reached the limits of growth within their domestic markets, and in order to preserve their strategic position, they had to be more aggressive in doing deals in foreign markets'.[50] An example of the breadth of some nations' commitment to cross-border acquisitions of US firms is the Netherlands' stock of direct investment in the United States. Recently, this amount exceeded the US$100 billion mark, equivalent to some 30 per cent of the Netherlands' annual gross domestic product. That investment total placed the Dutch on course to pass Japan as the second-largest investor in the United States, ranking only behind Britain.[51]

Firms in all types of industries are completing cross-border acquisitions. For example, in the wine industry, Foster's Brewing Group has used a series of acquisitions, such as the purchase of US wine giant Beringer Wine Estate, to make it the third-largest wine maker in the world.[52] In another part of the consumer goods industry, Kimberly-Clark, the world's largest producer of tissue products, intends to acquire primarily non-US companies to expand its disposable medical products lines and tissue and nappy businesses.[53]

Although used increasingly in multiple settings, financial services and telecommunications are industries in which cross-border mergers and acquisitions are prominent as a means of industry consolidation. For example, the Belgian–Dutch financial giant Fortis paid US$2.6 billion to acquire American Bankers Insurance Group. At the time, analysts labelled the transaction the latest in a spate of cross-border mergers and acquisitions in the insurance industry.

European pension funds are also expanding rapidly in the global market. A great deal of this growth is occurring through cross-border transactions, with more than two-thirds of 1999's mergers and acquisitions among these firms involving companies outside a firm's domestic market.

Activity in the telecommunications industry is equally brisk. Speaking to this issue for US firms, business writers suggested that 'with the consolidations in the U.S. reaching a peak, big American companies are likely to turn their attentions across the Atlantic to become global providers of telephone and Internet services. But instead of forging joint ventures or making small investments in European operators as they had in the past, with mixed results, U.S. telephone companies increasingly are likely to make big acquisitions in Europe.' European telecommunications companies are also looking to expand globally through the use of acquisitions. In 1998, Cable and Wireless PLC purchased 52.5 per cent of Australia's second-largest telecommunications company Optus. Since 1998, the value of the new company, Cable and Wireless Optus, has grown from $4 billion to over $10 billion.[54] Driving the interest in acquisitions among telecommunications firms is many companies' desire to own their networks rather than sharing or leasing them from competitors, as often is the case through joint ventures and other relationships. Ownership of network assets may help a firm reduce its costs of transporting voice and data traffic.[55]

The global automobile industry is also being consolidated through companies' strategic actions, including cross-border acquisitions. The Strategic Focus discusses what was reported as a merger between Daimler-Benz and Chrysler Corporation as an example of consolidation through cross-border acquisitions.

Strategic Focus International

Daimler-Benz and Chrysler Corporation: Will it be a successful union?

At the time of its announcement, the merger between Daimler-Benz and Chrysler Corporation was the world's largest. A horizontal merger, this cross-border transaction was intended to create market power and generate synergies on which the world's pre-eminent automotive, transportation and services company could be built. An immediate outcome of the merger was some additional consolidation of the global automobile industry.

Each of the former competitors had needs that the merger was supposed to address. Chrysler lacked the infrastructure and management depth required to be a truly global automobile company. Daimler-Benz executives concluded that increasingly intense competitive rivalry in its core luxury-car segment made it necessary for their firm to diversify its product line and distribution channels. Recognising these respective needs, some analysts believed that the two firms were a complementary fit for at least two reasons. First, Chrysler's dominant market position was in the United States, while Daimler's was in two regions – Europe and South America – where Chrysler lacked a meaningful presence. Second, the companies' product lines were complementary: The bulk of Chrysler's profitability was earned from sport utility vehicles and multipurpose vans, whereas luxury vehicles were the foundation of Daimler's automotive-based strategic competitiveness.

As discussed previously, horizontal acquisitions can create cost- and revenue-based synergies. Daimler and Chrysler expected to generate both types of synergies through their merger. For example, the integration of separate operations was expected to reduce costs by US$1.3 billion in 1999 alone. The decision to build the Mercedes M-Class cars and the Jeep Grand Cherokee on the same production line in Graz, Austria, is one of the integration projects that was started immediately in the combined firm. In fact, DaimlerChrysler wants the Graz facility to showcase its ability to generate cost-based synergies by integrating previously independent manufacturing operations. On the revenue side, the new firm seeks cross-selling synergies by integrating Daimler-Benz's competencies in technological innovations with Chrysler's ability to introduce new products into the marketplace rapidly.

Although framed around anticipated benefits, the Daimler-Chrysler cross-border transaction has been questioned and criticised. Some thought that integrating the firms' computer systems would be quite difficult, as would determining how product development decisions were to be made. However, in the short run, it appeared that Daimler's style of making decisions enabled Chrysler to get products to the marketplace quickly. Still, critics also argued that the companies' estimates of cost- and revenue-based synergies were far too optimistic. Compounding these issues was the perception that an acquisition had occurred, rather than a merger. Actions witnessed in the combined firm indicated to some that, in actuality, Daimler-Benz had acquired Chrysler Corporation. Regardless, the new firm's 1999 financial performance was encouraging: operating profit for the year was approximately 11 billion euros (US$10.72 billion), up from 8.6 billion euros in 1998. In addition, company officials were optimistic about the future, predicting that sales volume would climb from US$151 billion in 1999 to at least US$154 billion in 2000 and US$168 billion by 2002.

Positions articulated by DaimlerChrysler in 2000 suggested confidence in the results of the cross-border acquisition that formed the company, as well as a commitment to continue growing by using the same strategic option. Currently, DaimlerChrysler is the world's fifth-largest automobile manufacturer (behind General Motors, Ford, Toyota and Volkswagen). Company executives noted that a key objective was for their firm to become the largest transportation company in the world by 2003. To reach this objective, DaimlerChrysler intended to acquire other companies and to form an array of strategic alliances. By the start of 2001, however, it has become increasingly clear that the Daimler–Chrysler merger is more difficult to manage than first thought. Problems have begun to emerge on two fronts. First, differences in national culture between the two firms have led to difficulties in integrating management styles and HRM policies. Second, differences in time zones have made communications between the two firms difficult.

Sources: M. A. Hitt, J. S. Harrison and R. D. Ireland, 2001, *Creating Value through Mergers and Acquisitions: A Complete Guide to Successful M&As* (New York: Oxford University Press); J. Ball and S. Miller, 2000, 'Daimler profit accelerated 87 percent to $1.1 billion in 4th quarter', *Wall Street Journal*, 29 February, pp. A17, A19; J. Ball and S. Miller, 2000, 'DaimlerChrysler is aiming for top spot', *Wall Street Journal*, 14 January, p. A10; S. Miller, 2000, 'Daimler results climbed to top of expectations for last year', *Wall Street Journal*, 28 February, pp. A21, A23; J. Flint, 1999, 'A letter to Jürgen Schrempp', *Forbes*, 31 May, p. 168; R. Simison and S. Miller, 1999, 'Making "digital" decisions', *Wall Street Journal*, 24 September, pp. B1, B4.

Cost of new-product development

Developing new products internally and successfully introducing them into the marketplace often requires significant investments of a firm's resources, including time, making it difficult to earn a profitable return quickly.[56] Also of concern to firms' managers are estimates that almost 88 per cent of innovations fail to achieve adequate returns from the capital invested in them.[57] Perhaps contributing to these less-than-desirable rates of return is the fact that 60 per cent or so of innovations are successfully imitated within four years after patents are obtained. Because of outcomes such as these, managers often perceive internal product development as a high-risk activity.[58]

Acquisitions are another means through which a firm can gain access to new products and to current products that are new to the firm. Compared to internal product development processes, acquisitions provide more predictable returns as well as faster market entry. Returns are more predictable because the performance of the acquired firm's products can be assessed prior to completing the acquisition.[59] Pharmaceutical firms such as Watson Pharmaceuticals, Inc. frequently use acquisitions to enter markets quickly, to overcome the high costs of developing products internally and to increase the predictability of returns on their investments. For example, acquiring TheraTech, Inc. gave Watson access to more than 50 patents in advanced drug-delivery systems. Watson intends to use these patented systems to help it create opportunities for new products.[60]

In a broader context, evidence shows that acquisition activity is extensive throughout the pharmaceutical industry. According to business analysts, 'There's good reason' for this, in that 'patents on stalwart drugs – generating [US]$16 billion in annual revenue – are expiring' in the near future. Compounding the seriousness of this issue is the fact that 'Some companies don't have adequate substitutes in their research pipelines'. Without internally generated products, acquiring other firms, followed by cost reductions, is an attractive strategic option for many of these companies.[61] Recently, large pharmaceutical companies have chosen to acquire a number of small biotechnology firms. For example, Warner-Lambert acquired Agouron, a California biotech company, and Pharmacia & Upjohn bought Sugen, a San Francisco-based biotech firm specialising in cancer drugs. In addition to citing attractive prices, analysts suggest that these acquisitions are a way for large pharmaceuticals to 'fill their pipeline with projects from undervalued biotechnology companies and to get their hands on new products'.[62]

Increased speed to market

As indicated previously, compared to internal product development, acquisitions result in more rapid market entries.[63] In two researchers' words, 'Acquisitions remain the quickest route companies have to new markets and to new capabilities.'[64] Using new capabilities to pioneer new products and to enter markets quickly can create advantageous market positions.[65] As discussed in Chapter 5, the durability of the advantage created by an attractive market position is determined largely by rivals' competitive responses.[66]

Firms seek rapid market entry in many different industries. British Telecommunications, PLC (BT), for example, recently spent US$2.46 billion to acquire Esat Telecom Group, PLC, Ireland's second-largest phone company. The acquisition gives BT immediate access to 'Ireland's rapidly growing telecommunications market, including in the area of high-speed broadband delivery'.[67] Through its acquisition of Mildara Blass, the Foster's Brewing Group was automatically able to become the largest player in Australia's booming premium wine market.[68] In the consumer foods industry, Kraft Foods acquired meat alternative producer Boca Burger. This acquisition gave Kraft an immediate presence in the rapidly expanding market for soy-based products as alternatives to traditional meat offerings. The attractiveness of soy-based goods gained steam in the United States when the powerful US Food and Drug Administration decided to allow companies to equate soy-protein consumption with a reduced risk of heart disease.[69] At a cost of US$370 million, PC manufacturer Compaq Computer Corp. acquired the custom-assembly operations of Inacom Corp. Stimulating this purchase was new CEO Michael Capellas's conclusion that Compaq needed to be able to accelerate the speed with which it delivered products to major customers. According to Capellas, the 'purchase gives us the right capability quickly and cost-effectively'.[70] Increasing the speed of its distribution channel was necessary for Compaq to become more competitive with several rivals, especially Dell Computer Corp.

Lower risk compared to developing new products

As mentioned earlier, internal product development processes can be risky. Alternatively, because an acquisition's outcomes can be estimated more easily and accurately compared to the outcomes of an internal product development process, managers may view acquisitions as carrying lowering risk.[71]

The assessment of risk between an internal product development process and an acquisition may have taken place among managers at Procter & Gamble (P&G). Recently, P&G acquired the US premium dog- and cat-food manufacturer, Iams Co. Historically, Iams's customer base was pet-food chains and veterinary clinics. P&G intended to develop a first-time national advertising campaign for Iams to support the launch of its products into supermarket chains and mass merchandisers such as Wal-Mart. Company officials anticipated that broadening Iams's distribution channels would change the nature of competition in the pet-food industry.[72] Assessing Iams's performance before acquiring the company allowed P&G managers to have a reasonably high degree of confidence in the outcomes associated with their intended strategic actions. As a result, P&G managers may have considered entry into the premium pet-food market through acquisition to be less risky compared to entering the market through an internal product development process.

As with other strategic actions discussed in this book, caution must be exercised when a decision is made to acquire new products rather than to develop them internally. In the context of the issue of lower risk, for example, firms should be aware that research evidence suggests that acquisitions have become a common means of avoiding risky internal ventures (and therefore risky R&D investments). In fact, acquisition may become a substitute for innovation.[73] Thus, acquisitions are not a risk-free alternative to entering new markets through internally developed products.

Increased diversification

Based on experience and the insights resulting from it, firms typically find it easier to develop and introduce new products in markets served currently by the firm. In contrast, it is harder for companies to develop products – ones that differ from their current lines – for markets in which they lack experience. Thus, it is uncommon for a firm to develop new products internally as a means of diversifying its product lines.[74] Instead, a firm usually opts to use acquisitions as the means to engage in product diversification. Wesfarmers provides an example of a conglomerate that has been able to diversify its business through an acquisition strategy. Wesfarmers began as a cooperative of Western Australian farmers in 1914, providing merchandise and services to farmers in rural areas. Through a series of acquisitions, Wesfarmers was able to diversify their operations into a number of areas, such as energy, through the purchase of Kleenheat Gas and Western Collieries, and timber and hardware, through the purchase of the Bunnings Ltd hardware chain.[75] (See the Strategic Focus at the start of Chapter 9 for more details on Wesfarmers.)

Both related diversification and unrelated diversification strategies can be implemented through acquisitions. In addition, as discussed in Chapter 8, acquisitions are the most frequently used means for firms to diversify their operations into international markets.[76] Using acquisitions to diversify a firm seems appropriate, in that evidence suggests that acquisitions are the quickest and, typically, the easiest way to change a firm's portfolio of businesses.[77] Nevertheless, acquisitions that diversify a firm's product lines must be undertaken only after careful study and evaluation, in that the more related the acquired firm is to the acquiring firm, the greater is the probability that the acquisition will be successful. Thus, horizontal acquisitions (through which a firm acquires a competitor) and related acquisitions tend to contribute more to strategic competitiveness than do those through which a firm acquires a company operating in product markets that are quite different from those in which it currently competes.[78] This does not mean that all such moves are successful, as the failure of HIH Insurance's purchase of FAI Insurance indicates.[79]

Reshaping the firm's competitive scope

As discussed in Chapter 2, the intensity of competitive rivalry is an industry characteristic that affects a firm's profitability. To reduce the negative effect of an intense rivalry on its financial performance, the firm may use acquisitions as a way to restrict its dependence on a single or a few products or markets. Reducing a company's dependence on single products or markets alters the competitive scope of the company.

Increasingly, some of the world's automobile manufacturers are diversifying their operations to reduce their dependence on the intensely competitive global automobile markets. DaimlerChrysler, for example, 'is exploring opportunities to expand its presence in financial and computer services, aftermarket sales, and electronics and satellite systems'. Company officials believe that, in addition to affording more desirable operating margins, growth possibilities in these areas are now more attractive than are either alliances or acquisitions in car manufacturing.[80] Similarly, Ford CEO Jacques Nasser wants to make his company the world's leading consumer services business that specialises in the automotive sector. Nasser wants Ford to tap all sectors in the after-sales market, including repairs, replacement parts and product servicing. One of the first actions Ford took to reach this objective was the acquisition of Kwik-Fit, the UK automotive after-market group. To evaluate the success in its efforts to reshape the firm's competitive scope through diversification, 'Ford will measure itself against world-class consumer businesses in whatever business they operate rather than the traditional yardsticks of rival automakers'.[81]

Like DaimlerChrysler and Ford, Pacific Dunlop used a series of acquisitions in the late 1980s and early 1990s to decrease their reliance on the sale of rubber-based products, such as tyres. Two of Pacific Dunlop's most important acquisitions were that of Telectronic, the manufacturer of heart pacemakers and bionic ear implants, and Petersville Sleigh, one of Australia's leading food manufacturers, producing brands such as Edgell-Birds Eye, Latina, Vitari, Four 'n Twenty and Twinings.[82] Japan's largest electronics manufacturer, Hitachi Ltd, has US$3 billion that it intends to use either to purchase US and Japanese high-technology companies outright or to buy stakes in them. Recently, Hitachi studied 60 possible acquisitions, half in Japan and half in other nations. According to the president of the company, the acquisitions' primary purpose is to facilitate his objective of 'remaking' a firm that he believed had become a sprawling giant in order to increase its competitiveness in the global economy.[83]

As we have described, there are legitimate reasons for firms to use acquisition strategies as part of their efforts to increase strategic competitiveness and to improve the likelihood of being able to earn above-average returns. However, also as we have said, acquisition strategies are not risk free. In fact, on the basis of company experience and research findings, it has been suggested that 'less than 20 per cent of all mergers and acquisitions are successful'.[84] This success rate is consistent with the finding discussed earlier in the chapter that the average returns of acquisitions for acquiring firms hover close to zero.

Problems in achieving acquisition success

Reasons supporting the use of acquisition strategies, as well as potential problems accompanying their use, are shown in Figure 7.1. The potential problems are discussed in the sections that follow. A reasonable conclusion to draw from those discussions is that 'successful acquisitions involve a well thought out strategy in selecting the target, avoiding over-paying, and creating value in the integration process. [In addition], a good acquisition strategy combines the analytical with the intuitive, and the linear with the iterative.'[85]

Figure 7.1 | Reasons for acquisitions and problems in achieving success

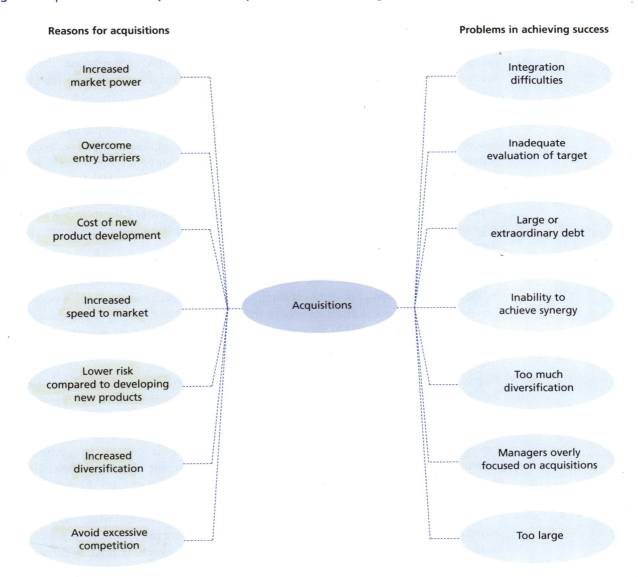

Integration difficulties

Integrating two companies following an acquisition can be quite difficult.[86] Integration issues include those of melding two disparate corporate cultures,[87] linking different financial and control systems, building effective working relationships (particularly when management styles differ), and resolving problems regarding the status of the newly acquired firm's executives.[88]

The importance of a successful integration should not be underestimated. Without it, a firm achieves financial diversification, but little else. Thus, as suggested by a researcher studying the process, 'managerial practice and academic writings show that the post-acquisition integration phase is probably the single most important determinant of shareholder value creation (and equally of value destruction) in mergers and acquisitions'.[89] In addition, firms should be aware of the large number of activities associated with integration processes. For instance, Intel acquired Digital Equipment Corporation's semiconductors division. On the day Intel began to integrate the acquired division into its operations, 6 000 deliverables were to be completed by hundreds of employees working in dozens of different countries.[90]

According to research completed by consulting firm Booz-Allen Hamilton, there is a positive relationship between the rapid integration of the acquiring and acquired firms and overall acquisition success. Intentions at the US firm Honeywell (AlliedSignal kept the Honeywell name after acquiring it) are consistent with this relationship. According to analysts, 'AlliedSignal and Honeywell have set an aggressive six-month timetable to merge their operations into a [US]$24 billion industrial powerhouse that makes everything from aircraft landing systems to home thermostats.'[91] To help integrate the two formerly independent firms within six months, Honeywell organised a team that was charged with developing and implementing an integration plan. Rapid integration is one of the guidelines that DaimlerChrysler CEO Jürgen Schrempp recommends companies follow to successfully integrate firms involved in a global merger or acquisition. Schrempp's other guidelines include dealing with unpopular issues immediately and being honest with people regarding the effects the integration will likely have on them.[92] In Australia, Macquarie Bank will spend $150 million to ensure a smooth integration between itself and the newly acquired Bankers Trust (BT). Part of the money will be spent exploring the structure, staff and culture of the two companies to identify possible sources of integration difficulties.[93]

According to some business writers, Cisco Systems 'wears the mantle of M&A king'.[94] One reason for this is the firm's ability to quickly integrate its acquisitions into its existing operations. Focusing on small companies with products and services related closely to its own, some analysts believe that the day after the company acquires a firm, employees in that firm feel as though they have been working for Cisco for decades.[95]

Inadequate evaluation of target

Due diligence is a process through which a firm evaluates a target firm for acquisition. An effective due-diligence process examines hundreds of items in areas as diverse as those of financing the intended transaction, differences in cultures between the acquiring and target firm, tax consequences of the transaction, and actions that would be necessary to successfully meld the two workforces. Due diligence is commonly performed by investment bankers, accountants, lawyers and management consultants specialising in that activity, although firms actively pursuing acquisitions may form their own internal due-diligence team.

The failure to complete an effective due-diligence process often results in the acquiring firm paying a premium – sometimes an excessive one – for the target company. In fact, research shows that without due diligence, 'the purchase price is driven by the pricing of other "comparable" acquisitions rather than by a rigorous assessment of where, when, and how management can drive real performance gains. [In these cases], the price paid may have little to do with achievable value.'[96] Premiums paid without effective due diligence may also account for research results indicating that the amount of the purchase premium does not predict acquisition success.[97]

The results of some acquisitions in a number of industries suggest a failure to perform adequate due diligence. In its hostile takeover of the GIO, AMP did not fully estimate the size of potential losses that would arise from the GIO's reinsurance business.[98, 99] As a consequence, the substantial losses made by the GIO after the takeover reduced AMP's share price from a high of $34 to a low of $14.[100] In a 1988 example, British retailer Marks & Spencer spent US$750 million to acquire Brooks Brothers of the United States. Even after more than 10 years, the acquisition remains unsuccessful. Initially, Marks & Spencer executives thought that renovating and 'upscaling' Brooks Brothers would attract customers and improve the chain's deteriorating performance. These efforts proved unsuccessful, and indeed, some believe that the premium Marks & Spencer paid to acquire Brooks Brothers precluded success, almost irrespective of any actions taken to reverse the chain's fortunes. At twice the sales volume and 75 times the earnings, the acquisition price was the highest a certain retail analyst had seen paid for a US retailer in his 35-year career. Another analyst called the purchase price 'insane'.[101] Effective due diligence might have resulted in a decision by Marks & Spencer not to buy Brooks Brothers.

An example of effective due diligence appears to be DaimlerChrysler's 1999 decision not to acquire Nissan Motor Company. DaimlerChrysler was interested in Nissan as a means of expanding Daimler's access to global automobile markets, especially those in Southeast Asia. The primary concern for analysts and, apparently, for DaimlerChrysler executives was Nissan's US$22 billion debt. Speaking to this possible acquisition, Robert Lutz, retired vice chairman of the former Chrysler Corporation, said that DaimlerChrysler 'might as well take [US]$5 billion in gold bullion, put it in a huge container, spray paint the word Nissan on the side and drop it into the middle of the Pacific Ocean'.[102] An adequate evaluation of the target firm through DaimlerChrysler's due-diligence process appears to be the cause of the company's decision not to acquire Nissan.

Large or extraordinary debt

To finance a number of acquisitions completed during the 1980s and 1990s, some companies significantly increased their levels of debt. Partly making this possible was a financial innovation called junk bonds,[103] a financing option through which risky acquisitions are financed with money (debt) that provides a large potential return to lenders (typically called bondholders). Because junk bonds are unsecured obligations (that is, they are not tied to specific assets such as collateral), interest rates for these high-risk debt instruments sometimes reached between 18 and 20 per cent during the 1980s.

Also supporting a decision to increase debt significantly during this period in order to acquire other companies was the belief that debt disciplined managers, causing them to act in shareholders' best interests. This view was grounded in work completed by finance scholars who argued that the constraints on spending possibilities created by the requirement to service debt obligations caused managers to be more prudent in allocating remaining funds and to behave less opportunistically. This logic resulted in managers sometimes being encouraged to utilise significant leverage to finance large acquisitions. Members of a firm's board of directors offered this type of encouragement, as did company finance officials.[104]

As the 21st century begins, junk bonds are being used less frequently to finance acquisitions. In addition, the conviction that debt disciplines managers is less strong than it was in the previous two decades. Nonetheless, some firms still take on too much debt to acquire companies. For example, AgriBioTech, Inc., in the United States, recently acquired dozens of small seed firms. These acquisitions were used to gain access to the skills necessary to develop genetically enhanced alfalfa and turf grasses and to gain the economies of scope required to distribute products nationwide. However, the firm's 'acquisition strategy got out of hand. AgriBioTech wound up issuing massive amounts of new shares. Debt, meanwhile, ballooned to [US]$135 million compared to annual revenues of about [US]$409 million.' Analysts concluded that the first order of business to turn the firm around was to 'clear up the debt mess'.[105]

In spite of the issues associated with too much of it, debt can discipline managerial actions because when debt is high, principal and interest payments reach levels that preclude other investments, some of which might be in managers' best interests (for example, greater amounts of diversification to reduce managerial employment risk). On the other hand, high debt levels increase the likelihood of bankruptcy, which can lead to a downgrade in the firm's credit rating from agencies such as Moody's and Standard & Poor's.[106] In addition, high debt precludes investments in activities that contribute to the firm's long-term success, including R&D, human resource training and marketing.[107]

Therefore, we conclude that the use of debt has positive and negative effects. On the one hand, leverage can be a positive force in a firm's development, allowing it to take advantage of attractive expansion opportunities. However, too much leverage (for example, extraordinary debt) can lead to negative outcomes, such as postponing or eliminating investments (for example, R&D expenditures), that are necessary to maintain strategic competitiveness over the long term. Partly because of debt's potential disadvantages and partly because of a generally favourable global economy, cash and equity offerings were frequently used instead of significant amounts of debt to complete acquisitions during the latter part of the 1990s and into the 21st century. For example, in a transaction between two Canadian firms, Abitibi-Consolidated, Inc. acquired Donohue, Inc. for US$4 billion in cash and stock. The transaction created market power for the new firm in that it became the world's largest newsprint maker, with 16.3 per cent of global newsprint capacity. (The next-largest market shareholder had 8.2 per cent.[108])

Inability to achieve synergy

Derived from the Greek word *synergos*, which means 'working together', synergy exists when the value created by units working together exceeds the value those units could create working independently (see Chapter 6). Another way of saying this is that synergy exists when assets 'are worth more when used in conjunction with each other than separately. Synergies can involve physical and non-physical assets'[109] such as human capital. For shareholders, synergy generates gains in their wealth that they could not duplicate or exceed through their own portfolio diversification decisions.[110] Being able to create synergy when using an acquisition strategy is important, in that doing so is a key justification for using such a strategy, which often results in a firm becoming more diversified.[111]

A firm develops a competitive advantage through an acquisition strategy only when a transaction generates private synergy, which is created when the combination and integration of the acquiring and acquired firms' assets yield capabilities and core competencies that could not be developed by combining and integrating either firm's assets with another company. Private synergy is possible when firms' assets are complementary in unique ways – that is, the unique type of asset complementarity is not possible by combining either company's assets with another firm's assets.[112]

Because of its uniqueness, private synergy is difficult for competitors to understand and imitate. However, private synergy is difficult to create. For example, Quaker Oats' executives believed that the company's ownership of Snapple, which came about through an acquisition, would create private synergy. The expectation was that integrating

Quaker's own Gatorade products with Snapple's would create complementarities that could not be created through any other combination of each firm's assets with the assets of any other company. However, that expectation was not realised, and after struggling with the acquisition, Quaker Oats finally divested Snapple. Analysts suggested that there was a lack of complementarity between the sales and marketing activities required by Gatorade's and Snapple's drinks.

Firms experience several expenses when trying to create private synergy through acquisitions. Called transaction costs,[113] these expenses are incurred when firms use acquisition strategies to create synergy. Direct costs include legal fees and charges from investment bankers who complete due diligence for the acquiring firm. Managerial time to evaluate target firms and then to complete negotiations is an example of an indirect cost, as is the loss of key managers and employees following an acquisition.[114] Affecting an acquisition's success, in terms of whether synergy is created, is a firm's ability to account for costs that are necessary to create anticipated revenue- and cost-based synergies. Of the two types of costs, firms tend to underestimate the sum of indirect costs when the value of the synergy that may be created by combining and integrating the acquired firm's assets with the acquiring firm's assets is calculated.

Too much diversification

As explained in Chapter 6, when used properly, diversification strategies lead to strategic competitiveness and above-average returns. In general, firms using related diversification strategies outperform those employing unrelated diversification strategies. However, conglomerates, formed by using an unrelated diversification strategy, also can be successful. For example, Thermo Electron, a US manufacturer of high-tech analytical instruments, is highly diversified, yet successful, as is Virgin Group, the UK-based firm with interests ranging from cosmetics to trains.[115]

At some point, firms can become over-diversified. The level at which this happens varies across companies. The reason for the variation is that each firm has different capabilities that are required to manage diversification successfully. Recall from Chapter 6 that related diversification requires more information processing than does unrelated diversification. The need for related diversified firms to be able to process more and more diverse information creates a situation in which they become over-diversified with a smaller number of business units, compared to firms using an unrelated diversification strategy.[116] Regardless of the type of diversification strategy implemented, however, declines in performance usually result from over-diversification,[117] after which different business units are divested. The pattern of excessive diversification followed by divestments of underperforming business units was observed frequently among US firms during the 1960s to 1980s. A similar pattern was followed by Australian businesses during the 1980s and early 1990s. Pacific Dunlop, for example, diversified into a number of business areas such as food (through the acquisition of Petersville Sleigh), batteries (through the acquisition of Chloride Group PLC) and heart pacemakers (through the acquisition of Telectronic), only to have to divest these businesses at a later date.[118, 119]

Even when a firm is not over-diversified, a high level of diversification can have a negative effect on the firm's long-term performance. For example, the scope created by additional amounts of diversification often causes managers to rely on financial rather than strategic controls to evaluate business units' performances.[120] (Financial and strategic controls are defined and explained in detail in Chapters 11 and 12.) Essentially, when top-level executives have the breadth and depth of information needed to understand each business unit's objectives and strategy, they are able to use strategic controls to monitor performance. Without such a rich understanding of business units' objectives and strategies, those same executives rely on financial controls to assess the performances of managers and their business units. Financial controls are based on

The costs associated with diversification may result in fewer allocations to innovative activities such as research and development. Without internal innovation skills, a firm may be forced to complete additional acquisitions to gain access to innovation.

objective evaluation criteria, such as the firm's return on investment (ROI). Executives' reliance on financial controls to judge managerial performance can cause individual business-unit managers to focus on short-term outcomes at the expense of long-term investments. When long-term investments are reduced to levels that jeopardise future success in order to boost short-term profits, a firm may have diversified to the point beyond which its diversification strategy can enhance overall strategic competitiveness.[121]

Another problem resulting from too much diversification is the tendency for acquisitions to become substitutes for innovation. Typically, managers do not intend acquisitions to be used in that way. However, a reinforcing cycle evolves. Costs associated with acquisitions may result in fewer allocations to activities (for example, R&D) that are linked to innovation. But without adequate support, a firm's innovation skills begin to atrophy. Without internal innovation skills, the only option available to a firm is to complete still additional acquisitions to gain access to innovation. Across time, though, it is difficult for firms to rely continuously on other companies' innovations as an important source of strategic competitiveness. In fact, evidence suggests that a firm that uses acquisitions as a substitute for internally developed innovations eventually encounters performance problems.[122]

Managers overly focused on acquisitions

Typically, a fairly substantial amount of managerial time and energy is required for acquisition strategies to contribute to a firm's strategic competitiveness. Activities with which managers become involved include (1) searching for viable acquisition candidates, (2) completing effective due-diligence processes, and (3) preparing for negotiations.

Top-level managers do not personally gather all data and information required to complete the activities that are part of an acquisition. However, upper-level executives do make final decisions regarding the firms to be pursued as targets, the nature of the negotiations to acquire a firm, and so forth. In a broader sense, the most important responsibility the top management team has in terms of acquisition strategies is to make certain that the firm is using them effectively. Company experiences show that being responsible for, and participating in, many of the activities that are part of an acquisition strategy can divert managerial attention from other matters (for example, thinking seriously about the firm's purpose and interacting effectively with board members and external stakeholders) that are linked with long-term competitive success.[123]

Another issue that concerns some analysts centres on the possibility that managers who are overly focused on acquisitions may fail to assess objectively the value of outcomes achieved through the use of the firm's acquisition strategy, compared with outcomes that might be achieved by concentrating on using the firm's other strategies more effectively. For example, it has been suggested that Ford Motor Company's acquisition strategy may not be enhancing the firm's strategic competitiveness. Consider the words of an individual who studies the automobile industry: 'Ford owns one-third of the stock of Mazda of Japan and essentially runs the company. There have been three Mazda presidents in three years (all from Ford). I wouldn't call that a sign of success. Ford pumped [US]$6 billion into Jaguar over the past decade, and there are signs that this may work out one day, but it will take a decade to earn back the investment. And I don't think Ford will ever earn back its Volvo investment.'[124] An option available to Ford is to rely on its technological skills to develop innovative engines, transmissions, suspension systems, and so forth. In other words, some believe that the firm might contribute more positively to its strategic competitiveness by focusing its time and attention on determining actions to take to increase the value of its own automobiles and trucks, instead of using managerial time and energy to expand the firm's product lines by acquiring competitors. Thus, upper-level executives should avoid focusing on the use of an acquisition strategy at the expense of a firm's long-term strategic competitiveness.

Acquisitions can consume significant amounts of managerial time and energy in target firms, as well as in the companies that acquire them. Because of the uncertainty that an acquisition creates, some suggest that target firms find themselves in a state of virtual suspended animation during an acquisition.[125] For example, while the target firm's day-to-day operations continue, albeit sometimes at a slower pace, most of the company's executives are hesitant to make decisions with long-term consequences, choosing to postpone such decisions until negotiations have been completed. Thus, evidence suggests that the acquisition process can create a short-term perspective and a greater aversion to risk among top-level executives in a target firm.[126]

Too large

Most acquisitions create a larger firm. In theory, the increased size should help a firm gain economies of scale in various organisational functions. These economies can then lead to more efficient operations. For instance, combining the R&D functions of two firms involved in an acquisition should create economies of scale that can be the stimulus to greater innovative output.

However, evidence suggests that a larger size creates efficiencies in various organisational functions only when the new firm is not *too* large. In other words, at some level, the additional costs required to manage the larger firm exceed the benefits of efficiency created by economies of scale. In addition, when faced with the complexities generated by the larger size, managers – especially those from the acquiring firm – typically decide that more bureaucratic controls should be used to manage the combined firms' operations. **Bureaucratic controls** are formalised supervisory and behavioural rules and policies that are designed to ensure consistency of decisions and actions across different units of a firm. Consistency in terms of decisions and actions can benefit the firm, primarily in the form of predictability and cost reductions. However, across time, relatively rigid and standardised managerial behaviour tends to be the product of strict adherence to formalised rules and policies. Certainly, in the long run, the diminished degree of flexibility that accompanies rigid and standardised managerial behaviour may produce less innovation. Because of innovation's importance to competitive success in the 21st-century landscape (see Chapters 1 and 2), the bureaucratic controls that are sometimes used when firms become too large through the use of an acquisition strategy can have a detrimental effect on performance.[127]

> **Bureaucratic controls** are formalised supervisory and behavioural rules and policies that are designed to ensure consistency of decisions and actions across different units of a firm.

Effective acquisitions

Earlier in the chapter, we noted that acquisition strategies do not consistently produce above-average returns for the acquiring firm's shareholders. Nonetheless, some companies are able to create value through the use of an acquisition strategy.[128] Results from a research study shed light on the differences between unsuccessful and successful acquisition strategies and suggest that there is a pattern of decisions and actions firms can follow which may improve the probability of acquisition strategy success.[129]

The study appears to show that when a target firm's assets are complementary to the acquired firm's assets, an acquisition is more successful. This is because, with complementary assets, integrating two firms' operations creates synergy. In fact, in the firms that were a part of the study, the researchers found that integrating two firms with complementary assets frequently produced unique capabilities and core competencies; a requirement for building strategic competitiveness, as previously described.[130] Thus, the acquisitions were generally highly related to the acquiring firm's businesses. In fact, the acquiring firm maintained its focus on core businesses and leveraged them with the complementary assets and capabilities from the acquired firm. Often, targets were selected and 'groomed' by establishing a working relationship sometime prior to the acquisition. Using a cooperative strategy between the two firms is one way to determine whether firms can work together effectively over an extended period. As discussed in Chapter 9, strategic alliances are sometimes used to test the feasibility of firms trying to work together to pursue mutual interests.[131]

The study's results also show that friendly acquisitions facilitate integration of the firms involved in an acquisition. Through friendly acquisitions, firms work together to find ways to integrate their operations so that positive synergy can be created. In hostile takeovers, animosity often results between the two top-management teams, a condition that in turn often affects relationships and methods of working in the newly created firm. As a result, more key personnel in the acquired firm may be lost, and those who remain may resist the changes necessary to integrate the two firms and create synergy.[132] With effort, cultural clashes can be overcome, and fewer key managers and employees will become discouraged and leave.[133] Thus, successful acquisitions tend to be friendly, although there are exceptions.

Another finding from the study is that a successful acquiring firm generally has conducted effective due-diligence processes that, at a minimum, involve the deliberate and careful selection of target firms and an evaluation of how negotiations should be conducted. Having financial slack (in the form of debt equity or cash) in both the acquiring and acquired firms also frequently contributed to success in acquisitions. Relatedly, continuing to maintain a low to moderate amount of debt in the newly created firm is an important attribute of acquisition success. Indeed, maintaining low or moderate debt was shown to be critical to success even in instances when a substantial amount of leverage was used to finance the acquisition. When substantial debt is used to finance the acquisition, companies with successful acquisitions reduced the debt quickly, partly by selling off assets from the acquired firm. Often, the assets that are sold are not complementary to the acquiring firm's businesses or are performing poorly. Also, the acquiring firm may sell its own lower-performing businesses after making an acquisition. In this way, high debt and debt costs are avoided. Therefore, the debt costs do not prevent long-term investments such as R&D, and managerial discretion in the use of cash flow is relatively flexible. Another attribute of successful acquisition strategies is an emphasis on innovation, as demonstrated by continuing investments in R&D activities. Significant R&D investments show a strong managerial commitment to innovation, a characteristic that is increasingly important to overall competitiveness, as well as acquisition success, in the 21st-century landscape.

Flexibility and adaptability are successful acquisitions' final two attributes. When both the acquiring and the target firms' executives have experience in managing change, they will be more skilled at adapting their capabilities to new environments. As a result, they will be more adept at integrating the two organisations, which is particularly important when firms have different organisational cultures. Adaptation skills allow the two firms to integrate their assets more quickly, efficiently and effectively. In turn, rapid, efficient and effective integration may quickly produce the desired synergy in the newly created firm.

The attributes and results of successful acquisitions are summarised in Table 7.1. Managers seeking acquisition success should emphasise the seven attributes that are listed. As explained in the Strategic Focus, Cisco Systems, Inc. uses an acquisition strategy quite successfully. While reading the Strategic Focus, notice how many of these attributes of effective acquisitions apply to this firm.

Table 7.1 | Attributes of successful acquisitions

	Attributes	Results
1	Acquired firm has assets or resources that are complementary to the acquiring firm's core business	High probability of synergy and competitive advantage by maintaining strengths
2	Acquisition is friendly	Faster and more effective integration; possibly lower premiums
3	Acquiring firm selects target firms and conducts negotiations carefully and deliberately	Firms with strongest complementarities are acquired and overpayment is avoided
4	Acquiring firm has financial slack (cash or a favourable debt position)	Financing (debt or equity) is easier and less costly to obtain
5	Merged firm maintains low to moderate debt position	Lower financing cost, lower risk (e.g. of bankruptcy) and avoidance of trade-offs associated with high debt)
6	Has experience with change and is flexible and adaptable	Faster and more effective integration facilitates achievement of synergy
7	Sustained and consistent emphasis on R&D and innovation	Maintain long-term competitive advantage in markets

[handwritten annotation next to item 3: "effective due diligence process"]

As we have learned, some acquisitions – particularly those characterised by the attributes shown in Table 7.1 – enhance strategic competitiveness. Certainly, this is the case with Cisco Systems, Inc. which earned US$2.1 billion in net income in fiscal-year 1999 on a sale volume of US$12.1 billion.[134] However, the majority of acquisitions that took place from roughly the 1970s to the 1990s did not enhance firms' strategic competitiveness. In fact, some researchers observe that 'history shows that anywhere between one-third [and] more than half of all acquisitions are ultimately divested or spun-off'.[135] Thus, firms often use restructuring strategies to correct for the failure of a merger or an acquisition. According to Peter Drucker, restructuring strategies are being used more frequently. To support his view, he observes that, on a single, yet typical, day in the business world, the *Wall Street Journal* reported that 'Hewlett-Packard was spinning off its [US]$8 billion business in test and measuring instruments, Procter & Gamble was selling its adult-incontinence business to a mid-sized company, and the Harris Co. was selling its entire semi-conductor business to a small company'.[136]

Restructuring

The failure of an acquisition strategy is often the driver of a restructuring strategy.[137] Among the famous restructurings taken to correct for an acquisition failure are: (1) AT&T's US$7.4 billion purchase of NCR and subsequent spin-off of the company to shareholders in a deal valued at US$3.4 billion; (2) Novell's purchase of WordPerfect for stock valued at US$1.4 billion and its selling of the company to Corel for US$124 million in stock and cash; and (3) SmithKline Beecham's purchase of Diversified Pharmaceutical Services for US$2.3 billion and its sale of Diversified to Express Scripts for US$700 million and US$300 million in tax benefits.[138] In other instances, however, firms use a restructuring strategy because of changes in their external and internal environments. For example, different opportunities sometimes surface in the external environment that are particularly attractive to the diversified firm in light of the core competencies that have been developed in its internal environment. In such cases, restructuring may be appropriate to position the firm so that it can create more value for stakeholders, given the environmental changes. In the United States, restructuring strategies are also used to gain the support of financial analysts – individuals who value firms' efforts to operate efficiently and effectively in the challenging global economy.[139] Regardless of the reason for its use, a restructuring strategy changes the composition of a firm's business portfolio.[140]

Strategic Focus Corporate

Successful acquisitions the Cisco Systems way

Cisco Systems, Inc. provides end-to-end networking solutions that customers use to connect to someone else's network or to build a unified information infrastructure of their own. Essentially, Cisco provides the hardware and software that are behind state-of-the-art Internet networks. Cisco, the global leader in networking for the Internet, generates over US$12 billion in annual sales, and, in early 2000, was recognised as the company creating the second-highest amount of capital for its shareholders.

Contributing significantly to Cisco's strategic competitiveness and its ability to consistently earn above-average returns is the company's acquisition strategy. CEO John Chambers, architect of that strategy, believes that advancing technology precludes Cisco from doing everything itself. As a result, corporate growth is achieved by acquiring firms with products and technologies the firm cannot or does not want to develop internally.

Cisco is highly active with its acquisition strategy. For example, during the six-and-a-half-year period ending in March 2000, Cisco had acquired 51 companies, with 21 of the acquisitions completed in the last 12 months of that period. Mid-year 2000 figures showed that the firm was on pace to complete at least 25 acquisitions in that year. Not every one of Cisco's acquisitions has been successful. CEO Chambers says that, of the dozens and dozens of acquisitions his firm has made, two or three have not met his expectations. But to prevent people who joined Cisco as part of a less-than-satisfactory acquisition experience from viewing their former top-level management team as a failure, Chambers chooses not to identify his acquisition disappointments. An overall evaluation of Cisco's acquisition strategy causes some analysts to suggest that 'Cisco has succeeded repeatedly in using acquisitions to reshape itself and plug holes in its product line'. Survey results identify Cisco as the most successful company using a merger and acquisition strategy. Yahoo! Inc. and US West, Inc. study Cisco's acquisition strategy, while competitors Lucent Technologies, Inc. and Nortel Networks Corp. attempt to mimic it.

What accounts for Cisco's successful acquisition strategy? Clearly, CEO Chambers deserves a great deal of credit. Appointed to the position in 1991, he conceived the strategy in 1993 and continues to fine-tune it today with the assistance of valued employees. With high expectations of those working with and for him, Chambers has been instrumental in the development of acquisition guidelines to which Cisco adheres rigorously. Although it is occasionally tempting to pass over one of the five inviolate guidelines to complete a prospective acquisition, Chambers says that 'it takes courage to walk. It really does. You can actually get caught up in winning the acquisition rather than making the thing successful.' Because of its commitment to the five acquisition guidelines, Cisco has refused to finalise a number of acquisitions.

Having a shared vision is the first of the five acquisition guidelines. Chambers believes that the acquiring company and the target firm must be in agreement regarding where the industry is going and the role each party is to play in the industry's anticipated future. Creating short-term wins for employees in the acquired firm is the second guideline. According to Chambers, these people must 'see a future. They've got to see a culture they want to be a part of. They have got to see an opportunity to really do what they were doing before or even more.' A company strategy that blends with Cisco's is the third guideline. In this context, the target firm's strategy must be one that, when integrated with Cisco's operations, will create value for shareholders, employees, customers and business partners. Cultural similarity and compatibility is the fourth guideline. Chambers and his colleagues are sceptical of efforts other companies take to integrate cultures that differ dramatically from one another. Finally, target firms must be geographically proximate to parts of Cisco's current operations with which they would be most closely associated. Geographic dispersion between units prevents the development of operational efficiencies, in Cisco's view.

Facilitating compliance with the five guidelines is the work of Cisco's integration team. Approximately three dozen Cisco employees work full-time 'shepherding newcomers into the fold'. Largely because of work this group completes before an acquisition is finalised, negotiations between Cisco and target companies tend to be brief. For example, only two-and-a-half hours of negotiations spread over three days were required for Cisco to finalise its US$7.2 billion acquisition of Cerent Corp. At the time, this was the largest dollar transaction of all acquisitions Cisco had completed during Chambers's tenure.

Sources: Cisco Systems, Inc., 2000, *Cisco Systems Home Page*, 4 March: www.cisco.com; S. Thurm, 2000, 'Under Cisco's system, mergers usually work: That defies the odds', *Wall Street Journal*, 1 March, pp. A1, A12; J. Daly, 1999, 'John Chambers: The art of the deal', *Business 2.0*, October, pp. 106–16; H. Goldblatt, 1999, 'Cisco's secrets', *Fortune*, 8 November, pp. 177–82; R. Karlgaard, 1999, 'Digital rules', *Forbes*, 14 June, p. 43.

Restructuring is a strategy through which a firm changes its set of businesses or financial structure.

Defined formally, **restructuring** is a strategy through which a firm changes its set of businesses or financial structure.[141] From the 1970s to the 1990s, divesting businesses from company portfolios and downsizing accounted for a large percentage of firms' restructuring strategies.[142]

Firms can adopt three types of restructuring strategies: downsizing, downscoping, and leveraged buyouts.

Downsizing

Once thought to be an indicator of organisational decline, downsizing is now recognised as a legitimate restructuring strategy.[143] **Downsizing** is a reduction in the number of a firm's employees and, sometimes, in the number of its operating units, but it may or may not change the composition of businesses in the company's portfolio. Thus, downsizing is an intentional proactive management strategy, whereas 'decline is an environmental or organizational phenomenon that occurs involuntarily and results in erosion of an organization's resource base'.[144] For example, Qantas Airways hopes to improve its profitability by reducing its workforce by 1500 and withdrawing flight services on unprofitable routes.[145]

The late 1980s and the decade of the 1990s saw the loss of thousands of jobs in private and public organisations throughout Australia and the United States. For example, one study estimates that 85 per cent of *Fortune* 1000 firms have used downsizing as a restructuring strategy.[146] Moreover, evidence suggests that, in spite of generally robust economic growth in many nations as the 21st century begins, 'the organisational downsizing juggernaut continues unabated'.[147]

Firms use downsizing as a restructuring strategy for different reasons. The most frequently cited reason is that the firm expects improved profitability from cost reductions and more efficient operations. For example, Bausch & Lomb, Inc. recently reduced its global workforce by 7 per cent in order to consolidate or restructure its contact-lens operations. The company expected these actions to produce at least US$30 million in payroll savings annually, beginning in 2001. Bausch & Lomb anticipated further savings through the phasing out of older equipment in favour of more efficient machinery. To restore sales growth and to 'revive a flagging culture of innovation', Procter & Gamble (P&G) decided to cut 15 000 jobs from its operations. The cuts, called for by the firm's Organization 2005 restructuring plan, accounted for 13 per cent of P&G's worldwide workforce. P&G expected annual savings of at least US$900 million by 2004 as a result of its downsizing decision. In Australia, a number of large firms have used downsizing to decrease costs and improve profitability. Three of the largest Australian downsizings during the 1990s were by Telstra (reducing its workforce from 81 000 to 66 000 employees), Foster's Brewing Group (reducing its workforce from 21 304 to 8 304 employees) and Mayne Nickless (reducing its workforce from 40 000 to 29 000 employees).[148]

In Japan, Malox, a logistics company and a unit of Mazda Motor Corp., tried for five years to restructure without layoffs. However, cost reductions and improvements in operational efficiency from these actions fell short of Mazda and Ford's expectations. Although downsizing was difficult because of the historical tradition in Japanese companies to avoid layoffs, Malox's executives finally decided to eliminate 100 of its 440 company-wide jobs as a key part of the firm's overall restructuring strategy.[149]

Downscoping

Compared to downsizing, downscoping has a more positive effect on firm performance.[150] **Downscoping** refers to divestiture, spin-off or some other means of eliminating businesses that are unrelated to a firm's core businesses. Commonly, downscoping is described as a set of actions that causes a firm to strategically refocus on its core businesses. A firm that downscopes often also downsizes simultaneously.[151] However, it does not eliminate key employees from its primary businesses in the process, because such action could lead to a loss of one or more core competencies. Instead, a firm

Chapter 7 Acquisition and restructuring strategies

that is simultaneously downscoping and downsizing becomes smaller by reducing the diversity of businesses in its portfolio. Following restructuring through downscoping, a firm can be managed more effectively by its top management team. Managerial effectiveness increases because the firm has become less diversified, allowing the top management team to better understand and manage the remaining businesses, primarily the core and other related businesses.[152]

In general, US firms use downscoping as a restructuring strategy more frequently than do European or Australian companies. Highlighting this reality are research findings indicating that 'there is a powerful post-war trend towards the building of more conglomerates among the top 100 domestically-owned French, German and British industrial companies'.[153] However, there has been an increase in downscoping by European firms. For example, RWE, the large German energy and industrial group, is restructuring through downscoping. Aiming to become a multi-energy, multi-utility company with a 15 per cent share of the European energy market by 2010, RWE intends to hold stakes in 'companies such as Hechtief, the construction group, E-Plus, the mobile telephone group, or Heidelberger printing machines, as pure financial investments, perhaps as a prelude to spin-offs'. Thus, by downscoping, RWE is abandoning the unrelated diversification strategy that drove the firm's growth during the 1980s and 1990s.[154]

Among the US-based firms using downscoping as a restructuring strategy, Walt Disney Co. sold its Fairchild Publications unit to Advance Publications, Inc. for US$650 million. Disney is also seeking to divest its baseball and hockey teams. As of the beginning of 2000, buyers had not been located for these units. According to analysts, sales of the sports teams and other operations (for example, a magazine called *Los Angeles*) 'would fit in with Disney's continuing drive to pare down or dispose of non-core operations. That drive [began in 1999], as Disney faced a deepening earnings slump.'[155] ConAgra performed well in the 1980s through the use of an unrelated diversification strategy. Implemented through an acquisition strategy, the diversification strategy resulted in ConAgra becoming a conglomerate with roughly 90 independent companies that make products from fertilisers to Slim Jim meat snacks. Analysts argue that the firm's recent

Walt Disney Co. is using downscoping as a restructuring strategy. The firm sold its Fairchild Publications unit and is seeking to divest its baseball and hockey teams. Hong Kong's CEO, Tung Chee-Hwa, is shown here in 1999 with Mickey Mouse at a press conference to announce a deal between the Hong Kong government and Disney for the building of a theme park.

profitability problems indicate that it is due for a serious downscoping effort. In response to its difficulties, the firm's top-level managers are restructuring their company's operations into 10 product groups under three main divisions – food service (restaurants), retail (grocery stores) and agricultural products.[156]

Downscoping emerged as a restructuring strategy among Australian firms during the late 1990s. Three of Australia's most diversified conglomerates – Boral, BHP and CSR – expressed their desire to increase their focus on core business units, divesting themselves of a number of their former business activities.[157] Downscoping has also become a strategic option for smaller Australian businesses, such as the Western Australian company, Bristle Ltd, which has sold its interest in timber milling to focus on its other core building products business.[158] This appears consistent with a trend in which Australian firms follow American firms after a lag of a number of years. Within Australia, downscoping has often led to assets being sold overseas. For example, when Pacific Dunlop moved out of food production, it sold its interest in Edgell to the American-based J. R. Simplot Company Limited.

Restructuring strategies may require a considerable amount of time before a firm is able to divest a sufficient number of operations so that it can refocus on its core business or businesses. This may or may not prove to be the case with Walt Disney Co. and ConAgra, though it has been for Ralston Purina, which intends to spin off its Eveready battery division, 'leaving the once highly-diversified group focused entirely on pet food'. However, Ralston has been restructuring almost since it purchased Eveready in 1986 and, analysts say, the firm's 'long-running restructuring has seen it dispose of bakeries, baby food [manufacture], animal feed [production], and ski resorts'.[159]

Leveraged buyouts

Commonly, leveraged buyouts are used as a restructuring strategy to correct for managerial mistakes or because managers are making decisions that primarily serve their own interests rather than those of shareholders.[160] A **leveraged buyout (LBO)** is a restructuring strategy whereby a party buys all of a firm's assets in order to take the firm private. Once the transaction is completed, the company's stock is no longer traded publicly. Usually, significant amounts of debt are incurred to finance an LBO. To support debt payments and to downscope the company so that managers can concentrate on the firm's core businesses, the owners of a firm created through an LBO may immediately sell, or attempt to sell, a number of assets.[161] It is not uncommon for those buying a firm through an LBO to restructure the firm to the point that it can be sold at a profit within a five- to eight-year period. A well-known finance scholar predicted that this restructuring strategy would become very prominent, but this has not proved to be the case.[162] In fact, as a percentage of the total merger and acquisition market in the United States, LBOs fell to 0.8 per cent towards the end of 1999, compared with 4.1 per cent in 1990.[163]

Management buyouts (MBOs), employee buyouts (EBOs) and whole-firm buyouts, in which one company or partnership purchases an entire company instead of a part of it, are the three types of LBOs. In part because of managerial incentives, MBOs, more so than EBOs and whole-firm buyouts, have been found to lead to downscoping, an increased strategic focus and improved performance.[164] As a case in point, Fender Musical Instruments, a unit of CBS, was performing poorly. In 1981, William Schultz was hired as the top-level executive and was charged with making decisions that would result in a turnaround at Fender. After four years of effort, Schultz decided to complete an MBO so that Fender could operate more independently than it was permitted to do under CBS

> A leveraged buyout (LBO) is a restructuring strategy whereby a party buys all of a firm's assets in order to take the firm private.

ownership. Heavily leveraged at the outset, with US$11 in debt for every US$1 in equity, the firm's performance improved steadily after the MBO was executed in 1985. More than 10 years later, Fender's annual volume reached US$300 million. In addition, Fender commanded almost 50 per cent of the guitar market, and is seen by electric guitar players as the brand to own, a mark of status in the world of 'garage bands'. The group Schultz assembled to complete the MBO thus saw its US$500 000 investment grow to more than US$100 million in value.[165]

Improvements at UAL (parent of United Airlines) and Avis Rent A Car are attributed to EBOs at those firms. The UAL arrangement appears to be working better than that at Avis. At UAL, there has been more of a cooperative spirit with gains in market share and above-average returns.[166] At Avis and other firms that have opted for EBOs, difficulties have surfaced between management and employees. Furthermore, few employee owners have been requested to sit on boards.[167] These problems are similar to problems experienced with EBOs in Russia: needed restructuring is hard to accomplish because of employee job security fears;[168] and when change is needed, more problems usually occur between managers and employees.

Whole-firm LBOs, on the other hand, often produce improvements through downsizing and retrenchment. This approach is illustrated by a buyout of Dr Pepper by Forsmann Little, an LBO specialist. Dr Pepper was successful enough to receive a new infusion of capital through an initial public offering. Subsequently, the firm was purchased by Cadbury Schweppes, PLC.[169]

Restructuring outcomes

The short- and long-term outcomes resulting from the three restructuring strategies are shown in Figure 7.2. As indicated, downsizing does not commonly lead to a higher firm performance. Commenting about this, two researchers noted that 'annual surveys conducted by the American Management Association show that only 41 per cent of downsizing companies have reported productivity increases, and only 37 per cent have realized any long-term gains in shareholder value'.[170] Still, in free-market-based societies at large, downsizing has generated a host of entrepreneurial opportunities for individuals to operate their own businesses. In fact, as discussed in Chapter 13, start-up ventures in the United States are growing at three times the rate of the national economy.[171]

Another researcher's findings about downsizing are also informative. This particular study showed that downsizing contributed to lower returns in both US and Japanese firms in the group of companies that was examined. In effect, these findings indicate that the stock markets in the firms' respective nations evaluated the downsizings negatively (that is, investors concluded that downsizing would have a negative effect on companies' ability to achieve strategic competitiveness in the long term). An interpretation of the findings is that downsizing occurs as a consequence of other problems in a company.[172] As an example, in 2000, Coca-Cola announced a reduction of 21 per cent of its 29 000-plus-strong global workforce, including what analysts saw as an 'astonishing 40 per cent at [the company's] headquarters'. The largest downsizing in the firm's history, this decision was viewed by some as an admission 'that the company had gone down the wrong road'.[173]

Coca-Cola's decision to reduce its workforce may also demonstrate another concern that often surfaces when firms use downsizing as a restructuring strategy. As shown in Figure 7.2, downsizing tends to result in a loss of human capital in the long term. Losing employees with many years – perhaps even decades – of experience with a firm creates a vacuum in terms of knowledge. As noted in Chapter 3, knowledge is the foundation for

Figure 7.2 | Restructuring and outcomes

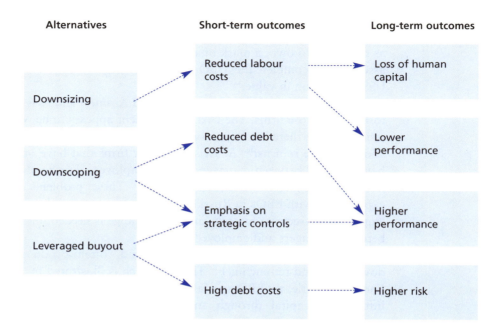

the type of organisational learning that is vital to competitive success in the global economy.[174] As regards Coca-Cola, it has been noted that 'analysts and company observers question whether [the firm] is cutting too many people in too many different places'.[175] Thus, in general, research evidence and corporate experience suggest that downsizing may be of more tactical (that is, short-term) than strategic (that is, long-term) value (see Chapter 5).

As Figure 7.2 indicates, downscoping leads to more positive outcomes in both the short and the long term than does downsizing or engaging in an LBO. Downscoping's desirable long-term outcome of contributing to higher performance is a product of the positive short-term benefits of reduced debt costs and the emphasis on strategic controls that becomes possible once a firm restructures itself to concentrate on its core businesses – businesses that are less diverse in nature and are more familiar to the top-management team. However, downscoping's positive short- and long-term outcomes are achieved only when the firm uses that restructuring strategy properly – that is, in ways that allow the company to refocus on its core business or businesses.[176]

While whole-firm LBOs have been hailed as a significant innovation in the financial restructuring of firms, there can be negative trade-offs. First, the large debt increases the financial risk of the firm, as is evidenced by the number of companies that filed for bankruptcy in the 1990s after having executed a whole-firm LBO. Sometimes, the intent of the owners to increase the efficiency of the bought-out firm and sell it within five to eight years creates a short-term and risk-averse managerial focus. As a result, many of these firms fail to invest in R&D or take other major actions designed to maintain or improve the company's core competence.[177] However, research suggests that in firms with an entrepreneurial mind-set, buyouts can lead to greater innovation.[178]

The strategic competitiveness spawned and above-average returns earned by GE during Jack Welch's tenure as CEO demonstrate the value that can be created by using restructuring strategies effectively. Downscoping was the primary restructuring strategy implemented by GE in this time. Indicators of GE's success since Welch was appointed CEO in 1981 include the fact that the firm was at or near the top of *Fortune* magazine's 'Most Admired Corporations' list while Welch was the firm's chief executive.[179] Towards the end of Welch's time as CEO, GE had become the ninth-largest and second-most-profitable company in the world.[180]

The GE of 1999 was substantially different from the GE of 1981, when Welch assumed the company's top executive position. Under Welch, GE was restructured almost continuously to create greater efficiencies, globalise operations, and develop world-class managers and top-level executives. During his final year as CEO, Welch was passionate about electronic commerce. Believing that electronic commerce was the biggest revolution in business in his lifetime, Welch thought that the Web would change how business was conducted on a global scale and how firms should be organised to compete successfully in light of those changes. Welch intended to include employees, suppliers and customers in various activities to gather information required to determine how GE should restructure itself to exploit Web-based opportunities.[181]

Strategic Focus Corporate

BHP Billiton: A resources giant is created

The merger between BHP and South African resources giant Billiton has created one of the biggest resources firms in the world. It was a triumph for BHP's chairman, Don Argus, and its (American) CEO, Paul Anderson, who won the big institutional shareholders' approval, which was essential for the deal to go ahead. The deal will remain controversial for some time – the 'big Australian' will now become a world corporation with a listing on the London Stock Exchange, and its American CEO will be succeeded in two years by the head of merger partner Billiton, the South African, Brian Gilbertson.

This is a very big move indeed for BHP, but as the analysis below by Ivor Ries indicates, it is one that has met with investor approval. While it is more advantageous from the point of view of the Billiton shareholders than BHP shareholders, it is good for both. The history of BHP since 1984 has been turbulent, but since the ultimately disastrous purchase of Magma Copper in 1990, it has focused on overseas growth. The BHP view was that 2001 was the time to get big in order to survive. Merger was the only available means to that end. Billiton had complementary resources, the acquisition was friendly, negotiations were fairly careful, and the merged firm has a moderate debt position. These factors indicate that the merger may be successful. On the other hand, there are major challenges in sorting out the new structure for the merged firm, and BHP does not have a good record for flexibility – either culturally or organisationally.

This merger presents you with a great opportunity to track a major change in the corporate landscape. We therefore present below some background material on the merger which will be relevant to topics raised in later chapters of this book.

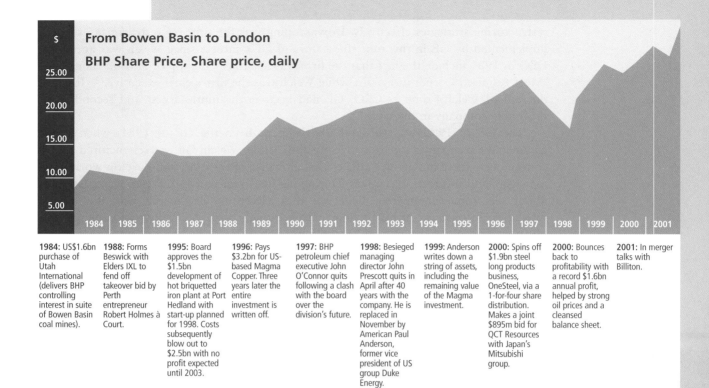

Dust settles but the hard yards lie ahead

BHP Billiton has silenced shareholder critics, but its success or failure will be judged on new projects, writes Ivor Ries.

Several thousand small shareholders met in Melbourne yesterday to grizzle and grumble about the loss of that quintessential icon of Australian industry and ingenuity – the Broken Hill Proprietary Company – to the forces of global capitalism.

But they need not have bothered. By the time the small shareholders of BHP trundled out of the Melbourne Concert Hall on Friday afternoon, global capitalism had already sealed the company's controversial merger with London-based Billiton plc with an $8 billion kiss.

Between March 16, the last day before the BHP Billiton merger was announced, and the close of yesterday's extraordinary general meeting, the combined value of the merging companies had risen by $8.1 billion. The steady rise in the share prices of both companies since the merger announcement – a ringing endorsement of the merger rationale by the world's professional fund managers – neutralised small shareholder and die-hard patriot concerns even before they were given a microphone.

Since the merger announcement, BHP shares have risen $2 a share, adding $3.4 billion to shareholder wealth. It was as if the darkest moment in BHP history – the $US3 billion wipeout on Magma Copper – had never happened.

While BHP shareholders are enjoying the company's record share price, they can also see clearly that they should have held Billiton shares. Billiton shares have risen 31 per cent in British pound terms and 24 per cent in $A terms, adding $4.7 billion to Billiton shareholder wealth.

That 57 per cent of the spoils (so far) of the biggest mining merger in history have gone to Billiton's shareholders – who theoretically own 42 per cent of the merged entity – displays clearly which group of shareholders got the better of the deal.

While the market likes the merger, the reality for BHP Billiton shareholders is that the merger will only deliver a real increase in shareholder wealth if the opportunities thrown up by the merger are seized and implemented. All the academic studies on mergers prove conclusively that post-merger integration and implementation of the merger plan are crucial if shareholders are to profit. Nine out of 10 mergers fail because implementation has been ignored.

Unfortunately for BHP boss Paul Anderson and his understudy, Brian Gilbertson, there are no textbooks on how to grow a $65 billion resources giant.

While there are dozens of larger companies around, there is only one other diversified resources giant in the same league: Rio Tinto.

Under chairman Bob Wilson, Rio Tinto's corporate strategy was essentially borrowed from Robert Holmes à Court: one takeover after another. The Rio strategy is essentially the same as that employed by Gilbertson at Billiton.

Analysts say that BHP's growth strategy will be a mixture of takeovers and organic growth from new projects.

Companies considered to be in BHP's takeover cross-hairs are nickel and copper giant WMC and Australia's leading oil and gas explorer-producer, Woodside Petroleum.

WMC would be a natural fit for BHP Billiton because Billiton has nickel and copper businesses. However, the downside is that half the value of WMC is made up of the company's 40 per cent stake in AWAC, an alumina giant controlled by Alcoa of the US. Because Alcoa and Billiton are the world's largest and fourth-largest aluminium producers respectively, competition regulators in Europe and the US would probably block a BHP Billiton takeover of WMC unless the company offloaded its most valuable asset.

Woodside is probably the easiest target for BHP. BHP has a large petroleum business (half of the Bass Straits field, one-sixth of the North-West Shelf and a large exposure to the Gulf of Mexico) that would marry perfectly with the Woodside portfolio. However, any deal with Woodside would necessitate striking a deal with Royal Dutch Shell, the company's 34 per cent shareholder.

While takeovers are expected to play a role in BHP Billiton's growth plans, analysts say that the merger will be judged a success or failure on how the merged company brings off new projects. One of the attractions cited by BHP in merging with Billiton was the latter company's suite of development projects.

Thanks to the US energy crisis – with power prices soaring to more than double long-term averages in some States – many US aluminium smelters are being forced to shut down.

The removal of 1 million to 2 million tonnes of aluminium capacity from world markets has created an opportunity for BHP Billiton to fast-track proposed expansions of its Mozal (Mozambique) and Hillside (South Africa) smelters. As Hillside and Mozal have low operating costs, any new capacity brought on stream would deliver instant profits.

A big expansion in BHP's steaming coal output is also on the cards. Billiton owns minority stakes in the Cerrejon Norte and Cerrejon Centrale coal deposits in Colombia, both earmarked for a big expansion, and analysts have speculated that Billiton would like to take a larger stake in both projects.

It took 118 years to build the company formerly known as the Big Australian. While the future that awaits BHP Billiton is undoubtedly big, most of the events that drive its fortunes certainly won't be Australian.

Source: *Australian Financial Review Weekend*, 19–20 May 2001, p. 13.

A deal short on great synergies

Trevor Sykes

Operationally, there are no great synergies to be gained from the merger of BHP and Billiton's mining assets.

It will be a merger of two groups of mining assets that have little in common geographically. The only synergies would appear to be whatever the groups can gain from their combined purchasing and selling power.

BHP said yesterday that benefits totalling $270 million had been identified in eliminating duplicated overheads, as well as efficiencies in procurement, exploration, marketing and technology. However, the $270 million benefits are not expected to be realised until the 2003 financial year, with more benefits to be realised afterwards.

While $270 million is a large number, it pales into insignificance in a $58 billion merger. Whether the combined group will have increased purchasing power is exceedingly doubtful. It might gain a little more leverage in coal talks with Japanese buyers, but only marginally.

The jewels in the BHP crown are – in no particular order – the Pilbara iron ore, the Queensland coalfields, Bass Strait oil, North-West Shelf gas, the Ekati diamond field in Canada and the Escondida copper mine in Chile. BHP also has a potentially huge sleeper in the deepwater Gulf of Mexico oil leases.

What does Billiton bring to the party to match these assets? It gets BHP into the aluminium business big time and gets it half of the great Richards Bay mineral sands deposit in South Africa; but after that it's a bit hard to find a third asset of the same quality.

Billiton's aluminium assets look pretty good. It has a majority interest in the Worsley alumina plant in Western Australia (most of it recently bought from Alcoa). It has aluminium smelters in South Africa and a smelter project in Mozambique. These would fill probably the largest gap in the BHP portfolio.

Richards Bay has for years been a dominant force in the mineral sand industry. It is the leading producer of titanium dioxide slag for the pigment industry, with high purity pig iron, zircon and rutile as important co-products. Billiton has a half interest in Richards Bay while the other half is owned by Rio Tinto, which is also the manager.

However, BHP's suite of assets appears far superior in all other areas. Also there are no places where Billiton and BHP have common operations for the same minerals, and where synergies can be easily seen.

In copper, the great asset is BHP's Escondida, producing 530,000 tonnes a year. BHP also has other good mines at Tintaya in Peru and Ok Tedi in Papua New Guinea.

In coal, the big producer would be Billiton's Ingwe Coal in South Africa, which controls eight mines. Billiton's share of production from Ingwe was some 60 million tonnes last year, but these appear to have been marginal operations, with most of Billiton's operating profit of $US59 million ($118 million) being made from its mines in NSW.

Ingwe looks a relatively low-margin operation compared to the profits generated from BHP's great Bowen Basin coalfields. There may be some synergies between the NSW coal operations of BHP and Billiton but they appear few as most of BHP's mines are in the Illawarra region whereas Billiton's main producer, Mount Arthur North, is near Muswellbrook at the north of the Hunter Valley.

BHP will be providing all the oil and gas operations which generated $2.7 billion revenue and $520 million profits last financial year before abnormals and tax. It will also provide all the iron ore assets, which generated $1.6 billion in sales last year and $640 million in profits.

The merger gets BHP into the nickel market, with production of some 53,000 tonnes a year from Yabulu in Queensland and Cerro Matoso in Colombia (which recorded its first profit last year). That's substantial, but barely half the output of WMC.

Those two divisions of BHP, incidentally, generated almost as much operating profit as the whole of Billiton for last financial year.

The country risk profile of the merged group will also be higher than for BHP alone. Many of Billiton's assets are in South Africa and South America.

The combined group will have 59 per cent of its net operating assets in those two regions. Of these, 21 per cent will be in South Africa, where BHP has no significant presence until now. Another 28 per cent will be in South America.

Source: *Australian Financial Review*, 20 March 2001, p. 14.

As we discuss in Chapter 9 and as was mentioned earlier in this chapter, cooperative strategies, such as strategic alliances, are an alternative to merger and acquisition strategies. Citing statistics, Peter Drucker suggests that alliances of all kinds, 'such as partnerships, a big business buying a minority stake in a small one, cooperative agreements in research or in marketing, joint ventures, and, often, handshake agreements with few formal and legally binding contracts behind them',[182] are being completed with greater frequency. When used because of a match between opportunities in the firm's external environment and the competitive advantages formed through its internal resources and capabilities, both cooperative strategies and merger and acquisition strategies can lead to competitive success.

Before examining cooperative strategies in detail in Chapter 9, however, we turn our attention to an analysis of international strategies. Because of the rapidly expanding global economy, international strategies are becoming more important drivers of strategic competitiveness for firms competing in all industries and countries.

Summary

- Acquisition strategies are increasingly popular among the world's firms. Because of globalisation, deregulation of multiple industries in many different economies and favourable legislation, among other factors, the number and size of domestic and cross-border acquisitions continues to increase.

- Firms use acquisition strategies to (1) increase market power, (2) overcome entry barriers to new markets or regions, (3) avoid the costs of developing new products internally and bringing them to market, (4) increase the speed of new market entries, (5) reduce the risk of entering a new business, (6) become more diversified, and (6) reshape their competitive scope through developing a different portfolio of businesses.

- Among the problems associated with the use of an acquisition strategy are (1) the difficulty of effectively integrating the firms involved, (2) incorrectly evaluating the target firm's value, (3) creating debt loads that preclude adequate investments (for example, R&D allocations) required for long-term success, (4) overestimating the potential for synergy between the companies involved, (5) creating a firm that is too diversified, given its core competencies and environmental opportunities, (6) creating an internal environment in which managers devote increasing amounts of their time and energy to analysing and completing additional acquisitions, and (7) developing a combined firm that is too large, necessitating an extensive use of bureaucratic, rather than strategic, controls.

- Although potentially problematic, acquisitions can contribute to a firm's strategic competitiveness. They do so when (1) the target firm is selected and purchased through careful, detailed analyses and negotiations, (2) the acquiring and target firms have considerable slack in the form of cash or debt capacity, (3) the acquiring firm has a low or moderate level of debt, (4) the newly created firm reduces its debt obligations quickly (especially the debts that were incurred to complete the acquisition) by selling off portions of the acquired firm or some of the acquiring firm's poorly performing companies, (5) the acquiring and target firms have complementary resources that can be the basis of core competencies in the newly created firm, (6) the acquiring and acquired firms have experience in terms of adapting to change (such experience increases the likelihood that the companies' operations will be integrated successfully), and (7) R&D and innovation are emphasised in the new firm.
- In the late 1980s and continuing into the present, restructuring is a strategy firms use to improve their performance by correcting for problems that were created by inappropriate or excessive diversification. Downsizing, a set of actions through which a firm's number of employees and hierarchical levels are reduced, is a restructuring strategy. Although it can lead to short-term cost reductions, they may be realised at the expense of long-term success. The reason for this is that once downsizing begins, the firm is unable to prevent an exodus of employees with skills required for strategic success. These employees might leave the focal firm to obtain positions with less uncertainty in other companies.
- With the goal of reducing the firm's level of diversification, downscoping is a second restructuring strategy. Often, it is accomplished by divesting unrelated businesses. As a result, the firm and its top-level managers are able to refocus on the core businesses. Firms sometimes downsize and downscope simultaneously, a comprehensive process that often yields better results than does downsizing.
- Leveraged buyouts (LBOs) are the third restructuring strategy. Through an LBO, a firm is purchased so that it can become a private entity. LBOs usually are financed largely through debt. There are three types of LBOs: management buyouts (MBOs), employee buyouts (EBOs), and whole-firm LBOs. Because they provide clear managerial incentives, MBOs have been the most successful of the three. Although EBOs have the potential to improve cooperation throughout the firm, power struggles are also a possibility. These struggles are more likely when significant change is required for a firm to improve its performance. In general, whole-firm LBOs have met with mixed success. Often, the intent is to improve efficiency and performance to the point where the firm can be sold successfully within five to eight years. However, the cost of debt incurred to finance the whole-firm LBO makes it difficult for companies to perform in ways that make them attractive candidates for purchase.
- Commonly, restructuring's primary goal is gaining or re-establishing effective strategic control of the firm. Of the three restructuring strategies, downscoping is aligned the most closely with establishing and using strategic controls. Once refocused on core businesses, as downscoping allows, managers can more easily control the firm because it is less diverse (in terms of products or markets) and the businesses that remain are those about which managers tend to be the most knowledgeable.

Review questions

1. Why are acquisition strategies popular in many firms competing in the global economy?
2. What specific reasons account for firms' decisions to use acquisition strategies as one means of achieving strategic competitiveness?
3. What are the seven primary problems that affect a firm's efforts to use an acquisition strategy successfully?
4. What are the attributes that have been found to be associated with the successful use of an acquisition strategy?
5. What is the restructuring strategy and what are its common forms?
6. What are the short- and long-term outcomes associated with the different restructuring strategies?

Application discussion questions

1. Evidence indicates that the shareholders of many acquiring firms gain little or nothing in value from the acquisitions. Why, then, do so many firms continue to use an acquisition strategy?
2. Of the problems that affect the success of an acquisition, which one do you believe is the most critical in the global economy? Why? What should firms do to make certain that they do not experience

such a problem when they use an acquisition strategy?
3. Use the Internet to read about acquisitions that are currently under way. Choose one of these acquisitions. Based on the firms' characteristics and experiences and the reasons cited to support the acquisition, do you think it will result in increased strategic competitiveness for the acquiring firm? Why or why not?
4. Using the Internet, study recent merger and acquisition activity that is taking place throughout the global economy. Are most of the transactions you found between domestic companies, or are they cross-border acquisitions? What accounts for the nature of what you found?
5. What is synergy, and how do firms create it through mergers and acquisitions? In your opinion, how often do acquisitions create private synergy? What evidence can you cite to support your position?
6. What can a top management team do to ensure that its firm does not become diversified to the point of earning negative returns from its diversification strategy?
7. Some companies enter new markets through internally developed products, while others do so by acquiring other firms. What are the advantages and disadvantages of each approach?
8. How do the Internet's capabilities influence a firm's ability to study acquisition candidates?

Ethics questions

1. Some evidence suggests that there is a direct and positive relationship between a firm's size and its top-level managers' compensation. If this is so, what inducement does that relationship provide to upper-level executives? What can be done to influence the relationship so that it serves shareholders' interests?
2. When a firm is in the process of restructuring itself by divesting some assets and acquiring others, managers may have incentives to restructure in ways that increase their power base and compensation package. Does this possibility explain at least part of the reason for the less-than-encouraging outcomes of acquisitions for shareholders of the acquiring firm?
3. When shareholders increase their wealth through downsizing, does this come, to some degree, at the expense of loyal employees – those who have worked diligently to serve the firm in terms of accomplishing its strategic mission and strategic intent? If so, what actions would you take to be fair to both shareholders and employees if you were charged with downsizing or 'smartsizing' a firm's employment ranks? What ethical base would you employ to make decisions regarding downsizing?
4. Are takeovers ethical? If not, why not?
5. Internet fever is mentioned in the Opening Case. Is it ethical for managers to acquire other companies just because industry competitors are doing so?

Internet exercise

Many interesting Internet sites, including the Australian Competition and Consumer Commission (ACCC) official site at www.accc.gov.au, offer information on mergers and acquisitions. With the increasing number of cross-border mergers and acquisitions, the ACCC has been required to work closely with enforcement agencies in other countries to regulate the new era of the global transaction.

e-project: Trace the history of some recent large mergers and acquisitions using the following Internet information sources: Daimler and Chrysler; BP Amoco and Arco; and Vodafone and Mannesmann. Use any other sources you find to obtain information on the official regulatory agencies that were involved in granting or denying permission for these mergers.

Notes

1. R. Whittington, 1999, 'In praise of the evergreen conglomerate', Mastering Strategy (Part Six), *Financial Times*, 1 November, pp. 4–6; M. A. Hitt, R. E. Hoskisson, R. D. Ireland and J. S. Harrison, 1991, 'Effects of acquisitions on R&D inputs and outputs', *Academy of Management Journal*, 34, pp. 693–706.
2. P. Moran and S. Ghoshal, 1999, 'Markets, firms, and the process of economic development', *Academy of Management Review*, 24, pp. 390–412.
3. T. A. Stewart, 2000, 'Managing risk in the 21st century', *Fortune*, 7 February, pp. 202–6.
4. R. Simons, 1999, 'How risky is your company?', *Harvard Business Review*, 77(3), pp. 85–94.
5. S. Sugawara, 1999, 'Merger mania spawns powerhouses as world enters new century', *Dallas Morning News*, 31 December, p. D11.
6. 'How M&A will navigate the turn into a new century', 2000, *Mergers & Acquisitions*, January, pp. 29–35.
7. B. Hale, 1999, 'Big aint necessarily beautiful', *Business Review Weekly*, 13 August, pp. 94–9.
8. 'How M&A will navigate', p. 30.
9. C. C. Markides, 1999, 'A dynamic view of strategy', *Sloan Management Review*, 40(3), pp. 55–63.
10. H. R. Greve, 1998, 'Managerial cognition and the mimetic adoption of market positions: What you see is what you do', *Strategic Management Journal*, 19, pp. 967–88.
11. B. Lowendahl and O. Revang, 1998, 'Challenges to existing strategy theory in a postindustrial society', *Strategic Management Journal*, 19, pp. 755–73.

12. D. L. Deephouse, 1999, 'To be different, or to be the same? It's a question (and theory) of strategic balance', *Strategic Management Journal*, 20, pp. 147–66.
13. M. A. Hitt, J. S. Harrison and R. D. Ireland, 2001, *Creating Value through Mergers and Acquisitions: A Complete Guide to Successful M&As* (New York: Oxford University Press); Hitt, Hoskisson, Ireland and Harrison, 'Effects of acquisitions', pp. 693–706.
14. A. Rappaport and M. L. Sirower, 1999, 'Stock or cash?', *Harvard Business Review*, 77(6), pp. 147–58.
15. Sugawara, 'Merger mania', p. D11.
16. 'M&A scorecard', 2000, *Mergers & Acquisitions*, January, pp. 40–2.
17. Hitt, Harrison and Ireland, *Creating Value*; K. C. O'Shaughnessy and D. J. Flanagan, 1998, 'Determinants of layoff announcements following M&As: An empirical investigation', *Strategic Management Journal*, 19, pp. 989–99.
18. J. Anand, 1999, 'How many matches are made in heaven', Mastering Strategy (Part Five), *Financial Times*, 25 October, pp. 6–7.
19. B. Deener, 1999, 'Mega-deals stifle shares, survey implies', *Dallas Morning News*, 30 November, pp. D1, D6.
20. N. Deogun and S. Lipin, 1999, 'Cautionary tales: When big deals turn bad', *Wall Street Journal*, 8 December, pp. C1, C28.
21. A. Ferguson, 1999, 'Time is up at Pacific Dunlop', *Business Review Weekly*, 1 February, pp. 72–8.
22. M. C. Jensen, 1988, 'Takeovers: Their causes and consequences', *Journal of Economic Perspectives*, 1(2), pp. 21–48.
23. Rappaport and Sirower, 'Stock or cash?', pp. 147–58.
24. Australian Competition and Consumer Commission, 1998, 'Coopers and Lybrand/Price Waterhouse merger not opposed', 13 March.
25. W. Mitchell, 1999, 'Recreating the company: Four contexts for change', Mastering Strategy (Part Ten), *Financial Times*, 29 November, pp. 4–7.
26. J. Kavanagh, 1999, 'AMP's hard slog', *Business Review Weekly*, 25 June, pp. 84–9.
27. M. Mellish, 2001, 'From among a deal's wreckage, a lesson for all', *Australian Financial Review*, 14 February, Supplement, p. 11.
28. S. Lipin, 1999, 'More big firms are ripe for hostile takeover bids', *Wall Street Journal*, 22 November, p. B10.
29. S. Tully, 2000, 'The new takeover target (Hint: It's in Detroit)', *Fortune*, 10 January, pp. 28–30.
30. Mitchell, 'Recreating the company', p. 7; D. K. Datta, G. E. Pinches and V. K. Naravyanan, 1992, 'Factors influencing wealth creation from mergers and acquisitions: A metaanalysis', *Strategic Management Journal*, 13, pp. 67–84; P. C. Haspeslagh and D. B. Jemison, 1991, *Managing Acquisitions: Creating Value Through Corporate Renewal* (New York: The Free Press).
31. M. L. Marks, 2000, 'Egos can make and unmake mergers', *Wall Street Journal*, 24 January, p. A26.
32. P. Haspeslagh, 1999, 'Managing the mating dance in equal mergers', Mastering Strategy (Part Five), *Financial Times*, 25 October, pp. 14–15.
33. Brambles Industries Limited, 2001, *Brambles Home Page*, 18 February: www.brambles.com.au.
34. L. Capron, 1999, 'Horizontal acquisitions: The benefits and risk to long-term performance', Mastering Strategy (Part Seven), *Financial Times*, 8 November, pp. 7–8.
35. L. Capron, 1999, 'The long-term performance of horizontal acquisitions', *Strategic Management Journal*, 20, pp. 987–1018.
36. Foster's Brewing Group, 2001, *Foster's Brewing Group Home Page*, 18 February: www.fosters.com.au.
37. K. Ramaswamy, 1997, 'The performance impact of strategic similarity in horizontal mergers: Evidence from the U.S. banking industry', *Academy of Management Journal*, 40, pp. 697–715.
38. L. B. Ward, 2000, 'Software companies to combine', *Dallas Morning News*, 15 February, pp. D1, D17.
39. Foster's Brewing Group, 2001, *Foster's Brewing Group Home Page*, 18 February: www.fosters.com.au.
40. Anand, 'How many matches', pp. 6–7.
41. R. Gertner and M. J. Knez, 1999, 'Vertical integration: Make or buy decisions', Mastering Strategy (Part Ten), *Financial Times*, 29 November, pp. 12–13.
42. M. Brannigan, 2000, 'Carnival agrees to buy Fairfield for stock, debt', *Wall Street Journal*, 25 January, p. A8.
43. M. Brannigan, 2000, 'Carnival, hit by stock dive, calls off talks to acquire Fairfield Communities', *Wall Street Journal*, 28 February, p. A15.
44. Australian Competition and Consumer Commission, 2001, 'ACCC Newsroom – ACCC rejects Qantas, Ansett revised proposal to acquire Hazelton', 18 January: www.accc.gov.au.
45. Australian Competition and Consumer Commission, 2001, 'ACCC Newsroom – ACCC to oppose acquisition of Australian Hospital Care by Mayne Nickless', 17 January: www.accc.gov.au.
46. J. Landers, 2000, 'Regulators increase scrutiny of mergers', *Wall Street Journal*, 4 February, pp. D1, D2.
47. T. Petzinger, Jr, 2000, 'So long, supply and demand', *Wall Street Journal*, 1 January, p. R31.
48. J. A. Gingrich, 1999, 'Five rules for winning emerging market consumers', *Strategy & Business*, 15, pp. 19–33.
49. Hitt, Harrison & Ireland, *Creating Value*, Chapter 10; D. Angwin and B. Savill, 1997, 'Strategic perspectives on European cross-border acquisitions: A view from the top European executives', *European Management Review*, 15, pp. 423–35.
50. N. Deogun, 1999, 'Made in U.S.A.: Deals from Europe hit record', *Wall Street Journal*, 25 October, pp. C1, C18.
51. G. Cramb, 1999, 'Off to New Amsterdam', *Financial Times*, 21 July, p. 12.
52. J. McCallum and M. Hannen, 2000, 'Foster's global wine push', *Business Review Weekly*, 10 November, pp. 72–8.
53. Bloomberg News, 1999, 'Kimberly-Clark planning acquisitions', *Dallas Morning News*, 1 December, p. D2; E. Robinson, 1999, 'Shiseido pursues M&A', *Financial Times*, 27 July, p. 14.
54. Cable and Wireless Optus, 2001, *Cable and Wireless Optus Home Page*, 19 February: www.cwo.com.au.
55. E. Portanger, 2000, 'Europe sets the stage for more megamergers', *Wall Street Journal*, 4 January, p. A17; 'Fortis to pay $2.6 billion for U.S. firm', *Wall Street Journal*, 8 March, p. A4; J. Martinson, 1999, 'Mergers spur expansion', *Financial Times*, 12 April, p. 3; S. Mehta and A. Raghavan, 1999, 'Europe is next frontier for U.S. telecom deals', *Wall Street Journal*, 25 October, p. B12.
56. J. K. Shank and V. Govindarajan, 1992, 'Strategic cost analysis of technological investments', *Sloan Management Review*, 34(3), pp. 39–51.
57. E. Mansfield, 1969, *Industrial Research and Technological Innovation* (New York: Norton).
58. Hitt, Harrison and Ireland, *Creating Value*; L. H. Clark, Jr and A. L. Malabre, Jr, 1988, 'Slow rise in outlays for research imperils U.S. competitive edge', *Wall Street Journal*, 16 November, pp. A1, A5; E. Mansfield, M. Schwartz and S. Wagner, 1981, 'Imitation costs and patents: An empirical study', *Economic Journal*, 91, pp. 907–18.
59. M. A. Hitt, R. E. Hoskisson, R. A. Johnson and D. D. Moesel, 1996, 'The market for corporate control and firm innovation', *Academy of Management Journal*, 39, pp. 1084–119.
60. M. Elvekrog, 2000, 'Watson Pharmaceuticals, Inc.', *Better Investing*, February, pp. 32–4.
61. R. Wherry, 1999, 'Pfizer's surpriser', *Forbes*, 29 November, p. 56.
62. D. Pilling, 1999, 'Big boys eye bite-sized bios', *Financial Times*, 15 July, p. 14.
63. K. F. McCardle and S. Viswanathan, 1994, 'The direct entry versus takeover decision and stock price performance around takeovers', *Journal of Business*, 67, pp. 1–43.
64. Rappaport and Sirower, 'Stock or cash?', p. 147.
65. M. Song, A. A. Di Benedetto and Y. L. Zhao, 1999, 'Pioneering advantages in manufacturing and service industries: Empirical evidence from nine countries', *Strategic Management Journal*, 20, pp. 811–36.
66. H. Lee, K. G. Smith, C. M. Grimm and A. Schomburg, 2000, 'Timing, order and durability of new product advantages with imitation', *Strategic Management Journal*, 21, pp. 23–30.
67. S. Stecklow, 2000, 'BT rides in to buy Ireland's Esat, topping bid by Norway's Telenor', *Wall Street Journal*, 12 January, p. A18.
68. McCallum and Hannen, 'Foster's global wine push'.
69. 'Kraft Foods agrees to buy Boca Burger, a soy-products firm', 2000, *Wall Street Journal*, 19 January, p. B7.
70. G. McWilliams, 2000, 'Compaq buying custom-PC lines of Inacom, with Dell in mind', *Wall Street Journal*, 15 January, p. B2.
71. M. A. Hitt, R. E. Hoskisson and R. D. Ireland, 1990, 'Mergers and acquisitions and managerial commitment to innovation in M-form firms', *Strategic Management Journal*, 11(Special Summer Issue), pp. 29–47.
72. S. Branch, 2000, 'P&G is out to fetch distribution gains for Iams pet foods', *Wall Street Journal*, 6 January, p. A6.
73. Hitt, Hoskisson and Ireland, 'Mergers and acquisitions'; J. Constable, 1986, 'Diversification as a factor in U.K. industrial strategy', *Long Range Planning*, 19, pp. 52–60.
74. Hitt, Hoskisson, Ireland and Harrison, 'Effects of acquisitions'; Hitt, Hoskisson and Ireland, 'Mergers and acquisitions'.

Chapter 7 Acquisition and restructuring strategies

75 Wesfarmers Limited, 2001, *Wesfarmers Home Page*, 19 February: www.wesfarmers.com.au.
76 J.-F. Hennart and S. B. Reddy, 2000, 'Digestibility and asymmetric information in the choice between acquisitions and joint ventures: Where's the beef?', *Strategic Management Journal*, 21, pp. 191–3.
77 D. D. Bergh, 1997, 'Predicting divestiture of unrelated acquisitions: An integrative model of ex ante conditions', *Strategic Management Journal*, 18, pp. 715–31.
78 J. Anand and H. Singh, 1997, 'Asset redeployment, acquisitions and corporate strategy in declining industries', *Strategic Management Journal*, 18 (Special Summer Issue), pp. 99–118.
79 HIH Insurance, 2001, *HIH Insurance Home Page*, 18 February: www.hih.com.au.
80 T. Burt, 1999, 'DaimlerChrysler looks to diversify', *Financial Times*, 3 August, p. 16.
81 J. Griffiths, 1999, 'Spotlight falls on Japanese', *Financial Times*, 27 May, p. 1; J. Griffiths, 1999, 'Fitter future for Ford as Nasser takes the driving seat', *Financial Times*, 13 April, p. 24.
82 G. Blainey, 1993, *Jumping Over the Wheel* (Sydney: Allen & Unwin).
83 P. Landers and R. A. Guth, 2000, 'Japan's Hitachi plans high-tech shopping spree', *Wall Street Journal*, 5 January, p. A19.
84 Marks, 'Egos can make', p. A26.
85 Anand, 'How many matches', p. 7.
86 Hitt, Harrison and Ireland, *Creating Value*; D. K. Datta, 1991, 'Organizational fit and acquisition performance: Effects of post-acquisition integration', *Strategic Management Journal*, 12, pp. 281–97.
87 A. J. Viscio, J. R. Harbison, A. Asin and R. P. Vitaro, 1999, 'Post-merger integration: What makes mergers work?', *Strategy & Business*, 17, pp. 26–33; H. Aaron, 1994, 'A poisoning of the atmosphere', *Wall Street Journal*, 29 August, p. A10; P. M. Elsass and J. F. Veiga, 1994, 'Acculturation in acquired organizations: A force field perspective', *Human Relations*, 47, pp. 453–71.
88 S. DeVoge and S. Spreier, 1999, 'The soft realities of mergers', *Across the Board*, December, pp. 27–32; A. F. Buono and J. L. Bowditch, 1989, *The Human Side of Mergers and Acquisitions* (San Francisco: Jossey-Bass).
89 M. Zollo, 1999, 'M&A the challenge of learning to integrate', Mastering Strategy (Part Eleven), *Financial Times*, 6 December, pp. 14–15.
90 Ibid., p. 14.
91 N. Knox, 1999, 'AlliedSignal, Honeywell plan rapid integration of companies', *Dallas Morning News*, 8 June, p. D4.
92 R. L. Simison and S. Miller, 1999, 'Making "digital" decisions', *Wall Street Journal*, 24 September, pp. B1, B4.
93 A. Ferguson, 'Culture is the key to BT merger', *Business Review Weekly*, 2 July, p. 83.
94 H. Goldblatt, 1999, 'Cisco's secrets', *Fortune*, 8 November, pp. 177–82.
95 Anand, 'How many matches', p. 7; K. Ohmae, 1999, 'The Godzilla companies of the new economy', *Strategy & Business*, 18, pp. 130–9.
96 Rappaport and Sirower, 'Stock or cash?', p. 149.
97 Viscio, Harbison, Asin and Vitaro, 'Post-merger integration', p. 27.
98 Kavanagh, 'AMP's hard slog'.
99 Mellish, 'From among a deal's wreckage, a lesson for all'.
100 Ibid.
101 R. C. Morais, 2000, 'Takeover bait', *Forbes*, 24 January, pp. 74–5.
102 Hitt, Harrison and Ireland, *Creating Value*.
103 G. Yago, 1991, *Junk Bonds: How High Yield Securities Restructured Corporate America* (New York: Oxford University Press), pp. 146–8.
104 M. C. Jensen, 1987, 'A helping hand for entrenched managers', *Wall Street Journal*, 4 November, p. A6; M. C. Jensen, 1986, 'Agency costs of free cash flow, corporate finance, and takeovers', *American Economic Review*, 76, pp. 323–9.
105 A. Osterland, 1999, 'False spring for a seed company', *Business Week*, 12 June, p. 130.
106 M. A. Hitt and D. L. Smart, 1994, 'Debt: A disciplining force for managers or a debilitating force for organizations?', *Journal of Management Inquiry*, 3, pp. 144–52.
107 Hitt, Harrison and Ireland, *Creating Value*.
108 C. J. Chipello, 2000, 'Abitibi agrees to purchase Donohue in $4 billion cash-and-stock accord', *Wall Street Journal*, 14 February, p. A32.
109 T. N. Hubbard, 1999, 'Integration strategies and the scope of the company', Mastering Strategy (Part Eleven), *Financial Times*, 6 December, pp. 8–10.
110 Hitt, Harrison and Ireland, *Creating Value*.
111 C. H. St. John and J. S. Harrison, 1999, 'Manufacturing-based relatedness, synergy, and coordination', *Strategic Management Journal*, 20, pp. 129–45.
112 Hitt, Hoskisson, Ireland and Harrison, 'Effects of acquisitions'; J. B. Barney, 1988, 'Returns to bidding firms in mergers and acquisitions: Reconsidering the relatedness hypothesis', *Strategic Management Journal*, 9 (Special Summer Issue), pp. 71–8.
113 O. E. Williamson, 1999, 'Strategy research: Governance and competence perspectives', *Strategic Management Journal*, 20, pp. 1087–108.
114 Hitt, Hoskisson, Johnson and Moesel, 'The market for corporate control'.
115 Whittington, 'In praise of', p. 4.
116 C. W. L. Hill and R. E. Hoskisson, 1987, 'Strategy and structure in the multiproduct firm', *Academy of Management Review*, 12, pp. 331–41.
117 R. A. Johnson, R. E. Hoskisson and M. A. Hitt, 1993, 'Board of director involvement in restructuring: The effects of board versus managerial controls and characteristics', *Strategic Management Journal*, 14 (Special Issue), pp. 33–50; C. C. Markides, 1992, 'Consequences of corporate refocusing: Ex ante evidence', *Academy of Management Journal*, 35, pp. 398–412.
118 A. Ferguson, 2000, 'Pacific Dunlop skids towards the parts yard', *Business Review Weekly*, 28 January, p. 36.
119 A. Ferguson, 'Time is up at Pacific Dunlop', *Business Review Weekly*, 1 February, pp. 72–8.
120 R. E. Hoskisson and M. A. Hitt, 1988, 'Strategic control systems and relative R&D investment in large multiproduct firms', *Strategic Management Journal*, 9, pp. 605–21.
121 Hitt, Hoskisson and Ireland, 'Mergers and acquisitions'.
122 Ibid.
123 Ibid.
124 J. Flint, 'No guts, no glory', *Forbes*, 7 February, p. 88.
125 Hitt, Hoskisson, Ireland and Harrison, 'Effects of acquisitions'.
126 R. E. Hoskisson, M. A. Hitt and R. D. Ireland, 1994, 'The effects of acquisitions and restructuring (strategic refocusing) strategies on innovation', in G. von Krogh, A. Sinatra and H. Singh (eds), *Managing Corporate Acquisitions* (London: Macmillan Press), pp. 144–69.
127 Hitt, Hoskisson and Ireland, 'Mergers and acquisitions'.
128 K. Ohmae, 2000, 'The Godzilla companies of the new economy', *Strategy & Business*, 18, pp. 130–9.
129 Hitt, Harrison and Ireland, *Creating Value*.
130 J. S. Harrison, M. A. Hitt, R. E. Hoskisson and R. D. Ireland, 1991, 'Synergies and post acquisition performance: Differences versus similarities in resource allocations', *Journal of Management*, 17, pp. 173–90; Barney, 'Returns to bidding firms'.
131 M. A. Lubatkin and P. J. Lane, 1996, 'Psst ... The merger mavens still have it wrong!', *Academy of Management Executive*, X(1), pp. 21–39.
132 J. P. Walsh, 1989, 'Doing a deal: Merger and acquisition negotiations and their impact upon target company top management turnover', *Strategic Management Journal*, 10, pp. 307–22.
133 L. S. Lublin, 1995, 'Strategies for preventing post-takeover defections', *Wall Street Journal*, 28 April, pp. B1, B8.
134 J. Daly, 1999, 'John Chambers: The art of the deal', *Business 2.0*, October, pp. 106–16.
135 Anand, 'How many matches', p. 6.
136 P. F. Drucker, 2000, 'The unrecognized boom', *Across the Board*, January, pp. 15–16.
137 R. E. Hoskisson, R. A. Johnson and D. D. Moesel, 1994, 'Divestment intensity of restructuring firms: Effects of governance, strategy and performance', *Academy of Management Journal*, 37, pp. 1207–51.
138 Deogun and Lipin, 'Cautionary tales', p. C1.
139 S. R. Fisher and M. A. White, 2000, 'Downsizing in a learning organization: Are there hidden costs?', *Academy of Management Review*, 25, pp. 244–51.
140 R. A. Johnson, 1996, 'Antecedents and outcomes of corporate refocusing', *Journal of Management*, 22, pp. 437–81.
141 J. E. Bethel and J. Liebeskind, 1993, 'The effects of ownership structure on corporate restructuring', *Strategic Management Journal*, 14 (Special Summer Issue), pp. 15–31.
142 A. Campbell and D. Sadtler, 1998, 'Corporate breakups', *Strategy & Business*, 12, pp. 64–73; E. Bowman and H. Singh, 1990, 'Overview of corporate restructuring: Trends and consequences', in L. Rock and R. H. Rock (eds), *Corporate Restructuring* (New York: McGraw-Hill).
143 Fisher and White, 'Downsizing in a learning organization', p. 244.
144 W. McKinley, J. Zhao and K. G. Rust, 2000, 'A sociocognitive interpretation of organizational downsizing', *Academy of Management Review*, 25, pp. 227–43.
145 M. Smith, 2001, 'Qantas considers no-frills option', *The Mercury*, 26 February, p. 4.

146 W. McKinley, C. M. Sanchez and A. G. Schick, 1995, 'Organizational downsizing: Constraining, cloning, learning', *Academy of Management Executive*, IX(3), pp. 32–44.

147 McKinley, Zhao and Rust, 'A sociocognitive interpretation', p. 227.

148 J. Kirby, 1999, 'Downsizing gets the push', *Business Review Weekly*, 22 March, pp. 50–4.

149 N. Shirouzu, 2000, 'Driven by necessity and by Ford Mazda downsizes, U.S.-style', *Wall Street Journal*, 5 January, pp. A1, A8; A. Edgecliffe-Johnson, 1999, 'Procter & Gamble to cut 15,000 jobs in restructuring', *Financial Times*, 10 June, p. 1; J. Hechinger, 1999, 'Bausch & Lomb to cut its work force, restructure contact-lens operation', *Wall Street Journal*, 3 December, p. B14.

150 Hoskisson and Hitt, 'Downscoping'.

151 J. S. Lublin, 1995, 'Spin offs may establish new companies, but they often spell the end of jobs', *Wall Street Journal*, 21 November, pp. B1, B8; J. Kose, H. P. Lang and J. Netter, 1992, 'The voluntary restructuring of large firms in response to performance decline', *Journal of Finance*, 47, pp. 891–917.

152 Johnson, Hoskisson and Hitt, 'Board of directors involvement'; R. E. Hoskisson and M. A. Hitt, 1990, 'Antecedents and performance outcomes of diversification: A review and critique of theoretical perspectives', *Journal of Management*, 16, pp. 461–509.

153 Whittington, 'In praise of', p. 4.

154 R. Atkins, 1999, 'German business giants evolve to meet new challenges', *Financial Times*, 24 June, p. 23.

155 B. Orwall and M. Rose, 2000, 'Disney may sell Los Angeles magazine as it pares down noncore operations', *Wall Street Journal*, 19 January, p. B7.

156 B. Copple, 2000, 'Synergy in ketchup?', *Forbes*, 7 February, pp. 68–9.

157 N. Tabakoff, 2000, 'Big spreads get down and focused', *Business Review Weekly*, 21 January, pp. 50–2.

158 M. Drummond, 2001, 'Timber sale lets Bristle chase core acquisitions', *Australian Financial Review*, 14 February, p. 18.

159 A. Edgecliffe-Johnson and M. Marsh, 1999, 'Ralston plans to spin off Eveready arm', *Financial Times*, 11 June, p. 18.

160 D. D. Bergh and G. F. Holbein, 1997, 'Assessment and redirection of longitudinal analysis: Demonstration with a study of the diversification and divestiture relationship', *Strategic Management Journal*, 18, pp. 557–71; C. C. Markides and H. Singh, 1997, 'Corporate restructuring: A symptom of poor governance or a solution to past managerial mistakes?', *European Management Journal*, 15, pp. 213–19.

161 M. F. Wiersema and J. P. Liebeskind, 1995, 'The effects of leveraged buyouts on corporate growth and diversification in large firms', *Strategic Management Journal*, 16, pp. 447–60.

162 M. C. Jensen, 1989, 'Eclipse of the public corporation', *Harvard Business Review*, 67(5), pp. 61–74.

163 'LBO signposts', 1999, *Mergers & Acquisitions*, November/December, pp. 47–56.

164 A. Seth and J. Easterwood, 1995, 'Strategic redirection in large management buyouts: The evidence from post-buyout restructuring activity', *Strategic Management Journal*, 14, pp. 251–74; P. H. Phan and C. W. L. Hill, 1995, 'Organizational restructuring and economic performance in leveraged buyouts: An ex-post study', *Academy of Management Journal*, 38, pp. 704–39.

165 M. Matzer, 1996, 'Playing solo', *Forbes*, 25 March, pp. 80–1.

166 S. Chandler, 1996, 'United we own', *Business Week*, 18 March, pp. 96–100.

167 A. Bernstein, 1996, 'Why ESOP deals have slowed to a crawl', *Business Week*, 18 March, pp. 101–2.

168 I. Filatochev, R. E. Hoskisson, T. Buck and M. Wright, 1996, 'Corporate restructuring in Russian privatizations: Implications for US investors', *California Management Review*, 38(2), pp. 87–105.

169 B. Ortega, 1995, 'Cadbury seeking a new king of pop to oversee no. 3 soft-drink business', *Wall Street Journal*, 30 January, p. B2.

170 Fisher & White, 'Downsizing in a learning organization', p. 244.

171 Petzinger, Jr, 'So long', p. R31.

172 P. M. Lee, 1997, 'A comparative analysis of layoff announcements and stock price reactions in the United States and Japan', *Strategic Management Journal*, 18, pp. 879–94.

173 H. Unger, 2000, 'Coke cutbacks show company went down wrong path', *Wall Street Journal*, 30 January, p. H6.

174 Fisher & White, 'Downsizing in a learning organization'.

175 Unger, 'Coke cutbacks', p. H6.

176 Johnson, 'Antecedents and outcomes'.

177 W. F. Long and D. J. Ravenscraft, 1993, 'LBOs, debt, and R&D intensity', *Strategic Management Journal*, 14 (Special Summer Issue), pp. 119–35.

178 M. Wright, R. E. Hoskisson, L. W. Busenitz and J. Dial, 2000, 'Entrepreneurial growth through privatizing: The upside of management tryouts', *Academy of Management Review*, in press.

179 Whittington, 'In praise of', p. 6.

180 T. A. Stewart, 1999, 'See Jack. See Jack run', *Fortune*, 27 September, pp. 124–36.

181 Ibid.

182 Drucker, 'The unrecognized boom', p. 15.

Chapter 8

International strategy

Objectives

After reading this chapter, you should be able to:

1. Explain traditional and emerging motives for firms to pursue international diversification.
2. Explore the four factors that lead to a basis for international business-level strategies.
3. Name and define generic international business-level strategies.
4. Define the three international corporate-level strategies: multi-domestic, global and transnational.
5. Discuss the environmental trends affecting international strategy.
6. Name and describe the five alternative modes for entering international markets.
7. Explain the effects of international diversification on firm returns and innovation.
8. Name and describe two major risks of international diversification.
9. Explain why the positive outcomes from international expansion are limited.

Technology and globalisation: A changing landscape in the 21st century

As described in Chapter 1, technology and the globalisation of business have created a new competitive landscape for the 21st century. In short, technology and globalisation have interacted to create an ongoing revolution. In particular, the development and use of new technology facilitate increasing globalisation. Two types of technology – the Internet and wireless communications – are having profound effects on the way business is conducted worldwide.

The Internet now allows rapid and effective communication and coordination of units and operations on a global basis. It also facilitates business-to-business (B2B) relationships (for example, between supplier and customer) and increases the speed with which innovations are diffused throughout the world. While the Internet revolution largely emanated from the United States, the rest of the world is participating as well. Although the United States accounted for approximately 75 per cent of e-commerce in 1998, it is expected to account for only about 50 per cent of global e-commerce by 2003. In Australia, e-commerce spending will grow from $17 billion in 2000 to $235 billion in 2005, with 22 per cent of inter-company transactions expected to be on-line. Further, consumer retailing purchases over the Internet are estimated to triple by 2003. Numbers of Internet hosts per 1 000 people provides an indication of different levels of Internet penetration in the OECD. (Hosts are computers connected to the Internet that provide data and services.) Finland leads with 122.8 hosts per 1 000 people, with the United States at 118.6. Australia has 60.8 hosts per 1 000, close to that of our neighbour New Zealand with 61.3. At the bottom of the table, Turkey and Mexico have only 2.1 hosts per 1 000 people, indicating considerable difficulty in using the Internet for sales in these countries.

Likewise, mobile phones are becoming ubiquitous and used for multiple purposes. For example, it is becoming increasingly common for school children (as young as 10 years old) to carry mobile phones in Sweden, and approximately 58 per cent of all people in Finland owned mobile phones in early 2000. Phones that allow people to connect to the Internet and perform many of the tasks normally confined to computers are becoming more widely available. In fact, mobile phone technology will bring the Internet to locations throughout the world that have been slow to adopt computer-based connections. The number of mobile phones in use is growing at more than twice the rate of new fixed (wired) telephone connections annually. This third generation of mobile telephony will dramatically increase the speed of data transmission and greatly enlarge the number of users of such phones globally. Mobile phones are a cheaper and easier (that is, more user-friendly) means of accessing the Internet than computers are and thus will be available to a larger number of people. Currently, the most wired nations are the United States and Western European countries, but the global potential for increased e-commerce is substantial. For example, although there were 4 million Internet users in China in 1999, it is predicted that the country will have 27 million users in 2001. The potential for this rapid increase in the number of Internet users in China rests with the introduction of mobile phone connections to the Internet.

For all of the preceding reasons, many firms are rushing to join the global e-commerce revolution. For instance, 7-Eleven Japan is leading the development of an e-commerce joint venture with seven other firms to offer goods and services through the Internet and multimedia portals in 8 000 Japanese 7-Eleven outlets. The goal is to expand this service to 7-Eleven stores globally. In 1999, Australia's Telstra Corporation identified that its mobiles, Internet and data, and international business segments were among its strategic growth areas.

Primarily domestic and multinational companies such as General Motors (GM) and Ford have joined the e-commerce revolution to extend their global reach. GM uses e-commerce to reach emerging markets. Firms in emerging-market countries such as Russia and Bulgaria in Eastern Europe are also increasing their use of e-commerce.

Another example is Ford and GM's competition to create increased global standardisation of parts through Web-based systems. Both GM (via its TradeXchange system) and Ford (via its AutoXchange) are seeking to dominate the Web-based marketplace for automobile manufacturers and suppliers.

Evidence of the increasing importance of e-commerce is shown by Intel's decision to develop 'server farms'. These server farms are intended to provide companies with the capability of conducting e-commerce. Intel located its first server farm in Reading, in England. This location houses 10 000 Internet servers and a staff of 170 people. These farms target small businesses that do not have the internal resources to support e-commerce activities. Intel projects that demand for servers will increase by 2 500 per cent by 2005. Accordingly, Intel expects to locate server farms throughout Europe to meet the fast-growing demand. Indeed, e-commerce activities will extend the reach of even small businesses across the globe.

In sum, two trends – the Internet and wireless telecommunication – as well as their combined use (Internet connections on mobile phones) are facilitating increased communications and e-commerce on a global basis. Although e-commerce initially spread rapidly in the United States and Western Europe because of those regions' dedicated telecommunication and computer infrastructures, it has now become a global revolution made possible by a broader availability and use of mobile communication devices.

www.ford.com
www.gm.com
www.intel.com
www.7dream.com
www.sej.co.jp
www.telstra.com.au

Sources: N. Shirouzu, 2000, 'Toyota may join Ford's web system', *Wall Street Journal*, 25 January, p. A13; S. Baker, 2000, 'Cell-phone central: Finland leads the wireless charge', *Businessweek Online*, 6 January: www.businessweek.com; J. Borzo, 2000, 'Court ruling in Russia may mean more order in Internet industry', *Wall Street Journal Interactive*, 6 January: www.interactive.wsj.com.articles; J. Dodge, 1999, 'Auto makers are shifting gears to accelerate a net revolution', *Wall Street Journal Interactive*, 13 July: www.interactive.wsj.com.articles; C. Grande, 1999, 'E-commerce: U.S to retain global lead': www.ft.com.nbearchive; C. Grande, 2000, 'Shopping: E-spending will triple by 2003', 17 January: www.ft.com.nbearchive; B. Groom, 2000, 'Intel: Berkshire hosts 90m server farm', 20 January: www.ft,com,nbearchive; R. Grover, 2000, 'Univision peers into Cyberspace', *Businessweek Online*, 9 January: www.businessweek.com; A. Kaiser, 2000, 'Bulgaria, LVMH strike deal to team up for online sales', *Wall Street Journal Interactive*, 6 January: www.interactive.wsj.com.articles; P. Landers, 1999, 'In Japan, the hub of E-Commerce is a 7-Eleven', *Wall Street Journal*, 1 November, pp. B1, B4; M. J. Mandel, 1999, 'The Internet economy: The world's next growth engine', *Businessweek Online*, 27 September; C. Matlack, J. Ewing, G. Edmondson and W. Echikson, 1999, 'Cashing in on an Internet bonanza', *Business Week*, 13 December, p. 62; N. Nakamae, 2000, 'Seven-Eleven: Online arm to launch', 7 January: www.ft.com.nbearchive; R. Quick, 2000, 'Federated to invest up to $200 million in web business; 2000 Stock takes dive', *Wall Street Journal Interactive*, 17 January: www.interactive.wsj.com.articles; 'Seven-Eleven Japan, NEC, Others JV called 7dream.com', 2000, *Wall Street Journal Interactive*, 6 January: www.interactive.wsj.com.articles; 'Seven-Eleven Japan reveals e-commerce joint venture', 2000, *Wall Street Journal Interactive*, 6 January: www.interactive.wsj.com.articles; 'The world in your pocket', 2000, *Economist.Com*, 6 January: www.economist.com/editorial; F. Warner, 1999, 'GM tests e-commerce plans in emerging markets', *Wall Street Journal*, 25 October, p. B4; B. Howarth, 2001, 'E-business 2006', *Business Review Weekly*, 9 February; A. Ferguson, 1999, 'Telstra's Master Plan', *Business Review Weekly*, 10 September; OECD, 2000, *OECD in Figures*.

In the 1980s, the dramatic success of Japanese firms and products, such as Toyota and Sony, in international markets provided a powerful jolt to managers and awakened them to the importance of international competition and global markets. In the 1990s, Russia and China represented potential major international market opportunities for firms from many countries, including the United States, Japan, Korea and European nations.[1] They also represented potentially formidable competitors – particularly China, in low-technology manufacturing industries. However, concerns have been expressed about the relative attractiveness of the Russian and Chinese markets for companies competing in the global marketplace. The economic crises in Russia in the latter 1990s lent credibility to these concerns. Some believe that, for at least a period of time, foreign investors will continue to favour China, because China is more orderly while Russian markets remain risky. Russia's movement to more of a free-market economy now seems more likely to depend on home-grown developments instead of foreign direct investments (FDI) and other modes firms use to internationalise their operations.²

The 21st century may find less focus on a particular region of the world and more emphasis on truly global markets. For geographic reasons, trade with Asian markets will remain important to Australian businesses in the short term, while companies like Foster's have now adopted a world focus (see the later Strategic Focus). An emphasis on global markets is facilitated by the developments in technology. Parallel developments in the Internet and mobile telephony facilitate communications all over the globe. Furthermore, these developments have led to the e-commerce revolution that is now prevalent in the business world. The global e-commerce phenomenon is exemplified by the venture led by 7-Eleven in Japan, whereby portals to the Internet to offer goods and services for sale are available in 8 000 7-Eleven stores. The interface between the Internet and mobile telephony is evidenced by Japanese firm, DoMoCo, which provides access to the Internet on mobile telephones. DoMoCo is taking this service global.

E-commerce is not restricted to large firms. Intel's server farms provide the technology necessary for small firms to participate in e-commerce. Thus, even small firms can sell their goods and services globally without having (bricks and mortar) facilities outside of their home location. Technology is promoting increasingly rapid globalisation of markets and business. This revolution is evident all over the world. For example, Brazil's Internet market is expanding quickly. Terra Brasil, an Internet provider controlled by Telefónica of Spain, acquired ZAZ, the second-largest Internet provider in Brazil. This action followed an announcement by two of Brazil's largest private banks to offer free Internet services. Other free Internet services are expected to enter the Brazilian market, some by way of the current largest service providers.³ In Australia, vibrant competition exists for Internet service provision among major telecommunications companies; many of these companies have significant foreign ownership.

Clearly, the international arena features both opportunities and threats for firms seeking strategic competitiveness in global markets. This chapter examines opportunities facing firms as they seek to develop and exploit core competencies by diversifying into global markets. In addition, we discuss different problems and complexities that can be associated with the implementation of a firm's chosen international strategies. National boundaries, cultural differences and geographical distances no longer pose barriers to business and entry into many markets. Business has become truly global, in markets ranging from drugs and tyres to publishing and engineering.⁴ Selecting and implementing appropriate international strategies allows the firm to become a global corporation. However, to mould their firms into truly global companies, managers must develop global mind-sets. Traditional means of operating with little cultural diversity and without global competition are no longer effective.⁵ Developing a global mind-set among managers without international experience and with little experience with cultural diversity is challenging. Of course, firms experiencing these challenges are slower to change. Providing international experiences may be required to more quickly build global mind-sets among a firm's managers.⁶ For example, Cemex rapidly changed from a domestic cement manufacturer in the Mexican market to a global producer of cement, largely through the acquisitions of cement firms in Latin America, Asia, North America and Europe. In fact, Cemex has played an important role in developing a global cement industry. For example, 60 per cent of Asia's cement market is now served by multinationals, up from only 20 per cent a few years ago. Cemex's managers had little experience with global markets, as its managers and those of the firms it acquired had focused primarily or solely on their domestic cement market. Thus, the company established an extensive management development program designed to help its managers build a global mind-set.[7] News Corporation, a company founded in Australia, now has global networks in the print and electronic media. Its global mind-set board members undertook strategic acquisitions in countries such as Britain and the United States to develop its global market reach.

As firms move into international markets, they develop relationships with suppliers, customers and partners, and they learn from these relationships. In fact, partners learn from each other and begin to develop more similar policies over time. Firms also learn from their competitors in international markets. In effect, they begin to imitate the policies of each other in order to compete more effectively in those markets.[8] Such activity is evident in the drug industry as firms compete against each other in global pharmaceutical markets.[9] Australia's only two domestic whitegoods makers are foreign-owned following Electrolux of Sweden's recent acquisition of Email, while Fisher & Paykel is a New Zealand company. Through industry standardisation and implementing quality manufacturing processes, Korean-produced whitegoods with some components sourced from China have higher selling margins in Australia than locally produced goods of equivalent quality. Australian producers will be forced to source components from similar countries to remain competitive.[10]

In this chapter, as illustrated in Figure 1.1 in Chapter 1, we discuss the importance of international strategy as a source of strategic competitiveness and above-average returns. The chapter focuses on the incentives to internationalise. Once a firm decides to compete internationally, it must select its strategy and choose a mode of entry into international markets. It may enter international markets by exporting from domestic-based operations, licensing some of its products or services, forming joint ventures with international partners, acquiring a foreign-based firm or establishing a new subsidiary. Such international diversification can extend product life cycles, provide incentives for more innovation and produce above-average returns. These benefits are tempered by political and economic risks and the problems of managing a complex international firm with operations in multiple countries. Figure 8.1 provides an overview of the various choices and outcomes. The relationships among international opportunities, and the exploration of resources and capabilities that result in strategies and modes of entry that are based on core competencies, are explored in this chapter.

Identifying international opportunities: The incentive to pursue an international strategy

An **international strategy** refers to the selling of products in markets outside a firm's domestic market.

An **international strategy** refers to the selling of products in markets outside a firm's domestic market.[11] One of the primary reasons for implementing an international strategy (as opposed to a strategy focused on the domestic market) is that international markets yield potential new opportunities. Raymond Vernon captured the classic rationale for international diversification.[12] He suggested that, typically, a firm discovers an innovation in its home-country market, especially in an advanced economy such as that found in the United States. Some demand for the product may then develop in other countries, and exports are provided by domestic operations. Increased demand in foreign countries justifies direct foreign investment in production capacity abroad, especially because foreign competitors also organise to meet increasing demand. As the product becomes standardised, the firm may rationalise its operations by moving production to a region where manufacturing costs are low. Vernon, therefore, suggests that firms pursue international diversification to extend a product's life cycle.

Figure 8.1 | Opportunities and outcomes of international strategy

Another traditional motive for firms to become multinational is to secure needed resources. Key supplies of raw material – especially minerals and energy – are important in some industries. For instance, aluminium producers need a supply of bauxite, tyre firms need rubber, and oil companies scour the world to find new petroleum reserves.

Others seek to secure access to low-cost factors of production. Clothing, electronics, watchmaking and many other industries have moved portions of their operations to foreign locations in pursuit of lower costs. For example, to enhance its cost competitiveness, GE in the United States began shifting some of its appliance-manufacturing operations to various locations throughout the world. All of the firm's gas ranges are now made in San Luis Potosí, Mexico, through the firm's joint venture with Mabe, a Mexican company. In all, GE employs over 24 000 people in Mexico, primarily to manufacture appliances.[13] The situation in Australia's whitegoods industry, described earlier, exemplifies the effect of low-cost factors of production on local competition.

Turkey's wage rates are among the lowest in Europe. In fact, the nation's hourly rates average half of those in Portugal, the poorest country in the European Union. Moreover, wages are lower than in some Eastern European countries and many developing nations. Because of these wage rates, coupled with the fact that workers' productivity is increasing by 3.6 per cent annually, compared to the OECD average of 2.8 per cent, many multinational companies are establishing operations in Turkey. In fact, foreign investments have caused Turkey's economy to grow at a rate that has actually created labour shortages.[14] Indonesia, Thailand and Vietnam are examples of countries in the Asia-Pacific region with relatively low wage rates.

Although these traditional motives persist, other emerging motivations have been driving international expansion (see Chapter 1). For instance, pressure has increased for a global integration of operations, mostly driven by more universal product demand. As nations industrialise, the demand for commodities appears to become more similar.[15] This nationless or borderless demand may be due to similarities in lifestyle in developed nations. Also, increases in global communication media facilitate the ability of people in different countries to visualise and model lifestyles in disparate cultures.[16]

In some industries, technology is driving globalisation because economies of scale necessary to reduce costs to the lowest level often require an investment greater than that needed to meet domestic market demand.[17] There is also pressure for cost reductions, achieved by purchasing from the lowest-cost global suppliers. For instance, R&D expertise for an emerging business start-up may not exist in the domestic market.[18]

New large-scale markets, such as China and India, also provide a strong incentive because of the potential demand in those countries. And, because of currency fluctuations, firms may desire to have their operations distributed across many countries in order to reduce the risk of devaluation in one country.[19] This desire notwithstanding, the unique nature of emerging markets, such as China, presents major growth opportunities. The uniqueness of those markets presents both opportunities and challenges.[20] China, for example, differs from Western countries in many respects, including culture, politics and the precepts of its economic system.[21] However, China offers a huge potential market. While its differences from Western countries are numerous, many international firms perceive Chinese markets as almost virgin markets, without exposure to many modern and sophisticated products. With such exposure, these firms believe that demand will develop. However, the differences pose serious challenges for Western competitive paradigms that emphasise the need for possession of the skills to manage financial, economic and political risks. Although a recent study found that the costs and availability of capital in China made it the worst country in the world to do business in, it is unlikely to deter foreign companies from accessing Chinese markets, given that it is preparing to enter the World Trade Organization.[22]

Many Australian businesses rely on exporting goods and services to Asian markets due to regional proximity and attractive demand conditions. Companies seeking to internationalise their operations should be aware of increased pressure on them to respond to local, national or regional customs, especially where goods or services require customisation because of cultural differences or effective marketing to entice customers

As an emerging market, China differs from Western countries in terms of culture, politics and economic system. Many international firms believe that demand will develop when virgin markets are exposed to modern and sophisticated products.

to try a different product.²³ For example, food products often have to be adapted to local tastes. However, Danone, an international French provider of food products, either acquires local companies to meet local needs or uses marketing in an attempt to help local customers acquire new tastes. In recent years, Danone has acquired local water companies in Indonesia, China and the United States. It has also acquired a number of local food providers in Latin America. In addition, the firm has attempted to overcome local dietary attitudes towards its products, such as yoghurt, with marketing. Danone is the global leader in providing dairy products, with particularly strong sales of its yoghurt worldwide. Because of its skill in adapting to international markets, Danone is among the top 10 food and beverage firms (in sales revenue) in the world.²⁴

The frequent need for local repair and service is another factor influencing an increased desire for local country responsiveness. This localisation may even affect industries that are seen as needing more global economies of scale, such as whitegoods.²⁵ Alternatively, it is becoming increasingly common for suppliers to follow their customers, particularly large ones, into international markets. When they do so, the need to find local suppliers is eliminated.²⁶ However, for large products, such as heavy earthmoving equipment, transportation costs are significant. Employment contracts and labour forces differ significantly as well. For example, it is more difficult to negotiate employee layoffs in Europe than in the United States, because of employment contract differences. Often, host governments demand joint ownership, which allows the foreign firm to avoid tariffs. Also, host governments frequently require a high percentage of local procurements, manufacturing and R&D. These issues increase the need for local investment and responsiveness, compared to seeking global economies of scale.

Given the traditional and emerging motivations for expanding into international markets, firms may achieve four basic benefits from international diversification: (1) increased market size; (2) greater returns on major capital investments or on investments in new products and processes; (3) greater economies of scale, scope or learning; and (4) a competitive advantage through location (for example, access to low-cost labour, critical resources or customers). These opportunities to enhance the firm's strategic competitiveness are examined relative to both the costs incurred to pursue them and the managerial challenges that accompany international diversification decisions. Higher coordination expenses, a lack of familiarity with local cultures, and limited access to knowledge about political influences in the host country are examples of costs firms incur when pursuing international diversification.²⁷

Increased market size

Firms can expand the size of their potential market, sometimes dramatically, by moving into international markets. In 2000, Telstra began negotiating a strategic alliance with Hong Kong-based Pacific Century CyberWorks (PCCW) allowing access to mobile telephone networks and the Internet in Asian markets such as Hong Kong and China. The Internet protocol backbone business encompassed in the proposal would create the world's second-biggest data carrier while giving Telstra access to a customer base many times larger than Australia.²⁸ The alliance appears to gain Telstra a strong presence and credibility in Asia.²⁹

Changing consumer tastes and practices linked to cultural values or traditions is not simple. For example, when the cereal market in the United States stagnated, the US cereal makers Kellogg and General Mills looked to international markets to revive their growth prospects. Initial efforts appeared to be successful. However, the dry cereal produced by these firms is not a staple in most European breakfasts. Thus, sales reached a peak, but then began to decline in the late 1990s. Kellogg had to close several manufacturing plants in Europe as its revenues and profits declined.[30]

Following an international strategy is a particularly attractive option to firms competing in domestic markets that have limited growth opportunities. For example, the US soft-drink industry is relatively saturated. Most changes in market share for any single firm must come at the expense of competitors' shares. Given this situation, two major soft-drink manufacturers, Coca-Cola and PepsiCo, entered international markets to take advantage of new growth opportunities. Pepsi moved into the former Soviet Union years ago; later, Coke entered China. Originally, each firm obtained an exclusive franchise in those countries; today, however, markets in Russia and China are more open. Coke gained competitive parity and has now surpassed Pepsi in Russia. Beyond this, Coke's volume exceeds Pepsi's in Europe, Latin America and Asia. In terms of overall volume, Coke outsells Pepsi almost three to one outside the United States. Recently, however, Coke suffered problems in several of its international markets, particularly in Europe. Because of these problems, Coke's profitability has declined and the company has begun to restructure.[31]

The size of a particular international market also affects a firm's willingness to invest in R&D to build advantages in that market. Larger markets usually offer higher potential returns and thus generally pose less risk for a firm's investments. The strength of the science base in the country in question also can affect a firm's foreign R&D investments. Most firms prefer to invest more heavily in those countries with the scientific knowledge and talent to produce more effective new products and processes from their R&D.[32]

In Chapter 5, we described the current transformation of the global automobile industry. As noted in that chapter, it is projected that only about six major automobile manufacturers will survive over time. The surviving firms will be large and wield considerable market power, thereby driving out smaller competitors. In fact, Renault's much-criticised acquisition of the troubled car maker Nissan was completed because of the need to build adequate market power in order to maintain a measure of competitive parity with the other large global car makers (for example, DaimlerChrysler, GM, Ford and Toyota). Analysts predict that eight to 10 years will be required before Renault realises a return on its investment in Nissan. Furthermore, if Nissan fails to perform, this investment may eliminate Renault's chances to survive as an independent company. Because of the importance of Nissan to Renault's future, the company has assigned the task of reviving it to tough, but successful, Brazilian-born executive Carlos Ghosn. In turn, he developed and implemented a drastic restructuring of the Japanese car maker that was designed to greatly reduce costs and increase efficiency in its manufacturing operations. Interestingly, Renault is also seeking to acquire other companies, particularly in Asia (especially Korea).[33] Australia's automotive assembly industry will undoubtedly face further structural change as the global manufacturing shake-out progresses.

Market size and a firm's market power do not guarantee success, however. For example, analysts argue that the merger between France's Seita and Spain's Tabacalera is unlikely to be successful. They suggest that the combination of two small, inefficient and poorly managed firms is likely to produce one large, inefficient and poorly managed firm.[34]

Return on investment

Large markets may be crucial for earning a return on significant investments, such as plant and capital equipment or R&D. Therefore, most R&D-intensive industries are international. For example, the aerospace industry requires heavy investments to develop new aircraft. To recoup their investments, aerospace firms may need to sell new aircraft in both domestic and international markets. This is the case for Boeing and Airbus Industrie. International sales are critical to the ability of each firm to earn satisfactory returns on its invested capital. Airbus is continuing to build its competitive ability. In fact, a merger in 1999 between two of its consortium owners, DASA (a DaimlerChrysler company) and Aerospatiale Matrais, was predicted to enhance the ability of Airbus to compete with Boeing in international markets. Boeing may need to take actions of its own, because Airbus captured more orders for civilian aircraft in 1999 than did Boeing.[35]

In addition to the need for a large market to recoup heavy investment in R&D, the development pace for new technology is increasing. As a result, new products become obsolete more rapidly. Therefore, investments need to be recouped more quickly. Beyond this, firms' abilities to develop new technologies are expanding, and because of different patent laws across country borders, imitation by competitors is more likely. Through reverse engineering, competitors are able to take apart a product, learn the new technology and develop a similar product that imitates the new technology (see Chapters 5 and 13). Because of competitors' abilities to do this relatively quickly, the need to recoup new-product development costs rapidly is increasing. Consequently, the larger markets provided by international expansion are particularly attractive in many industries (for example, computer hardware), because they expand the opportunity to recoup a large capital investment and large-scale R&D expenditures.[36] It must be emphasised, however, that the primary reason for making investments in international markets is to produce excellent returns on investments. Thus, expected returns from the investments represent a primary predictor of firms moving into international markets. Still, firms from different countries have different expectations and use different criteria to decide whether to invest in international markets.[37]

Economies of scale and learning

When firms expand their markets, they may be able to enjoy economies of scale, particularly in their manufacturing operations. Thus, to the extent that firms are able to standardise products across country borders and use the same or similar production facilities, thereby coordinating critical resource functions, they are likely to achieve more optimal economies of scale.[38] Economies of scale are critical in the global auto industry. As noted in Chapter 5 and earlier in the current chapter, only six global automobile firms are expected to survive because of the need for market power and efficiency to compete effectively. For instance, Honda has been a largely successful firm with substantial competencies in the manufacture of engines. However, it has problems competing against several larger and more resource-rich automobile manufacturers. Ford has US$23 billion in cash, whereas Honda has only about US$3.2 billion. GM invests approximately US$9 billion annually in R&D, while Honda can only invest about US$2.6 billion. As a result, Honda was not listed by PricewaterhouseCoopers as one of the expected surviving global six automobile manufacturers. A consultant for the firm suggested that Honda would have a chance if it could become large enough (to have adequate resources and gain comparable economies of scale). Honda has achieved economies of scale in the development and sale of its engines. It sells about 2 million automobiles annually, but sells 10 million engines (including lawn mower engines). Honda recently formed an alliance with GM to produce engines for some of its vehicles. Thus, perhaps Honda will survive as an independent engine manufacturer.[39] As noted in the preceding section, Australia's car assembly industry will need to remain efficient in light of the predicted changes.

Firms may also be able to exploit core competencies across international markets. This allows resource and knowledge sharing between units across country borders.[40] It generates synergy and helps the firm to produce higher-quality goods or services at lower cost. In addition, working across international markets provides an opportunity to learn. Multinational firms have substantial opportunities to learn from the different practices they encounter in separate international markets. Even firms based in developed markets can learn from operations in emerging markets.[41]

Location advantages

Firms may locate facilities in other countries to lower the basic costs of the goods or services they provide.[42] For example, they may have easier access to lower-cost labour, energy and other natural resources. Other location advantages include access to critical supplies and to customers. Once positioned favourably through an attractive location, firms must manage their facilities effectively to gain the full benefit of a location advantage.[43]

Telecommunications firms have sought specific location advantages in much of their international expansion efforts.[44] Deregulation in Australia's dairy sector and mergers of cooperative dairies in New Zealand have established the groundwork for a trans-Tasman milk products industry. The proposed Global Dairy Company has a significant shareholding in Australia's National Foods through one of its merger members, NZ Dairy Group. New Zealand earns 25 per cent of its export income from dairy products and its industry has become more efficient through merging small farms into larger properties. It appears that Australian companies like Australia's third-largest volume dairy company, Dairy Farmers in Sydney, are attractive potential alliance partners because of Australia's proximity and its efficient industry base on which to build further global competitiveness.[45]

As described in the Strategic Focus, the European Union is changing the competitive landscape in Europe and the world. It provides a large and unified market for European and foreign firms that is attracting considerable investment from international companies. In addition, European markets and firms are undergoing substantial changes to take advantage of economies of scale, economies of learning and advantages of location in the various European markets. The common currency and the integration of capital markets have reduced financial risks and made available significant amounts of capital that were previously unavailable in the separate country markets. Thus, European firms are growing in power and will challenge many of the world's prominent companies, including those from the United States and Asia.

Strategic Focus International

The decade of Europe: 2000–2010

Europe is undergoing a substantial transformation. Only a little more than a decade since the dramatic 'fall of the Berlin wall' and the collapse of the socialist regimes in Eastern Europe, a new economic and political architecture is emerging. The transformation is being shaped by technology and the globalisation of business, as described in Chapter 1. Economically, Europeans have made considerable gains. For instance, gross development product (GDP) in the new European Union (EU) increased by over 46 per cent during the decade of the 1990s, and the future is even brighter. During the same decade, inflation in the EU decreased by 77 per cent, automobiles per capita increased by 14.6 per cent, and even life expectancy increased, from 73 to 74 years. The EU produced a seamless market of over 290 million people. The introduction of the common currency, the euro, removed two barriers to economic development in Europe: the exchange rate risk and limited access to capital. The euro was introduced in 1999 and will be placed in full circulation in 2002. The use of the euro helps European firms to compete more effectively in global markets. A strong euro is welcomed in the rest of the world as well; it has helped to ease the economic crisis in Asia by increasing Asian firms' ability to compete in European markets. The strong euro also reduced the pressure on the US economy produced by the US trade deficit by helping US firms to compete more effectively in European markets. With the EU, Europe has joined the United States as a major driver of the world economy. Indeed, Europe has become a primary global growth engine. All but one of the EU members has adopted the euro (England is the sole hold-out). The EU has a US$6.5 trillion economy representing approximately 8.1 per cent of world trade.

The large pool and free flow of capital provides the means to finance large deals. Furthermore, to be competitive across the European markets and, externally, in global markets, firms needed to gain market power, achieve economies of scale and realise synergies. The implementation of the EU and the euro created and facilitated considerable incentives for large-scale mergers and acquisitions throughout Europe. In fact, one major business publication described the scene as consisting of mergers and acquisitions, American style, with hostile takeovers, substantial debt, and large fees for the investment bankers. Others described it as 'buyout fever'. European buyouts in 1999 were US$100 billion more than in 1998. Consolidation is the watchword in industries ranging from banking to telecommunications, most occurring across country boundaries (for example, the acquisition of Racal Electronics in the United Kingdom by the French firm Thomson-CSF). Consolidation also is exemplified by Cable & Wireless PLC's acquisition of eight Internet service providers throughout Europe. The companies that were acquired provide access primarily to business customers in Western Europe. The companies are located in Austria, Belgium, France, Italy, Spain and Switzerland. Cable & Wireless is a multinational firm controlling approximately 28 per cent of the Internet traffic in the United States as well.

While significant change engulfs most of Europe, resistance to change is also present. For example, four Italian top executives have forestalled change in their firms. These executives are well over the normal retirement age, and some refer to them as the 'corporate gerontocracy'. The four executives are Enrico Cuccia of Mediobanca, Cesare Romiti of Fiat, Giovanni Bazoli of Banco Ambrosiano and Alfonso Desiata of Assicurazioni Generali. These executives actually tightened their grip on power when analysts predicted changes that would likely reduce or even eliminate their power. However, their victory may be short lived as the EU comes into full bloom: these executives' firms may experience problems competing in the European markets, particularly against large, powerful and nimble rivals.

In some cases, the new Europe and its firms are gaining significant strength. These gains are exemplified by Airbus Industrie's besting of Boeing in 1999. Airbus garnered orders for 470 new commercial aircraft, compared to Boeing's 391 orders. Thus, Airbus captured 55 per cent of the global market for large commercial aircraft. In other sectors, the changes have not been kind to some venerable European competitors. For instance, Marks & Spencer, an old and formerly successful British retailer, is now experiencing significant problems. Marks & Spencer targets the 'middle market'. However, customers have been flocking to discounters and to the high-end market. Thus, Marks & Spencer's market has been shrinking, and the company has been unable to change its focus to other market niches. Marks & Spencer has tried to compete with the major discounters, but without success. It is also losing its traditional market to more attractive competitors, such as Gap and Next plc. In European banking, there has been considerable consolidation as well. However, prominent banks, such as Deutsche Bank, have reached beyond Europe. For example, Deutsche Bank acquired Bankers Trust in the United States. Deutsche Bank's goal is to become a universal bank. Of course, to do so, it must compete with the large and formidable US banks. In sum, there will be successes and failures in the new Europe. However, one can count on significant change, and, no doubt, the EU will be a prominent force in the world economy of the 21st century.

Sources: D. Ball, 2000, 'How old guard boardroom barons tightened their grip on new Italy', *Wall Street Journal Interactive*, 13 January: www.interactive.wsj.com.articles; E. Beck, 2000, 'Dixons, Marks & Spencer post weak results in a tough year', *Wall Street Journal Interactive*, 13 January: www.interactive.wsj.com.articles; P. Engardio and O. Ullmann, 1999, 'The Atlantic century', *Business Week*, 8 February, pp. 64–73; N. George, 2000, 'SDP backs Swedish entry to euro zone', 15 January: www.ft.com.nbearchive; T. Kamm, 1999, 'Europe's move into the free market spurs a massive corporate workout', *Wall Street Journal Interactive*, 30 December: www.interactive.wsj.com.articles; D. Michaels and J. Cole, 2000, *Wall Street Journal Interactive*, 13 January: www.interactive.wsj.com.articles; K. L. Miller, J. Ewing, S. Reed and G. Silverman, 1999, 'Fixing Deutsche Bank', *Business Week*, 19 July, pp. 56–8; G. Naik, 2000, 'Cable & Wireless announces purchase of eight Internet providers in Europe', *Wall Street Journal Interactive*, 13 January: www.interactive.wsj.com.articles; J. Peet, 1998, 'The year of Europe', *The Economist The World in 1999*, pp. 11–12; S. Reed, 1999, 'Buyout fever', *Business Week*, 14 June, pp. 60–1; S. Reed, 1999, 'We have liftoff!', *Business Week*, 18 January, pp. 34–7; S. Reed, J. Rossant and G. Edmondson, 1999, 'Deal', *Business Week*, 5 April, pp. 50–4; J. Rossant, 1999, 'Ten years after the wall', *Business Week*, 8 November, pp. 57–61; 'Thomson-CSF announces E1.32 bn Racal deal', 2000, 13 January: www.ft.com.nbearchive.

International strategies

In the previous section, we explored why international strategies may be important and examined some of their advantages. In this section, we describe the types and content of international strategies that might be formulated and then implemented.

An international strategy may be one of two basic types: business- or corporate-level strategy. At the business level, firms follow generic strategies: cost leadership, differentiation, focused cost leadership, focused differentiation or integrated cost leadership/differentiation. At the corporate level, firms can formulate three types of strategy: multi-domestic, global or transnational (a combination of multi-domestic and global). However, to create competitive advantage, each of these strategies must realise a core competence based on difficult-to-duplicate resources and capabilities.[46] As discussed in Chapters 4 and 6, firms expect to create value through the implementation of a business-level *and* a corporate-level strategy.[47]

International business-level strategy

Each business must develop a competitive strategy focused on its own domestic market. We discussed business-level generic strategies in Chapter 4 and competitive dynamics in Chapter 5. However, international business-level strategies have some unique features. In pursuing an international business-level strategy, the home country of operation is often the most important source of competitive advantage.[48] The resources and capabilities established in the home country frequently allow the firm to pursue the strategy into markets located in other countries.

Michael Porter developed a model that describes the factors contributing to the advantage of firms in a dominant global industry and associated with a specific country or regional environment.[49] His model is illustrated in Figure 8.2. The first dimension in the model, *factors of production*, refers to the inputs necessary to compete in any industry, such as labour, land, natural resources, capital and infrastructure (for example, highway, postal and communication systems). Of course, there are basic (for example, natural and labour resources) and advanced (for example, digital communication systems and a highly educated workforce) factors. There are also generalised (highway systems and the supply of debt capital) and specialised factors (skilled personnel in a specific industry, such as the workers in a port that specialises in handling bulk chemicals). If a country has both advanced and specialised production factors, it is likely to serve an industry well in spawning strong home-country competitors that can be successful global competitors as well. Ironically, countries often develop advanced and specialised factors because they *lack* critical basic resources. For example, some Asian countries, such as South Korea, lack abundant natural resources, but the country's strong work ethic, large number of engineers and systems of large firms have created an expertise in manufacturing. Similarly, Germany developed a strong chemical industry, partially because Hoechst and BASF spent years developing a synthetic indigo dye to reduce their dependence on imports. This was not the case in Britain, because large supplies of natural indigo were available in the colonies.[50]

Figure 8.2 | Determinants of national advantage

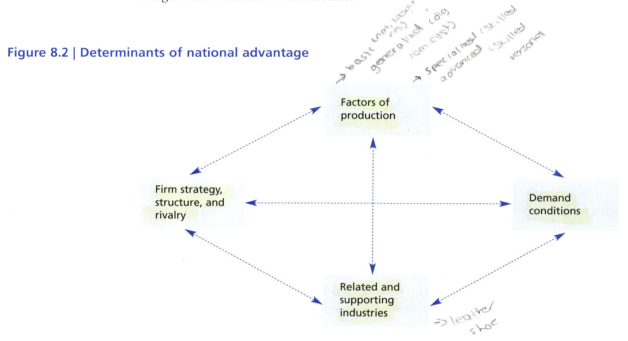

Source: Adapted with the permission of The Free Press, a Division of Simon & Schuster, Inc., from Michael E. Porter, *The Competitive Advantages of Nations*, p. 72. Copyright ©1990, 1998 by Michael E. Porter.

The second dimension, *demand conditions*, is characterised by the nature and size of buyers' needs in the home market for the industry's goods or services. The sheer size of a market segment can produce the demand necessary to create scale-efficient facilities. This efficiency could also lead to domination of the industry in other countries. Specialised demand may also create opportunities beyond national boundaries. For example, Swiss firms have long led the world in tunnelling equipment because of the need to tunnel through mountains for rail and highway passage in Switzerland. And Japanese firms have created a niche market for compact, quiet air conditioners. Small, but quiet, units are required in Japan because homes are often small and located close together.[51]

Related and supporting industries represent the third dimension in the model. Italy has become the leader in the shoe industry because of related and supporting industries. The leather supplies necessary to manufacture shoes are furnished by a well-established leather-processing industry. Also, many people travel to Italy to purchase leather goods. Thus, there is support in distribution. In addition, supporting industries in leather-working machinery and design services contribute to the success of the shoe industry. In fact, the design services industry supports many of its own related industries, such as ski boots, fashion apparel and furniture. In Japan, cameras and copiers are related industries. In Denmark, the dairy products industry is related to an industry focused on food enzymes.

Firm strategy, structure and rivalry, the final country dimension, also fosters the growth of certain industries. The pattern of strategy, structure and rivalry among firms varies greatly from nation to nation. Earlier, much attention was placed on examining US and then Japanese enterprise managers. Because of the excellent technical training system in Germany, there is a strong emphasis on methodological product and process improvement. In Japan, unusual cooperative and competitive systems have facilitated the cross-functional management of complex assembly operations. In Italy, the national pride of the country's designers has spawned strong industries in sports cars, fashion apparel and furniture. In the United States, competition among computer manufacturers and software producers has favoured the development of these industries.

The four basic dimensions of the 'diamond' model shown in Figure 8.2 emphasise the environmental or structural attributes of a national economy that contribute to national advantage. Government policy also clearly contributes to the success and failure of many firms and industries. This is exemplified in Japan, where the Ministry of International Trade and Investment has significantly affected the corporate strategies the country follows. Nevertheless, each firm must create its own success; not all firms survive to become global competitors – even those operating with the same country factors that spawned the successful firms. Therefore, the actual strategic choices managers make may be the most compelling reason for success or failure. Accordingly, the factors illustrated in Figure 8.2 are likely to produce competitive advantages for a firm only when an appropriate strategy is developed and implemented, one that takes advantage of distinct country factors. Hence, the next four subsections explain the cost leadership, differentiation, focused cost leadership, focused differentiation and integrated cost leadership/differentiation generic strategies (discussed in Chapter 4) in an international context.

International cost leadership strategy

The international low-cost strategy is likely to develop in a country with a large demand. Usually, the operations of such an industry are centralised in a home country, and obtaining economies of scale is the primary goal. Outsourcing of low-value-added operations may take place, but high-value-added operations are retained in the home country. Accordingly, products are often exported from the home country.

Through a variety of entry modes (entry modes are discussed in detail later in the chapter), Wal-Mart, too, follows an international cost leadership strategy as it continues to globalise its operations (explained in a Strategic Focus in Chapter 5). Wal-Mart has no stores in Australia, but, as described in Chapter 5, German grocery company Aldi has recently established stores and follows an international low-cost leadership strategy.

The essence of Wal-Mart's international low-cost strategy is demonstrated by founder Sam Walton's words: 'We'll lower the cost of living for everyone, not just in America.' One of the keys to implementing its low-cost strategy, both domestically and internationally, is the firm's advanced retail technology, which enables Wal-Mart to have the correct quantities of goods in the appropriate place at the right time while minimising inventory costs. The latest variation of this sophisticated system has employees carrying handheld computers that allow them to reorder merchandise. Simultaneously, backroom computers link each store with a sophisticated satellite system.

Wal-Mart started to internationalise its operations in 1991. Since then, the firm has already become the largest retailer in Canada and Mexico. Wal-Mart also operates stores in Argentina, Brazil, China and Indonesia through joint ventures. To continue diversifying internationally, Wal-Mart decided to enter the European market, as explained in Chapter 5. The process was started with the purchase of the Wertkauf hypermarket company in Germany. Wal-Mart has moved heavily into the British market. Its means of entering European markets have been different than entering other international markets. Previously, Wal-Mart usually entered international markets via a joint venture. However, it entered some European markets by acquiring existing large retail operations in each country. Combining its volume with the firm's logistics skills and merchandising savvy will help Wal-Mart to achieve strategic competitiveness in the European markets. Also, Wal-Mart emphasises customer service along with low prices, thereby changing the retailing culture in many European markets (for example, England).[52] Many analysts believe that Wal-Mart will be successful in European markets. If so, its resources and skills, along with its international cost leadership strategy, will have changed the retailing landscape in Europe and perhaps globally.[53]

There are, of course, risks associated with implementing the international low-cost strategy. A major risk for Wal-Mart is learning quickly how to compete successfully in Europe's unique retailing environment. Does Wal-Mart have the confidence it needs to make small adjustments to satisfy local tastes while maintaining the discipline required to keep prices low? Will European retailers retain their customers by learning how to create value either through differentiation strategies or by driving their costs lower relative to Wal-Mart's? These issues pose strategic challenges to Wal-Mart's executives; but the fact that the company hopes to generate one-third of its profit growth annually through international sales suggests its intentions in Europe and other world markets.[54] Aldi faces similar risks from entrenched market players in the Australian context.

Volkswagen AG is attempting to implement an international cost leadership strategy in China. Volkswagen plans to produce a low-price 'people's auto', reaching the huge mass market for automobiles in China. Few international manufacturers have been able to reach China's mass market, because most Chinese cannot afford expensive products such as automobiles. Foreign automobile manufacturers have been selling their vehicles chiefly to the government and corporations, a relatively small market. There are about 13 million automobiles in China, with only 30 per cent owned by individuals. However, Volkswagen built the original 'people's auto' in Germany, lovingly referred to as the 'bug' or 'beetle'. Volkswagen won approval from the Chinese government to produce a compact car over other hopeful firms, such as GM. The new automobile will be developed and produced by Shanghai Volkswagen, a joint venture with Shanghai Automotive Industrial Corp. formed in 1984. The company already owns 46 per cent of the Chinese market with its Santana model, used by many of the taxi fleets in China. The new car will have a small engine (1–1.6 litres) and sell for 100 000 yuan (about US$12 000). It is expected on the market by 2002.[55]

International differentiation strategy

Firms based in a country with advanced and specialised factor endowments are likely to develop an international differentiation strategy. Germany has a number of world-class chemical firms, for example. The differentiation strategy followed by many of these firms to develop specialised chemicals was possible because of the country's favourable conditions with respect to this industry. The Kaiser Wilhelm (later, Max Planck) Institutes and university chemistry programs were superior in research and provided the best chemistry education in the world. Also, Germany's emphasis on vocational education fostered strong apprenticeship programs for workers.[56] Today, German companies competing in retailing consumer goods are learning how to improve their services to battle against competitors (for example, Lands' End) implementing their international differentiation strategies in Germany.[57]

In Japan, DoMoCo is a wireless Internet service that has captured the Japanese market, but is planning to enter global wireless communication and Internet service markets. While Australians can connect to the Internet using wireless technology with their Palm Pilots, the DoMoCo technology is ahead of all competitors. Clearly, DoMoCo is following a differentiation strategy. It offers the only i-mode in the world that allows continuous access to the Internet by using a cell phone. While some predict that DoMoCo may be a global giant in wireless communications, it will have to continue to differentiate its product in ways that are attractive to the mass market, because it will face fierce competition in global markets from companies such as Vodafone AirTouch, AT&T and British Telecom. However, DoMoCo should have the resources to compete. In 1999, the company earned approximately US$5 billion on sales of US$36 billion, and it has access to the Japanese giant NTT, which owns 67 per cent of DoMoCo. DoMoCo is working on a third-generation technology called 3G to continue its differentiation in the market. 3G is a set of wireless protocols that will permit much higher communication speeds. To maintain its competitive advantage, DoMoCo strongly emphasises R&D.[58]

As described in Chapter 4, firms may differentiate their products and services through physical characteristics. However, they may also differentiate their products in the minds of the consumer. As the market for cigarettes in the industrialised world has decreased, international markets have become critical to tobacco companies. For example, generally, greater percentages of the population smoke in countries outside the OECD, and they tend to be less litigious. In those countries, cigarette companies compete largely on brand differences established through advertising.[59]

International focus strategies

Many firms remain focused on small market niches as they pursue international focus strategies.[60] The ceramic tile industry in Italy contains a number of medium-sized and small, fragmented firms that produce approximately 50 per cent of the world's tiles.[61] These firms, clustered in the Sassuolo area of the country, have formed a number of different focus strategies. Companies such as Marazzi, Iris, Cisa-Cerdisa and Flor Gres invest heavily in technology to improve product quality, aesthetics and productivity. The companies have close relationships with equipment manufacturers and tend to emphasise the focused cost leadership strategy, while maintaining a quality image. Another group, including Piemme and Atlas Concorde, attempts to compete more on image and design. Firms in this group invest heavily in advertising and showroom expositions. Because they try to appeal to selected customer tastes, they emphasise the focused differentiation strategy.[62]

The efficiency of the highly capitalised domestic institutions, coupled with their large branch networks and use of high-quality, sophisticated technologies, creates a retail banking environment in Spain in which it is difficult for foreign firms to compete successfully. Because of the domestic banks' competitive advantages, foreign rivals now concentrate on niche activities. Chase Manhattan, for example, focuses on a range of niches, including corporate finance, capital markets and derivatives businesses, and peseta- (euro) clearing activities. Based on its international focus strategy, Chase's recent performance in Spain is impressive – a return on earnings of 23 per cent and a return on assets of 5.9 per cent. As is highlighted in Chapter 10, Chase also owns very significant holdings in major Australian companies.

Because of what they envision as significant growth potential in terms of mutual and pension funds, UK-based Barclays and US-based Citibank are focusing on the private banking sector. Citibank has converted the 83 branches it operates in Spain into product advisory centres. In each location, customers have access to computer systems that help them to determine their desired risk levels; once these are known, a set of investment alternatives is recommended. Like Citibank, Barclays has 'scaled back its retail operations in Spain, concentrated on the big cities and focused on asset management of medium to big private accounts according to a carefully elaborated segmentation of potential clients'. Barclays operates 180 branches as it competes against Citibank and others to serve the unique needs of the private banking market segment in Spain.[63]

International integrated cost leadership/differentiation strategy

The integrated strategy has become more popular because of flexible manufacturing systems, improved information networks within and across firms, and total quality management systems (see Chapter 4). Because of the wide diversity of markets and competitors, following an integrated strategy has become critical in many global markets.[64] Therefore, competing in global markets requires sophisticated and effective management.[65] Komatsu illustrates a classic case where this strategy was well executed. Komatsu was able to gain on a strong competitor, Caterpillar, by pursuing the integrated cost leadership/differentiation strategy. Caterpillar had a very strong brand image in world markets, but Komatsu was able to overcome this differentiation advantage by improving its image and reducing its costs. It was able to do this initially because of low labour costs and low steel prices. Then, in the 1970s, the US dollar was strong, which allowed the company to implement a successful export strategy. Caterpillar continues to experience problems today because its competitors have been able to implement the integrated strategy more effectively than has Caterpillar. As a result, Caterpillar's competitors have been able to sell their differentiated products at lower prices than Caterpillar. Caterpillar's profits were down by 37.4 per cent in 1999 over 1998. Analysts and company spokespersons suggested that the next few years would continue to be challenging for Caterpillar.[66]

Compaq also is attempting to employ an integrated cost leadership differentiation strategy. It needs to maintain low costs so that it can standardise its prices to compete with firms like Dell. Compaq is doing so by reducing the number of products in its product line and by using the Internet both to purchase supplies from across the globe and to manage the distribution of its products. But Compaq also must continue to differentiate its products and meet domestic and international market requirements.[67]

International corporate-level strategy

The business-level strategies discussed previously are based at least partially on the type of international corporate-level strategy the firm is following. Some corporate strategies give individual country units the authority to develop their own business-level strategies; other corporate strategies largely dictate the business-level strategies used to accomplish standardisation of products and sharing of resources across countries. International corporate-level strategy focuses on the scope of a firm's operations through both product and geographic diversification.[68] International corporate-level strategy is required when the firm operates in multiple industries and multiple countries or regions.[69] The strategy is guided by the headquarters unit, rather than by business or country managers. The three international corporate-level strategies are multi-domestic, global and transnational, as shown in Figure 8.3.

Multi-domestic strategy

> A **multi-domestic strategy** is one in which strategic and operating decisions are decentralised to the strategic business unit in each country in order to tailor products to the local market.

A **multi-domestic strategy** is one in which strategic and operating decisions are decentralised to the strategic business unit in each country to allow the unit to tailor products to the local market.[70] A multi-domestic strategy focuses on competition within each country. It assumes that the markets differ and therefore are segmented by country boundaries. In other words, consumer needs and desires, industry conditions (for example, the number and type of competitors), political and legal structures, and social norms vary by country. Multi-domestic strategies provide the opportunity to customise products to meet the specific needs and preferences of local customers. Therefore, they should be able to maximise a firm's competitive response to the idiosyncratic requirements of each market.[71] The use of multi-domestic strategies usually expands the firm's local market share because of the attention paid to the needs of the local clientele. However, the use of these strategies also results in more uncertainty for the corporation as a whole, because of the differences across markets and thus the different strategies employed by local country units.[72] Moreover, multi-domestic strategies do not allow for the achievement of economies of scale and thus can be more costly. As a result, firms employing a multi-domestic strategy decentralise their strategic and operating decisions to the business units operating in each country. The multi-domestic strategy has been more commonly used by European multinational firms because of the varieties of cultures and markets found in Europe.

Figure 8.3 | International corporate-level strategies

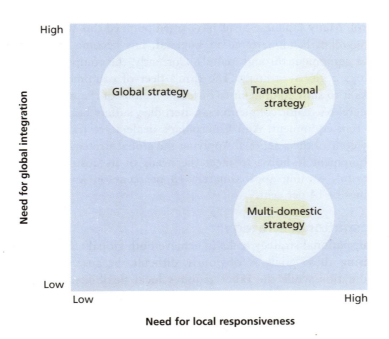

Sony's entertainment business recently changed its strategy from global to multi-domestic, with positive results. For example, Sony tried to penetrate the US entertainment market but never succeeded. While attempting to penetrate this market, the company distributed television programs and films produced for the US market to other markets across the world, the approach used by most large entertainment companies. Sony decided to change this approach and produce films and television programs itself for local markets around the world. To do so, it established production facilities and television channels in most larger Latin American and Asian countries. In 1999, Sony produced approximately 4 000 hours of foreign-language programs and about 1 700 hours of English-language programs. Sony now has 24 channels operating across 62 countries, and some of those channels are highly successful. In contrast, Sony's unit in China has lost money each of its three years of operation. Thus, this approach does not come without some uncertainty and risk.[73]

Global strategy

In contradistinction to a multi-domestic strategy, a global strategy assumes more standardisation of products across country markets.[74] As a result, competitive strategy is centralised and controlled by the home office. The strategic business units operating in each country are assumed to be interdependent, and the home office attempts to achieve integration across these businesses. Therefore, a **global strategy** is one in which standardised products are offered across country markets and the competitive strategy is dictated by the home office. Thus, a global strategy emphasises economies of scale and offers greater opportunities to utilise innovations developed at the corporate level or in one country in other markets. Accordingly, a global strategy produces lower risk, but may forgo growth opportunities in local markets, either because those markets are less likely to identify opportunities or because opportunities require that products be adapted to the local market.[75] In effect, the strategy is not responsive to local markets and is difficult to manage because of the need to coordinate strategies and operating decisions across country borders. Consequently, achieving efficient operations with a global strategy requires the sharing of resources and an emphasis on coordination and cooperation across country boundaries, and these in turn require centralisation and headquarters control. Many Japanese firms have often pursued this strategy with success.[76]

Aggreko, headquartered in England, has become the world's leading provider of power equipment through rentals. Currently, the company operates in 48 countries and employs a global strategy. The firm's fleet of equipment is integrated globally, which allows it to shift equipment to different regions of the world to meet specific needs. One of Aggreko's major competitors, Caterpillar, suffers because its dealers would rather sell than rent equipment. And Caterpillar's dealers are franchises, so the company cannot easily control their actions. Applying the global strategy, Aggreko designs and assembles its equipment in-house to meet the needs of its customers. Aggreko has been highly successful, earning approximately 18 per cent on invested capital with a growth in earnings of 14 per cent.[77]

> A **global strategy** is one in which standardised products are offered across country markets and the competitive strategy is dictated by the home office.

Transnational strategy

A **transnational strategy** seeks to achieve both global efficiency and local responsiveness. Realising these goals is obviously difficult, because one goal requires close global coordination while the other requires local flexibility. Thus, 'flexible coordination' – building a shared vision and individual commitment through an integrated network – is required to implement the transnational strategy.[78] In reality, it is difficult to achieve a pure transnational strategy because of the conflicting goals. On the positive side, the effective implementation of a transnational strategy often produces higher performance than either of the two other corporate strategies alone do.[79]

> A **transnational strategy** seeks to achieve both global efficiency and local responsiveness.

Until the mid-1990s, Ford used a multi-domestic strategy with separate, decentralised operations for North America and Europe. However, former CEO Alex Trotman implemented a global strategy in the mid-1990s. Applying this strategy, Ford attempted to build what it called a global automobile. The Mondeo was Ford's global car. Unfortunately, both the car and the strategy failed. The new CEO, Jacques Nasser, is now changing Ford's strategy to be transnational. Furthermore, Nasser is restructuring management so that it can respond flexibly to opportunities outside of the traditional automobile manufacturing business. Applying the transnational strategy, Ford is trying to standardise some of the components in its various automobiles – Ford, Lincoln, Jaguar and Volvo – but yet allow design and other differences that appeal to the customers served in the market segments at which each of those brands of automobile is targeted. Ford is trying to become consumer-oriented and be responsive to the various markets across the globe that it serves.[80] The transnational strategy requires that managers think globally, but act locally.[81]

Chapter 8 International strategy

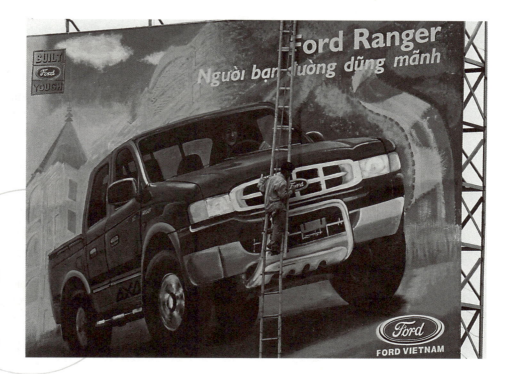

After its attempt to build a global automobile failed, Ford changed its strategy to be transnational instead of multi-domestic. The firm is trying to become consumer-oriented and responsive to various global markets.

The next Strategic Focus describes the changes in Asia's economic landscape. The world's largest continent in both area and population is awakening again. Many Asian firms used a global strategy before the 1998 economic crisis. Most, however, will have to adopt a transnational strategy to be competitive in the 21st-century landscape.

Strategic Focus International

Awakening of the Asian tiger

It looks as if the Asian tiger is awakening. Asia's economies are bottoming out and most are starting to grow again. For example, the economies in Malaysia, the Philippines, Korea, Japan and China experienced growth. Furthermore, the stock markets in most of these countries are on the upswing, portending economic growth. Singapore largely avoided the severe problems experienced by most other Asian countries. For most countries, 1998 was the year in which they incurred their greatest losses. Singapore's economy grew, albeit only 1.5 per cent. Still, Singapore is implementing reforms similar to those adopted by many of the other Asian countries to ensure continued economic prosperity. Asian countries must adapt as globalisation continues and powerful forces shape the world economy. The two most prominent of these forces, the Internet and wireless communications, were discussed in the Opening Case.

Japan has the largest economy in Asia and also has suffered significantly. The suffering is greater there because Japan was considered the economic miracle at one time and was imitated by many countries around the world. But Japan had what was referred to as a 'bubble economy', built on debt and interdependence, and the bubble eventually burst. Because of its economic difficulties, Japan has been subject to more outside influence than ever before. One of the best examples of Japan's fall is the problem experienced by Mitsubishi. The Mitsubishi *keiretsu* is huge and produces over 8 per cent of Japan's total output. In the late 1980s, Mitsubishi companies were feared because of their economic power and potential domination of global markets. Today, most of Mitsubishi's companies are trying to stem the tide of losses. The organisation had to obtain over US$2 billion in capital from its member companies to keep some of the other member firms from going bankrupt. Japanese companies were harmed severely by the economic problems throughout Asia. However, these firms are beginning to enjoy growth again as the Asian economies grow. Many foreign firms – particularly financial institutions – are gaining a foothold in Japan. Furthermore, analysts argue that Japan's assets are largely undervalued; thus, they are of substantial value to foreign investors. Some of Japan's best firms, including Honda, Sony, Bridgestone, Canon and Toyota, survived the crisis and even continued to achieve positive returns when many could not. In fact, these five firms experienced the largest growth in net profits among Japanese firms in 1999. Still, although most of them followed a global strategy, they will have to develop and implement a transnational strategy to compete effectively in global markets, because this strategy is being used increasingly by competitors from other regions of the world. Japan will have to become a larger participant in the Internet economy, particularly e-commerce. DoMoCo provides a good start, but more such firms are needed.

China has been the lone shining economic star in Asia, with a growing economy even during the crisis. China's GDP grew at 7.1 per cent in 1999, and the economy is expected to grow at 7.5 per cent annually for at least the foreseeable future. The country is also seeking to enter the World Trade Organization. Interestingly, Chinese firms manufacture products sold globally, but few people know about them. For example, Haier, a firm that manufactures and sells household appliances, is one of a small number of companies from China that sell their products outside of the local domestic market. Still, there are many more products made in China, but marketed under non-Chinese brand names. China leads the world in the export of toys, kitchenware and textile products. Magic Chef refrigerators, sold by Wal-Mart, are made by Haier. In many ways, China is undergoing an economic revolution. State enterprises are being transformed into private companies, and dynamic new entrepreneurial companies are growing dramatically. Some suggest that Chinese cities are flush with capital and entrepreneurs. While this is likely an overstatement, the economy does look bright. China has agreed to let many foreign firms enter Chinese markets, although usually requiring that they form a joint venture with a Chinese firm, similar to Volkswagen's venture with Shanghai Automotive Industrial Corp. The critical concern about China is the stability of its reforms. China still has an authoritarian communist government, and if economic reforms stall, economic growth may come to a halt. In particular, if the government becomes too heavy-handed, it could limit the inflow of foreign capital needed to fuel the country's economic growth. Also, many of the state firms have had problems privatising and breaking government ties.

The last of the 'big three' Asian economies is South Korea. A number of its companies suffered significant financial problems during the Asian economic crisis. In particular, Korean *chaebols* were caught with too much debt, were too diversified and were not flexible enough (primarily due to the massive debt and cross shareholdings). Several of the *chaebols* have been 'downscoping' (see Chapter 7) – ridding themselves of poorly performing diversified businesses. Samsung and Hyundai seem to be improving and likely will again become formidable competitors in global markets, but debate still surrounds the viability of Daewoo. In fact, Hyundai plans to be one of the six survivors in the global automobile industry during this decade; however, the company must reduce its large debt and improve its market capitalisation. Also, the South Korean economy remains fragile, and political problems – particularly those associated with dealing with the North Koreans – could spell trouble. South

Korea would have difficulty absorbing North Korea in the way West Germany absorbed East Germany, and the German reunification was itself fraught with severe problems during the adjustment.

Sources: B. Bremner, S. Prasso, J. Veale, J. Moore and J. Barnathan, 1999, 'Asia: How real is the recovery?', *Business Week*, 3 May, pp. 56–8; B. Bremner, E. Thorton and I. M. Kunii, 2000, 'Mitsubishi: Fall of a keiretsu', *Businessweek Online*, 6 January: www.businessweek.com; B. Bremner, E. Thornton, I. M. Kunii and M. Tanikawa, 1999, 'A new Japan', *Business Week*, 25 October, pp. 69–74; 'China at fifty: Can China change?', 1999, *The Economist*, 2 October, pp. 23–5; 'China's economy is expected to expand by 7.5% in 2000', 2000, *Wall Street Journal Interactive*, 13 January: www.interactice.wsj.com.articles; M. L. Clifford, M. Shari and B. Einhorn, 2000, 'Remaking Singapore Inc.', *Businessweek Online*, 6 January: www.businessweek.com; P. Engardio, J. Veale and M. L. Clifford, 1999, 'Boom or miracle?', *Business Week*, 8 November, pp. 50–1; B. Fulford and T. Y. Jones, 1999, 'Up from Lemons', *Forbes*, 14 June, pp. 122–4; J. Grant, 1998, 'Why Japan is undervalued', *Wall Street Journal*, 17 April, p. A14; J. E. Hilsenrath, 1999, 'The speed of change', *Wall Street Journal Interactive*, 25 October: www.interactive.wsj.com; 'Japan's growth companies', 1999, *The Economist*, 26 June, pp. 69–70; J. L. Lee, 1999, 'South Korea checks big business groups', *Wall Street Journal*, 23 July, p. A13; 'Out of the shadows', 1999, *The Economist*, 28 August, pp. 50–1; D. Roberts, 1999, 'China's new revolution', *Business Week*, 27 September, pp. 72–8; D. Roberts, 1999, 'Foreign carmakers get the green light', *Business Week*, 19 July, p. 63; D. Roberts, J. Barnathan, J. Moore and S. Prasso, 1999, 'Plans for reform are screeching to a halt as it enters a year of economic peril', *Business Week*, 22 February, pp. 48–50; J. Sapsford, 1999, 'U.S. financial firms delve deeper into Japan', *Wall Street Journal*, 26 January, p. A13; 'The Koreas: Yesterday's war, tomorrow's peace', 1999, *The Economist*, 10 July, pp. 3–16; E. Thornton and M Shari, 1999, 'Japan's Asian comeback', *Business Week*, 1 November, pp. 58–9; P. Wonacott and I. Johnson, 2000, 'Petrochina prepares to go public: changes fail to break its state ties', *Wall Street Journal Interactive*, 13 January: www.interactive.wsj.com.

Environmental trends

Although the transnational strategy is difficult to implement, emphasis on the need for global efficiency is increasing as more industries begin to experience global competition. To add to the problem, there is also an increased emphasis on local requirements: global goods and services often require some customisation to meet government regulations within particular countries or to fit customer tastes and preferences. In addition, most multinational firms desire to achieve some coordination and sharing of resources across country markets to hold down costs. Furthermore, some products and industries may be better suited for standardisation across country borders than others are. As a result, most large multinational firms with diverse products employ a multi-domestic strategy with certain product lines and a global strategy with others. Perhaps this type of flexibility will be required in many Asian firms if they are to be strategically competitive in the coming years. (See the Strategic Focus for a discussion of the Asian transformation.)

Regionalisation

Regionalisation is becoming more common in world markets. A firm's location can affect its strategic competitiveness.[82] Firms must decide whether to compete in all (or many) world markets or to focus on a particular region(s).[83] The advantages of attempting to compete in all markets centre on the economies that can be achieved because of the combined market size. However, if the firm is competing in industries where the international markets differ greatly (in which it must employ a multi-domestic strategy), it may wish to narrow its focus to a particular region of the world. In so doing, it can better understand the cultures, legal and social norms, and other factors that are important for effective competition in those markets. For example, a firm may focus on Far East markets only, rather than attempting to compete in the Middle East, Europe and the Far East simultaneously. Or the firm may choose a region of the world where the markets are more similar, and thus, some coordination and sharing of resources would be possible. In this way, the firm may be able not only to better understand the markets in which it competes, but also to achieve some economies, even though it may have to employ a multi-domestic strategy.

Regional strategies may be promoted by countries that develop trade agreements to increase the economic power of their regions. The European Union and the Association of Southeast Asian Nations (ASEAN) are collections of countries that developed trade agreements to promote the flow of trade across country boundaries within their respective regions.[84] Many European firms have been acquiring and integrating their businesses in Europe to better coordinate pan-European brands as the EU creates more unity in European markets. The North American Free Trade Agreement (NAFTA), signed by the United States, Canada and Mexico, is designed to facilitate free trade across country borders in North America and may be expanded to include other countries in South America, such as Argentina, Brazil and Chile.[85] NAFTA agreements loosen restrictions on international strategies within a region and provide greater opportunity to realise the advantages of international strategies. Of importance to Australia is the Closer Economic Relations (CER) agreement with New Zealand and its membership of the Asia Pacific Economic Cooperation (APEC) forum.[86]

Most firms enter regional markets sequentially, beginning in markets with which they are more familiar. However, they also enter these markets with their largest and strongest lines of business first, followed by their other lines of business after the first ones are successful.[87] After firms decide on their international strategies and whether to employ them in regional or world markets, they must decide how to accomplish such international expansion.[88] Accordingly, the next section discusses how to enter new international markets.

Choice of international entry mode

International expansion is accomplished through exporting products, licensing arrangements, strategic alliances, acquisitions and establishing new wholly owned subsidiaries. These means of entering international markets and their characteristics are shown in Table 8.1. Each has its advantages and disadvantages. Thus, choosing the appropriate mode of entering international markets is critical to the firms' financial performance in those markets.[89]

Table 8.1 | Global market entry: Choice of entry mode

Type of entry	Characteristics
Exporting	High cost, low control
Licensing	Low cost, low risk, little control, low returns
Strategic alliances	Shared costs, shared resources, shared risks, problems of integration (e.g. two corporate cultures)
Acquisition	Quick access to new market, high cost, complex negotiations, problems of merging with domestic operations
New wholly owned subsidiary	Complex, often costly, time consuming, high risk, maximum control, potential above-average returns

Exporting

Many industrial firms begin their international expansion by exporting goods or services to other countries.[90] Exporting does not require the expense of establishing operations in the host countries, but exporters must establish some means of marketing and distributing their products. Usually, exporting firms develop contractual arrangements with host-country firms. The disadvantages of exporting include the often high costs of transportation and possible tariffs placed on incoming goods. Furthermore, the exporter has less control over the marketing and distribution of its products in the host country and must either pay the distributor or allow the distributor to add to the price to recoup its costs and make a profit. As a result, it may be difficult to market a competitive product through exporting or to provide a product that is customised to each international market. However, evidence suggests that cost leadership strategies enhance the performance of exports in developed countries, whereas differentiation strategies are more successful in emerging economies.[91]

Firms export mostly to countries that are closest to their facilities, because of the lower transportation costs and the usually greater similarity between geographic neighbours. For example, the largest amount of exports from businesses located in Texas goes to Mexico, with which Texas shares a common border. In fact, exports from Texas to Mexico are greater than all of the other exports from Texas businesses combined.[92]

Small businesses are most likely to use the exporting mode of international entry. One of the largest problems with which small businesses must deal is currency exchange rates. Large businesses have specialists that help them manage the exchange rates, but small businesses rarely have this expertise. Thus, the change to a common currency in Europe actually is helpful to small businesses operating in European markets. Instead of trying to remain current with 12 different exchange rates (assuming that they are exporting to all EU countries), these firms only have to obtain information on one. However, small businesses still seem to have a concern about understanding the euro. Thus, small businesses continue to rely on the US dollar, but often must pay prohibitive surcharges in doing so. In general, small businesses operating in international markets must try to understand those markets and manage the business with a knowledge of foreign exchange rates to reduce their overall costs and remain competitive.[93]

Licensing

A licensing arrangement allows a foreign firm to purchase the right to manufacture and sell the firm's products within a host country or set of countries.[94] The licenser is normally paid a royalty on each unit produced and sold. The licensee takes the risks and makes the monetary investments in facilities for manufacturing, marketing and distributing the goods or services. As a result, licensing is possibly the least costly form of international expansion. As such, licensing is one of the forms of organisational networks that are becoming common, particularly among smaller firms.[95]

Licensing is also a way to expand returns based on previous innovations. For instance, Sony and Philips co-designed the audio CD and now license the rights to companies to make CDs. Sony and Philips collect 5 US cents for every CD sold.[96] As this example demonstrates, many firms can earn good returns on their past innovations. A continual focus on research and patent licensing allows a firm to gain strong returns from its innovations for many years into the future.[97]

Today, however, the returns to Sony and Philips from CD sales are being threatened. Cheap counterfeit disks imitating the original products are a growth business. Sales of counterfeit disks in China alone are estimated to exceed US$1 billion annually. Interestingly, technological advances are contributing to the severity of the problem. In fact, innovation makes it easier for counterfeiters to improvise. Pressing machinery used to manufacture disks is now so advanced and compact, that it can be operated in the smallest of quarters. Located commonly in housing tenements, counterfeiters' production lines are difficult for officials to find. Corporations are seeking legal remedies to this situation, but with limited success to date.[98]

Jakks Pacific, in the United States, has been named by *Forbes* magazine as one of the best 200 small companies to watch. Jakks's licensing strategy was developed by its two founders, Jack Friedman and Stephen Berman. On the basis of a 14-year licensing deal, the firm creates dolls representing World Wrestling Federation figures such as Stone Cold Steve Austin. The dolls are manufactured in China. Customers such as Wal-Mart, Toys 'R' Us and Kmart receive shipments directly from Chinese manufacturers, thereby keeping prices lower than those of comparable Mattel and Hasbro toys. Jakks, however, has been diversifying through licences for toy cars with the US National Hot Rod Association and the Indianapolis Motor Speedway, toy fishing rods with Bass (a sports equipment company), and toy hard hats and a matching tool belt with the Caterpillar logo. Through its licensing strategy, Jakks is close to becoming the fifth-largest toy company in the United States, and its stock price increased from US$7 to US$41 in 1999.[99]

Of course, licensing has its disadvantages. For example, it gives the firm very little control over the manufacture and marketing of its products in other countries. In addition, licensing provides the least potential returns, because returns must be shared between the licenser and the licensee. Worse, the international firm may learn the technology and produce and sell a similar competitive product after the licence expires. Komatsu, for example, first licensed much of its technology from International Harvester, Bucyrus-Erie and Cummins Engine in order to enter the earthmoving equipment business to compete against Caterpillar. Komatsu then dropped these licences and developed its own products using the technology it gained from the US companies.[100]

Strategic alliances

In recent years, strategic alliances have enjoyed popularity as a primary means of international expansion.[101] Strategic alliances allow firms to share the risks and the resources required to enter international markets.[102] Moreover, such alliances can facilitate the development of new core competencies that can contribute to a firm's future strategic competitiveness.[103] In addition, most strategic alliances are with a host-country firm that knows and understands the competitive conditions, legal and social norms, and cultural idiosyncrasies of the country, which should help the firm to manufacture and market a competitive product. In return, the host-country firm may find its new access to technology and innovative products attractive. Each partner in an alliance brings knowledge or resources to the partnership.[104] Indeed, partners often enter an alliance with the purpose of learning new capabilities. Common among those desired capabilities are technological skills.[105]

Alliances are involved in providing many products that we use each day. For example, a consulting partner for McKinsey & Company in the United States recently observed that the petrol he purchased for his car came from a joint venture between Royal Dutch Shell and Texaco. Furthermore, the credit card that he used to pay for the purchase was co-branded by Royal Dutch Shell and MasterCard.[106]

Not all alliances are successful; in fact, many fail. The primary reasons include selecting an incompatible partner and conflict between the partners.[107] International strategic alliances are especially difficult to manage.[108] Trust between the partners is critical. Trust did not have time to develop in the much-publicised telecommunications alliance called Global One, among Deutsche Telecom, French Telecom and MCI WorldCom. First, France Telecom became angry when it learned about Deutsche Telecom's attempt to take over Telecom Italia. When MCI WorldCom acquired Sprint without consulting its partners, the alliance was all but dead. Sprint is a member of another European alliance that is a rival of Global One.[109] Fortunately, research has shown that equity-based alliances, over which a firm has more control, tend to produce more positive returns.[110] (Strategic alliances are discussed in more depth in Chapter 9.)

Acquisitions

With free trade expanding more and more in global markets, cross-border acquisitions have been increasing significantly.[111] In recent years, cross-border acquisitions have comprised over 40 per cent of all acquisitions completed worldwide.[112] Acquisitions have been especially popular in Europe, as noted in an earlier Strategic Focus. Acquisitions are used by European firms to build their market power and extend their reach throughout the European Union. Also, foreign firms use acquisitions to enter the EU and gain a foothold in its commerce. For example, GE completed 133 acquisitions of European firms during the 1990s. As a result, GE employs about 90 000 people in Europe, and its European operations produce approximately US$24.4 billion in sales annually.[113] Similarly, Ford acquired Volvo in 1999 for about US$6 billion. Ford's goal, however, was not so much entry into the European market as gaining access to assets and products that would make Ford more competitive in global markets in general.[114]

As explained in Chapter 7, acquisitions can provide quick access to a new market. In fact, acquisitions may provide the fastest and often the largest initial international expansion of any of the alternatives. Although acquisitions have become a popular mode of entering international markets, they are not without their costs. International acquisitions carry some of the same disadvantages as domestic acquisitions (see Chapter 7). In addition, they can be expensive and often require debt financing (which also carries an extra cost). International negotiations for acquisitions can be exceedingly complex, generally more complicated than for domestic acquisitions. For example, it is estimated that, in the United States, only 20 per cent of the cross-border bids made lead to a completed acquisition, compared to 40 per cent for domestic acquisitions.[115] Dealing with the legal and regulatory requirements in the host country of the target firm and obtaining appropriate information to negotiate an agreement frequently present significant problems. Finally, the problems of merging the new firm into the acquiring firm often are more complex than in the case of domestic acquisitions. The acquiring firm must deal not only with different corporate cultures, but also with potentially different social cultures and practices. Therefore, while international acquisitions have been popular because of the rapid access to new markets they provide, they also carry with them important costs and multiple risks.

Wal-Mart, the world's largest retailer, has used several entry modes to globalise its operations. For example, in China, the firm used a joint-venture mode of entry. To begin the firm's foray into Latin American countries, Wal-Mart also used joint ventures. But in some cases it acquired its venture partner after entering the host country's market. As described earlier, Wal-Mart has used acquisitions to enter European markets. Thus, the most effective mode of entering a particular international market must be carefully considered and selected.

Interestingly, as mergers and acquisitions become more common in Europe, they are beginning to mirror such activity among US firms. For instance, the number of hostile European takeover attempts has increased greatly in recent years. Olivetti made a hostile takeover bid for Telecom Italia, which tried to fend off the takeover with a restructuring plan. Olivetti was not deterred and made a larger offer. Telecom Italia then agreed to be acquired by Deutsche Telekom, but Olivetti entered into a bidding war and eventually won the bid to acquire Telecom Italia. Likewise, Vodafone AirTouch (based in England) actively pursued a hostile takeover of Mannesmann, a German firm. However, Mannesmann actively fought the takeover attempt in almost any way possible.

Sometimes, takeover attempts become personal contests between the companies' executives, as opposed to taking the appropriate action for the shareholders.[116]

New wholly owned subsidiary

> A **greenfield venture** is one in which a new wholly owned subsidiary is established.

The establishment of a new wholly owned subsidiary is referred to as a **greenfield venture**. This is often a complex and potentially costly process, but it has the advantage of affording the firm maximum control and, therefore, if successful, has the most potential to provide above-average returns. This is especially true of firms with strong intangible capabilities that might be leveraged through a greenfield venture.[117] The risks are also high, however, because of the costs involved in establishing a new business operation in a new country. The firm may have to acquire the knowledge and expertise of the existing market by hiring either host-country nationals, possibly from competitive firms, or consultants (which can be costly). Still, the firm maintains control over the technology, marketing and distribution of its products. Alternatively, the company must build new manufacturing facilities, establish distribution networks, and learn and implement appropriate marketing strategies to compete in the new market.

Kmart, in the United States, used a greenfield venture to establish a store on the Pacific island of Guam. The 20 000-square-metre establishment was opened in 1995 and has been highly successful. Kmart took a risk, but research showed that the market was largely controlled by small retailers without the ability to carry the variety of merchandise handled by Kmart. Kmart's success in Guam continued even during the Asian economic crisis. The Kmart in Guam not only serves the residents of Guam, but also is a magnet for tourists. This Kmart sells more of Tengu beef jerky (made in California) than any other retailer in the world. Japanese tourists are particularly taken with the store. Thus, while Kmart took risks to establish its business in Guam, the investment has paid handsome dividends.[118]

Dynamics of mode of entry

A firm's choice of mode of entry into international markets is determined by a number of factors.[119] Initially, market entry will often be through export, because this requires no foreign manufacturing expertise and investment only in distribution. Licensing can facilitate the product improvement necessary to enter foreign markets, as in the Komatsu example. Strategic alliances have been popular because they allow a firm to connect with an experienced partner already in the targeted market. Strategic alliances also reduce risk through the sharing of costs. All three modes therefore are best for early market development tactics.

To secure a stronger presence in international markets, acquisitions or greenfield ventures may be required. Many Japanese automobile manufacturers, such as Honda, Nissan and Toyota, have gained a presence in the United States through both greenfield ventures and joint ventures. Toyota has particularly strong intangible production capabilities that it has been able to transfer through greenfield ventures.[120] Both acquisitions and greenfield ventures are likely to come at later stages in the development of an international diversification strategy. In addition, both strategies tend to be more successful when the firm making the investment has considerable resources, particularly in the form of valuable core competencies.[121] Large, diversified business groups, often found in emerging economies, not only gain resources through diversification, but also have specialised abilities in managing differences in inward and outward flows of foreign direct investment. In particular, Korean *chaebols* have been adept at making acquisitions in emerging economies.[122]

Thus, to enter a global market, a firm selects the entry mode that is best suited to the situation at hand. In some instances, the various options will be followed sequentially, beginning with exporting and ending with greenfield ventures. In other cases, the firm may use several, but not all, of the different entry modes, each in different markets. The decision regarding the entry mode to use is primarily a result of the industry's competitive conditions, the country's situation and government policies, and the firm's unique set of resources, capabilities and core competencies.

Strategic competitiveness outcomes

Once its strategy and mode of entry have been selected, a firm needs to be concerned about the overall success of its strategy. International expansion can be risky and may not result in a competitive advantage. This section examines a number of strategic competitiveness issues suggested by Figure 8.1.

International diversification and returns

International diversification is the primary international corporate-level strategy. In Chapter 6, we discussed the corporate-level strategy of product diversification. Through this strategy, the firm engages in the manufacture and sale of multiple diverse products. **International diversification** is a strategy through which a firm expands the sales of its goods or services across the borders of global regions and countries into different geographic locations or markets. The number of different markets in which it operates and their importance show the degree to which a firm is internationally diversified. The percentage of total sales is often used to measure a region's or country's importance to the firm.[123]

> **International diversification** is a strategy through which a firm expands the sales of its goods or services across the borders of global regions and countries into different geographic locations or markets.

As noted earlier, firms have numerous reasons to diversify internationally. Because of its potential advantages, international diversification should be related positively to firms' returns. Research has shown that, as international diversification increases, firms' returns increase.[124] In fact, the stock market is particularly sensitive to investments in international markets. Firms that are broadly diversified into multiple international markets usually achieve the most positive stock returns.[125] There are also many reasons for the positive effects of international diversification, such as potential economies of scale and experience, location advantages, increased market size and the opportunity to stabilise returns. The stabilisation of returns helps to reduce a firm's overall risk.[126] All of these outcomes can be achieved by smaller and newer ventures, as well as larger and established firms. Recently, it has been shown that new ventures can enjoy higher returns when they learn new technologies from their international diversification.[127]

Firms in the Japanese automobile industry have found that international diversification may allow them to better exploit their core competencies, because sharing knowledge resources between operations can produce synergy.[128] Also, a firm's returns may affect its decision to diversify internationally. For example, poor returns in a domestic market may encourage a firm to expand internationally in order to enhance its profit potential. In addition, internationally diversified firms may have access to more flexible labour markets, and may thereby benefit from global scanning for competition and market opportunities.[129] As a result, multinational firms with efficient and competitive operations are more likely to produce above-average returns for their investors and better products for their customers than are solely domestic firms.[130] However, as explained later, international diversification can be carried too far.

International diversification and innovation

In Chapter 1, we noted that the development of new technology is at the heart of strategic competitiveness. Michael Porter stated that a nation's competitiveness depends on the capacity of its industry to innovate and suggested that firms achieve competitive advantage in international markets through innovation. Eventually and inevitably, competitors outperform firms that fail to innovate and improve their operations and products. Therefore, the only way to sustain a competitive advantage is to upgrade it continually.[131]

International diversification provides the potential for firms to achieve greater returns on their innovations (through larger or more numerous markets) and thus lowers the often substantial risks of R&D investments. Therefore, international diversification provides incentives for firms to innovate. In addition, international diversification may be necessary to generate the resources required to sustain a large-scale R&D operation. An environment of rapid technological obsolescence makes it difficult to invest in new technology and the capital-intensive operations required to take advantage of it. Firms operating solely in domestic markets may find such investments problematic because of the length of time required to recoup the original investment. If the time is extended, it may not even be possible to recover the investment before the technology becomes obsolete.[132] As a result, international diversification improves a firm's ability to appropriate additional and necessary returns from innovation before competitors can overcome the initial competitive advantage created by the innovation. In addition, firms moving into international markets are exposed to new products and processes. If they learn about those products and processes and integrate this knowledge into their operations, further innovation can be developed.[133]

The relationship among international diversification, innovation and returns is complex. Some level of performance is necessary to provide the resources to generate international diversification, which in turn provides incentives and resources to invest in R&D. The latter, if done appropriately, should enhance the returns of the firm, which then provides more resources for continued international diversification and investment in R&D.

Because of the potential positive effects of international diversification on performance and innovation, some have argued that such diversification may even enhance returns in product-diversified firms. International diversification would increase market potential in each of these firms' product lines, but the complexity of managing a firm that is both product diversified and internationally diversified is significant. Therefore, it is likely that international diversification can enhance the returns of a firm that is highly product diversified, but only when it is managed well.

Asea Brown Boveri (ABB) may demonstrate these relationships. This US firm's operations involve high levels of both product and international diversification, yet ABB's performance is quite strong. Some believe that the firm's ability to effectively implement the transnational strategy contributes to its strategic competitiveness. To manage itself, ABB assembles culturally diverse corporate and divisional management teams, which are then used to facilitate the simultaneous achievement of global integration and local responsiveness. Evidence suggests that more culturally diverse top-management teams often have a greater knowledge of international markets and their idiosyncrasies.[134] (Top-management teams are discussed further in Chapter 12.) Moreover, an in-depth understanding of diverse markets among top-level managers facilitates intra-firm coordination and the use of long-term, strategically relevant criteria to evaluate the performance of managers and their units. In turn, this approach facilitates improved innovation and performance.[135]

Complexity of managing multinational firms

Although many benefits can be realised by implementing an international strategy, doing so is complex and can produce greater uncertainty.[136] For example, multiple risks are involved when a firm operates in several different countries. Firms can grow only so large and diverse before becoming unmanageable, or the costs of managing them exceed their benefits. Other complexities include the highly competitive nature of global markets, multiple cultural environments, potentially rapid shifts in the value of different currencies and the possible instability of some national governments.

Risks in an international environment

International diversification carries multiple risks.[137] International expansion is difficult to implement, and it is difficult to manage after implementation, because of these risks. The chief risks are political and economic. Taking these risks into account, highly diversified firms are accustomed to market conditions yielding competitive situations that differ from what was predicted. Sometimes, these situations contribute to the firm's strategic competitiveness; on other occasions, they have a negative effect on the firm's efforts.[138] Specific examples of political and economic risks are shown in Figure 8.4.

Figure 8.4 | Risks in the international environment

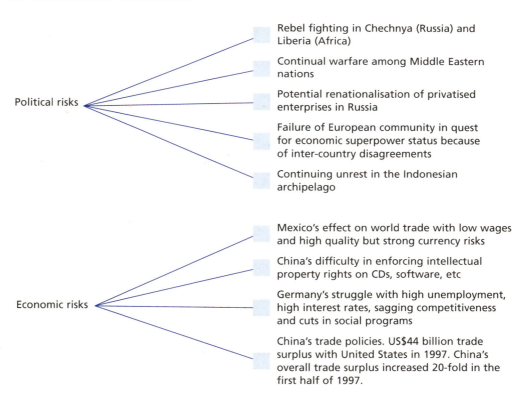

Sources: N. Banerjee, 1996, 'Russia's many regions work to attract funds from foreign investors', *Wall Street Journal*, 30 April, pp. A1, A8; P. Engardio and D. Roberts, 1996, 'Rethinking China', *Business Week*, 4 March, pp. 57–64; R. S. Greenberger, 1996, 'U.S. sharply attacks China over intellectual property', *Wall Street Journal*, 1 May, pp. A3, A4; A. D. Marcus, 1996, 'Israel seems to target Lebanon economy', *Wall Street Journal*, 17 April, p. A16; C. Rosett, 1996, 'Russian Communists target privatizers', *Wall Street Journal*, 13 February, p. A11; P. Stein, 1996, 'Hong Kong feels heavy hand of China', *Wall Street Journal*, 17 April, p. A16; J. Templeman, 1996, 'The economy that fell to earth', *Business Week*, 15 January, p. 46.

Strategic Focus International

Foster's worldwide wine

Competition in the global beer market is intensifying as globalisation creates borderless markets and homogeneity in consumer tastes emerges. Australian premium beer sales in 2000 were dominated by Foster's Brewing Group's Crown Lager and Lion Nathan's Tooheys Extra Dry. Yet during the latter part of 2000, Guinness Australasia launched an aggressive marketing campaign to reinforce its niche position as the top-selling international beer in Australia. Guinness aimed to build market share, given its consumers' traditional cultural links with Britain and Ireland while trying to increase consumption frequency among existing and new customers. Steady sales increases of 20 per cent per year over the last four years, and Guinness Australasia's ownership of the next bestseller in the international category, Kilkenny, guarantees its Australian niche in the short term. Clearly, Foster's faces aggressive competition in its home market.

Foster's is a well-known product name in beer sales in many countries outside Australia and is renowned for its innovative marketing. However, its push into global competitors' traditional markets should be viewed in a similar light to Guinness's Australian expansion strategy. Recent consolidation in the global beer industry has resulted in the world's seventh-largest brewer, Denmark's Carlsberg, stagnating while key rivals Heineken, Interbrew and Anheuser are building their market shares. For example, Belgium's Interbrew embarked on an international acquisition strategy in Britain to move from fifth- to second-largest global brewer to Anheuser-Busch. Scottish and Newcastle had a 28 per cent share of the British market and, through its acquisition of French brewer Kronenbourg, it now has an important strategic presence in Europe. It would appear that Carlsberg did not expand significantly outside its Scandinavian home market and failed to penetrate the lucrative North American market. Foster's strategic future lay elsewhere.

Consumer tastes are changing. Japan's largest brewers are experiencing declining earnings due to a shift towards consumption of non-beer, alcoholic drinks. Despite product differentiation strategies using low-malt brews, it has become apparent that Japanese beer sales will not show the same growth as other alcoholic products.

In 1999–2000, Foster's was also faced with low growth for its mainstream beer products in Australia, but it recognised that changing global demand for wine was a strategic opportunity to transform the company from an Australian brewer into a global beverage group. The brewing group acquired a Californian premium wines producer, Beringer, for $2.6 billion in September 2000. Through this international acquisition, the size of Foster's wine business has more than doubled and it is now in the top three global wine makers by sales volume. Although beer sales currently dominate earnings, it is planned that in five years' time wine growing will account for 50 per cent of Foster's group revenue. In the words of Foster's CEO, Ted Kunkel, 'It has totally redefined the company and it has given it a new impetus and growth horizon for the future.'

The global wine industry is likely to undergo a similar consolidation phase to that being seen in brewing. The strategic significance of Foster's wine business acquisition is more apparent if it can maintain its status in the top three wine makers as global consolidation progresses. The Beringer acquisition gives Foster's access to the difficult-to-enter US wine distribution network and the opportunity to sell its Australian premium wines in a growth market. In the United States Australian wines represent the third-largest by sales volume behind

France and Italy. Australian premium wines from Southcorp and Rosemount are in demand, and there is interest in a possible merger between the two companies to allow them to compete with larger global players. It is also significant that Foster's main Australian competitor, Lion Nathan, has embarked on a similar strategy by taking a 28 per cent share in New Zealand's largest wine company, Montano Group. Lion Nathan will rely on beer sales for the majority of its income in the short term, but, as with Foster's, it has experienced a downturn in beer consumption of its products in the Australian market in the months following the introduction of the GST. Despite the downturn, the Foster's Group has recently posted strong profits, showing the value of its change in strategic direction in the global wine industry.

Sources: J. McCallum and M. Hannen, 2000, 'Foster's global wine push', *Business Review Weekly*, 10 November; S. Evans, 2000, 'Wine sector lures the brewers', *Australian Financial Review*, 26 October; S. Evans, 2000, 'Beer giant starts mixing its drinks', *Australian Financial Review*, 20 October; R. Heller, 2000, 'Brewer droops', *Business Review Weekly*, 27 October; S. Lloyd, 2000, 'To be sure, Guinness sticks to a quirky campaign', *Business Review Weekly*, 15 September; Bloomberg, 2001, 'Japan's big brewers fall short of targets', *Australian Financial Review*, 20 February; S. Evans, 2001, 'Brewer relies on King in flat market', *Australian Financial Review*, 19 February; S. Evans, 2001, 'Race on to wind up Southcorp deal', *Australian Financial Review*, 19 February; S. Evans, 2001, 'Foster's surges after first taste of Beringer', *Australian Financial Review*, 13 February.

Political risks

> Political risks are related to instability in national governments and to war, both civil and international.

Political risks are related to instability in national governments and to war, both civil and international. Instability in a national government creates numerous problems. Among these are economic risks and uncertainty created by government regulation, the existence of many, possibly conflicting, legal authorities, and the potential nationalisation of private assets. For example, foreign firms that are investing in Russia may have concerns about the stability of the national government and what might happen to their investments or assets in that country should there be a major change in government.

Different concerns exist for foreign firms investing in China. They are less worried about the potential for major changes in China's national government than about the uncertainty of China's regulation of foreign business investments. For example, some analysts suggest that China has an unclear foreign-investor policy. Some of China's leaders worry about the flood of foreign investment and the potential for the government to lose control over the country's economy. Unfortunately, all debate on the topic is conducted in secrecy within the Chinese government and, thus, makes the situation even more unclear to potential foreign investors, creating further risk.[139]

Zeneca, a British chemical company, negotiated with Chinese government officials for five years for the right to build a large herbicide plant in the eastern province of Jiangsu. An even more direct example of political risk was the announced policy change in 1999 to reduce sales of cell phones by foreign companies. In addition, in 1999, a top Chinese official declared that ownership by a foreign company in the Chinese Internet was illegal.[140]

Economic risks

Economic risks are interdependent with political risks, as noted earlier. Chief among the economic risks of international diversification are the differences and fluctuations in the value of different currencies. With Australian firms, the value of the dollar relative to other currencies determines the value of their international assets and earnings; for example, an increase in the value of the Australian dollar can reduce the value of Australian firms' international assets and earnings in other countries. Furthermore, the value of different currencies can, at times, dramatically affect a firm's competitiveness in global markets because of its effect on the prices of goods manufactured in different

Brazil's economy underwent a major change to control inflation. As a result of the country's economic recovery, it is now more attractive to foreign investors.

countries. An increase in the value of the dollar can harm Australian firms' exports to international markets because of the price differential of the products.

Drypers experienced a strong decrease in sales due to the devaluation of Brazil's real in 1999. The devaluation reduced consumers' buying power and thus decreased Drypers' sales in Brazil. Its manufacturing facilities in Argentina became less viable, too, because they served the Brazilian market. The devaluation also hurt Argentina's economy. As a result, Drypers moved some of its manufacturing facilities from Argentina to Malaysia and Mexico. Still, while losing money in Latin America, Drypers wants to stay the course because of a higher fertility rate in that region of the world (2.9 children per mother), where there is a strong demand for baby products.[141]

Limits to international expansion: Management problems

Research has shown that firms tend to receive positive returns on early international diversification, but they often level off and become negative as the diversification increases past some point.[142] There are several reasons for the limits to the positive effects of international diversification. First, greater geographic dispersion across country borders increases the costs of coordination between units and the distribution of products. Second, trade barriers, logistical costs, cultural diversity and other differences by country (for example, access to raw materials and different employee skill levels) greatly complicate the implementation of an international diversification strategy.[143]

Institutional and cultural factors often represent strong barriers to the transfer of a firm's competitive advantages from one country to another. Marketing programs often have to be redesigned and new distribution networks established when firms expand into new countries. In addition, they may encounter different labour costs and capital charges. In general, it is difficult to implement, manage and control a firm's international operations effectively.[144]

Robert Shapiro, former CEO of Monsanto (now a part of Pharmacia), was once considered a genius for the development of NutraSweet and other positive strategic actions that he has taken. However, he made the fundamental mistake of assuming that Europe was similar to the United States. As a result of this miscalculation, Monsanto's genetically engineered seeds, such as herbicide-resistant soybeans, have been strongly rejected in Europe.[145] Similarly, Wal-Mart made significant mistakes in some Latin American markets. For example, Wal-Mart executives learned, surprisingly, that giant parking lots do not draw huge numbers of customers in a country where the shoppers do not have cars. The lots were so far away from the bus stops used by many Mexicans for travelling and shopping that potential customers did not come to Wal-Mart stores because they could not easily get their goods home.[146]

The amount of international diversification that can be managed will vary from firm to firm and according to the abilities of each firm's managers. The problems of central coordination and integration are mitigated if the firm diversifies into more friendly countries that have cultures similar to its own country's culture. In that case, there are fewer trade barriers, the laws and customs are better understood, and the product is easier to adapt to local markets. For example, US firms may find it less difficult to expand their operations into Canada and Western European countries than into Asian countries.[147]

Other management problems

One critical concern firms have is that the global marketplace is highly competitive. Firms that are accustomed to a highly competitive domestic market experience more complexities in international markets, caused not only by the number of competitors encountered, but also by the differences among those competitors. For instance, an Australian firm expanding its operations into an Asian country may encounter competitors not only from within Asia but from almost any Western country. Firms from each of these countries may enjoy different competitive advantages. Some may have low labour costs, others may have easy access to financing and low capital costs, and still others may have access to new high technology. Adapting to all these differences is neither simple nor easy. Finally, attempting to understand the strategic intent of a competitor is more complex because of all these different cultures and mind-sets.[148]

Another problem associated with international diversification focuses on the relationships between the host government and the multinational corporation. For example, while Japanese firms face few trade barriers in competing in US markets, US firms often encounter many barriers to selling their products and operating in Japanese markets.[149] These regulations have traditionally kept the yen high relative to the dollar by keeping out imports and reducing the value of Japanese exports. The latter, in turn, increases the price of Japanese products abroad. As noted earlier, the problem has been reversing itself somewhat, but much more remains to be done to reduce entry barriers. Many firms, such as Toyota and General Motors, are turning to strategic alliances to overcome those barriers. They do so to form inter-organisational networks that allow firms to share resources and risks, but that also help to build flexibility.[150]

Summary

- International diversification is increasing not only because of traditional motivations, but also for emerging reasons. Traditional motives include extending the product life cycle, securing key resources and having access to low-cost labour. Emerging motivations focus on the combination of the Internet and mobile telecommunications, which facilitates global transactions. Also, there is increased pressure for global integration as the demand for commodities becomes borderless, and yet pressure is also increasing for local country responsiveness.
- An international strategy usually attempts to capitalise on four important opportunities: an increased market size; the opportunity to earn a return on large investments, such as plant and capital equipment or research and development; economies of scale and learning; and advantages of location.
- International business-level strategies are similar to the generic business-level strategies and consist of international cost leadership, international differentiation, international focus, and international integrated cost leadership/differentiation strategies. However, each of these strategies is usually grounded in one or more home-country advantages, as Porter's diamond model suggests. The diamond model emphasises four determinants: factors of production, demand conditions, related and supporting industries, and patterns of firm strategy, structure and rivalry.
- There are three types of international corporate-level strategies. A multi-domestic strategy focuses on competition within each country in which a firm operates. Firms employing a multi-domestic strategy decentralise strategic and operating decisions to the strategic business units operating in each country, so that each can tailor its goods and services to the local market. A global strategy assumes more standardisation of products across country boundaries; therefore, competitive strategy is centralised and controlled by the home office. A transnational strategy seeks to combine aspects of both multi-domestic and global strategies in order to emphasise both local responsiveness and global integration and coordination. This strategy is difficult to implement, requiring an integrated network and a culture of individual commitment.
- Although the transnational strategy is difficult to implement, environmental trends are causing many multinational firms to consider the need for both global efficiencies and local responsiveness. Many large multinational firms – particularly those with many diverse products – use a multi-domestic strategy with some product lines and a global strategy with others.
- Some firms decide to compete only in certain regions of the world, as opposed to viewing all markets in the world as potential opportunities. Competing in regional markets allows firms and managers to focus their learning on specific markets, cultures, locations, resources, etc.
- Firms may enter international markets in one of several different ways, including exporting, licensing, forming strategic alliances, making acquisitions and establishing new wholly owned subsidiaries, often referred to as greenfield ventures. Most firms begin with exporting or licensing, because of their lower costs and risks, but later may expand to strategic alliances and acquisitions. The most expensive and risky means of entering a new international market is through the establishment of a new wholly owned subsidiary. On the other hand, such subsidiaries provide the advantages of maximum control by the firm and, if they are successful, the greatest returns.
- International diversification facilitates innovation in a firm, because it provides a larger market to gain more and faster returns from investments in innovation. In addition, international diversification may generate the resources necessary to sustain a large-scale R&D program.
- In general, international diversification is related to above-average returns, but this assumes that the diversification is implemented effectively and that the firm's international operations will be well managed. International diversification provides greater economies of scope and learning, which, along with greater innovation, help to produce above-average returns.
- Several risks are involved with managing multinational operations. Among these are political risks (for example, instability of national governments) and economic risks (for example, fluctuations in the value of a country's currency).
- There are also limits to the ability to manage international expansion effectively. International diversification increases coordination and distribution costs, and management problems are exacerbated by trade barriers, logistical costs and cultural diversity, among other factors.
- Finally, international markets are highly competitive, and firms must maintain an effective working relationship with the host government.

Review questions

1. What are the traditional and emerging motives that are causing firms to expand internationally?
2. What four factors provide a basis for international business-level strategies?
3. What are the generic international business-level strategies? How do they differ from each other?
4. What are the differences among the three corporate-level international strategies: multi-domestic, global and transnational?
5. What environmental trends are currently affecting international strategy?
6. What five modes of international expansion are available, and what is the normal sequence of their use?
7. What is the relationship between international diversification and innovation? How does international diversification affect innovation? What is the effect of international diversification on a firm's returns?
8. What are the risks involved in expanding internationally and managing multinational firms?
9. What are the factors that create limits to the positive outcomes of international expansion?

Application discussion questions

1. Given the advantages of international diversification, why do some firms choose not to expand internationally?
2. How can a small firm diversify globally using the Internet?
3. How do firms choose among the alternative modes for expanding internationally and moving into new markets (for example, forming a strategic alliance versus establishing a wholly owned subsidiary)?
4. Does international diversification affect innovation similarly in all industries? Why or why not?
5. What is an example of political risk in expanding operations into Indonesia or China?
6. Why do some firms gain competitive advantages in international markets? Explain.
7. Why is it important to understand the strategic intent of strategic alliance partners and competitors in international markets?
8. What are the challenges associated with pursuing the transnational strategy? Explain.

Ethics questions

1. As firms attempt to internationalise, there may be a temptation to locate their facilities where product liability laws are lax in testing new products. What are some examples in which this motivation is the driving force behind international expansion?
2. Regulations and laws regarding the sale and distribution of tobacco products are stringent in the Australian market. Use the Internet to investigate selected US tobacco firms to identify if sales are increasing in foreign markets compared to domestic markets. In what countries are sales increasing, and why? What is your assessment of this practice?
3. Some firms outsource production to foreign countries. Although the presumed rationale for such outsourcing is to reduce labour costs, examine the labour laws (for instance, the strictness of child labour laws) and laws on environmental protection in another country. What does your examination suggest from an ethical perspective?
4. Are there markets that the Australian government protects through subsidies and tariffs? If so, which ones and why? How will the continuing development of e-commerce potentially affect these efforts?
5. Should Australia seek to impose trade sanctions on other countries, such as China, because of human rights violations?
6. Latin America has been experiencing significant changes in both political orientation and economic development. Describe these changes. What strategies should foreign international businesses implement, if any, to influence government policy in these countries? Is there a chance that the political changes will reverse?

Internet exercise

As explained in the Opening Case, convenience stores in Japan, such as the corner 7-Eleven, and supermarkets in Britain are capitalising on Internet commerce by offering their customers easy access, e-service, and attractive prices and selections. Located at www.7dream.com, 7-Eleven allows shoppers to surf, order and pay for merchandise with cash, the most trusted method of payment in Japan, a country with a comparatively low crime rate. Locate the website of Britain's large supermarket chain, Tesco, at www.tesco.com. What types of services offered would appeal to you? What do you see as a deterrent to introducing these and other e-commerce services into supermarkets, hypermarkets and convenience stores in Australia?

e-project: This chapter explains the different methods of entering foreign markets. Using sources on the Internet provided by the Department of Foreign Affairs and Trade (www.dfat.gov.au) and private resources such as www.china-venture.com, plan the export of a new line of Australian surfwear clothing to Shanghai and Beijing, China. Assume that you plan to manufacture the clothing inside China and distribute them through local stores within those two cities.

Notes

1. T. Isobe, S. Makino and D. B. Montgomery, 2000, 'Resource commitment, entry timing and market performance of foreign direct investments in emerging economies: The case of Japanese international joint ventures in China', *Academy of Management Journal*, in press.
2. I. Filatotchev, T. Buck and V. Zhukov, 2000, "Downsizing in privatized firms in Russia, Ukraine and Belarus: Theory and empirical evidence', *Academy of Management Journal*, in press; P. Krantz, 2000, 'How Yeltsin blew Russia's big chance', *Business Week*, 17 January, p. 50.
3. J. Wheatley, 2000, 'TERRA: Brazil ISP launches free access', 21 January: http://news.ft.com/nbearchive.
4. J. B. White, 1998, 'There are no German or U.S. companies, only successful ones', *Wall Street Journal*, 7 May, pp. A1, A11.
5. B. L. Kedia and A. Mukherji, 1999, 'Global managers: Developing a mindset for global competitiveness', *Journal of World Business*, 34(3), pp. 230–51.
6. T. P. Murtha, S. A. Lenway and R. P. Bagozzi, 1998, 'Global mind-sets and cognitive shift in a complex multinational corporation', *Strategic Management Journal*, 19, pp. 97–114.
7. 'Bagged cement', 1999, *The Economist*, 18 June: www.economist.com/editorial.
8. B. R. Koka, J. E. Prescott and R. Madhaven, 1999, 'Contagion influence on trade and investment policy: A network perspective', *Journal of International Business Studies*, 30, pp. 127–48.
9. J. Carey, 1999, 'This drug's for you', *Business Week*, 18 January, pp. 98–100.
10. L. Colquhuon, 2000, 'Australia's foreign whitegoods industry', *Business Review Weekly*, 1 December.
11. C. W. L. Hill, 2000, *International Business: Competing in the Global Marketplace*, 3rd edition (Boston: Irwin/McGraw-Hill), pp. 378–80; B. J. Punnett and D. A. Ricks, 1997, *International Business*, 2nd edition (Cambridge, MA: Blackwell Publishers), p. 8.
12. R. Vernon, 1996, 'International investment and international trade in the product cycle', *Quarterly Journal of Economics*, 80, pp. 190–207.
13. A. Bernstein, S. Jackson and J. Byrne, 1997, 'Jack cracks the whip again', *Business Week*, 15 December, pp. 34–5.
14. 'Flexible and cheap', 1997, *Financial Times*, 12 December, p. II.
15. J. N. Kapferer, 1998, 'Making brands work around the world', in As Business Goes Global (Part One), *Financial Times*, 12–13 February.
16. Punnett and Ricks, *International Business*, pp. 334–7.
17. S. Batholomew, 1997, 'National systems of biotechnology innovation: Complex interdependencies in the global system', *Journal of International Business Studies*, 28, pp. 241–66; A. Madhok, 1997, 'Cost, value and foreign market entry mode: The transaction and the firm', *Strategic Management Journal*, 18, pp. 39–61.
18. W. Kuemmerle, 1997, 'Building effective R&D capabilities abroad', *Harvard Business Review*, 75(2), pp. 61–70; B. J. Oviatt and P. P. McDougall, 1995, 'Global start-ups: Entrepreneurs on a worldwide stage', *Academy of Management Executive*, IX(2), pp. 30–44.
19. J. J. Choi and M. Rajan, 1997, 'A joint test of market segmentation and exchange risk factor in international capital markets', *Journal of International Business Studies*, 28, pp. 29–49.
20. R. E. Hoskisson, L. Eden, C. M. Lau and M. Wright, 2000, 'Strategy in emerging economies', *Academy of Management Journal*, in press; D. J. Arnold and J. A. Quelch, 1998, 'New strategies in emerging markets', *Sloan Management Review*, 40, pp. 7–20.
21. S. Lovett, L. C. Simmons and R. Kali, 1999, 'Guanxi versus the market: Ethics and efficiency', *Journal of International Business Studies*, 30, pp. 231–48; J. L. Xie, 1996, 'Karasek's model in the People's Republic of China: Effects of job demands, control, and individual differences', *Academy of Management Journal*, 39, pp. 1594–618.
22. M. Dwyer, 2001, 'China tops the world as the worst place to do business', *Australian Financial Review*, 14 February.
23. Y. Luo and M. W. Peng, 1999, 'Learning to compete in a transition economy: Experience, environment and performance', *Journal of International Business Studies*, 30, pp. 269–95; M. A. Hitt, M. T. Dacin, B. B. Tyler and D. Park, 1997, 'Understanding the differences in Korean and U.S. executives' strategic orientations', *Strategic Management Journal*, 18, pp. 159–67.
24. G. Edmondson, 1999, 'Danone hits its stride', *Business Week*, 1 February, pp. 52–3.
25. Bernstein, Jackson and Byrne, 'Jack cracks the whip again'.
26. X. Martin, A. Swaminathan and W. Mitchell, 1999, 'Organizational evolution in the interorganizational environment: Incentives and constraints on international expansion strategy', *Administrative Science Quarterly*, 43, pp. 566–601.
27. S. Zaheer and E. Mosakowski, 1997, 'The dynamics of the liability of foreignness: A global study of survival in financial services', *Strategic Management Journal*, 18, pp. 439–64.
28. C. Lacey, 2000, 'Teltsra seeks third partner', *Australian Financial Review*, 17 October.
29. N. Shoebridge, 2000, 'Telstra's great helmsman holds course for Asia', *Business Review Weekly*, 6 October.
30. E. Beck and R. Balu, 1998, 'Europe is deaf to snap! crackle! pop!', *Wall Street Journal*, 22 June, pp. B1, B8.
31. B. Morris and P. Sellers, 2000, 'What really happened at Coke?', *Fortune*, 10 January, pp. 114–16.
32. W. Kuemmerle, 1999, 'The drivers of foreign direct investment into research and development: An empirical investigation', *Journal of International Business Studies*, 30, pp. 1–24.
33. K. L. Miller and J. Muller, 1999, 'Daimler Chrysler: The grace period is over', *Business Week*, 29 March, p. 50; E. Thornton, 1999, 'Remaking Nissan', *Business Week*, 15 November, pp. 70–6; D. Owen, 1999, 'Renault lifted by news of interest in Korean carmaker', 30 December: www.ft.com/nbearchive.
34. 'Smoke gets in your eyes', 1999, *The Economist*, 9 October, p. 83.
35. G. Edmondson, J. Rae-Dupree and K. Capell, 1999, 'How Airbus could rule the skies', *Business Week*, 2 August, p. 54; 'DASA, Aerospatiale to merge; Deal will also include Airbus', 1999, *Wall Street Journal Interactive*, 14 November: www.interactive.wsj.com/articles.
36. W. Shan and J. Song, 1997, 'Foreign direct investment and the sourcing of technological advantage: Evidence from the biotechnology industry', *Journal of International Business Studies*, 28, pp. 267–84.
37. L. G. Thomas, III and G. Waring, 1999, 'Competing capitalism: Capital investment in American, German and Japanese firms', *Strategic Management Journal*, 20, pp. 729–48.
38. A. J. Venables, 1995, 'Economic integration and the location of firms', *The American Economic Review*, 85, pp. 296–300.
39. E. Thornton, K. Kerwin and K. Naughton, 1999, 'Can Honda go it alone?', *Business Week*, 5 July, pp. 42–5.
40. H. Bresman, J. Birkinshaw and R. Nobel, 1999, 'Knowledge transfer in international acquisitions', *Journal of International Business Studies*, 30, pp. 439–62; J. Birkinshaw, 1997, 'Entrepreneurship in multinational corporations: The characteristics of subsidiary initiatives', *Strategic Management Journal*, 18, pp. 207–29.
41. Luo and Peng, 'Learning to compete in a transition economy'.
42. S. Makino and A. Delios, 1996, 'Local knowledge transfer and performance: Implications for alliance formation in Asia', *Journal of International Business Studies*, 27 (Special Issue), pp. 905–27.
43. K. Ferdows, 1997, 'Making the most of foreign factories', *Harvard Business Review*, 75(2), pp. 73–88.
44. M. B. Sarkar, S. T. Cavusgil and P. S. Aulakh, 1999, 'International expansion of telecommunication carriers: The influence of market structure, network characteristics, and entry imperfections', *Journal of International Business Studies*, 30, pp. 361–82.

45 R. Bromley, 2001, 'Kiwis chase cream', *The Australian*, 17 January.
46 D. J. Teece, G. Pisano and A. Shuen, 1997, 'Dynamic capabilities and strategic management', *Strategic Management Journal*, 18, pp. 509–33.
47 A. Campbell and M. Alexander, 1997, 'What's wrong with strategy?', *Harvard Business Review*, 75(6), pp. 42–51.
48 A. Rugman, 1998, 'Multinationals as regional flagships', in As Business Goes Global (Part One), *Financial Times*, 10–11 February, pp. 6–9.
49 M. E. Porter, 1990, *The Competitive Advantage of Nations* (New York: The Free Press).
50 Ibid., p. 84.
51 Ibid., p. 89.
52 A. Edgecliffe-Johnson, 1999, 'A friendly store from Arkansas', *Financial Times*, 19 June, p. 7.
53 N. D. Schwartz, 1998, 'Why Wall Street's buying Wal-Mart again', *Fortune*, 16 February, pp. 92–4.
54 Schwartz, 'Why Wall Street's buying Wal-Mart again', p. 94; 'Sam's travels', 1997, *Financial Times*, 19 December, p. 13.
55 C. S. Smith, 1999, 'Volkswagen AG plans to build low-price car to sell in China', *Wall Street Journal*, 30 June, p. A19.
56 Porter, *Competitive Advantage*, p. 133.
57 D. Woodruff, 1997, 'Service with a what?', *Business Week*, 8 September, pp. 130F–130H.
58 I. M. Kunii and S. Baker, 2000, 'Amazing DoCoMo', *Business Week Online*, 9 January: www.businessweek.com.
59 J. A. Byrne, 1999, 'Phillip Morris', *Business Week*, 29 November, pp. 176–92.
60 T. Burns, 1997, 'Niche goals bring away results', *Financial Times*, 17 November, p. II; Oviatt and McDougall, 'Global start-ups'.
61 Porter, *Competitive Advantage*, pp. 210–25.
62 M. J. Enright and P. Tenti, 1990, 'How the diamond works: The Italian ceramic tile industry', *Harvard Business Review*, 68(2), pp. 90–1.
63 Burns, 'Niche goals bring away results', p. 17.
64 D. Lei, M. A. Hitt and J. D. Goldhar, 1996, 'Advanced manufacturing technology: The impact on organization design and strategic flexibility', *Organization Studies*, 17, pp. 501–23.
65 R. D. Ireland and M. A. Hitt, 1999, 'Achieving and maintaining strategic competitiveness in the 21st century: The role of strategic leadership', *Academy of Management Executive*, 13(1), pp. 43–57.
66 N. Tait, 2000, 'Caterpillar: Low demand pulls profits', 22 January: www.ft.com/nbearchives.
67 K. J. Delaney, 1999, 'Compaq boosts role of internet sales, plans single pricing for firms in Europe', *Wall Street Journal*, 8 December, p. B2.
68 J. M. Geringer, S. Tallman and D. M. Olsen, 2000, 'Product and international diversification among Japanese multinational firms', *Strategic Management Journal*, 21, pp. 51–80.
69 M. A. Hitt, R. E. Hoskisson and R. D. Ireland, 1994, 'A mid-range theory of the interactive effects of international and product diversification on innovation and performance', *Journal of Management*, 20, pp. 297–326.
70 S. Ghoshal, 1987, 'Global strategy: An organizing framework', *Strategic Management Journal*, 8, pp. 425–40.
71 J. Taggart and N. Hood, 1999, 'Determinants of autonomy in multinational corporation subsidiaries', *European Management Journal*, 17, pp. 226–36.
72 T. T. Herbert, 1999, 'Multinational strategic planning: Matching central expectations to local realities', *Long Range Planning*, 32, pp. 81–7.
73 'The weakling kicks back', 1999, *The Economist*, 2 July: www.economist.com/editorial.
74 Ghoshal, 'Global strategy'.
75 Y. Luo, 1999, 'International strategy and subsidiary performance in China', *Thunderbird International Business Review*, 41, pp. 153–78.
76 J. K. Johaansson and G. S. Yip, 1994, 'Exploiting globalization potential: U.S. and Japanese strategies', *Strategic Management Journal*, 15, pp. 579–601.
77 'From desert to tundra, becoming a global power in rental', 1999, *Financial Times*, 20 October, p. 24.
78 C. A. Bartlett and S. Ghoshal, 1989, *Managing Across Borders: The Transnational Solution* (Boston: Harvard Business School Press).
79 Luo, 'International strategy and subsidiary performance in China'.
80 J. B. White, 1999, 'Ford's CEO Nasser ponders giving more authority to regional units', *Wall Street Journal Interactive*, 17 September: www.interactive.wsj.com/articles.
81 F. Rose, 1999, 'Think globally, script locally', *Fortune*, 8 November, pp. 157–60.
82 Govindarajan and Gupta, 'Setting a course'; A. Saxenian, 1994, *Regional Advantage: Culture and Competition in Silicon Valley and Route 128* (Cambridge, MA: Harvard University Press).
83 Rugman, 'Multinationals as regional flagships', p. 6.
84 Hill, *International Business: Competing in the Global Marketplace*.
85 J. I. Martinez, J. A. Quelch and J. Ganitsky, 1992, 'Don't forget Latin America', *Sloan Management Review*, 33 (Winter), pp. 78–92.
86 D. Mahoney, M. Trigg, R. Griffin and M. Pustay, 1998, *International Business: A Managerial Perspective* (Melbourne: Addison Wesley Longman).
87 J. Chang and P. M. Rosenzweig, 1998, 'Industry and regional patterns in sequential foreign market entry', *Journal of Management Studies*, 35, pp. 797–822.
88 V. Govindarajan and A. Gupta, 1998, ''How to build a global presence', in As Business Goes Global (Part One), *Financial Times*, 10–11 February; Madhok, 'Cost, value and foreign market entry mode', p. 41.
89 Y. Pan and P. S. K. Chi, 1999, 'Financial performance and survival of multinational corporations in China', *Strategic Management Journal*, 20, pp. 359–74.
90 Punnett and Ricks, *International Business*, pp. 249–50; G. M. Naidu and V. K. Prasad, 1994, 'Predictors of export strategy and performance of small- and medium-sized firms', *Journal of Business Research*, 31, pp. 107–15.
91 P. S. Aulakh, M. Kotabe and H. Teegen, 2000, 'Export strategies and performance of firms from emerging economies: Evidence from Brazil, Chile and Mexico', *Academy of Management Journal*, in press.
92 A. Dworkin, 1999, 'Texas exports pinched by global slowdown', *Dallas Morning News*, 10 March, pp. D1, D10.
93 J. H. Prager, 1999, 'Many small businesses continue to have "euro phobia"', *Wall Street Journal*, 6 April, p. B2.
94 Hill, *International Business*, pp. 436–7.
95 M. A. Hitt and R. D. Ireland, 2000, 'The intersection of entrepreneurship and strategic management research', in D. L. Sexton and H. Landstrom (eds), *The Blackwell Handbook of Entrepreneurship* (Oxford, UK: Blackwell Publishers, Ltd).
96 B. Schlender, 1995, 'Sony on the brink', *Fortune*, 12 June, p. 66.
97 J. R. Green and S. Schotchmer, 1995, 'On the division of profit in sequential innovation', *The Rand Journal of Economics*, 26, pp. 20–33.
98 B. Einhorn, 1997, 'China's CD pirates find a new hangout', *Business Week*, 15 December, p. 138F.
99 A. Marsh, 1999, 'Big Jakk attack', *Forbes*, 1 November, pp. 274–6.
100 C. A. Bartlett and S. Rangan, 1992, 'Komatsu Limited', in C. A. Bartlett and S. Ghoshal (eds), *Transnational Management: Text, Cases and Readings in Cross-Border Management* (Homewood, IL: Irwin), pp. 311–26.
101 A. Jan and M. Zeng, 1999, 'International joint venture instability: A critique of previous research, a reconceptualization, and directions for future research', *Journal of International Business Studies*, 30, pp. 397–414; A. C. Inkpen and P. W. Beamish, 1997, 'Knowledge, bargaining power, and the instability of international joint ventures', *Academy of Management Review*, 22, pp. 177–202; S. H. Park and G. R. Ungson, 1997, 'The effect of national culture, organizational complementarity, and economic motivation on joint venture dissolution', *Academy of Management Journal*, 40, pp. 279–307.
102 Y. Pan and D. K. Tse, 1996, 'Cooperative strategies between foreign firms in an overseas country', *Journal of International Business Studies*, 27 (Special Issue), pp. 929–46.
103 M. A. Hitt, B. W. Keats and S. M. DeMarie, 1998, 'Navigating in the new competitive landscape: Building strategic flexibility and competitive advantage in the 21st century', *Academy of Management Executive*, XII(4), pp. 22–42.
104 B. L. Simonin, 1999, 'Transfer of marketing know-how in international strategic alliances: An empirical investigation of the role and antecedents of knowledge ambiguity', *Journal of International Business Studies*, 30, pp. 463–90; M. A. Lyles and J. E. Salk, 1996, 'Knowledge acquisition from foreign parents in international joint ventures: An empirical examination in the Hungarian context', *Journal of International Business Studies*, 27 (Special Issue), pp. 877–903.
105 M. A. Hitt, M. T. Dacin, E. Levitas, J.-L. Arregle and A. Borza, 2000, 'Partner selection in emerging and developed market contexts: Resource based and organizational learning perspectives', *Academy of Management Journal*, in press; J. A. Mathews and D. S. Cho, 1999, 'Combinative capabilities and organizational learning in latecomer firms: The case of the Korean semiconductor industry', *Journal of World Business*, 34, pp. 139–56.

106. D. Sparks, 1999, 'The global rush to find partners', *Business Week Online*, 25 October: www.businessweek.com/bwarchive.
107. C. R. Fey and P. W. Beamish, 1999, 'Strategies for managing Russian international joint venture conflict', *European Management Journal*, 17, pp. 99–106.
108. M. T. Dacin, M. A. Hitt and E. Levitas, 1997, 'Selecting partners for successful international alliances: Examination of U.S. and Korean firms', *Journal of World Business*, 32, pp. 3–16.
109. A. C. Inkpen, 1999, 'Case study: Global one', *Thunderbird International Business Review*, 41, pp. 337–53.
110. Y. Pan, S. Li and D. K. Tse, 1999, 'The impact of order and mode of market entry on profitability and market share', *Journal of International Business Studies*, 30, pp. 81–104.
111. M. A. Hitt, R. E. Hoskisson and H. Kim, 1997, 'International diversification: Effects on innovation and firm performance in product-diversified firms', *Academy of Management Journal*, 40, pp. 767–98.
112. M. A. Hitt, J. S. Harrison and R. D. Ireland, 2001, *Creating Value through Mergers and Acquisitions* (New York: Oxford University Press).
113. T. A. Stewart, 1999, 'See Jack. See Jack run', *Fortune*, 27 September, pp. 124–36.
114. K. Naughton and S. Reed, 1999, *Business Week*, 8 February, p. 40.
115. 'French dressing', 1999, *The Economist*, 10 July, pp. 53–4.
116. A. Raghavan and S. Lipin, 1999, 'Europeans are learning mergers the American way', *Wall Street Journal*, 23 April, p. A12; J. Rossant, 1999, 'Germany is leading in the wrong direction', *Business Week*, 13 December, p. 66.
117. K. D. Brouthers and L. E. Brouthers, 2000, 'Acquisition or greenfield start-up? Institutional, cultural and transaction cost influences', *Strategic Management Journal*, 21, pp. 89–97.
118. C. S. Smith, 1999, 'The exotic sound of Guam: "Attention, Kmart shoppers"', *Wall Street Journal*, 12 July, pp. A17, A20.
119. W. C. Kim and P. Hwang, 1992, 'Global strategy and multinationals' entry mode choice', *Journal of International Business Studies*, 23, pp. 29–53.
120. D. K Sobek, II, A. C. Ward and J. K. Liker, 1999, 'Toyota's principles of set-based concurrent engineering', *Sloan Management Review*, 40(2), pp. 53–83.
121. H. Chen, 1999, 'International performance of multinationals: A hybrid model', *Journal of World Business*, 34, pp. 157–70.
122. M. Guillen, 2000, 'Business groups in emerging economies: A resource-based view', *Academy of Management Journal*, in press.
123. Hitt, Hoskisson and Kim, 'International diversification', p. 767.
124. A. Delios and P. W. Beamish, 1999, 'Geographic scope, product diversification, and the corporate performance of Japanese firms', *Strategic Management Journal*, 20, pp. 711–27.
125. C. Y. Tang and S. Tikoo, 1999, 'Operational flexibility and market valuation of earnings', *Strategic Management Journal*, 20, pp. 749–61.
126. J. M. Geringer, P. W. Beamish and R. C. daCosta, 1989, 'Diversification strategy and internationalization: Implications for MNE performance', *Strategic Management Journal*, 10, pp. 109–19; R. E. Caves, 1982, *Multinational Enterprise and Economic Analysis* (Cambridge, MA: Cambridge University Press).
127. S. A. Zahra, R. D. Ireland and M. A. Hitt, 2000, 'International expansion by new venture firms: International diversity, mode of market entry, technological learning and performance', *Academy of Management Journal*, in press.
128. B. Bremner, L. Armstrong, K. Kerwin and K. Naughton, 1997, 'Toyota's crusade', *Business Week*, 7 April, pp. 104–14.
129. S. J. Kobrin, 1991, 'An empirical analysis of the determinants of global integration', *Strategic Management Journal*, 12 (Special Issue), pp. 17–37.
130. M. Kotabe, 1989, 'Hollowing-out of U.S. multinationals and their global competitiveness', *Journal of Business Research*, 19, pp. 1–15.
131. Porter, *Competitive Advantage*.
132. M. Kotabe, 1990, 'The relationship between off-shore sourcing and innovativeness of U.S. multinational firms: An empirical investigation', *Journal of International Business Studies*, 21, pp. 623–38.
133. Y. Luo, 1999, 'Time-based experience and international expansion: The case of an emerging economy', *Journal of Management Studies*, 36, pp. 505–33.
134. S. Finkelstein and D. C. Hambrick, 1996, *Strategic Leadership: Top Executives and Their Effects on Organizations* (St. Paul, MN: West Publishing Company).
135. Hitt, Hoskisson and Kim, 'International diversification', p. 790.
136. W. G. Sanders and M. A. Carpenter, 1998, 'Internationalization and firm governance: The roles of CEO of compensation, top team composition and board structure', *Academy of Management Journal*, 41, pp. 158–78.
137. D. M. Reeb, C. C. Y. Kwok and H. Y. Baek, 1998, 'Systematic risk of the multinational corporation', *Journal of International Business Studies*, 29, pp. 263–79.
138. C. Pompitakpan, 1999, 'The effects of cultural adaptation on business relationships: Americans selling to Japanese and Thais', *Journal of International Business Studies*, 30, pp. 317–38.
139. D. Roberts, 1999, 'Logged on in limbo', *Business Week*, 15 November, p. 64.
140. J. Harding, 1999, 'Zeneca's long march', *Financial Times*, 16 March, p. 17; J. Kynge, 1999, 'Cell phone groups face big cut in China sales', 10 November: www.ft.com/nbearchives; M. Forney and L. Chang, 1999, 'Top Chinese official declares foreign net stakes are illegal', *Wall Street Journal Interactive*, 15 September: www.interactive.wsj.com/articles.
141. J. Moreno, 2000, 'Pursuing the bottom line overseas', *Houston Chronicle*, 23 January, pp. 1D, 4D.
142. Hitt, Hoskisson and Kim, 'International diversification'; S. Tallman and J. Li, 1996, 'Effects of international diversity and product diversity on the performance of multinational firms', *Academy of Management Journal*, 39, pp. 179–96; Hitt, Hoskisson and Ireland, 'A mid-range theory of interactive effects'; Geringer, Beamish and daCosta, 'Diversification strategy'.
143. Porter, *Competitive Advantage*.
144. Hitt, Hoskisson and Kim, 'International diversification'.
145. 'Grim reaper', 1999, *Economist Online*, 23 December: www.economist.com/editorial.
146. A. Sanders, 1999, 'Yankee imperialist', *Forbes*, 13 December, p. 56.
147. Hitt, Dacin, Tyler and Park, 'Understanding the differences'.
148. M. A. Hitt, B. B. Tyler and C. Hardee, 1995, 'Understanding strategic intent in the global marketplace', *Academy of Management Executive*, IX(2), pp. 12–19.
149. D. P. Hamilton, M. Williams and N. Shirouzu, 1995, 'Japan's big problem: Freeing its economy from over regulation', *Wall Street Journal*, 25 April, pp. A1, A6.
150. N. Athanassiou and D. Nigh, 1999, 'The impact of U.S. company internationalization on top management team advice networks: A tacit knowledge perspective', *Strategic Management Journal*, 20, pp. 83–92; P. C. Ensign, 1999, 'The multinational corporation as a coordinated network: Organizing and managing differently', *Thunderbird International Business Review*, 41, pp. 291–322; M. J. H. Oomens and F. A. J. van den Bosch, 1999, 'Strategic issue management in major European-based companies', *Long Range Planning*, 32, pp. 49–57.

Chapter 9

Cooperative strategy

Objectives

After reading this chapter, you should be able to:

1. Identify and define different types of cooperative strategy.
2. Explain the rationale for a cooperative strategy in three types of competitive situations: slow-cycle, standard-cycle and fast-cycle markets.
3. Understand the advantages and disadvantages of using business-level cooperative strategies.
4. Describe uses of cooperative strategies at the corporate level.
5. Discuss why international cooperative strategies are used in the form of cross-border alliances.
6. Describe the competitive risks of cooperative strategies.
7. Understand why trust is a strategic asset when using cooperative strategies.
8. Describe the two basic approaches that are used to manage strategic alliances.

Using cooperative strategies in the global automobile industry

Competition and competitive rivalry in the global automobile industry are dynamic and intense. Contributing to this situation is over-capacity on a global scale. With excess capacity, firms often seek to enter markets that are new to them or to expand sales in currently served, yet highly lucrative, markets. Both of these strategic decisions are made possible by excess resources in the firm's primary and support activities in which it creates value (see Chapters 6 and 7).

Using focus cost leadership strategies, Korean car manufacturers Hyundai Motors and Kia Motors Corp. announced intentions in 2000 to increase sales in both the US and Australian markets. Hyundai sought initially to increase its volume from 164 000 units in 1999 to 200 000 units in 2000 (or 18 per cent), although it actually managed an increase of some 23 per cent for that period. Kia concentrated on its hot-selling sports utility vehicle (SUV), the Sportage. Sales for this vehicle in the United States grew 82 per cent between 1998 and 1999. To increase sales in this general market segment, Kia introduced the Spectra, a four-door hatchback, into the market in April 2000. In total, Kia expected to sell 160 000 or more units in the United States and Australia in 2000 – up from 1999's volume of 134 000. The target customers for these firms' products are '... lower-income and middle-income buyers with cars that come loaded with features for under [US]$20 000, with some models starting well below [US]$10 000.' Analysts believe that for some customers, these cars, backed by long-term and comprehensive warranties, are substitutes for late-model used cars.

Increasingly, firms use cooperative strategies as one means of competing in the dynamic and challenging 21st-century competitive landscape. The nature and objectives of this type of strategy being used in the global automobile industry are quite varied. For example, Renault SA, France's leading automobile manufacturer, is investing US$400 million over a seven-year period in a production alliance with Nissan Motor Co. Through this alliance, Renault expects to produce roughly 25 000 additional vehicles annually by 2003, all of which are to be sold in Mexico. For the long term, Renault hopes to manufacture 80 000 vehicles per year under its name through this joint venture. The relationship between Renault and Nissan is an example of a complementary strategic alliance.

To improve its competitiveness in the small-car segment, business analysts – and company officials as well – thought that DaimlerChrysler might be forced to form alliances with other firms to manufacture some parts and platforms for a small car. The primary objective of such complementary alliances is for DaimlerChrysler and partner firms to use their resources, capabilities and core competencies to reduce development costs. Controlling product development costs is critical to operating profitably in the world's highly competitive small-car segment. In early 2000, PSA Peugeot Citroen was in talks with DaimlerChrysler regarding the possibility of forming an alliance to produce a small-car platform. It seems that collaborating with other companies to compete successfully in the small-car market segment against firms such as Korea's Hyundai Motors and Kia Motors might be an appropriate strategic direction for DaimlerChrysler to pursue.

General Motors (GM), the world's largest automobile manufacturer, is forming a number of alliances. With Toyota Motor Corp., GM has formed several technology development alliances. One of the objectives of this partnership is to cooperate on advanced environmental technology. In a more complicated cooperative arrangement, Honda Motor Co. and GM formed a basic agreement under which Honda sells low-emission gasoline engines to GM, and Isuzu (a Japanese manufacturer in which GM holds a 49 per cent equity stake) supplies fuel-efficient diesel engines to Honda. In early 2000, GM purchased a 20 per cent stake in Fuji Heavy Industries, the manufacturer of the Subaru line of vehicles, for approximately US$1.4 billion. When formed, this equity strategic alliance, one that is intended to reduce the uncertainty associated with GM's operations in Asia, involved the two companies exchanging technologies, including Fuji's four-wheel-drive systems and continuous variable transmission and GM's environmental technologies, such as its knowledge about fuel cell systems. According to analysts, these cooperative agreements are being developed because, 'GM is trying to boost its share of the auto market in the Asia-Pacific region to 10 per cent from just over 4 per cent currently. But the number one auto maker has elected to do so partly by forming strategic alliances.' Furthermore, an equity-based partnership with Fuji gives GM a presence in a different market segment as well as access to technologies such as the continuous variable transmission, which may be a source of competitive advantage for Fuji in the global automobile market. Thus, learning how to use cooperative strategies is becoming an important source of competitive advantage and strategic competitiveness for many of the world's automobile manufacturers.

www.citroen.com
www.daimlerchrysler.com
www.gm.com
www.honda.com
www.hyundai.com
www.kia.com
www.nissanmotors.com
www.renault.com
www.toyota.com

Sources: J. Flint, 2000, 'No guts no glory', *Forbes*, 7 February, p. 88; S. Freeman, 2000, 'Auto firms see a boost in sales for Korean cars', *Wall Street Journal*, 13 January, p. A6; G. L. White, 2000, 'GM stops making electric car, holds talks with Toyota', *Wall Street Journal*, 12 January, p. A14; B. S. Akre, 1999, 'Toyota alliance could lead to bigger things, GM exec hints', *Dallas Morning News*, 6 April, p. D6; A. Harney, 1999, 'Toyota seeks technology alliances', *Financial Times*, 19 July, p. 18; S. Miller and J. Ball, 1999, 'Daimler faces big test in small-car market', *Wall Street Journal*, 29 November, pp. A20, A25; S. Miller and D. Woodruff, 1999, 'Peugeot is set to aid Daimler on small car', *Wall Street Journal*, 10 December, p. A15; J. Millman, 1999, 'Renault to invest $400 million in Mexico in production alliance with Nissan', *Wall Street Journal*, 13 December, p. A28; R. L. Simison, 1999, 'GM nears agreement to buy 20 percent stake in Japan's Fuji Heavy for $970.2 million', *Wall Street Journal*, 8 December, p. A4; R. L. Simison and N. Shirouzu, 1999, 'GM may buy Honda gasoline engines: Both car makers consider other deals', *Wall Street Journal*, 11 December, p. B5; R. L. Simison and N. Shirouzu, 1999, 'GM pursues new links with Japanese', *Wall Street Journal*, 3 December, p. A3; http://global.hyundai-motor.com/hyundai/hd-subindex0201.htm.

As discussed in different parts of the book's first eight chapters (especially in Chapter 3), the characteristics of the 21st-century landscape make it necessary for firms to constantly re-create themselves to achieve competitive success.[1] Firms failing to do this risk decline and failure.[2] The Bendigo Bank is one Australian institution that employed just such a strategic approach. As late as 1997, the Bendigo Bank was a Victorian-based banking institution, with only one interstate office in Albury, New South Wales. Due to a period of rapid change in the financial markets between 1997 and 2000, Bendigo Bank was faced with the challenge of somehow maintaining its market share and profitability from new, and financially superior, market entrants. Bendigo Bank fundamentally changed the nature of its business, commencing its operations in all Australian states, and focusing upon rural/farm banking products (through a joint venture with Elders), and offering these products to rural communities through the use of pharmacies rather than bank branches. Within three years, Bendigo Bank transformed from a regional company that primarily serviced Victoria, into a bank with a national presence and a growing profit base. In general, how a firm re-creates itself is through use of newly developed competitive advantages and, more broadly, through the selection and implementation of different strategies or by using current strategies differently to increase the firm's effectiveness.[3]

To this point in the book, our focus has been competition among firms. The previous chapters facilitate an understanding of competitive advantage and strategic competitiveness through strong positions against external challenges, maximising of core competencies and minimising of weaknesses. This chapter focuses on gaining competitive advantage through cooperation with other firms.[4] This happens when firms find ways to combine their unique resources and capabilities to create core competencies that competitors find difficult to understand and imitate.[5]

Demonstrated by our discussion of the topics in this chapter is the fact that alliances are blurring the distinction between competitors and allies in some industries. For example, in the computer industry, IBM and Dell recently formed an alliance through which IBM will sell US$16 billion in parts to frequent competitor Dell over a seven-year period. Analysts say that this alliance 'positions IBM as a premier parts provider to one of the world's fastest growing computer firms. In exchange, people familiar with the matter said that Dell ... receives reduced royalty rates on technology it currently licenses from IBM at what are believed to be steep prices.'[6] Thus, the 21st-century landscape involves a complex web of competitive interactions and dynamics (see Chapter 5).

Since roughly the mid-1980s, cooperative strategies have become increasingly popular as a way for a firm to at least partially re-create itself by using different competitive advantages to pursue strategic competitiveness.[7] Some refer to this trend as 'coopetition' in that major competitors are forming cooperative arrangements to compete against competitors, often those from other nations.[8] The Internet's capabilities provide an interesting medium through which effective cooperative strategies are being formed.[9] For example, in August 2000, 14 of Australia's largest companies joined forces to form an 'on-line' buying operation (www.corprocure.com.au). The on-line alliance – between BHP, Foster's, Amcor, AMP, ANZ, Australia Post, Coca-Cola Amatil, Coles Myer, Goodman Fielder, Orica, Pacific Dunlop, Qantas, Telstra and Wesfarmers – will provide the companies with what is essentially $4 billion worth of consolidated buying power. Such an alliance is intended to supply the 14 firms with much greater purchasing power than each company enjoys individually, as well as to streamline the communications process between both new and existing buyers and suppliers to the group. It is expected that this alliance will result in cost savings of between 2 and 8 per cent for each of the companies, a figure that translates into savings of between $80 and $320 million for the alliance.[10]

Strategic alliances are a primary form of cooperative strategies. Speaking to the increasing popularity of strategic alliances as an important cooperative strategy, two researchers noted that an 'unprecedented number of strategic alliances between firms are being formed each year. [These] strategic alliances are a logical and timely response to intense and rapid changes in economic activity, technology, and globalization, all of which have cast many corporations into two competitive races: one for the world and the other for the future.'[11] Another indicator of the popularity of cooperative strategies is the fact that over 20 000 strategic alliances were formed in a recent two-year period on a worldwide basis; more than half of those alliances were between competitors.[12]

Although being used more frequently by companies headquartered within the same country, alliances are also increasingly popular with firms located in international markets. In this instance, alliances are formed between companies with headquarters in different countries. Discussed later in the chapter, these cooperative arrangements typically are called *cross-border alliances*. For example, in October 2000, the ANZ and National banks (as part of a 50-bank, worldwide cooperative strategy) formed an Internet-based foreign exchange 'portal' named Atriax, in an attempt to dominate the foreign exchange e-commerce market. Through such an alliance, both banks believe that they will have access to a much larger percentage of the potentially 'giant customer base' than they would as an individual Australian entity, especially once the technology is accepted in the global e-commerce marketplace.[13]

Even in light of the global economy's competitive realities, not all firms are positively predisposed to being involved with cooperative strategies. In the words of Takeshi Tanaka, president of Fuji Heavy Industries, 'We will always build cars with our own distinctive features. We are not interested in putting our engine in Nissan's cars and selling bigger and bigger volumes. We would rather build cars using our own capabilities, pushing capacity to its fullest or increasing it in certain areas, and strengthen the Fuji Heavy and Subaru brand.'[14] Shortly after articulating this position, Fuji entered into the strategic alliance with GM that we mentioned in the Opening Case. Thus, the realities of the 21st-century competitive landscape are such that firms may need to participate in cooperative strategies even if their preference is to avoid doing so.

As a prominent cooperative strategy, strategic alliances can serve a number of purposes. However, firms considering alliances must understand that managing them tends to be difficult.[15] Reflecting this difficulty is the fact that many alliances encounter trouble and that a number of them fail. In fact, evidence shows that two-thirds of all alliances have serious problems in their first two years and that as many as 70 per cent of them fail.[16] A corporate alliance mind-set increases the probability of an alliance succeeding. Shared among all organisational members, an effective alliance mind-set is one through which both the strengths and risks of a firm's entire set of alliance relationships are recognised and understood by all involved with alliance formation and use.[17]

Types of cooperative strategies

Strategic alliances are partnerships between firms whereby their resources, capabilities and core competencies are combined to pursue mutual interests in designing, manufacturing or distributing goods or services.

As previously noted, strategic alliances are a primary type of cooperative strategy. **Strategic alliances** are partnerships between firms whereby their resources, capabilities and core competencies are combined to pursue mutual interests in designing, manufacturing or distributing goods or services.[18] An important attribute of strategic alliances is that they allow firms to leverage their resources.[19] Thus, one of the theoretical foundations of strategic alliances resides in the resource-based view of the firm.[20] In Chapter 3's discussion on the resource-based view, we talked about the importance of a firm being able to leverage resources to achieve its strategic intent – that is, to achieve what at first may seem to be unattainable goals. At a broader level, some believe that strategic alliances will play an increasingly important role in the consolidation of industries that is anticipated in the 21st century. A reason for this is that through alliances, companies overcome barriers (for example, anti-competitive provisions) that sometimes prevent a firm's direct competitive entry into another nation's marketplace.[21]

A **joint venture** is when two or more firms create an independent company by combining parts of their assets.

Strategic alliances are explicit forms of relationships between firms. They come in three basic types. One type of strategic alliance is a **joint venture**, in which two or more firms create an independent company by combining parts of their assets. Joint ventures are effective in establishing long-term relationships and in transferring tacit knowledge, an important source of competitive advantage.[22] (See the discussion of this topic in Chapter 3.) Commonly, partner firms own an equal percentage of a joint venture's equity. In Australia, for example, Ecorp has undertaken a number of such 'equal percentage' joint ventures: ninemsn – a venture between Ecorp and Microsoft Corporation – represents the Nine Network's initial foray into Web-based entertainment and sales; and eBay Australia and New Zealand – a 50:50 joint venture between Ecorp and eBay Inc. of the United States – seeks to tap some of the potential in Internet commerce in these countries.[23]

Experience shows that joint ventures are framed around virtually any issue that is of common interest to the involved parties. GM and DaimlerChrysler, for example, initiated talks in late 1999 about forming a charter aircraft joint venture. To be called Air Automotive, the purpose of the venture is to share a company aircraft fleet in order to cut costs and improve usage rates.[24]

A second type of strategic alliance is an **equity strategic alliance**; here, partners own different percentages of equity in a new venture. Many foreign direct investments are completed through equity strategic alliances, such as those by Japanese and US companies in China.[25] Ford Motor Company and Mazda Motor Corporation formed an equity strategic alliance some time ago. Recently, four large Japanese companies formed this type of alliance to sell books through the Internet. Called e-shopping! Books, the partners hope to emulate Amazon.com's success by providing what they envision to be a Japanese version of that firm's operations. Softbank, a computer software and publishing company, holds the largest share (50 per cent) of the venture, while Yahoo! Japan and Tohan, a leading publisher and book distributor, each own 10 per cent. The remaining 30 per cent equity position in this venture is held by 7-Eleven Japan, the nation's largest convenience store operator.[26] Equity strategic alliances are considered more effective at transferring know-how between firms because they are closer to hierarchical control than are non-equity alliances.[27]

Non-equity strategic alliances are formed through contractual agreements given to a company to supply, produce or distribute a firm's goods or services without equity sharing. Other types of cooperative contractual arrangements concern marketing and information sharing. Because they do not involve the forming of a separate venture or equity investments, non-equity strategic alliances are less formal and demand fewer commitments from partners than do joint ventures and equity strategic alliances.[28] The attributes of non-equity alliances make them unsuitable for complex projects where success is to be influenced by effective transfer of tacit knowledge between partners.[29]

Our focus in this chapter is on the explicit forms of strategic alliances just discussed. However, firms sometimes engage in *implicit* cooperative arrangements. Tacit collusion is an example of an implicit cooperative arrangement. **Tacit collusion** exists when several firms in an industry cooperate tacitly to reduce industry output below the potential competitive level, thereby increasing prices above the competitive level.[30] Most strategic alliances, however, exist not to reduce industry output, but to increase learning, facilitate growth, or increase returns and strategic competitiveness.[31]

Cooperative agreements may also be explicitly collusive, which is illegal in Australia unless regulated by the government, as was the case in the telecommunications industries until recent deregulation. *Mutual forbearance* (another term for tacit collusion) is tacit recognition of interdependence, but it has the same effect as explicit collusion in that it reduces output and increases prices. Mutual forbearance is defined and explained in Chapter 6.

The following sections explain strategic alliances in depth. We first discuss reasons for engaging in strategic alliances. This is followed by an examination of strategic alliances at the business-unit level and then at the corporate and international levels. In addition, we describe network strategies where the cooperative relations among firms produce multiple alliances. Thus, we discuss how strategies among multiple alliance partnerships differ from those with two partner alliances. The main risks of pursuing the various alliance types are considered. Finally, we discuss the importance of trust as a strategic asset to foster cooperative strategies that create competitive advantage and approaches used to manage alliances.

Margin definitions:

An **equity strategic alliance** consists of partners who own different percentages of equity in a new venture.

Non-equity strategic alliances are formed through contractual agreements given to a company to supply, produce or distribute a firm's goods or services without equity sharing.

Tacit collusion exists when several firms in an industry cooperate tacitly to reduce industry output below the potential competitive level, thereby increasing prices above the competitive level.

Reasons firms develop strategic alliances

Different reasons support participation in strategic alliances.[32] The reasons for cooperation differ based on three types of basic market situations: slow cycle, standard cycle and fast cycle.[33] All three types were discussed in Chapter 5. As noted in the earlier chapter, *slow-cycle* markets refer to markets that are sheltered or near monopolies, such as railroads and, historically, telecommunications companies and utilities. Often, these companies cooperate to develop standards (for example, to regulate air or train traffic), but because they can also collude to reduce competition, the government usually provides significant regulation to avoid consumer price discrimination. *Standard-cycle* market cooperation can result from firms trying to avoid over-capacity, rather than attempting to increase their opportunities. These cooperative arrangements often focus on increasing firms' market power. *Fast-cycle* markets frequently involve entrepreneurial firms offering new goods or services with short life cycles that are imitated quickly. In these markets, a cooperative strategy is used to gain strategic competitiveness by increasing the speed of product development or market entry. The reasons for strategic alliances in each of these market types are listed in Table 9.1.

Table 9.1 | Reasons for strategic alliances by market type

Market	Reason
Slow cycle	• Gain access to a restricted market
	• Establish a franchise in a new market
	• Maintain market stability (e.g. establishing standards)
Standard cycle	• Gain market power (reduce industry over-capacity)
	• Gain access to complementary resources
	• Overcome trade barriers
	• Meet competitive challenges from other competitors
	• Pool resources for very large capital projects
	• Learn new business techniques
Fast cycle	• Speed up development of new goods or services
	• Speed up new market entry
	• Maintain market leadership
	• Form an industry technology standard
	• Share risky R&D expenses
	• Overcome uncertainty

Slow-cycle markets

Firms in *slow-cycle markets* tend to seek entry into markets that are restricted or try to establish franchises in new markets. For instance, many firms in slow-cycle markets consider cooperative strategic alliances in once highly regulated markets. A recent example of such a strategic move is that by New Zealand dairy giant, Global Dairy Co. The recent deregulation of Australia's $7 billion dairy market has opened up dialogue between Global Dairy and the Sydney-based Dairy Farmers Corporation, in what may become the first in a series of corporate alliances that will allow the New Zealand company access to once-protected Australian dairy revenues.[34]

Utility firms participating in energy-related industries also use strategic alliances. In the gas industry, for example, Woodside Energy, Tokyo Gas and Toho Gas recently formed a joint venture that calls for cross-investments between the three companies. The goal of this cooperative arrangement is to form a fourth, and world-largest, LNG production plant in the Pilbara region of Australia. The new plant is required to ensure that a prime customer of the alliance, the Osaka Gas Company, is supplied with 1 million tonnes of LNG a year for the next 30 years. It will require the partners to contribute upwards of $3 billion to finance the new plant and protect its customer base.[35]

Experience shows that achieving cooperation among partner firms in slow-cycle markets can be difficult. Near monopolies usually seek to be self-sustaining rather than be maintained jointly by partners. For example, as competition for telecommunication services emerges in Europe, a number of telecommunication firms that were previously state monopolies have sought to cooperate and form strategic alliances.

The Global One Alliance, formed initially in 1994 by France Telecom SA, Sprint Corp. and Deutsche Telekom AG, has been plagued by disagreements among the partners. One reason for this is that the partners often compete in multiple markets against each other. In early 2000, expectations were that Sprint would sell its stake to its two European partners. Analysts believed that following this transaction, 'The European companies would then conduct an auction in which each company places a bid for Global One with an independent party. The high bidder will buy out the remaining partner.'[36] Thus, although alliance opportunities exist in slow-cycle markets, they are not without managerial challenges and corporate risk.

As shown by our discussion of strategic actions being taken by firms competing in the telecommunications and energy industries, the 21st-century competitive landscape is one in which slow-cycle markets are becoming quite rare. Firms that historically have competed in slow-cycle markets should recognise that their future is one that in all likelihood will require them to learn how to compete in standard-cycle market conditions at a minimum, and perhaps even learn how to be successful in terms of fast-cycle market characteristics.

Standard-cycle markets

In *standard-cycle markets*, which are often large and oriented towards economies of scale (for example, automobile and commercial aerospace), alliances are more likely to be between partners with complementary resources, capabilities and core competencies (see Table 9.1). In markets where economies of scale are important for competitive parity or advantage, large international alliances are useful because national markets may be too small to support the scale-efficient nature of the businesses. Therefore, the increasing globalisation of markets presents opportunities to combine resources, capabilities and competencies. This is a primary reason for alliances between automobile firms such as the alliance formed by Ford and Mazda. However, recent evidence suggests that this alliance is not yielding totally positive strategic outcomes. Ford owns one-third of Mazda and essentially runs the company. Between 1997 and the end of 1999, Mazda had three presidents, all from Ford.[37] Nonetheless, because of potential synergies that are possible from this alliance, Ford remains committed to finding ways to derive the value it believes resides in the complementary resources possessed by the two companies.

Today, the Internet is shaping auto companies' international alliances. For example, in early 2000, GM held initial discussions with several companies, including Toyota and Honda, about joining its Internet marketplace for suppliers. Called GM TradeXchange, the Internet-based venture was intended to reduce costs for partner companies as they combined their purchases electronically to win larger discounts from suppliers.[38] Demonstrating the fluidity of alliances being considered by the world's automobile manufacturers is the fact that less than a month after being contacted by GM, Toyota accepted an invitation from Ford to consider participating in its Web-based marketplace venture. Called AutoXchange, Ford's Internet operation was a competitor to GM's

TradeXchange. As with the GM alliance, AutoXchange was designed to bring automobile manufacturers and suppliers together in efforts to reduce costs through increased efficiencies.³⁹

Firms also may cooperate in standard-cycle markets to gain market power and pool resources to meet capital needs (see Table 9.1). These two reasons support the alliance formed between Goodyear Tire and Rubber of the United States and Sumitomo Rubber Industries of Japan. The cooperative arrangement calls for the firms to organise four joint-venture-operating companies and two global service and support operations. By pooling resources in these fashions, the partners believe that operating synergies would result in savings of between US$300 and US$360 million in the first three years of the alliance's life. In addition, the deal calls for Sumitomo to help Goodyear gain better access to the crowded Japanese original equipment and after-tyre markets, while Goodyear is to facilitate Sumitomo's relaunch of its Dunlop brand into European markets.⁴⁰ In an effort to pool resources and enhance competitiveness, DuPont Co. is seeking partners 'to bring its small pharmaceuticals business to critical mass through strategic alliances'.⁴¹ Finally, firms in standard-cycle markets also may form alliances to overcome trade barriers (see Chapter 8) and to learn new business techniques.

Fast-cycle markets

Other companies, such as Global Crossing and Hutchison Whampoa, a Hong Kong-based conglomerate, use cooperative arrangements to compete differently in *fast-cycle markets*. To speed entry into a new market, these firms formed a joint venture (with each partner having a 50 per cent stake) called Hutchison Global Crossing. (This venture is mentioned in Chapter 5.) The venture's objective was to pursue fixed-line communications and Internet opportunities in Hong Kong and China, when permitted to do so by expected regulatory changes.⁴² This means of competing differs from Softbank Corporation and CMGI. These two firms use cooperative arrangements to sell Internet capacity and infrastructure equipment, rather than to operate Internet portals or provide media content. This competitive approach is in response to the global frenzy of Internet traffic.

Cooperative arrangements between firms competing in fast-cycle markets where significant levels of uncertainty exist can also lead to the development of standard products.⁴³ For instance, Sematech, a cooperative strategic alliance formed by multiple electronic and semiconductor firms, was quite important in establishing the adoption of the UNIX standard operating system for workstation computer producers.⁴⁴ Today, firms are forming alliances such as the one between Intel and Hewlett-Packard to develop an entirely new kind of microprocessor chip with the potential to establish a new industry standard. The fact that the alliance to develop this new chip, dubbed the Merced, is now in trouble shows the complexity of firms using alliances to set industry standards in fast-cycle markets.⁴⁵

Business-level cooperative strategies

As our discussion shows, many reasons support a firm's use of strategic alliances when pursuing strategic competitiveness, including the desire to use them as a substitute for vertical integration.⁴⁶ In this section, we explain four types of business-level cooperative strategies: complementary strategies, competition reduction strategies, competition response strategies, and uncertainty reduction strategies (see Figure 9.1). Following our discussion of these four business-level cooperative strategies is an assessment of the potential competitive advantages associated with each one.

Figure 9.1 | Types of business- and corporate-level strategic alliances

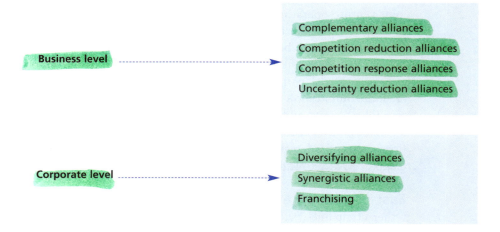

Complementary alliances

Complementary strategic alliances are designed to take advantage of market opportunities by combining partner firms' assets in complementary ways to create new value.[47] As shown in Figure 9.2, horizontal and vertical alliances are the two types of complementary strategic alliances.

Vertical complementary strategic alliances

A *vertical complementary strategic alliance* is formed between firms that agree to use their skills and capabilities in different stages of the value chain to create value (see Figure 9.2). Retailer Benetton, for example, has developed a number of successful vertical

> Complementary strategic alliances are designed to take advantage of market opportunities by combining partner firms' assets in complementary ways to create new value.

> Woolworths' Ezy Banking is a joint initiative of Woolworths Limited and the Commonwealth Bank of Australia. These two Australian companies are looking for ways to offer their customers choice through innovative products and services. This new banking service is aimed not only at offering choice in financial services, but at doing it in a way that increases its convenience and simplicity.

Figure 9.2 | Vertical and horizontal complementary strategic alliances

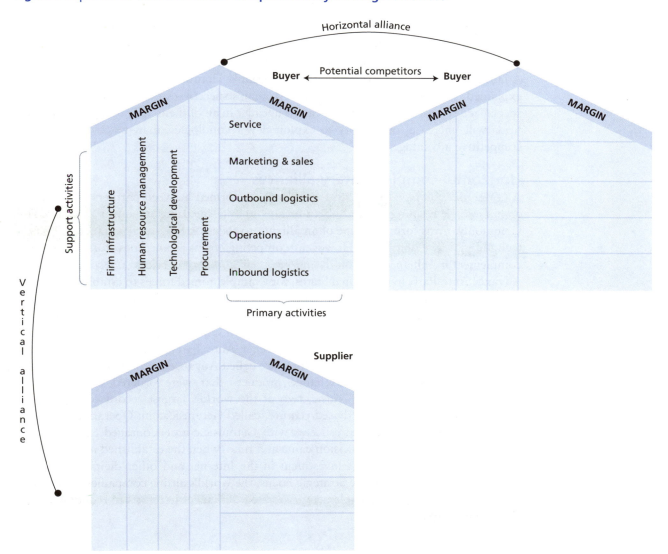

complementary alliances. Benetton has core competencies in the marketing and sales primary activities. However, the firm chooses not to attempt to develop a core competence in the manufacture of clothing. Instead, Benetton uses a number of alliances with companies that are competitively skilled in terms of being able to create value when manufacturing the high-fashion, trendy clothing items for which Benetton is widely known. Partly because of the project's scale and size, Boeing Company formed vertical complementary alliances with several firms that are involved with different stages of the value chain to design and build its 777 plane. Among the partners in this venture were United Airlines and five Japanese companies that supplied a number of the plane's components. According to one of the partners involved with this project, 'The development of the 777 was the fastest and most efficient construction of a new commercial aircraft ever.'[48]

Discussed in Chapter 3, *outsourcing* is the purchase of a value-creating primary or support activity from another organisation. A non-equity alliance, in which a contractual arrangement with another firm is developed to help in the design, manufacture or distribution of the firm's good or service, is the particular type of cooperative arrangement used to engage in outsourcing.[49] For example, in order to control costs and to remain abreast of the latest technologies, J.P. Morgan outsourced its information technology (IT) function to Pinnacle Alliance. Pinnacle is a consortium formed by Andersen Consulting, AT&T Solutions, Computer Sciences Corporation and Bell Atlantic Network Integration. As J.P. Morgan's chairman, Douglas A. Warner III, explained, 'Technology is critical to J.P. Morgan's success – so critical, and on so many specialized fronts, that no one firm can be a leader in all of them ... Teaming up with these firms will [increase] our ability to exploit new technologies, manage costs, and create competitive advantage.'[50]

Horizontal complementary alliances

A *horizontal complementary strategic alliance* is formed between partners who agree to combine their resources and skills to create value in the same stage of the value chain. Commonly, firms form this type of an alliance to focus on long-term product and service technology development.[51] However, competing firms sometimes form horizontal complementary alliances to jointly market their goods or services. CSK Auto Inc. and Advance Auto Parts in the United States, for example, joined forces to establish a separate company called PartsAmerica.com. This Web-based venture allows consumers and repair shops to buy parts on-line. An interesting competitive feature to this alliance is that customers can pick up parts ordered on-line from either company's local stores. (CSK operates stores under the trade names Checker Auto Parts, Shuck's Auto Supply and Kragen Auto Parts; Advance Auto's stores are called Advance Auto.) Customers can also use the stores to return or exchange products that were ordered on-line.[52] BMG Entertainment and Universal Music, two of the world's largest record companies, are expanding their joint Internet-based venture, called Getmusic.com. Operating initially in the United States, the partners' success with Getmusic.com encouraged expansion into international markets. This decision came at a time 'when the established music industry is aggressively stepping up its investment in the Internet and other digital distribution vehicles'.[53] As explained in the Strategic Focus, the world's airline companies are involved with a host of horizontal complementary strategic alliances in efforts to reduce costs and increase revenues.

Strategic Focus International

Horizontal alliances among airline companies: A route to increased strategic competitiveness?

As we noted in a Strategic Focus in Chapter 5, there is general consensus that the world's airline companies face difficult competitive conditions. Among the chief issues are the expenses associated with flying, maintaining and updating aircraft, and the stiff price competition among carriers that causes sales revenues to be under constant pressure. It is possible that through industry consolidation, airline companies would be able to increase sales revenue through new routes they would acquire and would be able to use their larger size to reduce costs. However, because of laws and regulations, airline companies are prevented from using cross-border merger and acquisition strategies to consolidate their industry. The specifics of legal constraints, however, vary by country or geographic region. In Australia, for example, the recent deregulation of the market has resulted in a number of new entrants to the national market, namely Virgin Blue, Impulse (until May 2001) and Spirit Airlines. The result has been a marked increase in the competitiveness of the domestic market and reduction of profitability for the 'traditional players'.

The realities of the political/legal segment of airline companies' general external environment (see Chapter 2) are a key driving force of the pattern of alliance activity occurring in the global airline industry. As previously noted, legal constraints prevent these companies from gaining economies of scale and economies of scope by using merger and acquisition strategies. Because they can result in some of the benefits of a merger or an acquisition, strategic alliances are a viable option for the world's airline companies. Describing the similarity of the benefits a firm can gain through a merger or acquisition and a strategic alliance, a business writer noted that through an alliance, 'If an airline does not fly to a destination, it can instead sell seats on an alliance partner's flight that does go there. The alliance partners can also pool their frequent flyer programs, encouraging passengers not to desert them for other carriers'. These practices are attempts to increase revenues for alliance partners with minimal capital investments; they also demonstrate airline companies' interest in being able to support their passengers' desire to reach a particular destination, even when they do not provide service to that destination.

As the Air New Zealand takeover of Ansett Australia demonstrates, alliances formed among airline companies have changed the competitive dynamics in their industry. In another instance, a comprehensive alliance between two European-based airline firms is thought to be an initial step towards a merger. KLM of the Netherlands and Italy's Alitalia agreed to an alliance calling for them to combine their management staffs and marketing and sales organisations and to jointly purchase aircraft. Executives from the two firms anticipated that two to three years would be required to complete the merger, even if it were to be approved by the European Commission. The two main obstacles to a full merger 'were that Alitalia was still not fully privatized and that Italy and the Netherlands had separate bilateral air agreements with the U.S. This meant that a half Dutch merged airline would not be able to fly from Italy to the U.S. A half Italian airline would have difficulty flying from the Netherlands.'

Previous to KLM and Alitalia's efforts to merge, an attempt to form a comprehensive alliance between UK-based British Airways (BA) and US-based American Airlines (AA) failed to gain regulatory approval. A key reason for this failure was a decision by US authorities and the European Commission that BA would have to relinquish hundreds of take-off and landing slots at London's Heathrow airport for the alliance with American to receive regulatory clearance. Regulators believed that operating jointly, BA's and AA's dominance at Heathrow, an airport to which many carriers desire to fly, would stifle competition. Because BA declined the Commission's requirement, the alliance was not approved. Nonetheless, consistent with regulations, BA and AA continue to engage in code-sharing practices and cross-use of their frequent flyer programs.

While proceeding with their intentions of forming a merger, KLM and Alitalia also simultaneously teamed with US-based Northwest and Continental in an alliance called Wings. Other global alliances among airline companies include (1) Oneworld (headed by BA and AA, but including other airlines – Cathay Pacific, Qantas, Finnair, LanChile, Iberia and Canadian), and (2) Star (headed by Lufthansa of Germany and United Airlines of the United States and including SAS, Air Canada, Thai Airways, Varig, Air New Zealand, Ansett Australia and All Nippon Airways). In late 1999 and early 2000, Air France and Delta, as primary partners, formed what at that time was an unnamed alliance with Sabena, Austrian and Swissair. This was the fifth global horizontal alliance formed among airline companies since 1997. The fourth-largest in the world, the alliance between Air France and Delta chose Havas Advertising's

Euro RSCG Worldwide to receive a US$30 million contract to establish an image for this alliance in the face of competition from the other airline global partnerships. The Air France/Delta alliance is expected to be a significant competitor of Oneworld, Star and Wings. An important reason for this, analysts note, is that the alliance links Delta's Atlanta hub, the world's largest, with Paris-Charles de Gaulle, 'the European hub offering the best potential for growth'. Data show that this alliance joins together a European airline with 37 million passengers, 210 aircraft, roughly 50 000 employees, and US$260 million in net income in 1998–9 with a US counterpart using 584 planes to serve 112 million passengers annually. Employing over 70 000 people, Delta had a 1999 net income of US$1.1 billion.

Are these cooperative strategies, in the form of horizontal complementary strategic alliances, improving airline partners' strategic competitiveness? Evidence is mixed, but encouraging. Typically, performances expected from alliances run high. Air France chairman Jean-Cyril Spinetta anticipated that his firm's alliance with Delta (and the other partners) would add about FFr1 billion (US$160 million) to the firm's results within two to three years – FFr700 million in revenue and FFr300 million from cost reductions. Studies of actual results from alliances indicate that partners' financial performances often do improve. Lufthansa, for example, generated an increase of DM500 million in 1998 through its participation in the Star alliance. However, alliances are proving less successful in terms of cost reductions. Stifling efforts among alliance partners to jointly purchase 'everything from toilet paper to aircraft' is the airline companies' failure to establish common computer systems and similar service standards.

Although airline horizontal complementary strategic alliances may not be yielding the robust results companies want, the 21st-century landscape seems to demand their formation. Commenting about this, an airline executive suggested that, 'In an environment of liberalized air transportation, every airline must be able to take advantage of the available chances.' One of these opportunities is the website that almost two dozen airlines from across the globe formed to offer tickets, including discounted Internet-only special fares. United Airlines, Delta Air Lines, Northwest Airlines and Continental Airlines created the website for this cooperative arrangement. The site is a competitive response to Travelocity.com, Expedia Inc. and other websites that appeal to independent-minded travellers – those willing to search websites to find the best fares. Thus, it appears that horizontal strategic alliances among airlines, ones through which complementary resources are combined to pursue mutual gains, will remain a viable and prominent strategic option in the 21st century for airline companies.

Sources: S. Carey, 2000, 'Nearly two dozen airlines will join planned Web site of four big carriers', *Wall Street Journal*, 13 January, p. B4; 'Euro RSCG will promote Air France/Delta alliance', 2000, *Wall Street Journal*, 25 January, p. B9; W. Hall, 1999, 'SAirGroup seeks promotion in global aviation league', *Financial Times*, 28 June, p. 20; D. Owen and M. Skapinker, 1999, 'Delta and Air France form alliance', *Financial Times*, 23 June, p. 8; D. Owen and M. Skapinker, 1999, 'Air France set to form fourth alliance', *Financial Times*, 18 June, p. 8; M. Skapinker, 1999, 'BA fails to land its alliance with American', *Financial Times*, 30 July, p. 3; M. Skapinker, 1999, 'KLM and Alitalia likely to merge', *Financial Times*, 30 July, p. 3; M. Skapinker, 1999, 'Airlines bent on bigamy ruffle alliances', *Financial Times*, 23 June, p. 8.

A final observation about trust's role in horizontal and vertical complementary strategic alliances is useful. Company experiences show that perceptions about partner trustworthiness tend to be different between the two types of complementary alliances. Accounting for this difference is the fact that horizontal alliance partners are simultaneously competitors. This is not the case in vertical alliances, where partners use their respective competitive advantages in different parts of the value chain to create mutually beneficial value. For example, the successful relationship Benetton has with the suppliers of its products is partly based on trust that has been developed across time as a result of positive outcomes from previous business transactions.

In contrast, the horizontal alliance between ANZ and the National Australia Bank may prove less successful, simply because the firms compete directly with one another in the banking and finance industry while cooperating through an Internet-based collaboration. In other words, simply because these two firms, as well as others involved in horizontal complementary alliances, are simultaneously cooperating and competing, there may be less of a basis for trust.

Similarly, the level of trust among the airline companies discussed in the Strategic Focus may be quite low because they continue to compete, even with their partners, on many routes. This may account in part for the evidence we mentioned previously about airline alliances; namely, that less than 30 per cent of the alliances between international air carriers have been successful. Thus, in general, horizontal alliances tend to be shorter in duration than are vertical complementary alliances. As such, it is somewhat difficult to develop a sustainable competitive advantage through horizontal complementary strategic alliances, especially when cooperation is to occur between former competitors. This does not devalue the importance of this alliance type; rather, it suggests that companies should enter such an alliance with an understanding of the likelihood that it is an impermanent cooperative arrangement.

Competition reduction strategies

In the heat of rivalry, many firms may seek to avoid destructive or excessive competition. One means of avoiding such competition is tacit collusion, or mutual forbearance (see Chapter 6). This may be accomplished in some markets through cartels, such as OPEC, that seek to manage the price and output of companies (for example, oil companies in member countries) in a specific industry. In countries around the world, governments develop policies that affect firms' efforts regarding competition reduction strategies. In Australia, for example, the Australian Competition and Consumer Commission (ACCC) is committed to finding ways to permit collaboration among rivals without violating any anti-competitive laws.

In general, governments seek to use competition-related policies that are consistent with the character of their nation's economics. This appears to be the case concerning a competitive situation in Russia. In the mid-1990s, Russia had a huge surplus of aluminium. When these aluminium-manufacturing firms were privatised, they began to export the metal in large quantities, an action that caused the world price to drop by as much as 50 per cent. The Aluminum Association, a trade association of aluminium manufacturers, met and called for the United States to file antidumping trade charges, claiming that Russia was 'dumping' aluminium below market rates. The Russians argued that they needed foreign hard currency to deal with a difficult transitional economy and to cut them off from foreign markets would create a difficult political problem. As a result, there was a meeting of government and industry officials in Brussels in 1994 that resulted in a government pact calling for 'voluntary' cuts in production. Although the politicians claimed this was not a cartel, it had the same result: production cuts to sustain a world price.[54] Aluminium prices in the late 1990s increased. Prices rose from near 50 US cents per pound (0.45 kilograms) to 65 US cents in 1996 and 72 US cents in 1997.[55]

Japan's economy entails a number of entrenched cartels and significant collusion. Even though economic and political forces have been working against cartels and collusion, approximately 50 per cent of the manufacturing industries in Japan engage in some form of price fixing on a historical basis. Because some cartels date back to the 1600s, such anti-competitive activity in Japan is accepted and tolerated, which makes it difficult to change cartels and collusive practices. Although the situation is complex, Eastman Kodak argues that cartels and collusion reduce competition substantially, giving Japanese competitors excessive returns against which it is difficult for international firms to compete. Kodak's market share for film in the United States continues to decrease while Fuji's increases. Partly in response to this competitive situation, Kodak is pursuing opportunities in other product areas. Early evidence from these actions is encouraging for Kodak, in that the firm's profits increased 75 per cent during the fourth quarter of 1999.[56]

Recent evidence suggests that Japan's economy is now more open to foreign investment. One reason for this could be increasing acceptance of the finding that across countries, protected markets such as Japan's lead to inefficiencies throughout both the manufacturing and service sectors that contribute to poor performance in international markets.[57] Thus, the effects of competition-reducing policies may be counterproductive in the long term.

Because of eases in market entry restrictions, investors from around the world are forming a more positive image of investment opportunities in Japan. In early 2000, a study revealed that corporate investors ranked Japan their 16th-favourite investment opportunity, up from 21st in June 1999. Moreover, analysts believed that significant investments in Japan's economy would continue at least through the 21st century's first 10 years. However, this 'doesn't mean it's always easy to do business [in Japan]. There has been some domestic backlash recently against deregulation in [Japan's] financial services sector, and Americans still invest less here than Japanese do in the U.S.' Thus, although caution is in order, global firms are becoming more confident of their ability to use their assets productively in Japan. Similarly, confidence in markets throughout Asia appears to be growing, at least as suggested by recent and dramatic increases in Asian equity markets. In 1999, for example, from 'Tokyo to Singapore, markets performed as if they were on speed; Korea's Kosdaq, which is similar in composition to Nasdaq, more than quadrupled.'[58]

Sometimes, firms collude directly to reduce competition, although this may have costly consequences for both the company and its directors. In 1999, for example, Sundaze Australia Pty Ltd was fined millions by the Federal Court for pursuing price maintenance policies with regular distributors of their Oakley range of sunglasses, and refusing to sell to outlets that would apply discounts to the range.[59] Similarly, Toys 'R' Us, a prominent toy retailer, was found to be in violation of US federal trade laws by colluding with toy manufacturers to not sell popular toy lines to its primary competitors such as warehouse clubs Price/Costco and Sam's Club.[60] In addition to the ethical implications of collusive alliances, companies should not expect long-term competitive success through their use.

Competition response strategies

Companies also use strategic alliances to respond to competitors' strategic, but typically not tactical, competitive actions and reactions (see Chapter 5). For example, SAirGroup, owner of Swissair Airlines, recently bought a 20 per cent stake in South African Airways. Although one of the top-quality airline names and recognised as a company with an effective top-level management team, Swissair, 'unlike Air France, Lufthansa or British Airways, does not have a big home market on which it can rely to help reserve a prime position in the fast-changing world of global aviation alliances' such as those discussed in a previous Strategic Focus and in the 'Ansett and Air NZ' case study later in this text. Also affecting the firm's competitive situation was Delta's decision to exit its alliance with Swissair in favour of forming one with Air France. In response to the pressures it feels from the array of strategic alliances its competitors are forming, Swissair considered other options in addition to the competitive possibilities that are associated with its investment in South African Airways, including the possibility of joining the OneWorld alliance dominated by AA and BA.[61]

Responding to increasing competition from Web-based ventures, some food companies are forming alliances with Internet companies. In the United States, Pillsbury Co., Kellogg Co., Quaker Oats Co., General Mills, Inc. and the US unit of Nestlé SA of Switzerland are participating in marketing-oriented alliances with Webvan Group Inc., a fast-growing Internet grocery store. An important benefit of such alliances is indicated by commentary from the director of e-business at Pillsbury: 'We want to work with Webvan to understand how to relate to consumers that buy online.' This is a critical objective, in that food manufacturers expect the 21st century to be a time during which the growth of on-line shopping will be explosive.[62] Similarly, to emulate Sun Microsystems Inc., its computer and server sales rival Hewlett-Packard (HP) formed an alliance with BEA Systems Inc. The two companies intend to work together to develop what is called middleware software products that firms can use to sell their goods or services via the Internet. Some analysts view the HP–BEA alliance 'as a clear response to Sun's recent alliance with America Online Inc. In that deal, Sun and the enterprise-software unit of the former Netscape Communications Corp. plan to provide their own integrated suite of middleware and network applications.'[63]

To improve its competitiveness in international mail operations, the US Postal Service formed an alliance with DHL Worldwide Express Inc. Through this cooperative arrangement, the firms jointly offer a two-day delivery service between 11 major US cities and any address in 18 European countries. The charges for these deliveries are significantly less than the prices of competitors FedEx, UPS and DHL's own trans-Atlantic operation. For the US Postal Service, this alliance is a response to the rapid transformation of the world's major post offices. In particular, as private delivery companies such as FedEx and UPS expand their global delivery services, demand for 'old-fashioned' international mail deliveries continues to decline.[64]

Uncertainty reduction strategies

Particularly in fast-cycle markets, strategic alliances are also used to hedge against risk and uncertainty.[65] Fearing the uncertainty of being able to obtain adequate exposure to a significant customer base, drkoop.com Inc. in the United States chose to pay America Online (AOL) US$89 million over a four-year period to become the firm's premiere health partner. Founded by former US Surgeon General C. Everett Koop, drkoop.com provides consumer health information to consumers. It is competing with other new ventures to become the dominant provider of Internet-based healthcare information and services. The firm's newly formed cooperative arrangement gives it access to AOL's large customer base. The investment community's positive response to the announcement of this alliance, as shown by a one-day increase of 56 per cent in the value of drkoop.com's shares, seems to suggest that the future of the start-up venture is less uncertain as a result of its cooperative arrangement with AOL.[66]

Global over-capacity and fierce cost competition affected the ability of Siemens and Fujitsu to compete successfully in the world's PC business. To reduce their risk in the business line, the two firms formed a joint venture called Fujitsu Siemens Computers. Europe's second-largest computer operation was created by this cooperative arrangement. Siemens gained economies of scale required to be a leader in this industry, while Fujitsu thought the alliance would allow it to reach its long-held goal of being one of Europe's five biggest computer producers.[67] At virtually the same time that this alliance was developed, Acer, the world's third-largest PC manufacturer, formed an alliance with IBM. A multibillion-dollar seven-year procurement and technology development alliance, this arrangement was intended to strengthen Acer's relationship with its most important customer.[68]

Thus, the rapidly changing 21st-century competitive landscape may create uncertain outcomes for firms as they form and use cooperative strategies to reduce their risks. It is possible that in a competitive dynamics context (see Chapter 5), one firm's alliances can create risks and uncertainty for competitors. For example, Wal-Mart's intention of becoming a dominant Internet retailer was disconcerting to a host of firms. In a business writer's words, 'Many online retailers are awaiting news of Wal-Mart's e-commerce plans with trepidation, given the unparalleled buying power of the Arkansas-based retail empire, its reputation for discount pricing and its well-established brand.'[69]

In other instances, firms form alliances to reduce the uncertainty associated with developing new product or technology standards. For example, NEC, the Japanese electronics conglomerate, and Hewlett-Packard are using an alliance to pool their expertise and technologies to further expand and develop their telecommunications applications. One purpose of the cooperative arrangement is to innovate the standard for next-generation communications networks.[70] In the global automobile industry, GM and Toyota formed a five-year R&D alliance that essentially makes the 'no. 1 U.S. auto maker and the no. 1 Japanese auto maker partners in the competition to develop alternative-power green cars' for the 21st century. Through this alliance, the two firms expect to be able to set the industry standard for environmentally friendly vehicles.[71] At the same time, GM and Toyota joined Ford, DaimlerChrysler and Renault SA in an alliance to develop an industry-wide standard through which their respective products would be able to accommodate the array of communications and entertainment equipment that the automobile industry was developing.[72]

Assessment of competitive advantage for business-level cooperative strategies

Different competitive outcomes tend to be associated with the strategic alliances we have discussed. For example, alliances used to reduce competition are more likely to achieve competitive parity and average returns rather than competitive advantage and above-average returns. Firms anticipate these outcomes, in that, typically, they choose to use competition-reducing strategies on a short-term basis in efforts to reduce the negative effects of competitors' strategic or tactical competitive actions and responses. Compared with competition-reducing cooperative arrangements, complementary alliances (especially vertical ones) are more likely to create competitive advantage and contribute to the firm's earning of above-average returns. These positive strategic outcomes are possible when firms combine complementary resources in ways that reduce costs or create new competitive advantages.

Because one of their objectives is to buffer firms from the uncertainty of aggressive marketplace competition, uncertainty-reducing strategies historically have resulted in competitive parity and average returns for partners involved with this type of alliance. However, using the Internet in these partnerships, as increasingly is the case, allows firms to have full rapid access to a host of competitively relevant information. For example, drkoop.com will have opportunities to gain important insights about customers through the use of AOL's information-gathering and information-processing capabilities. Thus, the Internet's capabilities, combined with firms' growing understanding of how to properly use cooperative strategies, suggest a trend of increasing effectiveness, in terms of competitiveness and returns, across all types of business-level cooperative strategies.

Corporate-level cooperative strategies

Corporate-level cooperative strategies are strategic alliances designed to facilitate product and/or market diversification.

Strategic alliances designed to facilitate product and/or market diversification (see Chapter 6) are called **corporate-level cooperative strategies**. As shown in Figure 9.1, the corporate-level strategic alliances are called diversifying, synergistic and franchising.

Diversifying strategic alliances

Diversifying strategic alliances allow a firm to expand into new product or market areas without completing a merger or acquisition.

In order to grow, firms may choose to expand into new product or market areas. **Diversifying strategic alliances** allow a firm to expand into new product or market areas without completing a merger or an acquisition. A corporate-level strategic alliance is a viable strategic option for a firm that wants to grow, but chooses not to merge with or acquire another company to do so.[73]

A reason that a diversifying strategic alliance is an attractive option to a merger or acquisition is that corporate-level alliances provide some of the potential synergistic benefits of a merger or acquisition, but with less risk and greater levels of flexibility. These benefits accrue to a firm because exiting a strategic alliance is easier and costs less than divesting an acquisition that did not contribute expected levels of strategic success. In addition, some governments restrict acquisitions, especially horizontal ones (in which companies combine their assets to gain market share by creating still more value in the same stage of the value chain). This is the case in the United States, a nation in which regulators tend to think of horizontal acquisitions as an action that fosters explicit collusion when companies combine their like assets.

Gianni Versace SpA, the Italian fashion group, intends to diversify. Resort development is the first business area that is of interest to the firm's top-level management team. The firm has organised a business unit, Versace Hotel and Condominium Resort Group, to focus on this business area. A corporate-level strategic alliance has been formed with Sunland Group, an Australian hotel developer, to help the Versace business unit begin its operations. The first hotel project to be completed by the alliance partners is in the Gold Coast tourism strip of Queensland.[74]

Firms might also form a diversifying alliance to determine whether a future merger would benefit both parties. For example, following the formation of one of the technology partnerships between GM and Toyota that we mentioned previously, Jack Pearce, GM's number-two executive, hinted that the cooperative arrangement could prove to be the prelude to a broader link-up between the automobile manufacturers. In Pearce's words, 'It would certainly be premature to talk about a merger. But I think it's important for both companies to have a very open mind in terms of where this kind of collaboration takes us.'[75] The fact that a merged GM and Toyota would account for 25 per cent of global automobile and truck sales demonstrates the market power the transaction would create. Sometimes, analysts think that a firm's alliance is an indication of a possible future merger when such may not be the case. Recently, Mitsubishi Motors formed an alliance with Fiat to jointly develop SUVs. In response to queries about the reason for this cooperative arrangement, especially in light of rumours that the two firms might merge their operations, a Mitsubishi executive observed that, 'Mergers are not our priority. We continue to seek mutually beneficial business collaborations, without capital tie-ups.'[76]

Synergistic strategic alliances

Synergistic strategic alliances create joint economies of scope between two or more firms. Similar to the horizontal complementary strategic alliance type that is used at the business level, synergistic strategic alliances create synergy across multiple functions or multiple businesses between partner firms. Two firms might, for example, create joint research and manufacturing facilities that they both use to their advantage and thus attain economies of scope without a merger.

In the financial services sector, Rabobank and DG Bank, the Dutch and German cooperative institutions, have formed a joint venture called DG-Rabo International. This equally owned venture combines the banks' respective strengths in the corporate and investment banking business areas. Viewed by some as 'one of the most important cross-border partnerships yet seen in European banking', the organisations intended to meld their skills to cooperate in other areas (for example, asset management transactions) in the future.[77] Through an array of technology-oriented synergistic alliances, Toyota is attempting to gain access to technologies that it has had difficulty developing on its own. Avoiding equity alliances, 'the carmaker has linked with General Motors for joint development of electric, hybrid, and fuel cell vehicles [as mentioned in the Opening Case], and Volkswagen for intelligent transportation systems, recycling and marketing. It also has a tie-up with Panasonic EV Energy for batteries.'[78]

Franchising

As discussed in Chapter 6, firms diversify when they can use excess resources, capabilities and core competencies to create value in other product or geographic markets or to reduce the risk of operating in a single business area. As with diversifying strategic alliances, franchising is a cooperative strategy a firm uses to spread risk and to use resources, capabilities and competencies productively, but without merging with or acquiring another company.[79]

As a cooperative strategy, franchising is based on a contractual relationship concerning a franchise that is developed between two parties: the franchisee and the franchisor. Thus, **franchising** is an alternative to diversification that is considered a cooperative strategy based on a contractual relationship. Defined more formally, a *franchise* is a 'contractual agreement between two legally independent companies whereby the franchisor grants the right to the franchisee to sell the franchisor's product or do business under its trademarks in a given location for a specified period of time'.[80]

The foundation for this cooperative strategy's success is the ability to gain economies of scale by forming multiple units while deriving operational efficiencies from the work of individual units competing in specific local markets.[81] Typically, the relationship between the franchisee and franchisor is seen as an entrepreneurial partnership, in that the parties work together to find new opportunities to achieve strategic competitiveness.[82] Franchising permits relatively strong centralised control and facilitates knowledge transfer without significant capital investment.[83] The brand name is thought to be the most effective competitive advantage for a franchise, in that, when powerful, it signals both tangible and intangible consumer benefits.[84]

Franchising is an increasingly popular strategic option on a global basis, accounting for 40 per cent of retail volume in the United States, 32 per cent in Great Britain, 25 per cent in Australia and 24 per cent in Brazil. Overall, data show that US companies dominate franchising internationally through the sheer number of franchisors and franchisees and that Canada, Japan and Australia have franchising sectors that are as well established, although not quite as large, as the US franchising sector.[85] Food establishments (for example, McDonald's, Burger King, Pizza Hut and Dunkin' Donuts)

Pizza Hut uses synergistic alliances between multiple franchises and partner firms to strive for market power in the fast-food industry.

and hotels (for example, Hilton International) use franchising as a cooperative strategy, as do a number of service firms.

As a cooperative strategy, franchising reduces financial risk, because franchisors commonly invest some of their own capital in the local venture. This capital investment motivates franchisors to perform well by reinforcing and emphasising the quality, standards and brand name that are associated with the franchisee's original business. Because of these potential benefits, franchising may provide growth at less risk than diversification. Of course, the franchising firm loses some control, but the franchise contract usually provides for performance and quality audits.

Assessment of competitive advantage for corporate-level cooperative strategies

As we have explained, firms use corporate-level cooperative strategies to develop competitive advantages and to reduce risk. However, corporate-level strategic decisions, such as cooperative strategies and diversification, can be influenced by managerial motives, as well as by the proper desire to achieve strategic competitiveness and earn above-average returns. (See Chapter 6 for a related discussion.)

In large diversified firms, incentives exist for managers to increase sales, particularly when firm performance falls short of the stakeholders' expectations. The incentive for managers is the increase in compensation that often is associated with larger firm size. A company's size can be increased through strategic alliances as it can be through diversification. Strong governance mechanisms (see Chapter 10) are required to verify that managerial use of cooperative strategies is in the best interests of shareholders in particular and other stakeholders as well. Without effective governance mechanisms in place to guard against opportunistic managerial behaviours, strategic alliances may be used for purposes that are inconsistent with shareholders' best interests and that do not contribute to enhanced strategic competitiveness.

Another risk of corporate-level cooperative strategies is that they may be based on an intricate set of relationships between members of a firm's top-level management team and their counterparts in other companies.⁸⁶ Managers, for example, may use the intricacy of alliance networks to enrich their own position in the firm. Alliances built on an upper-level manager's contacts and interpersonal relationships may be lost if that person leaves the company. He or she may be the only one who effectively understands the complex web of relationships existing in the corporate network of alliance partners.⁸⁷ These understandings can entrench the manager, making dismissal difficult.

Although risks exist, corporate-level cooperative strategies can also create value. We have described how this is done through our discussions of diversifying and synergistic alliances and of franchising. Beyond this, a firm can develop a competitive advantage at the corporate level through its ability to effectively manage a set of business-level and corporate-level cooperative strategies.

Recall from Chapter 6 that a corporate-level strategy is concerned with two key questions: what businesses the firm should be in, and how the corporate office should manage its group of businesses. A competitive advantage is created when a firm selects an appropriate set of businesses and when that set is managed in a manner that is difficult for competitors to imitate. Similarly, through use of the alliance mind-set that we mentioned previously in this chapter, a firm can form an appropriate set of strategic alliances and manage that alliance set in ways that are difficult for competitors to imitate. In fact, research shows that firms capable of learning from their cooperative collaborations develop know-how that can be distinguished from mere experience with strategic alliances.⁸⁸ Although networks of alliances can be used to diversify the firm and to create a competitive advantage, the cost and difficulty of managing them should not be underestimated. Monitoring these relationships and maintaining cordial and trusting relations require time and effort. Such costs should be considered before entering into numerous strategic alliances.⁸⁹

International cooperative strategies

Most strategic alliances are formed as either business-level or corporate-level cooperative strategies. This is because at the business level, cooperative strategies are used to help a firm create value for customers as it exploits its core competencies in specific, individual product markets. Firms use cooperative strategies at the corporate level as part of their process of selecting and managing a mix of businesses in a way that creates more value than would be created if the businesses were to operate as independent entities.

In addition to domestic collaborative arrangements, strategic alliances formed when using business-level or corporate-level cooperative strategies can involve a firm with companies that are headquartered in other countries⁹⁰ (as discussed in Chapter 8). Primarily because of increasing globalisation, *cross-border alliances* – ones in which firms with headquarters in different nations form a partnership – continue to increase in number and are becoming more important sources of strategic competitiveness.⁹¹

When using business-level and corporate-level cooperative strategies, the intent is to develop alliances that have a high probability of increasing the firm's strategic competitiveness. In this context, the interest is not to form only domestic or only cross-border alliances. Rather, either a domestic or a cross-border alliance is formed only when it is expected to contribute to successful use of the firm's business-level cooperative strategy or its corporate-level cooperative strategy. For four primary reasons, however, firms also choose to *focus* on forming cross-border alliances. When this happens, the firm has chosen explicitly to use an international cooperative strategy.

The first reason firms decide to use an international cooperative strategy to develop cross-border strategic alliances is that, in general, multinational corporations outperform firms operating on only a domestic basis.⁹² In the context of cooperative strategies, this general evidence suggests that a firm can form cross-border strategic alliances to leverage core competencies that are the foundation of its domestic success to expand into international markets.⁹³ For example, US-based Mellon Bank Corp. and France's Credit Lyonnais SA recently started discussions about forming an alliance in asset-management services. Commenting about this intended transaction, a business writer suggested that, 'For a midsize U.S. bank, Mellon has been unusually aggressive in seeking joint ventures and alliances to gain wider international distribution for its stable of mutual fund companies, which includes Dreyfus Corp. and Boston Co. Asset Management.'⁹⁴

Sometimes, cross-border alliances are used when opportunities to grow through acquisitions or alliances are limited within a firm's home nation. This is the case for Belgo-Dutch financial group Fortis. Noting that occasions to grow in its home markets were quite limited, especially in the Netherlands, a Fortis official said that, 'Our strength in Benelux has given us a strong platform to grow elsewhere.' Three geographic regions in which Fortis intends to use cross-border strategic alliances to grow are Asia, the United Kingdom and the United States. In the United States, Fortis is seeking alliances or acquisitions to concentrate on its successful niche market of funeral insurance.⁹⁵

The third reason firms choose to form cross-border alliances revolves around government policies. As discussed in Chapter 8, some countries regard local ownership as an important objective of national policy. In general, Western governments, though nervous about foreign ownership in some industries, are less concerned than many other governments. India, on the other hand, strongly prefers to license local companies, as opposed to foreign ownership and joint ventures with a local firm or wholly foreign-owned subsidiaries. Another example is South Korea, whose government recently increased the ceiling on foreign investment in South Korean firms from 15 to 18 per cent.⁹⁶ Thus, in some countries, managers may not have the full range of entry mode choices that we described in Chapter 8. Investment by foreign firms may only be allowed through cooperative agreements such as a cross-border alliance. This is often true in newly industrialised and developing countries with emerging markets. Cooperative arrangements can be helpful to foreign partners because the local partner can provide information about local markets, capital sources and management skills.

The fourth primary reason cross-border alliances are used is to help a firm transform itself in light of rapidly changing environmental conditions. GEC, a UK-based company, seeks to move from being 'a broadly focused group deriving much of its revenues from the defence budget to a full range telecommunications and information systems manufacturer'. Stimulating this intended transformation is the uncertainty associated with different nations' defence budgets. Relying on its status as a world leader in a number of technologies that are critical to the ongoing worldwide communications revolution, GEC is forming alliances as one means of transforming itself. One cross-border alliance completed in this regard is between GEC and NEC, the Japanese electronics giant. The alliance has both a commercial and technological focus in that NEC is distributing GEC products through its extensive marketing channels, while the two companies are collaborating in R&D efforts to develop new technologies.⁹⁷

In general, cross-border alliances are more complex and risky than domestic ones. Partly because of this complexity and risk, cross-border alliances have higher dissolution rates than do other modes that are used to enter international markets, such as a Greenfield venture, wherein the firm establishes a wholly owned subsidiary.⁹⁸ Although strategic alliances allow partner firms to share risks – and thus are less risky for each individual partner than a Greenfield venture – they are difficult to manage.⁹⁹ The need to coordinate and cooperate to share skills and knowledge requires significant processing of information on the part of all partner managers.¹⁰⁰ When significant demands are placed on partners' managers to achieve quick returns, the alliance has less of a chance of succeeding. Although difficult to attain, evidence shows that cross-border alliance success can be achieved as a result of careful partner selection and value-creating managerial practices.[101]

Strategic intent of partner

In the context of cooperative strategies, strategic intent denotes the most critical and important objectives a firm wants to achieve through collaborative arrangements. The competitive conditions of the 21st-century landscape – especially increasing globalisation – create a large set of objectives that drives why a firm develops its alliances, as well as how it intends to operate as an alliance partner. Some firms, for example, may intend to learn how to use a technology that belongs to a partner. Thus, it is important to assess potential partners' strategic intent when evaluating alliance possibilities. Many believe that Japanese firms 'are particularly good at learning from their partners'.[102] If a horizontal complementary alliance is the type through which knowledge about a technology is gained, the firm learning about the technology could become a competitor to the partner from whom it gained the insights required to successfully use that technology.[103] Other outcomes in these instances are for the firm that has acquired the knowledge it sought to exit the alliance quickly, or to acquire its partner through a merger or an acquisition.[104] Thus, the probability of alliance success is increased when firms understand each other's strategic intent as alliance partners.[105] Understanding intent requires careful selection of alliance partners. Factors influencing the selection of partners are discussed further in the Strategic Focus.

Strategic Focus | Corporate

The relationship between partner selection and strategic alliance success

Among the many factors influencing alliance success is partner selection. Choosing an appropriate partner calls for the firm to understand a great deal about another company, including the intent driving an interest to ally with the focal firm. Gaining these understandings typically requires multiple interpersonal interactions in that, in the final analysis, alliances are relationships between people, not institutions. As our discussion shows, one objective of virtually every alliance partner is to learn from its ally.

Several information sources can be of value to firms trying to better understand a potential partner's intent, historical methods of operating as an alliance partner, and trustworthiness. (Trust as an aspect of cooperative strategies is discussed further later in the chapter.) Industry analysts have information about how companies operate as alliance partners and the strategies they implement, as well as their future competitive objectives. This knowledge is acquired by studying industry-specific data and through interactions with peers to interpret it in competitively relevant ways.

Executive recruiters are a second source of information. The foundation of these individuals' knowledge is the insights they gain about a company when researching it to understand the qualifications and characteristics prospective employees should possess. The richness of recruiters' knowledge increases when their searches are completed to fill top-management team positions in a client firm. One of the hiring criteria for an upper-level managerial position could be, for example, a person's ability to successfully develop the type of strategic alliances at the business, corporate or international level that the firm uses as the core of its cooperative strategies. Business reporters and the articles they write are another source of information about firms and their intentions when they form strategic alliances.

Based on its experiences, the US firm Motorola Inc. developed a disciplined process that it uses to select alliance partners. The first step of the process calls for Motorola to specify the exact objectives it seeks through a possible alliance. The alliance objectives must be derived from the overall corporate or business unit objectives. In addition, the potential partner must possess complementary skills that can reinforce Motorola's value-creating capabilities, and it must have a strong desire to partner with Motorola. During discussions with potential partners, Motorola tries to gain a deep understanding of the potential partner's alliance intent.

Recent research findings inform our understanding of what firms can do to be aware of a potential alliance partner's strategic intent. In their study, Hitt, Dacin, Levitas, Arregle and Borza found that alliance partners are selected largely so the focal firm can gain access to the ally's resources and learn through participation in the alliance. Further refinement to this general expectation is also provided by the researchers' results. For example, when selecting partners, firms in emerging markets 'more strongly emphasize partners' financial assets, technical capabilities, intangible assets and willingness to share expertise than do developed market firms'. In contrast, firms in developed markets were found to emphasise partners' unique competencies and market knowledge and access more strongly than did emerging market firms. Thus, firms evaluating potential partners from emerging market countries can anticipate that the company likely will have strategic intentions that differ from the strategic intentions of possible allies from developed-market economies. These results provide additional evidence regarding the importance of trying to understand a potential partner's strategic intent before agreeing to form a cooperative strategy with it.

Sources: 'Full Armor and Entex announce strategic partnership', 2000, *Full Armor Home Page*, 31 January: www.fullarmour.com; M. A. Hitt, M. T. Dacin, E. Levitas, J.-L. Arregle and A. Borza, 2000, 'Partner selection in emerging and developed market conditions: Resource-based and organizational learning perspectives', *Academy of Management Journal*, in press; C. Caggiano, 1999, 'Hotlinks', *Inc.*, October, pp. 72–81; Y. L. Doz and G. Hamel, 1998, *Alliance Advantage: Creating the Art of Value through Partnering* (Boston: Harvard Business School Press); J. R. Harbison and P. Pekar, Jr, 1998, 'Institutionalizing alliance skills: Secrets of repeatable success', *Strategy & Business*, 11, pp. 79–94.

Network cooperative strategies

The focus of our discussion up to this point has been on cooperative arrangements between two firms.[106] Sometimes, however, companies participate in an alliance network, which is a set of identifiable and competitively relevant links between more than two relatively comparable firms.[107] Because it involves a firm with many strategic partnerships, an alliance network is the foundation for a network strategy.

> A **network strategy** is the alliance-related actions taken by a group of interrelated and comparable firms to serve the common interests of all partners.

A **network strategy** is the alliance-related actions taken by a group of interrelated and comparable firms to serve the common interests of all partners. The strategic intent of a network strategy is to serve the firms' common interests by increasing the performance of the alliance network itself.[108] Network strategies are particularly effective when formed among firms clustered together; this is the case in Silicon Valley in California and in Singapore's Silicon Island.[109] An alliance network's performance can be increased as a result of the mutual commitment partners make when a network is created and because of the mutual dependence the commitment creates, causing partners to work together to serve the common interests of all parties.[110] A network strategy can be used to form a stable network of alliances, a dynamic network of alliances, and even a network of alliances within an individual company.

Stable alliance networks are the foundation of a network strategy in mature industries that are characterised by largely predictable market cycles and demand. In Japan, these relationships usually include some shared ownership among the partners of the alliance network as part of a *keiretsu*.¹¹¹ This tends not to be the case in Australia, in that firms form their own alliance networks. For example, in the athletic footwear and apparel business, Nike has long-established relationships with a network of global alliance partners to supply and distribute its products throughout the world.

Dynamic alliance networks are the basis for using a network strategy in industries where rapid technological innovations are introduced frequently. Driving this pattern of competitive dynamics are the relatively short life cycles of goods and services in what are rapidly changing industries. Apple Computer employed a dynamic network with its innovative Newton, a personal digital assistant. Although Apple developed the product, Newtons are manufactured almost entirely by Sharp Corporation. Apple is also involved in an alliance with Motorola and IBM to develop a new microprocessor.¹¹² IBM, Microsoft, Intel, Fujitsu and NEC are examples of other technology firms that frequently form both individual alliances and alliance networks.

Internal alliance networks are formed within a company to facilitate the coordination of product and global diversity. For example, Asea Brown Boveri (ABB), the international electric products firm, buys and sells a wide range of products across many country boundaries. ABB has formed alliances inside the firm to coordinate its operations and to increase its efficiency as a result of doing so.¹¹³

Each of these network types has a focal *strategic centre firm*. Positioned at the centre of at least several bilateral alliances, the strategic centre firm manages a network of alliance relationships.¹¹⁴ Nike, Nintendo, Benetton, Apple, Sun Microsystems and IKEA (a Swedish furniture maker) are examples of strategic centre firms. Monsanto is a strategic centre firm with alliance networks in many areas, including seeds and biotechnology.¹¹⁵ Working at the centre of an alliance network, these companies are not 'virtual firms' where all central competence is outsourced;¹¹⁶ instead, they have capabilities and core competencies that allow them to shift important activities to other companies, which creates value when these companies are better able to perform such activities.¹¹⁷

In the Strategic Focus, we offer additional insights about why alliance networks are formed, as well as how to design and manage them.¹¹⁸ The discussion is expanded in the analysis of organisational structure in Chapter 11.

Strategic Focus Corporate

Alliance networks: Benefits and issues

The number of firms involved with multiple alliances and partners continues to increase. Several reasons account for firms' interest in using alliance networks as the foundation of a network cooperative strategy. Examples of these reasons include an opportunity to: (1) share complementary resources, capabilities and core competencies; (2) remain abreast of emerging technologies; and (3) share the risk and expenses that are part of a major capital outlay.

Beyond the benefits that can accrue from alliances with a single partner, forming an alliance network can help a firm to maintain pace with, and perhaps set, industry standards.

This benefit is especially crucial for companies in the telecommunications, software, computer and video game industries. Firms interested in these benefits are involved with dynamic alliance networks. As a researcher notes, 'The importance of alliances in standards-based industries stems from an essential characteristic of competitive dynamics in such markets: these industries often end up being dominated by a single standard, for example, as the Microsoft/Intel platform known as Wintel controls the major share of the PC market.' Partners in an alliance network that is committed to developing a new industry standard often have the influence and power to convince potential adopters of the probability that the standard produced by the alliance partners will likely dominate the market. A second reason for a firm to develop a network of alliances is to facilitate the introduction of major changes in the company's core activities. Through simultaneous cooperative relationships with multiple partners, a firm requiring change to remain competitive can be quickly exposed to an array of emerging technologies, allowing it to experiment with different strategic, technical and operational options. Using a network strategy for this purpose illustrates an approach for a firm to continuously reinvent itself. This issue was addressed at the beginning of the chapter as an important one for companies committed to achieving strategic competitiveness in the 21st century.

Firms should analyse several key issues as an alliance network is being formed. Chief among these issues are: (1) determining whether the alliance network will be horizontal (involving firms generating value in the same stage of the value chain) or vertical (involving companies generating value in different stages of the value chain); (2) assessing the number of firms that will foster the greatest levels of network effectiveness and efficiency; (3) identifying approaches to use to minimise conflicts among alliance partners; (4) specifying the alliance network's strategic intent in a manner that benefits all; and (5) determining how the network will be managed and selecting the strategic centre firm. Failure to carefully and deliberately evaluate these issues reduces the probability that the alliance network will succeed.

Despite the challenges of alliance networks, the 21st-century landscape creates conditions that likely will stimulate their further use by companies competing throughout the different sectors of the global economy. Thus, firms seeking strategic competitiveness should devote resources to understanding alliance networks and how to use them as the foundation for development of an effective network cooperative strategy.

Sources: T. E. Stuart, 1999, 'Network positions and propensities to collaborate: An investigation of strategic alliance formation in a high-technology industry', *Administrative Science Quarterly*, 43, pp. 668–98; T. E. Stuart, 1999, 'Alliance networks: View from the hub', Mastering Strategy (Part Eight), *Financial Times*, 15 November, pp. 4–7; K. P. Coyne and R. Dye, 1998, 'The competitive dynamics of network-based businesses', *Harvard Business Review*, 76(1), pp. 99–109; Y. L. Doz and G. Hamel, 1998, *Alliance Advantage: The Art of Creating Value through Partnering* (Boston: Harvard Business School Press).

Competitive risks with cooperative strategies

Cooperative strategies are not risk free, as shown by the risks included in Figure 9.3. One risk is that a partner may act opportunistically. Opportunistic behaviours surface either when formal contracts fail to prevent their occurrence, or when an alliance is based on a perception of partner trustworthiness that does not exist. As mentioned earlier in the chapter, understanding a partner's actual strategic intent reduces the likelihood that a partner will or can operate opportunistically.

Some cooperative arrangements dissolve when it is discovered that a partner has misrepresented the competencies it can bring to the alliance. This happens most

The Piaggio scooter is a good product that did well in India with an alliance. The alliance failed due to management differences that some trace back to different national cultures.

frequently when a partner conveys an intention of relying on intangible assets as its contribution to a cooperative relationship. Superior knowledge of local conditions is an example of an intangible asset that partners often fail to deliver. In a related instance, a firm may decide to end a relationship in order to pursue a related option for which it believes that its competencies are even more valuable.

Failure to make its complementary resources available to a partner is another competitive risk of cooperative strategies. This risk surfaces most commonly between partners located in different nations. Contractual arrangements can sometimes discourage this form of adverse behaviour. However, once a partner commits to and invests in a cooperative relationship with a firm located in a different global market, the local partner may hold those assets hostage if foreign countries do not have laws protecting the focal firm's investment.

Ineffective management skills or differences in managerial styles are a final risk to be mentioned. This issue caused the dissolution of a joint venture between Piaggio, the Italian scooter manufacturer, and LML, its partner located in India. Formed in 1990, the venture lasted for almost 10 years. At one level, it was successful in that the venture was producing approximately 300 000 scooters annually for the Indian market. This sales volume earned a 27 per cent market share for the venture. According to analysts, the venture ended because of 'increasingly sour management differences'.[119]

In addition to the moral hazards (potential cheating by partner firms), there are other risks. One of those risks is having the ability to form and manage a joint venture effectively. Prior experience, although obviously helpful, may not be adequate for collaborative strategies to endure.[120] Another risk is having the ability to collaborate. Alternatively, it may be difficult to identify trustworthy partners with which to collaborate.

Trust as a strategic asset

Trust between partners increases the likelihood that an alliance will succeed.[121] In fact, some believe that trust may be the most efficient mechanism for governing economic transactions.[122] Several conditions account for this efficiency. For example, trust creates confidence between partners that actions taken will serve both parties' interests. In addition, trust increases the probability that a firm will understand its partner's actual strategic intent as it participates in an alliance. Once intent is understood, it is also easier for a firm to predict the actions its partner will take as it encounters different situations requiring decisions to be made that will affect the alliance. When both partners are known to be trustworthy, an expectation of loyal behaviour exists for the parties as a cooperative arrangement is formed. Because of this expectation, firms are able to allocate fewer resources to monitor and control the alliance. In contrast, greater amounts of resources are required to monitor and control an alliance formed with a firm whose previous behaviour suggests that it can't be trusted.[123]

As explained in a Strategic Focus in Chapter 3, trust is valuable, rare, imperfectly imitable and often non-substitutable.[124] Thus, firms known to be trustworthy have a competitive advantage when it comes to forming and using cooperative strategies. One reason for this is that it is impossible to specify all operational aspects of a cooperative arrangement in a formal contract. Confidence that its partner can be trusted reduces the firm's concern about the inability to control or influence each operational aspect of an alliance through a contractual agreement.

Especially in developing countries, a government's actions can affect the level of trust associated in some manner with the use of cooperative strategies. Events experienced by Adolph Coors, the US brewer, demonstrate this situation. To compete in the Korean market, Coors formed a joint venture called Jinro Coors. The venture had several partners, including the majority owner, Jinro Group. The South Korean government placed the venture up for auction following Jinro Group's bankruptcy in 1997. To maintain involvement with its joint venture, Coors submitted a bid to buy Jinro Coors. However, Coors dropped out of the auction at the end of July 1999 because of a 'seriously flawed and unfair bidding process'. Beyond this, Coors said that it 'had no faith in the integrity of the process because of the questionable activities of a number of parties involved in the auction'.[125] Thus, the absence of trust about the role of a country's government regarding a joint venture created an untenable situation for a firm (for example, Adolph Coors) that wanted to engage in a cooperative strategy with partners in an international market.

Strategic approaches to managing alliances

Two primary approaches are used to manage cooperative strategies[126] (see Figure 9.3). In one instance, the firm develops formal contracts with its partners. These contracts specify how the cooperative strategy is to be monitored and how partner behaviour is to be controlled. The interest is to minimise the alliance's cost and to prevent opportunistic behaviour by a partner. The focus of the second managerial approach is on maximising value-creation opportunities as the partners participate in the alliance. In this instance, partners are prepared to take advantage of unexpected opportunities to learn from each other and to explore additional marketplace possibilities.[127] Trust-based relationships and complementary assets must exist between partners for this approach to be used successfully.

Figure 9.3 | Managing competitive risks in cooperative strategies

Although both managerial approaches can result in the creation of value, the amounts of monitoring costs to partner firms differ. Writing detailed contracts and using extensive monitoring mechanisms is expensive. Furthermore, protective contracts and monitoring systems shield parts of the organisation from both participating partners. Although monitoring systems can largely prevent opportunism and cheating by alliance partners, they also preclude positive responses to spontaneous opportunities that can surface as partners engage in alliance-related work. Thus, formal contracts and extensive monitoring systems tend to inhibit firms' efforts to maximise an alliance's value-creating potential.

When trust exists, partners' monitoring costs are reduced and opportunities to create value through the cooperative relationship are maximised. This managerial approach is referred to as *opportunity maximising* because alliance partners can pursue potential rent-generating opportunities that are not available to partners in more contractually restricted alliances.[128] It is important, then, for firms to consider both the assets and liabilities of monitoring systems that will be used to manage the alliance.[129] For example, AT&T entered an alliance with a much smaller credit card technology firm to develop a new credit card service. To ensure secrecy so that the alliance could maintain a critical lead in the industry, no contract was used for the first several months of this relationship. During this time, the firms worked collaboratively, sharing information and resources while relying on the character and goodwill of each other to guide the relationship. In examining this relationship, AT&T was more concerned with maximising the opportunities of the alliance than with the minimisation of potential opportunism within it.[130]

Our focus in the next major section of the book (Part 3) is the strategic actions firms take to implement the strategies they selected to pursue strategic competitiveness and above-average returns. Corporate governance, which is concerned with how firms align managers' interests with those of the shareholders and control managerial actions to assure alignment, is the first topic we address in Part 3.

Proper alignment of managers' interests with those of shareholders is also an issue in terms of strategic alliances. Because of a separation of ownership and control in modern corporations, an agency problem exists. (The agency problem is discussed in detail in the next chapter.) When the two parties' interests are not aligned, 'managers may enter strategic alliances when doing so may not be in the best interests of their firms. For example, managers may form alliances to protect jobs they might lose if there were a takeover, merger, or acquisition.'[131] Thus, as this brief discussion shows, and as is discussed in detail in the next chapter, the effective governance of firms is linked with strategic competitiveness and the earning of above-average returns across a broad range of managerial actions.[132]

Summary

- Strategic alliances are the primary form of cooperative strategies. A strategic alliance is a partnership between firms whereby resources, capabilities and core competencies are combined to pursue mutual interests. Joint ventures, equity strategic alliances and non-equity strategic alliances are the three basic types of strategic alliances.
- Other types of cooperative strategies are implicit rather than explicit. These include mutual forbearance, or tacit collusion, in which firms in an industry tacitly cooperate to reduce industry output below the potential competitive output level, thereby raising prices above the competitive level. Firms might also explicitly collude, which is an illegal practice unless it is sanctioned through government regulations such as in the case of electric and telecommunications utilities. With increasing globalisation, fewer government-sanctioned situations of explicit collusion are being observed.
- Four business-level cooperative alliances are frequently used. Through vertical and horizontal complementary alliances, companies combine their resources, capabilities and core competencies in ways that create value. Vertical complementary strategic alliances result when firms creating value in different parts of the value chain combine their assets to create new value. When outsourcing to create value, the firm may choose to form a non-equity strategic alliance with a partner that is distinctively capable of creating value in a part of the value chain in which the focal firm lacks the skills needed to create that value. Horizontal complementary strategic alliances are developed when firms combine their assets to create additional value in the same stage of the value chain. Common examples of horizontal alliances include marketing agreements and joint product-development arrangements between competitors (for example, domestic and international airlines).
- Competition reduction and competition response business-level cooperative strategies are formed in response to an industry's pattern of competitive dynamics among firms. Typically, with a short-term horizon, competition reduction alliances are used to avoid excessive competition while a firm marshals its resources to compete more successfully in light of changes in its competitive landscape. Competition response alliances are formed to deal directly with competitors' actions, especially strategic ones rather than tactical competitive actions.
- Firms use uncertainty and risk reduction cooperative strategies to hedge their risks when competing in dynamic and volatile markets or when attempting to form a new industry standard (for example, a new technology standard).
- Business-level cooperative strategies yield different strategic outcomes. In general, complementary strategic alliances are most likely to create strategic competitiveness, whereas competition reduction and competition response alliances are more likely to result in a firm achieving a condition of competitive parity with its competitors. Uncertainty reduction alliances may prevent a firm from experiencing below-average returns in the short run. However, when seeking to establish a new industry standard, an uncertainty reduction cooperative strategy can contribute to long-term strategic competitiveness.
- Corporate-level diversifying strategic alliances reduce risk, but, at the same time, tend to be highly complex. This alliance type can also be used when government policies prohibit or stifle horizontal mergers as an experimental step to determine whether a merger or an acquisition of an alliance partner would enhance the focal firm's strategic competitiveness.
- Corporate-level synergistic alliances create economies of scope. Such alliances facilitate the achievement of synergy across multiple businesses and functions at the corporate level.
- Franchising is an additional corporate-level cooperative strategy that provides an alternative to diversification. Firms following a franchising strategy can diversify their risk associated with a single business (even those in many markets) without adding new products.
- A number of firms use cross-border strategic alliances as the foundation for international cooperative strategy. These alliances are used for several reasons, including the performance superiority of firms competing in markets outside their domestic base and governmental restrictions on growth through mergers and acquisitions. International strategic alliances can be risky, especially when the firm fails to understand its partner's strategic intent in terms of being a party to an alliance.
- An alliance network is the foundation of a network cooperative strategy. Stable (primarily in mature industries), dynamic (witnessed mainly in rapidly changing industries) and internal (alliances within a single firm to coordinate its product and global diversity) are the three types of alliance networks. The

strategic intent of a network strategy is for partners to serve their common good as they cooperate to reach agreed-upon alliance objectives.
- Cooperative strategies are not risk-free strategy choices. If a contract is not developed appropriately, or if a potential partner firm misrepresents its competencies or fails to make available promised complementary resources, failure is likely. Furthermore, a firm may be held hostage through asset-specific investments made in conjunction with a partner, which may be exploited.
- Trust is an important asset in alliances. Firms recognise the value of partnering with companies possessing a reputation for trustworthiness. When trust exists, an alliance is managed to maximise the pursuit of opportunities between partners. Without trust, formal contracts and extensive monitoring systems are used to manage an alliance.

Review questions

1. What are the types of cooperative strategies that are described in this chapter, and how are they defined?
2. What are the different reasons that support a firm's use of cooperative strategies in slow-cycle, standard-cycle and fast-cycle markets?
3. What are the advantages and disadvantages of using the four types of business-level cooperative strategies: complementary alliances, competition reduction alliances, competition response alliances and uncertainty reduction alliances?
4. How are cooperative strategies used at the corporate level in a diversified firm? What are some potential problems when a firm uses cooperative strategies at the corporate level?
5. Why do firms use international cooperative strategies in the form of cross-border strategic alliances?
6. What are the four competitive risks of using cooperative strategies?
7. Why is trust important in cooperative strategies?
8. What are the differences between the cost-minimisation approach and the opportunity-maximisation approach to managing strategic alliances?

Application discussion questions

1. Using the Internet, go to the website for the *Australian Financial Review* (www.afr.com.au). Find three or four articles that discuss different firms' uses of cooperative strategies. What types of cooperative strategies are revealed in each article you found? What objective is each firm pursuing as it uses a particular cooperative strategy?
2. Use the Internet to find two articles describing firms' use of a cooperative strategy: one where trust is being used as a strategic asset, and another where contracts and monitoring are being emphasised. What are the differences between the managerial approaches being used in the two companies? Which of the cooperative strategies you examined has the highest probability of being successful? Why?
3. Choose one of Australia's top 100 firms that has a significant need to outsource a primary or support activity (such as information technology). Given the activity you believe the firm should outsource, can you justify a recommendation to the firm to form a non-equity strategic alliance to outsource the focal activity?
4. The possibility of DaimlerChrysler using cooperative strategies as the foundation for its small car strategy is discussed in the Opening Case. Use the Internet to determine whether the firm has formed strategic alliances to build its small cars. If these alliances have been formed, what factors caused this decision to be made? If alliances have not been formed for this purpose, why not?

Ethics questions

1. From an ethical perspective, how much information is a firm obliged to tell a potential strategic alliance partner about what it expects to learn from the cooperative arrangement?
2. 'A contract is necessary because most firms cannot be trusted to act ethically in a cooperative venture such as a strategic alliance.' In your opinion, is this statement true or false? Why? Does the answer vary by country? Why?
3. Ventures in foreign countries without strong contract law are more risky, because managers may be subjected to bribery attempts once their firms' assets have been invested in the country. How can managers deal with these problems?
4. The large number of international strategic alliances being formed by the world's airline companies is discussed in one of the chapter's Strategic Focus segments. Do these companies face any ethical issues as they participate in multiple alliances? If so, what are the issues? Are the issues different for airline companies headquartered in the United States than

for those with European or Australian/New Zealand home bases? If so, what are the differences, and what accounts for them?

5. Firms with a reputation for ethical behaviour in strategic alliances are likely to have more opportunities to form cooperative strategies than will companies that have not earned this reputation. What actions can firms take to earn a reputation for behaving ethically as a strategic alliance partner?

Internet exercise

As explained in the first Strategic Focus in this chapter, many airlines are forming global cooperative alliances. Explore two of these major alliances on the Internet: the OneWorld Alliance, which includes American Airlines and British Airways (www.oneworldalliance.com); and the Star Alliance, which includes Lufthansa and United Airlines (www.star-alliance.com). How do these alliances share competitive resources? Review the four competitive risks associated with using cooperative strategies. How does each alliance avoid these risks?

*e-project: Delta Airlines and its alliance partners commissioned an elite advertising firm to create an image for their airlines' network. As part of the team, you are hired to create the Web-based portion of the new advertising campaign. How would you design this new site? What features would you include to better define the alliance's strategic intent?

Notes

1. L. Capron, W. Mitchell and J. Oxley, 1999, 'Recreating the company: Four contexts for change', Mastering Strategy (Part Ten), *Financial Times*, 29 November, pp. 4–7.
2. M. S. Kraits, 1998, 'Learning by association? Interorganizational networks and adaptation to environmental change', *Academy of Management Journal*, 41, pp. 621–43.
3. Bendigo Bank Concise Annual Report 2000.
4. J. G. Combs and D. J. Ketchen, Jr, 1999, 'Explaining interfirm cooperation and performance: Toward a reconciliation of predictions from the resource-based view and organizational economics', *Strategic Management Journal*, 20, pp. 867–88; B. Gomes Casseres, 1996, *The Alliance Revolution: The New Shape of Business Rivalry* (Cambridge, MA: Harvard University Press).
5. J. H. Dyer and H. Singh, 1998, 'The relational view: Cooperative strategy and sources of interorganizational competitive advantage', *Academy of Management Review*, 23, pp. 660–79.
6. J. G. Auerbach and G. McWilliams, 1999, 'IBM will sell Dell $16 billion of parts', *Wall Street Journal*, 5 March, p. A3.
7. J. Kurtzman, 1999, 'An interview with Rosabeth Moss Kanter', *Strategy & Business*, 16, pp. 85–94; J. Child and D. Faulkner, 1998, *Strategies of Cooperation: Managing Alliance Networks and Joint Ventures* (New York: Oxford University Press); Y. L. Doz and G. Hamel, 1998, *Alliance Advantage: The Art of Creating Value through Partnering* (Boston: Harvard Business School Press); S. E. Human and K. G. Provan, 1997, 'An emergent theory of structure and outcomes in small-firm strategic manufacturing networks', *Academy of Management Journal*, 40, pp. 368–404.
8. A. N. Brandenburger and B. J. Nalebuff, 1996, *Co-opetition* (New York: Doubleday).
9. C. V. Callahan and B. A. Pasternack, 1999, 'Corporate strategy in the digital age', *Strategy & Business*, 15, pp. 10–18.
10. I. McIlwraith, 2000, 'Heavies form buying club', *Australian Financial Review*, 4 September, p. 14.
11. Doz and Hamel, *Alliance Advantage*, p. xiii.
12. J. R. Harbison and P. Pekar, Jr, 1998, 'Institutionalizing alliance skills: Secrets of repeatable success', *Strategy & Business*, 11, pp. 79–94.
13. A. Gome, 2000–1, 'Allies and enemies', *Business Review Weekly*, 15 December – 11 January.
14. A. Harney, 1999, 'Chief is slave to design, not fashion', *Financial Times*, 4 June, p. 20; A. Harney, 1999, 'Fuji Heavy considers alliance', *Financial Times*, 4 June, p. 21.
15. W. Mitchell, 1999, 'Alliances: Achieving long-term value and short-term goals', Mastering Strategy (Part Four), *Financial Times*, 18 October, pp. 6–7.
16. M. P. Koza and A. Y Lewin, 1999, 'Putting the S-word back in alliances', Mastering Strategy (Part Six), *Financial Times*, 1 November, pp. 12–13; S. H. Park and M. Russo, 1996, 'When cooperation eclipses competition: An event history analysis of joint venture failures', *Management Science*, 42, pp. 875–90.
17. Mitchell, 'Alliances', p. 7.
18. Combs and Ketchen, Jr, 'Explaining interfirm cooperation and performance', pp. 867–88.
19. Harbison and Pekar, Jr, 'Institutionalizing alliance skills', pp. 79–94.
20. R. Gulati, 1999, 'Network location and learning: The influence of network resources and firm capabilities on alliance formation', *Strategic Management Journal*, 20, pp. 397–420.
21. C. F. Freidheim, Jr, 1999, 'The trillion-dollar enterprise', *Strategy & Business*, 14, pp. 60–6.
22. P. E. Bierly, III and E. H. Kessler, 1999, 'The timing of strategic alliances', in M. A. Hitt, P. G. Clifford, R. D. Nixon and K. P. Coyne (eds), *Dynamic Strategic Resources: Development, Diffusion and Integration* (Chichester: John Wiley & Sons), pp. 299–345.
23. www.ecorp.com.au.
24. Wall Street Journal staff reporter, 2000, 'Dan River's ventures with Mexican textiler to eliminate U.S. jobs', *Wall Street Journal*, 13 January, p. B17; T. Burt, 1999, 'Car giants plan to take wing', *Financial Times*, 3 August, p. 16; J. Hechinger, 1999, 'Citigroup and State Street to form retirement-plan joint venture', *Wall Street Journal*, 8 December, p. A4.
25. Y. Pan, 1997, 'The formation of Japanese and U.S. equity joint ventures in China', *Strategic Management Journal*, 18, pp. 247–54.
26. N. Nakamae, 1999, 'Japanese giants join to sell books online', *Financial Times*, 4 June, p. 20.
27. D. C. Mowery, J. E. Oxley and B. S. Silverman, 1996, 'Strategic alliances and interfirm knowledge transfer', *Strategic Management Journal*, 17 (Special Winter Issue), pp. 77–92.
28. S. Das, P. K. Sen and S. Sengupta, 1998, 'Impact of strategic alliances on firm valuation', *Academy of Management Journal*, 41, pp. 27–41.
29. Bierly and Kessler, 'The timing of strategic alliances', p. 303.
30. J. B. Barney, 1997, *Gaining and Sustaining Competitive Advantage* (Reading, MA: Addison Wesley), p. 255.
31. Freidheim, Jr, 'The trillion-dollar enterprise'; B. Kogut, 1988, 'Joint ventures: Theoretical and empirical perspectives', *Strategic Management Journal*, 9, pp. 319–32.
32. D. Cyr, 1999, 'High tech-high impact: Creating Canada's competitive advantage through technology alliances', *Academy of Management Executive*, 13(2), pp. 17–26; A. A. Lado, N. G. Boyd and S. C. Hanlon, 1997, 'Competition, cooperation, and the search for rents: A syncretic model', *Academy of Management Review*, 22, pp. 110–41; F. J. Contractor and P. Lorange, 1988, 'Why should firms cooperate? The strategic and economic bases for cooperative strategy', in F. J. Contractor and P. Lorange (eds), *Cooperative Strategies in International Business* (Lexington, MA: Lexington Books).
33. J. R. Williams, 1998, *Renewable Advantage: Crafting Strategy Through Economic Time* (New York: Free Press); E. E. Bailey and W. Shan, 1995, 'Sustainable competitive advantage through alliances', in E. Bowman and B. Kogut (eds), *Redesigning the Firm* (New York: Oxford University Press); J. R. Williams, 1992, 'How sustainable is your competitive advantage?', *California Management Review*, 34(2), pp. 29–51.
34. R. Bromby, 2001, 'Kiwis chase cream', *The Australian*, 17 January; P. Kelly, 2001, 'Sacred cow disease', *The Weekend Australian*, 17 February.

35. C. Hoag, 1999, 'Oil duo plan energy alliance', *Financial Times*, 30 June, p. 17.
36. N. Harris and W. Boston, 2000, 'Three partners in Global One plan a statement', *Wall Street Journal*, 21 January, p. B6; D. Owen, 1999, 'Future of Global One comes under spotlight', *Financial Times*, 22 July, p. 17.
37. J. Flint, 2000, 'No guts, no glory', *Forbes*, 7 February, p. 88.
38. G. L. White and F. Warner, 2000, 'GM in talks for Web plan with Honda', *Wall Street Journal*, 12 January, p. A6.
39. N. Shirouzu, 2000, 'Toyota may join Ford's Web system', *Wall Street Journal*, 25 January, p. A13.
40. J. Griffiths, 1999, 'Tyre-makers sign up for strategic alliance', *Financial Times*, 14 June, p. 22.
41. S. Warren and C. Tejada, 1999, 'DuPont plans tracking stock for life sciences', *Wall Street Journal*, 11 March, p. A3.
42. 'Hutchison Whampoa and Global Crossing complete telecom joint venture in Hong Kong', 2000, *Global Crossing Home Page*, 12 January: www.globalcrossing.com.
43. C. W. L. Hill, 1997, 'Establishing a standard: Competitive strategy and technological standards in winner-take-all industries', *Academy of Management Executive*, XI(2), pp. 7–25.
44. R. Axelrod, W. Mitchell, R. E. Thomas, D. S. Bennett and E. Bruderer, 1995, 'Coalition formation in standard-setting alliances', *Management Science*, 41, pp. 1493–508; L. D. Browning, J. M. Beyer and J. C. Shetler, 1995, 'Building cooperation in a competitive industry: Sematech and the semiconductor industry', *Academy of Management Journal*, 38, pp. 113–51.
45. J. McHugh, 1999, 'No mercy for Merced', *Forbes*, 20 September, pp. 57–60.
46. J. T. Mahoney, 1992, 'The choice of organizational form: Vertical financial ownership versus other methods of vertical integration', *Strategic Management Journal*, 13, pp. 559–84.
47. S. H. Park and G. R. Ungson, 1997, 'The effect of national culture, organizational complementarity, and economic motivation on joint venture dissolution', *Academy of Management Journal*, 40, pp. 297–307; R. Johnston and P. Lawrence, 1988, 'Beyond vertical integration: The rise of the value adding partnership', *Harvard Business Review*, 66(4), pp. 94–101.
48. Freidheim, 'The trillion dollar enterprise', p. 62.
49. M. Delio, 1999, 'Strategic outsourcing', *Knowledge Management*, 2(7), pp. 62–8.
50. As quoted in P. Hapaaniemi, 1997, 'Side by side', *Chief Executive*, June, pp. S4–10.
51. M. Kotabe and K. S. Swan, 1995, 'The role of strategic alliances in high technology new product development', *Strategic Management Journal*, 16, pp. 621–36.
52. D. Clark, 2000, 'CSK, Advance Auto for firm to allow customers to purchase parts online', *Wall Street Journal*, 10 January, p. A8.
53. A. Rawsthorn, 1999, 'Internet music venture goes international', *Financial Times*, 11 June, p. 9.
54. E. Norton and M. DuBois, 1994, 'Foiled competition: Don't call it a cartel, but world aluminum has forged a new order', *Wall Street Journal*, 9 June, pp. A1, A6.
55. C. Adams, 1998, 'Aluminum companies earnings increased in the fourth quarter', *Wall Street Journal Interactive Edition*, 8 January: www.wsj.com.
56. A. Klein, 2000, 'Kodak posts gain of 75% in profit for fourth period', *Wall Street Journal*, 25 January, p. A4; D. P. Hamilton and N. Shirouzu, 1995, 'Japan's business cartels are starting to erode, but change is slow', *Wall Street Journal*, 4 December, pp. A1, A6.
57. G. Hundley and C. K. Jacobson, 1998, 'The effects of the Keiretsu on the export performance of Japanese companies: Help or hindrance?', *Strategic Management Journal*, 19, pp. 927–37.
58. J. Rohwer, 2000, 'Get rich quick – in Asia', *Fortune*, 24 January, pp. 30–2.
59. 'Oakley Sunglasses distributor penalised $500 000 for resale price maintenance', 1999, 7 November: www.accc.gov.au/media/mediar.htm.
60. J. M. Broder, 1997, 'Toys "R" Us led price collusion, judge rules in upholding FTC', *The New York Times on the Web*, 1 October: www.nytimes.com.
61. W. Hall, 1999, 'SAirGroup seeks promotion in global aviation league', *Financial Times*, 28 June, p. 20.
62. G. Anders, 2000, 'Several food companies to join Webvan in online grocery-marketing effort', *Wall Street Journal*, 25 January, p. B4.

63. D. P. Hamilton, 1999, 'H-P sets alliance with BEA Systems to pursue Internet goals', *Wall Street Journal*, 8 April, p. B9.
64. D. A. Blackmon, 1999, 'Postal service, DHL to form an alliance', *Wall Street Journal*, 2 March, p. A3.
65. R. G. McGrath, 1999, 'Falling forward: Real options reasoning and entrepreneurial failure', *Academy of Management Review*, 24, pp. 13–30; R. G. McGrath, 1997, 'A real options logic for initiating technological positioning investments', *Academy of Management Review*, 22, pp. 974–96; B. Kogut, 1991, 'Joint ventures and the option to expand and acquire', *Management Science*, 37, pp. 19–33.
66. A. Carrns, 1999, 'drkoop.com's shares jump on AOL link', *Wall Street Journal*, 7 August, p. B6.
67. U. Harnischfeger, 1999, 'Siemens and Fujitsu set for computer deal', *Financial Times*, 17 June, p. 26; U. Harnischfeger and B. Rahman, 1999, 'Fujitsu deal may give Siemens a computer break', *Financial Times*, 18 June, p. 22; M. Rose, 1999, 'Siemens, Fujitsu sign world-wide cooperation accord', *Wall Street Journal*, 17 June, p. A21.
68. M. Dickie, 1999, 'Acer agrees seven-year alliance with IBM', *Financial Times*, 8 June, p. 20.
69. A. Edgecliffe-Johnson, 1999, 'Wal-Mart in online bookstore alliance', *Financial Times*, 2 July, p. 19.
70. E. Kaneko, 1999, 'NEC, HP to extend alliance', *Financial Times*, 29 June, p. 16.
71. J. Ball, 1999, 'To define future car, GM, Toyota say bigger is better', *Wall Street Journal*, 20 April, p. B4.
72. J. Ball, 1999, 'Five of the world's top auto makers agree to develop technology standard', *Wall Street Journal*, 28 April, p. B6.
73. S. Chaudhuri and B. Tabrizi, 1999, 'Capturing the real value in high-tech acquisitions', *Harvard Business Review*, 77(5), pp. 123–30; J.-F. Hennart and S. Ready, 1997, 'The choice between mergers/acquisitions and joint ventures in the United States', *Strategic Management Journal*, 18, pp. 1–12.
74. G. Robinson, 1999, 'Versace joins $2bn resorts venture', *Financial Times*, 16 April, p. 17.
75. B. S. Akre, 1999, 'Toyota alliance could lead to bigger things, GM exec hints', *Dallas Morning News*, 20 April, p. D6.
76. T. Burt, 1999, 'Mitsubishi Motors to slim range', *Financial Times*, 26 July, p. 18.
77. C. Harris and G. Cramb, 1999, 'Seeking wider co-operation', *Financial Times*, 19 October, p. 20.
78. A. Harney, 1999, 'Toyota seeks technology alliances', *Financial Times*, 19 July, p. 18.
79. S. A. Shane, 1996, 'Hybrid organizational arrangements and their implications for firm growth and survival: A study of new franchisers', *Academy of Management Journal*, 39, pp. 216–34.
80. F. Lafontaine, 1999, 'Myths and strengths of franchising', Mastering Strategy (Part Nine), *Financial Times*, 22 November, pp. 8–10.
81. P. J. Kaufmann and S. Eroglu, 1999, 'Standardization and adaptation in business format franchising', *Journal of Business Venturing*, 14, pp. 69–85.
82. R. P. Dant and P. J. Kaufmann, 1999, 'Franchising and the domain of entrepreneurship research', *Journal of Business Venturing*, 14, pp. 5–16.
83. P. Ingram and J. A. C. Baum, 1997, 'Opportunity and constraint: Organizations' learning from the operating and competitive experience of industries', *Strategic Management Journal*, 18 (Special Summer Issue), pp. 75–98.
84. L. Wu, 1999, 'The pricing of a brand name product: Franchising in the motel services industry', *Journal of Business Venturing*, 14, pp. 87–102.
85. Lafontaine, 'Myths and strengths', p. 10.
86. S. L. Brown and K. M. Eisenhardt, 1998, *Competing on the Edge: Strategy as Structural Chaos* (Boston: Harvard Business School Press).
87. R. E. Hoskisson, W. P. Wan and M. H. Hanson, 1998, 'Strategic alliance formation and market evaluation: Effects of parent firm's governance structure', in M. A. Hitt, J. E. Ricart I Costa and R. D. Nixon, *Managing Strategically in an Interconnected World* (Chichester, UK: John Wiley & Sons), pp. 207–28.
88. B. L. Simonin, 1997, 'The importance of collaborative know-how: An empirical test of the learning organization', *Academy of Management Journal*, 40, pp. 1150–74.
89. P. J. Buckley and M. Casson, 1996, 'An economic model of international joint venture strategy', *Journal of International Business Studies*, 27, pp. 849–76; J. E. McGee, M. J. Dowling and W. L. Megginson, 1995, 'Cooperative strategy and new venture performance: The role of business strategy and management experience', *Strategic Management Journal*, 16, pp. 565–80.

90. J. J. Reuer and K. D. Miller, 1997, 'Agency costs and the performance implications of international joint venture internalization', *Strategic Management Journal*, 18, pp. 425–38.
91. M. A. Hitt, M. T. Dacin, E. Levitas, J.-L. Arregle and A. Borza, 2000, 'Partner selection in emerging and developed market contexts: Resource-based and organizational learning perspectives', *Academy of Management Journal*, in press; L. K. Mytelka, 1991, *Strategic Partnerships and the World Economy* (London: Pinter Publishers).
92. M. A. Hitt, R. E. Hoskisson and H. Kim, 1997, 'International diversification: Effects on innovation and firm performance in product diversified firms', *Academy of Management Journal*, 40, pp. 767–98; R. N. Osborn and J. Hagedoorn, 1997, 'The institutionalization and evolutionary dynamics of interorganizational alliances and networks', *Academy of Management Journal*, 40, pp. 261–78.
93. J. Hagedoorn, 1995, 'A note on international market leaders and networks of strategic technology partnering', *Strategic Management Journal*, 16, pp. 241–50.
94. P. Beckett and C. Fleming, 1999, 'Mellon Bank, Credit Lyonnais discuss strategic alliance, equity investment', *Wall Street Journal*, 8 March, p. A4.
95. I. Bickerton, 1999, 'Fortis seeks more link-ups', *Financial Times*, 27 May, p. 18.
96. M. Schuman, 1996, 'South Korea raises limit to 18% on foreign investment in firms', *Wall Street Journal*, 27 February, p. A12.
97. A. Cane, 1999, 'GEC and NEC in alliance talks', *Financial Times*, 11 May, p. 20.
98. J.-F. Hennart, D.-J. Kim and M. Zeng, 1998, 'The impact of joint venture status on the longevity of Japanese stakes in U.S. manufacturing affiliates', *Organization Science*, 9, pp. 382–95; J. Li, 1995, 'Foreign entry and survival: Effects of strategic choices on performance in international markets', *Strategic Management Journal*, 16, pp. 333–51.
99. J. M. Geringer, 1991, 'Measuring performance of international joint ventures', *Journal of International Business Studies*, 22(2), pp. 249–63.
100. R. Madhavan and J. E. Prescott, 1995, 'Market value impact of joint ventures: The effect of industry information-processing load', *Academy of Management Journal*, 38, pp. 900–15.
101. J. L. Johnson, J. B. Cullen and T. Sakano, 1996, 'Setting the stage for trust and strategic integration in Japanese–U.S. cooperative alliances', *Journal of International Business Studies*, 27, pp. 981–1004.
102. J.-F. Hennart, T. Roehl and D. S. Zietlow, 1999, '"Trojan horse" or "workhorse"? The evolution of U.S.–Japanese joint ventures in the United States', *Strategic Management Journal*, 20, pp. 15–29.
103. M. T. Dacin, M. A. Hitt and E. Levitas, 1997, 'Selecting partners for successful international alliances: Examinations of U.S. and Korean firms', *Journal of World Business*, 32(1), pp. 3–16; M. A. Hitt, M. T. Dacin, E. B. Tyler and D. Park, 1997, 'Understanding the differences in Korean and U.S. executives strategic orientations', *Strategic Management Journal*, 18, pp. 159–68; G. Hamel, 1991, 'Competition for competence and inter-partner learning with international strategic alliances', *Strategic Management Journal*, 12, pp. 83–103.
104. Hennart, Roehl and Zietlow, '"Trojan horse" or "workhorse"?', p. 16.
105. C. Caggiano, 1999, 'Hotlinks', *Inc.*, October, pp. 72–81; Koza and Lewin, 'Putting the S- word back', p. 12.
106. C. Jones, W. S. Hesterly and S. P. Borgatti, 1997, 'A general theory of network governance: Exchange conditions and social mechanisms', *Academy of Management Review*, 22, pp. 911–45; T. J. Rowley, 1997, 'Moving beyond dyadic ties: A network theory of stakeholder influences', *Academy of Management Review*, 22, pp. 887–910.
107. Doz and Hamel, *Alliance Advantage*, p. 222.
108. Rugman and D'Cruz, 1997, 'The theory of the flagship firm'; D. B. Holm, K. Eriksson and J. Johanson, 1996, 'Business networks and cooperation in international business relationships', *Journal of International Business Studies*, 27, pp. 1033–53.
109. S. S. Cohen and G. Fields, 1999, 'Social capital and capital gains in Silicon Valley', *California Management Review*, 41(2), pp. 108–30; J. A. Matthews, 1999, 'A silicon island of the east: Creating a semiconductor industry in Singapore', *California Management Review*, 41(2), pp. 55–78; M. E. Porter, 1998, 'Clusters and the new economics of competition', *Harvard Business Review*, 78(6), pp. 77–90; R. Pouder and C. H. St John, 1996, 'Hot spots and blind spots: Geographical clusters of firms and innovation', *Academy of Management Review*, 21, pp. 1192–225.
110. D. B. Holm, K. Eriksson and J. Johanson, 1999, 'Creating value through mutual commitment to business network relationships', *Strategic Management Journal*, 20, pp. 467–86.
111. M. L. Gerlach, 1992, *Alliance Capitalism: The Social Organization of Japanese Business* (Berkeley, CA: University of California Press).
112. H. Bahrami, 1992, 'The emerging flexible organization: Perspectives from Silicon Valley', *California Management Review*, 34(3), pp. 33–52.
113. J. Levine, 1996, 'Even when you fail, you learn a lot', *Forbes*, 11 March, pp. 58–62.
114. T. E. Stuart, 1999, 'Alliance networks: View from the hub', Mastering Strategy (Part Eight), *Financial Times*, 15 November, pp. 4–6; T. Nishiguchi and J. Brookfield, 1997, 'The evolution of Japanese subcontracting', *Sloan Management Review*, 39(1), pp. 89–101.
115. Ibid., p. 4.
116. W. Davidow and M. Malone, 1992, *A Virtual Corporation: Structuring and Revitalizing the Corporation of the 21st Century* (New York: HarperBusiness).
117. G. Lorenzoni and C. Baden-Fuller, 1995, 'Creating a strategic center to manage a web of partners', *California Management Review*, 37(3), pp. 146–63.
118. C. Shapiro and H. R. Varian, 1999, 'The art of standard wars', *California Management Review*, 41(2), pp. 8–32.
119. K. Merchant, 1999, 'Piaggio pulls out of Indian venture', *Financial Times*, 4 June, p. 20.
130. Simonin, 'The importance of collaborative know-how'.
121. Cyr, 'High-tech', p. 19; Doz and Hamel, *Alliance Advantage*, pp. 21–2; J. B. Barney and M. H. Hansen, 1994, 'Trustworthiness: Can it be a source of competitive advantage?', *Strategic Management Journal*, 15 (Special Winter Issue), pp. 175–203.
122. R. Gulati and H. Singh, 1998, 'The architecture of cooperation: Managing coordination costs and appropriation concerns in strategic alliances', *Administrative Science Quarterly*, 43, pp. 781–814; R. Gulati, 1996, 'Social structure and alliance formation patterns: A longitudinal analysis', *Administrative Science Quarterly*, 40, pp. 619–52.
123. M. J. Dollinger, P. A. Golden and T. Saxton, 1997, 'The effect of reputation on the decision to joint venture', *Strategic Management Journal*, 18, pp. 127–40; C. W. L. Hill, 1990, 'Cooperation, opportunism, and the invisible hand: Implications for transaction cost theory', *Academy of Management Review*, 15, pp. 500–13.
124. J. H. Davis, F. D. Schoorman, R. C. Mayer and H. H. Tan, 2000, 'The trusted general manager and business unit performance: Empirical evidence of a competitive advantage', *Strategic Management Journal*, in press; R. C. Mayer, J. H. Davis and F. D. Schoorman, 1995, 'An integrative model of organizational trust', *Academy of Management Review*, 20, pp. 709–34.
125. J. Burton, 1999, 'US brewer drops out of Korean auction', *Financial Times*, 30 July, p. 17.
126. J. H. Dyer, 1997, 'Effective interfirm collaboration: How firms minimize transaction costs and maximize transaction value', *Strategic Management Journal*, 18, pp. 535–56; M. Hansen, R. E. Hoskisson and J. B. Barney, 1997, 'Trustworthiness in strategic alliances: Opportunism minimization versus opportunity maximization', Working paper, Brigham Young University.
127. Mitchell, 'Alliances', p. 7.
128. P. Moran and S. Ghoshal, 1996, 'Theories of economic organization: The case for realism and balance', *Academy of Management Review*, 21, pp. 58–72.
129. A. Parke, 1993, 'Strategic alliance structuring: A game theoretic and transaction cost examination of interfirm cooperation', *Academy of Management Journal*, 36, pp. 794–829.
130. C. S. Sankar, W. R. Boulton, N. W. Davidson, C. A. Snyder and R. W. Ussery, 1995, 'Building a world-class alliance: The universal card–TSYS case', *Academy of Management Executive*, IX(2), pp. 20–9.
131. Das, Sen and Sengupta, 'Impact of strategic alliances', p. 30.
132. Hoskisson, Wan and Hanson, 'Strategic alliance formation'.

Part 3

Strategic actions: Strategy implementation

Chapter 10
Corporate governance

Chapter 11
Organisational structure and controls

Chapter 12
Strategic leadership

Chapter 13
Corporate entrepreneurship and innovation

Chapter 10

Corporate governance

Objectives

After reading this chapter, you should be able to:

1. Define corporate governance and explain why it is used to monitor and control managers' strategic decisions.
2. Explain how ownership came to be separated from managerial control in the modern corporation.
3. Define an agency relationship and managerial opportunism, and describe their strategic and organisational implications.
4. Explain how four internal corporate governance mechanisms – ownership concentration, the board of directors, executive compensation and the multi-divisional (M-form) structure – are used to monitor and control managerial decisions.
5. Discuss trends among the three types of compensation executives receive and their effects on strategic decisions.
6. Describe how the external corporate governance mechanism – the market for corporate control – acts as a restraint on top-level managers' strategic decisions.
7. Discuss the use of corporate governance in Australia, Germany and Japan.
8. Describe how corporate governance mechanisms can foster ethical strategic decisions and behaviours on the part of top-level executives.

Are CEOs worth their weight in gold?

Many years ago, Sultans were paid their weight in gold, thus beginning a traditional saying about individuals being worth their weight in gold. This statement is intended to be a positive assessment, and most of us would greatly value being paid our weight in gold. However, would most CEOs also value that opportunity? Given the current price of gold and the average weight of most CEOs, they would receive approximately $1.5 million per year. (All amounts are in Australian dollars for ease of comparison.) In the United States, average total compensation for CEOs was just under $20 million in 1999. Within Australia, the remuneration of some CEOs has begun to surpass this weight-based figure, trending towards those pay levels enjoyed by American CEOs. Given that this amount is about 12 to 13 times a CEO's weight in gold, few would take that option. Furthermore, some would suffer severe losses by taking their weight in gold. For example, Michael Eisner, CEO of Disney, had a total compensation over a recent five-year period of $1.2 billion. Other five-year totals included Stephen Hilbert, CEO of Conseco, with $712 million; Stephen Case, CEO of America Online, with $440 million; and Jack Welch, CEO of GE, with $328 million. The new CEO of Hewlett-Packard, Carly Fiorina, is said to have received an annual compensation package of $160–$180 million. Such large remuneration packages are not restricted to CEOs alone, and indeed, some justification of CEO remuneration levels have been made by comparing their pay to that of successful sporting stars. For example, Tiger Woods, the world's number one golf player, received an appearance fee some eight times the tournament total prize package (that is, he received $3.8 million just to play in the Dubai Open). Some argue that the CEO role has inherent to it a requirement of 'special skills' (akin to Tiger Woods, for example) and that such special skills are rare and valuable, and should be compensated for in a like manner.

Many US executives also receive highly attractive pay and severance packages when they leave a firm. For example, Frank Newman received $148 million when he left Banker's Trust after Deutsche Telecom found no place for him following its acquisition of Banker's Trust. David Coulter, former CEO of BankAmerica, received $58 million. Newman received a contract guaranteeing him $22 million per year, plus millions more in deferred compensation and additional compensation for five years, regardless of whether he stayed with the firm or not. He resigned approximately one month after the acquisition was finalised.

The exceptionally high compensation figure for US executives is not yet copied to the same extent outside of that country. The highest-paid executive outside of the United States is Edgar Bronfman, CEO of Seagrams, a Canadian company, at $9 million annually. Westfield CEO, Frank Lowry earns $7.6 million; and Dennis Eck, CEO of Coles Myer Limited, earns $4.1 million annually. The CEO of Japan's second-largest firm, Nippon Telegraph and Telephone, is paid approximately $600 000 annually. Thus, foreign companies do not pay executives as much as US companies do. Japan, for instance, has a tradition of relatively low pay for CEOs, while Australia is attracting American CEOs by giving them US-style remuneration packages.

Steve Jobs is an exception for US executives, as he only takes $2 (US$1) annually in pay. However, Apple's board of directors rewarded him for the strong performance of the company in recent years with approximately $180 million in stock options and perquisites in 1999. Part of his reward included a Gulfstream jet. He was remunerated handsomely because Apple's operating profit in 1999 was $356 million, or US$1.00 per share, which was much higher than the expected US$0.89 per share, increasing from US$0.29 per share in 1998. Jobs also received options to buy 10 million shares of Apple stock.

The action of Apple's board of directors is not that unique. The primary reason for the large differential in compensation between US CEOs and non-US CEOs is the shares or share options awarded to US CEOs based on the performance of their firms. There was a push in the late 1980s and into the 1990s to change the compensation of US CEOs to be tied more directly to performance, with Australian firms following with a lag of several years. Of particular importance was the linkage of their pay to the performance of the company's shares. Thus, it has become commonplace to award executives share options, which represent an option to purchase a certain number of the company's shares at a predetermined price. The intent is to provide the executive with incentives to improve the performance of the shares. Also, the executive who exercises the options becomes an owner of the firm and has an incentive to maintain the performance of the firm at a high level, because it now affects her or his personal wealth as well. An increasing number of CEOs have received 'mega-options' that are valued at over $20 million. Whereas options accounted for only 2 per cent of the total compensation paid to CEOs in the 1980s, they accounted for approximately 26 per cent of US executives' compensation in 1994 and well over 50 per cent of the total compensation paid to US CEOs in 1998 and 1999. In Australia, similar share options accounted for only 6 per cent of CEO compensation in 1987, 13 per cent in 1990 and 35 per cent in 1999. It would seem, therefore, that shareholders and boards of directors have been trying to motivate CEOs to act in the owners' best interests by increasing the value of the company, which in turn increases shareholders' wealth. Thus, executive compensation is a tool of corporate governance.

www.aol.com
www.apple.com
www.bankofamerica.com
www.coles.com.au
www.conesco.com
www.disney.go.com
www.ge.com
www.hewlett-packard.com
www.nippon.com
www.seagrams.com
www.westfield.com.au

Sources: G. Colvin, 2000, 'The big payoff: CEOs are getting pots of money just for getting out of the way', *Fortune*, 22 February, p. 78; 'Share and share unalike', 2001, *The Economist*, 7 February: www.economist.com; L. Kehoe, 2000, 'Jet for Jobs as Apple's profits surprise', 20 January: www.ft.com/nbearchives; T. W. Ferguson and J. Lee, 1999, 'Failing upward', *Forbes*, 19 October, p. 52; D. P. Hamilton, 1999, 'H-P values CEO's package at $80 to $90 million', *Wall Street Journal Interactive*, 22 September: www.interactive.wsj.com/articles; E. S. Hardy, S. DeCarlo, A. C. Anderson and J. Chamberlain, 1999, 'Compensation fit for a king', *Forbes*, 17 May, pp. 202–7; 'Top-paid foreign CEOs lag far behind Americans', 2000, *Houston Chronicle*, 5 May, p. 4C; G. L. O'Neill, 1999, 'Executive remuneration in Australia: An overview of trends and issues', a White Paper (Melbourne: Hay Group/AHRI); L. R. Gomez-Mejia and D. B. Balkin, 1992, 'Determinants of faculty pay: An agency theory perspective', *Academy of Management Journal*, 30(5), p. 921; 'Woods blows it on the last …', 2001, *The Age*, 6 March.

As the Opening Case illustrates, corporate governance is increasingly important as a part of the strategic management process.[1] If the board of directors makes the wrong decision in compensating the firm's strategic leader, the CEO, the whole firm suffers, as do its shareholders. Compensation is used to motivate CEOs to act in the best interests of the firm – in particular, the shareholders. When they do so, the firm's value should increase. Of course, some question what a CEO's actions are worth. The Opening Case suggests that they are worth a significant amount in the United States (considerably more than the CEO's weight in gold).

While some critics argue that CEOs are paid too much, the hefty increases in compensation they have received in recent years come from linking their pay to the performance of the firm. US firms have performed well compared with many others from different countries. Some research suggests that CEOs receive excessive compensation when the corporate governance is the weakest.[2]

Corporate governance represents the relationship among stakeholders that is used to determine and control the strategic direction and performance of organisations.[3] At its core, corporate governance is concerned with identifying ways to ensure that strategic

Corporate governance represents the relationship among stakeholders that is used to determine and control the strategic direction and performance of organisations.

decisions are made effectively.[4] In addition, governance can be thought of as a means used by corporations to establish order between parties (the firm's owners and its top-level managers) whose interests may be in conflict.[5] Thus, corporate governance reflects and enforces the company's values.[6] In modern corporations – especially those in the United States, the United Kingdom and Australia – the primary objective of corporate governance is to ensure that the interests of top-level managers are aligned with the interests of the shareholders. Corporate governance involves oversight in areas where owners, managers and members of boards of directors may have conflicts of interest. These areas include the election of directors, the general supervision of CEO pay and more focused supervision of director pay, and the corporation's overall structure and strategic direction.[7]

Corporate governance has been emphasised in recent years because some observers believe that corporate governance mechanisms have failed to adequately monitor and control top-level managers' strategic decisions.[8] This perspective is causing changes in governance mechanisms in corporations throughout the world, especially with respect to efforts intended to improve the performance of boards of directors.[9] This interest, however, is understandable for a second and more positive reason; namely, that evidence suggests that a well-functioning corporate governance and control system can result in a competitive advantage for an individual firm.[10] For example, one governance mechanism – the board of directors – has been suggested to be rapidly evolving into a major strategic force in firms.[11] Thus, in this chapter, we describe actions designed to implement strategies that focus on monitoring and controlling mechanisms. When used properly, these actions help to ensure that top-level managerial actions contribute to the firm's strategic competitiveness and its ability to earn above-average returns.

Effective corporate governance is also of interest to nations. As stated by one scholar,

> Every country wants the firms that operate within its borders to flourish and grow in such ways as to provide employment, wealth, and satisfaction, not only to improve standards of living materially but also to enhance social cohesion. These aspirations cannot be met unless those firms are competitive internationally in a sustained way, and it is this medium- and long-term perspective that makes good corporate governance so vital.[12]

Corporations around the world are making efforts to improve the performance of their boards of directors because corporate governance has failed to adequately monitor top managers' strategic decisions. A second reason is that a well-functioning governance and control system can result in a competitive advantage for a firm.

Corporate governance, then, reflects the standards of the company, which, in turn, collectively reflect societal standards.[13] Thus, in many individual corporations, shareholders are striving to hold top-level managers more accountable for their decisions and the results they generate. As with individual firms and their boards, nations that govern their corporations effectively may gain a competitive advantage over rival countries.

In OECD countries the fundamental goal of business organisations is to maximise shareholder value.[14] Traditionally, shareholders are treated as the firm's key stakeholders, because they are the company's legal owners. The firm's owners expect top-level managers and others influencing the corporation's actions (for example, the board of directors) to make decisions that will result in the maximisation of the company's value and, hence, of their own wealth.[15]

In the first section of this chapter, we describe the relationship providing the foundation on which the modern corporation is built; the relationship between owners and managers. The majority of this chapter is then devoted to an explanation of various mechanisms owners use to govern managers and ensure that they comply with their responsibility to maximise shareholder value.

Four internal governance mechanisms and a single external mechanism are used in the modern Western-style corporation (see Table 10.1). The four internal governance mechanisms examined herein are: (1) ownership concentration, as represented by types of shareholders and their different incentives to monitor managers; (2) the board of directors; (3) executive compensation; and (4) the multi-divisional (M-form) organisational structure. Next, we consider the market for corporate control, an external corporate governance mechanism. Essentially, this market is a set of potential owners seeking to acquire undervalued firms and earn above-average returns on their investments by replacing ineffective top-level management teams.[16] To this point, the discussion uses American and Australian material to explore the basic governance mechanisms. The chapter's focus then shifts to the issue of international corporate governance. We briefly describe governance approaches used in a number of countries and discuss the effect of these differences. Because the Australian system has unique legislative and culture-based patterns, we include a specific section on Australian corporate governance. Closing our analysis of corporate governance is a consideration of the need for these control mechanisms to encourage and support ethical behaviour in organisations.

Table 10.1 | Corporate governance mechanisms

Internal governance mechanisms

Ownership concentration
- Relative amounts of shares owned by individual shareholders and institutional investors

Board of directors
- Individuals responsible for representing the firm's owners by monitoring top-level managers' strategic decisions

Executive compensation
- Use of salary, bonuses and long-term incentives to align managers' interests with shareholders' interests

Multi-divisional structure
- Creation of individual business divisions to closely monitor top-level managers' strategic decisions

External governance mechanism

Market for corporate control
- The purchase of a firm that is underperforming relative to industry rivals in order to improve its strategic competitiveness

Importantly, the mechanisms explained in this chapter have the potential to influence positively the governance of the modern corporation. The modern corporation has placed significant responsibility and authority in the hands of top-level managers. The most effective of these managers understand their accountability for the firm's performance and respond positively to the requirements of the corporate governance mechanisms explained in this chapter.[17] In addition, the firm's owners should not expect any single mechanism to govern the company effectively over time. Rather, the use of several mechanisms allows owners to govern the corporation in ways that maximise strategic competitiveness and increase the financial value of their firm.[18] With multiple governance mechanisms operating simultaneously, it is also possible for some of the governance mechanisms to conflict.[19] Finally, we review how these conflicts can occur.

Separation of ownership and managerial control

Historically, firms were managed by the founder–owners and their descendants. In these cases, corporate ownership and control resided in the same person(s). As firms grew larger, 'the managerial revolution led to a separation of ownership and control in most large corporations, where control of the firm shifted from entrepreneurs to professional managers while ownership became dispersed among thousands of unorganized stockholders who were removed from the day-to-day management of the firm'.[20] These changes created the modern public corporation, which is based on the efficient separation of ownership and managerial control. Supporting the separation is a basic legal premise suggesting that the primary objective of a firm's activities is to increase the corporation's profit and, thereby, the financial gains of the owners (the shareholders).[21]

The separation of ownership and managerial control allows shareholders to purchase shares, which entitles them to income (residual returns) from the operations of the firm after expenses have been paid. This right, however, requires that they also take a risk that the firm's expenses may exceed its revenues. To manage this investment risk, shareholders seek to maintain a diversified portfolio by investing in several companies to reduce their overall risk.[22]

In small firms, managers often are the owners, so there is no separation between ownership and managerial control, but as firms grow and become more complex, owners–managers may contract with managerial specialists. These managers oversee decision making in the owner's firm and are compensated on the basis of their decision-making skills. Managers, then, operate a corporation through the use of their decision-making skills and are viewed as agents of the firm's owners.[23] In terms of the strategic management process (see Figure 1.1 in Chapter 1), managers are expected to form a firm's strategic intent and strategic mission and then formulate and implement the strategies that realise them. Thus, in the modern public corporation, top-level managers, especially the CEO, have primary responsibility for initiating and implementing an array of strategic decisions.

As shareholders diversify their investments over a number of corporations, their risk declines. The poor performance or failure of any one firm in which they invest has less overall effect. Thus, shareholders specialise in managing their investment risk, while managers specialise in decision making. Without management specialisation in decision making and owner specialisation in risk bearing, a firm probably would be limited by the abilities of its owners to manage and make effective strategic decisions. Therefore, the separation and specialisation of ownership (risk bearing) and managerial control (decision making) should produce the highest returns.

Shareholder value is reflected by the price of the firm's shares. As stated earlier, corporate governance, such as the board of directors or compensation based on the performance of a firm, is the reason that CEOs show general concern about the firm's share price. For example, according to a former senior executive at the Australian transport giant Mayne Nickless, former managing director of the company, Bob Dalziel's main problem was that he over-promised and under-delivered. 'Less than three years ago, he went to New York and told the market he would spin off the property division to reduce debt and improve cashflow. Whatever happened to that? In the past year, investors wanted reassurance.' He says another problem with Mayne Nickless is low morale: 'There have been so many changes and re-structurings and sales over the years that nobody feels safe or confident.' Poor morale and lack of share-market credibility led to Mayne Nickless shares falling to a record low of $2.90 on 10 March 2000. They rose to $3.86 on 10 July 2000 as the market absorbed news of a new management structure.[24]

Agency relationships

> An **agency relationship** exists when one or more persons (the principal or principals) hire another person or persons (the agent or agents) as decision-making specialists to perform a service.

The separation between owners and managers creates an agency relationship. An **agency relationship** exists when one or more persons (the principal or principals) hire another person or persons (the agent or agents) as decision-making specialists to perform a service.[25] Thus, an agency relationship exists when one party delegates decision-making responsibility to a second party for compensation (see Figure 10.1).[26] In addition to shareholders and top executives, other examples of agency relationships are consultants and clients and insured and insurer. Moreover, within organisations, an agency relationship exists between managers and their employees, as well as between top executives and the firm's owners.[27] In the modern corporation, managers must understand the links between these relationships and the firm's effectiveness.[28] Although the agency relationship between managers and their employees is important, in this chapter we focus on the agency relationship between the firm's owners (the principals) and top-level managers (the principals' agents), because this relationship is related directly to how strategies are implemented by managers.

Figure 10.1 | An agency relationship

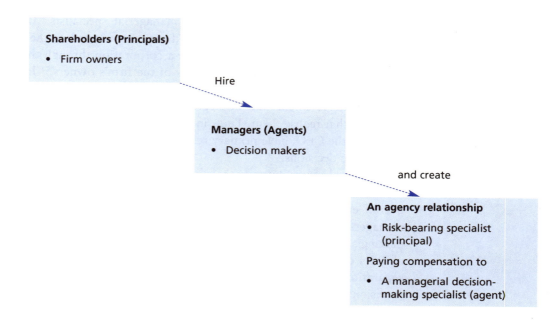

The separation between ownership and managerial control can be problematic. Research evidence documents a variety of agency problems in the modern corporation.[29] Problems can surface because the principal and the agent have different interests and goals, or because shareholders lack direct control of large publicly traded corporations. Problems arise when an agent makes decisions that result in the pursuit of goals that conflict with those of the principals. Thus, the separation of ownership and control *potentially* allows divergent interests (between principals and agents) to surface, which can lead to managerial opportunism.[30] **Managerial opportunism** is the seeking of self-interest with guile (that is, cunning or deceit).[31] Opportunism is both an attitude (for example, an inclination) and a set of behaviours (that is, specific acts of self-interest).[32] However, it is not possible for principals to know beforehand which agents will or will not engage in opportunistic behaviour. The reputations of top executives are an imperfect predictor, and opportunistic behaviour cannot be observed until it has occurred. Thus, principals establish governance and control mechanisms to prevent agents from acting opportunistically, even though only a few are likely to do so.[33] Any time that principals delegate decision-making responsibilities to agents, the opportunity for conflicts of interest exists. Top executives, for example, may make strategic decisions that maximise their personal welfare and minimise their personal risk.[34] Decisions such as these prevent the maximisation of shareholder wealth. Decisions regarding product diversification demonstrate these possibilities.

> **Managerial opportunism** is the seeking of self-interest with guile.

Product diversification as an example of an agency problem

As explained in Chapter 6, a corporate-level strategy to diversify the firm's product lines can enhance a firm's strategic competitiveness and increase its returns, both of which serve the interests of shareholders and the top executives. However, because product diversification can provide two benefits to managers that shareholders do not enjoy, top executives sometimes prefer more product diversification than do shareholders.[35]

Diversification usually increases the size of a firm, and size is positively related to executive compensation. Thus, increased product diversification provides an opportunity for top executives to increase their compensation through growth in firm size.[36]

In addition, product diversification and the resulting diversification of the firm's portfolio of businesses can reduce top executives' employment risk.[37] *Managerial employment risk* is the risk of job loss, loss of compensation and loss of managerial reputation. These risks are reduced with increased diversification, because a firm and its upper-level managers are less vulnerable to the reduction in demand associated with a single or limited number of product lines or businesses. Furthermore, a firm may have free cash flows over which top executives have discretion. *Free cash flows* are resources generated after investment in all projects that have positive net present values within the firm's current product lines.[38] In anticipation of positive returns, managers may decide to use these funds to invest in products that are not associated with the current lines of business, even if the investments increase the firm's level of diversification. The managerial decision to use free cash flows to over-diversify the firm is an example of self-serving and opportunistic managerial behaviour. In contrast to managers, shareholders may prefer that free cash flows be distributed to them as dividends, so that they can control how the cash is invested.[39]

Curve *S* in Figure 10.2 depicts the shareholders' optimal level of diversification. Owners seek the level of diversification that reduces the risk of the firm's total failure while simultaneously increasing the company's value through the development of economies of scale and scope (see Chapter 6). Of the four corporate-level diversification strategies shown in Figure 10.2, shareholders likely prefer the diversified position noted by point A on curve S – a position that is located between the dominant business and related-constrained diversification strategies. Of course, the optimum level of diversification sought by owners varies from firm to firm. Factors that affect shareholders' preferences include the firm's primary industry, the intensity of rivalry among competitors in that industry and the top management team's experience with implementing diversification strategies.

Figure 10.2 | Manager and shareholder risk and diversification

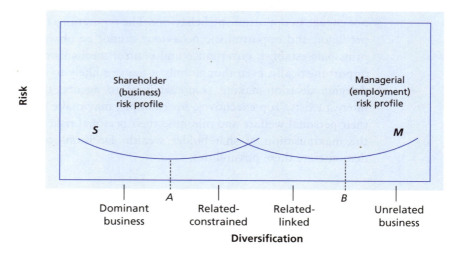

As with principals, upper-level executives – as agents – seek an optimal level of diversification. Declining performance resulting from too much product diversification increases the probability that a firm will be acquired in the market for corporate control. Once a firm is acquired, the employment risk for the firm's top executives increases substantially. Furthermore, a manager's employment opportunities in the external managerial labour market (discussed in Chapter 12) are affected negatively by a firm's poor performance. Therefore, top executives prefer diversification, but not to a point that it increases their employment risk and reduces their employment opportunities.

Curve M in Figure 10.2 shows that executives prefer higher levels of product diversification than shareholders. Top executives might prefer the level of diversification shown by point B on curve M. In general, shareholders prefer riskier strategies and more focused diversification. They reduce their risk through holding a diversified portfolio of equity investments. Alternatively, managers cannot work for a diverse portfolio of firms to balance their employment risk. Therefore, top executives may prefer a level of diversification that maximises firm size and their compensation and that reduces their employment risk. Product diversification, therefore, is a potential agency problem that could result in principals incurring costs to control their agents' behaviours.

Agency costs and governance mechanisms

The potential conflict illustrated by Figure 10.2, coupled with the fact that principals do not know which managers might act opportunistically, demonstrates why principals establish governance mechanisms. However, establishing and using the governance mechanisms create costs. **Agency costs** are the sum of incentive costs, monitoring costs, enforcement costs and individual financial losses incurred by principals because it is impossible to use governance mechanisms to guarantee total compliance by the agent.[40]

Agency costs are the sum of incentive costs, monitoring costs, enforcement costs and individual financial losses incurred by principals because it is impossible to use governance mechanisms to guarantee total compliance by the agent.

In general, managerial interests may prevail when governance mechanisms are weak, as is exemplified by allowing managers a significant amount of autonomy in making strategic decisions. If, however, the board of directors controls managerial autonomy, or if other strong governance mechanisms are used, the firm's strategies should better reflect the interests of the shareholders. However, recent research suggests that even using more governance mechanisms may produce major changes in strategies. This research showed, for example, that firms acquired unrelated businesses at approximately the same rate in the 1980s as they did in the 1960s, even though more governance mechanisms were employed in the 1980s. Thus, governance mechanisms represent an imperfect means of controlling managerial opportunism.[41] Alternatively, anecdotal evidence suggests that shareholders are not docile when they perceive that managers are not taking actions in their best interests. For example, in 2000, there was growing opposition among shareholders to limits on share ownership. In most cases, share ownership limits are put in place by state governments keen to offer takeover protection to large regional businesses. Most shareholders believe that these limits distort market prices and insulate companies from the usual market disciplines. An independent shareholder activist, Ray Proudley, has focused attention on the issue by standing for the board of the US gas utility, AGL, on a platform of removing the company's 5 per cent share ownership limit. Proudley missed out on election at the company's annual general meeting (AGM) on 17 October 1999, but he did succeed in prompting the board to acknowledge the issue. The AGL board has given a commitment to work towards removal of the restriction. Likewise, shareholders in Japan are becoming more active. Recently, shareholders of Dai-Ichi Kangyo Bank filed suits over payments that the bank made to racketeers known as *sokaiya*. The *sokaiya* commonly disrupted annual shareholders' meetings by jeering unless the firm made payments to them not to attend the meeting. The banks and other firms are worried about this new shareholder activism.[42]

In the sections that follow, we explain the effects of various means of governance on managerial decisions to formulate and implement the firm's different strategies.

Ownership concentration

Ownership concentration is defined by both the number of large-block shareholders and the total percentage of shares they own.

Large-block shareholders typically own at least 5 per cent of a corporation's issued shares.

The number of large-block shareholders and the total percentage of shares they own define **ownership concentration**. **Large-block shareholders** typically own a minimum of 5 per cent of a corporation's issued shares. Ownership concentration as a governance mechanism has received considerable interest because large-block shareholders are increasingly active in their demands that corporations adopt effective governance mechanisms to control managerial decisions.[43]

In general, *diffuse ownership* (a large number of shareholders with small holdings and few, if any, large-block shareholders) produces weak monitoring of managerial decisions. Among other problems, diffuse ownership makes it difficult for owners to coordinate their actions effectively. An outcome of weak monitoring might be the diversification of the firm's product lines beyond the shareholders' optimum level. Higher levels of monitoring could encourage managers to avoid strategic decisions that do not create greater shareholder value. In fact, research evidence shows that ownership concentration is associated with lower levels of firm diversification.[44] Thus, with high degrees of ownership concentration, the probability is greater that managers' strategic decisions will be intended to maximise shareholder value.

Concentration of ownership is a natural consequence of deregulated industries. For example, after the airline industry was deregulated in the United States, the ownership of the airlines became more concentrated.[45] Much of this concentration often has come from increasing equity ownership by institutional investors. In the Australian dairy industry, the removal of the Domestic Market Support (DMS) Scheme, coupled with the deregulation of the state milk markets on 30 June 2000, has resulted in many small dairy farmers leaving the industry. This exodus is a direct result of increased competition in the industry, which has led to a decline in milk prices at the farm gate.[46]

The growing influence of institutional owners

A classic work published in the 1930s argued that the 'modern' corporation had become characterised by a separation of ownership and control.[47] This change occurred as the growth of a firm prevented its founders–owners from maintaining their dual positions as owners and managers of their corporations. More recently, another shift has occurred: ownership of many modern corporations is now concentrated in the hands of institutional investors rather than individual shareholders.[48]

Institutional owners are financial institutions such as banks, mutual funds and superannuation funds that control large-block shareholder positions. Because of their prominent ownership positions, institutional owners, as large-block shareholders, are a powerful governance mechanism.[49] In Australia, the largest institutional investors tend to be the large corporate banks. As demonstrated by the cross-section of companies outlined in Table 10.2, it is common for banks to be large-block shareholders in Australia's largest companies. For example, the three largest shareholders in BHP, Brambles and Woolworths are Chase Manhattan Bank, Westpac and the National Australia Bank. Interestingly, Table 10.2 also indicates that one overseas institution, Chase Manhattan Bank, holds a stake in some of Australia's largest companies.

Thus, as the ownership percentages suggest, institutional owners have both the size and the incentive to discipline ineffective top-level managers and are able to influence significantly a firm's choice of strategies and overall strategic decisions.[50] Research evidence indicates that institutional and other large-block shareholders are becoming more active in efforts to influence a corporation's strategic decisions.

Initially, shareholders seemed to concentrate on the accountability of CEOs. After focusing on the performance of many CEOs, which has contributed to the ouster of a number of them, shareholder activists and institutional investors are targeting what they perceive as ineffective boards of directors. For example, Rupert Murdoch's trips to Adelaide for News Corporation's AGMs are occasions for a display of 'corporate triumphalism'. The global media tycoon returns to where it all started, to bask in the adulation of his most faithful shareholders. But at the meeting held on 18 October 2000, there were some dissident elements in attendance, determined to challenge the agenda of News Corporation's board. They represented big investment institutions and spoke for a substantial bloc of votes. A proposal to grant options to some senior News executives, including Lachlan Murdoch, Peter Chernin and David DeVoe, was passed with only 392.7 million votes for and 253.4 million against, a very narrow victory compared with previous experience. Institutional investors have complained in the past about the News board's practice of proposing a grant of executive options without spelling out the performance hurdles that have to be met before those options are vested. In 2000, some decided to do more than simply complain. A proposal to grant 24 million options to Rupert Murdoch, the company's executive chairman (the large number was explained by the fact that Murdoch had not been granted options since 1988), was passed with 478.5 million votes for and 112 million against. This was a bigger margin in favour but perhaps an even more serious challenge to the board than the vote on the executive options, given

> **Institutional owners** are financial institutions such as banks, mutual funds and superannuation funds that control large-block shareholder positions.

Table 10.2 | Top three large-block shareholders in a cross-section of listed Australian companies

Company	Top three large-block shareholders	Percentage
Amcor Limited	1 Westpac Custodian Nominees Limited	14.35
	2 Chase Manhattan Nominees Limited	9.69
	3 National Nominees Limited	8.47
BHP Limited	1 Chase Manhattan Nominees Limited	15.15
	2 Westpac Custodian Nominees Limited	10.58
	3 National Nominees Limited	10.11
Brambles Industries Limited	1 Chase Manhattan Nominees Limited	17.42
	2 Westpac Custodian Nominees Limited	15.52
	3 National Nominees Limited	11.92
Coles Myer Limited	1 MF Group	6.19
	2 Chase Manhattan Nominees Limited	5.55
	3 Premier Investments Limited	4.90
CSR Limited	1 Chase Manhattan Nominees Limited	14.22
	2 Westpac Custodian Nominees Limited	11.60
	3 National Nominees Limited	8.84
John Fairfax Holdings Limited	1 CPH Investment Corp.	14.92
	2 Chase Manhattan Nominees Limited	9.90
	3 National Nominees Limited	8.46
Publishing and Broadcasting Limited	1 Bareage Pty Limited	23.97
	2 Consolidated Press Holdings	12.52
	3 National Nominees Limited	5.26
Ranger Minerals Limited	1 Westpac Custodian Nominees Limited	12.47
	2 National Nominees Limited	10.64
	3 Chase Manhattan Nominees Limited	7.56
Qantas Airways Limited	1 British Airways Investments (Australia) Limited	25.00
	2 Chase Manhattan Nominees Limited	9.91
	3 National Nominees Limited	8.03
Woolworths Limited	1 Chase Manhattan Nominees Limited	8.51
	2 Westpac Custodian Nominees Limited	7.39
	3 National Nominees Limited	6.48

Source: Data on share ownership are drawn from each company's 2000 annual report.

that it was Murdoch's own remuneration that was at issue. In the end, all the board's resolutions were passed, but the strength of the opposition to some of them was a surprise. For those who would like to see more shareholder activism in Australia, the News Corporation meeting was an important event; it suggested that fund managers and superannuation fund trustees were starting to take corporate governance more seriously.[51]

The Strategic Focus examines how some shareholders in Australia have collectively formed an association, the Australian Shareholders Association (ASA), and how the actions by the association affect companies' actions. This also supports the argument that corporate governance is now being taken more seriously.

Strategic Focus Corporate

Institutional investors: ASA

The Australian Shareholders Association (ASA) ran a campaign against Pacific Dunlop chairman John Ralph, saying that the company was a chronic poor performer and needed some new blood on the board. Another of the ASA's targets was Ken Cowley, chairman of the magazine publisher, distributor and contract printer PMP Communications, who has presided over a steady decline in earnings per share since 1994. Ralph and Cowley were re-elected, but the activists believe they have made gains. Tony McLean, the ASA's executive officer, says he is not measuring the success of the organisation's AGM season campaign by counting scalps. 'Companies are getting the message,' McLean says. 'Our actions, along with the actions of a growing number of individual and institutional shareholders, are forcing directors and executives to make more contact with their shareholders and give commitment to improve performance. John Ralph is one chairman who has been doing the rounds during the past few weeks.' McLean says the increasing membership of the ASA indicates the level of interest in corporate governance among private investors. In the past five years, numbers have grown from 500 to 6 000, almost all of them retail investors. With a stronger membership base, the organisation has been able to devote resources to monitoring company performance and providing voting recommendations on issues that arise at company meetings.

Since 1999, the ASA has produced a list of poor performers, based on total shareholder returns over a three-year period. (Total shareholder return, a common performance benchmark in executive option planning, is a measure of the change in the sum of a company's share price and dividend payment.) The list published by the ASA in January 2000 had 44 names, including Amcor, AMP, CSR, David Jones, Mayne Nickless, PMP, Seven Network, St George Bank and Village Roadshow. The ASA has set up an AGM monitoring service on its website. Analysts review the resolutions that will be put to shareholders and make recommendations on how to vote. For example, the website recommended against a grant of options to Bruce Beeren, chief executive of Origin Energy, on the grounds that the company produced below-average returns. The ASA position is that executives should not be rewarded for performance that is below average. Despite this opposition, the resolution to grant options to Beeren was carried with 98.7 million votes in favour and 18.8 million against. Peter Morgan, head of Australian equities at Perpetual Investments, says the success of such campaigns should not be measured by counting resolutions defeated or chairmen deposed. He says the level of interest in corporate governance issues on the part of institutional and private shareholders has been so low that any increase in the level of activism is welcome.

'We are seeing more of these matters appearing in the public domain and that is a good thing,' Morgan says. 'There is some evidence of increased shareholder activism this year but it is coming off such a low base that you would not expect to see boards having their resolutions voted down. What is good is that we are seeing investors using the AGM as a forum for a serious discussion of the company's performance. I have never accepted the argument that it is better for an institution to express criticism of a company behind closed doors. I would like to see AGM discussions minuted.'

The ASA is opposed to an option plan proposed by the board of Energy Development, a developer and operator of power-generation projects, that would grant options to executives and non-executive directors with an exercise price that was below the prevailing market price. The position adopted by the ASA is that the exercise price is too low, and it argues that executive and non-executive directors should not receive incentive remuneration in the same form.

> **Activists showing their strength**
>
> Shareholder activists became more visible during year 2000's round of annual general meetings. They focused on a greater number of directors and a wider range of issues.
>
> - **Poor performance:** Top of the list, as it had been for the past few years, is Pacific Dunlop. Shareholders also asked questions of directors of PMP Communications, HIH Insurance (which has subsequently gone into liquidation), Arthur Yates & Company, Australian Pipeline Trust, News Corporation, Village Roadshow and a host of new-technology companies, including Melbourne IT.
> - **Executive remuneration:** Fund managers fought a losing battle over an executive option plan at News Corporation. They also took on directors at Brambles, AMP, Cable & Wireless Optus, One.Tel (which has subsequently gone into liquidation), Sausage Software, Grane Group, Origin Energy and Energy Development.
> - **Accounting policies:** Abnormals have become the norm at Goodman Fielder and PMP Communications. Investors called for clearer reporting of earnings.
> - **Conflict of interest:** Westfield and Brambles took advantage of a relaxation of the Corporations Law provisions on conflict of interest to give their directors the power to decide when a fellow director must withdraw from board discussion. Investors felt shareholders have nothing to gain from this.
> - **Disclosure:** The Australian Securities and Investments Commission (ASIC) criticised Travelshop, Isis Communications and Spike Networks for poor disclosure. ASIC says many technology companies do not realise that they have to keep the market informed.
> - **Share ownership limits:** The AGL board came under fire for not moving fast enough to remove an anachronistic 5 per cent share ownership limit. The issue was taken up by several institutions and has gained wider currency.
>
> Sources: J. Kavanagh, 2000, 'Shareholders bare their teeth', *Business Review Weekly*, 3 November; B. Adamson, 2000, 'Buy the blue sky', *Personal Investment*, 16(5), p. 34.

Sources: G. L. O'Neill, 1999, 'Executive remuneration in Australia: An overview of trends and issues', a White Paper (Melbourne: Hay Group/AHRI); Australian Shareholders Association, 20001, 'Executive options': www.asa.asn.au/ASALaunch/ExecutiveOptions.asp.

Shareholder activism: How much is possible?

Some analysts argue that greater latitude should be extended to those managing the funds of large institutional investor groups. Allowing these individuals to hold positions on companies' boards of directors in which their organisation has significant investments might enable fund managers to better represent the interests of those they serve.[52]

The type of shareholder and board-of-director activism used by institutional investors sometimes provokes reactions from top executives. Unintended and not always anticipated, these reactions require still further attention by those monitoring the decisions being made by the firm's managers. A reaction articulated by one American corporate CEO demonstrates this issue. When asked to evaluate results achieved through shareholder activism, the CEO suggested that at least some of the actions requested by shareholder activists exceeded the roles specified by the separation of ownership and managerial control. When this occurs, the CEO argued, owners and directors begin to micro-manage the corporation, which is not their job. Faced with such a situation, executives have incentives to take actions that reduce their employment risk. Implementing strategies with greater diversification, as explained earlier, is one path top executives can pursue to achieve their objective. The chairman of Heinz in the United States, Anthony O'Reilly, for instance, did not increase Heinz's diversification (even though at one stage he was a serious bidder for the Age/Sydney Morning Herald–Fairfax empire), but he held ownership positions and board responsibilities in a number of other enterprises.[53] In so doing, he was less dependent on his chairman position with Heinz. Of course, having the additional positions reduced the time O'Reilly was able to spend on Heinz's strategic issues.

A number of CEOs are now declining to be outside directors on other firms' boards because CEOs have been criticised for serving on outside boards, taking time away from their CEO responsibilities. Executives may take actions to protect themselves against employment risks when institutional investors have major investments in their firm. Besides the proactive protection of doing a better job, they may seek defensive protection from a possible acquisition. Evidence suggests that the number of executives receiving such protection is increasing. A *golden parachute*, a type of managerial protection that pays a guaranteed salary for a specified period in the event of a takeover and the loss of one's job, is sought by many top-level managers, particularly the CEO. A number of other provisions also allow a firm to defend against an attempted takeover.[54] A more recently developed protection is called the golden goodbye. A *golden goodbye* provides automatic payments to top executives if their contracts are not renewed, regardless of the reason for the non-renewal. In the extreme, golden goodbyes are being offered in the case of acquisitions. In general, though, the degree to which institutional investors can actively monitor the decisions being made in all of the companies in which they have invested is questionable. (Given limited resources, even large-block shareholders tend to concentrate on corporations in which they have significant investments. Thus, although shareholder activism has increased, institutional investors face barriers to the amount of active governance they can realistically employ.)[55]

Typically, shareholders monitor the managerial decisions and actions of a firm through the board of directors. Shareholders elect members to their firm's board. Those who are elected are expected to oversee managers and to ensure that the corporation is operated in ways that will maximise its shareholders' wealth.

Institutional activism should create a premium on companies with good corporate governance. However, sometimes trustees for these funds – particularly large private superannuation funds – have other business relationships with companies in the fund's portfolio. This prevents effective monitoring.[56] In addition, a recent phenomenon is the increase in managerial ownership of the firm's shares. There are many positive reasons for managerial ownership, including the use of share options to link managerial pay to the performance of a firm. However, an unexpected outcome in the United States has been reduced support for shareholder-sponsored proposals to repeal anti-takeover provisions. Institutional owners generally support the repeal of these provisions, while managerial owners generally oppose their repeal. Thus, managerial ownership provides managers with power to protect their own interests.[57] This suggests that other means of governance are needed. Next, we examine the board of directors as a governance mechanism.

Board of directors

*The **board of directors** is a group of elected individuals whose primary responsibility is to act in the owners' interests by formally monitoring and controlling the corporation's top-level executives.*

The **board of directors** is a group of elected individuals whose primary responsibility is to act in the owners' interests by formally monitoring and controlling the corporation's top-level executives.[58] This responsibility is a product of the legal system, which, in the United States and other advanced Western economies, 'confers broad powers on corporate boards to direct the affairs of the organization, punish and reward managers, and protect the rights and interests of shareholders'.[59] Thus, an appropriately structured and effective board of directors protects owners from managerial opportunism. Board members are seen as stewards of their company's resources, and the way they carry out these responsibilities affects the society in which their firm operates.[60]

Generally, board members (usually called 'directors') are classified into one of three groups (see Table 10.3). *Insiders* are active top-level managers in the corporation who are elected to the board because they are a source of information about the firm's day-to-day operations.[61] *Related outsiders* have some relationship with the firm – contractual or otherwise – that may create questions about their independence, but these individuals are not involved with the corporation's day-to-day activities. *Outsiders* are individuals elected to the board to provide independent counsel to the firm and may hold top-level managerial positions in another company or have been elected to the board prior to the beginning of the current CEO's tenure.[62] In Australia and the United Kingdom, outside directors are commonly referred to as *non-executive* or *independent* directors.

Table 10.3 | Classifications of boards of directors' members

Insiders
- The firm's CEO and other top-level managers

Related outsiders
- Individuals not involved with the firm's day-to-day operations, but who have a relationship with the company

Outsiders
- Individuals who are independent of the firm in terms of day-to-day operations and other relationships

Some analysts argue that many boards are not fulfilling their primary fiduciary duty to protect shareholders. Among other possibilities, it may be that boards are a managerial tool: they do not question managers' actions, and they easily approve managers' self-serving initiatives.[63] In general, those critical of boards as a governance device believe that inside managers dominate boards and exploit their personal ties with them. A widely accepted view is that a board with a significant percentage of its membership from the firm's top executives tends to provide relatively weak monitoring and control of managerial decisions.[64] Critics advocate reforms to ensure that independent outside directors represent a significant majority of the total membership of a board.[65] In Great Britain, the Cadbury Report on Corporate Governance advocated improvements in board accountability and performance. Furthermore, the architect of this report, Sir Adrian Cadbury, suggests that the reform of corporate governance has become a worldwide movement, because of the growth of global markets.[66]

Boards have become more active in recent years because of the emphasis on reform, because of shareholder lawsuits, and because of active institutional investors. One criticism has been that some boards wait too long before taking action to replace CEOs who are not performing well.

There is some disagreement over the most appropriate role of outside directors in a firm's strategic decision-making process.[67] Because of external pressures, board reforms have been initiated. To date, these reforms have generally called for an increase in the number of outside directors, relative to insiders, serving on a corporation's board. For example, in 1984, the New York Stock Exchange started requiring that listed firms have board audit committees composed solely of outside directors.[68] As a result of external pressures, boards of large corporations have more outside members. Research shows that outside board members can influence the strategic direction of companies. Thus, they play an important role on boards of directors.[69] Therefore, there are potential strategic implications associated with the movement towards having corporate boards dominated by outsiders.

Alternatively, a large number of outside board members can also present some problems. Outsiders do not have contact with the firm's day-to-day operations and thus do not have easy access to the rich information about managers and their skills that is required to evaluate managerial decisions and initiatives effectively. Valuable information may be obtained through frequent interactions with inside board members during board meetings. Insiders possess such information by virtue of their organisational positions. Thus, boards with a critical mass of insiders can be informed more effectively about intended strategic initiatives, the reasons for the initiatives and the outcomes expected from them.[70] Without this type of information, outsider-dominated boards may emphasise financial, as opposed to strategic, evaluations. Such evaluations shift risk to top-level managers, who, in turn, may make decisions to maximise their interests and reduce their employment risk. Reductions in R&D investments, additional diversification of the firm and the pursuit of greater levels of compensation are examples of managers' actions to achieve these objectives.

International differences in board structures

It is important to note that there are some important differences in board structures across countries. First, while the norm in many countries is to have one board for a company (referred to as the *unitary board model*), in some Western European countries the norm is to have two boards (often referred to as the *two-tier board model*). Perhaps the best-known national example of a two-tier board model is that of Germany – discussed in some detail later in this chapter. A second important difference concerns the issue of whether the chairman and CEO are separate roles. While the norm in the United States is for the chairman and CEO to be the same person, as Table 10.4 shows, this is not the case in Australia and the United Kingdom. A recent global study by the management-consulting firm Egon Zehnder International confirms the pattern demonstrated in Table 10.4. This survey of board practices and policies in 188 companies across 24 countries indicates that there is a clear difference between practices with regard to separating the roles of chairman and CEO in North America and Asia and the rest of the survey sample (see Table 10.5).

Table 10.4 | Board structures and director characteristics in various countries

Country	Chairman/CEO separate people	Average board size	Non-executive directors	Worker representation
Unitary board model				
Australia	Very high	8	75%	No
Belgium	High	15	78%	No
Brazil	Low	6	60%	No
Canada	66%	13	80%	No
France	Nil	13	82%	Yes
Hong Kong	Very low	8	15%	No
Italy	100%	11	73%	No
Singapore	Low			No
South Africa	50%	13	60%	
Spain	37%	12	71%	No
Sweden	High	9	85%	Yes
Switzerland	63%	5	89%	No
Taiwan	Low			No
United Kingdom	90%	12	50%	No
Two-tier board model				
France	100%	12	92%	Yes
Germany	100%	15	100%	Yes
The Netherlands	100%	7	100%	Yes

Note: Blank cells indicate that the data are not available.
Source: Adapted from an editorial in *Corporate Governance*, 1999, 7(2), p. 120.

Table 10.5 | Survey of company responses on separating the roles of chairman and CEO

	Total	Asia	Europe	North America	Latin America	Australia
Does the company separate the chairman and CEO roles?						
Yes – separate chairman and CEO roles	65%	43%	80%	42%	52%	94%
If yes, is the chairman a non-executive director?						
Yes	72%	89%	67%	61%	82%	94%

Source: Adapted from Board of Directors Global Study, Egon Zehnder International, 2000.

In pointing out differences in the way in which boards of directors are structured, we are not implying that one organisational structure is necessarily more efficient than another. Rather, we simply make the point that such differences must be considered when making international comparisons. It is widely recognised in most areas of comparative management research that a national framework of laws and regulations cannot be understood without an appreciation of its historical origin.[71]

Enhancing the effectiveness of the board of directors

Because of the importance of boards of directors in corporate governance, and as a result of increased scrutiny from shareholders – in particular, large institutional investors – the performances of individual board members and of entire boards are being evaluated more formally and with greater intensity.[72] Investors believe that directors fulfil their responsibilities more effectively when they act with prudence and integrity for the good of the entire firm and are committed to reaching independent judgements on an informed basis, rather than blindly supporting management's proposals.[73]

Given the demand for greater accountability and improved performance, many boards of directors have initiated voluntary changes. Among these changes are: (1) increases in the diversity of the backgrounds of board members (for example, a greater number of directors from public service, academic and scientific settings; a greater percentage of boards with ethnic minorities; and more boards with members from different countries); (2) the strengthening of internal management and accounting control systems; and (3) the establishment and consistent use of formal processes to evaluate the board's performance. Changes such as these should enhance the effectiveness of the board of directors as a means of control.

Boards are now becoming more involved in the strategic decision-making process, so they must work collaboratively. Research shows that boards working collaboratively make higher-quality strategic decisions, and they make them faster.[74] Boards also are becoming more involved in decisions regarding succession, as opposed to blindly supporting the incumbent's choice. In general, however, boards have relied on precedence (past decisions) for guidance in the selection process. Also, they are most likely to consider inside candidates before looking for outside candidates.[75] Increasingly, in the United States, outside directors are being required to own significant equity stakes as a prerequisite to holding a board position. A recent study also suggests that the performance of an inside director increases if she or he holds an equity position. The announcement of an inside director with less than 5 per cent ownership decreases shareholder wealth, but an insider with ownership of between 5 and 25 per cent *increases* shareholder wealth. Finally, an inside director's relationship to the CEO does not necessarily lead to entrenchment of that CEO if the inside director has a strong ownership position.[76] Interestingly, the use of a nominating committee for the selection of new board members is less likely with boards that have more inside members, particularly when those members have greater ownership in the company. Alternatively, boards with more independent outside members are more likely to use nominating committees to select new directors.[77] One of the problems associated with boards of directors within the Australian system is that it is common for able individuals to work concurrently on multiple boards of important companies. The major argument against this system is that it may become potentially rather difficult for such board members to understand in depth the activities of several major corporations. Another argument is that knowledge of multiple companies within a restricted market (such as Australia) may mean that conflicts of interests, at least in terms of 'insider strategic knowledge', can occur. To illustrate, consider Table 10.6, which lists individuals (names suppressed) that are on multiple boards in large Australian firms. The most important aspect of this listing is that it is not atypical; instead, such 'multiple-board' representation is quite the norm in Australia.

Table 10.6 | Examples of multiple board memberships in Australia

Individual A	Individual B	Individual C
Cable & Wireless Optus	BHP	Coles Myer
Comalco	CBA	Stockland
CSR	Foster's	QBE
Rio Tinto	Pacific Dunlop	BAT Aust.
Westpac	Pioneer	
	Telstra	

Given that individuals may undertake representative duties on multiple boards, and that this may represent 'conflict of interest' issues, the Strategic Focus examines some of the important characteristics of what constitutes both 'good' and 'bad' boards of directors. Furthermore, it provides examples of actions taken by good boards, thereby showing the importance of good boards of directors to effective corporate governance. The discussion is US-based, but presents arguments that are applicable in other countries using governance systems such as boards of directors.

Strategic Focus Corporate

The top and bottom of American boards of directors

In the summer of 2000, 18 people met to make a critical decision. They decided who will succeed Jack Welch of General Electric (GE), who many feel is the best CEO among active top executives. Welch has been referred to as 'the CEO of the 20th century'. The good news is that GE's board (making this critical decision) has been chosen as the best board of directors in the year 2000. The board was rated as the best through a survey conducted by *Business Week* of the largest investors on Wall Street and prominent experts in corporate governance. While GE's board received strong support as the best board, Disney's board was deemed the worst board of directors. It is not considered independent from Michael Eisner, and Disney's performance in recent years has been mediocre.

Some of the other top-rated boards are those of Johnson & Johnson, Campbell Soup, Compaq, Apria Healthcare, Intel and Texas Instruments. Alternatively, some other poorly rated boards were those of Rite Aid, First Union, Cendant, Dilliards, Starwood Hotel, Warnaco and Waste Management. The boards are rated on several criteria, including quality (for example, allowing an open debate in meetings), independence (for example, having a reasonable percentage of independent outside members), accountability (for example, directors having an ownership stake in the company) and firm performance. An example of quality is evidenced by the GE board meeting regularly with lower-level managers without Jack Welch present. Welch himself suggested this practice. At Disney, Eisner has agreed to some changes, but still has refused to make major alterations in the board's composition. Because of the firm's mediocre performance, he is coming under increasing pressure.

Effective boards are action-oriented. An example is the board's action at Baker Hughes, where the CEO was forced to resign because of several problems that culminated in poor company performance. While the CEO, Max Lukens, pledged to turn around the firm's performance, he was unable to do so in his three-year term in the job. Likewise, Coca-Cola's board encouraged its CEO of two years to resign, due to a series of disappointing problems and poorer-than-expected returns being reported. Warren Buffett argues that boards need to 'put some bite in their audit committees'. Buffett suggests that board audit committees cannot develop any meaningful knowledge of the firm's financial statements when they meet only a few hours annually. Rather, he suggests that they need to ensure that they know what the outside auditors know.

Others suggest that many board members do not understand their roles as directors. Thus, they advocate training for directors so that they are better prepared to perform their jobs as members of a board of directors. In other cases, new, independent and better-qualified directors are needed. After a number of large institutional investors banded together to file a suit against Columbia/HCA and its board for failing to exercise effective control, the company named three new board members. All are independent directors. General Motors' (GM) board was rated among the 25 worst boards in 2000. One of its members criticised the firm's unsuccessful efforts to restore its market share. He stated publicly that the firm's management had 'absolutely not delivered' on the commitments it had made. GM's US market share has continued to slide to about 27 per cent, compared with its once 50 per cent share of this market. Thus, shareholders have reason for concern. There is no magic formula; however, it is clear that the jobs of board members are more complex and challenging now than in previous years. The expectations from shareholders are high.

Sources: N. Antosh, 2000, 'Lukens is forced out at Baker Hughes', *Houston Chronicle*, 1 February, pp. 1C, 5C; B. McKay and J. S. Lublin, 2000, 'Behind Coke's massive cuts: An impatient board of directors', *Wall Street Journal Interactive*, 27 January: www.interactive.wsj.com; J. A. Byrne, 2000, 'The best and the worst boards', *Business Week*, 24 January, pp. 142–52; J. B. White and G. L. White, 1999, 'GM's Pearce pans market-share efforts', *Wall Street Journal*, 9 December, pp. A3, A8; 'Competence: Growing legal complexities an issue', 1999, *FT Director*, 28 October: www.ft.com/ftsurveys; 'Put bite into audit committees', 1999, *Fortune*, 2 August, p. 90; L. Lagnado, 1999, 'Columbia/HCA names three to board in face of continuing Medicare probe', *Wall Street Journal Interactive*, 27 March: www.interactive.wsj.com/archive.

Next, we discuss a highly visible corporate governance mechanism: executive compensation.

Executive compensation

As the Opening Case illustrates, the compensation of top-level managers, and especially of CEOs, generates a great deal of interest and strongly held opinions. The reason for this visibility and interest is depicted in the observations that while

> widespread interest in CEO pay can be traced to a natural curiosity about extremes and excesses ... it also stems from a more substantive reason. Namely, to observe CEO pay is to observe in an indirect but very tangible way the fundamental governance processes in large corporations. Who has power? What are the bases of power? How and when do owners and managers exert their relative preferences? How vigilant are boards? Who is taking advantage of whom?[78]

Executive compensation is a governance mechanism that seeks to align the interests of managers and owners through salaries, bonuses and long-term incentive compensation such as share options.[79] Share options are, at least theoretically, a mechanism used to link executives' performance to the performance of their company's shares.[80] Increasingly, long-term incentive plans are becoming a critical part of compensation packages in American firms, and to a lesser extent in Europe and Australia. The use of longer-term pay helps firms to cope with or avoid potential agency problems.[81]

Executive compensation is a governance mechanism that seeks to align the interests of managers and owners through salaries, bonuses and long-term incentive compensation such as share options.

Additionally, the stock market generally reacts positively to the introduction of a long-range incentive plan for top executives.[82] Sometimes the use of a long-term incentive plan prevents major stockholders (for example, institutional shareholders) from pressing for changes in the composition of the board of directors, because they assume that the long-term incentives will ensure that the top executives will act in the best interests of the shareholders. Alternatively, shareholders largely assume that top-executive pay and the permanence of a firm are more aligned when firms have boards that are dominated by outside members.[83] Effectively using executive compensation as a governance mechanism is particularly challenging in firms implementing international strategies. For example, preliminary evidence suggests that the interests of owners of multinational corporations are best served when there is less uniformity among the firm's foreign subsidiaries' compensation plans.[84] Developing an array of unique compensation plans requires additional monitoring and increases the firm's agency costs. Importantly, levels of pay vary by region of the world. For example, managers receive the highest compensation in the United States, as explained in the Opening Case of this chapter. Managerial pay is much lower in Asia. However, as firms acquire firms in other countries, the managerial compensation puzzle becomes more complex. For instance, when Daimler-Benz acquired Chrysler, the top executives of Chrysler made substantially more than the executives at Daimler-Benz. However, the Chrysler executives ended up reporting to the Daimler executives.[85]

A complicated governance mechanism

For several reasons, executive compensation – especially long-term incentive compensation – is complicated. First, the strategic decisions made by top-level managers are typically complex and non-routine, so direct supervision of executives is inappropriate for judging the quality of their decisions. Because of this, there is a tendency to link the compensation of top-level managers to measurable outcomes, such as the firm's financial performance. Second, an executive's decision often affects a firm's financial outcomes over an extended period, making it difficult to assess the effect of current decisions on the corporation's performance. In fact, strategic decisions are more likely to have long-term, rather than short-term, effects on a company's strategic outcomes. Third, a number of variables intervene between top-level managerial decisions and behaviour and the firm's performance. Unpredictable economic, social or legal changes (see Chapter 2) make it difficult to discern the effects of strategic decisions. Thus, although performance-based compensation may provide incentives to managers to make decisions that best serve shareholders' interests, such compensation plans alone are imperfect in their ability to monitor and control managers. Still, annual bonuses through incentive compensation represent a significant portion of many executives' total pay. For example, annual bonuses comprise an average of about 60 per cent of the CEO's total compensation in the United States, about 45 per cent in the United Kingdom, approximately 30 per cent in Canada, 19 per cent in France and only 14.5 per cent in Australia.[86] These figures underscore the differences in compensation across countries described in the Opening Case in this chapter.

Although incentive compensation plans may increase the value of a firm in line with shareholder expectations, such plans are subject to managerial manipulation. For instance, annual bonuses may provide incentives to pursue short-term objectives at the expense of the firm's long-term interests. Supporting this conclusion, some research has found that bonuses based on annual performance were negatively related to investments in R&D, which may affect the firm's long-term strategic competitiveness.[87] Although long-term performance-based incentives may reduce the temptation to under-invest in the

Charles Wang, CEO of Computer Associates, received the highest reported top executive compensation – more than $1.3 billion – in 1999.

short run, they increase executive exposure to risks associated with uncontrollable events, such as market fluctuations and industry decline.[88] The longer the focus of incentive compensation, the greater are the long-term risks borne by top-level managers.

The effectiveness of executive compensation

In recent times, many stakeholders, including shareholders, have been angered by the compensation received by some top-level managers, especially CEOs. For example, the top compensation received by an executive in 1998 was the equivalent of A$1.15 billion awarded to Michael Eisner, CEO of Disney. In 1999, the highest reported top executive compensation was more than $1.39 billion, for Charles Wang, CEO of Computer Associates. However, the firm lost a suit filed by a shareholder in which the award exceeded the amount provided by the company's long-range incentive compensation plan. The court ruled that Wang, along with the president and executive vice president of Computer Associates, had to return shares valued at about $19 million that had been awarded. The value of the shares returned was about $1.12 billion in total for the three executives. Interestingly, the 10th-highest-paid executive in 1997 was Douglas Ivestor, who was forced to resign his position as CEO of Coca-Cola in 2000.[89]

The primary component of such large compensation packages is share options and shares. In fact, the average amount of shares held by top executives and directors of firms reached 21 per cent in the 1990s, partly because of the long-term incentive plans that compensate executives in share options and shares.[90] The primary reasons for compensating executives in shares is that the practice affords incentives to keep the share price high. Hence, it should align the interests of managers and owners. However, there may be some unintended consequences: research has shown that managers who own more than 1 per cent of their firm's shares are less likely to be forced out of their jobs, even when the firm is performing poorly.[91]

Yahoo!'s CEO, Timothy Koogle, has unexercised share options worth approximately A$720 million and unvested options totalling about $368 million. Gap's CEO, Millard Drexler, has unvested share options worth approximately $1.26 billion. Dennis Eck, the CEO of Coles Myer, earned $4.14 million in 1999, of which half was in the form of 'realised' share options. While these are large figures, many of the shareholders of firms whose CEOs have received large payoffs have seen their shares gain significant value. For example, Gateway's CEO earned $294 million over a recent five-year period. However, the shareholders' share value increased an average of 48 per cent annually during this same period![92] Other CEOs who recently received substantial share options are Michael Dell of Dell Computer, with about $181.4 million; Stephen Hilbert of Conseco, with $83.6 million; and Duane Burnham of Abbott Laboratories, with $48.2 million.[93] The share option programs, while intended to tie executive compensation to firm performance, may be creating unintended benefits for executives. Some argue that executives with options have benefited by big increases in the overall value of their shares, even though their firm's shares underperformed the market.

A company's organisational structure also influences the alignment of principals' and agents' interests. As indicated in the next section, structure can be an especially valuable governance mechanism in diversified firms.

The multi-divisional structure

An organisational structure, particularly the multi-divisional (M-form) structure, serves as an internal governance mechanism by controlling managerial opportunism.[94] The corporate office that is a part of the M-form structure, along with the firm's board of directors, closely monitors the strategic decisions of managers responsible for the performance of the different business units or divisions of the corporation. Active monitoring of an individual unit's performance suggests a keen managerial interest in making decisions that will maximise shareholders' wealth. While the M-form may limit division managers' opportunistic behaviours, it may not limit corporate-level managers' self-serving actions. For example, research suggests that diversified firms using the M-form structure are likely to implement corporate-level strategies that cause them to become even more diversified.[95] In fact, one of the potential problems with divisionalisation in the M-form structure is that it is often used too aggressively.[96] Beyond some point, diversification serves managers' interests more than it serves shareholders' interests (see Chapter 6).

In addition, because of the diversification of product lines (breadth of businesses), top executives may not have adequate information to evaluate the strategic decisions and actions of divisional managers (depth). To complete their evaluations, they must focus on the resulting financial outcomes achieved by individual business units. While waiting for these financial outcomes, division managers may be able to act opportunistically.

Where internal controls are limited because of extensive diversification, the external market for corporate control and the external managerial labour market may serve as the primary controls on managers' decisions and actions, such as pursuing acquisitions to increase the size of their firm and their compensation.[97] Because external markets lack access to relevant information from inside the firm, they tend to be less efficient than internal governance mechanisms for monitoring the decisions and performance of top executives. Therefore, in diversified firms, corporate executive decisions can be controlled effectively only when other strong internal governance mechanisms (for example, the board of directors) are used in combination with the M-form structure. When used as a single governance mechanism, the M-form structure may actually facilitate over-diversification and inappropriately high compensation for corporate executives.[98]

Market for corporate control

> The **market for corporate control** is composed of individuals and firms that buy ownership positions in (or take over) potentially undervalued corporations so they can form new divisions in established diversified companies or merge two previously separate firms.

The market for corporate control is an external governance mechanism that becomes active when a firm's internal controls fail.[99] The **market for corporate control** is composed of individuals and firms that buy ownership positions in (or take over) potentially undervalued corporations so that they can form new divisions in established diversified companies or merge two previously separate firms. Because they are assumed to be the party responsible for formulating and implementing the strategy that led to poor performance, that team is usually replaced. Thus, when operating effectively, the market for corporate control ensures that managers who are ineffective or act opportunistically are disciplined. In either case, the firm performs more poorly than it should.[100] This governance mechanism should be activated by a firm's poor performance relative to the competitors in its industry. A firm's poor performance, often demonstrated by the firm's earning below-average returns, is an indicator that internal governance mechanisms have failed; that is, their use did not result in managerial decisions that maximised shareholder value. This market has been active for some time. The 1980s were known as a time of merger mania, with approximately 55 000 acquisitions valued at approximately US$1.3 trillion in the United States. However, there were many more acquisitions in the 1990s, and the value of mergers and acquisitions in that decade was more than US$10 trillion.[101]

Hostile takeovers are the major activity in the Australian market for corporate control (for example, AMP's bid for control of GIO Insurance). However, not all hostile takeovers are prompted by poorly performing targets. There may be other reasons, as the Pacific Dunlop case (in the cases section of this book) indicates. Pacific Dunlop diversified, often in a hostile manner, in order to buy innovators and gain further control of firms in Australia that fitted their immediate goals. Firms targeted for hostile takeovers may use multiple defence tactics to fend off the takeover attempt. Some of the managerial defence tactics available are discussed in the next section.

Managerial defence tactics

Historically, the increased use of the market for corporate control has enhanced the sophistication and variety of managerial defence tactics that are used to reduce the influence of this governance mechanism. The market for corporate control tends to increase risk for managers. As a result, managerial pay is often augmented indirectly through *golden parachutes* (wherein a CEO can receive up to three years' salary if his or her firm is taken over). Among other outcomes, takeover defences increase the costs of mounting a takeover, causing the incumbent management to become entrenched while reducing the chances of introducing a new management team.[102] Some defence tactics require the type of asset restructuring that results from divesting one or more divisions in the diversified firm's portfolio. Others necessitate only changes in the financial structure of the firm, such as repurchasing the firm's outstanding shares.[103] Some tactics (for example, reincorporation of the firm in another state) require shareholder approval, but the greenmail tactic (wherein money is used to repurchase shares from a corporate raider to avoid the takeover of the firm) does not. These defence tactics are controversial, and the research on their effects is inconclusive. Alternatively, most institutional investors oppose the use of defence tactics. However, some defence tactics may be appropriate. For example, shareholders of Canadian Occidental Petroleum approved a 'poison pill' designed to stop a takeover by the parent company, Occidental Petroleum. Canadian Occidental's managers claimed that the parent firm was trying to force Canadian

Occidental to give it the Canadian affiliate's lucrative oil operations in Yemen. The parent firm threatened to take over the firm with several partners and then divide and sell its assets. However, with the 'poison pill', the parent company cannot take over the firm and is likely to sell its 29 per cent stake in the Canadian firm.[104]

A potential problem with the market for corporate control is that it may not be totally efficient. A study of several of the most active corporate raiders in the 1980s showed that approximately 50 per cent of their takeover attempts targeted firms with above-average performance in their industry – corporations that were neither undervalued nor poorly managed.[105] The targeting of high-performance businesses may lead to acquisitions at premium prices and to decisions by managers of the targeted firm to establish what may prove to be costly takeover defence tactics to protect their corporate positions.

Although the market for corporate control lacks the precision possible with internal governance mechanisms, the fear of acquisition and influence by corporate raiders is an effective constraint on the managerial-growth motive.[106] The market for corporate control has been responsible for significant changes in many firms' strategies and, when used appropriately, has served the interests of the corporate owners – the shareholders. But this market and other means of corporate governance vary by region of the world and by country. Accordingly, we next address the topic of international corporate governance.

Strategic Focus Corporate

Corporate governance: Do shareholders' interests really matter?

Australia's $500 billion investment industry is under some significant levels of criticism from the Australian federal government, and from within its own ranks, for failing to get more involved with company directors over corporate governance issues. There is a growing concern – which manifested itself as a result of recent events in the AMP boardroom – that corporate directors are not being brought to account when they fail to act in the best interests of shareholders.

After spending the first few months of 2000 facing down criticism over his handling of several big issues, of which the acquisition of GIO was perhaps the most damaging, AMP chairman Ian Burgess announced his resignation on 3 April. Accompanying him are non-executive directors Kerry Roberts, Tim Crammond, Bruce Kean and Adrienne Clark.

The board has been criticised for giving its approval to former chief executive George Trumbull's takeover bid for GIO. A hostile bid, the GIO takeover turned into a rather drawn-out affair, and resulted in abnormal losses of $1.2 billion for AMP's shareholders. The board also came in for heavy criticism over its decision to pay Trumbull $13 million when he resigned from the company after this financial 'debacle' and before his employment contract had been discharged.

Of greatest note in the financial market was the criticism Burgess received from the National Australia Bank, which was effectively an effort by the bank in sounding out the AMP board's attitude to a subsequent merger. The bank raised the prospect of a $21-a-share offer, a substantial premium to AMP's share price shortly after the damage of the GIO acquisition was revealed to the market. Perhaps the most important question raised by this series of events is whether it indicates systemic failure by AMP's board – that is, a negligent attitude when it came to dealing with shareholders' interests.

Charles Macek, the chairman of County Investment Management, believed it did. He said of the situation: 'If there is a pattern of bad decisions, a general [corporate] governance issue arises. All these matters are ones over which a board has responsibility – the allocation of capital, appointment and termination of the chief executive, ensuring that there is proper due diligence when important matters arise.'

Macek believes another important corporate governance question deals with why so few 'institutional investors' are prepared to take up these issues with 'offending' companies' boards of directors. He estimated that no more than 10 per cent of 'investment managers' who run Australian equity portfolios take an active interest in corporate governance in situations where shareholder value is destroyed by management actions or omissions. He says: 'This is a very competitive industry with a lot of excess capacity. There is intensive scrutiny of investment returns. There is a lot of corporate activity occurring and changes to government regulation. The first priority of people in the industry is to meet the demands of their clients, keep up with a changing environment, and cope with very prescriptive regulation. They don't have time for corporate governance.'

Joe Hockey, the Minister for Financial Services and Regulation, expressed similar concerns more bluntly when he spoke at a meeting of the Securities Institute in Sydney on 23 March 2000. He essentially accused the 'investment industry' of being lazy, of 'running away from the tough task of holding directors accountable for their decisions' and of conducting their relationships with company directors 'with a wink and a nod'. Hockey stated: 'The responsibility of fund managers is to ensure we have liquid markets and to ensure their members get a good return. But they also have a responsibility to be good corporate citizens and good shareholders. It is not good enough for fund managers to be lazy at annual general meetings. Fund managers and trustees have to exercise their votes on behalf of their members in the best interests of the company.'

Lynn Ralph, CEO of the Investment and Financial Services Association (IFSA), the investment industry's peak body, refuted Hockey's comments as 'too simplistic'. Ralph stated: 'The annual general meeting is a forum for special-interest groups; it has long since ceased to be the primary means of interaction between a company and its shareholders. To think you can deal with substantial issues at an AGM is simplistic in the extreme.'

Ralph further suggested that when the corporate governance movement emerged in Australia at the start of the 1990s, there were a number of very public disputes between boards and investors, and that institutions have become more sophisticated in the way they deal with companies. She says that because there are fewer headlines, there is a perception that not as much attention is being given to the area. 'Having your dispute with a company turned into a brawl played out in the newspapers is not productive.'

Sandy Easterbrook, a director of the investment manager Independent Shareholder Services, which prepares corporate governance reports for institutional investors, stated that Ralph is wrong, and that fund managers are indeed paying less attention to corporate governance than is 'prudent'. Easterbrook believes IFSA is partly responsible for this situation in that the current IFSA executive has given corporate governance a low priority in its day-to-day operations.

Macek agrees that IFSA cannot effectively deal directly with a company's board of directors: 'It does not invest in these companies and therefore it has no place to be making recommendations to boards. But it can play another role; it can heighten awareness of the issue among its members and urge them to get more involved. It is not doing enough of that work.' He further believes Hockey's recent comment raised the stakes in the governance debate. 'The industry needs to improve its performance, or it will have changes forced upon it by the

Government.' Hockey says there are several proposals (that is, recommendations of parliamentary inquiries and regulatory reviews) that aim to increase investment management firms' involvement in corporate governance, one of which includes the introduction of compulsory voting by institutions at AGMs. He says: 'We are not inclined to follow this route, but we would like to see a greater involvement by all shareholders in annual general meetings. In Australia, fund managers and trustees hold just over 50 per cent of the shareholdings in publicly listed companies, yet only 30 per cent of the votes exercisable at annual meetings are, in fact, exercised. This figure is lower than that experienced in both the United States and the United Kingdom.' Ralph says the IFSA is undertaking a survey of its members to see just who does what. 'We want to put some facts out there so we can have an informed discussion.'

AMP's new caretaker chairman, Stan Wallis, unsurprisingly, does not concede that there was any systemic failure by the AMP board in protecting shareholder funds. He says: 'When you examine AMP's results for last year, you find there have been very significant improvements in assets, new business and funds under management. That goes across the board – in all our business areas and in all countries. Even allowing for the GIO [acquisition], there has been a very substantial increase in value.' (Wallis has been a director of AMP for 10 years.)

In response to the suggestion that Burgess acted negligently in his handling of the approach from National Australia Bank, Wallis says: 'That is rubbish. There was complete disclosure.' Indeed, Wallace does not expect the recent departures from the board to cause any disruption. 'We have got eight members very focused on what has to be done. I am encouraged. We have cleared the issues that made it hard for the board to function.'

Wallis also believes that most of the contact between investors and companies should occur at the management, rather than board, level. He says: 'It does not add a great deal to have the chairman involved in that process, although you get out there when there is a big issue. It is wrong to think that companies ignore investors' comments; you can't afford to do that.'

Sources: J. Kavanagh, 2000, 'Governance: Funds under fire for letting boards get out of line', *Business Review Weekly*, 22(14); S. Wallis, 2000, 'Corporate governance: Conformance or performance', *Journal of Banking and Financial Services*, 114(4), p. 14; M. J. Whincop, 'The institutional politics of corporate law in Australia: From Gambotto to DB Management', *Australian Journal of Corporate Law*, 11(3), pp. 247–59; S. Clyne, 'Modern corporate governance', *Australian Journal of Corporate Law*, 11(3), pp. 276–97.

International corporate governance

The discussion so far has been focused on the generic aspects of the Australian, US and UK systems for corporate governance. However, we now need to focus more closely upon specific national governance procedures. Accordingly, we briefly discuss the specific governance of Australian, German and Japanese corporations (and corporations in other countries) to illustrate that the nature of corporate governance throughout the world is being affected by the realities of the global economy and its competitive challenges.[107]

Corporate governance in Australia

We have already discussed the Australian system in general, with mention of institutional shareholders and CEO compensation as centrepieces. These are part of a governance system based upon the achievement of four main tenets:
- There must be protection for all shareholders (including those with a minority holding).

- Management must be held accountable to shareholders regularly.
- There must be transparency and full disclosure by each Australian Stock Exchange-listed company.
- Above all, there must be an active, and independent, board that oversees a corporation's management.[108]

In order to achieve these 'corporate governance goals', a number of Australian-specific laws and institutions have emerged in the period post-1970: legislative acts (in particular the *Trade Practices Act 1974* and the *Prices Surveillance Act 1983*); the Australian Competition and Consumer Commission (ACCC); the Australian Securities and Investments Commission (ASIC); the Australian Stock Exchange (ASX) and its company listing rules; shareholder activists; and influential 'financial media' attention. Each of these 'institutions' act together, although not necessarily directly, to apply the appropriate pressures to corporations (and their boards) to achieve important societal goals and the maximisation of returns on shareholder funding.

Legislation

Trade Practices Act. The objective of the *Trade Practices Act 1974* (TPA), as set out in the legislation, is to enhance the welfare of Australians through the promotion of competition and fair trading and provision for consumer protection. The main parts of the Act are essentially concerned with: curtailing anti-competitive practices; penalising unconscionable conduct; the enforcement of industry codes; policing country of origin claims; determining what constitutes 'product liability'; and penalising 'price exploitation' with regard to the implementation of the new GST system.[109]

Prices Surveillance Act. Similarly, under the *Prices Surveillance Act 1983* (PSA), the government has sought to control three pricing functions: (1) to vet the proposed price rises of any business organisation placed under prices surveillance; (2) to hold inquiries into pricing practices and related matters, and to report the findings to the responsible Commonwealth Minister; and (3) to monitor prices, costs and profits of an industry or business and to report the results to the relevant Minister.

Both the TPA and PSA, then, impose an important legal constraint upon the competitive actions of a corporate entity within Australia. Corporations, and indeed individual managers, are liable to considerable fines and gaol terms for actions that contravene these federal laws.

The Australian Competition and Consumer Commission

The Australian Competition and Consumer Commission (ACCC) was formed on 6 November 1995 by the merger of the Trade Practices Commission and the Prices Surveillance Authority. Its formation was an important step in the implementation of the national competition policy reform program agreed by the Council of Australian Governments.

An independent statutory authority, the ACCC administers the *Trade Practices Act 1974* and the *Prices Surveillance Act 1983* and has additional responsibilities under other legislation. Under the national competition policy reform program, the TPA has been amended so that, with state/territory application legislation, its prohibitions of anti-competitive conduct apply to virtually all businesses in Australia.

In broad terms, the Act covers anti-competitive and unfair market practices, mergers or acquisitions of companies, product safety/liability, and third party access to facilities of national significance. The ACCC is the only national agency dealing generally with competition matters and the only agency with responsibility for enforcement of the TPA and the associated state/territory application legislation.

The Commission's consumer protection work complements that of state and territory consumer affairs agencies, which administer the mirror legislation of their jurisdictions, and the Consumer Affairs Division of Treasury. The head of the ACCC, Professor Allan Fels, has been particularly active in scrutinising corporate behaviour. For example, by mid-2001 alone, under Fels' leadership, the ACCC had instigated investigations into (and subsequently had fined) five major Australian companies for anti-competitive actions. Most recently, a case against three animal vitamin suppliers (Roche Vitamins Australia Pty Ltd, BASF Australia Limited and Aventis Animal Nutrition) resulted in an indictment against the companies for price fixing. In total, the companies were fined some $26 million for their anti-competitive behaviour.[110]

The Australian Securities and Investments Commission

The Australian Securities and Investments Commission (ASIC) is another independent Commonwealth government body established by the *Australian Securities and Investments Commission Act 1989*. It was established in 1991 as the Australian Securities Commission, to administer the Corporations Law. It replaced the National Companies and Securities Commission (NCSC) and the Corporate Affairs offices of the states and territories. In July 1998 it received new consumer protection responsibilities and its current name. ASIC is the single national regulator of Australia's 1.2 million companies.

ASIC performs the following generic functions with regards to corporate governance: it protects investors, superannuants, depositors and insurance policy holders from financial harm arising from poor management practices; it regulates and enforces laws that promote honesty and fairness in financial markets, products and services and in Australian companies; it serves to underpin the strength, growth and international reputation of Australia's financial markets; and it maintains a public database on Australia's 1.2 million companies to provide certainty in commercial dealings.[111]

Australian Stock Exchange listing rules

The Australian Stock Exchange (ASX) imposes a series of important regulatory guidelines for all listed companies in Australia. In particular, in order for a company to be publicly listed, it must conform to a series of specific reporting procedures it would not be required to follow otherwise. For example, an ASX listed company must:
- institute a board of directors;
- undertake annual general meetings with shareholders;
- produce an annual report for all shareholders, as well as for the ASX; and
- undertake continuous and periodic disclosure of business activities.

The full listing of ASX rules and requirements can be found at www.asx.com.au/ListingRules/LRChps.shtm, and will provide an indication of the governance implications for all listed companies. In addition, and a result of the ASX's own listing upon the stock exchange, the ASX Supervisory Review company was formed. This ASX subsidiary body was established in order to dispel any perceived 'conflicts of interest' that may exist between the ASX (a regulatory body itself) and its own listing upon the ASX.

Shareholder activists

Shareholder activism refers to the extent to which individual shareholders (albeit as a group) are willing (or even perhaps able) to influence a corporation's board of directors. In Australia, the main organisation of such shareholders is the Australian Shareholders Association (ASA). In 2000, for example, the ASA established an annual general meeting monitoring service for its members, employing analysts to review corporate resolutions

and make recommendations on how to vote on same. Shareholder activists have become more visible during this year's round of annual general meetings. The focus has increased to include a greater number of directors and a wider range of issues. For example, the ASA now has policies that include the following areas of shareholder concern:
- poor performance;
- executive remuneration;
- accounting policies;
- conflict of interest;
- disclosure; and
- share ownership limits.[112]

The financial media

In the small Australian marketplace, the media are a powerful element of the governance system. Print news media, such as the *Australian Financial Review* and *Business Review Weekly*, along with television's *Business Sunday*, freely report Australian corporate activities. This attention provides an overarching control over corporate behaviour through mass exposure to newsworthy corporate actions and issues.

The preceding discussion serves to illustrate the complex 'web' of governance laws and institutions that are in place within the Australian market for corporate governance. Interestingly, issues such as CEO compensation levels, poor profit performance, poor targeting of acquisitions and 'conflicts of interest' remain commonplace in the Australian context. It has been argued that such issues remain the case because the 'web' of governance mechanisms is somewhat ineffective in their ability to deliver the four tenets discussed earlier. Alternately, it has been argued that it is due directly to the governance mechanisms that are in place that such issues remain at the forefront of corporate news, and therefore debate and control.[113, 114]

Corporate governance in Germany

In many private German firms, the owner and manager may still be the same individual. In these instances, there is no agency problem. Even in publicly traded corporations, there is often a dominant shareholder. Thus, the concentration of ownership is an important means of corporate governance in Germany, as it is in the United States.[115]

Historically, banks have been at the centre of the German corporate governance structure, as is also the case in many other European countries, such as Italy and France. As lenders, banks become major shareholders when companies they had financed earlier seek funding on the stock market or default on loans. Although the stakes are usually under 10 per cent, there is no legal limit on how much of a firm's shares banks can hold (except that a single ownership position cannot exceed 15 per cent of the bank's capital). Through their own shareholdings and by casting proxy votes for individual shareholders who retain their shares with the banks, three banks in particular – Deutsche, Dresdner and Commerzbank – exercise significant power. Although shareholders can tell the banks how to vote their ownership position, they generally elect not to do so. A combination of their own holdings and their proxies results in majority positions for these three banks in many German companies. Those banks, along with others, monitor and control managers, both as lenders and as shareholders, by electing representatives to supervisory boards.

German firms with more than 2 000 employees are required to have a two-tiered board structure. Through this structure, the supervision of management is separated from other duties normally assigned to a board of directors, especially the nomination of new board members. Thus, Germany's two-tiered system places the responsibility for monitoring and controlling managerial (or supervisory) decisions and actions in the

Banks are central to governance in many parts of the world because of the extent of their holdings in the economy. In Australia and Germany, banks are certainly the major players. In Australia, the US bank Chase Manhattan is one of the biggest players.

hands of a separate group.[116] While all the functions of direction and management are the responsibility of the management board – the *Vorstand* – appointment to the *Vorstand* is the responsibility of the supervisory tier – the *Aufsichtsrat*. Employees, union members and shareholders appoint members to the *Aufsichtsrat*.

Because of the power of banks in Germany's corporate governance structure, private shareholders rarely have major ownership positions in German firms. Large institutional investors, such as superannuation funds and insurance companies, are also relatively insignificant owners of corporate shares. Thus, at least historically, German executives generally have not been dedicated to the maximisation of shareholder value that is occurring in many countries. But corporate governance in Germany is changing, at least partially because of the increasing globalisation of business. Many German firms are beginning to gravitate towards the US system. For example, SGL Carbon AG lost in excess of US$71 million in the early 1990s. As a result, the corporation was restructured in an attempt to turn it around. In particular, the firm's governance structure was changed. Transparent accounting practices were adopted, and the goal of enhancing shareholder value was established. The firm's shares became listed on the US stock exchange, and English was adopted as the official language. Thereafter, the firm's performance improved dramatically, with many attributing the improvement to its changed governance structure.[117]

Corporate governance in Japan

Attitudes towards corporate governance in Japan are affected by the concepts of obligation, family and consensus. In Japan, an obligation 'may be to return a service for one rendered or it may derive from a more general relationship, for example, to one's family or old alumni, or one's company (or Ministry), or the country. This sense of particular obligation is common elsewhere but it feels stronger in Japan.'[118] As part of a company family, individuals are members of a unit that envelops their lives; families command the attention and allegiance of parties throughout corporations. Moreover, a *keiretsu* (a group of firms tied together by cross-shareholdings) is more than an economic concept; it, too, is a family. Consensus, an important influence in Japanese corporate governance, calls for the expenditure of significant amounts of energy to win the hearts and minds of people whenever possible, as opposed to issuing edicts from top executives. Consensus is highly valued, even when it results in a slow and cumbersome decision-making process.

As in Germany, banks in Japan play an important role in financing and monitoring large public firms. The bank owning the largest amount of the shares and the largest amount of debt – the main bank – has the closest relationship with the company's top executives. The main bank provides financial advice to the firm and also closely monitors managers. Thus, Japan has a bank-based financial and corporate governance structure, whereas the United States has a market-based financial and governance structure.

Aside from lending money, a Japanese bank can hold up to 5 per cent of a firm's total shares; a group of related financial institutions can hold up to 40 per cent. In many cases, main-bank relationships are part of a horizontal *keiretsu*. A *keiretsu* firm usually owns less than 2 per cent of any other member firm; however, each company typically has a stake of that size in every firm in the *keiretsu*. As a result, other members of the *keiretsu* own somewhere between 30 and 90 per cent of a firm. Thus, a *keiretsu* is a system of relationship investments.

As is the case in Germany, in Japan the structure of corporate governance is changing. For example, because of their continuing development as economic organisations, the role of banks in the monitoring and control of managerial behaviour and firm outcomes is less significant than in the past.[119] The Asian economic crisis in the latter part of the 1990s made the governance problems in Japanese corporations transparent. The problems were readily evidenced in the large and once-powerful Mitsubishi *keiretsu*. Many of its core members lost substantial amounts of money in the late 1990s.[120] Toyota's president was ousted by its board of directors because he demanded changes in its governance system and argued against rescuing other firms in the Toyota *keiretsu*.[121]

Still another change in Japan's governance system has occurred. In past years, the market for corporate control was nonexistent. However, the first hostile bid for another firm was advanced by Cable & Wireless plc of Great Britain in 1999 for International Digital Communications, Inc. In 2000, another hostile bid was made by a Japanese investment firm to take over Shoei Co., a large real-estate and electric parts firm. A 14 per cent premium was offered, but Shoei's board quickly rejected it. The CEO of the investment company criticised the passivity of Japanese shareholders.[122]

Global corporate governance

The 21st-century competitive landscape (see Chapters 1 and 5) and the global economy are fostering the creation of a relatively uniform governance structure that will be used by firms throughout the world.[123] As markets become more global and customer demands more similar, shareholders are becoming the focus of managers' efforts in an increasing number of companies. Investors are becoming more and more active throughout the world. Changes in governance are evident in many countries and are moving the governance models closer to that of the United States. For example, in France, anger has been growing over the lack of information on top executives' compensation. A recent report recommended that the positions of CEO and chairman of the board be held by different individuals; it also recommended reducing the tenure of board members and disclosing their pay.[124] In South Korea, changes went much further: principles of corporate governance were adopted that 'provide proper incentives for the board and management to pursue objectives that are in the interests of the company and the shareholders and facilitate effective monitoring, thereby encouraging firms to use resources more efficiently'.[125]

Even in transitional economies, such as those of China and Russia, changes in corporate governance are occurring. However, changes are implemented much more slowly in these economies. Chinese firms have found it helpful to use share-based compensation plans, thereby providing an incentive for foreign companies to invest in

China.[126] Because Russia has reduced controls on the economy and on business activity much more quickly than China has, the country needs more effective governance systems to control its managerial activities.[127]

Governance mechanisms and ethical behaviour

The governance mechanisms described in this chapter are designed to ensure that the agents of the firm's owners – the corporation's top executives – make strategic decisions that best serve the interests of the entire group of stakeholders, as described in Chapter 1. In the United States, shareholders are recognised as a company's most significant stakeholder. Thus, the focus of governance mechanisms is on the control of managerial decisions to ensure that shareholders' interests will be served, but product market stakeholders (for example, customers, suppliers and host communities) and organisational stakeholders (for example, managerial and non-managerial employees) are important as well.[128] Therefore, at least the minimal interests or needs of all stakeholders must be satisfied through the firm's actions. Otherwise, dissatisfied stakeholders will decide to withdraw their support from one firm and provide it to another. (For example, customers will purchase products from a supplier offering an acceptable substitute.)

John Smale, an outside member of the board of directors at General Motors, believes that all large capitalist enterprises must be concerned with goals, in addition to serving shareholders. In Smale's opinion, 'A corporation is a human, living enterprise. It's not just a bunch of assets. The obligation of management is to perpetuate the corporation, and that precedes their obligation to shareholders.'[129] The argument, then, is that the firm's strategic competitiveness is enhanced when its governance mechanisms are designed and implemented in ways that take into consideration the interests of all stakeholders. Although the idea is subject to debate, some believe that ethically responsible companies design and use governance mechanisms that serve all stakeholders' interests. There is, however, a more critical relationship between ethical behaviour and corporate governance mechanisms.

Evidence demonstrates that all companies are vulnerable to a display of unethical behaviours by their employees, including, of course, top executives. For example, HFS Inc., in the United States, acquired CUC International. Shortly after completing the transaction and attempting to merge the two businesses to create the newly named Cendant Corporation, significant accounting irregularities appeared in the figures provided by the former CUC executives. Investigations suggested fraud. When the accounting irregularities were announced, Cendant's share price fell from over US$47 per share to slightly more than US$12 per share. The company had to restate its financial results, reducing profits by hundreds of millions of dollars. A class-action lawsuit was filed by shareholders, claiming negligence by Cendant's executives and board of directors. In late 1999, Cendant settled the suit for a record US$2.83 billion. This is the primary reason that Cendant's board is rated as one of the worst, as reported earlier in the chapter.[130]

The decisions and actions of a corporation's board of directors can be an effective deterrent to unethical behaviours. In fact, some believe that the most effective boards participate actively in setting boundaries for business ethics and values.[131] Once formulated, the board's expectations related to ethical decisions and actions by all of the firm's stakeholders must be communicated clearly to the top executives. Moreover, these executives must understand that the board will hold them fully accountable for the development and support of an organisational culture that results in ethical decisions and behaviours. As explained in Chapter 12, CEOs can be positive role models for ethical behaviour.

It is only when the proper corporate governance is exercised that strategies are formulated and implemented to achieve strategic competitiveness and above-average returns. As the discussion in this chapter suggests, corporate governance mechanisms are a vital, yet imperfect, part of firms' efforts to develop and implement successful strategies.

Summary

- Corporate governance is a relationship among stakeholders that is used to determine a firm's direction and control its performance. How firms monitor and control top-level managers' decisions and actions, as called for by governance mechanisms, affects the implementation of strategies. Effective governance that aligns the interests of managers with those of shareholders can produce a competitive advantage for the firm.
- In the modern corporation, there are four internal governance mechanisms – ownership concentration, the board of directors, executive compensation and the multi-divisional structure – and one external governance mechanism, the market for corporate control.
- Ownership is separated from control in the modern corporation. Owners (principals) hire managers (agents) to make decisions that maximise the value of the firm. As risk specialists, owners diversify their risk by investing in an array of corporations. As decision-making specialists, top executives are expected by owners to make decisions that will result in earning above-average returns. Thus, modern corporations are characterised by an agency relationship that is created when one party (the firm's owners) hires and pays another party (top executives) to use its decision-making skills.
- Separation of ownership and control creates an agency problem when an agent pursues goals that are in conflict with the principals' goals. Principals establish and use governance mechanisms to control this problem.
- Ownership concentration is based on the number of large-block shareholders and the percentage of shares they own. With significant ownership percentages, such as those held by large mutual funds and superannuation funds, institutional investors often are able to influence top executives' strategic decisions and actions. Thus, unlike diffuse ownership, which tends to result in relatively weak monitoring and control of managerial decisions, concentrated ownership produces more active and effective monitoring of top executives. An increasingly powerful force in corporate America, institutional owners are actively using their positions of concentrated ownership in individual companies to force managers and boards of directors to make decisions that maximise a firm's value. These owners (for example, ASA) have caused executives in prominent companies to lose their jobs because of their failure to serve shareholders' interests effectively.
- In the United States and the United Kingdom, a firm's board of directors, composed of insiders, related outsiders and outsiders, is a governance mechanism that shareholders expect to represent their collective interests. The percentage of outside directors on many boards now exceeds the percentage of inside directors. The individuals from outside are expected to be more independent of a firm's top executives than are those selected from inside the firm.
- Executive compensation is a highly visible and often criticised governance mechanism. Salary, bonuses and long-term incentives are used to strengthen the alignment between managers' and shareholders' interests. A firm's board of directors has the responsibility of determining the degree to which executive compensation controls managerial behaviour.
- The multi-divisional (M-form) structure is intended to reduce managerial opportunism and to align principals' and agents' interests. The M-form structure makes it possible for the corporate office to monitor and control managerial decisions in the multiple divisions in diversified firms. However, at the corporate level, the M-form may actually stimulate managerial opportunism, resulting in top executives over-diversifying the firm.
- In general, evidence suggests that shareholders and boards of directors have become more vigilant in their control of managerial decisions. Nonetheless, these mechanisms are insufficient to govern managerial

behaviour in many large companies. Therefore, the market for corporate control is an important governance mechanism. Although it, too, is imperfect, the market for corporate control has been effective in causing corporations to combat inefficient diversification and to implement more effective strategic decisions.

- Corporate governance structures used in Germany and Japan differ from each other and from those used in Australia and the United States. Historically, the US and Australian governance structures have focused on maximising shareholder value. In Germany, employees, as a stakeholder group, have a more prominent role in governance. By contrast, until recently, Japanese shareholders played virtually no role in the monitoring and control of top-level managers. However, all of these systems are becoming increasingly similar, as are many governance systems in both developed countries, such as France and Italy, and transitional economies, such as Russia and China.

- Effective governance mechanisms ensure that the interests of all stakeholders are served. Thus, long-term strategic success results when firms are governed in ways that permit at least minimal satisfaction of capital market stakeholders (for example, shareholders), product market stakeholders (for example, customers and suppliers), and organisational stakeholders (managerial and non-managerial employees). Moreover, effective governance produces ethical behaviour in the formulation and implementation of strategies.

Review questions

1. What is corporate governance? What factors account for the considerable amount of attention corporate governance receives from several parties, including shareholder activists, business press writers and academic scholars? Why is governance necessary to control managerial decisions?
2. What does it mean to say that ownership is separated from control in the modern corporation? Why does this separation exist?
3. What is an agency relationship? What is managerial opportunism? What assumptions do owners of modern corporations make about managers as agents?
4. How are each of the four internal governance mechanisms – ownership concentration, boards of directors, executive compensation and the multi-divisional (M-form) structure – used to align the interests of managerial agents with those of the firm's owners?
5. What trends exist regarding executive compensation? What is the effect of the increased use of long-term incentives on executives' strategic decisions?
6. What is the market for corporate control? What conditions generally cause this external governance mechanism to become active? How does the mechanism constrain top executives' decisions and actions?
7. What is the nature of corporate governance in Australia, Germany and Japan?
8. How can corporate governance foster ethical strategic decisions and behaviours on the part of managerial agents?

Application discussion questions

1. The roles and responsibilities of top executives and members of a corporation's board of directors are different. Traditionally, executives have been responsible for determining the firm's strategic direction and implementing strategies to achieve it, whereas the board of directors has been responsible for monitoring and controlling managerial decisions and actions. Some argue that boards should become more involved with the formulation of a firm's strategies. How would the board's increased involvement in the selection of strategies affect a firm's strategic competitiveness? What evidence can you offer to support your position?
2. Do you believe that large Australian firms have been over-governed by some corporate governance mechanisms and under-governed by others? Provide an example of each.
3. How can corporate governance mechanisms create conditions that allow top executives to develop a competitive advantage and focus on long-term performance? Use the Internet to search the business press and give an example of a firm in which this occurred.
4. Some believe that the market for corporate control is not an effective governance mechanism. What factors might account for the ineffectiveness of this method of monitoring and controlling managerial decisions?
5. Assume that you overheard the following comment: 'As a top executive, the only agency relationship I am concerned about is the one between myself and the firm's owners. I think that it would be a waste of my

time and energy to worry about any other agency relationships.' What are these other agency relationships? How would you respond to this person? Do you accept or reject this view? Be prepared to support your position.

Ethics questions

1. As explained in this chapter, using corporate governance mechanisms should establish order between parties whose interests may be in conflict. Do owners of a firm have any ethical responsibilities to managers in a firm that uses governance mechanisms to establish order? If so, what are those responsibilities?
2. Is it ethical for a firm's owner to assume that agents (managers hired to make decisions in the owner's best interests) are averse to risk? Why or why not?
3. What are the responsibilities of the board of directors to stakeholders other than shareholders?
4. What ethical issues surround executive compensation? How can we determine whether top executives are paid too much?
5. Is it ethical for firms involved in the market for corporate control to target companies performing at levels exceeding the industry average? Why or why not?
6. What ethical issues, if any, do top executives face when asking their firm to provide them with either a golden parachute or a golden goodbye?
7. How can governance mechanisms be designed to ensure against managerial opportunism, ineffectiveness and unethical behaviours?

Internet exercise

The use of the Internet for buying and selling shares has opened up markets to an unprecedented number of people. With the click of a mouse, one can buy shares of the hottest stocks. Not always so, though, warns ACCC chairman Allan Fels. Orders are not necessarily processed at the moment they are sent, and by the time the stock is purchased, the price may have risen ten-fold. Read more about investing through the Internet and the ACCC's efforts to combat growing Internet-based investment fraud at www.accc.gov.au.

e-project: Go to the websites of two on-line trading venues: the more traditional Merrill Lynch at www.merrill-lynch.com and the new, highly successful E*Trade at www.etrade.com. How effectively do these companies communicate the risks of a volatile market to their customers? Looking at the recommendations outlined by the ACCC, how does each company rate?

Notes

1. R. D. Ward, 1997, *21st Century Corporate Board* (New York: John Wiley & Sons).
2. J. E. Core, R. W. Holthausen and D. F. Larcker, 1999, 'Corporate governance, chief executive officer compensation, and firm performance', *Journal of Financial Economics*, 51, pp. 371–406.
3. R. K. Mitchell, B. R. Agle and D. J. Wood, 1997, 'Toward a theory of stakeholder identification and salience: Defining the principle of who and what really counts', *Academy of Management Review*, 22, pp. 853–86.
4. J. H. Davis, F. D. Schoorman and L. Donaldson, 1997, 'Toward a stewardship theory of management', *Academy of Management Review*, 22, pp. 20–47.
5. M. M. Blair, 1999, 'For whom should corporations be run? An economic rationale for stakeholder management', *Long Range Planning*, 31, pp. 195–200; O. E. Williamson, 1996, 'Economic organization: The case for candor', *Academy of Management Review*, 21, pp. 48–57.
6. J. Magretta, 1998, 'Governing the family-owned enterprise: An interview with Finland's Krister Ahlstrom', *Harvard Business Review*, 76(1), pp. 112–23.
7. E. F. Fama and M. C. Jensen, 1983, 'Separation of ownership and control', *Journal of Law and Economics*, 26, pp. 301–25.
8. Ward, *21st Century Corporate Board*, pp. 3–144.
9. C. Arnold and K. Breen, 1997, 'Investor activism goes worldwide', *Corporate Board*, 18(2), pp. 7–12.
10. M. Kroll, P. Wright, L. Toombs and H. Leavell, 1997, 'Form of control: A critical determinant of acquisition performance and CEO rewards', *Strategic Management Journal*, 18, pp. 85–96; J. K. Seward and J. P. Walsh, 1996, 'The governance and control of voluntary corporate spinoffs', *Strategic Management Journal*, 17, pp. 25–39.
11. J. D. Westphal and E. J. Zajac, 1997, 'Defections from the inner circle: Social exchange, reciprocity and diffusion of board independence in U.S. corporations', *Administrative Science Quarterly*, 42, pp. 161–212; Ward, *21st Century Corporate Board*.
12. J. Charkham, 1994, *Keeping Good Company: A Study of Corporate Governance in Five Countries* (New York: Oxford University Press), p. 1.
13. A. Cadbury, 1999, 'The future of governance: The rules of the game', *Journal of General Management*, 24, pp. 1–14.
14. G. L. O'Neill, 1999, 'Executive remuneration in Australia: An overview of trends and issues', a White Paper (Melbourne: Hay Group/AHRI).
15. C. K. Prahalad and J. P. Oosterveld, 1999, 'Transforming internal governance: The challenge for multinationals', *Sloan Management Review*, 40(3), pp. 31–9.
16. M. A. Hitt, R. A. Harrison and R. D. Ireland, 2001, *Creating Value through Mergers and Acquisitions: A Complete Guide to Successful M&As* (New York: Oxford University Press); M. A. Hitt, R. E. Hoskisson, R. A. Johnson and D. D. Moesel, 1996, 'The market for corporate control and firm innovation', *Academy of Management Journal*, 39, pp. 1084–119; J. P. Walsh and R. Kosnik, 1993, 'Corporate raiders and their disciplinary role in the market for corporate control', *Academy of Management Journal*, 36, pp. 671–700.
17. Davis, Schoorman and Donaldson, 'Toward a stewardship theory of management'.
18. C. Sundaramurthy, J. M. Mahoney and J. T. Mahoney, 1997, 'Board structure, antitakeover provisions, and stockholder wealth', *Strategic Management Journal*, 18, pp. 231–46; K. J. Rediker and A. Seth, 1995, 'Boards of directors and substitution effects of alternative governance mechanisms', *Strategic Management Journal*, 16, pp. 85–99.
19. R. E. Hoskisson, M. A. Hitt, R. A. Johnson and W. Grossman, 2000, 'Conflicting voices: The effects of ownership heterogeneity and internal governance on corporate strategy', Paper presented at the Strategic Management Society, Vancouver, Canada.
20. G. E. Davis and T. A. Thompson, 1994, 'A social movement perspective on corporate control', *Administrative Science Quarterly*, 39, pp. 141–73.
21. M. A. Eisenberg, 1989, 'The structure of corporation law', *Columbia Law Review*, 89(7), p. 1461, as cited in R. A. G. Monks and N. Minow, 1995,

Corporate Governance (Cambridge, MA: Blackwell Business), p. 7.

22. R. M. Wiseman and L. R. Gomez-Mejia, 1999, 'A behavioral agency model of managerial risk taking', *Academy of Management Review*, 23, pp. 133–53.
23. E. E. Fama, 1980, 'Agency problems and the theory of the firm', *Journal of Political Economy*, 88, pp. 288–307.
24. A. Ferguson, 2000, 'Mayne's new man has got his orders', *Business Review Weekly*, 14 July: www.brw.com.au.
25. M. Jensen and W. Meckling, 1976, 'Theory of the firm: Managerial behavior, agency costs, and ownership structure', *Journal of Financial Economics*, 11, pp. 305–60.
26. H. C. Tosi, J. Katz and L. R. Gomez-Mejia, 1997, 'Disaggregating the agency contract: The effects of monitoring, incentive alignment, and term in office on agent decision making', *Academy of Management Journal*, 40, pp. 584–602; P. C. Godfrey and C. W. L. Hill, 1995, 'The problem of unobservables in strategic management research', *Strategic Management Journal*, 16, pp. 519–33.
27. P. Wright and S. P. Ferris, 1997, 'Agency conflict and corporate strategy: The effect of divestment on corporate strategy', *Strategic Management Journal*, 18, pp. 77–83.
28. T. M. Welbourne and L. R. Gomez-Mejia, 1995, 'Gainsharing: A critical review and a future research agenda', *Journal of Management*, 21, p. 577.
29. P. Wright, S. P. Ferris, A. Sarin and V. Awasthi, 1996, 'Impact of corporate insider, blockholder, and institutional equity ownership on firm risk taking', *Academy of Management Journal*, 39, pp. 441–63.
30. P. B. Frstenberg and B. G. Malkiel, 1994, 'The twenty-first century boardroom: Who will be in charge?', *Sloan Management Review*, Fall, pp. 27–35, as cited in C. M. Daily, 1996, 'Governance patterns in bankruptcy reorganizations', *Strategic Management Journal*, 17, pp. 355–75.
31. O. E. Williamson, 1996, *The Mechanisms of Governance* (New York: Oxford University Press), p. 6; O. E. Williamson, 1993, 'Opportunism and its critics', *Managerial and Decision Economics*, 14, pp. 97–107.
32. S. Ghoshal and P. Moran, 1996, 'Bad for practice: A critique of the transaction cost theory', *Academy of Management Review*, 21, pp. 13–47.
33. Godfrey and Hill, 'The problem of unobservables in strategic management research'.
34. Y. Amihud and B. Lev, 1981, 'Risk reduction as a managerial motive for conglomerate mergers', *Bell Journal of Economics*, 12, pp. 605–17.
35. R. E. Hoskisson and T. A. Turk, 1990, 'Corporate restructuring: Governance and control limits of the internal market', *Academy of Management Review*, 15, pp. 459–77.
36. S. Finkelstein and D. C. Hambrick, 1989, 'Chief executive compensation: A study of the intersection of markets and political processes', *Strategic Management Journal*, 16, pp. 221, 239; H. C. Tosi and L. R. Gomez-Mejia, 1989, 'The decoupling of CEO pay and performance: An agency theory perspective', *Administrative Science Quarterly*, 34, pp. 169–89.
37. Hoskisson and Turk, 1990, 'Corporate restructuring'.
38. M. S. Jensen, 1986, 'Agency costs of free cash flow, corporate finance, and takeovers', *American Economic Review*, 76, pp. 323–9.
39. C. W. L. Hill and S. A. Snell, 1988, 'External control, corporate strategy, and firm performance in research intensive industries', *Strategic Management Journal*, 9, pp. 577–90.
40. A. Sharma, 1997, 'Professional as agent: Knowledge asymmetry in agency exchange', *Academy of Management Review*, 22, pp. 758–98.
41. P. Lane, A. A. Cannella, Jr and M. H. Lubatkin, 1999, 'Agency problems as antecedents to unrelated mergers and diversification: Amihud and Lev reconsidered', *Strategic Management Journal*, 19, pp. 555–78.
42. H. Sender, 2000, 'Japan grapples with shareholder suits', *Wall Street Journal*, 7 January, p. A13.
43. J. A. Byrne, 1997, 'The CEO and the board', *Business Week*, 15 September, pp. 107–16.
44. R. E. Hoskisson, R. A. Johnson and D. D. Moesel, 1994, 'Corporate divestiture intensity in restructuring firms: Effects of governance, strategy, and performance', *Academy of Management Journal*, 37, pp. 1207–51.
45. S. R. Kole and K. M. Lehn, 1999, 'Deregulation and the adaptation of governance structure: The case of the U.S. airline industry', *Journal of Financial Economics*, 52, pp. 79–117.
46. Australian Dairy Council, 2001, 'Reviewing a turbulent but necessary year': www.dairy.com.au/adic/mm1.htr.
47. A. Berle and G. Means, 1932, *The Modern Corporation and Private Property* (New York: Macmillan).
48. M. P. Smith, 1996, 'Shareholder activism by institutional investors: Evidence from CalPERS', *Journal of Finance*, 51, pp. 227–52.
49. J. D. Bogert, 1996, 'Explaining variance in the performance of long-term corporate blockholders', *Strategic Management Journal*, 17, pp. 243–9.
50. Useem, 'Corporate leadership in a globalizing equity market'; R. E. Hoskisson and M. A. Hitt, 1994, *Downscoping: How to Tame the Diversified Firm* (New York: Oxford University Press).
51. J. Kavanagh, 2000, 'Shareholders bare their teeth', *Business Review Weekly*, 3 November.
52. M. J. Roe, 1993, 'Mutual funds in the boardroom', *Journal of Applied Corporate Finance*, 5(4), pp. 56–61.
53. Byrne, 'The CEO and the board', p. 114.
54. Sundaramurthy, Mahoney and Mahoney, 'Board structure, antitakeover provisions, and stockholder wealth'; C. Sundaramurthy, 1996, 'Corporate governance within the context of antitakeover provisions', *Strategic Management Journal*, 17, pp. 377–94.
55. B. S. Black, 1992, 'Agents watching agents: The promise of institutional investors voice', *UCLA Law Review*, 39, pp. 871–93.
56. R. A. G. Monks, 1999, 'What will be the impact of active shareholders? A practical recipe for constructive change', *Long Range Planning*, 32(1), pp. 20–7.
57. C. Sundaramurthy and D. W. Lyon, 1998, 'Shareholder governance proposals and conflict of interests between inside and outside shareholders', *Journal of Managerial Issues*, 10, pp. 30–44.
58. J. K. Seward and J. P Walsh, 1996, 'The governance and control of voluntary corporate spinoffs', *Strategic Management Journal*, 17, pp. 25–39.
59. P. Mallete and R. L. Hogler, 1995, 'Board composition, stock ownership, and the exemption of directors from liability', *Journal of Management*, 21, pp. 861–78.
60. D. P. Forbes and F. J. Milliken, 1999, 'Cognition and corporate governance: Understanding boards of directors as strategic decision-making groups', *Academy of Management Review*, 24, pp. 489–505.
61. B. D. Baysinger and R. E. Hoskisson, 1990, 'The composition of boards of directors and strategic control: Effects on corporate strategy', *Academy of Management Review*, 15, pp. 72–87.
62. E. J. Zajac and J. D. Westphal, 1996, 'Director reputation, CEO-board power, and the dynamics of board interlocks', *Administrative Science Quarterly*, 41, pp. 507–29.
63. J. D. Westphal and E. J. Zajac, 1995, 'Who shall govern? CEO/board power, demographic similarity, and new director selection', *Administrative Science Quarterly*, 40, pp. 60–83.
64. R. P. Beatty and E. J. Zajac, 1994, 'Managerial incentives, monitoring, and risk bearing: A study of executive compensation, ownership, and board structure in initial public offerings', *Administrative Science Quarterly*, 39, pp. 313–35.
65. A. Bryant, 1997, 'CalPERS draws a blueprint for its concept of an ideal board', *New York Times*, 17 June, p. C1.
66. A. Cadbury, 1999, 'What are the trends in corporate governance? How will they impact your company?', *Long Range Planning*, 32, pp. 12–19.
67. I. M. Millstein, 1997, 'Red herring over independent boards', *New York Times*, 6 April, p. F10; W. Q. Judge, Jr and G. H. Dobbins, 1995, 'Antecedents and effects of outside directors' awareness of CEO decision style', *Journal of Management*, 21, pp. 43–64.
68. I. E. Kesner, 1988, 'Director characteristics in committee membership: An investigation of type, occupation, tenure and gender', *Academy of Management Journal*, 31, pp. 66–84.
69. T. McNulty and A Pettigrew, 1999, 'Strategists on the board', *Organization Studies*, 20, pp. 47–74.
70. S. Zahra, 1996, 'Governance, ownership and corporate entrepreneurship among the Fortune 500: The moderating impact of industry technological opportunity', *Academy of Management Journal*, 39, pp. 1713–35.
71. See, for example, J. Schregle, 1981, 'Comparative industrial relations: Pitfalls and potential', *International Labor Review*, 120(1), pp. 15–30.
72. J. A. Conger, D. Finegold and E. E. Lawler, III, 1998, 'Appraising boardroom performance', *Harvard Business Review*, 76(1), pp. 136–48; J. A. Byrne and L. Brown, 1997, 'Directors in the hot seat', *Business Week*, 8 December, pp. 100–4.
73. H. Kaback, 1996, 'A director's guide to board behavior', *Wall Street Journal*, 1 April, p. A14.
74. C. A. Simmers, 2000, 'Executive/board politics in strategic decision making', *Journal of Business and Economic Studies*, 4, pp. 37–56.
75. W. Ocasio, 1999, 'Institutionalized action and corporate governance', *Administrative Science Quarterly*, 44, pp. 384–416.

76. S. Rosenstein and J. G. Wyatt, 1997, 'Inside directors, board effectiveness, and shareholder wealth', *Journal of Financial Economics*, 44, pp. 229–50.
77. N. Vafeas, 1999, 'The nature of board nominating committees and their role in corporate governance', *Journal of Business Finance & Accounting*, 26, pp. 199–225.
78. D. C. Hambrick and S. Finkelstein, 1995, 'The effects of ownership structure on conditions at the top: The case of CEO pay raises', *Strategic Management Journal*, 16, p. 175.
79. L. Gomez-Mejia and R. M. Wiseman, 1997, 'Reframing executive compensation: An assessment and outlook', *Journal of Management*, 23, pp. 291–374.
80. S. Finkelstein and B. K. Boyd, 1998, 'How much does the CEO matter? The role of managerial discretion in the setting of CEO compensation', *Academy of Management Journal*, 41, pp. 179–99.
81. O'Neill, 'Executive remuneration in Australia'.
82. J. D. Westphal and E. J. Zajac, 1999, 'The symbolic management of stockholders: Corporate governance reform and shareholder reactions', *Administrative Science Quarterly*, 43, pp. 127–53.
83. M. J. Conyon and S. I. Peck, 1998, 'Board control, remuneration committees, and top management compensation', *Academy of Management Journal*, 41, pp. 146–57; Westphal and Zajac, 'The symbolic management of stockholders'.
84. K. Roth and S. O'Donnell, 1996, 'Foreign subsidiary compensation: An agency theory perspective', *Academy of Management Journal*, 39, pp. 678–703.
85. S. Fung, 1999, 'How should we pay them?', *Across the Board*, June, pp. 37–41.
86. O'Neill, 'Executive remuneration in Australia'.
87. R. E. Hoskisson, M. A. Hitt and C. W. L. Hill, 1993, 'Managerial incentives and investment in R&D in large multiproduct firms', *Organization Science*, 4, pp. 325–41.
88. K. A. Merchant, 1989, *Rewarding Results: Motivating Profit Center Managers* (Cambridge, MA: Harvard Business School Press).
89. W. M. Bulkeley, 1999, 'Software firm executives ordered to return million in stock options', *Wall Street Journal Interactive*, 10 November: www.interactive.wsj.com/articles; J. Reingold and R. Grover, 1999, 'Executive pay', *Business Week*, 19 April, pp. 72–118.
90. C. G. Holderness, R. S. Kroszner and D. P. Sheehan, 1999, 'Were the good old days that good? Changes in managerial stock ownership since the Great Depression', *Journal of Finance*, 54, pp. 435–69.
91. J. Dahya, A. A. Lonie and D. A. Power, 1998, 'Ownership structure, firm performance and top executive change: An analysis of UK firms', *Journal of Business Finance & Accounting*, 25, pp. 1089–118.
92. E. S. Hardy, S. DeCarlo, A. C. Anderson and J. Chamberlain, 1999, 'Compensation fit for a king', *Forbes*, 17 May, pp. 202–7.
93. R. E. Silverman and J. S. Lublin, 1999, 'The going rate: Mega options', *Dallas Morning News*, 9 November, p. B20.
94. O. E. Williamson, 1985, *The Economic Institutions of Capitalism: Firms, Markets and Relational Contracting* (New York: Macmillan Free Press).
95. B. W. Keats and M. A. Hitt, 1988, 'A causal model of linkages among environmental dimensions, macro organizational characteristics, and performance', *Academy of Management Journal*, 31, pp. 570–98.
96. O. E. Williamson, 1994, 'Strategizing, economizing, and economic organization', in R. P. Rumelt, D. E. Schendel and D. J. Teece (eds), *Fundamental Issues in Strategy* (Cambridge, MA: Harvard Business School Press), p. 380.
97. Hoskisson and Turk, 'Corporate restructuring: Governance and control limits of the internal market'.
98. M. A. Hitt, R. E. Hoskisson and R. D. Ireland, 1990, 'Mergers and acquisitions and managerial commitment to innovation in M-form firms', *Strategic Management Journal*, 11 (Special Summer Issue), pp. 29–47.
99. Hitt, Hoskisson, Johnson and Moesel, 'The market for corporate control and firm innovation'; Walsh and Kosnik, 'Corporate raiders'.
100. Mallette and Hogier, 'Board composition', p. 864.
101. Hitt, Harrison and Ireland, *Creating Value through Mergers and Acquisitions*.
102. Sundaramurthy, Mahoney and Mahoney, 'Board structure, antitakeover provisions, and stockholder wealth'.
103. R. A. Johnson, R. E. Hoskisson and M. A. Hitt, 2000, 'The effects of environmental uncertainty on the mode of corporate restructuring', Working paper, University of Missouri.
104. T. Carlisle, 2000, 'Canadian oil firm sets defense against Occidental's takeover bid', *Wall Street Journal Interactive*, 6 February: www.interactive.wsj.com/articles.
105. Walsh and Kosnik, 'Corporate raiders'.
106. S. Johnston, 1995, 'Managerial dominance of Japan's major corporations', *Journal of Management*, 21, pp. 191–209.
107. Our discussion of corporate governance structures in Germany and Japan is drawn from Monks and Minow, *Corporate Governance*, pp. 271–99; Charkham, *Keeping Good Company*, pp. 6–118.
108. S. Wallis, 2000, 'Corporate governance: Conformance or performance?', *Journal of Banking and Financial Services*, 114(4), p. 14.
109. www.accc.gov.au.
110. Ibid.
111. www.asic.gov.au
112. Kavanagh, 'Shareholders bare their teeth'.
113. J. Milton-Smith, 1997, 'Business ethics in Australia and New Zealand', *Journal of Business Ethics*, 16(14), p. 1485.
114. Wallis, 'Corporate governance'.
115. E. R. Gedajlovic and D. M. Shapiro, 1998, 'Management and ownership effects: Evidence from five countries', *Strategic Management Journal*, 19, pp. 533–53.
116. S. Douma, 1997, 'The two-tier system of corporate governance', *Long Range Planning*, 30(4), pp. 612–15.
117. M. J. Rubach and T. C. Sebora, 1998, 'Comparative corporate governance: Competitive implications of an emerging convergence', *Journal of World Business*, 33, pp. 167–84.
118. Charkham, *Keeping Good Company*, p. 70.
119. J. Fiorillo, 2000, 'While Tokyo's commitment to reform waivers', *Wall Street Journal Interactive*, 12 January: www.interactive.wsj.com/articles.
120. B. Bremner, E. Thornton and I. M. Kunii, 1999, 'Fall of a keiretsu', *Business Week*, 15 March, pp. 87–92.
121. E. Thornton, 1999, 'Mystery at the top', *Business Week*, 26 April, p. 52.
122. P. Landers, 2000, 'Hostile bid for Tokyo's Shoei marks a milestone for Japan', *Wall Street Journal Interactive*, 6 February: www.interactive.wsj.com/articles; M. Almieda, 2000, 'Japanese hostile-takeover bid marks a departure from corporate model', *Wall Street Journal Interactive*, 6 February: www.interactive.wsj.com/articles.
123. J. B. White, 2000, 'The company we'll keep', *Wall Street Journal Interactive*, 17 January: www.interactive.wsj.com/articles.
124. S. Iskander, 1999, 'Salary disclosure in France: Transparency or voyeurism?', *Financial Times*, 26 July, pp. 11–12.
125. C. P. Erlich and D.-S. Kang, 1999, 'South Korea: Corporate governance reform in Korea: The remaining issues, Part I: Governance structure of the large Korean firm', *East Asian Executive Reports*, 21, pp. 11–14.
126. L. Chang, 1999, 'Chinese firms find incentive to use stock-compensation plans', *Wall Street Journal*, 1 November, p. A2.; T. Clarke and Y. Du, 1998, 'Corporate governance in China: Explosive growth and new patterns of ownership', *Long Range Planning*, 31(2), pp. 239–51.
127. T Buck, I. Filatotchev and M. Wright, 1998, 'Agents, stakeholders and corporate governance in Russian firms', *Journal of Management Studies*, 35, pp. 81–104.
128. E. Freeman and J. Liedtka, 1997, 'Stakeholder capitalism and the value chain', *European Management Journal*, 15(3), pp. 286–95.
129. A. Taylor, III, 1996, 'GM: Why they might break up America's biggest company', *Fortune*, 29 April, p. 84.
130. Hitt, Harrison and Ireland, *Creating Value through Mergers and Acquisitions*; 'Cendant reaches preliminary agreement to settle common stock securities class action for $2.83 billion', 1999, Cendant Press Release, 7 December.
131. R. F. Felton, A. Hudnut and V. Witt, 1995, 'Building a stronger board', *McKinsey Quarterly*, 2, p. 169.

Chapter 11

Organisational structure and controls

Objectives

After reading this chapter, you should be able to:

1. Explain the importance of integrating strategy implementation and strategy formulation.
2. Describe the dominant path of evolution from strategy to structure to strategy again.
3. Identify and describe the organisational structures used to implement different business-level strategies.
4. Discuss organisational structures used to implement different corporate-level strategies.
5. Identify and distinguish among the organisational structures used to implement three international strategies.
6. Describe organisational structures used to implement cooperative strategies.

The new structure of Microsoft

Although Microsoft has US$257 000 of income per employee, versus the average of US$17 000 for the Standard & Poor's 500 stock index, the company's top executives are restructuring the firm in a way that will barely resemble the one that got them to that position. Microsoft had its largest market capitalisation, US$414 billion, in 1999 and has had a revenue growth of 30 per cent annually. Why, then, does the firm feel that it must do something different to top this amazing performance for a 24-year-old company? In fact, Bill Gates is taking over as the chief software architect and stepping down as the CEO, and Steve Ballmer is taking over the top position.

In explaining why Microsoft is changing its leadership and structural arrangements, Bill Gates simply said, 'The Internet has changed everything. In order to respond to these changes, Microsoft needs to give people the power to do anything they want, anywhere they want and on any device.' Accordingly, the new vision, 'Microsoft Vision 2.0', is directed at giving Microsoft programmers freedom to develop programs that don't revolve around Windows software, and for Microsoft, that's a significant change. For example, although Microsoft lost to AT&T in the bid for MediaOne Group, Inc., a large American cable TV operation, it did receive a non-exclusive contract with MediaOne to provide set-top software for the interactive boxes that will facilitate using the Web through the home cable television platform, whereby consumers will also be able to hook up their PCs at lightning-fast speeds. In fact, MediaOne will have access to 8 per cent of American homes.

This Microsoft vision includes a new organisational structure that divides the company's product development into six different divisions. Two groups will target corporate leaders and knowledge workers. Two others emphasise home PC buyers and those who shop for computer and video games at stores. Still another is concerned with software developers. Finally, the last group is aimed at Web surfers and those who shop on the Web.

In the previous structure, products were split by technology, one focusing on Windows application software (such as Microsoft Word and associated software products) and the other on operating systems. The operating systems division focused on a range of systems, from Windows NT down to the stripped-down Win CE for handheld consumer devices. Accordingly, there was no distinction based on customers. Previously, this division had focused on technology for technology's sake and not on the basis of what consumers wanted. Thus, under the new structural arrangement, there will be fewer arcane technological features with the operating systems so that even less sophisticated consumers will obtain what they need and desire, without confusing them unnecessarily about technological aspects.

Previously, the power structure was such that Gates and Microsoft president Steven A. Ballmer made the division heads come to them for almost all decisions. With decisions large and small being funnelled through this top pair, there was a decision-making bottleneck. Thus, the structure was functionally oriented (focused on technology) and centralised. With 30 000 employees, 183 different products and at least five layers of management and staffers, there were significant complaints about bureaucratic red tape. Decision making was very slow, and many key employees were leaving because their ideas were not being heard. Additionally, there was little opportunity to develop them because of the centralised decision making. The new structure is closer to the multi-divisional structure adoption, which often follows increased product diversification.

Although the talent drain is one problem that Microsoft's restructuring is intended to slow down through more divisional independence and decentralisation, the loss of key employees will likely continue to be a competitive challenge. The hope is that the new structure will give the company an opportunity for fresh ideas to take hold and develop. Along these lines, Microsoft has been considering offering a 'tracking stock' (issues of shares focused on specific company assets) that would give its Internet properties a focus for investors. It would allow investors to cash in on the high Internet share valuations, but also protect their cash cow, the Windows software business, from wild price swings, because of the focus on the Internet. Furthermore, it would enable business-level managers to cash in on their entrepreneurial ideas. General Motors has had a tracking stock for Hughes that has risen much more rapidly than General Motors' ordinary shares, because of the DirectTV assets targeted by the tracking stock. Thus, the tracking stock allows better market value adjustment, given information on the type of asset, and provides an incentive for up-and-coming creative management talent to stay with Microsoft.

Whether such a structural change will work and whether Gates and Ballmer will be able to give up control are questions that will be tested over time. Those two executives are used to delving into every decision, but that approach has slowed decision making. Another potential pitfall is that the different product groups might undertake conflicting strategies now that they are ostensibly independent. However, if the change helps Microsoft to stay focused on its customers, it is likely to increase its already outstanding performance.

www.att.com
www.gm.com
www.mediaone.com
www.microsoft.com

Sources: *Microsoft Home Page*, 2000, 1 March: www.microsoft.com; D. J. Greene, 2000, 'A chat with the new guy in product development', *Business Week*, 31 January, p. 43; D. Bank, 1999, 'Microsoft will split into five divisions that deal with customers and rivals', *Wall Street Journal Interactive Edition*, 30 March: www.wsj.com; P. Gillin, 1999, 'Microsoft's Ballmer details reorg', *Computerworld*, 5 April, p. 12; M. Moeller, S. Hamm and T. J. Mullaney, 1999, 'Remaking Microsoft', *Business Week*, 17 May, pp. 106–14; M. Moeller and K. Rebello, 1999, 'Visionary-in-chief: A talk with Chairman Bill Gates on the world beyond Windows', *Business Week*, 17 May, pp. 114–16; E. Nee, 1999, 'Microsoft gets ready for a new game', *Fortune*, 26 April, pp. 107–12.

In the previous chapter, we described mechanisms companies use to govern their operations and to align various parties' interests – especially the interests of top-level executives – with those of the firm's owners. Governance mechanisms can influence a company's ability to implement formulated strategies successfully and thereby facilitate a competitive advantage.[1]

In this chapter, our focus is on the organisational structures and controls used to implement the strategies discussed previously (for example, business level, Chapter 4; corporate level, Chapter 6; international, Chapter 8; and cooperative, Chapter 9). Moreover, as the discussion in the Opening Case about actions taken at Microsoft suggests, the proper use of an organisational structure and its accompanying integrating mechanisms and controls can contribute to the firm's strategic competitiveness.[2] In fact, the most productive global competitors are those with effective product innovation skills and an organisational structure in place that facilitates successful and timely applications of internal capabilities and core competencies.[3] Thus, a firm's organisational structure influences its managerial work and the decisions made by top-level managers.[4]

Organisational structure alone, however, does not create a competitive advantage; rather, a competitive advantage is created when there is a proper match between strategy and structure.[5] For example, it may be that what makes 3M's competitive advantage somewhat sustainable 'is its unique blend of practices, values, autonomous structures, funding processes, rewards, and selection and development of product champions'.[6] Similarly, the Harvey Norman chain of retail outlets in Australia operates in such a unique fashion that 350 franchisees operate their own 'department stores' within the 101 Harvey Norman stores. That is, each department within a Harvey Norman store is a separate franchised business unit. A dedicated franchise manager, whose income is linked directly to their own department's sales performance, runs each of the departments. Harvey Norman head office provides the required advertising and financial bookkeeping support, and, as such, inventory and sales promotion control remain largely the responsibility of centralised head office. The transformation of the Harvey Norman retail group has been considered a success, with sales quadrupling to $2 billion between 1994 and 1999, store numbers increasing from 50 to 101, and market capitalisation increasing from $580 million to $3.1 billion over the same time period.[7]

On the other hand, ineffective strategy structure matches may result in rigidity and failure, given the complexity and need for rapid changes in the 21st-century competitive landscape.[8] Pacific Dunlop (see the Pacific Dunlop case study later in this text) provides an example of an ineffective divisional structure, where little integration of management and communication practices between corporate divisions has hindered their diversification for growth strategy over an extended period.[9] Effective strategic leaders (see Chapter 12) seek to develop an organisational structure and accompanying controls that are superior to those of their competitors.[10] Using competitively superior structures and controls explains in part why some firms survive and succeed while others do not.[11] Bill Gates and Steve Ballmer, the executives at Microsoft who have implemented the new structure outlined in the Opening Case, expect that the organisational structure will contribute to the firm's future success. As with the other parts of the strategic management process, top-level managers bear the final responsibility to make choices about organisational structures that will enhance a firm's performance.[12] Following its acquisition of Digital Equipment Corporation (DEC), Compaq Computer Corporation executives, for example, did not make good structural decisions, and a successful integration of DEC's businesses into their own continues to cause problems (see Strategic Focus in Chapter 1).

Selecting the organisational structure and controls that will implement chosen strategies effectively is a fundamental challenge for managers, especially those at the top. A key reason is that in the global economy, firms must be flexible, innovative and creative to exploit their core competencies in the pursuit of marketplace opportunities.[13] They also require a certain degree of stability in their structures so that day-to-day tasks can be completed efficiently. Accessible and reliable information is needed for executives to reach decisions regarding the selection of a structure that can provide the desired levels of flexibility and stability. By helping executives improve their decision making, useful information contributes to the formation and implementation of effective structures and controls.

This chapter first describes a pattern of growth and accompanying changes in an organisational structure experienced by strategically competitive firms. For example, the success of Microsoft mentioned in the Opening Case necessitated the proactive change in their structural arrangement. The chapter's second major section discusses organisational structures and controls that are used to implement different business-level strategies.

The implementation of corporate-level strategy is then described, with the transition from the functional to the multi-divisional structure highlighted. This major structural innovation took place in several firms during the 1920s, including DuPont. In fact, noted business historian Alfred Chandler cites DuPont as the innovator in both the strategy of diversification and the multi-divisional structure.[14] Specific variations of the multi-divisional structure are discussed in terms of their relationship with the effective implementation of the related and unrelated diversification strategies.

Because of the increasing globalisation of many industries, the number of firms implementing international strategies continues to grow. The trend towards globalisation is significant and pervasive. To cope successfully with the strategic challenges associated with discontinuous changes, the firm must develop and use organisational structures that facilitate meaningful conversations among all stakeholders regarding opportunities and threats facing the company at different points in time.[15] In the chapter's final two sections, we discuss the use of organisational structures to implement cooperative strategies and a few issues concerning organisational forms that should be of interest to those responsible for using a firm's strategic management process effectively.

Evolutionary patterns of strategy and organisational structure

All firms require some form of organisational structure to implement their strategies. Principally, structures are changed when they no longer provide the coordination, control and direction managers and organisations require to implement strategies successfully.[16] The ineffectiveness of a structure typically results from increases in a firm's revenues and levels of diversification. In particular, the formulation of strategies involving greater levels of diversification demands structural change to match each strategy. Some corporate-level strategies require elaborate structures and strategic controls, while others focus on financial control.

Organisational structure is a firm's formal role configuration, procedures, governance and control mechanisms, and authority and decision-making processes.[17] Influenced by situational factors, including company size and age, organisational structure reflects managers' determinations of *what* the firm does and *how* it completes that work, given its chosen strategies.[18] Strategic competitiveness can be attained only when the firm's selected structure is congruent with its formulated strategy.[19] Consequently, a strategy's potential to create value is reached only when the firm configures itself in ways that allow the strategy to be implemented effectively. Thus, as firms evolve and change their strategies, new structural arrangements are required. In addition, existing structures influence the future selection of strategies.[20] Accordingly, the two key strategic actions of strategy formulation and strategy implementation continuously interact to influence managerial choices about strategy and structure.

Figure 11.1 shows the growth pattern many firms experience. This pattern results in changes in the relationships between the firm's formulated strategies and the organisational structures used to support and facilitate their implementation.

> **Organisational structure** is a firm's formal role configuration, procedures, governance and control mechanisms, and authority and decision-making processes.

Simple structure

A **simple structure** is an organisational form in which the owner–manager makes all major decisions directly and monitors all activities, while the staff serves as an extension of the manager's supervisory authority. This structure involves little specialisation of tasks, few rules and limited formalisation. Although important, information systems are relatively unsophisticated, and owner–managers participate directly in the firm's day-to-day operations. Typically, firms offering a single product line in a single geographic market use the simple structure. The simple structure is used frequently in firms implementing either the focused cost leadership or focused differentiation strategy. Restaurants, repair businesses and other specialised enterprises are examples of firms

> A **simple structure** is an organisational form in which the owner–manager makes all major decisions directly and monitors all activities, while the staff serves as an extension of the manager's supervisory authority.

whose limited complexity calls for the use of the simple structure. In this structure, communication is frequent and direct, and new products tend to be introduced to the market quickly, which can result in a competitive advantage. Because of these characteristics, few of the coordination problems that are common in larger organisations exist.

Figure 11.1 | Strategy and structure growth pattern

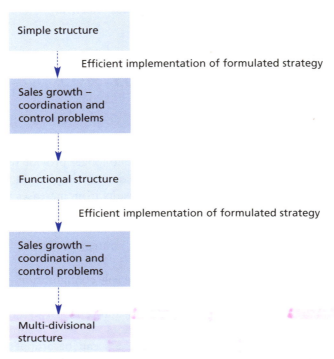

The simple structure, the operations it supports and the strategies implemented in companies that use it play important roles in the success of various economies. Data on job creation are one indicator of this importance. In Australia, for example, small companies (with between two and 100 employees) have become the largest job creators, and indeed are considered the 'engine room' for employment growth in this country during the 1990s. These small firms created approximately 92 per cent of the new jobs in Australia in the early to mid-1990s, and of the 5.5 million private-sector employees, more than 3.1 million are employed in small business.[21]

The value of small firms to the United Kingdom's economy has also been recognised: some analysts believe that, in that country, the simple organisational structure may result in competitive advantages for some small firms relative to their larger counterparts. A broad-based openness to innovation, greater structural flexibility and an ability to respond more rapidly to environmental changes are examples of these potential competitive advantages.[22] For example, large firms such as Nike have been overshadowed by a set of a dozen smaller firms at Super Show, the largest sporting-goods trade show in the United States. These smaller companies have endorsements by skateboarders, stunt bike riders and even rock stars, often with an extreme sports theme. 'With kids more interested in shoes worn on MTV than those worn in the NBA, and many youngsters preferring the X Games to the World Series, industry giants focusing on traditional sports are slumping.'[23] Nike's share price has slumped because of its executives' inability to adapt to this change as quickly as the smaller firms can.[24] Thus, although large corporations are indeed vital to the health of the world's economies, the importance of small firms should not be overlooked. The simple organisational structure properly supports the implementation of the focused strategies that are chosen most often by small firms (see Chapter 4).

However, as the small firm grows larger and more complex, managerial and structural challenges emerge. For example, the amount of competitively relevant information requiring analysis increases substantially. The ensuing more complicated information-processing needs place significant pressures on the simple structure and the owner–manager. Commonly, owner–managers lack the organisational skills and experience required to manage effectively the specialised and complex tasks involved with multiple organisational functions. Owner–managers, or the top-level managers employed by the small firm's owner, bear the responsibility to recognise inadequacies in the firm's organisational structure and the need to change to one that is consistent with the firm's strategy.[25]

In fact, this is what has happened to Nike. Phil Knight, Nike's CEO, indicated, 'We are becoming more of an international company than a U.S. company. That shift may be difficult to see for people who "grew up" with the company as it exploded in the United States.'[26] Nike's growth in Europe and Asia was 22 and 9.1 per cent, respectively. In the Americas, including Latin America and Canada, Nike grew in the double-digit range, but the firm's growth in the United States is expected to be in the single-digit range. Furthermore, retail department store consolidation in the United States creates an uncertainty that has also affected Nike's share price. Nike's growth has led to changes in the company's structure, as well as some inflexibility, as illustrated in the firm's failure to respond to the extreme-sports trend mentioned earlier. An appropriate structure for Nike in dealing with the pressures of growth would lead the company to move to a functional organisational structure or perhaps even one of the forms of the multi-divisional structure, given that Nike has apparel in addition to shoe products.

Functional structure

To coordinate more complex organisational functions, firms should abandon the simple structure in favour of the functional structure. The functional structure is used by larger firms implementing one of the business-level strategies and by firms with low levels of product diversification (for instance, companies implementing either the single- or dominant-business corporate-level strategy).

The **functional structure** consists of a chief executive officer and a limited corporate staff, with functional line managers in dominant organisational areas such as production, accounting, marketing, R&D, engineering and human resources. This structure allows for functional specialisation, thereby facilitating knowledge sharing and idea development.[27] Because the differences in orientation among organisational functions can impede communication and coordination, the central task of the CEO is to integrate the decisions and actions of individual business functions for the benefit of the entire corporation.[28] The functional structure also facilitates career paths and professional development in specialised functional areas.

An unintended negative consequence of the functional structure is the tendency for functional-area managers to focus on local versus overall company strategic issues. Such emphases cause specialised managers to lose sight of the firm's overall strategic intent and mission. When that happens, often the multi-divisional structure is implemented to overcome the difficulty.

Another condition that encourages a change in structure from the functional to the multi-divisional is greater diversification. Strategic success often leads to growth and

> The **functional structure** consists of a chief executive officer and a limited corporate staff, with functional line managers in dominant organisational areas such as production, accounting, marketing, R&D, engineering and human resources.

diversification. Deciding to offer the same products in different markets (market diversification) or choosing to offer different products (product diversification) creates control problems. The multi-divisional structure provides the controls required to deal effectively with additional levels of diversification. In fact, the firm's returns may suffer when increased diversification is not accompanied by a change to the multi-divisional structure, as shown in the Opening Case about Microsoft.

Multi-divisional structure

The CEO's limited ability to process increasing quantities of strategic information, the focus of functional managers on local issues and increased diversification are primary causes of the decision to change from the functional to the multi-divisional (M-form) structure. According to Alfred Chandler, 'The M-form came into being when senior managers operating through existing centralized, functionally departmentalized ... structures realized they had neither the time nor the necessary information to coordinate and monitor day-to-day operations, or to devise and implement long-term plans for the various product lines. The administrative overload had become simply too great.'[29]

The **multi-divisional (M-form) structure** is composed of operating divisions, each representing a separate business or profit centre in which the top corporate officer delegates responsibilities for day-to-day operations and business-unit strategy to division managers. Because the diversified corporation is the dominant form of business in the industrialised world, the M-form is being used in most of the corporations competing in the global economy.[30] However, only effectively designed M-forms enhance a firm's performance. Thus, for all companies, and perhaps especially for diversified firms, performance may be an important function of the 'goodness of fit' between strategy and structure.[31]

Chandler's examination of the strategies and structures of large American firms documented the M-form's development.[32] Chandler viewed the M-form as an innovative response to coordination and control problems that surfaced during the 1920s in the functional structures then used by large firms such as DuPont and General Motors.[33] Among other benefits, the M-form allowed firms to greatly expand their operations.

Use of the multi-divisional structure at DuPont and General Motors

Chandler's studies showed that firms such as DuPont began to record significant revenue growth through the manufacture and distribution of diversified products while using the functional structure. Functional departments (for example, sales and production), however, found it difficult to coordinate the conflicting priorities of the firm's new and different products and markets. Moreover, the functional structures that were in use allocated costs to organisational functions, rather than to individual businesses and products. This allocation method made it virtually impossible for top-level managers to determine the contributions of separate product lines to the firm's return on its investments. Even more damaging for large firms trying to implement newly formulated product diversification strategies through the use of a functional structure that was appropriate for small companies and for those needing proprietary expertise and economies of scale[34] was the increasing allocation of top-level managers' time and energies to solving short-term administrative problems. Focusing their efforts on these issues caused executives to neglect the long-term strategic issues that were their primary responsibility.

To cope with similar problems, General Motors CEO Alfred Sloan, Jr, proposed a reorganisation of the company.[35] Sloan conceptualised separate divisions, each representing a distinct business, that would be self-contained and have their own functional hierarchy. Implemented in 1925, Sloan's structure delegated day-to-day operating responsibilities to division managers. The small staff at the corporate level was responsible for determining the firm's long-term strategic direction and for exercising overall financial control of semi-autonomous divisions. Each division was to make its own business-level strategic decisions, but because the corporate office's focus was on the outcomes achieved by the entire corporation, rather than the performance of separate units, decisions made by division heads could be superseded by corporate office personnel. Sloan's structural innovation had three important outcomes: '(1) it enabled corporate officers to more accurately monitor the performance of each business, which simplified the problem of control; (2) it facilitated comparisons between divisions, which improved the resource allocation process; and (3) it stimulated managers of poor[ly] performing divisions to look for ways of improving performance.'[36] ANZ Bank have undertaken such a structure, establishing 21 autonomous business units from their once totally integrated operations. ANZ management use the expression 'portfolio management' to describe this structure, and utilise the form such that the central controlling body (ANZ head office) can ascertain which units perform well, as opposed to those that perform badly but are hidden in the consolidation of the corporate accounts. BP Australia is another example of such a structure. BP Australia 'tore up' its divisional structure and created 70 network-style business units, arguing that its markets were fragmenting and that there was 'no point having a business that was considerably larger than the markets it served'.[37]

The use of internal controls in the multi-divisional structure

The M-form structure holds top-level managers responsible for formulating and implementing overall corporate strategies; that is, they are responsible for the corporate-level acquisition and restructuring, international and cooperative strategies we examined in Chapters 6 to 9.

Strategic and financial controls are the two major types of internal controls used to support the implementation of strategies in larger firms.[38] Properly designed organisational controls provide clear insights regarding behaviours that enhance the firm's competitiveness and overall performance.[39] Diversification strategies are implemented effectively when firms use both types of controls appropriately. For example, as the Opening Case illustrates, Microsoft is implementing a multi-divisional structure. Currently, the company has good strategic control; however, it will need a better balance, with more of an emphasis on financial control, to create the appropriate incentives for managers of their new product-oriented divisions. If Ballmer and Gates do not allow division heads to develop stronger financial control of their divisions and evaluate the performance of those divisions with better financial controls (recall the idea of tracking stock, which could facilitate improved financial control and evaluation by the stock market), a control imbalance will remain, with Gates and Ballmer having too much centralised control.

Strategic control entails the use of long-term and strategically relevant criteria by corporate-level managers to evaluate the performance of division managers and their units. Strategic control emphasises largely subjective judgements and may involve intuitive evaluation criteria. Behavioural in nature, strategic controls typically require high levels of cognitive diversity among top-level managers. *Cognitive diversity* captures the differences in beliefs about cause–effect relationships and desired outcomes among top-level managers' preferences.[40] Corporate-level managers rely on strategic control to gain an operational understanding of the strategies being implemented in the firm's separate divisions or business units. Because strategic control allows a corporate-level

> Strategic control entails the use of long-term and strategically relevant criteria by corporate-level managers to evaluate the performance of division managers and their units.

evaluation of the full array of strategic actions – those concerned with both the formulation and implementation of a business-unit strategy – corporate-level managers must have a deep understanding of a division's or business unit's operations and markets.[41] The use of strategic controls also demands rich exchanges of information between corporate and divisional managers. These exchanges take place through both formal and informal (that is, unplanned) face-to-face meetings.[42] As diversification increases, strategic control can be strained.[43] Sometimes, the strain results in a commitment to reduce the firm's level of diversification. For example, Black & Decker's top-level managers decided recently to divest some divisions to reduce the firm's overall level of diversification. Units sold were the household products division in North America, Latin America and Australia; Emhart Glass (a maker of equipment for the manufacture of glass containers); and True Temper Sports (a manufacturer of golf club shafts). Difficulties encountered when the firm attempted to use strategic controls to evaluate the performance of those units and of the individuals managing them may have contributed to the divestment decisions. Coupled with a reduction in force of 3 000 jobs (10 per cent of the firm's workforce), the divestments were expected to generate annual savings of more than US$100 million.[44]

Financial control entails objective criteria (for example, return on investment) that corporate-level managers use to evaluate both the returns being earned by individual business units and the managers responsible for their performance. Because the units are oriented towards financial outcomes, an emphasis on financial controls requires each division's performance to be largely independent of that of other divisions.[45] Accordingly, when the firm chooses to implement a strategy calling for interdependence among the firm's different businesses, such as the related-constrained corporate-level strategy, the ability of financial control to add value to strategy implementation efforts is reduced.[46]

Implementing business-level strategies: Organisational structure and controls

As discussed in Chapter 4, business-level strategies establish a particular type of competitive advantage (typically, either low cost or differentiation) in a particular competitive scope (either an entire industry or a narrow segment of it). The cost leadership, differentiation and integrated cost leadership differentiation strategies are implemented effectively when certain modifications are made to the characteristics of the functional structure, based on the unique attributes of the individual business-level strategies.

Using the functional structure to implement the cost leadership strategy

The structural characteristics of specialisation, centralisation and formalisation play important roles in the successful implementation of the cost leadership strategy. *Specialisation* refers to the type and number of job specialities that are required to perform the firm's work.[47] For the cost leadership strategy, managers divide the firm's work into homogeneous subgroups. The basis for these subgroups is usually functional areas, products being produced or clients served. By dividing and grouping work tasks into specialities, firms reduce their costs through the efficiencies achieved by employees specialising in a particular and often narrow set of activities.

Centralisation is the degree to which decision-making authority is retained at higher managerial levels. Today, the trend in organisations is towards decentralisation – the movement of decision-making authority down to people in the firm who have the most direct and frequent contact with customers. However, to coordinate activities carefully across organisational functions, the structure used to implement the cost leadership strategy calls for centralisation. Thus, in designing this particular type of functional structure, managers strive to push some decision-making authority lower in the organisation, while remaining focused on the more general need for activities to be coordinated and integrated through the efforts of a centralised staff.

Because the cost leadership strategy is often chosen by firms producing relatively standardised products in large quantities, formalisation is necessary. *Formalisation* is the degree to which formal rules and procedures govern organisational activities.[48] To foster more efficient operations, R&D efforts emphasise improvements in the manufacturing process.

As summarised in Figure 11.2, successful implementation of the cost leadership strategy requires an organisational structure featuring strong task specialisation, the centralisation of decision-making authority and the formalisation of work rules and procedures. This type of functional structure encourages the emergence of a low-cost culture – a culture in which all employees seek to find ways to drive their firm's or unit's costs lower than rivals' costs. Using highly specialised work tasks, US airline industry cost leader Southwest Airlines strives continuously to increase the efficiency of its production and distribution systems. For example, Southwest was one of the first carriers to sell tickets on the Internet. A travel industry consultant concluded that Southwest's simple fares and schedule make it easy to sell travel directly to consumers on the Internet, a move that Impulse Airlines copied in Australia for their ultimately unsuccessful cost leadership strategy. Similarly, a number of European carriers have sprung up that follow Southwest's low-cost approach, including, for example, Richard Branson's discount carrier Virgin Blue's entry on to the Australian domestic market (see www.virginblue.com.au).

Figure 11.2 | Functional structure for implementation of a cost leadership strategy

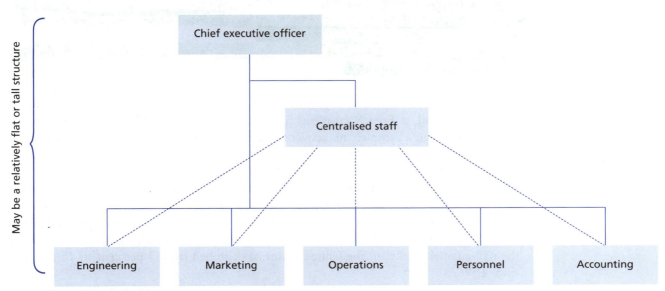

Notes:
- Operations is the main function
- Process engineering is emphasised, rather than new product R&D
- Relatively large centralised staff coordinates functions
- Formalised procedures allow for emergence of a low-cost culture
- Overall structure is mechanical; job roles are highly structured

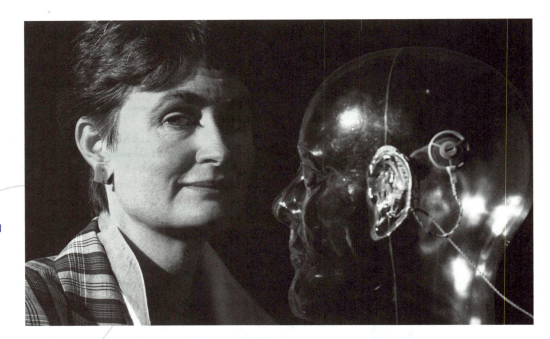

Cochlear are leaders in a key technical product arena. They are an Australian company that has prospered in a global market based on innovation. The picture, taken in March 1999, shows Catherine Livingstone, Cochlear MD.

Using the functional structure to implement the differentiation strategy

The differentiation strategy is implemented successfully when a functional structure is used in which decision-making authority is decentralised. Unlike the cost leadership strategy, in which the coordination and integration of organisational function activities occurs through centralisation of decision-making authority, the functional structure used to implement the differentiation strategy demands that people throughout the firm learn how to coordinate and integrate their activities effectively. In fact, the implementation of the differentiation strategy is facilitated if there is a consensus style of decision making among the top-management team members. Research suggests that the performance of a strategic business unit pursuing a differentiation strategy increases if a consensus style is used. This is particularly true when a differentiation strategy is implemented in a stable environment; it is more difficult to implement a consensus style when the market being pursued by the firm is dynamic and changing.[49]

The marketing and R&D functions are often emphasised in the differentiation strategy's functional structure. For example, because of L'Oreal's commitment to continuous product innovation across all of its operations, marketing and product R&D are emphasised in the company and in its recent acquisitions in beauty products. Recently, L'Oreal, a French cosmetic firm, acquired US firm Maybelline for US$758 million and began a complete makeover of the brand, including moving the headquarters from Memphis, Tennessee, to New York City. L'Oreal created the theme of 'urban American chic', which was posted on all Maybelline products to promote their US origins. Maybelline rolled out a radical new makeup line, heavy on unusual colours such as yellow and green. When L'Oreal marketers discovered that the moderately successful Great Finish nail enamel dried in one minute, they changed the name to Express Finish – and sold it heavily as a product used by urban women on the go. Maybelline's share of the nail-enamel market in the United States has climbed from 3 per cent to 15 per cent since 1996.[50]

Often, R&D and marketing need to be coordinated in order to implement the differentiation strategy. For example, L'Oreal's CEO, Lindsay Owen-Jones, recognised two prominent beauty cultures: French and American. After buying Maybelline, he decided to galvanise L'Oreal's Paris R&D operations by setting up a second creative headquarters in New York, with R&D as well as marketing and advertising teams. 'We set up a counter-power in New York with people that have a totally different mind-set, background, and creativity,'[51] said Owen-Jones.

Finally, to capitalise on emerging trends in key markets, the firm implementing the differentiation strategy often makes rapid changes based on ambiguous and incomplete information. Such changes demand that the firm use a relatively flat organisational structure to group its work activities. (In a relatively flat structure, workers are likely to have a number of tasks included in their job descriptions.) It is difficult to implement a differentiation strategy when the firm has extensive centralisation and formalisation, especially in a rapidly changing environment. Thus, the overall organisational structure needs to be flexible and job roles less structured. Additional characteristics of the form of the functional structure used to implement the differentiation strategy are shown in Figure 11.3.

Figure 11.3 | Functional structure for implementation of a differentiation strategy

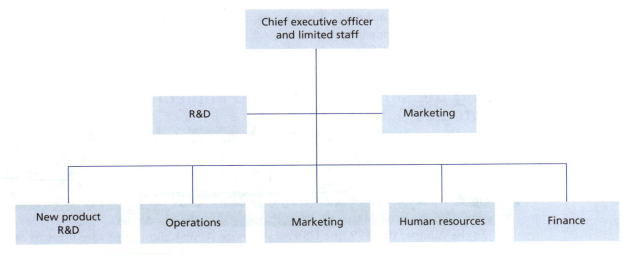

Notes:
- Marketing is the main function for keeping track of new product ideas
- New product R&D is emphasised
- Most functions are decentralised, but R&D and marketing may have centralised staffs that work closely with each other
- Formalisation is limited so that new product ideas can emerge easily and change is more readily accomplished
- Overall structure is organic; job roles are less structured

Using the functional structure to implement the integrated cost leadership/differentiation strategy

To implement the integrated cost leadership/differentiation strategy, companies seek to provide value which differs from that offered by the cost leader and the leading differentiated firm. They must be able to offer more differentiated features than the current cost leader. They must also be more able in the cost area than the leading differentiated firm.

The integrated cost leadership/differentiation strategy is being formulated more frequently, especially by global firms, even though it is difficult to implement. The primary reason for this is that the strategic and tactical actions required to implement the cost leadership and the differentiation strategies are not the same. For example, to achieve the low-cost position, relative to rivals, emphasis is placed on production and manufacturing process engineering, with infrequent product changes. In contrast, to achieve a differentiated position, marketing and new-product R&D are emphasised. But, as explained earlier, the structural characteristics used to emphasise new-product development differ from those needed to stress process engineering. Thus, to implement the integrated cost leadership/differentiation strategy successfully, managers are challenged to form an organisational structure that allows the development of differentiated product features, while costs, relative to those of rivals, are reduced. Often, the functional structure has to be supplemented by horizontal coordination, such as cross-functional teams and a strong organisational culture, to implement this strategy effectively.

Toyota Motor Corporation has been able to be a world leader in the automobile industry primarily because of its ability to implement cost leadership and differentiation simultaneously.[52] The key to Toyota's success has been the differentiated design and manufacturing process that the company has implemented concurrently through its integrated product design process. Toyota does this first by mapping the design space and defining feasible regions of overlap for product and process design. Second, it looks for intersections of feasible sets for this overlap. Finally, Toyota establishes the feasibility of the overlapping design before committing to it. Overall, comparing the Toyota system to others, one author concluded: 'Toyota considers a broader range of possible designs and delays certain decisions longer than other automotive companies, yet has what may be the fastest and most efficient vehicle development cycles in the industry.'[53]

Using the simple structure to implement focused strategies

As noted earlier, many focused strategies – strategies through which a firm concentrates on serving the unique needs of a narrow part or scope of the industry – are implemented most effectively through the simple structure. At some point, however, the increased sales revenues resulting from success necessitate changing from a simple to a functional structure. The challenge for managers is to recognise when a structural change is required to coordinate and control the firm's increasingly complex operations.

In the summer of 1999, the US Postal Service (USPS) allowed private firms to offer postage over the Internet. This regulatory change has spawned a number of small Internet operations, including Stamps.com, E-Stamp and Neopost's Simply Postage. These companies allow a firm to print USPS-verified address labels on envelopes. The Postal Service is targeting 22 million home offices and 7.5 million small businesses with fewer than 100 employees. Although there are likely to be other start-ups and new entrants, because the market potential of these firms is high, they will have to adjust their structures as growth occurs. However, at present, they have flexible operations with low levels of specialisation and formalisation associated with the simple structure.[54]

Movement to the multi-divisional structure

The above-average returns gained through the successful implementation of a business-level strategy often result in diversification of the firm's operations. This diversification can take the form of offering different products (product diversification) or offering the same or additional products in other markets (market diversification). As explained in Chapter 6, increased product or market diversification demands that firms formulate a corporate-level strategy, as well as business-level strategies for individual units or divisions. With greater diversification, the simple and functional structures must be discarded in favour of the more complex, yet increasingly necessary, multi-divisional structure.

Implementing corporate-level strategies: Organisational structure and controls

Effective use of the multi-divisional structure helps firms to implement their corporate-level strategy (diversification). In this section, we describe three M-form variations (see Figure 11.4) that are required to implement the related-constrained, related-linked and unrelated diversification strategies.

Figure 11.4 | Three variations of the multi-divisional structure

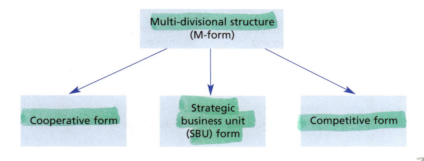

Using the cooperative form to implement the related-constrained strategy

To implement the related-constrained strategy, firms use the cooperative form of the multi-divisional structure. The **cooperative form** is an organisational structure that uses many integration devices and horizontal human resource practices to foster cooperation and integration among the firm's divisions. The cooperative form (see Figure 11.5) emphasises horizontal links and relationships more than the other two variations of the multi-divisional structure described later in the chapter. Cooperation among divisions that are formed around either products or markets served is necessary to realise economies of scope and to facilitate the transfer of skills.[55] Increasingly, it is important for these links to allow and support the sharing of a range of strategic assets, including employees' 'know-how', as well as tangible assets such as facilities and methods of operation.[56]

To facilitate cooperation among divisions that are either vertically integrated or related through the sharing of strategic assets, some organisational functions (for example, human resource management, R&D and marketing) are centralised at the corporate level. Work completed in these centralised functions is managed by the firm's central administrative, or headquarters, office. When the central office's efforts allow commonalities among the firm's divisions to be exploited in ways that yield a cost or differentiation advantage (or both) in the divisions, compared to undiversified rivals, the cooperative form of the multi-divisional structure is a source of competitive advantage for the diversified firm.[57]

Besides centralisation, a number of structural integration links are used to foster cooperation among divisions in firms implementing the related-constrained diversification strategy. Frequent direct contact between division managers encourages and supports cooperation and the sharing of strategic assets. Sometimes, liaison roles are established in each division to reduce the amount of time division managers spend facilitating the integration and coordination of their units' work. Temporary teams or

Figure 11.5 | Cooperative form of the multi-divisional structure for implementation of a related-constrained strategy

Notes:
- Structural integration devices create tight links among all divisions
- Corporate office emphasises centralised strategic planning, human resources, and marketing to foster cooperation between divisions
- R&D is likely to be centralised
- Rewards are subjective and tend to emphasise overall corporate performance, in addition to divisional performance
- Culture emphasises cooperative sharing

task forces may also be formed around projects and may require the efforts of many people from separate divisions to achieve desired levels of divisional coordination. Formal integration departments might be established in firms requiring the work of temporary teams or task forces on a continuous basis. Ultimately, a matrix organisation may evolve in firms implementing the related-constrained strategy. A *matrix organisation* is an organisational structure in which there is a dual structure combining both functional specialisation and business product or project specialisation.[58] Although complicated, effective matrix structures can lead to improved coordination among a firm's various divisions.[59]

As is implied by the horizontal procedures used for coordination that we described earlier, information processing must increase dramatically to implement the related-constrained diversification strategy successfully. But because cooperation among divisions implies a loss of managerial autonomy, division managers may not readily commit themselves to the type of integrative information-processing activities demanded by this organisational structure. Moreover, coordination among divisions sometimes results in an unequal flow of positive outcomes to divisional managers. In other words, when managerial rewards are based at least in part on the performance of individual divisions, the manager of the division that is able to derive the greatest marketplace benefit from the sharing of the firm's strategic assets might be viewed as receiving relative gains at others' expense. In these instances, performance evaluations are emphasised to facilitate the sharing of strategic assets. Furthermore, using reward systems that emphasise overall company performance, besides outcomes achieved by individual divisions, helps to overcome problems associated with the cooperative form.

The use of the cooperative form of the multi-divisional structure is illustrated in the Strategic Focus. Notice that IBM uses the related-constrained diversification strategy, which results in a match between strategy and structure within the firm.

Strategic Focus Corporate

IBM implements the cooperative M-form structure, facilitating e-commerce services

Before Louis Gerstner took over the CEO position at IBM, John Akers had a strategic plan to break up IBM into a loosely affiliated network of 'Baby Blues' built around different products. However, when Gerstner became the CEO, he determined that the company would be better off by keeping its businesses together. He felt that the corporation could offer the customers a lot more than just its name. Over the years since Gerstner has taken over, IBM has become the world's largest purveyor of technology services. The idea to pursue services was a 'bet the company' decision made in 1993 that's paying off significantly now. Through its vast array of services and products, IBM 'counsels customers on technology strategy, helps them prepare for mishaps, runs all their computer operations, develops their applications, procures their supplies, trains their employees, and even gets them into the dot com realm'.

IBM has always been a digital solutions company. However, in the past, its solutions depended primarily on its hardware products as well as software. Now services are driving growth in the company. In 1998, services accounted for 28 per cent of revenues. By 2003, it is expected that 46 per cent of IBM's revenues will be derived from services. 'It used to be that technology was strategic for IBM and services helped to sell technology. Now services-plus-software is more strategic. Services are IBM's primary form of account control.'

Outsourcing is a primary service business for IBM, but it is a low-margin business in the services area. Few customers trust IBM with full-scale reengineering projects and prefer to use such as Andersen Consulting, Pricewaterhouse Coopers and Ernst & Young. Thus, Sam Palmisano, who heads the services business, aims to move IBM's service focus into higher-margin businesses.

The whole system of interrelated businesses at IBM is held together by a cooperative M-form structure focused on serving e-commerce customers and providing total-solution services. The culture was supported early on by Gerstner, who shifted 25 per cent of IBM's R&D budget into Internet and e-commerce projects. He declared that every IBM product or service must be Internet-friendly. He also pushed the company's software development towards the Java programming language, which runs much of the software on the Web. Furthermore, he tried to tie Lotus Notes software tightly to the Web as well.

Gerstner saw early not just that the Internet was an information superhighway, but that it was about business doing transactions, not looking up information. Moreover, Gerstner is not just out to help set up e-tailers or cyber shops; rather, he is focusing on creating Internet operations in supply chain management, consumer service, logistics, procurement, and even training, using Web technology. He divides companies into two types: 'those who are above the e-line and those who are below it'. Those who are above, such as Charles Schwab, Dell and others who fully manage much of their operations through e-commerce techniques, have not been the traditional customers of IBM. Those who are below the e-line, IBM's traditional customer group, use IBM services and products more often than those above the line. Accordingly, IBM is focusing on getting into the latter businesses.

For instance, although Sun and Hewlett-Packard have significantly more market share than IBM in Web servers, IBM has maintained a lead in mainframe computers that continues to grow. The problem with mainframes, however, is that their cost is coming down rapidly, which will cut into IBM's margins. For now, though, IBM's margins in mainframes are quite good, although revenues are staying relatively flat. IBM is hoping that its services business will foster better sales in Web servers.

With IBM's ability to implement its strategy through its cooperative M-form structure and its cooperative culture, it is likely to be successful at the next challenge of Internet products. This market appears to be developing a strategy centred on devices, software and services that make the Internet accessible anywhere, any time. It may be through a cell phone or a Palm device. To get the right people to develop these new Internet products, IBM has developed a Web design office in Atlanta, Georgia, that it will try to use to change its old-style culture into more of an Internet culture. The Atlanta centre allows dogs, which are camped out alongside Web designers, and has an iguana. A ping-pong table doubles as a conference table, and there is a billiard table on an upper floor where workers can go to clear their heads after long hours toiling at their computers.

Like Intel and Cisco, IBM has invested US$60 million in venture capital funding. For instance, IBM invested US$45 million in Internet Capital Group, a holding company that funds B2B Internet companies. This investment took place just before the Internet Capital Group's public offering and is now worth US$619 million. Thus, not only has IBM done a good job in focusing its organisation and culture on Internet businesses, but it is also seeking to adjust this culture so that its future-oriented research centre and also its venture capital fund will create new businesses for the corporation. Truly, the company could be renamed 'Internet Business Machines'.

Sources: *IBM Home Page*, 2000, 1 March: www.ibm.com; P. Burroughs, D. Roks and D. Brady, 1999, 'Inside IBM: Internet business machines', 13 December, *Business Week e.biz*, eb20–eb38; D. Kirkpatrick, 1999, 'IBM: From Big Blue dinosaur to e-business animal', *Fortune*, 26 April, pp. 116–27; D. Lyons, 1999, 'Big iron, small iron', *Forbes.com*, 19 April: www.forbes.com; I. Sager, 1999, 'Big Blue at your service', *Business Week*, 21 June, pp. 130–2.

When there are fewer links or less constrained links among a firm's divisions, the related-linked diversification strategy should be implemented. As explained next, this can be done through the use of the strategic business unit form of the multi-divisional structure.

Using the strategic business unit form to implement the related-linked strategy

The strategic business unit (SBU) form of the multi-divisional structure consists of at least three levels, the top level being corporate headquarters, the next, SBU groups, and the final level, divisions grouped by relatedness (through either a product or a geographic market) within each SBU (see Figure 11.6). The firm's business portfolio is organised into those divisions related to one another within an SBU group and those unrelated to any division in other SBU groups. Thus, divisions within groups are related, but groups are largely unrelated to each other. Within the SBU structure, divisions with similar products or technologies are organised to achieve synergy. Each SBU is a profit centre that is controlled by the firm's headquarters office. An important benefit of this structural form is that individual decision makers, within their strategic business unit, look to SBU executives rather than headquarters personnel for strategic guidance.

Nobuyuki Idei, CEO of Sony, is taking the opportunity to restructure the great Japanese consumer products firm, given the trend towards restructuring in Japan. In fact, the job cuts have led to a postwar unemployment peak of 4.4 per cent in 1999. While Sony has had US$50 million in revenues due to flat-screen TVs, digital video cameras and many other differentiated products, its margins have not been significant relative to revenues. For example, Sony's PlayStation video games have contributed only 15 per cent of Sony's total sales, but make up 42 per cent of its operating profits. Accordingly, Idei

Figure 11.6 | SBU form of the multi-divisional structure for implementation of a related-linked strategy

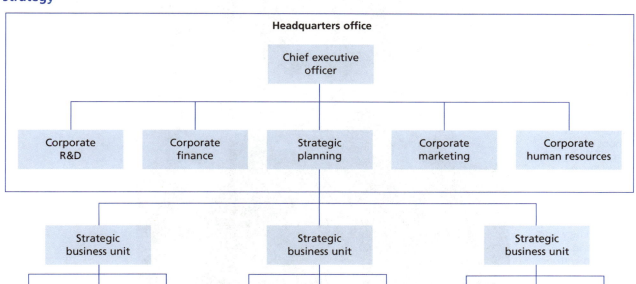

Notes:
- Structural integration among divisions within SBUs, but independence across SBUs
- Strategic planning may be the most prominent function in headquarters for managing the strategic planning approval process of SBUs for the chief executive officer
- Each SBU may have its own budget for staff to foster integration
- Corporate headquarters staff serve as consultants to SBUs and divisions, rather than having direct input to product strategy, as in the cooperative form

has been trying to shift the firm to make better use of software (for example, music, films and games) in its televisions and audio gear in order to increase Sony's profitability. To accomplish this, Sony's 10 internal companies are being regrouped 'into four autonomous units focused on products and networks'. In addition, Idei will cut headquarters staff from about 2 500 to several hundred over the next few years. Sony's global workforce of 170 000 will be cut by 10 per cent, and factories will go from 70 to 55 by the year 2003. The restructuring now matches the SBU structure with its 10 internal companies organised into four strategic business units. Each such unit will receive research funds and will be required to justify its existence on the basis of profitability. The units will also be required to cooperate among themselves within each strategic group.

The organisational structure of large diversified firms such as Sony can be complex. Their complexity is a reflection of the size and diversity of a diversified firm's operations. Consider the case of General Electric (GE). Implementing the related-linked corporate-level strategy, the firm called for integration among divisions within SBUs, but independence between SBUs. GE managers expect to be able to 'walk, think and talk' like a small firm and to make decisions and introduce innovative products at a pace that is equivalent to its smaller competitors.[60]

Recently, GE's structure featured 10 major SBUs. The company's Aircraft Engines business unit is the world's largest producer of large and small jet engines for commercial and military aircraft. The Appliances business unit produces Monogram, Profile Performance, Profile, GE and Hotpoint brands, as well as several private-label brands. Capital Services, a wholly owned subsidiary of GE, is a diversified financial services company that creates comprehensive solutions to increase client productivity and efficiency. Industrial Systems is a leading supplier of products used to distribute, protect, operate and control electrical power and equipment, as well as a supplier of services for commercial and industrial applications. The Lighting business unit is a leading supplier

Perhaps the bravest of Telstra's recent strategic moves is a major entry into the Asian market via an alliance with an offshoot of Hong Kong's richest family, the Li's. The risk is high, but the possible payoffs are attractive in an increasingly competitive industry dominated by world-scale telcos in comparison with which Telstra is a minnow.

of lighting products for global consumer, commercial and industrial markets. Medical Systems is a world leader in medical diagnostic imaging technology, services and healthcare productivity. NBC is a diverse global media company owned by GE. NBC in turn owns and operates the NBC Television Network, as well as 13 television stations. In the United States, NBC owns CNBC, operates MSNBC in partnership with Microsoft, and maintains equity interests in the A&E (Arts and Entertainment) Television Network and the History Channel. NBC also has an interest in Internet and new media businesses, holding equity stakes in CNET, Talk City, iVillage, Telescan, Hoover's and 24/7 Media. Several of NBC's Internet assets have merged with Snap.com and XOOM.com, Inc. to form NBCi, the seventh-largest Internet site and the first publicly traded Internet company integrated with a major broadcaster. GE's Plastics business unit is a world leader in versatile, high-performance engineered plastics used in the computer, electronics, data storage, office equipment, automotive, building and construction, and other industries. Power Systems is a world leader in the design, manufacture and servicing of gas, steam and hydroelectric turbines and generators for power production, pipeline and industrial applications. Transportation Systems manufactures more than half of the diesel freight locomotives in North America, and its locomotives operate in 75 countries worldwide.[61]

For firms as large as GE, structural flexibility is as important as strategic flexibility. (Recall the discussion in Chapter 5 indicating a need for firms to have strategic flexibility.) Through a combination of strategic and structural flexibility, GE is able to respond rapidly to opportunities as they emerge throughout the world. Amidst the company's flexibility, Welch sets precise performance targets and monitors them throughout the year. Thus, GE is run such that the bureaucracy is removed so that the company has a small-firm culture, but managers are held accountable by a leader who seeks to understand its many businesses.[62] In sum, one analyst noted that GE is not so much a collection of businesses as it is 'a repository of information and expertise that can be leveraged over a huge installed base'.[63]

Using the competitive form to implement the unrelated diversification strategy

Firms implementing the unrelated diversification strategy seek to create value through efficient internal capital allocations or by restructuring, buying and selling businesses.[64] The competitive form of the multi-divisional structure is used to implement the unrelated diversification strategy. The **competitive form** is an organisational structure in which the controls used emphasise competition between separate (usually unrelated) divisions for corporate capital. To realise benefits from efficient resource allocation, divisions must have a separate, identifiable profit performance and must be held accountable for such performance. The internal capital market requires organisational arrangements that emphasise *competition* rather than *cooperation* between divisions.[65]

To emphasise competitiveness among divisions, the headquarters office maintains an arm's-length relationship and does not intervene in divisional affairs, except to audit operations and discipline managers whose divisions perform poorly. In this situation, the headquarters office sets rate-of-return targets and monitors the divisional performance.[66] It allocates cash flow on a competitive basis, rather than automatically returning cash to the division that produced it. The competitive form of the multi-divisional structure is illustrated in Figure 11.7.

> The competitive form is an organisational structure in which the controls used emphasise competition between separate (usually unrelated) divisions for corporate capital.

Figure 11.7 | Competitive form of the multi-divisional structure for implementation of an unrelated strategy

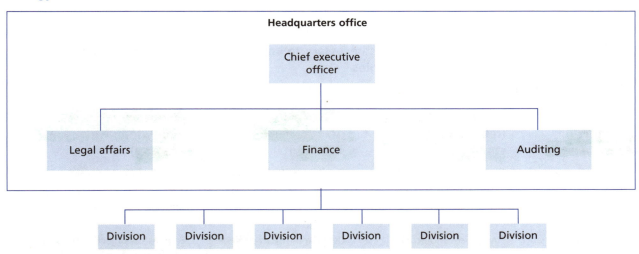

Notes:
- Corporate headquarters has a small staff
- Finance and auditing are the most prominent functions in the headquarters to manage cash flow and ensure the accuracy of performance data coming from divisions
- The legal affairs function becomes important when the firm acquires or divests assets
- Divisions are independent and separate for financial evaluation purposes
- Divisions retain strategic control, but cash is managed by the corporate office
- Divisions compete for corporate resources

One of Australia's most diversified companies, Pacific Dunlop, used the competitive form of the multi-divisional structure to implement its ongoing diversification strategy. The company's basic strategy was to market a multitude of brand-name consumer products as a mass retailer, with an emphasis on maximising their brand's equity and profitability.

Committed to growth by acquisition and divestment, Pacific Dunlop either added or removed product lines to each of the firm's six independent divisions. For example, to augment the success of their rubber products division (driven largely by the success of the Ansell Rubber Company), Pacific Dunlop acquired Smith & Nephew plc (a medical glove manufacturer) to further enhance their competency in the management within this industry. Similarly, in order to improve the management of their flagging foods division (created with the purchase of Petersville Sleigh in 1991), Pacific Dunlop acquired the Plumrose Food Company. Alternatively, Pacific Dunlop divested its GNB Batteries holdings due to its poor performance within the group, allowing the company access to funds that could potentially be used to greater effect elsewhere in the business.

In sum, there are three major forms of the multi-divisional structure, each of which is related to a particular corporate-level strategy. Table 11.1 shows the characteristics of these structures. Differences are seen in the degree of centralisation, the focus of the performance appraisal, the horizontal structures (integrating mechanisms) and the incentive compensation schemes necessary to implement the three corporate-level strategies – related-constrained, related-linked and unrelated diversification – successfully. The most centralised and most costly organisational form is the cooperative structure. The least centralised, with the lowest bureaucratic costs, is the competitive structure. The SBU structure requires partial centralisation and involves some of the mechanisms necessary to implement the relatedness between divisions. Also, the divisional incentive compensation awards are allocated according to both SBUs and corporate performance. In the competitive structure, the most important criterion is divisional performance.

Table 11.1 | Characteristics of the structures necessary to implement the related-constrained, related-linked and unrelated diversification strategies

OVERALL STRUCTURAL FORM

Structural characteristics	Cooperative M-form (related-constrained strategy)[a]	SBU M-form (related-linked strategy)[a]	Competitive M-form (unrelated diversification strategy)[a]
Centralisation of operation	Centralised at corporate office	Partially centralised (in SBUs)	Decentralised to divisions
Use of integrating mechanisms	Extensive	Moderate	Nonexistent
Divisional performance appraisal	Emphasises subjective criteria	Uses a mixture of subjective and objective criteria	Emphasises objective (financial or ROI) criteria
Divisional incentive compensation	Linked to overall corporate performance	Mixed linkage to corporate, SBU, and divisional performance	Linked to divisional performance

[a] Strategy implemented with structural form.

Earlier in the chapter, we indicated that, once formed, an organisational structure could influence a firm's efforts to implement its current strategy and the selection of future strategies. Using the multi-divisional structure as the foundation for the discussion, the next section examines the relationship between structure and strategy.

The effect of structure on strategy

As explained earlier, the M-form is a structural innovation that is intended to help managers deal with the coordination and control problems created by increasing product and market variety. Once established, however, the M-form structure has the potential to influence the firm's diversification strategy.[67] Strong and appropriate incentives that encourage managers to pursue additional marketplace opportunities, coupled with improved accountability and superior internal resource allocations from the corporate office, may stimulate additional diversification, which, in turn, can result in greater returns on the firm's investments.[68] Eventually, however, there is a tendency for the M-form to encourage inefficient levels of diversification. Following a comprehensive review, some researchers noted that there is a growing body of evidence which suggests that adoption of the M-form structure facilitates the pursuit of inefficient diversification.[69] Again, this cause–effect relationship – that is, the influence of the M-form on a firm's pursuit of additional diversification – is not inherently negative; the complicating factor is that at some point, the additional amounts of diversification stimulated by the M-form become inefficient, thereby reducing the firm's strategic competitiveness and its returns.

Other research suggests that once the M-form influences the pursuit of more diversification that yields inefficient strategic outcomes, the relationship between structure and strategy may reverse direction.[70] In other words, firms that become inefficiently diversified implement strategies that result in less efficient levels of diversification. One study found, for example, that half of the diversified acquisitions made by unrelated diversified firms were later divested because of their lack of focus.[71] Pacific Dunlop and Ansett provide an excellent example of just such corporate behaviour. Another discovered that a decrease in the diversified scope of M-form firms was associated with an improvement in shareholder wealth. This finding, too, suggests that these firms' diversification had become inefficient.[72]

An example of a firm that recently changed its diversification strategy to increase its efficiency and strategic competitiveness is Sony Corporation, as described earlier. As Sony tied its array of electronic product offerings to software and content, it shifted its organisational structure to the SBU M-form, to create better links between its diversified set of businesses. Our discussion now turns to an explanation of organisational structures used to implement the three international strategies explained in Chapter 8.

Implementing international strategies: Organisational structure and controls

Although important for many firms, competing successfully in global markets is perhaps especially critical for large companies. General Motors, for instance, is merging its manufacturing of cars and trucks in the United States. 'For GM, the merger is the latest step in a long series of moves aimed at taking a company that for decades had been run largely as individual fiefdoms into a single global organization.'[73] The move is designed to integrate the work of engineers with that of manufacturing and marketing personnel. International strategies such as those chosen by GM's top-level executives cannot be implemented successfully without using the proper organisational structure.[74]

Using the worldwide geographic area structure to implement the multi-domestic strategy

The *multi-domestic strategy* is a strategy in which strategic and operating decisions are decentralised to business units in each country in order to tailor products to local markets. However, it is sometimes difficult for firms to know how local their products should or can become. Lands' End, for example, is one of the American mail-order firms being lured by the promise of the European market for its products and services. Interested in adapting to local preferences, the firm's director of international operations observed that the most difficult part of achieving this objective is to know in which areas to be local.[75]

Firms implementing the multi-domestic strategy often attempt to isolate themselves from global competitive forces by establishing protected market positions or by competing in industry segments that are most affected by differences among local countries. The worldwide geographic area structure (see Figure 11.8) is used to implement the multi-domestic strategy. The **worldwide geographic area structure** emphasises national interests and facilitates managers' efforts to satisfy local or cultural differences.

> The **worldwide geographic area structure** emphasises national interests and facilitates managers' efforts to satisfy local or cultural differences.

Figure 11.8 | Worldwide geographic area structure for implementation of a multi-domestic strategy

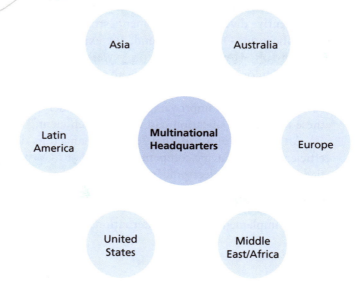

Notes:
- The perimeter circles indicate decentralisation of operations
- Emphasis is on differentiation by local demand to fit an area or country culture
- Corporate headquarters coordinates financial resources among independent subsidiaries
- The organisation is like a decentralised federation

The Body Shop, which pioneered the trend towards nature represented by 'green' cosmetics, has been changing its centralised structure to create a stronger focus on regions of the world. This restructuring to the worldwide geographic area structure was proposed after Patrick Cournay took over the CEO position from the company's founder, Anita Roddick. The change includes 'shifting centralized management from the company's base in Littlehampton [in the United Kingdom] to regional units in the U.K., Europe, the Americas and Australasia.'[76] Along with the structural change, The Body Shop is changing its approach to sourcing from local manufacturers linked to the regional centres. However, these manufacturers 'would have to uphold the company's ban on animal testing, and other "green" guidelines'.

Because implementing the multi-domestic strategy requires little coordination between different country markets, there is no need for integrating mechanisms among divisions in the worldwide geographic area structure. Hence, formalisation is low, and coordination among units in a firm's worldwide geographic area structure is often informal. Because each European country has a distinct culture, the multi-domestic strategy and the associated worldwide geographic structure were a natural outgrowth of the multicultural European marketplace. This type of structure often was developed originally by friends and family members of the main business who were sent as expatriates into foreign countries to develop the independent country subsidiary. The relationship to corporate headquarters by divisions took place through informal communication among 'family members'.[77]

The primary disadvantage of the multi-domestic strategy implemented through a worldwide geographic area structure is its inability to create global efficiency. As the emphasis on lower-cost products has increased in international markets, the need to pursue worldwide economies of scale and scope has also increased. These changes have fostered the use of the global strategy.

Using the worldwide product divisional structure to implement the global strategy

The *global strategy* is a strategy in which standardised products are offered across country markets and the firm's home office dictates competitive strategy. International economies of scale and scope are sought and emphasised when the international strategy is implemented. Because of the important relationship between economies of scale and scope, on the one hand, and successful implementation of the global strategy, on the other, some activities of the firm's organisational functions are sourced to the most effective worldwide providers.

The worldwide product divisional structure (see Figure 11.9) is used to implement the global strategy. The **worldwide product divisional structure** is an organisational form in which decision-making authority is centralised in the worldwide division headquarters to coordinate and integrate decisions and actions among disparate divisional business units. This form is the organisational structure of choice for rapidly growing firms seeking to manage their diversified product lines effectively.[78] Integrating mechanisms also create effective coordination through mutual adjustments in personal interactions. Among such mechanisms are direct contact between managers, liaison roles between departments, temporary task forces or permanent teams, and integrating roles. As managers participate in cross-country transfers, they become socialised in the philosophy of managing an integrated strategy through a worldwide product divisional structure. A shared vision of the firm's strategy and structure is developed through standardised policies and procedures (formalisation) that facilitate the implementation of this organisational form.

Two primary disadvantages of the global strategy and its accompanying worldwide product divisional structure are the difficulty involved with coordinating decisions and actions across country borders and the inability to respond quickly and effectively to local needs and preferences. As is explained in the Strategic Focus, Procter & Gamble is restructuring in order to use the worldwide product divisional structure to implement the global strategy. Notice that this structure is expected to contribute to the firm's efforts to improve its international operations and growth opportunities.

> The **worldwide product divisional structure** is an organisational form in which decision-making authority is centralised in the worldwide division headquarters to coordinate and integrate decisions and actions among disparate divisional business units.

Figure 11.9 | Worldwide product divisional structure for implementation of a global strategy

Notes:
- The headquarters circle indicates centralisation to coordinate information flow among worldwide products
- Corporate headquarters uses many intercoordination devices to facilitate global economies of scale and scope
- Corporate headquarters also allocates financial resources in a cooperative way
- The organisation is like a centralised federation

Strategic Focus International

Procter & Gamble restructures and implements a worldwide product divisional structure

Durk Jager, the CEO at Procter & Gamble (P&G), has implemented a restructuring plan to facilitate increased growth, the lack of which has been a problem at P&G. When P&G introduced Pampers disposable nappies in the 1970s, it achieved 70 per cent of the US market. In 1998, P&G's share of the nappies market was down to near 40 per cent, while that of Kimberly Clark, P&G's dominant competitor, was slightly above that mark. Also in the 1970s, P&G's Ivory brand soap had just under 50 per cent of the market. In 1998, Unilever's Dove brand soap had overtaken P&G's dominant share. Similarly, Crest toothpaste was recently overtaken by the Colgate brand in market share. These three dominant brands signal the basic problem at P&G: the company has stopped growing; revenues have flattened out.

To overcome this problem, P&G has reorganised its structure into seven worldwide product divisions, including baby care, beauty care, fabric and home care, feminine protection, food and beverage, and tissues and towels. Previously, P&G was organised regionally through a multi-domestic structure. Besides global product business units, P&G will have eight market development organisations that will work regionally to help prepare and market products created and managed by each global business unit. Jager hopes that this approach will move

P&G from an obsession with perfection and risk aversion to one of risk taking. The structure will have to keep successful products (such as the laundry detergent Tide) growing while expanding globally and producing new brand-category products. P&G has had many decades of rigid conformity in its culture, which, over time, has squelched entrepreneurship, creative types and freethinkers, who were labelled 'troublemakers'. Because of this culture, P&G may have lost some of the best business minds available. For instance, Bob Herbold at Microsoft began his career at P&G. Now the company hopes that the decentralisation to global product division structures will provide incentives for growth.

More than anything, P&G needs new products. The firm has a number of products with high potential, such as Termacare, a portable heat wrap; Fit, an antibacterial fruit-and-vegetable cleanser; Febreze, a spray-on odour eliminator; and its most recent and important entry, Dryel, a home dry-cleaning product that has been tested substantially and is now in supermarkets. P&G spends about 4 per cent of its sales annually on R&D. Fifteen per cent of its R&D budget is now devoted to major new projects involving products. Jager expects new products to generate another US$1 billion in sales a year. For instance, he expects Dryel sales to reach US$500 million, making it as big as Downy or Bounce. If these products are successful, they may create new global product divisions.

As part of its pursuit of growth, through an initiative of its beauty care division, P&G has launched a new website called reflect.com. The goal of this site was to introduce makeup and shampoos so personalised that no two individuals would get the same items. This strategy is similar to Dell's, which customises its brand-name PCs. However, rather than research the issue itself, P&G chose to team with Institutional Venture Partners, a venture capital firm famous for backing Internet pioneers such as Excite, Inc. The Silicon Valley venture capital firm was used to closing a deal in a day, but with P&G lawyers involved, it took three weeks. Nonetheless, P&G hopes it has found a way to turn one of the nation's largest corporations into a significant on-line Internet competitor. The venture will be a learning experience for P&G. None of P&G's brand-name lines, such as Cover Girl and Oil of Olay, will be for sale on this site, which will sell only custom-made cosmetics. Women can log on and craft their own beauty products that will be individually mixed and packaged and shipped to their homes. P&G's sales of cosmetics on-line may be a significant shock to other on-line consumer product sellers, such as drugstore.com, ibeauty.com and gloss.com.

P&G cannot afford to annoy its powerful retailer distributors, such as Wal-Mart, through this on-line selling initiative. Thus, reflect.com is only a small step in direct on-line selling. However, once someone figures out how to sell directly to somebody's home, the initiative may spread to other on-line projects by other global product divisions. Such initiatives are better carried out by global product divisions than by a geographic area structure, because on-line selling is not restricted by geographic markets.

In sum, P&G is seeking to reorganise itself into a worldwide product divisional structure wherein sales will be driven by growth in standard products, as well as new products such as Dryel. It is hoped that the 'most far-reaching changes in the history of P&G' will result in 'bigger innovation, faster speed to market, and greater growth'. Along with this process, P&G is eliminating about 15 000 jobs and shutting 10 factories. Thus, not only is P&G trying to boost increased revenues through the growth of successful, innovative products, but it is also seeking to boost its earning power through reduced operating costs.

Sources: K. Brooker, 2000, 'Plugging the leaks at P&G', *Fortune*, 21 February, pp. 44–8; N. Deogun and E. Nelson, 2000, 'P&G is on the move', *Wall Street Journal*, 24 January, pp. A1, A16; *Procter & Gamble Home Page*, 2000, 1 March: www.pg.com; K. Brooker, 1999, 'Can Procter & Gamble change its culture, protect its market share and find the next tide?', *Fortune*, 26 April, pp. 146–52; G. Fairclough, 1999, 'P&G to slash 15,000 jobs, shut ten plants', *Wall Street Journal*, 10 June, pp. A3, A4; P. Galuszka, J. Ott and D. Harbrecht, 1999, 'Procter and Gamble is set to shake itself up', *Business Week Online*, 4 June: www.businessweek.com; L. Himelstein and P. Galuszka, 1999, 'P&G gives birth to a web baby', *Business Week Online*, 27 September: www.businessweek.com; E. Neuborne, 1999, 'P&G could follow in Dell's net footsteps', *Business Week Online*, 27 September: www.businessweek.com.

Using the combination structure to implement the transnational strategy

The *transnational strategy* is an international strategy through which a firm seeks to provide the local responsiveness that is the focus of the multi-domestic strategy and to achieve the global efficiency that is the focus of the global strategy. The **combination structure** has characteristics and mechanisms that result in an emphasis on both geographic and product structures; thus, it has the multi-domestic strategy's geographic area focus and the global strategy's product focus. Ford is pursuing the combination structure to manage its international operations, as illustrated in the Strategic Focus.

> The combination structure has characteristics and mechanisms that result in an emphasis on both geographic and product structures.

Strategic Focus International

Ford implements the combination structure

Jacques Nasser, recently promoted to CEO at Ford, is seeking to implement a new structural arrangement in the firm that is aimed not only at changing the company's reporting relationships, but also at altering the mind-set of every employee. His vision is to reinvent the industrial giant into 'a growth-oriented consumer powerhouse for the twenty-first century'. As the battle for global market share continues, and only a few automobile giants are expected to emerge at the end of the competition, Nasser wants his organisation to be a nimble player in the global environment. 'He envisions a company in which executives run independent units cut loose from stifling bureaucracy and held more accountable for success and failure.'

Nasser started his career in the Australian division of Ford, which he left in 1987 to run a struggling unit in the Philippines. Although his boss in Australia warned him that he would never come back from the Philippines, Nasser did return to help turn the Australian unit around in 1990. Next, he moved into Europe and was able to turn its large organisational unit around as well. In 1994, Nasser became the head of product development at Ford's Dearborn headquarters. By that time, he had become skilled at a nimble entrepreneurial decision-making style that was developed in peripheral Ford organisational units, where there was much more opportunity for making entrepreneurial decisions without a lot of bureaucratic oversight from headquarters. His focus today is to regenerate Ford's employees such that a new mind-set emerges in which this entrepreneurial spirit allows Ford to be a much more decentralised and value-creating enterprise (like a multi-domestic structure). Nasser also views the market as valuing a global approach to business, where the company's units, divisions, teams, functions and regions are all tightly integrated and synchronised across borders (like the world product structure).

Traditionally, however, Ford has been organised into a 'collection of fiefdoms'. Nasser suggests that this structure is due to Ford's history, which can be segmented into three stages of evolution. From 1905 to the 1920s, Henry Ford, who focused on building a single car for use throughout the world, ran the organisation. Competition during that period was nonexistent and disorganised. The second period, from the late 1920s through to the late 1950s, was a period of intense nationalism. Accordingly, Ford established companies in the United Kingdom, France, Germany and Australia that built their own vehicles, tended towards nationalistic objectives and were tailored to the policies of the host country. Foreign strategy was implemented through exports from independent European or American operations. The third period, from the 1960s to the 1980s, was a period of regionalism, with the emergence of the

European Common Market and the North American Free Trade Agreement (NAFTA). Countries kept their own political systems and social values, but economic trading blocs were formed. Ford of Europe was fortunate to be evolving during this period. The units inside Ford decreased from 15 to four and competed in separate regions – one each in Europe, the United States, Asia and South America.

Currently, Nasser sees Ford in a fourth stage, in which the internationalisation of capital, communications, economic policy, trade policy, human resources, marketing, advertising and brands are forming around globally oriented markets or systems. Lately, globalisation is not a choice, but is demanded by the current stage of the market. 'You don't make money by downsizing or shutting plants or reducing your product line,' he says. 'You make money by building the company.' Accordingly, he is out to rebuild Ford and change its basic cultural approach through a combination structure that simultaneously matches localisation and global integration in the international automotive environment.

In Nasser's earlier days, the foreign units would get visitors from headquarters who would suggest new ways of thinking and doing things. The local managers would wine and dine them and nod yes at everything the visiting executives said. After the executives returned to Dearborn, the local managers would continue to run their division the way they saw fit. This can no longer be; there must be both decentralisation and centralisation to effect the integration that will meet the demands of the global marketplace. In the 1980s, Ford intended the Escort to be its first global product, and, accordingly, the car was engineered on two continents – North America and Europe. This made it possible to capitalise on global sourcing for components. But because each country wants its own individual variety of product, the advertising and message heard in each country was devised by a different advertising agency in order to get Ford's message across in the local culture. In one country it was a limousine, in another a sports vehicle. In comparison, the Mondeo (otherwise known as the Ford 'Focus' in the United States and Europe), the new Ford compact car, was engineered by one management team in Geneva and launched at one show in Paris. Journalists were brought in from all over the world, and there was only one advertising agency. The journalists who came all drove the Focus on the same roads in the same conditions and got the same technological presentation from the same people. Therefore, they got the same brand and product positioning delivered to them from the same marketing people.

This integration and shift from a fiefdom approach to a combination structure is being implemented through an education program to help facilitate the change in mind-set. Using the GE program built by Jack Welch as a model, Nasser is following a 'teachable point of view', in which a person writes out his or her version for the firm and teaches it to the leaders, who, in turn, teach it to their team members. Then the material becomes not just a manual for doing work, but a vision for why the business is approached the way it is. In the process of implementing the vision, managers and team members change their mind-set about how they have traditionally done their work at the company.

As part of the combination structure, Nasser hopes to package combinations of cars by using similar components, but still maintaining distinct brands. For example, he is seeking to combine the similar components of luxury cars in Lincoln, Jaguar and Volvo, each of which has a different consumer appeal. He expects to do the same in the car divisions of Ford, Mercury and Mazda. This is what Ford has done in its combinations of pickups and sport utility vehicles. Indeed, Ford has even used this platform to move into fancier versions, such as the SUV under the Lincoln brand. Such an approach can create significant savings on parts and drive costs down.

In sum, Ford has implemented the combination structure to change the centralised mind-set into one in which employees are taking more initiative. In addition, Ford is seeking to integrate across businesses to match these dual trends found in the automotive industry competitive environment. Besides the change in structure, Ford has brought in a lot of new outside management talent in key areas, such as design, and key regions, such as Europe, to manage the change. The focus is on education, as well as on the structural changes that have taken place. Managers are also receiving more incentive pay when they create value that will help realise an increased stock market capitalisation.

Sources: K. Kerwin, M. Stepanek and D. Welch, 2000, 'At Ford, e-commerce is job 1', *Business Week*, 28 February, pp. 74–8; 'Business: The revolution at Ford', 1999, *Economist*, 7 August, pp. 51–2; K. Kerwin and K. Naughton, 1999, 'Remaking Ford', *Business Week*, 11 October, pp. 132–40; N. Tichy, 1999, 'The teachable point of view: A primer', *Harvard Business Review*, 77(2), pp. 82–3; S. Wetlaufer, 1999, 'Driving change: An interview with Ford Motor Company's Jacques Nasser', *Harvard Business Review*, 77(2), pp. 77–81.

The fit between the multi-domestic strategy and the worldwide geographic area structure and between the global strategy and the worldwide product divisional structure is apparent. However, when a firm such as BHP seeks to implement both the multi-domestic and the global strategy simultaneously through a combination structure, the appropriate integrating mechanisms for the two structures are less obvious. The structure used to implement the transnational strategy must be simultaneously centralised and decentralised, integrated and non-integrated, and formalised and non-formalised. These seemingly opposite characteristics must be managed by an overall structure that is capable of encouraging all employees to understand the effects of cultural diversity on a firm's operations. Accordingly, there needs to be a strong educational component to change the whole culture of the organisation. If the cultural change is effective, the combination structure should allow the firm to learn how to gain competitive benefits in local economies by adapting its capabilities and core competencies, which often have been developed and nurtured in less culturally diverse competitive environments. As firms globalise and move towards the combination strategy, the idea of a corporate headquarters has become increasingly important in fostering leadership and a shared vision to create a stronger company identity.[79]

Implementing cooperative strategies: Organisational structure and controls

Increasingly, companies are developing multiple, rather than single, joint ventures or strategic alliances to implement cooperative strategies. Furthermore, the global marketplace accommodates many interconnected relationships among firms. Resulting from these relationships are networks of firms competing through an array of cooperative arrangements or alliances.[80] Managed effectively, cooperative arrangements can contribute to each partner's ability to achieve strategic competitiveness and earn above-average returns.

To facilitate the effectiveness of a *strategic network* – a grouping of organisations that has been formed to create value through their participation in an array of cooperative arrangements, such as a strategic alliance – a strategic centre firm may be necessary. A *strategic centre firm* facilitates management of a strategic network. Through its management, the centre firm creates incentives that reduce the probability of any company taking actions that could harm its network partners. Also, the strategic centre firm identifies actions that provide opportunities for each firm to achieve competitive success through its participation in the network.[81] Illustrated in Figure 11.10, the strategic centre firm is vital to the ability of companies to create value and increase their strategic competitiveness. The four critical aspects of the strategic centre firm's function are as follows:

1. *Strategic outsourcing.* The strategic centre firm outsources and partners with more firms than do the other network members. At the same time, the strategic centre firm requires partners to be more than contractors. Partners are expected to solve problems and to initiate competitive courses of action that can be pursued by the network.

2. *Capability.* The strategic centre firm has core competencies that are not shared with all network partners. To increase the network's effectiveness, the strategic centre firm attempts to develop each partner's core competencies and provides incentives for network firms to share their capabilities and competencies with partners.

3. *Technology.* The strategic centre firm manages the development and sharing of technology-based ideas among network partners.

4. *Race to learn.* The strategic centre firm emphasises to its partners that the principal dimensions of competition in competitive environments are between value chains and between networks of value chains. As a result, a strategic network is as strong as its weakest value-chain link and hence seeks to develop a competitive advantage in a primary or a support activity (see Chapter 3). The need for each firm to be strong for the benefit of the entire network encourages a friendly rivalry among the partners to learn rapidly and effectively.[82] The most effective strategic centre firms learn how to manage the learning processes that occur among network members.

Figure 11.10 | A strategic network

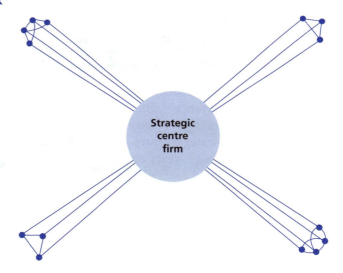

The dominant problem in single-venture cooperative arrangements is the difficulty they pose in controlling innovation and learning. However, a well-managed strategic network can overcome this problem. Therefore, as explained in the rest of this section, the managerial role of the strategic centre firm is critical to the successful implementation of business-level, corporate-level and international cooperative strategies.[83]

Implementing business-level cooperative strategies

As noted in Chapter 9, there are two types of complementary assets at the business level: vertical and horizontal. Vertical complementary strategic alliances are formed more frequently than horizontal alliances. Focused on buyer–supplier relationships, vertical strategic networks usually have a clear strategic centre firm. Japanese vertical *keiretsu*, such as those developed by Toyota Motor Company, are structured this way. Acting as the strategic centre firm, Toyota fashioned its lean production system around a network of supplier firms.[84]

A strategic network of vertical relationships in Japan, such as the network between Toyota and its suppliers, often involves a number of implementation issues. First, the strategic centre firm encourages subcontractors to modernise their facilities and provides them with technical and financial assistance if necessary. Second, it reduces its transaction costs by promoting longer-term contracts with subcontractors, so that supplier partners increase their long-term productivity. This approach is diametrically opposed to that of continually negotiating short-term contracts based on unit pricing. Third, the strategic centre firm enables engineers in upstream companies (suppliers) to have better communication with contractee companies for services. As a result, both the upstream companies and the strategic centre firms become more interdependent and less independent.[85]

The lean production system pioneered by Toyota has been diffused throughout much of the world's automotive industry. However, no automobile producer is able to duplicate the effectiveness and efficiency Toyota derives from the use of this manufacturing system.[86] A key factor accounting for Toyota's ability to derive a competitive advantage from the system is the cost other firms would incur to imitate the structural form used to support Toyota's application. In other words, Toyota's largely proprietary actions as the strategic centre firm in the network it created are actions that competitors are unable to duplicate easily.[87]

In vertical complementary strategic alliances, such as the one between Toyota and its suppliers, the company that should function as the strategic centre firm is obvious. However, this is not always the case with horizontal complementary strategic alliances. For example, the large airline alliances (discussed in a Strategic Focus in Chapter 9) have been quite unstable over the years, and a number of network partners have changed from one network to another or become partners in several networks.[88] Delta Airlines, for instance, recently changed allegiances in Europe from an affiliation with Swissair and Sabena to Air France.[89] This instability is usually caused by continuing rivalries among cooperating partners. A problem common to all of these ventures is the difficulty of selecting the strategic centre firm. The distrust that formed among the network airline companies through years of aggressive competition prevented them from agreeing on which firm should function as the strategic centre of a network. Thus, because who the dominant strategic centre firm should be is not evident in horizontal complementary strategic alliances, they tend to be far less stable than vertical complementary strategic alliances.

Implementing corporate-level cooperative strategies

In some types of corporate-level cooperative strategies, it is difficult to choose a strategic centre firm. For example, it is difficult for a strategic centre firm to emerge in a centralised franchise network. McDonald's is an example.

McDonald's has formed a centralised strategic network in which its corporate office serves as the strategic centre for its franchisees. Recently, McDonald's performance has been mediocre, and a new CEO, Jack M. Greenberg, has been trying to improve the network. However, without an improved menu and delivery system, no success is likely to last. Long a favourite of children, McDonald's does not inspire the same degree of enthusiasm in their parents.

To cope with its problems, McDonald's, as a strategic centre firm, initiated a series of actions. Framed around the need to improve the quality of its products and speed up their delivery, the company developed a 'just-in-time kitchen' concept for use by franchisees.

Chapter 11 Organisational structure and controls

The Australian Rules football code is now a world full of corporate activity, with clubs pursuing the corporate dollar in order to help pay for increasingly expensive player lists. The result is sponsorship deals that earn money and result in better-paid players, corporate boxes, sponsor-labelled jumpers, and logos on grounds. The football seems the same as ever, though.

This new production system is designed to move made-to-order sandwiches to customers without increasing the preparation time. As part of the system, a computer-monitored machine dumps frozen fries into a basket that in turn is dunked into hot oil for cooking. The machine then shakes the fries and dumps them into bins for serving. Simultaneously, robot machines quickly prepare drinks ordered by the customer. Preventing the full use of the system's capabilities, however, was the delay in supplying all franchisees with the equipment. Thus, as the strategic centre firm in its centralised franchise network, McDonald's still faces significant challenges.[90]

Unlike McDonald's corporate-level cooperative strategy, Corning's strategy has resulted in the implementation of a system of diversified strategic alliances that has required the company to implement a decentralised network. Over time, Corning has focused on intangible resources, such as a reliable reputation for being a trustworthy and committed partner, to develop competitively successful strategic partnerships. In this situation, the strategic network has loose connections between joint ventures or multiple centres, although Corning is typically the principal centre. However, the joint ventures are less dependent on the strategic centre firm and, consequently, require less managerial attention from it.[91]

Implementing international cooperative strategies

Competing in a number of countries dramatically increases the complexity associated with attempts to manage successful strategic networks formed through international cooperative strategies.[92] A key reason for this increased complexity is the differences among the various countries' regulatory environments. These differences are especially apparent in more regulated industries, such as telecommunications and air travel.

As shown in Figure 11.11, many large multinational firms form distributed strategic networks with multiple regional strategic centres to manage their array of cooperative arrangements with partner firms.[93] Among the large multinational firms, Swedish firms such as Ericsson (telecommunications exchange equipment) and Electrolux (white goods, washing machines) have strategic centres located in countries throughout the world, instead of only in Sweden, where they are headquartered. Ericsson, for example, is active in more than 100 countries and employs over 85 000 people. Divided into five business areas (public telecommunications, radio communications, business networks, components and microwave systems), the firm has cooperative agreements with companies throughout the world.

Figure 11.11 | A distributed strategic network

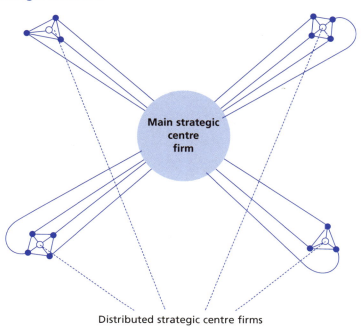

Distributed strategic centre firms

A world leader in electrical engineering, Asea Brown Boveri Group (ABB) is involved with a significant number of distributed strategic networks. Organised into four key business segments (power generation, power transmission and distribution, industrial and building systems, and financial services), ABB features 1 000 companies and 36 separate business areas. With a new global 11-member board of directors representing seven nationalities, ABB considers itself a truly global company, one that does not consider its home to be in any single country. The firm has formed strategic networks in five key world regions: the Americas, Europe (including the former Soviet Union), the Middle East and North Africa, sub-Saharan Africa and the Asia-Pacific rim.[94]

Contemporary organisational structures: A cautionary note

Contemporary organisational structures such as those used to implement international cooperative strategies emerge typically in response to social and technological advances.[95] However, the redesign of organisations throughout a society – indeed, globally – entails losses as well as gains.[96] For example, DuPont, the world's largest chemicals concern, decided recently to scrap most of its central support groups. Primarily, these groups provided information technology, communications and other services to the company's main operating divisions. The gains expected from this decision included the elimination of some corporate bureaucracy and reductions in the amount of time required for product innovations to reach the marketplace. The primary loss associated with the decision concerned personnel: while some workers were transferred to other positions, many lost their jobs.[97]

With new organisational forms, many workers become de-skilled – that is, their abilities are not up to the challenge posed by a new structure that often demands constant innovation and adaptation. This may be the case with some of the workers assigned to new positions within DuPont. The attitude towards learning that is a part of a new organisational form requires that each worker become a self-motivated, continuous learner.[98] At least in the short run, a number of employees lack the level of confidence necessary to participate actively in organisationally sponsored learning experiences. Moreover, the flatter contemporary organisational structures can seem intrusive as a result of their demand for more intense and personal interactions with internal and external stakeholders. Combined, these conditions may create stress for many.

In the face of all this, managers need not abandon efforts to adopt organisational structures that have the greatest probability of facilitating the successful implementation of a firm's strategies. The challenge is to develop and use organisational structures that will enhance the productivity of individuals and the firm.[99]

Summary

- A firm's organisational structure is a formal configuration that largely determines what the firm will do and how it will complete its work. Different structures are required to implement different strategies. A firm's performance increases when strategy and structure are properly matched.
- Business-level strategies are usually implemented through the functional structure. The cost leadership strategy requires a centralised functional structure, one in which manufacturing efficiency and process engineering are emphasised. The differentiation strategy's functional structure decentralises implementation-related decisions, especially those concerned with marketing, to those involved with individual organisational functions. Focus strategies, often used in small firms, require a simple structure until such time that a firm begins to compete in multiple markets or sells multiple products.
- The evolution from the functional structure to the three types of multi-divisional structure (M-form) occurred from the 1920s to the early 1970s. The cooperative M-form, used to implement the related-constrained corporate-level strategy, has a centralised corporate office and extensive integrating mechanisms. Divisional incentives are linked to overall corporate performance. The related-linked SBU M-form structure establishes separate profit centres within the diversified firm. Each profit centre may have divisions offering similar products, but the centres are unrelated to each other. The competitive M-form structure, used to implement the unrelated diversification strategy, is highly decentralised, lacks integrating mechanisms and utilises objective financial criteria to evaluate each unit's performance.
- Initially, an organisational structure is chosen in light of the kind of support required to implement a firm's strategy. Once established, however, structure influences strategy. This is observed most prominently in the M-form structure, stimulating additional diversification in the diversified firm.
- The multi-domestic strategy, implemented through the worldwide geographic area structure, emphasises decentralisation and locates all functional activities in the host country or geographic area. The worldwide product divisional structure is used to implement the global strategy. This structure is centralised in order to coordinate and integrate different functions' activities so as to gain global economies of scope and scale. Decision-making authority is centralised in the firm's worldwide division headquarters.
- The transnational strategy, a strategy through which the firm seeks the local responsiveness of the multi-domestic strategy and the global efficiency of the global strategy, is implemented through the combination structure. Because it must be simultaneously centralised and decentralised,

integrated and non-integrated, and formalised and non-formalised, the combination structure is difficult to organise and manage successfully.
- Increasingly important to competitive success, cooperative strategies are implemented through organisational structures framed around strategic networks. Strategic centre firms are critical to the management of such networks.

Review questions

1. Why is it important that strategy implementation and strategy formulation be integrated carefully?
2. What is the meaning of the following statement? 'In organisations, there is a consistent path of structure following strategy and then strategy following structure.'
3. What organisational structures are used to implement the cost leadership, differentiation, integrated cost leadership-differentiation and focused business-level strategies?
4. What organisational structures are used to implement the related-constrained, related-linked and unrelated corporate-level diversification strategies?
5. What organisational structures should be used to implement the multi-domestic, global and transnational international strategies?
6. What is a strategic network? What is a strategic centre firm? What roles do they play in organisational structures used to implement cooperative strategies?

Application discussion questions

1. Why do firms experience evolutionary cycles in which there is a fit between strategy and structure, punctuated with periods in which strategy and structure are reshaped? Provide examples of global firms that have experienced this pattern.
2. Select an organisation (for example, an employer, a social club or a non-profit agency) of which you currently are a member. What is this organisation's structure? Do you believe the organisation is using the structure that is appropriate, given its strategy? If not, what structure should it use?
3. Use the Internet to find a firm that uses the multi-divisional structure. Which form of the multi-divisional structure is the firm using? What is there about the firm that makes it appropriate for it to use the M-form?
4. Through reading of the business press, locate one firm implementing the global strategy and one implementing the multi-domestic strategy. What organisational structure is being used in each firm? Are these structures allowing each firm's strategy to be implemented successfully? Why or why not?
5. Identify a businessperson in your local community. Define strategic and financial controls for the person. Ask the person to describe the use of each type of control in his or her business. In which type of control do they have the greatest confidence? Why?

Ethics questions

1. When a firm changes from the functional structure to the multi-divisional structure, what responsibilities does it have to current employees?
2. Are there ethical issues associated with the use of strategic controls or financial controls? If so, what are they?
3. Are there ethical issues involved in implementing the cooperative and competitive M-form structures? If so, what are they? As a top-level manager, how would you deal with them?
4. Global and multi-domestic strategies call for different competitive approaches. What ethical concerns might surface when firms attempt to market standardised products globally? When they develop different products or approaches for each local market?
5. What ethical issues are associated with the view that the 'redesign of organisations throughout a society – indeed, globally – entails losses as well as gains'?

Internet exercise

Many retail industries, such as music sales, are ideal for Web-based organisational and selling structures. Visit the sites of some of the most popular venues: CDNow (www.cdnow.com), CD Quest (www.cdquest.com), CheckOut (www.checkout.com), Amazon.com (www.amazon.com) and European-based Front Stage (www.frontstage.com). Can you define the type of organisational structure each company uses? What attempts are being made by each to diversify and expand into other businesses?

*e-project: Suppose you want to launch your own CD sales company on the Internet that will have an immense global reach to the large Mandarin-speaking market around the world. Suppose, further, that you have hired a

Web design firm to construct a site for you. Based on your research of top sites, how will you describe your Web design and business-level strategy for this project? What organisational structure is appropriate to implement the business-level strategy selected?

Notes

1. R. A. Johnson and D. W. Greening, 1999, 'The effects of corporate governance and institutional ownership on types of corporate social performance', *Academy of Management Journal*, 42, pp. 564–756.
2. R. J. Kramer, 1999, 'Organizing for global competitiveness: The corporate headquarters design', *Chief Executive Digest*, 3(2), pp. 23–8; D. J. Teece, G. Pisano and A. Shuen, 1997, 'Dynamic capabilities and strategic management', *Strategic Management Journal*, 18, pp. 509–33.
3. A. Sharma, 1999, 'Central dilemmas of managing innovation in large firms', *California Management Review*, 41(3), pp. 146–64; C. Hales and Z. Tamangani, 1996, 'An investigation of the relationship between organizational structure, managerial role expectations and managers' work activities', *Journal of Management Studies*, 33, pp. 731–56.
4. S. E. Human and K. Provan, 1997, 'An emergent theory of structure and outcomes in small-firm strategic manufacturing networks', *Academy of Management Journal*, 40, pp. 368–403.
5. D. Miller and J. O. Whitney, 1999, 'Beyond strategy: Configuration as a pillar of competitive advantage', *Business Horizons*, 42(3), pp. 5–17; K. J. Euske and A. Riccaboni, 1999, 'Stability to profitabililty: Managing interdependencies to meet a new environment', *Accounting, Organizations & Society*, 24, pp. 463–81.
6. J. R. Galbraith, 1995, *Designing Organizations* (San Francisco: Jossey-Bass), p. 6.
7. L. Schmidt, 1999, 'Harvey Norman, a structured success', *Business Review Weekly*, 8 October.
8. A. Y. Ilinitch, R. A. D'Aveni and A. Y. Lewin, 1996, 'New organizational forms and strategies for managing in hypercompetitive environments', *Organization Science*, 7, pp. 211–20.
9. G. Blainey, 1993, *Pacific Dunlop: Jumping Over the Wheel* (Sydney: Allen & Unwin).
10. D. A. Nadler and M. L. Tushman, 1997, *Competing by Design: The Power of Organizational Architecture* (New York: Oxford University Press).
11. E. F. Suarez and J. M. Utterback, 1995, 'Dominant designs and the survival of firms', *Strategic Management Journal*, 16, pp. 415–30.
12. R. A. Heifetz and D. L. Laurie, 1997, 'The work of leadership', *Harvard Business Review*, 75(1), pp. 124–34; R. H. Hall, 1996, *Organizations: Structures, Processes, and Outcomes*, 6th edition (Englewood Cliffs, NJ: Prentice Hall), pp. 106–7.
13. H. W. Volberda, 1996, 'Toward the flexible form: How to remain vital in hypercompetitive environments', *Organization Science*, 7, pp. 359–74.
14. A. D. Chandler, Jr, 1990, *Scale and Scope: The Dynamics of Industrial Capitalism* (Cambridge: The Belknap Press of Harvard University Press), pp. 182–3.
15. J. A. Chesley and M. S. Wenger, 1999, 'Transforming an organization: Using models to foster a strategic conversation', *California Management Review*, 41(3), pp. 54–73.
16. C. H. Noble, 1999, 'The eclectic roots of strategy implementation research', *Journal of Business Research*, 45, pp. 119–34.
17. Galbraith, *Designing Organizations*, p. 13; R. R. Nelson, 1994, 'Why do firms differ, and how does it matter?', in R. P. Rumelt, D. E. Schendel and D. J. Teece (eds), *Fundamental Issues in Strategy* (Cambridge, MA: Harvard Business School Press), p. 259.
18. L. Donaldson, 1997, 'A positivist alternative to the structure-action approach', *Organization Studies*, 18, pp. 77–92; Hales and Tamangani, 'An investigation of the relationship', p. 738; Nelson, 'Why do firms ...?', p. 259.
19. B. C. Esty, 1997, 'A case study of organizational form and risk shifting in the savings and loan industry', *Journal of Financial Economics*, 44, pp. 57–76; C. W. L. Hill, 1994, 'Diversification and economics performance: Bringing structure and corporate management back into the picture', in R. P. Rumelt, D. E. Schendel and D. J. Teece (eds), *Fundamental Issues in Strategy* (Cambridge, MA: Harvard Business School Press), pp. 297–321.
20. W. B. Werther, Jr, 1999, 'Structure driven strategy and virtual organization design', *Business Horizons*, 42(2), pp. 13–18.
21. The Council of Small Business Organisations of Australia, 2001, 'Small business issues', 19 February: www.cosboa.com.au/smallbiz/22smlbiz.html#DEFINE.
22. V. Griffith, 1997, 'Lumbering giants', *Financial Times*, 15 December, p. 10.
23. Associated Press, 2000, 'Smaller companies and extreme sports conquer the sporting-goods industry', *Wall Street Journal*, 20 February, p. A9A.
24. P. Patterson, 2000, 'Market changes place demands on Nike Inc.', *Wall Street Journal*, 14 February, p. A9A.
25. J. J. Chrisman, A. Bauerschmidt and C. W. Hofer, 1998, 'The determinants of new venture performance: An extended model', *Entrepreneurship Theory & Practice*, 23, pp. 5–29; H. M. O'Neill, R. W. Pouder and A. K. Buchholtz, 1998, 'Patterns in the diffusion of strategies across organizations: Insights from the innovation diffusion literature', *Academy of Management Review*, 23, pp. 98–114.
26. Patterson, 'Market changes place demands on Nike, Inc.'.
27. Galbraith, *Designing Organizations*, p. 25.
28. P. Lawrence and J. W. Lorsch, 1967, *Organization and Environment* (Cambridge, MA: Harvard Business School Press).
29. A. D. Chandler, 1994, 'The functions of the HQ unit in the multibusiness firm', in R. P. Rumelt, D. E. Schendel and D. J. Teece (eds), *Fundamental Issues in Strategy* (Cambridge, MA: Harvard Business School Press), p. 327.
30. W. G. Rowe and P. M. Wright, 1997, 'Related and unrelated diversification and their effect on human resource management controls', *Strategic Management Journal*, 18, pp. 329–38; D. C. Galunic and K. M. Eisenhardt, 1996, 'The evolution of intracorporate domains: Divisional charter losses in high-technology, multidivisional corporations', *Organization Science*, 7, pp. 255–82.
31. G. G. Dess, A. Gupta, J.-F. Hennart and C. W. L. Hill, 1995, 'Conducting and integrating strategy research at the international, corporate, and business levels: Issues and directions', *Journal of Management*, 21, pp. 357–93.
32. A. D. Chandler, 1962, *Strategy and Structure: Chapters in the History of the American Industrial Enterprise* (Cambridge, MA: The MIT Press).
33. O. E. Williamson, 1994, 'Strategizing, economizing, and economic organization', in R. P. Rumelt, D. E. Schendel and D. J. Teece (eds), *Fundamental Issues in Strategy* (Cambridge, MA: Harvard Business School Press), pp. 361–401.
34. Galbraith, *Designing Organizations*, p. 27.
35. J. Greco, 1999, 'Alfred P. Sloan, Jr. (1875–1966): The original "organization" man', *Journal of Business Strategy*, 20(5), pp. 30–1.
36. R. E. Hoskisson, C. W. L. Hill and H. Kim, 1993, 'The multidivisional structure: Organizational fossil or source of value?', *Journal of Management*, 19, pp. 269–98.
37. D. Uren, 'Making divisions add up'.
38. Rowe and Wright, 'Related and unrelated diversification'.
39. C. M. Farkas and S. Wetlaufer, 1996, 'The ways chief executive officers lead', *Harvard Business Review*, 74(3), pp. 110–22.
40. C. C. Miller, L. M. Burke and W. H. Glick, 1998, 'Cognitive diversity among upper-echelon executives: Implications for strategic decision processes', *Strategic Management Journal*, 19, pp. 39–58; D. J. Collis, 1996, 'Corporate strategy in multibusiness firms', *Long Range Planning*, 29, pp. 416–18.
41. M. A. Hitt, R. E. Hoskisson, R. A. Johnson and D. D. Moesel, 1996, 'The market for corporate control and firm innovation', *Academy of Management Journal*, 39, pp. 1084–119.
42. R. E. Hoskisson, M. A. Hitt and R. D. Ireland, 1994, 'The effects of acquisitions and restructuring (strategic refocusing) strategies on innovation', in G. von Krogh, A. Sinatra and H. Singh (eds), *Managing Corporate Acquisitions* (London: Macmillan Press), pp. 144–69.
43. R. E. Hoskisson and M. A. Hitt, 1988, 'Strategic control and relative R&D investment in large multiproduct firms', *Strategic Management Journal*, 9, pp. 605–21.
44. R. Tomkins, 1998, 'Black & Decker plans to cut 3 000 jobs', *The Financial Times*, 28 January, p. 15.
45. Collis, 'Corporate strategy', p. 417.
46. M. A. Hitt, R. E. Hoskisson and R. D. Ireland, 1990, 'Mergers and acquisitions and managerial commitment to innovation in M-form firms', *Strategic Management Journal*, 11 (Special Summer Issue), pp. 29–47.
47. S. Baiman, D. F. Larcker and M. V. Rajan, 1995, 'Organizational design for business units', *Journal of Accounting Research*, 33, pp. 205–29; Hall, *Organizations*, p. 13.

48. Ibid.; Hall, *Organizations*, pp. 64–75.
49. C. Homburg, H. Krohmer and J.P. Workman, Jr, 1999, 'Strategic consensus and performance: The role of strategy type and market-related dynamism', *Strategic Management Journal*, 20, pp. 339–57.
50. G. Edmondson, E. Neuborne, A. L. Kazmin, E. Thornton and K. N. Anhalt, 1999, 'L'Oreal: The beauty of global branding', *BusinessWeek Online*, 28 June: www.businessweek.com.
51. Ibid.
52. P. S. Adler, B. Goldoftas and D. I. Levin, 1999, 'Flexibility versus efficiency? A case study of model changeovers in the Toyota production system', *Organization Science*, 10, pp. 43–68.
53. D. K. Sobek, II, A. C. Howard and J. K. Liker, 1999, 'Toyota's principles of set-based concurrent engineering', *Sloan Management Review*, 40(2), pp. 67–83.
54. D. Donovan, 2000, 'You just can't lick 'em', *Forbes*, 10 January, p. 174.
55. C. C. Markides and P. J. Williamson, 1996, 'Corporate diversification and organizational structure: A resource-based view', *Academy of Management Journal*, 39, pp. 340–67; C. W. L. Hill, M. A. Hitt and R. E. Hoskisson, 1992, 'Cooperative versus competitive structures in related and unrelated diversified firms', *Organization Science*, 3, pp. 501–21.
56. J. Robins and M. E. Wiersema, 1995, 'A resource-based approach to the multibusiness firm: Empirical analysis of portfolio interrelationships and corporate financial performance', *Strategic Management Journal*, 16, pp. 277–99.
57. C. C. Markides, 1997, 'To diversify or not to diversify', *Harvard Business Review*, 75(6), pp. 93–9.
58. Nadler and Tushman, *Competing by Design*, p. 99.
59. Hall, *Organizations*, p. 186; J. G. March, 1994, *A Primer on Decision Making: How Decisions Happen* (New York: The Free Press), pp. 117–18.
60. P. J. Frost, 1997, 'Bridging academia and business: A conversation with Steve Kerr', *Organization Science*, 8, p. 335.
61. *GE HomePage*, 2000, 1 March: www.ge.com.
62. J. A. Byrne, 1998, 'How Jack Welch runs GE', *BusinessWeek Online*, 8 June: www.businessweek.com.
63. T. A. Stewart, 1999, 'See Jack. See Jack run Europe', *Fortune*, 27 September, p. 127.
64. R. E. Hoskisson and M. A. Hitt, 1990, 'Antecedents and performance outcomes of diversification: A review and critique of theoretical perspectives', *Journal of Management*, 16, pp. 461–509.
65. C. W. L. Hill, M. A. Hitt and R. E. Hoskisson, 1992, 'Cooperative versus competitive structures in related and unrelated diversified firms', *Organization Science*, 3, pp. 501–21.
66. J. B. Barney, 1997, *Gaining and Sustaining Competitive Advantage* (Reading, MA: Addison-Wesley), pp. 420–33.
67. Williamson, 'Strategizing, economizing', p. 373.
68. B. W. Keats and M. A. Hitt, 1988, 'A causal model of linkages among environmental dimensions, macro organizational characteristics, and performance', *Academy of Management Journal*, 31, pp. 570–98.
69. Hoskisson, Hill and Kim, 'The multidivisional structure', p. 276.
70. R. E. Hoskisson, R. A. Johnson and D. D. Moesel, 1994, 'Corporate divestiture intensity: Effects of governance strategy and performance', *Academy of Management Journal*, 37, pp. 1207–51; R. E. Hoskisson and T. Turk, 1990, 'Corporate restructuring, governance and control limits of the internal capital market', *Academy of Management Review*, 15, pp. 459–71.
71. S. J. Chang and H. Singh, 1999, 'The impact of entry and resource fit on modes of exit by multibusiness firms', *Strategic Management Journal*, 20, pp. 1019–35; M. E. Porter, 1987, 'From competitive advantage to corporate strategy', *Harvard Business Review*, 65(3), pp. 43–59.
72. C. C. Markides, 1992, 'Consequences of corporate refocusing: Ex ante evidence', *Academy of Management Journal*, 35, pp. 398–412.
73. G. L. White, 2000, 'GM to unify manufacturing of cars, trucks', *Wall Street Journal*, 27 January, p. B22.
74. M. A. Hitt, M. T. Dacin, B. B. Tyler and D. Park, 1997, 'Understanding the differences in Korean and U.S. executives' strategic orientations', *Strategic Management Journal*, 18, pp. 159–67.
75. C. Rahweddeer, 1998, 'U.S. mail-order firms shake up Europe', *Wall Street Journal*, 6 January, p. A15.
76. E. Beck, 1999, 'Body Shop gets a makeover to cut costs', *Wall Street Journal*, 27 January, p. A18.
77. Bartlett and Ghoshal, *Managing Across Borders*.
78. Ibid.
79. Kramer, 'Organizing for global competitiveness'.
80. B. Gomes-Casseres, 1994, 'Group versus group: How alliance networks compete', *Harvard Business Review*, 72(4), pp. 62–74.
81. Werther, 'Structure driven strategy and virtual organization'; G. R. Jones, 1998, *Organizational Theory* (Reading, MA: Addison-Wesley), pp. 163–5.
82. P. Dussauge, B. Garrette and W. Mitchell, 2000, 'Learning from competing partners: Outcomes and duration of scale and link alliances in Europe, North America and Asia', *Strategic Management Journal*, 21, pp. 99–126; G. Lorenzoni and C. Baden-Fuller, 1995, 'Creating a strategic center to manage a web of partners', *California Management Review*, 37(3), pp. 146–63.
83. S. Harryson, 1998, *Japanese Technology and Innovation Management* (Northhampton, MA: Edward Elgar).
84. J. H. Dyer, 1997, 'Effective interfirm collaboration: How firms minimize transaction costs and maximize transaction value', *Strategic Management Journal*, 18, pp. 535–56.
85. T. Nishiguchi, 1994, *Strategic Industrial Sourcing: The Japanese Advantage* (New York: Oxford University Press).
86. W. M. Fruin, 1992, *The Japanese Enterprise System* (New York: Oxford University Press).
87. Sobek, Howard and Liker, 'Toyota's principles of set-based concurrent engineering'.
88. M. Skapinker, 1999, 'Airlines bent on bigamy ruffle alliances', *Financial Times*, 23 June, p. 8.
89. D. Harbrecht, 1999, 'A talk with Air France's pilot as he hooks up with Delta', *BusinessWeek Online*, 22 June: www.businessweek.com.
90. D. Leonhardt and A. T. Palmer, 1999, 'Getting off their McButts', *Business Week*, 22 February, pp. 84–8; S. Branch, 1997, 'What's eating McDonald's?', *Fortune*, 13 October, pp. 122–5.
91. *Corning Home Page*, 2000, 24 February: www.corning.com; J. R. Houghton, 1990, 'Corning cultivates joint ventures that endure', *Planning Review*, 18(5), pp. 15–17.
92. C. Jones, W. S. Hesterly and S. P. Borgatti, 1997, 'A general theory of network governance: Exchange conditions and social mechanisms', *Academy of Management Review*, 22. pp. 911–45.
93. R. E. Miles, C. C. Snow, J. A. Mathews, G. Miles and J. J. Coleman, Jr, 1997, 'Organizing in the knowledge age: Anticipating the cellular form', *Academy of Management Executive*, XI(4), pp. 7–20.
94. Kramer, 'Organizing for global competitiveness'; Nadler and Tushman, *Competing by Design*, p. 89.
95. Chandler, *Scale and Scope*.
96. B. Victor and C. Stephens, 1994, 'The dark side of the new organizational forms: An editorial essay', *Organization Science*, 5, pp. 479–82.
97. R. Waters, 1998, 'New DuPont shake-up to slash bureaucracy', *Financial Times*, 8 January, p. 3; A. Barrett, 1997, 'At DuPont, time to both sow and reap', *Business Week*, 29 September, pp. 107–8.
98. M. A. Hitt, B. W. Keats and S. M. DeMarie, 1998, 'Navigating in the new competitive landscape: Building competitive advantage and strategic flexibility in the 21st century', *Academy of Management Executive*, 12(4), pp. 22–42.
99. R. D. Ireland and M. A. Hitt, 1999, 'Achieving and maintaining strategic competitiveness in the 21st century: The role of strategic leadership', *Academy of Management Executive*, 13(1), pp. 43–57.

Chapter 12

Strategic leadership

Objectives

After reading this chapter, you should be able to:

1. Define strategic leadership and describe the importance of top-level managers as an organisational resource.
2. Define top management teams and explain their effects on the firm's performance and its ability to innovate and make appropriate strategic choices.
3. Describe the internal and external managerial labour markets and their effects on the development and implementation of a firm's strategy.
4. Discuss the value of strategic leadership in determining the firm's strategic direction.
5. Explain the role of strategic leaders in exploiting and maintaining core competencies.
6. Describe the importance of strategic leaders in developing a firm's human capital.
7. Define organisational culture and explain what must be done to sustain an effective culture.
8. Describe what strategic leaders can do to establish and emphasise ethical practices in their firms.
9. Discuss the importance and use of organisational controls.

Strategic leaders: The good, the bad and the ugly

Dennis Eck was imported from the United States to Australia and has been CEO of Coles Myer since 1997. When he took over, the organisation was struggling, particularly the supermarket division, and the company's share price was languishing at $3.80. By August 1999 it had risen to $9.25 and the supermarket division, as well as the rest of the organisation, was revitalised. Eck has made the stores more responsive to customers, giving managers more power but ensuring that they listen to staff and customers. Among other moves, Eck has repositioned Kmart, launched new 'category killer' superstores in home goods areas (Target Home), food (Let's Eat), and health and beauty (Essentially Me), and freshened up the Coles supermarket chain. He is receptive to new ideas and encourages staff to be innovative. Eck claims, 'It's very simple … Focus on customers, focus on your employees and get them involved, focus on your suppliers and get them involved, and focus on the community in which you do business. And if you get those few things right, what comes out for the shareholder is always right.' Eck took over Coles Myer at a good time to gain a reputation as a corporate turnaround champion. Coles was a poor performer and ridden with internal squabbles, but was equipped with excellent resources. The turnaround is nevertheless testament to the significance of leadership.

John F. (Jack) Welch, Jr, the renowned former CEO of General Electric (GE), provides another example of successful leadership because of the value that he has created for GE. Over the period from 1980 to 2000, more value has been created for GE shareholders than for any other company in the world. Early in his tenure as CEO of GE, Welch obtained the name 'Neutron Jack' for his infamous efficiency moves, including significant downsizing of employees. However, while still considered decisive and demanding, Welch enjoys much respect for what he has done at GE – namely, create one of the most successful management development programs in the world. Many firms try to raid GE's management ranks because they know these people have strong management skills. Welch believes and invests in building human capital. In a recent ranking of companies worldwide by the *Financial Times*, GE was ranked number one. Welch might be considered the master strategic leader. He retired on 31 December 2000. However, there are new, younger people to take Welch's place as excellent strategic leaders.

In the same survey that ranked GE as the number-one company in the world, Hewlett-Packard (HP) was ranked number 14. HP has not performed well in recent years, but it now has a new CEO, Carly Fiorina. During her tenure at Lucent Technologies, Fiorina was considered one of the world's most powerful women. In her current role, she *is* the most powerful woman. She has been described as having a silver tongue and an iron will. Fiorina has a challenge at HP: she must make the company more innovative without losing what made it great. She was chosen for HP's CEO position because of her ability to conceptualise and communicate sweeping strategies, her knowledge of operations to meet short- and long-term financial goals, her ability to create a need for change, and her capability to gain commitment to, and implement, a new vision for the company. Fiorina has the interpersonal skills that inspire loyalty from those who work with her. She also has savvy marketing skills and courts customers effectively. She can and will provide strong direction for HP.

Another new strategic leader is Jeff Bezos, the founder and CEO of Amazon.com. In 1999, Bezos was chosen as *Time*'s Person of the Year. Although a young firm, Amazon.com is a grandfather of the e-commerce age. Bezos developed a company selling books through the Internet, and initially most people paid little attention to him or his company. Those paying little attention included competitors Barnes & Noble and Borders. Now they pay attention. Barnes & Noble started barnesandnoble.com about two years after Amazon.com entered the market. However, Amazon.com had first-mover advantages (explained in Chapter 5). Bezos is innovative and willing to think entrepreneurially, a problem for some executives of large firms. Even as Amazon.com has grown, Bezos continues to think and act as an entrepreneur. He began expanding his on-line products by using the access to, and knowledge of, customers that he developed in the electronic business. In 1998, Amazon.com added music and films to its product offerings. Thereafter, the company began expanding into many product lines, such as pharmaceuticals and groceries. Today, Barnes & Noble is not considered Amazon.com's main competitor. Wal-Mart *is* a major competitor, but even it is scrambling to develop its Internet offerings to compete with Amazon.com. Clearly, Bezos has established a company with the best brand name in cyberspace.

Unfortunately, there are examples of less successful strategic leaders. Poppy King had spectacular success when she founded Poppy Industries in 1992. By 1995, it was a successful cosmetics business and King was Young Australian of the Year. She was the leader and figurehead of the company and had strong ideas about how the business should be conducted. In 1996, she tried to find capital to enable expansion into lingerie and into the US market. At the same time, turnover was falling and the Freid family purchased a half share in the business. When revenue continued to fall and King refused advice to distribute goods more widely, the investors and King quarrelled. In September 1998, the business was placed in receivership. King remains in the industry and is an innovative marketer, but she was unable, with Poppy Industries, to deliver on the vision she had for the brand.

Other strategic leaders have been successful by some standards, but may not be highly regarded for other reasons. Perhaps the best-known among these is Al Dunlap, sometimes referred to as 'Chain-saw Al'. Dunlap was known for taking the leadership reins of poorly performing companies and turning them around. He obtained his nickname because he often sold off businesses and retrenched many employees. He seemed to be successful with these actions in several companies, including the Packer firm, PBL, until his last CEO role with Sunbeam. There, he also sold off many of Sunbeam's businesses and tried to jump-start new growth with some acquisitions. Unfortunately, the additional businesses did not improve the firm's performance, but their acquisition substantially increased the firm's debt (by US$1.8 billion). The much higher debt led to a negative cash flow. With increased pressure from shareholders and creditors to improve the company's performance, Dunlap engaged in some possibly questionable actions, and Sunbeam's board of directors requested his resignation.

Another person trying to gain respect is Charles Wang, CEO of Computer Associates. By most accounts, Computer Associates has flourished under Wang's leadership. He has helped the company grow into a US$6.5 billion software firm. Much of the growth has come from acquiring competitors and firms in complementary product markets. So, why wouldn't people give respect to this CEO? When asked why no executives from the acquired firm remained afterwards, Wang replied, 'This dragon has only one head.' Some use the term 'ruthless' to describe both Wang and his actions. Overall, his methods can be described as harsh, but they produce positive results for the company. Wang doubled the size of the firm over a four-year period and, at the same time, maintained high profit margins. Computer Associates has approximately 31 per cent of the client server market, with IBM second at slightly over 11 per cent. In 1999, Computer Associates took a US$1.1 billion write-off to fund a grant in that

www.amazon.com
www.bn.com
www.borders.com
www.colesmyer.com.au
www.ge.com
www.hp.com
www.lucent.com
www.poppy.com.au
www.wal-mart.com

amount to its top three executives, a large share of which went to Wang. However, shareholders filed 10 separate suits, and a federal judge ruled that Wang had to give back approximately half of his US$670 million share. The bottom line is that Wang has been successful, but his methods are questioned and generally disliked.

Sources: M. A. Hitt, J. S. Harrison and R. D. Ireland, 2001, *Creating Value through Mergers and Acquisitions: A Complete Guide to Successful M&As* (New York: Oxford University Press); A. Bianco and Steve Hamm, 2000, 'Software's tough guy', *Business Week*, 6 March, pp. 133–44; 'Amazon.com, Inc.', 2000, *Wall Street Journal Interactive*, 15 February: www.interactive.wsj.com/articles; 'Grim reaper', 1999, *The Economist Online*, 25 December: www.economist.com; J. B. Cahill, 1999, 'Bank One's McCoy is quitting his posts of chairman, chief', *Wall Street Journal Interactive*, 22 December: www.interactive.wsj.com/articles; J. C. Ramo, 1999, 'Why the founder of Amazon.com is our choice for 1999', *Time Online*, 21 December: www.time.com; 'Ranking: World's top companies, 1999', 18 October: www.ft.com/ftsurveys; P. Burrows and P. Elstrom, 1999, 'The boss', *Business Week*, 2 August, pp. 76–84; L. Schmidt, 1999, 'Dennis Eck, Superstar?', *Business Review Weekly*, 10 December, pp. 72–5; A. Gome, 1998, 'Poppy Industries does a slow fade to black', *Business Review Weekly*, 12 October, pp. 36–40.

The examples in the Opening Case show some of the significant strategic challenges with which CEOs are confronted and emphasise the importance and outcomes of effective strategic leadership. Some of the leaders have been highly successful (for example, Eck, Welch, Fiorina and Bezos), while others may be successful for a while, but cannot sustain their success. Still others technically may be successful, but have less respect as leaders. It is difficult to build and maintain success over a sustained period of time. As this chapter makes clear, it is through effective strategic leadership that firms are able to use the strategic management process successfully (see Figure 1.1 in Chapter 1). Thus, as strategic leaders, top-level managers must guide the firm in ways that result in the formation of a strategic intent and strategic mission. This guidance may lead to goals that stretch everyone in the organisation to improve their performance.[1] Moreover, strategic leaders are then challenged to facilitate the development of appropriate strategic actions and determine how to implement them. These actions culminate in strategic competitiveness and above-average returns[2] (see Figure 12.1).

This chapter begins with a definition of strategic leadership and its importance as a potential source of competitive advantage. Next, we examine top management teams and their effects on innovation, strategic change and firm performance. Following this discussion is an analysis of the internal and external managerial labour markets from which strategic leaders are selected. Closing the chapter are descriptions of the six key components of effective strategic leadership: determining a strategic direction, exploiting and maintaining core competencies, developing human capital, sustaining an effective organisational culture, emphasising ethical practices, and establishing balanced organisational control systems.

The impermanence of success is well documented by the change in leadership at Compaq Computer. Compaq's former CEO, Eckhard Pfeiffer, had been highly successful in leading Compaq to the number-one position in the personal computer market. In 1998, Compaq seemed to be at the top of its game. However, problems ensued in 1999, and in a short period of time, Compaq became stagnant and was unseated as the number-one producer of personal computers by Dell. Compaq's board of directors forced Pfeiffer to resign. Pfeiffer's successor, Michael Capellas, is trying to re-energise the firm, to make it more innovative. He believes that this is necessary because, in the high-technology industry, the constant, substantial speed of change will relegate Compaq to a second-class seat. A short time after taking the job, Capellas made significant changes, restructuring the organisation and eliminating redundant and overlapping programs. Analysts believe that his actions are on track. One analyst observed that Compaq executives must 'start thinking outside the box and partner more with solution providers rather than box pushers'. Capellas is trying to do just that.[3]

Figure 12.1 | Strategic leadership and the strategic management process

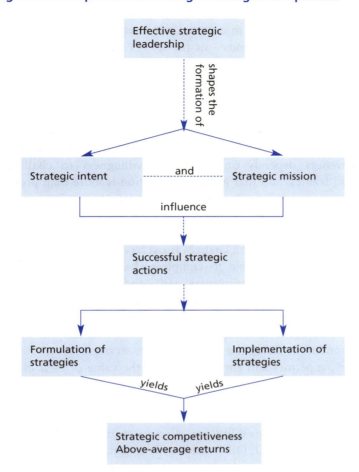

Strategic leadership

Strategic leadership is the ability to anticipate, envision, maintain flexibility and empower others to create strategic change as necessary.

Strategic leadership is the ability to anticipate, envision, maintain flexibility and empower others to create strategic change as necessary. Multi-functional in nature, strategic leadership involves managing through others, managing an entire enterprise rather than a functional sub-unit, and coping with change that seems to be increasing exponentially in the current competitive landscape. Because of the complexity and global nature of this landscape, strategic leaders must learn how to influence human behaviour effectively in an uncertain environment. By word or by personal example, and through their ability to envision the future, effective strategic leaders meaningfully influence the behaviours, thoughts and feelings of those with whom they work.[4] The ability to manage human capital may be the most critical of the strategic leader's skills.[5] In the opinion of a well-known observer of leadership, the key to competitive advantage in the 1990s and beyond 'will be the capacity of top leadership to create the social architecture capable of generating intellectual capital ... By intellectual capital, I mean know-how, expertise, brainpower, innovation [and] ideas.'[6] Competent strategic leaders also establish the context through which stakeholders (for example, employees, customers and suppliers) are able to perform at peak efficiency.[7] The crux of strategic leadership is the ability to manage the firm's operations effectively and sustain a high performance over time.[8]

> A **managerial mind-set** is the set of assumptions, premises and accepted wisdom that bounds – or frames – a manager's understanding of the firm, the industry(ies) in which it competes and the core competencies it uses in pursuit of strategic competitiveness.

In the 21st century, many managers working in nations throughout the world will be challenged to alter their mind-sets to cope with the rapid and complex changes occurring in the global economy. A **managerial mind-set** is the set of assumptions, premises and accepted wisdom that bounds – or frames – a manager's understanding of the firm, the industry(ies) in which it competes and the core competencies it uses in the pursuit of strategic competitiveness[9] (see Chapter 3).

A firm's ability to achieve strategic competitiveness and earn above-average returns is compromised when strategic leaders fail to respond appropriately and quickly to changes in the complex global competitive environment. The failure to respond quickly prompted Eckhard Pfeiffer's problems at Compaq. Research suggests that a firm's 'long-term competitiveness depends on managers' willingness to challenge continually their managerial frames' and that global competition is more than product versus product or company versus company: It is also a case of 'mindset versus mindset, managerial frame versus managerial frame'.[10] Competing on the basis of mind-sets demands that strategic leaders learn how to deal with diverse and cognitively complex competitive situations. One of the most challenging changes is overcoming one's own successful mind-set when that is required. Being able to complete challenging assignments that are linked to achieving strategic competitiveness early and frequently in one's career appears to improve a manager's ability to make appropriate changes to his or her mind-set.[11]

Effective strategic leaders are willing to make candid and courageous, yet pragmatic, decisions – decisions that may be difficult, but necessary in light of the internal and external conditions facing the firm.[12] Effective strategic leaders solicit corrective feedback from peers, superiors and employees about the value of their difficult decisions. Often, this feedback is sought through face-to-face communications. Unwillingness to accept feedback may be a key reason why talented executives fail, highlighting the need for strategic leaders to solicit feedback consistently from those affected by their decisions.[13]

The primary responsibility for effective strategic leadership rests at the top – in particular, with the CEO. Other commonly recognised strategic leaders include members of the board of directors, the top management team and divisional general managers. Regardless of their title and organisational function, strategic leaders have substantial decision-making responsibilities that cannot be delegated.[14]

Strategic leadership is an extremely complex, but critical, form of leadership. Strategies cannot be formulated and implemented to achieve above-average returns without effective strategic leaders. Because strategic leadership is a requirement of strategic success, and because organisations may be poorly led and over-managed, firms competing in the 21st-century competitive landscape are challenged to develop effective strategic leaders.[15]

Managers as an organisational resource

As the introductory discussion suggests, top-level managers are an important resource for firms seeking to formulate and implement strategies effectively.[16] A key reason for this is that the strategic decisions made by top managers influence how the firm is designed and whether goals will be achieved. Thus, a critical element of organisational success is having a top management team with superior managerial skills.[17]

Managers often use their discretion (or latitude for action) when making strategic decisions, including those concerned with the effective implementation of strategies.[18] Managerial discretion differs significantly across industries. The primary factors that determine the amount of a manager's (especially a top-level manager's) decision-making discretion include: (1) external environmental sources (for example, the industry structure, the rate of market growth in the firm's primary industry and the degree to which products can be differentiated); (2) characteristics of the organisation (for example, its size, age, resources and culture); and (3) characteristics of the manager (for example, commitment to the firm and its strategic outcomes, tolerance for ambiguity, skills in working with different people, and aspiration levels) (see Figure 12.2). Because strategic leaders' decisions are intended to help the firm gain a competitive advantage, the way in which managers exercise discretion when determining appropriate strategic actions is critical to the firm's success.[19] Top executives must be action-oriented; thus, the decisions that they make should spur the company to action. In fact, a renowned explorer of Africa, Dr Livingstone, believed that 'complacency is death'.[20]

Figure 12.2 | Factors affecting managerial discretion

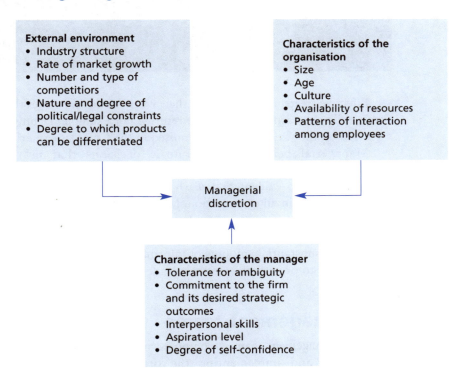

Source: Adapted from S. Finkelstein and D. C. Hambrick, 1996, *Strategic Leadership: Top Executives and Their Effects on Organizations* (St. Paul, MN: West Publishing Company).

In addition to determining new strategic initiatives, top-level managers develop the appropriate organisational structure and reward systems of a firm. In Chapter 11, we described how the organisational structure and reward systems affect strategic actions taken to implement different types of strategies. Furthermore, top executives have a major effect on a firm's culture. Evidence suggests that managers' values are critical in shaping a firm's cultural values.[21] Accordingly, top-level managers have an important effect on organisational activities and performance.[22] The significance of this effect should not be underestimated.

As the discussion that follows shows, the decisions and actions of some strategic leaders make those leaders a source of competitive advantage for their firm. In accordance with the criteria of sustainability discussed in Chapter 3, strategic leaders can be a source of competitive advantage only when their work is valuable, rare, costly to imitate and non-substitutable.

Strategic Management Competitiveness and Globalisation

Paul Anderson is the American-born and trained CEO of BHP, for a generation Australia's biggest corporation.

Effective strategic leaders focus their work on the key issues that ultimately shape the firm's ability to earn above-average returns. For example, Dennis Eck focused his initial attention on the way stock was organised in the Coles supermarket chain.

Managerial beliefs affect strategic decisions that in turn affect the firm's performance.[23] This causal chain is evident in James Strong's largely successful actions at Qantas. It is also evident that Carly Fiorina's self-confidence gives her the power to influence change in an organisation. Managers use their discretion to develop and utilise strategic resources to create value for the shareholders and to meet the other stakeholders' requirements.[24] However, the complexity of the challenges faced, and thus the need for substantial amounts of information and knowledge, require the use of teams of executives to provide the strategic leadership in most firms.

Top management teams

The **top management team** is composed of the key managers who are responsible for formulating and implementing the organisation's strategies. Typically, the top management team includes the officers of the corporation, as defined by the title of vice president and above or by service as a member of the board of directors.[25] The quality of the strategic decisions made by a top management team affects the firm's ability to innovate and engage in effective strategic change.[26]

The **top management team** is composed of the key managers who are responsible for formulating and implementing the organisation's strategies.

Top management team, firm performance and strategic change

The job of top-level executives is complex and requires a broad knowledge of the firm's operations, as well as the three key parts of the firm's external environment. Therefore, firms try to form a top management team that has the appropriate knowledge and expertise to operate the internal organisation, yet also deal with external stakeholders.[27] This normally requires a heterogeneous top management team. A **heterogeneous top management team** is composed of individuals with different functional backgrounds, experience and education. The more heterogeneous a top management team is, with varied expertise and knowledge, the more capacity it has to provide effective strategic leadership in *formulating* strategy. Members of a heterogeneous top management team benefit from discussing the different perspectives advanced by team members. In many

A **heterogeneous top management team** is composed of individuals with different functional backgrounds, experience and education.

cases, these discussions increase the quality of the top management team's decisions, especially when a synthesis emerges out of the clash among diverse perspectives that is generally superior to any one individual perspective.[28] For example, heterogeneous top management teams in the airline industry have the propensity to take stronger competitive actions and reactions than do more homogeneous teams.[29] The net benefit of such actions by heterogeneous teams was positive in terms of market share and above-average returns. Research shows that more heterogeneity among top management team members promotes debate, which often leads to better strategic decisions. In turn, better strategic decisions produce higher firm performance.[30]

It is also important that the top management team members function cohesively. In general, the more heterogeneous and larger the top management team is, the more difficult it is for the team to *implement* strategies effectively.[31] The fact that comprehensive and long-term strategic plans can be inhibited by communication difficulties among top executives who have different backgrounds and different cognitive skills may account for these implementation-related difficulties.[32] A group of top executives with diverse backgrounds may thus inhibit the process of decision making if it is not effectively managed. In these cases, top management teams may fail to comprehensively examine threats and opportunities, leading to a sub-optimal strategic decision.[33] Having members with substantive expertise in the firm's core functions and businesses is also important to the effectiveness of a top management team. In a high-technology industry, it may be critical for a firm's top management team to have R&D expertise, particularly when growth strategies are being implemented.[34]

The characteristics of top management teams are related to innovation and strategic change.[35] For example, more heterogeneous top management teams are associated positively with innovation and strategic change. The heterogeneity may force the team or some of the members to 'think outside of the box' and thus be more creative in making decisions.[36] Therefore, firms that need to change their strategies are more likely to do so if they have top management teams with diverse backgrounds and expertise. A top management team with various areas of expertise is more likely to identify environmental changes (opportunities and threats) or changes within the firms that require a different strategic direction.[37]

The CEO and top management team power

As suggested in Chapter 10, the board of directors is an important mechanism for monitoring a firm's strategic direction and for representing the interests of stakeholders, especially shareholders. In fact, higher performance normally is achieved when the board of directors is involved more directly in shaping a firm's strategic direction.[38]

Boards of directors, however, may find it difficult to direct the strategic actions of powerful CEOs and top management teams. In the United States, it is not uncommon for a powerful CEO to appoint a number of sympathetic outside board members or have inside board members who are on the top management team and report to the CEO. In Australia, the CEO and board are conceptually more separated, with the board appointing the CEO. The CEO is then normally part of the board as one of the 'inside directors' and consequently enjoys considerable authority. In either case, the CEO may have significant control over the board's actions. 'A central question is whether boards are an effective management control mechanism ... or whether they are a management tool ... a rubber stamp for management initiatives ... and often surrender to management their major domain of decision-making authority, which includes the right to hire, fire, and compensate top management.'[39] This concern is evident with the board of directors of Disney and its CEO, Michael Eisner. As explained in Chapter 10, several institutional shareholders have taken actions to pressure Eisner to change Disney's board. A more effective process of major shareholder pressure was evident in the AMP–GIO affair described in Chapter 10. Alternatively, recent research shows that social ties between the CEO and board members may actually increase board members' involvement in strategic decisions. Thus, strong relationships between the CEO and the board of directors may have positive or negative outcomes.[40]

CEOs and top management team members can also achieve power in other ways. Holding the titles of chairperson of the board and chief executive officer usually gives a CEO more power than one who is not simultaneously serving as chair of the firm's board.[41] Although the practice of CEO duality – that is, when the CEO and the chairperson of the board are the same – is rare in the Australian corporate world (except, perhaps, for non-listed companies), it has become more common in US businesses. In the United States, duality has come under heavy criticism, being blamed for poor performance and slow response to change in a number of firms.[42]

DaimlerChrysler's CEO, Jürgen Schrempp, holds the dual positions of chairman of the board and CEO. And Schrempp has substantial power in the firm. In fact, insiders suggest that he is purging those individuals who are outspoken and who represent potential threats to his dominance. In particular, former Chrysler executives are leaving the firm. The loss of some of these key executives, such as Thomas Stallkamp, who is credited with being the spiritual leader of the company's US operations and the leader of the integration efforts between the former Chrysler and Daimler operations, has worried investors. Without Stallkamp's leadership, investors worry that integration efforts may stall and the potential efficiencies and synergies may not be realised.[43]

Although it varies across industries, duality occurs most commonly in the largest US firms. Increased shareholder activism, however, has brought CEO duality under scrutiny and attack in both US and European firms. Historically, an independent board leadership structure in which one person did not hold the positions of CEO and chair was believed to enhance a board's ability to monitor top-level managers' decisions and actions, particularly in terms of the firm's financial performance.[44] Stewardship theory, on the other hand, suggests that CEO duality facilitates effective decisions and actions. In these instances, the increased effectiveness gained through CEO duality accrues from the individual who wants to perform effectively and desires to be the best possible steward of the firm's assets. Because of this person's positive orientation and actions, extra governance and the coordination costs resulting from an independent board leadership structure would be unnecessary.[45]

Top management team members and CEOs who have long tenure – on the team and in the organisation – have a greater influence on board decisions.[46] Long tenure is known to restrict the breadth of an executive's knowledge base. With the limited perspectives associated with a restricted knowledge base, long-tenured top executives typically develop fewer alternatives to evaluate in making strategic decisions.[47] However, long-tenured managers also may be able to exercise more effective strategic control, thereby obviating the need for board members' involvement because effective strategic control generally produces higher performance.[48]

In the final analysis, boards of directors should develop an effective relationship with the firm's top management team. The relative degrees of power to be held by the board and top management team members should be examined in light of an individual firm's situation. For example, the abundance of resources in a firm's external environment and the volatility of that environment may affect the ideal balance of power between boards and top management teams.[49] Through the development of effective working relationships, boards, CEOs and other top management team members are able to serve the best interests of the firm's stakeholders.

Managerial labour market

The choice of top executives – especially CEOs – is a critical organisational decision with important implications for the firm's performance.[50] Moreover, the selection of new members for a top management team represents an opportunity for the firm to adapt to changes occurring in its external environment – that is, in its general, industry and competitor environments (see Chapter 2).

Successful companies develop screening systems to identify those with managerial and strategic leadership potential. The most effective of these systems assesses people within the firm and gains valuable information about the capabilities of other firms' managers, particularly their strategic leaders. For current managers, training and development programs are provided in an attempt to pre-select and shape the skills of people who may become tomorrow's leaders. As noted earlier, the management development program at GE is considered one of the most effective in the world.

There are two types of managerial labour markets – internal and external – from which organisations select managers and strategic leaders. An **internal managerial labour market** consists of the opportunities for managerial positions within a firm, whereas an **external managerial labour market** is the collection of career opportunities for managers in organisations outside of the one for which they work currently. The discussion that follows focuses on how managerial labour markets are used to select CEOs.

Several benefits are thought to accrue to a firm when the internal labour market is used to select a new CEO. Because of their experience with the firm and the industry environment in which it competes, insiders are familiar with company products, markets, technologies and operating procedures. Also, internal hiring produces lower turnover among existing personnel, many of whom possess valuable firm-specific knowledge. When the firm is performing well, internal succession is favoured to sustain high performance. It is assumed that hiring from inside keeps the important knowledge necessary to sustain the performance. The CEO of Telstra, Ziggy Switowski, was an internal appointment. Switowski (who originally trained in science in California) gained credibility within the organisation in a number of senior management positions. For an inside move to the top to occur successfully, firms must develop and implement effective succession management programs. In that way, managers are developed such that one will eventually be prepared to ascend to the top.[51]

It is not unusual for employees to have a strong preference for using the internal managerial labour market to select top management team members and the CEO. The selection of insiders to fill top-level management positions reflects a desire for continuity and a continuing commitment to the firm's current strategic intent, strategic mission and chosen strategies. Thus, internal candidates tend to be valued over external candidates[52] in the selection of a firm's CEO and other top-level managers. In fact, outside succession to the CEO position 'is an extraordinary event for business firms [and] is usually seen as a stark indicator that the board of directors wants change'.[53]

Valid reasons exist for a firm to select an outsider as its new CEO. For example, research evidence suggests that executives who have spent their entire career with a particular firm may become 'stale in the saddle'.[54] There is also a rise in long tenure with a firm that seems to reduce the number of innovative ideas top executives are able to develop to cope with conditions facing their firm. Given the importance of innovation for a firm's success in the competitive landscape (see Chapter 13), an inability to innovate or to create conditions that stimulate innovation throughout a firm is a liability for a strategic leader. In contrast to insiders, CEOs selected from outside the firm may have

> An **internal managerial labour market** consists of the opportunities for managerial positions within a firm.
>
> An **external managerial labour market** is the collection of career opportunities for managers in organisations outside of the one for which they work currently.

broader, less limiting perspectives, leading them to encourage innovation and strategic change. These reasons, together with the restricted pool of senior managers in countries such as Australia, mean that searches for new managers extend beyond national boundaries. A belief that managers experienced in the competitive American market will do well in Australia has led to US-trained managers, such as Dennis Eck and BHP's CEO Paul Anderson, leading large Australian corporations. They promise to bring in new ideas and hold no allegiances within the established organisation.[55] Figure 12.3 shows how the composition of the top management team and CEO succession (managerial labour market) may interact to affect strategy. For example, when the top management team is homogeneous (for example, its members have similar functional experiences and educational backgrounds) and a new CEO is selected from inside the firm, the firm's current strategy is unlikely to change.

Figure 12.3 | Effects of CEO succession and top management team composition on strategy

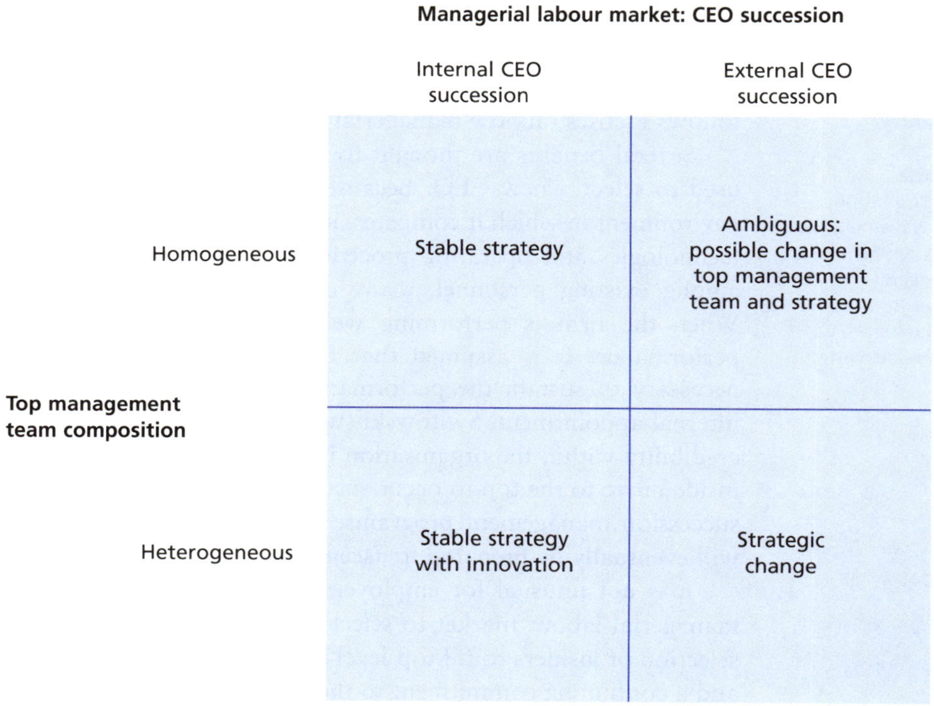

Top management team composition	Managerial labour market: CEO succession	
	Internal CEO succession	External CEO succession
Homogeneous	Stable strategy	Ambiguous: possible change in top management team and strategy
Heterogeneous	Stable strategy with innovation	Strategic change

On the other hand, when a new CEO is selected from outside the firm and the top management team is heterogeneous, there is a high probability that strategy will change. When the new CEO is from inside the firm, the strategy may not change, but with a heterogeneous top management team, innovation is likely to continue. An external CEO succession with a homogeneous team creates a more ambiguous situation.

To have an adequate number of highly qualified managers, firms must take advantage of a highly qualified labour pool, including one source of managers that has often been overlooked: women. Firms are beginning to utilise women's potential managerial talents with substantial success, as described in the Strategic Focus.

Strategic Focus Corporate

Shattering the glass ceiling: Women top executives

Clearly, Carly Fiorina broke the glass ceiling in her ascent to the CEO position at Hewlett-Packard. While she represents only a few women CEOs, more women are moving into key positions within major companies. In fact, Lew Platt, the CEO of HP when Fiorina was hired, decided that a woman CEO was what HP needed. Harriet Rubin, author of *Princessa: Machiavelli for Women*, suggests that 'we won't see great leaders until we see great women leaders'. While this is overstated, there is little doubt that there are many women who have been, are or will be great leaders. Margaret Thatcher and Golda Meir were both strong and great leaders.

Fewer women have been in business in the past only because of the glass ceiling, which, hopefully, is breaking. However, depending on who is counted, about 10–12 per cent of the top executive positions in US corporations are now held by women, an increase of approximately 48 per cent over a five-year period. Debra Meyerson, from Stanford University, suggests that 'It's not the ceiling holding women back; it's the whole structure of the organizations in which we work: the foundation, the beams, the walls, the very air.' While this statement may seem a little extreme, it does reflect the reality of the past and the frustration felt by the many talented women leaders. Perhaps Carly Fiorina's selection to be HP's CEO will break the barrier. The first woman CEO of a *Fortune* 50 or Dow 30 firm, Fiorina does not seem to believe as strongly in the barriers as some others. She suggested that competitive industries do not have time for glass ceilings. Her advice is to 'believe in yourself and invest in yourself and ignore the naysayers'.

Arlene Blum, a mountain climber and consultant, states, 'If you cannot picture it, you will not make it.' Thus, leaders must know where they are and where they are headed. Blum also recommends 'choosing your companions as if your life depended on it'.

Karen McCleod, head of Human Resources for Rio Tinto (which has recently acquired North Limited and Comalco), grew up in Weipa in Far North Queensland. She believes in developing a pool of top management people, in the virtues of collaboration and in a well-balanced personal life. Clearly, her influence as HR manager on Rio Tinto is considerable.

Gillian Franklin, the managing director of a company in a highly competitive industry, shares this same philosophy. Franklin works around 70 hours a week, travels overseas four or five times a year and makes regular trips interstate. She also has a busy family life: she and her husband have three girls, aged 12, 10 and eight. And she says her life is balanced. Indeed, Franklin, who heads up the toiletries and cosmetics company Creative Brands, insists that the demands of an exacting career can not only dovetail with family life, but enhance it. 'I have asked the girls if they would ever like me to give up the job, and they just look at me in amazement,' she says. Franklin admits her frenetic lifestyle is not for everyone. She gets to her office in Melbourne's southeast at around 7.15 am, is rarely home before 7 pm, and works some nights and weekends. 'I've been criticized by other women for adopting the work habits of some senior men executives. And I acknowledge there are women executives out there who do an excellent job working 40 to 50 hours a week. But that's just not me. To work to my optimum, I need 60 to 70 hours a week.'

Sources: P. LaBarre, 2000, 'Here's how to make it to the top', *Fast Company Online*, 1 March: www.fastcompany.com; L. Goldberg, 2000, 'A woman who became a high flier/Continental executive is still a pilot', *Houston Chronicle*, 26 February, p. 1B; P. W. Lauro, 2000, 'Ad woman of year changed small planet's view of

IBM', *Houston Chronicle*, 1 January, p. 2B; 'Glass ceiling still difficult to break/Just 10 percent of senior managers for Fortune 500 are women', 2000, *Houston Chronicle*, 7 January, p. 3B; H. Rubin, 2000, 'Living dangerously', *Fast Company Online*, 7 January: www.fastcompany.com; P. Burrows and P. Elstrom, 1999, 'The boss', *Business Week*, 2 August, pp. 79–84; A. Orr, 1999, 'Hewlett-Packard picks Lucent exec as CEO', *Houston Chronicle*, 20 July, p. 1B; N. Way, 1999, 'Profiles: Executives' stress', *Business Review Weekly*, 21(4): www.brw.com.au/newsadmin/stories/brw/19991022/3883.htm.

As noted earlier, the type of strategic leadership that results in the successful implementation of strategies is exemplified by several key actions. The most critical of these are shown in Figure 12.4. The remainder of this chapter is devoted to explaining each action. Note that many of the actions interact with each other. For example, developing human capital through executive training contributes to establishing a strategic direction, fostering an effective culture, exploiting core competencies, using effective organisational control systems and establishing ethical practices.

Figure 12.4 | Exercise of effective strategic leadership

Determining strategic direction

Determining the strategic direction of a firm involves developing a long-term vision of the firm's strategic intent.

Determining the **strategic direction** of a firm involves developing a long-term vision of the firm's strategic intent. Normally, a long-term vision looks at least five to 10 years into the future. A philosophy with goals, and a long-term vision, is the ideal image and character the firm seeks.[56] The ideal long-term vision has two parts: a core ideology and an envisioned future. While the core ideology motivates employees through the company's heritage, the envisioned future encourages employees to stretch beyond their expectations of accomplishment and requires significant change and progress in order to be realised.[57] The envisioned future serves as a guide to many aspects of a firm's strategy implementation process, including motivation, leadership, employee empowerment and organisational design. For firms competing in numerous industries, evidence suggests that the most effective long-term vision is one that has been accepted by those affected by it.[58]

To determine the firm's long-term vision, managers must take a sufficient amount of time to think about how it should be framed. Areas requiring executive thought include an analysis of the firm's external and internal environments and its current performance. Most top executives obtain inputs from many people with a range of skills to help them analyse various aspects of the firm's operations.

Brett Blundy, CEO of Australia's Brazin, has a vision of success in Australia's overcrowded coffee industry. Brazin, which also controls Sanity record stores and Bras 'n Things, have created the Gosh chain of coffee shops to compete with Perth-based Dome Coffee, the myriad of high-quality single unit coffee shops and the other new entrant, American giant Starbucks.[59] Likewise, Minoru Arakawa, president of Nintendo's US operations, had a vision. His vision was of enthusiasm in the United States for Pokémon, a Japanese video game with 150 collectible monsters. Market research produced conclusions that American children did not like the game. Arakawa decided to import it anyway. Pokémon's sales in the US exceeded US$1 billion between 1998 and 2000.[60] It has also proved immensely successful in Australia, where the Pokémon craze was well established by the end of 2000. Thus, both Blundy and Arakawa followed a philosophy similar to the advice provided by Carly Fiorina. They believe in their visions and ignored the naysayers. Once the vision is determined, CEOs must motivate employees to achieve it. Some, but not all, top executives are thought to be charismatic strategic leaders. Theory suggests that charisma comes through interactions between leaders and followers. Among these interactions is the creation and management of impressions, in which the strategic leader's framing, scripting, staging and performing lead to their being characterised as charismatic.[61] Although charisma is perceived as helpful, it is not a requirement for successful strategic leadership. Non-charismatic people often have other skills and traits – intelligence, vision, ambition and toughness, for example – that provide benefits similar to those gained when one is thought to be charismatic.[62] In certain situations, charismatic CEOs might facilitate a better performance by followers; in others, charisma might diminish a leader's credibility. Jack Welch, General Electric's former CEO, combined self-confidence, a high-strung passion for ideas he unabashedly borrowed and an unforgiving candour.[63]

A charismatic CEO may help gain employees' commitment to a new vision and strategic direction. Nonetheless, it is important not to lose sight of the strengths of the organisation in making changes required by a new strategic direction. In addition, executives must structure the firm effectively to help achieve their vision.[64] The goal is to balance the firm's short-term need to adjust to a new vision while maintaining its long-term survivability by emphasising its current and valuable core competencies.

Exploiting and maintaining core competencies

Examined in Chapters 1 and 3, *core competencies* are resources and capabilities that serve as a source of competitive advantage for a firm over its rivals. Typically, core competencies relate to an organisation's functional skills, such as manufacturing, finance, marketing, and research and development. As shown by the descriptions that follow, firms develop and exploit core competencies in many different functional areas to implement their strategies. Strategic leaders must verify that the firm's competencies are emphasised in strategy implementation efforts. Intel, for example, has core competencies of competitive agility (an ability to act in a variety of competitively relevant ways) and competitive speed (an ability to act quickly when facing environmental and competitive pressures).[65]

In many large firms, and certainly in related diversified ones, core competencies are exploited effectively when they are developed and applied across different organisational units (see Chapter 6). Alternatively, Amazon.com, built by Jeff Bezos, has a core competence that creates synergies across its multiple and diversified *product lines*. Amazon's core competencies are in its customer knowledge base, which, in turn, contributes to another competence: customer service. These competencies translate into a significant asset for a diversified e-commerce business: 17 million customers. Also, because of the company's knowledge of its customers and emphasis on customer service, 73 per cent of Amazon.com's sales are repeat business.[66] Core competencies cannot be developed or exploited effectively without developing the capabilities of human capital.[67]

Developing human capital

Human capital refers to the knowledge and skills of a firm's entire workforce.

Human capital refers to the knowledge and skills of a firm's entire workforce. From the perspective of human capital, employees are viewed as a capital resource that requires investment. Much of the development of industry can be attributed to the effectiveness of its human capital. In support of this conclusion, it is noted that 'as the dynamics of competition accelerate, people are perhaps the only truly sustainable source of competitive advantage'.[68] This statement suggests that the role of human resource management should be increasing in importance.[69] In turn, the effective development and management of the firm's human capital – that is, of all of the firm's managerial and non-managerial personnel – may be the primary determinant of a firm's ability to formulate and implement strategies successfully.[70]

Finding the human capital necessary to run an organisation effectively is a difficult problem that many firms attempt to solve by using temporary employees. Other firms try to improve their recruiting and selection techniques. Solving the problem, however, requires more than hiring temporary employees; it requires building effective commitment to organisational goals as well. Hiring star players is also insufficient; rather, a strategic leader needs to build an effective organisational team committed to achieving the company's vision and goals, as the Strategic Focus indicates.

Strategic Focus International

Competitive advantage powered by human capital

Consolidated Diesel's manufacturing plant in the United States does not look extraordinary. The equipment is the same as its competitors'. However, Consolidated produces exceptional results, powered by the firm's human capital, which is captured and released through its team-based system. To ensure the effective use of the company's human capital, employees are cross-trained on several jobs. Furthermore, employees are involved in developing solutions to problems. For example, with customer demand high, the plant had to add significant overtime and a third shift. However, after enlisting the aid of team leaders to help resolve the problem, Consolidated developed a more flexible scheduling system that cut the shifts back to eight hours, but the work continued to be completed. Similarly, MTW, an e-commerce applications firm, places high importance on its employees' needs. Like Consolidated Diesel, it uses teams. In addition, MTW attempts to create an environment in which people like to work. In so doing, the company has grown from a firm with 50 employees and US$8 million in annual sales to one with 200 employees and US$31 million in sales. In this environment, teams of employees make many of the operational decisions that affect the whole company. While decisions take longer in teams, the company gains the employees' confidence, trust and commitment.

Warren Buffett is known as one of the world's most successful investors. One of the criteria he uses in investing in firms is their managerial talent and human capital. The firms in which he invests heavily, such as Coca-Cola, American Express and Disney, are known to rely heavily on their human capital.

The importance of human capital also is shown in mergers and acquisitions, many of which are not successful (see Chapter 7). There are a number of reasons for these failures, a prime one of which is the loss, or failure to take advantage, of human capital from the acquired firm. Often, there is significant turnover in the acquired firm before and after the two firms are merged. Frequently, the most talented managers and employees leave because they have attractive opportunities and are uncertain whether they will have the same opportunities in the new company. Certainly, they are unlikely to have opportunities if their firm is acquired by Computer Associates, Charles Wang's company. Wang is notorious for firing many of the managers and technical talent of a firm he acquires immediately after the acquisition is consummated. Dennis Kozlowski, CEO of Tyco, analyses the managerial talent of potential target firms in his quest for acquisitions. He targets only those firms with substantial managerial skills and capabilities. In fact, he considers his review of the human capital of a firm a part of the due-diligence process.

Among the substantial number of under-utilised sources of human capital are under-represented groups, such as women and minorities. We discussed women in managerial roles in the previous Strategic Focus. According to Luci Li, partner of Wang & Li Asia Associates, there is a glass ceiling in the United States for many expatriate Chinese and Chinese Americans as well. These workers have many technical and other skills and a host of capabilities that can be developed, but frequently are not. Some suggest that the new types of distance learning using Internet courses can help firms to develop their human capital without significant costs. Clearly, the real-time environment of Internet instruction could revolutionise the means of developing human capital, particularly by promoting continuous learning within companies. In large and small firms, there are tremendous economic returns to human capital. In fact, human capital is critical to the implementation of a number of a firm's strategies.

Sources: G. Gendron, 2000, 'Editors tackle the question, what makes a good start-up?', *Wall Street Journal Interactive*, 16 February: www.interactive.wsj.com/archive; J. Rosenfeld, 1999, 'MTW puts people first', *Fast Company Online*, December: www.fastcompany.com; C. Sittenfeld, 1999, 'Powered by the people', *Fast Company Online*, July–August: www.fastcompany.com; G. S. Becker, 1999, 'How the web is revolutionizing learning', *Business Week Online*, 5 July: www.businessweek.com; J. Pfeffer and J. F. Veiga, 1999, 'Putting people first for organizational success', *Academy of Management Executive*, 13(2), pp. 37–48; J. Reingold and P. Elstrom, 1999, 'Big headhunter is watching you', *Business Week Online*, 1 March: www.businessweek.com; J. O'C. Hamilton, 1999, 'Have tech business, will travel', *Business Week Online*, 8 February: www.businessweek.com.

Amazon.com, founded by Jeff Bezos (shown here with a Pokémon doll), has a core competence that created synergies across its multiple product lines. Amazon.com's core competencies are in its customer knowledge base and customer service, and they translate into a significant asset of 17 million customers.

Actively participating in company-sponsored programs to develop one's abilities is highly desirable, because upgrading one's skills continuously leads to more job and economic security.[71] Increasingly, part of the development necessary for strategic leaders is international experience. As one business analyst noted, 'With nearly every industry targeting fast-growing foreign markets, more companies are requiring foreign experience for top management positions.'[72] Thus, companies committed to the importance of competing successfully in the global economy are wise to provide opportunities for their future strategic leaders to work in locations outside of their home nation. Also, because international management capabilities are becoming important, managing 'inpatriation' (the process of transferring host-country or third-country national managers into the domestic market of multinational firms) has become an important means of building global core competencies.[73]

Effective training and development programs increase the probability that a manager will be a successful strategic leader. These programs have grown progressively important as knowledge has become more integral to gaining and sustaining a competitive advantage.[74] Additionally, such programs build knowledge and skills, inculcate a common set of core values, and offer a systematic view of the organisation, thus promoting the firm's strategic vision and organisational cohesion. The programs also contribute to the development of core competencies.[75] Furthermore, they help strategic leaders to improve skills that are critical to completing other tasks associated with effective strategic leadership (for example, determining the firm's strategic direction, exploiting and maintaining the firm's core competencies and developing an organisational culture that supports ethical practices). Thus, building human capital is vital to the effective execution of strategy.[76]

Strategic leaders must acquire the skills necessary to help develop human capital in their areas of responsibility. This is an important challenge, given that most strategic leaders need to enhance their human resource management abilities. For example, firms that place value on human resources and have effective reward plans for employees obtained higher returns on their initial public offerings.[77] When human capital investments are successful, the result is a workforce capable of learning continuously. Continuous learning and leveraging the firm's expanding knowledge base are linked with strategic success.[78] When asked to specify what accounts for Johnson & Johnson's competitive success, the firm's CEO answered that his company was 'not in the product business, [but] in the knowledge business'.[79]

Programs that achieve outstanding results in the training of future strategic leaders become a competitive advantage for a firm. As noted in the Opening Case, General Electric's system of training and development of future strategic leaders is comprehensive and thought to be among the best.[80] Accordingly, it may be a source of competitive advantage for the firm.

A number of interesting changes are occurring in the corporate education market. Most training and development is conducted in-house, but firms are increasingly outsourcing this activity to private companies and to university outreach programs. Many of the firms have been pleased with the results.[81] Another trend is an increasing demand for on-line education programs. For example, GM has developed an on-line training program for its 175 000 employees at 7 500 dealerships. This program will save GM millions of dollars (for example, in travel, housing and food costs for the normal training programs at corporate headquarters). The program also saves time, as all employees can be reached in less than one week, whereas the normal training process required at least four months to include all of them.[82]

In the 1990s, millions of managers, strategic leaders and non-managerial personnel lost jobs through restructuring and downsizing in many companies (see Chapter 7). These processes are continuing into the 21st century, with Telstra announcing in May 2000 that it would downsize by 8 000 workers, while in October of that year a drop in its share price led to leaked announcements that up to 30 per cent of staff were to be shed. These moves should reduce the firm's costs and thus increase its profits over time. However, it is not clear how this action will increase the firm's growth, because, regardless of the cause, layoffs can result in a significant loss of knowledge that is possessed by a firm's human capital. A leaked e-mail to management from CEO Ziggy Switowski indicated that the emphasis was on cost cutting rather than protection of knowledge. 'Let me urge you onto greater efforts … The head count progress is temporarily slowing, and the [next generation cost reduction] projects are not far enough developed. Please note we have no room for forgiveness or negotiation re this …'[83] Although it is also not uncommon for restructuring firms to reduce their expenditures on, or investments in, training and development programs, restructuring may be an important time to increase investments in these programs. Restructuring firms have less slack and cannot absorb as many errors; moreover, many employees may be placed into positions without all of the skills or knowledge necessary to perform the required tasks effectively.[84] In the final analysis, a view of employees as a resource to be maximised, rather than a cost to be minimised, facilitates the successful implementation of a firm's strategies. The implementation of such strategies also is more effective when strategic leaders approach layoffs in a manner that employees believe is fair and equitable.[85]

As described next, human capital is an important part of a firm's ability to develop and sustain an effective organisational culture.

Sustaining an effective organisational culture

An organisational culture consists of a complex set of ideologies, symbols and core values that is shared throughout the firm and influences the way it conducts business. Evidence suggests that a firm can develop core competencies both in terms of the capabilities it possesses and the way the capabilities are used to produce strategic actions. In other words, because it influences how the firm conducts its business and helps regulate and control employees' behaviour, the organisational culture can be a source of competitive advantage.[86] Thus, shaping the context within which the firm formulates and implements its strategies – that is, shaping the organisational culture – is a central task of strategic leaders.[87]

BHP, for most of the last generation Australia's biggest corporation, has specifically recognised the need for a change to its corporate culture. This 'Big Australian' has a 'masculine' culture focused on Australia, but is now trying to become a more globalised and culturally sensitive corporation. They have been badly affected by long-running and highly publicised environmental issues at their Ok Tedi mine in Papua New Guinea, deaths at the Moura mine and falling share prices. Their corporate reputation has suffered while the culture focused on resource extraction and short-term gains. The culture they are trying to establish, under new CEO Paul Anderson, is more globally-oriented and more focused on win–win relationships, safety and environmental responsibility.[88]

Entrepreneurial orientation

An organisational culture often encourages (or discourages) the pursuit of entrepreneurial opportunities, especially in large firms. IBM produces a handbook designed to infuse an entrepreneurial spirit into its culture. The handbook is called *Changing the World* and is filled with tips designed to break mental barriers and to enable employees to be more creative in their jobs. For example, one tip states, 'Remember, if you don't exceed your authority at least once a week, you probably aren't doing your job.' Another tip states, 'Brainstorm with someone 10 years older and someone 10 years younger.'[89]

Successful outcomes derived through employees' pursuit of entrepreneurial opportunities are a major source of growth and innovation for firms.[90] These benefits are exemplified by the culture and activities at Oakley, Inc., the US manufacturer of sunglasses and sneakers. The company's culture combines 'a passion for design with a lust for combat'. The culture places a strong importance on being entrepreneurial, to challenge the norms. Oakley's sales flourished in the late 1990s, growing substantially. The company continues to introduce wild and different designs in its products, and it finds a market for them.[91]

Five dimensions characterise a firm's entrepreneurial orientation.[92] In combination, these dimensions influence the activities a firm uses in efforts to be innovative and launch new ventures. Discussed in Chapter 13, one of the key ways in which new ventures are launched in large firms is through corporate entrepreneurship. Particularly for firms seeking first-mover advantages (see Chapter 5), an entrepreneurial orientation among employees is critical.

Autonomy is the first of an entrepreneurial orientation's five dimensions. An active part of a firm's culture, autonomy allows employees to take actions that are free of stifling organisational constraints and permits individuals and groups to be self-directed. The second dimension, *innovativeness*, 'reflects a firm's tendency to engage in and support new ideas, novelty, experimentation, and creative processes that may result in new products, services, or technological processes'.[93] Cultures with a tendency towards innovativeness encourage employees to think beyond existing knowledge, technologies and parameters in efforts to find creative ways to add value. *Risk taking* reflects a willingness by employees and their firm to accept risks in the pursuit of marketplace opportunities. These risks can include assuming significant levels of debt and allocating large amounts of other resources (for example, people) to projects that may not be completed. Often, a firm accepts risks in order to seize marketplace opportunities that can substantially increase the firm's strategic competitiveness and its returns. The fourth dimension of an entrepreneurial orientation, *proactiveness*, describes a firm's ability to be a market leader rather than a follower. Proactive organisational cultures constantly use processes to anticipate future market needs and to satisfy them before competitors learn

Janet Holmes à Court is a significant businessperson controlling extensive assets, many based in Western Australia. She maintains a low public profile but is an active patron of the arts as well as an astute strategic thinker.

how to do so. Finally, *competitive aggressiveness* is a firm's propensity to take actions that allow it to outperform its rivals consistently and substantially. In summary, the key dimensions that characterise an entrepreneurial orientation are autonomy, a willingness to innovate and take risks, and a tendency to be aggressive towards competitors and proactive relative to marketplace opportunities.[94]

Changing the organisational culture and business reengineering

Changing a firm's organisational culture is more difficult than maintaining it, but effective strategic leaders recognise when change is needed. Incremental changes to the firm's culture typically are used to implement strategies.[95] However, more significant and, sometimes, even radical changes to a company's organisational culture are designed to support the selection of strategies that differ from the ones the firm has implemented historically. Regardless of the reasons for change, shaping and reinforcing a new culture requires effective communication and problem solving, along with the selection of the right people (those who have the values desired for the organisation), effective performance appraisals (establishing goals and measuring individual performance towards goals that fit in with the new core values) and appropriate reward systems (rewarding the desired behaviours that reflect the new core values).[96]

Evidence suggests that cultural changes succeed only when they are supported actively by the firm's CEO, other key top management team members and middle-level managers.[97] In fact, for large-scale changes, approximately one-third of middle-level managers need to be effective change agents possessing 'a nice balance of capabilities: They are technically skilled people who are also very capable in personal relationships. They're an odd combination. On the one hand, they're tough decision-makers who are highly disciplined about performance results. But they also know how to get lots of people energized and aligned in the same direction.'[98]

One catalyst for changing an organisation's culture, particularly for critical changes, is the selection of new top management team members from outside the corporation. Dell Computer Corporation founder and CEO Michael Dell, who pioneered direct marketing of computers to customers, recruited executives from companies such as Motorola, Hewlett-Packard and Apple Computer to deal with problems the firm encountered in late 1993 and early 1994.[99]

Transforming an organisation and its culture is challenging, as the current BHP experience indicates. The 'Big Australian' tag is continually reinforced by Australian media, and associated ideas are well established in the organisation. Change is slow. In another example, in 1997, top executives at Sara Lee decided to change the firm from a capital-intensive manufacturer to a less asset-intensive brand manager. Thus, the company had to sell its manufacturing facilities, find excellent suppliers to replace products manufactured in-house and change the firm's internal culture to focus on brand management. However, by 2000, Sara Lee had reduced its ratio of fixed assets to net working capital from 31 per cent to 24 per cent. Also, it had become an unwieldy conglomerate, unable to capture many synergies across product lines. Local managers were suspicious of managers in other product units or profit centres and thus would not cooperate with them to gain economies. The decentralised culture that developed at Sara Lee disallowed any centralisation (for example, of payroll or computer systems). Worse, the firm has not yet developed brand management as a core competence. Thus, the changes that accrued from the culture and strategy have not produced the end results desired; a different culture evolved than was intended.[100]

Pacific Dunlop is in an even more difficult position. In early 2000, its shares were at a 14-year low, and as a classic conglomerate, an unrelated diversified firm, it struggled with managing numerous brands as well as manufacturing facilities. Pacific Dunlop had, at that time, four divisions – GNB Batteries, South Pacific Tyres, Ansell condoms (their star) and Pacific Brands (a variety of branded goods). Its attempted sale of GNB Batteries was failing and brand management was a weakness rather than a core competency.[101]

Alternatively, the US firm Continental Airlines successfully changed its culture, building a system of teamwork that has paid handsomely through increased returns. Gordon Bethune, Continental's CEO, describes the importance of the teamwork culture that he and his managers have created at the company. Bethune suggests that Continental is not composed of cross-functional teams. Rather, he compares Continental's operation to that of a watch: if one part fails, the whole watch quits working. He notes that the firm is composed of multiple functions that have value when they all work cooperatively. In this way, all functions are important. Thus, Continental managers made cooperation a part of everyone's job, and employees are rewarded for cooperating and working as a team. Continental also developed a means of rewarding specific behaviours that it desired. For example, it provided bonuses to all employees each month that the company met its deadline. Prior to Bethune, Continental had suffered through 10 CEOs and two bankruptcies.[102] Essentially, a company's reputation is linked to its culture and its strategy,[103] and in that regard, Continental's reputation has been vastly improved.

Emphasising ethical practices

The effectiveness of processes that implement strategy increases when the processes are based on ethical practices. Ethical companies encourage and enable people at all organisational levels to exercise ethical judgement. Alternatively, if unethical practices evolve in an organisation, they become like a contagious disease.[104] To properly influence employees' judgement and behaviour, ethical practices must shape the firm's decision-making process and be an integral part of an organisation's culture. In fact, research has found that a value-based culture is the most effective means of ensuring that employees comply with the firm's ethical requirements.[105] As discussed in Chapter 10, in the absence of ethical requirements, *managerial opportunism* allows managers to take actions that are in their own best interests, but not in the firm's best interests. In other words, managers take advantage of their positions and therefore make decisions that benefit them to the detriment of the owners (shareholders).[106] Problems that have been documented include questionable hiring practices and a willingness to commit fraud by understating write-offs that reduce corporate returns.[107] Sometimes, very high CEO compensation is a sign of opportunism being pursued by those in top management (for example, the court order to Charles Wang to return almost 50 per cent of the US$670 million compensation awarded him in 1999).[108]

Another set of studies sheds light on these issues. Research examining managers' ethical values and beliefs in the mid-1980s and again in the early 1990s showed little change. In both of those years, managers emphasised utilitarian goals – that is, the achievement of economic gains for the organisation's stakeholders. In fact, the earlier survey found that one of the primary reasons managers emphasised ethical practices was to achieve greater profits. Some argue that the managerial and organisational gains are mutually beneficial. In other words, firms that establish and maintain ethical practices are more likely to achieve strategic competitiveness and earn above-average returns. A key reason for this is that a reputation for ethical practices attracts loyal customers.[109]

On the other hand, other evidence suggests that at least some individuals from different groups – including top-level executives and business students – may be willing to commit either illegal actions (for example, fraud) or actions that many think are unethical. In one American study, researchers found that 47 per cent of upper-level executives, 41 per cent of controllers, and 76 per cent of graduate-level business students expressed a willingness to commit fraud (as measured by a subject's willingness to misrepresent his or her company's financial statements). Moreover, these researchers discovered that 87 per cent of the managers made at least one fraudulent decision in seven situations requiring a decision. Another of their findings is that the more an individual valued a comfortable life or pleasure, and the less he or she valued self-respect, the greater was the probability that a fraudulent decision would be made.[110]

Another study's results appear to have important implications for organisations and those who manage them.[111] The study found that, although cheating was observed, there was reluctance to report it. An unwillingness to report wrongdoing calls for the development of comprehensive organisational control systems to assure that individuals' behaviours are consistent with the firm's needs and expectations.

These studies' findings suggest the need for firms to employ ethical strategic leaders – leaders who include ethical practices as part of their long-term vision for the firm, who desire to do the right thing and for whom honesty, trust and integrity are important.[112] Strategic leaders who consistently display these qualities inspire employees as they work with others to develop and support an organisational culture in which ethical practices are the expected behavioural norms.

Unfortunately, not all people in positions of strategic leadership display the ethical approach described. The actions explained in the next Strategic Focus suggest the need for vigilance in guarding against unethical actions taken by those in key managerial positions within companies.

Strategic Focus Corporate

Lies, managed earnings and conflicts of interest – the ethics of strategic leaders

A case of 'managed earnings' occurred at Sunbeam Corporation in the United States, where the problems involved Al Dunlap, a well-known and often controversial CEO. Dunlap, popularly known in the Australian press as 'Chainsaw Al' because of his role in downsizing companies such as Packer's PBL, had been successful in turning around the performance of several companies (although his methods had been criticised) prior to his role with Sunbeam. He took actions similar to those he took with previous firms, such as selling off assets and laying off employees, but was unable to reach the performance targets desired by Sunbeam investors. He attempted to sell the company, but could not find a buyer. So instead, he acquired three other firms in an effort to jump-start Sunbeam's performance. Partly because of a massive accrual of debt to finance the acquisitions (and because of the accompanying cost of the debt), Sunbeam's performance deteriorated even further. The company reported a net loss in the first quarter of 1998. However, close examination suggested that the books had been 'cooked' in 1997 to create a false turnaround. Most believe that this was done to facilitate the sale of Sunbeam. Unfortunately for Dunlap, the firm did not sell, and he had to live with the consequences. The results for 1997 were restated, and it was discovered that Sunbeam actually incurred a loss of US$6.4 million in that year. Sunbeam's board of directors fired Al Dunlap for his actions.

A similar incident occurred at Cendant Corporation, also in the United States, but it was discovered several months after an acquisition was completed. HFS Incorporated had acquired CUC International to form Cendant. A review of the accounts revealed that CUC executives had been overstating the firm's profits for approximately three years prior to the acquisition. The earnings had to be restated by US$511 million less than previously reported. Upon the announcement of the restatement, Cendant's share price fell from US$41 to less than US$10, and the company lost US$29 billion in value. Later, shareholders settled with Cendant for the largest shareholder settlement in history to that point, US$335 million.

In 2000, it was reported that the US Securities and Exchange Commission accused PricewaterhouseCoopers of over 8 000 violations. The most serious of the allegations was having employees and officers owning shares in companies that were auditing clients of the firm. Five per cent of the firm's employees, including 31 of 43 senior partners, were charged with violations. Five partners were asked to resign, and five managers and other staff were also dismissed.

Other examples involving ethical concerns include a price-fixing investigation at Sotheby's, an auctioneering company, and managers at British Nuclear Fuels (BNFL) who overlooked safety violations. Sotheby's share price declined significantly after the investigation was announced, and the firm's top two officers resigned. BNFL fired managers whom it suspected of ignoring safety violations in order to meet the company's timetable for privatisation. These actions of questionable ethics and their outcomes suggest that they are undertaken with considerable risk. The consequences may be great if the practices are uncovered.

Sources: M. A. Hitt, J. S. Harrison and R. D. Ireland, 2001, *Creating Value Through Mergers and Acquisitions: A Complete Guide to Successful M&As* (New York: Oxford University Press); K. Brown and M. Jones, 2000, 'BNFL to cull managers in fall-out from safety scandal', 29 February: www.ft.com; J. Chaffin, 2000, 'Sotheby's shares slide amid scandal', 23 February: www.ft.com; A. Peers and D. Costello, 2000, 'Top executives quit Sotheby's amid price-fixing investigation', *Wall Street Journal Interactive*, 23 February: www.interactive.wsj.com/archive; P. L. Moore, 2000, 'The PWC scandal changes everything', *Business Week Online*, 28 February: www.businessweek.com; M. Schroeder and E. MacDonald, 1999, 'SEC enforcement actions target accounting fraud', *Wall Street Journal Interactive*, 29 September: www.interactive.wsj.com/articles.

Strategic leaders are challenged to take actions that increase the probability that an ethical culture will prevail in their organisation. One means of doing this that is gaining favour in companies is to institute a formal program to manage ethics in the organisation. While such programs operate much like control systems, they help to inculcate values throughout the organisation as well.[113] Therefore, when these efforts are successful, the practices associated with an ethical culture become institutionalised in the firm; that is, they become the set of behavioural commitments and actions accepted by most of the firm's employees and other stakeholders with whom employees interact. Further actions that strategic leaders can take to develop an ethical organisational culture include: (1) establishing and communicating specific goals to describe the firm's ethical standards (for example, developing and disseminating a code of conduct); (2) continuously revising and updating the code of conduct, based on inputs from people throughout the firm and from other stakeholders (for example, customers and suppliers); (3) disseminating the code of conduct to all stakeholders to inform them of the firm's ethical standards and practices; (4) developing and implementing methods and procedures to use in achieving the firm's ethical standards (for example, using internal auditing practices that are consistent with the standards); (5) creating and using explicit reward systems that recognise acts of courage (for example, rewarding those who use proper channels and procedures to report observed wrongdoings); and (6) creating a work environment in which all people are treated with dignity.[114] The effectiveness of these actions increases when they are taken simultaneously, thereby making them mutually supportive. When managers and employees do not engage in such actions – perhaps because an ethical culture has not been created – problems are likely to occur. These problems are exemplified in the Strategic Focus on ethically questionable practices. Formal organisational controls may then be needed to prevent further problems.

Establishing balanced organisational controls

Organisational controls have long been viewed as an important part of strategy implementation processes. Controls are necessary to help ensure that firms achieve their desired outcomes of strategic competitiveness and above-average returns.[115] Defined as the 'formal, information-based ... procedures used by managers to maintain or alter patterns in organizational activities', controls help strategic leaders to build credibility, demonstrate the value of strategies to the firm's stakeholders, and promote and support strategic change.[116] Most critically, controls provide the parameters within which strategies are to be implemented, as well as corrective actions to be taken, when implementation-related adjustments are required. In this chapter, we focus on two organisational controls – strategic and financial – that were introduced in Chapter 11. Our discussion of organisational controls here emphasises strategic and financial controls, because strategic leaders are responsible for their development and effective use.

Evidence suggests that, although critical to the firm's success, organisational controls are imperfect. Consider the example of PricewaterhouseCoopers, in which many of the partners and employees owned shares in companies that the firm audited. This conflict of interest could provide incentives for taking an inappropriate action in audits. If, for example, an audit discovered a major impropriety in which the profits were overstated, revealing the problem could harm the firm's share price. The problem at PricewaterhouseCoopers could be described as a *control failure*. Control failures such as this have a negative effect on the firm's reputation and divert managerial attention from actions that are necessary to use the strategic management process effectively.

As explained in Chapter 11, financial control is often emphasised in large corporations. Financial control focuses on short-term financial outcomes. In contrast, strategic control focuses on the *content* of strategic actions, rather than their *outcomes*. Some strategic actions can be correct, but poor financial outcomes may still result because of external conditions, such as a recession in the economy, unexpected domestic or foreign government actions, or natural disasters.[117] Therefore, an emphasis on financial control often produces more short-term and risk-averse managerial decisions, because financial outcomes may be due to events beyond managers' direct control. Alternatively, strategic control encourages lower-level managers to make decisions that incorporate moderate and acceptable levels of risk because outcomes are shared between the business-level executives making strategic proposals and the corporate-level executives evaluating them.

Successful strategic leaders balance strategic control and financial control (they do not *eliminate* financial control), with the intent of achieving more positive long-term returns.[118] In fact, most corporate restructuring is designed to refocus the firm on its core businesses, thereby allowing top executives to re-establish strategic control of their separate business units.[119] Thus, both types of controls are important.

The effective use of strategic control by top executives frequently is integrated with appropriate autonomy for the various sub-units so that they can gain a competitive advantage in their respective markets. Strategic control can be used to promote the sharing of both tangible and intangible resources among interdependent businesses within a firm's portfolio. In addition, the autonomy provided allows the flexibility necessary to take advantage of specific marketplace opportunities. As a result, strategic leadership promotes the simultaneous use of strategic control and autonomy.[120]

Diversified business firms often have trouble in balancing the two types of control. Because large diversified firms have not maintained this balance, many throughout the world are restructuring their operations. For instance, the recent currency crisis in Southeast Asia has revealed significant problems in the diversification strategies of large diversified firms in South Korea. Among the South Korean firms that had to restructure are Samsung, LG Group, Hyundai, Sangyong and Daewoo (the last with considerable acrimony and, indeed, street violence).

Family-owned companies of expatriate Chinese run many of the business groups in Southeast Asia. Traditionally, these firms have been in consumer industries that are non-technical, such as shipping; commodity trading; hotel, real estate and financial services; and other light industries. As these firms sought to move into high-tech industries, such as chemicals and electronics, they have had to move away from the family-managed business concept to more professional managerial techniques. This adjustment was partly due to the change in capital markets, where more transparency is now required and where contracting law is becoming more prominent. Strategic leaders of those firms, mostly family members and friends, ran the business operations before the economic shocks occurred. They are now being forced to implement better and more professional control systems, as have other diversified business groups throughout the world.[121]

As our discussion in this chapter suggests, organisational controls establish an integrated set of analyses and actions that reinforce one another. Through the effective use of strategic controls, strategic leaders increase the probability that their firms will gain the benefits of carefully formulated strategies, but not at the expense of the financial control that is a critical part of the strategy implementation process. Effective organisational controls provide an underlying logic for strategic leadership, focus attention on critical strategic issues, support a competitive culture, and provide a forum that builds commitment to the firm's strategic intent.

Summary

- Effective strategic leadership is required to use the strategic management process successfully, including the strategic actions associated with the implementation of strategies. Strategic leadership entails the ability to anticipate events, envision possibilities, maintain flexibility and empower others to create strategic change.
- Top executives are an important resource for firms to develop and exploit competitive advantages. In addition, these strategic leaders can be a source of competitive advantage.
- The top management team is composed of key managers who formulate and implement strategies. Generally, they are officers of the corporation or members of the board of directors.
- There is a relationship among the top management team's characteristics, a firm's strategy and a firm's performance. For example, a top management team that has significant marketing and R&D knowledge often enhances the firm's effectiveness in the implementation of growth strategies. Overall, most top management teams are more effective when they have diverse skills.
- When boards of directors are involved in shaping firms' strategic direction, those firms generally improve their strategic competitiveness. Alternatively, boards may be less involved in decisions regarding strategy formulation and implementation when CEOs have more power. CEOs obtain power when they appoint people to the board and when they simultaneously serve as the CEO and board chair.
- Strategic leaders are selected from either the internal or the external managerial labour market. Because of their effect on firm performance, the selection of strategic leaders from these markets has implications for a firm's effectiveness. Valid reasons exist to use

both labour markets when selecting strategic leaders and managers with the potential to become strategic leaders. In the majority of cases, the internal market is used to select the firm's CEO. Outsiders often are selected to initiate needed change.
- Effective strategic leadership has six components: determining the firm's strategic direction, exploiting and maintaining core competencies, developing human capital, sustaining an effective organisational culture, emphasising ethical practices, and establishing balanced organisational controls.
- A firm must develop a long-term vision of its strategic intent. A charismatic leader can help to realise that vision.
- Strategic leaders must ensure that their firm exploits its core competencies, which are used to produce and deliver products that create value for customers, through the implementation of strategies. In related diversified and large firms in particular, core competencies are exploited by sharing them across units and products.
- A critical element of strategic leadership and the effective implementation of strategy is the ability to develop a firm's human capital. Effective strategic leaders and firms view human capital as a resource to be maximised, rather than as a cost to be minimised. Resulting from this perspective is the development and use of programs intended to train current and future strategic leaders to build the skills needed to nurture the rest of the firm's human capital.
- Shaping the firm's culture is a central task of effective strategic leadership. An appropriate organisational culture encourages the development of an entrepreneurial orientation among employees and an ability to change the culture as necessary. In ethical organisations, employees are encouraged to exercise ethical judgement and to behave ethically at all times. Ethical practices can be promoted through several actions, including setting specific goals to describe the firm's ethical standards, using a code of conduct, rewarding ethical behaviours, and creating a work environment in which all people are treated with dignity.
- The final component of effective strategic leadership is the development and use of effective organisational controls. It is through such controls that strategic leaders provide the direction the firm requires to flexibly, yet appropriately, use its core competencies in the pursuit of marketplace opportunities. The best results are obtained when there is a balance between strategic and financial controls.

Review questions

1. What is strategic leadership? In what ways are top executives considered important resources for an organisation?
2. What is a top management team, and how does it affect a firm's performance and its abilities to innovate and make appropriate strategic changes?
3. What are the differences between the internal and external managerial labour markets? What are the effects of each type of labour market on the formulation and implementation of firm strategy?
4. How does strategic leadership affect the determination of the firm's strategic direction?
5. Why is it important for strategic leaders to make certain that their firm exploits its core competencies in the pursuit of strategic competitiveness and above-average returns?
6. What is the importance of human capital and its development for strategic competitiveness?
7. What is organisational culture? What must strategic leaders do to develop and sustain an effective organisational culture?
8. As a strategic leader, what actions could you take to establish and emphasise ethical practices in your firm?
9. What are organisational controls? Why are strategic controls and financial controls an important part of the strategic management process?

Application discussion questions

1. Choose a CEO of a prominent firm you believe exemplifies the positive aspects of strategic leadership. What actions does this CEO take that demonstrate effective strategic leadership? What are the effects of those actions on the firm's performance?
2. Select a CEO of a prominent firm you believe does *not* exemplify the positive aspects of strategic leadership. What actions did this CEO take that are inconsistent with effective strategic leadership? How have those ineffective actions affected the firm's performance?
3. What are managerial resources? What is the relationship between managerial resources and a firm's strategic competitiveness?
4. Examine some articles in the popular press, and select an organisation that recently went through a significant strategic change. Collect as much information as you can about the organisation's top

management team. Is there a relationship between the top management team's characteristics and the type of change the organisation experienced? If so, what are the nature and outcome of that relationship?

5   Read some articles in the popular press and identify two new CEOs, one from the internal managerial labour market and one from the external labour market. Why do you think these individuals were chosen? What do they bring to the job, and what strategy do you think they will implement in their respective organisations?

6   Based on your reading of this chapter and accounts in the popular press, select a CEO you feel has exhibited vision. Has this CEO's vision been realised? If so, what have its effects been? If the vision has not been realised, why not?

7   Identify a firm in which you believe strategic leaders have emphasised and developed human capital. What do you believe are the effects of this emphasis and development on the firm's performance?

8   Select an organisation that you think has a unique organisational culture. What characteristics of that culture make it unique? Has the culture had a significant effect on the organisation's performance? If so, what is that effect?

9   Why is the strategic control exercised by a firm's strategic leaders important for long-term competitiveness? How do strategic controls differ from financial controls?

Ethics questions

1   As discussed in this chapter, effective strategic leadership occasionally requires managers to make difficult decisions. In your opinion, is it ethical for managers to make these types of decisions without obtaining feedback from employees about the effects of those decisions? Be prepared to justify your response.

2   As an employee with less than one year of experience in a firm, what actions would you pursue if you encountered unethical practices by a strategic leader?

3   Are firms ethically obligated to promote employees from within, rather than relying on the external labour market to select strategic leaders? What reasoning supports your position?

4   What ethical issues, if any, are involved with a firm's ability to develop and exploit a core competence in the manufacture of goods that may be harmful to consumers (for example, cigarettes)?

5   As a strategic leader, would you feel ethically responsible for developing your firm's human capital? Why or why not? Do you believe that your position is consistent with the majority or minority of today's strategic leaders?

6   Select an organisation, social group or volunteer agency of which you are a member that you believe has an ethical culture. What factors caused this culture to be ethical? Are there any events that would cause the culture to become less ethical? If so, what are they?

Internet exercise

*e-project: Amazon.com has revolutionised the Internet shopping industry, a fact that can, in large part, be accredited to Jeff Bezos, America's number-one CEO of an Internet-based company. Learn about Bezos's background through the Amazon home page and other Web resources. What was his initial strategy in creating Amazon? Was he able to implement the strategy effectively? What successes spurred him to expand and diversify his Web-based business?

Notes

1   K. R. Thompson, W. A. Hochwarter and N. J. Mathys, 1997, 'Stretch targets: What makes them effective?', *Academy of Management Executive*, XI(3), pp. 48–59.

2   R. D. Ireland and M. A. Hitt, 1999, 'Achieving and maintaining strategic competitiveness in the 21st century: The role of strategic leadership', *Academy of Management Executive*, 12(1), pp. 43–57; D. Lei, M. A. Hitt and R. Bettis, 1996, 'Dynamic core competencies through meta-learning and strategic context', *Journal of Management*, 22, pp. 547–67.

3   D. Silverman, 2000, 'CEO brings new life to stagnant Compaq/Capellas moves firm back to profitability', *Houston Chronicle*, 25 January, p. 1B.

4   Ireland and Hitt, 'Achieving and maintaining strategic competitiveness'.

5   M. A. Hitt, B. W. Keats and S. DeMarie, 1998, 'Navigating in the new competitive landscape: Building competitive advantage and strategic flexibility in the 21st century', *Academy of Management Executive*, XI(4), pp. 22–42; J. B. Quinn, P. Anderson and S. Finkelstein, 1996, 'Managing professional intellect: Making the most of the best', *Harvard Business Review*, 74(2), pp. 71–80.

6   M. Loeb, 1994, 'Where leaders come from', *Fortune*, 19 September, pp. 241–2.

7   M. F. R. Kets de Vries, 1995, *Life and Death in the Executive Fast Lane* (San Francisco: Jossey-Bass).

8   T. Kono, 1999, 'A strong head office makes a strong company', *Long Range Planning*, 32, pp. 225–46.

9   R. Nixon, M. A. Hitt and J. E. D. Ricart I Costa, 1998, 'New managerial mindsets and strategic change in the new frontier', in M. A. Hitt, J. E. Ricart and R. D. Nixon (eds), *New Managerial Mindsets* (New York: John Wiley & Sons).

10 G. Hamel and C. K. Prahalad, 1993, 'Strategy as stretch and leverage', *Harvard Business Review*, 71(2), pp. 75–84.

11 R. Calori, G. Johnson and P. Sarnin, 1994, 'CEOs' cognitive maps and the scope of the organization', *Strategic Management Journal*, 15, pp. 437–57.

12 U. S. Daellenbach, A. M. McCarthy and T. S. Schoenecker, 1999, 'Commitment to innovation: The impact of top management team characteristics', *R&D Management*, 29, pp. 199–208.

13 M. Hammer and S. A. Stanton, 1997, 'The power of reflection', *Fortune*, 24 November, pp. 291–6.
14 S. Finkelstein and D. C. Hambrick, 1996, *Strategic Leadership: Top Executives and Their Effects on Organizations* (St. Paul, MN: West Publishing Company), p. 2.
15 E. Weldon and W. Vanyhonaker, 1999, 'Operating a foreign-invested enterprise in China: Challenges for managers and management researchers', *Journal of World Business*, 34, pp. 94–107; J. A. Byrne and J. Reingold, 1997, 'Wanted: A few good CEOs', *Business Week*, 11 August, pp. 64–70.
16 H. P. Gunz and R. M. Jalland, 1996, 'Managerial careers and business strategy', *Academy of Management Review*, 21, pp. 718–56.
17 C. M. Christensen, 1997, 'Making strategy: Learning by doing', *Harvard Business Review*, 75(6), pp. 141–56; M. A. Hitt, B. W. Keats, H. E. Harback and R. D. Nixon, 1994, 'Rightsizing: Building and maintaining strategic leadership and long-term competitiveness', *Organizational Dynamics*, 23, pp. 18–32; R. L. Priem and D. A. Harrison, 1994, 'Exploring strategic judgment: Methods for testing the assumptions of prescriptive contingency theories', *Strategic Management Journal*, 15, pp. 311–24.
18 M. J. Waller, G. P. Huber and W. H. Glick, 1995, 'Functional background as a determinant of executives' selective perception', *Academy of Management Journal*, 38, pp. 943–74; N. Rajagopalan, A. M. Rasheed and D. K. Datta, 1993, 'Strategic decision processes: Critical review and future directions', *Journal of Management*, 19, pp. 349–84.
19 Finkelstein and Hambrick, *Strategic Leadership*, pp. 26–34; D. C. Hambrick and E. Abrahamson, 1995, 'Assessing managerial discretion across industries: A multi-method approach', *Academy of Management Journal*, 38, pp. 1427–41; D. C. Hambrick and S. Finkelstein, 1987, 'Managerial discretion: A bridge between polar views of organizational outcomes', in B. Staw and L. L. Cummings (eds), *Research in Organizational Behavior* (Greenwich, CT: JAI Press), pp. 369–406.
20 C. Sittenfeld, 2000, 'Leader on the edge', *Fast Company Online*, 1 March: www.fastcompany.com.
21 R. C. Mayer, J. H. Davis and F. D. Schoorman, 1995, 'An integrative model of organizational trust', *Academy of Management Review*, 20, pp. 709–34.
22 D. A. Waldman and F. Yammarino, 1999, 'CEO charismatic leadership: Levels of management and levels of analysis effects', *Academy of Management Review*, 24, pp. 266–85; N. Rajagopalan and D. K. Datta, 1996, 'CEO characteristics: Does industry matter?', *Academy of Management Journal*, 39, pp. 197–215.
23 P. Chattopadhyay, W. H. Glick, C. C. Miller and G. P. Huber, 1999, 'Determinants of executive beliefs: Comparing functional conditioning and social influence', *Strategic Management Journal*, 20, pp. 763–89.
24 M. A. Hitt, R. D. Nixon, P. G. Clifford and K. P. Coyne, 1999, 'The development and use of strategic resources', in M. A. Hitt, P. G. Clifford, R. D. Nixon and K. P. Coyne (eds), *Dynamic Strategic Resources* (New York: John Wiley & Sons).
25 H. A. Krishnan, 1997, 'Diversification and top management team complementarity: Is performance improved by merging similar or dissimilar teams?', *Strategic Management Journal*, 18, pp. 361–74; J. G. Michel and D. C. Hambrick, 1992, 'Diversification posture and top management team characteristics', *Academy of Management Journal*, 35, pp. 9–37.
26 A. L. Iaquito and J. W. Fredrickson, 1997, 'Top management team agreement about the strategic decision process: A test of some of its determinants and consequences', *Strategic Management Journal*, 18, pp. 63–75; K. G. Smith, D. A. Smith, J. D. Olian, H. P. Sims, Jr, D. P. O'Bannon and J. A. Scully, 1994, 'Top management team demography and process: The role of social integration and communication', *Administrative Science Quarterly*, 39, pp. 412–38.
27 N. Athanassiou and D. Nigh, 1999, 'The impact of U.S. company internationalization on top management team advice networks: A tacit knowledge perspective', *Strategic Management Journal*, 20, pp. 83–92.
28 D. Knight, C. L. Pearce, K. G. Smith, J. D. Olian, H. P. Sims, K. A. Smith and P. Flood, 1999, 'Top management team diversity, group process, and strategic consensus', *Strategic Management Journal*, 20, pp. 446–65.
29 D. C. Hambrick, T. S. Cho and M. J. Chen, 1996, 'The influence of top management team heterogeneity on firms' competitive moves', *Administrative Science Quarterly*, 41, pp. 659–84.
30 T. Simons, L. H. Pelled and K. A. Smith, 1999, 'Making use of difference, diversity, debate, and decision comprehensiveness in top management teams', *Academy of Management Journal*, 42, pp. 662–73.
31 Finkelstein and Hambrick, *Strategic Leadership*, p. 148.
32 C. C. Miller, L. M. Burke and W. H. Glick, 1998, 'Cognitive diversity among upper-echelon executives: Implications for strategic decision processes', *Strategic Management Journal*, 19, pp. 39–58.
33 Ibid.
34 D. K. Datta and J. P. Guthrie, 1994, 'Executive succession: Organizational antecedents of CEO characteristics', *Strategic Management Journal*, 15, pp. 569–77; M. A. Hitt and R. D. Ireland, 1986, 'Relationships among corporate-level distinctive competencies, diversification strategy, corporate structure, and performance', *Journal of Management Studies*, 23, pp. 401–16; M. A. Hitt and R. D. Ireland, 1985, 'Corporate distinctive competence, strategy, industry, and performance', *Strategic Management Journal*, 6, pp. 273–93.
35 W. Boeker, 1997, 'Strategic change: The influence of managerial characteristics and organizational growth', *Academy of Management Journal*, 40, pp. 152–70; W. Boeker, 1997, 'Executive migration and strategic change: The effect of top manager movement on product-market entry', *Administrative Science Quarterly*, 42, pp. 213–36.
36 A. Tomie, 2000, 'Fast Pack 2000', *Fast Company Online*, 1 March: www.fastcompany.com.
37 M. E. Wiersema and K. Bantel, 1992, 'Top management team demography and corporate strategic change', *Academy of Management Journal*, 35, pp. 91–121; K. Bantel and S. Jackson, 1989, 'Top management and innovations in banking: Does the composition of the top team make a difference?', *Strategic Management Journal*, 10, pp. 107–24.
38 W. Q. Judge, Jr and C. P. Zeithaml, 1992, 'Institutional and strategic choice perspectives on board involvement in the strategic decision process', *Academy of Management Journal*, 35, pp. 766–94; J. A. Pearce II and S. A. Zahra, 1991, 'The relative power of CEOs and boards of directors: Associations with corporate performance', *Strategic Management Journal*, 12, pp. 135–54.
39 J. D. Westphal and E. J. Zajac, 1995, 'Who shall govern? CEO/board power, demographic similarity, and new director selection', *Administrative Science Quarterly*, 40, p. 60.
40 J. D. Westphal, 1999, 'Collaboration in the boardroom: Behavioral and performance consequences of CEO-board social ties', *Academy of Management Journal*, 42, pp. 7–24.
41 Ibid., p. 66; E. J. Zajac and J. D. Westphal, 1995, 'Accounting for the explanations of CEO compensation: Substance and symbolism', *Administrative Science Quarterly*, 40, pp. 283–308.
42 B. K. Boyd, 1995, 'CEO duality and firm performance: A contingency model', *Strategic Management Journal*, 16, p. 301.
43 J. Muller, K. Kerwin and J. Ewing, 1999, 'DaimlerChrysler's Schrempp: Man with a plan', *Business Week Online*, 4 October: www.businessweek.com.
44 C. M. Daily and D. R. Dalton, 1995, 'CEO and director turnover in failing firms: An illusion of change?', *Strategic Management Journal*, 16, pp. 393–400.
45 R. Albanese, M. T. Dacin and I. C. Harris, 1997, 'Agents as stewards', *Academy of Management Review*, 22, pp. 609–11; J. H. Davis, F. D. Schoorman and L. Donaldson, 1997, 'Toward a stewardship theory of management', *Academy of Management Review*, 22, pp. 20–47.
46 J. D. Westphal and E. J. Zajac, 1997, 'Defections from the inner circle: Social exchange, reciprocity and diffusion of board independence in U.S. corporations', *Administrative Science Quarterly*, pp. 161–83; A. K. Buchholtz and B. A. Ribbens, 1994, 'Role of chief executive officers in takeover resistance: Effects of CEO incentives and individual characteristics', *Academy of Management Journal*, 37, pp. 554–79.
47 Rajagopalan and Datta, 'CEO characteristics', p. 201.
48 R. A. Johnson, R. E. Hoskisson and M. A. Hitt, 1993, 'Board involvement in restructuring: The effect of board versus managerial controls and characteristics', *Strategic Management Journal*, 14 (Special Summer Issue), pp. 33–50.
49 B. K. Boyd, 1995, 'CEO duality and firm performance: A contingency model', *Strategic Management Journal*, 16, pp. 301–12.
50 T. A. Stewart, 1998, 'Why leadership matters', *Fortune*, 2 March, pp. 71–82.
51 W. C. Byham, 1999, 'Grooming leaders', *Executive Excellence*, 16, p. 18.
52 Datta and Guthrie, 'Executive succession', p. 570.
53 Finkelstein and Hambrick, *Strategic Leadership*, pp. 180–1.
54 D. Miller, 1991, 'Stale in the saddle: CEO tenure and the match between organization and environment', *Management Science*, 37, pp. 34–52.

55 B. Gaylord, 2000, 'Meeting the men from Uncle Sam', *The Age*, 16 November, p. 5; M. Davis, 1998, 'After Prescott a quick-fire effort', *Business Review Weekly*, 20 March, pp. 24–8; L. Schmidt, 1999, 'Dennis Eck, Superstar?', *Business Review Weekly*, 10 December, pp. 72–75.

56 J. E. Ettlie, 1996, Review of E. Bowman (ed.), *The Perpetual Enterprise Machine: Seven Keys to Corporate Renewal through Successful Product and Process Development* (New York: Oxford University Press), in *Academy of Management Review*, 21, pp. 294–8; Hitt et al., 'Rightsizing', p. 20.

57 J. C. Collins and J. I. Porras, 1996, 'Building your company's vision', *Harvard Business Review*, 74(5), pp. 65–77.

58 C. M. Falbe, M. P. Kriger and P. Miesing, 1995, 'Structure and meaning of organizational vision', *Academy of Management Journal*, 39, pp. 740–69.

59 S. Lloyd, 2000, 'Big beans', *Business Review Weekly*, 1 September, pp. 30–3.

60 'Pokémon patriarch', 2000, *Businessweek Online*, 10 January: www.businessweek.com.

61 W. L. Gardner and B. J. Avolio, 1998, 'The charismatic relationship: A dramaturgical perspective', *Academy of Management Review*, 23, pp. 32–58.

62 Finkelstein and Hambrick, 1996, *Strategic Leadership*, pp. 69–72; P. Sellers, 1996, 'What exactly is charisma?', *Fortune*, 15 January, pp. 68–75.

63 T. Smart, 1996, 'Jack Welch's encore', *Business Week*, 28 October, pp. 154–60.

64 R. M. Hodgetts, 1999, 'Dow Chemical's CEO William Stavropoulos on structure and decision making', *Academy of Management Executive*, 13(4), pp. 29–35.

65 P. R. Nayyar and K. A. Bantel, 1994, 'Competitive agility: A source of competitive advantage based on speed and variety', in P. Shrivastava, A. Huff and J. Dutton (eds), *Advances in Strategic Management*, 10A (Greenwich, CT: JAI Press), pp. 193–222.

66 R. D. Hof, H. Green and D. Brady, 2000, 'Suddenly, Amazon's books look better', *Business Week*, 21 February, pp. 78–84.

67 C. A. Lengnick-Hall and J. A. Wolff, 1999, 'Similarities and contradictions in the core logic of three strategy research streams', *Strategic Management Journal*, 20, pp. 1109–32.

68 S. A. Snell and M. A. Youndt, 1995, 'Human resource management and firm performance: Testing a contingency model of executive controls', *Journal of Management*, 21, pp. 711–37.

69 D. Ulrich, 1998, 'A new mandate for human resources', *Harvard Business Review*, 76(1), pp. 124–34.

70 Snell and Youndt, 'Human resource', p. 711; K. Chilton, 1994, *The Global Challenge of American Manufacturers* (St Louis, MO: Washington University, Center for the Study of American Business); J. Pfeffer, 1994, *Competitive Advantage through People* (Cambridge, MA: Harvard Business School Press), p. 4.

71 H. W. Jenkins, Jr, 1996, 'What price job security?', *Wall Street Journal*, 26 March, p. A19.

72 J. S. Lublin, 1996, 'An overseas stint can be a ticket to the top', *Wall Street Journal*, 29 January, pp. B1, B2.

73 M. G. Harvey and M. R. Buckley, 1997, 'Managing inpatriates: Building a global core competency', *Journal of World Business*, 32(1), pp. 35–52.

74 D. M. DeCarolis and D. L. Deeds, 1999, 'The impact of stocks and flows of organizational knowledge on firm performance: An empirical investigation of the biotechnology industry', *Strategic Management Journal*, 20, pp. 953–68.

75 J. Sandberg, 2000, 'Understanding human competence at work: An interpretative approach', *Academy of Management Journal*, 43, pp. 9–25.

76 J. Lee and D. Miller, 1999, 'People matter: Commitment to employees, strategy and performance in Korean firms', *Strategic Management Journal*, 20, pp. 579–93.

77 T. M. Welbourne and L. A. Cyr, 1999, 'The human resource executive effect in initial public offering firms', *Academy of Management Journal*, 42, pp. 616–29; J. Pfeffer and J. F. Veiga, 1999, 'Putting people first for organizational success', *Academy of Management Executive*, 13(2), pp. 37–48.

78 DeCarolis and Deeds, 'The impact of stocks and flows of organizational knowledge'.

79 H. Rudnitsky, 1996, 'One hundred sixty companies for the price of one', *Forbes*, 26 February, pp. 56–62.

80 'Live wire Welch', 2000, *Business Week*, 10 January, p. 71; L. Grant, 1995, 'GE: The envelope, please', *Fortune*, 26 June, pp. 89–90.

81 W. C. Symonds, 2000, 'Education', *Business Week*, 10 January, pp. 138–40.

82 'Log on for company training', 2000, *Business Week*, 10 January, p. 140.

83 C. Lacy and S. Lewis, 2000, 'Telstra: No more cost cuts', *Australian Financial Review*, 11 October, pp. 1, 14; G. Elliott and M. Gilchrist, 2000, 'Paper loss mounts in share dive', *The Australian*, 4 May, p. 1.

84 M. A. Hitt, R. E. Hoskisson, J. S. Harrison and B. Summers, 1994, 'Human capital and strategic competitiveness in the 1990s', *Journal of Management Development*, 13(1), pp. 35–46; C. R. Greer and T. C. Ireland, 1992, 'Organizational and financial correlates of a contrarian human resource investment strategy', *Academy of Management Journal*, 35, pp. 956–84.

85 C. L. Martin, C. K. Parsons and N. Bennett, 1995, 'The influence of employee involvement program membership during downsizing: Attitudes toward the employer and the union', *Journal of Management*, 21, pp. 879–90.

86 C. M. Fiol, 1991, 'Managing culture as a competitive resource: An identity-based view of sustainable competitive advantage', *Journal of Management*, 17, pp. 191–211; J. B. Barney, 1986, 'Organizational culture: Can it be a source of sustained competitive advantage?', *Academy of Management Review*, 11, pp. 656–65.

87 S. Ghoshal and C. A. Bartlett, 1994, 'Linking organizational context and managerial action: The dimensions of quality of management', *Strategic Management Journal*, 15, pp. 91–112.

88 D. Hanson and H. Stuart, 2000, 'Failing the reputation test: The case of BHP', Corporate Reputation conference, June, Copenhagen, Denmark.

89 L. Zack, 1999, 'How IBM gets unstuck', *Fast Company Online*, October: www.fastcompany.com.

90 C. A. Bartlett and S. Ghoshal, 1997, 'The myth of the generic manager: New personal competencies for new managerial roles', *California Management Review*, 40(1), pp. 92–116.

91 P. Roberts, 1999, 'The empire strikes back', *Fast Company Online*, February: www.fastcompany.com.

92 G. T. Lumpkin and G. G. Dess, 1996, 'Clarifying the entrepreneurial orientation construct and linking it to performance', *Academy of Management Review*, 21, pp. 135–72.

93 Ibid., p. 142.

94 Ibid., p. 137.

95 'Gradual process: One that cannot be pushed', 1999, 28 October: www.ft.com.

96 Ireland and Hitt, 'Achieving and maintaining strategic competitiveness'.

97 J. E. Dutton, S. J. Ashford, R. M. O'Neill, E. Hayes and E. E. Wierba, 1997, 'Reading the wind: How middle managers assess the context for selling issues to top managers', *Strategic Management Journal*, 18, pp. 407–25.

98 S. Sherman, 1995, 'Wanted: Company change agents', *Fortune*, 11 December, pp. 197–8.

99 A. E. Serwer, 1997, 'Michael Dell turns the PC world inside out', *Fortune*, 8 September, pp. 76–86.

100 'Branded goods 2-Fashion victim', 2000, *Economist Online*, 26 February: www.economist.com.

101 A. Shand 2000, 'Ralph's PacDun woes worsen', *Australian Financial Review*, 29–30 July, p. 11; A. Ferguson, 2000, 'Pacific Dunlop skids towards the parts yard', *Business Review Weekly*, 28 January, p. 28.

102 S. M. Puffer, 1999, 'Continental Airlines' CEO Gordon Bethune on teams and new product development', *Academy of Management Executive*, 13(3), pp. 28–35.

103 E. R. Gray and J. M. Balmer, 1998, 'Managing corporate image and corporate reputation', *Long Range Planning*, 31, pp. 695–702.

104 D. J. Brass, K. D. Butterfield and B. C. Skaggs, 1998, 'Relationships and unethical behavior: A social network perspective', *Academy of Management Review*, 23, pp. 14–31.

105 L. K. Trevino, G. R. Weaver, D. G. Toffler and B. Ley, 1999, 'Managing ethics and legal compliance: What works and what hurts', *California Management Review*, 41(2), pp. 131–51.

106 C. W. L. Hill, 1990, 'Cooperation, opportunism, and the invisible hand: Implications for transaction cost theory', *Academy of Management Review*, 15, pp. 500–13.

107 D. Blalock, 1996, 'Study shows many execs are quick to write off ethics', *Wall Street Journal*, 26 March, pp. C1, C3; A. P. Brief, J. M. Dukerich, P. R. Brown and J. F. Brett, 1996, 'What's wrong with the Treadway Commission Report? Experimental analysis of the effects of personal values and codes of conduct on fraudulent financial reporting', *Journal of Business Ethics*, 15, pp. 183–98; G. Miles, 1993, 'In search of ethical profits: Insights from strategic management', *Journal of Business Ethics*, 12, pp. 219–25.

108 Zajac and Westphal, 'Accounting for the explanations of CEO compensation'.
109 S. R. Premeaux and R. W. Mondy, 1993, 'Linking management behavior to ethical philosophy', *Journal of Business Ethics*, 12, pp. 219–25.
110 Brief et al., 'What's wrong?'.
111 B. K. Burton and J. P. Near, 1995, 'Estimating the incidence of wrongdoing and whistle blowing: Results of a study using randomized response technique', *Journal of Business Ethics*, 14, pp. 17–30.
112 J. Milton-Smith, 1995, 'Ethics as excellence: A strategic management perspective', *Journal of Business Ethics*, 14, pp. 683–93.
113 G. R. Weaver, L. K. Trevino and P. L. Cochran, 1999, 'Corporate ethics programs as control systems: Influences of executive commitment and environmental factors', *Academy of Management Journal*, 42, pp. 41–57.
114 Brief et al., 'What's wrong?', p. 194; P. E. Murphy, 1995, 'Corporate ethics statements: Current status and future prospects', *Journal of Business Ethics*, 14, pp. 727–40.
115 L. J. Kirsch, 1996, 'The management of complex tasks in organizations: Controlling the systems development process', *Organization Science*, 7, pp. 1–21.
116 R. Simons, 1994, 'How new top managers use control systems as levers of strategic renewal', *Strategic Management Journal*, 15, pp. 170–1.
117 K. J. Laverty, 1996, 'Economic "short-termism": The debate, the unresolved issues, and the implications for management practice and research', *Academy of Management Review*, 21, pp. 825–60.
118 M. A. Hitt, R. E. Hoskisson and R. D. Ireland, 1990, 'Mergers and acquisitions and managerial commitment to innovation in M-form firms', *Strategic Management Journal*, 11 (Special Summer Issue), pp. 29–47.
119 R. A. Johnson, 1996, 'Antecedents and outcomes of corporate refocusing', *Journal of Management*, 22, pp. 437–81; R. E. Hoskisson and M. A. Hitt, 1994, *Downscoping: How to Tame the Diversified Firm* (New York: Oxford University Press).
120 Ireland and Hitt, 'Achieving and maintaining strategic competitiveness'.
121 M. Weidenbaum, 1996, 'The Chinese family business enterprise', *California Management Review*, 38(4), pp. 141–56.

Chapter 13

Corporate entrepreneurship and innovation

Objectives

After reading this chapter, you should be able to:

1. Define and describe the importance of innovation, entrepreneurship, corporate entrepreneurship and entrepreneurs.
2. Discuss the three stages of the innovation process.
3. Discuss the two forms of internal corporate venturing: autonomous strategic behaviour and induced strategic behaviour
4. Discuss how the capability to manage cross-functional teams facilitates the implementation of internal corporate ventures.
5. Explain how strategic alliances are used to produce innovation.
6. Discuss how a firm creates value by acquiring another company to gain access to that company's innovations or innovative capabilities.
7. Explain how large firms use venture capital to increase the effectiveness of their innovation efforts.
8. Describe the resources, capabilities and core competencies of small versus large firms in producing and managing innovation.

Innovation, competition and competitive success in the global automobile industry

Innovation drives competitive success in many companies, including global automobile manufacturers. However, when thinking about innovations, we typically recall product innovations. But organisations can be innovative in other ways, such as with their organisational structure. For example, as discussed in Chapter 11, the multi-divisional organisational structure that was developed by Alfred Sloan during his tenure as General Motors' CEO in the United States was an innovative response to coordination and control problems. These difficulties surfaced during the 1920s in a number of large US firms (for example, DuPont and GM) that were using the functional structure. For many years, most of the world's dominant automobile firms, including General Motors, Ford Motor Company and Chrysler Corporation, among others, used the multi-divisional structure as an innovative way of coordinating and controlling their diversified operations.

In part, the merger or acquisition between Daimler-Benz and Chrysler Corporation (see Chapter 7) was an innovative structural response to the need to create economies of scope to compete successfully in global automobile markets. Another objective of that transaction was to integrate the R&D functions of the formerly independent Daimler-Benz and Chrysler Corporation to enhance the quality and innovativeness of each product the combined firm produces. Innovation is especially critical to DaimlerChrysler's minivan. Developed initially by Chrysler, the minivan has a large profit margin that plays a key role in DaimlerChrysler's attempts to earn above-average returns.

Innovations are viewed as the pathway to reverse a decline in DaimlerChrysler's share of the US minivan market, from 40.3 per cent in 1998 to 36 per cent in 1999. Analysts note that DaimlerChrysler's 2001 model 'will up the ante in the minivan-gadget game, adding features such as a power-lift tailgate, an electrified console that can power a cellular phone and can be moved between the front and middle seats, and side doors that aren't merely powered, but are equipped with sensors that stop the doors in their tracks if they detect that an object – say, a child's head – is in the way'. By contrast, minivan competitors Honda Motor Company, General Motors and Mazda Motor Company believe that these innovations are relatively risk free and fail to provide customers with functions or capabilities that create significant value. Incremental innovations, such as those for each new generation of Holden Commodores, are less risky, but also have a lower probability of contributing substantially to a firm's strategic competitiveness.

Historically, General Motors' Cadillac is a product line in which new technologies have been used as a source of innovation. Night Vision is a recent example of an innovation that is a US$2 000 option on the Cadillac DeVille DTS. Night Vision is based on thermal-imaging technology. Developed initially by Raytheon Systems for the US military, this technology was adapted for GM after being declassified in 1993. Through the use of 76 800 infrared detectors mounted in a camera on the middle of the DTS's grille, the night-time driving conditions are improved, and for a good reason, according to analysts: 'You're three times as likely to die driving at night, and this is one case where the usual rule that younger drivers are more dangerous does not hold. A 40-year-old needs ten times as much light to see a given object as a 20-year old.' Other innovations in the automobile industry that are expected to facilitate night-time vision include infrared beams, ultrasonic pulses, xenon gas-filled headlights that emit a purplish hue, and headlights that emit ultraviolet rays.

The Holden Special Vehicle (HSV) unit provides another example of incremental innovation. It produces modified Holden cars. Based on the Holden Commodore, the HSV team produces fast, sports handling, street-tough cars that have an excellent reputation throughout the Australian sports car culture. The CEO says: 'I think we're light years ahead of anyone else in the technology used in special vehicles and racing.'

Hybrid vehicles are an example of a radical, rather than an incremental, product innovation. Unlike Chrysler's minivan, Cadillac's Night Vision product and the HSV, Ford Motor Company's THINK, a new brand for cars and bicycles, uses clean-battery and fuel-cell propulsion technology. Norwegian made, the THINK City car was to become available to consumers during 2001's fourth quarter, through Ford Electric vehicle dealerships in California and New York. Already being sold in Norway, the City is a battery-powered electric two-seater that has a top speed of 90 kilometres per hour and a maximum cruising range of 85 kilometres. Among other THINK products, two electric-powered bicycles, retailing for US$1000 to US$1200, were introduced in June 2000. These products are sold directly to consumers through THINK Mobility, an Internet-based electronic-commerce system, as well as through Ford dealers.

www.daimerchrysler.com
www.dupont.com
www.ford.com
www.ge.com
www.gm.com
www.holden.com.au
www.honda.com
www.mazda.com

Sources: J. Ball, 2000, 'DaimlerChrysler fights to retain minivan dominance', *Wall Street Journal*, 11 January, p. B4; T. Box, 2000, 'A new breed', *Dallas Morning News*, 11 January, pp. D1, D4; S. Freeman, 2000, 'Ford introduces THINK brand for cars, bikes', *Wall Street Journal*, 11 January, p. A10; M. Murphy, 2000, 'Boogies lights', *Forbes*, 7 February, p. 208; M. Murphy, 2000, 'The Packard is back', *Forbes*, 7 February, pp. 108–10; T. Powers, 2000, 'Auto company merger good idea', *Newswire*, 13 March: www.newswise.com; A. Taylor, III, 2000, 'Detroit: Every silver lining has a cloud', *Fortune*, pp. 92–3; B. Tuckey, 2000. 'HSV's new surge', *Business Review Weekly*, 6 October, p. 45.

The Opening Case suggests that innovation is related to a firm's strategic competitiveness and ability to earn above-average returns. In many industries, including the world's automobile industry, conditions of the global economy make it increasingly easy to commoditise products. Over-capacity, multiple competitors, intense competitive rivalries, rapidly changing technologies and market conditions, and the ability to standardise production methods in manufacturing firms and delivery mechanisms in service businesses are examples of these conditions.[1] Innovations are critical to companies' efforts to differentiate their goods or services from competitors in ways that create additional or new value for customers.[2] For example, in 1990, Australian agricultural entrepreneur John Raff commercialised (and profited from) the introduction of disease-resistant canola oil seeds to the rural market. Raff (along with three others) formed a company called Dovuro after observing that the production of this new disease-resistant canola seed was not accompanied by a means to retail it to the farmers that would most benefit. Although getting the initial message of this new product's benefits across to farmers proved extremely difficult, by 1994, Dovuro was selling 300 000 tonnes of canola product per year. In 1999, revenues from this single product line were $15 million.[3] Thus, as a corporate capability, innovation can be a vital source of competitive advantage as firms seek to compete in the arenas created by the global economy's characteristics.[4] For example, the automobile company that is able to use innovation as the foundation to manufacture fuel-efficient, environmentally friendly products may be able to establish a competitive advantage over its rivals in the 21st century's first few years.

As our discussion in this chapter suggests, and as is indicated in Figure 1.1 in Chapter 1, producing and managing innovation is a capability that is vital to a firm's efforts to implement its strategies successfully. For example, this is the case in terms of two business-level strategies, as product innovations are linked with the successful use of the product differentiation strategy, while process innovations are linked to the effective use of the cost leadership strategy. In addition to the role they play in strategy implementation, innovations developed by a firm in the course of using its strategies may affect its choice of future strategies. This possibility is shown by the feedback loop in Figure 1.1. Moreover, as suggested by the events described in the Opening Case, innovation has a strong effect on an industry's competitive dynamics.[5]

To describe how firms produce and manage innovation, we examine several topics in this chapter. To set the stage, we speak about innovation in general; then we define terms that are central to the chapter: innovation, entrepreneurship, corporate entrepreneurship and entrepreneurs. In defining these terms, we examine their importance and links to a firm's strategic competitiveness. Next, we discuss international entrepreneurship, a phenomenon reflecting the increased use of entrepreneurship in countries throughout the world. Internally, firms innovate through either autonomous or induced strategic behaviour. After our descriptions of these internal corporate venturing activities, we discuss actions firms take to implement the innovations resulting from those two types of strategic behaviour. In addition to innovating through internal activities, firms can gain access to other companies' innovations or innovative capabilities through strategic alliances and acquisitions. Following our discussion of these topics is a description of entrepreneurship in start-up ventures and smaller firms. This section closes both the chapter and our analysis of actions firms take to successfully implement strategies.

Innovation, entrepreneurship, corporate entrepreneurship and entrepreneurs

Peter Drucker argues that 'innovation is the specific function of entrepreneurship, whether in an existing business, a public service institution, or a new venture started by a lone individual in the family kitchen'. Moreover, Drucker suggests that innovation is 'the means by which the entrepreneur either creates new wealth-producing resources or endows existing resources with enhanced potential for creating wealth'.[6] Thus, entrepreneurship and the innovation resulting from it are important for large and small firms, as well as start-up ventures, as they compete in the 21st-century competitive landscape. In the words of several researchers, 'Entrepreneurship and innovation are central to the creative process in the economy and to promoting growth, increasing productivity and creating jobs.'[7]

Innovation is as vital to the development of competitive advantages in the service sector as it is in the manufacturing sector. Data processing, healthcare, transportation, financial planning and telecommunications are examples of service areas that are growing in size and in which firms are able to develop competitive advantages through innovation.[8] Telecommunications giant, Deutsche Telekom, suggests that innovation is the firm's competitive advantage: 'Innovation – we use it to our advantage. Today, our innovation pipeline is full. From 50-megabit transfers in the telephone network, to applications for the intelligent home, to our pioneering work in wireless/Internet integration, innovation is at the heart of our competitive strategy.'[9]

Although certainly important today, innovation has long been recognised as vital to competitive success. For example, Henry Ford, founder of Ford Motor Company, observed that 'Competition whose motive is merely to compete, to drive some other fellow out, never carries very far. The competitor to be feared is one who never bothers about you at all, but goes on making his own business better all the time. Businesses that grow by development and improvement do not die. But when a business ceases to be creative, when it believes it has reached perfection and needs to do nothing but produce – no improvement, no development – it is done.'[10]

Partly because it is intended to disrupt the status quo, entrepreneurship is not risk free.[11] However, the characteristics of the 21st-century competitive landscape (see Chapters 1 and 2) generate significant risks that firms cannot avoid while competing in the global economy. In fact, not seeking to innovate through entrepreneurship may be riskier than are actions taken to match a firm's capabilities and core competencies with its external environmental opportunities in order to innovate. In one sense, decisions some automobile manufacturers make about the Formula One racing season demonstrate the risk of innovating and competing on the basis of that innovation with the risks of not innovating. According to companies involved with Formula One racing, developing a losing car can actually damage a brand. To avoid this outcome, companies sometimes spend 'a fortune trying to give their entries a technological edge'. In describing this matter, the head of Ford's Premier Auto Group states, 'This sport is about perfection. Formula One is the No. 1 communication tool if you have the right brand. But it can backfire if you show that you tried to do something and failed.'[12] For Ferrari in 2000, the winning of the world championship with driver Michael Schumacher was an even bigger win for the brand.

Thus, in the rapidly changing global economy, firms simultaneously encounter risk and opportunity in terms of innovation. The Internet is an instructive example of these twin conditions. Dell Computer Corporation's chairman, Michael Dell, suggests that, for almost all firms, the Internet will be their business. Describing the risk the Internet creates for many businesses, Dell observes that 'If your business isn't enabled by information, if your business isn't enabled by customers and suppliers having more information and being able to use it, you're probably already in trouble.' Moreover, Dell believes that 'the Internet is like a weapon sitting on a table ready to be picked up by either you or your competitors'.[13] However, for the agile and responsive firm that is committed to innovation and the change that it brings, the Internet is an incredible source of opportunity and competitive advantage. In this book's first 12 chapters, we have offered numerous examples of firms that are innovating through the Internet's capabilities and moving towards competitive success as a result of doing so.

According to Michael Dell, 'The Internet is like a weapon sitting on a table ready to be picked up by either you or your competitors.' For a firm that is committed to innovation, the Internet is an incredible source of opportunity and competitive advantage.

Innovation

As noted earlier, innovation is a key outcome firms seek through entrepreneurship and is often the source of competitive success for firms competing in the global economy. In Rosabeth Moss Kanter's words, 'Winning in business today demands innovation. Companies that innovate reap all the advantages of a first mover.'[14] Thus, innovation is intended to enhance a firm's strategic competitiveness and financial performance.[15] Academic studies also highlight innovation's importance. For example, research results show that firms competing in global industries that invest more in innovation also achieve the highest returns.[16] In fact, investors often react positively to the introduction of a new product, thereby increasing the price of a firm's stock. Innovation, then, is an essential feature of high-performance firms.[17] The fact that firms differ in their propensity to produce value-creating innovations, as well as in their ability to protect innovations from imitation by competitors, is another indicator of innovation's ability to be a source of competitive advantage.[18] In other words, because 'innovation is relatively rare in organizations, compared to normal administrative routines', the firm that is able to innovate consistently and effectively is well positioned to rely on its innovative skill as a competitive advantage.[19]

In his classic work, Joseph Schumpeter argued that firms engage in three types of innovative activity.[20] **Invention** is the act of creating or developing a new product or process. **Innovation** is the process of creating a commercial product from an invention. In the 21st-century competitive landscape, 'innovation may be required to maintain or achieve competitive parity, much less a competitive advantage in many global markets'.[21] Moreover, innovation success is influenced by a firm's ability to absorb and evaluate external environmental information.[22] Because they typically are built by integrating knowledge and skills from multiple sources, every innovation creates opportunities for additional innovations.[23] Thus, an invention brings something new into *being*, while an innovation brings something new into *use*. Accordingly, technical criteria are used to determine the success of an invention, whereas commercial criteria are used to determine the success of an innovation.[24] Finally, **imitation** is the adoption of an innovation by similar firms. Imitation usually leads to product or process standardisation, and products based on imitation often are offered at lower prices, but without as many differentiated features.

The array of innovative products that have been and may be created from invention is intriguing. Previous product innovations, as well as future ones, are described in the Strategic Focus, which also discusses the importance of R&D as the source of all product innovations.

> **Invention** is the act of creating or developing a new product or process.
>
> **Innovation** is the process of creating a commercial product from an invention.
>
> **Imitation** is the adoption of an innovation by similar firms.

Strategic Focus International

Surprise, surprise, surprise! What might be tomorrow's innovative products, and what will be the source of their development?

As defined in the text, innovation is the process of creating a commercial product or process from an invention. Thus, in terms of creating value, an invention's potential is reached only when a firm develops and sells a product that satisfies customers' current or unmet needs.

One way to think of the value created by previous product innovations is to group them by functionality. For example, some innovative products have created value for consumers in their homes. The vacuum cleaner, invented by James Murray Spangler in 1907, 1918's Frigidaire refrigerator, Permacel duct tape in 1942, the introduction of Tupperware products in 1946, and the invention, in the same year, of the Australian icon, the Hills Hoist, by Lance Hill, are recognised as important innovations in the home environment. RCA's radio in 1921 and television in 1939 were significant innovations in communication that history may show pale in comparison to the value created by 1991's establishment of the World Wide Web. The paper clip, Xerox's photocopier and fax machine, Intel's microprocessor and Apple's Macintosh personal computer all changed the nature of work. Each of these products was the commercialisation of an invention.

What about the future? With regard to the energy sector of the economy, environmentally friendly products are expected to become more prominent. A diversified energy provider, TXU Corporation in the United States is trying to develop products from renewable energy sources through which significant amounts of energy can be delivered to customers. Currently, TXU is devoting considerable efforts to windmills and solar-powered energy sources as the foundation of its future delivery mechanisms. For personal residences, future home appliances probably will be linked through tethered and wireless connections. Experts believe that 'the day will come when you can order a book from a restaurant, preheat the oven from the office and start the dishwasher over the telephone'. As regards financial investments, individual consumers will have access to vast quantities of data and information that were once the purview of professional advisers only. In addition, investors will be able to use videoconferencing to attend shareholders' meetings and to cast their ballots on a real-time basis, rather than by submitting a written proxy through the mail. Even toilets are undergoing innovation: Japan's Matsushita has developed a high-tech toilet that reads an individual's weight, body temperature and blood pressure. By 2003, the product will also be able to check the amount of glucose and protein in a user's urine.

It is interesting to recall earlier product innovations and to think about those to come. But from a strategic management perspective, it is more important to recognise that, in some form or fashion, R&D activities are the source of all innovations. This fact is widely accepted in many Japanese corporations. For example, Samsung Electronics Co. Ltd tripled its investment in R&D in 2000 to support the development of new products. Viewing the company's actions, a business writer suggested that 'If you are beginning to think that Japan has lost its flair for product innovation and global marketing, think again. No matter how far down Japan's economy may be, its R&D divisions and factories are far from out.' Supported by national policies and firm-level commitments to R&D, Japanese companies continue to develop innovations that yield a large number of patents, an important indicator of R&D productivity. In 1998, the US Patent Office granted 32 119 US patents to Japanese firms, an increase of 32 per cent over the 1997 figure.

Finland has also become a world leader in innovation, particularly in communications technology where Nokia is their best performer. Finland has increased its total R&D expenditure in both the public and private arenas consistently since 1985. In 1985, total R&D expenditure as a proportion of GDP was 1.5 per cent, in 1995 it was 2.35 per cent, and in 1999 it was 3.1 per cent. The words of Erkki Tuomioja, Finnish Minister of Trade and Industry, make interesting reading for Australians concerned about a lack of government commitment to R&D and innovation:

> We have always invested in knowledge and skills and we will continue to do so – after all, apart from forests, we have hardly any other natural resources on which to base out industrial and commercial activities. We believe this is Finland's way to succeed also in the global marketplace of the future. Naturally, all this requires an efficient and comprehensive general education system.

Evidence shows, however, that companies throughout the world are committed to innovation through R&D. Australian company Cochlear was founded in 1981. On the basis of university research by Professor Graeme Clark, and others in Melbourne, it has continued, via constant innovation, to be the international leader in implanted hearing systems for the seriously hearing impaired. It strives to retain position by 'investing in research and development to provide high quality products' and from its Sydney office sells worldwide. Their most recent innovation, the Nucleus 24 Contour, was launched in February 2000 after five years of collaborative research and received the Year 2000 Australian Design Award. (Their systems work with a number of miniaturised components: sound is received by a microphone at the top of a person's ear and goes to a speech processor; this is encoded into meaningful information by a chip and is sent to a transmitter, then across the skin to a device implanted in the ear that stimulates the ear's nerve fibres, producing the sensation of hearing.) Thus, companies committed to innovation must be willing to devote considerable resources to R&D. Indeed, the most successful of these firms develop R&D as a source of competitive advantage.

Sources: AEA Technology, 2000, 'Who we are', *AEA Technology Home Page*, 10 March: www.aeat.com; K. Fairbank, 2000, 'Beyond 2000', *Dallas Morning News*, 2 January, pp H1, H2; Staff Reports, 2000, 'TXU to expand wind, solar power program', *Dallas Morning News*, 25 January, p. D7; C. Chen and T. Carvell, 1999, 'Products of the century', *Fortune*, 22 November, pp. 134–40; A. Paul, 1999, 'Made in Japan', *Fortune*, 6 December, pp. 190–200; E. Ramstad, 1999, 'Samsung to pour money into R&D, new ad campaign', *Wall Street Journal*, 11 November, p. B6; Cochlear, 2000, Annual Report; R. Batterham (Chief Scientist, Australian Government), 2000, *The Chance to Change* (Canberra: AGPS); M. Fyfe, 2001, 'Bionic Ear still delights its maker', *The Age*, 31 March.

Many companies are able to create ideas that lead to inventions, but commercialising those inventions through innovation has, at times, proved difficult. This is a merger problem in countries such as Australia. To turn an invention into a commercial application requires money, referred to in such cases as venture capital. In the United States, venture capital funds are far more readily available than in Australia. The US has more than 1 300 venture capital companies, fed by major pension funds. This has led a range of innovative Australian companies to move to the US. For example, Hypercom Corporation, a point-of-sale performance systems producer, moved to the US in the early 1990s because they could not find venture capital in Australia. More recently, in 1997, Res-Med, a producer of respiratory equipment, was unable to obtain venture capital in Australia and also moved to the US. Both companies are now listed on the US Nasdaq – which is now effectively the world's technology stock exchange.[25]

Entrepreneurship

Schumpeter viewed entrepreneurship as a process of 'creative destruction', through which existing products or methods of production are destroyed and replaced with new ones.[26] Thus, entrepreneurship is 'concerned with the discovery and exploitation of profitable opportunities'.[27] Formerly, *entrepreneurship* was defined as 'any attempt at new business or new venture creation, such as self-employment, a new business organization, or the expansion of an existing business, by an individual, a team of individuals, or an established business'.[28] As this definition suggests, entrepreneurship is an important mechanism for creating changes, as well as for helping firms adapt to changes created by others.[29] Firms that encourage entrepreneurship are risk takers, are committed to innovation and act proactively[30] (that is, they try to create opportunities rather than waiting to respond to those created by others).

Corporate entrepreneurship

> **Corporate entrepreneurship** is a process whereby an individual or group in an existing organisation creates a new venture or develops an innovation.

An organisational process that contributes to a firm's survival and performance, **corporate entrepreneurship** is a process whereby an individual or a group in an existing organisation creates a new venture or develops an innovation.[31] Another important perspective is that corporate entrepreneurship is the sum of a firm's innovation, renewal and venturing efforts.[32] Evidence suggests that corporate entrepreneurship practices are facilitated through the effective use of a firm's strategic management process.[33] One of the issues addressed when a firm uses the strategic management process to facilitate corporate entrepreneurship is determining how to harness the ingenuity of a firm's employees and reward them for it while retaining some of the rewards of the entrepreneurial efforts for the shareholders' benefit.[34]

Entrepreneurs

Evidence shows that entrepreneurs are primary agents of economic growth, introducing new products, new production methods and other innovations that stimulate economic activity.[35] Seeking to create the future, organisational entrepreneurs, engaging in corporate entrepreneurship, take risks and act aggressively and proactively in their firms.[36] Moreover, entrepreneurs sense opportunities before others do and take risks in the face of uncertainty to establish new markets, develop new products, or form innovative production processes or service delivery mechanisms.[37] These characteristics and evidence suggest that **entrepreneurs** are individuals, acting independently or as part of an organisation, who create a new venture or develop an innovation and take risks entering them into the marketplace.[38]

> **Entrepreneurs** are individuals, acting independently or as part of an organisation, who create a new venture or develop an innovation and take risks in entering them into the marketplace.

Entrepreneurs surface at any organisational level. Thus, top-level managers, middle- and first-level managers, staff personnel, and those producing the company's good or service can all be entrepreneurs. In the highly successful company Incat Tasmania, producer of high-speed, wave-piercing passenger catamarans, the CEO Bob Clifford is the entrepreneur.[39] Suggesting the importance of each person in a firm acting as an entrepreneur is the following opinion expressed by a corporate executive: 'In the future – the not-too-distant future – only two groups of people will be in the world of work: entrepreneurs and those who think like entrepreneurs.'[40]

Although all members of a firm can be entrepreneurs, expectations of their entrepreneurship vary by organisational level. Top-level managers, for example, should try to establish an entrepreneurial culture that inspires individuals and groups to engage in corporate entrepreneurship.[41] Apple Computer's Steve Jobs is committed to this effort, believing one of his key responsibilities is to help Apple become 'more entrepreneurial and start-up like'.[42] Top-level executives at 3M have emphasised innovation through entrepreneurship for years. George Allen, retired vice president of research and development at 3M, states, '3M innovates for the same reason that cows eat grass. It is a part of our DNA to do so.'[43] Middle- and first-level managers are promoters and caretakers of organisational efficiency. Their work is especially important once an idea for a product has been commercialised and the organisation necessary to support and promote the product has been formed.[44] Because of their close contacts with customers, suppliers and other sources of external information, first-level managers are vital to efforts to absorb and evaluate information from outside the firm that signals insights about potentially successful innovations. Because they work with procedures, staff personnel have the knowledge required to develop innovative processes that can increase organisational efficiency. Similarly, those producing a good or service have the experience necessary to propose process innovations, as well as the knowledge of customers' needs required to facilitate a firm's efforts to design and produce product innovations.

Accordingly, innovation, entrepreneurship, corporate entrepreneurship (as one form of entrepreneurship) and the work of entrepreneurs affect a firm's efforts to achieve strategic competitiveness and earn above-average returns. As we shall see in the next section, entrepreneurship and corporate entrepreneurship are being practised more commonly in countries throughout the global economy.

International entrepreneurship

Entrepreneurship is at the top of public policy agendas in many of the world's countries, including Finland, Germany, Israel, Ireland and France, among others. In Northern Ireland, for example, the minister for enterprise, trade and investment told businesspeople that their current and future commercial success would be affected by the degree to which they decided to emphasise R&D and innovation (critical components of entrepreneurship).[45]

According to some researchers who study economies throughout the world, virtually all industrial nations 'are experiencing some form of transformation in their economies, from the dramatic move from centrally planned to market economies in East-central Europe ... to the efforts by Asian countries to return to their recent high growth levels'.[46] Entrepreneurship and corporate entrepreneurship can play central roles in those transformations, in that they have strong potential to fuel economic growth, create employment and generate prosperity for citizens.[47] For example, in a comprehensive study in which entrepreneurial activity was assessed in 10 countries (Canada, Denmark, Finland, France, Germany, Israel, Italy, Japan, the United Kingdom and the United States), researchers discovered that 'variation in rates of entrepreneurship may account for as much as one-third of the variation [in countries'] economic growth'.[48]

Australian government and businesses are currently concerned about the problem of facilitating innovation and entrepreneurship. A National Innovation Summit was held in February 2000 by the federal government and the Business Council of Australia, but was then criticised for lack of focus and ideas. The head of iiiglobal.com, a website dedicated to linking innovators, called the summit communiqué 'bland and weak-kneed', while the head of the summit's implementation committee has criticised the focus on stories of 'hero entrepreneurs'. In response to these (and other) concerns, the Coalition government announced a new innovation plan in early 2001. It included a range of initiatives, such as:

- A tax concession of 175 per cent on R&D labour costs for companies that undertake R&D above existing levels. This is in addition to the existing 125 per cent R&D tax concession, but is only available to companies that have spent three years using the 125 per cent rate. Many companies will therefore be ineligible to claim this extended tax concession.
- Companies with turnover of less than $5 million will be eligible (for the first $1 million) of an R&D expenditure rebate of 37.5 per cent on every dollar spent.
- An R&D START program that provides up to 50 per cent funding for 'approved projects'.
- An extra $40 million for the commercialising of early technologies, which is in response to the call for help by small firms.
- A postgraduate loan scheme that will cost $995 million over five years. This may attract more postgraduates, particularly those willing to have a large debt from study.
- A range of other education initiatives indicating an aim for 21 000 extra science/technology university places.

- More funding to the Australian Research Council and the Cooperative Research Centres system.

It may well be several years before the impact of these changes is apparent. Difficulties in attracting foreign venture capital remain – in 1998, the pool of venture capital in Australia from foreign investors represented 12 per cent of the total, while in Britain it was 57 per cent. Fundamentally, the pool of venture capital will continue to be minuscule compared to that of large economies at the 'centre' of the world economy. In the United States, venture capital exceeds the equivalent of A$40 billion, compared to the $400 million available in Australia.[49]

Australia still does not have the aggressive approach to innovation taken by the Israeli government. Israel has attempted to model itself on California's Silicon Valley. The government has actively sought US venture capital funds and has set up good links between industry and universities using 'innovation incubators' (organisations that foster innovation by providing infrastructure and facilitating the flow of ideas). They also have business working with an active military force (a good source of R&D and ideas) and the luxury of employing 10 000 engineers and scientists who have arrived recently from Russia. These highly skilled people moved to Israel to create a new life, but have turned out to be significant resources for innovation.[50]

A society's cultural characteristics also influence a nation's rate and practice of entrepreneurship. In the late 1970s, for example, Chinese economic reforms facilitated the use of market forces as an important, but not exclusive, driver of economic activity in Mainland China. With increased economic freedom, some businesspeople used entrepreneurship as the foundation to initiate and then operate a start-up venture. In other cases, corporate entrepreneurship was introduced into existing companies to improve their performance.[51]

However, tension surfaced among Chinese workers between the need for individualism to promote entrepreneurship and the more traditional Chinese cultural characteristic of collectivism: 'Individualism refers to a self-orientation, an emphasis on self-sufficiency and control, and a value system where people derive pride from their own accomplishments. [In contrast, collectivism] involves the subordination of personal interests to the goals of the larger work group, an emphasis on sharing ... a concern with group welfare, and antipathy towards those outside the group.'[52] How the tension between individualism and collectivism is handled is important, because research shows that entrepreneurship declines as collectivism is emphasised. Simultaneously, however, research results suggest that exceptionally high levels of individualism might be dysfunctional for entrepreneurship. Viewed collectively, these results appear to call for a balance to be established between individual initiative and the spirit of cooperation and group ownership of innovation. For firms to achieve corporate entrepreneurship, they must provide appropriate autonomy and incentives for individual initiative to surface, but also promote cooperation and group ownership of an innovation if it is to be implemented successfully. Thus, corporate entrepreneurship often requires teams of people with unique skills and resources, especially perhaps with cultures in which collectivism is a valued historical norm.[53]

The importance of balancing individualism and collectivism for entrepreneurship is exemplified by the success of Asian entrepreneurs in North America. Some have argued that the success of those of Chinese and Korean origin in North America is due to their industriousness, perseverance, frugality and emphasis on family. Research shows, however, that other traits also promote their success. In North America, these individuals are allowed the autonomy necessary for creativity and entrepreneurial behaviour. In addition, the emphasis on collectivism afforded by their cultural background helps them to promote cooperation and group ownership of innovation.[54]

Interestingly, Chinese entrepreneurs (operating in China) have several character traits that are similar to those of Western entrepreneurs, including ambitiousness, independence and self-determination. But the two sets of entrepreneurs also have different characteristics, particularly those most influenced by Confucian social philosophy.[55] Entrepreneurs of Chinese and Korean descent who operate in the United States exhibit differences from all other entrepreneurs in the country. For example, Chinese and Korean entrepreneurs conducting business in the United States invest more equity, obtain more capital from family and friends, and receive fewer loans from financial institutions. Furthermore, they achieve higher profits than their non-Asian counterparts.[56] In contrast, a study of Israeli women showed that industry experience, business skills and achievement were related to their performance, much the same as with other entrepreneurs in the Western nations. But, unlike those other entrepreneurs, Israeli women entrepreneurs could attribute their success to their affiliation with a network for support and advice. When they were affiliated with multiple networks, by contrast, their performance suffered, possibly because of too much and potentially conflicting advice.[57]

Internal corporate venturing

Internal corporate venturing is the set of activities used to create inventions and innovations through internal means.[58] Spending on R&D is linked to success in internal corporate venturing. Put simply, firms are unable to invent or innovate without significant R&D investments. Australian firms are lagging behind competitors in commitment to R&D. This is clear in a recent OECD analysis of what is referred to as 'business R&D intensity' – that is, business expenditure on R&D as a percentage of industrial value added. The results are presented in Figure 13.1.

Autonomous strategic behaviour

Autonomous strategic behaviour is a bottom-up process in which product champions pursue new ideas, often through a political process, by means of which they develop and coordinate the commercialisation of a new good or service until it achieves success in the marketplace. A **product champion** is an organisational member with an entrepreneurial vision of a new good or service who seeks to create support for its commercialisation. Evidence suggests that product champions play critical roles in moving innovations forward.[59] Autonomous strategic behaviour is based on a firm's wellsprings of knowledge and resources that are the sources of the firm's innovation. Thus, a firm's capabilities and competencies are the basis for new products and processes.[60]

General Electric (GE) is a company in which autonomous strategic behaviour occurs regularly. Essentially, 'the search for marketable services can start in any of GE's myriad businesses. [For example], an operating unit seeks out appropriate technology to better do what it already does. Having mastered the technology, it then incorporates it into a service it can sell to others.' In response to frequent crisis calls and requests from customers, GE's Industrial Systems division took six months to develop a program that uses artificial intelligence to help assign field engineers to customer sites. Quite sophisticated, the program handles thousands of constraints while making assignments.

Autonomous strategic behaviour is a bottom-up process in which product champions pursue new ideas, often through a political process, by means of which they develop and coordinate the commercialisation of a new good or service until it achieves success in the marketplace.

A **product champion** is an organisational member with an entrepreneurial vision of a new good or service who seeks to create support for its commercialisation.

Figure 13.1 | Intensity of business R&D in domestic product of industry, 1997 or latest year available

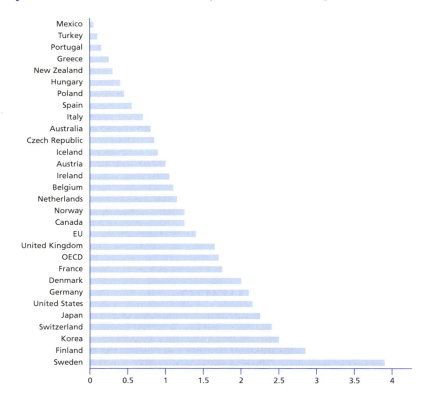

Source: OECD, 2000, *The Knowledge-based Economy: A Set of Facts and Figures*, Meeting of the Committee for Scientific and Technological Policy, 22–23 June, p. 13.

As shown in Figure 13.2, there are two forms of internal corporate venturing: autonomous strategic behaviour and induced strategic behaviour. We discuss each form separately.

Figure 13.2 | Model of internal corporate venturing

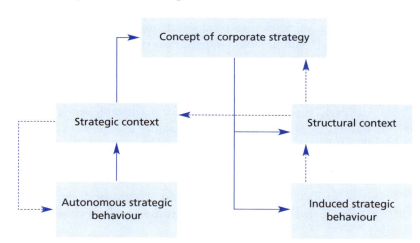

Source: Adapted from R. A. Burgelman, 1983, 'A model of the interactions of strategic behavior, corporate context, and the concept of strategy', *Academy of Management Review*, 8, p. 65.

The division's customer relationship manager was a champion for this product. The manager observed that the program 'reduced the average time to dispatch an engineer from 18 hours to 4 hours'.[61] In addition to facilitating the operations of one of GE's units, the program is being sold as a marketable item that developed through autonomous strategic behaviour.

Changing the concept of corporate-level strategy through autonomous strategic behaviour results when a product is championed within strategic and structural contexts (see Figure 13.2). The strategic context is the process used to arrive at strategic decisions (often requiring political processes to gain acceptance). The best firms keep changing their strategic context and strategies because of the continuous changes in the 21st-century competitive landscape (see Chapter 1). Thus, some believe that the most competitively successful firms reinvent their industry or develop a completely new one across time as they engage in competition with current and future rivals.[62]

Callaway Golf Co. may be a firm with a capability to reinvent the industry in which it competes. For example, Callaway reinvented the oversized club part of the golf club industry through the introduction of its 'Big Bertha' (the biggest-selling driver in Australia on its release). Callaway now seeks to reinvent the golf ball segment of the golfing industry. Using state-of-the-art-technology and relying in part on autonomous strategic behaviour among some of the firm's personnel, Callaway claims that its golf ball, introduced in February 2000, 'will be as revolutionary to balls as the Big Bertha was to clubs'. Called the Rule 35, two versions (the Firmfeel and the Softfeel) of Callaway's golf ball were introduced initially. Callaway engineers and scientists spent more than three years in R&D activities to innovate the Rule 35 golf ball.[63]

Induced strategic behaviour

Induced strategic behaviour is a top-down process whereby the firm's current strategy and structure foster product innovations that are associated closely with that strategy and structure.

The second of the two forms of internal corporate venturing, **induced strategic behaviour**, is a top-down process whereby the firm's current strategy and structure foster product innovations that are associated closely with that strategy and structure. In this situation, the strategy in place is filtered through a matching structural hierarchy. Innovations developed, or being developed, through induced strategic behaviour as a form of internal corporate venturing are described in the Strategic Focus.

Strategic Focus International

Product innovations and induced strategic behaviours: Personal computers, video games and other delights

According to analysts, competitors likely chuckled to themselves, at least privately, when they heard in 1996 that Sony Corporation intended to introduce another PC line, called the Vaio series. One reason for this reaction was that the firm had endured four previous short-lived efforts to establish Sony in brand-name computers. Today, however, through the success of the Vaio line of PCs, Sony is one of four major PC brands remaining on US retailers' shelves. An edict from Sony CEO Nobuyuki Idei to 'build a Sony-style personal computer' was the foundation through which the firm's current strategy fostered a product innovation. Managers listening to their CEO heard a challenge to develop a PC 'whose design would be as distinctive as Sony's televisions, Walkman and digital cameras'. The product evolved from work completed at Sony's main research facility in Japan. Engineer Susumu Ito and designer Teiyu Goto combined their visions and efforts to develop what has become a successful product innovation. Observers believe that the Vaio's sleek looks and design compensate for what the product lacks in cutting-edge technical performance.

Sony's current strategy and structure also induced strategic behaviours through which the PlayStation 2 came into being. Introduced into Japan in March 2000 and into Europe, Australia and North America in the autumn of that year, the PlayStation 2 was viewed by Sony officials 'as a sort of Trojan horse that will enter the house as a videogame player and then become a secret weapon to access the Internet, play movies and download music, rivaling the PC as the hub of entertainment in the home'. The PlayStation 2's introduction into Japan was nothing short of sensational, with 980 000 initial units sold in record time. Ken Kutaragi, CEO of Sony Computer Entertainment, the video-game unit of Sony Corporation, stimulated the innovation of the PlayStation. This strategic leader's objective was to use the firm's current strategy and structure to develop a product that would move Sony to a position of being able to dominate a new wave of Internet gadgets and services. Thus, Sony views its PlayStation 2 as a viable entertainment platform for the home. Interestingly, Sony is currently the world's only company that offers consumers all three devices – the PC, television and video-game machine – around which homes could be wired with networks of digital products. Moreover, the firm's penetration in markets around the world through these three products is impressive.

Executives at Nissan Motor Company are not abandoning their firm's innovation strategy. Instead, they intend to continue to rely on Nissan's internal innovation capabilities to develop and introduce four new products into North America, a market that is vital to Nissan's success. By 2003, plans call for Nissan to launch a large sport-utility vehicle, a new minivan, a new Z-series sports car, and a fourth vehicle that had not yet been specified by mid-2000. In addition, Nissan executives decided to use the firm's innovation skills to complete changeovers of six other models.

Sources: R. A. Guth, 2000, 'Inside Sony's Trojan horse', *Wall Street Journal*, 25 February, pp. B1, B4; C. Taylor, 2000, 'Game wars', *Time*, 20 March, pp. 44–5; Nissan Motor Co., 2000, 15 March: www.nissan.com; N. Shirouzu, 2000, 'Nissan may launch new SUV, minivan for North America in product revamp', *Wall Street Journal*, 14 February, p. A18; Sony Home Page, 2000, 13 March: www.sony.com; R. A. Guth and E. Ramstad, 1999, 'How Sony turned a skinny laptop into an unlikely PC success', *Wall Street Journal*, 12 November, pp. B1, B6.

Implementing internal corporate ventures

Innovation is a necessary, but insufficient, condition for competitive success. Having processes and structures in place through which a firm can successfully implement the outcomes of internal corporate ventures is as vital as the innovations themselves. The successful introduction of innovations into the marketplace reflects implementation effectiveness. In the context of internal corporate ventures, processes are the 'patterns of interaction, coordination, communication, and decision making employees use'[64] to convert the innovations resulting from either autonomous or induced strategic behaviours into successful market entries. Organisational structures are the sets of formal relationships supporting organisational processes.

To facilitate the implementation of product innovations and to identify opportunities to engage in still more innovation that can create value for customers, IBM is creating a network of innovation centres. Devoted to IBM's e-commerce services, these centres are locales 'where business customers can visit with Web designers, software engineers, business strategists and marketing people under the same roof'. The purpose of the centres is to foster collaborative relationships among IBM personnel, technologists, business experts and customers to develop and implement product innovations.[65]

Effective integration among the various functions involved with either autonomous or induced strategic innovation behaviour processes – from engineering to manufacturing and, ultimately, market distribution – is required to implement (that is, to effectively use) the innovations that result from internal corporate ventures. Increasingly, product development teams are being used as a means of integrating the activities associated with different organisational functions. The outcome sought by using product development teams is commonly called *cross-functional integration*, a concept that is concerned with coordinating and applying the knowledge and skills of different functional areas in order to maximise innovation.[66]

Using product development teams to achieve cross-functional integration

Cross-functional integration's importance has been recognised for some time.[67] Cross-functional teams facilitate efforts to integrate activities associated with different organisational functions, such as design, manufacturing and marketing. In addition, new product development processes can be completed more quickly when cross-functional teams work effectively.[68] Through the work of cross-functional teams, product development stages are grouped into parallel or overlapping processes. Doing this allows the firm to tailor its product development efforts to its unique core competencies and to the needs of the market. In addition, the cross-functional integration that results from the work of such teams helps a firm learn how to mass-produce a successful new product.[69]

Horizontal organisational structures support the use of cross-functional teams in their efforts to integrate innovation-based activities across organisational functions. In a *horizontal organisation*, managing changes in organisational processes across functional units is more critical than managing up and down functional hierarchies.[70] Therefore, instead of being built around vertical hierarchical functions or departments, the

Cross-functional teams facilitate efforts to integrate activities associated with different organisational functions, such as design, manufacturing and marketing. Effective cross-functional teams also expedite new product development processes.

organisation is built around core horizontal processes that are used to produce and manage innovations. As noted earlier, processes are the patterns of interaction, coordination, communication and decision making personnel use to transform resources into outputs (for example, product innovations). Some of the core horizontal processes that are critical to innovation efforts are formal – defined and documented as procedures and practices. More commonly, though, these processes are informal: 'They are routines or ways of working that evolve over time.'[71] Often invisible, informal processes are critical to successful product innovations and are supported properly through horizontal organisational structures more so than through vertical organisational structures.

As we discuss next, barriers sometimes exist that must be overcome for a firm to use cross-functional teams as a means of integrating organisational functions.

Barriers to integration

The two primary barriers that may prevent the successful use of cross-functional teams as a means of integrating organisational functions are independent frames of reference of team members and organisational politics.[72]

Personnel working within a distinct specialisation (that is, a particular organisational function) typically have common backgrounds and experiences. Because of these similarities, people within individual organisational functions tend to view situations similarly and are likely to use the same decision criteria to evaluate issues such as those having to do with product development efforts. In fact, research results suggest that departments around which organisational functions are framed vary along four dimensions: time orientation, interpersonal orientation, goal orientation and formality of structure.[73] Thus, individuals from different functional departments that have different orientations on these dimensions can be expected to understand separate aspects of product development in different ways. Accordingly, they place emphasis on separate design characteristics and issues. For example, a design engineer may consider the characteristics that make a product functional and workable to be the most important of the product's characteristics. Alternatively, a person from the marketing function may hold characteristics that satisfy customer needs most important. These different orientations can create barriers to effective communication across functions.[74] Although functional specialisation may be damaging to the horizontal relationships necessary to successfully implement innovations produced from internal corporate venturing efforts, such specialisation has an important purpose in creating an efficient organisation. Therefore, eliminating functional specialisation to overcome barriers to cross-functional integration may do more harm than good to the organisation.

Organisational politics is the second potential barrier to the effective integration of organisational functions through use of cross-functional teams. In some organisations, considerable political activity may centre on allocating resources to different functions. Inter-unit conflict may result from aggressive competition for resources among those representing different organisational functions. Of course, dysfunctional conflict between functions creates a barrier to their integration.[75] Methods must be found through which cross-functional integration can be promoted without excessive concurrent political conflict and without simultaneously changing the basic structural characteristics necessary for task specialisation and efficiency.

Facilitating integration

Shared values are the first of four methods firms use to achieve effective cross-functional integration.[76] Highly effective shared values are framed around the qualities that make the firm unique compared to its rivals.⁷⁷ Moreover, when linked clearly with a firm's strategic intent and mission, shared values reduce political conflict and become the glue that promotes coupling among functional units. Hewlett-Packard (HP), for example, has remained an accomplished technological leader because it has established the 'HP way'. In essence, the HP way refers to the firm's esteemed organisational culture that promotes unity. Australia's BHP is pursuing a similarly useful culture.

Leadership is a second method of achieving cross-functional integration. Effective strategic leaders remind organisational members continuously of the value of product innovations. In the most desirable situations, this value-creating potential becomes the basis for the integration and management of functional department activities. BHP CEO Paul Anderson has as one of his main aims the integration between BHP's business units. He claimed in late 2000 that the firm has good assets but poor information flow, pointing to the need for greater integration within Australia's leading multinational.⁷⁸ In May 2001, the problem obviously increased with the merger with Billiton that created a A$60 billion global resources firm. (See the Strategic Focus on BHP Billiton in Chapter 7.) The new firm will need a new management structure, a new global system of business units and a revamped communication system. This is a huge challenge that will be difficult to meet.

A third method of achieving cross-functional integration is concerned with *goals and budgets*. This method calls for firms to formulate goals and allocate the budgetary resources necessary to accomplish them. These goals are specific targets for the integrated design and production of new goods and services. Effective horizontal organisations – those in which accomplishments are expected in terms of processes, as well as outcomes such as product innovations – reinforce the importance of integrating activities across organisational functions.

An *effective communication system* is a fourth method used to facilitate cross-functional integration. Some key beneficial outcomes of effective communication are increased motivation, more and better information, and the sharing of knowledge among cross-functional team members.⁷⁹ Free-flowing communications between those working within different organisational functions are important, but effective communication within cross-functional teams is critical to the successful implementation of a new product. Without such communication, members of a cross-functional team would find it difficult to integrate their individual function's activities in ways that create synergy. Shared values and leadership practices shape the communication systems that are developed to support the work of cross-functional product development teams.

Appropriating (gaining) value from innovation

Internal corporate-venturing implementation efforts are designed to help a company gain competitive benefits from its product innovations. Another way of saying this is that implementation efforts are used to help a firm appropriate or gain value from activities undertaken to innovate (that is, commercialise) inventions.

The model in Figure 13.3 shows how value can be appropriated, or gained, from internal corporate-venturing processes. As mentioned earlier, cross-functional integration is required for innovation's value to be tapped fully. Cross-functional teams increase the likelihood of cross-functional integration, in that their effective use helps to overcome barriers to integration. Also helping a firm's efforts to overcome these barriers are four facilitators of integration: shared values, visionary leadership, supportive budgets and allocations, and effective communication systems.

Figure 13.3 | Appropriating (gaining) value from internal firm innovation

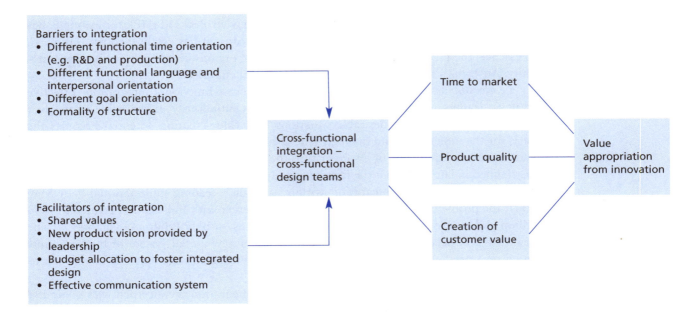

Source: Adapted from M. A. Hitt, R. E. Hoskisson and R. D. Nixon, 1993, 'A mid-range theory of interfunctional integration, its antecedents and outcomes', *Journal of Engineering and Technology Management*, 10, pp. 161–85.

The model highlights three desirable outcomes of achieving cross-functional integration: time to market, product quality and the creation of customer value. In several earlier chapters, we described the competitive value of the rapid entry of a product into the marketplace; we highlighted evidence which suggests that a firm can gain a competitive advantage when it is able to develop innovative goods or services and transfer them to the marketplace faster than competitors can.[80] In fact, some argue that developing products rapidly in the global economy has a strong and positive effect on a firm's profitability.[81] But product quality is also important.[82] Although shorter time-to-market cycles that result from the rapid entry of a product into a marketplace have the potential to help a firm appropriate value from its innovations, unacceptable levels of product quality may contribute to expensive recalls, product performances that fail to meet customers' expectations, and exposure to product liability charges. In the final analysis, customer value is created when product innovations *with acceptable levels of quality* are introduced rapidly into the marketplace. Thus, as our discussion of the model in Figure 13.3 suggests, internal corporate ventures must be effectively managed to facilitate cross-functional integration so that a firm will be able to appropriate maximum value from its product design and commercialisation efforts.[83]

Strategic alliances: Cooperating to produce and manage innovation

It is difficult for a firm to possess all the knowledge required to compete successfully in its product areas over the long term. Complicating this matter is the fact that the knowledge base confronting today's organisations is not only vast, but also increasingly specialised. As such, the knowledge needed to commercialise inventions is frequently embedded within different corporations located in various parts of the global economy.

In Chapter 9, we discussed why and how firms use *strategic alliances* (partnerships between firms whereby resources, capabilities and core competencies are combined to pursue common interests and goals)[84] to gain either competitive parity or competitive advantage relative to rivals. Used with increasing frequency,[85] alliances are often formed to produce or manage innovations. To innovate through a cooperative relationship such as a strategic alliance, firms share their knowledge and skills.[86] Forming alliances for this purpose is appropriate, in that value is created through the effective formation and use of an alliance.[87]

Porsche AG and Volkswagen AG recently formed an alliance to develop an innovative sport-utility vehicle (SUV) that was to appear as a year-2002 model. Because of a conviction that their product had to be unique compared to existing SUVs, both firms committed significant resources to R&D activities. Although some components (for example, a core platform) were to be shared, the partners also were seeking to produce their own individualised versions of the jointly developed product. For example, a Porsche executive noted that his firm was 'going to great lengths to differentiate the two versions and [to] guard Porsche's brand image'. The historically cooperative relationship between the two companies was expected to enhance the probability of the alliance's success.[88]

In the United States, a major alliance was formed between industry and the federal government. Called Partnership for a New Generation of Vehicles (PNGV) and featuring participation between GM, Ford, DaimlerChrysler and the federal government, this alliance was developed to improve the US automobile industry's competitive position compared to the Japanese automobile manufacturers which had increased their share of the US automobile market during the 1980s with cars that were fuel-efficient and desired by customers.

The three automobile manufacturers involved in PNGV showed test cars in 2000 and announced that they would have ready-to-build prototypes in 2004. All of the parties to the alliance hoped that innovative products would be developed from these prototypes that could achieve marketplace success. However, at least in terms of rapid market entry, the initial results were not encouraging. In early 2000, for example, Honda Motor Company introduced its Insight into the marketplace. The Insight is a two-seat hybrid car that uses an auxiliary electric motor to achieve a fuel economy rating of about 3 litres/100 kilometres. Similarly, Toyota Motor Corporation launched its Prius hybrid in the United States in the latter part of 2000. As noted earlier in the chapter, the rapid introduction of product innovations into the marketplace helps firms to appropriate, or gain, value from their innovations. Thus, PNGV participants were already at a disadvantage relative to Japanese competitors with respect to this performance criterion.

Although the final results of the PNGV alliance are not known at this time, experience shows that alliances can be used successfully to produce and manage innovations. The cooperative relationship between Porsche and Volkswagen described earlier may help both firms to create value for their customers. However, alliances formed for the purpose of innovation are not without risks. An important risk is that a partner will appropriate a firm's technology or knowledge and use it to enhance its own competitive abilities. To prevent, or at least minimise, this risk, a firm – particularly a start-up venture – needs to select its partner carefully.[89] The ideal partnership is one in which the firms have complementary skills, as well as compatible goals and strategic orientations.[90] Two other risks include a firm becoming dependent on its partner for the development of core competencies, and the loss of skills that can result when they are not used regularly to produce or manage innovations.

In sum, building successful strategic alliances to produce and manage innovation requires focusing on knowledge, identifying core competencies and developing strong human resources to manage those core competencies. Expecting to gain financial benefits in the short run may lead to unintended consequences in the long run. Also, firms may view their collaboration with other companies as an indirect form of competition for knowledge.[91]

Acquisitions and venture capital: Buying innovation

In this section, we focus on acquisitions and venture capital, activities representing the third approach firms use to produce and manage innovation.

Acquisitions

Acquiring innovative companies is a common way for corporations that strive to remain innovative. It is also common that Australian innovative firms are acquired overseas. For example, Radiata Communications was recently purchased by US Cisco Systems for A$570 million. Radiata was an Australian flagship 'new-economy' firm specialising in wireless technology developed by scientists at Macquarie University in Sydney. It was one of the relatively rare commercial successes to come out of Australian universities. Andrew Sneddon, the head of PricewaterhouseCoopers' emerging technology practice in Australia, said of this situation: 'There is some brilliant technology in universities and in the CRCs [Cooperative Research Centres]. There are lots more Radiatas out there – probably hundreds of technology opportunities – that haven't been commercialised.' Because of the lack of local venture capital (discussed earlier in the chapter), lack of federal government funding for universities, and lack of expertise in commercialising product by universities, this situation is likely to continue, and as good ideas develop, there is a good chance they will drift overseas.[92]

Meritor Automotive, Inc. is emerging as an ambitious and competitively successful participant in the global automobile parts manufacturing industry, an industry that is being consolidated rapidly. They also demonstrate movement of new ideas to the powerful US economy. A spin-off from Rockwell International Corporation, Meritor has a strategy built around specialisation, modular assembly operations, innovation, global acquisitions and globalisation.

Recently, Meritor designed an integrated roof system that DaimlerChrysler is using in Europe with its Smart car. According to analysts, Meritor's design is unique because the car goes through the entire assembly process without a roof. This gives assembly-line workers greater access to the car's interior. The roof is bolted on at the end of the process. Other recent Meritor product innovations include a fully integrated door module and a modular assembly that incorporates struts, brakes and other suspension components in a single package.

To continuously strengthen its ability to innovate, Meritor completes strategic acquisitions. The purchases of Euclid Industries, a supplier of replacement parts for trucks, the European heavy-truck axle business of Sweden's AB Volvo, and the heavy-vehicle brake business of LucasVarity plc, of the United Kingdom are three of Meritor's recent acquisitions. By integrating the capabilities of these acquisitions with those of companies it owns already, Meritor intends to continue producing and managing innovations in ways that create value for customers. As an indication that firms often seek innovation through more than one of the three approaches available to produce and manage innovations (that is, internal corporate ventures, alliances and acquisitions), we note that Meritor also formed a joint venture with Germany's ZF Friedrichshafen AG to produce transmissions.[93] Thus, the firm is using alliances and acquisitions in efforts to appropriate what it hopes will be full value from its innovation activities.

Similar to internal corporate venturing and strategic alliances, acquisitions are not a risk-free approach to producing and managing innovations. A key risk of acquisitions is that a firm may substitute an ability to buy innovations for an ability to produce innovations internally. As discussed next, research results suggest that this substitution may not be in the firm's best interests.[94]

Figure 13.4 shows that firms gaining access to innovations through acquisitions risk reductions in both R&D inputs (as measured by investments in R&D) and R&D outputs (as measured by the number of patents received). The curves indicate that the R&D-to-sales ratio drops after acquisitions have been completed and that the patent-to-sales ratio drops significantly after companies have been involved with large acquisitions. Additional research shows that firms engaging in acquisitions introduce fewer new products into the market.[95] Thus, firms appear to substitute acquisitions for internal corporate-venturing processes. This substitution may take place because firms lose strategic control and emphasise financial control of original, and especially of acquired, business units.[96] Although reduced innovation may not always result, managers of firms seeking to make acquisitions should be aware of this potential outcome.

Figure 13.4 | Evidence of R&D inputs (expenditures) and outputs (number of patents) per dollar of sales before and after large acquisitions

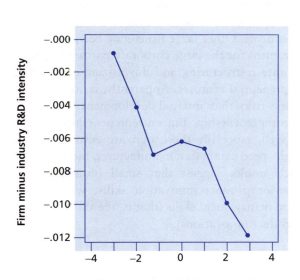
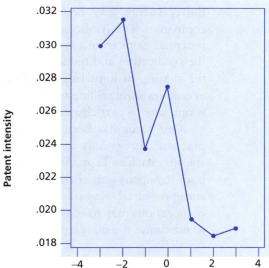

Years before and after acquisition
Difference between pre- and post-acquisition observations is statistically significant at $p<.01$.

Source: M. A. Hitt, R. E. Hoskisson, R. D. Ireland and J. S. Harrison, 1991, 'Are acquisitions a poison pill for innovation?', *Academy of Management Executive*, 5(4), pp. 24–5.

Venture capital

Venture capital is a resource that is typically allocated to entrepreneurs who are involved in a project with high growth potential. The intent of venture capitalists is to help achieve a high rate of return on the funds they invest.[97] Increasingly, venture capital is being used to facilitate the earning of high rates of return by supporting the acquisition of innovations. To provide such support, some firms establish their own venture capital divisions. These divisions carefully evaluate other companies to identify those with innovations or innovative capabilities that might yield a competitive advantage. In other instances, a firm might decide to serve as an internal source of capital for innovative product ideas that can be spun off as independent or affiliated firms. New enterprises that are backed by venture capital provide an important source of innovation and new technology. As mentioned in earlier discussion, the lack of venture capital in economies such as Australia is a major inhibitor to innovation.

Historically, the venture capital business has been associated primarily with independent venture capital firms, but both domestic and foreign corporations have discovered that investing in venture capital adds a new dimension to their corporate development strategies and can produce an attractive return on their investments.[98] A major strategic benefit to a corporation is the ability to invest early and observe what happens to the new venture. This may lead to subsequent acquisitions, the licensing of technology, product marketing rights and, possibly, the development of international opportunities. Large firms often view venture capital as a window on future technological development. Participation by corporations can take many forms, but usually begins with investment in several venture capital funds as a limited partner and evolves into direct investments in new business ventures. Many firms begin this strategy by forming a venture development division.

The disdain of large corporations by outside entrepreneurs can be a potential pitfall. Entrepreneurs may be wary of large corporations that seek to dominate fledgling companies. The syndication of venture funds to reduce risk may also be a factor limiting potential gains from venture capital investments. Other large firms may become part of the syndication and reduce the potential returns for the large corporate partner (through the sharing of knowledge).[99] With corporate restructuring and downsizing continuing, executives seem willing to try more entrepreneurial ventures. Apparently, venture capital is one way to participate, and it may be less risky than internal development.[100]

Our focus has been on corporate entrepreneurship. But entrepreneurship may be practised successfully in small firms as well, especially those that are entrepreneurial ventures such as Tasmania's successful high-speed catamaran manufacturer, Incat. In fact, both company experiences and research results suggest that small businesses and entrepreneurial ventures may have superior product innovation skills, while larger corporations may have superior innovation management skills (that is, the skills required to maximise the marketplace return of product innovations).

Entrepreneurship in small businesses and entrepreneurial ventures

Small businesses and entrepreneurial ventures based in countries throughout the global economy are awarded a large number of US patents, a measure of excellent early success.[101] Although 80 per cent of the world's R&D activity in developed nations is concentrated in firms with 10 000 or more employees, these large firms account for under half of the world's technological activity, as measured by US patents awarded. The data suggest that, while large firms are important for technological advances, small businesses, entrepreneurial ventures and individual entrepreneurs account for a significant share of today's innovative activity and the technological progress resulting from it. Concurrently, smaller nations are contributing meaningfully to the global economy's innovative activity.

One business writer observed recently that, 'Many of the most important innovations in cell-phone technology have come from some of the smallest economies in the developed world, in Scandinavia. Even though a pharmaceutical company may spend billions shepherding a new product through the regulatory process, the spark of innovation behind new drugs comes increasingly from college labs and biotech start-ups.'[102]

Executives and women are two sometimes-related categories of workers who are changing their employment venue in large numbers. Evidence suggests, for example, that 'Executives leaving large companies are taking jobs with smaller firms, including Internet start-ups. The latest figures from outplacement firm Challenger, Gray & Christmas show that seven out of 10 job-switching executives and managers are signing on with smaller firms.'[103] Moreover, at least in developed countries, 'the greatest and most rapid gain in firm start-ups will be achieved by increasing the participation of women in the entrepreneurial process'.[104] Collectively, these data suggest that small businesses and entrepreneurial ventures are rapidly becoming an important part of the mainstream economy and business activity, most certainly in developed countries.[105] As mentioned earlier in the chapter, entrepreneurship and corporate entrepreneurship are assuming increasing levels of importance in emerging economies as well.

Previously, we stated that small businesses and entrepreneurial ventures tend to outperform large organisations in terms of *producing* innovations. A reason for this is that entrepreneurs have been found to be more innovative than managers of large firms. The increased level of innovative capability that entrepreneurs possess is at least partly a function of their tendency to use more heuristics in making decisions than do those managing large organisations.[106] However, successfully *managing* innovations is more difficult for small firms and entrepreneurial ventures than it is for large established companies. Integrating and coordinating the work required to fund the introduction of an innovation to the marketplace (work that includes writing a strategic plan as well as a marketing plan, and establishing effective production and distribution systems) typically challenges what are often constrained resources in small and entrepreneurial firms. The disadvantages notwithstanding, small and entrepreneurial ventures are proving vital to the growth of several industries, such as semiconductors, communications, biotechnology and the entire Internet phenomenon, among others.[107] In these industry settings, some small businesses and entrepreneurial ventures seem to be demonstrating their capacity to excel in terms of producing *and* managing innovation. For example, Sydney firm Newport Scientific has been successful in the production of innovative instruments for the food sector, taking advantage of scientific capabilities and the robust demand conditions of the large Sydney market.[108]

Strategic Focus Corporate

Innovation as a key source of value creation

In Chapter 4, we discussed the relationship between value creation and strategic competitiveness. As we noted there, *value* consists of the performance characteristics and attributes that a company offers in the form of a good or service for which customers are willing to pay. Thus, the ability to create value is at the core of a firm's competitive success. In this chapter, the importance of innovation to a firm's success in the global economy has been emphasised. In fact, innovation, which is the process of creating a commercial good or service from an invention, is *critical* to competitive success for today's firms.

Combining value with innovation yields an interesting term called *value innovation*. According to researchers Kim and Mauborgne, 'Value innovation makes the competition irrelevant by offering fundamentally new and superior value in existing markets and by enabling a quantum leap in buyer value to create new markets.' Through value innovation, a firm seeks to commercialise each invention so that a new good or service is able to offer performance characteristics to customers that exceed their expectations or that actually create a new market through the use of unique product characteristics or attributes. Thus, effective value innovation creates radically different or greater value for customers, rather than producing incremental value enhancements. To make this possible, a firm must learn consistently and effectively and must be able to convert what is learned into knowledge that can become the foundation for developing new core competencies.

The actions of firms in numerous industries have resulted in value innovation. In the manufacturing tools and equipment industry. For example, SolidWorks Corporation developed the SolidWorks 2000, which is the leading mainstream computer-aided-design (CAD) solution for various design problems. Some argue that this product has allowed customers to substantially reduce errors and the amount of rework they must perform, as a result of its ability to permit rapid and simple changes to parts, drawings and assemblies simultaneously through modelling techniques. Earlier, we learned about Callaway Golf Company's Big Bertha golf club, which created, at a minimum, fundamentally new and superior buyer value. The Big Bertha was unlike competitors' golf clubs at the time of its introduction. Essentially, Callaway Golf Company innovated a product with a larger head that made playing golf less difficult and more enjoyable, particularly for 'weekend warriors' – relatively poor golfers who aspire to hit the ball longer distances without actually increasing their skill level. Through this value innovation, Callaway's product captured a large share of existing players and drew new players into the market. Other organisations recognised for their value innovations include IKEA (in the retailing of home furnishings), Dyson (in vacuum cleaners) and the Australian SBS television network (which has a world reputation in the provision of global news). Product development teams can be instrumental in helping a firm to appropriate or gain maximum value from its value innovations.

In the final analysis, value innovation challenges firms to develop their knowledge-generating capabilities. With knowledge as the foundation for the shaping and nurturing of core competencies, a firm has the capacity to produce and manage innovations that have the potential to create new markets or significantly expand current ones.

Sources: Callaway Golf Company, 2000, *Callaway Golf Company Home Page*, 22 March: www.callaway.com; SolidWorks, 2000, 'SolidWorks 2000', 16 March; M. A. Hitt, R. D. Nixon, R. E. Hoskisson and R. Kochhar, 1999, 'Corporate entrepreneurship and cross-functional fertilization: Activation, process and disintegration of a new product design team', *Entrepreneurship: Theory and Practice*, 23(3), pp. 147–67; W. C. Kim and R. Mauborgne, 1999, 'Strategy, value innovation, and the knowledge economy', *Sloan Management Review*, 40(3), pp. 41–4; S. A. Zahra, A. P. Nielsen and W. C. Bogner, 1999, 'Corporate entrepreneurship, knowledge, and competence development', *Entrepreneurship: Theory and Practice*, 23(3), pp. 169–89.

Producing more innovation in large organisations

Full value from innovation is achieved when a firm is able to produce *and* manage innovation effectively. As we have mentioned, large organisations are less effective than small and entrepreneurial ventures in producing innovations. Given their deficiency relative to smaller and more entrepreneurial ventures, what can large firms do to act small and improve their ability to produce innovations?

Several actions can be taken to deal with this issue. First, greater levels of individual autonomy can be created through the restructuring of a firm into smaller and more manageable units (see Chapter 7). The additional amounts of creativity and innovation that tend to be witnessed among those granted more autonomy stimulates autonomous strategic behaviour when a firm purses innovation through internal corporate ventures.[109] Simultaneously, a firm can reengineer its operations to develop more efficient work-related processes and to form channels through which customers' interests can be expressed with greater clarity and intensity.[110] The cross-functional work teams described earlier also provide opportunities for personnel to think and act creatively. Handled effectively, even downsizing (see Chapter 7) can create arrangements through which a firm is able to better focus its efforts on key tasks, such as those required to produce innovations.[111] Other actions a firm can take to stimulate the production of innovations are allocating significant levels of resources to R&D and using cooperative arrangements effectively.

Thus, both large and small firms can innovate. Until the skills required to both produce and manage innovation are mastered by either large organisations or small businesses and entrepreneurial ventures, cooperative arrangements will be an attractive option. Through effective collaborations, the small partner has an opportunity to concentrate on producing an innovation that the large partner can manage to marketplace success.[112] As the Strategic Focus above shows, regardless of the approach used to produce and manage innovations, a firm may be able to appropriate or gain the greatest amount of value when its innovations create exceptional value for customers.

Summary

- Firms engage in three types of innovative activity. Invention is the act of creating and developing an idea for a new product or process. Innovation is the process of commercialising the products or processes that surfaced through invention. Imitation is the adoption of an innovation by others, often the firm's competitors. Imitation usually leads to product or process standardisation and market acceptance.
- Increasingly, entrepreneurship and corporate entrepreneurship are being practised in many countries. As used by entrepreneurs, entrepreneurship and corporate entrepreneurship are strongly related to a nation's economic growth. This relationship is a primary reason for the increasing use of entrepreneurship and corporate entrepreneurship in countries throughout the global economy.
- Three basic approaches are used to produce and manage innovation: internal corporate venturing, strategic alliances, and acquisitions. Autonomous strategic behaviour and induced strategic behaviour are the two processes of internal corporate venturing. Autonomous strategic behaviour is a bottom-up process through which a product champion facilitates the commercialisation of an innovative good or service. Induced strategic behaviour is a top-down process in which a firm's current strategy and structure facilitate product or process innovations that are associated with them. Thus, induced strategic behaviour is driven by the organisation's current corporate strategy, structure, and reward and control systems.
- Increasingly, cross-functional integration is vital to a firm's efforts to appropriate or gain value from its internal corporate venturing efforts. Facilitated by cross-functional teams, cross-functional integration can reduce the time a firm needs to introduce innovative products into the marketplace. Cross-functional integration also can improve product quality and, ultimately, create value for customers.
- In the complex global economy, it is difficult for an individual firm to possess all the knowledge needed to innovate consistently and effectively. To gain access to the kind of specialised knowledge that often is required to innovate, firms may form a cooperative relationship such as a strategic alliance with others – sometimes even with competitors.
- Acquisitions are the third basic approach firms use to produce and manage innovation. Innovation can be acquired either through direct acquisition or through indirect investment. Examples of indirect investment are the formation of a wholly owned venture capital division and the use of private placement of venture capital. Buying innovation, however, comes with the risk of reducing a firm's internal invention and innovative capabilities.
- Small firms are particularly well suited for fostering

innovations that do not require large amounts of capital. Small firms have therefore become a vibrant part of industrialised nations, accounting for more job creation than large firms during the last decade.
- Large firms are needed to foster innovation due to capital requirements. Small firms are often found to be better at creating speciality products and diffusing the innovation through spin-offs from large corporations. Thus, collaborations between large and small firms often lead to successful product innovation processes.

Review questions

1. What is innovation? What is entrepreneurship? What is corporate entrepreneurship? Who are entrepreneurs? What is the importance of these terms for firms competing in the global economy?
2. What are the three stages of the innovation process, and why are the differences among them important?
3. What is autonomous strategic behaviour? What is induced strategic behaviour?
4. Some believe that, when managed successfully, cross-functional teams facilitate the implementation of internal corporate ventures and a firm's innovation efforts. How should cross-functional teams be managed to achieve these desirable outcomes?
5. How do firms use strategic alliances to help them produce innovation?
6. How can a firm create value when it acquires another company to gain access to its innovations or its ability to produce innovations?
7. How do large firms use venture capital to produce innovations and to identify new product opportunities?
8. What are the differences in the resources, capabilities and core competencies of large and small firms to produce and manage innovation?

Application discussion questions

1. Is there a relationship between the wave of acquisitions and the increase in available venture capital?
2. In your opinion, is the term 'corporate entrepreneurship' an oxymoron? In other words, can corporations, especially large ones, be innovative?
3. Have you observed a product champion supporting an innovation in a corporation? If so, what were the results of the champion's efforts?
4. The economies of countries such as Russia and China have historically been operated through centralised bureaucracies. What can be done to infuse such economies with a commitment to corporate entrepreneurship and the innovation resulting from it?
5. Use the Internet to find an example of two corporate innovations, one brought about through autonomous strategic behaviour and one developed through induced strategic behaviour. Which innovation do you believe holds the most promise for commercial success and why?
6. Are strategic alliances a way to enhance a firm's technological capacity, or are they used more commonly to maintain pace with technological developments in a company's industry? In other words, are strategic alliances a tool of firms that have a technological advantage, or are they a tool of technologically disadvantaged companies?

Ethics questions

1. Is it ethical for a company to purchase another firm to gain ownership of its product innovations and innovative capabilities? Why or why not?
2. Do firms encounter ethical issues when they use internal corporate-venturing processes to produce and manage innovation? If so, what are these issues?
3. Firms that are partners in a strategic alliance may legitimately seek to gain knowledge from each other. At what point does it become unethical for a firm to gain additional and competitively relevant knowledge from its partner? Is this point different when a firm partners with a domestic firm as opposed to a foreign firm? If so, why?
4. Small firms often have innovative products. When is it appropriate for a large firm to buy a small firm for its product innovations and new product ideas?

Internet exercise

The World Wide Web has made it both possible and necessary for many traditional businesses to market and sell their goods and services on-line. Consumer goods and services such as banking, clothing, holidays and grocery items can be ordered through the Internet. Creating new, safe and reliable methods to access, pay for and deliver goods and services via the Web has added to the list of innovations and management strategies that corporate entrepreneurs need to explore to be successful. To find out more about entrepreneurship and innovation, explore the following website: The Kauffman Foundation's EntreWorld at: www.entreworld.org.

e-project: Australia's most successful pizza delivery chains, including Domino's, Pizza Hut and other regional businesses, have long relied on phone orders for delivery. How can the Internet's capabilities be integrated into their business? Weighing the pros and cons of ordering pizza on-line, make a list of 10 management concerns and techniques that you would need to consider to successfully promote, develop and run an on-line business in this lucrative market.

Notes

1. A. Taylor, III, 2000, 'Detroit: Every silver lining has a cloud', *Fortune*, 24 January, pp. 92–3.
2. R. D. Ireland and M. A. Hitt, 1999, 'Achieving and maintaining strategic competitiveness in the 21st century: The role of strategic leadership', *Academy of Management Executive*, 13(1), pp. 43–57; M. D. Nevins and S. A. Stumpf, 1999, '21st century leadership: Redefining management education', *Strategy & Business*, 16, pp. 41–51.
3. A. Gome, 1999, 'The good oil on science: Growing a new business', *Business Review Weekly*, November, pp. 175–9.
4. M. A. Hitt, R. D. Nixon, P. G. Clifford and K. P. Coyne, 1999, 'The development and use of strategic resources', in M. A. Hitt, P. G. Clifford, R. D. Nixon and K. P. Coyne (eds), 1999, *Dynamic Strategic Resources: Development, Diffusion and Integration* (Chichester: John Wiley & Sons), pp. 1–14.
5. H. Lee, K. G. Smith, C. M. Grimm and A. Schomburg, 2000, 'Timing, order and durability of new product advantages with imitation', *Strategic Management Journal*, 21, pp. 23–30.
6. P. F. Drucker, 1998, 'The discipline of innovation', *Harvard Business Review*, 76(6), pp. 149–57.
7. P. D. Reynolds, M. Hay and S. M. Camp, 1999, *Global Entrepreneurship Monitor, 1999 Executive Report* (Babson Park, MA: Babson College).
8. M. H. Meyer and A. DeTore, 1999, 'Product development for services', *Academy of Management Executive*, 13(3), pp. 64–76.
9. Deutsche Telekom, 2000, 'The new millennium with a capital "T"', *Forbes*, 24 January, p. 81.
10. H. Ford, 2000, 'Noteworthy quotes', *Strategy & Business*, 18, p. 154.
11. S. A. Zahra, D. F. Kuratko and D. F. Jennings, 1999, 'Guest editorial: Entrepreneurship and the acquisition of dynamic organizational capabilities', *Entrepreneurship: Theory and Practice*, 23(3), pp. 5–10.
12. S. Miller, 2000, 'Formula One racing gets riskier – for its sponsors', *Wall Street Journal*, 25 February, pp. B1, B4.
13. D. Roth, 1999, 'Dell's big new act', *Fortune*, 6 December, pp. 152–5.
14. R. M. Kanter, 1999, 'From spare change to real change: The social sector as Beta site for business innovation', *Harvard Business Review*, 77(3), pp. 122–32.
15. M. A. Mone, W. McKinley and V. L. Barger, III, 1998, 'Organizational decline and innovation: A contingency framework', *Academy of Management Review*, 23, pp. 115–32.
16. R. Price, 1996, 'Technology and strategic advantage', *California Management Review*, 38(3), pp. 38–56; L. G. Franko, 1989, 'Global corporate competition: Who's winning, who's losing and the R&D factor as one reason why', *Strategic Management Journal*, 10, pp. 449–74.
17. G. T. Lumpkin and G. G. Dess, 1996, 'Clarifying the entrepreneurial orientation construct and linking it to performance', *Academy of Management Review*, 21, pp. 135–72; K. M. Kelm, V. K. Narayanan and G. E. Pinches, 1995, 'Shareholder value creation during R&D innovation and commercialization stages', *Academy of Management Journal*, 38, pp. 770–86.
18. P. W. Roberts, 1999, 'Product innovation, product-market competition and persistent profitability in the U.S. pharmaceutical industry', *Strategic Management Journal*, 20, pp. 655–70.
19. Mone, McKinley and Barker, 'Organizational decline', p. 117.
20. J. Schumpeter, 1934, *The Theory of Economic Development* (Cambridge, MA: Harvard University Press).
21. M. A. Hitt, R. D. Nixon, R. E. Hoskisson and R. Kochhar, 1999, 'Corporate entrepreneurship and cross-functional fertilization: Activation, process and disintegration of a new product design team', *Entrepreneurship: Theory and Practice*, 23(3), pp. 145–67.
22. D. L. Deeds, D. DeCarolis and J. Coombs, 2000, 'Dynamic capabilities and new product development in high technology ventures: An empirical analysis of new biotechnology firms', *Journal of Business Venturing*, 15, pp. 211–29.
23. T. Petzinger, Jr, 2000, 'So long, supply and demand', *Wall Street Journal*, 1 January, p. R31.
24. P. Sharma and J. L. Chrisman, 1999, 'Toward a reconciliation of the definitional issues in the field of corporate entrepreneurship', *Entrepreneurship: Theory and Practice*, 23(3), pp. 11–27; R. A. Burgelman and L. R. Sayles, 1986, *Inside Corporate Innovation: Strategy, Structure, and Managerial Skills* (New York: Free Press).
25. N. Talsarkoff and T. Featherstone, 1999, 'R&D Australia', *Business Review Weekly*, 2 June, pp. 53–7.
26. Schumpeter, *The Theory of Economic Development*.
27. S. Shane and S. Venkataraman, 2000, 'The promise of entrepreneurship as a field of research', *Academy of Management Review*, 25, pp. 217–26.
28. Reynolds, Hay and Camp, *Global Entrepreneurship Monitor*, p. 3.
29. A. Zacharakis, P. D. Reynolds and W. D. Bygrave, 1999, *Global Entrepreneurship Monitor, National Entrepreneurship Assessment, United States of America* (Babson Park, MA: Babson College).
30. B. R. Barringer and A. C. Bluedorn, 1999, 'The relationship between corporate entrepreneurship and strategic management', *Strategic Management Journal*, 20, pp. 421–44.
31. Sharma and Chrisman, 'Toward a reconciliation', p. 18.
32. S. A. Zahra, 1995, 'Corporate entrepreneurship and financial performance: The case of management leveraged buyouts', *Journal of Business Venturing*, 10, pp. 225–47.
33. Barringer and Bluedorn, 'The relationship between', p. 421.
34. S. D. Sarasvathy, 2000, 'Seminar on research perspectives in entrepreneurship (1997)', *Journal of Business Venturing*, 15, pp. 1–57.
35. Barringer and Bluedorn, 'The relationship between', p. 422; R. W. Smilor, 1997, 'Entrepreneurship: Reflections on a subversive activity', *Journal of Business Venturing*, 12, pp. 341–6.
36. Lumpkin and Dess, 'Clarifying the entrepreneurial orientation construct'.
37. Reynolds, Hay and Camp, *Global Entrepreneurship Monitor*, p. 7.
38. Sharma and Chrisman, 'Toward a reconciliation', p. 17.
39. C. Thomas, 1999, '"Dunce" leaves the rest in his wake', *Business Review Weekly*, May, pp. 70–7.
40. Fast Company, 2000, 8 March: www.fastcompany.com.
41. J. Birkinshaw, 1999, 'The determinants and consequences of subsidiary initiative in multinational corporations', *Entrepreneurship: Theory and Practice*, 24(1), pp. 9–36.
42. B. Schlender, 2000, 'Jobs' Apple', *Fortune*, 24 January, pp. 66–76.
43. J. Bowles, 1997, 'Best practices: Driving growth through innovation, alliances, and stakeholder symbiosis', *Fortune*, 14 November, pp. S3–24.
44. S. W. Floyd and B. Wooldridge, 1999, 'Knowledge creation and social networks in corporate entrepreneurship: The renewal of organizational capability', *Entrepreneurship: Theory and Practice*, 23(3), pp. 123–43; J. P. Kotter, 1990, *A Force for Change* (New York: The Free Press).
45. Staff reporter, 2000, 'Business innovation urged', *Irish Times*, p. 23.
46. J. E. Jackson, J. Klich and V. Kontorovich, 1999, 'Firm creation and economic transitions', *Journal of Business Venturing*, 14, pp. 427–50.
47. Reynolds, Hay and Camp, *Global Entrepreneurship Monitor*, p. 7.
48. Ibid., p. 3.
49. B. Howarth, 2000, 'Aussies in Wonderland', *Business Review Weekly*, 25 August, pp. 6–7; T. Skotnicki, 2001, 'A little help, a little hindrance', *Business Review Weekly*, 1 February, pp. 52–5.
50. D. James, 2000, 'No clear view from innovation summit', *Business Review Weekly*, 16 June, pp. 58–62.
51. F. N. Pieke, 1995, 'Bureaucracy, friends and money: The growth of capital socialism in China', *Comparative Studies in Society and History*, 37, pp. 494–518.
52. M. H. Morris, 1998, *Entrepreneurial Intensity: Sustainable Advantages for Individuals, Organizations, and Societies* (Westport, CT: Quorum Books), pp. 85–6.

53. Ibid.; M. H. Morris, D. L. Davis and J. W. Allen, 1994, 'Fostering corporate entrepreneurship: Cross-cultural comparisons of the importance of individualism versus collectivism', *Journal of International Business Studies*, 25, pp. 65–89.
54. P. S. Li, 1993, 'Chinese investment and business in Canada: Ethnic entrepreneurship reconsidered', *Pacific Affairs*, 66, pp. 219–43.
55. D. H. Holt, 1997, 'A comparative study of values among Chinese and U.S. entrepreneurs: Pragmatic convergence between contrasting cultures', *Journal of Business Venturing*, 12, pp. 483–505.
56. T. Bates, 1997, 'Financing small business creation: The case of Chinese and Korean immigrant entrepreneurs', *Journal of Business Venturing*, 12, pp. 109–24.
57. M. Lerner, C. Brush and R. Hisrich, 1997, 'Israeli women entrepreneurs: An examination of factors affecting performance', *Journal of Business Venturing*, 12, pp. 315–39.
58. R. A. Burgelman, 1983, 'A model of the interaction of strategic behavior, corporate context, and the concept of strategy', *Academy of Management Review*, 8, pp. 61–70.
59. R. Leifer and M. Rice, 1999, 'Unnatural acts: Building the mature firm's capability for breakthrough innovation', in M. A. Hitt, P. G. Clifford, R. D. Nixon and K. P. Coyne (eds), *Dynamic Strategic Resources: Development, Diffusion and Integration* (Chichester: John Wiley & Sons), pp. 433–53.
60. M. A. Hitt, R. D. Ireland and H. Lee, 2000, 'Technological learning, knowledge management, firm growth and performance', *Journal of Engineering and Technology Management*, in press; D. Leonard-Barton, 1995, *Wellsprings of Knowledge: Building and Sustaining the Sources of Innovation* (Cambridge, MA: Harvard Business School Press).
61. S. S. Rao, 2000, 'General Electric, software vendor', *Forbes*, 24 January, pp. 144–6.
62. G. Hamel, 1997, 'Killer strategies that make shareholders rich', *Fortune*, 23 June, pp. 70–88.
63. F. M. Biddle, 2000, 'Fore! Callaway Golf, maker of Big Bertha clubs, tees up a new ball', *Wall Street Journal*, 4 February, p. B1; Callaway Golf Co., 2000, 'The history of Callaway Golf Company', 13 March: www.callawaygolf.com.
64. C. M. Christensen and M. Overdorf, 2000, 'Meeting the challenge of disruptive change', *Harvard Business Review*, 78(2), pp. 66–77.
65. A. Goldstein, 1999, 'IBM plans e-commerce network', *Dallas Morning News*, 16 November, pp. D1, D11.
66. P. S. Adler, 1995, 'Interdepartmental interdependence and coordination: The case of the design/manufacturing interface', *Organization Science*, 6, pp. 147–67.
67. B. L. Kirkman and B. Rosen, 1999, 'Beyond self-management: Antecedents and consequences of team empowerment', *Academy of Management Journal*, 42, pp. 58–74.
68. A. R. Jassawalla and H. C. Sashittal, 1999, 'Building collaborative cross-functional new product teams', *Academy of Management Executive*, 13(3), pp. 50–63.
69. Hitt, Nixon, Hoskisson and Kochhar, 'Corporate entrepreneurship', p. 146.
70. J. A. Byrne, 1993, 'The horizontal corporation: It's about managing across, not up and down', *Business Week*, 20 December, pp. 76–81.
71. Christensen and Overdorf, 'Meeting the challenge', p. 68.
72. Hitt, Nixon, Hoskisson and Kochhar, 'Corporate entrepreneurship', pp. 149–50.
73. A. C. Amason, 1996, 'Distinguishing the effects of functional and dysfunctional conflict on strategic decision making: Resolving a paradox for top management teams', *Academy of Management Journal*, 39, pp. 123–48; P. R. Lawrence and J. W. Lorsch, 1969, *Organization and Environment* (Homewood, IL: Richard D. Irwin).
74. D. Dougherty, L. Borrelli, K. Muncir and A. O'Sullivan, 2000, 'Systems of organizational sensemaking for sustained product innovation', *Journal of Engineering and Technology Management*, in press; D. Dougherty, 1992, 'Interpretive barriers to successful product innovation in large firms', *Organization Science*, 3, pp. 179–202; D. Dougherty, 1990, 'Understanding new markets for new products', *Strategic Management Journal*, 11 (Special Summer Issue), pp. 59–78.
75. Hitt, Nixon, Hoskisson and Kochhar, 'Corporate entrepreneurship', p. 150.
76. E. C. Wenger and W. M. Snyder, 2000, 'Communities of practice: The organizational frontier', *Harvard Business Review*, 78(1), pp. 139–44; J. D. Orton and K. E. Weick, 1990, 'Loosely coupled systems: A reconsideration', *Academy of Management Review*, 15, pp. 203–23.
77. J. Champy, 2000, 'Only a few sea turtles survive', *Forbes*, 21 February, p. 96.
78. J. Kavanagh, 2000, 'Chief executives – pin up boys', *Business Review Weekly*, 20 October, p. 87.
79. G. Rifkin, 1998, 'Competing through innovation: The case of Broderbund', *Strategy & Business*, 11, pp. 48–58.
80. K. M. Eisenhardt, 1999, 'Strategy as strategic decision making', *Sloan Management Review*, 40(3), pp. 65–72.
81. B. B. Flynn and E. J. Flynn, 2000, 'Fast product development', *Newswise*, 23 March: www.newswise.com.
82. S. A. Zahra and W. C. Bogner, 2000, 'Technology strategy and software new ventures' performance: Exploring the moderating effect of the competitive environment', *Journal of Business Venturing*, 15, pp. 135–73.
83. S. W. Fowler, A. W. King, S. J. Marsh and B. Victor, 2000, 'Beyond products: New strategic imperatives for developing competencies in dynamic environments', *Journal of Engineering and Technology Management*, in press.
84. P. Kale, H. Singh and H. Perlmutter, 2000, 'Learning and protection of proprietary assets in strategic alliances: Building relational capital', *Strategic Management Journal*, 21, pp. 217–37.
85. R. Gulati, N. Nohria and A. Zaheer, 2000, 'Strategic networks', *Strategic Management Journal*, 21 (Special Issue), pp. 203–15.
86. Hitt, Ireland and Lee, 'Technological learning'.
87. B. N. Anand and T. Khanna, 2000, 'Do firms learn to create value? The case of alliances', *Strategic Management Journal*, 21 (Special Issue), pp. 295–315.
88. S. Miller, 1999, 'Porsche profits may leave the fast lane', *Wall Street Journal*, 9 December, p. A21.
89. J. A. C. Baum, T. Calabrese and B. S. Silverman, 2000, 'Don't go it alone: Alliance network composition and startups' performance in Canadian biotechnology', *Strategic Management Journal*, 21 (Special Issue), pp. 267–94.
90. M. T. Dacin, M. A. Hitt and E. Levitas, 1997, 'Selecting partners for successful international alliances: Examination of U.S. and Korean firms', *Journal of World Business*, 32(1), pp. 3–16; M. A. Hitt, M. T. Dacin, B. B. Tyler and D. Park, 1997, 'Understanding the differences in Korean and U.S. executives' strategic orientations', *Strategic Management Journal*, 18, pp. 159–67.
91. G. Hamel, 1991, 'Competition for competence and interpartner learning within international strategic alliances', *Strategic Management Journal*, 12, pp. 83–103.
92. B. Quinliven, 2001, 'Big science, little money', *Business Review Weekly*, 23 February, pp. 68–71.
93. M. Yost, 1999, 'Innovation lifts Meritor's profile in auto-parts business', *Wall Street Journal*, 15 November, p. B4.
94. M. A. Hitt, R. E. Hoskisson, R. A. Johnson and D. D. Moesel, 1996, 'The market for corporate control and firm innovation', *Academy of Management Journal*, 39, pp. 1084–119; M. A. Hitt, R. E. Hoskisson, R. D. Ireland and J. S. Harrison, 1991, 'Effects of acquisitions on R&D inputs and outputs', *Academy of Management Journal*, 34, pp. 693–706.
95. Hitt et al., 'The market for corporate control'.
96. M. A. Hitt, J. S. Harrison and R. D. Ireland, 2001, *Creating Value through Mergers and Acquisitions: A Complete Guide to Successful M&As* (New York: Oxford University Press); M. A. Hitt, J. S. Harrison, R. D. Ireland and A. Best, 1998, 'Attributes of successful and unsuccessful acquisitions of U.S. firms', *British Journal of Management*, 9, pp. 91–114.
97. J. A. Timmons, 1999, *New Venture Creation: Entrepreneurship for the 21st Century*, 5th edition (New York: Irwin/McGraw-Hill), p. 440.
98. T. E. Winters and D. L. Murfin, 1988, 'Venture capital investing for corporate development objectives', *Journal of Business Venturing*, 3, pp. 207–22.
99. G. F. Hardymon, M. J. DeNino and M. S. Salter, 1983, 'When corporate venture capital doesn't work', *Harvard Business Review*, 61(3), pp. 114–20.
100. U. Gupta, 1993, 'Venture capital investment soars, reversing four-year slide', *Wall Street Journal*, 1 June, p. B2.
101. Paul, 'Made in Japan', pp. 190–200.
102. Petzinger, Jr, 'So long', p. R31.
103. R. Poe and C. L. Courter, 2000, 'Small is beautiful again', *Across the Board*, January, p. 9.

104 Reynolds, Hay and Camp, *Global Entrepreneurship Monitor*, p. 4.
105 A. L. Anna, G. N. Chandler, E. Jansen and N. P. Mero, 2000, 'Women business owners in traditional and non-traditional industries', *Journal of Business Venturing*, 15, pp. 279–303.
106 L. W. Busenitz, 1997, 'Differences between entrepreneurs and managers in large organizations: Biases and heuristics in strategic decision making', *Journal of Business Venturing*, 12, pp. 9–30.
107 A. Goldstein, 2000, 'Culture of money', *Dallas Morning News*, 30 January, pp. H1, H2.
108 Industry Research and Development Board, 2000, *R&D Scorecard 1998*.
109 R. A. Melcher, 1993, 'How Goliaths can act like Davids', *Business Week* (Special Bonus Issue), pp. 192–201.
110 Champy, 'Only a few', p. 96.
111 M. A. Hitt, B. W. Keats, H. F. Harback and R. D. Nixon, 1994, 'Rightsizing: Building and maintaining strategic leadership and long-term competitiveness', *Organizational Dynamics*, 23(2), pp. 18–32.
112 M. A. Hitt, B. W. Keats and S. M. DeMarie, 1998, 'Navigating in the new competitive landscape', *Academy of Management Executive*, 12(4), pp. 22–42.

Case Studies

INTRODUCTION Preparing an effective case analysis C-3

CASE 1 ABB in China, 1998 C-16

CASE 2 Ansett Airlines and Air New Zealand: A flight to oblivion? C-31

CASE 3 BP–Mobil and the restructuring of the oil refining industry C-44

CASE 4 Compaq in crisis C-67

CASE 5 Gillette and the men's wet-shaving market C-76

CASE 6 Incat Tasmania's race for international success: Blue Riband strategies C-95

CASE 7 Kiwi Travel International Airlines Ltd C-105

CASE 8 Beefing up the beefless Mac: McDonald's expansion strategies in India: C-120

CASE 9 Nucor Corporation and the US steel industry C-128

CASE 10 Pacific Dunlop: Caught on the half volley C-157

CASE 11 Philip Morris C-173

CASE 12 Pisces Group of Singapore C-188

CASE 13 Raffles, Singapore's historic hotel C-194

CASE 14 Southwest Airlines, 1996 C-205

Introduction

Preparing an effective case analysis

In most strategic management courses, cases are used extensively as a teaching tool.[1] A key reason is that cases provide active learners with opportunities to use the strategic management process to identify and solve organisational problems. Thus, by analysing situations that are described in cases and presenting the results, active learners (that is, students) become skilled at effectively using the tools, techniques and concepts that combine to form the strategic management process.

The cases that follow are concerned with actual companies. Presented within the cases are problems and situations that managers and those with whom they work must analyse and resolve. As you will see, a strategic management case can focus on an entire industry, a single organisation or a business unit of a large, diversified firm. The strategic management issues facing not-for-profit organisations also can be examined using the case analysis method.

Basically, the case analysis method calls for a careful diagnosis of an organization's current conditions (as manifested by its external and internal environments) so that appropriate strategic actions can be recommended in light of the firm's strategic intent and strategic mission. Strategic actions are taken to develop and then use a firm's core competencies to select and implement different strategies, including business-level, corporate-level, acquisition and restructuring, international and cooperative strategies. Thus, appropriate strategic actions help the firm to survive in the long run as it creates and uses competitive advantages as the foundation for achieving strategic competitiveness and earning above-average returns. The case method that we are recommending to you has a rich heritage as a pedagogical approach to the study and understanding of managerial effectiveness.[2]

As an active learner, your preparation is critical to successful use of the case analysis method. Without careful study and analysis, active learners lack the insights required to participate fully in the discussion of a firm's situation and the strategic actions that are appropriate.

Instructors adopt different approaches in their application of the case analysis method. Some require active learners/students to use a specific analytical procedure to examine an organisation; others provide less structure, expecting students to learn by developing their own unique analytical method. Still other instructors believe that a moderately structured framework should be used to analyse a firm's situation and make appropriate recommendations. Your lecturer or tutor will determine the specific approach you take. The approach we are presenting to you is a moderately structured framework.

We divide our discussion of a moderately structured case analysis method framework into four sections. First, we describe the importance of understanding the skills active learners can acquire through effective use of the case analysis method. In the second section, we provide you with a process-oriented framework. This framework can be of value in your efforts to analyse cases and then present the results of your work. Using this framework in a classroom setting yields valuable experiences that can, in turn, help you to successfully complete assignments that you will receive from your employer. The third section is where we describe briefly what you can expect to occur during in-class case discussions. As this description shows, the relationship and interactions between instructors and active learners/students during case discussions are different than they are during lectures. In the final section, we present a moderately structured framework that we believe can help you to prepare effective oral and written presentations. Written and oral communication skills also are valued highly in many organisational settings; hence, their development today can serve you well in the future.

Skills gained through use of the case analysis method

The case analysis method is based on a philosophy that combines knowledge acquisition with significant involvement from students as active learners. In the words of Alfred North Whitehead, this philosophy 'rejects the doctrine that students had first learned passively, and then, having learned should apply knowledge'.[3] In contrast to this philosophy, the case analysis method is based on principles that were elaborated upon by John Dewey:

> *Only by wrestling with the conditions of this problem at hand, seeking and finding his own way out, does [the student] think ... If he cannot devise his own solution (not, of course, in isolation, but in correspondence with the teacher and other pupils) and find his own way out he will not learn, not even if he can recite some correct answer with a hundred percent accuracy.*[4]

The case analysis method brings reality into the classroom. When developed and presented effectively, with rich and interesting detail, cases keep conceptual discussions grounded in reality. Experience shows that simple fictional accounts of situations and collections of actual organisational data and articles from public sources are not as effective for learning as fully developed cases. A comprehensive case presents you with a partial clinical study of a real-life situation that faced managers as well as other stakeholders, including employees. A case presented in narrative form provides motivation for involvement with and analysis of a specific situation. By framing alternative strategic actions and by confronting the complexity and ambiguity of the practical world, case analysis provides extraordinary power for your involvement with a personal learning experience. Some of the potential consequences of using the case method are summarised in Exhibit 1.

As Exhibit 1 suggests, the case analysis method can assist active learners in the development of their analytical and judgement skills. Case analysis also helps you learn how to ask the right questions. By this we mean questions that focus on the core strategic issues that are included in a case. Active learners/students with managerial aspirations can improve their ability to identify underlying problems rather than focusing on superficial symptoms as they develop skills at asking probing yet appropriate questions.

The collection of cases your instructor chooses to assign can expose you to a wide variety of organisations and decision situations. This approach vicariously broadens your experience base and provides insights into many types of managerial situations, tasks and responsibilities. Such indirect experience can help you to make a more informed career decision about the industry and managerial situation you believe will prove to be challenging and satisfying. Finally, experience in analysing cases definitely enhances your problem-solving skills, and research indicates that the case method for this class is better than the lecture method.[5]

Furthermore, when your instructor requires oral and written presentations, your communication skills will be honed through use of the case method. Of course, these added skills depend on your preparation as

Exhibit 1 | Consequences of student involvement with the case method

1. Case analysis requires students to practise important managerial skills—diagnosing, making decisions, observing, listening and persuading—while preparing for a case discussion.
2. Cases require students to relate analysis and action, to develop realistic and concrete actions despite the complexity and partial knowledge characterising the situation being studied.
3. Students must confront the *intractability of reality*—complete with absence of needed information, an imbalance between needs and available resources, and conflicts among competing objectives.
4. Students develop a general managerial point of view—where responsibility is sensitive to action in a diverse environmental context.

Source: C.C. Lundberg and C. Enz, 1993, 'A framework for student case preparation', *Case Research Journal*, 13 (Summer), p. 134.

well as your instructor's facilitation of learning. However, the primary responsibility for learning is yours. The quality of case discussion is generally acknowledged to require, at a minimum, a thorough mastery of case facts and some independent analysis of them. The case method therefore first requires that you read and think carefully about each case. Additional comments about the preparation you should complete to successfully discuss a case appear in the next section.

Student preparation for case discussion

If you are inexperienced with the case method, you may need to alter your study habits. A lecture-oriented course may not require you to do intensive preparation for *each* class period. In such a course, you have the latitude to work through assigned readings and review lecture notes according to your own schedule. However, an assigned case requires significant and conscientious *preparation before class*. Without it, you will be unable to contribute meaningfully to in-class discussion. Therefore, careful reading and thinking about case facts, as well as reasoned analyses and the development of alternative solutions to case problems, are essential. Recommended alternatives should flow logically from core problems identified through study of the case. Exhibit 2 shows a set of steps that can help you to familiarise yourself with a case, identify problems and propose strategic actions that increase the probability that a firm will achieve strategic competitiveness and earn above-average returns.

Exhibit 2 | An effective case analysis process

Step 1: Gaining familiarity	a.	In general – determine who, what, how, where and when (the critical facts of the case).
	b.	In detail – identify the places, persons, activities and contexts of the situation.
	c.	Recognise the degree of certainty/uncertainty of acquired information.
Step 2: Recognising symptoms	a.	List all indicators (including stated 'problems') that something is not as expected or as desired.
	b.	Ensure that symptoms are not assumed to be the problem (symptoms should lead to identification of the problem).
Step 3: Identifying goals	a.	Identify critical statements by major parties (e.g. people, groups, the work unit, etc.).
	b.	List all goals of the major parties that exist or can be reasonably inferred.
Step 4: Conducting the analysis	a.	Decide which ideas, models and theories seem useful.
	b.	Apply these conceptual tools to the situation.
	c.	As new information is revealed, cycle back to sub-steps (a) and (b).
Step 5: Making the diagnosis	a.	Identify predicaments (goal inconsistencies).
	b.	Identify problems (discrepancies between goals and performance).
	c.	Prioritise predicaments/problems regarding timing, importance, etc.
Step 6: Doing the action planning	a.	Specify and prioritise the criteria used to choose action alternatives.
	b.	Discover or invent feasible action alternatives.
	c.	Examine the probable consequences of action alternatives.
	d.	Select a course of action.
	e.	Design an implementation plan/schedule.
	f.	Create a plan for assessing the action to be implemented.

Source: C. C. Lundberg and C. Enz, 1993, 'A framework for student case preparation', *Case Research Journal*, 13 (Summer), p. 144.

Gaining familiarity

The first step of an effective case analysis process calls for you to become familiar with the facts featured in the case and the focal firm's situation. Initially, you should become familiar with the focal firm's general situation (for example, who, what, how, where and when). Thorough familiarisation demands appreciation of the nuances, as well as the major issues, in the case.

Gaining familiarity with a situation requires you to study several situational levels, including interactions between and among individuals within groups, business units, the corporate office, the local community and the society at large. Recognising relationships within and among levels facilitates a more thorough understanding of the specific case situation.

It is also important that you evaluate information on a continuum of certainty. Information that is verifiable by several sources and judged along similar dimensions can be classified as a *fact*. Information representing someone's perceptual judgement of a particular situation is referred to as an *inference*. Information gleaned from a situation that is not verifiable is classified as *speculation*. Finally, information that is independent of verifiable sources and arises through individual or group discussion is an *assumption*. Obviously, case analysts and organisational decision makers prefer having access to facts over inferences, speculations and assumptions.

Personal feelings, judgements and opinions evolve when you are analysing a case. It is important to be aware of your own feelings about the case and to evaluate the accuracy of perceived 'facts' to ensure that the objectivity of your work is maximised.

Recognising symptoms

Recognition of symptoms is the second step of an effective case analysis process. A symptom is an indication that something is not as you or someone else thinks it should be. You may be tempted to correct the symptoms instead of searching for true problems. True problems are the conditions or situations requiring solution before the performance of an organisation, business unit or individual can improve. Identifying and listing symptoms early in the case analysis process tends to reduce the temptation to label symptoms as problems. The focus of your analysis should be on the *actual causes* of a problem, rather than on its symptoms. Thus, it is important to remember that symptoms are indicators of problems; subsequent work facilitates discovery of critical causes of problems that your case recommendations must address.

Identifying goals

The third step of effective case analysis calls for you to identify the goals of the major organisations, business units and/or individuals in a case. As appropriate, you should also identify each firm's strategic intent and strategic mission. Typically, these direction-setting statements (goals, strategic intents and strategic missions) are derived from comments made by central characters in the organisation, business unit or top management team as described in the case and/or from public documents (for example, an annual report).

Completing this step successfully can sometimes be difficult. Nonetheless, the outcomes you attain from this step are essential to an effective case analysis because identifying goals, intent and mission helps you to clarify the major problems featured in a case and to evaluate alternative solutions to those problems. Direction-setting statements are not always stated publicly or prepared in written format. When this occurs, you must infer goals from other available factual data and information.

Conducting the analysis

The fourth step of effective case analysis is concerned with acquiring a systematic understanding of a situation. Occasionally cases are analysed in a less-than-thorough manner. Such analyses may be a product of a busy schedule or of the difficulty and complexity of the issues described in a particular case. Sometimes you will face pressures on your limited amounts of time and may believe that you can understand the situation described in a case without systematic *analysis* of all the facts. However, experience shows that familiarity with a case's facts is a necessary, but insufficient, step in the development of effective solutions – solutions that can enhance a firm's strategic competitiveness. In fact, a less-than-thorough analysis typically results in an emphasis on symptoms, rather than on problems and their causes. To analyse a case effectively, you should be sceptical of quick or easy approaches and answers.

A systematic analysis helps you to understand a situation and determine what can work and probably what will not work. Key linkages and underlying causal networks based on the history of the firm become apparent. In this way, you can separate causal networks from symptoms.

Also, because the quality of a case analysis depends on applying appropriate tools, it is important that you use the ideas, models and theories that seem to be useful for evaluating and solving individual and unique situations. As you consider facts and symptoms, a useful theory may become apparent. Of course, having familiarity with conceptual models may be important in the effective analysis of a situation. Successful students and successful organisational strategists add to their intellectual tool kits on a continual basis.

Making the diagnosis

The fifth step of effective case analysis – diagnosis – is the process of identifying and clarifying the roots of the problems by comparing goals with facts. In this step, it is useful to search for predicaments. Predicaments are situations in which goals do not fit with known facts. When you evaluate the actual performance of an organisation, business unit or individual, you may identify over- or underachievement (relative to established goals). Of course, single-problem situations are rare. Accordingly, you should recognise that the case situations you study probably will be complex in nature.

Effective diagnosis requires you to determine the problems affecting longer-term performance and those requiring immediate handling. Understanding these issues will aid your efforts to prioritise problems and predicaments, given available resources and existing constraints.

Doing the action planning

The final step of an effective case analysis process is called action planning. *Action planning* is the process of identifying appropriate alternative actions. In the action planning step, you select the criteria you will use to evaluate the identified alternatives. You may derive these criteria from the analyses; typically, they are related to key strategic situations facing the focal organisation. Furthermore, it is important that you prioritise these criteria to ensure a rational and effective evaluation of alternative courses of action.

Typically, managers 'satisfice' when selecting courses of action; that is, they find *acceptable* courses of action that meet most of the chosen evaluation criteria. A rule of thumb that has proved valuable to strategic decision makers is to select an alternative that leaves other plausible alternatives available if the one selected fails.

Once you have selected the best alternative, you must specify an implementation plan. Developing an implementation plan serves as a reality check on the feasibility of your alternatives. Thus, it is important that you give thoughtful consideration to all issues associated with the implementation of the selected alternatives.

What to expect from in-class case discussions

Classroom discussions of cases differ significantly from lectures. The case method calls for instructors to guide the discussion, encourage student participation and solicit alternative views. When alternative views are not forthcoming, instructors typically adopt one view so that students can be challenged to respond to it thoughtfully. Often students' work is evaluated in terms of both the quantity and the quality of their contributions to in-class case discussions. Students benefit by having their views judged against those of their peers and by responding to challenges by other class members and/or the instructor.

During case discussions, instructors listen, question and probe to extend the analysis of case issues. In the course of these actions, peers or the instructor may challenge an individual's views and the validity of alternative perspectives that have been expressed. These challenges are offered in a constructive manner; their intent is to help students develop their analytical and communication skills. Instructors should encourage students to be innovative and original in the development and presentation of their ideas. Over the course of an individual discussion, students can develop a more complex view of the case, benefiting from the diverse inputs of their peers and instructor. Among other benefits, experience with multiple-case discussions should help students to increase their knowledge of the advantages and disadvantages of group decision-making processes.

Student peers as well as the instructor value comments that contribute to the discussion. To offer *relevant* contributions, you are encouraged to use independent thought and, through discussions with your peers outside of class, to refine your thinking. We also encourage you to avoid using 'I think', 'I believe' and 'I feel' to discuss your inputs to a case analysis process. Instead, consider using a less emotion-laden phrase, such as 'My analysis shows'. This highlights the logical nature of the approach you have taken to complete the six steps of an effective case analysis process.

When preparing for an in-class case discussion, you should plan to use the case data to explain your assessment of the situation. Assume that your peers and instructor know the case facts. In addition, it is good practice to prepare notes before class discussions and use them as you explain your view. Effective notes signal to classmates and the instructor that you are prepared to engage in a thorough discussion of a case. Moreover,

Exhibit 3 | Types of thinking in case preparation: Analysis and synthesis

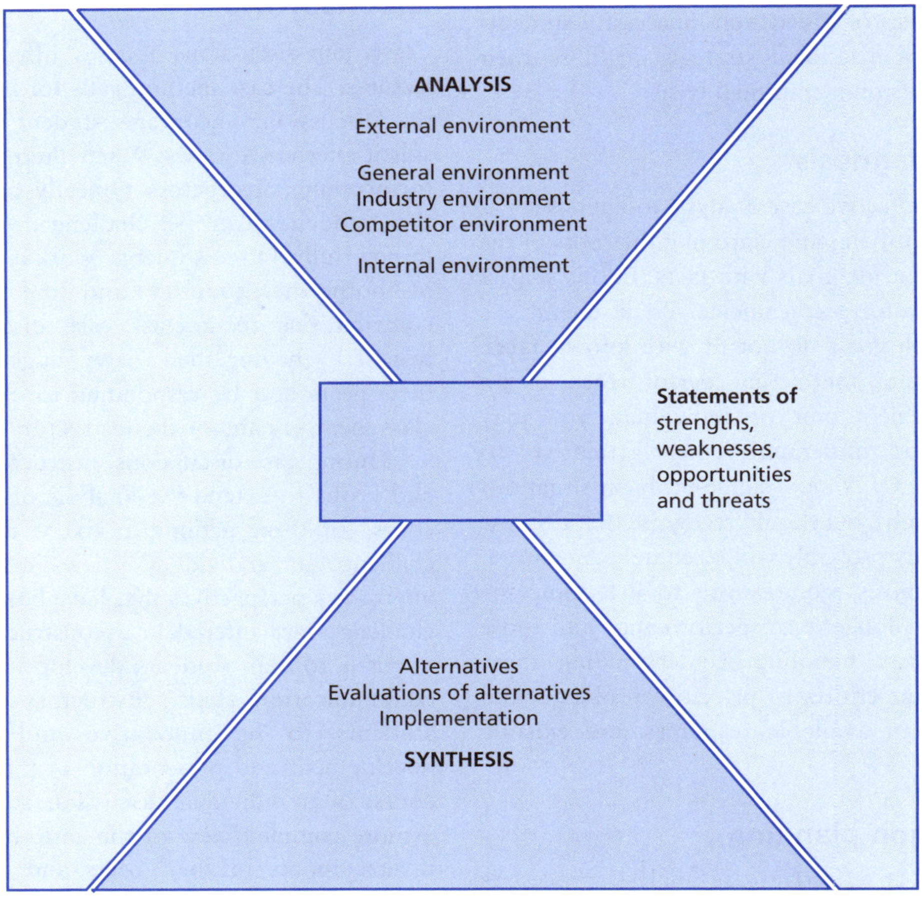

ANALYSIS

External environment

General environment
Industry environment
Competitor environment

Internal environment

Statements of strengths, weaknesses, opportunities and threats

Alternatives
Evaluations of alternatives
Implementation

SYNTHESIS

thorough notes eliminate the need for you to memorise the facts and figures needed to discuss a case successfully.

The case analysis process just described can help you prepare to effectively discuss a case during class meetings. Adherence to this process results in consideration of the issues required to identify a focal firm's problems and to propose strategic actions through which the firm can increase the probability that it will achieve strategic competitiveness.

In some instances, your instructor may ask you to prepare either an oral or a written analysis of a particular case. Typically, such an assignment demands even more thorough study and analysis of the case contents. At your instructor's discretion, oral and written analyses may be completed by individuals or by groups of two or more people. The information and insights gained through completing the six steps shown in Exhibit 2 are often of value in the development of an oral or written analysis. However, when preparing an oral or written presentation, you must consider the overall framework in which your information and inputs will be presented. Such a framework is the focus of the next section.

Preparing an oral/written case strategic plan

Experience shows that two types of thinking are necessary to develop an effective oral or written presentation (see Exhibit 3). The upper part of the model in Exhibit 3 outlines the *analysis* stage of case preparation.

In the analysis stage, you should first analyse the general external environmental issues affecting the firm. Next, your environmental analysis should focus on the particular industry (or industries, in the case of a diversified company) in which a firm operates. Finally, you should examine the competitive environment of the focal firm. Through study of the three levels of the external environment, you will be able to identify a firm's opportunities and threats. Following the external environmental analysis is the analysis of the firm's

Exhibit 4 | Strategic planning process

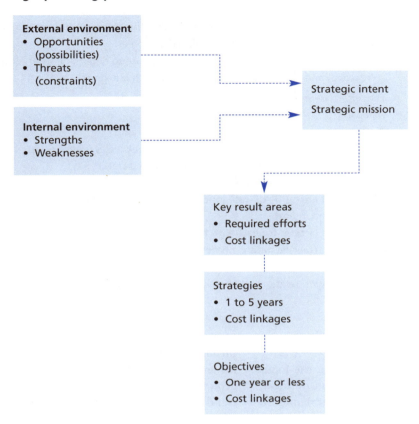

internal environment, which results in the identification of the firm's strengths and weaknesses.

As noted in Exhibit 3, you must then change the focus from analysis to *synthesis*. Specifically, you must *synthesise* information gained from your analysis of the firm's internal and external environments. Synthesising information allows you to generate alternatives that can resolve the significant problems or challenges facing the focal firm. Once you identify a best alternative, from an evaluation based on predetermined criteria and goals, you must explore implementation actions.

Exhibits 4 and 5 outline the sections that should be included in either an oral or a written strategic plan presentation: introduction (strategic intent and mission), situation analysis, statements of strengths/weaknesses and opportunities/threats, strategy formulation and implementation plan. These sections, which can be completed only through use of the two types of thinking featured in Exhibit 3, are described in the following discussion. Familiarity with the contents of your textbook's 13 chapters is helpful because the general outline for an oral or a written strategic plan shown in Exhibit 5 is based on an understanding of the strategic management process detailed in those chapters.

External environment analysis

As shown in Exhibit 5, a general starting place for completing a situation analysis is the external environment. The *external environment* is composed of outside (external) conditions that affect a firm's performance. Your analysis of the environment should consider the effects of the *general environment* on the focal firm. Following that evaluation, you should analyse the *industry and competitor environmental* trends.

These trends or conditions in the external environment shape the firm's strategic intent and mission. The external environment analysis essentially indicates what a firm *might choose to do*. Often called an *environmental scan*, an analysis of the external environment allows a firm to identify key conditions that are beyond its direct control. The purpose of studying the external environment is to identify a firm's opportunities and threats. *Opportunities* are conditions in the external environment that appear to have the potential to contribute to a firm's success. In essence, opportunities represent *possibilities*. *Threats* are conditions in the external environment that appear to

Exhibit 5 | Strategic planning and its parts

- *Strategic planning* is a *process* through which a firm determines what it seeks to accomplish and the actions required to achieve desired outcomes
  - ✓ *Strategic planning*, then, is a *process* that we use to determine *what* (outcomes to be reached) and *how* (actions to be taken to reach outcomes)
- The effective *strategic plan* for a firm would include statements and details about the following:
  - ✓ *Opportunities* (possibilities) and *threats* (constraints)
  - ✓ *Strengths* (what we do especially well) and *weaknesses* (deficiencies)
  - ✓ *Strategic intent* (an indication of a firm's ideal state)
  - ✓ *Strategic mission* (purpose and scope of a firm's operations in product and market terms)
  - ✓ *Key result areas* (KRAs) (categories of activities where efforts must take place to reach the mission and intent)
  - ✓ *Strategies* (actions for each KRA to be completed within one to five years)
  - ✓ *Objectives* (specific statements detailing actions for each strategy that are to be completed in one year or less)
  - ✓ *Cost linkages* (relationships between actions and financial resources)

have the potential to prevent a firm's success. In essence, threats represent potential *constraints*.

When studying the external environment, the focus is on trying to *predict* the future (in terms of local, regional, and international trends and issues) and to *predict* the expected effects on a firm's operations. The external environment features conditions in the broader society *and* in the industry (area of competition) that influence the firm's possibilities and constraints. Areas to be considered (to identify opportunities and threats) when studying the general environment are listed in Exhibit 6. Many of these issues are explained more fully in Chapter 2.

Once you analyse the general environmental trends, you should study their effect on the focal industry. Often the same environmental trend may have a significantly different impact on separate industries. Furthermore, the same trend may affect firms within the same industry differently. For instance, with deregulation of the airline industry in the United States, older, established airlines had a significant decrease in profitability, while many smaller airlines, such as Southwest Airlines, with lower cost structures and greater flexibility, were able to aggressively enter new markets.

Porter's five forces model is a useful tool for analysing the specific industry (see Chapter 2). Careful study of how the five competitive forces (that is, supplier power, buyer power, potential entrants, substitute products and rivalry among competitors) affect a firm's strategy is important. These forces may create threats or opportunities relative to the specific business-level strategies (that is, differentiation, cost leadership, focus) being implemented. Often a strategic group's analysis reveals how different environmental trends are affecting industry competitors. Strategic group analysis is useful for understanding the industry's competitive structures and firm constraints and possibilities within those structures.

Firms also need to analyse each of their primary competitors. This analysis should identify competitors' current strategies, strategic intent, strategic mission, capabilities, core competencies and a competitive response profile. This information is useful to the focal firm in formulating an appropriate strategic intent and mission.

Internal environment analysis

The *internal environment* is composed of strengths and weaknesses internal to a firm that influence its strategic competitiveness. The purpose of completing an analysis of a firm's internal environment is to identify its strengths and weaknesses. The strengths and weaknesses in a firm's internal environment shape the strategic intent and strategic mission. The internal environment essentially indicates what a firm *can do*. Capabilities or skills that allow a firm to do something that others cannot do or that allow a firm to do something better than others do it are called strengths. *Strengths* can be categorised as something that a firm does especially well. Strengths help a firm to take advantage of external opportunities or overcome

Exhibit 6 | Sample general environmental categories

Technology	■ Information technology continues to become cheaper and have more practical applications.
	■ Database technology allows organisation of complex data and distribution of information.
	■ Telecommunications technology and networks increasingly provide fast transmission of all sources of data, including voice, written communications and video information.
Demographic trends	■ Computerised design and manufacturing technologies continue to facilitate quality and flexibility.
	■ Regional changes in population due to migration
	■ Changing ethnic composition of the population
	■ Ageing of the population
	■ Ageing of the 'baby boom' generation
Economic trends	■ Interest rates
	■ Inflation rates
	■ Savings rates
	■ Trade deficits
	■ Budget deficits
	■ Exchange rates
Political/legal environment	■ Antitrust enforcement
	■ Tax policy changes
	■ Environmental protection laws
	■ Extent of regulation/deregulation
	■ Developing countries privatising state monopolies
	■ State-owned industries
Socio-cultural environment	■ Increasing number of women in the workforce
	■ Awareness of health and fitness issues
	■ Concern for the environment
	■ Concern for customers
Global environment	■ Currency exchange rates
	■ Free trade agreements
	■ Trade deficits
	■ New or developing markets

external threats. Capabilities or skill deficiencies that prevent a firm from completing an important activity as well as others do it are called weaknesses. *Weaknesses* have the potential to prevent a firm from taking advantage of external opportunities or succeeding in efforts to overcome external threats. Thus, *weaknesses* can be thought of as something the firm needs to improve.

Analysis of the primary and support activities of the value chain provides opportunities to understand how external environmental trends affect the specific activities of a firm. Such analysis helps to highlight strengths and weaknesses. (See Chapter 3 for an explanation of the value chain.) For the purposes of preparing an oral or written presentation, it is important to note that strengths are internal resources and capabilities that have the potential to be core competencies. Weaknesses, on the other hand, have the potential to place a firm at a competitive disadvantage relative to its rivals.

When evaluating the internal characteristics of the firm, your analysis of the functional activities emphasised is critical. For instance, if the strategy of the firm is primarily technology-driven, it is important to evaluate the firm's R&D activities. If the strategy is market-driven, marketing functional activities are of paramount importance. If a firm has financial difficulties, critical financial ratios would require careful evaluation. In fact, because of the importance of financial health, most cases require financial analyses.

The appendix lists and operationally defines several common financial ratios. Included are exhibits describing profitability, liquidity, leverage, activity and shareholders' return ratios. Other firm characteristics that should be examined to study the internal environment effectively include leadership, organisational culture, structure and control systems.

Identification of strategic intent and mission

Strategic intent is associated with a mind-set that managers seek to imbue within the company. Essentially, a mind-set captures how we view the world and our intended role in it. Strategic intent reflects or identifies a firm's ideal state. Strategic intent flows from a firm's opportunities, threats, strengths and weaknesses. However, the major influence on strategic intent is a firm's *strengths*. Strategic intent should reflect a firm's intended character and a commitment to 'stretch' available resources and strengths in order to reach strategies and objectives. Examples of strategic intent include:

- The relentless pursuit of perfection (Lexus).
- To be the top performer in everything that we do (Phillips Petroleum).
- We are dedicated to being the world's best at bringing people together (AT&T).

The strategic mission flows from a firm's strategic intent; it is a statement used to describe a firm's unique intent and the scope of its operations in product and market terms. In its most basic form, the strategic mission indicates to stakeholders what a firm seeks to accomplish. An effective strategic mission reflects a firm's individuality and reveals its leadership's predisposition(s). The useful strategic mission shows how a firm differs from others and defines boundaries within which the firm intends to operate. For example:

- Cochlear's mission is to have 'clinical teams and recipients embrace Cochlear as their partner in hearing for life'; and
- Coca-Cola Amatil's mission is to have market leadership in every territory.

Hints for presenting an effective strategic plan

There may be a temptation to spend most of your oral or written case analysis on results from the analysis. It is important, however, that the *analysis* of a case should not be over-emphasised relative to the *synthesis* of results gained from your analytical efforts – what does the analysis mean for the organisation (see Exhibit 3)?

Strategy formulation: Choosing key result areas

Once you have identified strengths and weaknesses, determined the firm's core competencies (if any), and formulated a strategic intent and mission, you have a picture of what the firm is and what challenges and threats it faces.

You can now determine alternative key result areas (KRAs). Each of these is a category of activities that helps to accomplish the strategic intent of the firm. For example, KRAs for Cochlear may include to remain a leader in hearing implant technology and to build links with hearing clinicians in Southeast Asia. Each alternative should be feasible (that is, it should match the firm's strengths, capabilities and, especially, core competencies), and feasibility should be demonstrated. In addition, you should show how each alternative takes advantage of the environmental opportunity or avoids/buffers against environmental threats. Developing carefully thought-out alternatives requires synthesis of your analyses and creates greater credibility in oral and written case presentations.

Once you develop a strong set of alternative KRAs, you must evaluate the set to choose the best ones. Your choice should be defensible and provide benefits over the other alternatives. Thus, it is important that both the alternative development and evaluation of alternatives be thorough. The choice of the best alternative should be explained and defended. For the two Cochlear KRAs presented earlier, the strategies are clear and in both cases they take advantage of competencies within the company and opportunities in the external environment.

Key result area implementation

After selecting the most appropriate KRAs (that is, those with the highest probability of enhancing a firm's strategic competitiveness), you must consider effective implementation. Effective synthesis is important to ensure that you have considered and evaluated all critical implementation issues. Issues you might consider include the structural changes necessary to implement the new strategies and objectives associated with each KRA. In addition, leadership changes and new controls or incentives may be necessary to implement these strategic actions. The implementation actions you recommend should be explicit and thoroughly explained. Occasionally, careful evaluation of implementation actions may show the strategy to be less favourable than you originally thought. (You may find that the capabilities required to implement the strategy are absent and unobtainable.) A strategy is only as good as the firm's ability to implement it effectively. Therefore, expending the effort to determine effective implementation is important.

Process issues

You should ensure that your presentation (either oral or written) has logical consistency throughout. For example, if your presentation identifies one purpose, but your analysis focuses on issues that differ from the stated purpose, the logical inconsistency will be apparent. Likewise, your alternatives should flow from the configuration of strengths, weaknesses, opportunities and threats you identified through the internal and external analyses.

Thoroughness and clarity also are critical to an effective presentation. Thoroughness is represented by the comprehensiveness of the analysis and alternative generation. Furthermore, clarity in the results of the analyses, selection of the best alternative KRAs and strategies, and design of implementation actions are important. For example, your statement of the strengths and weaknesses should flow clearly and logically from the internal analyses presented, and these should be reflected in KRAs and strategies.

Presentations (oral or written) that show logical consistency, thoroughness and clarity of purpose, effective analyses, and feasible recommendations are more effective and will receive more positive evaluations. Being able to withstand tough questions from peers after your presentation will build credibility for your strategic plan presentation. Furthermore, developing the skills necessary to make such presentations will enhance your future job performance and career success.

Appendix: Financial analysis in case studies

Exhibit A-1 Profitability ratios

Ratio	Formula	What it shows
1 Return on total assets	$\dfrac{\text{Profits after taxes}}{\text{Total assets}}$ or $\dfrac{\text{Profits after taxes + interest}}{\text{Total assets}}$	The net return on total investment of the firm or The return on both creditors' and shareholders' investments
2 Return on shareholders' equity (or return on net worth)	$\dfrac{\text{Profits after taxes}}{\text{Total shareholders' equity}}$	How effectively the company is utilising shareholders' funds
3 Return on ordinary equity	$\dfrac{\text{Profit after taxes} - \text{preference share dividends}}{\text{Total shareholders' equity} - \text{par value of preference shares}}$	The net return to ordinary shareholders
4 Operating profit margin (or return on sales)	$\dfrac{\text{Profits before taxes and before interest}}{\text{Sales}}$	The firm's profitability from regular operations
5 Net profit margin (or net return on sales)	$\dfrac{\text{Profits after taxes}}{\text{Sales}}$	The firm's net profit as a percentage of total sales

Exhibit A-2 Liquidity ratios

Ratio	Formula	What it shows
1 Current ratio	$\dfrac{\text{Current assets}}{\text{Current liabilities}}$	The firm's ability to meet its current financial liabilities
2 Quick ratio (or acid-test ratio)	$\dfrac{\text{Current assets} - \text{inventory}}{\text{Current liabilities}}$	The firm's ability to pay off short-term obligations without relying on sales of inventory
3 Inventory to net working capital	$\dfrac{\text{Inventory}}{\text{Current assets} - \text{current liabilities}}$	The extent to which the firm's working capital is tied up in inventory

Exhibit A-3 Leverage ratios

Ratio	Formula	What it shows
1 Debt-to-assets	$\dfrac{\text{Total debt}}{\text{Total assets}}$	Total borrowed funds as a percentage of total assets
2 Debt-to-equity	$\dfrac{\text{Total debt}}{\text{Total shareholders' equity}}$	Borrowed funds versus the funds provided by shareholders
3 Long-term debt-to-equity	$\dfrac{\text{Long-term debt}}{\text{Total shareholders' equity}}$	Leverage used by the firm
4 Times-interest-earned (or coverage ratio)	$\dfrac{\text{Profits before interest and taxes}}{\text{Total interest charges}}$	The firm's ability to meet all interest payments
5 Fixed charge coverage	$\dfrac{\text{Profits before taxes and interest} + \text{lease obligations}}{\text{Total interest charges} + \text{lease obligations}}$	The firm's ability to meet all fixed-charge obligations, including lease payments

Exhibit A-4 Activity ratios

Ratio	Formula	What it shows
1 Inventory turnover	$\dfrac{\text{Sales}}{\text{Inventory of finished goods}}$	The effectiveness of the firm in employing inventory
2 Fixed assets turnover	$\dfrac{\text{Sales}}{\text{Fixed assets}}$	The effectiveness of the firm in utilising plant and equipment
3 Total assets turnover	$\dfrac{\text{Sales}}{\text{Total assets}}$	The effectiveness of the firm in utilising total assets
4 Accounts receivable turnover	$\dfrac{\text{Annual credit sales}}{\text{Accounts receivable}}$	How many times the total receivables have been collected during the accounting period
5 Average collection period	$\dfrac{\text{Accounts receivable}}{\text{Average daily sales}}$	The average length of time the firm waits to collect payments after sales

Exhibit A-5 Shareholders' return ratios

Ratio	Formula	What it shows
1 Dividend yield on ordinary shares	$\dfrac{\text{Annual dividends per share}}{\text{Current market price per share}}$	A measure of return to ordinary shareholders in the form of dividends.
2 Price-earnings ratio	$\dfrac{\text{Current market price per share}}{\text{After-tax earnings per share}}$	An indication of market perception of the firm. Usually, the faster-growing or less risky firms tend to have higher PE ratios than the slower-growing or more risky firms.
3 Dividend payout ratio	$\dfrac{\text{Annual dividends per share}}{\text{After-tax earnings per share}}$	An indication of dividends paid out as a percentage of profits.
4 Cash flow per share	$\dfrac{\text{After-tax profits + depreciation}}{\text{Number of ordinary shares outstanding}}$	A measure of total cash per share available for use by the firm.

Endnotes

1. M. A. Lundberg, B. B. Levin and H. I. Harrington, 2000, *Who Learns What from Cases and How? The Research Base for Teaching and Learning with Cases* (Englewood Cliffs, NJ: Lawrence Erlbaum Associates).
2. L. B. Barnes, A. J. Nelson and C. R. Christensen, 1994, *Teaching and the Case Method: Text, Cases and Readings* (Boston: Harvard Business School Press); C. C. Lundberg, 1993, 'Introduction to the case method', in C. M. Vance (ed.), *Mastering Management Education* (Newbury Park, Calif.: Sage); C. Christensen, 1989, *Teaching and the Case Method* (Boston: Harvard Business School Publishing Division).
3. C. C. Lundberg and E. Enz, 1993, 'A framework for student case preparation', *Case Research Journal*, 13 (Summer), p. 133.
4. J. Solitis, 1971, 'John Dewey', in L. E. Deighton (ed.), *Encyclopedia of Education* (New York: Macmillan and Free Press).
5. F. Bocker, 1987, 'Is case teaching more effective than lecture teaching in business administration? An exploratory analysis', *Interfaces*, 17(5), pp. 64–71.

Case 1

ABB in China, 1998

Suzanne Uhlen
Lund University

Michael Lubatkin
University of Connecticut

'I want to make ABB a company that encourages and demands innovation from all of its employees, and a company that creates the environment in which teamwork and innovation flourish,' declares ABB's CEO Göran Lindahl. In seeking new growth, Lindahl is escaping the long shadow of his predecessor, Percy Barnevik. The former CEO of ABB was argued to be one of the most successful international managers in Europe.

ABB, the world leader in electrical engineering, is a US$35 billion electrical engineering group, with companies all over the globe. It operates primarily in the fields of reliable and economical generation, transmission and distribution of electrical energy.[1] Much has been written about the worldwide company. In 1996, ABB was ranked in the top 40 listed by *Fortune* 500. Recently, the company announced its newest reorganisation, making it more up to date with the global world, as the current CEO, Göran Lindahl, expressed.[2] In 1997, Lindahl took over from Barnevik as CEO of the technology giant and is feeling the demanding market and shareholder pressures.

ABB has different priorities in different markets. Western Europe and North America are the company's biggest markets. However, the high-potential markets are the Middle East, Africa, Latin America and Asia. These markets are growing fast, and ABB expects to have half of its customers in these regions not long into the 21st century. The priority is on building local manufacturing, engineering and other forms of added value. ABB wants to integrate these operations into the global networks to obtain full synergy effects and economies of scale.

During 1998, it was shown that the industrial production in OECD countries, in which ABB performs about 75 per cent of its total business, continues to grow, although at a slower pace than the strong growth rates of the previous year. Overall, industrial production in Europe is lower than the year before, but still high compared with historical levels. Current economic activity in North America is slowing compared with the strong economy of recent years. In Latin America, high interest rates are delaying the financial closing of projects in an environment of reduced economic activity. The Indian economy is slowing due to reduced exports as a result of its strong currency compared with others in the region. Southeast Asia is gradually stabilising at a low level, with reduced consumption and investments.

As a result of the ongoing economic uncertainty, overall global demand is forecast to remain soft in the near future. ABB expects to benefit with its well-established local presence around the world from higher demand in various industries and world markets. Appropriate cost cutting, continued selective tendering and successful working capital reduction programs are expected to continue contributing positively to the ABB Group results. The company recognises that the world is rapidly changing and increasingly unpredictable. Efforts have paid off and the group has taken its opportunities in Asia and positioned itself for future growth in what is seen to be 'the world's most dynamic market over a long term – China'.[3]

The interest in China is growing steadily, and companies in Japan, the Western European countries, the United States and elsewhere today view the Chinese market as having enormous potential. With a population of a billion and a growing economy, it seems to be worthwhile to gain a foothold in the market.[4] On

---

This case is to serve as a basis for classroom discussion rather than to illustrate either effective or ineffective handling of an administrative situation.

Case 1 ABB in China, 1998

the one hand, China represents a huge and largely untapped market. The Chinese market alone is potentially bigger than that of the United States, the European Community and Japan combined! On the other hand, China's new firms are proving to be very competitive, and China's culture is quite different from that of the West. However, the Chinese market growth remains relatively good for enterprises such as Procter & Gamble, Motorola, Nestlé and ABB. This market acts as a lifeboat to many worldwide companies suffering from the financial crisis in the rest of Southeast Asia. Nevertheless, discussions exist about China devaluing its currency, which might also drag China down into the crisis. Yet the country has not shown any visible scratches from the surrounding crisis. China seems to be unshakeable, and analysts are still valuing China as the country of the future.[5] Thus, the changes in China are creating both opportunities and threats for established worldwide companies. This is a country that, according to *Management Today*, will be one of the top 10 economies in the world by the year 2010.[6]

Chinese influence

> China will enter the next century as the rising power in Asia after two decades of astonishing economic growth that has transformed the country and that has given rise to new challenges.[7]

Many cities in China have more than 5 million inhabitants. It is a country that has had a growing economy which cannot be compared to that of any other country during almost three decades.[8] It is argued that China is not like any other developing country, due to the rapid changes that are taking place in certain areas. In some areas, such as with home electronics,[9] the development has surpassed that in Western countries, while in other areas, China lags far behind.

The Chinese culture and society is more than 5 000 years old, with a unique cultural heritage of philosophy, science and technology, societal structures and traditional administrative bureaucracy.[10] With this in mind, it is no wonder, according to researchers, that conflicts often occur between Chinese and foreign cultures. This is caused by foreign managers being accustomed to other values and norms, some of which are not acceptable in China.[11]

In the current half-year reports from worldwide companies, a distinct trend is noticed, according to *Dagens Industri*.[12] The more focus that the companies have put on basic industry, the more the Asian crisis tends to affect these companies. However, China can save these companies and others, especially those companies operating in the business of infrastructure.[13] Now that the Cold War with China has ended, economic growth is stabilising and the country is demanding a speedy reconstruction. The country has begun to enjoy unprecedented strategic latitude for the first time in 200 years, and it no longer faces the threat of aggression from superior powers.[14] This has enabled the country to focus on economic developments as the driving force of both its domestic and foreign policies. According to Professor Yahuda, China's leaders are basing their legitimacy on providing stability and continued high levels of prosperity. The need for economic development is fuelled by many other factors, such as providing employment for a vast population that increases by some 15 million people a year. In addition, there are significant regional inequalities that can be addressed only by further economic development.[15]

China is expected to evolve into a hybrid system of authoritarianism, democracy, socialism and capitalism. Also recognised are the internal problems the country faces, such as environmental disasters, political struggles, and tensions between the emerging entrepreneurial economy and the vast parts of China still under state control.[16] Today, China receives the most direct investment and foreign aid of any developing country. Many companies are eager to establish their presence in China, which, it is argued, attracts more than its proportionate share of investments.[17] However, 'westerners cannot expect to know how China will develop and need to expect that the Chinese will always be different from them. Instead of trying to change China, they should look for positive steps that take their differences into account'.[18]

According to China's Premier, Zhu Rongji, China is indeed the largest market in the world. However, due to the problem of duplicate construction, there is a problem of over-supply in some areas. Nevertheless, the Premier states that the market is far from being saturated.[19] Since China opened up its doors to the outside world in the late 1970s, a large number of foreign investors have gained rich returns from their investments, yet some have ended in failure. Some guiding keys to ensuring successful business in China, according to *China Daily*, include:[20]

- Making long-term strategies for the Chinese market. Competition is intensifying and market exploitation needs time and patience. Foreign companies eager to get a quick return are usually disappointed at the results.

- Localising staff. They are familiar with the local business environment.
- Being aware of changes in policies and regulation. China is in the process of transforming from a planned economy to a market economy. Various policies and regulations are being revised and replaced, while new ones are being issued. Foreign investors must keep informed of the ongoing changes.
- Undertaking practical market research. Due to social, economic and cultural differences, practical and down-to-earth market research is a must before and during investment in China.

Chinese cultural influence

There is a consensus among several authors that China has a traditional respect for age, hierarchy and authority.[21] This originates from the Confucian concept of *li* (rite, propriety), which plays an important role in maintaining a person's social position. *Li* can be seen today in the existing traditional bureaucracy and in vertical relationships concerning centralisation of decision making, and in corruption to some extent, which is acceptable in such a cultural context.[22]

Second, the family is viewed as an essential social unit and there is a strong tendency to promote the collective or the group. Members within the family or group must maintain harmonious relationships, and these social relations are seen as more important than the individual.[23] Thus, the family or clan norms are adopted as the formal code of conduct, and members are bound to these standards. Other research found that in modern China, business and industrial enterprises were perceived as an extension of the family system.[24]

Third, the concept of 'face' (*mianzi*) is seen as an important characteristic. As Ju noted, the general idea of *mianzi* is related to 'a reputation achieved through getting on in life through success and ostentation'.[25] *Mianzi* also serves to enhance harmony within the family or group, so that the positive is expressed publicly and any conflicts remain private.[26] Hong has found that the concept of *mianzi* still plays an important role in social relationships and organisational behaviour.[27] However, Yuan points out that there are two sides to this concept.[28] The first includes the individual's moral character, and the strong fear of losing this limits the person's behaviour. The second aspect of *mianzi* involves assertions about a person, which is not seen quite as seriously as the former type of loss of face.[29]

The importance of personal relations (*guanxi*) is the fourth characteristic. According to Hong, persons with *guanxi* usually share a common birthplace, lineage, surname or experience, such as attending the same school, working together or belonging to the same organisation.[30] A comparative study of decision making in China and Britain has revealed that Chinese managers use their personal *guanxi* more widely to exchange information, negotiate with planning authorities and accelerate decision-making processes than do managers from British firms.[31] As it is, the network transmits information, and because contacts and cooperation are built on trust, it is seen as very serious if that trust is broken. If a trust is broken, the whole network will soon know about the incident and it is maintained that the person involved will have a hard time doing business again.[32]

A company that has been doing business in the Chinese market since 1919 is ABB. At that time this was the first product delivery to China, and it was not until 1979 that ABB established its first permanent office. Almost 11 years later, the heart of almost every chairman of an energy company started to pound with excitement if it heard the words 'Asia' and 'electricity'. There were billions to be had from the booming demand for electricity in Asia.[33] But in recent years, the emerging Asian market has slowed down due to the financial crisis in the area. At the moment, it seems as if China is the only country not affected by this financial crisis, and consequently, there are many companies that are now trying to be successful in China.

ABB is argued to be a company with a good position in the Chinese market, due to good performance, delivery, autonomy and its good name. Today the company has nine representative offices and 15 joint ventures, and the number of employees in China has grown in four years from approximately 1 000 to 6 000.

Local roots

The strategy of ABB is to use its global strength to support the needs of its local customers around the world. However, in China, ABB has a fairly high import duty on its products, which limits how much the company can sell. The idea of setting up local production in China was to increase the market share, as most Chinese customers do not have foreign currency[34] and are consequently forced to buy locally produced goods with the local currency. Furthermore, the reason for ABB to localise in China was not to achieve lower production costs, as some locally supplied components are actually more expensive in China than elsewhere. Rather, it was to be closer to the local market, and therefore facilitate a few local modifications to the products and provide shorter delivery times to the customer.

Case 1 ABB in China, 1998

The phrase 'think global, act local' is said to reflect ABB's fundamental idea of strong local companies working together across borders to gain economies of scale in many areas.[35] In spite of ABB's claims to respond swiftly and surely to market conditions,[36] some of the products in China are not truly adapted to the local market. Most of the products are designed for the IEC – the international standard association based in Europe. The company manufactures products that have to be tested according to different norms and standards. For example, North America ABB follows the ANSI standard, and Canada ABB follows the CSA standard.

However, some of ABB's products would not pass a type test based on the Chinese standards. That is not because the quality is too low; on the contrary, the quality of ABB products is sometimes too high. The quality of some of the products has evolved far beyond the requirements of Chinese standards; therefore, these ABB products cannot meet local Chinese standards. The Chinese standards are based on what the local manufacturer can produce, because the country does not have much other information. As one manager at ABB in China stated,

> We are not going to redesign our products in order to meet the standards, for the obvious reasons: Why should we take our quality out? Why shall we take the advances out? It does become an issue from time to time. Chinese are very risk averse, if we have not done the type test in China. It is more to cover themselves in case something goes wrong.

Some managers feel that when ABB tries to adapt the products to the Chinese local standard, there is a negative response. The customer regards Western standards as superior and is actually asking for the superior product. The Chinese customers are seen as tough and sometimes demand more tests than ABB's products have gone through. Another reason put forward is insufficient feasibility studies when setting up new joint ventures in China. This delays the work when new information has to be collected about the market conditions. This aspect originates from the speed of changes in China and the difficulty for the company to catch up with what is going on.

However, when the so-called type tests of the product have been done, the company cannot change the design, due to the high costs involved in this test. Some criticism has been heard that ABB should adapt more to the Chinese situation, which the company cannot respond to concerning the technical design, because then the tests have to be done all over again. Of course, it is different from product to product; for some of the products, as one manager said,

> We have to adapt to the configurations the customers have a demand for, because they have an option – go to the competitor.

Still, in most cases, the local ABB companies in China are not allowed to change the products other than according to agreements with the licensee. The reason for this is that the technology partners[37] have the overall view of the quality and performance. The ABB corporation definitely does not want to have different product performance from different countries. The products must have the same descriptions, so that they are seen as the same product all over the world. Consequently, the local ABB company can only do a few modifications to the standard product for specific customers and cannot change the technology involved. The technology partners have a few alternatives that meet the demands of the Chinese customers, and these products are also tested, but do not necessarily meet the Chinese standards.

The local ABB company tries to follow the ABB Group's policy, to be close to the customer and responsive to their needs.[38] In China, however, contracts are not commonly used, and this frequently obstructs satisfying many customer demands.

> They keep on saying this is China and you should adapt to the Chinese way: OK, if you want to buy a Chinese product that's fine, but this is our product – here are the terms and conditions. You can't just give in to that; otherwise you will kill your company, because they expect you to accept unlimited liability and lifetime warranty, and the risks to which you would expose your company would eventually lead to its shutting down, so you just cannot do that.

ABB feels that to be close to the customer is the best guarantee that local requirements are met.[39] However, the headquarters in Zurich has also set up some rules about the kind of contracts that the local subsidiaries shall sign worldwide. In China, contracts are something rather new, and many Chinese customers do not want it that way. The consequence is that some ABB companies in China do not use the standard ABB contract and are actually responsive to the customers' needs. When another ABB company comes to the same customer to set up a standard contract, the customer will refer them to the previous ABB company who did not seem to find the contract necessary. The question asked by the confused customer is said to be,

Why do you then have to use a standard contract when the other ABB didn't?

Profit centres

ABB's strategy is to take full advantage of its economies of scale and at the same time be represented by national companies in many home markets where some 5 000 entrepreneurial profit centres are attentive to every local customer. These companies are independent and have to stand on their own economically. The individual company's profit can easily be compared to revenue. The individual ABB company is measured on its own performance and needs. It is recognised that the profit centres are efficient for decentralisation and that the organisation can act relatively fast. This enables the company to be sensitive and responsive to potential problems. Each company has a fair amount of autonomy, making the individual company flexible. Even though ABB brochures state that the strategy of having profit centres enables the easy transfer of know-how across borders,[40] the direction is pretty much one way – from the technology partners, business areas and country level, to the subsidiary – rather than a two-way exchange.

Nevertheless, some conflicts of interest have occurred because the local ABB company and all other licensees are more or less dependent on their licensors in Europe.[41] In the local ABB company's case, one of their technology partners is measured like the others, on performance and profit. If it gives the local ABB company support, it will cost the former money, and likewise, if it sells the local ABB company components, it wants to make a profit. The consequence is that it is charging the local ABB company 25–100 per cent over and above the cost of its parts.

So in the end you end up calling them as little as possible and we end up buying parts from local suppliers that probably we should not buy from local suppliers. And we reduce our quality. They have great profit figures; we have some profit figures, but there are some real serious problems along the way.

The technology partner argues that the prices are high because first it has to buy from its supplier and then sell to the local ABB company. This makes the products more expensive. The technology partners also pay for the type tests and all the product development.[42]

Conflicts of this sort have been occurring for a long time within ABB, but nobody has yet found a solution. It is difficult for a company like ABB, which is working with so many different products, markets, and in different cultures, to have anything other than sole profit centres. If the profit centres did not aim for a profit when selling within the ABB Group, then the companies would no longer be independent companies. Being independent is seen as a strength, and therefore it would be against the laws of nature if the companies were not always aiming for a profit. Nonetheless, between these independent companies with profit centres there are some extreme examples:

Our partner in Y-country was selling the finished product in China before. Now he sells the parts to the joint venture in China and wants to charge more for the parts than he did for the finished product, and that is because it is in his interest and he will be evaluated on his performance. If he does not do that, his profits will be too low and he will be blamed for it. So he has got to do what he has got to do. That is what he is motivated to do and that is what he is going to do.

To some extent, the technology partners are selling indirectly to the Chinese market using non-official agents to avoid a high import tax and the high market price that exists on the Chinese market. ABB China is trying to force ABB companies to use only two official channels for ABB goods into the Chinese market – the locally produced by the local ABB company and the directly imported from a technology partner.

Structure

ABB is a huge enterprise with dispersed business areas which encompass the three segments of Power Generation, Transmission and Distribution, and Industrial Building Systems. However, this recently has been changed and divided into six segments. Before the reorganisation, every country had its national ABB head office, dealing with all the company business in that particular country. The other dimension of the matrix structure reflects the clustering of the activities of the enterprise into 36 Business Areas (BAs). Each BA represents a distinct worldwide product market. Simplified, each BA is responsible for worldwide market allocation and the development of a worldwide technical strategy for that specific product line. Additional responsibilities for the BA are to coordinate who shall supply or deliver where, and also to work as a referee in potential disagreements between companies within the ABB Group.

However, in China, as in most developing countries, there is no BA in place and the decision power of the country management is consequently closer at hand. The power of the decision making tends to rest more heavily on the country level than on the BA level. Disagreements between licensees in Western countries and subsidiaries in China have been, and are, occurring, due to different business orientations. The local subsidiary in China has two or more licensors in Western countries, from which they buy components. Some of the licensees sold these components themselves before the local subsidiary was set up in China. In some cases, the licensee feels that the market in China was taken from them and that they therefore can compensate for potentially lost sales only by charging the Chinese subsidiary a higher cost. Consequently, if the disagreeing partner seeks the BA as a referee in this kind of case, the following happens, as explained by one manager:

The BA is looking at the global business – we can increase our global business if we set up a joint venture in China. But the technology partner can't increase their business if we set up a joint venture in China. If we set up a joint venture in China the technology partner wants to increase its business also, they are going to do some work, and of course want something for it. The BA is really powerless to push those along.

To date, the licensors have been paying for all the technology development, which is the reason for charging a higher price for the components they are selling. Since the enterprise is divided into 5 000 profit centres and because each of these profit centres wants a profit when selling a component or product, there have been some shortcomings in the coordination and cooperation between the licensors and the local Chinese subsidiary.

The licensor in X-country makes the same breakers that the local ABB company does and faces the same problems with quality. For example, in Germany, they do not inform their licensee in China, who will also run into the same problem with quality in the near future. The problem is also discussed at the local ABB company, but if it suggests changes to the licensor, the licensor will evaluate on the basis of benefits to itself. Since they are going to invest their own resources, they are, of course, going to invest in areas beneficial to themselves first, or else charge the local ABB company extra. The consequences are thus summarised as follows:

We have had some things that would really help us here in China. But I don't even bother, because I know the reaction.

Over 80 per cent of what the Centres of Excellence produce is going to be exported,[43] making it important that the partners of the licensor manage the contemporary challenges and opportunities that can emerge. However, the BA divides the world markets into different areas in which the specific ABB companies are to be a first source.[44] Between some of the licensors and the local ABB company, this has resulted in certain disputes. For example,

We are responsible for the People's Republic of China's market and are supposed to be the sole source (or, rather, first source) because we have the expertise for this market. Our technology partner in X-country quotes into this market on a regular basis, does not inform us, and competes against us, and takes orders at a lower price. This can destroy our position in the marketplace.

According to the licensor, it does not quote in the local ABB company's market because a customer with foreign currency will prefer imported products. The licensor argues that it does not go into the Chinese market and offer its products, but does get enquiries from ABB in Hong Kong and delivers to it. Hong Kong sells the products directly to the Chinese customer after having increased the original price so that it is several times higher in China than in Europe. It is a decision of the ABB China management that the Hong Kong coordinated sales force shall sell the local ABB company's products on the Chinese market among imported products and locally joint venture produced products. It helps to have sales coordination when deciding whether the products should be imported or not.

The technology is owned today by the Centres of Excellence in Europe or so-called licensors who pay for all the product development. ABB has chosen these licensees to be responsible for the company's world source of this specific technology. These units are responsible for developing new products and look after the quality. They arrange technical seminars about the technology, and by keeping special technology parts at only their factory. The strategic decision to keep special parts and the drawings of these parts at only one chosen factory enables the company to secure itself against competitors copying its products. Consequently, these parts will not be localised or purchased in China. However, for one products group (THS) there has been an organisational change, including the establishment of a unit called CHTET, which shall now own all new technology that is developed and also pay for the product development. This change now involves all product groups.

Multicultural

The current fashion, exemplified by ABB, is for the firms to be 'multicultural multinationals' and be very sensitive to national differences.[45] Barnevik did debate that a culturally diverse set of managers can be a source of strength. According to Barnevik, managers should not try to eradicate these differences and establish a uniform managerial culture. Rather, they should seek to understand these cultural differences, to empathise with the views of people from different cultures, and to make compromises for such differences. Barnevik believes that the advantage of building a culturally diverse cadre of global managers is to improve the quality of managerial decision making.[46]

ABB in China is typified by a culturally diverse set of managers with a mixture of managerial ideas, derived from the managers' different national backgrounds, different values and different methods of working. It then depends on which stage in personal development the manager has reached if he or she is going to be influenced and absorb the new climate. Or, as one manager said,

> If you are close to being retired you might not change so much; there isn't much point. But you can't work in the same way as you do at home – it just wouldn't work.

According to another manager, ABB is a very international company with a great deal of influence from Scandinavian culture. However, it is a mixture of many cultures and it really depends on where the ABB company is located. In China, the ABB culture is influenced by Chinese culture, by the environmental circumstances and by the laws. It is stricter in China than it is, for example, in Europe, because there are more rules. In spite of that, the managers do not feel that the result is a subculture of the ABB culture, rather a mixture of managers from different cultures – 'we are a multi-domestic company'.

However, the top level of the ABB management is seen to be far away from the daily life at the subsidiary level in China, such as at the local ABB company. Or as one manager expressed it, 'Between that level and here, it's like the Pacific Ocean.' All the managers agree that what the top level, including Barnevik and Lindahl,[47] says sounds very good and that is how it should be. Some managers continued the discussion and expressed this difference:

> Sounds like I'm working for a different ABB than these guys are. What they talk about is really good and that is how it should be. But then when I sit back and go into the daily work, that's not at all how it is. Somewhere along the line something gets lost between the theory and ideas at that level which is quite good. But when you get down to the working level and have to make it work, something really gets lost along the way.

Expatriates

It is the BA with its worldwide networks that recommends, after suggestions from local offices, who is going to be sent as an expatriate to China or any other country. Thereafter, it is a cooperation between the BA and the country level, but it is the latter that finally decides which potential foreign expatriate is appropriate. However, it is important that an expatriate be able to fit into the system when coming to China, given the high costs involved in being there. It is estimated that an expatriate costs the company about US$250 000 a year, due to the high taxes the company is paying to have a foreign employee.

ABB's identity is supported by a coordinating executive committee and an elite cadre of 500 global managers, which the top management shifts through a series of foreign assignments. Their job is intended to knit the organisation together, to transfer expertise around the world and to expose the company's leadership to differing perspectives.[48]

However, ABB in China is not yet a closely tied country unit, for several reasons. First, the expatriates come from the outside and most of their contacts are back in the home country. Most expatriates feel that the home office does not understand how difficult it can be to work abroad and that they need support. 'Sometimes it just feels like I'm standing in the desert screaming,' one expatriate expressed. The home office feels that the expatriates can be a burden because they need so much

Case 1 ABB in China, 1998

support. It is the home office, along with the BA, that selects candidates for foreign placement, even though it has brief or no knowledge of how it is to work in that country. However, it would be impossible to have insights into how the working conditions are in the other operating countries.

Concerning growing a strong country unit, the expatriates are stationed in China on assignments for a relatively short time period, and are thus less able to build up informal networks. Few efforts are put into establishing an informal network, because the few contact persons the managers have today will eventually return home after a while and there is no formal way of contacting the replacing person. Of course, there is the formal LOTUS Notes®, which is a computer-based network with all managers worldwide included, but it is said to be deficient in building the preferred strong country unit within China. Finally, the managers do not feel they can offer the time to establish informal networks, due to the replacement of expatriates every two to three years. A worldwide policy within the company limits the expatriates to operating as such for not more than five years at a time. Executives have questioned this policy, saying that

> It is during the first year you learn what is going on and get into your new clothes. During the second year you get to know the people and the system, the third year you apply what you learned and the fourth year you start to make some changes – and this is very specific for developing countries.

Three years ago, the expatriates did not get any information or education about the country-specific situation before being sent out to ABB's subsidiaries in China. Today, when there are about 100 expatriates with 25 different nationalities in China, it has changed, but it is mostly up to the individual to collect material and prepare for the acclimatisation. Within the worldwide corporation, there is no policy of formal training before one is sent out as an expatriate; rather, it is up to the home office of the expatriates to prepare the managers for the foreign assignments. Some argue that 'you could never prepare for the situation in China anyway, so any education wouldn't help'. Others say that this has resulted in a lot of problems with the expatriates, which results in even higher costs for the company if the expatriate fails.

When the expatriate's contract time is finished, he or she may feel unsure about placement back home. Thus, it is important for the expatriate to have close contact with the home office and to make use of the free trips home. In most cases, the expatriates do not know what will happen when the contract expires and they are to return home.

The Chinese challenge

According to ABB, they prefer to send out managers with 10–15 years of experience. However, the task is difficult when the location may be in a rural area overseas and most managers with 10–15 years' experience have families who are less likely to want to move to these areas. Sometimes a manager gets sent to China when the company does not want to fire him.

> So instead they send the manager to where the pitfalls are greater and challenges bigger and potential risks are greater.

It is found throughout the research that most expatriates have strong feelings about living in and adapting to the new environment in China. Newly arrived expatriates seem to enjoy the respect they get from the Chinese, as several managers delightedly expressed:

> I love it here, and how could you not? You get a lot of respect just because you're a foreigner and life is just pleasant.

Other expatriates that have stayed a bit longer disliked the situation to a great extent and a number of expatriates have asked to leave because their expectations about the situation in China have not been fulfilled.[49]

One country-specific situation is how to teach the Chinese employees to work in teams. The worldwide company ABB is especially focusing on creating an environment that fosters teamwork and promotes active participation among its employees.[50] This is a big challenge for Western managers (the expatriates) because the Chinese employees have a hard time working in a group, due to cultural and historical reasons. Some of the local ABB companies have failed in their attempt with team working, ad hoc groups and the like, because they have been in too much of a hurry. Or, as one manager said,

> Here in China the management needs to encourage the teamwork a little bit, because it is a little against the culture and the nature of the people. This is not a question of lack of time for the managers, but I do not think we have the overall

commitment to do it. Some of us feel strongly that we should, others that we can't.

Another consequence is that expatriate management does not have the understanding or the commitment to teach local employees the company values, a situation that has resulted in unacceptable quality at some companies.

ABB has a great advantage in comparison to other worldwide companies due to its top priority of building deep local roots by hiring and training local managers who know their local markets.[51] Replacing expatriates with local Chinese employees, where the local employees are set to be successors to the expatriates after a certain number of years, shows the commitment to the philosophy of having a local profile. However, as the Chinese employees are coming from an extremely different system from the Western expatriates, it takes quite a long time for the former to get exposed to Western management practices. To ease this problem and to teach Western management style, ABB China, among other companies, has recently set up an agreement with a business school in Beijing to arrange training for Chinese employees with good management potential. This is specific for ABB China, because in developed countries the employees are responsible for their own development.[52] Recently ABB had its own school in Beijing for Chinese employees to learn ABB culture and management. Unfortunately, this school had to close due to the profit-centre philosophy, where even the school had to charge the individual ABB companies for teaching their employees.

ABB is sending about 100 local Chinese employees to an ABB company in a Western country every year. After problems with several employees quitting after training, ABB has set up precautions with a service commitment. The employee (or new employer) has to pay back the training investment if he or she quits, or the employee signs an agreement that he or she will continue working for ABB for a certain number of years. The problem with local employees quitting after ABB's investment in training has also been experienced in India and Thailand. It is shown in the personnel turnover rate, approximately 22 per cent within ABB China, that many local employees are aiming for the experience of working for an international company such as ABB and then move on to a better-paying job.

However, by having local employees, the local ABB company is responsive to local conditions and sensitive to important cultural objectives such as the Chinese *guanxi*.[53] It has been decided that the local employees should take care of the customer contact, since the expatriates are usually stationed for only a few years at one location and are consequently not able to build up strong connections with customers.

Reorganisation

The organisation is decentralised based on delegated responsibility and the right to make decisions in order to respond quickly to customers' requirements. In the core of this complex organisation are two principles: decentralisation of responsibility, and individual accountability. These principles have been very relevant in China, which is a relatively young country for ABB to be operating in.[54] Decentralisation is highly developed, and the expatriate[55] managers have a wide responsibility that would normally demand more than one specialist in a Western company. However, in some instances the organisation is criticised for being too centralised.

The changes in China happen very quickly and, according to ABB brochures, the greatest efficiency gains lie in improving the way people work together.[56] Within the ABB China region, communication has its shortcomings. Companies with overlapping products or similar products do not exchange information to any large degree or coordinate their marketing strategies. On the technical side, communication is used frequently, which can be seen when a manager usually receives up to 100 e-mails a day from other ABB employees. However, tactics for building up effective informal communication are lacking between most ABB companies operating in China. The distances are large and, accordingly, a meeting demands greater efforts than in almost any other country in the world.

According to the former CEO, Percy Barnevik, the purpose with the matrix organisation is to make the company more bottom-heavy than top-heavy – 'clean out the headquarters in Zurich and send everybody out; have independent companies operating in an entrepreneurial manner', as one respondent mentioned. It is further maintained in the company brochures that these entrepreneurial business units have the freedom and motivation to run their own business with a sense of personal responsibility.[57]

However, the result from the matrix organisation in China is that ABB subsidiaries have ABB China's objectives (the country level) as well as the BA's objectives to follow. ABB China is measuring how the different companies are performing within China. The BA, on the other hand, is measuring how the specific products are performing on a worldwide basis and what the profitability is for the products. Each BA has a financial controller, and each country level has one also.

Case 1 ABB in China, 1998

Rarely are the two coordinated, or do they meet. So you end up with one set of objectives from each ... Duplication! Which one shall you follow?

According to the ABB mission book, the roles in the two dimensions of the ABB matrix must be complementary.[58] It demands that both the individual company and the headquarters level are flexible and strive for extensive communication. This is the way to avoid the matrix interchange becoming cumbersome and slow. It is seen to be the only way to 'reap the benefits of being global (economies of scale, technological strength, etc.) and of being multidomestic (a high degree of decentralization and local roots in the countries in which we operate)'.

For many years, ABB was widely regarded as an exemplary European company, yet it is undergoing a second major restructuring within four years. CEO Göran Lindahl says that restructuring is aimed at making the organisation faster and more cost-efficient.[59] Due to the demands of a more global market, there are reasons for getting rid of the regional structure and concentrating more on the specific countries. The reorganisation has basically dismantled one half of the matrix: the country management. Henceforth, the BAs will manage their businesses on a worldwide basis and there will no longer be the confusion caused by BA and country management setting different objectives. At the same time, segments are split up (many BAs form a segment) to make them more manageable (for example, the Transmission and Distribution segment has been split into two segments: Transmission and Distribution). To conclude, the general managers of the individual joint ventures and other units will have only one manager above them in the organisation that has a global view of the business. In China, it also means the dismantling of the Hong Kong organisation as well as the Asia-Pacific organisation.

According to Göran Lindahl, the reorganisation is preparation for a much faster rate of change in the markets and for the company to be able to respond more effectively to the demands of globalisation. It is seen as an aggressive strategy to create a platform for future growth.

Future vision

CEO Göran Lindahl was appointed in 1997 to be the new president and chief executive of ABB. His view of the future is that it can no longer be extrapolated, but can be forecast by creativity, imagination, ingenuity and innovation – action based not on what was, but on what could be. The corporate culture needs to be replaced by globalising leadership and corporate values. ABB is focusing on this by creating a unified organisation across national, cultural and business borders.

On the path towards the 21st century, ABB will focus on several essential elements: a strong local presence; a fast and flexible organisation; the best technology and products available; and excellent local managers who know the business culture, who are able to cross national and business borders easily, and who can execute your strategy faster than the competition.[60]

We are living in a rapidly changing environment, and our competitors will not stand still. In the face of this great challenge and opportunity, enterprises that adapt quickly and meet customer needs will be the winner, and this is the ultimate goal of ABB.[61]

Appendix

Motorola

Motorola was involved in Russia and faced some problems with Glasnost and the decline of the country. At that time, the founder of the company, Galvin, realised that there was no future in Russia and declared that China was the country where the growth was to be. Consequently, Motorola established its first representative office in China in 1987 and has grown very quickly ever since. Today, China generates more than 10 per cent of Motorola's sales and the company has its major businesses in China.

Motorola has found that modernisation in China happens quickly and all their competitors are present in the country. They still predict China to be the potential leader in Asia for their business. The customers also have high expectations of the products Motorola is offering, because the products are regarded as being very expensive. However, the problem the company is facing in China is that the company is growing too quickly, or as expressed another way:

... it is like chasing a speeding train and trying to catch up with it.

Presently, Motorola has 12 000 employees and 200 expatriates in China, where the goal is that Chinese successors will take over the jobs of the expatriates. The expatriates are sent out on assignments for two to three years, with the possibility of renewal with a one–two rotation, but limited to a maximum of six years as an expatriate. High demands are set on the expatriates, especially concerning the difficulties experienced in teaching teamwork to local employees. This is very important within the company, since all the strategy planning is done in teams. When the contract time for the expatriate has expired, the following is expressed:

> You have done your job when the time comes and you have left the company and everything is working smoothly, but if everything is falling apart, you are a failure as an expatriate and have not taught a successor.

However, progress has been made in developing the company's local employees. Motorola has set up training abroad. The training, nevertheless, is preferably held within China, with rotation assignments and training at Motorola University. This company university was set up in 1994 when the company found that the Chinese universities did not turn out sufficiently well-trained students. Within the company, there is, however, a requirement that every employee worldwide shall have at least 40 hours of training, which is exceeded in China. There must be a combination of good training and mentor development. Motorola admits that it does not provide enough training for foreign expatriates before they come to China.

> You get more understanding if you look like a foreigner and make some mistakes than if you don't. Overseas Chinese are measured through other standards than other foreigners.

Some expatriates just cannot handle the situation in China. If an expatriate fails, it has to be handled with care, otherwise the person loses face when coming back to the home office. The company also has pointed out that it needs expatriates with 10–15 years of experience in order to teach the local employees the company values and to transfer company knowledge. However, the people that are willing to change addresses and move to China are the younger employees with less than five years' experience.

The expatriates are often responsible for transferring technology knowledge and helping to start projects, especially the newly set-up Center of Excellence in Tianjin, where US$750 million was invested. This was Motorola's first manufacturing research laboratory outside the United States. The company has invested US$1.1 billion in China and has plans to invest another US$1–1.5 million. Motorola has also set up two branches of worldwide training universities to educate customers, suppliers and government officials, as well as its own employees. The invested money in China is from the earnings within the whole enterprise, with the motivation that the Chinese market is going to be huge. Sincere commitment has been made and the present CEO, Gary Tucker, expressed the following:

> When Motorola has come to your country they never leave … We manufacture in China, because this is where our market is. We get wealth by going to a lot of countries around the world and then doing well in that country.

The expansion strategy in China is through joint ventures. However, it is important that the Chinese partners bring something of value, which means that the partners have to be approved by the CEO. The company has become 'so decentralized that it has become bad', and it desires to reorganise more along customer than product lines. A practical reorganisation has taken place to move everybody operating in Beijing to the same newly built headquarters. However, entrepreneurial activities are also of importance, but difficult, due to financial motivation and autonomy.

In China, the products are localised with Chinese characters on the cellular phones and pagers. In 1987, Motorola started selling pagers and thought there would not be a big market because the telephone-net was not well established. The company invented codebooks, which enabled two-way communication. Fortunately, this also worked in Hong Kong, Singapore and Taiwan. After five years of operation in China, the company does not have deep roots in the market. Motorola has invested huge sums in sponsoring environmental protection, providing scholarships to students, building labs at universities, and donating money to primary schools in rural areas.[62]

The worldwide organisation is a 'pyramid', with the corporate office on top and business units underneath – 'then put the apex at the bottom'. The corporate office works as the glue that holds the organisation together. In 1997, Motorola conducted a reorganisation to better reflect the global nature of the business.[63] The coordination is safeguarded by this new formal structure. However, the informal information flow is better, but it is overused. The information flow is mostly through e-mails. A manager gets approximately 70–100 e-mails a day, of which less than 30 per cent are really useful. Regarding communication, the following was expressed:

> Some days it feels like we have all these opportunities and we do not really communicate.

All the controllers or general managers in the joint ventures get together quarterly to solve problems and to counsel and support each other. Information is encouraged, but no system is developed to track what is going on in all the six districts in China where the company is operating. Competition between the different units is a common problem Motorola is experiencing, which results in the customers becoming confused. This is a problem that has no solution, due to the matrix organisation:

> We do not have the answers, because if we are too centralised then we miss new opportunities. How do you encourage creativity and yet keep people from competing with each other?

What makes Motorola a worldwide company is a set of key common beliefs or guiding principles from the role model and father figure of the company, Galvin: 'Uncompromising integrity and constant respect for people – that is what makes us Motorola.' This is the principal code of conduct that Motorola practises, and which the management has to reread and sign every two years.

Motorola notes that it 'obviously' has to change because it is operating in the Chinese market – for example, show face, build relations and go to ceremonial meetings. It is essential that the partner is reliable, that the business makes sense and that it is legal. However, Motorola always looks the same all over the world, but it is the expatriates and their families who have made an effort to adapt to the surrounding changes.

The challenge for Motorola is doing business in China. China is very difficult for a company like Motorola

> ... because they would like to control the system and everything takes a long time because they will make sure that you are not cheating. You must be able to work with all the people that come from different departments and to let them trust you. Ordinary things like getting water, electricity, etc., is a huge problem. Doing business in the Chinese system is a challenge and therefore creates pressure because you get frustrated.

Procter & Gamble

In August 1998, China's largest international employer had been in China for 10 successful years. Procter and Gamble (P&G) has approximately 5 000 employees and 100 expatriates spread over 11 joint ventures and wholly owned enterprises in the country. P&G was ranked this year [1998] on *Fortune* magazine's 'World's Most Admired Companies' list. Currently, the biggest market for the company is China, where new companies are being established. However, before companies were established in China, a feasibility study was done. As with most other feasibility studies done in China, the information was outdated even though it was only one year old, and people were criticised for not having sufficient knowledge about the country's specific situation.

The expatriates sent to China for the P&G account are no more prepared for the situation, except for knowing that the company has a deep culture that will support them. Furthermore, a continuous effort exists within the company to put different cultural backgrounds together. Cultural values are also written down and are consistent all over the world. However, the different expatriates have a wide variety of cultural backgrounds, and their culture is coloured by their management style. This mixture of management styles might confuse the local Chinese employees.

The main benefit gained for an expatriate is the one offered in the daily work. One exception is made: for the expatriate salespeople, who get a whole year of orientation training and language training. In line with the localisation demands, the number of expatriates is decreasing. Due to the high costs involved in having expatriates, who are mostly three to four levels up in the organisation, one key strategy is to develop local employees. Everybody who is an expatriate for P&G has a sponsor, or contact, back home. It is essential to keep contact with the sponsor so that it is not just a name on a paper, and people are encouraged to go back home once a year at the company's cost. There is no official limit in expatriate policy within the company; however, most expatriates are on a three-year contract. The expatriate network is not yet an issue; however, the expatriates are said to be a very close group: 'We are all in this together and we have a common vision.'

The optimal goal for P&G is to develop the organisation so that it can be a Chinese-run company. Today, everything is made in the Chinese P&G factories for internal use, and the company opened up a research centre in Beijing, in cooperation with a prominent university.[64] If the company has developed a good idea in China, the company will analyse how to reapply the idea in the rest of the world.

Counterfeits are the greatest competition for the company and an extensive problem. However, not all the products from P&G are sold in China and the quality of the products sold is not as high as it is in Western countries. The Chinese customers are unable to pay for better value; nevertheless, the company is trying to offer a consistency of quality to Chinese consumers.

In the Chinese P&G organisation, fewer layers are developed and the decision making takes a shorter time within the organisation. Because the company evolved very quickly and the market is so dynamic and changing, it has not had the time to implement the layers – it has 'only tried to understand the market'. Consequently, the Chinese organisation and structure are not the same as in other countries, but it is more efficient. P&G will implement some of the ideas from China in other countries. At the current time, a reorganisation is taking place within the worldwide P&G Group where the organisation is being changed along with the culture and reward system – all to make the company more flexible.[65]

As for the Chinese situation, *guanxi* is mentioned, which is difficult for the expatriates to establish, and consequently the company relies on the local staff. On the other hand, the local employees get an immense amount of education at P&G's own school. Also, some of the company's expatriates have an explicit responsibility to deal with company principles and values, and all the technical specifics for P&G. The company falls short with the expatriates, because 'they are so into running the business that sometimes the coaching of the locals is not possible'.

One of the challenges Procter & Gamble faces in China is the difficulty in dealing with the government. The company has dealt with this by searching for a sophisticated government-relations manager who shall report not only to the head of operations in China but also to the chief executive of the company.[66]

Nestlé

In the beginning of the 1980s, China asked the world's largest food company – Nestlé – to come and build 'milk streets' in the country. China was unfamiliar with how to produce milk and turned to Nestlé, whose core business is actually milk powder. From that time the company has grown strongly in China and now has almost 4 000 employees, 200 of them foreign expatriates.

Today, Nestlé is regarded as having come from Swiss roots and turned into a transnational corporation.[67] Nestlé is argued to have its foundation in its history for being locally adaptive. During the First World War, Nestlé gave its local managers increasing independence to avoid disruptions in distribution.[68] This resulted in a great deal of Nestlé's operations being established at other locations than its headquarters in Switzerland. Another cause was the company's belief that the consumers' tastes were very local and that there were no synergy effects to be gained by standardising the products. However, in 1993, the company started to rethink its belief in localisation, due to the increasing competition in the industry. Nestlé has acquired several local brands, influenced by its own country's culture, causing Nestlé to standardise where it is possible.[69]

However, although the company is growing in China, it is not always selling products with as much margin as desired. The downside is that they must have lower margins in order to be competitive, which might not always be profitable. On the question, 'Why does Nestlé have to be in China?', the following was expressed:

It is because China is a large country and if you have a company that is present in more than 100 countries, you see it as a must for all international companies to be present there. We supply all over the world and it is our obligation to bring food to the people – which is the company's priority.

Nestlé entered China with a long-term strategy to focus on the long-run perspective. Nestlé's overall approach is stated to be 'Think global and act local!' The company's strategy is guided by several fundamental principles, such as the following:

Nestlé's existing products will grow through innovation and renovation while maintaining a balance in geographic activities and product lines.[70]

With regard to the local Chinese employees, they receive a few days of Nestlé education to learn about the Nestlé culture, but the expatriates have less training going to another country. It is up to the home country to decide if it is necessary to train expatriates before sending them on an often three-year foreign assignment. However, the leadership talent is highly valued within the company and consequently Nestlé has developed courses for this. The managers can independently develop their leadership talent without any connection with the specific company style or culture. Community centres have been developed to help expatriates with their contacts, supporting these expatriates psychologically and even offering language training.

In 1997, Nestlé's *The Basic Nestlé Management and Leadership Principles* was published, aimed at making 'the Nestlé spirit' of the company generally known throughout the organisation by discussions, seminars and courses.[71] According to the CEO of Nestlé China, Theo Klauser, this publication is the key factor in Nestlé's corporate culture and started the company's international expansion 130 years ago.[72]

Within the organisation of Nestlé China, the company has developed a specific structure, due to the joint venture configuration. The information flow is easy and smooth between these regions, thanks to the company concentrating its activities in only three regions in China. However, communication is said to be on a high level; yet, it is not even necessary to get all levels involved. As an example, only one unit in China takes care of all the marketing. At the same time, each Nestlé company in China is responsible for its own turnover rate, which creates the flexible and decentralised company Nestlé is today. Quite unique for a worldwide company, Nestlé does not have any external e-mail network; this is believed to concentrate the flow of information within the company.

A major challenge indicated for Nestlé in China is in building long relationships to establish Nestlé as the leading food company. A difficulty is to bring the products to a more acceptable level in terms of profitability. Legal difficulties are also more important than in any other country. Other challenges are the issues concerning change, about which the following was expressed:

> *Change happens every couple of months here – that is how the environment is. A lot of employees come from other more stable countries and sometimes find it difficult with all the changes. Change is how things are in China – it is normal. When something doesn't change, that is when you get worried! It is expected to change! This is different from other countries where changes can be difficult to get.*

Endnotes

1. *100 Years of Experience Ensures Peak Technology Today*, ABB STAL AB, Finspong.
2. *Dagens Industri*, 13 August 1998, p. 25.
3. Ibid.
4. J.-C. Usunier, *Marketing across Cultures*.
5. *Dagens Industri*, 2 July 1998.
6. D. Smith, 1996, *Management Today*, April, p. 49.
7. Professor Michael Yahuda, 'Preface', in M. Ahlquist (ed.), *The Recruiter's Guide to China*.
8. *Bizniz*, 30 September 1997.
9. Examples include VCD-players, CD-ROM players, mobile telephones, beepers and video cameras.
10. J. E. Garten, 1998, 'Opening the doors for business in China', *Harvard Business Review*, May–June, pp. 160–72.
11. *Månadens Affärer*, 11 November 1996, searched through AFFÄRSDATA via www.ad.se/bibsam/.
12. *Dagens Industri*, 19 August 1998, searched through AFFÄRSDATA via www.ad.se/bibsam/.
13. Ibid.
14. Yahuda, 'Preface'.
15. Ibid.
16. Garten, 'Opening the doors for business in China', pp. 167–71.
17. See report from *The Economist*, October 1998: www.economist.com.
18. Hong Yung Lee, 'The implications of reform for ideology, state and society in China', *Journal of International Affairs*, 39(2), pp. 77–90.
19. An interview with Premier Zhu Rongji in *China Daily*, 20 March 1998, p. 2.
20. *China Daily, Business Weekly*, 18(5479), 29 March–4 April 1998, p. 2.
21. S. K. Hoon-Halbauer, *Management of Sino-Foreign Joint Ventures*; Yuan Lu, *Management Decision-making in Chinese Enterprises*.
22. Ibid.
23. Jun Ma, *Intergovernal Relations and Economic Management in China*.
24. O. Laaksonen, *Management in China During and After Mao in Enterprises, Government, and Party*.
25. Yanan Ju, *Understanding China*, p. 45.
26. Quanyu Hwang, *Business Decision Making in China*.
27. Hong Yung Lee, 'The implications of reform for ideology, state and society in China'.
28. Yuan Lu, *Management Decision-making in Chinese Enterprises*.
29. Ibid.
30. Hong Yung Lee, 'The implications of reform for ideology, state and society in China'.
31. Yuan Lu, *Management Decision-making in Chinese Enterprises*.
32. *Månadens Affärer*, 11 November 1996.
33. *The Economist*, 28 October 1995: www.economist.com.
34. Due to China still being a quite closed country, Chinese people are not able to obtain foreign currency, other than in very limited amounts.
35. ABB, 'The art of being local' (ABB Corporate Communications, Ltd).
36. ABB brochure, 'You can rely on the power of ABB' (Zurich: ABB Asea Brown Boveri, Ltd, Department CC-C).
37. Technology partner (in this case) = Center of Excellence (CE) = Licensors.
38. *ABB's Mission, Values, and Policies*, 1991 (Zurich).
39. HV Switchgear, ABB, ABB Business Area H. V. Switchgear.
40. ABB Asea Brown Boveri, Ltd, 'You can rely on the power of ABB' (Zurich: Department CC-C).
41. Licensing is defined here as a form of external production where the owner of the technology or proprietary right (licensor) agrees to transfer this to a joint venture in China which is responsible for local production (licensee).
42. During the study this has changed to some degree, due to a unit called CHTET being introduced.
43. www.abb.se/swg/switchgear/index.htm, November 1997.
44. First source = you are the first source, but if you cannot meet the customers' requirements, the second source steps in.
45. *The Economist*, 6 January 1996: www.economist.com.
46. Ibid.
47. Göran Lindahl is the present CEO, chairman of the board.
48. *The Economist*, 6 January 1996: www.economist.com.
49. There are two types of common, but false, expectations expatriates have when coming to China. They believe either that they are going to make a lot of money, or that they are going to experience the old Chinese culture – a culture that, most of the time, does not correspond to the culture of today in China.
50. *ABB's Mission, Values, and Policies*.
51. ABB, 'The art of being local'.
52. *ABB's Mission, Values, and Policies*.
53. *Guanxi* = connections, relations.
54. ABB set up its first office, a representative office, in 1979.
55. An expatriate is a person who has a working placement outside the home country.

56 ABB Asea Brown Boveri, Ltd, 'You can rely on the power of ABB'.
57 Ibid.
58 *ABB's Mission, Values, and Policies.*
59 *Dagens Industri*, 13 August 1998, p. 25.
60 'Meeting the challenges of the future', Presentation given to the Executives Club of Chicago, 16 October 1997.
61 ABB, 'Leading the way in efficient and reliable supply of electric power' (Hong Kong: ABB Transmission and Distribution, Ltd.)
62 Garten, 'Opening the doors for business in China', pp. 174–5.
63 *Motorola Annual Report*, 1997.
64 Qinghua University.
65 *Procter & Gamble Annual Report*, 1998.
66 Garten, 'Opening the doors for business in China', pp. 173–5.
67 www.Nestlé.com/html/home.html, September 1998.
68 J. A. Quelch and E. J. Hoff, 1986, 'Customizing global marketing', *Harvard Business Review*, 3, May–June, pp. 59–60.
69 Brorsson, Skarsten, Torstensson, 1993, *Marknadsföring på den inre markanden—Standardisering eller Anpassning*, Thesis, Lund University.
70 www.Nestlé.com/html/h2h.html, September 1998.
71 *Nestlé Management Report*, 1997.
72 Interview with CEO of Nestlé China, Theo Klauser, *Metro*, July 1998, p. 27.

Case 2

Ansett Airlines and Air New Zealand: A flight to oblivion?

Megan Woods
Peter Dowling
Dallas Hanson
University of Tasmania

In February 2001, less than a year after acquiring the major stake in Ansett, Air New Zealand admitted that it 'probably paid too much' for Ansett, but that the purchase was 'absolutely necessary to strategic growth'.[1] For Air New Zealand, the takeover was an opportunity to expand into the Australian domestic market, as well as to obtain ownership of a brand with a high level of international recognition and a strong service reputation. For Ansett, it meant financial and operational support for an airline still learning how to compete in a deregulated market, while struggling with cost inefficiencies and a dire need to re-equip its fleet. Much-needed capital and network support had been provided for Air New Zealand when Singapore Airlines acquired a 25 per cent stake in that airline, and also through the membership of both Ansett and Air New Zealand in the Star Alliance network, a global marketing and travel logistics alliance. The challenge now was to improve Ansett's competitiveness in the Australian market, develop the group's domestic, regional and global presence, and maximise the benefits that could be achieved through the alliance network. How had Ansett come to this point? Could it be done?

Ansett takes off

The history of Ansett Airlines (summarised in Exhibit 1) began in Victoria in 1936 when the airline was founded by Reginald Ansett as a complement to his road transport company. In 1937, the company was incorporated in order to fund the purchase of new aircraft and the expansion of flight services across interstate routes in competition with the established national carriers, Airlines of Australia and Australian National Airlines (ANA).[2] Over the next 10 years, Ansett expanded its facilities at Essendon Airport in Melbourne, won contracts to service planes for the Royal Australian Air Force and the United States Air Force, and continued to build a competitive presence against the newly integrated ANA–Airlines of Australia network.

Limited horizons: Ansett under the two-airline policy

By the end of the Second World War, the Australian federal government had decided that its own involvement in the aviation industry should extend beyond regulation to the actual provision of flight services. With the passing of the *Australian National Airlines Act 1945,* the Australian National Airlines Commission was established as the statutory body responsible for aviation regulation in Australia and the provider of domestic flight services under the operating name of Trans Australian Airways (TAA). Constitutional limitations meant that as a Commonwealth agency, TAA was able to fly between states but not to operate services within individual states, and would therefore be unable to be established as the sole provider of flight services across Australia. So, the two-airline policy was developed, whereby any route or service which could not be handled by TAA would be handled by private airlines.[3]

Although the two-airline policy was promoted as providing the 'best of both worlds' between public service and private competition, in fact the Commission operated a virtual monopoly over Australian aviation. The Commission regulated the importation of aircraft into Australia, set fare levels, determined the passenger volume to be serviced on trunk routes, and decided which routes would be flown by TAA or by private airlines. In its initial form, the *Australian National*

Exhibit 1 | Ansett's company timeline

1936:	Ansett Airways founded by Reginald Ansett as an expansion of road transport services.
1937:	Ansett was incorporated and began flying interstate flight services in competition with Australian National Airlines (ANA) and Airlines of Australia.
1945:	Federal government passed the *Australian National Airlines Act* empowering the Australian National Airlines Commission to regulate Australian domestic aviation as well as provide flight services operating as Trans Australian Airways. The Commission acquired Qantas Airlines in 1947 and gave the airline exclusive rights to operate all international services to and from Australia.
1948:	Ansett Airways renamed as Ansett Transport Industries Ltd (ATI). The company expanded its transport and other businesses, including hotels, resort development and freight delivery.
1957:	Ansett purchased ANA and became Australia's major private carrier.
1979:	ATI acquired by News Limited and TNT, who each purchased a 50 per cent stake in the business. Reg Ansett continued as chairman.
1981:	Peter Abeles, CEO of TNT, became chairman of Ansett and continued to pursue the company's policy of diversification while expanding the airline's fleet of aircraft.
1990:	The Australian aviation market was officially deregulated.
1992:	Peter Abeles resigned as chairman of Ansett Holdings.
1996:	TNT sold its stake in Ansett Holdings Ltd to Air New Zealand for A$325 million.
1997:	Rod Eddington became chief executive of Ansett, launched his Great Business Plan to cut costs and improve profitability, and began merging Ansett operations with those of Air New Zealand.
1999:	Ansett joined the Star Alliance global network.
2000:	Air New Zealand bought the remaining stake in Ansett Holdings from News Corporation for A$650 million.
2001:	Ansett has a safety fiasco of major importance.

Airlines Act 1945 also contained two sections which allowed the Commission to invalidate the licences of private carriers to provide flight services simply by establishing a TAA service on the route (section 46) and prohibited private carriers from providing the same interstate services as TAA (section 47). When the Act was passed, Ansett and two other airlines mounted a legal challenge against these two sections, arguing that they prevented competition and established a monopoly over domestic air services. Their challenge was successful and they won the right to provide interstate services so long as these did not directly duplicate those offered by TAA.[4]

With TAA's entry into the industry, Ansett and ANA both lost the contracts they had previously held for the provision of governmental services such as freight and mail delivery. In 1947, competitive opportunities for Ansett and the other private airlines were constrained further when the federal government announced that it would acquire Qantas Airways Limited to be operated as the exclusive provider of all international services to and from Australia.[5] Unable to expand internationally or compete directly against the Commission, Ansett began to develop a number of strategies to circumvent or overcome TAA's opposition and strengthen its position against ANA in the passenger travel market.

In the passenger market, Ansett differentiated itself by offering lower fares than ANA, as well as two classes of seating. To avoid duplicating TAA's interstate services, Ansett scheduled all flights to make at least one stop between capital cities,[6] and in this way was able to expand its flight network without engaging in head-to-head competition with the Commission. Ansett also began acquiring smaller state-based airlines, which were then integrated into the Ansett service network.

Ansett's acquisition strategy was adopted as a response to actions by TAA, who was at that time attempting to extend its own services. Unlike the other airlines, TAA did not require permission from the Commission to purchase new aircraft and was able to use this position to build commercial relationships with other airlines. TAA purchased a number of planes and resold or leased them to other carriers in return for cooperation on aligning flight services and the establishment of long-term strategic relationships.[7] Ansett, operating outside these relationships, responded by purchasing many of the remaining airlines. Further alliances with TAA were prevented, and Ansett was able to spread overhead costs over divisions, achieve economies of scale in support functions such as engineering and marketing, and generate a strong enough position to prevent another independent carrier from seeking to establish a similar foothold in the Australian market.[8]

To offset the pressures faced by the airline, Reg Ansett began expanding his transport network and moving into other business areas, again through acquisitions and mergers. Ansett Airways was renamed Ansett Transport Industries Ltd (ATI), and a subsidiary operation, Ansett Hotels, was established to build and operate hotels for the accommodation of passengers from the company's coach and airline services. In 1947, Ansett Hotels began developing resorts in the Barrier Reef so that the company could move into the holiday market, and by 1948 was the largest hotel operator in Australia.[9]

By 1952, a change in federal government saw a reconsideration of TAA's privileged position within Australian aviation. When efforts to amalgamate TAA and ANA proved unrealisable, the government negotiated the first 'Airlines Agreement' with ANA in an attempt to strengthen the airline's financial position and maintain TAA and ANA as the two major airline operators in Australia.[10] The agreement allowed ANA equal access with TAA to mail carriage, government business, lease of Commonwealth equipment and government security for loans for re-equipment, but failed to restore ANA to commercial health. In 1957, ATI bought out the struggling ANA and became the major private airline in Australia.[11]

Although now the main competitor against TAA, Ansett was still constrained in its ability to improve its competitiveness against TAA or to differentiate its service from other carriers. TAA's position as a government-subsidised enterprise was one contributing factor, because Ansett was forced to operate with higher cost structures than TAA and this impacted on the airline's profitability.[12] The two-airline agreement was another limitation, because under the agreement, airlines had to offer the same fare structure and advise competitors of any schedule changes.[13] This meant that in most cases, new services or schedules by one airline would be matched almost immediately by competitors, so there was little incentive or opportunity to develop distinctive points of competitive difference in core service areas.

By 1979, ATI had expanded into a variety of different business areas, some of which are listed in Exhibit 2. The diversity of operations contributed to an eventual takeover by TNT (who wanted the company's transport divisions) and News Limited (who wanted the television interests) in 1979. Both bought a 50 per cent

Exhibit 2 | Subsidiary operations of Ansett Transport Industries by 1979[14]

Subsidiary	Operations
Ansair	Manufacture of coaches and airport buses
Ansett Hotels	Largest hotel operator in Australia
Barrier Reef Islands Ltd	Resort management on Hayman and Daydream Islands
Ansett Travel Service	Retail travel services
Ansett Freight Express	Road freight services
Ansett Roadlines of Australia	Interstate coach services
Transport Industries Insurance	Insurance coverage for the transport divisions
Wridgways Holdings Ltd	Furniture removal
Albury Border Transport	Removalists
Avis Rent-A-Car	Automobile rental
Ownership interests	
ATV Channel 0 (later Channel 10) (ATI also held interests in four other TV stations around Australia)	Television broadcasting
Australian franchise of Diners Club International	Charge card services
Associated Securities Ltd	Finance (collapsed 1978)
Biro Bic (Australia and New Zealand)	Stationery and office supplies

stake in ATI, but Reg Ansett continued as chairman of the company until his death in 1981.[15]

A new navigator: ATI under Peter Abeles

Although ATI was highly diversified by the 1980s, Reg Ansett maintained a managerial style of tight control, characterised by his insistence on having a profit and loss report produced every Friday night in order to be able to track the company's operations. Known for being 'very demanding', Reg Ansett was also characterised as a 'tremendously loyal' man who 'knew his staff, his aircraft and the airline industry'.[16] According to Ted Forrester, general manager of Ansett Airlines in 1986 and with the company for over 40 years, the key to Ansett's success was the level of control Reg Ansett held over the airline, along with his understanding of the industry's labour- and capital-intensiveness.[17]

After Reg Ansett's death, the CEO of TNT, Peter Abeles, took over as chairman of ATI. He continued to diversify the company, as well as to make plans for international expansion. In 1981, Ansett Airlines was relaunched with a new logo, new livery, refurbished terminals and upgraded in-flight services. Although Qantas still held exclusive rights to all international services out of Australia, Ansett began pursuing international expansion by negotiating to fly routes under the Qantas flight designator and by taking on the management of very small overseas airlines such as Air Vanuatu and Polynesian Airlines. In 1986, Ansett also signed an agreement with Qantas to operate joint travel centres and to establish Ansett as Qantas's preferred domestic carrier.[18]

Abeles invested in a wide range of new aircraft for the airline, which prompted one commentator to make a comparison with a child collecting Matchbox cars.[19] The airline had always been a technological leader and introduced many new aircraft into Australia, but under Abeles, Ansett came to possess almost every available model of aircraft. As a result, Ansett was forced to spend far more on servicing, maintaining and flying its aircraft than its competitors did, at a time when it was already facing an increase in competitive pressure from established opponents and the growing possibility of new players entering the Australian market.

In 1985, James Strong became CEO of TAA. He instituted a program of significant cultural change to move the airline away from its image as a dowdy, public service enterprise. The airline was renamed Australian Airlines, and Strong began focusing on ways to target the market for business travel, such as providing more convenient scheduling, upgrading airport terminals and investing heavily in staff training. The business travel segment of the market became the focus for stiff competition between Ansett and Australian, and by March 1988, Australian had achieved a market share of 44 per cent compared to 36 per cent held by Ansett.[20] In response, Abeles announced a major relaunch of Ansett in May 1989, which included the introduction of business-class travel. Abeles had previously argued that introducing a business class to Ansett was unnecessary because 'our economy product was of the same standard as our competitors' business class'.[21]

The turbulence of deregulation

At the end of the 1980s, the federal government announced that it was deregulating the domestic aviation industry in order to encourage increased competition and responsiveness in the industry.[22] Fares, importation of aircraft, passenger capacity and route assignment would no longer be subject to government regulation, and new entrants would be encouraged to move into the Australian market.[23]

Almost immediately, Ansett and Australian began establishing their position in the new environment. Negotiations with the newly formed Federal Airports Commission culminated in a series of long-term leases for airport terminals, and the decision by both airlines to join the Galileo computer reservation system established Galileo membership as a key competitive factor

in the aviation industry.[24] Further changes began in 1989 with a wage claim by the airline pilots for a pay increase of almost 30 per cent. The airlines had identified cost reductions and productivity improvements as critical to success in deregulated competition, so the pay increase was rejected. To force the airlines to negotiate, the pilots resigned en masse, but the government then passed legislation which allowed international airlines and the Royal Australian Air Force to carry domestic passengers, so the domestic carriers were able to continue to operate without having to re-employ the pilots. The dispute finally ended in April 1990 when the airlines offered the pilots new contracts, but the contracts required the pilots to fly almost twice the number of hours per month as they had previously. As a result, the airlines only had to re-employ half as many pilots as they had hired previously.[25]

The pilots' strike had a number of powerful consequences for the airline industry. The most immediate was the cost savings and efficiency increases which the airlines achieved with the new contracts. The second consequence was the disempowerment of the Australian Federation of Airline Pilots as an influence over the employment conditions of the industry. This gave the airlines greater freedom in their operating policies and employment negotiations. However, the strike also damaged the tourism industry in Australia by making air travel seem unreliable,[26] which was a particularly heavy blow for Ansett because of the company's high level of investment in the tourism industry.

Tough times on the tarmac

Deregulation in 1990 brought new competitive pressures into Australian aviation almost immediately, from Compass Airlines and East West Airlines. Compass Airlines opened for business in October 1990, with an operating strategy of using only one type of aircraft to provide a one-class air service for the Australian holiday market, and offering lower fares than the major airlines. The airline only had access to two gates at Sydney and Melbourne airports, so Compass decided to operate with the largest possible aircraft and maximise the number of passengers per flight. The airline concentrated on a small number of key routes between Adelaide, Brisbane, Cairns, Melbourne, Sydney and Perth, and based its operations at Melbourne airport to achieve greater efficiencies in crew turnaround between flights.[27] Using only one aircraft type meant that training costs for pilots were lowered,[28] and the larger aircraft were more fuel-efficient and less costly to maintain than those used by Qantas or Ansett.[29]

At around the same time, East West Airlines announced that it would soon begin building its own presence in the Australian domestic industry. East West Airlines had been a subsidiary of Ansett Transport Industries since 1987 but operated as an independent airline out of Sydney.[30] The only intrastate airline to compete with Ansett and Qantas on interstate services, East West announced in 1990 that it was repositioning itself as a leisure airline and aimed to become the top leisure carrier by 1993 by capturing key holiday markets and combining direct flight services with resort holiday packages.[31] This was particularly threatening for Ansett, because it would involve increased competition in the markets for resort accommodation and travel packages as well as flight services.

In response to these new competitive pressures, Ansett and Qantas began an intense period of competition on fares and aggressive advertising which had not been seen before in Australian aviation.[32] The fiercest competition with Compass was in the business market, the most profitable market segment.[33] Ansett and Australian wooed corporate customers with discounts and upgraded facilities, as well as matching Compass and East West on all discounted fares.[34] Compass had already encountered difficulties with refuelling facilities, delays in aircraft delivery from manufacturers, and reservations systems,[35] and eventually the economic recession, coupled with Compass's inadequate capital levels and failure to gain a hold in the business market, forced the airline to cease operations in 1991.[36] Despite being relaunched the following year as Compass II, the airline failed to strengthen its position and was declared bankrupt in

1993. East West continued to compete in the leisure markets as an independent airline until 1993, when it was merged with several other ATI subsidiaries.[37]

Qantas climbs while Ansett loses altitude

As Ansett and Australian adjusted to intensified competition, the federal government announced that Qantas would be privatised and would purchase Australian Airlines in order to compete on both international and domestic fronts. Competition on international flight routes to and from Australia would be open to all airlines, who would also now be able to invest in each other. Soon after the announcement, British Airways purchased a 25 per cent stake in Qantas, and an improvement program to develop Qantas's competitiveness was launched. ATI responded by regrouping its various airline companies into Ansett Australia and Ansett International in order to consolidate services and reduce overheads.[38]

Over the next five years, Qantas began cutting costs and building efficiencies through its alliance with British Airways, while Ansett focused on building its route network throughout Asia.[39] As Ansett dealt with aggressive competition from Qantas over domestic flight frequency, fare discounts and frequent flyer loyalty, Qantas capitalised on Ansett's decision to relinquish its hold on Melbourne and Brisbane and used these bases as international gates to build its overseas flight network.[40] By November 1996, Qantas held almost 40 per cent of the international market, while Ansett held just over 2.5 per cent.[41] When the Asian financial crisis hit in the late 1990s, Ansett's competitiveness was undermined even further because the airline was heavily committed to its Asian service network. Qantas had already withdrawn many of its services throughout Asia and had redirected capacity towards more profitable markets such as North America and Europe.[42]

Continued diversification of Ansett's business interests and escalating fleet management costs eventually sent Ansett into what one commentator described as 'financial free fall'.[43] In the financial year 1996–7, Ansett generated only $39 million in revenue from its domestic operations, while the international operations made a loss of over $41 million.[44] By this time, both News Corporation and TNT had expressed interest in selling their stakes in Ansett, and in an effort to improve performance, the company began to refocus on aviation and divest itself of non-core subsidiary operations, including Ansett Freight Express and Turbine Components Australia.[45] In 1996, Air New Zealand purchased TNT's stake in Ansett Australia Holdings for $325 million and Rod Eddington was established as chief executive of the airline to turn the company around and begin the process of integration with Air New Zealand.[46]

Now boarding: Australian aviation in the late 1990s

In 1999, Australian airports handled over 50.5 million passengers, of which almost 15 million were international arrivals and departures.[47] Australian domestic travel offers one of the highest levels of unit revenue on domestic routes in the world,[48] as well as a springboard into the Asia-Pacific region, through which airline passenger traffic is predicted to grow by around 7 per cent per year for the next 20 years.[49] At the end of June 2000, Qantas, Ansett and new entrant Impulse held 83 per cent of the domestic market between them,[50] a segment that currently increases by 3–7 per cent annually.[51] Although officially deregulated in 1990, the competitive dynamics of the industry have really only begun to change over the last five years with the arrival of new entrants into the market and, with them, new competitive pressures for Ansett and Qantas.

New entrants crowd the runway

Over the past five years, three new airlines began operating in the Australian market – Virgin Blue, Impulse Airlines and Spirit Airlines. (See Exhibit 3 for a brief background on each.) All began by offering low fares. Since the new entrants began operating, analysts estimate that the lower fares being offered have expanded rather than redivided the market for air travel because they have prompted discretionary travel as well as attracting customers who might otherwise have used alternative transport.[52] However, slowing economic conditions and the increased passenger-carrying capacity of new aircraft are predicted to see fiercer competition develop as all five airlines seek to strengthen their positions and carve out greater market share.[53] A combination of rising fuel prices, savage fare reductions and competitors with deeper financial reserves have severely damaged Impulse's profitability and seen the airline's key institutional backers (Singapore firm CIG Investment) withdraw their financial support. To avoid the airline's collapse, founder Gerry McGowan sold Impulse to Qantas in May 2001, which has begun integrating the new acquisition into Qantas's network. Qantas's own competitiveness has been enhanced by the acquisition of

Exhibit 3 | New entrants in the Australian domestic aviation market

Impulse Airlines: Founded as a dedicated freight carrier for the Fairfax newspaper group, Impulse expanded into passenger services in 1993 and at its peak serviced 15 destinations across Victoria, New South Wales and Queensland.[54] Using only Boeing 717s, Impulse used smaller aircraft and more frequent services to target the business market, particularly small businesses and owner-operators who pay their own fares rather than hold a corporate account. Pushing Internet booking, Impulse also had an exclusive partnership agreement with Flight Centre, an Australia-wide low-cost travel agency.[55]

Spirit Airlines: Spirit originally operated a 'flying coach' service along the east coast of Australia but now also flies services to Perth, Adelaide and Hobart. Offering budget fares but no advance bookings, Spirit only takes bookings through a direct phone line but offers the choice of paper or electronic ticketing, whereby passengers present photo identification at the check-in counter rather than be issued with a paper ticket.[56]

Virgin Blue: A sister airline to Virgin Atlantic and Virgin Express, Virgin Blue currently flies from Brisbane to Sydney, Melbourne and Adelaide, and between Sydney and Adelaide. Presented as the 'fun' airline, Virgin, like Spirit, offers no-frills service where ticket prices cover only the cost of the flight. Virgin promotes the fact that passengers do not pay for extra features like airport lounge facilities, in-flight meals or frequent flyer programs in their ticket price, although passengers are able to purchase food and drinks during the flight.[57]

additional planes and slots, so although the fare wars may cease in the industry, the competition is likely to remain fierce.

Yields and deals

Domestic airline fares in Australia are grouped into five separate categories: business, full economy, and economy with small, middle and deep discounts.[58] In order to generate the most revenue possible per flight, yield management or revenue management systems are used to market seats on flights as perishable products. Sophisticated computer systems use historical information and analyses of market demand to adjust the price of a seat depending on the number of seats available, any discounts which may apply, and the timing of demand, such as whether the seat is being booked four weeks or two days before the actual flight. Analysts compare actual with predicted booking levels to determine whether prices need to be adjusted for demand, and how many seats per flight should be allocated for various segments of the market.[59]

While Ansett and Qantas use very sophisticated yield management systems to set fare levels, Virgin currently offers set fares on one-way and return tickets without advance purchase conditions, as well as 'walk-up' fares which can be purchased for the next available flight.[60] The new fare arrangements, coupled with aggressive price competition on several key east coast routes, are predicted to affect the market for business travel as well as discretionary travel, as corporate clients force Ansett and Qantas to match the fare structures offered by competitors.[61]

Slotting in: The battle for Hazelton Airlines

An airline's ability to improve the competitiveness of its flight services and scheduling depends upon the number of slots it controls at different airports. A slot is a period of time that an airline can use for landing or takeoff and is the mechanism by which airports control the amount of traffic at various times of the day. In Australia, slots cannot be traded or sold, so the only way that an airline can increase the slots it can access is to buy another airline.

For this reason, ownership of Hazelton Airlines, a regional carrier in New South Wales, sparked a fierce bidding war in early 2001 between Qantas and Ansett. Adding Hazelton's slots to their own would have given either carrier over 50 per cent of the slots at Sydney airport, and would have affected their own ability to schedule flight services as well as the ability of other airlines to offer equally competitive scheduling arrangements. For this reason, the Australian Competition and Consumer Commission (ACCC) initially refused to allow either airline to gain ownership of Hazelton, and Qantas withdrew from the bidding.

Ansett persisted, and in March 2001 the ACCC announced that Ansett had addressed these concerns in its bid for ownership and the purchase would be approved.[62]

Rewarding frequent flyers and frequent buyers

Frequent flyer programs are loyalty reward programs whereby customers are rewarded for the level of custom they provide for the airline. By November 2000, Ansett's Global Rewards program had 2.2 million members, while Qantas's Frequent Flyer program had 2.4 million. For each flight, customers earn reward points (Ansett) or miles (Qantas) which can then be redeemed for free flights, hotel accommodation and other benefits. Points have to be redeemed within five years,[63] and customers are graded according to the number of points they accumulate. Qantas, for example, has silver, gold or platinum tier status, but members must re-earn their status every 15 calendar months.[64] Members also accrue points through use of certain credit cards and affiliated organisations such as medical benefits funds and telephone companies.[65]

Impulse and Virgin both targeted customers from the lower-yield end of the market, because the customer loyalty generated by frequent flyer programs in the higher end was too strong to compete with.[66] However, Impulse launched its own reward program whereby travellers received one free flight for every 10 full-fare flights they purchased, a move that was designed to attract smaller business customers.[67]

The two main benefits of frequent flyer programs for airlines are customer loyalty and a database of detailed customer information that can be used to improve the effectiveness of marketing programs,[68] but there have also been difficulties associated with them. In June 2000, the ACCC announced that in response to numerous complaints about the schemes, an investigation would be launched to investigate, among other things, whether frequent flyer programs discouraged competition by preventing new entrants from establishing a competitive presence in the industry,[69] and whether customers were being adequately informed of the conditions of point redemption, such as limited seat availability on certain flight services.[70]

Worldwide travel with the World Wide Web

Until deregulation, air travel was most commonly booked through travel agencies, usually at the same time as a customer booked accommodation, car hire and other travel arrangements. In 1997, there were over 3 200 dedicated retail travel agents in Australia,[71] but since deregulation, cost pressures have seen many airlines establish direct booking facilities through call centres, and now Internet booking services, to reduce overhead costs and avoid paying a commission to travel agents. On-line ticket sales are currently estimated to account for around 3 per cent of all airline ticket sales, but this is predicted to reach 15 per cent by 2005.[72] For Qantas and Ansett, Internet bookings currently account for only 3–5 per cent of ticket sales, but Virgin Blue transacts around 35 per cent of its business over the Internet (and Impulse did more than 60 per cent), while Spirit Airlines only offers telephone bookings.[73]

Expanding horizons with oneworld and the Star Alliance

Perhaps the most important development in the Australian, and indeed global, aviation industry in recent years has been the development of the Star Alliance and oneworld global networks. Both were launched in 1998 and grew quickly. Exhibit 4 shows the

Exhibit 4 | Partner airlines of the Star Alliance[74] and oneworld alliances[75]

Star Alliance	Star Alliance partner airlines	oneworld
Ansett Australia	South African Airways	AerLingus
Air Canada	Virgin Atlantic Airways	American Airlines
Air New Zealand	SAS	British Airways
Australian Airlines	Singapore Airlines	Cathay Pacific
British Midland	Thai Airways International	Finnair
Lauda-Air	Tyrolean Airways	Ibena
Lufthansa	United Airlines	LanChile
Mexicana	VARIG	Qantas

member airlines of each at January 2001. Partners share flight codes, facilities such as airport terminals and passenger lounges, and marketing programs, while passengers belonging to any member's frequent flyer program are also credited for journeys on partner airlines.

The alliances were originally promoted by member airlines as an opportunity to extend flight networks, increase access to new markets and develop cost efficiencies through shared facilities, joint marketing efforts and strategic purchasing.[76] However, conflicts between some member airlines over promised membership benefits and the development of smaller alliance groups such as Qualiflyer suggest that the major alliance blocks may yet splinter if members feel that they would achieve increased benefits and more control over management of the alliances through smaller strategic networks.[77]

Ansett/Air New Zealand fly a new formation

Eddington pilots the Great Business Plan

When Rod Eddington joined Ansett in 1997, he pronounced it a 'great airline but a poor business'[78] and set about improving the airline's profitability and ability to compete. During the sale negotiations between TNT and Air New Zealand, News Corporation indicated that it was interested in selling its share in Ansett Holdings, so when Eddington took over the management of Ansett Australia, another change of ownership in the near future was almost assured. To increase Ansett's attractiveness as an acquisition, Eddington began targeting cost reductions and improvements in profitability, which were predominantly achieved through the merging of operations with Air New Zealand and the development of commercial partnerships with other airlines such as Singapore Airlines (SIA). Exhibit 5 illustrates the improvements in Ansett's financial performance that had been achieved under Eddington's leadership by the end of the 1999 financial year.

Eddingon also began refocusing Ansett from being an 'airline with planes' to a 'brand with customers'.[79] Ansett was promoted as a 'virtual airline' which would help allied airlines to offer 'global travel solutions' by providing services in the Australian/Asian region that partner airlines could or would not offer.[80] In 1997, an alliance was formed between Ansett Australia, Ansett International, Air New Zealand and Singapore Airlines so that the airlines could provide more competitive international travel options and greater access to airline facilities for customers, as well as develop more efficient arrangements for fleet re-equipment and joint operations.[81] The scope for benefits was extended in 1998 when all four airlines joined the Star Alliance network.[82]

Flight teams and fuel crews: The merging of support functions

From 1997, Ansett and Air New Zealand began merging various support functions, including catering, ground handling, freight handling, information technology and marketing, in shared pursuit of cost savings and greater operational efficiencies.[83] They also formed a joint venture called Newco to operate as an independent aircraft maintenance and engineering company and to tender for contracts with Ansett and Air New Zealand as well as other airlines, thus obviating the need for in-house engineering and maintenance facilities.[84]

Exhibit 5 | Ansett Holdings performance data, 1994–5 to 1998–9[85]

Group profit and loss account	1994–5	1995–6	1996–7	1997–8	1998–9
Total revenue	3 129.8	3 301.3	3 395.6	3 505.4	3 511.3
Total expenses	3 031.3	3 319.9	3 376.0	3 445.6	3 363.7
Earnings before interest and tax	198.6	80.9	114.1	377.4	432.5
Trading profit	99.3	(13.5)	(0.3)	27.8	140.8
Sale of non-core assets and foreign exchange	(0.8)	(5.1)	19.9	32.0	6.8
Net profit after tax	52.6	58.4	(35.0)	29.5	156.8
Group balance sheet					
Total assets	3 675.5	3 748.8	3 908.6	4 145.1	3 689.1
Total debt	1 942.6	1 719.2	1 690.7	1 786.7	1 314.8
Total equity	316.0	377.1	540.7	537.2	697.4

New bearings on human resource management

At the time of Eddington's arrival at Ansett, the key challenge for Ansett's human resource management was addressing the low morale and high turnover which had developed during the previous years of ownership uncertainty.[86] As part of the response to this problem, there was a radical restructure of employee benefits packages. Previously, employee benefits, such as use of a company car and the structure of compensation packages, had been determined according to a rigid hierarchy of entitlements and linked to rank within the company. The new policy, designed to be more flexible and to give employees more control over their compensation, included choices over make and model of company-funded transport and flexibility over superannuation contributions, and contributed to a reduction in voluntary turnover over the next three years.[87]

At the same time, Ansett was also facing the issue of reducing its staffing levels. In 1996, Ansett employed almost 18 000 employees, but by 1999, staff levels had fallen to less than 15 000 people. Most of these employees left under Eddington's 'job bank program' in which employees throughout the organisation were able to register their interest in voluntary redundancy before job cuts were announced. Further reductions were achieved through each level of management by requiring people to re-bid for a smaller number of positions.[88] When Air New Zealand purchased the remaining stake in Ansett in 2000, 13 board positions were also cut between the two airlines and over 250 middle management positions were eliminated, with Ansett executives predicting that 'only savage staff cuts will restore profitability and our ability to compete'.[89]

Shedding the excess baggage: Fleet re-equipment

Ansett's wide assortment of aircraft types made fleet re-equipment a pressing issue for the airline and was the first area in which Ansett and Air New Zealand attempted to develop synergies between the two companies. As well as having too many different types of aircraft, Ansett also faced pressures from competitors who had upgraded to smaller, faster jet models, and from the impact of escalating fuel costs on the airline's profitability.[90] Originally intending to follow Qantas's lead and purchase the new aircraft it required, Ansett instead negotiated lease agreements for most of its new aircraft with Air New Zealand and Singapore Airlines. To expand Kendall Airlines, an Ansett subsidiary, 12 new 50-seat Canadair-Regional Jet Series 200 aircraft were ordered and two Boeing 747-400 aircraft leased from Singapore Airlines to replace two of its B747-300s used by Ansett International.[91]

Benefits to Ansett included lower re-equipment costs, joint purchasing of engineering and maintenance services with Air New Zealand, and reduced costs related to training and licensing staff to operate a variety of aircraft.[92] However, Ansett's reliance on its commercial partners and on the maintenance of good relationships between Ansett, Air New Zealand and Singapore Airlines also increased. This had the potential to influence Ansett's future options to replace the three B747-300s currently leased from Singapore Airlines with smaller wide-bodied jets such as 777s and A340s, which offered improved fuel efficiency and roomier cabin facilities for passengers. The airline also had to begin planning how it would respond to the expected introduction of the 550-seater Airbus A3XX in 2006. The new aircraft design had been predicted to see aircraft size and in-flight service facilities become the focus of competition for international service networks,[93] and Ansett/Air New Zealand needed to ensure that it was well positioned to benefit from those recently ordered by Singapore Airlines.

Domesticating services in the Australian market

To revamp services in the Australian domestic market, Ansett and Air New Zealand developed new strategies for all of its newly acquired airlines (see Exhibit 6). Following in Air New Zealand's footsteps, Ansett began to pursue improved profitability by matching jet size to route demand and increasing flight frequency on higher-yield services.[94] New planes were ordered for Kendall Airlines so that Kendall's service frequencies and capacity could be expanded and it could continue to take on services for rural routes and below-100-seat markets from Ansett Australia.[95] Unprofitable routes in Queensland and the Northern Territory were taken over by independent carriers.[96] Kendall predicted that by May 2001, it would have around 90 southeastern flights operating on routes which were less than profitable for Ansett.[97]

With all five domestic airlines competing on east-coast routes in Australia, frequency of services was set to become a key competitive issue for Ansett in the business travel market. To increase its appeal to business travellers, Ansett began focusing on increasing service frequencies and improving in-flight amenities, as well as scheduling more convenient connections with international services.⁹⁸ In October 2000, Ansett admitted that their main competitive concern was fighting Qantas for the corporate market, the most profitable market sector.⁹⁹ After losing corporate travel accounts with the ANZ Bank,¹⁰⁰ BHP and the Department of Defence,¹⁰¹ Ansett decided to concentrate on maximising the benefits it could cultivate from deliberately targeting corporate clients during its sponsorship of the Sydney 2000 Olympic Games.¹⁰²

Going the long haul: International expansion

Shortly after purchasing the remaining stake in Ansett, Air New Zealand announced that Ansett Australia would continue to build flight services to North America under its own banner, but that Air New Zealand would do so by developing the network serviced by Ansett International. Holding only a 49 per cent stake in Ansett International, Air New Zealand nevertheless decided that it would develop services under Ansett's banner, rather than its own, in order to take advantage of the Ansett brand's higher level of international recognition and strong reputation for service quality.¹⁰³ With airline passenger traffic in the Asia-Pacific region forecasted to increase by 7 per cent per year for the next two decades,¹⁰⁴ Air New Zealand also announced that Ansett Australia and Air New Zealand would both increase services in the Asian region. The services would be provided using planes leased from Singapore Airlines¹⁰⁵ and according to 'whether … commercial objectives are best served by having (the routes) flown by (Star Alliance) partners or by including an Ansett product in the options'.¹⁰⁶

Ansett/Air New Zealand tests its wings

As well as addressing the internal changes of the merger, Ansett and Air New Zealand also had to consider how to respond to new external challenges in the local and global aviation industries. Locally, Qantas continued to hold a greater share of the Australian domestic business travel segment than Ansett, with the competition within the Australian market set to toughen as all parties sought increases to their market share.¹⁰⁷

One of the biggest challenges facing Ansett and Air New Zealand would be Ansett's recovery from severe damage to its reputation for safety. Failures in Ansett's safety and maintenance procedures saw the airline face two major safety crises between late 2000 and early 2001. Despite a warning from the Civil Aviation and Safety Authority (CASA) that Ansett needed to change its entire culture regarding safety,¹⁰⁸ the airline failed to act on a recommendation from Boeing to check the engine pylon mounts of their 767s, and the failure was only discovered when Ansett realised that compulsory inspections of its 767-200s had been overlooked. The planes were grounded over Christmas 2000 to conduct the inspections, which also damaged Ansett's reputation for reliability. The second crisis came in April 2001, when CASA grounded Ansett's entire fleet of 767s over the Easter holiday.¹⁰⁹ The delayed checks on the engine pylon mounts had found cracks in three of the planes,

Exhibit 6 | Ownership structure of Ansett/Air New Zealand¹¹⁰

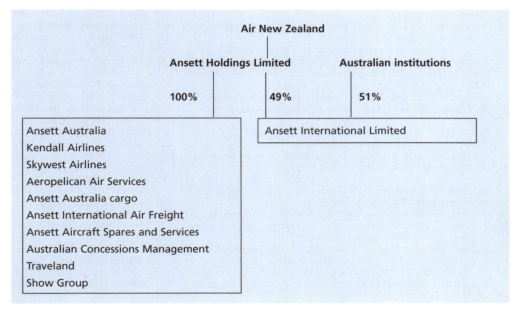

and when this was compounded by a report that Ansett had unknowingly flown one of the planes on eight flights with a defective emergency slide, CASA gave Ansett 14 days to show why its operational licence should not be revoked.

As well as being a public relations nightmare, the grounding was a financial disaster for Ansett. Forced to lease planes from Air New Zealand, Air Canada and Qantas in order to transport its grounded passengers over the Easter period, Ansett also had to facilitate inspection of its entire maintenance and safety system, as well as deal with a nationwide customer response to the grounding. In defensive mode, Ansett launched an extensive media campaign to attribute the safety failures to the previous management team, and to convince customers that the airline had already begun extensive changes to its maintenance processes and culture. Ansett also spent $30 million on an advertising campaign featuring celebrity endorsements of the airline, but whether this would restore customer confidence remained to be seen.

With the stage set for tougher competition in the Australian domestic market, Air New Zealand/Ansett needed to consider whether to develop its own no-frills service to compete at the lower end of the Australian market, or to focus on competing with service quality at the higher end of the market. If the latter option was adopted, how might the market for business travel be affected by developments in Internet and telephone technology designed to facilitate 'virtual conferencing'? Would this prompt reductions in business travel similar to those which resulted from the economic recession in the early 1990s?[111]

In the longer term, the airline also had to consider whether to maintain both the Ansett and Air New Zealand brands, or pursue the development of a single trans-Tasman brand.[112] Some analysts had predicted that the formation of the Star and oneworld alliances would lead to the lobbying of national governments and aviation authorities to allow jets owned by one airline to enter a country under one partner's flight codes, fly some domestic routes under the auspices of another partner, and fly out again under a third carrier's banner.[113] If approved, the number of services provided by each partner airline (and therefore the revenues generated within the alliance) might come to be determined by which partner has the most valuable brand equity. In such circumstances, which brand was positioned to provide the best value to the airline?

The decisions made by the top-management of Ansett/Air New Zealand would determine not only whether the airlines would ever achieve the benefits expected from the merger, but whether in fact they could continue to compete in what had now become a highly competitive industry. Would the strategic alliances result in the growth of the airline's own service network, or would the airline's future lie in feeding regional travellers in the global networks of other airlines? Only time would tell.

Endnotes

1. S. Creedy, 2001, 'Fuel costs cruel Air New Zealand', *The Australian*, 21 February.
2. Ansett Holdings Corporate Affairs, 1999, *Ansett Milestones* (Melbourne: Ansett Holdings Pty Ltd).
3. H. W. Poulton, 1982, *Law, History and Politics of the Australian Two-Airline System* (Melbourne: H. W. Poulton).
4. G. Hubbard, 1999, 'The deregulation of the Australian domestic airline industry', in G. Lewis and A. Morkel (eds), *Australian and New Zealand Strategic Management: Concepts, Context and Cases* (Sydney: Prentice Hall).
5. Hubbard, 'The deregulation of the Australian domestic airline industry'.
6. Poulton, *Law, History and Politics of the Australian Two-Airline System*.
7. Ibid.
8. Ibid.
9. Ansett Holdings Corporate Affairs, *Ansett Milestones*.
10. Poulton, *Law, History and Politics of the Australian Two-Airline System*.
11. Ansett Holdings Corporate Affairs, *Ansett Milestones*.
12. Ibid.
13. Hubbard, 'The deregulation of the Australian domestic airline industry'.
14. Ansett Holdings Corporate Affairs, *Ansett Milestones*.
15. Hubbard, 'The deregulation of the Australian domestic airline industry'.
16. G. Thomas, 2000, 'Staggering under the weight of Abele's excess baggage', *Sydney Morning Herald*, 19 February.
17. Hubbard, 'The deregulation of the Australian domestic airline industry'.
18. Ansett Holdings Corporate Affairs, *Ansett Milestones*.
19. C. Colquhuon, 2000, 'Strategy: Newcomers score in dogfight's early rounds', *Business Review Weekly*, 13 October.
20. Hubbard, 'The deregulation of the Australian domestic airline industry'.
21. Ibid.
22. Bureau of Transport and Communications Economics, 1991, *Deregulation of Domestic Aviation – The First Year*, Report 73 (Canberra: AGPS).
23. Hubbard, 'The deregulation of the Australian domestic airline industry'.
24. Ibid.
25. T. Keenoy and D. Kelley, 1998, *The Employment Relationship in Australia*, 2nd edition (Sydney: Harcourt Brace).
26. Hubbard, 'The deregulation of the Australian domestic airline industry'.
27. Bureau of Transport and Communications Economics, *Deregulation of Domestic Aviation – The First Year*.
28. Hubbard, 'The deregulation of the Australian domestic airline industry'.
29. Bureau of Transport and Communications Economics, *Deregulation of Domestic Aviation – The First Year*.
30. Ansett Holdings Corporate Affairs, *Ansett Milestones*.
31. Hubbard, 'The deregulation of the Australian domestic airline industry'.
32. Ibid.
33. Ibid.
34. Ibid.
35. Bureau of Transport and Communications Economics, *Deregulation of Domestic Aviation – The First Year*.
36. N. Shoebridge, 2000, 'Cut-price flights no way to make business soar', *Business Review Weekly*, 11 August.
37. Ansett Holdings Corporate Affairs, *Ansett Milestones*.
38. Ibid.
39. B. Sandilands, 2000, 'Ansett chief promises to wield branding iron', *Business Review Weekly*, 20 July.
40. R. Gottliebsen and L. Schmidt, 1998, 'Fight for the skies', *Business Review Weekly*, 12 October.

41. C. Falvey, 1996, 'Reluctant romance: Air New Zealand and Ansett Australia muddle towards inevitable mergers as grousing by their governments grows', *Air Transport World*, 33(5), pp. 57–60.
42. Gottliebsen and Schmidt, 'Fight for the skies'.
43. P. Lewis, 1997, 'Starring role: Ansett is being propelled on to the international stage, with its strategic partnership with ANZ and SIA', *Flight International*, 152(4581), p. 27.
44. T. Ballantyne, 1997, 'Business revolution', *Airline Business*, 13(8), pp. 28–31.
45. Falvey, 'Reluctant romance'.
46. Ansett Holdings Corporate Affairs, *Ansett Milestones*.
47. Australian Bureau of Statistics, 2000, *Australian Bureau of Statistics Home Page*: www.abs.gov.au, 31 January.
48. *South China Morning Post*, 17 April 2000.
49. S. Creedy, 2000, 'Airline traffic set for take-off', *Australian Financial Review*, 25 May.
50. Australian Bureau of Statistics, 2000, *Australian Bureau of Statistics Home Page*: www.abs.gov.au, 31 January.
51. L. Colquhoun, 2001, 'Sunshine in the open sky', *Business Review Weekly*, 23 February.
52. Colquhoun, 'Strategy'.
53. Colquhoun, 'Sunshine in the open sky'.
54. Impulse Airlines, 2001, *Impulse Airlines Home Page*: www.impulseairlines.com.au, 4 February
55. Colquhoun, 'Strategy'.
56. Spirit Airlines, 2001, *Spirit Airlines Home Page*: www.spiritairlines.com.au, 4 February.
57. Virgin Blue, 2001, *Virgin Blue Home Page*: www.virginblue.com.au, 4 February.
58. S. Creedy, 2000, 'Air fair', *The Weekend Australian*, 26 August.
59. D. Macken, 1999, 'Fare go', in C. H. Lovelock, P. G. Patterson and R. H. Walker (eds), *Services Marketing in Australia and New Zealand* (Sydney: Prentice Hall).
60. D. Kitney, 2000, 'Air fare war as Qantas, Ansett take on Impulse', *Australian Financial Review*, 12 May.
61. Creedy, 'Air fair'.
62. Australian Competition and Consumer Commission (ACCC), 2001, *ACCC Home Page*: www.accc.gov.au/media/mediar.htm, 2 April.
63. I. Thomas, 2000, 'Frequent flyers reap rewards in battle for the airways', *Australian Financial Review*, 8 November.
64. Lovelock, Patterson and Walker, *Services Marketing in Australia and New Zealand*.
65. Thomas, 'Frequent flyers reap rewards in battle'.
66. G. Carman, 2000, 'Competition: Airline challengers taxi for takeoff', *Business Review Weekly*, 31 March.
67. J. Boyle, 2000, 'Revamp for Impulse to woo flyers', *Australian Financial Review*, 23 October.
68. G. Kingshott, 2001, 'Building loyalty that lasts', Unisys client profile: www.unisys.com.au, 2 March.
69. K. Cummins and J. Boyle, 2000, 'ACCC to probe frequent flyer loyalty schemes', *Australian Financial Review*, 6 June.
70. Australian Competition and Consumer Commission (ACCC), 2001, *ACCC Home Page*: www.accc.gov.au, 2 March.
71. Australian Bureau of Statistics, 1998, *Travel Agency Services Industry, Australia, 1996–1997*.
72. M. Hanlon, 2000, 'Airlines flying high on web sales surge', *Australian Financial Review*, 8 November.
73. Colquhoun, 'Strategy'.
74. Ansett Holdings Limited, 2001, *Travelling Life: Ansett Rewards* (Melbourne: Ansett Holdings Limited).
75. oneworld, 2001, *oneworld Home Page*: www.oneworldalliance.com, 4 February.
76. *AsiaPulse News*, 3 May 1999.
77. B. Sandilands, 2000, 'Cracks in oneworld as AA loses faith', *Australian Financial Review*, 5 September.
78. B. Sandilands, 1998, 'Ansett chief promises to wield the branding iron', *Business Review Weekly*, 16 November.
79. Sandilands, 'Ansett chief promises to wield the branding iron'.
80. B. Sandilands, 1999, 'Aviation: Ansett's "virtual" global future', *Business Review Weekly*, 9 April.
81. *Ansett Holdings Limited Annual Review, 1997* (Melbourne: Ansett Holdings Limited).
82. Ansett Holdings Corporate Affairs, *Ansett Milestones*.
83. Ballantyne, 'Business revolution'.
84. *AsiaPulse News*, 20 August 1999.
85. *Ansett Holdings Limited Annual Review, 1999* (Melbourne: Ansett Holdings Limited).
86. M. Laurence, 1998, 'Employees have a sky-high level of choice', *Business Review Weekly*, 23 March.
87. Ibid.
88. A. Kohler, 2000, 'Toomey scrambles for dogfight', *Australian Financial Review*, 17 September.
89. *Airline Industry Information*, 6 November 2000.
90. Ballantyne, 'Business revolution'.
91. *Ansett Holdings Limited Annual Review 1999*.
92. Ballantyne, 'Business revolution'.
93. B. Sandilands, 2000, 'Massive flights of fancy', *Australian Financial Review*, 20 October.
94. R. Chapman, 1999, 'En route to sustained profitability', *Business Review Weekly*, 1 December.
95. Kendall Airlines, 2001, *Kendall Airlines Home Page*: www.kendall.com.au, 31 January.
96. S. Penney, 2000, 'Ansett 747 acquisition to raise long-haul capacity', *Flight International*, 6 June.
97. J. Boyle, 2000, 'Kendall looks for 12 new jets', *Australian Financial Review*, 31 May.
98. D. Knibb, 2000, 'Cash injection planned for Ansett', *Airline Business*, 1 October, p. 30.
99. Colquhoun, 'Strategy'.
100. J. Boyle, 2000, 'Ansett gets $250m boost to fight slump', *Australian Financial Review*, 30 August.
101. Kohler, 'Toomey scrambles for dogfight'.
102. *Airline Industry Information*, 26 October 2000.
103. D. Knibb, 2000, 'New owners discuss change at Ansett', *Airline Business*, December, p. 24
104. Creedy, 'Airline traffic set for take-off'.
105. Knibb, 'New owners discuss change at Ansett'.
106. Sandilands, 'Ansett chief promises to wield the branding iron'.
107. Colquhoun, 'Sunshine in the open sky'.
108. Australian Broadcasting Corporation, 2 February 2001.
109. B. Sandilands, 2001, 'Ansett tale of woe', *Australian Financial Review*, 17 April, p. 5.
110. *Ansett Holdings Limited Annual Review, 1999*.
111. Hubbard, 'The deregulation of the Australian domestic airline industry'.
112. Ballantyne, 'Business revolution'.
113. Sandilands, 'Aviation'.

Case 3

BP–Mobil and the restructuring of the oil refining industry

Karel Cool
Jeffrey Reuer
Ian Montgomery
Francesca Gee
INSEAD

On 29 February 1996, British Petroleum (BP) and Mobil surprised investors and competitors with an unexpected announcement: after six months of secret talks, the two oil companies had agreed to merge their refining and retail sales operations in a pan-European joint venture.

The move was a new approach to confronting long-standing problems in the European oil market. In refining, international companies had been confronted with low returns, excess capacity and high exit costs; in retail, competition was heating up, especially from a new category of players: supermarkets. For years, major players had practised increasingly stringent cost cutting. Yet, none had attempted anything as ambitious as Mobil and BP.

When presenting the deal, Mobil and BP stressed their shared focus on financial performance and discipline and said that the combination provided an excellent fit in terms of geographic spread and quality of assets which would give them leadership in key markets. By pooling their US$5 billion in European assets, BP and Mobil figured they could save US$400–500 million a year. They said their combined market share in Europe would amount to 12 per cent in fuels, hard on the heels of market leaders Exxon and Shell, and 18 per cent in lubricants.

While oil industry analysts praised BP and Mobil for acting decisively, they also expressed some doubts about the joint venture. Was an alliance the best response to the industry's troubles at a time when other players were leaving the market altogether? 'It's an original deal,' said an investment banker, 'but it puts them right in the middle: they are not niche players but they are not the leaders either. I wonder whether they are quite big enough.' To reap the dramatic savings they were announcing, Mobil and BP would have to close down more refineries and petrol stations and lay off thousands – an unpopular move in unemployment-stricken Europe.

The oil industry value chain

Oil was the world's main source of energy. Its end products were used in a variety of ways: transport by land, water and air (petrol,[1] diesel, jet propulsion fuels), heating (heating oil), lubricants (mainly in rolling mills, car engines, machinery and precision instruments), building materials (asphalt), etc. About 12 per cent of crude oil was converted into plastics and synthetic fibres. Crude oils varied substantially in looks, composition, density and flow properties, due to their different formation conditions. Crude from Libya and Algeria, for instance, was thin-bodied and yellowish with virtually no sulphur content. Venezuelan heavy oils, by contrast, were viscous, almost solid and dark black in colour with a lot of sulphur. Normal petroleum products could be made from all oils, but good crude (thin-bodied, low-sulphur) was easier to refine.

Upstream operations

Upstream operations, the generic name for all activities related to crude oil before refining, included exploration and production. Oil was found in underground reservoirs, surrounded by rock formations which geologists studied to identify the presence of oil. They used increasingly sophisticated and expensive tools, from surface mapping and aerial surveys to seismic soundings. Advanced drilling techniques had made it

---

This case is intended to be used as a basis for classroom discussion rather than to illustrate either effective or ineffective handling of an administrative situation.
Copyright © 1999 INSEAD, Fontainebleau, France. All rights reserved.

possible to explore new areas such as the seabeds of the Gulf of Mexico and the North Sea. Exploratory wells could reach 2 500 metres below the surface of the ocean. By 1996, world production averaged 65 million barrels per day (bpd).[2] While the world's largest oil fields were in the Middle East, part of production had moved to the North Sea and the Americas, the result of a switch to politically safer areas.

After a series of nationalisations, mostly in the 1970s, the upstream industry became dominated by major producers which owned most of the world's proven reserves. Aramco of Saudi Arabia was the biggest; other important players were Petroleos de Venezuela, Pemex of Mexico, the Kuwait Petroleum Company and Statoil of Norway. Exhibit 1 shows their share in world production.

Downstream operations

Downstream operations included transportation and storage of crude oil, processing, refining and marketing of final products to customers. Refining (described in Exhibit 2) essentially breaks down crude into various components which are then reconfigured into new products. While refineries could handle different qualities of crude and produce various end products, the more sophisticated refineries were better able to upgrade crude into high-value products. Although the product mix could not be changed completely, the way plants were configured and the quality of crude afforded some flexibility.

Global refining capacity in 1996 stood at 78 million bpd. Refining was carried out in about 700 refineries which were evenly distributed between North America, Europe, Asia and the rest of the world. The average capacity was 100 000 bpd.[3] Most of these plants had been planned before the 1973 oil shock when demand had been expected to grow almost indefinitely. Opening a new refinery took a long time and cost billions of dollars. Running it was comparatively inexpensive, but closing it down entailed substantial clean-up costs (estimated to be as high as US$100 million) and redundancy costs. For these reasons, owners usually operated existing plants, even in a situation of over-capacity. Exhibit 3 shows the worldwide trend in refining.

In marketing, the largest volumes sold were petrol at the pump. Initially, service stations had been operated by large oil companies and small, independent operators. Lately, large out-of-town supermarkets had been joining the fray. Profitability was determined by the number and location of service stations and by supply logistics. Oil companies also offered specific services to industrial customers, supplies of jet fuel and bunkering (marine fuels, diesel oil and gas oil). These were usually delivered direct from the refinery.

Exhibit 1 | Distribution of control of world oil production and refining, 1970–91

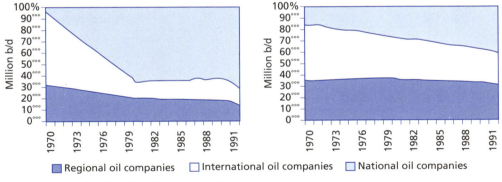

Source: Booz-Allen & Hamilton, 'Dinosaurs can fly'.

Exhibit 2 | Refining processes and product flows

	Input	Intermediate	Output
Products	Crude oil	Kerosene, naphtha, gas oils, distillate	Gasoline, distillate, jet fuel, liquefied petroleum gas (LPG), and residuals
Processes	Crude distillation	Coker, hydrotreater, catalytic cracker, alkylation, hydrocracker, reformer	Distribution and retailing

Exhibit 3 | World refining capacity, 1980–96 (millions of tonnes)

Region	1980	1993	1994	1995	1996 (est.)
Western Europe	1 000.0	704.5	706.7	701.4	704.1
Middle East	205.8	255.0	266.2	264.8	269.8
Africa	107.4	145.9	144.2	144.1	145.3
North America	1 025.0	851.1	861.3	860.1	864.2
Latin America	436.3	375.4	367.8	371.0	372.6
Far East	572.0	682.9	720.9	740.2	814.3
Eastern Europe and FSU	769.7	642.3	642.6	636.6	632.5
Total	4 116.2	3 657.1	3 709.7	3 718.2	3 802.8

Source: Union Francaise des Industries Petrolieres (Bilan, 1996).

Exhibit 4 | Relative positions of large companies at various stages of the oil industry value chain, 1995

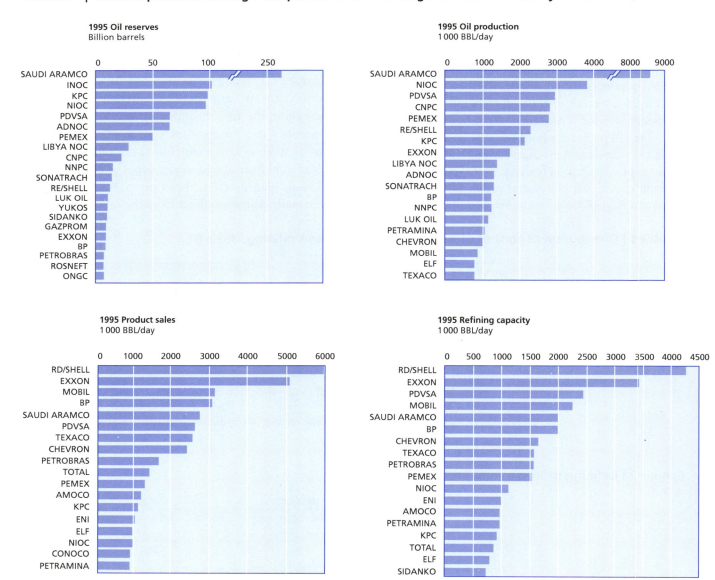

Source: National statistics; oil company annual reports.

Case 3 BP–Mobil

Large integrated companies were dominating downstream operations. These included Shell, BP, Texaco, Gulf, Exxon, Mobil and Chevron. The last three had been formed after an antitrust decision to break up John D. Rockefeller's Standard Oil in 1911. These giant multinationals engaged in all aspects of the oil and gas business, from exploration and production to refining and marketing. Exhibit 4 shows their relative position in terms of reserves, output and sales.

Customer demand

Historically, the main driver of demand for oil had been the rate of economic growth. Demand also followed an annual cycle, peaking during the Northern Hemisphere's winter and falling in summer and stood at about 65 million bpd in 1996. The global oil market was still growing, albeit at a slower pace than in the 1960s and 1970s. After the Second World War, demand

Exhibit 5 | European energy market (existing and projected), 1995 and 2005

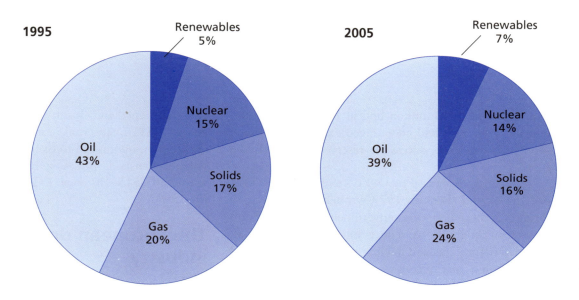

Exhibit 6 | Increase in automobile fuel efficiency, 1970–88

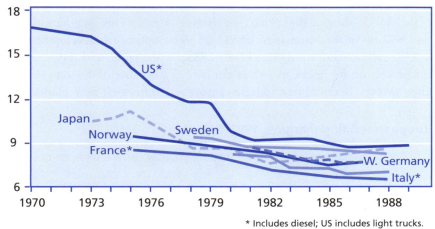

* Includes diesel; US includes light trucks.

Source: International Energy Studies, LBL.

Exhibit 7 | Worldwide and European refining capacity and demand (throughput), 1968–96

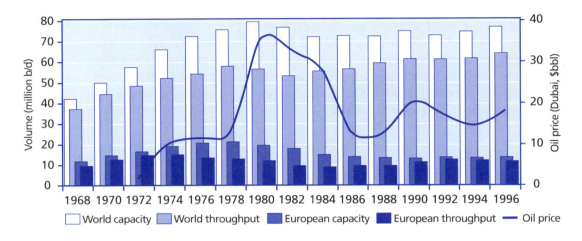

Source: *BP Statistical Review of World Energy, 1997.*

had surged from 10 million bpd in 1945 to 60 million bpd in 1970. This had encouraged exploration, which soon unveiled large, accessible reserves in the Middle East.

The oil shock caused by OPEC's embargo in 1973–4 and the second shock in 1979 wrought such havoc to Western economies that governments embarked on long-term programs to reduce oil dependence. Coal, liquefied natural gas and nuclear power were developed as substitutes; energy conservation and efficiency gains were encouraged. (Exhibit 5 shows the expected shift away from oil until 2005; Exhibit 6 shows fuel savings achieved by car manufacturers.) The result was that between 1978 and 1985, oil's share of the total energy market in industrial countries fell to 43 per cent from 53 per cent.

The oil shocks, government programs and the cyclical nature of demand caused wide swings in oil prices. After the 1973 shock, the price per barrel increased from US$2.90 in the summer to US$11.65 in December. By 1979, it had shot up to US$34. In 1985, OPEC stopped protecting its prices to regain demand. The Bellwether West Texas Intermediate futures contract immediately lost two-thirds of its value to trade below US$10. Internal conflict within OPEC and cheating on quotas led to over-production. While more volatility ensued, prices stabilised in the mid-1990s within a US$15–18 range. Exhibit 7 plots spot prices in the 1990s.

The European downstream industry

Refining

In recession-hit Europe in the mid-1990s, demand was nearly flat with growth forecasts of 0.5 per cent per annum until 2005. The market was depressed by fuel efficiency gains, higher duties, taxes (which governments often justified on environmental grounds), and increased supplies of nuclear power and natural gas. This stagnation was in stark contrast to the optimistic development programs prior to 1973 when demand had been expected to grow exponentially. Because of the long lead times for planning and building refineries, new plants had come onstream, resulting in

Exhibit 8 | European refining margins, 1991–6

| | DOLLAR MARGIN ON A BARREL OF COMPLEX NWE BRENT | | | | | |
	1991	1992	1993	1994	1995	1996
Quarter 1	6.28	2.2	1.81	2.17	1.35	1.56
Quarter 2	3.37	1.92	2.26	1.43	1.67	1.75
Quarter 3	2.88	1.94	2.34	1.74	1.64	
Quarter 4	−2.89	1.92	2.4	1.67	1.46	

Source: Woods Mackenzie.

Exhibit 9 | European refining margins and utilisation, 1985–96

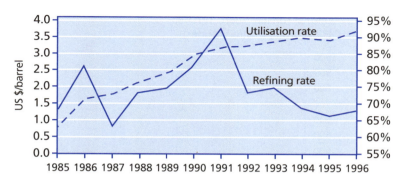

Source: Woods Mackenzie.

significant over-capacity in some parts of Europe. Exhibit 8 shows margins during the 1990s.

High exit costs, as well as governments' industrial and employment policies, were often blamed for the industry's failure to tackle over-capacity. There was also fragmented ownership of firms. The European refining industry had a mix of state-owned, integrated and independent companies. In most national markets, up to a dozen of these companies shared half the total capacity.

Over-capacity was also exacerbated by productivity improvements. Until 1991, capacity utilisation and margins had grown in parallel but this was no longer true, as Exhibit 9 shows. Demanding new regulations, often dictated by environmental concerns, had resulted in capacity creep. As margins declined, all producers were working to incrementally increase their capacity. Exhibit 10 shows capacity utilisation for major European oil companies.

The problem of over-capacity was aggravated by mismatches between the configuration of refineries (which had been planned for heavy Middle East crude) and actual supplies (often, lighter North Sea oil). Demand for diesel also had grown much faster than expected, so that many refineries operating at capacity for diesel had spare capacity for petrol. Demand for fuel oil also had declined as supplies of natural gas became available. Exhibit 11 shows changes in the European demand mix.

Although oil companies generally aggregated into their published accounts their refining and marketing results, it was known that refining was far less profitable than marketing. Geographic differences in refining margins persisted. Margins had been higher in Asia where refining units were larger and yielded greater market power. In Europe, they were lower than in the United States where cheap prices for divested plants had enabled independent refiners to acquire assets which they operated at about 15 per cent return on capital. (Tosco, for instance, had bought refineries and retail sites from both Exxon and BP.) More lenient environmental laws, a flexible labour market, less price competition in a more consolidated industry, and the absence of direct central government control also helped

Exhibit 10 | Refining capacity utilisation rate, 1993–6

EUROPEAN REFINERS' UTILISATION RATE				
	1993	1994	1995	1996
Agip	78%	79%	74%	75%
Exxon	86	84	79	89
Repsol	86	87	87	84
Shell	100	100	98	102
Total	89	94	90	104
BP-Mobil	95	92	99	94
European average	86	88	88	91

Source: Woods Mackenzie.

Exhibit 11 | Demand mix

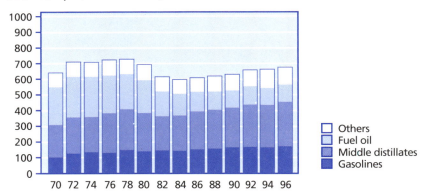

Regional consumption, 1970–96
OECD Europe (million tonnes)

Legend: Others, Fuel oil, Middle distillates, Gasolines

Note: 'Middle distillates' refers to diesel.
Source: *BP Statistical Review of World Energy*, 1997.

make US downstream players more profitable than European ones.

Beyond these concerns, the European downstream industry was bracing itself for a huge bill following the European Commission's 1993 Auto-Oil program, which aimed at reducing levels of urban atmospheric pollution by the year 2010. The industry would probably need huge investments to improve the quality of diesel and petrol. This was likely to cost the industry a total of US$16 billion over a 15-year period.

Marketing

Some 300 billion litres of petrol and other retail products were sold every year in Western Europe. The leaders, Shell and Exxon, each had about 12 per cent market share. There were some 120 000 service stations operated by the major integrated companies, supermarkets and independent retailers. Their number was falling rapidly (as shown in Exhibit 12). In France, there were 18 000 petrol stations left, compared with 47 000 in 1976, and a further 5 500 were expected to close. Germany too had 18 000, down from a peak of 46 700. In the United Kingdom, their number was forecast to fall below 10 000 by 2005, from 16 000 in 1996.

The Western European market was characterised by weak brands and changes in distribution channels, where supermarkets increasingly displaced small dealer networks while integrated companies and national players were trying to turn service station forecourts

Exhibit 12 | The trend in petrol retailing sites, 1987–96

	AVERAGE NUMBER OF RETAIL SITES			
	United Kingdom	Germany	France	Benelux
1987	20 197	20 751	31 100	15 510
1988	20 016	20 198	29 000	15 150
1989	19 756	19 802	27 700	14 699
1990	19 465	19 351	25 700	13 937
1991	19 247	18 898	23 700	13 211
1992	18 549	18 836	21 700	12 668
1993	17 969	18 464	20 000	11 820
1994	16 971	18 300	19 013	11 022
1995	16 244	17 957	18 406	10 490
1996	14 748	17 660	17 974	10 030

Source: Woods Mackenzie.

Exhibit 13 | Comparative average throughput per site, 1995

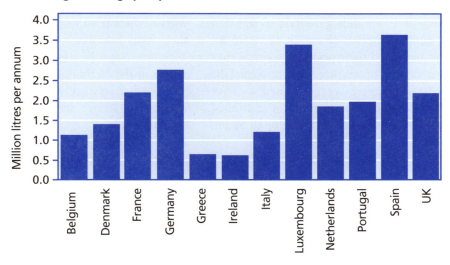

Source: Woods Mackenzie.

into convenience stores. (Exhibits 13 to 20 describe various characteristics of national markets.) Petrol was increasingly perceived as a commodity product, with gross sales margins of 2–4 per cent. Consumers bought mainly on convenience (proximity) and price. Even the 'majors' now competed on price. Brands remained weak and undifferentiated despite efforts to build them up; independent surveys showed that brand value, measured by the additional margin compared with an unbranded product, was minimal.

The weakness of brands had favoured the entry and growth of supermarkets. Huge shopping centres had sprung up near major cities and enjoyed many advantages. They had acres of free parking, and customers had become used to visiting them every week. Filling up was just part of 'one-stop shopping'. In 1996, their market share was already high in France (over 50 per cent), the United Kingdom (over 20 per cent) and Germany (over 10 per cent).

The average supermarket service station sold much more fuel than other service stations. In Britain, for example, the 664 supermarket stations had 20 per cent of the whole market. As 'bulk' buyers, they could negotiate lower prices for supplies. They could also take advantage of imbalances between supply and demand in their region. As a result, the supermarkets often paid lower wholesale prices than the integrated oil companies' own marketing divisions.

Exhibit 14 | Retail petrol margins, 1995 and 1996

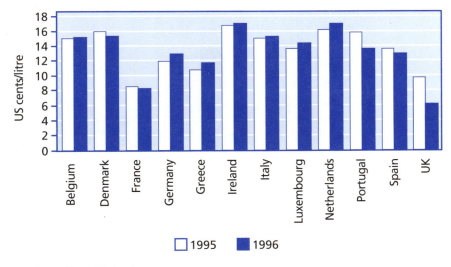

Source: Woods Mackenzie.

Supermarkets also seemed to operate on smaller margins than traditional service stations. Competitors grumbled that supermarkets didn't hesitate to sell at a loss in order to capture market share. In fact, French supermarkets had increased their prices as soon as they had established a degree of market power. While the growth of out-of-town supermarkets seemed to have peaked in the United Kingdom and France, it continued in Germany and Italy and was only starting up in Spain, Portugal and Ireland.

Independent retailers that could no longer compete went out of business. Other retailers tried to rise to the challenge: they consolidated their networks, keeping only the more profitable locations, and engaged in price wars. Others tried to turn old rivals into allies, opening their own branded outlets on supermarket premises. This was Repsol's strategy in Spain with El Corte and Shell's in the Netherlands with Ahold.

Another strategy was to develop convenience stores in existing service stations. Taking advantage of long opening hours and dedicated car parks, these new 'corner shops' offered goods and services such as cigarettes, newspapers, food and drinks, automated bank tellers, fax, photocopiers, post office, lottery and photo shops,

Exhibit 15 | Retail diesel margins, 1995 and 1996

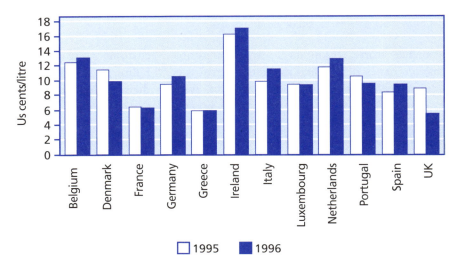

Source: Woods Mackenzie.

Exhibit 16 | Comparative total gross margin per site, 1995

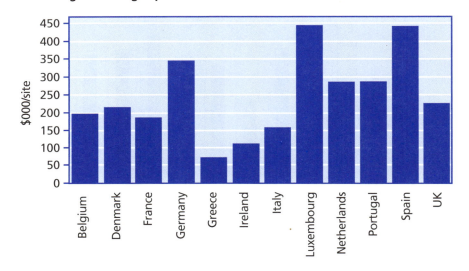

Source: Woods Mackenzie.

reducing the dependence of retailers on petrol sales. It was hoped that, in the longer term, forecourts would become shopping areas in their own right, maybe in partnership with established food retailers.

Opportunities in Eastern Europe

The stagnation of the Western European retail market was encouraging oil companies to look east. The collapse of communism in 1989 had left a dilapidated infrastructure and limited distribution networks, but upbeat forecasts for economic growth suggested that the downstream oil market would grow quickly. Oil companies could enter this new market in two ways. First, existing oil assets could be purchased at bargain-basement rates. However, their low prices often reflected poor quality and under-investment; cleaning up the sites and meeting potential environmental liabilities could turn out to be enormously costly. Second, firms could build new refineries and retail networks. This was less uncertain, but it would take a long time and be hugely expensive. While these risks had made investment slower than expected, all the integrated oil companies had plans for Eastern Europe, with Shell, Exxon and Total leading the pack.

Exhibit 17 | Comparison of European countries – selected variables

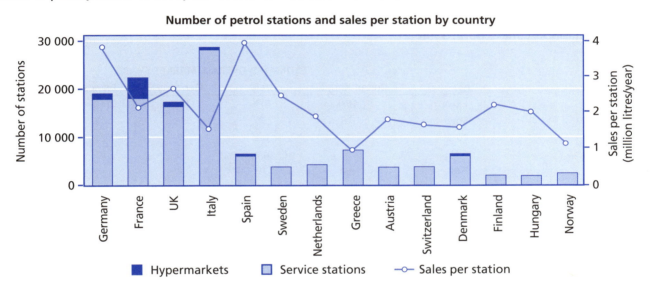

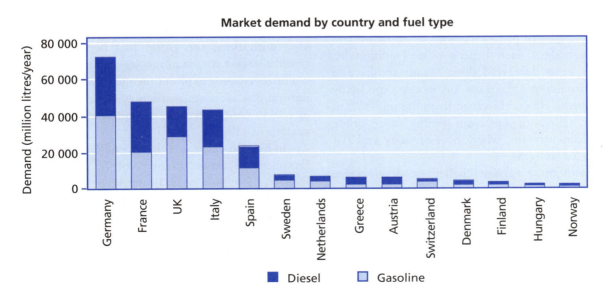

Sources: *Petroleum Review*, June 1997; UFIP; national oil industry associations.

Exhibit 18 | The economics of selling petrol across Europe

	REFINING NET PROFITABILITY ANALYSIS			
	United Kingdom	Italy	Germany	France
Retail costs				
Distribution	0.8	23.5	2.2	8
Advertising and promotion	0.5	15	1.4	4.5
Other marketing	1.3	33.5	3.4	11.5
Retail site costs	3.4	66	8.5	19
Retail revenue				
Unit margin	6.2	223	17.8	43
Non-fuel sources	1.5	12	4.3	4.5
	pence/litre	lire/litre	pfenning/litre	centimes/litre

Source: Woods Mackenzie.

Exhibit 19 | Market share data, 1996

	ESTIMATED OVERALL MARKET SHARE				
	United Kingdom	Italy	Germany	France	Benelux
Exxon	16%	10%	11%	11%	16%
Shell	16	3	13	12	19
Total	5	n/a	2	21	6
Elf	3	n/a	6	21	n/a
Agip	n/a	19	2	1	n/a

Source: Woods Mackenzie

BP and Mobil's competitors in Europe

Historically, integrated companies had been able to mitigate the impact of price variations as upstream and downstream hedged each other's risk. Traditionally, high crude prices depressed downstream results and boosted upstream profits. Low oil prices supposedly had the opposite effect. However, from the mid-1980s, profitability fell both upstream (with lower crude prices) and downstream, where over-capacity and flat demand eroded margins.

Faced with these various challenges, downstream companies had taken steps to restructure, often in alliance with competitors. Overall, however, restructuring in Europe had remained less ambitious than in North America. The European players tended to only sell or swap assets. Their profitability was also lower, as illustrated in Exhibit 21.

Royal Dutch/Shell

Royal Dutch/Shell, the European market leader, had been founded in 1907 by merging a British and a Dutch group in order to counter the dominance of Standard Oil. With time, the group had become one of the world's largest corporations. Its operations in over 100 countries covered exploration and production of oil and natural gas, refining, marketing and chemicals, as well as coal mining, polymers, crop protection products and various metals.

In Europe, Shell was the second-largest refiner after Exxon, with annual capacity of 70 million tons and sales of 65 million tons. In marketing, it had been the leader with a 12 per cent market share and 8 500 retail sites. After the 1990–1 Gulf War, Shell had found itself with large inventories just as prices fell. The drop in profits had prompted a round of internal restructuring that had left analysts generally unimpressed. In 1996,

Case 3   BP–Mobil

Exhibit 20 | Western European oil consumption, 1987–96

	1987	1988	1989	1990	1991	1992	1993	1994	1995	1996
Austria	9 359	9 145	8 948	9 489	10 158	9 913	9 984	10 074	10 136	10 816
Belgium	17 486	17 788	17 205	17 022	18 559	19 240	18 656	19 188	18 884	21 262
Denmark	8 997	8 351	7 898	7 704	7 879	7 648	7 665	8 100	7 847	8 128
Finland	9 810	9 561	9 410	9 371	9 058	8 786	8 541	8 913	8 664	8 960
France	77 528	77 616	80 518	79 636	84 124	84 337	82 718	82 984	84 234	85 871
Germany	120 020	120 172	112 954	117 617	125 062	126 134	127 451	126 102	126 210	128 358
Greece	10 351	10 948	11 379	11 328	12 133	12 190	12 072	12 541	13 273	14 212
Ireland	3 895	3 675	3 715	4 199	4 419	4 678	4 655	5 112	5 266	5 454
Italy	82 842	82 126	85 593	85 412	84 224	85 686	83 841	84 279	86 865	85 694
Luxembourg	1 285	1 316	1 450	1 585	1 848	1 897	1 892	1 884	1 736	1 808
Netherlands	17 902	18 680	18 293	17 537	18 038	17 840	16 923	17 365	18 264	17 295
Portugal	8 208	8 566	10 993	10 776	10 940	12 192	11 475	11 335	12 267	11 841
Spain	36 415	41 060	41 063	40 672	40 570	41 882	44 997	48 504	50 613	49 272
Sweden	15 032	16 119	15 122	13 735	13 941	14 570	14 161	15 058	15 330	17 719
United Kingdom	67 703	72 316	73 029	73 941	74 507	75 472	75 790	74 957	73 836	75 241
EU total	486 833	497 439	497 570	500 024	515 460	522 465	520 821	526 396	533 425	541 931
Iceland	608	596	538	540	565	561	718	729	731	780
Norway	7 402	7 087	6 909	6 737	6 599	6 560	6 147	6 407	6 442	7 171
Switzerland	12 211	12 247	11 774	12 612	12 790	12 969	12 117	12 508	11 577	11 923
Turkey	20 387	20 436	20 763	21 326	20 905	22 020	25 412	24 016	26 725	27 889
Western Europe Total	527 441	537 805	537 554	541 239	556 319	564 575	565 215	570 056	578 900	589 694

Thousands of metric tonnes.
Source: National statistics.

Exhibit 21 | Comparative financial data, 1991–6

	ROACE (91–96)	ROE (91–96)	Average NI (91–96)	Average CAPEX (91–96)	Average Market Cap (91–96)	Average P/E (91–96)	Price to Book (91–96)	Net Income 1996	Balance Sheet 1996	
British Petroleum	6.8%	8.2%	1 501	5 092	38 378	15.4	2.1	3 025	12 914	(£m)
Mobil	8.6	10.2	1 823	4,288	34 886	21.7	2.0	3 043	19 118	(£m)
Royal Dutch/Shell	20.6	10.7	6 028	9 848	100 752	18.1	1.8	5 591	39 299	(£m)
Exxon	12.1	15.4	5 788	7 081	87 849	15.3	2.3	6 975	45 456	(US$m)
Agip	6.9	9.1	1 289	874	34 487	12.1	2.2	4 829	27 407	(LIT b)
Elf	4.3	4.6	744	4 167	19 592	24.0	1.3	7 518	99 709	(FF m)
Total	7.0	7.7	713	2 028	12 918	20.4	1.3	4 795	61 479	(FF m)
Repsol	13.9	15.7	769	1 332	8 967	12.1	1.9	120 932	986 886	(Ptas m)
Norsk Hydro	8.4	11.1	548	1 182	7 681	1.9	1.7	6 991	42 808	(NKR m)
Tosco	8.3	7.5	60	123	4 127	34.9	6.1	146	1 070	(US$m)
Lyondell	26.2	61.9	167	342	1 858	37.4	4.1	96	1 040	(US$m)
			(US$mn)	(US$mn)	(US$mn)					

Shell was planning to sell its Swiss refinery, close down lubricant plants and reduce its retail workforce.

An early mover into central and Eastern Europe, Shell had formed a joint venture with Agip and Conoco to take a 49 per cent stake in two Czech refineries. In 1996, it had swapped 38 of its sites in western Germany for 44 total sites in eastern Germany. It had also invested in some smaller markets such as Romania, Bulgaria and Slovenia.

Two recent public relations crises had damaged Shell's image. In 1995, it was forced to shelve plans to dump its used Brent Spar oil installation into the North Sea after vocal complaints led by Greenpeace and consumer boycotts orchestrated across Germany and the rest of Europe. And when Nigeria executed a leading dissident, human rights campaigners accused Shell of supporting a military dictatorship in contempt of minority rights.

Exxon

Exxon, the former Standard Oil of New Jersey (Esso), was the world's largest oil company in terms of revenue. After many of its Middle Eastern oil fields and facilities had been nationalised, Exxon had aggressively expanded exploration and production in safer regions in the 1980s. It suffered a major setback in 1989 when the *Exxon Valdez* tanker ran aground in Alaska, spilling 11 million gallons of oil. The initial clean-up bill was US$3.6 billion with a lawsuit seeking US$16.5 billion in compensatory and punitive damages still pending.

In Europe, Exxon had a retail market share of about 11 per cent. It had cut back on refining investments and was focusing on reducing costs. In refining, the size and integration of its assets gave it a cost advantage. In marketing, it had started a fierce price war in Britain with its 'Price Watch' campaign, which promised to match any competitor's prices within 5 kilometres.

Eastern Europe was a major area of new investment for Exxon. It had formed marketing joint ventures in Hungary (with state company AFOR) and in Poland (with a German partner). By 1996, 35 Esso stations were operating in Hungary, Poland, the Czech Republic and Slovakia.

National companies

Agip, the leading Italian integrated oil company, was part of the ENI Group. It had production and downstream activities in 13 countries and downstream activities only in a further 13 countries. However, most of its refining and marketing operations were in Italy (which accounted for 41 per cent of 1995 sales). Agip's strategy was to maintain a strong presence in the attractive Italian market while gradually expanding elsewhere in Europe. In Italy, it wanted to increase return on capital by reducing excess capacity in refining and by closing down less profitable retail sites.

Elf Aquitaine, France's largest industrial company, had been formed in 1965 by merging several small state companies. It was gradually being privatised; the government still had a 13.3 per cent stake. Elf was a diversified conglomerate with interests in health and hygiene products and was refocusing on oil. Under a new chief executive, explicit goals had been set in terms of cost savings, debt reduction and return on capital; non-core assets were sold, resulting in a US$1 billion net loss of 1994 from write-downs. Its new strategy was to focus on the upstream business, limiting downstream operations to France, Spain and Germany where Elf had a strong position. There were plans to leave the British market. Elf was expanding in Eastern Europe, although with mixed success. A joint venture with a Russian consortium and German public authorities to acquire 1 000 petrol stations in eastern Germany had proven expensive and unprofitable and Elf now wanted to sell.

Repsol, Spain's largest industrial company, had a 60 per cent share of the domestic oil market. The government, which had formed Repsol in 1987 to consolidate the fragmented Spanish oil industry, retained a 10 per cent stake. The company was expanding its natural gas business through acquisitions, mostly, but not solely, in Spain. Repsol's strategy was to defend its domestic position while expanding natural gas exploration and production. Targets for international expansion included Latin America as well as Portugal, southern France and northern Africa.

Total, Europe's fourth-largest oil and gas producer, had over 10 000 retail stations across the continent. It was listed on the New York Stock Exchange, yet the French government retained a 5 per cent stake. The company had invested aggressively upstream in exploration, especially in the former Soviet Union. Efforts to restore downstream profitability had included cost cutting and selling off less profitable assets (for example, refineries in Portugal and the Czech Republic were sold in 1995). In France, competition from the supermarkets had hurt profitability, prompting the company to trim retailing costs and launch an aggressive effort to regain market share.

Total wanted to expand in high-growth regions such as central and Eastern Europe, Portugal and Turkey, with a focus on marketing and distributing motor fuel. Total had invested FF 700 million in Hungary and the Czech Republic between 1992 and 1994. A joint venture with Benzina, owned by the Czech government, had been disappointing in terms of sites and market share. In Hungary, Total had 25 per cent of the LPG market after acquiring two marketing companies, Egaz and Kogaz, in 1993.

BP and Mobil

British Petroleum

One of the world's largest petroleum and petrochemical groups, BP had operations in some 70 countries, more than 56 000 employees and annual revenues of US$79 billion. It had been fully privatised in 1987 when the British government sold its 51 per cent stake and had gradually become more diversified and decentralised.

Upstream, BP focused on oil exploration, with production facilities in Alaska, the Gulf of Mexico, Colombia and the North Sea. (Exhibit 22 summarises BP's upstream activities.) Downstream, BP had a weak position in the United States. Aggressive restructuring and asset disposals had not quite solved the problem of high costs and asset quality.

The company, however, had forced the admiration of industry watchers by staging a remarkable recovery under the successive CEOs David Simon and John Browne. In 1992, an unprecedented quarterly loss had caused it to nearly default on interest payments. Since then, BP increased earnings to US$3.2 billion (from US$900 million), while the share price had more than doubled. (See Exhibit 22 for an overview of cumulative returns.) By 1995, dividend payments were back above their 1992 level. (Exhibits 23 and 24 give financial data.) Analysts expected financial improvement to continue until at least the year 2000, thanks to higher output (by 5 per cent per annum on average) and a better product mix.

BP was seen as a leader in cutting costs: It had halved its total workforce to 56 500 in 1995 from 111 900 four years earlier. The company also sought greater efficiency through consolidation, reorganisation, and optimisation of storage and logistics. In refining, its strategy was to sell or close unprofitable refineries, upgrade others and generally improve operating reliability. It had recently spent £171 million on a five-year, worldwide rebranding effort, with mixed success.

Europe was BP's main market, with 48 per cent of refinery capacity and 49 per cent of sales. The company had downstream operations in 18 countries. It employed some 15 500 people, including 4 000 service station staff, and owned, wholly or in part, eight European refineries with combined capacity of 760 000 bpd. (The planned sale of the Lavera plant in southern France would reduce this to 575 000 bpd.) BP and partner Texaco had also announced the closure of their Pernis refinery and the consolidation of their joint refining at BP's Europort plant in Holland. (Exhibit 25 has data on BP's refineries.)

BP sold 825 000 bpd of oil products through 5 600 retail sites. Its market share, 8 per cent in both fuels and lubricants, had been steady for years. (Exhibit 26 shows BP's market performance.)

In marketing, its two-pronged strategy was to upgrade facilities at prime retail sites to improve petrol throughput and increase non-fuel revenue and to pursue expansion in Eastern Europe where it planned to quadruple its 100 service stations. In the last two years, BP had sold 90 service stations in southwestern France to Repsol, 60 other French sites to PetroFina and eight Austrian sites to Shell. In the United Kingdom, it had acquired independent fuel distributor Charringtons.

BP's success in cost cutting had spawned imitators and had not produced notable gains in its market share. Analysts believed that European oil companies (including BP) had cut 'all the fat and some of the muscle' and doubted whether any further cost reductions were possible.

Mobil

Mobil, founded as Standard Oil of New York, was the world's third-largest oil company after Exxon and Shell. It operated in over 100 countries with 50 000 employees and annual revenues of US$73 billion; it owned 21 refineries and 28 tankers and shared ownership in over 58 000 kilometres of pipeline. Its response to the 1970s' oil shock had been to diversify. This had culminated in the acquisition of the Montgomery Ward department stores. Mobil later sold that business to concentrate once more on oil.

The company had worldwide earnings of US$2.9 billion in 1995, nearly double the 1992 level of US$1.5 billion. It had not suffered as badly as BP from the Gulf

Exhibit 22 | BP's upstream activities, 1990–6

War, but its performance had not improved as dramatically either. Analysts saw potential for more cost cutting and increased production. Exhibit 27 summarises Mobil's financial results.

Upstream, Mobil was a major player in both oil and natural gas. Output, which had dropped in 1994, was expected to increase 2–3 per cent annually in the medium term. A significant share of Mobil's revenue came from international exploration and production in Indonesia, Qatar, Nigeria, the North Sea and Canada, where it had a share in the Hibernia offshore oil field.

Mobil had a strong downstream position in the United States, especially in terms of market share and retail network. It was the world's leader in finished lubricants, with large market share in all regions. As part of its global strategy, Mobil had made considerable R&D investments in lubricants, and it was recognised as a quality brand in this business.

In Europe, Mobil's downstream operations had remained relatively weak despite extensive rationalisation. Analysts wondered whether it would have to leave the market. Mobil owned, wholly or in part, six European refineries with capacity of 350 000 bpd (about 16 per cent of its total capacity) but was planning to close its Woerthe plant in Germany. It made 25 per cent of its sales in Europe where its market share in fuels was only 4 per cent. In lubricants, however, it had 10 per cent share (Exhibit 28 has details). In 1996, Mobil's 8 000 workforce sold 550 000 bpd of oil products. About 2 000 service station staff operated 3 300 service stations in 22 European countries. In the last two years, Mobil had swapped 18 of its French service stations for eight Repsol stations in southern Spain.

In Germany, Mobil did not sell any retail fuels under its own brand but it was a major supplier to Aral, a joint venture with German group Veba Oel in which Mobil had a 28 per cent stake. Aral, which had by far the largest network of service stations in Germany, with a 20 per cent market share, had been one of the first German retailers to open convenience stores. It was energetically expanding non-fuel retailing and considered selling McDonald's hamburgers. For some products, however, and in other countries, Mobil competed with Aral.

The alliance

Discussions between Mobil and BP had begun in the summer of 1995; lawyers had become involved in October. The two companies had decided to form a partnership, with no changes in ownership of assets or equity. Setting up a traditional joint venture would have taken much longer because of the complex business of valuing assets, technologies and trademarks. Both BP and Mobil were familiar with using partnerships in their upstream activities.

The partnership would operate refineries, buy crude oil and other feedstocks for these refineries, refine and convert downstream products such as lubricants, and market them, both to retail and to industrial and

Exhibit 23 | British Petroleum earnings summary, 1991–6

	1991	1992	1993	1994	1995	1996E
Exploration and production						
United Kingdom	870	795	1 086	1 527	1 492	1 636
Rest of Europe	423	483	399	257	330	304
United States	1 673	1 607	1 277	920	1 251	1 246
Rest of world	54	91	123	169	386	437
Total	3 020	2 976	2 885	2 873	3 459	3 623
Refining and marketing						
United Kingdom	115	−132	36	119	92	13
Rest of Europe	407	175	245	189	−22	280
United States	211	2	270	173	43	250
Rest of world	586	416	582	509	528	591
Total	1 319	461	1 133	990	641	1 134
Chemicals						
United States	−19	64	26	35	216	175
Non-US	76	−106	−128	350	−216	750
Total	57	−42	−102	385	0	925
Other and corporate	−199	−60	−164	−79	−61	−13
Replacement cost operating profit	4 197	3 335	3 752	4 169	4 039	5 669
Gain/(loss) from asset sales	428	124	−60	55	−5	−11
Restructuring costs	−103	−1 884	−300	0	−1 525	0
Inventory gain/(loss)	−1 113	−187	−426	95	4	95
Historical cost operating profit	3 409	1 388	2 966	4 319	2 513	5 753
Interest expense	−1 280	−1 190	−1 013	−829	−787	−600
Pre-tax income	2 129	198	1 953	3 490	1 726	5 153
Income tax	−1 451	−1 000	−1 027	−1 059	−1 310	−1 476
Minority interest	57	−9	−7	−18	8	−20
Historical cost income	735	−811	919	2 413	424	3 657
Exploration and production						
US capital employed	7 639	7 237	7 064	7 017	7 124	7 480
US adjusted earnings	931	883	682	546	828	674
Foreign capital employed	11 199	9 912	9 787	10 594	11 502	12 422
Foreign adjusted earnings	843	784	969	1 042	1 322	1 441
Refining and marketing						
US capital employed	3 697	3 482	2 802	2 775	1 571	1 602
US adjusted earnings	139	1	176	112	59	162
Foreign capital employed	6 317	5 784	5 476	5 947	5 663	5 890
Foreign adjusted earnings	720	308	578	577	553	592

All numbers are in millions of dollars.
Source: Merrill Lynch, 1996, 'BP and Mobil – similar in size but different in the way they are'.

Exhibit 24 | BP Refining and marketing profitability, 1992–6

	1992	1993	1994	1995	1996	Average
Net profit after tax (£ million)						
Refining	20	180	6	–68	194	66.4
Marketing	240	575	640	474	485	482.8
Total	260	755	646	406	679	549.2
Operating capital (£ million)						
Total	6 137	5 593	5 591	4 637	5 137	5 419
Refining	53%	56%	61%	54%	43%	53.4%
Marketing	47	44	39	46	57	46.6
Return on average capital employed (ROACE)						
Refining	0.6%	5.6%	0.2%	–2.3%	8.2%	2.5%
Marketing	8.3	21.5	27.6	22.0	19.2	19.7
Total	4.2	12.9	11.6	7.9	13.9	10.1

Source: BP financial and operating information, 1992–6.

Exhibit 25 | Summary of BP downstream activity, 1991–5

Crude oil sources[i]	Thousand barrels per day				
	1991	1992	1993	1994	1995
Produced from own reserves[ii]					
United Kingdom	359	364	370	429	403
Rest of Europe	81	87	88	81	69
United States	738	688	627	605	572
Rest of world	37	23	32	32	56
	1 215	1 162	1 117	1 147	1 100
Produced from associated undertakings					
Abu Dhabi	141	131	125	118	113
Total production	**1 356**	**1 293**	**1 242**	**1 265**	**1 213**
Purchased					
United States	358	427	568	572	728
Rest of world	1 474	2 016	2 087	2 434	2 648
	1 832	2 443	2 655	3 006	3 376
Total	**3 188**	**3 736**	**3 897**	**4 271**	**4 589**

[i] Crude oil in respect of which royalty is taken in cash is shown as a purchase: royalty oil taken in kind is excluded from both production and purchased oil.

[ii] Oil production includes natural gas liquids and condensate.

Crude oil sales	Thousand barrels per day				
	1991	1992	1993	1994	1995
United Kingdom	1 167	1 301	1 378	1 860	2 004
Rest of Europe	40	88	82	90	116
United States	391	479	497	534	693
Rest of world	27	33	30	15	24
Total	**1 625**	**1 901**	**1 987**	**2 499**	**2 837**

(Continues)

REFINERY THROUGHPUTS AND UTILISATION

Refinery throughputs[i]	Thousand barrels per day				
	1991	1992	1993	1994	1995
United Kingdom	194	185	184	183	193
Rest of Europe	525	570	617	593	661
United States	701	711	717	621	713
Rest of world	297	307	327	339	332
	1 717	1 773	1 845	1 736	1 899
For BP by others	21	13	11	9	10
Total	1 738	1 786	1 856	1 745	1 909
Crude distillation capacity at 31 December	2 066	2 020	1 963	2 004	2 000
Crude distillation capacity utilisation[ii]	90%	94%	97%	94%	104%

[i] Includes actual crude oil and other feedstock input both for BP and third parties.

[ii] Crude distillation capacity utilisation is defined as the percentage utilisation of capacity per calendar day over the year after making allowance for average annual shutdowns at BP refineries (net rated capacity).

Crude oil input	Thousand barrels per day				
	1991	1992	1993	1994	1995
Low sulphur crude	69%	62%	63%	72%	71%
High sulphur crude	31	38	37	28	29

Refinery yield[i]	Thousand barrels per day				
	1991	1992	1993	1994	1995
Aviation fuels	171	186	184	192	194
Gasolines	659	712	676	668	704
Middle distillates	530	549	603	574	548
Fuel oil	220	245	282	214	215
Other products	212	218	230	196	286
Total	1 792	1 910	1 975	1 844	1 947

[i] Refinery yields exceed throughputs because of volumetric expansion.

Exhibit 26 | BP's pre-alliance market share, 1991–5

	ESTIMATED MARKET SHARE					
	1991	1992	1993	1994	1995	Rank
Benelux	12.1%	12.2%	12.0%	12.3%	12.6%	4
France	7.8	8.1	8.0	8.5	8.0	5
Germany	8.2	8.6	8.5	8.8	8.8	6
Italy						
Spain/Portugal	8.4	8.1	6.9	6.9	6.7	3
United Kingdom	12.5	12.0	11.9	11.5	11.5	3
Ireland	12.6					
Austria	9.4	8.9	9.1	9.2	9.3	4
Switzerland	13.5	13.1	12.4	18.0	18.6	2
Denmark						
Norway						
Sweden	7.1	2.6	2.0	0.1	0.1	
Finland						
Greece	12.8	13.2	13.4	13.0	13.5	1
Turkey	8.0	8.0	8.0	8.1	8.1	

Source: Woods Mackenzie.

Exhibit 27 | Mobil earnings summary, 1991–6

	1991	1992	1993	1994	1995	1996E
US Petroleum						
Exploration and production	189	348	363	125	−107	444
Refining and marketing	116	−145	151	241	226	448
Total	305	203	514	366	119	892
Foreign Petroleum						
Exploration and production	1 094	1 042	1 289	951	952	1 150
Refining and marketing	819	329	554	−33	447	846
Total	1 913	1 371	1 843	918	1 399	1 996
Total Petroleum	2 218	1 574	2 357	1 284	1 518	2 888
Chemicals	217	136	44	102	1 164	375
Financing	−385	−316	−127	−209	−295	−240
Other and corporate	−130	−86	−190	−98	−11	−150
Accounting changes	0	−446	0	0	0	0
Net income	1 920	862	2 084	1 079	2 376	2 873
Exploration and production						
US capital employed	6 443	5 670	4 925	4 420	4 035	4 116
US adjusted earnings	189	423	432	306	332	444
Foreign capital employed	3 760	3 621	3 836	4 076	4 474	4 832
Foreign adjusted earnings	1 045	1 066	1 098	1 018	1 065	1 150
Refining and marketing						
US capital employed	4 705	5 286	5 071	5 155	5 128	5 231
US adjusted earnings	212	−17	296	273	330	448
Foreign capital employed	7 362	7 193	7 464	7 356	7 770	8 159
Foreign adjusted earnings	805	370	792	681	805	846

All numbers are in millions of dollars.

Source: Merrill Lynch, 1996, 'BP and Mobil – similar in size but different in the way they are'.

Exhibit 28 | Mobil's pre-alliance market share, 1991–5

	ESTIMATED MARKET SHARE					
	1991	1992	1993	1994	1995	Rank
Benelux	2.3%	2.2%	2.2%	2.3%	2.9%	8
France	5.5	5.3	4.5	4.6	4.3	6
Germany	7.1	7.4	7.5	7.3	7.1	7
Italy						
Spain/Portugal	2.2	2.0	2.1	2.8	2.6	6
United Kingdom	5.0	5.2	4.9	5.2	5.3	6
Ireland						
Austria	12.0	12.4	12.2	13.0	12.9	3
Switzerland	2.7	2.8	2.8	2.6	2.0	8
Denmark						
Norway	6.6	3.1	0.1	0.1	0.1	
Sweden						
Finland						
Greece	11.9	12.2	11.2	11.1	11.4	3
Turkey	10.9	10.8	12.6	12.9	12.6	3

Source: Woods Mackenzie.

Exhibit 29 | Structure of the BP–Mobil alliance

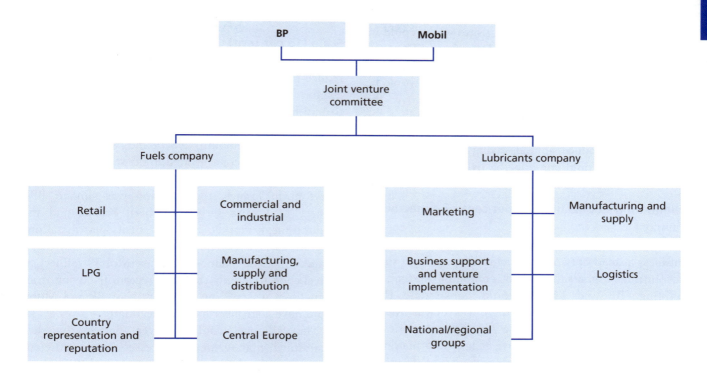

commercial customers, in Western and Eastern Europe (including west Russia), as well as in Turkey and Cyprus. The deal did not extend to international operations such as exploration and production, international trading, and basic research and development. Aviation fuels and lubricants, marine fuels and lubricants, and shipping, as well as natural gas marketing and chemicals, were also excluded.

In each country, Mobil and BP would combine their fuel and lubricant businesses through two separate partnerships, one for fuels, one for lubricants. BP would operate the fuels business as a whole, while Mobil would operate the lubricants business. All 8 000 service stations in the combined network would be rebranded with BP colours. They would display the alliance's logo and distribute Mobil oils.

BP as Fuels Operator and Mobil as Lubricants Operator would be controlled by a supervisory committee which would approve business plans, major acquisitions, closures, disposals and investments, and oversee the national Fuels and Lubricants partnerships. BP and Mobil would have the power to veto any of the committee's decisions. Exhibit 29 shows the alliance's organisational design.

BP and Mobil would have different equity stakes in each business: in fuels, BP would have 70 per cent and Mobil 30 per cent; in lubricants, Mobil would hold 51 per cent and BP 49 per cent. This reflected the value of the two partners' assets in February 1996 as well as their strength and expertise across Europe. Profits and losses in each partnership would be shared in the same proportion as the firms' equity stakes. If either partner contributed less assets than the agreed ratio in a given country, it would have to bridge the gap through cash.

BP and Mobil would hand over all relevant fuels and lubricants assets to the joint venture (including 10 refineries, terminals, retail sites, pipelines and truck fleets). BP would transfer its lubricants activities to Mobil, and Mobil would transfer its fuels activities to BP. Even though the ownership of assets would not be transferred, the joint venture would enjoy indefinite and exclusive use of those assets. Employees would transfer from one company to the other where appropriate. Central services (such as information technology, human resources, legal and accounting management) would be merged under BP management. The new structure was expected to be fully implemented by mid-1998.

The expected benefits

The alliance would have US$5 billion in assets (US$3.4 billion from BP) and sales of US$20 billion, with an estimated 12 per cent market share in fuel retail (10 per cent according to the European Commission) and 18 per cent in lubricants. Combining the two retail networks would lead to redundant sites which could be sold without affecting overall sales volume. This and other asset disposals would produce one-off revenues of US$200 million. However, this one-off benefit would be more than offset by exceptional charges to cover the costs of the alliance in its first year (US$490 million for BP and US$330 million for Mobil). The deal was also expected to produce annual savings of US$400–500 million (most would come in the five largest markets) from three main sources.

Eliminating duplication (60 per cent of expected savings)

Most of the savings would come from operating as one business instead of two. This included operating a single accounting organisation and computer system. In refining, BP and Mobil would consolidate their portfolio, selling assets where there was a clear overlap in capacity (this was the case for three refineries in Bavaria, among others), a move that would maximise capacity utilisation. Both companies had found it difficult to find buyers for individual refineries in the past, but they hoped that a range of assets would be easier to sell.

Synergies (25 per cent)

These would arise from the complementarity of the two partners' downstream organisations. In terms of geography, a bigger network of stations with the right spread across Europe would cut distribution costs. In the United Kingdom, for instance, Mobil's network in the south of England complemented BP's strong presence in Scotland. In terms of product range, BP's strength in fuels complemented Mobil's leadership in lubricants. Duplicated storage and distribution facilities would be eliminated. The alliance would manage fuel storage at a pan-European level, ensuring a better balance relative to demand and reducing dependence on expensive external storage.

Thousands of jobs across Europe were earmarked for cuts, many from closing down overlapping service stations. In particular, between 2 000 and 3 000 non-service-station jobs (out of a total 17 500) would be cut. BP and Mobil were already the industry's cost leaders in petrol retailing; they had built increasingly large self-service stations and their combined network had lower costs than the small operators. Many competitors (especially national companies such as Total, Elf, Agip and Repsol) were thought to be unable to match those cuts. Their governments, opposed to layoffs and fearing to lose control of a 'strategic' industry, were unlikely to let them merge or enter cost-cutting alliances.

Scale (15 per cent)

More refineries spread across major markets would reduce high transport costs to the retail site (shown in Exhibit 30). In many cases, this would obviate the need to buy from competitors.[4] In the United Kingdom, BP had been forced to buy from other refiners because its refinery at Grangemouth, in Scotland, was too far from its retail network concentrated in the south of England. The alliance would now source from Mobil's refinery at Coryton. In France, the situation was similar: BP's refinery at Lavera served southern France and the Mediterranean market, but most of its petrol stations were in the Paris area. This forced it to buy from competitors. The alliance could use Mobil's refinery at Gravenchon to supply the Paris region. If buying from competitors was still necessary, at least BP and Mobil would have a stronger hand to negotiate.

The alliance could deliver better logistics, streamlined management processes, more efficient procurement, and economies of scale which BP saw as vital in the downstream industry. Together, Mobil and BP would be able to compete on prices with the largest European players. In particular, greater power in procurement, especially in lubricants packaging and non-fuel retail site supplies, was an obvious benefit.

Beyond cash savings

The two partners also expected other advantages from combining their operations. 'The key issue is competitive performance,' said John Browne, CEO of BP. 'BP and Mobil were number three and four in the European market; now we will be up there with the big players.' Together, they would be able to enter new markets, especially in central and Eastern Europe. They would achieve economies of scale in investment and logistics to enter these attractive markets. They would be in a better position to buy privatised companies, since governments favoured large investors.

A larger distribution network would also help attract food-retailing partners in new forecourt convenience stores and be better able to counter the supermarkets' negotiating power. Additional capacity to implement environmental investments would also be welcome. Finally, a wider geographic spread would make the joint venture less vulnerable to cyclical downturns as market conditions differed across Europe. For example, a strong, diversified pan-European player would be less affected by price wars in the United

Exhibit 30 | Transportation costs of petrol

Transportation	Cost
German rail	$4.34 per mt + $0.034 per km per mt
Polish rail	$2.38 per mt + $0.028 per km per mt
German road	$0.046 per km per mt
Czech pipe	$0.02 per km per mt
United Kingdom pipeline	$0.013 to $0.02 per km per mt
Rhine barge	$0.022 to $0.04 per km per mt

All amounts are in US dollars.
mt = metric tonne
Source: BP.

Kingdom or domineering supermarkets in France. Size was seen as an important advantage, since it could smooth out some of the competitive conditions across Europe.

The uncertain future

Analysts' initial reaction to the deal was largely favourable. Most saw the alliance as an innovative response to the industry's problems; they underlined the advantages in terms of market power and brand power, as well as the complementariness of the two businesses. Both partners would gain from the deal: BP would be able to further cut costs and continue its expansion. For Mobil, it was an opportunity to reaffirm its position in the European market. 'The subtext of this BP-Mobil deal is that you need a 10 per cent market share to survive in the European market,' commented investment bank Morgan Stanley.

But there were some negative interpretations as well. In a sense, the alliance was an admission of failure: BP and Mobil were acknowledging their inability to achieve economies of scale on their own. Since neither could grow big enough and neither wanted to leave the market, they had to compromise. Another concern was that the deal still left Mobil and BP in a middle position, stuck between the national players (each strong in its own domestic market) and overall leaders Shell and Exxon. Some analysts also questioned the extent of possible synergies, considering that the two companies were not a perfect fit. 'A merger isn't a catch-all solution for the industry's fundamental problems,' said one. 'When you combine weak resources and low-quality assets, you do not make a strong company.'

While BP and Mobil had deliberately avoided an acquisition, the partnership still raised governance issues. Both partners had to give up a measure of control and flexibility. The supervisory committee had considerable operational independence, but it remained subject to a veto from either company. While Mobil and BP both had a lot of experience in managing upstream alliances, no oil company had ever attempted such an ambitious deal downstream. Initially, their interests seemed aligned, but questions about the longer term remained.

There was also the tricky Aral issue. Mobil was now allied with two competing groups. Given the strength of the BP-Mobil marketing network, Aral was the clear loser. Some analysts felt that Mobil should sell its stake to enable Aral to find another partner. Others criticised Mobil's ability to manage complex alliances as the European Commission began investigating the two joint ventures.

The daunting task of actually merging operations still lay ahead. BP and Mobil executives were aware that most large mergers, no matter their strategic logic, failed to create value for shareholders. The challenges involved in bringing together different products, services, management systems and cultures, as well as workforces, while competing in the marketplace often precluded benefits. These issues could be even more problematic in this deal, because BP and Mobil continued to compete as independent corporations in petrol and other businesses elsewhere in the world.

Analysts also wondered how the relationship between the two partners would evolve over time. What if the deal turned out to be a half-hearted compromise that neither side was fully satisfied with? Neither was there a guarantee that European Union regulators would approve the deal. The combined market share of the two companies gave them a strong presence in several countries. Determined to root out anti-competitive behaviour, the European Commission was targeting large, headline-grabbing mergers. If the alliance was shown to establish a dominant position that significantly restricted competition, the Commission could stop the deal. To overcome this hurdle, BP and Mobil had to provide enough information for the Commission to make a quick decision and they had to demonstrate that there was no threat to competition.

Commentators were already speculating about how BP and Mobil's competitors would respond to the move. Was it the beginning of industry-wide realignment? The next few years could be crucial. What would the two companies have to do to turn their deal into a success? Was the deal a masterstroke, or insufficient as some claimed? What would Mr Browne have to do to keep the performance of BP on track?

Endnotes

1. Known as gasoline in the United States. We use the word 'petrol' throughout to refer to retail motor fuels (petrol, diesel and other refinery products), unless otherwise specified.
2. One barrel equals 42 US gallons, or 159 litres.
3. The world's largest refinery was at Yukong in South Korea (770 000 bpd).
4. Because even the integrated oil companies didn't have refineries near all their major markets, they were often faced with a difficult choice: either they bought fuels internally and paid the cost of shipment, or they purchased from competitors. For this reason, major refining players such as Shell and Exxon often managed to extract high prices from retailers.

Case 4

Compaq in crisis

Adrian Elton

Eckhard Pfeiffer was named CEO of Compaq Computer Corporation in 1991. Since 1991, Compaq's annual revenues have increased almost ten times (see Exhibit 1) and its stock price has increased 1 072 per cent.[1] Compaq became the world's largest PC vendor in 1994 – two years ahead of schedule. In 1998, it was named Company of the Year by *Forbes* magazine. 'As long as Pfeiffer is at the wheel, Compaq will continue to execute with relentless efficiency,' said *Fortune* magazine in 1996.[2] In 1998, *The Economist* declaimed, 'Compaq's rivals now fall into two categories: those it is leaving behind and those whose corporate markets it threatens.'[3]

On 18 April 1999, Eckhard Pfeiffer was unceremoniously fired by Compaq's board of directors. How did the man who turned Compaq around in 1991 and built it into the premier PC vendor end up in such a position? What strategic decision during his tenure led to his downfall? What problems has he bequeathed to the CEO who follows him?

Company history

Compaq was founded in 1982 by three former Texas Instruments executives, Rod Canion, Jim Harris and Bill Murto. Their guiding idea was to build a 'portable' version of the IBM PC. They persuaded Benjamin Rosen of Sevin Rosen Management Company to fund a prototype, and later the company, and Compaq, was born. Rod Canion was its first president and Rosen became chairman of the board.

Compaq had two major advantages. First, it built an IBM-compatible machine that could run IBM software right out of the box. Demand for PCs was so great that IBM couldn't keep up, and dealers were happy to have Compaq fill the gaps.[4] Second, Compaq didn't develop its own sales force and so its dealers didn't have any direct competition from the company. This was in stark contrast to the other major computer makers of the time, IBM and Apple.[5]

Compaq began setting records in its first year of operation with sales of US$111 million. This was a record in first-year sales for a new business in any industry. In 1983, it began to sell in Europe and shipped its 100 000th PC. In 1985, the company began trading on the New York Stock Exchange and earned a place on the *Fortune* 500 list. No other company has grown so fast.

In 1986, Compaq became a serious threat to IBM by introducing a computer that used Intel's new 386 processor nine months before IBM did. Sales continued to increase, breaking US$1 billion in 1987. Compaq introduced the first battery-powered laptop in 1988, and revenues that year were US$2.1 billion, twice what they were the previous year. In 1990, international sales topped US sales for the first time, making Compaq a truly global corporation. Total sales were US$3.2 billion, second only to IBM. All this in less than a decade.

In 1991, Compaq experienced its first hard times. There was a general industry downturn, and Compaq had the first layoffs in its history, releasing 12 per cent of its workforce. On 24 October, a day after reporting Compaq's first quarterly loss, Rod Canion was 'unexpectedly removed'[6] from his position as CEO, and Eckhard Pfeiffer succeeded him.

This case was prepared under the direction of Professor Robert E. Hoskisson. The case is intended to be used as the basis for class discussion rather than to illustrate either effective or ineffective handling of an administrative or strategic situation.

Exhibit 1 | Compaq's revenue growth, 1983–98 (US$mn)

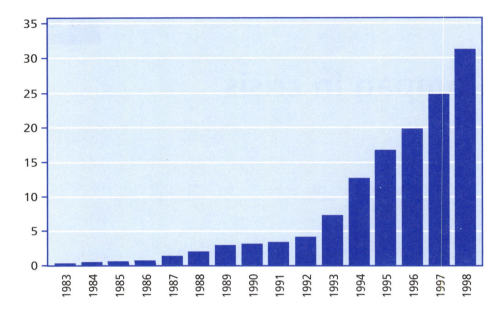

Sources: *Compaq Home Page*, Financial Highlights: www.compaq.com/corporate/1998ar; P. Burrows, 1994, 'Compaq stretches for the crown', *Business Week*, 11 July, p. 140; 'Compaq reports record 1992 sales', 1993, *Business Wire*, 26 January; 'Compaq's history', 1991, *The Atlanta Journal and Constitution*, p. C3; 'Compaq Computer financial results', 1989, *Business Wire*, 1 February; 'Compaq Computer financial results', 1986, *Business Wire*, 1 February; 'Compaq Computer financial results', 1985, *Business Wire*, 11 February; *Christian Science Monitor*, 1984; 'Compaq wins by thinking big', *The San Diego Union-Tribune*, 19 April, p. D6.

Ben Rosen indicated that Canion's dismissal was not a knee-jerk reaction to bad quarterly results. He indicated that the board had been discussing creating an 'office of the president' to be shared by Canion and Pfeiffer, but Canion was not pleased by the idea. Forced to choose between them, the board opted in favour of Pfeiffer, mainly because of his international experience in a rapidly globalising industry.[7]

Michael Swavely, former president of Compaq's North American operations who retired in July 1991, commented, 'Change was overdue at Compaq.' Past success had generated a 'self-satisfied view of the world' that produced a reluctance to change, a fatal attribute in any industry, but especially in computer technology.[8] The reasons Rosen gave for Compaq's falling sales and declining market share were tardiness in lowering prices and not enough emphasis on its core market, desktop PCs.[9] Rod Canion had believed that Compaq could sell at a higher price based on its brand reputation for quality, and the company quickly found that was a fallacy.[10]

Compaq under Eckhard Pfeiffer

Eckhard Pfeiffer began his career at Compaq in 1983 when he left Texas Instruments to launch Compaq's European operation. He was very successful, opening 20 subsidiaries and increasing sales in Europe, accounting for 54 per cent of Compaq's revenues in 1990.[11] Rod Canion brought Pfeiffer to Houston in January 1991 to be chief operating officer, and he succeeded Canion as CEO in October of 1991.

The first thing Pfeiffer did as CEO was cut the gross margins from 35 to 27 per cent[12] by slashing prices and effectively declaring war on the companies who built clones, which at that time held 60 per cent of the market.[13] He also fired 25 per cent of the workforce and increased the number of resellers.[14] Even amid restructuring, Compaq still managed to finish the year with increased revenue of US$3.3 billion, slightly up from US$3.1 billion the year before. Pfeiffer, with vision and determination, set a goal: Compaq will be the world's biggest PC producer in 1997 – in only six years. Industry analysts didn't think he could do it in such a short time.[15]

The first Compaq computers were high in performance and high in price, and they sold well until competitors introduced lower-priced machines with fewer extras.[16] Compaq regrouped and in 1992 introduced a new low-cost PC called the ProLinea. There was 'a lot of doubt', Pfeiffer recalls. 'Would we … bastardize the Compaq name?'[17] Instead, the ProLinea put Compaq back on track for continued growth, rapidly becoming the company's best-selling PC.[18] Compaq nearly doubled its US market share to 23 per cent, surpassing both IBM and Apple. It also emerged as the favoured PC supplier in Europe, holding 10.3 per cent market share.[19] Revenues continued to rise, reaching US$4.1 billion at the end of the year.[20]

In August 1993, Compaq took another giant stride forward and introduced the Presario, another PC directed towards individual consumers, especially those with little or no previous computing experience. The Presario broke all the records at Compaq, selling twice as fast as the ProLinea in the first 60 days.[21] The Presario quickly became, and has remained, Compaq's mainstay, and the company finished the year with US$7.2 billion in revenues.

In January 1994, the business world was shocked when Compaq announced that it would no longer exclusively use Intel's microprocessor chips in its computers. In explaining the choice to buy from Advanced Micro Devices (AMD), Compaq told the press that AMD was more than just an Intel clone; it also had products that would potentially fill some holes where Intel did not compete.[22] Compaq also began to sell the Presario in Japan in 1995, traditionally a tough market for American companies.

Pfeiffer convened a company meeting in an arena in Houston in January 1995 where, in front of 16 000 employees and their families, he announced, 'We are No. 1! We made it in 1994! We've replaced IBM as the world's top PC vendor!'[23] Compaq had reached a six-year goal in only two years. Although Compaq products were not all that original, it had realised this accomplishment through exceptional execution. When Pfeiffer took over, he began by cutting prices and costs, not by looking for brilliant new engineering. He said, 'A ground rule is to set very aggressive cost goals to get very attractive entry-level products.'[24] Compaq finished 1994 with US$10.9 billion in sales.

Having conquered the PC market, Compaq shifted its strategic focus slightly in 1995. It began to add value to the computers it sold, emphasising built-in networking and system management features.[25] The company also launched a worldwide service and support system to assure information technology workers that Compaq systems could reliably run business-critical applications and that the company could deliver the service and support they required. This brought Compaq one step closer to becoming a computer company rather than just a PC company.[26] Deciding to operate in the service sector as well as the hardware sector put the company in more direct competition with industry giants Hewlett-Packard and IBM.

Compaq also decided to move into the networking business and signed a joint venture deal with Cisco Systems to build low-cost gear to connect servers to networks. Likewise, it signed a marketing agreement with Germany's ITK, which produces modems that link portable PCs to servers. It also closed a deal with Thomas-Conrad Co., a manufacturer of local-network cards for PCs. The final transaction in November 1995 was the acquisition of NetWorth, Inc., a company that makes high-speed network gear. All of this gave Compaq the technology to offer a complete networking package to its customers.[27] Revenues continued to rise, and the company finished the year with US$14.8 billion in sales.[28]

In 1996, Compaq landed two big contracts, one with Smith Barney and the other with General Motors. The contracts included purchase of both PCs and servers, a major step forward for enterprise-wide client-server computing.[29] Compaq's ProLiant server captured nearly 80 per cent of the Pentium server market, and Compaq shipped its 1 millionth server in November 1996, the first company in the industry to reach this milestone.[30]

However, things were beginning to strain. In March, Pfeiffer had to warn analysts that Compaq might not meet its first-quarter earnings estimates, and the stock plunged. He acted quickly, ordering incentives for dealers and price cuts to lift demand. Revenues for the quarter jumped 42 per cent, and the stock recovered. This should have been cause for celebration, but the cost to the company of hitting the growth target was a drop in profit margin to 20 per cent – the lowest it had ever been. A troubling fact emerged: Compaq had been running twice as fast just to stay in place. Sales and revenues had increased, but profits hadn't moved. Pfeiffer wanted the company to continue growing at the rapid rate of the past years and reach US$40 billion in revenues by the year 2000. Following a meeting with managers from around the world, a new strategy was forged: move aggressively into new product areas that will make Compaq a full-line information-technology company, capable of competing with IBM and Hewlett-Packard.[31] Also, a new strategic approach was needed because IBM had reversed the trend and begun to take PC market share from Compaq.[32]

In May 1997, Compaq announced another step into the networking business by acquiring Microcom, Inc., a company that makes networking gear. The line between the networking business and the computer business had become increasingly blurry, as computer companies rushed to increase sales in the lucrative industry. Also, in June, Compaq announced that it was expanding by purchasing Tandem Computers, another computer maker, which helped the company expand its line to include more powerful servers and parallel commercial systems.[33]

More symptoms of internal problems cropped up in 1997, as Pfeiffer had to make an extra effort to soothe its resellers after Compaq officials said they wanted a 'more direct relationship with customers'. Because of the inroads that Dell Computer had made into Compaq's sales, many resellers interpreted the remark to mean that Compaq was seriously considering turning to the direct on-line business model practised by Dell. Pfeiffer had to summon distributors to the company's Houston headquarters and reassert his commitment to Compaq's traditional distribution channels.[34]

In October 1997, Compaq paid its first dividend and finished the year with sales of US$24.5 billion.[35] However, its next move surprised the industry; in 1998, Compaq acquired Digital Equipment Company (DEC) for US$9.6 billion – the largest computer buyout in history.[36] Digital, which was founded in 1957, was one of IBM's original competitors. It helped to bring computers out of back offices and into the hands of the general public, giving birth to the minicomputer market. When Compaq was formed, Digital was second only to IBM. However, bad leadership and bad technology decisions had made Digital into a second-tier player.[37]

The acquisition of Digital considerably filled out Compaq's product line. Digital specialised in higher-end computers: workstations and Internet servers. More important, Digital brought to Compaq an excellent, large service and support organisation used to working with big companies and provided Compaq with the entrance into an upper-scale big business market that it had been trying to achieve for several years.[38] Additional assets were the Alta Vista Web search engine (which was later sold to KPMG) and the blazingly fast Alpha 64 bit processor chip. Analysts expected Compaq to bring its low-cost, no-holds-barred PC economics into the high-end computing markets that were dominated by IBM, Hewlett-Packard and Sun Microsystems. Such an approach could have potentially revolutionised the high-end computing business, and would make Compaq's regular PC business more competitive with Dell and Gateway 2000. Although some commentators raised concerns about the difference between the corporate cultures at Digital and Compaq, the merger moved forward and was finalised on 11 June 1998.

At the 1998 PC Expo trade show, Pfeiffer was invited to give the keynote address. In his speech, he discussed the five key areas that Compaq's strategy was focused on and what it was doing to accomplish each:

- *Industry standard computing*: 'Anywhere there is standards-based computing, Compaq wants to be the driver, whether it's in your home, your business or your car.'
- *Business critical computing*: Compaq will continue to invest in high-performance 64-bit computing with its Alpha chip.
- *Global service and support*: Compaq now has more than 25 000 service professionals around the world who can give customers support and availability services, systems integration and operations management. This gives customers a single point of accountability and lowers the cost and risk of ownership.
- *Cost-effective solutions for the enterprise*: 'We will focus on solutions that build on our leadership in enterprise platforms, expertise in key markets, service capabilities, and partnerships with industry-leading companies.'
- *Customers*: Compaq will leverage the account-based customer relationships nurtured by Digital and Tandem and combine them with Internet-based selling to provide customers with the most flexibility and choice. Compaq wants to be 'a strategic partner whose mission is to give you what you need, when you need it, and how you want it, at the lowest total cost'.[39]

At the end of 1998, Compaq had US$31.2 billion in sales revenues and, with the acquisition of Digital, was one of the largest computer companies in the world. It had a definite strategy, and although build-to-order companies were beginning to take away market share, it still had commanding market share.

The firing

On 9 April 1999, Pfeiffer announced to Wall Street that Compaq would probably not meet earnings expectations for the quarter; that they would in fact be about half of what analysts predicted. Compaq's stock plummeted on the news.[40]

Benjamin Rosen, chairman of Compaq's board of directors, called a board meeting without Pfeiffer, and the board voted him out. On 18 April, Pfeiffer handed in his resignation to Compaq's board of directors. Rosen and two other board members, Frank P. Doyle and Robert T. Enloe, formed the Office of the Chief

Executive to run the company while they searched for another CEO. This office was not intended to be a passive caretaker of the company. Rosen said, 'The board is committed to move quickly to select the right Chief Executive Officer to lead the next era of Compaq's growth and development. In the interim, we will move decisively to take those actions that are indicated.'[41]

So where did Pfeiffer go wrong? What grave mistakes did he make that merited his removal as CEO? When he announced the quarterly results (or lack thereof), he attempted to blame Compaq's poor performance on a generally weak demand in the PC industry, lower profit margins and competitive pricing.

As with Rod Canion, he was not removed for simply having a bad quarter. The bad quarterly results were merely symptomatic of larger internal problems. Pfeiffer's complaints about weak demand, lower profit margins and competitive pricing were valid, but the other major PC makers (IBM, Dell, Hewlett-Packard and Gateway) were not struggling in the same way as Compaq. Even Rosen had said as much when he commented that Compaq itself was largely at fault for its disappointing financial performance.[42] He also added that problems at Compaq were more severe than at first glance, and he wished they'd replaced Pfeiffer a year earlier.[43]

To arrive at this point, Pfeiffer had begun to isolate himself from employees, even some of his own vice presidents and higher executives. He oversaw the construction of an executive parking garage at a company where parking places had never been reserved, visibly separating himself from the other employees. Security on the executive floor was repeatedly increased and access increasingly restricted. Pfeiffer and his inner circle worked out the acquisition of Digital, and the rest of the senior executives only found out about it the night before it was announced to the press. Apparently, Pfeiffer had become too insular, not open to feedback and new ideas from those below.[44]

When he replaced Canion as CEO in 1991, Pfeiffer's aggressive initiatives changed Compaq's fortunes and turned the company around. But he seemed to have become less definite about making decisions. 'He was paralyzed by the speed with which the market was changing, and he couldn't make the difficult decisions,' says one former executive.[45]

As a result of his indecision, there was a failure to execute as effectively as Compaq had in the past. 'Pfeiffer is not supposed to be the guy who fails on implementation,' says Jonathon Eunice, an analyst at Illuminata Inc. 'Everyone talks about keeping the CEO accountable; almost no one does it. But [Rosen's] not afraid to fire his main guy and move on.' Eunice continues, 'The operations have been so sloppy for the second year in a row that it's almost staggering how off those numbers have been.'[46] The reason the office is called 'Chief Executive Officer' is because the CEO should execute strategy. Pfeiffer was no longer following through, getting things done, delivering on commitments. Benjamin Rosen told the press, 'The change [will not be in] our fundamental strategy – we think that strategy is sound – but in execution. Our plans are to speed up decision-making and make the company more efficient.'[47]

Over time, Pfeiffer began to focus on being number one and forgot about understanding the customer. Long-time chief strategist Robert Stearns, who left Compaq in June 1998, says, 'In his quest for bigness, he lost an understanding of the customer and built what I call empty market share – large but not profitable.'[48] The acquisitions of Tandem Computers and especially of Digital Equipment were indicative of this flaw. Against the advice of some of the senior executives, Pfeiffer and his tiny inner circle negotiated for Digital and presented it to the rest of the company after it was already completed. 'Buying Digital played into Eckhard's fantasy, but it's turning out to be a beast that's consuming the company,' said one former executive.[49] Digital had proved to be tougher to integrate than predicted: the corporate cultures were more incompatible than first thought, and Compaq seemed to have lost its way, although it was likely to reach Pfeiffer's ambitious goal of US$40 billion in earnings by 2000.

While Pfeiffer bears extensive blame for the company's poor performance, he should also be given a great deal of credit. Since becoming CEO in 1991, he turned Compaq around more than once and helped it grow into a tremendous power in the PC industry. 'Eckhard Pfeiffer oversaw a period of stunning growth in Compaq's history,' said Rosen. 'All those who benefited from that growth owe him a debt of gratitude.'[50] (See Exhibit 2 for Compaq's financial performance from 1994 to 1998.)

Wanted: CEO for a large *Fortune* 500 company

The board's search for a new CEO went on for three months. Rumours were rampant as many different people were considered for the job. Finally, on 22 July

Exhibit 2 | Compaq consolidated income statement, 1994–8 (year ended 31 December)

	1998	1997	1996	1995	1994
Revenue					
• Products	$27 372	24 122	19 611	16 308	12 274
• Services	3 797	462	398	367	331
Total:	31 169	24 684	20 009	16 675	12 605
Cost of sales					
• Products	$21 383	17 500	14 565	12 026	8 671
• Services	2 597	333	290	265	214
Total:	$23 980	17 833	14 855	12 291	8 885
Other total costs	9 851	3 993	3 271	3 058	2 367
Income (loss) before taxes	(2 662)	2 758	1 883	1 326	1 353
Income taxes	81	903	565	43	365
Net income (loss)	(2 743)	1 855	1 318	893	988

All amounts are in US$mn.

Source: Compaq Home Page, 1998 Annual Report: www.compaq.com/corporate/1998ar/financials/5yr_summary_nf.html.

1999, Rosen called a press conference and announced that Michael A. Cappellas, the chief operating officer at Compaq, had been offered the job and accepted.

Cappellas joined Compaq in August 1998 as the chief information officer and became the acting chief operating officer in June 1999. Before coming to Compaq, he had worked at Schlumberger, an oil service company, for 15 years as an executive which included the company's first corporate director for information systems. In 1996, he moved to SAP America as the director of supply chain management, and in 1997 he joined Oracle Corporation as senior vice president before moving to Compaq.[51]

One of the first problems Cappellas faced as CEO was convincing shareholders and customers that he was capable of filling the job. Industry analysts were concerned by the appointment of an 'insider' who had been at the company for less than a year and who did not have any CEO experience. Many shared concerns about his ability to lead a large company like Compaq.[52] This issue didn't bother Cappellas, who told the press, 'Strategy is about solving business problems. I've been in IT for many years, [so] I'm confident that I can do that.'[53]

On the other hand, others were glad to see someone with a great deal of information technology experience appointed CEO. 'The companies that put marketing and sales people in as CEO never had to run a full enterprise infrastructure, and they have no idea what our [IT] problems are,' says Mike May, vice president of IT at Teknion Furniture Systems, a Compaq customer.[54] And an analyst at J.P. Morgan & Co. comments, 'He is not well-known, but in terms of his qualifications, he's as credible as any of the other candidates we were hearing about.'[55] Cappellas's experience in information technology could prove to be an asset for Compaq. However, he faces a set of strong rivals.

Competition

Compaq competes with four other major competitors: Dell, IBM, Hewlett-Packard and Gateway. These companies will challenge Cappellas's capabilities in strategic leadership. (See Exhibit 3 for the PC market shares of Compaq and its dominant competition.)

Dell Computer

Dell was founded in 1985 by Michael Dell in Round Rock, Texas, with a unique premise: selling directly to the customer and bypassing resellers. Because it sells direct, Dell has greatly reduced inventory cost and turnover time. (Currently, turnover is every six days.) In 1996, Dell began to sell directly over the Internet, which now accounts for approximately 50 per cent of orders. Dell has used the Internet to offer specially catered customer service to its large corporate customers by constructing a personal web page for each. Dell has been increasing its high-profit product line for big business. Corporate sales account for most of Dell's revenue. In October 1999, Dell outsold Compaq for the first time in the PC market, increasing its market share to 18.1 per cent while Compaq's fell to 15.9 per cent.[56]

Exhibit 3 | PC market share (first quarter 1999)

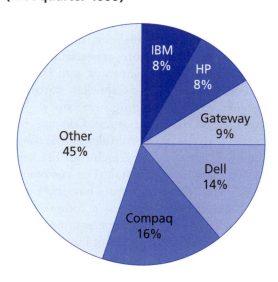

Source: PC Week Online, Archives: www.zdnet.com/pcweek/stories/jumps/0.4270,2263744,00.html.

IBM (International Business Machines)

IBM was incorporated in 1911. It was the first and biggest computer company, and pioneered the introduction of the PC in 1981. IBM faltered in the mid-1980s when confronted with Compaq and other rivals. In 1996, IBM began to regain market share in the PC market and came back to be second in the United States, after Compaq.[57] In 1999, it had US$81.7 billion in revenues.

Despite its turnaround in the PC sector, IBM has shifted its focus to its more profitable services division and is marketing itself as an 'e-business', emphasising how it can help other companies get their companies on-line to take advantage of the Internet. This allows it to emphasise services such as high-end servers which also drives its hardware sales into a higher profit margin than PCs.[58] Currently, it holds 7.5 per cent of the PC market share in the United States.[59]

Hewlett-Packard

Hewlett-Packard (HP) was founded by two engineers, Bill Hewlett and Dave Packard, in 1938 in a garage in Palo Alto, California. HP was incorporated the following year and has never stopped growing. Hewlett and Packard developed a remarkable corporate culture that encouraged communication and innovation, and their company has performed accordingly. HP began by building oscillators and evolved with the technology, building the scientific calculator that made slide rules obsolete, and eventually computers and other hardware.[50]

HP gradually diversified into many areas, including communications and medical technology. In 1999, HP launched a new company, Agilent, consisting of its industry-leading test-and-measurement products, semiconductor products and chemical-analysis medical businesses. HP could now focus on its core business of computers and hardware, including printers. HP had computer-related revenue of US$39.5 billion in its 1998 fiscal year[61] and had 8 per cent of the PC market.[62]

Gateway Computers

Gateway Computers was founded in 1985 by Ted Waitt. Like Dell, Gateway's business model is based on direct customised selling. In 1996, it began to sell computers on the Internet. Gateway has begun experimenting with various ways to earn more revenues from its customers. It opened 'Gateway Country Stores', bricks-and-mortar stores that are owned by the company; the stores carry no inventory but provide customer service and facilitate shopping for first-time customers by giving them the opportunity to test machines before buying. Gateway has also started up its own Internet service provider, which has taken off this past year, with half a million subscribers. At 9 per cent,[63] Gateway has more US PC market share than either IBM or HP.

Future challenges

Michael Cappellas has quite a formidable task in front of him. Although Compaq has many problems, it has just as many opportunities. The merger with Digital must be completed and assimilated into Compaq.[64]

Buying Digital was to help Compaq grow into a full-line computer company offering a large range of products that would be driven by service solutions. Cappellas said, 'We underestimated the cultural issues and just the hard work it takes to integrate two companies like Compaq and Digital. And that drains a lot of energy in the field .... The core PC business was coming under attack, and the market was shifting just as the integration was draining management attention. So the timing was really bad.'[65]

Completing Digital's integration will allow Compaq to expand into the profitable services business by leveraging Digital's admirable services arm. This will put it into direct competition with Hewlett-Packard and IBM. Business users are buying all-in-one packages of products and services. However, the solutions business at Compaq is not functioning well, while at the same time, margins in the PC business are falling.[66]

To compete with Dell, Compaq must develop a better on-line strategy.[67] PCs depreciate approximately 1 per cent per week, and a company mustn't continually be caught with back inventory on its hands. To reduce the costs of back inventory, it needs to move to a more direct sales model.[68] When IBM tried selling direct, its dealers complained and IBM backed off; the company currently doesn't sell on-line. Compaq may need to find a happy medium between on-line and retail selling.

In May, a month after Pfeiffer's departure, Compaq announced a restructuring of the sales channel, reducing the number of places that it ships to from 29 to four. This new 'Distributor Alliance Program' will reduce shipping and transaction costs.[69] It will also reduce inventories and thus cut the associated costs. All this will boost the bottom line, as well as open up many more opportunities and make Compaq a more viable competitor with Dell.

Cappellas stated, 'We did not do a good job of telling our story. We had fragmented marketing messages. Compaq had stood for the world's most powerful personal computing brand. Then we added the very high-end Tandem side, and then we brought in Digital. The customer lost track of who we were.'[70] Compaq has the opportunity to reinvent itself once more as a comprehensive computer company that can offer an enormous services benefit to its customers, instead of just being the 'world's top PC vendor'.[71] This is a chance to realign the company's focus and become a computing behemoth like IBM.

In an interview, Cappellas was asked, 'Who do you worry about more, Dell or IBM?' He responded, 'I worry about IBM. They have done a very good job of positioning themselves around e-business. They sell the entire suite. They have a great solutions mindset. I have a great respect for them as a competitor.'[72] At first glance, an observer would think that surely Dell should be Cappellas's big worry. However, as the quote indicates, Cappellas may seek to pursue a strategy similar to IBM's. Whatever strategic approach is taken, he has a significant challenge.

Endnotes

1. 'Eckhard's gone but the PC rocks on: Compaq's CEO blames his ouster on a savagely competitive industry', 1999, *Fortune*, 24 May, p. 153.
2. D. Kirkpatrick, 1996, 'Fast times at Compaq', *Fortune*, 1 April, pp. 121–8.
3. 'Compaq goes after Big Blue', 1998, *The Economist*, 31 January, p. 66.
4. 'How Compaq's portable leaped ahead of the pack', 1983, *Business Week*, 15 August, p. 89.
5. Ibid.
6. E. Richards, 1991, 'Compaq ousts president who founded firm', *The Washington Post*, 26 October, p. C1.
7. L. Kehoe, 1991, 'Compaq founder fired because board "had to make choice"', *Financial Times*, 28 October, p. 19.
8. Ibid.
9. Ibid.
10. 'And the losers are ...', 1994, *The Economist*, 17 September, p. 6.
11. Kirkpatrick, 'Fast times at Compaq'; H. Preston, 1994, 'Compaq's winning ways', *International Business*, September, p. 56.
12. E. Nee, 1998, 'Company of the year – Compaq Computer Corp.', *Forbes*, 12 January, p. 90.
13. 'Selling computers is easy – the hard bit is making a profit', *The Economist*, 1994, p. 6.
14. Nee, 'Company of the year – Compaq Computer Corp.'.
15. M. Loeb, 1995, 'Leadership lost – and regained', *Fortune*, 17 April, p. 217.
16. J. Jones, 1993, 'Compaq builds sales, profits with aggressive price policy', *Investor's Business Daily*, 27 May, p. 32.
17. S. Higgins, 1993, 'Executive update', *Investor's Business Daily*, 7 June, p. 4.
18. 'Compaq Presario 425 is fastest-selling new PC in company's history', 1993, *Business Wire*, 26 October.
19. 'Compaq's Pfeiffer sees significant growth opportunities for U.S. computer industry', 1992, *Business Wire*, 7 December.
20. 'Compaq reports record 1992 sales', 1993, *Business Wire*, 26 January.
21. Reuters, 1993, 'Compaq says its new PC set sales record', *The New York Times*, 27 October, p. D3.
22. J. Burgess, 1994, 'Compaq goes with clone over Intel chip', *The Washington Post*, 27 January, p. D11.
23. Loeb, 'Leadership lost – and regained'.
24. P. Burrows, 1994, 'Compaq stretches for the crown', *Business Week*, 11 July, p. 140.
25. L. Spiegelman and M. Mehler, 1995, 'Compaq's new PCs mark a shift in strategic focus', *Investor's Business Daily*, 9 March, p. A6.
26. 'Compaq launches world-class enterprise service and support capability', 1995, *Business Wire*, 16 October.
27. G. McWilliams, 1995, 'Compaq hooks up with a networking wizard', *Business Week*, 20 November, p. 48.
28. *Compaq Home Page*, 1999, 1995 Annual Report: www.compaq.com/corporate/1995ar, 17 November.
29. 'Compaq, Microsoft announce major contracts with EDS to revolutionize General Motors dealer service', 1996, *Business Wire*, 4 June; 'Compaq, Microsoft awarded $17 million contract to supply PCs, servers, software to Smith Barney', 1996, *Business Wire*, 17 April.
30. 'Compaq first company in world to ship one million industry-standard servers', 1996, *Business Wire*, 19 November.
31. G. McWilliams, 1996, 'Compaq at the "crossroads"', *Business Week*, 22 July, p. 70.
32. N. Alster, 1996, 'IBM's silver-medal win: Sign of a PC power shift?', *Investor's Business Daily*, 5 August, p. A6.
33. *Compaq Home Page*, 1997, Press Release Archives: www.compaq.com/newsroom/pr/1997/pr230697a, 18 November.
34. R. Britt, 1997, 'Compaq soothes resellers, but will the détente last?',

Investor's Business Daily, 3 June, p. A6.
35. *Compaq Home Page*, 1999, 1995 Annual Report: www.compaq.com/corporate/1995ar, 17 November; D. Silverman, 1997, 'Compaq Computer to pay first dividend', *Investor's Business Daily*, 17 October.
36. D. Abrahms, 1998, 'Compaq agrees to purchase Digital in largest computer buyout in history', *The Washington Times*, 27 January.
37. E. Ramstad and J. Auerbach, 1998, 'Behind Digital's downfall: It's the story of modern computing, and how a mega-giant has stumbled in recent years', *The Ottawa Citizen*, 28 January, p. C3.
38. T. Quinlan, 1998, 'Texas-based Compaq to acquire Digital for $9.6 billion', *San Jose Mercury News*, 27 January; G. McWilliams, 1998, 'Power play', *Business Week*, 9 February, p. 90.
39. 'Compaq president and CEO Pfeiffer outlines vision for "new world of computing"', 1998, *Business Wire*, 16 June.
40. D. Einstein, 1999, 'Compaq stock tumbles on profit warning', *The San Francisco Chronicle*, 13 April, p. C1.
41. 'Compaq board of directors forms office of the chief executive under leadership of chairman Benjamin Rosen; Eckhard Pfeiffer and Earl Mason resign as CEO and CFO', 1999, *Business Wire*, 18 April.
42. G. Balfour, 1999, 'Pfeiffer: How Compaq's mighty CEO has fallen', *ComputerWorld Canada*, 7 May, p. 1.
43. Company profile, 1999, 'The lion in winter', *Business Week*, 26 July, p. 108; '"I was an asset ... rather than a meddler"', *Business Week*, 26 July, p. 116.
44. 'Eckhard's gone but the PC rocks on'; L. DiCarlo, 1999, 'Eye of the storm: Compaq executive turmoil traced to Pfeiffer's inner circle', *PC Week*, 24 May, p. 1.
45. DiCarlo, 'Eye of the storm'.
46. Balfour, 'Pfeiffer: How Compaq's mighty CEO has fallen'.
47. R. Charan and G. Colvin, 1999, 'Why CEOs fail', *Fortune*, 21 June, p. 69.
48. 'Eckhard's gone but the PC rocks on'.
49. DiCarlo, 'Eye of the storm'..
50. 'Compaq board of directors forms office of the chief executive'.
51. J. Darwin, 1999, 'Surprising week shakes up Compaq', *Houston Business Journal*, 30 July, p. 1.
52. L. Kehoe and R. Taylor, 1999, 'Compaq faces "Internet speed" change', *The Financial Times*, 26 July, p. 20; L. DiCarlo, 1999, 'New Compaq, HP CEOs: A contrast', *PC Week*, 26 July, p. 1; Darwin, 'Surprising week shakes up Compaq'; L. DiCarlo and M. R. Zimmerman, 1999, 'Initial reactions vary on new Compaq CEO', *PC Week*, 2 August, p. 40; L. Hawkins, 1999, 'Compaq Computer selects company insider as CEO', *Knight-Ridder/Tribune Business News*, 23 July; R. Taylor, 1999, 'Compaq promotes Cappellas to top job', *The Financial Times*, 23 July, p. 21.
53. Dicarlo, 'New Compaq, HP CEOs'.
54. Ibid.
55. Dicarlo and Zimmerman, 'Initial reactions vary on new Compaq CEO'.
56. *Dell Home Page*, 1999: www.dell.com; A. Goldstein, 1999, 'Dell outpaces Compaq in U.S. sales of personal computers', *Knight-Ridder/Tribune Business News*, 25 October; 'Eckhard's gone but the PC rocks on'.
57. N. Alster, 1999, 'IBM's silver-medal win: Sign of PC power shift?', *Investor's Business Daily*, 5 August, p. A6.
58. *IBM Home Page*, 1998 Annual Report: www.ibm.com/annualreport/1998/letter/ibm98arlsen01.
59. *PC Week Online*, Archives: www.zdnet.com/pcweek/stories/jumps/0,4270,2263744,00.html; 'Eckhard's gone but the PC rocks on'.
60. *Hewlett-Packard Home Page*, History: www.hp.com/abouthp/history.
61. *Hewlett-Packard Home Page*, Press Releases: www.hp.com/pressrel/jul99/28jul99.htm.
62. *PC Week Online*, Archives: www.zdnet.com/pcweek/stories/jumps/0,4270,2263744,00.html.
63. 'Eckhard's gone but the PC rocks on'; *Gateway Home Page*, 1999, History: www.gateway.com/about/info; *PC Week Online*, Archives: www.zdnet.com/pcweek/stories/jumps/0,4270,2263744,00.html.
64. S. Gibson, 1999, 'Compaq, customers need common ground', *Fortune*, 10 May, p. 85.
65. D. Kirkpatrick, 1999, 'Superior performance is the key to independence', *Fortune*, 16 August, p. 126.
66. S. Deck, 1999, 'Compaq counts its losses', *Computerworld*, 28 June, p. 30.
67. 'Compaq looks inside for salvation: Can Michael Capellas make the PC giant into a Web master?', 1999, *Fortune*, 16 August, p. 124.
68. Ibid.
69. T. Campbell, 1999, 'Compaq tries to reboot', *Sales & Marketing Management*, July, p. 20.
70. Kirkpatrick, 'Superior performance is the key to independence'.
71. Loeb, 'Leadership lost – and regained'.
72. Kirkpatrick, 'Superior performance is the key to independence'.

Gillette and the men's wet-shaving market

Lew G. Brown
Jennifer M. Hart
University of North Carolina at Greensboro

SAN FRANCISCO

On a spring morning in 1989, Michael Johnson dried himself and stepped from the shower in his San Francisco Marina District condominium. He moved to the sink and started to slide open the drawer in the cabinet beneath the sink. Then he remembered that he had thrown away his last Atra blade yesterday. He heard his wife, Susan, walk past the bathroom.

'Hey, Susan, did you remember to pick up some blades for me yesterday?'

'Yes, I think I put them in your drawer.'

'Oh, okay, here they are.' Michael saw the bottom of the blade package and pulled the drawer open.

'Oh, no! These are Trac II blades, Susan, I use an Atra.'

'I'm sorry. I looked at all the packages at the drugstore, but I couldn't remember which type of razor you have. Can't you use the Trac II blades on your razor?'

'No. They don't fit.'

'Well, I bought some disposable razors. Just use one of those.'

'Well, where are they?'

'Look below the sink. They're in a big bag.'

'I see them. Wow, 10 razors for $1.97! Must have been on sale.'

'I guess so. I usually look for the best deal. Seems to me that all those razors are the same, and the drugstore usually has one brand or another on sale.'

'Why don't you buy some of those shavers made for women?'

'I've tried those, but it seems that they're just like the ones made for men, only they've dyed the plastic pink or some pastel colour. Why should I pay more for colour?'

'Why don't you just use disposables?' Susan continued. 'They are simpler to buy, and you just throw them away. And you can't beat the price.'

'Well, the few times I've tried them they didn't seem to shave as well as a regular razor. Perhaps they've improved. Do they work for you?'

'Yes, they work fine. And they sure are better than the heavy razors if you drop one on your foot while you're in the shower!'

'Never thought about that. I see your point. Well, I'll give the disposable a try.'

Engraph Corporation provided a grant to UNCG to support development of the case. Gillette's management cooperated in the field research for the case, which was written solely for the purpose of stimulating student discussion; the authors also drew from secondary sources. All incidents and events are real, but individual names were disguised at Gillette's request.

Copyright © 1992 by the Case Research Journal and Lew G. Brown.

History of shaving

Anthropologists do not know exactly when or even why men began to shave. Researchers do know that prehistoric cave drawings clearly present men who were beardless. Apparently these men shaved with clamshells or sharpened animal teeth. As society developed, primitive men learned to sharpen flint implements. Members of the early Egyptian dynasties as far back as 7 000 years ago shaved their faces and heads, probably to deny their enemies anything to grab during hand-to-hand combat. Egyptians later fashioned copper razors and, in time, bronze blades. Craftsmen formed these early razors as crescent-shaped knife blades, like hatchets or meat cleavers, or even as circular blades with a handle extending from the centre. By the Iron Age, craftsmen were able to fashion blades that were considerably more efficient than the early flint, copper and bronze versions.

Before the introduction of the safety razor, men used a straight-edged, hook-type razor and found shaving a tedious, difficult and time-consuming task. The typical man struggled through shaving twice a week at most. The shaver had to sharpen the blade (a process called stropping) before each use and had to have an expert cutler hone the blade each month. As a result, men often cut themselves while shaving; and few men had the patience and acquired the necessary skill to become good shavers. Most men in the 1800s agreed with the old Russian proverb: 'It is easier to bear a child once a year than to shave every day.' Only the rich could afford a daily barber shave, which also often had its disadvantages because many barbers were unclean.

Before King C. Gillette of Boston invented the safety razor in 1895, he tinkered with other inventions in pursuit of a product which, once used, would be thrown away. The customer would have to buy more, and the business would build a long-term stream of sales and profits with each new customer.

'On one particular morning when I started to shave,' wrote Gillette about the dawn of his invention, 'I found my razor dull, and it was not only dull but beyond the point of successful stropping and it needed honing, for which it must be taken to a barber or cutler. As I stood there with the razor in my hand, my eyes resting on it as lightly as a bird settling down on its nest, the Gillette razor was born.' Gillette immediately wrote to his wife, who was visiting relatives, 'I've got it; our fortune is made.'

Gillette had envisioned a 'permanent' razor handle on to which the shaver placed a thin, razor 'blade' with two sharpened edges. The shaver would place a top over the blade and attach it to the handle so that only the sharpened edges of the blade were exposed, thus producing a 'safe' shave. A man would shave with the blade until it became dull and then would simply throw the used blade away and replace it. Gillette knew his concept would revolutionise the process of shaving; however, he had no idea that his creation would permanently change men's shaving habits.

Shaving in the 1980s

Following the invention of the safety razor, the men's shaving industry in the United States grew slowly but surely through the First World War. A period of rapid growth followed, and the industry saw many product innovations. By 1989, US domestic razor and blade sales (the wet-shave market) had grown to a US$770 million industry. A man could use three types of wet shavers to remove facial hair. Most men used the disposable razor – a cheap, plastic-handled razor that lasted for eight to 10 shaves on average. Permanent razors, called blade and razor systems, were also popular. These razors required new blades every 11 to 14 shaves. Customers could purchase razor handles and blade cartridges together, or they could purchase packages of blade cartridges as refills. The third category of wet shavers included injector and double-edge razors and accounted for a small share of the razor market. Between 1980 and 1988, disposable razors had risen from a 22 per cent to a 41.5 per cent market share of dollar sales. During the same period, cartridge systems had fallen from 50 per cent to 45.8 per cent and injector and double-edge types had fallen from 28 per cent to 12.7 per cent. In addition, the development of the electric razor had spawned the dry-shave market, which accounted for about US$250 million in sales by 1988.

Despite the popularity of disposable razors, manufacturers found that the razors were expensive to make and generated very little profit. In 1988, some industry analysts estimated that manufacturers earned three times more on a razor and blade system than on a disposable razor. Also, retailers preferred to sell razor systems because they took up less room on display racks and the retailers made more money on refill sales. However, retailers liked to promote disposable razors to generate traffic. As a result, US retailers allocated 55 per cent of their blade and razor stock to disposable razors, 40 per cent to systems and 5 per cent to double-edge razors.

Electric razors also posed a threat to razor and blade systems. Unit sales of electric razors jumped from

6.2 million in 1981 to 8.8 million in 1987. Low-priced imports from the Far East drove demand for electric razors up and prices down during this period. Nonetheless, fewer than 30 per cent of men used electric razors, and most of these men also used wet-shaving systems.

Industry analysts predicted that manufacturers' sales of personal care products would continue to grow. However, the slowing of the overall US economy in the late 1980s meant that sales increases resulting from an expanding market would be minimal and companies would have to fight for market share to continue to increase sales.

The Gillette Company dominated the wet-shave market with a 60 per cent share of worldwide razor market revenue and a 61.9 per cent share of the US market as of 1988. Gillette also had a stake in the dry-shave business through its Braun subsidiary. The other players in the wet-shave market were Schick with 16.2 per cent of market revenues, BIC with 9.3 per cent, and others, including Wilkinson Sword, with the remaining 12.6 per cent.

The Gillette Company

King Gillette took eight years to perfect his safety razor. In 1903, the first year of marketing, the American Safety Razor Company sold 51 razors and 168 blades. Gillette promoted the safety razor as a saver of both time and money. Early ads proclaimed that the razor would save US$52 and 15 days' shaving time each year and that the blades required no stropping or honing. During its second year, Gillette sold 90 884 razors and 123 648 blades. By its third year, razor sales were rising at a rate of 400 per cent per year, and blade sales were booming at an annual rate of 1 000 per cent. In that year, the company opened its first overseas branch in London.

Such success attracted much attention, and competition quickly developed. By 1906, consumers had at least a dozen safety razors from which to choose. The Gillette razor sold for US$5, as did the Zinn razor made by the Gem Cutlery Company. Others, such as the Ever Ready, Gem Junior and Enders, sold for as little as US$1.

With the benefit of a 17-year patent, Gillette found himself in a very advantageous position. However, it was not until the First World War that the safety razor gained wide consumer acceptance. One day in 1917, King Gillette had a visionary idea: have the government present a Gillette razor to every soldier, sailor and marine. In this way, millions of men just entering the shaving age would adopt the self-shaving habit. By March 1918, Gillette had booked orders from the US military for 519 750 razors, more than it had sold in any single year in its history. During the First World War, the government bought 4 180 000 Gillette razors as well as smaller quantities of competitive models.

Although King Gillette believed in the quality of his product, he realised that marketing, especially distribution and advertising, would be the key to success. From the beginning, Gillette set aside 25 cents per razor for advertising and by 1905 had increased the amount to 50 cents. Over the years, Gillette used cartoon ads, radio shows, musical slogans and theme songs, prizes, contests and cross-promotions to push its products. Perhaps, however, consumers best remember Gillette for its Cavalcade of Sports programs that began in 1939 with the company's sponsorship of the World Series. Millions of men soon came to know Sharpie the Parrot and the tag line, 'Look Sharp! Feel Sharp! Be Sharp!'

Because company founder King Gillette invented the first safety razor, Gillette had always been an industry innovator. In 1932, Gillette introduced the Gillette Blue Blade, which was the premier men's razor for many years. In 1938, the company introduced the Gillette Thin Blade; in 1946, it introduced the first blade dispenser that eliminated the need to unwrap individual blades; in 1959, it introduced the first silicone-coated blade, the Super Blue Blade. The success of the Super Blue Blade caused Gillette to close 1961 with a commanding 70 per cent share of the overall razor and blade market and a 90 per cent share of the double-edge market, the only market in which it competed.

In 1948, Gillette began to diversity into new markets through acquisition. The company purchased the Toni Company to extend its reach into the women's grooming-aid market. In 1954, the company bought Paper Mate, a leading marker of writing instruments. In 1962, it acquired the Sterilon Corporation, which manufactured disposable hospital supplies. As a result of these moves, a marketing survey found that the public associated Gillette with personal grooming as much as, or more than, with blades and razors.

In 1988, the Gillette Company was a leading producer of men's and women's grooming aids. Exhibit 1 lists the company's major divisions. Exhibits 2 and 3 show the percentages and dollar volumes of net sales and profits from operations for each of the company's major business segments. Exhibits 4 and 5 present income statements and balance sheets for 1986–8.

Despite its diversification, Gillette continued to realise the importance of blade and razor sales to the company's overall health. Gillette had a strong foothold in the razor and blade market, and it intended to use this dominance to help it achieve the company's goal – 'sustained profitable growth'. To reach this goal, Gillette's mission statement indicated that the company should pursue 'strong technical and marketing efforts to assure vitality in major existing product lines; selective diversification, both internally and through acquisition; the elimination of product and business areas with low growth or limited profit potential; and strict control over product costs, overhead expenses, and working capital'.

Gillette introduced a number of innovative shaving systems in the 1970s and 1980s as part of its strategy to

Exhibit 1 | Gillette product lines by company division, 1988

Blades and razors	Stationery products	Toiletries and cosmetics	Oral B products	Braun products
Trac II	Paper Mate	Adorn	Oral B toothbrushes	Electric razors
Atra	Liquid Paper	Toni		Lady Elegance
Good News	Flair	Right Guard		Clocks
	Waterman	Silkience		Coffee grinders
	Write Bros.	Soft and Dri		and makers
		Foamy		
		Dry Look		
		Dry Idea		
		White Rain		
		Lustrasilk		
		Aapri skin care products		

Exhibit 2 | Gillette's sales and operating profits by product line, 1986–8 (US$mn)

	1988		1987		1986	
Product line	Sales	Profits	Sales	Profits	Sales	Profits
Blades and razors	$1 147	$406	$1 031	$334	$903	$274
Toiletries and cosmetics	1 019	79	926	99	854	69
Stationery products	385	56	320	34	298	11
Braun products	824	85	703	72	657	63
Oral B	202	18	183	7	148	8
Other	5	(0.1)	4	2	48	(1)
Totals	$3 582	$643	$3 167	$548	$2 908	$424

Source: Gillette Company Annual Reports, 1985–8.

Exhibit 3 | Gillette's net sales and profit by business, 1984–8 (per cent)

	Blades and razors		Toiletries and cosmetics		Stationery products		Braun products		Oral B products	
Year	Sales	Profits	Sales	Profits	Sales	Profits	Sales	Profits	Sales	Profits
1988	32	61	28	14	11	9	23	13	6	3
1987	33	61	29	18	10	6	22	13	6	2
1986	32	64	30	16	11	3	20	15	5	2
1985	33	68	31	15	11	2	17	13	6	3
1984	34	69	30	15	12	3	17	12	3	2

Source: Gillette Company Annual Reports, 1985–8.

sustain growth. Gillette claimed that Trac II, the first twin-blade shaver, represented the most revolutionary shaving advance ever. The development of the twin-blade razor derived from shaving researchers' discovery that shaving causes whiskers to be briefly lifted up out of the follicle during shaving, a process called 'hysteresis' by technicians. Gillette invented the twin-blade system so that the first blade would cut the whisker and the second blade would cut it again before it receded. This system produced a closer shave than a

Exhibit 4 | Gillette income statements, 1986–8 (US$mn except for per share data)

	1988	1987	1986
Net sales	$3 581.2	$3 166.8	$2 818.3
Cost of sales	1 487.4	1 342.3	1 183.8
Other expenses	1 479.8	1 301.3	1 412.0
Operating income	614.0	523.2	222.5
Other income	37.2	30.9	38.2
Earnings before interest and tax	651.2	545.1	260.7
Interest expense	138.3	112.5	85.2
Non-operating expense	64.3	50.1	124.0
Earnings before tax	448.6	391.5	51.5
Tax	180.1	161.6	35.7
Earnings after tax	268.5	229.9	15.8
Earnings per share	2.45	2.00	.12
Average common shares outstanding, 000	109 559	115 072	127 344
Dividends paid per share	$0.86	$0.785	$0.68
Stock price range			
High	$49	$45 7/8	$34 1/2
Low	$29 1/8	$17 5/8	$17 1/8

Source: Gillette Company Annual Reports, 1986–8.

Exhibit 5 | Gillette balance sheets, 1986–8 (US$mn)

		1988	1987	1986
Assets	Cash	$ 156.4	$ 119.1	$ 94.8
	Receivables	729.1	680.1	608.8
	Inventories	653.4	594.5	603.1
	Other current assets	200.8	184.5	183.0
	Total current assets	1 739.7	1 578.2	1 489.7
	Fixed assets, net	683.1	664.4	637.3
	Other assets	445.1	448.6	412.5
	TOTAL ASSETS	2 867.9	2 731.2	2 539.5
Liabilities and equity	Current liabilities*	965.4	960.5	900.7
	Long-term debt	1 675.2	839.6	915.2
	Other long-term liabilities	311.9	331.7	262.8
	Equity†	$ (84.6)	$ 599.4	$ 460.8

* Includes current portion of long-term debt: 1988 = $9.6, 1987 = $41.0, 1986 = $7.6.
† Includes retained earnings: 1988 = $1 261.6, 1987 = $1 083.8, 1986 = $944.3.

Source: Gillette Company Annual Reports, 1986–8.

traditional one-blade system. Gillette also developed a clog-free, dual-blade cartridge for the Trac II system.

Because consumer test data showed a 9-to-1 preference for Trac II over panellists' current razors, Gillette raced to get the product to market. Gillette supported Trac II's 1971 introduction, which was the largest new product introduction in shaving history, with a US$10 million advertising and promotion budget. Gillette cut its advertising budgets for its other brands drastically to support Trac II. The double-edge portion of the advertising budget decreased from 47 per cent in 1971 to 11 per cent in 1972. Gillette reasoned that growth must come at the expense of other brands. Thus, it concentrated its advertising and promotion on its newest shaving product and reduced support for its established lines.

Gillette launched Trac II during a World Series promotion and made it the most frequently advertised shaving system in America during its introductory period. Trac II users turned out to be predominantly young, college-educated men who lived in metropolitan and suburban areas and earned higher incomes. As the fastest-growing shaving product on the market for five years, Trac II drove the switch to twin blades. The brand reached its peak in 1976 when consumers purchased 485 million blades and 7 million razors.

Late in 1976, Gillette, apparently in response to BIC's pending entrance into the US market, launched Good News!, the first disposable razor for men sold in the United States. In 1975, BIC had introduced the first disposable shaver in Europe; and by 1976 BIC had begun to sell disposable razors in Canada. Gillette realised that BIC would move its disposable razor into the United States after its Canadian introduction, so it promptly brought out a new blue plastic disposable shaver with a twin-blade head. By year's end, Gillette also made Good News! available in Austria, Canada, France, Italy, Switzerland, Belgium, Greece, Germany and Spain.

Unfortunately for Gillette, Good News! was really bad news. The disposable shaver delivered lower profit margins than razor and blade systems, and it undercut sales of other Gillette products. Good News! sold for much less than the retail price of a Trac II cartridge. Gillette marketed Good News! on price and convenience, not performance; but the company envisioned the product as a step-up item leading to its traditional high-quality shaving systems.

This contain-and-switch strategy did not succeed. Consumers liked the price and the convenience of disposable razors, and millions of Trac II razors began to gather dust in medicine chests across the country. Many Trac II users figured out that for as little as 25 cents, they could get the same cartridge mounted on a plastic handle that they had been buying for 56 cents to put on their Trac II handle. Further, disposable razors created an opening for competitors in a category that Gillette had long dominated.

Gillette felt sure, however, that disposable razors would never gain more than a 7 per cent share of the market. The disposable razor market share soon soared past 10 per cent, forcing Gillette into continual upward revisions of its estimates. In terms of units sold, disposable razors reached a 22 per cent market share by 1980 and a 50 per cent share by 1988.

BIC and Gillette's successful introduction of the disposable razor represented a watershed event in 'commoditisation' – the process of converting well-differentiated products into commodities. Status, quality and perceived value had always played primary roles in the marketing of personal care products. But consumers were now showing that they would forgo performance and prestige in a shaving product – about as close and personal as one can get.

In 1977, Gillette introduced a new blade and razor system at the expense of Trac II. It launched Atra with a US$7 million advertising campaign and over 50 million US$2 rebate coupons. Atra (which stands for Automatic Tracking Razor Action) was the first twin-blade shaving cartridge with a pivoting head. Engineers had designed the head to follow a man's facial contours for a closer shave. Researchers began developing the product in Gillette's UK research and development lab in 1970. They had established a goal of improving the high-performance standards of twin-blade shaving and specifically enhancing the Trac II effect. The company's scientists discovered that moving the hand and face was not the most effective way to achieve the best blade-face shaving angle. The razor head itself produced a better shave if it pivoted so as to maintain the most effective shaving angle. Marketers selected the name 'Atra' after two years of extensive consumer testing.

Atra quickly achieved a 7 per cent share of the blade market and about one-third of the razor market. The company introduced Atra in Europe a year later under the brand name 'Contour'. Although Atra increased Gillette's share of the razor market, 40 per cent of Trac II users switched to Atra in the first year.

In the early 1980s, Gillette introduced most new disposable razors and product enhancements. Both Swivel (launched in 1980) and Good News! Pivot (1984) were disposable razors featuring movable heads. Gillette announced Atra Plus (the first razor with the patented Lubra-smooth lubricating strip) in 1985 just as

BIC began to move into the United States from Canada with the BIC shaver for sensitive skin. A few months later, Gillette ushered in Micro Trac – the first disposable razor with an ultra-slim head. Gillette priced the Micro Trac lower than any other Gillette disposable razor. The company claimed to have designed a state-of-the-art manufacturing process for Micro Trac. The process required less plastic, thus minimising bulk and reducing manufacturing costs. Analysts claimed that Gillette was trying to bracket the market with Atra Plus (with a retail price of US$3.99 to US$4.95) and Micro Trac (US$0.99), and protect its market share with products on both ends of the price and usage scale. Gillette also teased Wall Street with hints that, by the end of 1986, it would be introducing yet another state-of-the-art shaving system that could revolutionise the shaving business.

Despite these product innovations and introductions in the early 1980s, Gillette primarily focused its energies on its global markets and strategies. By 1985, it was marketing 800 products in more than 200 countries. The company felt a need at this time to coordinate its marketing efforts, first regionally and then globally.

Unfortunately for Gillette's management team, others noticed its strong international capabilities. Ronald Perelman, chairman of the Revlon Group, attempted an unfriendly takeover in November 1986. To fend off the takeover, Gillette bought back 9.2 million shares of its stock from Perelman and saddled itself with additional long-term debt to finance the stock repurchase. Gillette's payment to Perelman increased the company's debt load from US$827 million to US$1.1 billion, and put its debt-to-equity ratio at 70 per cent. Gillette and Perelman signed an agreement preventing Perelman from attempting another takeover until 1996.

In 1988, just as Gillette returned its attention to new product development and global marketing, Coniston Partners, after obtaining 6 per cent of Gillette's stock, engaged the company in a proxy battle for four seats on its 12-person board. Coniston's interest had been piqued by the Gillette-Perelman US$549 million stock buyback and its payment of US$9 million in expenses to Perelman. Coniston and some shareholders felt Gillette's board and management had repeatedly taken actions that prohibited its shareholders from realising their shares' full value. When the balloting concluded, Gillette's management won by a narrow margin – 52 to 48 per cent. Coniston made US$13 million in the stock buyback program that Gillette offered to all shareholders, but Coniston agreed not to make another run at Gillette until 1991. This second takeover attempt forced Gillette to increase its debt load to US$2 billion and pushed its total equity negative to (US$84.6 million).

More importantly, both takeover battles forced Gillette to 'wake up'. Gillette closed or sold its Jafra Cosmetics operations in 11 countries and jettisoned weak operations such as Misco, Inc. (a computer supplies business), and S.T. Dupont (a luxury lighter, clock and watchmaker). The company also thinned its workforce in many divisions, such as its 15 per cent staff reduction at the Paper Mate pen unit. Despite this pruning, Gillette's sales for 1988 grew 13 per cent to US$3.6 billion, and profits soared 17 per cent to US$268 million.

Despite Gillette's concentration on fending off takeover attempts, it continued to enhance its razor and blade products. In 1986, it introduced the Contour Plus in its first pan-European razor launch. The company marketed Contour Plus with one identity and one strategy. In 1988, the company introduced Trac II Plus, Good News! Pivot Plus and Daisy Plus – versions of its existing products with the Lubra-smooth lubricating strip.

Schick

Warner-Lambert's Schick served as the second major competitor in the wet-shaving business. Warner-Lambert, incorporated in 1920 under the name William R. Warner & Company, manufactured chemicals and pharmaceuticals. Numerous mergers and acquisitions over 70 years resulted in Warner-Lambert's involvement in developing, manufacturing and marketing a widely diversified line of beauty, health and well-being products. The company also became a major producer of mints and chewing gums, such as Dentyne, Sticklets and Trident. Exhibit 6 presents a list of Warner-Lambert's products by division as of 1988.

Warner-Lambert entered the wet-shave business through a merger with Eversharp in 1970. Eversharp, a long-time competitor in the wet-shave industry, owned the Schick trademark and had owned the Paper Mate Pen Company prior to selling it to Gillette in 1955. Schick's razors and blades produced US$180 million in revenue in 1987, or 5.2 per cent of Warner-Lambert's worldwide sales. (Refer to Exhibit 7 for operating results by division, and Exhibits 8 and 9 for income statement and balance sheet data.)

In 1989, Schick held approximately a 16.2 per cent US market share, down from its 1980 share of 23.8 per cent. Schick's market share was broken down as follows: blade systems, 8.8 per cent; disposable razors,

4.1 per cent; and double-edged blades and injectors, 3.3 per cent.

Schick's loss of market share in the 1980s occurred for two reasons. First, even though Schick pioneered the injector razor system (it controlled 80 per cent of this market by 1979), it did not market a disposable razor until mid-1984 – eight years after the first disposable razors appeared. Second, for years Warner-Lambert had been channelling Schick's cash flow to its research and development in drugs.

In 1986, the company changed its philosophy; it allocated US$70 million to Schick for a three-year period and granted Schick its own sales force. In spite of Schick's loss of market share, company executives felt they had room to play catch-up, especially by exploiting new technologies. In late 1988, Schick revealed that it planned to conduct 'guerrilla warfare' by throwing its marketing resources and efforts into new technological advances in disposable razors. As a result, Warner-Lambert planned to allocate the bulk of its US$8 million razor advertising budget to marketing its narrow-headed disposable razor, Slim Twin, which it introduced in August 1988.

Schick believed that the US unit demand for disposable razors would increase to 55 per cent of the market by the early 1990s from its 50 per cent share in 1988. Schick executives based this belief on their feeling that men would rather pay 30 cents for a disposable

Exhibit 6 | Warner-Lambert product lines by company division, 1988

Ethical pharmaceuticals	Gums and mints	Non-prescription products	Other products
Parke-Davis drug	Dentyne	Benadryl	Schick razors
	Sticklets	Caladryl	Ultrex razors
	Beemans	Rolaids	Personal Touch
	Trident	Sinutab	Tetra Aquarium
	Freshen-up	Listerex	
	Bubblicious	Lubraderm	
	Chiclets	Anusol	
	Clorets	Tucks	
	Certs	Halls	
	Dynamints	Benylin	
	Junior Mints	Listerine	
	Sugar Daddy	Listermint	
	Sugar Babies	Efferdent	
	Charleston Chew	Effergrip	
	Rascals		

Exhibit 7 | Warner-Lambert's net sales and operating profit by division, 1985–8 (US$mn)

Division		Net sales				Operating profit/(loss)			
		1988	1987	1986	1985	1988	1987	1986	1985
Healthcare	Ethical products	$1 213	$1 093	$ 964	$ 880	$ 420	$ 351	$ 246	$ 224
	Non-prescription products	1 296	1 195	1 077	992	305	256	176	177
	Total healthcare	2 509	2 288	2 041	1 872	725	607	422	401
	Gums and mints	918	777	678	626	187	173	122	138
	Other products*	481	420	384	334	92	86	61	72
Divested businesses									(464)
	R&D					(259)	(232)	(202)	(208)
	Net sales and operating profit	3 908	3 485	3 103	3 200	745	634	599	(61)

* Other products include Schick razors, which accounted for US$180 million in revenue in 1987.

Source: Warner-Lambert Company Annual Report, 1987; *Moody's Industrial Manual*.

razor than 75 cents for a refill blade. In 1988, Schick held an estimated 9.9 per cent share of dollar sales in the disposable razor market.

Schick generated approximately 67 per cent of its revenues overseas. Also, it earned higher profit margins on its non-domestic sales – 20 per cent versus its 15 per cent domestic margin. Europe and Japan represented the bulk of Schick's international business, accounting for 38 per cent and 52 per cent, respectively, of 1988's overseas sales. Schick's European business consisted of 70 per cent systems and 29 per cent disposable razors, but Gillette's systems and disposable razor sales were 4.5 and 6 times larger, respectively.

However, Schick dominated in Japan. Warner-Lambert held over 60 per cent of Japan's wet-shave market. Although Japan had typically been an electric shaver market (55 per cent of Japanese shavers use electric razors), Schick achieved an excellent record and reputation in Japan. Both Schick and Gillette entered the Japanese market in 1962; and their vigorous competition eventually drove Japanese competitors from the industry, which by 1988 generated US$190 million in sales. Gillette's attempt to crack the market flopped because it tried to sell razors using its own salespeople, a strategy that failed because Gillette did not have the distribution network available to Japanese companies. Schick, meanwhile, chose to leave the distribution to Seiko Corporation. Seiko imported razors from the United States and then sold them to wholesalers nationwide. By 1988, Schick generated roughly 40 per cent of its sales and 35 per cent of its profits in Japan. Disposable razors accounted for almost 80 per cent of those figures.

BIC Corporation

The roots of the BIC Corporation, which was founded by Marcel Bich in the United States in 1958, were in France. In 1945, Bich, who had been the production manager for a French ink manufacturer, bought a factory outside Paris to produce parts for fountain pens and mechanical lead pencils. In his new business, Bich became one of the first manufacturers to purchase presses to work with plastics. With his knowledge of inks and experience with plastics and moulding machines, Bich set himself up to become the largest pen manufacturer in the world. In 1949, Bich introduced his version of the modern ballpoint pen, originally invented in 1939, which he called 'BIC', a shortened, easy-to-remember version of his own name. He supported the pen with memorable, effective advertising; and its sales surpassed even his own expectations.

Realising that a mass-produced disposable ballpoint pen had universal appeal, Bich turned his attention to the US market. In 1958, he purchased the Waterman-Pen Company of Connecticut and then incorporated as Waterman-BIC Pen Corporation. The company changed

Exhibit 8 | Warner-Lambert income statements, 1986–8 (US$000)

		1988	1987	1986
Net sales		$3 908 400	$3 484 700	$3 102 918
Cost of sales		1 351 700	1 169 700	1 052 781
Other expenses		2 012 100	1 819 800	1 616 323
Operating income		544 600	495 200	433 814
Other income		61 900	58 500	69 611
Earnings before interest and tax		606 500	553 700	503 425
Interest expense		68 200	60 900	66 544
Earnings before tax		538 300	492 800	436 881
Tax		198 000	197 000	136 297
Non-recurring item		—	—	8 400
Earnings after tax		340 000	295 800	308 984
Retained earnings		1 577 400	1 384 100	1 023 218
Earnings per share		5.00	4.15	4.18
Average common shares outstanding (000)		68 035	71 355	73 985
Dividends paid per share		2.16	1.77	1.59
Stock price range	High	$79 1/2	$87 1/2	$63 1/8
	Low	$59 7/8	$48 1/4	$45

Source: *Moody's Industrial Manual*.

Exhibit 9 | Warner-Lambert balance sheets, 1986–8 (US$000)

		1988	1987	1986
Assets	Cash	$ 176 000	$ 24 100	$ 26 791
	Receivables	525 200	469 900	445 743
	Inventories	381 400	379 000	317 212
	Other current assets	181 300	379 600	720 322
	Total current assets	1 264 500	1 252 600	1 510 068
	Fixed assets, net	1 053 000	959 800	819 291
	Other assets	385 300	263 500	186 564
	Total assets	2 702 800	2 475 900	2 515 923
Liabilities and equity	Current liabilities*	1 025 200	974 300	969 806
	Current portion long-term debt	7 100	4 200	143 259
	Long-term debt	318 200	293 800	342 112
	Equity	$ 998 600	$ 874 400	$ 907 322

*Includes current option of long-term debt.
Source: *Moody's Industrial Manual*.

its name to BIC Pen in 1971 and finally adopted the name BIC Corporation for the publicly owned corporation in 1982.

After establishing itself as the country's largest pen maker, BIC attacked another market – the disposable lighter market. When BIC introduced its lighter in 1973, the total disposable lighter market stood at only 50 million units. By 1984, BIC had become so successful at manufacturing and marketing its disposable lighters that Gillette, its primary competitor, abandoned the lighter market. Gillette sold its Cricket division to Swedish Match, Stockholm, the manufacturer of Wilkinson razors. By 1989, the disposable lighter market had grown to nearly 500 million units, and BIC lighters accounted for 60 per cent of the market.

Not content to compete just in the writing and lighting markets, BIC decided to enter the US shaving market in 1976. A year earlier, the company had launched the BIC Shaver in Europe and Canada. BIC's entrance into the US razor market started an intense rivalry with Gillette. Admittedly, the companies were not strangers to each other – for years they had competed for market share in the pen and lighter industries. Despite the fact that razors were Gillette's primary business and an area where the company had no intention of relinquishing market share, BIC established a niche in the US disposable-razor market.

BIC, like Gillette, frequently introduced new razor products and product enhancements. In January 1985, following a successful Canadian test in 1984, BIC announced the BIC Shaver for Sensitive Skin. BIC claimed that 42 per cent of the men surveyed reported that they had sensitive skin, while 51 per cent of those who had heavy beards reported that they had sensitive skin. Thus, BIC felt there was a clear need for a shaver that addressed this special shaving problem. The US$10 million ad campaign for the BIC Shaver for Sensitive Skin featured John McEnroe, a highly ranked and well-known tennis professional, discussing good and bad backhands and normal and sensitive skin. BIC repositioned the original BIC white shaver as the shaver men with normal skin should use, while it promoted the new BIC Orange as the razor for sensitive skin.

BIC also tried its commodity strategy on sailboards, car-top carriers and perfume. In 1982, BIC introduced a sailboard model at about half the price of existing products. The product generated nothing but red ink. In April 1989, the company launched BIC perfumes with US$15 million in advertising support. BIC's foray into fragrances was as disappointing as its sailboard attempt. Throughout the year, Parfum BIC lost money, forcing management to concentrate its efforts on reformulating its selling theme, advertising, packaging and price points. Many retailers rejected the product, sticking BIC with expensive manufacturing facilities in Europe. BIC found that consumers' perceptions of commodities did not translate equally into every category. For example, many women cut corners elsewhere just to spend lavishly on their perfume. The last thing they wanted to see was their favourite scent being hawked to the masses.

Despite these failures, BIC Corporation was the undisputed king of the commoditisers. BIC's success with pens and razors demonstrated the upside potential

Exhibit 10 | BIC Corporation's net sales and income before taxes, 1986–8 (US$mn)

		1988	1987	1986
Net sales	Writing instruments	$118.5	$106.7	$91.7
	Lighters	113.9	120.0	115.0
	Shavers	51.9	47.1	49.6
	Sport	10.6	16.8	11.3
	Total	294.9	290.6	267.6
Profit/(loss) before taxes	Writing instruments	$16.7	$17.5	$15.0
	Lighters	22.9	28.2	28.5
	Shavers	9.4	8.5	8.0
	Sport	(4.7)	(3.5)	(3.6)
	TOTALS	44.3	50.7	47.9

Source: BIC Annual Reports, 1986–8.

Exhibit 11 | BIC Corporation consolidated income statements, 1986–8 (US$000)

	1988	1987	1986
Net sales	$294 878	$290 616	$267 624
Cost of sales	172 542	165 705	147 602
Other expenses	81 023	73 785	67 697
Operating income	41 313	51 126	52 325
Other income	4 119	1 836	7 534
Earnings before interest and tax	45 432	52 962	59 859
Interest expense	1 097	2 301	11 982
Earnings before tax	44 335	50 661	47 877
Tax	17 573	21 944	24 170
Extraordinary credit	—	—	2 486*
Utilisation of operating loss carry forward	2 800	—	—
Earnings after tax	$ 29 562	$ 28 717	$ 26 193
Retained earnings	159 942	142 501	121 784
Earnings per share	2.44	2.37	2.16
Average common shares outstanding (000)	12 121	12 121	12 121
Dividends paid per share	0.75	0.66	0.48
Stock price range High	$30 3/8	$34 7/8	$35
Low	$24 3/8	$16 1/2	$23 1/4

*Gain from elimination of debt.
Source: Moody's Industrial Manual; BIC Annual Reports.

of commoditisation, while its failures with sailboards and perfumes illustrated the limitations. BIC concentrated its efforts on designing, manufacturing and delivering the 'best' quality products at the lowest possible prices. And although the company produced large quantities of disposable products (for example, over 1 million pens a day), it claimed that each product was invested with the BIC philosophy: 'maximum service, minimum price'.

One of BIC's greatest assets was its retail distribution strength. The high profile the company enjoyed at supermarkets and drugstores enabled it to win locations in the aisles and display space at the checkout – the best positioning.

Even though BIC controlled only the number three spot in the wet-shaving market by 1989, it had exerted quite an influence since its razors first entered the US market in 1976. In 1988, BIC's razors generated US$52

Exhibit 12 | BIC Corporation balance sheets, 1986–8 (US$000)

		1988	1987	1986
Assets	Cash	$ 5 314	$ 4 673	$ 5 047
	Certificates of deposit	3 117	803	6 401
	Receivables, net	43 629	41 704	32 960
	Inventories	70 930	59 779	50 058
	Other current assets	37 603	47 385	34 898
	Deferred income taxes	7 939	6 691	5 622
	Total current assets	168 532	161 035	134 986
	Fixed assets, net	74 973	62 797	58 385
	Total assets	243 505	223 832	193 371
Liabilities and equity	Current liabilities*	55 031	54 034	45 104
	Current portion long-term debt	157	247	287
	Long-term debt	1 521	1 511	1 789
	Equity	$181 194	$164 068	$142 848

*Includes current portion of long-term debt.
Source: *Moody's Industrial Manual*.

million in sales with a net income of US$9.4 million; BIC held a 22.4 per cent share of dollar sales in the disposable razor market. Exhibit 10 presents operating data by product line, and Exhibits 11 and 12 give income statement and balance sheet data.

The introduction of the disposable razor revolutionised the industry and cut into system razor profits. However, despite the low profit margins in disposable razors and the fact that the industry leader, Gillette, emphasised razor and blade systems, BIC remained bullish on the disposable razor market. In 1989, a spokesperson for BIC claimed that BIC 'was going to stick to what consumers liked'. The company planned to continue marketing only single-blade, disposable shavers. BIC stated that it planned to maintain its strategy of underpricing competitors, but it would also introduce improvements such as the patented metal guard in its BIC Metal Shaver. Research revealed that the BIC Metal Shaver provided some incremental, rather than substitute, sales for its shaver product line. BIC executives believed that the BIC Metal Shaver would reach a 5–8 per cent market share by 1990.

Wilkinson Sword

Swedish Match Holding Incorporated's subsidiary, Wilkinson Sword, came in as the fourth player in the US market. Swedish Match Holding was a wholly owned subsidiary of Swedish Match AB, Stockholm, Sweden. The parent company owned subsidiaries in the United States that imported and sold doors, produced resilient and wood flooring, and manufactured branded razors, blades, self-sharpening scissors and gourmet kitchen knives. (Exhibits 13 and 14 present income statement and balance sheet data on Swedish Match AB.)

A group of swordsmiths founded Wilkinson in 1772, and soldiers used Wilkinson swords at Waterloo, at the charge of the Light Brigade and in the Boer War. However, as the sword declined as a combat weapon, Wilkinson retreated to producing presentation and ceremonial swords. By 1890, Wilkinson's cutlers had begun to produce straight razors, and by 1898 it was producing safety razors similar to King Gillette's. When Gillette's blades became popular in England, Wilkinson made stroppers to resharpen used blades. Wilkinson failed in the razor market, however, and dropped out during the Second World War.

By 1954, Wilkinson decided to look again at the shaving market. Manufacturers used carbon steel to make most razor blades at that time, and such blades lost their serviceability rapidly due to mechanical and chemical damage. Gillette and other firms had experimented with stainless steel blades; but they had found that despite their longer-lasting nature, the blades did not sharpen well. But some men liked the durability; and a few small companies produced stainless steel blades.

Wilkinson purchased one such small German company and put Wilkinson Sword blades on the market in 1956. Wilkinson developed a coating for the stainless blades (in the same fashion that Gillette had coated the Super Blue Blade) that masked their rough

Exhibit 13 | Swedish Match AB income statements, 1986–8 (US$000)

		1988	1987	1986
Net sales		$2 814 662	$2 505 047	$1 529 704
Cost of sales		N/A	N/A	N/A
Operating expenses		2 541 128	2 291 023	1 387 360
Other expenses		108 206	95 420	48 711
Earnings before interest		165 328	118 604	93 633
Interest expense		5 386	19 084	21 618
Earnings before tax		159 942	99 520	72 015
Tax		57 612	29 996	39 165
Earnings after tax		102 330	69 554	32 850
Dividends paid per share		0.53	0.51	1.75
Stock price range	High	22.53	19.65	66.75
	Low	$ 15.00	$ 11.06	$ 22.00

Source: *Moody's Industrial Manual.*

Exhibit 14 | Swedish Match AB balance sheets, 1986–8 (US$000)

		1988	1987	1986
Assets	Cash and securities	$ 159 616	$ 117 027	$323 993
	Receivables	611 372	561 479	297 321
	Inventories	421 563	415 116	258 858
	Total current assets	1 192 551	1 093 622	880 172
	Fixed assets, net	707 664	671 409	397 411
	Other assets	161 085	132 799	93 211
	Total assets	2 061 300	1 897 830	370 794
Liabilities and equity	Current liabilities	996 214	905 778	576 534
	Current portion long-term debt			
	Long-term debt	298 505	316 542	244 118
	Equity			

Source: *Moody's Industrial Manual.*

edges, allowing the blades to give a comfortable shave and to last two to five times longer than conventional blades. Wilkinson called the new blade the Super Sword-Edge. Wilkinson introduced the blades in England in 1961 and in the United States in 1962, and they became a phenomenon. Schick and American Safety Razor followed a year later with their own stainless steel blades, the Krona-Plus and Personna. Gillette finally responded in late 1963 with its own stainless steel blade; and by early 1964 Gillette's blades were outselling Wilkinson, Schick and Personna combined. Wilkinson, however, had forever changed the nature of the razor blade.

In 1988, Wilkinson Sword claimed to have a 4 per cent share of the US wet-shave market; and it was predicting a 6 per cent share by mid-1990. Industry analysts, however, did not confirm even the 4 per cent share; they projected Wilkinson's share to be closer to 1 per cent. Wilkinson introduced many new products over the years, but they generally proved to be short-lived. The company never really developed its US franchise.

However, in late 1988, Wilkinson boasted that it was going to challenge the wet-shave category leader by introducing Ultra-Glide, its first lubricating shaving system. Wilkinson designed Ultra-Glide to go head-to-head with Gillette's Atra Plus and Schick's Super II Plus and Ultrex Plus. Wilkinson claimed that Ultra-Glide represented a breakthrough in shaving technology because of an ingredient, hydromer, in its patented lubricating strip. According to Wilkinson, the Ultra-

Glide strip left less residue on the face and provided a smoother, more comfortable shave by creating a cushion of moisture between the razor and the skin.

Wilkinson introduced Ultra-Glide in March 1989 and supported it with a US$5 million advertising and promotional campaign (versus the Atra Plus US$80 million multimedia investment in the United States). Wilkinson priced Ultra-Glide 5–8 per cent less than Atra Plus. Wilkinson was undaunted by Gillette's heavier advertising investment, and it expected to cash in on its rival's strong marketing muscle. Wilkinson did not expect to overtake Gillette but felt its drive should help it capture a double-digit US market share within two to three years.

Many were sceptical about Wilkinson's self-predicted market share growth. One industry analyst stated, 'Gillette dominates this business. Some upstart won't do anything.' One Gillette official claimed his company was unfazed by Wilkinson. In fact, he was quoted as saying, in late 1988, 'They [Wilkinson] don't have a business in the US; they don't exist.'

Nonetheless, Gillette became enraged and filed legal challenges when Wilkinson's television ads for Ultra-Glide broke in May 1989. The ads stated that Ultra-Glide's lubricating strip was six times smoother than Gillette's strip and that men preferred it to the industry leader's. All three major networks had reservations about continuing to air the comparison commercials. CBS and NBC stated that they were going to delay airing the company's ads until Wilkinson responded to questions they had about its ad claims. In an 11th-hour counterattack, Wilkinson accused Gillette of false advertising and of trying to monopolise the wet-shave market.

GILLETTE'S SOUTH BOSTON PLANT

Robert Squires left his work station in the facilities engineering section of Gillette's South Boston manufacturing facility and headed for the shave test lab. He entered the lab area and walked down a narrow hall. On his right were a series of small cubicles Gillette had designed to resemble the sink area of a typical bathroom. Robert opened the door of his assigned cubicle precisely at his scheduled 10 a.m. time. He removed his dress shirt and tie, hanging them on a hook beside the sink. Sliding the mirror up as one would a window, Robert looked into the lab area. Rose McCluskey, a lab assistant, greeted him.

'Morning, Robert. See you're right on time as usual. I've got your things all ready for you.' Rose reached into a recessed area on her side of the cubicle's wall and handed Robert his razor, shave cream, aftershave lotion and a clean towel.

'Thanks, Rose. Hope you're having a good day. Anything new you've got me trying today?'

'You know I can't tell you that. It might spoil your objectivity. Here's your card.' Rose handed Robert a shaving evaluation card (see Exhibit 15).

Robert Squires had been shaving at the South Boston Plant off and on for all of his 25 years with Gillette. He was one of 200 men who shaved every work day at the plant. Gillette used these shavers to compare its products' effectiveness with competitors' products. The shavers also conducted R&D testing of new products and quality control testing for manufacturing. An additional seven to eight panels of 250 men each shaved every day in their homes around the country, primarily conducting R&D shave testing.

Like Robert, each shaver completed a shave evaluation card following every shave. Lab assistants like Rose entered data from the evaluations to allow Gillette researchers to analyse the performance of each shaving device. If a product passed R&D hurdles, it became the responsibility of the marketing research staff to conduct consumer-use testing. Such consumer testing employed 2 000 to 3 000 men who tested products in their homes.

From its research, Gillette had learned that the average man had 30 000 whiskers on his face that grew at the rate of half an inch (1.3 centimetres) per month. He shaved 5.8 times a week and spent three to four minutes shaving each time. A man with a life span of 70 years would shave more than 20 000 times, spending 3 350 hours (130 days) removing 27.5 feet (8.4 metres) of facial hair. Yet, despite all the time and effort involved in shaving, surveys found that if a cream were available that would eliminate facial hair and shaving, most men would not use it.

Robert finished shaving and rinsed his face and shaver. He glanced at the shaving head. A pretty good shave, he thought. The cartridge had two blades, but it seemed different. Robert marked his evaluation card and slid it across the counter to Rose.

William Mazeroski, manager of the South Boston shave test lab, walked into the lab area carrying computer printouts with the statistical analysis of last week's shave test data.

Exhibit 15 | Gillette shaving evaluation card

NUMB. _____ CODE _____ STA TEST# _____ NAME _____ EMP.# _____ DATE _____

IN-PLANT SHAVE TEST SCORECARD

INSTRUCTIONS: Please check one box in each column

Overall evaluation of shave	Freedom from nicks and cuts	Caution	Closeness	Smoothness	Comfort
❏ Excellent	❏ Excellent	❏ Exceptionally safe	❏ Exceptionally close	❏ Exceptionally smooth	❏ Exceptionally comfortable
❏ Very good	❏ Very good	❏ Unusually safe	❏ Very close	❏ Very smooth	❏ Very comfortable
❏ Good	❏ Good	❏ Average	❏ Average	❏ Average	❏ Average comfort smoothness
❏ Fair	❏ Fair	❏ Slight caution needed	❏ Fair	❏ Slight pull	❏ Slight irritation
❏ Poor	❏ Poor	❏ Excessive caution needed	❏ Poor	❏ Excessive pull	❏ Excessive irritation

Source: The Gillette Company.

Noticing Robert, William stopped. 'Morning, Robert. How was your shave?'

'Pretty good. What am I using?'

'Robert, you are always trying to get me to tell you what we're testing! We have control groups and experimental groups. I can't tell you which you are in, but I was just looking at last week's results, and I can tell you that it looks like we are making progress. We've been testing versions of a new product since 1979, and I think we're about to get it right. Of course, I don't know if we'll introduce it or even if we can make it in large quantities, but it looks good.'

'Well, that's interesting. At least I know I'm involved in progress. And, if we do decide to produce a new shaver, we'll have to design and build the machines to make it ourselves because there is nowhere to go to purchase blade-making machinery. Well, I've got to get back now; see you tomorrow.'

Thirty-Seventh Floor, The Prudential Center

Paul Hankins leaned over the credenza in his 37th-floor office in Boston's Prudential Center office building and admired the beauty of the scene that spread before him. Paul felt as though he were watching an impressionistic painting in motion. Beyond the green treetops and red brick buildings of Boston's fashionable Back Bay area, the Charles River wound its way towards Boston Harbor. Paul could see the buildings on the campuses of Harvard, MIT and Boston University scattered along both sides of the river. Soon the crew teams would be out practising. Paul loved to watch the precision with which the well-coordinated teams propelled the boats up and down the river. If only, he thought, we could be as coordinated as those crew teams.

Paul had returned to Boston in early 1988 when Gillette created the North Atlantic Group by combining what had been the North American and the European operations. Originally from Boston, he had attended Columbia University and earned an MBA at Dartmouth's Tuck School. He had been with Gillette for 19 years. Prior to 1988, he had served as marketing director for Gillette Europe from 1983 to 1984, as the country manager for Holland from 1985 to 1986, and finally as manager of Holland and the Scandinavian countries.

During this 1983–7 period, Paul had worked for Jim Pear, vice president of Gillette Europe, to implement a pan-European strategy. Prior to 1983, Gillette had organised and managed Europe as a classic decentralised market. To meet the perceived cultural nuances within each area, the company had treated each country as a separate market. For example, Gillette offered the same products under a variety of sub-brand names. The company sold its Good News! disposable razors under the name 'Blue II' in the United Kingdom,

'Parat' in Germany, 'Gillette' in France and Spain, 'Radi e Getta' (shave and throw) in Italy, and 'Economy' in other European markets.

Jim Pear believed that in the future Gillette would have to organise across country lines, and he had developed the pan-European idea. He felt that shaving was a universal act and that Gillette's razors were a perfect archetype for a 'global' product.

Gillette had launched Contour Plus, the European version of Atra Plus, in 1985–6 and had experienced greater success than the US launch which took place at the same time. The pan-European strategy seemed to be both more efficient and more effective. Colman Mockler, Gillette's chairman, noticed the European success and asked Pear to come to Boston to head the new North Atlantic Group. Paul had come with him as vice president of marketing for the Shaving and Personal Care Group.

Paul turned from the window as he heard people approaching. Sarah Kale, vice president of Marketing Research; Brian Mullins, vice president of marketing, Shaving and Personal Care Group; and Scott Friedman, business director, Blades and Razors, were at his door.

'Ready for our meeting?' Scott asked.

'Sure, come on in. I was just admiring the view.'

'The purpose of this meeting,' Paul began, 'is to begin formulating a new strategy for Gillette North Atlantic, specifically for our shaving products. I'm interested in your general thoughts and analysis. I want to begin to identify options and select a strategy to pursue. What have you found out?'

'Well, here are the market share numbers you asked me to develop,' Scott observed as he handed each person copies of tables he had produced (see Exhibits 16 and 17). Like Paul, Scott had earned an MBA from the Tuck School and had been with Gillette for 17 years.

'These are our US share numbers through 1988. As you can see, Atra blades seem to have levelled off and Trac II blades are declining. Disposable razors now account for over 41 per cent of the market, in dollars, and for over 50 per cent of the market in terms of units. In fact, our projections indicate that disposable razors will approach 100 per cent of the market by the mid- to late 1990s given current trends. Although we have 56 per cent of the blade market and 58 per cent of the disposable razor market, our share of the disposable razor market has fallen. Further, you are aware that every 1 per cent switch from our system razors to our disposable razors represents a loss of US$10 million on the bottom line.'

'I don't think any of this should surprise us,' Sarah Kale interjected. Sarah had joined Gillette after graduating from Simmons College in Boston and had been with the firm for 14 years. 'If you look back over the 1980s, you'll see that we helped cause this problem.'

'What do you mean by that?' asked Paul.

'Well, as market leader, we never believed that the use of disposable razors would grow as it has. We went along with the trend, but we kept prices low on our disposable razors, which made profitability worse for both us and our competition because they had to take our price into consideration in setting their prices. Then, to compensate for the impact on our profitability from the growth of the disposable razor market, we were raising the prices on our system razors. This made disposable razors even more attractive for price-sensitive users and further fuelled the growth of disposable razors. This has occurred despite the fact that our market research shows that men rate system shavers significantly better than disposable razors. We find that the weight and balance contributed by the permanent handle used with the cartridge contributes to a better shave.'

Exhibit 16 | Gillette market share of dollar sales, 1981–8 (per cent)

Product or category	1981	1982	1983	1984	1985	1986	1987	1988
Atra blades	15.4	17.3	19.4	18.7	20.2	20.9	20.0	20.5
Trac II blades	17.5	16.4	15.2	14.6	14.1	13.5	11.8	11.4
Gillette blades	47.3	48.9	52.1	54.2	55.8	57.1	54.1	56.0
Gillette disposables	14.3	15.4	17.4	20.0	21.1	22.7	22.2	24.0
All disposables	23.0	23.2	27.0	30.6	32.7	34.9	38.5	41.1
Gillette disposables as % of all disposables	67.9	66.9	64.7	65.7	64.6	64.2	57.6	58.4
Gillette razors	50.3	52.5	54.9	58.8	62.2	67.6	64.1	61.0

Source: Prudential-Bache Securities.

Exhibit 17 | Gillette system cartridges, 1971–88 (dollar share of US blade market)

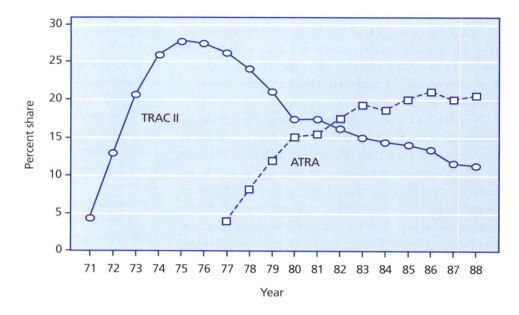

Source: The Gillette Company; Prudential-Bache Securities.

'Yes, but every time I tell someone that,' Paul added, 'they just look at me as if they wonder if I really believe that or if it is just Gillette's party line.'

'There's one other thing we've done,' Scott added. 'Look at this graph of our advertising expenditures in the US over the 1980s [see Exhibit 18]. In fact, in constant 1987 dollars, our advertising spending has fallen from US$61 million in 1975 to about US$15 million in 1987. We seem to have just spent what was left over on advertising. We are now spending about one-half of our advertising on Atra and one-half on Good News!. Tentative plans call for us to increase the share going to Good News!. Our media budget for 1988 was about US$43 million. Further, we've tried three or four themes, but we haven't stuck with any one for very long. We're using the current theme, "The Essence of Shaving", for both system and disposable products. Our advertising has been about 90 per cent product-based and 10 per cent image-based.'

'Well, Scott's right,' Sarah noted, 'but although share of voice is important, share of mind is what counts. Our most recent research shows a significant difference in how we are perceived by male consumers based on their age. Men over 40 still remember Gillette, despite our reduced advertising, from their youth. They remember Gillette's sponsorship of athletic events, like the Saturday Baseball Game of the Week and the Cavalcade of Sports. They remember "Look Sharp! Feel Sharp! Be Sharp" and Sharpie the Parrot. They remember their fathers loaning them their Gillette razors when they started shaving. There is still a strong connection between Gillette and the male image of shaving.'

'How about with younger men?' asked Brian. Brian had joined Gillette in 1975 after graduating from Washington and Lee University and earning a master's degree in administration from George Washington University.

'Younger men's views can be summed up simply – twin blade, blue and plastic,' Sarah reported.

'Just like our disposable razors!' Paul exclaimed.

'Precisely,' Sarah answered. 'As I say, we've done this to ourselves. We have a "steel" man and "plastic" man. In fact, for males between 15 and 19, BIC is better known than Gillette with respect to shaving. Younger men in general – those under 30, these "plastic" men – feel all shavers are the same. Older men and system users feel there is a difference.'

'Yes,' Paul interjected, 'and I've noticed something else interesting. Look at our logos. We use the Gillette brand name as our corporate name, and the brand name is done in thin, block letters. I'm not sure it has the impact and masculine image we want. On top of that, look at these razor packages. We have become so product-focused and brand-manager-driven that we've lost focus on the brand name. Our brands look tired: there's nothing special about our retail packaging and display.'

Exhibit 18 | Blade and razor media spending, United States, 1975–87

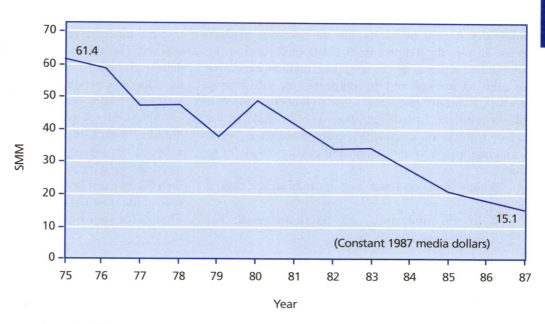

Source: The Gillette Company.

'Speaking of the male image of shaving, Sarah, what does your research show about our image with women?' asked Brian.

'Well, we've always had a male focus and women identify the Gillette name with men and shaving, even those who use our products marketed to women. You know that there are more women wet shavers than men in the US market, about 62 million versus 55 million. However, due to seasonability and lower frequency of women's shaving, the unit volume used by women is only about one-third that of the volume used by men. Women use about eight to 12 blades a year versus 25 to 30 for men. It is still very consistent for us to focus on men.'

'Well, we've got plenty of problems on the marketing side, but we also have to remember that we are part of a larger corporation with its own set of problems,' Brian suggested. 'We're only 30 per cent or so of sales but we are 60 per cent of profits. And, given the takeover battles, there is going to be increased pressure on the company to maintain and improve profitability. That pressure has always been on us, but now it will be more intense. If we want to develop some bold, new strategy, we are going to have to figure out where to get the money to finance it. I'm sure the rest of the corporation will continue to look to us to throw off cash to support diversification.'

'This can get depressing,' Paul muttered as he looked back at the window. 'I can sense the low morale inside the company. People sense the inevitability of disposability. We see BIC as the enemy even though it is so much smaller than Gillette. We've got to come up with a new strategy. What do you think our options are, Scott?'

'Well, I think we're agreed that the "do-nothing" option is out. If we simply continue to do business as usual, we will see the erosion of the shaving market's profitability as disposable razors take more and more share. We could accept the transition to disposable razors and begin to try to segment the disposable razor market based on performance. You might call this the "give up" strategy. We would be admitting that disposable razors are the wave of the future. There will obviously continue to be shavers who buy based on price only, but there will also be shavers who will pay more for disposable razors with additional benefits, such as lubricating strips or movable heads. In Italy, for example, we have done a lot of image building and focused on quality. Now, Italian men seem to perceive that our disposable razors have value despite their price. In other words, we could try to protect the category's profitability by segmenting the market and offering value to those segments willing to pay for it. We would de-emphasize system razors.

'Or, we could try to turn the whole thing around. We could develop a strategy to slow the growth of disposable razors and to reinvigorate the system razor market.'

'How does the new razor system fit into all this?' Paul asked.

'I'm pleased that we have continued to invest in R&D despite our problems and the takeover battles,' Brian answered. 'Reports from R&D indicate that the new shaver is doing well in tests. But it will be expensive to take to market and to support with advertising. Further, it doesn't make any sense to launch it unless it fits in with the broader strategy. For example, if we decide to focus on disposable razors, it makes no sense to launch a new system razor and devote resources to that.'

'What's the consumer testing indicating?' asked Scott.

'We're still conducting tests,' Sarah answered, 'but so far the results are very positive. Men rate the shave superior to both Atra or Trac II and superior to our competition. In fact, I think we'll see that consumers rate the new shaver as much as 25 per cent better on average. The independently spring-mounted twin blades deliver a better shave, but you know we've never introduced a product until it was clearly superior in consumer testing on every dimension.'

'Okay. Here's what I'd like to do,' Paul concluded. 'I'd like for each of us to devote some time to developing a broad outline of a strategy to present at our next meeting. We'll try to identify and shape a broad strategy then that we can begin to develop in detail over the next several months. Let's get together in a week, same time. Thanks for your time.'

References

Adams, R. B. Jr, 1978, *King Gillette: The Man and His Wonderful Shaving Device* (Boston: Little, Brown).

BIC Annual Report, 1989.

Caminiti, S., 1989, 'Gillette gets sharp', *Fortune*, 8 May, p. 84.

Dewhurst, P., 1981, 'BICH = BIC', *Made in France International*, Spring, pp. 38–41.

Dunkin, A., Baum, L. and Therrein, L., 1986, 'This takeover artist wants to be a makeover artist, too', *Business Week*, 1 December, pp. 106, 110.

Dun's Million Dollar Directory, 1989.

Fahey, A. and Sloan, P., 1988, 'Gillette: $80M to rebuild image', *Advertising Age*, 31 October, pp. 1, 62.

Fahey, A. and Sloan, P., 1988, 'Wilkinson cuts in', *Advertising Age*, 28 November, p. 48.

Fahey, A. and Sloan, P., 1989, 'Kiam gets some help: Grey sharpens Remington ads', *Advertising Age*, 13 November, p. 94.

Gillette Annual Corporate Reports, 1985–8.

Hammonds, K., 1987, 'How Ron Perelman scared Gillette into shape', *Business Week*, 12 October, pp. 40–1.

Hammonds, K., 1989, 'At Gillette disposable is a dirty word', *Business Week*, 29 May, pp. 54–5.

Jervey, G., 1984, 'New blade weapons for Gillette-BIC war', *Advertising Age*, 5 November, pp. 1, 96.

Jervey, G., 1985, 'Gillette and BIC spots taking on sensitive subject', *Advertising Age*, 18 March, p. 53.

Jervey, G., 1985, 'Gillette, Wilkinson heat up disposable duel', *Advertising Age*, 10 June, p. 12.

Kiam V., 1987, 'Remington's marketing and manufacturing strategies', *Management Review*, February, pp. 43–5.

Kiam V., 1989, 'Growth strategies at Remington', *Journal of Business Strategy*, January/February, pp. 22–6.

Kummel, C. M. and Klompmaker, J. E., 1980, 'The Gillette Company – Safety Razor Division', in D. W. Cravens and C. W. Lamb (eds), *Strategic Marketing: Cases and Applications* (Homewood, Ill.: Irwin), pp. 324–45.

McGeehan, P., 1988, 'Gillette sharpens its global strategy', *Advertising Age*, 25 April, pp. 2, 93.

Newport, J. P., 1988, 'The stalking of Gillette', *Fortune*, 23 May, pp. 99–101.

North American Philips Corporation Annual Report, 1987.

Pereira, J., 1988, 'Gillette's next-generation blade to seek new edge in flat market', *The Wall Street Journal*, 7 April, p. 34.

Raissman, R., 1984, 'Gillette pitches new throwaway', *Advertising Age*, 9 July, p. 12.

'Razors and blades', 1989, *Consumer Reports*, May, pp. 300–4.

Rothman, A., 1988, 'Gillette, in a shift, to emphasize cartridge blades over disposables', *The Wall Street Journal*, 18 November, p. B6.

Sacharow, S., 1982, *Symbols of Trade* (New York: Art Direction Book Company).

Shore, A., 1989, *Gillette Report* (New York: Shearson Lehman Hutton), 19 October.

Shore, A., 1990, *Gillette Company Update* (New York: Prudential-Bache Securities), May 18.

Sloan, P., 1985, 'Marschalk brains land Braun', *Advertising Age*, 18 March, p. 53.

Sloan, P., 1988, 'Remington gets the edge on Gillette', *Advertising Age*, 16 May, pp. 3, 89.

Sutor, R., 1988, 'Household personal care products', *Financial World*, 27 December.

The Europa World Year Book 1990, vol. II.

Trachtenberg, J. A., 1986, 'Styling for the masses', *Forbes*, 10 March, pp. 152–3.

Warner-Lambert Annual Corporate Report, 1987.

Weiss, G., 1986, 'Razor sharp: Gillette to snap back from a dull stretch', *Barron's*, 25 August, pp. 15, 37.

Case 6

Incat Tasmania's race for international success:
Blue Riband strategies

Mark Wickham
Dallas Hanson
University of Tasmania

In 1999, Robert Clifford (aged 56) entered the *Business Review Weekly*'s 'Richest 200 Australians' for the first time, qualifying for the elite group with an estimated net worth of some $150 million.[1] Clifford is the founder and chairman of Incat Tasmania, a highly successful catamaran manufacturer in Hobart. His far-sightedness as a ship-builder, alongside his ability to manage innovation, enabled his small boat-building business (and river-ferry operation) to become a world force in the high-speed catamaran market, exporting to Europe, Asia and the Americas. So successful has the Incat operation been that, in 1999, it directly employed over 1 000 people, generated $250 million in revenue and accounted for approximately 20 per cent of Tasmania's total export earnings.[2] The success and wealth that Clifford has generated through his catamaran business is a far cry from his somewhat 'humble' beginnings.

Robert Clifford a.k.a. 'Judge Dredge'

Robert (Bob) Clifford's start in the business world was founded upon what may be best described as a 'relatively unsuccessful scholarly career'. Indeed, during his high-school years at the exclusive Hutchins Boys School, a rash of subject failures resulted in his crowning as a 'dunce' by his teachers.[3] Clifford, in his semi-autobiography, recalls an incident whereby he was also failed in his favourite subject, woodwork. The failure was awarded to Clifford when his teachers failed to believe (perhaps not unreasonably) that he could have possibly built, all by himself, a 14-foot (4.3-metre) yacht in his bedroom. Although the yacht was presented to the teachers for marking, it was a consensus view that he must have received considerable help from his family. It was an assumption that was only true to a point. (His father did help to get his mother out of the house so that Clifford could remove windows and frames and actually get the boat out of the house!4)

After Clifford finished his tour of duty at school, he entered the workforce as a printing apprentice, a position that he soon resigned in favour of a family-oriented job as a fisherman. His job as a fisherman involved helping his father manage five crayfish and scalloping boats, which he had also helped to build. The family business was run on a tight budget and, as such, the firm's boat manufacturing premises equated to vacant land adjacent to their residential property. It was in such ship-building yards that Bob Clifford, with the help of his father and siblings, toiled from dawn until dusk in order to build their fleet. The resulting boats were named the *Moana*, *Dolphin*, *Gazelle*, *Lanzig* and *Leillateah*, and ranged from 10 metres to 15 metres in length.[5]

Their first boat, the *Moana*, was also the shortest in length and was built utilising the 'state of the art' fishing technologies of the day. However, the backbreaking, and at times very dangerous, scallop dredging process motivated the young Bob Clifford to redesign certain aspects of the operation. In particular, he was worried that the 'traditional' dredging process, whereby three individuals were required to place themselves in precarious positions from which to empty the dredging nets, was potentially hazardous to life and limb. To overcome this hazard, which stemmed from a dredging net that became rather difficult to manage with the added weight of a substantial catch, Clifford sought to innovate the process with a 'self-tipping net'. In an effort to make this much simplified, and much safer, dredging process a reality, Clifford constructed numerous models made from lightweight balsa wood held together by glue and pins. With the help of his family, he successfully engineered a dredge that would 'self-tip' its cargo, removing the need for many dangerous moving parts and potentially hazardous human intervention. In order to implement a full-scale trial of this new system, the Cliffords built their second vessel, the *Dolphin*, with the new dredging design. After several real-life tests, further modifications were undertaken and a new and improved version was fitted to their third boat, the 54-foot (16.5-metre) *Gazelle*.[6]

The Clifford scallop boats were the only users of this new dredging technology for quite some time, with many other fishermen reluctant to change a dredging process that they were fully familiar with, and which heralded back some 50 years to their fathers and grandfathers. Times changed, however, as did occupational health and safety regulations. Today, scallop boats in Australia are universally fitted with virtually the same 'self-tipping' dredging system that was developed by Bob Clifford for his *Gazelle* in 1965.

The Clifford family business decided to expand its catchment area in late 1965 to include the rugged west coast of Tasmania. In keeping with previous efforts to expand their rewards through an improvement in their methods, Clifford decided to design a boat specifically for the region, rather than simply build 'another typical sailing craft common in Tasmania'. Unlike the eastern fishing regions, the west coast of Tasmania experiences winds that are affectionately known as 'the roaring forties', a number that refers to the wind speeds in the area. To help overcome these rather extreme conditions, Clifford designed the new boat (named the *Lanzig*) with a reinforced hull and an increased engine hold capable of housing a more powerful diesel engine. Expecting excellent catches from this region, he also included in the design a system of 'powerful bilges, capable of carrying a good load of fish a long distance'.[7]

Another opportunity to improve the family business's profitability arose in 1968 when a rival fisherman's vessel was sunk on a reef on the west coast of Tasmania. This loss of a vessel meant that the opportunities for an increased share in the new, and very promising, southern crayfishing season were available to those that supplied ships to the region. Having enjoyed entrepreneurial success previously, Clifford attempted to take advantage of the opportunity by designing and building the family's largest boat to date: the 15-metre *Leillateah*.

Due to the sheer size and scale of the *Leillateah* project, Clifford was forced to abandon the family's traditional methods for boat building. Instead of using vacant blocks and various family back yards, Clifford utilised the Battery Point boat-building sheds of a new maritime friend, Max Creese. Creese was one of Tasmania's best-known boat builders, and provided Clifford with access to valuable materials, labour and 'experience' in the boat manufacturing process. The size of the new boat project was considerable, and required that a team of builders work 'around the clock' in order to complete the boat before the season opened. Clifford himself states that 'the importance of timing to an entrepreneurial business venture has been proven many times over'.[8] The project was a success, and the *Leillateah* was completed on the Sunday before the season opened the following Wednesday. The effort proved to be very profitable for the Clifford family business, with the *Leillateah* returning one week after the season's opening with some five tonnes of crayfish in its hold.

From 1968 to 1972, the Cliffords' fishing business maintained a fleet of five vessels. As with most businesses, the profitability of the venture surged. At its most successful, the five vessels were returning with significant catches, the best of which yielded 81 dozen crayfish, three tonnes of shark and 150 bags of scallops. At its least successful, the business sent its fleet on a three-month, 6 000-nautical mile journey to the Gulf of Carpentaria for a return of two prawns.

During this time, there was little need for further innovations to be undertaken, and by late 1971, Bob Clifford had become somewhat dissatisfied with life as a Tasmanian fisherman. It was agreed early in 1972 to dissolve the family fishing business that had been created some seven years earlier. The father–son partnership had proved to be very successful over the years, with the pair generating enough revenue by 1972 to form what would prove to be a pivotal business partnership.

Clifford and Clifford Incorporated: Don't pay the ferrymen …

During the early 1970s, there had been some talk of reintroducing a 'Trans-Derwent' ferry service, one that would predominantly serve Tasmania's tourist population.[9] As had happened with the sinking of a rival's vessel some four years earlier, Clifford sensed an opportunity to re-employ his entrepreneurial skill and capture a 'new' market through the implementation of valuable innovations. He was extremely keen to initiate this business opportunity, and in 1972 Bob and his father formed the Sullivan's Cove Ferry Company on the Derwent River.[10] So keen had Clifford been that, simultaneously, he approached the Marine Construction

Company (a boat-building venture in Rokeby, Hobart) with some preliminary design plans for his proposed 'Derwent River ferry'. As with the *Leillateah*, Clifford was keen to have production under way nearly immediately, and in fact, the details of the ferry's design were worked out by the builder and Clifford as construction progressed. By mid-1972, construction of Clifford's first ferry, the 20-metre steel-hulled *Matthew Brady* (named after a famous Australian bushranger) was completed. Armed with a suitable vessel to handle a ferry service across the Derwent River, all that the Sullivan's Cove Ferry Company had to accomplish was a successful bid for the rights to service the market. The company indeed was successful in its bid, and began operations late in 1972.

Business proved to be good in the early stages of the newly formed ferry service, with tourists and locals alike taking advantage of this novel attraction. In order for Clifford to generate sales growth, and indeed protect his source of income, he prudently decided to build a second ferry in case the *Matthew Brady* was unable to sail. A second ferry was designed, commissioned and built in 1973 (by the same Rokeby ship-building yard as the *Matthew Brady*). The Cliffords' new ferry, the *James McCabe*, was again named after a notorious Australian bushranger. Technologies had improved since the construction of the *Matthew Brady*, and the new ferry was somewhat faster and more comfortable than the mother ship. The decision to construct a second ferry was a rather fortuitous one, given the tragic events in early 1975.

On 5 January 1975, at 9.27 p.m., the bulk ore carrier *Lake Illawarra* crashed into the 19th pier of the Tasman Bridge, claiming 12 lives and severing the Eastern Shore's link with Hobart by knocking out an 80-metre section of the bridge.[11] Many tens of thousands of motorists and cyclists were now unable to travel easily to their required destinations, be it for work or pleasure. Bob Clifford found himself in the enviable position of 'being in the right place at the right time'.

...'til they get you to the other side: Transportation returns to Van Dieman's Land

In response to the increased demand for transport that resulted from the Tasman Bridge tragedy, Clifford hurriedly built a third ferry, the *Martin Cash*. Such was the priority of the project that 'records were broken in the rush to get the craft into service quickly'.[12] The construction process was aided somewhat by the fact that the new ferry was a sister ship to the original *Matthew Brady*, and therefore no new designs or alterations were required.

Although the ferry service now boasted three boats, demand still exceeded supply, and in late 1975 a fourth ferry was commissioned. Given the urgency of demand in the market, the latest ferry, the *Lawrence Kavanagh* (again a famous bushranger), was constructed in record time. As with the *Martin Cash*, there was little fanfare at its launch, simply a push into the Derwent River on her way to pick up a load of customers. The four 'bushrangers' were to serve as the west–east link for some three years while repairs to the Tasman Bridge were under way. In this time, Clifford's ferries transported in excess of 9 million paying passengers.

These 9 million passengers, forced to utilise the ferry service, provided Clifford with significant revenues, but they didn't come from the sale of transport tickets alone. Indeed, after finding a loophole in the Tasmanian licensing laws, Clifford was able to serve both counter meals and alcoholic beverages on his ferry rides, even though he did not possess what the law required – a dedicated dining area. It would appear that the law makers of the day had not considered the possibility that a ferry service would undertake such additional services. At its zenith, Clifford's 'bushranger fleet' was the largest licensee in Australia, averaging sales of 3 800 litres of beer per week; the sales from beer and food were so great that they accounted for more than 50 per cent of the entire revenues generated by the business.[13]

In order to improve customer service and increase the business's revenues, Clifford hired a new British-built fast-ferry, the *Michael Howe*. The *Michael Howe* was twice as fast and twice as comfortable as the 'bushranger fleet' owned by Clifford, and was an instant success with the general public. Unfortunately, the *Michael Howe* was also a maintenance-intensive investment, with 75 per cent of all company maintenance expenditure spent on the new 'hired hand'. Clifford was understandably unimpressed with the boat's design and maintenance requirements, despite the public's obvious delight with the faster service. The flaws that Clifford observed in the boat's design and structure (the mechanics were far too complicated and labour-intensive to be viable in the long term) once again reignited his innovative flair: 'If the English can sell 34 heaps of rubbish like this [around the world], how many properly engineered fast ships could we sell from Tasmania?'[14] With this marketing opportunity well in his grasp, the Clifford business began its initial foray into the fast-ferry industry.

Clifford: Licensed to keel

The question for Clifford now concerned how to develop a boat with the speed and passenger appeal of a fast-moving vessel (such as a hovercraft), while maintaining the basic economies of a conventional ferry. Clifford studied the merits of numerous low-resistance hovercraft and the catamaran-style 'sidewall' hovercraft was chosen as the best available design template. Clifford utilised this hovercraft design, but altered it to include twin-hulls (somewhat wider than the norm for catamarans at the time) and to exclude altogether the 'air-lift equipment' that was standard to the hovercraft. The newly designed boat was described as 'thought-provoking' by naval engineering experts, and indeed, the prototype model was not sanctioned by the maritime authorities as a 'legal means for general public transportation'. This rejection was primarily due to a recent change in the maritime laws in Tasmania.

Under new legislation, Clifford (and every other boat manufacturer) was forced to seek the services of a qualified naval architect to endorse any new design – a time-consuming and rather expensive task given that no such professional practised in the state at the time. In order to get the required endorsement, Clifford had to travel to New South Wales to meet a certified naval architect, Phil Hercus, who resided in Sydney. The plans were checked for design flaws, and after a 'clean bill of health' was awarded by Hercus, the *Jeremiah Ryan* was conceived with the blessing of the authorities.

The *Jeremiah Ryan* was built in a Tasmanian government-owned wharf shed at Prince of Wales Bay in September 1977, and, according to Clifford, it could only have been described as 'ugly as sin'. Construction of the vessel was undertaken by collaboration between Clifford employees and a number of contracted 'expert' tradesmen. Although not as aesthetically pleasing as Clifford may have liked, the steel catamaran was considered a major breakthrough, achieving some 26 knots in initial speed trials, considerably more than the 18 originally hoped for in the design stage. After the success of the *Jeremiah Ryan*, Clifford and Hercus entered into a partnership to form International Catamarans Pty Ltd of Australia and launch the predecessor of one of Tasmania's most successful businesses ever.[15]

International Catamarans (Incat) Pty Ltd, buoyed by the success of their original catamaran design and construction, continued to employ innovative design and construction processes.[16] To achieve this end, the company restructured its management team, which now 'professionally employed' the functional services of an offshore project manager (Graeme Freeman) and the strategic services of three company directors (Bob Clifford, Phil Hercus and Kerry Sturmey).

By 1979, in an effort to reduce the weight of their boats, the company did away with the traditional steel-based catamaran designs in favour of an experiment with aluminium super-structures. The first steel-aluminium catamaran to be sold by Incat was the *James Kelly* in June 1979, which serviced ferry passengers across Macquarie Harbour. The project was considered 'highly important', as it was the initial foray into new ship-building technologies and processes, the most important of which is arguably the perfection of aluminium-based welding. However radical the design and building processes were, the end result was that the operators found the ferry to be much faster and cheaper to run than traditional ferry designs. Consequently, the operators considered the *James Kelly* a great success. The commercial success of the *James Kelly* soon became the talk of the maritime industry and resulted in the first orders for all-aluminium catamarans.[17]

In keeping with the innovative nature of the business to date, Clifford was only too happy to attempt this new all-aluminium catamaran. The lighter, and more aesthetically pleasing, vessel also proved to be a great success for the purchasers and was very popular with their customers. Clifford comments that, with this first effort (eventually named the *Fitzroy*), 'We had overcome our fear of the unknown and built an excellent aluminium vessel at out first try.'[18] He also learned an important marketing lesson: a fast ship must *look* fast! In an effort to impress Incat's customers, the delivery voyage was used as an opportunity to show off the tremendous speed the boat had to offer. So impressed were the customers by the speed at which their new boat arrived that they immediately ordered five more similar vessels on the spot. Positive word of mouth soon followed, as did orders from all over Australia.

The majority of the interstate orders originated from Queensland, where operators were greatly interested in faster transport for their customers between islands, across bays and between reefs. For example, before the 'fast catamarans' serviced the outer Barrier Reef, only dedicated reef enthusiasts could visit the Great Barrier Reef on slow fishing vessels. Incat's new fast-catamarans essentially opened up the reef as a multimillion-dollar market to both domestic and international tourists.

A pivotal, and unplanned, marketing moment occurred on New Year's Eve 1981, when the 20-metre catamaran the *Tangalooma* was filmed cruising at full speed through two-metre seas on its way to a year's end party. The media coverage was apparently very impressive and resulted in further orders being place from around the nation. When it became clear that the Hobart facility could not keep up with consumer demand, the decision was undertaken to license others to construct catamarans to Incat's designs. This decision would constitute Incat's initial foray into the internationalisation process.[19] Licences were granted to three ship-building yards in New Zealand, two in the United States, and one in each of the United Kingdom, China and Singapore. Interestingly, each of the firms licensed by Clifford in this period were located in areas of relatively high unemployment. Collectively, the licensing agreements resulted in the construction of 80 catamarans outside of Australia's borders. With the exception of the New Zealand and Singapore contracts, each of the licensees have since prospered, a result of strong world demand for specialised catamaran transport.

Changing tack: Incat's move from people to people and cargo

The increased demand for Incat's fast-ferries was accompanied by changes in consumer preferences. Although the market for people carriers was still characterised by strong demand, additional requests were being made for 'fast cargo carriers'. Clifford was once again faced with an opportunity to utilise his innovative skills, this time to build a catamaran that remained fast, yet was large enough to stow mass cargo.

Returning to the drawing board, Clifford created the blueprints for a new 30-metre catamaran, which was larger by far than anything previously designed or built. The new vessel, the *Spirit of Roylen*, had the capacity to transport 250 passengers in spacious comfort, as well as accommodate their luggage and the supplies needed by the holiday resort it serviced. Once again, the new vessel was a huge success, with both the purchaser and their passengers very satisfied with the quality and speed of the new service. The success also did not go unnoticed by those outside the maritime community. In late 1982, for example, orders were placed by the government-run Hydro-Electric Commission for a high-speed catamaran capable of transporting 150 workers or 30 tonnes of cargo to the newly planned 'Gordon below Franklin' power scheme site. At their request, Incat designed and built the *Trojan* fast-catamaran. The vessel was launched on 30 March 1983 in time to service the new electricity project; however, it was soon 'unemployed', due to the successful protest of environmental groups against the damming scheme.

By 1984, Incat's catamarans had proved their worth, servicing the islands in Queensland's north through the speedy transportation of both people and cargo. An order by the resort operators on Keppel Island, however, would require that Clifford once again return to the drawing board, this time to overcome a rather difficult problem that presented itself for his, and indeed anyone's, boats – the resort had no jetty. The result was the design and construction of the *Keppel Cat 1* and its well-named successor, the *Keppel Cat 2*. These 'new cats' had the ability to dock on the beach and be unloaded of passengers and cargo via specially designed ramps. Needless to say, this design feature was highly valued by the Keppel Island holiday resort, as well as by the customers, as it sped up the trip to and from the island markedly. The *Keppel Cat 1* was a 'personal milestone' for International Catamarans as well, as it was the first vessel to be built by the company in a yard that was fully owned and operated by the firm.

By 1985, orders for Incat's range of products were coming from several international companies. Sealink, a British ferry company, ordered two 30-metre passenger catamarans (*Our Lady Patricia* and *Our Lady Pamela*) for their Portsmouth to Ryde service across The Solent in England. The British purchasers were more than impressed with the boats' performance during the delivery stage from Belgium to Portsmouth: a journey that usually took three days was completed in just one.[20]

In 1986, another major marketing opportunity arose for Incat in the form of the 1987 defence of the America's Cup. By this stage, Incat was able to buy back *Keppel Cat 2* from the Keppel Island resort owners, due to diminishing demand for a dual boat service. Incat took up the offer to re-buy the boat and refurbish the vessel as an official media boat for the full six-month period of the America's Cup trials and finals. The exposure of the vessel to the world's media, especially given its sterling performance during the entire competition, was invaluable advertising for Incat. Clifford was not waiting for the market to react to this exposure, however, and before the America's Cup challenge was run and lost by Australia, he had already begun work on what he believed to be the next generation of saleable catamaran – the 'wave piercer'.

Clifford first advanced the idea of the wave-piercing catamaran in 1983, at which stage he had completed the construction of an eight-metre model for practical appraisal. The quality of the 'ride' experienced by the maximum of six passengers on the new vessel was quoted as being 'unprecedented in choppy seas'. It took until 1986 for the designs and construction material requirements to be finalised through Incat's planning and design process. On 20 December 1986, the *Tassie Devil 2001* was launched and hurriedly fitted out on its way to Fremantle for the running of the America's Cup finals. On the delivery voyage across the Great Australian Bight, it was noted how easily the vessel could 'surf' down the rising seas. During its time as the premier passenger vessel of the series, the *Tassie Devil 2001* provided fast, smooth rides and an excellent standard of comfort. It was more economical than many of Incat's competitor craft, and the viewing world took notice. It was on the basis of the *Tassie Devil 2001* that the decision to go ahead with the design and construction of wave-piercing, car-carrying vessels was made.

The period from 1986 to 1988 saw the construction of two further innovative catamarans, the *Starship Genesis* and the wave-piercing *2000*. The *Starship Genesis* was built as part of experiments to improve the economy of the propulsion systems of the catamaran fleet. Although the novel approach to propulsion, which involved new 'surface-piercing' propellers, was successful, the idea has not been followed up on any further vessels. The *2000* was built following the great success of the *Tassie Devil 2001*, and was much improved with regards to its carpets, seating and timber-work finishes. The *2000* was purpose-built for the Hamilton Island resort complex, and, as with their other catamarans, was a complete success for their business.

International Catamarans: The end of the line

International Catamarans Pty Ltd was formed in 1977 as a partnership between Clifford and Hercus, a partnership that lasted for some 11 creative and profitable years. On 29 February 1988, the partners agreed to split the business to allow each to concentrate on their individual areas of expertise.[21] The partnership dissolution resulted in the two halves of the business (that is, licensing and manufacturing) separating to operate as individual firms; one dealing with the design and manufacture of the catamarans, the other with licensing and 'other legal matters'. Needless to say, Bob Clifford undertook the operation of the manufacturing business, a move that was to see the formation of Incat Tasmania.

In order to modernise its operations and reduce costs, the construction of Incat's new fully owned catamaran-manufacturing site, at Bender Drive on Prince of Wales Bay, began in 1988. Work that had already started on the latest catamaran project continued, with one the new sheds actually being built around the burgeoning vessel. In all, three new manufacturing sheds were constructed on the site between 1988 and 1991, and would include features such as a dry dock and a dedicated catamaran assembly line.[22]

The new site also incorporated a partially government-funded 'college of aluminium training' from which workers could gain certification of their skills under the Technical and Further Education scheme (TAFE). This educational 'service' also provided scholarships for staff to attend the Faculty of Engineering at the University of Tasmania, some of which resulted in engineering doctorates for Incat staff.[23] By 1997, the training program had been so successful that a dedicated purpose-built 'educative centre' was completed near the shipyard. The new centre employed 17 training staff, had a floor space capacity of some 3 500 square metres, and featured 50 welding bays able to cater for 400 apprentices and trainees.[24] The Incat-based training program significantly contributed to Incat's broad skill-base by multi-skilling their actual (and potential) workers in the two primary areas of catamaran manufacture: aluminium welding and fabrication. Through government-subsidised training and development, Incat found itself with access to a highly skilled workforce with practically 'nowhere else to go'.

Clifford's first major project for the newly formed company was the construction of what was originally to be a 66-metre catamaran for the British company, Sea Containers. The design and construction of the car-carrying ferry would take nearly two years, a result of ongoing design changes (the boat would stretch to be a 74-metre giant by its end) and a troublesome change in Incat's manufacturing location. Originally named the *Christopher Columbus*, sea trials for the *Hoverspeed Great Britain* began just prior to Easter 1990. The boat, the largest built by Clifford to date, was in essence a compilation of the preceding 20 years of ship-building experience. Clifford said, 'In all imaginable ways the ship was a journey into the future. Never before had a ship of this size been built of aluminium. Never before had a ship carried cars at 40 knots.'

Despite the high praise of its creator, *Hoverspeed Great Britain* experienced major and simultaneous failures almost immediately it was put on sea trial. Some of the most severe failures included electrical overloads (which disabled important navigation devices), fires in

Case 6 Incat Tasmania's race for international success

the hold and an 'unplanned' grounding upon rocks. The setbacks, however, failed to deter Clifford from continuing the sea trials of the vessel once tug boats had successfully freed it from its rocky prison some hours later.

After the sea trials were completed, and the technical errors defined and eliminated, the *Hoverspeed Great Britain* was indeed a sight to behold. So impressive was the sight that it was suggested to the president of the British company purchasing the vessel, James Sherwood, that the vessel would be capable of winning the Hales Trophy. The 'Blue Riband' Hales Trophy is awarded to the commercial vessel that undertakes the fastest crossing of the Atlantic Ocean, a record that in 1990 was held by the liner the SS *United States*. To win the trophy (a Blue Riband award), Clifford's vessel would have to cross the Atlantic in less than three days, 10 hours and 40 minutes.

The crossing attempt was a media event that generated a great deal of worldwide interest in both the Hales Trophy and, perhaps more importantly, Clifford's business. The *Hoverspeed Great Britain* was never in doubt to break the record and win the trophy, given that its average speed during the sea trials was in excess of that required. Once again, however, technical failures dogged the *Hoverspeed Great Britain*'s journey, this time in the form of water-jet failure. Despite the problem, the *Hoverspeed Great Britain* managed to cross the finish line with an average speed exceeding the previous record by 1.1 knots per hour. Clifford had achieved a marketing triumph: he had managed to break a long-standing world record with a state-of-the-art, 74-metre aluminium catamaran, a vessel that utilised new technologies, new materials and an innovative design. And the world was there to see it.[25]

The successful crossing fuelled demand for the new breed of large car-carrying catamarans. Within three years, Incat Tasmania filled eight orders for its 74-metre catamarans. The vessels were built for:

France: *Hoverspeed France*
Denmark: *Hoverspeed Denmark*
Scotland: *Hoverspeed Scotland*
South America: *Patricia Olivia* and *Juan L*
New Zealand: *Condor 10*
Wales and Ireland: *Stena Sea Lynx*
Tasmania and Victoria: *SeaCat Tasmania*

In order for Incat Tasmania to maintain its profitability and growth rate, Clifford once again resorted to drawing board innovations. This time, he was to design a catamaran with an even greater carrying capacity, one that would hopefully attract more orders from larger operators. The result was the construction of the first 78-metre catamaran, the *Stena Sea Lynx 2*. This new vessel was capable of carrying 600 passengers and 150 cars. The point of difference in this catamaran was the innovative mezzanine car deck, a deck that was connected to the main vehicle deck by hydraulically operated ramps and stored an additional 41 cars. The boat was named the *Stena Sea Lynx 2* after it was purchased by the same Wales and Ireland transport company to replace the *Stena Sea Lynx*.

The success of the new 78-metre vessel, once again, did not go unnoticed by the marketplace. In 1994, Holyman sought to take advantage of the new carrier type and contracted with Incat Tasmania to build a second 78-metre vessel, the *Condor 11*. As with the *Hoverspeed Great Britain*, the sea trials of the *Condor 11* were not incident-free. In fact, *Condor 11*'s trial in the waters south of Hobart would 'go down as a significant part of Hobart's maritime history'. On 8 October 1994, a navigational error and radar malfunction led to the *Condor 11* coming to an abrupt halt upon Black Jack Rock. It took the ship a full boat length to stop, with both the stern and the portside hull clear of the water. The media attention that the incident received (including a special seven-page feature story in the *Hobart Mercury* newspaper) was testimony to the magnitude of the event. Indeed, the *Condor 11* remained in the news for some six weeks, as rescue attempt after rescue attempt failed to free the ship.[26]

At 7.40 a.m. on Sunday, 20 November (some 42 days after the incident), the final rescue attempt was undertaken. Using tugboats and a complex system of ropes and pulleys, the *Condor 11* was freed from the rocks and slipped back into the water. Despite damage to 10 of the 16 watertight compartments, the vessel floated on a near normal waterline, and was easily towed to Incat's newly completed dry dock for repairs. The incident did a lot to prove the structural integrity of the craft and the inherent safety features of the design. That a ship could withstand such maltreatment with a minimum of damage greatly impressed the maritime world.

Incat Tasmania: Eighty metres and beyond

By 1995, the world market for high-speed ferries had grown to generate sales revenues of just under A$1.6 billion annually.[27] Not surprisingly, a significant number of businesses had entered the international catamaran industry to gain a share of this substantial revenue opportunity. By 1995, Clifford was faced with direct, and intensifying, competition from both domestic firms (such as Austal Limited, Sea Wind, Venturer, Commercial Catamarans and Aussie Cat) and UK- and US-based firms (such as the US Catamaran Company and Prout Catamarans). Of greatest concern to Incat was the fact that these competitors were also newly internationalising firms, with access to similar resources (that is, revenues from international markets, raw materials and trained staff), and had likewise based their growth on the manufacture of innovative high-speed vessels. A number of Incat's competitors had also targeted the potentially lucrative Chinese market for fast-ferries, somewhat threatening Clifford's most immediate and highly prioritised internationalising strategy. It would appear that Incat Tasmania no longer had a monopoly in the world's high-speed catamaran market, nor the innovation and expertise required for success therein.

Clifford was well aware of the need to maintain Incat's revenue growth and protect its market share in the face of this increasingly competitive industry. As had been the case in the past, Clifford once again returned to the drawing board to design a 'new and improved catamaran' for the world's markets. The result was Incat's (and indeed the world's) first 80-metre-plus catamaran, the *Condor 12*. The innovative changes introduced by Clifford this time around would focus on 'passenger and crew safety', an important point of differentiation, given the spate of ferry disasters occurring in Europe at the time.[28]

The *Condor 12* was equipped with four of the world's most advanced safety systems (known as the Marine Evacuation System, or MES). The MES ensures that the entire passenger population of the *Condor 12* (some 700 people) can be evacuated in an emergency in under 12 minutes, a time significantly less than that required by the peak international maritime safety body, the International Maritime Organisation. In addition to the MES, the *Condor 12* was fitted with an advanced and lightweight fire protection system, as well as single-leafed hinged fire doors, single and double sliding fire doors, engine room fire dampers, fire hatches and smoke baffles. These new features, combined with structural fire protection, formed the best fire protection system available for a high-speed aluminium craft. The safety features were well received by the new owners of the boat, which in 1996 was to serve as a major transport vessel for passengers crossing the English Channel.

The success of the *Condor 12* was once again evident to those in the market that provide a fast-ferry service. Between 1996 and 1998, Incat was to produce a number of 80-metre-plus catamarans for the European market. As with the Incat tradition, the new catamarans became larger in size, with greater levels of comfort and safety, and the adoption of new and innovative technologies. The completed catamarans during this period are as follows:

> *Stena Lynx 3*: 81 metres, English Channel ferry
> *Holyman Express*: 81 metres, England–Belgium run
> *Condor Express*: 86 metres, 800-passenger, 200-car capacity ferry for the UK
> *Sicilia Jet*: 86 metres, Mediterranean Sea crossing vessel
> *Condor Vitesse*: 86 metres, UK summer season ferry carrier
> *Incat 045*: 86 metres, Bass Strait carrier
> *Cat-Link IV*: 91 metres, Scandinavia
> *Catalonia*: 91 metres, Spain

During this period, Incat averaged the construction and launch of one catamaran every 10 weeks. The most notable boat of the latest generation was the *Catalonia*, a 91-metre wave-piercing catamaran destined for Spain. Although the *Catalonia* was completed over-schedule (due to the inability of the company to physically perform the tasks required given the workload), it remained very much the latest 'showpiece' of the Incat empire. Unlike previous efforts, the *Catalonia* was fitted out with a duty-free shop and a number of extra luxurious features (such as staircases and plush carpeting). The more luxurious fit-out meant that she was noticeably heavier than other similarly sized catamarans. However, the *Catalonia* remained capable of travelling at a respectable 48 knots as a lightship, and 43 knots fully loaded. Despite the *Catalonia*'s size and weight, Clifford was confident that the craft was significantly advanced, and was therefore faster than the record-breaking *Hoverspeed Great Britain*. With this thought in mind, as well as the implications for marketing and sales growth, Clifford decided to revisit the Hales Trophy glory of 1990, this time using the *Catalonia* to secure a second 'Blue Riband vessel' for the company.

Incat's Hales Trophy defence: *Catalonia* and the Atlantic Ocean crossing

In mid-May of 1998, the *Catalonia* left Hobart, bound for New York from where the latest record attempt would begin. On Saturday, 6 June, the *Catalonia* hauled anchor and set sail for the United Kingdom in an attempt to set a new record for the Hales Trophy, as well as a new record for the greatest distance travelled by a ship in a given 24-hour period. Once again, the mass media were on hand to witness the great feats undertaken by Clifford and his Incat team. Once again, the media, and the rest of the interested world, were treated to a triumph. The *Catalonia* had, in only its second international voyage, managed to become the first boat in history to cover in excess of 1 000 nautical miles in a 24-hour period. She had also crossed the Atlantic faster than any commercial vessel before her, establishing a new world record for Clifford and Incat.

While this journey was under way, the Incat manufacturing plant was putting the finishing touches on a new 91-metre catamaran named the *Cat-Link V*. Built for the Scandinavian company Scandlines, the boat was also to undertake a record-breaking attempt at the Atlantic Ocean crossing. Within weeks of the *Catalonia*'s efforts, the *Cat-Link V* successfully rewrote the record books and claimed the Hales Trophy and Blue Riband certification. What was most important for Clifford was the fact that now three Incat vessels had managed to break the speed records once held by a US vessel for 50 years, and to do it in absolute comfort.

Strong demand for Incat's wave-piercing catamarans resulted in the development of an important joint venture agreement with Afai Ships of Hong Kong. The joint venture was important, as it provided Incat with an initial foray into the high-potential Chinese market, as well as helping the company to keep up with the huge global demand for its vessels. The Chinese yard started work on its first vessel early in 1998, under the supervision of Graeme Freeman, an Incat manager. Most of the materials for the ships were supplied through the Tasmanian yard, and a constant team of Incat personnel and subcontractors travelled to Hong Kong to supervise each stage of construction.[29] The joint venture proved successful, with the first ship completed by May 1988 and a second ship's construction already under way. As with any licensing agreement, a major risk for Incat lies in the potential theft of its intellectual property, and therefore, potentially, the company's core competency of innovative catamaran design. Perhaps an indication of the innovative drive within the company, Incat management said of such concerns: 'We haven't really worried too much about the theft of our intellectual property. We work on the theory that whatever our licensees are stealing, they are stealing yesterday's work anyway.'[30]

Growth into the future: Incat and the continued internationalisation of a Tasmanian icon

The main issue facing Bob Clifford and his team at Incat in 2001 is ensuring the continued growth of the company through innovation, diversification and globalisation in the face of increasing competition and tough global economic times. The history of successful marketing exercises, the constant flow of innovation throughout the organisation, and the ability of Incat to foster international relationships have, at least to date, seen the company rise from obscurity to a global leader in boating excellence. While there seems to be little change in the strength of global demand for high-speed vessels, cash flow problems did arise in early 2001 when six ships built by the company remained unsold for an extended period of time. The amount of money tied up in six idle ships equated to a substantial cutting back in employee overtime and other 'non-essential company expenditure'.

This cutback in 'non-essential' expenditure, unfortunately for Incat's workforce, apparently extended to include a 15 per cent pay-rise claim by the two major unions operating in the shipyard (the Australian Manufacturing Workers Union and the Construction, Forestry, Mining and Energy Union). Clifford's response to the pay claim was to dismiss it entirely, stating that pay increases at Incat will only result from an increase in catamaran sales. Given the state of the company's sales at the time (having six completed, but as yet unsold, vessels on the books), the pay claim appeared to be doomed to failure. In response to Clifford's statement that it would be easier for the union to 'get blood from a stone' than a pay rise based merely upon a 'cost-of-living' adjustment, industrial action was undertaken by some 650 workers in the form of a 24-hour strike. Clifford was forewarned of this imminent industrial action and acted immediately to release a statement to this sector of his workforce that branded some as 'donkeys with not enough brains to make their heads ache'.[31] He continued to suggest that 'as "intelligent leaders" in tough economic times, Incat has no choice but to "cull the donkey population" for the good of the majority, and in doing so get rid of "The Weakest Links"'.[32]

Incat's management, it seemed, was less than perturbed by this economic anomaly, and indeed undertook yet more design innovations along their way to planning the construction of the first 120-metre catamaran. In 2001, 'tentative plans' were also announced to construct catamarans for a totally unrelated market – the US military service. It was lauded that the US government had a potential US$10 billion to spend on new 'tactical response' vehicles, vehicles the service lacked for quick response to situations of armed conflict. Incat, rather fortuitously, had provided the Australian defence force with the use of a catamaran (the HMAS *Jervis Bay*) for such duties in the East Timor peace-keeping mission, and were therefore well positioned to bid for the US contract. Should the company indeed win the US contract, it would once again have to innovate its designs to accommodate the specific needs of the US military, as well as, once again, license out its manufacturing processes to an overseas construction company.[33]

The business of building fast-ferries remains a relatively new one, and as such there is considerable scope for still further market development (continued catamaran-based construction) and market diversification (that is, new product lines). Given Incat's capabilities with its innovative aluminium products, an opportunity may indeed exist to manufacture a range of aluminium-based products other than just catamaran hulls. Clifford may be able to diversify Incat's product range further to include products such as 'run-about' boats, storage sheds and perhaps even small-aircraft fuselage. As Clifford himself states: 'There are always problems to be solved that will require the design of both new and innovative products. It is coming up with ideas that is essential, and for that you need people with their brains in gear. Likewise, new markets will emerge to be served, and our team is constantly working to "improve the breed". If there is one thing that I'm proud of, it is [Incat's] ability to solve problems and expand our horizons.'[34] Although this ability seems to have always existed at Incat under Clifford's leadership, the question arises as to whether it will provide a continued source of competitive advantage into the future, given the similarly innovative capabilities of Incat's similarly 'internationalising' competition.

Endnotes

1. T. Thomas, 1999, '"Dunce" leaves the rest in his wake', *Business Review Weekly*, 28 May.
2. T. Skotnicki, 2000, 'Exports: Full throttle', *Business Review Weekly*, 18 August.
3. R. Clifford, 1998, *Incat – The First 40 Years* (Melbourne: Baird Publications).
4. Ibid.
5. Ibid.
6. Ibid.
7. Ibid.
8. Ibid.
9. Ibid; Thomas, '"Dunce" leaves the rest in his wake'.
10. Thomas, '"Dunce" leaves the rest in his wake'.
11. 'The Tasman Bridge disaster', 2000, *Clarence City Home Page*: www.ccc.tas.gov.au/clarence/about/history/bridgedisaster, 16 March.
12. Clifford, *Incat – The First 40 Years*, p. 18.
13. Clifford, *Incat – The First 40 Years*.
14. Ibid., p. 22.
15. Skotnicki, 'Exports: Full throttle'.
16. S. L. McCaughey, P. W. Liesch and D. Poulson, 2000, 'An unconventional approach to intellectual property protection: The case of an Australian firm transferring shipbuilding technologies to China', *Journal of World Business*, 35(1), pp. 1–22.
17. Clifford, *Incat – The First 40 Years*.
18. Ibid.
19. Thomas, '"Dunce" leaves the rest in his wake'.
20. Clifford, *Incat – The First 40 Years*.
21. Ibid.
22. Ibid.
23. Ibid.
24. Ibid.
25. Ibid.
26. S. Dalley, 1994, 'Repair work is well advanced on catamaran', *The Mercury*.
27. Austral Limited information memorandum, 2000.
28. Clifford, *Incat – The First 40 Years*.
29. McCaughey, Liesch and Poulson, 'An unconventional approach to intellectual property protection'.
30. Ibid.
31. M. Haley, 2001, 'Incat's "cull" starts with strike', *The Mercury*, 4 April.
32. R. Clifford, 2001, 'The intelligent worker', an address to staff at Incat Tasmania, 3 April.
33. Clifford, *Incat – The First 40 Years*.
34. Ibid.

Case 7

Kiwi Travel International Airlines Ltd

Jared W. Paisley
University of Manitoba

In recognition of his 'raw determination and tenacity' in cutting through red tape and surmounting huge obstacles to set up an airline – in the face of direct competition from industry giants Qantas and Air New Zealand – Ewan Wilson (29) was awarded the 1996 Young Entrepreneur of the Year Award.

Accepting the award, Ewan remarked, 'It's been a bumpy flight for the past couple of years, but we've changed the way New Zealanders will fly across the Tasman. If people won't concede anything else, they have to acknowledge that fares have been influenced by Kiwi International. People still make the mistake of saying I can't do something, but that only adds fuel to the fire and some of those people must be feeling pretty silly now. If I asked you to give me $1 000 because I had a good idea for a business, it would be smart to give it to me.'

Ewan Wilson, CEO

The son of a psychiatrist and a nurse, Ewan Wilson was born in the small South Island town of Timaru, New Zealand. His two brothers have five university degrees between them, one sister is a newspaper editor, and his other sister a lab technician. Family members suspect that Ewan's drive to succeed stems in part from the fact that, in a highly academic family, he had his share of problems at school. According to one of his sisters, 'It would have been very hard in my family, where everybody else who went through school sort of soared. He's the youngest and always felt like he had to run to keep up with the rest of us. Although he is not an academic, he's proved that he's got a business acumen that I can only describe as startling.'

'For a while they thought I was dyslexic,' stated Ewan. 'Obviously I'm not, but even today I will avoid at all costs having to write.' After leaving school at age 16, he worked as an Air Force steward and as a 'go-fer' for a small regional airline. He says he inherited his love for ports and airports from his father, and managed to get his pilot's licence ('I had a terrible job passing all the academic exams'). Ewan worked for a short time in Australia and at a pub in Yorkshire, England, and he spent six months washing cars in Montreal, Canada, where, in 1986, he married his French-Canadian wife, Monique.

Kiwi Travel

Ewan finally found his thing – selling airline tickets and arranging charter flights. He set up his own Montreal travel agency in 1988 and ran escorted tours to the Brisbane Expo. Shortly thereafter he sold the business to his brother-in-law, and, with his wife and twin daughters, moved from Montreal to Hamilton, New Zealand, where his parents lived.

Fresh from the cutthroat competition of North America, Ewan set about establishing his own Hamilton-based travel agency, Kiwi Travel, in 1990. 'I was not exactly Mr Popularity with the other travel agents,' commented Ewan, 'We were quite aggressive in our retail operation. We discounted; we *really* discounted.' Unlike the vast majority of the country's travel agents, Kiwi Travel was not a member of the

---

This case was prepared as a basis for classroom discussion rather than to illustrate either effective or ineffective handling of an administrative situation. The cooperation of Kiwi Travel International Airlines and the Department of Strategic Management and Leadership – University of Waikato is gratefully acknowledged. Some of the historical information presented in this case was obtained from an article by Paul Panckhurst in the November 1995 issue of *North and South* magazine. Used with permission.

Copyright © 1998 by South-Western College Publishing and Thomson Learning Custom Publishing (ISBN: 0-324-03795-3). For information regarding this and other CaseNet® cases, please visit CaseNet® on the World Wide Web at casenet.thomson.com.

Travel Agents' Association of New Zealand, which demanded a bond, qualified staff and financial reporting.

According to Ewan, the Association refused him membership because he and his staff did not have the required qualifications. 'That was b— s—! I was a bloody good travel agent who learned at the coalface, as did every one of my employees.' Always looking for his main chance, Wilson hooked up with three other young strivers and set up a company called Kiwi Travel Air Charters Ltd, later renamed Kiwi Travel International Airlines Ltd.

The air charter business takes off

Besides Ewan Wilson and his wife Monique, the directors of the new airline company were:

- Mike Tournier (30), an air traffic controller, ex-army, formerly from Hamilton but now living and working in Auckland;
- Mike Park (29), a friend of Tournier's and a pilot for Air New Zealand. Park later resigned his position as director of Kiwi Airlines, because his employer was 'not comfortable' with him holding a management position with a rival business; and
- Patrick Pruett (29), a University of Tennessee business graduate, formerly a travel agent in the United States. Pruett met Ewan Wilson when they roomed together for an airline computer reservation course in Houston, Texas, and later travelled to New Zealand for a 'working holiday' in Wilson's travel agency with, he says, 'US$400 and a lot of ambition'. Wilson calls Pruett 'level headed and conservative – everything that I'm not – and my best friend.'

Each of the partners chipped in about NZ$1 000 and, with a grand total of NZ$5 000, chartered an old DC3 in June 1994 to transport passengers from Auckland and Wellington to Hamilton's National Agricultural Field Days. In Ewan's words: 'We made no money, but we had a hell of a lot of fun.'

In August and September 1994, they decided to 'go international', and offered flights on four consecutive Sundays from Hamilton to Brisbane, using a chartered Air Nauru plane. In December 1994, the group offered what Ewan termed a series of 'hugely profitable' charter flights to Western Samoa and Tonga. 'These were what really set us up,' said Pat Pruett, 'We could make NZ$30 000 on each of those flights.'

Red tape and tight deadlines

In March 1995, New Zealand's Ministry of Transport advised Ewan that he could not run weekly charter flights indefinitely without an air service licence, because they effectively amounted to a scheduled service. But the Ministry was not in a hurry to close down the fledgling airline and gave him until January 1996 to make the switch. That extension allowed Kiwi Travel to start offering weekly Sunday charter flights from Hamilton to Brisbane, and sometimes other Australian destinations such as Cairns, Rockhampton, Coolangatta and Townsville. On the subject of market research, Ewan had this to say: 'We didn't do any. I just had a gut feeling it would work.'

Shortly thereafter, Ewan closed his travel agency so that he could concentrate on the airline business. A couple of months later, he decided to work towards launching a scheduled air service, and initially planned a fairly 'relaxed' implementation schedule, to meet the Ministry's January 1996 deadline. However, in early June 1995, Ewan and his partners got wind of a Boeing 737 available for lease from Adelaide-based National Jet Systems. It was a cargo plane which could be reconfigured to take passengers.

To proceed with the deal and to convince the Ministry of Transport that Kiwi Travel was 'a sound and viable operator', the four shareholders (Monique is not a shareholder) had to come up with more money. Pruett, Tournier and Park each set out to raise another NZ$64 000. Pat Pruett had to borrow from his family in Nashville. By using funds from the sale of his house in Canada, and borrowing from his parents' life savings, Wilson was able to come up with NZ$250 000. Altogether, including profits from charter operations, the group was able to increase Kiwi Travel International Airlines' paid-up capital from NZ$200 to NZ$778 000. This took three weeks. A summary of each shareholder's stake is shown in Exhibit 1.

The Bank of New Zealand (BNZ) provided an overdraft account on the strength of a registered security over the company, making the bank first in line if the company went broke. The BNZ did not, however, provide any start-up capital. In late June 1995, with the tentative National Jet Systems agreement in hand, Kiwi Travel began advertising and selling tickets for their scheduled Hamilton–Dunedin to Sydney–Brisbane flights to commence on 23 August 1995. Unfortunately, the deal fell through in July, when it became clear that National Jet Systems would not be able to convert the plane to passenger use in time for the 23 August launch

Exhibit 1 | Kiwi Travel International Airlines Ltd

Summary of shareholders, June 1995

Shareholder	$ Holdings	Paid capital (NZ$)
Ewan Wilson	49%	381 220
Mike Park	17	132 260
Patrick Pruett	17	132 260
Mike Tournier	17	132 260
TOTAL	100%	NZ$778 000

date. 'I guess we should have looked at that deal more carefully,' commented Pat Pruett. So there they were – six weeks before their first scheduled flight and no aircraft. Ewan recalled the rush that ensued:

We started faxing everywhere in the Pacific looking for a plane. At the end of July, I went off to the States and Europe and met with four or five operators. They said they needed 90 days, and I said I don't have bloody 90 days, I have less than five weeks!

Ewan finally came across a family-owned aircraft charter company called AvAtlantic, in Savannah, Georgia (Forrest Gump territory). They were willing to supply a Boeing 727, which could carry about 50 more passengers than the 737 but had a significant disadvantage in that it would have to refuel in Auckland before heading across to Australia. This extra 30-minute wait that passengers would have to endure was not something that Kiwi Airlines had planned on or mentioned in their advertisements. Returning to Hamilton from Georgia, Ewan interviewed prospective flight attendants over a weekend in early August, hired them on Monday, and four days later sent them packing off to Savannah for training.

With three weeks to go before their inaugural flight, Ewan Wilson had managed to line up an aircraft, but he still didn't have the licences his airline needed to fly. This involved negotiations with government organisations in the United States, Australia and New Zealand. As for the political approval, Kiwi Airlines required an air service licence from the New Zealand Ministry of Transport (MOT). AvAtlantic needed an air service certificate from New Zealand's Civil Aviation Authority (CAA) as the safety approval. The *International Air Services Licensing Act* required, among other things, an investigation of Kiwi Airlines' financial viability.

According to the head of the CAA:

At times the relationship was not easy. Mr Wilson did not really understand the depth and breadth of the safety requirements to get a licence, and would not sit still long enough to find out. We suggested Kiwi spend a day with us to allow full explanations of what was required of them, but Mr Wilson spent just 15 minutes.

The CAA was faced with the extra hassle of dealing with the media, with what it says were Wilson's unfounded claims of unfair treatment. Wilson acknowledged:

I hyped it up and put so much pressure on them, they decided to be very thorough with their investigations of AvAtlantic's application. They came over as arrogant as I am. I now know why it's so frustrating dealing with people like me, but it's not every day you get somebody calling you up saying you want to start a second international airline, and of course you take it as a joke. They think I'm pulling their leg, but I'm not. The feeling was 'Look, you're a travel agent, you're wasting our time', and I said, 'Well hold on, you're a government department and I'm a taxpayer, that's what you get paid for.'

Ewan claims that he would have loved to have spent a day with the CAA, but didn't know that the invitation existed.

There was doubt within the CAA as to whether the licence would be issued in time. Altogether, they had less than four weeks to complete investigations which normally take two to three months. They sent a staff member to Savannah and Ft Lauderdale to check on AvAtlantic's charter operations and maintenance facilities, and Ewan made sure he was on the same flight.

On 22 August 1995, the day before Kiwi's first scheduled flight, Ewan Wilson arrived back in Hamilton aboard the freshly painted Boeing 727. A crowd of several hundred spectators cheered as Patrick Pruett ran up the steps of the aircraft waving the CAA approval which had just come in. The final international approval from the Australian authorities came in a short time later, and New Zealand's Transport Minister had already promised that an airservice licence would be granted, subject to CAA approval.

When asked whether it was responsible of Kiwi Travel to take bookings before the airline had a plane or the required licences, Ewan had this to say:

I knew I was going to have a plane and I knew the licences to fly would be granted. We had faith. If the licences had not been granted in time, we would have operated the scheduled flights as charter flights.

On 23 August 1995, the morning of Kiwi Travel's inaugural flight to Australia, Hamilton's airport was buzzing with excitement. Ewan Wilson had paint on his trousers, and the newly built check-in counter was still not completely dry. Behind the counter were Ewan's wife, Monique (known within the company as 'Fluffy'), working long days for no pay, and Pat Pruett, with bags under his eyes. Finally, everyone was loaded aboard, and the big silver bird sporting the new 'KIWI' logo took off over Hamilton amid applause and cheers from the passengers. New Zealand now had two international airlines. A chronology of events in Kiwi Travel's brief history is summarised in Exhibit 2.

'Peanuts and Cola' class

Ewan Wilson came up with the idea of offering at least 50 seats per flight at bargain-basement return fares of NZ$349 (Hamilton–Sydney) and NZ$399 (Hamilton–Brisbane), when other airlines were charging NZ$629 (for example, Auckland). He dubbed these no-meal, no-bar service fares as 'Peanuts and Cola' class, which turned out to be a stroke of marketing genius. The media quickly latched on to the term, which gained national publicity and jammed the phone lines at Kiwi Travel's office.

In the early days, Kiwi Travel International Airlines wasn't getting much support from local travel agents, and they showed very little interest in booking Kiwi flights. Perhaps this was because they wanted to see if Kiwi would survive, or perhaps they were getting pressure from the major airlines; probably both. To get around this problem, Kiwi took the innovative step of setting up their own toll-free 800 number to handle bookings directly, which also meant they didn't have to pay commissions to travel agents. Kiwi set up their own reservations centre with an initial complement of 30 staff.

All went well until 18 October 1995, when two tyres blew out as the Boeing 727 landed in Hamilton. Damage to the aircraft was minimal, and under the terms of their lease, AvAtlantic was to provide all service and repairs. Unfortunately, there were delays, caused in part by AvAtlantic's failure to provide parts locally, and Ewan even travelled to Georgia to personally escort the required parts back to New Zealand. In all, the plane was grounded for 10 days, at a cost to Kiwi of NZ$500 000, as they had to book their passengers on other airlines.

Kiwi Travel attempted to sue AvAtlantic to recover their loss, and as a result, their business relationship soured. In November 1995, Ewan was able to source a nearly-new Boeing 757 from the British-based charter company Air 2000, and sent AvAtlantic's older 727 back. This new arrangement had several advantages for Kiwi:

1 The 757 could fly direct to Australia without having to stop in Auckland to fill up.
2 Their 'ACMI' lease required Air 2000 to assume all aircraft, crew, maintenance and insurance costs. This included provision of some NZ$5 million in spare parts in New Zealand, four flight crews, three aircraft maintenance engineers and an operations supervisor.
3 As a large Northern Hemisphere operator, Air 2000 had the flexibility to provide Kiwi Travel with additional aircraft that might be required to cope with demand during the Southern Hemisphere's 'high season'.

Within one year (April 1995 – March 1996), Kiwi Travel International Airlines had grown from five staff to almost 200. In their first 10 months of operation, Kiwi's before-tax profit of NZ$1.2 million was almost double their earlier forecasts. One airline analyst considered the company's financial performance 'stunning' (refer to Exhibit 3). Meanwhile, their chief rival, Air New Zealand, announced a 4 per cent decline in profit to NZ$135 million for the six months ending December 1995, compared to NZ$140 million for the same period the previous year.

Kiwi Travel's passenger movements increased from 256 per week in August 1994, to 1 500 in August 1995, to 3 500 in December 1995. Cargo grew from nothing in August 1995, to 14 tons per week in December of the same year. Managing this exponential growth has been no small feat for Ewan and his general manager, Patrick Pruett.

Exhibit 2 | Kiwi Travel International Airlines Ltd

Chronology of events, 1990–April 1996

1990: Ewan Wilson establishes a travel agency called Kiwi Travel in Hamilton, New Zealand.

June 1994: Ewan, his wife Monique, and three partners set up a company called Kiwi Travel Air Charters Ltd. They charter a DC3 to transport passengers from Auckland and Wellington to Hamilton's Agricultural Field Days.

August 1994: The company charters an Air Nauru jet. Offers four Sunday flights from Hamilton to Brisbane.

December 1994: A series of charter flights is offered to Western Samoa and Tonga.

March 1995: Ministry of Transport advises Kiwi that it required an air service licence if it wished to offer scheduled flights. Extension granted until January 1996.

April 1995: Scheduled weekly charters are offered from Hamilton to various destinations in Queensland: Brisbane, Cairns, Rockhampton, Coolangatta and Townsville.

May 1995: Ewan closes the travel agency to concentrate on the airline business. Company name changed to Kiwi Travel International Airlines Ltd.

June 1995: Ewan signs a lease for a Boeing 737 from National Jet Systems in Adelaide. Advertising begins for trans-Tasman service, scheduled to commence on 23 August.

July 1995: National Jet Systems deal falls through. Kiwi scrambles to find another plane. Boeing 727 leased from Georgia-based charter company AvAtlantic.

August 1995: Flight attendants interviewed, hired and sent to Georgia for training. CAA operating approval granted one day before scheduled flights to begin.

August 23: Kiwi's inaugural flight to Australia takes off on schedule.

October 1995: Boeing 727 blows two tyres on landing. AvAtlantic is unable to supply parts and the plane is grounded for 10 days, at a cost to Kiwi of NZ$500 000.

November 1995: Kiwi leases a nearly-new Boeing 757 from British-based charter company Air 2000 and sends the 727 back to AvAtlantic.

February 1996: Services begin from Dunedin.

March 1996: Kiwi Airlines' staff complement grows to almost 200, including 60 reservations staff, and company profits are described as 'stunning'. Competition heats up as Air New Zealand subsidiary Freedom Air offers more flights on Kiwi's routes.

April 1996: Air 2000 requests an early return of the Boeing 757. In its place, Kiwi leases a 737–400 and a 737–300.

The organisational structure was viewed internally as being 'fairly flat, project-oriented and floating'. For example, someone might be given the task of organising an in-flight magazine and would be responsible for that project from start to finish, reporting directly to Ewan or Patrick. Someone else might be put in charge of setting up an office in Christchurch. A general organisation chart (subject to change) is shown in Exhibit 4. The average age of Kiwi's employees was 27. 'Ours is a very young company,' stated Pat Pruett, 'I've been here almost two years – which makes me one of the old-timers.'

Many of Kiwi Travel's operations were contracted out, which allowed the airline to minimise capital investments while maximising their ability to expand quickly. The aircraft came with three flight crews and maintenance staff as part of the lease agreement. Catering and ground services, including baggage handling, were contracted. Flight attendants were Kiwi's employees, as were about 60 staff at their Hamilton reservation centre.

Kiwi planned to lease a second aircraft in June 1996 – an Airbus A320, which, at 180 seats, was slightly smaller than the Boeing 757 but still capable of direct trans-Tasman service. The A320 was to be leased through Orix, a Japanese bank and leasing firm, and was, according to Ewan, 'the most modern passenger aircraft in the world'. In New Zealand, a Christchurch destination was to be added with a feeder service[1] to Hamilton. Melbourne and Perth would be added to their Australian destinations (refer to Exhibit 5).

The competition heats up

'She's a tough old world out there, and we don't intend to let the grass grow under our feet in terms of addressing them or any other competitor,' were the words of Bob Matthew, chairman of Air New Zealand, when asked in a television interview for his thoughts on Kiwi Travel – New Zealand's second international airline.

There was no doubt in anybody's mind that the big airlines like Air New Zealand and Qantas could, as one

Exhibit 3 | Kiwi Travel International Airlines Ltd

Kiwi Airline's profit 'stunning' says analyst
by Andrea Fox

A [NZ]$1.2 million before-tax profit announced by Hamilton's new Kiwi trans-Tasman airline is a 'stunning' result, says an aviation financial analyst.

The one-aircraft privately owned, no-frills airline yesterday said it had almost doubled its forecast profit of [NZ]$700 000 for the 10 months from April 1995 to January.

In this period Kiwi's gross sales from tickets were [NZ]$13.5 million – [NZ]$2.5 million better than the airline's own predictions.

Chief executive Ewan Wilson said Kiwi had flown more than 50 000 people.

The broking house analyst, who would not be named because of possible repercussions from Air New Zealand, said if the announcement was correct, the recorded profit was stunning because Kiwi only had shareholder funds of [NZ]$700 000.

The analyst took a 'cautious' approach to announcements from any company wanting to list on the Stock Exchange. Kiwi is preparing a prospectus for a possible September public share issue.

Kiwi, which started as a trans-Tasman charterer in 1994, became a scheduled international carrier last August. Today it has 155 staff in New Zealand and Australia.

The analyst said a small 'start-up' airline faced several perils, and Kiwi had encountered and apparently survived some of them.

'You can go out the back door very quickly if things go wrong. From the start he (Ewan Wilson) said he didn't intend to be a price setter. And it's clear Air New Zealand and Qantas (his trans-Tasman competitors) decided to drop their fares very quickly (to match) so things could have gone very wrong if he didn't get the yields.'

Another peril was only having one jet when mechanical failures struck. Kiwi was grounded for 10 days shortly after launching as a scheduled airline because of a serious tyre blowout. Mr Wilson said if not for the grounding the profit could have been [NZ]$500 000 higher.

Kiwi had also been involved in rows – another peril. It's recent run-in with a Cook Islands agency over charters to Rarotonga could have cost it dearly.

Another risk was growing too quickly. The analyst was concerned at Kiwi's plan to build an [NZ]$8 million building after its sharefloat.

Source: *Waikato Times*, 17 February 1996.

---

aviation analyst put it, 'squash Kiwi like a bug', should a price war develop. Ewan recognised this risk but remained philosophical:

If it gets too hot in the kitchen, we'll just get out of that kitchen. We'll keep coming up with new niches such as flying out of other provincial airports, but I believe we have a trump card – public support for the little guy. People still support the spirit of entrepreneurship. I think the public appreciates what is likely to happen to airfares if we're forced out of the market.

By early 1996, the kitchen was certainly getting warm (refer to Exhibit 6). Freedom Air, a subsidiary of Air New Zealand, was competing head-on with Kiwi Travel, by offering direct flights from Hamilton to Sydney for NZ$299, or to Brisbane for NZ$349. This compared to NZ$329 (Sydney) and NZ$379 (Brisbane) for Kiwi's 'Nuts and Cola' flights. In addition, Freedom's customers could, for an additional NZ$9, choose between two nights' accommodation or two days' car rental in Australia.

Ewan Wilson filed a complaint with New Zealand's Commerce Commission, citing 'predatory pricing by Air New Zealand in an attempt to blast Kiwi out of the skies'. In response, legal counsel for Air New Zealand categorically denied that it had been involved in unlawful predatory pricing 'on certain Tasman routes, or indeed other predatory behaviour designed to eliminate a competitor'. Ewan disagreed, citing information on lease costs and passenger loadings which, he said, clearly showed that Freedom Air was operating well below cost.

To make matters worse, in April 1996 Ewan accused Freedom Air of 'poaching' his staff by offering flight attendants an expense allowance of NZ$55 per flight in addition to their regular salary of NZ$24 000 to NZ$30 000 per year. He commented on this new development:

It's a case of Freedom deliberately targeting every one of our flight attendants. They want our staff because they are well trained and well qualified. I really feel hurt. Four of our flight attendants quit to work for Freedom Air, and three of them were from our original group.

Case 7 Kiwi Travel International Airlines Ltd

Exhibit 4 | Kiwi Travel International Airlines Ltd

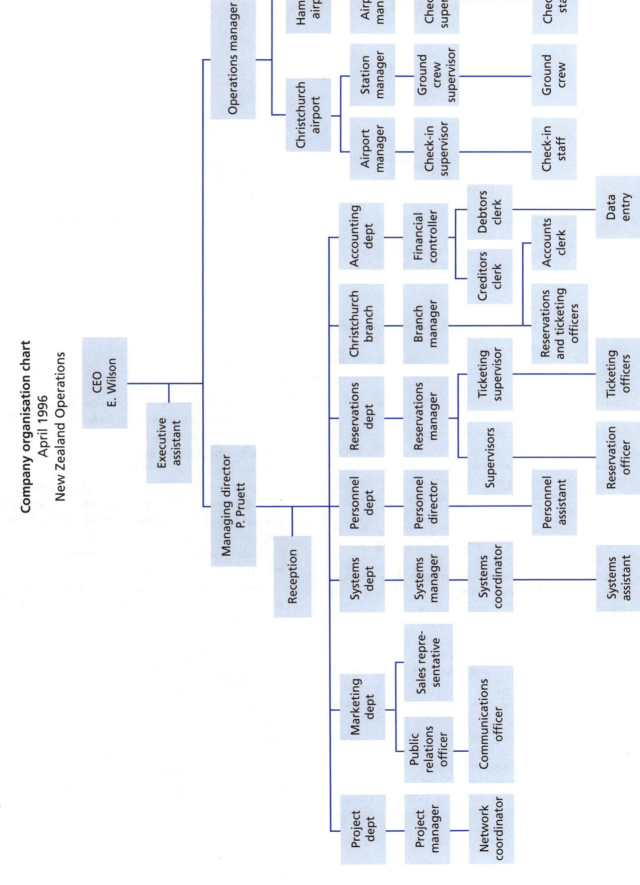

Company organisation chart
April 1996
New Zealand Operations

Exhibit 5 | Kiwi Travel International Airlines Ltd

Current and proposed flight route map, April 1996.

- - - - Proposed flights
———— Scheduled flights

Exhibit 6 | Kiwi Travel International Airlines Ltd

Freedom Air turns up heat on city rival
by Andrea Fox

Crunch time is looming for Hamilton's trans-Tasman airline industry.

Air New Zealand-connected Freedom Air yesterday announced it was increasing its limited Hamilton-trans-Tasman operations to seven days a week with low fares. It signals the acid test on Waikato's ability to support two high-frequency trans-Tasman airlines and keep the city's own airline Kiwi flying.

Freedom started in December, flying charters to Brisbane and Sydney from Hamilton, Dunedin, Auckland, Christchurch and Wellington.

Yesterday it announced a new schedule from late April, with more flights from Hamilton and Dunedin, and introducing Palmerston North as a gateway.

Auckland, Christchurch and Wellington would now be served on special dates with specific fares.

Introductory return fares between all Freedom's New Zealand gateways and Sydney would be [NZ]$299 and Brisbane [NZ]$349.

Kiwi chief executive Ewan Wilson, who pioneered Hamilton-trans-Tasman flights, said today Freedom's move was 'very nasty'. Kiwi's outlook was bleak without regional support.

'I can tell you now we can't match those fares if they continue them until the end of the year.'

Kiwi's Hamilton–Sydney return is [NZ]$329, rising to [NZ]$349 next month. Hamilton–Brisbane return is [NZ]$379, rising to [NZ]$399 next month.

May to September was the traditional money-spinning period for a trans-Tasman airline, before the low season of October–November, he said.

Freedom management did not respond to *Waikato Times*' calls.

Regional aviation sources said Freedom loadings have been small, with sometimes only 12 people flying out on its 233-seat Boeing 757. The sources said Kiwi's Boeing 757 has had minimum loads of 150.

Freedom spokesman Stuart Eastman recently said Hamilton was the airline's 'soft spot'.

Hamilton airport chief executive Barry O'Connor said whether the region could support two full-time trans-Tasman airlines was 'anybody's guess'.

Waikato Development Foundation chief, Frank van der Velden, said Freedom's move was a 'classic case' of a big company 'using predatory tactics to take out competition that is hurting its bottom line'.

Consumers' Institute spokesman Peter Sutton said competition was good provided it was sustained. Waikato Chamber of Commerce president Gail Jones predicted Freedom would pull out immediately if Kiwi failed.

Air NZ last week reported a slight decline in its six-monthly financial result on the corresponding period last year. It cited trans-Tasman trade as a contributing factor.

Source: *Waikato Times*, 1 March 1996.

Exhibit 7 | Kiwi Travel International Airlines Ltd

Assumptions used in financial projections, 12 months ending 31 May 1997

Aircraft

1. Boeing B757
   - Capacity: 192 passengers
   - ACMI lease cost: US$3 235 per hour for the first 250 hours, US$2 805 per hour thereafter
   - Fuel consumption: 10.24 litres per mile

   Airbus A320
   - Capacity: 180 passengers. In service commencing 1 July 1996
   - ACMI lease cost: US$3 361 per hour for first 250 hours, US$2 726 per hour thereafter
   - Fuel consumption: 825 gallons per hour

2. Fuel cost: US$0.90 per gallon

3. Landing fees:
   - New Zealand = NZ$585 per landing
   - Australia = A$731 per landing

   Terminal charges:
   - New Zealand = NZ$1 per passenger
   - Australia = A$10 per passenger

4. Aircraft ferry costs: US$50 000 delivery and return charge per aircraft

5. Supplementary aircraft rental: Payable at US$65 000 per month for the first six months of the A320 lease term

Revenue

6. Passenger: 50% of passengers on 'Nuts and Cola' fares

7. Cargo:
   - B757 = 3 000 kg per sector at NZ$0.50 per kg
   - A320 = 2 000 kg per sector at NZ$0.50 per kg

8. Duty free sales: NZ$11.00 per passenger per flight

Other costs

9. Catering: NZ$6.60 per person per rotation
   Beverages: NZ$2.58 per person per rotation

10. GST: 12.5%. Applicable to domestic (NZ) expenses and income only
    Income tax: 33%

Other assumptions

11. Exchange rates:
    - NZ$1.00 = US$0.647
    - NZ$1.00 = A$0.871

12. Depreciation:
    - Office equipment = 35% DV
    - Motor vehicles = 26% DV
    - Furniture & fittings = 9.5% DV

Exhibit 8 | Kiwi Travel International Airlines Ltd

Proposed flight schedules, 12 months ending 31 May 1997

AIRBUS A320

Destination		Mon	Tues	Wed	Thur	Fri	Sat	Sun
4	HLZ→BNE→HLZ→MEL→HLZ				✈			
3	BNE→HLZ→SYD→HLZ			✈				
5	HLZ→SYD→DUD→SYD→HLZ					✈		
2	BNE→SYD→HLZ→SYD→BNE		✈					
6	HLZ→SYD→HLZ→MEL→PER						✈	
1	BNE→DUD→BNE	✈						
7	PER→MEL→HLZ→BNE→HLZ→BNE							✈

BOEING B757 (or alternative)

Destination		Mon	Tue	Wed	Thur	Fri	Sat	Sun
8	HLZ→CHC→SYD→CHC	✈						
9	CHC→MEL→PER→MEL→CHC		✈					
10	CHC→BNE→CHC→MEL→CHC			✈				
11	CHC→SYD→MEL→CHC				✈			
12	CHC→BNE→CHC					✈		
13	CHC→BNE→DUD→BNE→CHC						✈	
14	CHC→SYD→DUD→SYD→CHC→HLZ							✈

Destination Codes: BNE – Brisbane; CHC – Christchurch; DUD – Dunedin; HLZ – Hamilton; MEL – Melbourne; PER – Perth; SYD – Sydney.

Ewan was quick to point out that his airline's initial marketing strategy was based upon location rather than price. They were trying to appeal to a niche market by offering direct air service to Australia from cities (such as Hamilton and Dunedin) which were not served by the other airlines. For example, prior to the arrival of Kiwi, Hamilton residents had no choice but to travel to Auckland if they wanted to catch a plane to Australia. The company's initial target market was the Central North Island region (approximate population of 650 000), and the Lower South Island region (approximately 250 000 people).

When Kiwi Travel announced its plans to expand service to Christchurch, Freedom Air responded by offering its own Australia-direct discount fares from that city. Christchurch was different from Hamilton and Dunedin in that it was already served by Qantas and Air New Zealand. This was clearly moving away from Kiwi's initial strategy of operating out of centres that did not have direct trans-Tasman air service. This move was explained by Rodney Macdonald, Kiwi's communications officer:

Moving into Christchurch is moving into Air New Zealand's territory, but they've already moved into our territory by offering Freedom Air flights out of Hamilton. But they have actually shot themselves in the foot. In Christchurch, Air New Zealand staff complained that Freedom Air was taking their customers!

In effect, Air New Zealand ended up competing with themselves in the Christchurch market through their subsidiary Freedom Air.

March 1996

Considering that Kiwi Travel International Airlines and its competitive environment were changing, almost on a daily basis, the traditional exercise of 'long-range strategic planning' was almost impossible. Nevertheless, a major accounting firm was given the task of developing financial projections for the 12-month period from 1 June 1996 to 31 May 1997. These projections were made using historical information available at the time (if you consider seven months of scheduled airline operation 'historical') and other assumptions based upon company and industry experience. Refer to Exhibits 7–13 for a summary of these projections and related assumptions.

Exhibit 9 | Kiwi Travel International Airlines Ltd

Projected balance sheet, 31 May 1997 (NZ$)

Assets	
Current assets	
Cash	$22 588 346
Deposits with suppliers	2 508 953
GST balance	1 533 705
Prepayments	25 000
Shareholders' current accounts	233 428
	$26 889 432
Fixed assets (depreciated value)	
Furniture & fittings	6 145
Motor vehicles	39 731
Office equipment	204 288
Total fixed assets	$ 250 164
Total assets	$27 139 596
Liabilities & equity	
Current liabilities	
Bond – flight attendants	$ 45 000
Flight deposits	6 979 742
Taxation balance	5 767 754
Accounts payable	1 784 993
Total current liabilities	$14 577 489
Term liabilities	
Hire-purchase account payable	21 165
Authorised, issued & paid-up capital	778 000
Retained earnings	11 762 942
Total liabilities & equity	$27 139 596

Source: Unaudited company records.

The projections mentioned above assume the lease of an Airbus A320 aircraft commencing July 1996, to complement the existing aircraft, and the addition of new routes to include Christchurch, Melbourne and Perth. A net profit of NZ$9.3 million on total revenue of NZ$72.4 million was forecast for the period. According to Ewan Wilson:

> We aim to become the number one independent airline in New Zealand, operating a variety of low-cost services and taking travel to a wide sector of the world market. Synergy will be sought with other airline and tour operators worldwide, to capitalise on seasonal reciprocity and global asset management. Part of our aims are to establish a strong presence in Hamilton, and develop vertical integration of our business in areas such as ground handling, catering, cargo and hangar facilities.

April 1996

In true Kiwi Airlines fashion, the company's situation once again 'changed overnight'. Their British leasing company, Air 2000, requested an early return of the Boeing 757. Instead of extending the lease as Kiwi had originally planned, Air 2000 wanted it back at the end of April. Ewan commented on this latest development:

> Kiwi has an excellent relationship with Air 2000, so when they asked for the return of the 757 earlier than originally agreed, to accommodate a busier European summer than expected, we felt obliged to work with them.

In short order, Ewan managed to source two more aircraft to replace the 757. A 126-seat Air Nauru Boeing 737-400, scheduled to arrive at the end of April,

Exhibit 10 | Kiwi Travel International Airlines Ltd

Projected statement of income and expenses, 12 months ending 31 May 1997 (NZ$)

Income		
Sales		$87 328 380
Less: direct costs		66 115 668
Gross profit		$21 212 712
Expenses		
ACC levy		$ 18 000
Accounting & legal fees		18 000
Advertising & promotion		1 575 004
Aircraft ferry expenses		308 892
Cleaning & maintenance		24 000
Communication		379 500
Computer expenses		96 000
Contingency		200 004
Depreciation		124 606
Flight consumable		114 000
Freight		18 000
Fringe benefit tax		10 000
Insurance		996
Interest & bank charges		48 648
Miscellaneous expenses		24 000
Office costs:	Brisbane office	456 000
	Sales office	666 000
	General expenses	22 800
Rent		54 300
Salaries, wages, benefits		1 805 928
SITA reservation system fees		276 000
Staff recruitment, seminars, training		346 000
Stationery & subscriptions		38 400
Supplementary aircraft rental		602 316
Travel & entertainment		54 000
Utilities		12 000
Vehicle expenses		36 000
Total expenses		$ 7 329 394
Profit before taxation		$13 883 318
Taxation (33%)		4 581 495
Net profit after tax		$ 9 301 823

Source: Unaudited company records.

Exhibit 11 | Kiwi Travel International Airlines Ltd

Projected monthly income and expenses, 12 months ending 31 May 1997 (NZ$)

	June	July	Aug	Sept	Oct	Nov	Dec	Jan	Feb	March	April	May	Total
Total sales	3 588 394	8 243 234	8 243 234	8 000 786	7 588 092	7 364 912	8 243 234	8 243 234	6 495 099	7 177 085	6 965 994	7 177 085	87 328 380
Less: direct costs	2 824 377	5 873 231	5 873 231	5 763 299	5 785 072	5 677 732	5 873 231	5 873 231	5 411 687	5 755 685	5 649 159	5 755 685	66 115 668
Gross profit	762 017	2 370 003	2 370 003	2 237 487	1 803 020	1 687 180	2 370 003	2 370 003	1 083 412	1 421 400	1 316 785	1 421 400	21 212 712
Less: expenses	599 851	595 851	674 051	703 050	701 051	637 050	532 665	556 415	556 415	569 665	602 665	600 665	7 329 394
Profit before taxation	162 166	1 774 152	1 695 952	1 534 437	1 101 969	1 050 130	1 837 338	1 813 588	526 997	851 735	714 120	820 735	13 883 318
Less: tax @ 33%	55 515	585 470	559 664	506 364	363 650	346 543	606 322	598 484	173 909	281 073	235 660	270 843	4 581 495
Net profit after tax	108 651	1 188 682	1 136 288	1 028 073	738 319	703 587	1 231 016	1 215 104	353 088	570 662	478 460	549 892	9 301 823

Note: One additional aircraft projected to commence July 1996. June figures reflect the operation of only one aircraft.

Exhibit 12 | Kiwi Travel International Airlines Ltd

Projected current account summary, 12 months ending 31 May 1997 (NZ$)

	June	July	Aug	Sept	Oct	Nov	Dec	Jan	Feb	March	April	May
Opening bank balance	5 364 760	10 591 181	11 612 425	13 538 345	13 932 775	15 681 968	16 803 118	19 413 338	18 778 308	20 857 004	20 784 872	22 513 688
Total net cash movement	5 226 421	1 021 244	1 925 919	394 430	1 749 193	1 121 151	2 610 220	(635 030)	2 078 696	(72 132)	1 728 816	74 658
Closing bank balance	10 591 181	11 612 425	13 538 345	13 932 775	15 681 968	16 803 118	19 413 338	18 778 308	20 857 004	20 784 872	22 513 688	22 588 346

Exhibit 13 | Kiwi Travel International Airlines Ltd

Projected statement of contribution to profit per destination, 12 months ending 31 May 1997 (NZ$)

Rotation destination	1	2	3	4	5	6	7	8	9	10	11	12	13	14	Total
Avg. aircraft costs per rotation															
ACMI	27 945	34 687	36 012	53 551	48 991	54 837	68 166	28 577	55 572	52 024	31 160	26 648	54 299	52 988	
Fuel	11 097	12 273	13 940	18 806	18 696	18 150	18 806	14 161	18 751	20 771	14 511	11 097	22 194	21 088	
Handling	4 018	12 114	7 010	9 079	8 958	9 809	9 079	7 448	13 102	10 436	8 666	5 218	10 436	12 896	
Landing charges	1 331	3 522	1 992	2 859	2 492	2 471	2 859	3 046	3 298	3 980	2 588	2 102	3 980	4 695	
Airway charges	3 968	8 997	4 810	6 759	6 932	7 154	6 759	3 564	7 888	7 562	3 594	3 968	7 562	7 188	
Aircrew	918	1 709	1 183	1 759	1 609	1 801	1 753	1 423	2 767	2 590	1 551	1 327	2 703	2 638	
Total	49 277	73 302	64 947	92 813	87 678	94 222	107 422	58 219	101 378	97 363	62 070	50 360	101 174	101 493	
Other costs per year															
Commission	280 449	358 488	392 235	556 751	519 840	461 311	625 826	282 631	386 159	513 504	294 782	258 814	513 504	496 614	5 940 908
Catering	97 346	194 693	149 020	194 693	194 693	194 693	243 366	134 598	179 464	179 464	134 598	89 732	179 464	224 330	2 387 154
Beverages	38 054	76 107	57 080	76 107	76 107	76 107	95 134	52 616	70 154	70 154	52 616	35 077	70 154	87 693	933 160
Total	415 849	629 288	595 335	827 551	790 640	732 111	964 326	469 845	635 777	763 122	481 996	383 623	763 122	808 637	9 261 222
Flight hours per rotation	7.17	8.9	9.24	13.75	12.57	14.07	17.49	7.41	14.41	13.49	8.08	6.91	14.08	13.74	
Number of rotations	52	52	52	52	52	52	52	48	48	48	48	48	48	48	
Avg. capacity loading	78.58%	78.58%	78.58%	78.58%	78.58%	78.58%	78.58%	74.0%	74.0%	74.0%	74.0%	74.0%	74.0%	74.0%	
Total seat capacity	180	180	180	180	180	180	180	192	192	192	192	192	192	192	
Avg. ticket income per head	$532.33	$680.33	$744.33	$1 056.33	$986.33	$875.33	$1 187.33	$582.09	$795.09	$1 057.09	$607.09	$533.09	$1 057.09	$1 086.09	
Other revenue															
Duty free sales	81 122	81 122	81 122	81 122	81 122	81 122	74 777	74 777	74 777	74 777	74 777	74 777	74 777	74 777	1 091 293
Net cargo revenue	104 200	208 400	156 300	208 400	208 400	208 400	260 500	215 145	286 890	286 860	215 145	143 430	286 860	358 575	3 147 505
Contribution summary:															
Total revenue	4 107 687	5 303 346	5 723 229	8 076 243	7 560 013	6 741 418	9 094 432	4 242 799	5 762 462	7 543 505	4 412 746	3 837 988	7 543 505	7 379 007	87 328 380
Total direct costs	2 982 291	4 290 953	3 977 899	5 661 423	5 357 050	5 639 377	6 559 205	3 253 720	5 480 756	5 416 299	3 448 548	2 790 442	5 598 459	5 659 246	66 115 668
Gross profit	1 125 396	1 012 393	1 745 330	2 414 820	2 202 963	1 102 041	2 535 227	989 079	281 706	2 127 206	964 198	1 047 546	1 945 046	1 719 761	21 212 712

Source: Unaudited company records.

and a 148 seat Boeing 737-300 from a leasing company called Aviareps, to commence service on 1 June 1996.

This is yet another exciting time for Kiwi. We are going from our current one aircraft with a seat capacity of 233 passengers, to a total of three aircraft with a seat capacity of 454. Life does not get any easier in the airline business, and we have to be proactive to keep our customers happy. The additional aircraft will allow us to offer a wider variety of flight schedules, including special flights for major events, and will give us greater depth in the area of aircraft backup. These changes will give Kiwi more flexibility to combat competition from Freedom Air.

Over the 'long term', Kiwi Airlines was considering a number of new initiatives:

- Establishment of New Zealand's first on-line booking system, which would allow Kiwi's customers to book their own flights using a home computer and a credit card number. The company had recently launched their own website,[2] which was proving extremely popular.
- A public share float on the New Zealand Stock Exchange. Ewan had recently sold 10 000 of his shares to some friends, which had the effect of lowering his holdings from 49 per cent to about 47 per cent. Kiwi's own employees were considered good potential customers for some shares.
- Obtaining its own air operating certificate, and purchasing two new aircraft in May 1997.

Endnotes

1. It is important to note that Kiwi Travel's air service licence did not, at present, permit them to operate scheduled flights between points within New Zealand. They were only permitted to ferry their own international passengers to connection points for overseas flights. Kiwi planned to offer 'free' flights between Christchurch and Hamilton for their Kiwi class (full economy) passengers booked on international flights.
2. As of October 1997, Kiwi's web address was: www.kiwi-travel.co.nz/.

Case 8

Beefing up the beefless Mac: McDonald's expansion strategies in India*

Nitin Pangarkar
Saroja Subrahmanyan
National University of Singapore

Background

In March 2001, the McDonald's Corporation's Indian operation was at a critical juncture in its evolution. Over the previous few months, the company had expanded its retail base from Mumbai (10 outlets) and Delhi (14 outlets) to Bangalore (one outlet), Pune (one outlet), Jaipur (one outlet) and the Delhi-Agra highway (one outlet). During 2001, McDonald's had plans to open 15 more outlets with one each in Ludhiana and Ahmedabad (see Exhibit 1 for a brief profile of the different cities and Exhibit 2 for a map showing their locations in India) and the rest in cities where it already had a presence. By 2003, the company planned to increase the number of outlets to 80 and the cumulative investment in India to more than Rs 10 billion. (The approximate exchange rate in March 2001 was Rs 46.50 = US$1.) This would represent a threefold increase over the cumulative investment until June 2000 (Rs 3.5 billion). Three other cities (Agra, Baroda and Chandigarh) would also have at least one McDonald's outlet by 2003.

The Indian venture had been operational for more than four years and had recorded healthy growth but no profits. Commenting on the progress until that point in time, Vikram Bakshi (McDonald's partner in Delhi) said: 'Our growth and expansion in India over the last three years has definitely been very encouraging.' Only a few months previously, Amit Jatia (McDonald's other partner in charge of the Mumbai outlets) had said: 'We are still to recover our investment. You need a very large base and break-even is normally after seven to ten years.' Despite the venture's lack of profits, Jatia also showed his enthusiasm for expansion when he said, 'Having cracked the Indian market, McDonald's is ready to leverage its initial investments in infrastructure to rapidly expand.'

Observers were wondering about the appropriateness of McDonald's bold strategic move. Was the additional investment wise, especially in view of the lack of profitability of the existing operations? Since many of the new cities to be entered were less Westernised than Mumbai or Delhi, many observers doubted whether the demand potential would be sufficient to justify the economic operation of outlets. The cost and availability of prime real estate in major Indian cities was another issue. Opening a new outlet required an average investment of Rs 30 million. In Mumbai and Delhi, where prime real estate was expensive, the investments could be higher. Finally, some analysts doubted whether McDonald's could afford to spend big amounts on advertising to create a strong brand-name reputation if its outlet base and customer base remained relatively narrow.

McDonald's – the global fast-food powerhouse

McDonald's is, by far, the world's biggest marketer of fast food. In 2000, it operated nearly 30 000 restaurants and had 1.5 million people serving 45 million customers each day in 120 countries. The company had built an impressive set of financial figures, with US$40.2 billion in system-wide sales (out of which US$24.5 billion was accounted for by franchised

---

This case was written as a basis for class discussion rather than to illustrate effective of ineffective handling of an administrative or business situation.

Exhibit 1 | Profile of the Indian cities targeted by McDonald's

Place	Population (000s) 1991	Population (000s) 2001	Remarks	State	Annual per capita income in Rs (1997–8)[1]	Annual per capita income in Rs (1997–8)[2]
Agra	892	1 076	Tourist attraction; home to the Taj Mahal	Uttar Pradesh	7 263	5 890
Jaipur	1 459	1 893	Major tourist attraction	Rajasthan	9 356	7 694
Chandigarh	504	790	Capital city of two northern states, Punjab & Haryana	Punjab & Haryana	19 500	14 457
Ahmedabad	2 955	3 823	Major business centre in western India	Gujarat	16 251	13 709
Vadodara/Baroda	1 031	1 454	Business centre	Gujarat	16 251	13 709
Mumbai	9 926	12 903	Commercial capital of India	Maharashtra	18 365	16 217
Pune	1 567	2 004	Satellite town of Mumbai; manufacturing centre	Maharashtra	18 365	16 217
Ludhiana	1 043	1 482	Textile manufacturing centre in northern India	Punjab	19 500	1 457
Delhi	9 119	13 661	Capital city, seat of the central government	Delhi	22 687	19 091
Bangalore	2 660	3 637	India's Silicon Valley	Karnataka	11 693	11 153

Notes:
1 Income data from Per Capita Income (State-wise) – Maps of India. The figures refer to the whole state and not the particular cities. Income levels for cities are likely to be somewhat higher than the figures for the whole states.
2 Income data from the Associated Chambers of Commerce and Industry of India (http://203.122.1.245/assocham/prels/04181.asp\). The figures refer to the whole state and not the particular cities. Income levels for cities are likely to be somewhat higher than the figures for the whole states.

Sources: Population data from www.world-gazetteer.com/fr/fr_in.htm.

restaurants), US$21.7 billion in assets, US$3.3 billion in operating profits and US$2 billion in net profits. (See Exhibit 3 for a geographic analysis of McDonald's operations.) It was also routinely cited by the business press as being a savvy marketer. In June 1999, with a value of US$26.231 billion, the McDonald's brand was rated as being the eighth most valuable brand in the world, ahead of well-known brands such as Sony, Nokia and Toyota.

McDonald's has had a long history in Asia. It entered the Japanese market in 1971, which was followed by entry into other newly industrialising economies (such as Singapore and Hong Kong, among others) in Asia. Entry into China occurred only in 1990. McDonald's entered India in 1996. (See Exhibit 4 for McDonald's start-up dates in East Asian and South Asian countries.) The late entry could be attributed to several factors, such as the fact that a significant percentage of India's population is vegetarian, the limited purchasing power of the population and the closed nature of the economy.

The Indian market

India is a vast subcontinent with an area one-quarter of that of the United States, and a population almost four times that of the US, at about 950 million. The per capita GDP is quite low, at US$390 in 1999. However, after adjusting for purchasing power parity, India was ranked the fifth-largest economy in the world (ranking above France, Italy, the UK and Russia) with the third-largest GDP in Asia in 1999. (See Exhibit 5 for income distribution in India.) Among emerging economies, India is often considered second only to China.

India's economic diversity is matched by its social diversity. There are more than 20 major spoken languages and over 200 dialects. The Indian currency (Rupee) has its denomination spelt out not only in English and Hindi, but also in 13 other languages. About 50 per cent of the population is considered to be illiterate, and advertising reaches them via billboards and audiovisual means. For national launches, at least eight languages are used. In addition, the country faces

Exhibit 2 | McDonald's outlets in India (existing and planned)

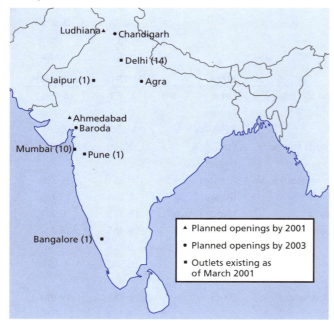

a poor infrastructure with frequent power outages, even in New Delhi (the capital city) and Bangalore (India's Silicon Valley).

In terms of political system, India is a democracy. Since independence from the British in 1947, the economic system has historically been modelled on the socialist style. Under this system, the government strictly controls the entry and exit of domestic as well as multinational corporations (MNCs) into different sectors. MNCs also face a variety of other restrictions. Since 1991, India has started deregulating the economy. However, the socialist mind-set cannot be erased overnight. A Member of Parliament said of fast-food chains such as McDonald's and KFC, 'We want computer chips and not potato chips.'

The country has a few anti-Western factions, which have opposed the entry of MNCs in general. The mistrust of MNCs could be at least partially attributed to the fact that the British rule of India was rooted in the entry of the British East India Company (for trading purposes) into the country. There are also several small

Exhibit 3 | Geographic analysis of McDonald's operations and performance (financial year 2000)

		Geographic breakdown				
	Total	USA	Europe	Asia-Pacific	Latin America	Others
Revenues	14 243	5 259	4 754	1 987	949	1 294
Operating income	3 330	1 773	1 180	442	102	94
Total assets	21 684	7 877	7 084	2 790	1 856	1 069
Capital expenditures	1 945	469	798	224	246	161
Depreciation & amortisation	1 011	418	297	121	69	61

Notes:
- All figures in US$ millions.
- Corporate accounted for US$262 million (loss) to operating income, US$1 009 million of assets, US$48 million of capital expenditures, and US$46 million of depreciation and amortisation.
- Figures may not add up, due to rounding.

Source: www.mcdonalds.com.

but vocal groups of health activists and environmentalists that are opposed specifically to the entry of fast-food giants such as McDonald's and KFC. When KFC opened its restaurant in Bangalore in 1995, local officials found that KFC had excessive levels of monosodium glutamate (MSG) in its food and closed the outlet. The outlet soon reopened, however. Said Vandana Shiva, a vocal exponent of environmental and animal welfare issues, in an audio interview with McSpotlight,

The McDonald's experience, which is really the experience of eating junk while thinking you are in heaven, because of the golden arches, which is supposed I guess to suggest that you enter heaven, and the clown Ronald McDonald, are experiences that the majority of the Indian population would reject. I think our people are too earthy. First of all, it would be too expensive for the ordinary Indian – for the peasant, or the person in the slums. It's an experience that a very tiny elite would engage in, and most of that elite – which knows what good food is all about – would not fall for it. McDonald's is doing no good to people's health, and in a country like India where first of

Exhibit 4 | Dates of McDonald's entry into East and South Asian markets

Year	Country
1971	Japan
1975	Hong Kong
1979	Singapore
1980	Philippines
1981	Malaysia
1984	Taiwan
1985	Thailand
1988	South Korea
1990	China (Shenzhen Special Economic Zone)
1991	Indonesia
1992	China (Beijing)
1996	India
1998	Pakistan
1998	Sri Lanka

Sources: J. L. Watson (ed), 1997, *Golden Arches East* (Stanford, CA: Stanford University Press), Table 2; *Food and Drink Weekly*, 26 October 1998.

all, we are not a meat culture, and therefore our systems are ill-adapted to meat in the first place, and where people are poorer – shifting to a diet like this will have an enormous impact.

Since 1991, when the Indian economy began opening up to foreign investments, many multinationals have rushed in – lured by the attraction of serving a large middle class, estimated at 300 million. However, even some of the well-known global brands failed with their initial strategies and were forced to reposition, including, in some cases, drastic reduction of prices. Some multinationals (for example, Peugeot) even had to close shop. Kellogg's, which entered with high-priced cereals (several orders of magnitude more expensive than a traditional Indian breakfast), faced a lack of demand. KFC initially failed to realise that Indians were repulsed by chicken skin, which was vital for the Colonel's secret batter to stick. Thus, apart from a lack of understanding of the local tastes, a combination of circumstances – including overestimation of the demand potential, rosy assumptions about the dismantling of bureaucratic hurdles to doing business, infrastructural inadequacies and, finally, inappropriate firm strategies (for example, pricing) – led to many failures and disappointments.

McDonald's entry strategy in India

McDonald's India was incorporated as a wholly owned subsidiary in 1993. In April 1995, the wholly owned subsidiary entered into two 50:50 joint ventures: with Connaught Plaza Restaurants (Vikram Bakshi) to own and operate the Delhi Restaurants; and Hardcastle Restaurants (Amit Jatia) to own and operate the Mumbai outlets.

Although McDonald's had done product adaptation to suit local tastes and cultures in several previous ventures, such as the Teriyaki Burger in Japan, rice dishes in Indonesia, noodles in Manila and McLox Salmon sandwiches in Norway, the degree of adaptation required in India was significantly greater. McDonald's replaced its core product, the Big Mac, with the Maharaja Mac. The latter had a mutton patty (instead of the beef patty in the Big Mac), to avoid offending the sensibilities of Hindus (80 per cent of the population), who consider killing cows as sacrilegious, and Muslims (12 per cent of the population), for whom pork is taboo. In addition, since 40 per cent of the market is estimated to be vegetarian, the menu included the McAloo Burger (based on potato), a special salad sandwich for vegetarians, and the McChicken kebab sandwich. It also

Exhibit 5 | Income distribution in India

Classification	Number of people (millions)	Households (millions)	Income in US$
The Deprived	763	131	<600
The Aspirants	120	20	1 000–3 000
The Climbers	45	8	3 000–6 000
The Strivers	25	5	6 000–12 500
The Rich (total)	2.18	0.3545	>12 500
The Near Rich	1.55	0.25	12 500–25 000
The Clear Rich	0.444	0.074	25 000–50 000
The Sheer Rich	0.144	0.024	50 000–125 000
The Super Rich	0.039	0.0065	>125 000

Sources: Income figures are approximate and based on A. Chatterjee, 1998, 'Marketing to the superrich', *Business Today* (Living Media India Ltd), 22 April; W. Berryman and J. McManus, 1998, 'India: Turning the elephant economy', *Independent Business Weekly*, 24 June.

offered spicier sauces, such as McMasala and McImli (made from tamarind). Other elements of the menu, such as chicken nuggets, fillet fish sandwiches, fries, sodas and milkshakes, were in common with the rest of the McDonald's system.

In 1998, McDonald's India set up a menu development team to collect consumer feedback. Subsequently, the team came up with its menu vision, and new products since then have been based on this vision.

The adaptation of the strategy went well beyond the menu, encompassing many aspects of the restaurant management system. Two different menu boards were displayed in each restaurant – green for vegetarian products and purple for non-vegetarian products. Behind the counter, restaurant kitchens had separate, dedicated preparation areas for the meat and non-meat products. The kitchen crew (in charge of cooking) had different uniforms to distinguish their roles and did not work at the vegetarian and non-vegetarian stations on the same day, thus ensuring clear segregation. The wrapping of vegetarian and non-vegetarian food took place separately. These extra steps were taken to assure Indian customers of the wholesomeness of both products and their preparation. To convince Indian customers that the company would not serve beef and would respect the culinary habits of its clientele, McDonald's printed brochures explaining all these steps and took customers on kitchen tours.

McDonald's positioned itself as a family restaurant. The average price of a 'Combo' meal, which included burger, fries and Coke, varied from Rs 76 for a vegetarian meal to Rs 88 for a Maharaja Mac meal. This could be compared with KFC meal prices at Rs 59 (Crispy Burger, regular fries and large Pepsi) and Rs 79 (KFC Chicken, Colonel Burger and regular Pepsi). McDonald's Happy Meal, which included a complimentary toy, was priced at Rs 46. The prices in India were lower than in Sri Lanka or Pakistan, and even the price of the Maharaja Mac was 50 per cent less than an equivalent product in the United States.

To fight its premium image among the public, the company undertook selective price cutting and ran some periodic promotions. In February 1999, the company was offering 'economeals' for as low as Rs 29. The company reduced the price of vegetable nuggets from Rs 29 to Rs 19 and that of its soft-serve ice-cream cone from Rs 16 to Rs 7. Apparently, this still afforded McDonald's a healthy margin (40 per cent for cones). As Vikram Bakshi, explained, 'I will never become unaffordable, as I will not then be able to build up volumes.' The lower price could be attributed to two factors: the pricing strategies of MNC rivals as well as mid-range local restaurants, and the development of a local (low-cost) supply chain.

McDonald's pricing strategies, as well as special promotions, were influenced by rivals. In February 1999, several competitors were running special promotions, with KFC offering a meal inclusive of chicken, rice and gravy for Rs 39. For Rs 350, Pizza Hut was offering a whole family meal, including two medium pizzas, bread and Pepsi. Wimpy's was offering mega meals at Rs 35. A typical vegetarian 'set meal', or 'thali' (which included Indian breads, rice, vegetables and yogurt) at a mid-range restaurant cost around Rs 50, which was considerably lower than a McDonald's meal.

Some analysts believed that that by introducing loss leaders (for example, cones), McDonald's wanted to highlight good value for all its products. Whether customers attracted by special promotions pay repeat visits to McDonald's remains to be seen.

In October 2000, the company introduced two new Indianised products to its menu – the Chicken McGrill and the Veg Pizza McPuff. At that point in time, 75 per cent of the menu in India was unique – that is, different from the rest of the McDonald's system. The Chicken McGrill had a grilled chicken patty topped with onions and mint sauce, to give it an Indian flavour. The Veg Pizza was a takeoff on the popular Indian samosa (potato-based curry puff) with differences in shape (rectangular) and stuffing (capsicum, onions and Mozarella cheese with tomato sauce). In keeping with the low pricing strategy in India, these items were priced at Rs 25 and Rs 16, respectively.

With its value pricing and localised menu, McDonald's had attracted some loyal customers. One such customer said, 'A normal kebab, with all the trimmings, at a regular restaurant would cost more than Rs 25 and if the new McGrill is giving us a similar satisfaction with its mint chutney (sauce), then we'd rather eat in a lively McDonald's outlet than sitting in a cramped car on the road.'

Some elements of the promotional strategy remained the same as in other parts of the world. One instance of this included the emphasis on attracting children. A Happy Meal film was consistently shown on the Cartoon Network and the Zee (a local channel) Disney Hour. McDonald's also teamed up with Delhi Traffic Police and the Delhi Fire Service to highlight safety issues, again trying to create goodwill among schoolchildren. In October 1999, in conjunction with The Walt Disney Company and UNESCO, McDonald's launched a search for Millennium Dreamers. The program would bring together 2 000 young people from around the globe who had made a positive and significant impact on their communities. Based on the number of its outlets, India was allocated two representatives.

By June 2000, the company had started rolling out its first national campaign, as it was expanding beyond Mumbai and New Delhi. The campaign, budgeted at Rs 100 million, was expected to highlight (in phased order) the brand (the experience that there is something special about McDonald's), food quality and variety. The company also ran special promotions during festivals, and 'vegetarian' days, and was even developing garlic-free sauces to bring in 'hard-core' vegetarian traffic.

In terms of the selection of cities, McDonald's followed the same strategy in India as in the rest of the world. Its initial focus on Mumbai and Delhi was driven by the following factors: they were the two largest cities in India; their citizens enjoyed relatively high income levels compared to the rest of the country; and they were exposed to foreign food and culture. After establishing a presence in the leading cities, McDonald's then moved to smaller satellite towns near the metropolitan cities (for example, from Delhi to Gurgaon and Noida, both suburbs of Delhi, and from Mumbai to Pune). McDonald's often found that there were positive spillover effects, in terms of its reputation, from the metropolitan cities to the satellite towns. In Jaipur, the company was hoping to attract foreign tourists.

Developing the supply chain

McDonald's search for Indian suppliers started as early as 1991. Its initial challenge was to develop local suppliers who could deliver quality raw materials, regularly and on schedule. In the five-and-a-half years until start-up, McDonald's spent as much as Rs 500 million (US$12.8 million) to set up a supply network, distribution centres and logistics support. By mid-2000, some estimates placed the total investment in the supply chain at almost Rs 3 billion. Local suppliers,

Exhibit 6 | McDonald's supply chain in India

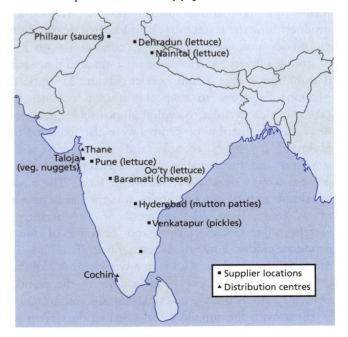

distributors and joint venture partners and employees had to match the restaurant chain's quality and hygiene standards before they became part of its system.

McDonald's experience in identifying and cultivating the supplier of lettuce provided an excellent illustration of the difficulties involved. In 1991, hardly any iceberg lettuce was grown in India, except for a small quantity grown around Delhi during the winter months. McDonald's identified a lettuce supplier (Mangesh Kumar from Ootacamund in Tamilnadu, a southern state) and helped him in a broad range of activities, from seed selection to advice on farming practices. In the case of several other suppliers, such as Cremica Industries which supplied the sesame seed buns, McDonald's helped them to gain access to foreign technology. In another instance, it encouraged Dynamix, the supplier of cheese, to establish a program for milk procurement by investing in bulk milk collection and chilling centres. This, in turn, led to higher milk yields and overall collections, as well as to an improvement in milk quality. McDonald's ended up with a geographically diverse sourcing network, with buns coming from northern India, chicken and cheese from western India, and lettuce and pickles from southern India. There were as many as 40 suppliers in the company's supply chain. (See Exhibit 6 for McDonald's supply chain.)

A dedicated distribution system was established to match the suppliers' production and delivery schedules with the restaurant's needs. The first two centralised distribution centres were set up near Mumbai and at Cochin (in the southernmost part of India) in joint ventures with two local retailers, both of whom had to learn from international distributors of McDonald's products how the restaurant chain handled distribution worldwide and, especially, how to enhance the quality of storage operations. The company estimated that each distribution centre could service about 25 outlets. McDonald's strove to keep the storage volumes of products high in order to exploit all possible economies of scale. The distribution centres were also expected to maintain inventory records and to interact with suppliers and the logistics firm to ensure that their freezers were well stocked. Said Amit Jatia, 'The most important part of our operations was the development of a cold chain [the process of procurement, warehousing, transportation and retailing of food products under controlled temperatures]. There is practically no need for a knife in any restaurant. All the chopping and food processing is done in the plants. Only the actual cooking takes place in the restaurants.'

Even with the suppliers and distribution system in place, McDonald's needed a distribution link to move raw materials to its restaurants. Logistics management was contracted out to AFL Logistics – itself a 50:50 joint venture between Air Freight (a Mumbai-based firm) and FX Coughlin of the United States, McDonald's international logistics provider. AFL logistics was responsible for the temperature-controlled movement of all products (by rail, road or air, as appropriate) from individual suppliers to the regional distribution centres.

McDonald's had to work extremely hard at inculcating a service orientation in its employees, especially those involved in physical logistics, since the freshness of the food was at stake. The truck operators had to be explicitly and clearly instructed not to switch off the truck's refrigeration system to save on fuel or electricity. The corporation went to the extent of installing trapping devices, which would show the temperature chart through the entire journey.

Since 1999, McDonald's had started using India as an export base for cheese, lettuce and other products that went into its burgers. Exports had already begun to Sri Lanka, where it had opened in October 1998, and trial shipments had commenced to Hong Kong and the Middle East. Said Amit Jatia, 'Things are becoming global in nature. Once you set up a supply chain in a strategic location, it can service other countries as well.'

Past performance and planned strategies

During its first 12 months of operations, McDonald's opened seven outlets (four in Delhi and three in Mumbai), had 6 million customer visits and served 350 000 Maharaja Macs. By the end of 1998, the number of outlets had gone up to 14, and, by mid-2000, it had expanded to 25 outlets with an outlet in Pune and Jaipur. The estimates for average daily customer visits to a McDonald's outlet differed widely. According to a mid-range estimate (conservative estimates were half as much, whereas generous estimates could be about 40 per cent higher), in June 2000, McDonald's outlets were doing (on average) about 1 500 transactions (or bills raised) a day, serving over 3 500 visitors. This was a significant improvement over 1998 when a typical McDonald's restaurant was doing only 900 transactions per day (according to the same source). Industry sources, however, were in agreement that the spending per customer visit at McDonald's was around Rs 45.

The growth rate in McDonald's sales had been 70 per cent over the previous two years (1998–2000) and was expected to be sustained until 2002. This growth rate included the effect of starting up new outlets. Even with this growth, analysts were expecting that the

Indian operation would take three to four more years to break even overall. This was attributable to the heavy investments made in vendor development, infrastructure and brand building.

One gratifying aspect of McDonald's success was the fact that, by mid-2000, it derived as much as 50 per cent of its revenues from vegetable food items, thus disproving its critics – especially those who were sceptical of its ability to serve food that suited Indian palates. In 1997, customers rated McDonald's food as bland. By September 2000, the perception had changed, however. Customers thought that McDonald's food had a unique taste.

To exploit the opportunities created due to its better brand awareness and customer acceptance, McDonald's was following a three-pronged strategy: increase the seating capacity in existing outlets to cater to additional traffic; open new outlets in Mumbai and Delhi; and, finally, penetrate new cities.

McDonald's was also in talks with Delhi Metro Rail Corporation, Airports Authority of India, Indian Railways and Delhi Development Authority to open smaller McDonald's outlets in airports and railway stations, among others. The investments required to open these smaller outlets were only half that of the regular outlets.

High real estate prices were a thorny issue in nationwide expansion. In metropolitan cities such as Mumbai, prime real estate was extremely expensive and sometimes not available at all. The costs were also high in other cities such as Bangalore. 'Our expansion plans are always relative to the availability of real estate,' Bakshi said.

McDonald's also had plans to set up several outlets along the Delhi-Agra national highway in a tie-up with a major petroleum refining and marketing organisation, Bharat Petroleum Corporation Limited. Jatia said, 'We feel both local tourists and foreigners travelling by road don't have many reliable eating options right now.' The first such outlet, a project estimated at Rs 35 million, was already in operation. The company proposed to offer highway travellers parking space and a play area for children. The emphasis on quality, service, cleanliness and value (QSCV) had been quite successful in drawing highway travellers in its home market (the United States). Some analysts, however, believed that highway travellers in India, who were typically truck and bus drivers, would not be willing to go in for the type of food or prices that McDonald's currently offered. In addition, McDonald's was looking at tie-ups with other oil companies, as well as retail vehicles such as malls, multiplexes or cinema halls.

Endnote

* This case was first published, in an earlier form, in Kulwant Singh, Nitin Pangarkar and Gaik Eng Lim (eds), 2001, *Business Strategy in Asia: A Casebook* (Singapore: Thomson Learning).

References

Ad Age, 'Daily World Wire', 1998 (Crain Communications Inc.), 1 April.
Avertino, M., 2000, 'McDonald's to stir up adjusted menus in break-even hunt', *Business Standard*, 22 June.
Berryman, W. and J. McManus, 1998), 'India: Turning the elephant economy', *Independent Business Weekly*, 24 June.
Business Line, 1998, 'Where McDonald's buys its stuff', 15 July.
Business Line, 1998, 'Big Mac woos Indian palates with homegrown menus', *The Hindu*, 6 November.
Business Line, 1999, 'Dinner on discount', 25 February.
Business Line, 1999, 'India: Mac, Disney look out for millennium kids', 29 October.
Business Line, 2000, 'India-McDonald's shifts to product-focussed ads', 8 September.
Business Line, 2000, 'McDonald's goes for media splash', 3 April.
Business Line, 2001, 'India: Big Mac sets eyes on the south', 20 February.
Chaterjee, A., 1998, 'Marketing to the superrich', *Business Today* (Living Media India Ltd), 22 April.
Connect Magazine, 1998, Worldwide Feedback Form: www.connectmagazine.com/June 1998/Junepgshtml/June98Wwind.html.
DeGarmo, K., 1998, 'Mulan Happy Meal goes worldwide', *The Fort Worth Star Telegram*, 16 June.
Deshpande, V., 'McDonald's goes more Indian': www.financialexpress.com/fe/daily/20000910/faf10031.html.
The Ecologist, 1995, 'Kentucky Fried Chicken protests in India', October.
The Economist, 1997, 'Spice with everything', 22 November.
Happy Birthday, 'Maharaja Mac! One year later: McDonald's in India': www.media.mcdonalds.com/secured/products/international/maharajamac.html.
Independent Business Weekly, 1998, 'Of Swadeshiwallahs and Saffronomics: India seeks economic salvation in its past', 17 June.
'India to be McDonald's export base': www.indian-express.com/ie/daily/19990704/ibu04020.html.
Jain, S., 2000, 'Big Mac to serve highway travelers', *Business Standard*, 21 July.
Kadaba, S. L., 1998, 'Line up for Maharaja Mac', *Chicago Tribune*, 22 April.
Markets Asia Pacific, 1997, 'Indian market is culturally diverse', 1 January.
Masih, A., 1999, 'McJatia tickles Bombay's taste buds, builds an empire, all in two years', *Rediff Business Special*: www.rediff.com/business/1999/apr/29jatia.htm.
Masih, A., 1999, 'Jatia forayed into McDonald's by chance', Part I: www.rediff.com/business/1999/ apr/29jatia1.htm
Matthew, J., 1997, 'McDonald's realty proposals in a jam', *Business Standard*, 10 February.
'McDonald's India to invest Rs 7.5 billion': http://biz.indiainfo.com/news/june19/india.html.
'McDonald's plans major investments in India': http://news.sawaal.om/21-Jun-2000/Business/50.htm.
'McDonald's reworks its menu': www.indiatoday.com/btoday/20000607/c6.html.
Pande, B. and A. Dua, 2000, 'Big Mac's appetite for growth', *Business Standard*, 29 August.
PTI News Agency, 1999, 'Indian board approves foreign investment including McDonald's outlet', 20 February.
Raghunath, P., 1998, 'VHP may act against McDonald's outlet', *Gulf News* (Al Nasir Publishing LLC), 14 April.
Singh, N., 1998, 'McDonald's plans to move outlets', *Indian Express*, 27 January.
South China Morning Post, 1997, 'Beefless Mac arrives', 26 January.
The Times of India, 2000, 'McDonalds comes to town', 22 June.
The Times of India, 2000, 'What next, McDosas?', 9 September.
The Wall Street Journal, 1999, 'Brand names are of equal rank as productive equipment and very important assets', June.

Case 9

Nucor Corporation and the US steel industry

Brian K. Boyd
Steve Gove
Arizona State University

Darlington, South Carolina, 1969. Making steel is a technically demanding, complex and dangerous process. Nucor Corp.'s initial foray into steel production was the latter. Instead of staffing the plant with seasoned steel veterans, Nucor hired farmers, mechanics and other intelligent, motivated workers. Those employees along with company executives and dignitaries in attendance at Nucor's mill opening fled the plant as the inaugural pour resulted in molten steel pouring on to the mill floor and spreading towards the crowd. Onlookers and employees alike were left wondering if Nucor would ever successfully produce steel.[1]

The steel industry, a classic example of a market in the late stages of maturity, traces its roots to colonial-era blacksmiths who forged basic farm and household equipment. The industry grew (and consolidated) rapidly in the first half of the 20th century, with worldwide demand growing throughout the 1960s. However, a series of shifts in market dynamics led to dramatic industry-wide declines in growth and profitability. The dominant players faced the same problems as leaders of other mature industries – Ford and General Motors, for example: obsolete production facilities, bureaucratic management systems, heavily unionised workers and hungry foreign competitors. Due to its centrality in the economy, the decline of the steel industry was cited by some observers as evidence of the decline of the overall US economic system.

While foreign competition played a significant role in changing the US steel industry, an even larger factor emerged during the 1970s: minimill technology. Traditional 'integrated mills' rely on large-scale vertical integration including integrated coke and ore production. 'Minimills' used a new technology to recycle scrap steel and quickly stole most of the commodity steel market away from integrated producers. This enabled minimills to enter a geographic market with a distinct cost advantage: they typically require a capital investment of US$300 to US$500 million, or 5–10 per cent of that required for an integrated mill. The minimill revolution has resulted in a dramatic dispersion of the steel manufacturers from the 'rust belt' to the primary population and growth areas of the United States. The impact of minimills on the industry is best demonstrated by looking at the former industry leader US Steel (now USX Corp.). In 1966, US Steel controlled 55 per cent of the American steel market; in 1986 it controlled only 17 per cent.

Despite its inauspicious foray into steel, Nucor Corp. has become the benchmark for both the US steel industry and US industry in general. Nucor is one of the fastest growing and most efficient steel producers in the world. Despite declining demand for steel, Nucor's growth has been phenomenal. Since pouring its first batch of steel in the 1960s to support in-house operations, the company has become one of the top five producers of steel in the United States. Without an R&D department, Nucor has repeatedly achieved technological feats other steel producers thought impossible. Their hourly pay is among the lowest in the industry, yet they have the highest productivity per worker of any steel producer in the US and near zero employee turnover. How has Nucor achieved such phenomenal success? Can it continue to do so?

US steel industry history

Steel has been a part of the domestic economic system since the colonial era, when iron (the parent of steel) was smelted and forged. The early 19th century, with the advent of steam engines, cotton gins and farming

Exhibit 1 | Comparative trends: GDP, steel industry output and Nucor output, 1980–96

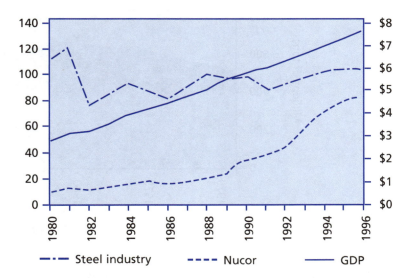

Note: Information is overall trends; it is not to scale for comparison. GDP is scaled on right axis in trillions of 1992$. Industry is scaled on left axis in million tons. Nucor is scaled on left axis in million tons, but shown at 10X.

combines, advanced iron as a commodity of progress. The addition of carbon to iron yielded a material with additional strength, elasticity, toughness and malleability at elevated temperatures. The Civil War provided the impetus for the industry to organise, consolidate, expand and modernise to supply the vast quantities of steel required for warfare.

Following the Civil War, the construction of new transportation systems, public works projects, automobiles, bridges, ships and large buildings all fuelled a torrid expansion of the industry lasting through the turn of the century. Domestic economic expansion and two world wars maintained an unquenchable appetite for steel both in the United States and around the world in the first half of the 20th century. Even in the aftermath of the Second World War, America's steel industry prospered as it supplied an ever-expanding domestic economy and the rebuilding of war-ravaged infrastructures. This windfall for the domestic industry was in actuality one of the root causes for its eventual decline. US plants, left idle by the end of the war, were reactivated to support the Marshall Plan and MacArthur's rebuilding of Japan. The war-torn nations of the world, however, rebuilt their industrial facilities from the ground up, incorporating the latest production technology. Conversely, domestic producers were content with older, formerly inactivated facilities.

Global demand for steel expanded continuously throughout the 1960s; domestic producers elected not to meet this demand, choosing only to match domestic consumption requirements. This presented an opportunity for up-start foreign producers to rejuvenate and strengthen themselves without directly competing against US producers. Throughout this expansion, the relationship between management and labour soured. In 1892, Henry Clay Frick's Pinkerton guards attacked striking workers, setting the stage for a contentious relationship between management and labour. Labour, represented by the United Steel Workers of America (USWA), and management began negotiating three-year collective bargaining agreements beginning in 1947. These negotiations frequently collapsed, and strikes following the third year of a contract became commonplace. Firms dependent on steel soon initiated a pattern of accumulating 30-day 'strike hedge' inventories to feed operations during strike shutdowns. In 1959, the USWA walked out for 116 days. In 1964, another strike required presidential intervention. The impact of these strikes reverberated throughout the economy. Major customers began to look for stable supplies of steel from foreign producers who, in 1959, met only 3 per cent of domestic demand. Fuelled by excess capacity and strike-induced demand, foreign producers were providing 18 per cent of domestic demand by the time a long-term labour accord was reached in the early 1970s. Foreign producers currently supply 20–25 per cent of the steel used in the United States.

Protectionists are quick to blame the Japanese for the decimation of the American steel industry. However, other countries have an even stronger presence in the US market: since 1991, for example, Canada has exported

Exhibit 2 | World capacity, production and idle capacity, 1970–90

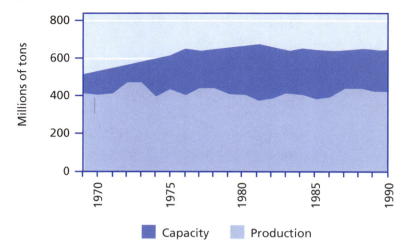
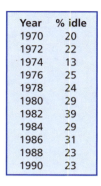

Year	% idle
1970	20
1972	22
1974	13
1976	25
1978	24
1980	29
1982	39
1984	29
1986	31
1988	23
1990	23

more steel to the United States than has Japan. By 1994, Europe and other regions accounted for the bulk of steel imports. While foreign producers maintain a strong presence in the United States, the same cannot be said for American steel firms abroad. Exports by US firms have traditionally been minuscule, 1 per cent of production in the mid-1980s, but have grown to 3–5 per cent of production during the 1990s.

While the labour accords reached in the 1970s stabilised the supply of domestic steel, the cost of living adjustments (COLAs) and automatic wage adjustments included in the accords would prove to be detrimental to the industry's cash position during periods of reduced demand for steel. Such a situation was experienced in the 1970s when the domestic automobile industry, historically the largest consumer of steel in the United States, began to decline. Domestic producers attempted to remedy the resulting cash flow crisis with layoffs and price hikes, but the price hikes came at the expense of further market share erosion to low-cost foreign producers. While the industry claimed productivity improvements, these were often the result of layoffs and shutdowns, as opposed to process efficiency improvements.

The slowdowns and closures of the 1970s set the stage for the steel industry's 'dark ages' – the period from 1980 to 1986 when steel output declined from 115 to 80 million tons despite an increase in real GDP. The energy crisis led to demand for smaller, lighter cars which require less steel, also resulting in less required tonnage. R&D in the steel industry led to stronger blends of steel. New materials, such as petroleum-based materials (plastics), organics (wood/pulp) and synthetic materials (fibreglass, epoxies) became significant threats in several applications customarily met by steel. Overall employment in steel fell from 535 000 in 1979 to 249 000 in 1986.

Despite this decline, this was also a period of shakeout and dynamic activity in the industry. Slowly, and with the help of the federal government (primarily in tax and regulatory relief and enforcement of Uruguay Trade Agreements/Voluntary Restraining Agreements), some firms were able to revitalise their operations by streamlining production, selecting better markets, focusing production (minimills), improving facilities, stabilising labour contracts, and reducing labour content through plant modernisation, dollar devaluation and a reprieve from the onslaught of substitute materials. This gave the surviving firms an opportunity to recover and prosper.

Historically, demand for steel fluctuates in both the US and international markets due to its close ties to durable and capital goods, markets which suffer more acutely during austerity and are more prosperous during economic expansions. Economic swings notwithstanding, there has been little appreciable growth in steel demand between the 1950s and the 1990s. Current domestic production is approximately 100 million tons per year, far less than the 120 million tons of 1981. Decline in demand has led to substantial excess capacity. In 1980, for example, domestic producers had 25 per cent idle capacity. While the industry now operates at 90 per cent of capacity, this has come as a result of reduced capacity, not increased output; total domestic capacity declined by 30 per cent between 1980 and 1994. Capacity reduction in the steel industry is expensive, particularly for integrated producers. USX Corp., for example, eliminated 16 per cent of its capacity in 1983

Exhibit 3 | US production, 1974 and 1994

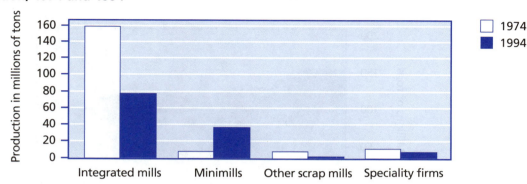

	1974	1994	% Change
Integrated mills	158	77	−51
Minimills	8	37	363
Other scrap mills	7	1	−86
Speciality firms' production in millions of tons	12	8	−33

at a cost of US$1.2 billion. Still, by 1987, USX had 40 per cent idle capacity.

While large-scale, integrated producers such as USX were shedding excess capacity, a new type of competitor, 'minimills', was entering the market. Minimills utilise recycled steel (in the form of junk cars, scrap, etc.) as a primary ingredient. Unlike the integrated producers, minimills are less capital intensive, smaller and have historically focused on producing low-technology, entry-level products. Unlike integrated mills, which have seen production decline, minimills have seen explosive growth, with numerous plants opening in the late 1980s and 1990s.

Overall, the steel industry has all of the characteristics of a highly competitive market: stagnant demand, excess capacity and numerous global competitors. The ability of the largest firm to use its power to set prices is gone. Above-average industry margins are quickly targeted by other firms. These factors are compounded by a largely commodity-like product that minimises switching costs and customer loyalty. Not surprisingly, the profit performance of the industry has been weak; the industry as a whole lost money during much of the 1980s. In 1987, the first (albeit small) industry-wide profit in eight years was posted. With the exception of the 1990–1 recession, domestic producers have gradually improved the return on assets to a value of 6.1 per cent in 1994. A flurry of exits and Chapter 11 reorganisations led to an improved profit potential for remaining firms by the mid-1990s. The success is more pronounced in the minimill sector, although the integrated producers are presently healthy and now represent a new threat to the minimills.

Emerging industry trend

While in many ways the industry appears to have stabilised, a number of emerging trends threaten to cause further disruption within the industry to both integrateds and minimills.

Minimill over-capacity

Starting in 1989, only one company, Nucor, was capable of producing flat-rolled steel using minimill technology. However, competing firms have started using similar technology and there were expected to be 10 new flat-roll minimills on-line by 1997, adding 13 million tons of production capacity – about 10 per cent of 1996 production – to the industry. This new capacity should become available just as steel consumption is expected to decline.

Scrap prices

Due to growing demand for scrap metal, its cost has become increasingly volatile in the 1990s. In 1994, for example, prices climbed as much as US$50/ton to US$165–170/ton, while 10 million tons of American scrap were exported to offshore customers. In 1996, prices reached US$200/ton, and were expected to climb, but instead declined to US$170–180/ton by the end of 1997.

Euro production

While growth has improved in recent years, demand for steel is still weak in much of Europe, particularly in Eastern European nations. Western Europe alone had 20 million tons of excess capacity in 1994, and Russian

Exhibit 4 | Domestic capacity and production, 1980–96

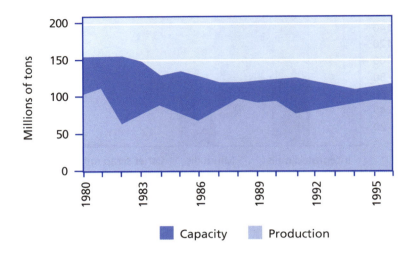

mills were operating at 65 per cent of capacity. Additionally, many European mills are state-owned and subsidised. Faced with weak performance and idle capacity, many of these mills are aggressively pursing export opportunities in China and other parts of Asia. Russian steel exports approached US$4 billion in 1993, double their 1992 level.

Antidumping rulings

US integrated steel producers filed 72 charges of dumping against foreign competitors – primarily the Germans and Japanese. In 1993, the International Trade Commission concluded that there was some justification for these charges, but not for others, and ruled that foreign steel caused no harm in 40 of the 72 cases. Stock prices for US producers (in aggregate) declined US$1.1 billion in the 90 minutes following the announcement of the ruling.

Industry economic structure

The domestic steel industry, until recent technological changes, was essentially composed of two vertically integrated sectors. The first was the raw steel production sector which encompassed steel-making operations from the unearthing of ores and coke to the basic ore reduction and smelting. The outcome or product of this sector was ingots, billets and slabs which are standard steel shapes. These products were then sent to finishing mills (the second sector) which conducted various heat treating and shaping processes to produce finished steel products such as bars, tubes, castings, forgings, plates, sheets and structural shapes. These two sectors were typically housed under a single facility but as two distinct operations in what was termed the 'integrated' producer. Traditionally, steel manufacturers used batch processing, which involved heating a furnace of steel and pouring the entire furnace full of molten steel into billets, ingots and slabs. These intermediate products were then processed and the process was repeated. The onset of continuous casting technology (a process in which ores are reduced and poured into final shapes without the intermediate production of slabs and ingots) in the late 1970s has blurred the classical two-sector demarcation. Most producers today use the continuous casting process for producing isometric shapes, but raw steel must still be shipped to finishing mills for manufacture of more complex products.

The suppliers to the steel industry can be broadly assigned to three major classes: ore, energy and transportation. Since a preponderance of the final production cost is tied up in these input items, many producers have vertically integrated backwards by acquiring ore and coal/coke mining firms and transportation networks (rail and barge). The supply factors of production (transformation factors) are labour to operate plants, capital facilities and land. Recent modernisation has significantly substituted technology for labour in steel production.

Minimills are a significant force of change in the industry, as their supplier and customer requirements differ from the integrated mills. First, ore supplies are, to differing degrees, replaced by a need for access to large quantities of scrap steel. Second, minimills, while still large consumers of electricity, consume far less power than their integrated mill counterparts. This,

Exhibit 5 | Steel demand by market sector, 1972 and 1998

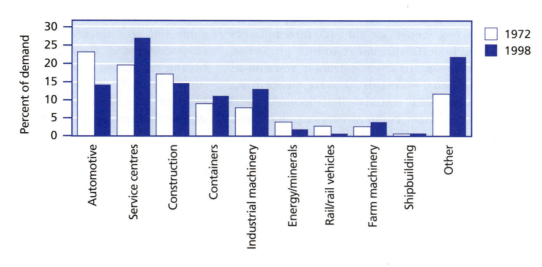

along with the lower output capacity of each plant, allows for placement of the mills closer to the third factor: the changing customer base. This has resulted in a radical shift in steel production in recent years from western Pennsylvania and Ohio to a much broader dispersion of steel mills throughout the United States. By one estimate, steel mills can now be found in over half of the US states.

The principal markets and customers for steel are the classical markets. Some sectors are on the decline, while others are fairly stable. The automotive sector was historically the largest consumer of steel in peacetime. Construction materials is now the largest sector, followed by the automobile and container industries, energy equipment, industrial machinery, farming equipment, car/rail production and various military applications. The reduced demand by the automobile industry is the result of the lower steel content in a modern automobile, a trend steel producers are aggressively trying to counter by banding together to form the Steel Alliance which is running a US$100 million advertising campaign targeted at consumers and touting the advantages of steel for automobile design (and house construction).

Service centres are playing an increased role in the industry, acting as major distributors and wholesalers for finished steel products to steel consumers (construction firms, shipbuilders, machine fabricators, etc.). With the exception of the automobile and automobile part manufacturers (who contract directly with producers), most finished steel is delivered to end users via the steel service centre, moving some of the inventory management burden to the service centres for a marginal mark-up to the end user. This presents a forecasting complication to planners and strategists, as all demand for steel is a derived demand. The forecaster must be able to look into the macro forces affecting an economy and project steel's role in the broader economic system from which a consumer demand pattern could be ascertained.

Steel production technology

Any attempt to consolidate steel and steel production technology into a few paragraphs would be doing the topic a disservice. However, two major issues deserve additional attention: production factors and substitutes. Automation has improved the competitive position of the industry by reducing its exposure to volatile labour markets and labour costs. It has also increased the flexibility of producers to shift product output and incorporate the continuous casting process. Closely related is the elimination of the old open-hearth furnace in favour of the blast-oxygen furnace and electric arc furnaces which are far more efficient, more easily automated and require less manpower. These furnaces also reduce stack emissions, a critical environmental requirement (and a concern that many foreign producers do not face). While technology has been a driver of change, labour agreements and relations have not always made it possible to fully exploit the benefits of technological improvements.

The proliferation of substitute materials is an important issue. It is important to note, however, that while substitutes have made significant inroads into steel markets over the last 30 years, they will likely never replace steel as the commodity of choice for many applications. Steel will not be displaced (with very minor exceptions) as a material in strength applications: plastic is not strong enough; graphite-reinforced plastics and epoxies lack steel's thermal resistance properties; wood is not as strong or environmentally resistant as steel; and titanium remains a rare, expensive, strategically controlled material. Furthermore, steel comes in many different compositions (stainless, tool, high-strength, galvanised). The industry's R&D efforts have continued to evolve steel to meet the demands of customers. In short, steel remains – and is likely to remain – the material of choice in most applications.

Nucor Corporation

Nucor Corp. began life as the Nuclear Corporation of America. The latter was a highly diversified and marginally profitable company; its products included instruments, semiconductors, rare earths and construction. One of its potential acquisitions was Coast Metals, a family-owned producer of speciality metals. When the acquisition fell through, Nuclear hired one of Coast's top engineers as a consultant to recommend other acquisition targets. The engineer – Ken Iverson – had strong technical skills (including a graduate degree in metallurgy from Purdue University) and general management experience. Based on Iverson's recommendation, Nuclear acquired a steel joist company in South Carolina. Subsequently, Iverson joined Nuclear as a vice president in 1962. Nuclear built a second joist plant in Nebraska the following year. Iverson was responsible for supervising the joist operations as well as the research, chemical and construction segments. By 1965, the diversified company had experienced another string of losses, although the joist operations were profitable, and Iverson was promoted to president.

Recognising that its most valuable skills lay in its joist operations, Nuclear became Nucor Corp. and divested non-joist operations. New joist plants soon followed, including one in Alabama in 1967 and another in Texas in 1968. As a joist company, Nucor was dependent on American and foreign steel producers for its key input. Iverson decided to integrate backwards into steel making in the hopes of stabilising supply and lowering input costs for the joist business. So, Nucor began construction on its own steel mill in Darlington, South Carolina – a location close to an existing joist operation. The Darlington plant used the then new minimill technology. When the plant opened on 12 October 1969, the pouring of the first batch of steel resulted in molten steel cascading out of the mould and across the floor of the plant. Despite the mishap, Nucor quickly became adept at minimill technology. In addition to supplying its own joist operations, it began competing with integrateds and other minimills in the commodity steel business. Iverson and Nucor soon became recognised as the 'Southwest Airlines' of steel: a simple, no-frills organisation, with a unique culture, highly motivated workers and the lowest cost structure of the industry. Some indicators of Nucor's success include:

- It is the only major player in the industry that can boast of 22 years of uninterrupted quarterly dividends (Nucor began paying quarterly dividends in 1973) and 30 years of continuous quarterly profits, despite numerous slumps and downturns in the industry (see Exhibits 6–14).
- Between 1980 and 1990, Nucor doubled in size. In comparison, the six main integrated producers reduced their steel-making capacity from 108 to 58 million tons during this period.
- In 1990, Nucor had six steel plants and a total annual capacity of 3 million tons. By 1995, it had added a seventh plant, and its overall capacity neared 8 million tons.
- In 1994, Nucor generated US$1.50 in sales for every dollar in property, plant and equipment. The industry average was US$0.95 before depreciation expenses. After depreciation, these ratios are US$2.18 and US$1.83 respectively.
- Nucor continues to be the industry leader in cost efficiency. In 1990, it produced 980 tons of steel per employee each year, at a net cost of US$60/ton, compared to the industry average of 420 tons per employee at a cost of US$135/ton. In 1994, Nucor's conversion cost was US$170/ton, roughly US$50–75 less than its competitors.

Nucor has primary mills located in Arkansas, Nebraska, Utah, South Carolina, Texas and Indiana. Additional operating facilities located in Fort Payne, Alabama; Conway, Arkansas; Saint Joe and Waterloo, Indiana; Wilson, North Carolina; and Swansea, South Carolina are all engaged in the manufacture of steel products. During 1997, the average utilisation rate of all operating facilities was more than 85 per cent of production capacity. Nucor competes in a number of distinct product segments, and the emphasis on these segments has changed substantially in recent years. Historically, the largest segment was the Nucor Steel division, which produces bar and light structural steel products. In 1991, this was its largest segment (measured by product volume). However, by 1995, sheet steel, once considered to be an exclusive product

Case 9 Nucor Corporation and the US steel industry

Exhibit 6 | Historical data, 1955–96

Year	Net sales	Earnings Operations	Earnings Other	Earnings Net	EPS Operations	EPS Other	EPS Net	Total assets	Stockholders' equity Amount	Stockholders' equity per share	Shares outstanding	Common stock Per Share	Common stock Amount
PRIOR MANAGEMENT													
1955	415 658	(39 359)	—	(39 359)	LOSS	—	LOSS	1 630 644	930 188	0.06	16 355 402	0.48	7 850 593
1956	1 653 007	(355 293)	—	(355 293)	LOSS	—	LOSS	1 881 385	848 934	0.04	20 573 241	0.23	4 731 845
1957	1 925 462	(546 270)	—	(546 270)	LOSS	—	LOSS	1 908 337	1 052 664	0.03	33 803 241	0.17	5 746 551
1958	2 020 886	(521 827)	—	(521 827)	LOSS	—	LOSS	1 717 335	672 638	0.02	35 628 981	0.21	7 482 086
1959	1 859 034	(260 161)	—	(260 161)	LOSS	—	LOSS	1 783 598	502 454	0.01	36 532 149	0.28	10 229 002
1960	2 182 204	(367 149)	(261 829)	(628 978)	LOSS	LOSS	LOSS	1 837 102	647 565	0.01	44 023 275	0.44	19 370 241
1961	4 014 416	379 006	(16 021)	362 985	0.01	LOSS	0.01	5 630 178	2 307 566	0.04	55 267 743	0.43	23 765 129
1962	9 100 958	24 095	(683 323)	(659 228)	—	LOSS	LOSS	7 184 395	1 952 764	0.03	56 646 415	0.23	13 028 675
1963	15 374 487	260 710	240 000	500 710	0.01	0.00	0.01	8 324 759	2 453 474	0.04	56 646 415	0.18	10 196 355
1964	17 485 319	33 264	30 000	63 264	—	—	—	10 337 955	2 796 719	0.05	57 809 552	0.18	10 405 719
1965	22 310 595	(431 013)	(1 803 748)	(2 234 761)	LOSS	LOSS	LOSS	6 937 251	762 380	0.01	58 695 962	0.26	15 260 950
PRESENT MANAGEMENT													
1966	23 006 483	698 900	635 000	1 333 900	0.01	0.01	0.02	8 109 190	2 239 882	0.04	59 310 011	0.23	13 641 303
1967	23 600 093	822 424	880 832	1 703 256	0.01	0.02	0.03	11 546 498	6 581 876	0.10	66 836 275	0.64	42 775 216
1968	35 544 913	1 002 954	1 235 982	2 238 936	0.01	0.02	0.03	16 501 866	9 288 771	0.14	68 078 687	0.78	53 101 376
1969	46 321 797	1 210 083	1 125 000	2 335 083	0.02	0.01	0.03	24 655 801	11 938 178	0.17	68 935 656	0.45	31 021 045
1970	50 750 546	1 140 757	—	1 140 757	0.02	—	0.02	28 800 183	13 101 313	0.19	69 001 709	0.27	18 630 461
1971	64 761 634	2 740 694	—	2 740 694	0.04	—	0.04	33 168 014	15 892 357	0.23	69 245 150	0.41	28 390 512
1972	83 576 128	4 668 190	—	4 668 190	0.07	—	0.07	47 537 247	20 929 525	0.30	70 353 577	0.54	37 990 932
1973	113 193 617	6 009 042	—	6 009 042	0.09	—	0.09	67 550 110	26 620 195	0.38	70 302 597	0.41	28 824 065
1974	160 416 931	9 680 083	—	9 680 083	0.14	—	0.14	82 038 748	37 103 939	0.50	73 712 586	0.30	22 113 776
1975	121 467 284	7 581 788	—	7 581 788	0.10	—	0.10	92 639 413	44 549 735	0.59	75 010 113	0.41	30 754 146
1976	175 768 479	8 696 891	—	8 696 891	0.11	—	0.11	119 095 581	54 084 970	0.70	77 790 707	0.74	57 565 123
1977	212 952 829	12 452 592	—	12 452 592	0.16	—	0.16	128 010 982	66 295 405	0.84	78 807 784	1.02	80 383 940
1978	306 939 667	25 848 849	—	25 848 849	0.33	—	0.33	193 454 693	92 129 119	1.15	80 261 028	1.74	139 654 189
1979	428 681 778	42 264 537	—	42 264 537	0.52	—	0.52	243 111 514	133 257 816	1.64	81 046 524	3.32	269 074 460
1980	482 420 363	45 060 198	—	45 060 198	0.55	—	0.55	291 221 867	177 603 690	2.16	82 199 964	5.82	478 403 790
1981	544 820 621	34 728 966	—	34 728 966	0.42	—	0.42	384 782 127	212 376 020	2.54	83 562 084	4.98	416 139 178
1982	486 018 162	22 192 064	—	22 192 064	0.27	—	0.27	371 632 941	232 281 057	2.77	83 951 292	5.21	437 386 231
1983	542 531 431	27 864 308	—	27 864 308	0.33	—	0.33	425 567 052	258 129 694	3.05	84 541 086	7.13	602 777 943
1984	660 259 922	44 548 451	—	44 548 451	0.53	—	0.53	482 188 465	299 602 834	3.53	84 966 474	5.38	457 119 630
1985	758 495 374	58 478 352	—	58 478 352	0.68	—	0.68	560 311 188	357 502 028	4.16	85 890 030	8.98	771 292 469
1986	755 228 939	46 438 888	—	46 438 888	0.54	—	0.54	571 607 644	383 699 454	4.54	84 525 192	7.72	652 534 482
1987	851 022 039	50 534 450	—	50 534 450	0.60	—	0.60	654 090 139	428 009 367	5.05	84 784 352	9.91	840 212 928
1988	1 061 364 009	70 881 020	38 558 822	109 439 842	0.83	0.46	1.29	949 661 710	532 281 449	6.25	85 150 764	11.94	1 016 700 122
1989	1 269 007 472	57 835 844	—	57 835 844	0.68	—	0.68	1 033 831 512	584 445 479	6.83	85 598 480	15.06	1 289 113 109
1990	1 481 630 011	75 065 261	—	75 065 261	0.88	—	0.88	1 035 886 060	652 757 216	7.59	85 950 696	15.50	1 332 235 788
1991	1 465 456 566	64 716 499	—	64 716 499	0.75	—	0.75	1 181 576 798	711 608 991	8.23	86 417 804	22.34	1 930 573 741
1992	1 619 234 876	79 225 703	—	79 225 703	0.92	—	0.92	2 507 382 255	784 230 713	9.04	86 736 700	39.19	3 399 211 273
1993	2 253 738 311	123 509 607	—	123 509 607	1.42	—	1.42	1 829 268 322	902 166 939	10.36	87 073 478	53.00	4 614 894 334
1994	2 975 596 456	226 632 844	—	226 632 844	2.60	—	2.60	2 001 920 165	1 122 610 257	12.85	87 333 313	55.50	4 846 998 872
1995	3 462 045 648	274 534 505	—	274 534 505	3.14	—	3.14	2 296 141 333	1 382 112 159	15.78	87 598 517	57.13	5 004 503 276
1996	3 647 030 387	248 168 948	—	248 168 948	2.83	—	2.83	2 619 533 406	1 609 290 193	18.33	87 795 947	51.00	4 477 593 297

Source: Nucor Corporation Web page (www.nucor.com/h_historicaldata.htm) 04/09/98.

Exhibit 7 | Annual balance sheets, 1977–96

Note – all US$mn

	Dec-96	Dec-95	Dec-94	Dec-93	Dec-92	Dec-91	Dec-90	Dec-89
Assets								
Cash & equivalents	104.40	201.80	101.93	27.26	25.55	38.30	51.65	32.55
Net receivables	292.64	283.21	258.13	202.18	132.14	109.46	126.75	106.95
Inventories	385.80	306.77	243.03	215.02	206.41	186.08	136.64	139.45
Prepaid expenses	0.00	0.00	0.00	0.00	0.00	0.00	0.00	0.00
Other current assets	45.54	38.97	35.61	23.79	0.52	0.47	0.09	1.08
Total current assets	828.38	830.74	638.70	468.23	364.62	334.29	315.13	280.03
Gross plant property & equipment	2 698.75	2 212.89	1 977.58	1 820.99	1 574.10	1 261.53	1 086.37	1 048.01
Accumulated depreciation	907.60	747.49	614.36	459.95	448.34	414.25	363.12	294.22
Net plant property & equipment	1 791.15	1 465.40	1 363.22	1 361.04	1 125.77	847.28	723.25	753.80
Investments at equity	0.00	0.00	0.00	0.00	0.00	0.00	0.00	0.00
Other investments	0.00	0.00	0.00	0.00	0.00	0.00	0.00	0.00
Intangibles	0.00	0.00	0.00	0.00	0.00	0.00	0.00	0.00
Deferred charges	0.00	0.00	0.00	0.00	0.00	0.00	0.00	0.00
Other assets	0.00	0.00	0.00	0.00	0.00	0.00	0.00	0.00
Total assets	2 619.53	2 296.14	2 001.92	1 829.27	1 490.38	1 181.58	1 038.38	1 033.83
Liabilities								
Long-term debt due in one year	0.75	0.15	0.25	0.20	0.20	2.00	2.21	2.27
Notes payable	0.00	0.00	0.00	0.00	0.00	0.00	0.00	0.00
Accounts payable	224.37	214.56	182.85	165.74	119.30	93.76	78.72	89.75
Taxes payable	10.29	11.30	15.51	14.27	10.46	11.07	10.65	13.20
Accrued expenses								
Other current liabilities	230.25	221.12	183.86	170.29	142.02	122.34	134.00	88.34
Total current liabilities	465.65	447.14	382.47	350.49	271.97	229.17	225.58	193.56
Long-term debt	152.60	106.85	173.00	352.25	246.75	72.78	28.78	155.98
Deferred taxes	50.00	51.00	63.00	53.00	18.82	21.10	25.82	18.82
Investment tax credit	0.00	0.00	0.00	0.00	0.00	0.00	0.00	0.00
Minority interest	265.71	220.66	175.99	143.09	140.50	124.05	105.44	81.02
Other liabilities	76.28	88.38	84.86	28.27	28.11	22.87	0.00	0.00
Total liabilities	1 010.24	914.03	879.31	927.10	706.15	469.97	385.62	449.39
Equity								
Preferred stock – redeemable	0.00	0.00	0.00	0.00	0.00	0.00	0.00	0.00
Preferred stock – non-redeemable	0.00	0.00	0.00	0.00	0.00	0.00	0.00	0.00
Total preferred stock	0.00	0.00	0.00	0.00	0.00	0.00	0.00	0.00
Common stock	35.95	35.90	35.80	35.70	17.78	8.86	8.82	8.78
Capital surplus	55.05	48.67	39.27	29.91	39.41	42.81	37.67	34.23
Retained earnings	1 535.95	1 315.85	1 065.80	854.86	745.26	678.16	624.66	559.90
Less: treasury stock	17.66	18.30	18.26	18.31	18.23	18.23	18.39	18.46
Common equity	1 609.29	1 382.11	1 122.61	902.17	784.23	711.61	652.76	584.45
Total equity	1 609.29	1 382.11	1 122.61	902.17	784.23	711.61	652.76	584.45
Total liabilities & equity	2 619.53	2 296.14	2 001.92	1 829.27	1 490.38	1 181.58	1 038.38	1 033.83
Common shares outstanding	87.80	87.60	87.33	87.07	86.74	86.42	85.95	85.60

Source: Compustat.

	Dec-88	Dec-87	Dec-86	Dec-85	Dec-84	Dec-83	Dec-82	Dec-81	Dec-80	Dec-79	Dec-78	Dec-77
	26.38	72.78	128.74	185.14	112.71	79.06	44.89	8.71	21.75	36.65	27.42	7.10
	97.43	80.08	61.27	70.87	66.87	58.17	38.34	48.70	43.52	40.21	31.90	23.39
	123.22	81.50	105.60	78.64	73.80	56.56	48.83	73.00	49.60	40.01	41.55	30.41
	0.00	0.00	0.00	0.00	0.00	0.00	0.00	0.00	0.00	0.00	0.00	0.00
	0.74	0.36	0.14	0.11	0.08	0.11	0.48	0.98	0.49	0.50	0.25	0.26
	247.76	234.72	295.74	334.77	253.45	193.89	132.54	131.38	115.37	117.36	101.11	61.16
	942.27	618.54	452.26	376.23	359.97	338.66	322.85	318.86	219.10	160.46	115.25	86.67
	240.37	199.16	181.43	150.95	131.87	107.36	83.78	66.25	46.02	35.88	26.72	20.73
	701.90	419.37	270.83	225.28	228.10	231.31	239.07	252.62	173.07	124.58	88.53	65.94
	0.00	0.00	0.00	0.00	0.00	0.00	0.00	0.00	0.00	0.00	0.00	0.00
	0.00	0.00	0.00	0.00	0.00	0.00	0.00	0.00	0.00	0.00	0.00	0.00
	0.00	0.00	0.00	0.00	0.00	0.00	0.00	0.00	0.00	0.00	0.00	0.00
	0.00	0.00	0.00	0.00	0.00	0.00	0.00	0.00	0.00	0.00	0.00	0.00
	0.00	0.00	5.04	0.27	0.63	0.37	0.02	0.78	2.78	1.17	3.81	0.92
	949.66	654.09	571.61	560.31	482.19	425.57	371.63	384.78	291.22	243.11	193.46	128.01
	2.21	2.21	3.05	2.40	2.40	2.40	1.60	1.66	1.70	1.25	0.46	0.44
	0.00	0.00	0.00	0.00	0.00	0.00	0.00	0.00	0.00	0.00	0.00	0.00
	93.17	68.46	53.17	35.47	32.69	37.14	22.95	32.24	36.64	26.42	24.15	12.08
	35.80	24.34	14.31	27.60	23.71	14.81	12.54	10.73	4.36	15.91	15.64	4.44
	84.92	52.46	47.91	55.78	41.74	34.14	29.02	28.41	23.79	19.96	15.54	13.35
	216.11	147.47	118.44	121.26	100.53	88.49	66.10	73.03	66.49	63.54	55.79	30.30
	113.25	35.46	42.15	40.23	43.23	45.73	48.23	83.75	39.61	41.40	41.47	28.13
	15.32	19.32	27.32	41.32	38.82	33.22	25.02	15.62	7.52	4.92	4.02	2.62
	0.00	0.00	0.00	0.00	0.00	0.00	0.00	0.00	0.00	0.00	0.00	0.00
	72.71	23.83	0.00	0.00	0.00	0.00	0.00	0.00	0.00	0.00	0.00	0.00
	0.00	0.00	0.00	0.00	0.00	0.00	0.00	0.00	0.00	0.00	0.04	0.66
	417.38	226.08	187.91	202.81	182.59	167.44	139.35	172.41	113.62	109.85	101.33	61.72
	0.00	0.00	0.00	0.00	0.00	0.00	0.00					
	0.00	0.00	0.00	0.00	0.00	0.00	0.00	0.00	0.00	0.00	0.00	0.00
	0.00	0.00	0.00	0.00	0.00	0.00	0.00	0.00	0.00	0.00	0.00	0.00
	8.74	8.70	8.67	5.73	5.67	5.64	2.80	2.79	2.74	2.70	1.78	1.25
	30.54	27.38	25.19	24.30	18.99	17.02	17.70	16.24	12.91	10.67	10.41	9.55
	511.46	410.51	367.58	327.82	275.04	235.57	211.92	193.36	161.95	119.89	79.94	55.50
	18.46	18.58	17.73	0.35	0.09	0.10	0.14					
	532.28	428.01	383.70	357.50	299.60	258.13	232.28	212.38	177.60	133.26	92.13	66.30
	532.28	428.01	383.70	357.50	299.60	258.13	232.28	212.38	177.60	133.26	92.13	66.30
	949.66	654.09	571.61	560.31	482.19	425.57	371.63	384.78	291.22	243.11	193.46	128.01
	85.15	84.78	84.52	85.89	84.97	84.54	83.95	83.57	82.20	81.05	80.26	78.80

Exhibit 8 | Annual cash flow statement, 1977–96

Note – all US$mn

	Dec-96	Dec-95	Dec-94	Dec-93	Dec-92	Dec-91	Dec-90	Dec-89
Indirect operating activities								
Income before extraordinary items	248.17	274.54	226.63	123.51	79.23	64.72	75.07	57.84
Depreciation and amortization	182.23	173.89	157.65	122.27	97.78	93.58	84.96	76.57
Extraordinary items and disc. operations	0.00	0.00	0.00	0.00	0.00	0.00	0.00	0.00
Deferred taxes	(8.00)	(15.00)	(2.00)	1.00	(3.00)	(4.00)	7.00	3.50
Equity in net loss (earnings)	0.00	0.00	0.00	0.00	0.00	0.00	0.00	0.00
Sale of property, plant, and equipment and sale of investments – loss (gain)	0.00	0.00	0.00	0.00	0.00	0.00	0.00	0.00
Funds from operations – other	82.57	48.18	17.67	9.75	23.17	26.11	29.71	8.32
Receivables – decrease (increase)	(9.43)	(25.07)	(55.96)	(70.03)	(22.69)	14.80	(19.80)	(9.52)
Inventory – decrease (increase)	(79.03)	(63.75)	(28.01)	(8.61)	(20.33)	(49.43)	2.81	(16.24)
Accounts payable and accrued liabs – inc (Dec)	9.81	31.72	17.11	46.44	25.53	11.54	(11.03)	(3.43)
Income taxes – accrued – increase (decrease)	(1.01)	(4.21)	1.24	3.81	(0.61)	0.42	(2.55)	(22.60)
Other assets and liabilities – net change	25.30	26.87	90.60	43.67	26.32	15.66	48.16	3.56
Operating activities – net cash flow	450.61	447.16	424.95	271.79	205.41	173.40	214.33	98.00
Investing activities								
Investments – increase	0.00	0.00	0.00	0.00	0.00	0.00	0.00	0.00
Sale of investments	0.00	0.00	0.00	0.00	0.00	0.00	0.00	0.00
Short-term investments – change	0.00	0.00	0.00	0.00	0.00	0.00	0.00	0.00
Capital expenditures	537.44	263.42	185.32	364.16	379.12	217.72	56.75	130.20
Sale of property, plant, and equipment	1.59	0.92	5.22	1.30	2.12	0.55	0.83	1.26
Acquisitions	0.00	0.00	0.00	0.00	0.00	0.00	0.00	0.00
Investing activities – other	0.00	0.00	0.00	0.00	0.00	0.00	0.00	0.00
Investing activities – net cash flow	(535.84)	(262.50)	(180.11)	(362.86)	(377.00)	(217.17)	(55.92)	(128.95)
Financing activities								
Sale of common and preferred stock	7.07	9.67	9.50	8.51	5.60	5.35	3.59	3.86
Purchase of common and preferred stock	0.00	0.22	0.00	0.17	0.08	0.00	0.04	0.14
Cash dividends	28.06	24.49	15.69	13.91	12.13	11.22	10.30	9.40
Long-term debt – issuance	46.50	24.00	0.00	105.70	183.90	46.00	0.00	45.00
Long-term debt – reduction	0.15	90.25	179.20	0.20	11.73	2.20	127.27	2.21
Current debt – changes				0.00				
Financing activities – other	(37.52)	(3.51)	15.22	(7.16)	(6.73)	(7.51)	(5.29)	0.00
Financing activities – net cash flow	(12.16)	(84.79)	(170.17)	92.77	158.84	30.42	(139.31)	37.11
Exchange rate effect	0.00	0.00	0.00	0.00	0.00	0.00	0.00	0.00
Cash and equivalents – change	(97.40)	99.87	74.68	1.71	(12.75)	(13.35)	19.10	6.17
Direct operating activities								
Interest paid – net	6.95	9.21	16.06	10.74	9.14	3.42	8.58	16.03
Income taxes – paid	152.90	176.50	124.37	57.52	40.82	34.68	31.70	46.90

CF—combined figure
NA—not available
NC—not calculable

Source: Compustat.

	Dec-88	Dec-87	Dec-86	Dec-85	Dec-84	Dec-83	Dec-82	Dec-81	Dec-80	Dec-79	Dec-78	Dec-77
	70.88	50.53	46.44	58.48	44.55	27.86	22.19	34.73	45.06	42.27	25.85	12.45
	56.27	41.79	34.93	31.11	28.90	27.11	26.29	21.60	13.30	9.71	7.46	5.93
	0.00	0.00	0.00	0.00	0.00	0.00	0.00	0.00	0.00	0.00	0.00	0.00
	(4.00)	(8.00)	(14.00)	2.50	5.60	8.20	9.40	8.10	2.60	0.90	1.40	0.80
	0.00	0.00	0.00	0.00	0.00	0.00	0.00	0.00	0.00	0.00	0.00	0.00
	0.00	0.00	NA	NA	NA	NA	NA	NA	NA	NA	NA	NA
	0.00	0.00	0.00	0.00	0.00	0.00	0.00	0.00	0.00	0.00	0.00	0.00
	(18.93)	NA	NA	NA	NA	NA	NA	NA	NA	NA	NA	NA
	(44.65)	NA	NA	NA	NA	NA	NA	NA	NA	NA	NA	NA
	25.36	NA	NA	NA	NA	NA	NA	NA	NA	NA	NA	NA
	(8.54)	NA	NA	NA	NA	NA	NA	NA	NA	NA	NA	NA
	71.33	NA	NA	NA	NA	NA	NA	NA	NA	NA	NA	NA
	147.71	NA	NA	NA	NA	NA	NA	NA	NA	NA	NA	NA
	0.00	0.00	0.00	0.00	0.00	0.00	0.00	0.00	0.00	0.00	0.00	0.00
	0.00	0.00	0.00	0.00	0.00	0.00	0.00	0.00	0.00	0.00	0.00	0.00
	0.00	NA	NA	NA	NA	NA	NA	NA	NA	NA	NA	NA
	345.63	188.99	81.43	29.07	26.08	19.62	14.79	101.52	62.44	45.99	31.59	15.95
	0.40	3.69	0.94	0.79	0.38	0.27	2.05	0.38	0.65	0.23	1.54	0.02
	0.00	0.00	0.00	0.00	0.00	0.00	0.00	0.00	0.00	0.00	0.00	0.00
	78.50	NA	NA	NA	NA	NA	NA	NA	NA	NA	NA	NA
	(266.73)	NA	NA	NA	NA	NA	NA	NA	NA	NA	NA	NA
	3.33	2.34	3.96	5.39	2.01	2.20	1.46	3.37	2.29	1.33	1.52	1.02
	0.0	0.96	17.52	0.27	0.00	0.00	0.12	0.00	0.00	0.16	0.13	0.22
	8.49	7.60	6.68	5.70	5.08	4.22	3.63	3.33	3.00	2.31	1.41	1.04
	80.00	0.00	4.91	0.00	0.00	0.00	7.50	46.40	0.00	1.14	13.90	0.00
	2.21	6.69	3.00	3.00	2.50	2.50	43.02	2.25	1.79	1.21	0.56	3.54
		0.84	(0.65)	0.00	NA	NA	NA	NA	NA	NA	NA	NA
	0.00	NA	NA	NA	NA	NA	NA	NA	NA	NA	NA	NA
	72.62	NA	NA	NA	NA	NA	NA	NA	NA	NA	NA	NA
	0.00	NA	NA	NA	NA	NA	NA	NA	NA	NA	NA	NA
	(46.40)	(55.96)	(56.41)	72.43	33.66	CF	CF	CF	CF	CF	CF	CF
	3.65	NA	NA	NA	NA	NA	NA	NA	NA	NA	NA	NA
	49.24	NA	NA	NA	NA	NA	NA	NA	NA	NA	NA	NA

Exhibit 9 | Annual income statement, 1977–96

Note – all US$mn

	Dec-96	Dec-95	Dec-94	Dec-93	Dec-92	Dec-91	Dec-90	Dec-89
Sales	3 647.03	3 462.05	2 975.60	2 253.74	1 619.24	1 465.46	1 481.63	1 269.01
Cost of goods sold	2 956.93	2 726.28	2 334.11	1 843.58	1 319.60	1 209.17	1 208.12	1 028.68
Gross profit	690.11	735.77	641.49	410.16	299.64	256.29	273.51	240.33
Selling general & administrative expense	120.39	130.68	113.39	87.58	76.80	66.99	70.46	66.99
Operating income before deprec.	569.72	605.09	528.10	322.57	222.84	189.30	203.05	173.34
Depreciation depletion & amortization	182.23	173.89	156.65	122.27	97.78	93.58	84.96	76.57
Operating profit	387.49	431.20	370.45	200.31	125.06	95.73	118.09	96.77
Interest expense	7.55	9.28	14.59	14.32	9.03	2.60	8.10	16.88
Non-operating income/expense	7.84	10.41	1.08	1.12	1.30	2.69	1.23	5.74
Special items	0.00	0.00	0.00	0.00	0.00	0.00	0.00	0.00
Pretax income	387.77	432.34	356.93	187.11	117.33	95.82	111.22	85.64
Total income taxes	139.60	157.80	130.30	63.60	38.10	31.10	36.15	27.80
Minority interest								
Income before extraordinary items & discontinued operations	248.17	274.54	226.63	123.51	79.23	64.72	75.07	57.84
Preferred dividends	0.00	0.00	0.00	0.00	0.00	0.00	0.00	0.00
Available for common	248.17	274.54	226.63	123.51	79.23	64.72	75.07	57.84
Savings due to common Stock equivalents	0.00	0.00	0.00	0.00	0.00	0.00	0.00	0.00
Adjusted available for common	248.17	274.54	226.63	123.51	79.23	64.72	75.07	57.84
Extraordinary items	0.00	0.00	0.00	0.00	0.00	0.00	0.00	0.00
Discontinued operations	0.00	0.00	0.00	0.00	0.00	0.00	0.00	0.00
Adjusted net income	248.17	274.54	226.63	123.51	79.23	64.72	75.07	57.84
Earnings per share (primary) – excluding extra items & disc op	2.83	3.14	2.60	1.42	0.92	0.75	0.88	0.68
Earnings per share (primary) – including extra items & disc op	2.83	3.14	2.60	1.42	0.92	0.75	0.88	0.68
Earnings per share (fully diluted) excluding extra items & disc op	2.83	3.13	2.59	1.41	0.91	0.75	0.87	0.68
Earnings per share (fully diluted) including extra items & disc op	2.83	3.13	2.59	1.41	0.91	0.75	0.87	0.68
EP from operations	2.83	3.14	2.60	1.42	0.92	0.75	0.88	0.68
Dividends per share	0.32	0.28	0.18	0.16	0.14	0.13	0.12	0.11

Source: Compustat.

	Dec-88	Dec-87	Dec-86	Dec-85	Dec-84	Dec-83	Dec-82	Dec-81	Dec-80	Dec-79	Dec-78	Dec-77
	1 061.36	851.02	755.23	758.50	660.26	542.53	486.02	544.82	482.42	428.68	306.94	212.95
	832.88	671.55	575.45	569.69	510.83	434.62	382.32	434.61	356.12	305.98	220.50	162.32
	228.49	179.47	179.78	188.80	149.43	107.91	103.70	110.21	126.30	122.71	86.44	50.63
	62.08	55.41	65.90	59.08	45.94	33.99	31.72	33.53	38.16	36.72	28.66	19.73
	166.40	124.06	113.88	129.72	103.49	73.93	71.98	76.69	88.14	85.98	57.78	30.90
	56.27	41.79	34.93	31.11	28.90	27.11	26.29	21.60	13.30	9.71	7.46	5.93
	110.14	82.27	78.95	98.62	74.59	46.82	45.69	55.09	74.84	76.27	50.33	24.98
	9.18	3.94	5.32	4.36	4.62	4.80	8.41	10.67	3.53	4.30	2.87	2.82
	6.63	4.91	10.61	11.92	8.58	5.55	0.52	0.42	4.75	2.79	1.00	0.10
	0.00	0.00	0.00	0.00	0.00	0.00	0.00	0.00	0.00	0.00	0.00	0.00
	107.58	83.23	84.24	106.18	78.55	47.56	37.79	44.83	76.06	74.77	48.45	22.25
	36.70	32.70	37.80	47.70	34.00	19.70	15.60	10.10	31.00	32.50	22.60	9.80
	70.88	50.53	46.44	58.48	44.55	27.86	22.19	34.73	45.06	42.27	25.85	12.45
	0.00	0.00	0.00	0.00	0.00	0.00	0.00	0.00	0.00	0.00	0.00	0.00
	70.88	50.53	46.44	58.48	44.55	27.86	22.19	34.73	45.06	42.27	25.85	12.45
	0.00	0.00	0.00	0.00	0.00	0.00	0.00	0.00	0.00	0.00	0.00	0.00
	70.88	50.53	46.44	58.48	44.55	27.86	22.19	34.73	45.06	42.27	25.85	12.45
	0.00	0.00	0.00	0.00	0.00	0.00	0.00	0.00	0.00	0.00	0.00	0.00
	38.56	0.00	0.00	0.00	0.00	0.00	0.00	0.00	0.00	0.00	0.00	0.00
	70.88	50.53	46.44	58.48	44.55	27.86	22.19	34.73	45.06	42.27	25.85	12.45
	0.83	0.60	0.54	0.69	0.53	0.33	0.27	0.42	0.55	0.52	0.33	0.16
	1.29	0.60	0.54	0.69	0.53	0.33	0.27	0.42	0.55	0.52	0.33	0.16
	0.83	0.60	0.54	0.68	0.53	0.33	0.27	0.42	0.54	0.52	0.32	0.16
	1.28	0.60	0.54	0.68	0.53	0.33	0.27	0.42	0.54	0.52	0.32	0.16
	0.83											
	0.10	0.09	0.08	0.07	0.06	0.05	0.04	0.04	0.04	0.03	0.02	0.01

Exhibit 10 | Annual ratios, 1977–96

Note – all ratios

	Dec-96	Dec-95	Dec-94	Dec-93	Dec-92	Dec-91	Dec-90	Dec-89
Liquidity								
Current ratio	1.78	1.86	1.67	1.34	1.34	1.46	1.40	1.45
Quick ratio	0.85	1.08	0.94	0.65	0.58	0.64	0.79	0.72
Working capital per share	4.13	4.38	2.93	1.35	1.07	1.22	1.04	1.01
Cash flow per share	4.90	5.12	4.40	2.82	2.04	1.83	1.86	1.57
Activity								
Inventory turnover	8.54	9.92	10.19	8.75	6.72	7.49	8.75	7.83
Receivables turnover	12.67	12.79	12.93	13.48	13.40	12.41	12.68	12.42
Total asset turnover	1.48	1.61	1.55	1.36	1.21	1.32	1.43	1.28
Average collection period (days)	28.00	28.00	28.00	27.00	27.00	29.00	28.00	29.00
Days to sell inventory	42.00	36.00	35.00	41.00	54.00	48.00	41.00	46.00
Operating cycle (days)	71.00	64.00	63.00	68.00	80.00	77.00	70.00	75.00
Performance								
Sales/net property, plant & equip	2.04	2.36	2.18	1.66	1.44	1.73	2.05	1.68
Sales/stockholder equity	2.27	2.50	2.65	2.50	2.06	2.06	2.27	2.17
Profitability								
Operating margin before depr (%)	15.62	17.48	17.75	14.31	13.76	12.92	13.70	13.66
Operating margin after depr (%)	10.62	12.46	12.45	8.89	7.72	6.53	7.97	7.63
Pretax profit margin (%)	10.63	12.49	12.00	8.30	7.25	6.54	7.51	6.75
Net profit margin (%)	6.80	7.93	7.62	5.48	4.89	4.42	5.07	4.56
Return on assets (%)	9.47	11.96	11.32	6.75	5.32	5.48	7.23	5.59
Return on equity (%)	15.42	19.86	20.19	13.69	10.10	9.09	11.50	9.90
Return on investment (%)	12.24	16.06	15.40	8.84	6.76	7.12	9.54	7.04
Return on average assets (%)	10.10	12.77	11.83	7.44	5.93	5.83	7.24	5.83
Return on average equity (%)	16.59	21.92	22.39	14.65	10.59	9.49	12.13	10.36
Return on average investment (%)	13.28	17.26	15.80	9.62	7.62	7.63	9.33	7.51
Leverage								
Interest coverage before tax	52.35	47.60	25.46	14.07	13.99	37.85	14.73	6.07
Interest coverage after tax	33.87	30.59	16.53	9.63	9.77	25.89	10.27	4.43
Long-term debt/common equity (%)	9.48	7.73	15.41	39.04	31.46	10.23	4.41	26.69
Long-term debt/shrhldr equity (%)	9.48	7.73	15.41	39.04	31.46	10.23	4.41	26.69
Total debt/invested capital (%)	7.56	6.26	11.77	25.22	21.08	8.23	3.94	19.26
Total debt/total assets (%)	5.85	4.66	8.65	19.27	16.57	6.33	2.98	15.31
Total assets/common equity	1.63	1.66	1.78	2.03	1.90	1.66	1.59	1.77
Dividends								
Divident payout (%)	11.31	8.92	6.92	11.26	15.31	17.34	13.72	16.25
Divident yield (%)	0.63	0.49	0.33	0.30	0.36	0.58	0.77	0.73

NC – not calculable
Source: Compustat.

Dec-88	Dec-87	Dec-86	Dec-85	Dec-84	Dec-83	Dec-82	Dec-81	Dec-80	Dec-79	Dec-78	Dec-77
1.15	1.59	2.50	2.76	2.52	2.19	2.01	1.80	1.74	1.85	1.81	2.02
0.57	1.04	1.60	2.11	1.79	1.55	1.26	0.79	0.98	1.21	1.06	1.01
0.37	1.03	2.10	2.49	1.80	1.25	0.79	0.70	0.59	0.66	0.56	0.39
1.49	1.09	0.96	1.04	0.86	0.65	0.58	0.67	0.71	0.64	0.41	0.23
8.14	7.18	6.25	7.47	7.84	8.25	6.28	7.09	7.95	7.50	6.13	NC
11.96	12.04	11.43	11.01	10.56	11.24	11.17	11.81	11.52	11.89	11.10	NC
1.32	1.39	1.33	1.46	1.45	1.36	1.29	1.61	1.81	1.96	1.91	NC
30.00	30.00	31.00	33.00	34.00	32.00	32.00	30.00	31.00	30.00	32.00	NC
44.00	50.00	58.00	48.00	46.00	44.00	57.00	51.00	45.00	48.00	59.00	NC
74.00	80.00	89.00	81.00	80.00	76.00	90.00	81.00	77.00	78.00	91.00	NC
1.51	2.03	2.79	3.37	2.89	2.35	2.03	2.16	2.79	3.44	3.47	3.23
1.99	1.99	1.97	2.12	2.20	2.10	2.09	2.57	2.72	3.22	3.33	3.21
15.68	14.58	15.08	17.10	15.67	13.63	14.81	14.08	18.27	20.06	18.83	14.51
10.38	9.67	10.45	13.00	11.30	8.63	9.40	10.11	15.51	17.79	16.40	11.73
10.14	9.78	11.15	14.00	11.90	8.77	7.78	8.23	15.77	17.44	15.78	10.45
6.68	5.94	6.15	7.71	6.75	5.14	4.57	6.37	9.34	9.86	8.42	5.85
7.46	7.73	8.12	10.44	9.24	6.55	5.97	9.03	15.47	17.38	13.36	9.73
13.32	11.81	12.10	16.36	14.87	10.79	9.55	16.35	25.37	31.72	28.06	18.78
9.87	10.37	10.91	14.70	12.99	9.17	7.91	11.73	20.74	24.20	19.35	13.19
8.84	8.25	8.21	11.22	9.81	6.99	5.87	10.27	16.87	19.36	16.08	NC
14.76	12.45	12.53	17.80	15.97	11.36	9.98	17.81	28.99	37.50	32.63	NC
11.76	11.07	11.28	15.79	13.78	9.54	7.70	13.53	23.00	27.42	22.67	NC
12.72	22.11	16.83	25.35	18.00	10.91	5.49	5.20	22.55	18.40	17.86	8.88
8.72	13.82	9.73	14.41	10.64	6.81	3.64	4.25	13.77	10.84	9.99	5.41
21.28	8.29	10.98	11.25	14.43	17.72	20.76	39.44	22.30	31.07	45.02	42.44
21.28	8.29	10.98	11.25	14.43	17.72	20.76	39.44	22.30	31.07	45.02	42.44
16.08	7.73	10.61	10.72	13.31	15.84	17.77	28.84	19.01	24.42	31.39	30.26
12.16	5.76	7.91	7.61	9.46	11.31	13.41	22.20	14.18	17.54	21.68	22.32
1.78	1.53	1.49	1.57	1.61	1.65	1.60	1.81	1.64	1.82	2.10	1.93
11.98	15.04	14.38	9.74	11.41	15.13	16.34	9.58	6.66	5.46	5.46	8.38
0.84	0.91	1.03	0.74	1.12	0.70	0.83	0.80	0.63	0.86	1.03	1.30

Exhibit 11 | Comparative income statements – SIC 3312

Note – all US$mn	NUCOR CORP Dec-96	BETHLHM STL Dec-96	BIRM STEEL Jun-96	CARPNTR TCH Jun-96	CHAPARR STL May-96	INLAND STL Dec-96	STEEL DYNAM Dec-96	USX-US STL Dec-96
Sales	3 647.0	4 679.0	832.5	865.3	607.7	2 397.3	252.6	6 547.0
Cost of goods sold	2 956.9	4 168.2	730.4	601.6	480.6	2 156.1	201.2	6 005.0
Gross profit	690.1	510.8	102.0	263.8	127.1	241.2	51.5	542.0
Selling general & administrative expense	120.4	105.5	37.7	112.9	26.1	54.7	13.8	−169.0
Operating income before deprec.	569.7	405.3	64.3	150.9	101.0	186.5	37.6	711.0
Depreciation depletion & amortization	182.2	268.7	34.7	35.2	29.5	124.6	19.4	292.0
Operating profit	387.5	136.6	29.6	115.6	71.5	61.9	18.2	419.0
Interest expense	7.6	60.3	18.5	19.3	10.0	50.7	23.7	97.0
Non-operating income/expense	7.8	12.9	10.4	−3.8	4.3	2.5	2.9	51.0
Special items	0.0	−465.0	−23.9	2.7	0.0	−26.3	0.0	−6.0
Pretax income	387.8	−375.8	−2.4	95.2	65.8	−12.6	−2.6	367.0
Total income taxes	139.6	−67.0	−0.2	35.0	23.8	−3.5	0.0	92.0
Minority interest	CF	CF	0.0	0.0	CF	0.0	0.0	CF
Income before extraordinary items & discontinued operations	248.2	−308.8	−2.2	60.1	42.0	−9.1	−2.6	275.0
Preferred dividends	0.0	41.9	0.0	1.6	0.0	25.8	0.0	22.0
Available for common	248.2	−350.7	−2.2	58.6	42.0	−34.9	−2.6	253.0
Savings due to common Stock equivalents	0.0	0.0	0.0	0.0	0.2	0.0	0.0	0.0
Adjusted available for common	248.2	−350.7	−2.2	58.6	42.2	−34.9	−2.6	253.0
Extraordinary items	0.0	0.0	0.0	0.0	0.0	−8.8	−7.3	−2.0
Discontinued operations	0.0	0.0	0.0	0.0	0.0	0.0	0.0	0.0
Adjusted net income	248.2	−350.7	−2.2	58.6	42.2	−43.7	−9.8	251.0

Source: Compustat.

Case 9 Nucor Corporation and the US steel industry

Exhibit 12 | Comparative balance sheets – SIC 3312

Note – all US$mn	NUCOR CORP Dec-96	BETHLHM STL Dec-96	BIRM STEEL Jun-96	CARPNTR TCH Jun-96	CHAPARR STL May-96	INLAND STL Dec-96	STEEL DYNAM Dec-96	USX-US STL Dec-96
Assets								
Cash & equivalents	104.4	136.6	6.7	13.2	20.0	0.0	57.5	23.0
Net receivables	292.6	311.6	111.6	137.1	49.5	225.6	32.5	580.0
Inventories	385.8	1 017.3	196.8	160.5	121.8	182.0	65.9	648.0
Prepaid expenses	0.0	0.0	1.4	0.0	7.8	0.0	0.0	0.0
Other current assets	45.5	22.9	11.6	13.8	0.0	18.6	1.6	177.0
Total current assets	828.4	1 488.4	328.0	324.5	199.1	426.2	157.4	1 428.0
Gross plant property & equip.	2 698.8	6 344.0	678.2	809.7	493.5	4 011.4	356.1	8 347.0
Accumulated depreciation	907.6	3 924.2	134.2	390.2	279.4	2 642.7	16.8	5 796.0
Net plant property & equipment	1 791.2	2 419.8	544.0	419.5	214.1	1 368.7	339.3	2 551.0
Investments at equity	0.0	50.0	0.0	9.8	0.0	221.4	0.0	412.0
Other investments	0.0	NA	0.0	0.0	0.0	0.0	0.0	209.0
Intangibles	0.0	160.0	46.1	18.8	59.2	0.0	0.0	39.0
Deferred charges	0.0	0.0	CF	91.5	2.0	CF	12.4	1 734.0
Other assets	0.0	991.7	9.9	48.0	1.0	326.5	13.2	207.0
TOTAL ASSETS	2 619.5	5 109.9	928.0	912.0	475.3	2 342.8	522.3	6 580.0
Liabilities								
Long-term debt due in one year	0.8	49.3	0.0	7.0	12.4	7.7	11.2	73.0
Notes payable	0.0	0.0	0.0	19.0	0.0	272.5	0.0	18.0
Accounts payable	224.4	410.4	83.2	75.8	34.1	217.7	41.2	667.0
Taxes payable	10.3	67.9	0.4	13.7	0.0	69.2	0.0	154.0
Accrued expenses	CF	313.3	32.8	56.5	15.9	73.3	9.2	387.0
Other current liabilities	230.2	116.5	0.0	0.0	0.0	3.9	0.0	0.0
Total current liabilities	465.7	957.4	116.4	172.0	62.4	644.3	61.6	1 299.0
Long-term debt	152.6	497.4	307.5	188.0	66.7	307.9	196.2	1 014.0
Deferred taxes	50.0	0.0	50.3	84.5	CF	0.0	0.0	0.0
Investment tax credit	0.0	0.0	0.0	0.0	CF	0.0	0.0	0.0
Minority interest	265.7	CF	0.0	0.0	0.0	0.0	0.0	0.0
Other liabilities	76.3	2 689.1	5.6	158.4	51.3	1 179.8	0.0	2 637.0
Equity								
Preferred stock – redeemable	0.0	0.0	0.0	0.0	0.0	0.0	0.0	0.0
Preferred stock – non-redeemable	0.0	14.1	0.0	5.8	0.0	0.0	0.0	7.0
Total preferred stock	0.0	14.1	0.0	5.8	0.0	0.0	0.0	7.0
Common stock	36.0	113.9	0.3	97.7	3.0	0.0	0.5	85.0
Capital surplus	55.0	1 886.3	331.4	13.5	178.5	1 194.5	303.8	NA
Retained earnings	1 535.9	(988.6)	137.6	256.6	126.9	(983.7)	(39.8)	NA
Less: treasury stock	17.7	59.7	21.1	64.5	13.4	0.0	0.0	0.0
Common equity	1 609.3	951.9	448.2	303.3	295.0	210.8	264.6	1 559.0
TOTAL EQUITY	1 609.3	966.0	448.2	309.1	295.0	210.8	264.6	1 566.0
TOTAL LIABILITIES & EQUITY	2 619.5	5 109.9	928.0	912.0	475.3	2 342.8	522.3	6 580.0

Source: Compustat.

Exhibit 13 | Comparative ratios – SIC 3312

	BETHLHM STL Dec-96	BIRM STEEL Jun-96	CARPNTR TCH Jun-96	CHAPARR STL May-96	INLAND STL Dec-96	IPSCO INC Dec-96	NUCOR CORP Dec-96	STEEL DYNAM Dec-96	USX-US STL Dec-96	WEIRTON Dec-96
Liquidity										
Current ratio	1.55	2.82	1.89	3.19	0.66	2.98	1.78	2.56	1.10	2.14
Quick ratio	0.47	1.02	0.87	1.12	0.35	1.92	0.85	1.46	0.46	0.98
Working capital per share	4.75	7.40	9.18	4.76	−218099.97	9.48	4.13	2.01	1.52	7.31
Cash flow per share	−0.36	1.14	5.74	2.49	115499.99	2.76	4.90	0.35	6.68	0.32
Activity										
Inventory turnover	4.22	3.95	4.78	4.31	11.33	4.17	8.54	5.06	9.62	4.99
Receivables turnover	13.64	7.48	6.76	12.01	10.27	8.18	12.67	15.51	10.97	9.08
Total asset turnover	0.87	0.99	0.99	1.29	1.02	0.62	1.48	0.60	1.00	1.06
Average collection per (days)	26.00	48.00	53.00	30.00	35.00	44.00	28.00	23.00	33.00	40.00
Days to sell inventory	85.00	91.00	75.00	84.00	32.00	86.00	42.00	71.00	37.00	72.00
Operating cycle (days)	112.00	139.00	129.00	114.00	67.00	130.00	71.00	94.00	70.00	112.00
Performance										
Sales/net PP&E	1.93	1.53	2.06	2.84	1.75	1.07	2.04	0.74	2.57	2.27
Sales/stockholder equity	4.84	1.86	2.80	2.06	11.37	1.02	2.27	0.95	4.18	8.25
Profitability										
Oper. margin before depr (%)	8.66	7.73	17.44	16.61	7.78	15.78	15.62	14.89	10.86	4.24
Oper. margin after depr. (%)	2.92	3.56	13.36	11.76	2.58	13.39	10.62	7.21	6.40	0.05
Pretax profit margin (%)	−8.03	−0.28	11.00	10.82	−0.53	15.13	10.63	−1.01	5.61	−4.00
Net profit margin (%)	−6.60	−0.26	6.95	6.91	−0.38	10.35	6.80	−1.01	4.20	−3.22
Return on assets (%)	−6.86	−0.23	6.42	8.83	−1.49	5.93	9.47	−0.49	3.84	−3.42
Return on equity (%)	−36.84	−0.49	19.31	14.23	−16.56	10.53	15.42	−0.97	16.23	−29.83
Return on investment (%)	−23.96	−0.29	11.78	11.61	−6.73	7.08	12.24	−0.56	9.57	−7.43
Return on average assets (%)	−6.49	−0.26	6.72	8.88	−1.49	6.37	10.10	−0.61	3.86	−3.40
Return on average equity (%)	−32.23	−0.48	20.78	14.86	−15.31	11.01	16.59	−1.56	17.47	−25.59
Return on average invest.(%)	−21.59	−0.32	12.26	11.78	−5.95	7.62	13.28	−0.69	10.17	−7.29
Leverage										
Interest coverage before tax	−5.23	0.87	5.92	7.57	0.75	6.27	52.35	0.89	4.78	−0.22
Interest coverage after tax	−4.12	0.88	4.11	5.19	0.82	4.60	33.87	0.89	3.84	0.02
Long-term debt/common eq. (%)	52.25	68.61	61.99	22.61	146.06	48.73	9.48	74.15	65.04	288.89
Long-term debt/shrhldr eq. (%)	51.49	68.61	60.83	22.61	146.06	48.73	9.48	74.15	64.75	256.97
Total debt/invested cap. (%)	37.36	40.69	43.05	21.86	113.38	32.89	7.56	45.00	41.79	71.99
Total debt/total assets (%)	10.70	33.14	23.47	16.63	25.10	27.57	5.85	39.70	16.79	33.12
Total assets/common equity	5.37	2.07	3.01	1.61	11.11	1.77	1.63	1.97	4.22	8.72
Dividends										
Dividend payout (%)	0.00	−524.80	37.10	13.88	0.00	15.62	11.31	0.00	33.60	0.00
Dividend yield (%)	0.00	2.42	4.13	1.37	@NA	1.26	0.63	0.00	3.19	0.00

Note – all ratios.
Source: Compustat.

Exhibit 14 | Steel companies (SIC 3312) sorted by sales

Company name	SIC	1996 Sales	1996 Assets
Broken Hill Proprietary – ADR	3312	$15 260.90	$28 113.50
British Steel PLC -ADR	3312	$11 882.00	$12 939.60
Pohang Iron & Steel Co – ADR	3312	$11 140.60	$18 967.60
USX-US Steel Group	3312	$6 547.00	$6 580.00
Bethlehem Steel Corp	3312	$4 679.00	$5 109.90
LTV Corp	3312	$4 134.50	$5 410.50
Allegheny Teledyne Inc	3312	$3 815.60	$2 606.40
Nucor Corp	3312	$3 647.03	$2 619.53
National Steel Corp – CL B	3312	$2 954.03	$2 547.06
Inland Steel Co	3312	$2 397.30	$2 342.80
AK Steel Holding Corp	3312	$2 301.80	$2 650.80
Armco Inc	3312	$1 724.00	$1 867.80
Weirton Steel Corp	3312	$1 383.30	$1 300.62
Rouge Steel Co – CL A	3312	$1 307.40	$681.95
WHX Corp	3312	$1 232.70	$1 718.78
Texas Industries Inc	3312	$985.67	$847.92
Lukens Inc	3312	$970.32	$888.75
Grupo IMSA SA DE CV – ADS	3312	$953.00	$1 404.00
Algoma Steel Inc	3312	$896.47	$983.47
Quanex Corp	3312	$895.71	$718.21
Carpenter Technology	3312	$865.32	$911.97
Birmingham Steel Corp	3312	$832.49	$927.99
Oregon Steel Mills Inc	3312	$772.82	$913.36
Republic Engnrd Steels Inc	3312	$746.17	$640.58
Geneva Stl Co – CL A	3312	$712.66	$657.39
Highvld Stl & Vanadium – ADR	3312	$695.36	$957.28
Northwestern Stl & Wire	3312	$661.07	$442.52
Tubos de Acero de Mex – ADR	3312	$645.16	$1 027.85
Titan International Inc	3312	$634.55	$558.59
Florida Steel Corp	3312	$628.40	$554.90
J & L Specialty Steel	3312	$628.02	$771.93
Chaparral Steel Company	3312	$607.66	$475.34
Ipsco Inc	3312	$587.66	$1 025.00
Talley Industries Inc	3312	$502.70	$280.39
NS Group Inc	3312	$409.38	$300.03
Laclede Steel Co	3312	$335.38	$331.11
Keystone Cons Industries Inc	3312	$331.18	$302.37
Huntco Inc – CL A	3312	$264.09	$222.44
Steel Dynamics Inc	3312	$252.62	$522.29
Roanoke Electric Steel Corp	3312	$246.29	$167.02
Grupo Simec-Spon ADR	3312	$214.64	$509.72
Bayou Steel Corp – CL A	3312	$204.43	$199.27
New Jersey Steel Corp	3312	$145.21	$151.37
China Pacific Inc	3312	$123.50	$114.33
Kentucky Electric Steel Inc	3312	$98.32	$78.43
Steel of West Virginia	3312	$95.33	$79.30
UNVL Stainless & Alloy Prods	3312	$60.26	$42.10
Consolidated Stainless Inc	3312	$50.82	$51.25
Stelax Industries Ltd	3312	$0.73	$16.76

of integrated producers, accounted for the largest production volume. Heavy structural beams from a joint venture with Yamato Steel of Japan were the third-largest segment, followed by the Vulcraft joist division. Remaining products – including grinding balls, fasteners, ball bearings and prefabricated steel buildings – each account for relatively small proportions of total output.

While Nucor's first experience with steel was the result of backward integration by the Vulcraft joist division, the manufacture of steel has become the central focus of the firm. That focus has broadened to include sheet steel (1989) and heavy structural beams (1988). The company has also extended its focus to several downstream products, including fasteners and ball bearings (both in 1986) and prefabricated metal buildings (1988). With the exception of the ball bearings mill, which was acquired, new business segments are developed internally. Roughly 15 per cent of steel output is used internally for downstream operations. More recently, Nucor has chosen to integrate backwards from steel with a plant in Trinidad. This backward integration is aimed at lowering production costs; the plant produces iron carbide, which is expected to become an alternative to scrap in the minimill process.

Nucor's strategy

Nucor has chosen to avoid the formalised planning processes that are typically found in *Fortune* 500 firms. This lack of formalisation also extends to the company's mission statement, which is non-existent but known to all employees. The company does not have a formal mission statement, as management believes that most mission statements are developed in isolation, never seen or conveyed to employees, and have little in common with what the firm really does and how it operates. Nonetheless, all Nucor employees can tell you what their job entails and what the objective of the organisation is: the production of high volumes of quality, low-cost steel.[2] Nucor and its employees recognise that all the steel produced must meet industry standards for quality. In fact, Nucor frequently exceeds quality standards. High levels of production per man-hour result in low-cost and, subsequently, prices among the lowest in the industry.

Nucor's strategic intent is clearly known by employees, customers and its competitors. Each year, the business review of the annual report gives this succinct description of its scope of operations: 'Nucor Corporation's business is the manufacture of steel products.' The annual letter to shareholders gives this picture of the company:

> *Your management believes that Nucor is among the nation's lowest cost steel producers. Nucor has operated profitably for every quarter since 1966. Nucor's steel products are competitive with those of foreign imports. Nucor has a strong sense of loyalty and responsibility to its employees. Nucor has not closed a single facility, and has maintained stability in its work force for many years ... Productivity is high and labor relations are good.*[3]

As with the mission, goals at Nucor are equally streamlined. Iverson has noted that in some companies planning systems are as much ritual as reality, resulting in plans and budgets that are inappropriate and unrealistic.[4] Nucor has both long- and short-range goals. However, they are handled differently than at many firms. Short-term plans focus on budget and production for the current and next fiscal year. The plans are zero-based – created from actual needs and estimates for specific projects – not an updated copy of a prior year's budget. Long-range plans are a combination of the plans of different divisions and plant – a bottom-up approach to planning. The long-range plans are seen as guides – not gospel. The plans incorporate relative goals instead of specific milestones that the firm expects managers to achieve. Division and plant managers set their target goals knowing that they will be rewarded for meeting them, but not punished if for unexpected reasons they are not met.

Similarly, even plans for specific projects are minimalist. For example, the company handles new mill construction largely internally. Many aspects of the plant design are done 'on the fly' to save time. The company does not create finely detailed construction plans for new plants. Instead, it uses this experience as a guide for starting construction. It then fills in the details as construction proceeds.[5] This approach allows Nucor to construct plants both faster and at less cost than their competitors. The Hickman, Arkansas, mill was completed six months ahead of schedule, going from groundbreaking to first commercial shipment in a mere 16 months.

By 1995, Nucor had become the fourth-largest domestic steel producer. CEO John Correnti targets annual growth at between 15 and 18 per cent – substantially above the 1–2 per cent rate of growth for the industry. Given Nucor's size and the industry's maturity, growth for Nucor requires taking market share away from the integrated producers. Most experts

Exhibit 15 | Nucor annual sales, 1986–97

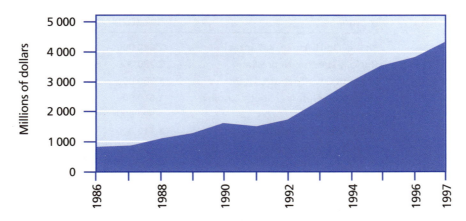

agree that Nucor is well positioned to achieve such growth and sustain profitability, given its industry-leading cost structure. Steel industry analysts attribute Nucor's ability to grow in a constricting market to the firm's aggressive style of management, its innovative and revolutionary technologies, and a solid understanding of the dynamics and cost-drivers of the steel industry.

Nucor can trace its low-cost position to a combination of three factors: technological innovation, continuous process refinement and a strong corporate culture. Investments in any of the three alone is insufficient; the three elements must work together for the firm to be productive and successful.

Technological innovation at Nucor

Historically, the main distinction between minimills and integrated producers has been the range of products offered. While minimill technology is less capital intensive, the production process is also limited to commodity steel products: bars, angles and structural steel beams. Integrated producers largely retreated from these commodity products and concentrated on sheet steel, which was presumably safe from encroachment by the minis. Strategically, though, Nucor more closely resembles the integrated producers versus other minimills in terms of product offerings. Innovative use of technology is key to this strategy.

A prime example of Nucor's innovation was its foray into sheet steel. By the mid-1980s, Iverson had anticipated the coming shake-out among minimills; the lure of easy pickings from dinosaurs like Bethlehem Steel had drawn many firms into the minimill business, resulting in over-supply. Integrated mills produce steel sheet by starting with 10-inch-thick slabs of steel and repeatedly processing the slab through rollers to reduce thickness and increase width. Multiple rolling machines result in a production line hundreds of yards long. Conventional wisdom said that it was impossible to produce the 10-inch-thick steel slabs needed to roll sheet steel in a minimill; their small electric arc furnaces simply did not have the same capability as the blast furnace used by an integrated mill. Nucor carefully researched emerging technology. Rather than develop a proprietary system, they licensed and modified a new German caster and began a US$270 million experiment. This new plant – in Crawfordsville, Indiana – started up in 1987. The process was very different from making sheet steel in an integrated plant. Nucor's system involves the highly controlled continuous pouring of molten steel into a narrow mould and on to a conveyor belt to form a continuous two-inch-thick ribbon of semi-solid steel – pouring steel much in the same manner as frosting an endless cake using a pastry tube. The process requires sophisticated computer technology and monitoring to ensure constant quality and to avert costly and dangerous spills. This precisely sized ribbon of steel is then rolled to the specific thickness using a few, smaller-sized rolling machines. This results in a much smaller and less expensive plant than a traditional mill for the production of sheet steel.

The technical challenges of producing steel using this method are the basic requirements of entry into the minimill market. Profitability, however, is achieved through efficiency. Labour costs constitute a large portion of the cost of steel. Integrated producers can take up to four to five man-hours per ton to produce sheet steel, with three hours/ton on a productivity benchmark. In comparison, Nucor's Crawfordsville plant took only 45 man-minutes per ton. Such efficiency gave Nucor a US$50–75 cost advantage per ton, a savings of nearly 25 per cent compared to their

Exhibit 16 | Nucor's principal manufacturing locations, 1997

Location	Size (ft2)	Products
Blytheville-Hickman, Arkansas	2 880 000	Steel shapes, flat-rolled steel
Norfolk-Stanton, Nebraska	2 280 000	Steel shapes, joists, deck
Brigham City-Plymouth, Utah	1 760 000	Steel shapes, joists
Darlington-Florence, South Carolina	1 610 000	Steel shapes, joists, deck
Grapeland-Jewett, Texas	1 500 000	Steel shapes, joists, deck
Crawfordsville, Indiana	1 410 000	Flat-rolled steel
Berkeley, South Carolina	1 300 000	Flat-rolled steel

competitors. By 1996, Nucor had production time down to 36 minutes per ton with additional savings expected. A second sheet plant was added in 1992, and capacity was expanded at both plants in 1994. Production capacity was 1 million tons in 1989, and 3.8 million tons in 1995.

Not content with the sheet steel market, Nucor chose to enter a new strategic segment in 1995: speciality steel. The Crawfordsville plant was modified to produce thin slab stainless steel – another 'impossible' feat for a minimill. Through experimentation, it was able to produce 2-inch-thick stainless steel slabs. It shipped 16 000 tons in 1995, 50 000 tons in 1996, and expects to hit a production capacity of 200 000 tons annually. Coincidentally, perhaps, its projected capacity mirrors the volume of stainless sheet imported to the United States – about 10 per cent of stainless steel demand in the United States.

Another example of technological innovation was Nucor's entry into the fastener steel segment. Fasteners include hardware such as hex and structural bolts and socket cap screws, which are used extensively in an array of applications, including construction, machine tools, farm implements and military applications. Dozens of American fastener plants shuttered their doors in the 1980s, and foreign firms captured virtually all of this business segment. After a year of studying the fastener market and available technology, Nucor built a new fastener plant in Saint Joe, Indiana. Productivity was substantially higher than that at comparable US plants, and a second fastener plant came on-line in 1995. The fastener plants receive most of their steel from the Nucor Steel division. With a production capacity of 115 000 tons – up substantially from 50 000 tons in 1991 – Nucor has the capacity to supply nearly 20 per cent of this market.

A final example of technological innovation concerns upstream diversification. Scrap steel is a critical input for minimills. Quality differences in scrap types coupled with insufficient supply have led to large fluctuations in scrap costs. Frank Stephens, a mining engineer, had developed a technology to improve the efficiency of steel making through the use of iron carbide. Stephens had tried – unsuccessfully – to sell this process to US Steel, National Steel and Armco, among others.[6] In comparison, to Nucor, iron carbide appeared to be an opportunity to reduce its reliance on the increasingly volatile scrap steel market. After speaking with the inventor of the process and touring an iron carbide pilot plant in Australia, Nucor made preliminary plans to construct an iron carbide pilot plant.[7] The location selected – Trinidad – would provide the large quantities of low-cost natural gas needed for iron carbide production. Nucor estimated that establishing the pilot plant would require US$60 million. However, as the process was unproven, Nucor would, in essence, be making a gamble that would yield an industry-revolutionising process or be investing US$60 million in a plant that would be virtually worthless. To Nucor, the investment constituted a measured risk; while the investment to determine the feasibility was significant, if the process failed it would not cripple the firm. In 1994, Nucor opened the iron carbide pilot plant at a cost of US$100 million – almost double expectations. At the end of 1995, the plant was operating at only 60 per cent of capacity. Still, Nucor was betting big on this opportunity. Nucor estimates that the use of iron carbide would allow them to reduce their steel-making costs by US$50 per ton – a 20 per cent reduction. Additionally, Nucor is working on a joint venture with US Steel to manufacture steel directly from iron carbide, which could revolutionise the steel industry.

Process refinement at Nucor

Much of the business press focuses on the high-profile quantum advances made at Nucor, such as the creation of flat-rolled steel in an electric arc furnace and the use of iron carbide as a substitute for scrap. However, an emphasis on continuous innovation is felt throughout the organisation and is equally important. A manager from Nucor's Crawfordsville mill observed that most of the innovation comes not from management, but from equipment operators and line supervisors. The job of management, says the manager, is to make sure the innovations can be implemented.[8] For example, workers discovered that they could fine-tune surface characteristics of their galvanised steel (a benefit valued by many customers) simply by making small adjustments to the air pressure of a coating process. Changes such as these do not require management review or approval. Instead, equipment operators and line supervisors are authorised to innovate and implement processes that improve production. Such innovation is routine enough at Nucor that management does not track individual improvements. Rather, Nucor tracks innovation by looking at the end result – reductions in the amount of labour required to produce each ton of steel.

Employee innovation is driven by two factors. First, the company's bonus system means that any substantial improvements to efficiency will contribute to both the plant's performance and individual pay cheques. Second, the corporate culture emphasises how experiments – even failed ones – keep Nucor as the perennial benchmark for industry productivity. Experiments are conducted both at the time of mill start-up and on an ongoing basis. Typical of most mill start-ups, the start-up of Nucor's Hickman plant was fraught with problems. The high rate of the production line resulted in 'breakouts' – bad pours – of the 'ribbon' of steel for thin-slap casting. Though initially occurring at the rate of several per day, breakouts have been declining since the plant became operational. The high rates of production still result in two to five breakouts per week and Nucor continues to make modifications to the equipment to reduce this level.

Focusing on clean-steel practices, the melt-shop people are developing mould powders that can handle the high-speed, thin-slab casting. Mould powders insulate, lubricate, aid uniform heat transfer, and absorb inclusions, all of which makes for cleaner steel. Unfortunately, no existing mould powders can handle hot steel at the rate Nucor could potentially produce it: 200 inches a minute. To reduce inclusions (impurities in the steel), Nucor is working to standardise all operating practices in the two furnaces and two ladle furnaces.

The Nucor philosophy towards innovation is that attempts at improvement will be accompanied by failures. Tony Kurley, a Nucor plant manager, recalls Nucor chairman Ken Iverson's expectation that success is making the correct decision 60 per cent of the time. What's important isn't the mistakes that are made, says Iverson, but the ability to learn from the 20 per cent that are truly mistakes and the 20 per cent that are sub-optimal decisions.[9]

This willingness to modify on the fly and 'shoot from the hip', as one melt-shop supervisor puts it, makes Nucor an exciting place to work. The lean, flexible workforce is continually trying new things, doing different jobs. Employees continue to engage in risk taking because the company rewards success and does not punish for failures. The result is that employees, from top managers to hourly personnel, are willing to take risks to achieve innovation and take ownership in their jobs.

At Nucor, the tolerance levels for failure are apparently high. In the 1970s, a Nucor plant manager was considering the replacement of the electric arc furnace in the plant with an induction furnace. At

Exhibit 17 | Nucor annual worker productivity, 1990–7

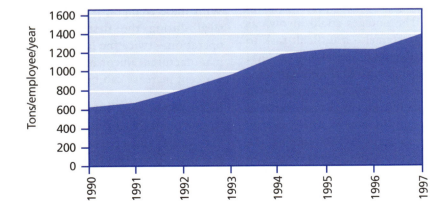

Nucor, the plant manager has the authority to select the type of furnaces used in his plant. There was no clearly right or wrong answer. A discussion yielded strong arguments in favour of the switch from some plant managers and equally enthusiastic arguments against the switch from others. The plant manager elected to make the switch at a cost to Nucor of US$10 million. From the start, the new furnaces failed to live up to expectations and resulted in repeated shutdowns. Discussion shifted to the pluses and minuses of removing the furnace and within a year the furnace was removed. When the manager told Iverson of his decision, Iverson supported him, saying he had made the right decision – there was no sense in leaving the reminder of a bad decision laying around.[10]

Despite the price tag on this particular learning experience, management was unfazed. Iverson's comment on this failure was that the true problem is people *not* taking risks. Nucor has a saying: 'Don't study an idea to death in a dozen committee meetings; try it out and make it work.'

Through incremental advances, employees are continually able to streamline and refine the steel-making process. The data suggests that Nucor employees have not come close to exhausting these enhancements. Productivity, as measured in tons produced per employee, doubled from 1990 to 1995 (626 tons/worker and 1 269 tons/worker, respectively) and continues to climb. In 1997, productivity exceeded 1 400 tons/worker. How is Nucor able to realise such productivity gains in this mature industry? The following examples highlight incremental innovations.

Preventive maintenance

Preventive maintenance is a crucial but time-consuming task at a minimill. At Nucor-Yamato, a joint venture between Nucor and Yamato Kogyo, a Japanese steel producer, the plant had week-long shutdowns three times a year. During these periods, outside contractors – as many as 800 at a time – would strip, service and replace worn machinery. The outages could involve as many as 800 contractor personnel – a difficult task to manage. Further exacerbating the situation was the level of skill and low level of productivity of some contractor personnel. Aside from the challenges of hunting down missing contractors, the plant (and employees) suffered from the three weeks without production. The company addressed both of these concerns by eliminating the week-long shutdowns, instead tackling specific areas of the mill in focused, 24-hour shutdowns. This new process has several advantages, including spreading the maintenance costs over a wider window and being able to use a smaller in-house staff that operates continually. Some maintenance jobs are large enough to still require multiple-day shutdowns, but the number of outside contractors has been reduced from 800 to 150. Through this program, downtime at the plant has fallen from 10 per cent to near 1 per cent. Some improvements are less dramatic, but significant nonetheless. A young engineer at a Nucor plant was concerned that too much was being spent to lubricate and maintain a series of supporting screws under a rolling line. He had a better idea. The screws, part of the original manufacturer's design, were replaced with metal shims, achieving an annual savings of over US$1 million.

Reduced melt times

At the Crawfordsville plant, workers made a series of small changes, such as replacing an exhaust pipe and tinkering with the chemistry of the melt. By doing so, they reduced the melt time from 72 minutes to 65 minutes. While this may seem a small improvement, it meant that an additional 25 tons of steel could be poured in a single shift.

Revitalisation of outdated equipment

When Nucor bought a casting line from a German supplier, an obsolete reversing mill, which is used to reduce the thickness of steel, was thrown in as an afterthought to sweeten the deal. The capacity of the reducing mill was rated as 325 000 tons a year by the supplier. Nucor employees immediately began fiddling with the mill; the following are among the improvements and results:

- Changing the way the steel was fed into the machine increased capacity from 360 to 1 960 feet per minute.
- Changes reduced the time to thread the machine from five minutes to 20 seconds.
- Nucor changed the type and grade of lubricating oil and installed a bigger motor.

With these changes, Nucor processed 650 000 tons of steel during the first year the equipment was in operation – twice the machine's capacity as rated by its manufacturer. Nucor anticipates that an additional 10 per cent increase can be achieved.[11]

New galvanising line

At one point, Nucor decided to install a galvanising line that coats finished steel to enhance its durability. Engineers from US$17.8-billion USX Corp. visited the plant before the foundation for the line had even been poured, and Nucor engineers told them they would have the line running by year's end. The USX visitors laughed because they had started building a similar line a year earlier and it still wasn't operational. The day after Christmas, USX ran its first coil through its new galvanising line. Twelve hours later, Nucor's US$25 million galvanising line was operational. No other firm had constructed such a line for less than US$48 million.[12]

Continuous production

In most minimills, the conversion of scrap to a finished product is a discontinuous process. Scrap is converted to ingots, for instance, which are then stockpiled for further conversion. When building their new Hickman plant in the early 1990s, Nucor tried an experiment: continuous production. All steps of the steel-making process are coordinated, from picking up the raw scrap, to melting it, forming it and laying down a finished coil. Continuous production is both faster (three to four hours from inputs to finished product) and more efficient. The downside? This just-in-time approach eliminates all slack or buffers in the process; problems at any point in the production line shut the entire operation down. How well has this new process worked? As with other Nucor plants, virtually none of the employees had ever worked in a steel mill before. Still, plant performance within one year of start-up was competitive with more established mills: 0.66 man-hours per ton, and a 91 per cent yield (percentage of scrap converted to finished product, a measure of efficiency). In late July 1993, the Hickman plant shipped 8 804 tons, setting a new Nucor record for the most tons shipped from a single plant in a day.[13]

Culture at Nucor

A key ingredient in any effective corporate culture is people. It is not surprising that many organisations, especially manufacturing firms, have dysfunctional cultures given the fear and distrust experienced by many workers, frequent layoffs and an 'us versus them' mentality. Executives of Bethlehem Steel, for example, constructed a golf course using corporate funds, then built a second and third course for middle managers and employees, respectively. Ken Iverson questioned how a company with a culture so dysfunctional as to require the construction of three golf courses to maintain the hierarchical distinction between executives, managers and line employees could ever expect to improve its operations.[14]

Nucor differs dramatically from its competitors. At Nucor, 'us versus them' clearly implies management and workers united against competitors. One melt-shop supervisor described a sense of personal responsibility not only for his own job but also for the firm. He described his position at Nucor as being much like running his own company – a typical comment given the entrepreneurial environment Nucor has created. Decentralised authority and a sense of individual responsibility are a key part of that structure. John Correnti explains that he does not want to micro-manage the firm's operations. Doing so, he feels, would result in employees placing blame when things go wrong instead of taking responsibility and finding solutions. This, Correnti feels, results in line personnel having a realistic ability to control their own job environment, increase productivity and increase their pay.[15]

Still, Nucor is anything but a 'workers' paradise'. The standards for employee productivity are extremely high, and there are a number of painful reminders of this emphasis. For example, the steelworker who is 15 minutes late loses his production bonus for the day – as much as half of the day's pay. Thirty minutes late and the bonus for the entire week is forfeited. Workers are not paid for sicknesses less than three days, or for production downtime due to broken machinery. However, by most measures, Nucor is the employer of choice. There is extreme competition for new positions. The Darlington plant has routinely received 1 000 applications from a single job posting in the newspaper. Similarly, the new plant in Jewett, Texas (population 435), received 2 000 applications. Employee turnover rates are among the lowest in the industry. For example, the Crawfordsville, Indiana, plant lost a total of four employees between 1988 and 1994: two for drug use and two for poor performance. Nucor is a non-union shop with much of the opposition to unions coming from Nucor employees who feel that union rules would hurt productivity and subsequently their pay cheques. According to company folklore, there has been one labour dispute outside the mill gates, and plant supervisors had to protect union pamphleteers from angry employees!

How does Nucor achieve such levels of motivation and dedication? Iverson suggests that corporate America has confused the ideas of motivation and manipulation. Manipulation stipulates a one-sided relationship wherein management convinces employees to do things in the interest of management. Motivation involves getting employees to do things that are in the best interest of both parties. In the long term, Iverson says, motivation yields a strong company whereas manipulation destroys a company. With this in mind,

Nucor has identified the following elements as critical to effective employee motivation:

1. Everyone must know what is expected of them, and goals should not be set too low.
2. Everyone must understand the rewards, which must be clearly delineated and not subjective.
3. Everyone must know where to go to get help. The company must have a system that clearly tells the employee who to talk to when confused or upset.
4. Employees must have real voices. They must participate in defining the goals, determining the working conditions and establishing production processes.
5. The company must provide a feedback system so that employees always know how they, their group and the company are doing.[16]

The approach appears to work. A long-time Nucor employee recalls when the Darlington, South Carolina, plant could produce 30 tons of steel a day. The same plant now produces 100 tons of steel an hour. The worker says that, given the can-do attitude of employees and the focus on constant improvement, the 'sky is the limit' for additional improvements.[17]

While Nucor is a merit-oriented company, it also makes it clear that there are no 'classes' of employees. Top managers receive the same benefits as steel-makers on everything from vacation time to health insurance. There are no preferred parking spaces, and the 'executive dining room' is the delicatessen across the street. Incidentally, the corporate headquarters is located in a dowdy strip mall in Charlotte, North Carolina. Not surprisingly, there is no corporate jet or executive retreat in the Caymans. Officers travel in coach class on business trips, and the organisation is rife with legends of corporate austerity – such as Iverson travelling via subway when on business in New York City (true, incidentally). This emphasis on egalitarianism is an integral part of the Nucor culture. Iverson, wanting to eliminate even the smallest distinctions between personnel, ordered everyone to wear the same colour hardhat. In many plants, the colour of your hardhat is a highly visible signal of your level in the company hierarchy. Even at Nucor, some managers thought that their authority rested not in their expertise and management ability, but in the colour of their hat. This goal of egalitarianism has not been completely without problems. When it was brought to Iverson's attention that workers needed to be able to quickly identify maintenance personnel, Iverson admitted his mistake and at Nucor plants everyone wears green hardhats except maintenance personnel who wear yellow so that they can be easily spotted.[18]

This approach appears transferable and the motivational effects are contagious. Iverson recalls when Nucor purchased a plant and immediately sold the limousine and eliminated executive parking spaces in favour of a first-come, first-serve system. Iverson greeted employees on their way into the plant and recalls one employee who parked in what was the boss's reserved spot and commented that the simple changes in the parking system made him feel much better about the company.[19]

Compensation and bonus system

Leadership by example can only induce so much behaviour; one of the more visible aspects of Nucor's culture is its compensation system, particularly the prominent bonus system. 'Gonna make some money today?' is a common greeting on the plant floor, and discussion of company financials is as common in the lunchroom as basketball scores. The bonus system is highly structured, consisting of no special or discretionary bonuses. The company is divided based on production teams of 25–50 individuals who are responsible for a complete task (such as a cold rolled steel fabrication line). The group includes everyone on that line, from scrap handlers to furnace operators, mould and roller operators, and even finish packagers. Managers get together and, based on the equipment being used, set a standard for production. This standard is known to everyone in advance and doesn't change unless the company makes a significant investment in capital equipment. With the standard in mind, employees make whatever changes they see fit to increase production. A bonus is paid for all production over the standard and there is no limit as to how much bonus can be paid. The only qualifier is that the production must be good – that is, of sufficient quality for sale. No bonus is paid for bad production. At the end of the week, all employees on a particular line get the same production bonus, which is issued along with their weekly cheques.[20]

With bonuses, Nucor employees typically earn as much as their unionised counterparts in the integrated plants. Weekly bonuses have, in recent years, averaged 100–200 per cent of base wages. Typical production workers earn US$8 to US$9 in base pay plus an additional US$16 per hour in production bonuses and averaged US$60 000 in 1996, making them the highest-paid employees in the industry. Since Nucor locates its plants in rural locations, employee salaries are well above the norm for any specific area, making Nucor jobs highly desirable.

Nucor also offers several other benefits to help motivate and retain employees. In the 1980s, it shifted to a work week of four 12-hour days. Workers take four days off and then resume another intensive shift – a practice borrowed from the oil industry. While this practice results in a lot of expensive overtime – Crawfordsville alone paid out an extra half a million dollars in 1995 due to the compressed work week – management feels that the ensuing morale and productivity gains pay for themselves. The company has also disbursed special US$500 bonuses (four times in the last 20 years) in exceptionally good years. They also provide four years worth of college tuition support (up to US$2 000/year) for each child of each employee – excluding only the children of corporate officers.

Job security

Listening to Nucor managers, it is difficult to determine which fact they are most proud of: 30 years of uninterrupted quarterly profits or 20 years since they have last had to lay off an employee. Nucor locates in rural areas and there are often few other employment opportunities, let alone other jobs at similar pay scales, so Nucor feels a strong responsibility for keeping workers employed, even during economic downturns.

Popular impressions aside, Iverson is clear to note that Nucor does not have a no-layoff policy. He cautions that Nucor will lay off employees as a last resort if the survival of the company is at stake.[21] But during prior downturns, the company has chosen to ride out slowdowns with its 'Share the Pain' program, which involves reduced work weeks and plant slowdowns instead of layoffs. What is most unusual with the program is that the brunt of poor performance is felt most heavily at upper parts of the organisation, particularly as long-term compensation is an integral part of the executive pay system. During a period of reduced demand for steel, the plants reduce their operations. For line personnel and foremen, this reduces their income by about 20 per cent. For department heads, who are covered by a bonus plan based on the profitability of their plant, slowdowns result in a reduction of about one-third of their pay. Nucor's top managers have their pay based largely on return on shareholders' equity – the measure most important to shareholders. This is hit the hardest and top managers see their pay decline the most – as much as two-thirds or three-quarters of their income is lost.[22] This structure serves a number of purposes. First, the line personnel don't feel that they are bearing the brunt of a downturn. Second, there is a great deal of motivation to further reduce the cost per ton so that Nucor can underprice any other producer and keep its mills active even during an economic downturn. Lastly, while the shareholders may not be happy with a reduced ROI, they at least know that management has an incentive to improve company performance. As an example, Iverson notes that in 1961 – a good year – he made US$460 000 including bonuses. In 1982, though, Nucor fell shy of its 8 per cent return on equity and Iverson earned only US$108 000.[23]

Exhibit 18 | Nucor profitability vs. industry, 1981–95

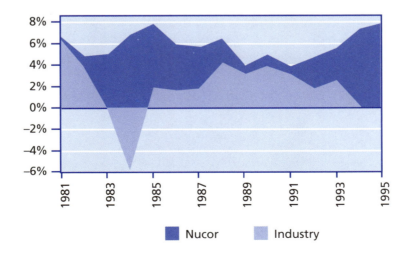

Summary

How important is the corporate culture to Nucor's success? Management is free to point out that their advantage does not stem from proprietary technology. After all, most of their innovations – including thin-slab casting and the use of iron carbide – are based on technology developed by other firms. While they pioneered the modifications to make thin-slab casting possible, numerous other minimills are hot on their heels in this product segment. Nucor's plants are open to firms seeking to benchmark their operations, including other steel producers. When other firms tour a plant, they may see the same equipment as in their plant. Many comment on the culture of the plant. One visitor from an integrated producer commented that at his plant the culture is adversarial, management versus employee, with no trust between the parties. 'Us versus them' refers to workers versus management and production. In contrast, at Nucor, workers are seen striving together as a team, helping each other and working towards a common goal: the production of a high volume of low-cost, quality steel.[24]

Iverson explains Nucor's success as being based on a combination of the technology used and the culture of the organisation. He is unsure if technology is 20, or 30, or even 40 per cent – but he's sure it is less than half of the formula for Nucor's achievements. The culture that Nucor instills is focused primarily on the long-term health of the organisation. For example, debt is avoided, start-up costs are not capitalised but rather are expensed in the current period, and depreciation and write-offs lean towards the detriment of short-term earnings. Iverson is adamant about not bowing to short-term pressures to manage earnings or spread dividends evenly over a quarterly basis. He refuses to do it. He compares companies that try endlessly to meet short-term projections at the expense of a long-term approach to dogs on a leash – trying to perform a trick to satisfy the stock market. He admonishes short-term share speculators to stay away from the company. He compares Nucor to an eagle and invites long-term investors to soar with the company.[25]

Endnotes

1. J. L. McCarthy, 1996, 'Passing the torch at big steel', *Chief Executive*, 111, p. 22.
2. K. Iverson, 1993, 'Changing the rules of the game', *Planning Review*, 21(5), pp. 9–12.
3. Nucor Corp., 1996 Annual Report.
4. K. Iverson, 1993, 'Effective leaders stay competitive', *Executive Excellence*, 10(4), pp. 18–19.
5. G. McManus, 1992, 'Scheduling a successful startup', *Iron Age New Steel*, 8(7), pp. 14–18.
6. S. Carey and E. Norton, 1995, 'Blast from the past: Once scorned, a man with an idea is wooed by the steel industry', *Wall Street Journal*, 29 December, Sec A, p. 1, col. 6.
7. R. S. Ahlbrandt, R. J. Fruehan and F. Giarratani, 1996, *The Renaissance of American Steel* (New York: Oxford University Press).
8. T. Kuster, 1995, 'How Nucor Crawfordsville works', *Iron Age New Steel*, 11(12), pp. 36–52.
9. B. Berry, 1993, 'Hot band at 0.66 manhours per ton', *Iron Age New Steel*, 1(1), pp. 20–6.
10. K. Iverson, 1998, *Plain Talk: Lessons from a Business Maverick* (New York: John Wiley & Sons).
11. E. O. Welles, 1994, 'Bootstrapping for billions', *Inc.*, 16(9), pp. 78–86.
12. Ibid.
13. Berry, 'Hot band at 0.66 manhours per ton'.
14. Iverson, *Plain Talk*.
15. Ahlbrandt, Fruehan and Giarratani, *The Renaissance of American Steel*.
16. Iverson, 'Changing the rules of the game'.
17. Ibid.
18. J. Isenberg, 1992, 'Hot steel and good common sense', *Management Review*, 81(8), pp. 25–7.
19. Iverson, *Plain Talk*.
20. Iverson, 'Changing the rules of the game'.
21. Iverson, *Plain Talk*.
22. Isenberg, 'Hot steel and good common sense'.
23. Iverson, 'Changing the rules of the game'.
24. B. Berry, 1996, 'The importance of Nucor', *Iron Age New Steel*, 12(7), p. 2.
25. Iverson, *Plain Talk*.

Case 10

Pacific Dunlop: Caught on the half volley

Stuart Crispin
Mark Wickham
Dallas Hanson
University of Tasmania

Introduction

Time is not on Rod Chadwick's side. As managing director of Pacific Dunlop, he has one of the toughest jobs in Australia: trying to extract value from a conglomerate that is worth more 'dead than alive'. By January 2000, Pacific Dunlop's share price languished at a 14-year low, its market capitalisation value had dropped from $3 billion to $1.1 billion, and investors and analysts were calling for major restructuring within the company. Of greatest concern to all was the fact that the share price was now $1.50 below the 'break-up' valuation for the company, making it a prime target for acquisition and dissolution for quick profit. At the core of Rod Chadwick's problems was a history of frequent acquisition by Dunlop, without any attempts to achieve synergies between business units, or indeed undertake any integration in management systems. Chadwick's position was not made any easier by the fact that the company's business units (with the exception of Ansell) operated in mature, low-growth and highly competitive markets. How had Pacific Dunlop come to be in such a precarious position, and how was Chadwick to improve the performance, and perhaps even ensure the survival, of this 'corporate dinosaur'?

Genesis, 1888–1920

The origins of Pacific Dunlop can be traced back to Belfast, Northern Ireland, where in 1888 a Scottish-born veterinarian by the name of John Boyd Dunlop invented the first pneumatic bicycle tyre. Before this time, bicycle tyres had been made out of solid rubber, ensuring a slow and uncomfortable ride for the cyclist. Dunlop's pneumatic tyre had an air-filled inner tube, which provided cyclists with a much more comfortable ride and allowed them to travel at much faster speeds. The potential benefits of the pneumatic tyre to cyclists led Dunlop to patent his invention, and with a syndicate of business associates he formed the Dunlop Pneumatic Tyre Company in November 1889. Soon after its formation, the company moved production to a factory in Coventry, England.

The company's business grew steadily, with pneumatic tyres being exported to continental Europe, the United States and Australia. By 1891 the growing demand for Dunlop pneumatic tyres was so great that the company opened factories in France, Germany and North America. In 1893 it opened its first Australian factory in Tattersall's Lane, Melbourne. From its beginnings in Australia, the company was driven by a belief in the value of marketing and strong brand names. The company appointed its first 'publicity man' in 1895, long before such a position was common to Australian businesses. It also advertised widely in magazines, newspapers and on billboards, and was actively involved in the promotion of cycle racing, often sponsoring record-breaking long-distance bike rides. Such a strong marketing focus had the effect of making the Dunlop brand name synonymous with cycling and tyres in Australia.

While the growing popularity of cycling and cycle racing at the end of the 19th century was fuelling the worldwide demand for pneumatic tyres, the Dunlop Pneumatic Tyre Company had fallen into financial difficulties. A takeover of the Dunlop Pneumatic Tyre Company in 1896, and a major downturn in Dunlop's tyre sales both in Britain and in export markets such as the United States, had left the company in a poor financial position. To counter this, the company decided to sell its overseas holdings, and in 1899 a syndicate, led

Exhibit 1 | PDP, Pacific Dunlop Limited, company directors, 2000

Mr John T. Ralph (Chairman)
Mr Rodney L. Chadwick (Managing director)
Mr Anthony B. Daniels
Ms S. Carolyn H. Kay
Mr Robert J. McLean
Professor David G. Penington
Mr Ian E. Webber

by Canadian businessmen Richard Garland and John Palmer, bought the company's Australian and New Zealand operations and formed the Dunlop Pneumatic Tyre Company of Australasia Ltd. It was this company that was to be the forerunner of what is today Pacific Dunlop.

The first decade of the 20th century saw the arrival of the motorcar in Australia, and the newly formed Dunlop Pneumatic Tyre Company, with its core competencies in production of pneumatic tyres, was positioned strongly to be a major producer of tyres for the automotive industry. As it had previously done with bicycle tyres, Dunlop actively promoted motoring, sponsoring both motor races as well as attempts to set long-distance driving records. In fact, Dunlop's first advertising manager, Harry James, was at times himself the holder of several world long-distance driving records. At the same time, bicycle riding continued to be a popular pastime for many Australians. The growing demand for both bicycle and car tyres led the company to open a new factory in the Melbourne bayside suburb of Montague in August 1902.

The first years of the 20th century also proved to be highly competitive in the Australian tyre industry, providing a catalyst for what was to be one of the first of many acquisition strategies by Dunlop. The main source of competition for Dunlop came from the Pioneer Rubber Company, which was owned by Barnett Glass, who in 1876 had essentially founded the Australian rubber industry. Pioneer was the producer of a range of rubber goods, including tyres, and had significant advantages over Dunlop with regard to tyre quality control and reduced cost structures. Faced with a highly competitive market where profitability was low, Dunlop had two choices. The first was to compete with Pioneer and other tyre manufactures on price and quality, a difficult proposition given that the quality of tyre produced at Dunlop's Montague factory was relatively inferior. The second option was for Dunlop to purchase its competitor. As would become Dunlop's trademark strategy in the future, Dunlop's management decided to purchase the Pioneer Rubber Company.

The purchase of the Pioneer Rubber Company served to strengthen Dunlop's position in the Australian tyre industry. Between 1905 and the beginning of the First World War in 1914, Dunlop's business continued to burgeon, with sales and profitability increasing markedly. In particular, the arrival of the 'Model-T' Ford in Australia made owning a car affordable for the average middle-class Australian and subsequently increased the demand for car tyres. In addition, the purchase of Pioneer enabled Dunlop to diversify into the manufacture of a range of rubber-based products. Dunlop also continued to produce Pioneer's range of wet-weather clothing, hot water bottles, shoes, mats, valves and washers, and increased sales and profitability through product innovation, such as the first Australian-made conveyor belts and moulded rubber hoses.

Interestingly, Dunlop divested Pioneer's condom operations, selling the operations to one of its employees, Eric Ansell. Ansell created the Ansell Rubber Company with an initial capital base of $60. The company operated out of a factory in the Melbourne suburb of Richmond, and grew by the 1960s to become Australia's largest producer of condoms and rubber gloves. In 1969, Dunlop would buy back the Ansell operation, and grow this into a business with annual sales of $1.2 billion and a capital value of $1.1 billion. Today, Ansell is a core business unit for Dunlop, generating more sales revenue than that of their tyre division.

While the First World War impacted on Dunlop's sales figures and supplies of skilled labour, the company emerged from the war reasonably unaffected. Although the first post-war years were chaotic, both economically and socially, Dunlop remained profitable. In two out of every three years from 1908 to 1920, Dunlop had managed to maintain high ('super-economic') profits, but this ratio would not be repeated again until the 1950s.

Turmoil I, 1920–50

The period from 1920 to 1950 was characterised by economic upheaval and catastrophic social change due to the effects of war. During this period, there would be the economic boom of the Roaring Twenties, the economic bust of the Great Depression and the social destruction of the Second World War. This period would see the introduction of massive increases in tariff protection for Australian manufacturers in an effort by the government to 'prop-up' the economy and create employment. This protection was greatest in industries such as tyre production and clothing, industries where Dunlop had a very strong presence. While these tariffs shielded Dunlop from overseas imports, it would have the long-term effect of reducing Dunlop's ability to compete successfully in the global marketplace.

During the 1920s the Australian tyre industry again became highly competitive. Competition came from both Australian tyre manufacturers, such as the Perdriau Rubber Company and a newly formed Barnett Glass Rubber Company, as well as from international manufacturers such as Goodyear. This competition threatened Dunlop's share of the Australian tyre market, as well as adversely affecting the profitability of the industry as a whole. As in the past, Dunlop had spent little on research and development, and their factories were not employing the latest in tyre production technology. Consequently, Dunlop tyres were again relatively inferior in quality to those of their competitors. Dunlop was again faced with stiff competition on price and quality, and with the challenge of making tough strategic choices.

Initially, in an effort to counter their problems with quality, Dunlop Australasia turned to England, and in return for a 25 per cent stake in the Dunlop Pneumatic Tyre Company of Australia Ltd, Dunlop England provided the company with new tyre technology. Unfortunately for the company, this technological support did little to improve quality standards, with many of the British tyre designs being unsuitable for Australian conditions. As a result, Dunlop once again sought to overcome the threat to their viability through a strategy based on acquisition. Dunlop approached both Perdriau and Barnett Glass with offers of a takeover, with Perdriau accepting the offer. In June 1929 the Dunlop Perdriau Rubber Company Ltd was established, and the company subsequently purchased a controlling interest in Barnett Glass. While these purchases had the effect of reducing competitive pressure in the Australian tyre market, Dunlop did little to integrate the operations of the three companies. In fact, apart from the name change, the three companies continued to operate as completely separate entities.

Although Dunlop had been vulnerable in the tyre industry during the 1920s, it remained competitive in the production and sale of many other rubber goods, becoming the market leader in the production of rubber belting, hoses and clothing. In addition, Dunlop manufactured the first Australian-made balloon tyres for cars and aircraft tyres. It was during this period that Dunlop began the production of its famous sport shoe, the Dunlop Volley. Much of Dunlop's success with these products was again due to its strong marketing orientation, coupled with a tariff barrier that decreased the sales of imported products.

Within six months of acquiring Perdriau and Barnett Glass, the world plunged into the economic depression which began in 1929. Stock markets collapsed, banks closed, and businesses were forced to cease operations. Tyres and tubes were the first rubber goods to experience a major slump in demand. Sales of new cars fell dramatically, and those people who already owned cars reduced their usage equally dramatically in favour of horses and walking. People who continued to use their cars during the Depression favoured retreads over new tyres, further worsening demand and Dunlop's profitability. Although tyre sales were badly affected, the sale of Dunlop's other innovative rubber products fared considerably better.

To counter the effects of the Depression on their tyre revenues, Dunlop commenced an efficiency (cost-minimisation) drive in 1930. Hard decisions were made to rationalise operations, and some factories were closed. Relief also came from the political arena, with the election of a federal Labor government, which further raised tariffs on imported tyres. By 1932 the economic depression showed signs of lifting, and sales of Dunlop's other rubber products (for example, golf balls and clothing) had turned the company around. Dunlop, however, still faced considerable competition in the Australian tyre market, in particular from the Goodyear Tyre Company. While Goodyear had also suffered during the Depression, their ability to draw on the skills and expertise of their parent company in the United States meant that they emerged from the Depression as Australia's premier tyre wholesaler. Goodyear was able to 'poach' market share away from

Dunlop in the post-Depression period, with 50 per cent of new cars produced during the period 1930–3 being fitted with Goodyear tyres as the standard.

Dunlop was faced with the need to recapture the market share lost to Goodyear. However, the problem for Dunlop was that it had developed a habit of purchasing its major competitors rather than beating them in head-on competition. Unfortunately for Dunlop, Goodyear was not for sale. To overcome this problem, Dunlop opened up a dialogue with Goodyear. Both companies had been adversely affected by the precarious profitability of the industry during the Depression, and in February 1933 they agreed, quite legally at the time, to sell their tyres at a fixed price to dealers in order to shore up the profitability of the two companies.

However, by October, two factors within the tyre market would again place pressure on Dunlop. First, a shift in consumer demand away from high-quality tyres meant that savvy tyre dealers were able to sell cheap tyres far more easily and profitably. Consequently, the price fixing deal between Dunlop and Goodyear collapsed as prices fell. Second, the entry of Sir Frank Beaurepaire's Olympic Tyre and Rubber Company created increased competitive pressures in the tyre industry. These factors greatly affected Dunlop's sales and profitability, so much so that by the start of 1935 Dunlop's share price had fallen in value by one-fifth.

The performance of Olympic, and Dunlop's inability to compete in the Australian tyre industry, perplexed the board of Dunlop, especially as Dunlop had an extensive range of tyres sold under the Dunlop, Barnett Glass and Perdriau brand names. In theory, Dunlop, with its extensive range of tyres, should have been a dominant force in the market. However, Dunlop was a complacent and inefficient organisation. In effect, the purchase of Perdriau and Barnett Glass had been a phantom merger, with no attempt made to integrate the operations of the three companies, each continuing as a separate firm with its own factory, sales force and brand of tyres.

Slowly, the Dunlop board began to realise that their competitive problems stemmed from this basic inefficiency and its triplication of costs. The only way the company could restore its share price and position in the market was to address these problems. In December 1935, Wallace Andrew Bartlett was appointed the new general manager of the company, with a mandate to improve the competitive performance of the company via streamlining of operations and the rationalisation of company resources.

With the appointment of Bartlett, Dunlop would never be the same again. Between 1935 and the start of the Second World War in 1939, Bartlett would drastically restructure the company by reducing the size of its sales force, merging tyre production facilities and eliminating bureaucratic triplication. Bartlett's aim was to become less reliant on tyres, which had been the main source of Dunlop's problems in the past. It was his aim to make Dunlop a universal producer of rubber goods, focusing on a wider range of products such as foam rubber, upholstery, latex and cushions. Interestingly, in his restructuring of the company, Bartlett divested Dunlop's loss-making plastics division, even though the company was the market leader. The division was sold to John Derham and Partners, who would grow this business into Nylex, one of Australia's top 100 firms today.

War was again to impact on the company, but this time in a much more detrimental manner. By 1941, the Japanese invasion of Southeast Asia denied Dunlop access to vital raw materials, forcing the company to be innovative in the use of synthetic and recycled rubber in its products. In addition, the government, in an attempt to ensure sufficient supplies of rubber for the war effort, placed restrictions on the sale of rubber products to the general public. Dunlop became a large producer of products for the war effort, providing the Allied forces with tyres, bullets, inflatable boats, and gas masks. During the war the company removed Perdriau from its name, becoming Dunlop Rubber Australia Limited.

By the start of 1946 the war was over, and the restrictions on the sale of rubber products had been removed. Production freed up and sales of Dunlop's products began to increase. Once again, Dunlop would have to rely on market forces rather than government contracts and military requirements to drive sales. In 1948 the company was briefly thrown into chaos with the death of Wallace Bartlett. Bartlett had given the company focus and renewed vigour, and many on the board were concerned that his passing might herald a new era of uncertainty for the company. After careful consideration, Robert Blackwood was selected to be the new managing director. Unlike previous managing directors, Blackwood had his background in research and development, not sales and production, leading many to question how he would perform in the role.

The last years of the 1940s proved to be a time of renewed economic activity. After the dark times of the Second World War, business was again booming and markets were again rife with competitive action. The 1950s would prove to be a time of great prosperity, and one of the most successful periods in the history of the company.

Consolidation and expansion, 1950–66

Blackwood came to Dunlop with a belief in the virtues of 'simplification' and an attitude that 'small is best'. While the measures undertaken by Bartlett had gone some of the way to improving Dunlop's position, Blackwood and the board believed that more still needed to be done to restructure the company and improve its performance. Of highest priority was the streamlining of Dunlop's production process by reducing the size of the factories employed in the manufacture of Dunlop's range of products. Dunlop's main factories at Drummoyne (Sydney) and Montague (Melbourne) had been built at the start of the century, and were now largely employing outdated technologies. Blackwood believed that new, smaller factories with current technologies (located closer to the main markets that they wished to serve) would provide Dunlop with the greatest flexibility in production and, therefore the greatest potential profits.

Blackwood was also keen to further diversify the company's product range away from tyres. At the beginning of the 1950s, and despite all of the company's previous efforts in product diversification, tyres still accounted for 70 per cent of Dunlop's revenue. The Dunlop board was highly concerned with this reliance upon an industry with high tariff protection, protection that was in no way guaranteed into the future. In almost every month of the 1950s, Dunlop was tempted to manufacture a new range of goods. Its formal policy was to be less dependent on tyres and to diversify into related areas. Dunlop once again turned to corporate acquisition in order to achieve its goals. Between 1952 and 1960, Dunlop had made a number of significant purchases:

- Moulded Hair of Australia (a manufacturer of foam rubber);
- a 75 per cent holding in Trilby (ladies' footwear);
- Kenworth Rubber Limited;
- Slazenger Australia (sporting goods);
- Buesst and Bills (bedding);
- Sleepmaker (mattresses);
- B.B.B Pty Ltd (mattresses);
- John Bull Rubber Company; and
- a joint venture with Olympic to form Wheels and Rims Australia.

During this period, Dunlop also redeveloped a chain of tyre retreading stores that it had purchased during the war into retail distribution outlets for its range of tyres. This distribution network enabled Dunlop to compete more successfully with the Olympic Rubber Company, which distributed its tyres through the Beaurepaire chain of tyre centres. As a result of these acquisitions and redevelopments, the 1950s proved to be one of the most successful and profitable periods in Dunlop's history. Dunlop was able to grow its business and profitability to such an extent that dividends of 10 per cent were easily paid on preference and ordinary shares, leaving large unpaid surpluses to help finance the expansion of factories and tyre depots.

Post-war prosperity was to experience its first serious downturn, however, in 1961. During that year, the Australian economy experienced a serious balance of payments problem, and the federal government imposed a 'credit squeeze' to curtail consumer demand. New car sales fell markedly as a result of this government policy, directly affecting Dunlop's tyre revenues. Dunlop was also coming under increasing market pressure with the influx of cheap imported tyres, which by 1967 accounted for one in six tyre replacements.

While the 'credit squeeze' policy and the threat posed by imported tyres adversely affected Dunlop's performance in the tyre market, their diversification enabled the organisation to weather the economic downturn relatively unscathed. In 1966, Blackwood stepped down as general manager. Without fanfare, he had turned Dunlop into one of Australia's top five manufacturing companies, enjoying one of its most profitable periods in its history. Dunlop was now to enter a new phase in its history under the guidance of Eric Dunshea.

Turmoil II, 1966–80

Eric Dunshea had been the driving force behind Dunlop in the last three years of Blackwood's reign. As company secretary, he had been responsible for overseeing the 1963 reorganisation of the company into five divisions: Automotive (tyres); Industrial; Footwear and Weatherproof Clothing; Flooring; and Sporting Goods. Under this reorganisation, each division was run as an autonomous group, with its own general manager. In a sense, the Dunlop Group was once again divided into separate entities. It was Dunshea's success in this restructuring effort that persuaded the board to appoint him as Blackwood's successor.

One of Dunshea's first efforts was to develop a 12-year plan for the company, which he believed would enable the firm to hold international competitors at bay. The plan was based on a massive capital works campaign, the largest ever conceived by an Australian company. This program was designed to improve Dunlop's existing stock of capital and allow it to produce greater amounts of quality goods at a much lower cost. This strategy proved to be successful from the very start, with Dunlop enjoying significant profit increases through both increased sales and cost minimisation.

By 1968, Dunshea's capital works campaign had been so successful that new projects were sought. Dunshea became 'obsessed' with the notion that Dunlop needed to seek new business opportunities in new industries that offered significant growth potential. Consequently, the incremental profitability generated by the capital improvement was channelled into a renewed acquisition strategy. Such was the fervour of the acquisition strategy that the capital improvements program, the goose laying the golden eggs, was effectively forgotten. Between 1968 and 1970, Dunshea would drive Dunlop into an unprecedented period of acquisition. In December 1968, it was decided that the company would buy a controlling interest in the following firms:

- Ernest-Hiller Holdings;
- Taft Australia;
- Julius Marlow Holdings;
- S.A. Rubber Holdings;
- Halandia Shoes; and
- Frankwell Engineering Industries.

On the first Friday in May 1969, the company decided to purchase the following additional firms:

- Pelaco;
- Yarra Falls;
- Universal Textiles;
- Warrnambool Woollen Mills;
- Qualitaire Holdings; and
- Ansell Rubber Company.

Dunlop's thirst for acquisitions became the talk of Australian business, and Dunshea's power over the board enabled him to implement this arguably excessive pursuit unhindered. It appeared to be Dunshea's goal to transform Dunlop into a conglomerate that would rival those of the Japanese *zaibatsu*. Unfortunately, the effects of Dunshea's buying spree would be somewhat detrimental to the company, and be felt many years into the future. By mid-1971, the unthinkable was almost certain to occur: Dunlop was running out of cash. There were calls from within the company for each of the five divisions to cut their expenditure in favour of a cash-saving strategy. Concerns were also voiced about the lack of integration within the business, and the manner in which this affected both communication and efficiency within Dunlop.

While Dunlop was now far less dependent upon the tyre industry than it once was, the company as a whole was now faced with the double-edged sword of its diversification strategy: accumulated debt. By the end of 1971, Dunlop's debt problem peaked, with debt of $1.25 for each $1 of equity. In early 1972, Dunshea died, and control of the company changed: Leith Jarman was appointed CEO, and Robert Blackwood was recalled to the company as chairman of the board. It was felt that Blackwood had served the company well in his last managerial role, and was best suited to manage the firm back to health. At this time, the debt crisis had eased to $1.18 debt to each $1 of equity, but there were still grave fears that liquidators would be called in to deal with the situation. By mid-1973, Blackwood and Jarman had undertaken a massive course of pruning and streamlining of operations. Their efforts were hampered somewhat by the oil crisis of late 1973, a crisis that had presented the Western world with the economic effect of 'stagflation'. Stagflation affected Dunlop's sales across all of its product lines, which in turn plunged it back into negative sales growth and debt servicing issues.

Dunlop's initial response to the new crisis was to eliminate its fashion holdings from the corporate whole, as it was felt the company had no competence in this area and was paying too high an opportunity cost for the capital it had tied up in that industry. During this time, Dunlop also began to explore the cost minimisations available in the offshore production of its footwear into countries such as China and the Philippines. Dunlop was able to weather the economic conditions raised by the oil crisis, through both rationalisation and cost minimisation and the fact that one of its divisions – in particular, the Ansell Rubber Company – had become a major profit centre. By 1977 the company had emerged from the long storm. By the end of 1977, Dunlop had reduced its debt by $18 million and increased its cash reserves to serviceable levels. To further improve Dunlop's performance, the company was given permission to go ahead with a capital hand-back. This had the effect of reducing the number of Dunlop shares in the marketplace, thus increasing the share price as well as increasing the reportable earnings-per-share figures.

After successfully managing the company for a second period, Blackwood stood down from the chairman's position, having done more good for the company than perhaps any other individual. Unfortunately, Dunlop still held interests in a number of unattractive industries, made more so by the fact that the government of the day had flagged the end of tariff protection for those in manufacturing. The next 15 years would see Dunlop again employ a policy of diversification, this time into a plethora of unrelated industries.

Appetite for acquisition, 1980–91

In 1980 there were major changes in the top management of Dunlop. The new chairman of the board, Sir Brian Massy-Greene, replaced the departing Robert Blackwood, and John Gough took the position of CEO. Both men had been with the company for over 10 years, with Gough as the managing director of the footwear division, and Massy-Greene a board member. Their previous history with the company ensured a shared understanding between the two men of the need to continue restructuring the company.

A major factor to shape their thinking was their awareness that Dunlop mainly operated in highly protected industries. Since the 1920s the Australian government had established a 'Fortress Australia' policy, where the labour-intensive manufacturing sector had been artificially protected from international competition by a wall of tariffs and import duties. However, since the mid-1970s the government had progressively dismantled protectionist policies, and this agenda was to continue into the future.

Both men were aware of the deleterious effects that an end to tariff protection would have on the company's profitability. With its reliance on tariff-protected industries such as tyres, clothing and footwear, Dunlop had much to fear. Consequently, the company, under Gough and Massy-Greene, sought to lessen its exposure by a concerted move into non-tariff protected industries. Such a move would require Dunlop over the next 15 years to pursue an aggressive strategy of diversification, often into industries unrelated to their present operations. As the company would later find, such unrelated diversification had both positive and negative consequences.

Given the company's desire to diversify into new areas, it was interesting (if not ironic) that the first action taken by Dunlop in 1980 was to buy the Olympic Tyre and Rubber Company. Since forming in 1933, Olympic had been a thorn in the side of Dunlop, consistently outperforming them in tyre quality and sales. In addition, Olympic's distribution arm, the Beaurepaire Tyre Centres, had allowed Olympic to spread its reach across the country. However, the increasing maturity of the Australian tyre industry, coupled with the growing pressures from imported tyres, meant that the market could only support a few large manufacturers.

In May 1980, Dunlop approached Olympic to discuss the possibility of a takeover. However, Ian Beaurepaire, head of Olympic, rejected the initial offer out of hand. Beaurepaire felt that to sell to Dunlop would diminish his father's accomplishments. Dunlop, however, was determined that the sale should go ahead, and some weeks later Gough made a personal approach to Beaurepaire to discuss this possibility. Gough and Beaurepaire had been old family friends, and after several nights of long and intimate discussion, Beaurepaire relented and withdrew his opposition to the sale. After further negotiations, the deal was finally agreed to in May 1980, with Dunlop assuming a controlling interest in Olympic. After the takeover, the company changed its name to Dunlop Olympic Ltd.

No sooner was the takeover completed than the new entity itself would become a target for acquisition. In December 1980, mining and investment company North Broken Hill Ltd offered to buy the company. Rather than offering to pay cash for Dunlop, North offered Dunlop shareholders one North share for every Dunlop share. As North shares were superior in value to Dunlop share, this offer was very attractive to shareholders. The attractiveness of the offer depended on the relative value of the two companies' shares, and Dunlop decided that the best strategy to ward of this takeover was to employ delaying tactics, hoping for the desired change in the respective share values. Dunlop's prayers were answered when in 1981 there was a fall in mineral prices on the world market, consequently reducing the value of North shares and thus the attractiveness of their takeover offer. By the end of this campaign, North had only succeeded in acquiring approximately 20 per cent of Dunlop's shares, which it subsequently sold to institutional investors.

With the threat from North dissipating, Dunlop could concentrate on the integration of Olympic into

their corporate structure. During the integration process, it was discovered that Olympic had a core competency (and therefore a competitive advantage) in the production of tyres. With this realisation, the decision was taken to close Dunlop's Montague rubber works, with the bulk of tyre production being moved to Olympic's Footscray factory. While this move improved the quality of Dunlop's tyres, problems on the human resources front began to emerge. Ex-Montague employees relocating to the Olympic factory had problems adjusting, and for years in-fighting occurred between the two groups of employees, who continued to view each other as competitors. Dunlop, however, did little to rectify this situation.

In purchasing Olympic, Dunlop had acquired a 50 per cent holding in Olex Cable. Olex was a manufacturer of electrical cabling, and had been operated as a joint venture between Olympic and Nylex. Olex was already a highly profitable operation, and when the opportunity arose in 1982, Dunlop purchased the remaining 50 per cent of the company from Nylex. In 1983, Dunlop ventured further into the electrical industry with the purchase initially of Spinaway Cable, and the subsequent purchase of Lawrence and Hanson, Australia's oldest chain of electrical retailers. Electrical goods would eventually become a core business unit of Dunlop, growing to become the most profitable group in the company by 1986.

In the early 1980s, Dunlop made a number of other purchases. In 1982 it purchased Slumberland, the manufacturer of a range of bedding products. Dunlop already had a stake in the bedding industry through its Sleepmaker range, and it hoped that the purchase of Slumberland would improve this position. In the same year, Dunlop also purchased a 75 per cent stake in Winestock Footwear. This purchase made Dunlop one of the largest footwear customers of the People's Republic of China, and complemented its already substantial links with that country.

The process of acquisitions continued in 1984, with Dunlop Olympic purchasing Dunlop New Zealand Ltd (tyre manufacturer and retailing, industrial products and sporting goods), Olex Canzac Cables, Harpain (insulated panels), David Galt Industries (maker of Tontine pillows) and Pacific Polymers (manufacturers of industrial goods). Later that same year, Dunlop Olympic severed its ties with England, purchasing back Dunlop UK's 25 per cent share in the company. Shortly after the sale, Dunlop UK itself was bought out by BTR, making Dunlop Olympic the flagship of the Dunlop name worldwide.

While continuing to make acquisitions, Dunlop also attempted to increase its profitability through the introduction of the innovative 'Pulsar Battery' in 1984. Dunlop had first manufactured batteries in 1949, then had slowly increased its focus on batteries, first through a joint venture with Oldhams in 1960, and second through the purchase of Marshall (Batteries) Holdings Pty Ltd in 1967. The arrival of the Pulsar battery was much heralded. It had taken the company 17 years of research and development to develop the Pulsar, at a cost in excess of $32 million. The Pulsar was thought to have many advantages over existing batteries, in that it was much smaller, lighter and technologically advanced. Dunlop commenced mass production of the Pulsar in 1985, building a new factory at Geelong to service the Australian market, and purchasing North American battery manufacturer Chloride Group plc for its US and Canadian production. In 1986 the Pulsar was awarded the Australian Product Design Award, and it appeared that it would be a successful product for the company.

While it had taken Dunlop 17 years to develop the Pulsar, it would take just 17 months for them to realise it was not the success they had expected. The Pulsar was inefficient and costly to produce, with a rejection rate of around 15 per cent at the Geelong factory. In addition, the Pulsar had been designed for the larger vehicles common to the 1970s, not the smaller, streamlined cars of the 1980s. The cost of retooling the factories to accommodate the need for different battery sizes was found to be prohibitive. In addition, the market did not perceive the Pulsar battery to offer a point of difference. To counter this problem, Dunlop introduced the Switch battery, which was effectively two Pulsar batteries combined into the one unit, with a switch allowing the consumer to switch cells should the main cell go 'flat'. While the Switch proved more successful than the Pulsar, it still failed to prevent further factory closures and reductions in stock levels.

The failure of the Pulsar battery scheme was not considered a major financial disaster for Dunlop, given that profit levels remained healthy due to the excellent economic conditions that prevailed at the time of its launch. In 1985, acquisitions continued, with Dunlop purchasing outright the Hamilton Shoe Company, Apair Ltd (latex gloves), Flexible Hose Ltd, Celluform (manufacturer of polystyrene boxes), Futurform (plastic compounds), Lamprecht (industrial gloves), Kelga (industrial gloves) and Pharmaseal (surgeons' gloves). Controlling interests in Chemtron (an electrical wholesaler) and lesser shares in Holeproof Industries Ltd (clothing) were also acquired. Dunlop also entered into a joint venture with M.S. Mcleod to distribute tyres in South Australia and Western Australia.

In 1986, after a further series of acquisitions (including Joubert & Joubert (foam), Hallmark industries (fibre products), Frank Allen Tyres, R.D. Park and Solomon Bros (electrical distribution), A.J. Clader & Hoey Fry (industrial) and Desco (footwear)), watershed financial highlights were achieved by Dunlop, with sales exceeding $2 billion and profit exceeding $100 million for the first time. By 1986, Dunlop had truly become an acquisition-driven company. Indeed, as the chairman himself reports in the annual financial statement, 'acquisitions help growth'. Importantly for Dunlop, profits from their international operations exceeded 25 per cent of the total profit figure. Such a strong performance signalled Dunlop's emergence as a significant international manufacturer. From this point, it would become an objective of Dunlop's management to have 30 per cent of their total company profits derived from their international operations.

In line with its move towards an international focus, Dunlop engaged in a series of joint ventures with leading Chinese manufacturers to produce their ever-expanding range of products. This series of joint ventures was to provide Dunlop with access to cheaper production, thus enabling it to compete more effectively in the global marketplace, while providing Dunlop with a foothold in the potentially lucrative Chinese market.

While Dunlop disclosed high profitability in its 1986 annual report, there were some financial indicators that could potentially undermine its performance in the future. The first major financial issue was its debt to equity ratio. While hard measures had had to be taken in the mid-1970s to reduce Dunlop's debt and ward off the liquidators, its spending spree of the 1980s had again returned Dunlop to a potentially precarious position, owing more than it owned. By 1985, for example, the ratio of debt to equity was 131.7 per cent, improving slightly in the following year to 122.2 per cent. Although this ratio should perhaps have been of great concern to management, only passing attention was given to the fact in the 1986 annual report.

A second issue was that of the structure of the Dunlop Corporation. In 1986, Dunlop controlled operations in six separate divisions:

- International Battery Group;
- Electrical Products;
- Consumer Products;
- Latex and Medical Products;
- Tyre Retailing; and
- Tyre Manufacturing.

As it had done in the past, Dunlop operated these divisions as autonomous entities, both between the divisions themselves, as well as between the business units within the divisions. The only requirement Dunlop placed upon its acquisitions strategy through the 1980s was that the target firm be profitable. In growth markets, little attention was given to whether a target firm could actually add synergistic value to the Dunlop Group. As a result, very few synergies were sought, or achieved, between and within Dunlop's many business units. This acquisition strategy was found to be effective in times of economic growth. However, in times of economic downturn and lower earnings, the lack of synergistic efficiencies within Dunlop meant that the firm was relatively unable to achieve cost savings and to compete efficiently in the majority of its markets.

At the end of 1986, Dunlop again decided to change its corporate name, this time to better reflect its position in Australia and its significance as a player in the international marketplace. The name selected was Pacific Dunlop. The 'Dunlop' name was retained as it represented a link to its past, while 'Pacific' was added as it indicated not only its main region of operations, but also complied with an image of a 'fresh and clean' start to a new era.

The 'new era' began with a continuation of the past. Dunlop embarked upon yet another round of acquisitions, with one of its major purchases being Bonds, Coats, Patons Ltd (the manufacturer of such brands as Gotcha, Bonds, Dry-Glo and Cotton-Tails). This purchase made it the largest manufacturer of clothing in Australia – a long way from its beginnings as a tyre manufacturer. Increasingly, Dunlop's acquisition strategy focused on the purchase of leading brand names. According to CEO John Gough, Dunlop's business was the 'management of outstanding brands with high public awareness'. By this stage it already had a strong stable of brands, such as Adidas, Slazenger, Olympic, Ansell, Sleepmaker, Marshall, Bonds and Holeproof.

In addition, Dunlop entered into a joint venture with Goodyear in an effort to combine their Australian, New Zealand and Papua-New Guinea operations. This venture was given the corporate title of the South Pacific Tyre Company Ltd, and effectively reduced the competitive nature of the tyre industry by assimilating a number of major tyre brands into the one corporate group.

Management problems began to emerge in 1987, by which stage the company was operating 163 factories and over 1 000 retail outlets in countries throughout the globe. The company's head office was relatively small, with most of the key decisions delegated to the individual divisions, business units and subsidiary companies. The decentralisation of control ensured that there was little cooperative effort throughout the company. To counter this issue, further restructuring of its divisions was undertaken. The six-division structure was maintained as a framework; however, the composition of these divisions was changed:

- Batteries;
- Consumer Products;
- Electrical Products;
- Latex and Medical Products;
- Industrial Products; and
- Tyre Manufacturing and Retailing.

The restructure was viewed as a success, gauged by the increasing profitability of the firm. Dunlop managed to increase its profits of the previous year by 34 per cent, as well as to exceed a 20 per cent return on shareholder funds for the first time. International operations were still delivering excellent returns, accounting for 33 per cent of the group's total profit margin. On the back of the company's record-breaking profit margins, John Gough decided to 'call it a day', resigning his CEO position at the end of 1987, and undertaking the lesser position of deputy chairman. His replacement was Phillip Brass, who, like Gough, was a company insider, transferring from the general manager position in the footwear division.

Although Dunlop undertook a number of acquisitions in 1988, arguably the most important were those of Nucleus Ltd and Telectronics. These two companies were the leading manufacturers of cutting-edge medical technologies, namely heart pacemakers and bionic (Cochlear) implants. Dunlop believed that such purchases would enable the group to reap the rewards of the new life-saving technologies, while further diversifying the company away from its reliance on rubber. Dunlop also strengthened its position in the automotive spare-parts and servicing industry through its purchase of Repco Auto Parts, Trader's Auto, and Check-Point Brake and Clutch. In total, Dunlop spent $424 million on acquisitions in 1988, while only $147 million was spent on capital improvements. To fund this buying spree, Dunlop had borrowed a further $267 million, compared with $62 million the previous year.

By 1988, it was becoming apparent to Dunlop that its Ansell operations were fast becoming the major contributor of profit to the company. While many of Dunlop divisions still operated in mature markets with low growth potential, Ansell was a world leader in the production of such items as surgical gloves, medical gloves, household gloves, balloons and condoms. Much of the growth in Ansell's sales, both in medical gloves and condoms, had been driven by the worldwide fear of the HIV epidemic. To support the growth of Ansell, one of the capital works programs undertaken by Dunlop was the establishment of a new Ansell factory in Sri Lanka.

The five-year period 1985–9 had been a period of exceptional performance for Dunlop. During this time, earnings per share had exceeded a compound growth of 18 per cent per year and a return on shareholder equity exceeding 20 per cent. The company was continuing to generate funds from a much more diverse basis of operation. This basis was further expanded in 1989 by the purchases of Nicolet (hearing aids) and 3M's pacemaker implant business. These acquisitions were designed to build on the foundation provided for by Nucleus in the medical technology arena. In line with its expansion into a wider range of business activities, Dunlop restructured its operating divisions, replacing its six-division structure with a seven-division structure comprised of:

- Ansell International;
- Distribution Group;
- GNB Batteries;
- Medical Group;

- Pacific Brands;
- Industrial Foam, Fibre and Cable; and
- South Pacific Tyres.

The good times continued for Dunlop in 1990, with profits reaching a record high of $300 million, on the back of total company sales of over $5 billion. The company made a further round of acquisitions, purchasing the Roberts Group (market leaders in floor coverings), Vita Pacific (manufacturer of bedding and outdoor furniture) and Burton Cables (manufacturer of the Click brand of electrical accessories). Dunlop also entered into a second joint venture with Goodyear, this time in industrial rubber products. Through this joint venture, the two companies would increase their production of both steel-cord and fabric conveyer belting.

By the start of 1991, Dunlop's program of acquisitions had achieved the desired effect of reducing the company's exposure to the tyre industry, with only 10 per cent of revenue now derived from tyres. However, many on the board of Dunlop were still concerned that these acquisitions had not gone far enough, with many of the company's businesses operating in markets that were expected to mature by 1995. In a bold attempt to improve this situation, Dunlop would undertake its most ambitious takeover to date, with the 1991 purchase of Petersville Sleigh. Petersville Sleigh was a giant in the food industry, controlling highly visible brands such as Peters, Pauls, Edgell, Birds Eye, Four 'n' Twenty Pies, Wedgwood and Herbert Adams pies, cakes and pastries, and Robur and Twinings teas. In addition to their food interests, Petersville Sleigh bought Banbury Engineering (sellers of heavy earthmoving equipment), two retail chains (Hardy's and Robb Brown), a group of sawmills, and half of shipping company Patrick Sleigh.

Dunlop saw many similarities between itself and Petersville Sleigh. Both were manufacturers, both were Australian-owned, both were marketing-led companies, and both had strong ties with their retailers. Certainly, Petersville Sleigh had highly recognisable brands and excellent market share in most of its product markets. By Dunlop's estimations, Petersville controlled 40 per cent of the ice cream market, 35 per cent of frozen foods, 40 per cent of pies and pastries, and 20 per cent of the baby food market. By purchasing Petersville Sleigh, Dunlop would automatically become one of the largest players in the Australian food industry, an industry it perceived to have considerable growth potential.

The problem for Dunlop was that the share market did not share its enthusiasm for the Petersville Sleigh takeover. Many questioned Dunlop's estimation that the food market was a growth industry, highlighting that growth in this industry was largely tied to population and Australia's population growth had stagnated. Questions were also raised about Dunlop's view of the similarities between the two companies, failing to see the links between pacemakers and ice cream (except, perhaps, that too much of one would lead to dependence later in life on the other). The financial position of Petersville Sleigh was also a cause for concern. Under the control of previous owner Adsteam, considerable amounts of the company's funds had been channelled into somewhat 'dubious' investments and servicing the debt of the Adsteam Group.

In spite of these opposing views, Dunlop went ahead with the takeover, paying over $390 million for Petersville Sleigh. With this takeover complete, Dunlop had spent $1.5 billion on acquisitions in just four years. This had, however, come at a cost, with the company's debt to equity ratio now running at 165.8 per cent, representing an outstanding debt of $572 million. As a result of this acquisition, Dunlop again changed its corporate structure, moving from seven to five operating divisions, these being:

- Consumer Products (Pacific Brands, Pacific Brands Food Groups);
- Healthcare (Medical Group and Ansell International);
- Automotive (GND Batteries and South Pacific Tyres);
- Building and Construction; and
- Distribution.

Each of these divisions continued to operate autonomously, each with their own managing directors responsible for the performance of that group. Increasingly, the company's actions were driven by a belief in the value of strong brands, and that strong brands would provide the springboard to further growth.

Skidding into decline, 1991–2000

In late 1991 and early 1992 the Australian economy went into a recession that 'we had to have'. With Dunlop's exposure to building and construction, and to consumer markets such as clothing, footwear and food, the recession had a major impact on the company's profitability, reducing total company profit by over 10 per cent. At the same time, the company's accumulated debt increased from $572 million to $711 million, a figure that represented an 11-fold increase over 1987 debt levels. The combined effect of the economic downturn and the recent purchase of Petersville Sleigh brought Dunlop's acquisitions spree forcibly to a halt.

Rather than purchasing more firms, Dunlop turned its attention to consolidating its recent acquisitions. In particular, considerable attention was given to improving the performance of Petersville Sleigh. Closer inspection of the company (after acquisition) revealed that although it was generating cash and owned brands that were market leaders, its plant and equipment were underinvested to such a point that these same brands were basically profitless. Had the equipment been at a current standard, an extra $34 million in profit could have been generated from its food operations. Dunlop also found that what profit was being made by Petersville Sleigh was coming from the company's comparatively small non-food operations.

Problems also began to emerge for Dunlop in its Telectronics business. Telectronics was a leading manufacturer of pacemakers, designed to regulate the heartbeat of patients with cardiac problems. However, during 1992, doctors began to report design problems with Telectronics' pacemakers, some even citing them as the cause of patient death. The problems from Telectronics would cost Dunlop dearly. Over the next four years, six deaths and 36 injuries were attributed to the Telectronic heart pacemaker, and would cost the company in excess of $400 million in lawsuits and out-of-court settlements. In 1996, Dunlop sold its holdings in Telectronics to distance itself from the major issues arising from its operations. Unfortunately, the damage had already been done to Dunlop's reputation and bank balance.

By 1993, the Australian economy began to show signs of recovery, with Dunlop's profits improving by 15 per cent over the previous year, and the company being successful in winning two contracts to supply fibre-optic cable to the value of $125 million. While Dunlop had regained some of the ground lost to the recession, the Dunlop board expressed concerns that the company's range of products and global markets had not protected Dunlop from the ravages of the recession, as hoped. The blame for the company's worse-than-expected performance was placed squarely by analysts upon the continuing lack of integration between business units and divisions.

In order to overcome such criticism, and to improve the performance of its Pacific Brands Food Group, Dunlop purchased Plumrose Food Australia and New Zealand. Plumrose controlled such brands as Yoplait, Petit Miam, Leggo's, Harvest and Plumrose. It was expected that the addition of Plumrose would enable Dunlop to achieve 'significant synergies' in its food operations and to overcome some of the problems they had in food production. The purchase of Plumrose also increased the 'stable of leading Australian brands' controlled by Dunlop.

By 1994, Dunlop management claimed that the strength of the company came from both the diversity of its product range and its global operations. Management believed that further product innovation and market development would generate still greater growth in the future. This philosophy was put into practice by a number of joint ventures and licensing agreements with Asian countries. The bulk of this activity was centred upon China, a country once thought of by Dunlop as largely a base for cheaper production, but now viewed as a high-potential market for sales and profit growth. Dunlop planned to double its investment in China over the next five years, increasing its total assets in that country to $400 million. Of greatest note for this financial year was the company's success in achieving a contract to provide fibre-optic cabling for the Chinese government. This project would enable telecommunications between the east and west of the country to improve to world-best standards.

Dunlop, despite the purchase of Plumrose, still experienced problems with its food division. To further improve the profitability of the division, the company invested money in a new 'state of the art' chip manufacturing plant at Ulverstone in Tasmania. Unfortunately, due to the design of the plant, any fault along the production line would result in the total shutdown of all factory operations. As Murphy's Law would suggest, the plant experienced major production stoppages early in its life. Although the factory did overcome some teething difficulties, and had increased the profitability of the group, sales figures failed to achieve much over half of the projected $100 million forecast by management.

The poor performance of the company's food operations in 1994 was to act as a precursor for the particularly difficult year that the entire company would experience in 1995. Under the weight of apparent inefficiencies and spiralling debt (now running at some $1.2 billion), Dunlop's profit for the year ran at some 20 per cent below the previous year. The share price fell accordingly, and pressure was put to bear on management to take immediate and corrective action to prevent the company from sliding even further into decline. As a result, the board decided to adopt a new 'strategy' to focus on what were now to be considered 'core business areas': GNB Technologies, Pacific Industries, Pacific Brands and Distribution. In line with this strategy, Pacific Brands Food was sold. Dunlop also divested its Cochlear operations to avoid any further damage to its reputation from impending and potential lawsuits against that subsidiary. To support what the company viewed as its 'new core businesses', a number of new acquisitions were made: Smith & Nephew plc (medical gloves) and Boydex Outerwear (a clothing manufacturer). It was hoped that by focusing on a few 'core business areas', Dunlop could become far more streamlined than in the recent past and finally achieve synergies between its operations.

Despite the major restructuring and divestment undertaken by the company throughout 1994 and 1995, the pressure on Brass to step down as CEO grew to such an extent, that in February 1996 he resigned his position, with Rod Chadwick assuming the role. It was widely viewed that Brass's biggest mistakes were to buy into businesses (such as medical and food) that were outside Pacific Dunlop's core activities of clothing, rubber, cables and industrial products. Indeed, media coverage had described Pacific Dunlop as 'just another bloated and hopelessly over-diversified conglomerate'. In accepting the role of CEO, Chadwick cited the need to rebuild consumer confidence in Pacific Dunlop within 18 months or face the real possibility of takeover – or perhaps even liquidation.

Chadwick recognised that Ansell International had proved to be the company's 'shining light', and that an improvement in Pacific Dunlop's performance as a whole would require further funding for this business unit. To achieve this end, the only major acquisitions undertaken by Pacific Dunlop in 1996–7 were those of JK Chemicals (in 1996), an Indian condom manufacturer, and Golden Needles Knitting (in 1997), the world's leading safety gloves manufacturer.

By mid-1997, the market was warming to Chadwick's focus, and Dunlop's share price and profitability were both beginning to improve. Chadwick's vision and efforts to change the corporate culture within Pacific Dunlop impressed market analysts. As part of Chadwick's plans, the seemingly impenetrable walls between the company's divisions and business units were dismantled by moving people between divisions and promoting cross-divisional communications. This was a revolutionary new approach for Dunlop, which, in the past, had believed that the divisions and business units were best run as single and autonomous entities.

It was also part of Chadwick's vision that unprofitable or underperforming business units be divested from the company, and that operations should be further streamlined through factory closures. Increasingly, attention was focused on GNB Batteries, which was one area of operation performing well below expectations. While the company was happy to hold on to GNB for the time being, the possibility that this unit would be divested was only dependent upon the location of a buyer.

Chadwick's popularity with market analysts and the stock market soon came to an end. While promising much improvement by way of streamlining and divestments, profit levels slumped drastically during 1998, resulting in a subsequent fall in share price. Apart from Ansell, all of Pacific Dunlop's businesses performed poorly. Further divestments were forthcoming in a 'last ditch' effort to achieve improved performance. Most notable was the sale of Olex to a US corporation, removing Pacific Dunlop from the cabling industry altogether.

Ironically, for Pacific Dunlop, its most profitable activities at this time were to emanate from the rubber industry, the industry on which it had always attempted to lessen its reliance. Ansell, the world leader in latex rubber products, was the standout performer for Pacific Dunlop. Ansell's earnings for 1998 exceeded $150 million (41 per cent of the company's total), while its individual value was put at $2.5 billion (75 per cent of Pacific Dunlop's market capitalisation value). The potential of Ansell to add value to Pacific Dunlop was well recognised by market analysts and Pacific Dunlop's management. The company adopted a strategy that no further large acquisitions would be undertaken, in favour of a series of small purchases aimed to strengthen Ansell's position in the world market.

Despite the sound approach undertaken by Chadwick, Pacific Dunlop's performance on the stock market continued to decline rapidly. Few major industrial stocks had performed as badly as Pacific Dunlop in the mid- to late 1990s, its share price halving in the period post-1995 and wiping a staggering $1.4 billion from shareholder value. Potential investors were obviously sceptical about Pacific Dunlop's ability to perform – even to survive – into the near future. In fact, the company itself was actively scouting the world for potential buyers for its non-rubber industry divisions. The problem for Pacific Dunlop, however, was that apart from Ansell, its 'for sale' divisions were not attractive, as they represented underperforming entities in mature, low-growth industries. In fact, discounting Ansell from the company, the remaining business divisions were valued at a mere $10 million each. Arguably its most saleable division was its distribution

Exhibit 2 | PDP, Pacific Dunlop Limited, balance sheets, 2000

Balance sheets of Pacific Dunlop Limited and Controlled Entities for the year ended 30 June 2000

($mn)	Notes	Consolidated 2000	Consolidated 1999	Consolidated 1998	The Company 2000	The Company 1999	The Company 1998
Current assets							
Cash	11	1 077.9	1 072.3	997.3	28.0	30.7	31.2
Receivables	12	784.7	987.5	978.7	2 798.0	2 404.1	2 243.4
GNB assets held for sale		591.2	—	—	18.8	—	—
Inventories	13	848.7	952.2	1 021.9	162.8	175.8	210.7
Prepayments		41.5	58.9	58.5	21.8	28.1	13.6
Total current assets		3 344.0	3 070.9	3 056.4	3 029.4	2 638.7	2 498.9
Non-current assets							
Receivables	12	39.2	45.8	69.8	29.7	34.5	48.6
Investments	14	127.6	148.4	166.9	2 853.6	3 034.6	3 065.2
Property, plant and equipment	15	658.2	1 065.8	1 257.7	93.0	120.9	212.1
Intangibles	16	627.8	607.8	683.4	18.5	14.5	46.4
Future income tax benefit	17	272.0	280.2	363.8	145.3	154.5	142.4
Other		16.9	—	—	16.4	—	—
Total non-current assets		1 741.7	2 148.0	2 541.6	3 156.5	3 359.0	3 514.7
Total Assets		5 085.7	5 218.9	5 598.0	6 185.9	5 997.7	6 013.6
Current Liabilities							
Accounts payable	18	566.4	725.7	795.8	1 881.2	1 957.5	1 853.6
Borrowings	19	1 889.4	1 340.3	1 419.4	1 485.7	1 107.1	1 167.0
Provisions	20	403.9	508.3	562.4	203.8	209.3	230.6
Other	21	3.3	7.1	2.4	1.4	2.9	2.6
Total current liabilities		2 863.0	2 581.4	2 780.0	3 572.1	3 276.8	3 253.8
Non-current liabilities							
Accounts payable	18	5.7	14.0	14.2	0.4	0.4	0.7
Borrowings	19	627.7	781.0	848.1	626.0	627.0	656.1
Provisions	20	71.8	174.9	228.2	5.7	4.6	5.9
Other	21	17.6	33.3	35.8	17.6	18.9	20.3
Total non-current liabilities		722.8	1 003.2	1 126.3	649.7	650.9	683.0
Total liabilities		3 585.8	3 584.6	3 906.3	4 221.8	3 927.7	3 936.8
Net assets		1 499.9	1 634.3	1 691.7	1 964.1	2 070.0	2 076.8
Shareholders' equity							
Share capital	5	1 617.2	1 776.0	514.9	1 617.2	1 776.0	514.9
Reserves	6	(31.2)	(102.1)	1 188.9	10.2	10.0	1 266.0
(Accumulated losses)/retained profits	6	(103.6)	(65.4)	(38.2)	336.7	284.0	295.9
Shareholders' equity attributable to Pacific Dunlop Limited shareholders		1 482.4	1 608.5	1 665.6	1 964.1	2 070.0	2 076.8
Outside equity interests in controlled entities	10	17.5	25.8	26.1	—	—	—
Total shareholders' equity		1 499.9	1 634.3	1 691.7	1 964.1	2 070.0	2 076.8

The above balance sheets should be read in conjunction with the accompanying notes.

Exhibit 3 | PDP, Pacific Dunlop Limited, profit and loss statements, 2000

**Profit and Loss Statements
of Pacific Dunlop Limited and Controlled Entities
for the year ended 30 June 2000**

($mn)	Notes	Consolidated 2000	1999	1998	The Company 2000	1999	1998
Revenue							
Sales revenue		5 725.8	5 680.0	5 473.0	1 691.2	1 933.1	2 004.5
Other revenue	4	88.4	333.8	122.9	266.7	466.5	314.5
Total revenue		5 814.2	6 013.8	5 595.9	1 957.9	2 399.6	2 319.0
Costs and expenses							
Cost of goods sold		4 080.2	3 951.8	3 806.5	1 060.0	1 246.1	1 339.6
Selling general and administrative		1 395.3	1 662.4	1 410.0	530.9	973.2	949.2
Total costs and expenses		5 475.5	5 614.2	5 216.5	1 590.9	2 219.3	2 288.8
Interest expense	3	146.4	142.9	153.6	122.2	110.2	113.4
Operating profit/(loss) before abnormal items and income tax		192.3	256.7	225.8	244.8	70.1	(83.2)
Abnormal items before income tax	7	(244.9)	(94.0)	(157.5)	(235.8)	54.8	(15.4)
Operating profit/(loss) before income tax		(52.6)	162.7	68.3	9.0	124.9	(98.6)
Income tax attributable to operating profit/(loss)	8	29.8	51.2	44.5	13.0	(8.5)	(91.7)
Operating profit/(loss) after income tax		(82.4)	111.5	23.8	(4.0)	133.4	(6.9)
Outside equity interests in operating profit after income tax		4.1	5.7	(1.0)	—	—	—
Operating profit/(loss) after income tax attributable to Pacific Dunlop Limited shareholders		(86.5)	105.8	24.8	(4.0)	133.4	(6.9)
(Accumulated losses)/Retained profits at the beginning of the financial year		(65.4)	(38.2)	116.1	284.0	295.9	449.8
Adjustment to retained profits at the beginning of the financial year on initial adoption of revised AASB1016 Accounting for Investments in Associates	1	—	—	(23.3)	—	—	—
Amount transferred from share capital	6	160.0	—	—	160.0	—	—
Aggregate of amounts transferred from reserves	6	(8.4)	12.1	(11.6)	—	(0.8)	(2.8)
Total available for appropriation		(0.3)	79.7	106.0	440.0	428.5	440.1
Dividends provided for or paid							
Redemption of Bonds Preference Shares		—	0.6	—	—	—	—
Interim and final dividends	9	103.3	144.4	144.1	103.3	144.4	144.1
Under provision for prior year interim and final dividends		—	0.1	0.1	—	0.1	0.1
(Accumulated losses)/retained profits at end of financial year		(103.6)	(65.4)	(38.2)	336.7	284.0	295.9
Summary of operating profit for the year							
Operating profit/(loss) after income tax attributable to Pacific Dunlop Limited shareholders		(86.5)	105.8	24.8	(4.0)	133.4	(6.9)
Abnormal items after income tax attributable to Pacific Dunlop Limited shareholders							
Operating profit after income tax before abnormal items attributable to Pacific Dunlop Limited shareholders		140.9	199.8	180.8	225.1	78.5	8.5
Earnings per share based on operating profit after income tax attributable to Pacific Dunlop Limited shareholders							
					cents	cents	cents
Basic earnings per share before goodwill amortisation and abnormal items					17.5	23.2	21.1
Basic earnings per share before abnormal items					13.6	19.4	17.6
Basic earnings per share inclusive of abnormal items					(8.4)	10.3	2.4

The above profit and loss statements should be read in conjunction with the accompanying notes.

arm, consisting of Repco and the wholesale distributors of Pacific Dunlop's electrical and automotive parts, which was still exhibiting a reasonable return.

Chadwick's challenge, 2001–

Certainly, it can be said that Pacific Dunlop has had more than its share of bad luck, stemming back to the 1920s when it purchased Perdriau and Barnett Glass just before a depression decimated the tyre market. It had also been unlucky in 1992, just after the major purchase of Petersville Sleigh, to encounter the economic downturn of the 'recession that Australia had to have'. Pacific Dunlop, however, could also be accused of habitual bad management, manifesting itself in spectacular acquisitions (primarily undertaken by Dunshea and Brass) and an ongoing failure to achieve synergies between any of its operations and divisions.

Chadwick, as CEO entrusted with the job of improving Dunlop's performance and standing in the market, was forced to ask himself the question: 'Is the predicament facing Pacific Dunlop a result of bad luck or bad management?' and, regardless of the answer, how was he to turn things around? Should Chadwick actively listen to the advice of contemporary market analysts, he would find himself faced with several important strategic choices. The first would be to consolidate the business units as they exist, and to attempt (through further restructuring) to better integrate their operations such that the firm could actually harness any available synergistic advantages. The second choice would be for Dunlop to undertake further acquisition measures, as it had done in the past reasonably successfully, in order to purchase its way back to profitability – surely the bad luck of the 1990s could not continue forever. A third choice, and perhaps most popularly advanced, is the divestment of all businesses with the exception of the Ansell Group, the one truly excellent profit centre that the company possesses.

Whichever strategic decision Chadwick undertakes, it would seem that he can ill afford to ignore the effects of the external economic forces at play. Throughout its entire history, it would seem that Pacific Dunlop's management has operated in a virtual vacuum, seemingly oblivious to the external economic environment and the effect that this environment has had on the company. Will this external environment enforce a liquidation of Pacific Dunlop, or will Chadwick be able to reverse the decades of bad luck and bad management and see the company continue into the third millennium as a force to be reckoned with?

References

Blainey, G., 1993, *Jumping Over the Wheel* (Sydney: Allen & Unwin).
Burge, G., 1999, 'Lowly PacDun looks to chairman Ralph', *Australian Financial Review*, 2 July.
Deans, A., 1995, 'Tripped up by a pacemaker', *Australian Financial Review*, 3 February.
Durie, J., 1998, 'PacDun's battery goes flat', *Australian Financial Review*, 20 October.
Durie, J., 1999, 'Waiting for PacDun to deliver', *Australian Financial Review*, 28 April.
Ferguson, A., 1999, 'Time's up for Pacific Dunlop', *Business Review Weekly*, 21(3).
Ferguson, A., 2000, 'Pacific Dunlop skids towards the parts yard', *Business Review Weekly*, 22(3).
Guy, R., 1999, 'PacDun knows the value of protection', *Australian Financial Review*, 20 February.
Hewett, J., 1993, *Australian Financial Review*, 1 October.
McLachlan, C., 1991, 'Crossroads for Pacific Dunlop', *Australian Financial Review*, 8 August.
McLean, T., 2001, 'Time to put PacDun dinosaur out of its misery', *The Australian*, 6 March.
Pacific Dunlop Annual Reports, 1992–2000.
Parkinson, G., 1998, 'PacDun needs a conjuring act', *Australian Financial Review*, 7 July.
Porter, I., 1995, 'How PacDun struggled to get its food strategy right', *Australian Financial Review*, 3 November.
Porter, I., 1997, 'Market applauds PacDun's revival', *Australian Financial Review*, 13 September.
Porter, I., 1998, 'Corporate focus', *Australian Financial Review*, 13 March.
Price, G., 1999, 'The unlucky company', *The Australian*, 23 August.
Ries, I., 1994, 'Potato humbles PacDun', *Australian Financial Review*, 6 December.
Ries, I., 1996, 'Two majors on the brink', *Australian Financial Review*, 15 May.
Ries, I., 1998, 'Rod returns to rubber', *Australian Financial Review*, 3 October.
Tilston, J., 1988, 'John Gough shares success story', *Australian Financial Review*, 29 July.
Webb, R., 1992, 'Pacific Dunlop weathers storm', *Australian Financial Review*, 22 September.
Wood, L., 1992, 'PacDun, BTR still gloomy on recovery hopes', *Australian Financial Review*, 23 March.

Case 11

Philip Morris

Rhonda Fronk
Bill Pilgrim
Bill Prosser
Regan Urquhart
Monte Wiltse
University of Oklahoma

Introduction

After the second quarter of 1998, Philip Morris chairman and chief executive officer Geoffrey C. Bible could look back upon both positive and negative occurrences within the tobacco industry that had an impact on his company during the first half of the year. In its favour, the industry avoided comprehensive federal tobacco legislation in 1998. Such legislation was avoided primarily for two reasons. First, an advertising campaign linking the legislation to tax increases for government spending spurred conservative opposition to the proposed legislation. Second, the President was involved in an investigation regarding possible felony violations. The investigation forced the President to focus his energies on events other than the tobacco legislation.

Philip Morris, however, was still concerned with the continued prospect of future federal legislation that might have a severe impact upon the profitability of the firm's domestic operations. Additionally, there were significant and numerous legal actions being taken against Philip Morris by parties claiming damages caused by tobacco products. On the operations side, the company had seen a decline of almost 6 per cent in cigarette shipments in the second quarter due in part to price increases and consumer promotions.[1]

Given this background, there are a number of ethical, legal and operational issues facing Philip Morris. As the health risks associated with the use of tobacco have become more evident, public sentiment against tobacco companies is becoming increasingly negative. Many feel that the companies have a responsibility to eliminate nicotine from their products and to discontinue marketing to minors. Others claim that management's only responsibility is to shareholders and not to the public at large. How can Philip Morris continue its success in the midst of pending and threatened litigation and negative public sentiment both in the United States and abroad?

This case begins with an overview of the tobacco industry and a brief history of Philip Morris Company to provide background for the current legal situation. The case will also discuss current Philip Morris competitors such as B.A.T. Industries plc and Gallaher Group plc. Philip Morris business units will be discussed and their financial performance will be addressed. Once the current competitive and internal situations are described, the case will end with a discussion of the legal issues facing Philip Morris and a summary of the future strategic issues the company will face.

Overview of the tobacco industry

The Mayan people first introduced tobacco to Native North Americans in the 15th century. Tobacco use quickly spread throughout Europe and Russia, and by the 17th century it had reached China, Japan and the western coast of Africa.[2] Early proponents claimed that medicinal properties could be found in tobacco.

Tobacco fields were found in colonial America as early as 1615. Tobacco quickly became the staple crop and principal currency in the colony of Jamestown. After 1776, the tobacco business spread to North Carolina and as far west as Missouri. By the late 1880s, the United States was the second-largest tobacco producer after China and was responsible for about 9 per cent of world production.[3]

This case was prepared under the direction of Professor Robert E. Hoskisson. The case is intended to be used as the basis for class discussion rather than to illustrate either effective or ineffective handling of an administrative situation.

About 50 million people in the United States currently smoke a total of 570 billion cigarettes each year.[4] For the first part of the 20th century, society's general attitude was that smoking relieved tensions and produced no ill effects. As recently as the 1940s, smoking was considered harmless, but laboratory and clinical research have proven that smoking can be harmful.[5]

Because of a dramatically noticeable rise in previously rare lung cancer, the American Cancer Society and other organisations began studies comparing death among smokers and non-smokers over a period of several years. All such studies found increased mortality among smokers. As a result of this information, the government became involved in the early 1960s, and ongoing reports and warnings have been issued since that time. All cigarette advertising was banned from radio and television starting in 1971.[6] Research suggests that smokers crave the effect of nicotine. In a 1988 report, the Surgeon General declared nicotine to be an addictive drug comparable to other addictive substances in its ability to induce dependence.[7] A 1989 report stated that smoking definitely did cause cancer and therefore warranted substantial investigation.[8]

Medical studies have established that the overall mortality rate is twice as high among middle-aged men who smoke as among those who do not. The American Cancer Society estimated that cigarettes are responsible for 30 per cent of all US cancer mortality. Cigarette smoke is also estimated to be responsible for 83 per cent of all lung cancer mortality in the United States. Lung cancer is seven times as likely to strike a smoker as a non-smoker. Smoking can also be tied to a number of other forms of cancer and disease, such as strokes and emphysema. While this information, combined with awareness campaigns, has reduced the number of male smokers, there has been a rise in female and teenage smokers despite the Surgeon General's reports.

Cigarette consumption, which accounts for most tobacco use in the United States, dropped slightly after 1964, when a special report to the US Surgeon General linked cigarette smoking with lung cancer, coronary artery disease and other ailments. Since 1987, US cigarette consumption has been slipping by about 2 per cent per year (also see Exhibit 1).[9] This has resulted in two major industry strategies: diversify at home and pursue international business. According to Robert Miles, author of *Coffin Nails and Corporate Strategies*, diversification was the most substantial strategy implemented by the tobacco companies in response to the decreasing consumption.[10] The companies pursuing international business found the formerly communist regions of Eastern Europe and China to be ideal markets for American cigarette makers. Also, tobacco consumption is rising rapidly in developing countries, where tobacco use is projected to increase 2.8 per cent annually. This is supported by a 1974 to 1987 US tobacco export increase from US$650 million to US$3.4 billion.[11]

Exhibit 1 | Tobacco products, United States' per-capita consumption

| | Units | | | Pounds | | |
Year	Cigarettes	Large cigars and cigarillos#	Smoking tobacco#	Chewing tobacco#	Snuff*	Total tobacco products*
1996[P]	2 482	32.7	0.1	0.6	0.31	4.70
1995[R]	2 505	27.5	0.1	0.7	0.31	4.70
1994[R]	2 524	25.3	0.2	0.7	0.32	4.90
1993[R]	2 543	23.4	0.2	0.7	0.30	5.37
1992	2 641	24.5	0.2	0.8	0.29	5.30
1991	2 720	25.1	0.2	0.8	0.28	5.54
1990	2 826	26.4	0.2	0.8	0.28	5.62
1989	2 926	27.9	0.2	0.8	0.27	5.68
1988	3 096	29.1	0.3	0.9	0.26	6.11
1987	3 197	31.7	0.3	0.9	0.25	6.30

* Consumption per capita, 18 years and over.
# Consumption per male, 18 years and over.
P Preliminary.
R Revised.

Source of information: Department of Agriculture.
Source: Standard and Poor's, 1997, 'Alcoholic beverages and tobacco', *Standard and Poor's Industry Survey*, 11 September, p. 12.

The US tobacco industry is highly profitable. It is estimated that one in four Americans smoke, and the average smoker spends US$260 per year on tobacco products.[12] Leaders in the market maintain a monopolistic position because of extremely difficult barriers to entry. Tobacco companies also enjoy almost no capital, research or advertising costs. The product sells as is, leaving no incentive for change. The demand for the product has driven itself, resulting in minimal advertising requirements. Social consciousness alone has greatly reduced the industry's advertising budgets.

Brief history of Philip Morris

In 1847, Philip Morris opened a tobacco shop in London. It was in this London shop that he began making cigarettes. After Morris's death before the turn of the century, the company was sold to William Thomson. Mr Thomson introduced cigarettes to the United States in 1902.

During this same period, the American Tobacco Trust controlled 92 per cent of the world's tobacco.[13] A 1911 US Supreme Court decision broke the trust into four separate companies. Those companies would become American Tobacco (now B.A.T. Industries), R. J. Reynolds, Loews' Lorillard unit and Liggett & Meyers (now Brooke Group subsidiary Liggett Group).

In 1919, American investors purchased Philip Morris and US production began in 1929. Shortly thereafter, the original companies of the American Tobacco Trust began to raise their prices. Philip Morris successfully took advantage of this situation by offering its product at a lower price.

Philip Morris's success can be attributed to its expertise in sales and marketing. The company's early growth was tied to its close alliances with tobacco wholesalers and retailers along the East Coast. As the market evolved, Philip Morris became more dependent on its advertising campaigns. Early on, Philip Morris was promoted as a milder cigarette. Later the company claimed that its English blend did not cause something referred to as 'cigarette hangover'.[14] The company's 1955 introduction of the 'Marlboro man' enabled it to capitalise on the American cowboy image.

Today, Philip Morris is the world's largest cigarette maker. The company leads the cigarette industry in market share, followed by RJR Nabisco and B.A.T. subsidiary, Brown & Williamson. Marlboros account for about a third of all US sales. At the same time, the company gets almost half of its revenues (but only one-third of its profits) from food and beer subsidiaries that include Kraft and Miller Brewing Company. Miller is ranked number two among US beer makers after Anheuser-Busch (see Exhibit 2). The company also operates a financial service and operated a real estate investment division until its sale in 1997.

Overview of competitors

The following overview provides a description of each of Philip Morris's major competitors. Ultimately, this will provide a background to discuss how individual firms might respond to the legal threat considered later.

B.A.T. Industries plc

B.A.T. Industries plc is the world's second-largest tobacco company. It owns both Brown & Williamson (the third-largest tobacco company in the United States) and British-American Tobacco. B.A.T. controlled 16 per cent of the US cigarette market share in 1997.[15] It is planning to spin off the tobacco portion of its business in September or October. In 1997, sales by segment were as follows: tobacco, 71 per cent (53 per cent operating profit); insurance, 29 per cent (47 per cent operating profit).[16] BAT owns 40 per cent of Imasco, which is a Canadian business centred around tobacco and banking. The company has 164 000 employees.[17] Return on equity for the five years including 1993–7 has ranged from 25.2 to 30.0 per cent.[18] Its major tobacco brands are GPC Approved, Kool and Lucky Strike. The chief executive officer (CEO) is Martin Broughton and the company is headquartered in London, England. Shares are traded on the American Stock Exchange (ASE) under the symbol BTI.

Gallaher Group plc

Gallaher Group plc is the largest manufacturer of tobacco products in the United Kingdom, with 39.6 per cent of the market in 1997.[19] In 1997, sales by region were as follows: UK, 87 per cent (84 per cent operating profit); outside UK, 13 per cent (16 per cent operating profit).[20] The company currently has about 3 600 employees.[21] Its major tobacco brands are Silk Cut, Berkeley, Mayfair, Sovereign and Sobranie. Gallaher's lower-priced offerings, Mayfair and Sovereign, are selling well mostly because consumers faced with higher prices due to increased taxation are switching to less expensive brands. The CEO is Peter Wilson and the company is headquartered in the UK. Shares are traded on the New York Stock Exchange (NYSE) under the symbol GLH.

Exhibit 2 | Philip Morris products

Tobacco

Marlboro	Cambridge	Caro	Lark	Next
Benson & Hedges	Basic	Chesterfield	L&M	Peter Jackson
Virginia Slims	*Selected international*	Diana	Longbeach	Petra
Merit	*brands**	f6	Multifilter	Philip Morris
Parliament	Bond Street	Klubowe	Muratti	

Food
Grocery aisles
Beverages
Coffee
  Maxwell House
  Sanka
  Yuban
  General Foods
  International
    Coffees
  Maxim
Soft drinks
  Country Time
  Crystal Light
  Kool-Aid
  Tang
  Capri Sun
Post cereals
  Alpha-Bits
  Banana Nut Crunch
  Blueberry Morning
  Cranberry Almond
    Crunch
  Frosted Shredded
    Wheat
  Fruit & Fiber
  Grape-Nuts
  Great Grains
  Honey Bunches of
    Oats
  Honeycomb
  Honey Nut Shredded
    Wheat
  Natural Bran Flakes
  Pebbles
  Raisin Bran
  Shredded Wheat
  Shredded Wheat 'n
    Bran
  Spoon Size Shredded
    Wheat
  Toasties
  Waffle Crisp
  100% Bran
Condiments & sauces
  Kraft mayonnaise
  Kraft barbecue sauces
  Miracle Whip
  Bull's-Eye barbecue
    and grilling sauces

Sauceworks
  cocktail,
  horseradish,
  sweet 'n sour
  and tartare
  sauces
Confectioneries
  Altoid's mints
  Callard &
    Bowser toffees
  La Vosgienne
  Toblerone
  and Tobler
  chocolates
Dry desserts
  D-Zerta
  Jell-O
  Minute brand tapioca
Dry grocery
  Baker's
    chocolate and
    coconut
  Calumet baking
    powder
  Oven Fry
    coatings
  Shake 'N Bake
  Sure-Jell and
    Certo pectins
Ethnic foods
  Taco Bell
    dinner kits,
    salsa and meal
    components
Meals/side dishes
  Kraft macaroni
    & cheese
  Minute rice
  Stove Top
  Velveeta shells &
    cheese
Salad dressings
  Good Seasons
    mixes
  Kraft
  Seven Seas
Snacks
  Handi-Snacks
Toppings
  Dream Whip

  whipped
  topping mix
  Kraft dessert
  toppings
Refrigerated case
Cheese
  Parmesan/Romano
  Kraft
  Kraft Free
  Di Giorno
  Natural
  Cracker Barrel
  Harvest Moon
  Processed American
    cheese
  Kraft Deluxe
  Kraft Singles
  Kraft Super Slice
  Kraft Cheez
  Whiz
  Light n' Lively
  Old English
  Velveeta
  Cream cheese
  Philadelphia
  Philly Flavors
  Temp-Tee
  Other cheeses
  Althenos
  Chumy
  Di Giorno
  Hoffman
  Polly-O
Dairy products
  Breakstone's
    sour cream and
    cottage cheese
  Breyer's yogurt
  Jell-O yogurt
  Knudsen sour
    cream and
    cottage cheese
  Light n' Lively
    low-fat cottage
    cheese, yogurt
  Sealtest cottage
    cheese, dips and
    sour cream
Desserts
  Ready-to-eat Jell-O

Fresh pasta & sauces
  Di Giorno
Processed meats
  Oscar Mayer
    hot dogs, cold
    cuts and bacon
  Oscar Mayer
    Lunchables
  Louis Rich turkey
    products (hot
    dogs, cold cuts
    and bacon).
  Louis Rich
    Carving Board
    sliced meats
Pickles & sauerkraut
  Claussen
Freezer case
Desserts
  Cool Whip
Pizza
  Di Giorno
  Jack's
  Tombstone
Selected
  international
  *brands**
Cheese
  Dairylea
  El Caserio
  Eden
  Invernizzi
  Philadelphia
  Sottilette
  P'tit Quebec
Coffee
  Blendy
  Carte Noire
  Gevalia
  Grand' Mere
  Kaffee HAG
  Jacobs Kronung
  Jacobs Monarch
  Jacques Vabre
  Kenco
  Maxim
  Nabob
  Saimaza
  Splendid
Confectioneries

  Aladdin
  Africana
  Cote d'Or
  Daim
  Figaro
  Freia
  Hollywood
  Korona
  Marabou
  Milka
  Peanott
  Poiana
  Prince Polo
  Suchard
  Sugus
  Terry's of York
  Toblerone
Other
  Estrella snacks
  Frisco beverages
  Kraft ketchup,
    peanut butter
  Magic Moments
  Miracle Whip
  Miracoli
  Simmenthal
  Vegemite
Beer
  Miller Lite
  Miller High Life Best
  Molson non-alcohol
  Miller Lite Ice
  Miller Beer
  Meister Brau
  Foster's brew
  Miller Genuine
  Red Dog
  Leinenkugel's
  Asahi
  Magnum
  Draft
  Icehouse
  Celis Presidente malt
    liquor
  Miller Genuine
  Lowenbrau
  Shipyard
  Sharp's
  Draft Light
  Milwaukee's

*Not generally available in the United States as Philip Morris products.

Source: Philip Morris Annual Report, inside back cover.

Imasco Ltd

Imasco Ltd is the dominant company in the Canadian cigarette industry with almost 65 per cent of the Canadian market.[22] Tobacco accounts for more than 50 per cent of the company's operating profit.[23] Return on equity for the five years including 1993–7 ran between 13.7 and 17.3 per cent.[24] The company's major tobacco brands are Players and du Maurier. These brands continue to do well even with the virtual ban on tobacco advertising in Canada, which confirms an industry belief that advertising restrictions 'freeze' market positions. Restrictions make it harder for smaller rivals or new entrants to persuade consumers to switch brands. The CEO is Brian Levitt and the company is headquartered in Montreal, Canada.

RJR Nabisco Holdings Corporation

RJR Nabisco, formerly R. J. Reynolds, is the second-largest US producer of cigarettes with about 25 per cent of the market.[25] The company has major positions in both the food and tobacco industries. Food products include Oreo, Chips Ahoy!, Ritz, Wheat Thins, Cream of Wheat and LifeSavers. The company has approximately 80 000 employees.[26] Return on equity for the four years including 1994–7 ran between 7.0 and 9.5 per cent.[27] Its major tobacco brands include Winston, Salem, Camel, Doral, Vantage and More. RJR is test marketing a new tobacco brand named Eclipse in several markets in the United States. Eclipse – which primarily heats tobacco rather than burning it – reduces second-hand smoke by 80 per cent and leaves practically no ash, stains or lingering odour.[28] The CEO is Steven Goldstone and the company is headquartered in New York City. Shares are traded on the NYSE under the symbol RN.

Loews Corporation

Loews is a diversified investment company. Its primary business segments are a multi-line insurance company (85 per cent of 1997 revenues, 81 per cent operating profit)[29] and tobacco segment (12 per cent of 1997 revenues, 29 per cent operating profit).[30] In 1997, Loews held around 8 per cent of the US cigarette market.[31] The company employs approximately 35 000 people.[32] Return on equity for the five years including 1993–7 ran between 5.0 and 21.4 per cent.[33] The company's major tobacco brands include Newport, Kent and True. The CEO is L. A. Tisch and the company is headquartered in New York City. Shares are traded on the NYSE under the symbol LTR.

UST Inc.

UST Inc. is the leading US producer of smokeless tobacco with approximately a 75 per cent share of the moist smokeless segment.[34] Smokeless tobacco products accounted for 86 per cent of sales as well as 97 per cent of the company's profits.[35] The company has approximately 4 500 employees.[36] Return on equity for the five years including 1993–7 ran between 74.9 and 164.5 per cent.[37] Its major brands include Copenhagen, Skoal, Borkum Riff and Don Tomas pipe tobacco. The company has been able to price its products at a premium to the market. It is now beginning to face serious competition from discounters that can deliver similar products for about half the price UST is charging. UST is reluctant to compete in the discount market for fear of cannibalising sales from their premium brands. UST has started a promotional initiative that puts a 'made date' on cans of Copenhagen that indicates the freshness of the product to the consumer. This has led to an increase in the number of cans being returned. The CEO is Vincent Gierer, Jr, and the company is headquartered in Greenwich, Connecticut. Shares are traded on the NYSE under the symbol UST.

Universal Corporation

Universal Corporation, formerly known as Universal Leaf Tobacco, is the largest leaf tobacco exporter/importer in the world. It purchases, processes and sells tobacco to manufacturers. Because many of the other competitors are vertically integrated, Universal is a direct competitor in supply and otherwise indirectly affects competition. The company has approximately 25 000 employees.[38] Return on equity for the five years including 1993–7 was between 9.3 and 21.5 per cent.[39] The CEO is A. B. King and the company is headquartered in Richmond, Virginia. Shares are traded on the NYSE under the symbol UVV.

Philip Morris's business units

Philip Morris understood the need to diversify long before the introduction of the current formal tobacco litigation. Philip Morris and R. J. Reynolds were among the first to begin a serious program of diversification only a few years after the 1964 Surgeon General's Report.[40] Major acquisitions began in 1969 with the purchase of Miller Brewing Co. and continued through the late 1980s with the acquisition of Kraft Foods. After the 1985 acquisition of General Foods, former Philip Morris CEO Hamish Maxwell said, 'We wanted to lessen our dependence on cigarettes as our earnings source, and to spur growth.'[41] By making several major diversification efforts, Philip Morris was able to invest a portion of its cash and diversify the risk of what it perceived to be an inevitable tobacco liability. The resulting family of products created by these acquisitions is delineated in Exhibit 2.

Tobacco

Philip Morris USA (PMUSA) holds the nation's largest market share in retail tobacco sales with 51 per cent. According to *The Maxwell Consumer Report* issued by Wheat, First Securities, Inc., Philip Morris USA has been the leading cigarette company in the US market since 1983.[42] This claim is founded upon the strength of the brand name of its leading cigarette, Marlboro. Marlboro itself holds 35.2 per cent market share in domestic sales.[43] Other Philip Morris tobacco brand names include Basic, Merit, Benson & Hedges, Parliament and Virginia Slims. In 1997, domestic tobacco provided 38 per cent of domestic operating revenue, while providing for 47 per cent of domestic operating income. Operating income margins were 24 per cent in 1997, down significantly from 33 per cent in 1996.

Philip Morris International (PMI) has a cigarette market share of at least 15 per cent in more than 40 markets, including Argentina, Australia, Belgium, the Canary Islands, the Czech Republic, Finland, France, Germany, Hong Kong, Italy, Japan, the Netherlands, the Philippines, Poland, Singapore, Spain, Switzerland and Turkey.[44] Marlboro is the largest-selling brand internationally as well, with 6 per cent of the world market. Philip Morris maintains brands internationally that include Bond Street, Parliament, L&M and Chesterfield. PMI utilises a practice of expanding into new international markets by acquiring existing local brands.[45] This practice has recently been used in Poland, Portugal and Mexico. PMI operating revenues are much more dependent upon tobacco, with 70 per cent of operating revenues coming from tobacco sales, but it has much lower profitability than its domestic counterpart, with only a 17 per cent operating income margin.

Food

Kraft Foods, Inc. (KFI) is the largest processor and marketer of retail packaged food in the United States. KFI is a combination of General Foods Corp., which was acquired in September 1985 for US$5.75 billion,[46] and Kraft Foods, Inc., which was acquired through a hostile takeover in December 1988 for US$12.9 billion.[47] The investment community questioned Philip Morris at the time of these acquisitions for investing in businesses with significantly smaller operating income margins than the traditional tobacco margins. At the time of the General Foods acquisition, analyst David A. Goldman of Dean Witter was quoted as saying, 'Those turkeys, ... this is dumb.'[48] Philip Morris has been able to increase the operating margins on the food business by utilising superior marketing skills, capitalising on the industry knowledge of key personnel from both Kraft and General Foods, and reducing expenses by leveraging common resources across the entire food business.

KFI owns trademarks to major brand names, which include Jell-O, Oscar Mayer, Maxwell House, Post Cereals, Kool-Aid, DiGiorno Pizza and Altoids. In 1997 the domestic division of KFI generated 48 per cent of domestic operating revenues and 41 per cent of domestic operating margins. KFI has shown significant growth in operating income margins, from 14 per cent in 1995 to 17 per cent in 1997.

Internationally, the food business unit has been a globalisation of the existing Kraft and General Foods brand names as well as the acquisition of large international brands. Subsidiaries and affiliates of KFI manufacture and market a wide variety of coffee, confectionery, cheese, grocery and processed meat products in Europe, the Middle East, Africa and the Asia-Pacific region. The international portion of the food business provided an operating income margin of 12 per cent in 1997.

Beer

Philip Morris acquired Miller Brewing in 1969 from W. R. Grace.[49] In 1969, Miller sales placed seventh in the domestic beer market. In less than six years, Miller moved from seventh to fourth place in domestic beer sales and it currently holds the number two position behind Anheuser-Busch. This growth is attributed to the superior marketing expertise of Philip Morris and the overlapped target customer segments for both product categories.

In 1997, the Miller Brewing Company provided Philip Morris with only 3.7 per cent of operating income at a margin of 11 per cent, significantly less than both the tobacco and food business units. The international portion of this business represents only 6 per cent of the volume of the beer business. Philip

Morris has decided to keep the beer business mainly domestic. This was demonstrated when Miller sold its 20 per cent equity stake in Molson Breweries in Canada, but retained majority ownership of Molson USA, LLC, in order to maintain importing, marketing and distribution rights for Molson and Foster's brands in the United States.

Philip Morris's financial performance

The diversification practices of Philip Morris Companies Inc., combined with its ongoing market dominance of the tobacco industry, have yielded tremendous growth in earnings for the company. Exhibit 3 highlights selected financial data of Philip Morris Companies Inc. during the past 11 years. One illustration of the company's growth is its increase in net earnings. This number grew from US$1.8 billion in 1987 to US$6.3 billion in 1997, with an average annual increase of 25 per cent.

Exhibits 4 and 5 show the Philip Morris Companies Inc. balance sheets and results of operations for the six months ending 30 June 1998 and for the years ended 31 December 1995–7. Comparisons of operating results between reporting periods and items of significant impact on operating results are discussed in the following three sections. The discussion will highlight general (consolidated) operations, discuss operating results of the domestic tobacco and international tobacco business segments, and conclude with summary results.

Results of operations – general

As Exhibit 5 illustrates, for the first six months of 1998, operating revenues were in excess of US$37 billion. This represented a 2 per cent increase over the comparable 1997 period for the combined Philip Morris Companies Inc. This increase was primarily the result of an increase in sales of domestic tobacco, international tobacco and North American food operations. Financial services and real estate operating revenues decreased due to the sale of the real estate business in 1997.[50]

Several unique events affected income during the first six months of 1998. In February 1998, the company announced voluntary early retirement and separation programs for salaried and hourly employees, which resulted in pre-tax charges of US$327 million. During the same six-month period, the company recorded pre-tax charges of US$806 million related to the settlement of healthcare cost recovery litigation in Minnesota and US$199 million related to 'Most Favored Nation' clauses in previous state settlement agreements with the states of Mississippi and Texas. Excluding these charges, as well as results from operations divested in 1997, underlying operating income increased 7.4 per cent, or US$484 million, over the first six months of 1997.[51]

Operating revenues in 1997 were approximately US$72 billion, as seen in Exhibits 5 and 6. This was an increase of US$2.9 billion, or 4.1 per cent, over 1996. This improvement was due primarily to sales increases in domestic and international tobacco and North American food operations. Operating profit, however, showed a slight decline of 0.2 per cent, or US$25 million, in comparison to the 1996 results.[52]

Operating results in 1997 were also affected by several singular events. The operating profit decrease was the result of several pre-tax charges. These included US$1.5 billion paid by Philip Morris Incorporated, the company's domestic tobacco subsidiary, for settlement of healthcare cost recovery litigation in Mississippi, Florida and Texas; a one-time charge from a Florida class action suit settlement; and a US$630 million charge for realignment of the international food operations. Operating profit included a US$774 million pre-tax gain on the sale of ice cream businesses in Brazil and a US$103 million pre-tax gain on the sale of real estate operations.[53]

Results of operations – domestic tobacco

During the first six months of 1998, operating revenues of US$7.01 billion for Philip Morris Inc. represented an increase of 10.1 per cent over 1997, due to pricing and improved product mix, partially offset by lower volume. In the same 1998 period, this segment recorded pre-tax charges of over US$1 billion related to tobacco litigation settlements (mentioned previously), and US$309 million related to voluntary early retirement and separation programs for salaried and hourly employees. Operating income decreased 53.6 per cent from the comparable 1997 period, due primarily to the aforementioned tobacco litigation settlement charges; higher marketing, administration and research costs; charges for the voluntary early retirement and separation programs; and lower volume.[54]

In 1997, operating revenues of US$13.5 billion in this business segment (Exhibit 6) represented an increase of 8.2 per cent over 1996 because of pricing, higher volume and an improved product mix. This category sustained the US$1.5 billion charge for litigation settlement mentioned previously. Operating profit for

Exhibit 3 | Philip Morris Companies Inc. and subsidiaries, selected financial data – 11-year review (US$mn, except per share data)

	1997	1996	1995	1994	1993	1992	1991	1990	1989	1988	1987
Operating revenues	72 055	69 204	66 071	65 125	60 901	59 131	56 458	51 169	44 080	31 273	27 650
Cost of sales	26 689	26 560	26 685	28 351	26 771	26 082	25 612	24 430	21 868	13 565	12 183
Operating income	11 663	11 769	10 526	9 449	7 587	10 059	8 622	7 946	6 789	4 397	3 990
Net earnings (including cumulative effect of accounting changes)	6 310	6 303	5 450	4 725	3 091	4 939	3 006	3 540	2 946	2 337	1 842
Total assets	55 947	54 871	53 811	52 649	51 205	50 014	47 384	46 569	38 528	36 960	21 437
Total long-term debt	12 430	12 961	13 107	14 975	15 221	14 583	14 213	16 121	14 551	16 812	5 983
Stockholders' equity	14 920	14 218	13 985	12 786	11 627	12 563	12 512	11 947	9 571	7 679	6 823
United States export sales	6 705	6 476	5 920	4 942	4 105	3 797	3 061	2 928	2 288	1 863	1 592
Federal excise taxes on products	3 596	3 544	3 446	3 431	3 081	2 879	2 978	2 159	2 140	2 127	2 085
Foreign excise taxes on products	12 345	11 107	9 486	7 918	7 199	6 157	5 416	4 687	3 608	3 755	3 331
Basic EPS (including per-share cumulative effect of accounting changes)	2.61	2.57	2.17	1.82	1.17	1.82	1.08	1.28	1.06	0.84	0.65
Diluted EPS (including per-share cumulative effect of accounting changes)	2.58	2.54	2.15	1.81	1.17	1.80	1.07	1.27	1.05	0.83	0.64
Dividends declared per share	1.60	1.47	1.22	1.01	0.87	0.78	0.64	0.52	0.42	0.34	0.26
Book value per common share outstanding	6.15	5.85	5.61	5.00	4.42	4.69	4.53	4.30	3.43	2.77	2.40
Market price per common share at year end	45.25	37.67	30.08	19.17	18.54	25.71	26.75	17.25	13.88	8.50	7.13

Source: Philip Morris Companies Inc. 1998 Exhibit 13 *Annual 10-K Report to Security Holders for 1997* 6 March p. 35.

Exhibit 4 | Philip Morris Companies Inc. and subsidiaries, consolidated balance sheets (US$mn)

ASSETS	(a) 30 June 1998	(b) 31 December 1997	(b) 31 December 1996
Consumer products:			
Cash and cash equivalents	4 605	2 282	240
Receivables, net	5 293	4 294	4 466
Inventories:			
Leaf tobacco	4 166	4 348	4 143
Other raw materials	1 910	1 689	1 854
Finished product	3 043	3 002	3 005
Total inventories	9 119	9 039	9 002
Other current assets	1 840	1 825	1 482
Total current assets	20 857	26 479	24 192
Property, plant and equipment, at cost:			
Land and land improvements		666	664
Buildings and building equipment		5 114	5 168
Machinery and equipment		12 667	12 481
Construction in progress		1 555	1 659
Sub-total	20 595	20 002	19 972
Less accumulated depreciation	(8 740)	(8 381)	(8 221)
Total property, plant and equipment	11 855	11 621	11 751
Goodwill and other intangible assets, net of accumulated amortization of 5 087; 4 814; and 4 391	17 557	17 789	18 998
Other assets	3 023	3 211	3 015
Total consumer products assets	53 292	50 061	48 954

LIABILITIES	(a) 30 June 1998	(b) 31 December 1997	(b) 31 December 1996
Consumer products:			
Short-term borrowings	847	157	260
Current portion of long-term debt	1 577	1 516	1 846
Accounts payable	2 505	3 318	3 409
Accrued liabilities:			
Marketing	2 148	2 149	2 106
Taxes, except income taxes	1 667	1 234	1 331
Employment costs		1 083	942
Accrued settlement charges	1 790		
Other	3 467	3 780	2 726
Income taxes	1 000	862	1 269
Dividends payable	975	972	978
Total current liabilities	15 976	15 071	14 867
Long-term debt	12 289	11 585	11 827
Deferred income taxes	920	889	731
Accrued post-retirement healthcare costs	2 506	2 432	2 372
Other liabilities	6 630	6 218	5 773
Total consumer products liabilities	38 321	36 195	35 570
Financial services and real estate:			
Short-term borrowings	103		173
Long-term debt	838	845	1 134
Deferred income taxes	3 933	3 877	3 636
Other liabilities	146	110	140
Total financial services and real estate liabilities	5 020	4 832	5 083
Total liabilities	43 341	41 027	40 653

Exhibit 4 | Philip Morris Companies Inc. and subsidiaries, consolidated balance sheets (US$mn) *(continued)*

	(a) 30 June 1998	(b) 31 December 1997	(b) 31 December 1996
Financial services and real estate:			
Finance assets, net	5 900	5 712	5 345
Other assets	171	174	572
Total financial services and real estate assets	6 071	5 886	5 917
TOTAL ASSETS	59 363	55 947	54 871

	(a) 30 June 1998	(b) 31 December 1997	(b) 31 December 1996
STOCKHOLDERS' EQUITY			
Common stock, par value 0.33–1/3 per share (2 805 961 317 shares issued)	935	935	935
Earnings reinvested in the business	26 111	24 924	22 478
Currency translation adjustments	(1 330)	(1 109)	192
Sub-total	25 716	24 750	23 605
Less cost of repurchased stock 374 902 778; 380 474 028; and 374 615 043 shares)	(9 694)	(9 830)	(9 387)
Total stockholders' equity	16 022	14 920	14 218
TOTAL LIABILITIES AND STOCKHOLDERS' EQUITY	59 363	55 947	54 871

(a) Source: Philip Morris Companies Inc., 1998, Form 10Q, *Quarterly Report for the Quarterly Period Ended June 30, 1998*, 31 July, pp. 2–3.
(b) Source: Philip Morris Companies Inc., 1998, Exhibit 13, *Annual 10-K Report to Security Holders for 1997*, 6 March, pp. 36–8.

Exhibit 5 | Philip Morris Companies Inc. and subsidiaries, consolidated statements of earnings (US$mn, except per share data)

	(a) Six months ended 30 June 1998 (Unaudited)	(b) For the years ended 31 December		
		1997	1996	1995
Operating revenues	$37 361	$72 055	$69 204	$66 071
Cost of sales	13 590	26 689	26 560	26 685
Excise taxes on products	8 419	15 941	14 651	12 932
Gross profit	15 352	29 425	27 993	26 454
Marketing, administration and research costs	8 354	15 720	15 630	15 337
Settlement charges	1 005	1 457		
Amortization of goodwill	290	585	594	591
Operating income	5 703	11 663	11 769	10 526
Interest and other debt expense, net	482	1 052	1 086	1 179
Earnings before income taxes and cumulative effect of accounting changes	5 221	10 611	10 683	9 347
Provision for income taxes	2 103	4 301	4 380	3 869
Earnings before cumulative effect of accounting changes	3 118	6 310	6 303	5 478
Cumulative effect of accounting changes	0	0	0	(28)
Net earnings	$3 118	$6 310	$6 303	$5 450
Per-share data:				
Basic earnings per share before cumulative effect of accounting changes	$1.28	$2.51	$2.57	$2.18
Cumulative effect of accounting changes				(0.01)
Basic earnings per share	$1.28	$2.61	$2.57	$2.17
Diluted earnings per share before cumulative effect of accounting changes	$1.28	$2.58	$2.54	$2.16
Cumulative effect of accounting changes				(0.01)
Diluted earnings per share	$1.28	$2.58	$2.54	$2.15

(a) Source: Philip Morris Companies Inc., 1998, Form 10Q, *Quarterly Report for the Quarterly Period Ended June 30, 1998*, 31 July, p. 4.
(b) Source: Philip Morris Companies Inc., 1998, Exhibit 13, *Annual 10-K Report to Security Holders for 1997*, 6 March, p. 39.

1997 decreased 22.3 per cent from 1996, due to litigation charges; higher marketing, administration and research costs; higher fixed manufacturing costs; higher volume; and the improved product mix. Excluding the impact of litigation settlement charges, Philip Morris Inc.'s operating profit for 1997 increased 12.3 per cent over 1996.[55]

Results of operations – international tobacco

During the first six months of 1998, operating revenues of Philip Morris International were US$14.3 billion, an increase of 4.5 per cent over the comparable 1997 period, including excise taxes. Increases were caused by price increases, favourable volume/mix and the consolidation of previously unconsolidated subsidiaries. Operating income for this period increased 11.1 per cent over the comparable 1997 period for primarily the same reasons.[56]

During 1997, tobacco operating revenues of this segment were US$26.3 billion (Exhibit 6) which is US$2.2 billion over 1996, including a US$1.2 billion increase in excise taxes. Excluding excise taxes, operating revenues increased US$1 billion, due primarily to price increases; favourable volume/mix; and the consolidation of previously unconsolidated and newly acquired subsidiaries. Operating profit for 1997 increased 12.6 per cent over 1996, because of these same factors.[57]

Exhibit 6 | Philip Morris Companies Inc. and subsidiaries, consolidated operating results

	Operating revenues (US$mn)[a]			Operating revenue (%)		
	1997	1996	1995	1997	1996	1995
Tobacco						
Domestic	$13 485	$12 462	$11 493	18.7%	18.0%	17.4%
International	26 339	24 087	20 823	36.6	34.8	31.5
Total tobacco	39 824	36 549	32 316	55.3	52.8	48.9
Food	27 690	27 950	29 074	38.4	40.4	44.0
Beer	4 201	4 327	4 304	5.8	6.3	6.5
Financial services	340	378	377	0.5	0.5	0.6
Operating revenues	$72 055	$69 204	$66 071	100.0%	100.0%	100.0%

	Operating income (US$mn)[b]			Operating income (%)			Operating income margins (%)		
	1997	1996	1995	1997	1996	1995	1997	1996	1995
Tobacco	$7 830	$8 263	$7 177	64.1%	67.4%	65.4%	19.7%	22.6%	22.2%
Food	3 647	3 362	3 188	29.8	27.4	29.1	13.2	12.0	11.0
Beer	456	437	444	3.7	3.6	4.0	10.9	10.1	10.3
Financial services	296	192	164	2.4	1.6	1.5	87.1	50.8	43.5
Operating income	$12 229	$12 254	$10 973	100.0%	100.0%	100.0%			

	Assets[c] (US$mn)			Return on assets (%)		
	1997	1996	1995	1997	1996	1995
Tobacco	$14 820	$13 314	$11 196	52.8%	62.1%	64.1%
Food	$30.926	$32 934	$33 447	11.8	10.2	9.5
Beer	$1 455	$1 707	$1 751	31.3	25.6	25.4
Financial services	$5 886	$5 917	$5 632	5.0	3.2	2.9

[a] Source: Philip Morris Companies Inc., 1998, Exhibit 13, *Annual 10-K Report to Security Holders for 1997*, 6 March, p. 20.
[b] Source: Philip Morris Companies Inc., 1998, Exhibit 13, *Annual 10-K Report to Security Holders for 1997*, 6 March, p. 26.
[c] Source: Philip Morris Companies Inc., 1998, Exhibit 13, *Annual 10-K Report to Security Holders for 1997*, 6 March, p. 48.

Summary results

A summary of operating results for Philip Morris Companies, Inc. indicates that the tobacco business segment provides a substantial portion of the company's revenues. For the six months ended 30 June 1998, domestic tobacco sales of US$7.011 billion represented 32.9 per cent of tobacco revenues and 18.8 percent of operating revenues, while international tobacco sales of US$14.325 billion represented 67.1 per cent of tobacco revenues and 38.3 per cent of total operating revenues.[58] For the year ended 31 December 1997, domestic tobacco sales of US$13.485 billion represented 33.9 per cent of tobacco revenues and 18.7 per cent of total operating revenues, while international tobacco sales of US$26.339 billion represented 66.1 per cent of tobacco revenues and 36.6 per cent of total operating revenues.[59]

Philip Morris legal issues

In recent years, tobacco companies have been faced with significant legal threats, as noted in the previous financial results section. In the past, tobacco companies were able to maintain defence. Things started to change in 1988, when Liggett was ordered to pay the first award in a liability suit.[60] Later, in 1994, Florida passed a law making it legal to sue cigarette makers for reimbursement of Medicaid expenses from smoking-related illnesses. A total of 39 states have filed suit seeking compensation for healthcare costs. Adding to tobacco firms' potential problems, the US President declared nicotine a drug and placed it under the jurisdiction of the Federal Drug Administration.[61]

Philip Morris faces a tremendous amount of tobacco-related litigation both in and outside the United

Exhibit 7 | Overview of pending tobacco-related litigation against Philip Morris Companies Inc. as of 1 August 1998

Category	Approximate number of cases pending	
	In the United States	Outside the United States
(1) Smoking and health cases alleging personal injury brought on behalf of INDIVIDUAL plaintiffs	400	20
(2) Smoking and health cases alleging personal injury brought on behalf of a CLASS of individual plaintiffs	65	4
(3) Health care cost recovery cases brought by state and local governments and similar entities seeking reimbursement for health care expenditures allegedly caused by cigarette smoking	140	1

Source: This information was obtained from Philip Morris Companies Inc., Form 10Q, *Quarterly Report for the Quarter Ended June 30, 1998* and filed 31 July 1998. For a detailed listing of the pending litigation for categories (2) and (3) above, please refer to Exhibit 99 of the aforementioned Form 10Q.

States. The pending legal proceedings pertain to many different issues, but generally fall into three basic categories: individual smoking and health cases, class action smoking and healthcare cost recovery cases.[62]

The smoking and health cases vary according to the claim being made. Claims such as negligence, gross negligence, strict liability, fraud, misrepresentation, design defect, failure to warn, breach of express and implied warranties, breach of special duty, conspiracy, concert of action, violations of deceptive trade practice laws and consumer protection statutes, and claims under the federal and state *Racketeer Influenced and Corrupt Organization Act* (RICO) statutes are common among the pending legal proceedings.[63] Currently, approximately 400 smoking and health cases have been filed and served against Philip Morris in the United States and approximately 25 cases are pending outside of the United States. Of the 400 cases, only 22 allege personal injuries as a result of exposure to environmental tobacco smoke.[64]

The healthcare cost recovery cases mostly seek reimbursement for Medicaid and/or other healthcare-related costs allegedly incurred through the fault of tobacco companies. Some of the recovery cases seek future damages as well (Exhibit 7).[65] Approximately 140 healthcare cost recovery cases are currently pending against Philip Morris. Of the 140 cases, 37 were filed by states, 70 were filed by unions, six were filed by HMOs, eight were filed by city and county governments, five by Native American tribes, and five by federal and state taxpayers.[66]

Other tobacco-related claims are also common. For instance, one claim asserts that Philip Morris allegedly failed to manufacture a fire-safe cigarette when they possessed knowledge of a technology that would produce a cigarette that was less likely to cause fires. Cigarette price-fixing claims and suits filed by former asbestos manufacturers also add to the list of tobacco-related cases against Philip Morris.[67]

In an effort to increase stability and decrease uncertainties in the tobacco industry, Philip Morris and other tobacco companies have adopted a Memorandum of Understanding (referred to as the Resolution). The purpose of the Resolution is to address the majority of the legal and regulatory issues that the tobacco industry faces. Issues discussed in the Resolution include: advertising and marketing, product warning and labelling, underage smoking reduction goals, enforcement of no sales to underage consumers by the states, and surcharges against the industry for failure to reduce underage smoking.[68]

Philip Morris has proposed its own form of legislation safeguarding against sales to minors. Steve Parrish, Philip Morris's senior vice president of corporate affairs, and Richard H. Verheij, UST executive vice president and general counsel, presented the plan. The plan includes a ban on outdoor advertising within 1 000 feet of a school or playground and also calls for a minimum age of 18 for the sale of

Exhibit 8 | Actual and/or proposed regulations on the tobacco industry

- Excise tax increases
- Federal regulatory controls
- Requirements regarding disclosure of cigarette ingredients and other proprietary information
- Requirements regarding disclosure of the yields of tar, nicotine and other components of cigarette smoke
- Governmental and grand jury investigations
- Increased smoking and health litigation
- Federal, state and local governmental and private bans and restrictions on smoking
- Restrictions on tobacco manufacturing, marketing, advertising and sales
- Legislation and regulations to require substantial additional health warnings on cigarette packages and in advertising
- Elimination of the tax deductibility of tobacco advertising and promotional costs
- Legislation or other governmental action seeking to ascribe to the tobacco industry responsibility and liability for the purported adverse health effects associated with smoking

Source: Philip Morris Companies Inc., 1998, Form 10Q, *Quarterly Report for the Quarterly Period Ended June 30, 1998*, 31 July, p. 26.

tobacco products. The plan would ban vending sales by requiring face-to-face sales and would ban the sale of single cigarettes and mini packs (fewer than 20 cigarettes to a pack). Cigarette sampling would also be banned in areas where minors are allowed to enter.[69]

It is difficult for Philip Morris to predict the uncertain outcome of the litigation it is facing, and it is unable to estimate potential losses that may result from an unfavourable outcome. It is also hard to predict the effect that the pending litigation will have upon current smokers and cigarette sales. The company does feel that it has valid and concrete defences against the pending litigation, and the officers stress their willingness to continue to defend the company.[70]

The future

What must Philip Morris Companies, Inc. do in the future to maintain its financial success in light of ongoing tobacco litigation, proposed legislation and increasing public sentiment against smoking? A recent comment from *The Wall Street Journal* states: 'Even as the 30 stocks making up the Dow Jones industrial average have been pummeled over the past month, one company has managed to stand out: Philip Morris Co.'s.'[71] Philip Morris continues to outdistance its competitors in the tobacco industry and to show marked success in its beer and packaged food divisions. In the United States and abroad, many actual and/or proposed regulations are pending. These regulations (listed in Exhibit 8), along with the aforementioned potential liabilities arising from unfavourable outcomes of litigation, could have negative effects on the future operating results of Philip Morris Companies, Inc. as well as its competitors.

How will the current litigation affect the nature of competition? How will competitors choose to manage their own litigation threat?

How can Philip Morris balance social responsibility with business success? Do legislation and litigation present imminent threats to the company's tobacco segment? What business strategies can Philip Morris use to hedge against possible adverse effects on or elimination of this segment of its operations?

Endnotes

1. P. H. Roth, 1998, *Investment Survey* (Value Line Publishing, Inc.), 14 August, p. 1581.
2. *Microsoft Encarta 96 Electronic Encyclopedia on CD-ROM*, Microsoft Corporation, 1996, search Life Science, Plants, Tobacco, History.
3. Ibid.
4. Ibid., search Life Science, Medicine, Smoking, Introduction.
5. Ibid.
6. Ibid., search Life Science, Medicine, Smoking, History.
7. Ibid., search Life Science, Medicine, Smoking, Smoking Cessation.
8. R. M. Jones, 1997, *Strategic Management in a Hostile Environment, Lessons from the Tobacco Industry* (Westport, CT: Greenwood Publishing Group), p. 12.
9. Ibid.
10. R. H. Miles, 1982, *Coffin Nails and Corporate Strategy* (Englewood Cliffs, NJ: Prentice Hall), p. 138.
11. *Microsoft Encarta 96 Electronic Encyclopedia on CD-ROM*, Microsoft Corporation, 1996, search Life Science, Plants, Tobacco, Use.
12. Byron Sachs, 'Industry zone, industry snapshot: Tobacco', *Hoover's Online*, p. 2.
13. Ibid.
14. Philip Morris Companies Inc., 1998, *International Directory of Company Histories*, p. 417.

15. New Content Copyright, 1998, *PBS Online*, accessed 28 September 1998: www.pbs.org/wgbh/pages/frontline/shows/settlement/big/owns.html, p. 2.
16. N. Primavera, 1998, *Investment Survey* (Value Line Publishing, Inc.), 14 August, p. 1578.
17. New Content Copyright, 1998, *PBS Online*.
18. Primavera, *Investment Survey*.
19. Ibid., p. 1579.
20. Ibid.
21. Ibid.
22. Roth, *Investment Survey*, p. 1580.
23. Ibid.
24. Ibid.
25. New Content Copyright, 1998, *PBS Online*.
26. Market Guide, Inc., accessed November 1998: http://research.web.aol.com/data/marketguide/stock/r/rn.htm.
27. Primavera, *Investment Survey*, p. 1582.
28. RJR Nabisco, 1997, Annual Report: www.rjrnabisco.com/annual97/whatsup.htm.
29. J. W. Milner, 1998, *Investment Survey* (Value Line Publishing, Inc.), 4 September, p. 2151.
30. Ibid.
31. New Content Copyright, 1998, *PBS Online*.
32. Ibid.
33. Milner, *Investment Survey*.
34. Roth, *Investment Survey*, p. 1583.
35. Ibid.
36. New Content Copyright, 1998, *PBS Online*.
37. Roth, *Investment Survey*, p. 1583.
38. Primavera, *Investment Survey*.
39. Ibid.
40. Miles, *Coffin Nails and Corporate Strategy*, p. 138.
41. J. Sasseen, 1985, 'The General Foods deal may not be so sweet', *Business Week*, 14 October, pp. 40–1.
42. Philip Morris, 1994, 10K, p. 2.
43. Philip Morris, 1997, Annual Report, p. 6.
44. Philip Morris, 1996, 10K, p. 3.
45. Philip Morris, 1997, Annual Report, p. 9.
46. Sasseen, 'The General Foods deal may not be so sweet'.
47. S. P. Sherman, 1989, 'How Philip Morris diversified right', *Fortune*, 23 October, pp. 120–2.
48. Sasseen, 'The General Foods deal may not be so sweet'.
49. 'Make way for Miller', 1976, *Forbes*, 15 May, pp. 45–7.
50. Philip Morris Companies Inc., 1998, Form 10Q, *Quarterly Report for the Quarterly Period Ended June 30, 1998*, 31 July, p. 24.
51. Ibid.
52. Philip Morris Companies Inc., 1998, Exhibit 13, *Annual 10-K Report to Security Holders for 1997*, 6 March, p. 21.
53. Ibid.
54. Philip Morris Companies Inc., 1998, Form 10Q, *Quarterly Report for the Quarterly Period Ended June 30, 1998*, 31 July, pp. 33.
55. Philip Morris Companies Inc., 1998, Exhibit 13, *Annual 10-K Report to Security Holders for 1997*, 6 March, pp. 27–8.
56. Philip Morris Companies Inc., 1998, Form 10Q, *Quarterly Report for the Quarterly Period Ended June 30, 1998*, 31 July, p. 34.
57. Philip Morris Companies Inc., 1998, Exhibit 13, *Annual 10-K Report to Security Holders for 1997*, 6 March, p. 28.
58. Philip Morris Companies Inc., 1998, Form 10Q, *Quarterly Report for the Quarterly Period Ended June 30, 1998*, 31 July, p. 33.
59. Philip Morris Companies Inc., 1998, Exhibit 13, *Annual 10-K Report to Security Holders for 1997*, 6 March, p. 27.
60. Sachs, Industry Zone, Industry Snapshot.
61. Ibid.
62. Philip Morris, 1997, Annual Report, p. 51.
63. Ibid., pp. 52–3.
64. www.sec.gov/Archives/edgar/data/764180/0001047469-98-031299.txt, accessed 4 October 1998, pp. 10–11.
65. Philip Morris, 1997, Annual Report, p. 54.
66. www.sec.gov/Archives/edgar/data/764180/0001047469-98-031299.txt, accessed 4 October 1998, p. 15.
67. Ibid., p. 56.
68. Ibid., p. 57.
69. A. Kaplan, 1998, 'Tobacco cos. propose federal legislation', *CSNews Online*, accessed 4 October 1998: http://macfadden.com/csnews/news/bn_52.html.
70. Ibid., pp. 20–1.
71. 'Philip Morris a bright spot in Dow Industrials', 1998, *WSJ Interactive Edition*, 31 August, accessed 31 August 1998: www.wsj.com.

Case 12

Pisces Group of Singapore*

Siah Hwee Ang
Kulwant Singh
National University of Singapore

Introduction

China, Malaysia, Saudi Arabia, Singapore, Thailand. Retailing, department stores, electronic manufacturing, optics, transportation, hotels, trading, garment manufacturing and retailing, textiles and electronics component manufacturing, property development, industrial parks, transportation, optical products, food, travel and entertainment. In a few short years, Pisces Holdings had rapidly expanded from its single small clothing store in Singapore to become a diversified firm with multiple ventures spread over several countries. Its aggressive expansion suggested a strong commitment to its announced target of turning a family-owned firm into a public company. Yet this expansion also suggested the need for the firm to rationalise its businesses and to build its organisation to support its strategy for long-term success. In late 1996, it was clear that the Pisces Group needed to make fundamental decisions on its strategy for future success.

Pisces traced its roots to a small *pasar malam* (night market) stall in Singapore in the early 1970s. This was a small family venture, run by the eldest son of the Ang family, Ang Chin Thian. The small, makeshift operation comprised a display table that would be moved to different parts of the city on different nights, to sell low-end clothing to casual shoppers. The early going was difficult, but gradually it developed into a reasonably successful, if unglamorous, operation. However, as Singapore developed rapidly, night markets fell in popularity and had almost ceased to exist by the late 1970s. The need to find an alternative business, and their relative success in selling clothes, encouraged the family to focus on the retail clothing business.

Ang Chin Thian and his four brothers started Pisces with a single retail store in the Chinatown shopping district of Singapore in 1986. The store essentially replicated their night market stall format, selling a range of value-for-money clothing to price-conscious customers. Over time, the range of products sold expanded to include household items, and the store's format evolved into that of a clothing and household goods-oriented department store. However, the focus continued to be on low-end products, and the range of items sold was relatively limited. Almost all goods sold in the store were sourced from China. This format proved to be successful and sales grew steadily throughout the 1980s. By 1989, the operation was so successful that Pisces started limited manufacturing of its own garments in China. By 1991, Pisces had achieved an annual turnover of S$50 million and was a well-known outlet in the Chinatown area of Singapore.

Pisces appeared to have a simple formula for success: 'We focus on value-for-money garments and have a niche market in the mid-lower income group. The question is whether you know the target audience, are able to get what they want and sell the products to them at the right price,' Seah Hwee Hock, a senior manager at Pisces, pointed out. Pisces believed that its long experience in garment retailing gave it the experience to source and manufacture the right products at low cost. In addition, Pisces' smaller store size and low rental were 'good for local shoppers' and made it easier for the stores to break even. Despite its success, Pisces believed that it would be difficult to grow sales by about 20 per cent annually in a mature store location in Singapore. This concern appeared to be the major driver behind the strategy adopted in the early 1990s, of rapidly expanding its businesses by establishing new stores.

Transformation and growth

With its first retail outlet successfully established, Pisces went on an expansion spree between 1992 and 1993, establishing three more department stores in various parts of Singapore. These were based on the same department store format of its original store. This was quickly followed by the opening of several small outlets in the middle-class housing estates, in which the majority of Singapore's population resided. These stores provided easy access to the middle-class, price-sensitive, retail-clothing segment that Pisces targeted. By 1993, Pisces had transformed itself into a retail chain with 16 stores accounting for a total retail space of about 100 000 square feet.

The firm subsequently explained the rationale for its rapid expansion in retailing as follows: 'By expanding the number of stores, we can achieve greater economies of scale,' said Seah Hwee Hock. 'The ideal location for us is in housing estates where we can capture the local crowd.' The firm also prided itself on its flexibility and speed, as reflected in what it called, a 'hit and run' strategy. 'We never stayed in one housing estate for more than four months. After we sold our goods, we packed up and went to another estate. What's the point of staying? All the goods that people in the neighbourhood wanted to buy from you, they would have done so already,' explained Ang Chin Thian.

In February 1994, Pisces announced plans to enter a new niche in the retail sector, investing S$1 million in renovations for its first large discount store. This store, PMart, was located on Singapore's high-end Orchard Road tourist belt. An additional discount store was to be opened in Singapore in 1995, and two more in Malaysia in the next two years. This new large discount store format appeared to have become popular in Singapore at that time, as the giant US discounter, Kmart, had set up the first of its three new stores in 1994. Market rumours abounded that other large discounters would soon establish operations in the country. In April 1994, Pisces acquired four small retail outlets in housing estates for S$5 million.

In September 1994, Pisces acquired 40 per cent of Circuits Plus, a 15-year-old manufacturer of printed circuit boards (PCBs). The acquisition for more than S$10 million was made through a newly established subsidiary, Pisces Technologies Holdings (PTH). PTH identified its core businesses as PCB manufacturing, electronics components trading, and the development and engineering of data communication products.

PTH announced its intention to buy other companies that had complementary capabilities to that of Circuits Plus. It also aimed to undertake turnkey projects, as well as to enter the original equipment manufacturing business. In addition, it was planning to set up PCB manufacturing plants in China by 1995. Shortly thereafter, Pisces announced that it had invested S$7.6 million in a joint venture with a Singapore firm to set up a transport and chartering business.

Pisces' group general manager, Koh Hee Hiong, explained the rationale for the diversification as follows: 'Traditionally, we have been in retail and garment manufacturing. This is the first time we are getting into areas like transport and hotels. This is to turn the company from a family-owned interest to a public company.' He further explained that the investment in the Singapore transport company was designed to help the firm build its expertise in preparation for entry into the inland transportation business in China. Similarly, the purchase of a stake in Circuits Plus was part of its plan to build a factory in this business in China.

These investments foreshadowed several new ventures over the next few months, reflecting what appeared to be a major change of strategy. The key element of this strategy was a major focus on foreign expansion. The timing of the expansion was fortuitous, as the Singapore retail market experienced a significant slowdown from 1994. Tourist shopping expenditures, which accounted for much of the high-end retail clothing market, had begun to decline. This trend, overbuilding in the high-end shopping belt and a slowdown in regional tourism were starting to hurt the retail clothing and department store businesses. The year 1994 also saw the first of several closures of major department stores in Singapore, and the emergence of a much more difficult retailing environment.

Foreign expansion

Pisces' foreign ventures had a quiet start in June 1992, when it was invited to the Middle East on a business mission organised by the Arab Business Center. During that trip, it clinched a deal to sell its consumer products at Happy Family Department Store in Saudi Arabia. Under the agreement, Pisces was required to reorganise and manage the store. In addition, it was to display more than US$3 million (S$4.86 million) worth of goods such as clothing and sportswear at the store each year. The Saudi Arabian company's chairman announced that Pisces' business strategy, management style and range of consumer products suited the store. Pisces' general manager believed that Pisces could help the Happy Family store, as it was poorly organised and lacked the purchasing and marketing expertise that Pisces possessed. For a small but ambitious operation, this endeavour represented an impressive achievement. It presaged what was to become an important part of the Pisces model, foreign expansion.

In September 1993, Pisces announced a S$20 million purchase of a 75 per cent stake in Kingdom Corporation, a Singapore-based firm that traded optical products such as spectacle frames and sunglasses. Earlier in August 1993, Kingdom had closed its five-year-old manufacturing plant in Singapore and relocated it to China, as it was too expensive to operate in Singapore. The new US$1 million (S$1.58 million) facility near Shanghai was expected to commence operations by the end of 1993. Kingdom was majority-owned by Thailand's textile and fashion group TTI, although the acquisition by Pisces would reduce its stake in Kingdom to 9 per cent.

Pisces announced that it intended to use TTI's connections in China to accelerate its penetration into the Chinese market and to support its intention to obtain a listing on the Singapore stock market. Pisces believed that joint ownership of Kingdom with TTI would allow it to tap into TTI's extensive contacts in China. Pisces also announced that it would sell Kingdom's products in China, in its newly established 130 000-square-foot department store in Guilin and in other stores it planned to set up with TTI. TTI would also supply the garments and textiles for Pisces' stores in China. The links between Pisces and TTI were further strengthened by TTI's subsequent announcement that it planned to sell to Pisces 10 per cent of its subsidiary garment company, Lu Thai Textiles. This sale had received the approval of Lu Thai Textile's equal owner, the Chinese provincial government. Lu Thai Textiles had an annual turnover of US$23.5 million, and had received approval for a stock listing in China, a relatively rare event in China in the early 1990s.

In December 1993, Pisces formed a joint venture, Qintraco Resources Development, with Chinese company Five Rings Holdings to carry out bilateral trading and investment activities. Five Rings, which was awaiting approval for listing on the Shanghai bourse, was a textile manufacturer that exported more than 60 per cent of its products to more than 40 countries. The first effort of this joint venture was to set up a S$10 million garment plant in Malaysia, with each firm investing an equal share of S$5 million.

In May 1994, Pisces announced a second venture with Five Rings, to be run by Qintraco. Shaanxi Speeding Transportation was a US$1.82 million (S$2.84 million) venture to transport goods from Xian to Shanghai using a fleet of 40 container lorries and tankers. Pisces claimed that this was the first operation of its kind in the area. The same month, a US$2 million joint venture with Zhao Feng Real Estate Development Company was formed to operate 50 taxis in Shanghai.

In August 1994, Pisces Land (a wholly owned subsidiary of Pisces) committed to a 75 per cent share of a S$30 million (US$17 million) joint venture with China-based Beihai Port Authority to build and operate for 50 years an industrial park in Guangxi Province. Pisces' investment would be financed from borrowing and internal reserves, while its Chinese partner's stake came from granting the 50-year land lease. Pisces explained that its motivation for the investment in Beihai was its strategically located port in the south part of China, where it could be a gateway to and from the southern land-locked provinces. Pisces expected the project to start generating returns by mid-1996.

The Guangxi industrial park was the group's fourth property development in China. The others were investments in a S$20 million housing estate in Shanghai, a S$10 million industrial park in Quanzhou, Fujian, and a S$10 million residential bungalow project in Chengdu. The last venture was 55 per cent owned by Pisces, with the rest held by a Chinese entrepreneur. With 12 of the 31 units sold, Pisces announced the development of another 40 units in the same project in 1995.

In addition, two other projects, a 43-unit landed development in Shanghai and a 24-hectare township project in Quanzhou, would be launched in 1995.

Later in 1994, Pisces expanded its real estate efforts, making the following three hotel investments in China:

- S$4.6 million in Zhejiang Province;
- S$4.9 million to purchase a hotel on Hainan Island from Five Rings; and
- S$8 million to purchase 54 per cent of a 400-room hotel on Qingdao Island.

As its property portfolio grew, Pisces announced in late 1994 that it would focus on property development, predominantly in China, over the next few years. Pisces explained that this diversification into property was a result of the soft retail market in Singapore. Much of its future focus would be on its China businesses, where 40 per cent of its operations were based.

Despite the range of these ventures, Pisces continued to expand its retail operations. Together with another Singapore firm, it opened three department stores in

China – in Xiamen, Fuzhou and Suzhou – for a total investment of S$5 million. Pisces also announced discussions with a Chinese company to open another three outlets in Qingdao, Shanghai and Hunan.

Structure and ownership

To keep up with its expansion, Pisces expanded the number of its directors from five to 12. It also hired more people with wider expertise and experience. 'This is no longer a family-run organisation, so we have increased the number of board seats to reflect the professional-run nature of the business ... We are no longer a retail and garment company but a diversified, international company, as our venture in China shows,' Koh Hee Hiong, Pisces' general manager, explained. Yet Pisces retained the essence of a family-based firm, being driven by the Ang brothers while apparently retaining the flexibility and informality associated with such firms.

Pisces also indicated that it intended to continue its aggressive expansion and faced relatively few constraints. Funding its acquisitions was not a problem, as internal sources, other shareholders, venture capital companies and investors were 'more than willing' to fund projects. Instead, the problem was to find suitable acquisitions.

In July 1994, Pisces sold 30 per cent of the ownership in Pisces Group (its parent holding company) for S$18 million to Chinese firm Shenzhen Gintian. Shenzhen Gintian was a diversified company engaged through more than 40 wholly owned or joint venture subsidiaries in sectors ranging from real estate, textiles and securities trading, to high-tech industrial and commercial services. In 1988, Shenzhen Gintian had been the first state-owned enterprise in China to obtain a public listing on the Shanghai bourse, and it subsequently obtained a second listing in Hong Kong. In 1993, it had a turnover of S$220 million (RMB $1.099 billion) and operating profit of S$27 million. It was believed to possess good *guanxi* (connections) with the authorities in China, which would facilitate the extensive approval process required for major business ventures in the country. Pisces explained that this link would provide it with greater China expertise, and would enhance its chances of obtaining a main board listing in Singapore, a target it hoped to achieve by 1997. Observers believed that Shenzhen Gintian invested in Pisces to access Singapore's financial markets and to acquire knowledge of Singapore's very well-regarded public housing program.

Further changes in the company's capital structure took place towards the end of 1994 when Transpac Capital, a venture capital management company, invested S$10 million in convertible loans issued by the company. The loan would be convertible into an 18 per cent stake in Pisces at the option of Transpac. It was believed that Transpac was attracted in part by the valuation of Pisces for about S$55 million, which appeared conservative relative to the company's projected 1995 net profits after tax of about S$9 million. The entry valuation of six times the prospective price/earning ratio was considered low in the light of the then booming stock market conditions and Pisces' foray into technology-related investments. This investment was hailed by Pisces as recognition that it had made the transition from a family-run business into a professionally managed conglomerate.

Then, in January 1995, Pisces sold a 15.2 per cent ownership stake to Pacific Can Investment Holdings for S$6.68 million. Pacific Can was a Singapore-listed company whose principal activities included investment holdings and the provision of management services to related companies. Its intention was to use Pisces' network of business contacts in China and the region for its own expansion. Pacific Can had been linked to Pisces indirectly since 1994, through its 13 per cent ownership of Kingdom, the first foreign investment made by Pisces.

Further growth and transformation

The year 1995 saw a change in the direction, though not in the speed, of Pisces' expansion. The acquisition strategy appeared to shift towards technology-oriented ventures, particularly through its technology arm, Pisces Technologies Holdings (PTH).

In January 1995, Pisces was ready to expand its PCB manufacturing business beyond Singapore. It did this through an agreement with Chinese shoe manufacturer Double Star Corporation to set up a S$7.35 million plant in Qingdao to manufacture PCBs. Pisces, holding a 55 per cent stake, would provide management know-how, while Double Star would contribute the land and working capital. Pisces would then distribute Double Star's other products when the Chinese company set up its regional office in Singapore in 1996.

Further supporting its PCB manufacturing effort, Pisces invested S$5.7 million in a PCB manufacturing plant in Malaysia. The factory, which it bought at a discount, was expected to bring in S$15–20 million in revenues for Pisces. Pisces also announced that it would double its capacity at its Singapore PCB operation by mid-1996. Revenue from PCB operations was expected to double to S$30 million by 1996 as a result of these investments.

In August 1995, Pisces bought General Electronics & Instrumentation Corporation (GEIC) through a share swap with its shareholders. GEIC specialised in the distribution of electrical and electronic equipment and components, and the provision of hardware and software engineering. It had an annual turnover of S$30 million. As Pisces paid for its stake through shares in subsidiary PTH, this had the effect of reducing the group's shareholding in its technology arm from 56 per cent to 25 per cent.

At about the same time, Pisces paid S$0.3 million for a 30 per cent stake in Falco Technologies, a technology start-up that made automatic printer and computer sharing devices. Falco intended to diversify into liquid crystal displays, electronic components manufacturing, factory automation and system integration. Pisces' management recognised that although their acquisition of Falco did not exactly fit into their diversification plans, as Falco's products were further downstream, it believed that Falco's design team would bring PTH closer to being a provider of engineering solutions.

Pisces then signed a preliminary agreement for its third technology acquisition, for 30 per cent of Hongguan Technologies through a share swap. Hongguan was a machinery maker and system integrator. The 30 per cent purchase was to be concluded at the end of 1995. However, Pisces indicated that it would increase its stake over time, until it took over full ownership of Hongguan.

As a result of these acquisitions, PTH was expected to contribute 20 per cent of group revenue, while garment manufacturing, wholesaling and retailing would comprise 42 per cent of turnover. The balance would come from its property and transport division. Pisces projected group turnover of S$100 million in 1995, up 53.8 per cent from S$65 million in 1994. It forecasted a bright future, and expected to grow by 20 per cent annually over the next few years. Perhaps the only worrying sign was that in mid-1995, Ang Chin Thian, Pisces' founder and main driving force, resigned as chairman because of poor health. His four brothers jointly took over the leadership of the firm.

The situation in 1996

After a brief stay of two years and a loss of S$12.6 million, American discount giant Kmart decided to pull out of Singapore in June 1996. Although Kmart said that its decision to close its three stores was part of an internal worldwide consolidation, the move was widely viewed as reflecting a lack of confidence in the Singapore retail market.

Nevertheless, Pisces' two PMart department stores were operating well, as were its other retail outlets in Singapore. Exhibit 1 provides a summary of the performance of Pisces' various clothing and department store operations in Singapore. According to Pisces, its

Exhibit 1 | Pisces Group: Retail and wholesale trading (S$ million)

	Pisces Group			PMart International			Pisces Chain Store			Pisces Garments			Cheap & Good Trading		
	1996	1995	1994	1996	1995	1994	1996	1995	1994	1996	1995	1994	1996	1995	1994
Sales	7.55	9.01	1.66	10.59	5.10		7.3	8.43	4.68	15.45	15.00	25.12	13.13	14.02	16.15
Profit after tax	−0.79	−1.21	0.03	0.30	0.07	−0.03	−0.45	0.07	0.33	0.56	0.59	1.37	−0.31	0.10	1.05
Total assets	89.48	77.37	41.97	5.43	3.25	0.23	4.81	4.56	3.10	12.70	13.16	14.78	15.07	16.54	16.90
Current assets	37.76	22.18	7.07	4.47	2.63	0.15	4.50	4.27	2.86	11.18	11.31	12.51	12.03	13.32	13.52
Total liabilities	50.06	41.54	11.36	4.59	2.71	0.26	3.66	2.96	1.57	5.55	6.57	8.78	10.53	11.69	12.15
Current liabilities	38.84	27.58	8.16	4.32	2.55	0.26	3.62	2.92	1.55	5.02	5.78	7.80	9.99	10.85	11.32
Shareholders' funds	39.42	35.83	30.61	0.84	0.54	−0.03	1.15	1.60	1.53	7.15	6.59	6.00	4.54	4.85	4.75
Working capital ratio	0.97	0.80	0.87	1.03	1.03	0.58	1.24	1.46	1.84	2.23	1.96	1.60	1.20	1.23	1.19
Total debt/ equity ratio	55.95	53.69	27.07	84.52	83.46	115.03	76.10	64.85	50.66	43.69	49.90	59.39	69.86	70.68	71.88

PMart International, Pisces Chain Store, Pisces Garments and Cheap & Good Trading are subsidiaries under the retail and wholesale trading division of Pisces Group.

combined retail operations would have a turnover of S$40 million in 1997 and all its stores would be profitable.

Yet, Pisces' success was dependent on much more than its retail operations in Singapore. It was clear that Pisces had undergone a radical transformation. From a largely Singapore-based retailer, Pisces had in the space of little more than two years transformed itself into a diversified conglomerate with more than 50 subsidiaries in textiles, electronics component manufacturing, property development, industrial parks, hotels, transportation, trading and optical products. In addition, it had other smaller ventures in food, travel and entertainment. Observers wondered how well it would integrate these operations, how well it would perform, and what its strategy would be in future. Would its spate of acquisitions continue? In that case, would it continue its diversification?

Endnote

* This case was first published in Kulwant Singh, Nitin Pangakar and Gaik Eng Lim (eds), 2001, *Business Strategy in Asia: A Casebook* (Singapore: Thomson Learning).

References

The Business Times, 1994, 'Local retailer Pisces ventures into transport business in China', 11 May.
The Straits Times, 1992, 'Pisces wins deal to manage Saudi store, sell its goods', 3 June.
The Straits Times, 1993, 'Pisces buys stake in optical company', 24 September.
The Straits Times, 1993, 'Pisces Group signs joint venture deal with Chinese firm', 24 December.
The Straits Times, 1994, 'Pisces' $30-million plan', 21 April.
The Straits Times, 1994, 'China's Shenzhen Gintian Industry buys 30% of Pisces', 22 July.
The Straits Times, 1994, 'Retailer Pisces continues drive into China property market', 17 August.
The Straits Times, 1994, 'Pisces buys PCB manufacturer in move to diversify', 17 September.
The Straits Times, 1995, 'Pacific Can issuing 6m shares to pay for 15% stake in Pisces', 4 January.
The Straits Times, 1995, 'Retailer Pisces takes 30% stake in Falco Tech', 30 January.

Case 13

Raffles, Singapore's historic hotel*

Kulwant Singh
Nitin Pangarkar
Gaik Eng Lim
Ng Seok-Hui
National University of Singapore

History

The story of Raffles Hotel really began in 1869, when, with the opening of the Suez Canal, travelling abroad for pleasure became a new passion of aristocrats and the super-rich. Together with their wives, fiancées or lovers, they took long cruises on P&O and Lloyd Triestino ships to exotic cities around the globe, where they stayed in hotels of unsurpassed class, such as Cairo's Shepherd Hotel, Bombay's Taj Mahal Hotel and Rangoon's Strand Hotel.

It did not take long for four Armenian brothers,[1] Aviet, Arshak, Martin and Tigran Sarkies, to see the opportunities that lay in accommodating these well-heeled travellers. On 1 December 1887, after an eight-day search, they found a favourable location – an old bungalow on the south waterfront of Singapore island. It had plenty of space for shady gardens, and was close enough to the Padang[2] yet remote enough from the hubbub of the harbour. A deal was struck with the bungalow's Arab owner with a yearly payment of 127 Spanish dollars. The Sarkies then began renovations to construct a 20-room hotel that was a cross between a Florentine palazzo and a French chateau. It was built using deeply coursed plasterwork with rusticated columns, arches, and a wide verandah running completely around all four sides of the building. Lofty rooms were built to suit the tropical climate.

The brothers named it 'Raffles Hotel', after the island's founder, Sir Stamford Thomas Raffles, who had established a trading post in Singapore for the British East India Company in 1819. His free trade policy had enabled Singapore to flourish as a commercial and trading centre.

The early 20th century was the golden age of world travel and Raffles Hotel soon attracted royalty, the rich and the powerful. It became a social hub of the well-heeled from the East and West – Crown princes, dukes, and local notables such as Sir Frank Swettenham and Sir Henry Keppel, along with a great many colonial military and civil bigwigs. Raffles was referred to as the 'Rendezvous of the Elite'. Tigran Sarkies, quick to capitalise on the human penchant for rubbing shoulders with the rich and famous, would publish lists of the celebrities who stayed at Raffles. Tigran was an irrepressible promoter of Raffles. Once, Rudyard Kipling, having stayed at Raffles, was prompted to write: 'Feed at Raffles and sleep at the Hotel de l'Europe'[3] and '... where the food is as excellent as the rooms are bad'.[4] Tigran blithely turned these sentiments to the hotel's advantage by extracting the words, 'Feed at Raffles – where the food is excellent.' Another brother, Arshak, loved to delight guests with jokes and party tricks. One of his all-time favourites was to balance a glass of whisky on his bald head, and waltz around the ballroom without spilling a drop.

Raffles underwent constant renovation and expansion to keep up with the business boom over the years. Its 1899 reopening was a brilliant affair. The whole hotel was illuminated by 800 bulbs and five arched lights that blazed at the main entrance. Raffles was Singapore's first hotel to have electricity, which it generated from its own dynamos. It was also the first private enterprise to have a telephone and attached bathroom with running water in each room.

During the years 1929–31, Arshak Sarkies embarked on extravagant renovations which resulted in a bankruptcy court suit. The renovation had unfortunately coincided with the Malayan rubber slump and the Great Depression. However, despite

*This case was funded by a grant from the National University of Singapore.

problems with creditors, Raffles survived with the help of a few hopeful investors. Between the 1920s and 1940s, Raffles began to show its age. Guests complained about leaking roofs, broken windows, cracked pillars and peeling plaster. The Sarkies, ever sanguine, saw it differently and increased advertising in the *Daily News* that read, 'For a taste of genuine antiquity, stay at Raffles Hotel.'

On 15 February 1942, Singapore fell to the invading Japanese army. Raffles was appropriated during the Japanese Occupation and turned into military quarters for senior Japanese officers. By the 1970s and 1980s, Raffles was showing its age badly – with run-down, roach-infested rooms, creaky doors, rattling windows and leaking taps. When Roberto Pregarz, an Italian, took over as general manager in 1972, 115 out of the hotel's 127 rooms were vacant.[5] Raffles was also losing some S$250 000 a year. Around it, old shophouses and colonial buildings were being razed to make way for the country's development. Raffles' seafront was soon replaced by reclaimed land for commercial development. Next to it, the Westin Stamford, the tallest hotel in Asia, soared proudly. Raffles stuck out like a derelict, decaying grandeur in the hustle and bustle of modern Singapore, and was regarded by many locals as an overrated colonial relic. There was talk of tearing down the hotel, but the intervention of a few concerned, influential individuals, as well as a growing appreciation among the nation's governing technocrats of the importance of preserving historical artifacts, led to Raffles being officially gazetted as a historical landmark on 3 March 1987 – the grand old hotel.

Two years later, the hotel was closed for a two-and-a-half-year restoration at a cost of S$160 million. The restoration work was a delicate affair. Care was taken to preserve the original colonial architecture of the three-storey building. Each of its 104 spacious and luxurious suites had 14-foot moulded ceilings, overhead fans, central air-conditioning, furnishings, marble bathrooms and hand-woven oriental rugs on teakwood floors. Raffles' suites, which recreated the style and ambience of the hotel's heyday at the turn of the century, had modern amenities skilfully blended in.

The new Raffles

Raffles Hotel's suites cost between S$650 and S$6 000 a night in 1995 (Exhibit 1). For S$6 000 a night, the most expensive in Singapore,[6] one could enjoy a colonial ambience, a luxurious 260-square-metre suite, which included sitting and dining rooms, two bedrooms, three bathrooms with a changing area, a private balcony, jacuzzis, and a 24-hour valet service. Comparatively, the presidential suites of other neighbouring top-end hotels,[7] which were usually taken up by heads of state, royalty, top corporate staff, celebrities and millionaires, went for between S$2 700 and S$4 960 a day.

Guests came predominantly from the United States (30 per cent) and Europe (30 per cent), with Japan and Australia making up about 25 per cent. Asians and visitors from a few other countries formed the remaining 15 per cent. Corporate clients represented 30

Exhibit 1 | Suite rates at Raffles Hotel effective from 1 April 1995

Suites	S$
Courtyard	650
Bras Basah	700
Palm Court	750
Gallery	750
Personality	800
Noel Coward	950
Somerset Maugham	950
Grand Hotel	4 000
Sarkies	from 6 000
Raffles	from 6 000

Note: All rates (except Grand Hotel) are for single occupancy and are subject to 10 per cent service charge, 1 per cent government tax and 3 per cent goods and services tax. Additional person charge S$50 up to a maximum of two additional persons.

Source: *The Tariff Schedule*, 1995, Raffles Hotel.

per cent of all occupants, while well-heeled, prominent travellers (including celebrities and politicians) comprised 65 per cent. The remaining 5 per cent of the hotel's guests were independently wealthy and wanted to commemorate special occasions with a stay at Raffles.

The hotel arcade

The hotel owned the Raffles Arcade which housed 12 food-and-beverages (F&B) outlets, six function areas, a mini-museum, a theatre playhouse, and 70 retail shops which included speciality stores such as Tiffany's, Hour Glass, Louis Vuitton, Jim Thompson, Hanae Mori and Donna Karan. The museum, opened free to the public, displayed photographs of famous guests such as Charlie Chaplin and Douglas Fairbanks Sr, a collection of 19th-century photographs of Singapore and Southeast Asia, and a safe in which the original maker of the cocktail concoction, the Singapore Sling, Ngiam Tong Boon, allegedly kept his secret recipe.

Raffles ran five of the speciality shops, selling a range of 500 merchandise items from coffee, spices and jams to notepads, T-shirts, shorts, caps and gold cufflinks. All these items were specially designed for the hotel and bore the Raffles name.

About 8 000 local people visited Raffles' F&B outlets each day. The food, costing between S$5 and S$10, was affordable and comparable to many other food centres.

Management

Raffles Hotel was managed by Raffles International Group, a wholly owned subsidiary of DBS Land which had a 56.67 per cent stake in Raffles. Raffles Investments Limited owned the remaining 43.33 per cent. Besides managing Raffles Hotel, Raffles International also offered tourism consultancy services, including hotel development, marketing and management, heritage conservation and restoration.

After renovation, Raffles Hotel changed in more than just appearance. For the first time in its history, Raffles' general manager was a Singaporean and a woman – Jennie Chua. All previous general managers had been European males – from Italy, Switzerland and Britain. Chua, an urbane and articulate woman, held a postgraduate degree from Cornell University in the United States and had over 25 years of hotel experience.

Raffles had a staff strength of 870, including about 130 executives. Until 1987, staff and their family members used to work at the hotel for generations. With the closing of the hotel for restoration, many were asked to leave. Hotel rules were strict – doormen, porter boys, chambermaids and waiters were required to undergo rigorous training. Doormen wore military uniforms that were meant to evoke memories of Raffles' early heyday.[8] Half of the staff wore designer uniforms. Others wore batik clothes with motifs of the orchid, Singapore's national flower, as well as the traveller's palm tree. Staff were trained to observe and attend to the smallest needs of individual guests – for example, a painting in a suite would be taken down if it was observed that a guest disliked it.

Raffles sought to recreate the old-world charm and ambience of its illustrious past. For Raffles, nostalgia and old-world service go hand in hand. Management's rule of thumb was 'the older the better'. Its mission was 'to delight patrons with many memorable experiences'.

Marketing

Marketing Raffles had always involved building upon its rich history and colourful events. One poignant tale had the last tiger of Singapore shot dead under a billiard table at Raffles in 1902. The real story was that the tiger was, in fact, a circus escapee, and anyone would have been very happy to see it shot. The tiger episode was now a part of the history of the hotel and lent itself well to promoting Raffles' exoticism. Besides the tiger in that era, there had been encounters with a python, a pig and a wild boar, so much so that *The Straits Times*, Singapore's local paper, was prompted to write: 'No sportsman in Asia should miss paying a visit to Raffles …'[9]

Another story Raffles used in promoting the hotel's exceptional service was that of the 70-year-old guest who refused to sleep in her room unless a mosquito net was set over her bed, just the way it was in her earlier stay at the hotel in 1937. Although the use of such mosquito nets had long been abandoned as all the suites were installed with air-conditioners, the staff nonetheless spent all night dutifully sewing her a fresh one from remnants of cloth found in a storeroom.

Raffles had been a respite for some of the most famous writers in English literature – Rudyard Kipling, Joseph Conrad and Noel Coward. Many of their handwritten letters and manuscripts were found in the hotel's museum. Raffles had used this fact to their advantage in their advertising. The hotel boasted of Somerset Maugham spending a whole morning writing under a frangipani tree in the hotel's Palm Court. Raffles continued to encourage this tradition by inviting well-known travel writers and journalists to Raffles to experience its ambience and personalised service.

Raffles Hotel, well-aware of the power of the visual medium in capturing the public imagination, had often volunteered its unique setting for films[10] and television productions. After all, as one writer wrote, 'There may be a hundred other luxury hotels, Hiltons, Sheratons, and Westins; but there is only one Raffles.'[11] The hotel also used network marketing and word of mouth, as well as calling on prospective and current corporate clients, in selling its rooms.

Raffles' ratings

Institutional Investor Magazine, in a 1993 hotel survey of the world's best hotels, ranked Raffles Hotel 18th in the world and seventh in the Asia-Pacific region.[12] It was rated highly for its excellent, professional service, security, and amenities such as huge American king-size beds, Persian carpets, interesting furniture, attractive bathrooms with old Peranakan-style[13] tiles, good disposable toothbrushes, soap and shampoo specially

Exhibit 2 | Raffles Hotel's balance sheet at 31 December 1992 and 1993

	1993 S$000	1992 S$000
FIXED ASSETS	162 661	171 678
INVESTMENT PROPERTY	175 300	175 300
INVESTMENTS	2 678	2 654
DEFERRED EXPENDITURE	6 544	7 496
CURRENT ASSETS		
Stocks	1 715	1 591
Trade debtors less provision S$189 819 (1992: S$174 326)	3 660	3 096
Other debtors and prepayments	696	385
Fixed deposits	3 916	4 281
Cash and bank balances	128	233
	10 115	9 586
CURRENT LIABILITIES		
Trade creditors	3 746	3 558
Other creditors and accrued charges	19 646	26 186
Due to related companies (non-trade)	209	189
Provision for income tax	90	24
Proposed final dividend	243	243
Bank overdraft (unsecured)	6 614	605
	30 548	30 805
NET CURRENT LIABILITIES	20 433	21 219
NON-CURRENT LIABILITIES		
Bank loans	130 500	147 100
Loan from holding company	17 000	17 488
Loan from shareholder	13 000	13 373
	166 250	157 948
SHARE CAPITAL		
Authorised: 100,000 ordinary shares of S$1 each	100 000	100 000
Issued and fully paid: 66 600 000 ordinary share of S$1 each	66 600	66 600
RESERVES		
Investment revaluation reserve	89 246	87 234
Unappropriated profit	10 404	4 114
	99 650	91 348
	166 250	157 948

Source: Raffles Hotel.

packaged for Raffles by Floris of London, and fruit trays. However, Raffles did not fare well on a number of items. Drain-holes in the showers were too small and occasionally caused flooding. Rooms in the S$600 range were a trifle small to be suites. There was no comprehensive minibar range, or coffee or tea service, while breakfast had to be ordered by phone. Toiletry items were limited (for example, body lotion, which is usually available in most hotels, is not provided) and bathrobes were oversized for women guests.

Financial performance

Raffles Hotel reported brisk business barely a month after its reopening. Initial occupancy rate was about 60 per cent, but management reported about 79 per cent – the industry average in 1994. Its 12 F&B outlets were booked in advance to up to 80 per cent of their capacity during meal-times,[14] with 70 per cent of the bookings done by locals. For Raffles, 90 cents on the dollar were earned for each room, while F&B outlets earned on average 35 cents on the dollar before taxes. At least one function a night was booked at the hotel's banquet halls until the end of the year. Raffles Hotel's balance sheet, profit and loss, and changes in financial position statements for 1992 and 1993 are shown in Exhibits 2–4.

The Asian financial crisis

In late 1997, the vibrant economies of Asia crumbled one after another as the full force of the Asian financial crisis hit the countries of Thailand, Indonesia, South Korea, Malaysia and Hong Kong, causing their economies to dive into a recession. Currencies plunged, with the Indonesian rupiah being affected the worst, diving in January 1998 to Rp 15 000 to US$1 from Rp 2 000 to US$1 before the crisis. Civil and political unrest ensued in Indonesia. Singapore was not spared, although the impact of the crisis hit it less severely

Exhibit 3 | Raffles Hotel's profit and loss statement at 31 December 1992 and 1993

	1993 S$000	1992 S$000
TURNOVER	65 682	64 446
PROFIT BEFORE TAXATION	6 623	5 903
After charging the following:		
Auditors remuneration	30	29
Depreciation of fixed assets	7 297	7 259
Director's fee	26	24
Amortisation of deferred expenditure	1 182	1 117
Provision for doubtful trade debts	36	136
Interest expense		
—holding company	512	—
—related companies	391	—
—others	4 474	6 151
And after crediting the following:		
Interest income	80	109
TAXATION	(90)	(90)
PROFIT AFTER TAXATION	6 533	5 813
Dividends	(243)	(243)
PROFIT FOR THE YEAR RETAINED	6 290	5 570
UNAPPROPRIATED PROFIT/(LOSS) BROUGHT FORWARD	4 114	(1 456)
UNAPPROPRIATED PROFIT CARRIED FORWARD	10 404	4 114

Source: Raffles Hotel.

Exhibit 4 | Raffles Hotel's changes in financial position at 31 December 1992 and 1993

	1993 S$000	1992 S$000
SOURCE OF FUNDS		
Profit before taxation	6 623	5 903
Adjustments for item not involving the movements of funds:		
Amortisation of deferred expenditure	1 182	1 117
Depreciation of fixed assets	7 297	7 259
	8 479	8 376
TOTAL GENERATED FROM OPERATIONS	15 102	14 279
FUNDS FROM OTHER SOURCES		
Bank loans	—	11 700
	15 102	25 979
OTHER APPLICATIONS		
Dividends paid	243	—
Income tax paid	90	—
Purchase of fixed assets	428	4 237
Purchase of investments	24	82
Payment of bank loans	16 600	—
Increase/(decrease) in working capital	(2 283)	21 660
	15 102	25 979
INCREASE/(DECREASE) IN WORKING CAPITAL		
Inventory	124	437
Deferred expenditure	230	496
Debtors	875	910
Creditors	2 126	14 993
Amount owing to/by related companies	841	1 234
	4 196	18 070
Increase/(decrease) in net liquid funds:	(470)	(31)
Fixed deposits, cash and bank balances	(6 009)	3 621
Bank overdraft	(6 479)	3 590
	(2 283)	21 660

Source: Raffles Hotel.

than other countries. Its economy contracted, with tens of thousands of workers being laid off in 1998, the trough of the recession. By 1999, the worst was over for most of the countries, although problems still remained. Many people were still unemployed, political unrest still existed and economic restructuring had yet to be completed. The tourism and hotel industry was badly hit.

The Asian financial crisis and the Singapore hotel industry

The crisis caused a drop in the tourism industry in Singapore. It did not help that, even before the Asian financial crisis was precipitated in August, the region had experienced thick smog caused by the indiscriminate burning of forests by logging and plantation companies in Sumatra, Indonesia. In 1997 and 1998, visitor arrivals dropped to 7.19 million and 6.24 million, respectively, from 7.29 million in 1996. Total revenue from tourism dropped to S$8.3 billion in 1998, bringing revenue back to the level in 1990.

Hotels in Singapore suffered a 32 per cent decrease in revenue per available room (RevPar) from S$143.74 in 1997 to S$97.97 in 1998. The RevPar registered a further decline to S$89.86 by end-1999. However, the 1999 RevPar was accompanied by an increase in occupancy levels of 74.7 per cent – that is, a 3.4 per cent increase compared to the 1998 level. By the end of June 2000, five-star hotels enjoyed an occupancy level of 82.9 per cent. The higher occupancy levels resulting from the region's recovery from the crisis were reflected in the increased visitor arrivals in 1999 of 6.96 million. As the region continued to recover from the crisis, visitor arrivals in Singapore were expected to remain healthy.

Raffles Hotel: Performance

In the years of the Asian economic crisis, Raffles Hotel suffered from the lower tourist arrivals in Singapore. In 1997 and 1998, Raffles Hotel registered a lower turnover and profit. In 1997, its profit declined by S$1.2 million. The decline in turnover and profit persisted in 1998. Raffles Hotel's turnover booked a decline of S$10.9 million. The hotel topped the industry, with an average room rate of S$599 in 1997 and above S$580 in 1998. In the first half of 1999, the average room rate for the industry fell approximately 17 per cent compared to the first half of 1998. Raffles Hotel's decrease for the first half of 1999 was approximately 4 per cent.

Its revenue from F&B, which had contributed significantly to overall revenues, was affected as a result of lower local spending. Rental revenue from the Raffles Hotel Arcade was also adversely affected. In spite of the recession years, capital expenditures for Raffles Hotel in 1997 and 1998 were approximately S$2.13 million and S$1.99 million, respectively.

Raffles continued to be rated well internationally. In 1998, it was in the *Conde Naste Traveler* list of the 'Top Hotels in the World' and was ranked among the top 25 hotels in the world in the 'Readers Select World's Best Hotels' survey in *Institutional Investor* magazine.

Competition

Between 1996 and 1999, the vicinity of Raffles Hotel saw the completion of Suntec City, a huge complex of office buildings, exhibition centres and shopping mall; Chjmes, a sprawling turn-of-the-century convent girls' school now housing shops, restaurants and galleries; two malls, the up-market Millenia Walk and the underground mall CityLink; and two high-end hotels, the Ritz-Carlton Millennia and the Conrad International. While the new shopping malls and office buildings brought more visitors and tourists into the area, the two hotels posed new competition for Raffles.

A survey of room rates by the consulting company Arthur Anderson concluded that room rates in Singapore should be higher. In 1999, Singapore's average room rate was S$161, compared to Hong Kong's S$209. It should have been on a par with Hong Kong's, but for the intense competition in the hotel industry. According to Conrad International's sales and marketing director, Theresa Choo, 'Each time any hotel decides to raise room rates, a competitor hotel of a higher standard either matches or lowers theirs.'[15]

This situation was not helped by the fact that 65–75 per cent of total room supply in Singapore was in the up-scale and deluxe hotels – defined to be the business, business and pleasure, and meetings, incentives, convention and exhibition visitors – while the market for such hotels is limited to around 30 per cent of total visitor arrivals.[16]

Ownership[17]

Raffles Hotel was 56.7 per cent owned by Raffles Holdings Limited, which in turn was 45 per cent owned by DBS Land Limited (DBSL), one of the largest property groups in Singapore (Exhibit 5). Raffles Holdings was listed on the Singapore Stock Exchange in December 1999.

Raffles Holdings had expanded locally and internationally. As of 1999, it owned 2 626 deluxe hotel rooms and suites representing approximately 10 per cent of the deluxe hotel rooms available in Singapore. Its international expansion was marked in 1997 by the purchases of hotels in London and Hamburg, in Germany, as well as the establishment of two hotels in Cambodia. Among the hotels owned by Raffles Holdings, the Raffles Hotel Singapore was positioned as the flagship product (Exhibit 6).

In building its hotel portfolio, Raffles Holdings developed a three-tiered branding strategy. All of its hotels were marketed using the Raffles International master brand, capitalising on the distinctive Raffles name. However, there were some distinctions among the hotels' targeting and positioning strategies. Hotels marketed under the Raffles brand were targeted at affluent and leisure travellers and were luxury landmark hotels or distinctive properties located in gateway cities. These included Raffles Hotel; Brown's Hotel, London; Hotel Vier Jahreszeiten, Hamburg; and Hotel Le Royal, Phnom Penh, Cambodia. In 1994, Raffles Hotel formed a joint venture with the owner of the 19th-century Galle Face Hotel, Colombo, Sri Lanka, to restore and redevelop the historic hotel. A year later, the deal was called off because the cost of the facelift was more expensive than estimated. The distinctive positioning of the hotels belonging to this category, vis-à-vis other top international hotels, was their 'memorable experience'.

The Raffles Resort brand comprised luxury resorts in locations with strong appeal to the leisure market, including individual, family, incentive and special interest travellers. The resort hotels were designed to take their distinctive form and character from their local culture, history and natural environment. Raffles Holdings owned and operated the Grand Hotel d'Angkor, a Raffles Resort in Siem Reap, Cambodia, near the Angkor Temple complex, and was developing Raffles Resorts in Mallorca, Spain, and on the islands of Bali and Bintan in Indonesia.

The third category was marketed under the Merchant Court brand name and targeted at the middle and upper mid-level market segments and designed to appeal to both business and leisure travellers.

Besides hotels, which contributed approximately 70 per cent to the group's turnover, Raffles Holdings also owned and managed the Raffles City complex, a 337 384-square-metre mixed-use property located in Singapore's central business district. The Raffles City complex comprised the Westin Stamford and Westin Plaza hotels, the Raffles City Convention Center, and a retail and office complex. These two hotel properties were leased out to RC Hotels through Raffles Holdings' wholly owned subsidiary, Raffles City (Pte) Limited. Raffles City (Pte) Limited received rental fees from RC Hotels. The Westin Hotel Company managed and operated the two hotels under the Westin brand name and received a management fee based on a percentage of gross operating profits.

Raffles Holdings' strategy was to 'build upon the Raffles international master brand name to create a diversified group of luxury hotels and resorts in strategic locations throughout the world'.

In addition to expansion, they also formed a cross-marketing alliance with three top-ranked hotels in Europe. Raffles Holdings was also part of Global

Exhibit 5 | Raffles Holdings' hotel portfolio, June 1999

Hotel	Location	Total no. of rooms
Raffles Brand		
Raffles Hotel	Singapore	104 suites
Brown's Hotel	London, England	118
Hotel Vier Jahreszeiten	Hamburg, Germany	158
Hotel Le Royal	Phnom Penh, Cambodia	208
Raffles Resort Brand		
Grand Hotel d'Angkor	Siem Reap, Cambodia	128
Merchant Court Brand		
Merchant Court Singapore	Singapore	476
Asset Managed Hotels		
Westin Stamford	Singapore	1 263
Westin Plaza	Singapore	783

Source: Raffles Hotel.

Exhibit 6 | Raffles Holdings Limited, principal operating companies

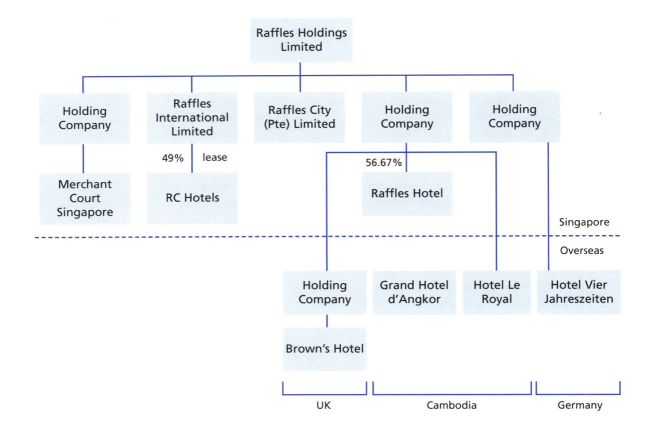

Exhibit 7 | Distribution of visitor arrivals by residence, 1993–8

Residence	1993	1994	1995	1996	1997	1998
Americas	6.06	6.20	5.97	6.30	6.40	6.82
Asia	69.57	71.30	73.30	72.94	72.26	67.67
ASEAN	30.71	31.62	31.15	31.30	32.56	30.12
China	3.51	2.39	2.83	3.11	3.27	4.70
Hong Kong SAR	3.93	3.93	3.92	3.96	3.68	4.38
Japan	15.58	16.08	16.52	16.07	15.20	13.52
S. Korea	3.09	4.20	4.92	5.27	4.15	1.59
Taiwan	6.65	7.40	7.89	7.25	6.94	5.81
Others	6.10	5.68	6.07	5.98	6.46	
Europe	15.87	14.74	13.53	13.75	13.72	15.74
Oceania	6.97	6.29	5.98	5.91	6.43	8.33
Africa	1.52	1.46	1.22	1.09	0.98	1.27
Not stated	0.01	0.01	0.00	0.00	0.21	0.18
Total %	100	100	100	100	100	100
Total arrivals	6 425 778	6 898 951	7 137 255	7 292 521	7 197 963	6 242 153

Note:
* Oceania includes Australia, New Zealand and other countries in Oceania.
Source: *Singapore Annual Report on Tourism Statistics*, 1998, Table 3.

Exhibit 8 | Statement of operations based on number of rooms, 1998

	Less than 350 rooms Ratio to revenue	351 to 500 rooms Ratio to revenue	501 rooms & above Ratio to revenue
Revenues			
Room department	56.1%	54.8%	55.1%
Food department	27.8	28.9	29.2
Beverage department	8.4	8.6	10.3
Telephone department	2.0	1.4	1.6
Other operated department	1.0	1.0	1.1
Rentals and other income	4.7	4.6	2.6
Total revenues	100%	100%	100%
Departmental costs & expenses*			
Room department	24.9%	28.1	20.6
Food & beverage department	78.7	85.6	73.0
Telephone department	113.7	111.9	103.4
Total cost & expenses	44.8%	49.8	42.2
Total operated departments income	55.2%		
Undistributed operating expenses	55.2	71.9	79.4
Administrative & general	10.7%	14.4	27.0
Marketing & guest entertainment	5.9%	5.9	4.0
Property operation & maintenance	5.4%	6.0	8.7
Energy costs	5.4%	5.4	4.0
Total undistributed expenses	27.3%	26.1	55.7
Income before management fees & fixed charges**	28.0%	19.5%	34.6%

Notes:
* The ratio of departmental costs and expenses to revenues generated by the respective departments. For example, the costs and expenses of the room department amount to 24.9 per cent of revenues generated by the room department for hotels with less than 350 rooms.
** Fixed charges include property tax, insurance, rent, interest, depreciation, etc.

Source: *1998 Singapore Hotel Industry Survey of Operations*, Singapore Hotel Association

Distribution Systems, a major reservations system used by travel agents for flights and accommodation.

Raffles Holdings believed that it should capitalise on its management expertise and master brand name through securing management contracts for properties owned by third parties. By securing management contracts, it could improve its return on capital and enhance its management fee income.

F&B and service were considered critical to its success. As such, it established the Culinary Academy at Raffles Hotel, which served as a test kitchen for Raffles Holdings' new food concepts and as a training site for its culinary employees. It also provided F&B appreciation programs to hotel guests as well as interested locals. It developed a proprietary training program, 'Excel Through Training', which was used in its training centres in Singapore, Cambodia and Germany. It recently collaborated with the Cambodian government to establish the Cambodia Hotel and Tourism Academy to provide training in the hotel industry.

The future

Raffles Holdings believed that there was really no competition for Raffles Hotel, although it acknowledged that their hotels competed for guests with other hotels in the highly competitive lodging industry in various countries. How can Raffles Holdings help its flagship hotel, Raffles Hotel, compete better in this very competitive industry? How should Raffles Holdings itself pursue its growth strategy?

Exhibit 9 | Labour cost, 1998

	Hotel industry ($)	Ratio to revenue (%)	Analysis by number of rooms		
			Less than 350 rooms Ratio to revenue (%)	351 to 500 rooms Ratio to revenue (%)	501 & above rooms Ratio to revenue (%)
*Labour cost per available room					
Room department	5 287	8.1	8.5	9.6	5.8
Food & beverage department	9 828	14.8	13.8	16.5	12.5
Telephone department	310	0.5	0.5	0.5	0.4
Administrative & general department	3 441	6.3	6.3	5.5	4.1
Marketing department	1 467	2.2	2.2	2.6	1.7
Property operation & maintenance department	1 519	2.3	2.5	2.6	1.7
Total labour cost	21 852	34.2	33.8	36.7	26.2

Note:
* Total payroll and related expenses (salaries and wages, including vacations and employees' benefits).
Source: *1998 Singapore Hotel Industry Survey of Operations*, Singapore Hotel Association.

Exhibit 10 | Comparison of rates of selected hotels, 2000

	Single/double rooms	Suite
Raffles	—	$650–$6 000
Four Seasons	$435–$500	$580–$4 500
Shangri-La	$375–$550	$500–$3 200
Westin Stamford	$340–$380	$450–$1 700
Westin Plaza	$360–$400	$700–$2 100
Hyatt Regency	$450–$530	$1 200–$3 800
Ritz-Carlton	$430–$475	$550–$5 000
Conrad International	$360–$400	$550–$3 300

Endnotes

* This case was first published as two separate cases ('Raffles Hotel (A)' and 'Raffles Hotel (B)') in Kulwant Singh, Nitin Pangarkar and Gaik Eng Lim (eds), 2001, *Business Strategy in Asia: A Casebook* (Singapore: Thomson Learning).
1. The Sarkies brothers also owned the Strand Hotel in Rangoon.
2. A large rectangular assembly ground for national events in those days, enclosed by important government administrative buildings and commerce buildings on its northern side and the waterfront on its southern side.
3. A European competitor hotel of Raffles, also in the vicinity of the waterfront.
4. At that point in time, Raffles had previously served as a boarding house for schoolgirls.
5. N. Ghosh, 1989, 'The selling of Raffles', *Business Times*, 9–10 November.
6. 'Raffles Hotel will boast the dearest suites in August', 1991, *The Straits Times*, 27 March.
7. Top-end hotels are equivalent to five-star hotels based on the amount of amenities and quality of services provided. In Singapore, hotels are categorised according to the number of rooms they have. Examples of top-end hotels include the Westin Stamford & Westin Plaza, Four Seasons, Shangri-La and Hyatt Regency.
8. 'Re-opening of Raffles will see most staff in designer uniforms', 1991, *The Straits Times*, 22 July.
9. K. Chopard, 1987, *The Tiger's Tale* (Singapore: Landmark Books).
10. One such film is *Pretty Polly*, which starred Trevor Howard and Hayley Mills in 1967.
11. I. Sharp, 1986, *There is Only One Raffles* (London: Souvenir Press).
12. 'Raffles Hotel voted one of the world's best', 1993, *Business Times*, 12 October.
13. Tiles that affect the style favoured by Peranakan Chinese (that is, Chinese born in the Straits Settlements of Peninsular Malaysia).
14. 'Rooms 79% occupied, F&B outlets 80% booked at meal-times', 1991, *Business Times*, 14 October.
15. K. Boo, 2000, 'It's a price war out there in the hospitality industry', *The Straits Times*, 30 August.
16. C. Khoo, 2000, 'Address hotel sector's imbalance holistically', *Business Times*, 31 August, p. 12.
17. Raffles Holding Limited Prospectus, 1 December 1999.

Case 14

Southwest Airlines, 1996

Andrew Inkpen
Valerie DeGroot
Thunderbird, The American Graduate School of International Management

In January 1996, Southwest Airlines (Southwest) entered the Florida and southeastern US markets. The company planned to operate 78 daily flights to Tampa, Fort Lauderdale and Orlando by August of the following year. With the expansion into Florida, the northeast remained the only major US air traffic region where Southwest did not compete. The northeast US market had generally been avoided by low-fare airlines such as Southwest because of airport congestion, air traffic control delays, frequent inclement weather and dominance by a few major airlines. Airports such as Logan International in Boston, J.F.K. International in New York, and Newark International were among the busiest and most congested airports in the country. Continental Airline's attempt to introduce widespread, low-fare operations in the East during 1994–5 was a financial disaster.

With the move into Florida and the potential challenges associated with the northeastern market, questions were being raised about Southwest's ability to maintain its position as America's most consistently profitable airline. In particular, there were concerns whether Southwest was growing too fast and deviating from its proven strategy. Would entry into the Florida market, and possibly the northeastern market, jeopardise 25 years of success? Success resulted in a focused strategy based on frequent flights, rapid turnarounds at airport gates, and a careful selection of markets and airports that avoided ground and air traffic control delays. Herb Kelleher, the charismatic president, co-founder and chief executive officer of the airline, wrote to his employees in 1993: 'Southwest has had more opportunities for growth than it has airplanes. Yet, unlike other airlines, it has avoided the trap of growing beyond its means. Whether you are talking with an officer or a ramp agent, employees just don't seem to be enamored of the idea that bigger is better.'[1]

The US airline industry

The nature of the US commercial airline industry was permanently altered in October 1978 when President Jimmy Carter signed the *Airline Deregulation Act*. Before deregulation, the Civil Aeronautics Board regulated airline route entry and exit, passenger fares, mergers and acquisitions, and airline rates of return. Typically, two or three carriers provided service in a given market, although there were routes covered by only one carrier. Cost increases were passed along to customers, and price competition was almost nonexistent. The airlines operated as if there were only two market segments: those who could afford to fly and those who couldn't.[2]

Deregulation sent airline fares tumbling and allowed many new firms to enter the market. The financial impact on both established and new airlines was enormous. The fuel crisis of 1979 and the air traffic controllers' strike in 1981 contributed to the industry's difficulties, as did the severe recession that hit the United States during the early 1980s. During the first decade of deregulation, more than 150 carriers, many of them new start-up airlines, collapsed into bankruptcy. Eight of the major 11 airlines dominating the industry in 1978 ended up filing for bankruptcy, merging with other carriers or simply disappearing from the radar screen. Collectively, the industry made enough money during this period to buy two Boeing 747s (Exhibit 1).[3] The three major carriers that survived

© Copyright 1997 Thunderbird, The American Graduate School of International Management. All rights reserved. This case was prepared for the basis of classroom discussion only and is not intended to illustrate either effective or ineffective management.

Exhibit 1 | Airline operating data, 1986–94

Seat-miles flown

	American	America-West	Continental	Delta	Eastern	Northwest	Pan-American	Southwest	TransWorld	United	USAir	Total All Majors
1994	110 658	17 852	49 762	98 104		52 110	0	29 624	27 938	95 965	58 311	540 324
1993	117 719	16 980	49 690	99 852		52 623	0	34 759	25 044	98 652	55 918	551 237
1992	114 418	18 603	49 143	100 904		52 430		21 371	30 483	89 605	56 027	532 984
1991	104 616	19 460	48 742	94 350		48 847	9 042	18 440	29 684	88 092	56 470	517 743
1990	102 864	18 139	48 385	87 748	25 299	47 210	12 157	16 456	33 942	86 085	58 014	536 299
1989	98 638	13 523	47 107	82 440	15 489	44 372	11 670	14 788	35 246	82 758	40 652	486 683
1988	88 620	11 994	53 343	79 719	41 126	39 349	10 331	13 370	35 024	84 240	28 234	485 350
1987	77 724	10 318	54 626	71 504	50 156	41 499	8 217	11 457	33 566	86 246	20 014	465 327
1986	66 901	4 296	27 778	50 448	52 556	27 561	8 901	9 712	29 534	78 568	18 254	374 509
Total	882 158	131 165	428 576	765 069	184 626	406 001	60 318	169 977	280 461	790 211	391 894	4 490 456

Revenue per passenger-miles (RPMs) (in cents)

	American	America-West	Continental	Delta	Eastern	Northwest	Pan-American	Southwest	TransWorld	United	USAir
1994	13.11	10.81	11.50	13.93		13.93	0	11.65	12.67	11.81	15.92
1993	13.65	11.13	11.97	14.66		13.06	0	11.92	12.78	12.49	17.94
1992	12.03	10.36	11.01	14.02		12.21	0	11.78	11.13	11.88	16.97
1991	13.11	10.00	11.79	14.30		12.79	10.02	11.25	11.31	12.21	16.93
1990	12.86	11.14	12.48	14.21		13.24	11.65	11.48	12.34	12.71	16.37
1989	12.27	11.84	12.04	13.91	11.71	13.02	11.98	10.49	12.10	12.18	15.83
1988	11.92	10.52	10.61	13.52	12.00	12.54	10.94	10.74	11.47	10.86	15.33
1987	11.06	9.66	9.34	13.11	11.02	11.73	9.97	10.02	11.02	10.10	14.91
1986	10.23	9.90	8.56	13.54	11.26	10.48	10.12	10.59	10.07	9.87	14.93

Passenger load factor (per cent)

	American	America-West	Continental	Delta	Eastern	Northwest	Pan-American	Southwest	TransWorld	United	USAir
1994	62.35	67.99	62.48	64.68		64.88	0.00	66.80	62.73	69.80	62.02
1993	59.21	65.56	62.20	61.52		63.51	0.00	68.09	62.38	63.80	58.59
1992	63.12	61.62	63.14	60.59		62.24	0.00	64.52	62.94	66.15	58.60
1991	60.86	64.94	61.80	59.95		62.90	60.53	61.14	60.94	64.23	58.22
1990	61.48	60.99	58.42	57.98	60.80	62.53	60.00	60.60	58.90	63.85	59.54
1989	63.6	57.7	60.3	63.6	61.9	60.9	61.2	62.7	59.4	65.4	61.2
1988	63.1	57.9	58.8	57.6	61.8	61.8	63.4	57.7	59.9	67.4	61.3
1987	63.7	56.1	60.7	55.5	65.3	61.8	64.1	58.9	62.0	65.0	65.3
1986	65.6	61.0	62.7	57.4	60.6	54.9	51.4	58.3	59.5	65.6	61.1

Case 14   Southwest Airlines, 1996

Operating revenues (US$mn)

	American	America-West	Continental	Delta	Eastern	Northwest	Pan-American	Southwest	TransWorld	United	USAir	Total All Majors
1994	10 631	1 414	4 091	9 514		5 325		2 417	2 555	8 966	6 394	51 307
1993	10 828	1 332	4 128	9 653		4 928		2 067	2 325	8 794	6 364	50 419
1992	9 902	1 281	3 840	9 164		4 464		1 685	2 510	7 861	5 974	46 681
1991	9 429	1 359	4 014	8 593		4 356	596	1 314	2 464	7 790	5 895	45 810
1990	9 203	1 322	4 036	7 697		4 298	946	1 187	2 878	7 946	6 085	45 598
1989	8 670	998	3 896	7 780	1 295	3 944	957	1 015	2 918	7 463	4 160	43 096
1988	7 548	781	3 682	6 684	3 423	3 395	804	860	2 777	7 006	2 803	39 763
1987	6 369	577	3 404	5 638	4 054	3 328	625	699	2 668	6 500	2 070	35 932
1986	5 321	330	1 676	4 245	4 093	1 815	553	620	2 064	5 727	1 787	28 231
Total	77 901	9 394	32 767	68 968	12 865	35 853	4 481	11 864	23 159	68 053	41 532	

Net operating income/(loss) (US$mn)

	American	America-West	Continental	Delta	Eastern	Northwest	Pan-American	Southwest	TransWorld	United	USAir	Total All Majors
1994	432	146	(145)	123		725		290	(81)	262	(466)	1 286
1993	357	121	56	335		268		281	(63)	184	(143)	1 396
1992	(251)	(64)	(183)	(225)		(203)		182	(191)	(354)	(397)	(1 686)
1991	40	(79)	(218)	(115)		17	(186)	62	(233)	(412)	(233)	(1 357)
1990	103	(32)	(191)	(176)		(132)	(280)	82	(134)	(34)	(437)	(1 231)
1989	709	48	124	677	(666)	57	(118)	98	10	302	(239)	1 002
1988	794	18	(87)	441	(187)	19	(181)	86	113	461	144	1 621
1987	483	(35)	(56)	383	66	72	(260)	41	79	97	263	1 133
1986	378	4	91	212	61	(25)	(283)	81	(77)	51	164	657
Total	3 045	127	(609)	1 655	(726)	798	(1 308)	1 203	(577)	557	(1 344)	

Source: Department of Transportation.

intact – Delta, United and American – ended up with 80 per cent of all domestic US air traffic and 67 per cent of trans-Atlantic business.[4]

Competition and lower fares led to greatly expanded demand for airline travel. By the mid-1990s, the airlines were having trouble meeting this demand. Travel increased from 200 million travellers in 1974 to 500 million in 1995, yet only five new runways were built during this time period. During the 1980s, many airlines acquired significant levels of new debt in efforts to service the increased travel demand. Long-term debt-to-capitalisation ratios increased dramatically: Eastern's went from 62 to 473 per cent, TWA's went from 62 to 115 per cent, and Continental's went from 62 to 96 per cent. In contrast, United and Delta maintained their debt ratios at less than 60 per cent, and American Airline's ratio dropped to 34 per cent.

Despite the financial problems experienced by many fledgeling airlines started after deregulation, new firms continued to enter the market. Between 1992 and 1995, 69 new airlines were certified by the FAA. Most of these airlines competed with limited route structures and lower fares than the major airlines. The new low-fare airlines created a second tier of service providers that save consumers billions of dollars annually and provided service in markets abandoned or ignored by major carriers. One such start-up was Kiwi Airlines, founded by former employees of the defunct Eastern and Pan Am airlines. Kiwi was funded largely by employees: pilots paid US$50 000 each to get jobs and other employees paid US$5 000.

Despite fostering competition and the growth of new airlines, deregulation created a significant regional disparity in ticket prices and adversely affected service to small and remote communities. Airline workers generally suffered, with inflation-adjusted average employee wages falling from US$42 928 in 1978 to US$37 985 in 1988. About 20 000 airline industry employees were laid off in the early 1980s, while productivity of the remaining employees rose 43 per cent during the same period. In a variety of cases, bankruptcy filings were used to diminish the role of unions and reduce unionised wages.

Industry economics

About 80 per cent of airline operating costs were fixed or semi-variable. The only true variable costs were travel agency commissions, food costs and ticketing fees. The operating costs of an airline flight depended primarily on the distance travelled, not the number of passengers on board. For example, the crew and ground staff sizes were determined by the type of aircraft, not the passenger load. Therefore, once an airline established its route structure, most of its operating costs were fixed.

Because of this high fixed-cost structure, the airlines developed sophisticated software tools to maximise capacity utilisation, known as *load factor*. Load factor was calculated by dividing RPM (revenue passenger miles – the number of passengers carried multiplied by the distance flown) by ASM (available seat miles – the number of seats available for sale multiplied by the distance flown).

On each flight by one of the major airlines (excluding Southwest and the low-fare carriers), there were typically a dozen categories of fares. The airlines analysed historical travel patterns on individual routes to determine how many seats to sell at each fare level. All of the major airlines used this type of analysis and flexible pricing practice, known as a *yield management system*. These systems enabled the airlines to manage their seat inventories and the prices paid for those seats. The objective was to sell more seats on each flight at higher yields. (Total passenger yield was passenger revenue from scheduled operations divided by scheduled RPMs.) The higher the ticket price, the better the yield.

Although reducing operating costs was a high priority for the airlines, the nature of the cost structure limited cost-reduction opportunities. Fuel costs (about 13 per cent of total costs) were largely beyond the control of the airlines, and many of the larger airlines' restrictive union agreements limited labour flexibility. Although newer aircraft were much more fuel-efficient than older models, most airlines had sharply lowered their new aircraft orders to avoid taking on more debt. At the end of June 1990, US airlines had outstanding orders to buy 2 748 aircraft. At the end of June 1996, orders had fallen to 1 111.[5] (A new Boeing 737 cost about US$28 million in 1995.)

To manage their route structures, all of the major airlines (except Southwest) maintained their operations around a 'hub-and-spoke' network. The spokes fed passengers from outlying points into a central airport – the hub – where passengers could travel to additional hubs or their final destination. For example, to fly from Phoenix to Boston on Northwest Airlines, a typical route would involve a flight from Phoenix to Northwest's Detroit hub. The passenger would then take a second flight from Detroit to Boston.

Establishing a major hub in a city like Chicago or Atlanta required an investment of as much as US$150 million for gate acquisition and terminal construction.

Although hubs created inconveniences for travellers, hub systems were an efficient means of distributing services across a wide network. The major airlines were very protective of their so-called fortress hubs and used the hubs to control various local markets. For example, Northwest controlled more than 78 per cent of the local traffic in Detroit and 84 per cent in Minneapolis. When Southwest entered the Detroit market, the only available gates were already leased by Northwest. Northwest subleased gates to Southwest at rates 18 times higher than Northwest's costs. Southwest eventually withdrew from Detroit, one of only three markets the company had abandoned in its history. (Denver and Beaumont, Texas, were the other two.)

Recent airline industry performance

US airlines suffered a combined loss of US$13 billion from 1990 to 1994 (Exhibit 1).[6] High debt levels plagued the industry. In 1994, the earnings picture began to change, with the industry as a whole reducing its losses to US$278 million.[7] Overall expansion and health returned to the industry in 1995 and 1996. In 1996, net earnings were a record US$2.4 billion. (See Exhibit 2 for 1995 airline performance and Exhibit 3 for 1995 market share ratings.) For 1996, revenue forecasts were US$7.2 billion with a net profit of US$3 billion.

In 1996, for the first time in 10 years, the industry had a profitable first quarter (US$110 million). Numerous statistics indicated that the industry was in good shape: load factors were up to 68–69 per cent in 1996; fares were up 5 per cent; and yields were up to 13.52 cents per passenger-mile. The break-even load factor fell 2.5 points to about 65 per cent and unit costs dropped by 0.4 per cent in 1995.[8] The expiration of a 10 per cent domestic ticket tax resulted in net lower-priced tickets to customers despite increased fares. Traffic growth outpaced the 1.7 per cent industry rise in capacity.

Future pressures on the industry

Despite the recent positive financial performance, concerns over fare wars, over-capacity in some markets, increased fuel prices and the possibility of economic recession created significant uncertainty about the future. In particular, cost pressures were expected from several factors:

1 *Labour costs.* The average salary per airline employee from 1987 to 1996 rose at a rate faster than the increase in the CPI index (4.4 per cent increase in

Exhibit 2 | Airline performance

	Revenue ($000s)	Net profit ($000s)	RPM (000s)	ASM (000s)
American	15 501 000	167 000	102 900 000	155 300 000
United	14 943 000	349 000	111 811 000	158 569 000
Delta	12 194 000	510 000	86 400 000	130 500 000
Northwest	9 080 000	392 000	62 500 000	87 500 000
USAir	7 474 000	119 000	37 618 000	58 163 000
Continental	5 825 000	224 000	40 023 000	61 006 000
TWA	3 320 000	(227 400)	25 068 683	38 186 111
Southwest	2 872 751	182 626	23 327 804	36 180 001
America West	1 600 000	53 800	13 300 000	19 400 000
Alaska	1 417 500	17 300	9 335 000	15 299 000
American Trans Air	715 009	8 524	4 183 692	5 951 162
Tower Air	490 472	10 689	1 208 001	1 455 996
Mesa	454 538	14 012	1 179 397	2 310 895
Conair	418 466	N/A	1 187 706	2 274 695
ValuJet	367 800	67 800	2 600 000	3 800 000
Hawaiian	346 904	(5 506)	3 171 365	4 238 320
Atlantic Southeast	328 725	51 137	763 000	1 700 000
Midwest Express	259 155	19 129	1 150 338	1 794 924
Reno Air	256 508	1 951	2 090 017	3 322 475

Source: *Business Travel News*, 27 May 1996, and *Air Transport World*, March 1996.

Exhibit 3 | Airline market shares

1995 Company rankings	% Market share	1985 Company rankings	% Market share
United	21.0	American	13.3
American	19.3	United	12.5
Delta	16.0	Eastern	10.0
Northwest	11.7	TWA	9.6
Continental	7.5	Delta	9.0
USAir	7.2	Pan Am	8.1
TWA	4.7	NWA	6.7
Southwest	4.4	Continental	4.9
America West	2.5	People Express	3.3
American Trans Air	1.2	Republic	3.2
Others	4.5	Others	19.4
Total	100.0	Total	100.0

Sources: Department of Transportation and Standard & Poor's, cited by *Industry Surveys*, 1 February 1996.

labour costs compared with a 3.7 per cent CPI increase over the same period).[9] Pressure from labour was expected to increase as employees sought a share of the airlines' recent record profits. The possibility of new federal regulations concerning aircrew flight and duty time requirements were also an issue. It was estimated that the potential costs from regulation changes could be as high as US$1.2 billion in the first year and US$800 million in each subsequent year.

2 *Aircraft maintenance*. The ageing of the general aircraft population meant higher maintenance costs and eventual aircraft replacement. The introduction of stricter government regulations for older planes placed new burdens on those operating them.

3 *Debt servicing*. The airline industry's debt load of approximately 65 per cent greatly exceeded US industry averages of about 40 per cent.

4 *Fuel costs*. Long-term jet fuel cost was uncertain. Prices had risen 11 cents per gallon from July 1995 to May 1996. Proposed fuel taxes could cost the industry as much as US$500 million a year.

5 *Air traffic delays*. Increased air traffic control delays caused by higher travel demand and related airport congestion were expected to negatively influence airlines' profitability.

Southwest Airlines' background

In 1966, Herb Kelleher was practising law in San Antonio when a client named Rollin King proposed starting a short-haul airline similar to California-based Pacific Southwest Airlines. The airline would fly the 'Golden Triangle' of Houston, Dallas and San Antonio and by staying within Texas, avoid federal regulations. Kelleher and King incorporated a company, raised initial capital and filed for regulatory approval from the Texas Aeronautics Commission. Unfortunately, the other Texas-based airlines – namely, Braniff, Continental and Trans Texas (later called Texas International) – opposed the idea and waged a battle to prohibit Southwest from flying. Kelleher argued the company's case before the Texas Supreme Court, which ruled in Southwest's favour. The US Supreme Court refused to hear an appeal filed by the other airlines. In late 1970, it looked as if the company could begin flying.

Southwest began building a management team and purchased three surplus Boeing 737s. Meanwhile, Braniff and Texas International continued their efforts to prevent Southwest from flying. The underwriters of Southwest's initial public stock offering withdrew and a restraining order against the company was obtained two days before its scheduled inaugural flight. Kelleher again argued his company's case before the Texas Supreme Court, which ruled in Southwest's favour a second time, lifting the restraining order. Southwest Airlines began flying the next day, 18 June 1971.[10]

When Southwest began flying to three Texas cities, the firm had three aircraft and 25 employees. Initial flights were out of Dallas's older Love Field Airport and Houston's Hobby Airport, both of which were closer to downtown than the major international airports. Flamboyant from the beginning, original flights were staffed by flight attendants in hot-pants. By 1996, the flight attendant uniform had evolved into khakis and polo shirts. The 'Luv' theme was a staple of the airline from the outset and became the company's ticker symbol on Wall Street.

Southwest management quickly discovered that there were two types of travellers: convenience, time-oriented business travellers and price-sensitive leisure travellers. To cater to both groups, Southwest developed a two-tiered pricing structure. In 1972, Southwest was charging US$20 to fly between Houston, Dallas and San Antonio, undercutting the US$28 fares of the other carriers. After an experiment with US$10 fares, Southwest decided to sell seats on weekdays until 7 p.m. for US$26 and after 7 p.m. and on weekends for US$13.[11] In response, in January 1973, Braniff Airlines began charging US$13 for its Dallas–Houston Hobby flights. This resulted in one of Southwest's most famous ads, which had the caption 'Nobody's going to shoot Southwest out of the sky for a lousy $13.' Southwest offered travellers the opportunity to pay US$13 or US$26 and receive a free bottle of liquor. More than 75 per cent of the passengers chose the US$26 fare and Southwest became the largest distributor of Chivas Regal scotch whisky in Texas. In 1975, Braniff abandoned the Dallas–Houston Hobby route. When Southwest entered the Cleveland market, the unrestricted one-way fare between Cleveland and Chicago was US$310 on other carriers; Southwest's fare was US$59.[12] One of Southwest's problems was convincing passengers that its low fares were not just introductory promotions but regular fares.

Southwest's operations

Although Southwest grew to be one of the largest airlines in the United States, the firm did not deviate from its initial focus: short-haul (less than 500 miles), point-to-point flights; a fleet consisting only of Boeing 737s; high-frequency flights; low fares; and no international flights. In 1995, the average Southwest one-way fare was US$69. The average stage length of Southwest flights was 394 miles, with flights of 600 miles making up less than 2.5 per cent of the airline's capacity. Kelleher indicated in an interview that it would be unlikely that the company's longer flights (those more than 600 miles) would ever exceed 10 per cent of its business.[13] On average, Southwest had more than 40 departures per day per city, and each plane flew about 10 flights daily, almost twice the industry average.[14] Planes were used an average of 11.5 hours a day, compared with the industry's 8.6 hours per day average.[15] Southwest's cost per available seat-mile was the lowest in the industry (Exhibit 4) and the average age of its fleet in 1995 was 7.9 years, the lowest for the major carriers. Southwest also had the best safety record in the airline business.

Southwest was the only major airline to operate without hubs. Point-to-point service provided maximum convenience for passengers who wanted to fly between two cities, but insufficient demand could make such non-stop flights economically unfeasible. For that reason, the hub-and-spoke approach was generally assumed to generate cost savings for airlines through operational efficiencies. However, Southwest saw it another way: hub-and-spoke arrangements resulted in planes spending more time on the ground waiting for customers to arrive from connecting points.

Turnaround time – the time it takes to unload a waiting plane and load it for the next flight – was 15 minutes for Southwest, compared with the industry average of 45 minutes. This time saving was accomplished with a gate crew 50 per cent smaller than that of other airlines. Pilots sometimes helped to unload bags when schedules were tight. Flight attendants regularly assisted in the cleaning of planes between flights.

Relative to the other major airlines, Southwest had a 'no frills' approach to services: reserved seating was not offered and meals were not served. Customers were handed numbered or colour-coded boarding passes based on their check-in order. Seating was first come, first served. As a cost-saving measure, the colour-coded passes were reusable. As to why the airline did not have assigned seating, Kelleher explained: 'It used to be we only had about four people on the whole plane, so the idea of assigned seats just made people laugh. Now the reason is you can turn the airplanes quicker at the gate. And if you can turn an airplane quicker, you can have it fly more routes each day. That generates more revenue, so you can offer lower fares.'[16]

Unlike some of the major carriers, Southwest rarely offered delayed customers a hotel room or long-distance telephone calls. Southwest did not use a computerised reservation system, preferring to have travel agents and customers book flights through its reservation centre or vending machines in airports. Southwest was the first national carrier to sell seats from an Internet site. Southwest was also one of the first airlines to use ticketless travel, first offering the service on 31 January 1995. By June 1996, 35 per cent of the airline's passengers were flying ticketless, at a cost savings of US$25 million per year.[17] The company was a 1996 Computerworld Smithsonian Awards Finalist for the

Exhibit 4 | Cost per available seat-mile data

Short-haul costs*
(Based on standardised seating, 500-mile hop)

Company	Plane	Cost (in cents)	Per cent
American	F-100	12.95	202
USAir	F-100	12.05	187
USAir	737-300	11.49	179
United	737-300	11.17	174
American	MD-80	11.02	171
Continental	737-300	10.18	158
Northwest	DC-9-30	10.18	158
TWA	DC-9-30	9.67	150
Continental	MD-80	9.58	149
Delta	MD-80	8.77	136
Northwest	MD-80	8.76	136
TWA	MD-80	8.29	129
America West	737-300	7.96	124
Alaska	MD-80	7.59	118
ValuJet	DC-9-30	6.58	102
Reno Air	MD-80	6.53	102
Southwest	737-300	6.43	100

Long-haul costs
(Based on standardised seating, 1 400-mile hop)

Company	Plane	Cost (in cents)	Per cent
USAir	757	6.72	134
American	757	6.70	134
United	757	6.51	130
Northwest	757	5.83	116
Continental	757	5.70	114
Delta	757	5.61	112
American Trans Air	757	5.40	108
America West	757	5.02	100

* Second quarter 1995 data.
Source: Roberts Roach & Associates, cited in Air *Transport World*, June 1996, p. 1.

rapid development and installation of its ticketless system within a four-month time frame.

Over the years, Southwest's choice of markets resulted in significant growth in air travel at those locations. In Texas, traffic between the Rio Grande Valley (Harlingen) and the 'Golden Triangle' grew from 123 000 to 325 000 within 11 months of Southwest's entering the market.[18] Within a year of Southwest's arrival, the Oakland–Burbank route became the 25th-largest passenger market, up from 179th. The Chicago–Louisville market tripled in size 30 days after Southwest began flying that route. Southwest was the dominant carrier in a number of cities, ranking first in market share in more than 50 per cent of the largest US city-pair markets. Exhibit 5 shows a comparison of Southwest in 1971 and 1995.

Southwest's performance

Southwest bucked the airline industry trend by earning a profit in 23 consecutive years. (See Exhibit 6 for Southwest's financial performance.) Southwest was the only major US airline to make a profit in 1992. Even taking into account the losses in its first two years of operation, the company averaged an annual 12.07 per cent return on investment. In 1995, for the fourth year in a row, Southwest received the coveted Triple Crown award given by the US Department of Transportation for having the best on-time performance, best luggage handling record and fewest customer complaints. No other airline achieved that record for even one month.

Southwest accomplished its enviable record by challenging accepted norms and setting competitive thresholds for the other airlines to emulate. The company had established numerous new industry standards. In 1991, Southwest flew more passengers per employee (2 318 versus the industry average of 848) than any other airline, while at the same time having the fewest number of employees per aircraft (79 at Southwest, compared with the industry average of 131).[19] Southwest maintained a debt-to-equity ratio much lower than the industry average. The ratio was 50 per cent in 1995, with cash holdings of US$400 million. In addition, Southwest had a credit rating of 'A', with a US$460 million line of credit in 1995. Southwest was the only airline with an investment-grade credit rating.

Southwest's fleet of 737s had grown to 224 by 1995, up from 106 in 1990 and 75 in 1987. New aircraft deliveries were expected to average 22 per year until 2000, split equally between purchases and leases.[20] Revenues more than doubled between 1987 and 1995. Profits grew even faster during the same period. In 1994, Southwest tripled annual capacity growth, measured by available seat-miles, to 30 per cent and flew to 46 cities in 22 states. The number of flights per day in 1995 was 2 065 serving 46 cities, up from 1 883 flights in 1994.

Herb Kelleher

Southwest's CEO, Herb Kelleher, managed the airline with a leadership style of flamboyance and fun and a fresh, unique perspective. Kelleher played Big Daddy-O in one of the company videos, appeared as the King of Rock (Elvis Presley) in in-flight magazine advertisements, and earned the nickname 'High Priest of Ha-Ha' from *Fortune* magazine.[21] Although Kelleher was unconventional and a maverick in his field, he led his company to consistently new standards for itself and for the industry. Sincerely committed to his employees, Kelleher generated intense loyalty to himself and the company. His ability to remember employees' names and to ask after their families was just one way he earned respect and trust. At one point, Kelleher froze his salary for five years in response to the pilots agreeing to do the same. Often when he flew, Kelleher would help the ground crew unload bags or help the flight crew serve drinks. His humour was legendary and served as an example for his employees to join in the fun of working for Southwest. He was called 'a visionary who leads by example – you have to work harder than anybody else to show them you are devoted to the business'.[22]

Although Kelleher tried to downplay his personal significance to the company when questions were raised about succession, many analysts following Southwest credited the airline's success to Kelleher's unorthodox personality and engaging management style. As one analyst wrote, 'The old-fashioned bond of loyalty between employees and company may have vanished elsewhere in corporate America, but it is stronger than ever at Southwest.'[23]

The Southwest spirit

Customer service far beyond the norm in the airline industry was not unexpected at Southwest and had its own name – Positively Outrageous Service. Some examples of this service included: a gate agent

Exhibit 5 | Southwest 25-year comparison, 1971 and 1995

	1971	1995
Size of fleet	4	224
Number of employees at year end	195	19 933
Number of passengers carried	108 554	44 785 573
Number of cities served	3	45
Number of trips flown	6 051	685 524
Total operating revenues	2 133 000	2 872 751 000
Net income (losses)	(3 753 000)	182 626 000
Stockholders' equity	3 318 000	1 427 318 000
Total assets	22 083 000	3 256 122 000

Source: K. Freiberg and J. Freiberg, 1996, *Nuts: Southwest Airlines' Crazy Recipe for Business and Personal Success* (Austin, TX: Band Press), p. 326.

Exhibit 6 | Southwest Airlines 10-year financial summary, 1986–95

Selected consolidated financial data[1]
(in thousands except per share amounts)

	1995	1994	1993	1992	1991	1990	1989	1988	1987	1986
Operating revenues:										
Passenger	$2 760 756	$2 497 765	$1 144 421	$973 568	$1 267 897	$1 144 421	$973 568	$828 343	$751 649	$742 287
Freight	65 825	54 419	42 897	33 088	26 428	22 196	18 771	14 433	13 428	13 621
Charter and other	46 170	39 749	37 434	146 063	84 961	70 659	65 390	17 658	13 251	12 882
Total operating revenues	2 872 751	2 591 933	2 296 673	1 802 979	1 379 286	1 237 276	1 057 729	860 434	778 328	768 790
Operating expenses	2 559 220	2 275 224	2 004 700	1 609 175	1 306 675	1 150 015	955 689	774 454	747 881	679 827
Operating income	313 531	316 709	291 973	193 804	72 611	87 261	102 040	85 980	30 447[9]	88 963
Other expenses (income) net	8 391	17 186	32 335	36 361	18 725	(6 827)[6]	(13 696)[7]	620[8]	1 374[10]	23 517
Income before income taxes	305 140	299 523	259 637	157 443	53 886	80 434	115 736	85 360	29 073	65 446
Provision for income taxes[3]	122 514	120 192	105 353	60 058	20 738	29 829	41 231	27 408	8 918	15 411
Net income[3]	$182 626	$179 331	$154 284[4]	$97 385[5]	$33 148	$50 605	$74 505	$57 952	$20 155	$50 035
Income per common and common equivalent share[3]	$1.23	$1.22	$1.05[4]	$.68[5]	$.25	$.39	$.54	$.41	$.14	$.34
Cash dividends per common share	$.04000	$.04000	$.03867	$.03533	$.03333	$.03223	$.03110	$.02943	$.02890	$.02890
Total assets	$3 256 122	$2 823 071	$2 576 037	$2 368 856	$1 854 331	$1 480 813	$1 423 298	$1 308 389	$1 042 640	$1 061 419
Long-term debt	$661 010	$583 071	$639 136	$735 754	$617 434	$327 553	$354 150	$369 541	$251 130	$339 069
Stockholders' equity	$1 427 318	$1 238 706	$1 054 019	$879 536	$635 793	$607 294	$591 794	$567 375	$514 278	$511 850
Consolidated financial ratios[1]										
Return on average total assets	6.0%	6.6%	6.2%[4]	4.6%[5]	2.0%	3.5%	5.5%	5.1%	1.9%	4.8%
Return on average stockholder's equity	13.7%	15.6%	16.0%[4]	12.9%[5]	5.3%	5.4%	12.9%	10.3%	4.0%	10.3%
Debt as a percentage of invested capital	31.7%	32.0%	37.7%	45.5%	49.3%	35.0%	37.4%	39.4%	32.8%	39.8%

Case 14 Southwest Airlines, 1996

Consolidated operating statistics:[2]	1995	1994	1993	1992	1991	1990	1989	1988	1987	1986
Revenue passengers carried	44 785 573	42 742 602[11]	36 955 221[11]	27 839 284	22 669 942	19 830 941	17 958 263	14 876 582	13 503 242	13 637 515
RPMs (000s)	23 327 804	21 611 266	18 827 288	13 787 005	11 296 183	9 958 940	9 281 992	7 676 257	7 789 376	7 388 401
ASMs (000s)	36 180 001	32 123 974	27 511 000	21 366 642	18 491 003	16 411 115	14 796 732	13 309 044	13 331 055	12 574 484
Load factor	64.5%	67.3%	68.4%	64.5%	61.1%	60.7%	62.7%	57.7%	58.4%	58.8%
Average length of passenger haul	521	506	509	495	498	502	517	516	577	542
Trips flown	685 524	624 476	546 297	438 184	382 752	338 108	304 673	274 859	270 559	262 082
Average passenger fare	$61.64	$58.44	$59.97	$58.33	$55.93	$57.71	$54.21	$55.68	$55.66	$54.43
Passenger revenue yield per RPM	11.83¢	11.56¢	11.77¢	11.78¢	11.22¢	11.49¢	10.49¢	10.79¢	9.65¢	10.05¢
Operating revenue yield per ASM	7.94¢	8.07¢	8.35¢	7.89¢	7.10¢	7.23¢	6.86¢	6.47¢	5.84¢	6.11¢
Operating expenses per ASM	7.07¢	7.08¢	7.25¢[12]	7.03¢	6.76¢	6.73¢	6.20¢	5.82¢	5.61¢	5.41¢
Fuel cost per gallon (average)	55.22¢	53.92¢	59.15¢	60.82¢	65.69¢	77.89¢	59.46¢	51.37¢	54.31¢	51.42¢
Number of employees at year end	19 933	16 818	15 175	11 397	9 778	8 620	7 760	6 467	5 765	5 819
Size of fleet at year end[13]	224	199	178	141	124	106	94	85	75	79

[1] The Selected Consolidated Financial Data and Consolidated Financial Ratios for 1989–92 have been restated to include the financial results of Morris. Years prior to 1989 were immaterial for restatement purposes.
[2] Prior to 1993, Morris operated as a charter carrier; therefore, no Morris statistics are included for these years.
[3] Pro forma for 1989–92 assuming Morris, an S-Corporation prior to 1993, was taxed at statutory rates.
[4] Excludes cumulative effect of accounting changes of US$15.3 million (US$.10 per share).
[5] Excludes cumulative effect of accounting changes of US$12.5 million (US$.09 per share).
[6] Includes US$2.6 million gains on sales of aircraft and US$3.1 million from the sale of certain financial assets.
[7] Includes US$10.8 million gains on sales of aircraft, US$5.9 million from the sale of certain financial assets, and US$2.3 million from the settlement of a contingency.
[8] Includes US$5.6 million gains on sales of aircraft and US$3.6 million from the sale of certain financial assets.
[9] Includes TranStar's results to 30 June 1987.
[10] Includes US$10.1 million net gains from the discontinuance of TranStar's operations and US$4.3 million from the sale of certain financial assets.
[11] Includes certain estimates for Morris.
[12] Excludes merger expenses of US$10.8 million.
[13] Includes leased aircraft.

volunteering to watch a dog (a Chihuahua) for two weeks when an Acapulco-bound passenger showed up at the last minute without the required dog crate; an Austin passenger who missed a connection to Houston, where he was to have a kidney transplant operation, was flown there by a Southwest pilot in his private plane. Another passenger, an elderly woman flying to Phoenix for cancer treatment, began crying because she had no family or friends at her destination. The ticket agent invited her into her home and escorted her around Phoenix for two weeks.[24]

Southwest Airlines' customers were often surprised by the 'Southwest Spirit'. On some flights, magazine pictures of gourmet meals were offered for dinner on an evening flight. Flight attendants were encouraged to have fun: songs, jokes and humorous flight announcements were common. One flight attendant had a habit of popping out of overhead luggage compartments as passengers attempted to stow their belongings, until the day she frightened an elderly passenger who called for oxygen.[25] Herb Kelleher once served in-flight snacks dressed as the Easter Bunny.

Intense company communication and camaraderie were highly valued and essential to maintaining the *esprit de corps* found throughout the firm. The Southwest Spirit, as exhibited by enthusiasm and extroverted personalities, was an important element in employee screening conducted by Southwest's People Department. Employment at Southwest was highly desired. When the company held a job fair in Oklahoma City, more than 9 000 people attended in four days.[26] In 1995, 5 444 employees were hired from the 124 000 applications received and 38 000 interviews held.[27] Once landed, a job was fairly secure. The airline had not laid off an employee since 1971. Employee turnover hovered around 7 per cent, the lowest rate in the industry.[28] More than half of Southwest's 22 000 employees had been hired after 1990. In 1990, Southwest had only 8 600 employees and less than 6 000 in 1987.

During initial training periods, efforts were made to share and instill Southwest's unique culture. New employee orientation, known as the new-hire celebration, included Southwest's version of the Wheel of Fortune, scavenger hunts, and company videos including the 'Southwest Airlines Shuffle' in which each department introduced itself, rap style, and in which Kelleher appeared as Big Daddy-O.

Advanced employee training regularly occurred at the University of People at Love Field in Dallas. Various classes were offered, including team building, leadership and cultural diversity. Newly promoted supervisors and managers attended a three-day class called 'Leading with Integrity'. Each department also had its own training department focusing on technical aspects of the work. 'Walk-a-Mile Day' encouraged employees from different departments to experience first hand the day-to-day activities of their co-workers. The goal of this program was to promote respect for fellow workers while increasing awareness of the company.[29]

Employee initiative was supported by management and encouraged at all levels. For example, pilots looked for ways to conserve fuel during flights, employees proposed designs for ice storage equipment that reduced time and costs, and baggage handlers learned to place luggage with the handles facing outward to reduce unloading time.

Red hearts and 'Luv' were central parts of the internal corporate culture, appearing throughout the company literature. A mentoring program for new hires was called CoHearts. 'Heroes of the Heart Awards' were given annually to one behind-the-scenes group of workers, whose department name was painted on a specially designed plane for a year. Other awards honoured an employee's big mistake through the 'Boner of the Year Award'. When employees had a story about exceptional service to share, they were encouraged to fill out a 'LUV Report'.

Southwest placed great emphasis on maintaining cooperative labour relations. Within the firm, almost 90 per cent of all employees were unionised. The company encouraged the unions and their negotiators to conduct employee surveys and to research their most important issues prior to each contract negotiation. Southwest had never had a serious labour dispute. The airlines' pilot union, SWAPA, represented 2 000 pilots. At its 1994 contract discussion, the pilots proposed a 10-year contract with stock options in lieu of guaranteed pay increases over the first five years of the contract. In 1973, Southwest was the first airline to introduce employee profit sharing.

Southwest's imitators

Southwest's low-fare, short-haul strategy spawned numerous imitators. By the second half of 1994, low fares were available on more than one-third of the industry's total capacity.[30] Many of the imitators were new start-up airlines. The Allied Pilots Association (APA) claimed that approximately 97 per cent of start-ups resulted in failures. According to the APA, only two of 34 start-up airlines formed between 1978 and 1992 were successful, with success defined as surviving 10 years or longer without bankruptcy. The two successful firms, Midwest Express and America West, had both been through Chapter 11 bankruptcy proceedings. APA's prognosis for newer airlines was equally pessimistic, with only Frontier and Western Pacific of the 19 start-ups formed since 1992 perceived as having good prospects for long-term survival.[31] Three of the 19 had already folded by 1996, and ValuJet was grounded after its May 1996 crash in the Florida Everglades.

The major airlines had also taken steps to compete directly with Southwest. The Shuttle by United, a so-called airline with an airline, was started in October 1994. United's objective was to create a new airline owned by United with many of the same operational elements as Southwest: a fleet of 737s, low fares, short-haul flights and less restrictive union rules. Although offering basically a no-frills service, the Shuttle provided assigned seating and offered access to airline computer reservation systems. United predicted that the Shuttle could eventually account for as much as 20 per cent of total United US operations.

United saturated the West Coast corridor with short-haul flights on routes such as Oakland–Seattle, San Francisco–San Diego and Sacramento–San Diego. Almost immediately, Southwest lost 10 per cent of its California traffic. Southwest responded by adding six aircraft and 62 daily flights in California. In April 1995, United eliminated its Oakland–Ontario route and proposed a US$10 fare increase on other flights. By January 1996, United had pulled the Shuttle off routes that did not feed passengers to its San Francisco and Los Angeles hubs. In early 1995, United and Southwest competed directly on 13 per cent of Southwest's routes. By 1996, that number was down to 7 per cent.[32]

Cost was the major problem for United in competing with Southwest. The Shuttle's cost per seat-mile remained at about 8 cents, whereas Southwest's cost was close to 7 cents. Two factors were largely responsible for the Shuttle's higher costs. First, many passengers booked their tickets through travel agents, which resulted in commission fees. Second, many of the Shuttle's flights were in the San Francisco and Los Angeles markets, both of which were heavily congested and subject to costly delays. In addition, the Shuttle was unable to achieve the same level of productivity as Southwest. Nevertheless, by launching the Shuttle, United was able to gain market share in the San Francisco and Los Angeles markets, largely at the expense of American, USAir and Delta.

Continental Lite (CALite) was an effort by Continental Airlines to develop a low-cost service and revive the company's fortunes after coming out of bankruptcy in April 1993. CALite began service in October 1993 on 50 routes, primarily in the southeast. Frequency of flights was a key part of the new strategy. Greenville–Spartanburg got 17 flights a day and in Orlando, daily departures more than doubled. CALite fares were modelled after those of Southwest and meals were eliminated on flights of less than 2.5 hours.

In March 1994, Continental increased CALite service to 875 daily flights. Continental soon encountered major operational problems with its new strategy.[33] With its fleet of 16 different planes, mechanical delays disrupted turnaround times. Various pricing strategies were unsuccessful. The company was ranked last among the major carriers for on-time service, and complaints soared by 40 per cent. In January 1995, Continental announced that it would reduce its capacity by 10 per cent and eliminate 4 000 jobs. By mid-1995, Continental's CALite service had been largely discontinued. In October 1995, Continental's CEO was ousted.

Delta was developing its 'Leadership 7.5' campaign, intended to cut costs by US$2 billion by mid-1997 and lower its ASM costs to 7.5 cents. Western Pacific (WestPac) was one of the newest domestic start-up airlines building on Southwest's formula, while adding its own twists. WestPac began flying out of a new airport in Colorado Springs in April 1995. WestPac's fleet consisted of 12 leased Boeing 737s. The airline started with 15 domestic destinations on the West Coast, East Coast, southwest and midwest, and all medium-length routes. Offering an alternative to the expensive Denver International Airport, business grew quickly. The company made a profit in two of its first four months of operation. Load factors averaged more than 60 per cent in the first five months of operation, and were 75.9 per cent in August. Operating cost per available seat-mile averaged 7.37 cents during the early months and dropped to 6.46 cents within five months. The Colorado Springs Airport became one of the country's fastest growing as a result of WestPac's market entry. WestPac had one-third of the market share and had flown almost 600 000 passengers during its first seven months.

One of WestPac's most successful marketing efforts was the 'Mystery Fare' program. As a way to fill empty seats, US$59 round-trip tickets were sold to one of the airline's destinations, but which one remained a mystery. Response greatly exceeded the airline's expectations; thousands of the mystery seats were sold. 'Logo jets', also known as flying billboards, were another inventive approach by the start-up company. Jets painted on the outside with client advertising raised more than US$1 million in fees over a one-year period. The airline also benefited from recent advances in ticketless operations. A healthy commission program to travel agents and a diverse, non-union workforce were other features of WestPac operations.[34]

Morris Air, patterned after Southwest, was the only airline Southwest had acquired. Prior to the acquisition, Morris Air flew Boeing 737s on point-to-point routes, operated in a different part of the United States than Southwest and was profitable. When Morris Air was acquired by Southwest in December 1993, seven new markets were added to Southwest's system.

Southwest's move into Florida

In January 1996, Southwest began new flights from Tampa International to Fort Lauderdale, Nashville, New Orleans, St. Louis/Lambert International Airport, the Birmingham, the Houston/Hobby Airport and the Baltimore/Washington International Airport. Saturation and low initial fares were part of Southwest's expansion strategy. Some of the routes would have as many as six daily flights. In April, service began from Orlando International Airport, with 10 flights headed to five different airports. Southwest's goal was to operate 78 daily flights to Tampa, Fort Lauderdale and Orlando.

Availability of assets and staff was a potential restriction on the airline's expansion possibilities. Ground crews were being transferred from other Southwest locations, with pilot and flight attendants coming from Chicago and Houston bases to cover the Florida expansion. Ten new Boeing jets were on order for the Florida routes.

Expansion into the northeast

With Southwest established as a leader in many aspects of the industry, continued success was hard to doubt. Yet, Southwest had shown itself to be vulnerable, at least for a short time, to the well-planned competition from Shuttle by United on the West Coast. New airlines, such as WestPac, had also proved capable of innovating and quickly becoming profitable.

The proposed entry into the northeastern region of the United States was, in many respects, the next logical move for Southwest. The northeast was the most densely populated area of the country and the only major region where Southwest did not compete. New England could provide a valuable source of passengers to Florida's warmer winter climates. Southwest's entry into Florida was exceeding initial estimates. Using a low-fare strategy, ValuJet had, until its crash, built a strong competitive base in important northeastern markets.

Despite the large potential market, the northeast offered a new set of challenges for Southwest. Airport congestion and air traffic control delays could prevent efficient operations, lengthening turnaround time at airport gates and wreaking havoc on frequent flight scheduling. Inclement weather posed additional challenges for both air service and car travel to airports. Southwest had already rejected some of the larger airports as too crowded, including LaGuardia, J.F.K. International and Newark International airports. Some regional airports lacked facilities required by a high-volume airline. For example, Stewart International Airport, near Newburgh, New York and north of New York City, lacked basic facilities such as gates and ticket counters.

The critical question for Southwest management was whether expansion to the northeast, and particularly New England, was premature. Or, would the challenge bring out the best in a firm with a history of defying conventional wisdom and doing things its own way?

Endnotes

1. K. Freiberg and J. Freiberg, 1996, *Nuts: Southwest Airlines, Crazy Recipe for Business and Personal Success* (Austin, TX: Bard Press), p. 61.
2. Ibid., p. 28.
3. P. S. Dempsey, 1984, 'Transportation deregulation: On a collision course', *Transportation Law Journal*, 13, p. 329.
4. W. Goralski, 1996, 'Deregulation déjà vu', *Telephony*, 17 June, pp. 32–6.
5. A. Bryant, 1996, 'US airlines finally reach cruising speed', *New York Times*, 20 October, Section 3, p. 1.
6. *Business Week*, 7 August 1995, p. 25.
7. C. A. Shifrin, 1996, 'Record US airline earnings top $2 billion', *Aviation Week & Space Technology*, 29 January, p. 46.
8. P. Proctor, 1996, 'ATA predicts record year for US airline profits', *Aviation Week & Space Technology*, 13 May, p. 33.
9. Ibid.
10. Freiberg and Freiberg, *Nuts*, pp. 14–21.
11. Ibid., p. 31.
12. Ibid., p. 55.
13. 'More city pairs await Southwest', 1995, *Aviation Week & Space Technology*, 7 August, p. 41.
14. K. Labich, 1994, 'Is Herb Kelleher America's best CEO?', *Fortune*, 2 May, p. 47.
15. Freiberg and Freiberg, *Nuts*, p. 51.
16. Herb Kelleher: www.iflyswa.com/cgi-bin/imagemap/swagate 530.85.
17. *Computerworld*, 23 June 1996, p. 98.
18. Freiberg and Freiberg, *Nuts*, p. 29.
19. 'Southwest Airlines charts a high-performance flight', 1995, *Training & Development*, June, p. 39.
20. A. L. Velocci, 1995, 'Southwest adding depth to short-haul structure', *Air Transport*, 7 August, p. 39.
21. Labich, 'Is Herb Kelleher America's best CEO?', p. 45.
22. '24th Annual CEO Survey: Herb Kelleher, Flying his own course', 1995, *IW*, 20 November, p. 23.
23. Labich, 'Is Herb Kelleher America's best CEO?', p. 46.
24. '24th Annual CEO Survey'.
25. B. O'Brian, 1992, 'Flying on the cheap', *Wall Street Journal*, 26 October, p. A1.
26. B. P. Sunoo, 1995, 'How fun flies at Southwest Airlines', *Personnel Journal*, June, p. 66.
27. Freiberg and Freiberg, *Nuts*, p. 72.
28. 'Southwest Airlines charts a high-performance flight'.
29. A. Malloy, 1996, 'Counting the intangibles', *Computerworld*, June, pp. 32–3.

30 'Industry surveys', 1996, *Aerospace & Air Transport*, 1 February, p. A36.
31 E. H. Phillips, 1996, 'GAO study: Demographics drive airline service', *Aviation Week & Space Technology*, 13 May, p. 37.
32 S. McCartney and M. J. McCarthy, 1996, 'Southwest flies circles around United's Shuttle', *Wall Street Journal*, 20 February, p. B1.
33 B. O'Brian, 1995, 'Heavy going: Continental's CALite hits some turbulence in battling Southwest', *Wall Street Journal*, 10 January, pp. A1, A16.
34 'Rapid route growth tests WestPac's low-fare formula', 1995, *Aviation Week & Space Technology*, 4 December, pp. 37–8.

Glossary

A

above-average returns are returns in excess of what an investor expects to earn from other investments with a similar amount of risk. *5*

acquisition is a strategy through which one firm buys a controlling, or 100 per cent, interest in another firm with the intent of using a core competence more effectively by making the acquired firm a subsidiary business within its portfolio. *232*

agency costs are the sum of incentive costs, monitoring costs, enforcement costs and individual financial losses incurred by principals because it is impossible to use governance mechanisms to guarantee total compliance by the agent. *354*

agency relationship exists when one or more persons (the principal or principals) hire another person or persons (the agent or agents) as decision-making specialists to perform a service. *352*

autonomous strategic behaviour is a bottom-up process in which product champions pursue new ideas, often through a political process, by means of which they develop and coordinate the commercialisation of a new good or service until it achieves success in the marketplace. *465*

average returns are returns equal to those an investor expects to earn from other investments with a similar amount of risk. *5*

B

board of directors is a group of elected individuals whose primary responsibility is to act in the owners' interests by formally monitoring and controlling the corporation's top-level executives. *361*

bureaucratic controls are formalised supervisory and behavioural rules and policies that are designed to ensure consistency of decisions and actions across different units of a firm. *249*

business-level strategy is an integrated and coordinated set of commitments and actions designed to provide value to customers and gain a competitive advantage by exploiting core competencies in specific, individual product markets. *125*

C

capability is the capacity for a set of resources to integratively perform a task or an activity. *20*

combination structure has characteristics and mechanisms that result in an emphasis on both geographic and product structures. *412*

competitive action is a significant competitive move made by a firm that is designed to gain a competitive advantage in a market. *167*

competitive dynamics results from a series of competitive responses among firms competing within a particular industry. *159*

competitive form is an organisational structure in which the controls used emphasise competition between separate (usually unrelated) divisions for corporate capital. *405*

competitive response is a move taken to counter the effects of an action by a competitor. *169*

competitive rivalry exists when two or more firms jockey with one another in the pursuit of an advantageous market position. *161*

competitor intelligence is the ethical gathering of needed information and data about competitors' objectives, strategies, assumptions and capabilities. *70*

complementary strategic alliances are designed to take advantage of market opportunities by combining partner firms' assets in complementary ways to create new value. *318*

cooperative form is an organisational structure that uses many integration devices and horizontal human resource practices to foster cooperation and integration among the firm's divisions. *399*

core competencies are resources and capabilities that serve as a source of competitive advantage for a firm over its rivals. *22*

corporate entrepreneurship is a process whereby an individual or group in an existing organisation creates a new venture or develops an innovation. *462*

corporate governance represents the relationship among stakeholders that is used to determine and control the strategic direction and performance of organisations. *348*

corporate-level cooperative strategies are strategic alliances designed to facilitate product and/or market diversification. *327*

corporate-level strategy is an action taken to gain a competitive advantage through the selection and management of a mix of businesses competing in several industries or product markets. *196*

cost leadership strategy is an integrated set of actions designed to produce or deliver goods or services at the lowest cost, relative to competitors, with features that are acceptable to customers. *132*

costly-to-imitate capabilities are those that other firms cannot develop easily. *101*

D

demographic segment is concerned with a population's, size, age, structure, geographic distribution, ethnic mix and income distribution. *46*

differentiation strategy is an integrated set of actions designed to produce goods or services that customers perceive as being different in ways that are important to them. *132*

diversifying strategic alliances allow a firm to expand into new product or market areas without completing a merger or acquisition. *327*

downscoping refers to divestiture, spin-off or some other means of eliminating businesses that are unrelated to a firm's core businesses. *254*

downsizing is a reduction in the number of a firm's employees and, sometimes, in the number of operating units, but it may or may not change the composition of businesses in the company's portfolio. *254*

E

economic environment refers to the nature and direction of the economy in which a firm competes or may compete. *48*

economies of scope are cost savings attributed to transferring the capabilities and competencies developed in one business to a new business. *203*

entrepreneurs are individuals, acting independently or as part of an organisation, who create a new venture or develop an innovation and take risks in entering them into the marketplace. *462*

equity strategic alliance consists of partners who own different percentages of equity in a new venture. *314*

executive compensation is a governance mechanism that seeks to align the intersts of managers and owners through salaries, bonuses and long-term incentive compensation such as share options. *366*

external managerial labour market is the collection of career opportunities for managers in organisations outside of the one for which they work currently. *433*

F

fast-cycle markets a competitive advantage cannot be sustained; firms attempt to gain temporary competitive advantages by strategically disrupting the market. *182*

financial control entails objective criteria (that is, return on investment) that corporate-level managers use to evaluate both the returns being earned by individual business units and the managers responsible for their performance. *394*

financial economies are cost savings realised through improved allocations of financial resources based on investments inside or outside the firm. *210*

first mover is a firm that takes an initial competitive action. *167*

first-mover advantage is an early competitive advantage that allows firms to anticipate customers' needs and shape their industry's future. *130*

focus strategy is an integrated set of actions designed to produce or deliver goods and services that serve the needs of a particular competitive segment. *141*

franchising in an alternative to diversification that is considered a cooperative strategy based on a contractual relationship. *328*

functional structure consists of a chief executive officer and a limited corporate staff, with functional line managers in dominant organisational areas such as production, accounting, marketing, R&D, engineering and human resources. *391*

G

general environment is composed of elements in the broader society that influence an industry and the firms within it. *42*

global economy is one in which goods, services, people, skills and ideas move freely across geographic borders. *11*

global mind-set is the capacity to appreciate the beliefs, values, behaviours and business practices of individuals and organisations from a variety of regions and cultures. *26*

global segment includes relevant new global markets, existing ones that are changing, important international political events, and critical cultural and institutional characteristics of global markets. *55*

global strategy is one in which standardised products are offered across country markets and the competitive strategy is dictated by the home office. *288*

greenfield venture is one in which a new wholly owned subsidiary is established. *296*

H

heterogeneous top management team is composed of individuals with different functional backgrounds, experience and education. *430*

human capital refers to the knowledge and skills of a firm's entire workforce. *438*

I

imitation is the adoption of an innovation by similar firms. *459*

induced strategic behaviour is a top-down process whereby the firm's current strategy and structure foster product innovations that are associated closely with that strategy and structure. *467*

industry is a group of firms producing products that are close substitutes. *58*

industry environment is the set of factors – the threat of new entrants, suppliers, buyers, product substitutes and the intensity of rivalry among competitors – that directly influences a company and its competitive actions and responses. *43*

innovation is the process of creating a commercial product from an invention. *459*

institutional owners are financial institutions such as banks, mutual funds and superannuation funds that control large-block shareholder positions. *356*

intangible resources include assets that are rooted deeply in the firm's history and that have accumulated over time. *91*

internal managerial labour market consists of the opportunities for managerial positions within a firm. *433*

international diversification is a strategy through which a firm expands the sales of its goods or services across the borders of global regions and countries into different geographic locations or markets. *297*

international strategy refers to the selling of products in markets outside a firm's domestic market. *273*

invention is the act of creating or developing a new product or process. *459*

J

joint venture is when two or more firms create an independent company by combining parts of their assets. *313*

L

large-block shareholders typically own at least 5 per cent of a corporation's issued shares. *355*

late mover is a firm that responds to a competitive action, but only after considerable time has elapsed after the first mover's action and the second mover's response. *169*

leveraged buyout (LBO) is a restructuring strategy whereby a party buys all of a firm's assets in order to take the firm private. *256*

M

managerial mind-set is the set of assumptions, premises and accepted wisdom that bounds – or frames – a manager's understanding of the firm, the industry(ies) in which it competes and the core competencies it uses in pursuit of strategic competitiveness. *428*

managerial opportunism is the seeking of self-interest with guile. *353*

market for corporate control is composed of individuals and firms that buy ownership positions in (or take over) potentially undervalued corporations so they can form new divisions in established diversified companies or merge two previously separate firms. *370*

market power exists when a firm is able to sell its products above the existing competitive level or reduce the costs of its primary and support activities below the competitive level, or both. *207*

market segmentation is a process through which people with similar needs are clustered into individual and identifiable groups. *127*

merger is a strategy through which two firms agree to integrate their operations on a relatively co-equal basis because they have resources and capabilities that together may create a stronger competitive advantage. *232*

multi-divisional (M-form) structure is composed of operating divisions, each representing a separate business or profit centre in which the top corporate officer delegates responsibilities for day-to-day operations and business-unit strategy to division managers. *392*

multi-domestic strategy is one in which strategic and operating decisions are decentralised to the strategic business unit in each country in order to tailor products to the local market. *286*

multi-point competition occurs when firms compete against each other simultaneously in several product or geographic markets. *162*

mutual interdependence among firms means that strategic competitiveness and above-average returns result only when companies recognise that their strategies are not implemented in isolation from their competitors' actions and responses. *161*

N

network strategy is the alliance-related actions taken by a group of interrelated and comparable firms to serve the common interests of all partners. *333*

non-equity strategic alliances are formed through contractual agreements given to a company to supply, produce or distribute a firm's goods or services without equity sharing. *314*

non-substitutable capabilities are those that do not have strategic equivalents. *102*

O

opportunity is a condition in the general environment that may help a company achieve strategic competitiveness. *43*

organisational culture refers to the complex set of ideologies, symbols and core values shared throughout the firm and that influences the way it conducts business. It is the social energy that drives – or fails to drive – the organisation. *30*

organisational structure is a firm's formal role configuration, procedures, governance and control mechanisms, and authority and decision-making processes. *389*

outsourcing is the purchase of a value-creating activity from an external supplier. *109*

ownership concentration is defined by both the number of large-block shareholders and the total percentage of shares they own. *355*

P

political risks are related to instability in national governments and to war, both civil and international. *301*

political/legal segment is the arena in which organisations and interest groups compete for attention, resources and a voice in overseeing the body of laws and regulations guiding the interaction among nations. *50*

primary activities are involved with a product's physical creation, its sale and distribution to buyers, and its service after the sale. *105*

product champion is an organisational member with an entrepreneurial vision of a new good or service who seeks to create support for its commercialisation. *465*

Q

quality involves meeting or exceeding customer expectations in the goods or services offered. *177*

R

rare capabilities are those possessed by a few, if any, current or potential competitors. *100*

resources are inputs into a firm's production process, such as capital equipment, the skills of individual employees, patents, finance and talented managers. *20*

restructuring is a strategy through which a firm changes its set of businesses or financial structure. *253*

risk is an investor's uncertainty about the economic gains or losses that will result from a particular investment. *5*

S

second mover is a firm that responds to a first mover's competitive action, often through imitation or a move designed to counter the effects of the action. *168*

simple structure is an organisational form in which the owner–manager makes all major decisions directly and monitors all activities, while the staff serves as an extension of the manager's supervisory authority. *389*

slow-cycle markets' products reflect strongly shielded resource positions wherein competitive pressures do not readily penetrate a firm's sources of strategic competitiveness. *180*

socio-cultural segment is concerned with a society's attitudes and cultural values. *51*

stakeholders are the individuals and groups who can affect, and are affected by, the strategic outcomes achieved and who have enforceable claims on a firm's performance. *24*

standard-cycle markets' products reflect moderately shielded resource positions where competitive interaction penetrates a firm's sources of strategic competitiveness; but with improvement of its capabilities, the firm may be able to sustain a competitive advantage. *181*

strategic action represents a significant commitment of specific and distinctive organisational resources; it is difficult to implement and to reverse. *170*

strategic alliances are partnerships between firms whereby their resources, capabilities and core competencies are combined to pursue mutual interests in designing, manufacturing or distributing goods or services. *313*

strategic business unit (SBU) form of the multi-divisional structure consists of at least three levels, the top level being corporate headquarters, the next, SBU groups, and the final level, divisions grouped by relatedness (through either a product or a geographic market) within each SBU. *402*

strategic control entails the use of long-term and strategically relevant criteria by corporate-level managers to evaluate the performance of division managers and their units. *393*

strategic direction of a firm is determined by developing a long-term vision of the firm's strategic intent. *436*

strategic flexibility is a set of capabilities firms use to respond to various demands and opportunities that are a part of dynamic and uncertain competitive environments. *18*

strategic group is a group of firms in an industry following the same or a similar strategy along the same strategic dimensions. *68*

strategic intent is the leveraging of a firm's internal resources, capabilities and core competencies to accomplish the firm's goals in the competitive environment. *22*

strategic leadership is the ability to anticipate, envision, maintain flexibility and empower others to create strategic change as necessary. *427*

strategic management process is the full set of commitments, decisions and actions required for a firm to achieve strategic competitiveness and earn above-average returns. *5*

strategic mission is a statement of a firm's unique purpose and the scope of its operations in product and market terms. *23*

strategy is an integrated and coordinated set of commitments and actions designed to exploit core competencies and gain a competitive advantage. *124*

support activities provide the support necessary for the primary activities to take place. *105*

sustained, or sustainable, competitive advantage occurs when a firm implements a value-creating strategy of which other companies are unable to duplicate the benefits or find it too costly to imitate. *5*

synergistic strategic alliances create joint economies of scope between two or more firms. *328*

synergy exists when the value created by business units working together exceeds the value those same units create when working independently. *217*

T

tacit collusion exists when several firms in an industry cooperate tacitly to reduce industry output below the potential competitive level, thereby increasing prices above the competitive level. *314*

tactical action is taken to fine-tune a strategy; it involves fewer and more general organisational resources and is relatively easy to implement and reverse. *170*

takeover is a type of acquisition strategy wherein the target firm did not solicit the acquiring firm's bid. *232*

tangible resources are assets that can be seen and quantified. *91*

technological segment includes the institutions and activities involved with creating new knowledge and translating that knowledge into new outputs, products, processes and raw materials. *53*

threat is a condition in the general environment that may hinder a company's efforts to achieve strategic competitiveness. *44*

top management team is composed of the key managers who are responsible for formulating and implementing the organisation's strategies. *430*

total quality management is managerial innovation that emphasises an organisation's total commitment to the customer and to continuous improvement of every process through the use of data-driven, problem-solving approaches based on empowerment of employee groups and teams. *178*

transnational strategy seeks to achieve both global efficiency and local responsiveness. *288*

valuable capabilities are those that create value for a firm by exploiting opportunities or neutralising threats in the firm's external environment. *100*

value consists of the performance characteristics and attributes provided by companies in the form of goods or services for which customers are willing to pay. *87*

vertical integration exists when a company is producing its own inputs (backward integration) or owns its own source of distribution of outputs (forward integration). *209*

worldwide geographic area structure emphasises national interests and facilitates managers' efforts to satisfy local or cultural differences. *408*

worldwide product divisional structure is an organisational form in which decision-making authority is centralised in the worldwide division headquarters to coordinate and integrate decisions and actions among disparate divisional business units. *409*

Name index

Abbott Laboratories 369
Abitibi-Consolidated Inc. 246
Accenture 30, 209–10
Acer Computer Corporation 8, 135, 325
Adidas 80, 81
Adolph Coors 337
Advance Auto Parts 320
Aggreko 288
AGL 355, 359
AgriBioTech, Inc. 246
Air Canada 321
Air France 321, 322, 324, 416
Air New Zealand 163, 321, 324
Airbus Industrie 173, 174, 278, 280
Aircraft Engines 403
Akers, John 401
Aldi 97, 132–3, 158, 208, 283
Alitalia 321
All Nippon Airways 321
Allen, George 462
Aluminium Association 323
Amazon.com 3, 4, 5, 21, 63, 64–5, 80, 82, 121, 122, 127, 158, 230, 425, 437–8, 439
Amcor 312, 357, 358
America Online Inc. 28, 157, 185–6, 221–3, 229, 325, 347
American Airlines 321
American Express 79, 80, 439
American Radio Systems 201
Amgem 28
AMP 79, 232, 245, 312, 358, 359, 370, 371–2, 373, 432
ampers 80
Anderson & Associates 104
Anderson, Paul 58, 259, 430, 434, 471
Anheuser-Busch 206
Ansell Rubber Company 9, 406, 444
Ansett Airlines 81, 109, 161, 162, 163–4, 235, 321, 324, 407
Ansett, Reg 81
ANZ 124, 163, 312–13, 322–3
AOL 80, 221–3
Apple Computers 3, 28, 80, 84, 175, 185, 334, 348, 443, 460, 462
Apria Healthcare 365
Arakawa, Minoru 28, 437
Argus, Don 259

Arnault, Bernard 28
Arthur Yates & Company 359
Asea Brown Boveri 298, 334
AT&T 11, 17, 80, 110, 159, 208, 222, 252, 285, 320, 338, 386
Atlantic Richfield Co. 235–6
Australia Post 3, 4, 5, 7, 124, 312
Australian Pipeline Trust 359
Austrim Nylex 198
AutoXchange 316–17
Avis Rent A Car 257
Avon 52–3, 169

Baan 145
Bacardi 80
Baker Hughes 365–6
Ballmer, Steven A. 386, 387, 388
BankAmerica 347
Banker's Trust 244, 347
Barbie 80, 93
Barclays 285
Barnes & Noble 21, 63, 64–5, 122, 127, 158, 425
BASF 282
Bausch & Lomb 254
Bazoli, Giovanni 280
BEA Systems 325
Beeren, Bruce 358
Bell Atlantic 208
Bendigo Bank 311
Benetton 318–19, 322, 334
Berman, Stephen 294
Bertelsmann 122
Bethune, Gordon 444
Betta Milk 166
Bezos, Jeff 64–5, 425, 426, 437, 439
BHP 7, 14, 23, 29, 58, 176, 198, 209, 256, 312, 356, 357, 414, 430, 434, 443, 471
BHP Billiton 259–63, 471
Bijur, Peter 28
Bi-Lo 157
Binder, Gordon 28
Biota Holdings 7, 149
Blank, Arthur 28
Blockbuster 149, 174
Blum, Arlene 435
Blundstone Boots 97
Blundy, Brett 437
BMG Entertainment 320

BMW 80
Body Shop, The 97, 143, 408–9
Boeing Company 72, 73, 174, 217, 218, 278, 280, 319
Bond Brewing 161
Books-A-Million 123–4
Boonstra, Cor 221
Boral 256
Borders Books & Music 425
Borders, Louis H. 72
Bower, Marvin 101
BP Amoco 80, 235–6
Brady Corporation 98
Brambles Industries 14, 198, 233, 356, 357, 359
Branson, Richard 81, 163, 395
Brazin 437
Bristle Ltd 256
British Airways 321
British Nuclear Fuels 446
British Telecommunications 51, 178, 240, 285
Bronfman, Edgar 347
Budweiser 80
Buffett, Warren 366, 438–9
Bunnings 194
Burger King 65, 80, 173, 328–9
Burgess, Ian 371
Burnham, Duane 369
Burns Philp 14

Cable and Wireless 238, 280
Cadbury Schweppes 200, 257
Callaway Golf Co. 467, 478
Campbell Soup 200, 365
Canadian Airlines 321
Canadian Occidental Petroleum 370–1
Canon 23
Capellas, Michael 98, 241, 426
Capital Services 403
Carlton Communications 159
Carlton United 161
Carnival Corp. 234, 235
Carrefour 133, 156, 175
Cascade 182
Case, Stephen 28, 222, 347
Caterpillar 127, 136, 286, 288, 336
Cathay Pacific 321
CBS Corp. 28, 201, 256

I-1

Cemex 272–3
Cendant Corporation 365, 379, 446
Chadwick, Rod 9
Chambers, John 28, 252–3
Chandler, Alfred 388
Chanel 80
Chaney, Michael 196
Chaparral Steel 111, 112
Charles Schwab 127, 147, 148
Chase Manhattan 285, 356
Chernin, Peter 356
Chrysler Corporation 455
Ciba-Geigy Ltd 204
Cisco Systems 28, 122, 141–2, 183, 244, 251, 252–3, 402, 474
Citibank 79, 80, 285
Clark, Adrienne 371
Clark, Graeme 461
Clifford, Bob 462
Clifford, Leigh 39, 40
CNBC 404
CNET 404
Coca-Cola 60, 69, 79, 80, 81, 105, 112, 144, 165–6, 170–1, 181, 234, 257, 258, 277, 312, 366, 368, 439
Cochlear 9, 52, 97, 112, 396, 461
Coles Myer 27, 69, 97, 121, 124, 155, 157, 158, 208, 312, 347, 357, 368–9, 424, 430
Colgate 80
Colonial 7
Columbia/HCA 366
Comalco 39, 435
Commerzbank 376
Commonwealth Bank of Australia 11, 109, 127, 318
Compaq Computer Corporation 4, 16–17, 18, 56, 98, 141, 157, 166, 171, 175, 241, 286, 365, 426, 428
CompuServe 185
Computer Associates International 233, 368, 425–6, 439
Computershare Limited 101
ConAgra 255–6
Connect Credit Union 230
Conseco 347, 369
Consolidated Diesel 438
Continental Airlines 321, 322, 444
Coopers Beer 182
Corning 97, 417
corProcure 40, 124
Coulter, David 347
Country Road Limited 81, 94, 97, 136
County Investment Management 372
Cournay, Patrick 408
Coventry Group 198
Cowley, Ken 358
Crammond, Tim 371
Credit Lyonnais 331
CSK Auto Inc. 320
CSL 98
CSR Limited 198, 256, 357, 358
CUC International 446
Cuccia, Enrico 280
Curvey, Jim 28

D'Aveni, Richard A. 11
Daewoo 171, 290, 448
DaimlerChrysler 13, 45–6, 49, 171–2, 174, 176, 216–17, 238–9, 242, 244, 245, 310–11, 314, 367, 432, 455, 473, 474
Dairy Farmers 279, 315
Dalziel, Bob 352
Danone 276
David Jones 83, 358
Deere & Co. 87
Dell Computer Corporation 3, 4, 5, 16, 18, 54–5, 56–7, 61, 80, 84, 86, 91, 101, 109, 157, 169, 171, 175, 312, 369, 401, 411, 426, 443, 458
Dell, Michael 54–5, 56, 84, 86, 175, 369, 443, 458
Delta Airlines 321, 322, 324, 416
Deming, W. Edwards 178–9
Desiata, Alfonso 280
Desmarest, Thierry 28
Deutsche Bank 136, 280–1, 376
Deutsche Telecom 294, 295, 316, 347, 457
DeVoe, David 356
DG Bank 328
DG-Rabo International 328
DHL Worldwide Express Inc. 325
Dick Smith Foods 137, 205
Dilliards 365
Dinnair 321
Disco SA 133, 167–8
Disney 80, 81, 102, 196, 210, 222, 255, 256, 347, 365, 368, 431, 439
Disney, Walt 81
DoMoCo 272, 284–5, 290
Dovuro 456
Dow Chemical 72–3
Dresdner Bank 376, 377

Drexler, Millard 368
drkoop.com Inc. 325
Drucker, Peter 251, 263, 457
Drypers 302
Dunford, Richard 107
Dunkin' Donuts 328
Dunlap, Al 425, 445–6
DuPont 45, 317, 388, 418–19, 455
Dymocks 127
Dyson 97, 478

E*Trade 127
Easterbrook, Sandy 372
Eastman Kodak 323
eBay 3
Ebbers, Bernie 28
Eck, Dennis 27, 158, 347, 368–9, 424, 426, 430, 434
Ecorp 313
Eisner, Michael 347, 365, 368, 431
Electrolux 12, 273, 417–18
Eli Lilly 59
Email 198
Energy Development 358–9
Engibous, Tom 28
Enron 28
Envirosell 69
Ericsson 80, 83, 177, 417–18
e-shopping!Books 314
Esprit 143
Euclid Industries 474
Excite, Inc. 411
Exxon 159

FedEx 325
Feigenbaum, Armand 178–9
Fender Musical Instruments 256–7
Ferrari 143, 458
Fiat 280, 327
Fidelity Investments 28
Fingerhut 5
Fiorina, Carly 93, 347, 424–5, 426, 430, 435, 437
First Union 365
Fisher & Paykel 273
Flight Centre 87–8, 106, 107–8
Ford Motor Company 4, 13, 23, 45–6, 49, 80, 86, 98, 109, 111, 124, 171, 176, 242, 249, 271, 278–9, 288–9, 295, 314, 316–17, 412–14, 455, 457, 473
Ford, Henry 86, 412, 413, 457–8
Forsmann Little 257
Fortis 238, 331

Name index

Foster's Brewing Group 233, 234, 237, 240, 254, 300–1, 312
Fox, Lindsay 81
Foxtel 11
Franklin, Gillian 435
Franklins 8, 157
Friedman, Jack 294
Frigidaire 460
Fuji Heavy Industries 311, 313
Fujitsu 325, 334
Fujitsu Siemens Computers 325
Futuris Corporation 198

Gap, Inc. 9, 10, 80, 368
Gates, Bill 185, 386, 387, 388
Gateway 171, 369
Gazal Corp. 140
GEC 331
General Electric 29, 40, 44, 80, 83, 102, 167, 200, 209, 258–9, 274, 295, 331, 347, 365, 403, 424, 433, 437, 440, 465
General Mills, Inc. 276–7, 325
General Motors 43, 45–6, 49, 62, 111, 124, 126, 171, 174, 176, 182, 232, 271, 278, 303, 311, 313, 314, 316–17, 327, 328, 366, 379, 387, 440, 455–6, 473
Gent, Christopher 28, 208
Gerstner, Lou 130, 401
Ghosn, Carlos 277
Gianni Versace SpA 327
Gilbertson, Brian 259
Gillette 97
GIO 232, 245, 370, 371, 432
Glaxo Smithkline 204
Glaxo Wellcome 204
Global Crossing 167, 317
Global Dairy Company 279, 315
Global Mining Initiative 39
Global One Alliance 294, 316
GNB Batteries 9, 406, 444
Gofish.com 127
Goldman Sachs 79
Goodman Fielder 312, 359
Goodyear Tire and Rubber 317
Goto, Teiyu 138
Grane Group 359
Greater Union 172
Greenberg, Jack M. 416
GroceryWorks.com 72
GroPep 23, 94
Grove, Andrew 3, 10, 15
Gudinski, Michael 102

Guinness 80
GWA International 198

Haas, Robert 9
Haier 290
Haley, Steve 146
Hancock and Gore 198
Hanson plc 200–1
Harley-Davidson 61, 93–4, 168
Harvey Norman 83, 102, 387–8
Harvey World Travel 108
Hazelton Airlines 235
Hefner, Hugh 81
Heineken 80
Heinz 80, 360
Herbold, Bob 411
Hertz 80
Hewlett-Packard 4, 17, 56, 80, 93, 97, 102, 123, 130–1, 141, 166, 251, 317, 325, 347, 401, 424, 435, 443, 471
HFS Incorporated 379, 446
HIH Insurance 242, 359
Hilbert, Stephen 347, 369
Hill, Lance 460
Hills Industries 198, 460
Hilton 80, 142, 329
Hitachi Ltd 242
Hockey, Joe 372
Hoechst 199, 282
Holmes à Court, Janet 442
Home Depot 28
Honda Motor Co. 13, 23, 45, 61, 80, 171, 206, 216–17, 278, 296, 311, 316, 455, 473
Honeywell 98, 244
Hoover 404
Howard Smith 198
Hoyts 172
Hutchison Whampoa 167, 317
Hyundai Motors 290, 310, 448

i2 Technologies 126
Iams Co. 241
Iberia Airlines 321
IBM 4, 15, 16, 44, 56, 80, 84, 109, 110, 123, 130, 141, 169, 171, 175, 180, 181, 312, 325, 334, 401–2, 468–9
Iceland 62
Idei, Nobuyuki 138, 402–3, 467–8
Ikea 80, 142–3, 478
Impulse Airlines 107, 161, 163–4, 167, 234, 321, 395

Incat 12, 462
Industrial Systems 403
Infoseek 196
Intel 3, 10, 23, 80, 175, 183, 244, 271, 272, 317, 334, 365, 402, 460
Internet Capital Group 402
Investment and Financial Services Association 372
Isis Communications 359
Isuzu 311
Ivestor, Douglas 166, 368
iVillage 404

J. Boag and Son Brewery 100, 182
J.B. Were 108
J.D. Edwards 145
J.P. Morgan 320
Jackson, Margaret 52
Jacobs, Irwin 28
Jager, Durk 177, 410, 411
Jakks Pacific 294
Jinro Group 337
Jobs, Steve 28, 84, 175, 185, 248, 462
John Fairfax Holdings 357
Johnnie Walker 80
Johnson & Johnson 200, 207, 365, 440
Jordan, Michael 81
Jordan, Michael H. 201
Jung, Andrea 52
Juran, Joseph 178

Kanter, Rosabeth Moss 459
Karmazin, Mel 28, 201
Kean, Bruce 371
Kelleher, Herbert 175
Kellogg Co. 80, 200, 276–7, 325
Kelly, Jim 28
Kendrick, John 93
Ker Conway, Jill 52
KFC 81, 234
Kia Motors 310
Kimberly-Clark 237, 410
King Island Dairy 81–2
King, Poppy 425
Kleenex 80
KLM 321
Kmart 296, 424
Knight, Phil 81, 391
Kodak 32, 80, 97, 138, 323–4
Komatsu 286, 294, 296
Koogle, Timothy 28, 368

Kozlowski, Dennis 439
Kraft Foods 22, 137, 208, 240–1
Krauer, Alex 204
Kroc, Ray 81
Kunkel, Ted 300
Kutaragi, Ken 468

LanChile 321
Larsen, Ralph 207
Lavis, Peter 124
Lay, Ken 28
Lend Lease Corporation 52
Leophairatna, Prachai 213
Leschly, Jan 204
Levi Strauss 8, 9–10, 33, 145
Levin, Gerald 222, 223
Lexis-Nexis 15
LG Group 448
Li, Luci 439
Linfox 81
Linux 186
Lion Nathan 50, 161, 300, 301
Livermore, Ann 131
Livingstone, Catherine 52, 396
Lloyds TSB Group 136
LML 336
Lockheed Martin 215–16
L'Oreal 140, 396–7
Louis Vuitton 80
Lowry, Frank 347
LucasVarity plc 474
Lucent Technologies 253, 424
Lufthansa 321, 322
Lukens, Max 366
Lutz, Robert 245
LVMH 28

McCleod, Karen 435
McDonald's 65, 66, 69, 80, 81, 97, 98, 173, 328–9, 416
Macek, Charles 372–3
McGowan, Gerry 163, 234
McKinsey & Co. 98, 101, 136, 140, 209, 294
McLean, Tony 358
McPherson's 198
Macquarie Bank 244
Malox 254
Mambo 97, 137, 140
Mannesmann 183, 199, 208, 229, 295
Marks & Spencer 245, 280
Marlboro 80
Marriott 80

Matsushita 460
Maybelline 140, 396–7
Mayne Nickless 235, 254, 352, 358
Mazda Motor Corp. 97, 171, 249, 254, 314, 316, 455
MCI WorldCom 28, 183, 229, 294
MediaOne Group, Inc. 386
Medical Systems 404
Meir, Golda 435
Melbourne IT 359
Mellon Bank Corp. 331
Mercedes 80
Merck & Company 59, 102
Meritor Automotive Inc. 474
Merrill Lynch 147–9
Metro AG 155
Microsoft 7, 8, 11, 23, 79, 80, 84, 94, 167, 176, 180, 181, 183, 185–6, 313, 386–7, 404, 411
Mildara Blass 233, 240
Miller Brewing 205–6, 207
Ming, Jenny 28
Mitsubishi Electric 166, 172
Mitsubishi Motors 8, 172, 217, 290, 327
Mobil 159
Moet & Chandon 80
Monet, Marc 204
Monsanto 8, 204, 303, 334
Morgan, Peter 358
Morita, Akio 81
Motorola Inc. 8, 14, 51, 80, 145, 221, 333, 334, 443
MP3.com 135
MTW 438
Murdoch, Lachlan 356
Murdoch, Rupert 356, 357
Mushroom Records 102
Myerson, Debra 435

Nasser, Jacques 86, 121, 242, 288, 412
National Australia Bank 7, 200, 312–13, 322–3, 356, 371, 373
NBC 209, 404
NBCi 404
NEC 166–7, 331, 334
Nescafé 80
Nestlé 62, 82, 325
Netscape 185, 325
New Balance Inc. 169
Newman, Frank 347
Newport Scientific 477
News Corporation 26, 273, 356–7, 359
NextCard 4
Nike 65, 69, 80, 81, 109, 169, 334, 390
Nintendo 28, 334, 437
Nippon Telegraph and Telephone 347
Nissan 13, 109, 110, 171, 172, 245, 277, 296, 310, 468
Nokia 80, 177, 221, 460
Nonaka, Ikujiro 96
Nordstrom Inc. 17
Norska Skog 4
Nortel Networks 183, 253
North Forest Products 39
North Limited 7, 39, 435
Northwest Airlines 321, 322
Novartis 204
Nucor Corporation 133

O'Reilly, Anthony 360
Oakley Inc. 442
Okuda, Hiroshi 171
Old Navy 28
Olivetti 208, 295
One.Tel 359
Oneworld 321, 322, 324
OPSM 141
Optus 238
Oracle 145
Orange 208
Ord Minnett 108
Orica 312
Origin Energy 358, 359
Owen-Jones, Lindsay 396–7

Pacific Century CyberWorks 159, 229, 276
Pacific Dunlop 7, 8, 9, 29, 198, 209, 232, 242, 247, 256, 312, 358, 359, 370, 388, 405–6, 407, 444
Pacifica Group 198
Packard Bell NEC 166
Palmer, Ian 107
Palmisano, Sam 401
Panasonic EV Energy 328
Partnership for a New Generation of Vehicles 473
Pasona 53
PBL 425, 445
Pearce, Jack 327
PeopleSoft 145
PepsiCo 60, 80, 97, 105, 165–6, 181, 234, 277

Name index

Perpetual Investments 358
Petersville Sleigh 9, 242, 247, 406
Pfeiffer, Eckhard 16–17, 26, 428
Pharmacia & Upjohn 8, 204, 240
Philip Morris 22, 81, 137, 205–6, 207–8
Philips Electronics 221, 293
Phillips Petroleum Company 23
Piaggio 336
Pillsbury Co. 325
Pinnacle Alliance 320
Pirelli SpA 108
Pitman, Sir Brian 136
Pivotpoint 146
Pizza Hut 234, 328–9
Platt, Lew 435
Playboy Enterprises 81
Plumrose Food Company 406
PMP Communications 358, 359
Poppy Industries 425
Porsche 136, 473
Porter, Michael 87, 281, 298
Power Systems 404
Prahalad, C.K. 157
Pratt Industries 14, 97
PricewaterhouseCoopers 232, 446, 447, 474
Procter & Gamble 12, 177, 200, 204, 241, 251, 254, 409, 410–11
Proudley, Ray 355
Pubco 234
Publishing & Broadcasting Limited 357
Pura Milk 166

Qantas Airways 52, 161, 162, 163–4, 234, 235, 254, 312, 321, 357, 430
Quaker Oats Co. 246–7, 325
Qualcomm 28

R.M. Williams 81, 88, 97
Rabobank 328
Radiata Communications 474
Raff, John 456
Ralph Lauren 80
Ralph, John 26, 358
Ralph, Lynn 372
Ralston Purina 256
Ranger Minerals 357
RCA 460
Real 155–6
Red Earth 143
Redstone, Sumner M. 201

Reebok 65, 69, 109, 169
Renault 161, 171, 172, 174, 277, 310
Reuben Central Design Bureau 217
Riggio, Len 64
Riggio, Steve 64
Rio Tinto 7, 39–40, 86–7, 176, 435
Rite Aid 365
RJR 208
Roberts, Kerry 371
Roddick, Anita 143, 408–9
Rolex 80
Rolls Royce Motor Cars 128
Romiti, Cesare 280
Rosen, Benjamin M. 16
Ross, Steven J. 31
Royal Ahold 156, 167
Rubin, Harriet 435
RWE 255

Sabena 321, 416
Sage, Lee 86
Sainsbury 156, 173, 175
St George Bank 358
Samsung Electronics Co. Ltd 14, 29, 200, 290, 448, 460
Sanders, Colonel 81
Sandoz Ltd 204
Sangyong 448
SAP 145–6
Sara Lee 443
SAS 321
Sausage Software 359
SBS 478
Schrempp, Jürgen 13, 49, 216, 244, 432
Schultz, William 256–7
Schumacher, Michael 458
Schumpeter, Joseph 167, 175, 459, 461
Schwab, Charles 401
Schweppes 170
Seagrams 347
SecureNet 104
Seita 277
Sematech 317
Seven Network 358
7-Eleven, Japan 271, 272, 314
SGL Carbon AG 377
Shapiro, Robert 303
Sharp Corporation 334
Shell 80
Siebel Systems 28
Siebel, Thomas 28

Siemens 96, 97, 199, 325
Silicon Graphics 17
Singapore Airlines 97
Sizzler International Inc. 98–9
Sloan, Alfred 455
Smale, John 379
Smirnoff 80
Smith & Nephew plc 406
SmithKline Beecham 59, 204, 252
Smorgon Steel 198
Snap.com 404
Sneddon, Andrew 474
Snelling Personnel Services 53
Softbank 29, 167, 314, 317
SolidWorks Corporation 478
Son, Masayoshi 29
Sony 11, 80, 81, 97, 100, 102, 137–8, 210, 221, 271, 287, 293, 402–4, 407, 467–8
Sotheby's 446
South African Airways 324
South Pacific Tyres 9, 444
Southcorp 198
Southwest Airlines 163, 175, 395
Spangler, James Murray 460
Spike Networks 359
Spinetti, Jean-Cyril 322
Spirit Airlines 321
Spotless Group Limited 109–10
Sprint 183, 229, 294, 316
STA Travel 108
Stallkamp, Thomas 432
Star Alliance 321, 322
Starbucks 69
Starwood Hotel 365
Station Inn 142
Stax Research Inc. 110
Steamships Trading 198
Sterling Software 233
Stewart, Martha 29
Strong, James 430
Sumitomo Rubber Industries 317
Sun Microsystems Inc. 4, 16, 31, 176, 180, 185, 325, 334, 401
Sunbeam Corporation 425, 445–6
Sundaze Australia Pty Ltd 324
Sunland Group 327
Susumu Ito 468
Swissair 321, 324, 416
Switowski, Ziggy 433, 441
Sykes, Richard 204

Tabacalera 277
Tachikawa, Keiji 29

Taiwan Semiconductor Manufacturing Co. 14
Takeuchi, Hirotaka 96
Talk City 404
Tanaka, Takeshi 313
Teets, Peter B. 216
Teiyu Goto 468
Telectronic 242, 247
Telescan 404
Telstra Corporation 51, 159, 167, 176, 183, 229, 254, 271, 276, 312, 404, 433, 440–1
Tesco 145, 155, 173, 175
Texaco 28
Texas Instruments 28, 365
Thai Airways 321
Thai Petrochemical Industry 213
Thatcher, Margaret 435
The Limited, Inc. 111
The Nine Network 11
Thermo Electron 175, 247
3M 112, 387, 462
Thurow, Lester 85
Time Warner 31, 186, 221–3, 229
Tioxide 30
Toho Gas 315–16
Tokyo Gas 315–16
tom.com 3
Tonic 143
Totalfina 28
Toyota 45, 80, 123, 161, 171, 172, 174, 176, 271, 296, 303, 311, 316, 327, 328, 398, 415–16, 473
Toys 'R' Us 324
TradeXchange 316–17
Transatlantic Business Dialogue 49, 50
Transportation Systems 404
Traveland 108
Travelshop 359
Tricon 234
Tripac International (Australia) 109
Trotman, Alex 288
Trumbull, George 371

Tuomiojo, Erkki 460
Tupperware 460
24/7 Media 404
TXU Corporation 460
Tyco 439

UAL 257
Unifi Inc. 133, 134–5, 145
Unilever 62, 410
United Airlines 319, 321, 322
United Microelectronics 14
United News and Media 159
United Parcel Service 28
Universal Music 320
UPS 325
US Postal Service 325, 398
US West, Inc. 253

Varig 321
Vasella, Daniel 204
Veba 199, 208
Velox Investment Co. 167
Vernon, Raymond 273–4
Viacom 201
Viag 199
Victoria Power 41
Village Roadshow 172, 358, 359
Virgin 79, 206, 247
Virgin Atlantic 81
Virgin Blue 107, 161, 163–4, 321, 395
Vodafone Airtouch 28, 183, 208, 229, 285, 295
Volkswagen 45, 80, 130, 157, 171, 172, 284, 328, 473
Volvo 13, 171, 249, 295, 474

Wallace, George 155
Wallis, Stan 373
Wal-Mart 5, 12, 14, 62, 100, 123–4, 133, 155–6, 158, 159, 170, 173, 175, 241, 283–4, 295, 303, 411, 425
Walt Disney Co. 80, 81, 102, 196, 210, 222, 255, 256, 347, 365, 368, 431, 439
Walton, Sam 155, 283
Wang & Li Asia Associates 439
Wang, Charles 368, 425–6, 439, 444
Warnaco 365
Warner, Douglas A., III 320
Warner-Lambert 240
Waste Management 365
Watson Pharmaceuticals 240
Webvan Group Inc. 72, 325
Welch, Jack 29, 40, 83, 258, 259, 347, 365, 404, 413, 424, 426, 437
Wells Fargo & Co. 136
Wendy's 173, 234
Wesfarmers 194–6, 198, 201, 241, 312
Westfield 347, 359
Westinghouse 201
Westpac 7, 356
Wexner, Leslie 111
Whirlpool Corporation 12, 122–3, 126
Williams Companies 206–7
Williams, R.M. 81
Wilson, Robert 87
Wings 321, 322
Wm Wrigley Jr Co. 80, 200, 215
Woodruff, Robert 80
Woodside Energy 315–16
Woolworths 11, 69, 121, 155, 157, 158, 170, 208, 318, 356, 357
Wozniak, Steve 84, 175

Xerox 80, 175, 200, 460
XOOM.com 404

Yahoo! 3, 5, 28, 80, 121, 147, 175, 222–3, 230, 253, 314, 368
Yun Jong Yong 29

Zeneca 301

Subject index

above-average returns 6, 7
   definition of 5
   I/O model of 18–20
   resource-based model of 20–2
access to distribution channels 60–1
acquisitions 474–5
   adaptation skills, need for 152
   BP Amoco & Atlantic Richfield 235–6
   Cisco, success of 252–3
   and complementary assets 250
   cross-border 231, 237–9, 295–6
   definition 232
   due diligence over 244–5, 250
   and economies of scale 229
   effective 243, 250–2
   friendly 250
   guidelines for 253
   horizontal 205, 233, 238–9, 242
   and human capital 439
   and innovation 241, 248–9, 250
   integration difficulties 244
   for international expansion 292, 295–6
   Internet, role of 229–30, 231
   and large firm inefficiencies 249
   managerial input 248–9
   objective evaluation of 249
   and overdiversification 247–8
   private synergy created 246–7
   problems 230–2, 243–9, 252
   reasons for 231, 233–43
   related 234–5, 239
   and restructuring 252
   stopping 235–6
   successful 243, 250–3
   and venture capital 474–5
   vertical 234
activity sharing 202, 203, 204–5
age of population, analysis of 47
agency costs 354–5
agency relationships 352–3
alliances
   competition reduction 318, 323–4
   competition response 318, 324–5
   complementary 318–23
   cross-border 231, 237, 312–13, 330–2
   diversifying 318, 327
   dynamic 334
   equity strategic 294, 314
   global 159
   horizontal complementary strategic 319, 320–3, 416
   internal 334
   non-equity 319–20
   to overcome trade barriers 317
   stable 334
   strategic approaches to managing 337–8
   synergistic strategic 318, 328, 329
   uncertainty reduction 319, 325–6
   vertical complementary strategic 318–20, 321, 322, 323
ASEAN 292
Asia
   economies 11–12, 14, 289–91
   financial crisis 11–12, 157, 212, 213, 290, 378, 448
Asia-Pacific Economic Co-operation (APEC) group 49, 292
attack, likelihood 167–9
Australian Competition and Consumer Commission (ACCC) 212, 235, 323, 374–5
Australian Securities and Investments Commission (ASIC) 359, 375
Australian Shareholders Association 26, 357, 358–9, 375–6
Australian Stock Exchange listing rules 212, 375
autonomous strategic behaviour 465–7
autonomy and entrepreneurship 442
average returns 5

B2B (business-to-business) 40, 124, 125, 270
backward integration 209
barriers to market entry 59–61, 236–8
benchmarking 179
board of directors
   and CEO 431–2
   classifications of 361–2
   deterrent to unethical behaviour 379
   duality 362, 363, 432
   enhancing effectiveness of 364–6
   'good and bad' 365–6
   international differences in 362–4
   multiple board memberships 364–5
   non-executive directors 363
   responsibility of 361
   and shareholders 356, 360
   size of 363
   and top management teams 431
   worker representation 363
borderless commerce 49–50
brand
   individual as 81
   intangible resource 79, 93
   source of competitive advantage 79–85, 93–4
   top global brands (1999) 80
brand loyalty 126, 139–40, 141, 168
brand mechanics 81
brand umbrella 82
business-level cooperative strategies 317
   assessing competitive advantage of 326
   competition reduction alliances 318, 323–4
   competition response alliances 318, 324–5
   complementary alliances 318–23
   implementing 415–16
   uncertainty reduction alliances 319, 325–6
business-level strategy 32
   and customer relationships 125, 126–7
   definition 125
   focus strategy 109
   and Internet 121–4, 142
   organisational structure and controls 394–8
   types of 131–49
business-level strategy, international
   cost leadership strategy 283–4
   differentiation strategy 284–5
   focus strategies 285
   integrated cost leadership/differentiation strategy 286
   and national advantage 281–3
buyers *see* customers

capabilities 20, 22, 94–7
   combination outcomes 104–5
   costly-to-imitate 99, 101–2
   non-substitutable 99, 102
   rare 99, 100–1
   valuable 99, 100
capital market allocation, internal 210–14
capital market stakeholders 24–6

see also shareholders
capital requirements as entry barrier 60
cartels 323
cash flow
    and diversification 217
    free 353
centralisation 395
CEO 8
    and board of directors 431–2
    compensation 347–8, 366
    duality 362, 363, 432
    E-CEO 3
    good and bad 424–6
    on outside boards 360
    responsibilities 58, 351, 380, 443–4
    selection of 433–6
    share options 348, 368–9
    and share price 350, 352
    and top management team 431–2, 434
    women 435–6
change, resistance to 90–1
chief knowledge officer 95–6
chief learning officer 95–6
China 55
    Dell's success in 56–7
    entrepreneurs 465–6
    and globalisation 271–2, 275, 277
    joint ventures with 290
Closer Economic Agreement 292
cognitive diversity 393
collusion 314, 323–4
combination structure (Ford) 412–14
competencies *see* core competencies
competition
    and e-commerce 3–5
    five forces model of 19, 41, 42–3, 58–67, 131
    intensity of rivalry 58, 63–7, 133, 139–40
    multi-point 162, 197, 207–8
    new entrants 58, 59–61, 135, 140
    reduction strategies 318, 323–4
    regulations and diversification 215
    response strategies 318, 324–5
    and strategic choices 32
    see also competitive rivalry
competitive action 167, 170
competitive advantage 15, 17, 20, 90, 181
    of brands 79–85, 93–4
    through cooperative strategies 312–13, 316, 329–30
    of core competencies 22, 84, 88–9, 93, 98–9, 168
    definition 5

of first mover 21, 130, 167–8, 425, 442
of home country 281–3
of human capital 27, 83, 94–6, 429, 438–9
of innovation 455–6, 457
and international strategy 85
of Internet 458
new paradigm 182–3
of organisational culture 30
competitive asymmetry 161
competitive dynamics
    definition 159
    dependence on market 172–4
    and industry evolution outcomes 184–6
    innovation encouraged 176–7, 180
    market commonality 162–4
    model of 160–7
    and product quality 177–80
    resource similarity 162, 164–7
    and size of firm 174–5, 180
    speed of action and response 175–6
    types of 170
    Wal-Mart example 155–6
    see also competitive rivalry
competitive form of multi-divisional structure 399, 405–6
competitive landscape 7, 270
    changes in 156, 158–9
    characteristics of 11–18
    and creation of uniform corporate governance structure 378
    and EU 279
    increased rivalry 157
    role of innovation 459
    slow-cycle markets 316
competitive response 160, 162, 169–74
competitive rivalry
    ability to act and respond 174–80
    in airline industry 163–4, 167
    definition 161
    likelihood of attack 167–9
    likelihood of response 169–74
    model of 160–7
    outcomes of 160, 161, 180–6
competitive scope, reshaping 242–3
competitor analysis 43, 69–73
competitor awareness 161–2
competitor environment 41, 69
competitor intelligence 70–3
complementary assets 250
complementary strategic alliances
    horizontal 319, 320–3
    role of trust 322–3
    vertical 318–20, 321, 322, 323

conflict of interest 359
conglomerates 215, 255
    using unrelated diversification strategy 200–1, 214, 247
    Wesfarmers 194–6
consensus-style decision-making 377, 396
consolidation
    in automobile industry 171
    in Europe 280
    trend to 156, 159
constraints 44
contingency workers 53
cooperative form of multi-divisional structure
    at IBM 401–2
    for implementing related-constrained strategy 399–400, 406
cooperative strategies 263
    business-level 317–26, 415–16
    competitive advantage of 312–13, 316, 329–30
    competitive risks with 335–7, 338
    corporate level 318, 327–30, 416–17
    cross-border alliance 312–13, 330–2
    in global car industry 310–11
    international 330–3, 417–18
    means to recreate firms 311, 312
    network 167, 333–5
    opportunity maximising 338
    organisational structure and controls 414–18
    strategic approaches to managing 337–8
    trust in 332, 335–6, 337
    types of 313–17
'coopetition' 312
core competencies
    of Amazon.com 439
    cautions and reminders 111–12
    as competitive advantage 22, 84, 88–9, 93, 98–9, 168
    criteria 99–105
    definition 22
    how many 98–9
    recognising 87, 89
    and resources 93
    role of managers in maintaining 437–8
    to satisfy customer needs 124, 130–1
    transferring 205–7
core rigidities 111
corporate education 440
corporate entrepreneurship 462
corporate gerontocracy 280

Subject index

corporate governance 347–50
  and agency costs 354–5
  managerial opportunism 353, 355, 369, 444
  separating ownership and managerial control 351–5
  and shareholders' interests 371–3
corporate governance mechanisms
  and agency costs 354–5
  board of directors 348, 349, 350, 356, 361–6
  and ethical behaviour 379–80
  executive compensation 347–8, 350, 366–9
  and managerial opportunism 355
  market for corporate control 350, 370–3
  multi-divisional structure 350, 369
  ownership concentration 350, 355–60
corporate governance, international
  Australia 364–5, 373–6
  financial media 376
  Germany 362, 376–7
  global 378–9
  Japan 377–8
  legislation 374–5
  United States 362, 365–6, 379
corporate intelligence firms 72
corporate mind-set 86–7
corporate relatedness 202, 203, 205–7
corporate-level cooperative strategies
  assessing competitive advantage 329–30
  diversifying strategic alliances 318, 327
  franchising 318, 328–9, 388
  implementing 416–17
  synergistic strategic alliances 318, 328, 329
corporate-level strategy 32
  and diversification 196–7
  international 281, 286–91
  organisational structure and controls 399–406
cost disadvantages as entry barrier 61
cost leadership strategy 19, 131, 132–5
  associated value-creation 134
  competitive risks of 136
  focus strategy 142–3
  functional structure for implementation 394–5
  international 283–4
cost leadership/differentiation strategy 397–8
costly-to-imitate capabilities 99, 101–2

counterfeiting 141, 293
'creative destruction' 175
cross-border acquisitions 231, 237–9, 295–6
cross-border alliances 231, 237, 295–6, 312–13, 330–2
cross-border electronic telecommuters 53
cross-functional integration
  barriers to 70
  outcomes of 472
  using product development teams 469–71
cultural change in organisation 414
cultural similarity and acquisition 253
culture of firm 429
customer loyalty 60, 126, 139–40, 141, 168
customer segmentation 127–9
customer value 87–8, 472
customers
  affiliation dimension 127
  anticipating needs of 126, 127, 128, 129, 130–1, 141–2
  average customer 127
  bargaining power of 58, 62, 134–5, 140
  competitively relevant groups 129
  reach dimension 127
  richness dimension 127
  value for 87–8, 123
  who, what and how 125–31
customised products 60

debt levels and acquisitions 245–6
decision-making
  conditions affecting 89–91
  consensus style 377, 396
  decentralisation of 395, 396
de-conglomeration 198
de-escalation strategy 170
de-mergering 198
demographic segment of general environment 42, 46–8
dependence on single products 242
dependence on the market 172–4
deregulated industries 199, 279, 355–6
differentiation strategy 19, 131, 132, 136
  associated value-creation 139
  competitive risks of 141
  focus strategy 143
  functional structure for implementation 396–7
  and governance mechanisms 221

international 284–5
  at Sony Corp. 137–8
diffuse share ownership 255
directors see board of directors
disclosure 359
diseconomies of scope 209
distributed strategic network 417–18
diversification
  Australian boom 198
  and acquisition strategy 241–2
  as agency problem 353–4
  business-level strategy 196, 197
  corporate-level strategy 196–7
  history of 197–9
  incentives for 214–18, 220
  international 198, 297, 298, 299–303
  levels of 199–201, 220
  and M-form structure 407
  optimal level of 220, 353–4
  overdiversification 14, 247–8, 353, 369
  and performance 215–17, 220–1
  reasons for 201–3, 219–20, 353–4
  related 196, 200, 202, 203–10, 242
  related-constrained firm 200
  resources for 218, 220
  and strategic competitiveness 201–2
  unrelated 199, 200–1, 202, 203, 210–14, 247
  value-creating strategies 202–3
diversifying strategic alliances 318, 327
diversity of business and downscoping 255
dominant business strategy 197, 199, 200
downscoping 253, 254–6, 258–9
downsizing 253, 254, 257, 258
duality (CEO/chairman) 362, 363, 432
due diligence 244–5, 250
dynamic alliance networks 334

e-businesses 15, 16
E-CEO 3
e-commerce 15, 17, 49
  changing the nature of competition 3–5
  degrees in 44, 54
  global 272
  growth of 270–1
  and IBM's cooperative M-form structure 401–2
  regulation of 50–1
economic environment, analysis of

48–50
economic segment of general environment 42, 48–50
economies of scale 209, 288
 as entry barrier 59–60
 and international strategy 278–9
 and merger and acquisition strategies 229
 and related diversification 203
economies of scope 203, 205, 209, 217
effective acquisitions 243, 250–2
electronic telecommuters 53
e-mail 15
 snagging 71
emerging economies, implementing unrelated business strategy 211–13
employee
 as competitive advantage 27, 83, 94–6, 429, 438–9
 contingency 53
 electronic telecommuters 53
 representative on board 363
 as stakeholders 24, 25, 27
 women 52–3, 425–6
employee buyout 256
enterprise resource planning software systems 145–6
entrepreneurial actions 185
entrepreneurship
 Chinese 464–5
 corporate 462
 definition 461
 and innovation 442, 457
 international 463–5
 and organisational culture 441–3
 proactiveness in 442–3
 in small business 476–8
 and society 464
entry barriers to market 59–61, 236–7
environmental trends 291–2
equity strategic alliance 294, 314
ethical practices
 CEO role models 380
 and corporate governance mechanism 379–80
 in gathering competitor intelligence 70–1
 of strategic decisions 33
 of strategic leaders 444–7
ethnic population mix analysis 48
Europe (2000–2010) 279–81
European Union (EU) 49, 172, 199, 233, 279–80, 281, 292, 295
executive compensation 347, 350
 and diversification 353–4
 effectiveness of 368–9
 as governance mechanism 366–9
 incentives 366–8
 managerial opportunism 355
 questioned by shareholders 359, 368
 as shares 348, 356–7, 360, 366, 368–9
exit barriers 67
explicit knowledge 96
exporting for expansion 292–3, 296
external environment 7
 analysis of 30, 43–6, 85, 95
 competitor environment 41, 69–73
 Dell in China 56–7
 as determinant of strategies 18–20
 forecasting 43, 45
 and managerial discretion 429
 Rio Tinto and 39–40
 understanding 40–1
external managerial labour market 433
external market capital allocation 211

fast-cycle markets 180, 182–4, 315, 317, 318
financial controls 394
 and diversification 247–8
 strategic 447–8
financial economies 210
financial media 376
financial resources 92
first mover
 advantages 21, 130, 167–8, 425, 442
 disadvantages 168
five forces model of competition 19, 41, 42–3, 58–67, 131
flexible manufacturing systems 145
focus strategy 131, 141
 business-level 109
 competitive risks of 143–4
 cost leadership 142–3
 differentiation 143
 international 285
 simple structure to implement 398
formalisation in implementing cost leadership strategy 395
forward integration 209
fragmented markets 185
franchises 318, 328–9, 388
 strategic centre firm 416–17
free cash flow 353
free trade 49–50

friendly acquisitions 250
functional organisational structure 391–2
 to implement cost leadership strategy 394–5
 to implement differentiation strategy 396–7
 to implement focused strategies 398
 to implement integrated cost leadership/differentiation strategy 397–8

general environment 41
 demographic segment 42, 46–8
 economic segment 42, 48–50
 global segment 42, 55
 opportunities 43
 political/legal segment 42, 50–1
 socio-cultural segment 42, 51–3
 technological segment 42, 53–5
 threats 44
geographic distribution, analysis of 47
glass ceiling 435–6
global alliances 159
global economy 11–12, 85
global markets 55
 entry mode 292–7
 rate of growth 237
global mind-set 26, 272–3
global segment of general environment 42, 55
global strategy 287–8
 implementing worldwide product divisional structure 409–11
globalisation 12–13, 49, 156, 270
 and Asian economies 289
 Chinese and Russian markets 271–2, 275, 277
 and employment 14
 joint ventures for 295
 Rio Tinto 39–40
 and technology 272, 275
goals and cross-functional integration 471
golden goodbye 360
golden parachute 360, 370
governance mechanisms
 agency costs 354–5
 and differentiation 221
 effective 338
 and implementation of strategies 387
government policy as entry barrier 61
greenfield venture 296, 297
growth-oriented actions 185

Subject index

heterogeneous top management team 430–1, 434
home country advantage 281–3
homogeneous top management team 430, 434
horizontal acquisitions 205, 233, 238–9, 242
horizontal alliances 319, 416
   airlines 320–3
horizontal organisational structures 469–70
hostile takeovers 214, 232, 295–6
human capital
   competitive advantage of 27, 83, 94–6, 429, 438–9
   intangible resource 92
   role of managers in developing 438–41
hyper-competition 11, 31

I/O model of above-average returns 18–20
imitation 459
   cost of 180
   of cost leadership strategy 136
income distribution analysis 48
induced strategic behaviour 466, 467–8
industrial markets, customer segmentation 128
industry 58
   deregulated 199, 279, 355–6
   life cycle 184–6
industry environment 41, 42–3, 58–67
infoglut 72
infomediaries 45
information age 15–16
information networks across firms 145–6
innovation
   acquisition as access to 241, 248–9, 250
   Australian initiatives 463–4
   and bureaucratic controls 249
   and choice of CEO 433–4
   commercialising 461
   as competitive advantage 455–6, 457
   and counterfeiting 293
   diffusion and Internet 270
   encouragement of 176–7
   and entrepreneurship 442, 457
   in global automobile industry 455–6
   importance of 459

   as intangible resource 92
   and international diversification 298
   in large organisations 478–9
   management of 477, 478
   process 457
   products 457, 459–61
   and risk 458
   role of strategic alliances 472–4
   in small businesses 477, 479
   and value creation 471–2, 477–8
   venture capital for 461
insider strategic knowledge 364–5
institutional investors 372
institutional owners 356–9, 360
institutional venture partners 411
intangible resources 91, 92, 94
   brand names 79, 93
   and diversification 218
integrated cost
   leadership/differentiation strategy 131, 144–5
   competitive risks of 146–7
   functional structure to implement 397–8
   international 286
   Merrill Lynch 'stuck in the middle' 147–9
integrating organisational functions 469–71
integration difficulties with acquisitions 244
inter-firm rivalry see competitive rivalry
internal alliance networks 334
internal capital market allocation 210–14
internal corporate venturing
   autonomous strategic behaviour 465–7
   implementing 468–72
   induced strategic behaviour 466, 467–8
   model of 466
internal environment
   analysis of 7, 30, 85–90
   as determinant of strategies 20–2
internal managerial labour market 433
international cooperative strategies 318
   and cross-border alliances 330–2
   implementing 417–18
   strategic intent of partner 332–3, 335–6
international diversification 198
   and innovation 298
   management problems 302–3

   and returns 297
international entrepreneurship 463–5
international environment
   Europe (2000–2010) 279–81
   opportunities 274–5
   regionalisation 291–2
   risks in 14, 299–303
international markets, entry mode
   acquisition 292, 295–6
   dynamics of 296–7
   exporting 292–3, 296
   licensing 292, 293–4, 296
   new wholly owned subsidiary 292, 296, 297
   strategic alliances 292, 294–5, 296
International Monetary Fund (IMF) 50, 213
international strategy 85, 263
   benefits of 276–81
   business-level 281–6
   corporate-level 281, 286–91
   economies of scale 278–9
   incentive to pursue 273–80, 302
   and local limited growth 277
   location advantages 279
   management problems 302–3
   market entry mode 292–7
   and market size increase 276–7, 278
   organisational structure and controls 407–14
   rationale for 273–4
   return on investment 277–8
   risks 299
   strategic competitive outcomes 274, 297–9
   and universal product demand 274–5
Internet 3–4, 40, 123
   access equality 121
   and business-level strategy 121–4, 142
   Compaq 16–17
   and conduct of global business 270–1
   for cooperative arrangements 312, 316
   driving mergers and acquisitions 229–30, 231
   infomediaries 45
   intelligence for competitors 71–3
   potential of 54–5
   source of competitive advantage 458
intranet 4
invention 459

joint ventures 166–7, 313–14
   with China 290

for globalisation 295
strategic centre firm 417
junk bonds 245

knowledge as competitive advantage 17, 95–6
knowledge base and outsourcing 110

labour markets for managers 433–6
large firm inefficiencies 249
large-block shareholders 355, 357
late movers 169
leverage 246, 313
leveraged buyouts 253, 256–7, 258
'liability of foreignness' 14
licensing 292, 293–4, 296
likelihood of attack 167–9
likelihood of response 169–70
location, advantages of 253, 278, 279, 291–2
low performance and diversification 215–17
low-cost culture 395
low-cost production 274

managed earnings 445–6
management buyouts 256
manager 27, 437
and acquisitions 248–9
and agency relationships 352–3
and culture of firm 429
and diversification 219–20
and human capital development 438–41
as organisational resource 428–32
role 351
as strategists 29–31
top management teams 430–6
top managers (1999) 28–9
managerial competencies 22
managerial decisions, conditions affecting 89–91
managerial defence tactics 370–1
managerial discretion 428–9
managerial employment risk 353
managerial labour market 433–6
managerial mind-set 428
at Ford 413
managerial opportunism 353, 355, 369, 444
managerial ownership 360
managerial risk 103
manufacturing execution system 145

market
barriers to entry 59–61, 236–8
for corporate control 350, 370–3
fast-cycle 180, 182–4, 315, 317, 318
fragmented 185
global 55, 237, 292–7
industrial 128
oligopolistic 181–2
slow-cycle 180–1, 315–16
standard-cycle 181–2, 315, 316–17
see also international markets, entry mode
market commonality 162–4
market dependence 172–4
market expansion 276–7
market niches 61
market power
as reason for acquisition 233–6
and related diversification 207–10
and size of firm 174
market segmentation 127–9
market size 276–7, 278
market-power actions 186
matrix organisation 400
merger
AOL-Time Warner 221–3
BHP Billiton 259–63
definition 232
and economies of scale 229
failure 231–2
and human capital 439
increasing use of 230–63
Internet and 229–30
merger mania 215, 231, 370
metalearning 87
M-form organisational structure see multi-divisional organisational structure (M-form)
mixed related business 200
mobile phone technology 270–1
monopoly positions 180–1
motivation 162
multi-divisional organisational structure (M-form)
competitive form of 399, 405–6
cooperative form of 399–402, 406
and diversification strategy 407
at DuPont and GM 392–3
at IBM 401–2
as internal governance mechanism 350, 369
movement to 386–7
and overdiversification 369
strategic business unit form of 399, 402–4, 406

multi-domestic strategy 286–7, 408–9
multi-market competition 164
multi-point competition 162, 197, 207–8
mutual forbearance 208, 314, 323–4
mutual interdependence 161

national advantage 281–3
network cooperative strategies 167, 333–5
new entrants
barriers to 135, 140
threat of 58, 59–61
new product development 240, 241
new wholly owned subsidiary 292, 296, 297
non-equity alliance 319–20
non-equity strategic alliances 314
non-strategic team of resources 100, 110
non-substitutable capabilities 99, 102
North American Free Trade Agreement (NAFTA) 49, 292, 413

oligopolistic markets 181–2
on-line retailing 159
OPEC 323
open-book management 104
operational relatedness 202, 203, 204–5
opportunistic behaviour 335–6, 353
opportunities, maximising 338
organisational culture 101
changing 23, 29, 443–4
and competitive response 173–4
definition 30
entrepreneurial orientation 441–3
ethics of 33
source of competitive advantage 30
sustaining 441–4
as tangible resource 92
organisational resources 92
managers as 428–32
organisational risk 103
organisational stakeholders 24, 25, 27
organisational strategists
characteristics of 30–1
role 29–30
top managers (1999) 28–9
organisational structure
cautions 418–19
definition 389
effect on strategy 389–93, 407

Subject index

flexibility 404
functional structure 391–2
horizontal 469–70
and implementing business-level strategies 394–8
and implementing cooperative strategies 414–18
and implementing corporate-level strategies 399–406
and implementing international strategies 407–14
Microsoft, changes to 386–7, 388
simple structure 389–91, 398
see also multi-divisional organisational structure (M-form)
outsiders 361–2
outsourcing 109–10, 123, 319–20
overdiversification 247–8
 internationally 14
 and M-form structure 369
 using free cash flows 353
ownership concentration 350, 355–60

partners
 selection of 332–3
 strategic intent of 332, 335–6
 trust between 337
patents 15, 240
performance and diversification 215–17, 220–1
perpetual innovation 15
physical resources 92
political risks in international environment 299, 301
political/legal segment of general environment 42, 50–1
population analysis 46
price predators 171
Prices Surveillance Act 1983 215, 374
primary activities 105–6
privatisation 41, 51
proactiveness and entrepreneurship 442–3
process innovation 457
product champion 465, 467
product development (new) 240, 241
product differentiation
 as agency problem 353–4
 as entry barrier 60
 and substitute products 63
product market stakeholders 24, 25, 27
 see also customers
product obsolescence 278

product quality 14, 177–80, 472
product substitutes 58, 63, 135, 140
product-related competencies 22

quality of product 177–80, 472

rare capabilities 99, 100–1
regionalisation 291–2
related acquisitions 234–5, 239
related diversification 196, 200, 202, 203–10, 242
related outsiders 361
related-constrained firm 200
related-constrained strategy 199, 400, 401–2, 406
related-linked strategy 196, 199, 200, 201, 402–4, 406
reputation 92, 170–1
resource
 capability 20
 competitive advantage of 20, 22
 component of internal analysis 88
 costly to imitate 22
 definition 20
 for differentiation 218, 220
 and diversification 218
 financial 92
 intangible 91, 92, 93–4
 as motive for international strategy 274
 non-strategic team of 100, 110
 non-substitutable 22
 physical 92
 rare 22
 strategic value of 92–3
 tangible 91, 92–3, 94, 218, 220
 valuable 22
resource dissimilarity 164
resource similarity 162, 164–7
resource-based model of above-average returns 20–2
response, likelihood of 169–70
restructuring
 definition 253
 downscoping 253, 254–6, 258–9
 downsizing 253, 254, 257, 258
 and failure of acquisition 252
 following diversification 198–9, 214
 leveraged buyouts 253, 256–7, 258
 outcomes 257–63
returns on investment
 and international diversification 297
 from international strategy 277–8

reverse engineering 168, 278
risk 5
 of cooperative strategies 335–7, 338
 of cost leadership strategy 136
 of differentiation strategy 141
 and entrepreneurship 442
 of first movers 168
 and innovation 14, 458
 of integrated cost leadership/differentiation strategy 146–7
 in international environment 14, 299–303
 managerial 103
 of new product development 241
 organisational 103
rivalry with competitors 58, 63–7, 133, 139–40

scanning external environment 43, 44–5
second movers 168–9
server farms 271, 272
service quality, dimensions of 178
share ownership limits 355, 359
shared values and cross-functional integration 470–1
shared vision and acquisition success 253
shareholders 24–5
 of acquired firms 232
 of acquiring firms 232
 activism 355, 356–7, 358–60, 375–6
 Australian Shareholders Association 26, 357, 358–9, 375–6
 and board of directors 356, 360
 and diversification 353
 entitlements 351
 and executive compensation 359, 368
 institutional owners 356–9, 360
 investment risks 351
 large-block shareholders 355, 357
 neglect of interests 371–3
 ownership concentration 350, 355–6
 of poor-performing companies 358, 359
 total shareholder return 358
sheltered markets 180–1, 315–16
short-term win and acquisition success 253
simple organisational structure 389–91, 398
single business strategy 197, 199,

I–13

200
size of firm 174–5, 180
skill transference 205–7
slow-cycle markets 180–1, 315–16
small businesses 29, 389–91
　entrepreneurship in 476–8
　and innovation 477, 479
socio-cultural segment of general environment 42, 51–3
specialisation 394
speed of competitive actions and responses 31, 175–6
speed to market 15, 240–1
stable alliance networks 334
stakeholders 7
　capital market 24–6
　classification of 24–7
　definition 23–4
　employees as 24, 25, 27
　organisational 24, 25, 27
　product market 24, 25, 27
　see also shareholders
standard products 317
standard-cycle markets 181–2, 315, 316–17
start-up ventures 257
statistical process control 178
stocks, best and worst (in 2000) 8
strategic actions 5, 6, 124, 170
strategic alliances 159
　competition reduction strategies 318, 323–4
　competition response strategies 318, 324–5
　complementary 318–23
　corporate-level cooperative strategies 318, 327–30, 416–17
　equity-based 295, 314
　form of cooperative strategy 312–13
　and innovation 472–4
　international 292, 294–5, 296
　joint ventures 166–7, 290, 295, 313–14, 417
　non-equity 314
　partner selection 332–3
　to produce and manage innovation 472–4
　reasons for developing 315–17
　tacit collusion 208, 314, 323–4
　trust 294
　uncertainty reduction strategies 319, 325–6
　see also cooperative strategies
strategic assets 98
strategic business unit form of multi-divisional structure 399, 402–4, 406

strategic capabilities see core competencies
strategic centre firm 334, 414–15, 416–17, 418
strategic competitiveness 5, 6, 7, 87, 170, 201–2, 274, 297–9
strategic controls 247, 393–4, 447–8
strategic direction 436–7
strategic flexibility 18, 144–6, 404
strategic focus: corporate
　acquisitions: success of Cisco 252–3
　air wars: competitive rivalry in Australia 163–4
　alliance networks: benefits and issues 334–5
　Amazon.com/Barnesandnoble.com rivalry 64–5
　American boards of directors: top and bottom 365–6
　competitive intelligence and the Internet 72–3
　Compaq and Internet technology 16–17
　cooperative M-form structure and e-commerce at IBM 401–2
　corporate governance and shareholders' interests 371–2
　differentiation strategy: Sony Corporation 137–8
　diversification merger: AOL-Time Warner 221–3
　ethics of strategic leaders 445–6
　food retailing in Australia 157–8
　innovation: key source of value creation 477–8
　institutional investors: ASA 358–9
　knowledge management and competitive advantage 95–6
　mergers: BHP Billiton 259–63
　partner selection and strategic alliance success 332–3
　success: difficulties of 9–10
　transfer skills: Williams Companies 206–7
　trust 102–4
　value adding: Flight Centre 107–8
　women top executives 435–6
strategic focus: international
　acquisitions: BP Amoco and Atlantic Richfield 235–6
　Asia: changing economies 289–91
　car wars 171–2
　cola wars 165–6
　combination structure: Ford 412–14
　competitive advantage and human capital 438–9
　cross-border acquisition: Daimler-Benz and Chrysler 238–9

　Dell direct business model in China 56–7
　Europe (2000–2010) 279–81
　Foster's worldwide wine 300–1
　horizontal alliances among airlines 320–2
　innovative products of tomorrow 459–61
　Merrill Lynch: differentiation and on-line strategies 147–9
　product innovations and induced strategic behaviours 467–8
　refocusing large diversified business groups in emerging economies 211–13
　worldwide product divisional structure: Procter & Gamble 410–11
strategic group analysis 68, 69
strategic inputs 5, 6, 32, 124
strategic intent 6, 7, 22–3, 30, 40, 31, 85, 112, 113
　of partner 332–3, 335–6
strategic leadership
　and balanced organisational controls 447–8
　and core competencies 437–8
　definition of 427
　ethical practices 444–7
　good and bad 424–6
　and human capital 427, 438–41
　and innovation 433–4
　international experience 440
　and management process 427
　managerial labour market 433–6
　managers as organisational resource 428–32
　qualities 427–8, 437
　source of competitive advantage 429
　and strategic direction 436–7
　sustaining organisational culture 441–4
　top management teams 430–6
　training and development programs 440
strategic management
　challenge of 6, 7–10
　and e-commerce 5
　process 5–6, 31–3
strategic mission 6, 7, 23, 31, 40, 85, 112, 113
strategic orientation 23, 30
strategic outcomes 5, 6, 124
strategic reorientation 18
strategy
　definition of 124
　difficulties with: Pacific Dunlop & Levi Strauss 9–10
　effect of structure on 389–93, 407

Subject index

and external environment 18–20
   formulation 6, 32
   implementation 6, 32, 387
   and organisational structure 407
structure *see* organisational structure
substitute products 14, 58, 63, 135, 140
suppliers 58, 61–2, 121–3, 135, 140
support activities 105, 106–7
sustainability 180
sustained (sustainable) competitive advantage *see* competitive advantage
switching costs 60, 66
synergistic strategic alliances 318, 328, 329
synergy
   between business units 217–18
   BHP-Billiton merger 262–3
   created with acquisitions 246–7
   transaction costs 247

tacit collusion 208, 314, 323–4
tacit knowledge 96, 313
tactical action 170
takeover 232
talent drain 387
tangible resources 91, 92–3, 94
   and diversification 218, 220
target evaluation and acquisition 244–5
tax laws and diversification 215
technological resources 92
technological segment of general environment 42, 53–5
technology 270–1

change and diffusion 15–18
and changes in competitive environment 158–9
and globalisation 272, 275
threats in general environment 44
time to market 175–6, 472
top management teams
   and CEO 431–2, 434
   and corporate governance mechanisms 351
   culturally diverse 298
   definition 430
   heterogeneous 430–1, 434
   homogeneous 430, 434
   women 435–6
   see also manager
top managers (1999) 28–9
total quality management systems 146, 178–9
total shareholder return 358
tracking stock 387
Trade Practices Act 1974 215, 374
transaction costs 247
transnational strategy 288–91, 412–14
transparency 199
'triad' competition 162
trust 30, 102–4, 294, 322–3, 335–6, 337
two-tiered board of directors 362, 363

uncertainty reduction strategies 319, 325–6
unions and multinationals 39–40
unitary model board of directors 362, 363

universal product demand 274–5
unrelated diversification 199, 200–1, 202, 203, 210–14, 247
   through acquisitions 242

valuable capabilities 22, 99, 100
value chain analysis 105–9, 133, 138–9
value for customers 87–8, 123
value innovation 477–8
value-creation 105–8
venture capital 461, 464, 474–6
vertical acquisitions 234
vertical complementary strategic alliances 318–20, 321, 322, 323
vertical integration 201, 203, 209
vertical strategic networks/alliances 318–20, 321, 322, 323, 415–16

web-spying services 72–3
whole-firm buyouts 256
wireless communication 270–1
women in the workforce
   equal pay 52
   executives 52–3, 435–6
workforce diversity 52–3
World Trade Organization (WTO) 49, 55, 275, 290
worldwide geographic area structure to implement multi-domestic strategy 408–9
worldwide product divisional structure to implement global strategy 409–11

Photo credits

The authors and publishers would like gratefully to credit or acknowledge permission to reproduce the following photographs:

AAP Image, pp. 86, 144, 185, 204, 216, 229, 289, 336, 424, 430, 439, 455; Ansell Healthcare, p. C-166; Australian Picture Library/Corbis, pp. 302, 329, 458; Coo-ee Picture Library, pp. 13, 155, 417; Dick Smith Foods Pty Ltd, p. 137; Fairfax Photo Library/Kylie Pickett, p. 347, /Joe Castro, p. 442; Hewlett Packard Office Machines, p. 53; Image Addict, pp. 29, 52, 121, 368, 377, 386, 469; Newspix, pp. 24, 39, 79, 234, 255, 396, 404, C-34, C-35, C-164; PhotoDisc, pp. 129, 310; photolibrary.com, pp. 3, 95, 248, 270, 275, 349; Qantas, p. 162; Stock Photos/Masterfile, p. 194; Woolworths, p. 318.

Every attempt has been made to trace and acknowledge copyright holders. Where the attempt has been unsuccessful, the publisher welcomes information that would redress the situation.